# BEYOND POWER

*On Women, Men, and Morals*

*Also by Marilyn French*

THE BOOK AS WORLD: JAMES JOYCE'S *ULYSSES*
THE WOMEN'S ROOM
THE BLEEDING HEART
SHAKESPEARE'S DIVISION OF EXPERIENCE

# BEYOND POWER

*On Women, Men, and Morals*

## MARILYN FRENCH

BALLANTINE BOOKS • NEW YORK

Library of Congress Catalog Card Number: 85-91512

ISBN: 0-345-33405-1

This edition published by arrangement with Summit
Books, a division of Simon & Schuster, Inc.

Manufactured in the United States of America

First Ballantine Books Trade Edition: June 1986

10   9   8   7   6   5   4

For
Charlotte Sheedy
and
with constant memory
of
William Hull

# Acknowledgments

No book covering so many areas and disciplines can be written without enormous help from others. Most of the people who helped in the writing of this book are unacquainted with it—they are the scholars and thinkers whose work illuminated my thinking, even when I disagreed with it. Their names appear in the notes. But a great many people gave me not only their scholarly work but their time and encouragement as well. Primary among these is JoAnn McNamara, who patiently read two full drafts of the first three chapters, and made generous and useful comments. Rayna Rapp also read these chapters and, in addition to making many good suggestions, took the trouble to educate me in anthropological dos and don'ts. Jean Jackson also generously commented on my anthropology. Sarah Pomeroy offered help with the Egyptians, Greeks, and Romans; Claudia Koonz read many drafts of the material on Nazi women, clarifying my confusions; Karen Gottschang was very helpful with China; and Blanche Cook and Janet Murray offered good comments and suggestions for further reading on the entire history chapter.

For Chapter Five too, I consulted a group of experts, among them Alan Sadovnik on education, Robert Engler on corporations, Renny Fulco on political theory, Joel Kovel on medicine and psychology, Judith Fleisher, Elsa First, and Janet Younng on psychology, and Kathleen Paratis on law. Françoise Basch read and commented on Chapter Six. Myra Jehlen read the entire book in an early draft, and made many good suggestions. Each of these people too was generously helpful. However, it should be understood that errors that may remain in the book are my responsibility alone.

Some people kindly responded to questions mailed to them by a stranger: John Money, Barbara Lerner, Stephen Jay Gould, and Fritjof Capra. Others suggested various readings or sent me articles: Benjamin Barber, Nancy Wechsler, and other friends.

Jamie French and Robert French III found books and other materials for me, and helped greatly with research. Rosemary Beaumont and the rest of the staff at the tiny library in Riviera Beach, Florida, were invariably cordial and efficient in obtaining for me somewhat arcane volumes. Barbara Haspel helped in many ways—shielding me from the telephone when I worked, finding books and articles, typing innumerable drafts, making corrections and suggestions, and, finally, managing to draw lucid sense out of messy reworked pages with unmatching notes.

   Hilde Hein and Barbara Greenberg read a short early version of this book
and were kind about it, as was Jim Silberman, who also allowed himself to be
pressed into service reading later versions, and continued to encourage me.
Charlotte Sheedy has supported me throughout: from the first she saw what I
was trying to do and has never wavered in her faith in it.

# Contents

# Introduction

There seems to be a rhythm in human affairs. Although human marking of time is utterly arbitrary, many cultures have created myths about ages of time, periods with predetermined characteristics. According to one Western tradition, the decades surrounding a new millennium are periods of severe disruption and cultural transformation. No doubt many periods could be so described, but it is true that many of us feel we are living through the death throes of what has been called Western civilization.

Apocalyptic vibrations charge the thinking of cults preparing for the end of the world, and of writers and film makers fascinated by cataclysm. Lurking in the background of most apocalyptic visions, however, is an idyllic dream of "purity," a new beginning cleansed of the horror and grime of past and present. But there is no idyllic vision in the popular imagination, nothing but threadbare traditional images of human versus nature in a newly pristine frontier, however that frontier may be presented.[1] These images, found in film and novels, offer only the past wiped clean; and the past as it was can lead only to the present as it is. In every dimension of life there is a sense of old molds cracked or cracking, of the precious—or rancid—contents spilling out; but there is no vision of a human future.

There are realistic grounds for our sense that we are living through a period of severe disruption, that, indeed, we may be shuddering our way to the end of the world. People of the fourteenth century, visited by continuous wars and the black plague, also believed the end of the world was at hand. But they did not themselves possess the means to accomplish that end: we do. And human history does not provide us with grounds for assurance that that means will not be used.

Humans have reached a stage from which it is almost impossible to imagine a future. This has not been true in the past. Those who anticipated the end of the world, a final day of judgment, also envisioned an afterlife in paradise, with their enemies properly installed in hell. The past few centuries have entertained dreams of progress, in which technology would free the human race from its burdens. If the future imagined by people of past ages was not the future that actually evolved, the two bore some resemblance to each other. But we cannot envision even a continuation of the present: we are utterly bankrupt of vision. And the barrenness of our imagination, our hope and faith, could result in the annihilation of our race. No matter where we turn our minds, we find no realistic ground for confidence in any vision, any alternative except atomic war, a planet made sterile by pollution, or world totalitarianism.

This book rests on the assumptions that our present lack of vision as well as the present condition of the world is the result of a failure of our morality; that it is possible for humans to create and live by a different morality; and that only by adopting a new morality can we restore enough emotional, physical, and intellectual equilibrium to create a more felicitous society.

The term *morality* is out of favor. Ethicists are quick to disavow connections between their discipline and actual life, and critics scorn "moral" judgments of literature, painting, or other arts. For many people, morality means a set of rules governing the disposition of one's genital organs; or a set of injunctions against lying, stealing, or killing except when such acts are sanctioned by church or state. On the other hand, many people think morality means specific value systems—the commandments of a given church—Catholic or Protestant Christianity, Orthodox or Reform Judaism, Sunni or Shi'ite Moslemism, for example.

But morality is a neutral term: it has no specific content. It refers to the set of values by which we judge, which guide our behavior and even our emotions. Morals are our real values—not qualities we claim to revere, to which we give lip service and not much more. Our moral system is a system of priorities, or, rather, a texture, an interlocking set of shifting, ambivalent, and conditional goods and ills. Our morality manifests itself in our choices—how we live, to what we devote our time and money, the kinds of friends we make, the way we spend our leisure, and above all, the kind of person we become, the kind of person we want to be. The morality of a society also manifests itself in its choices: how much it spends on what; its language and art; its mode of production and what it produces; its mode of ordering itself and the kind of order deemed desirable.

Morality is a personal and communal affair; when it reaches the public realm, it is called politics. The relation of the two is not like two sides of a coin, but like the inner and outer skins of a balloon; that is, it is the same thing, seen from inside or outside. Rousseau claimed that separating morality from politics made both disciplines incomprehensible. Alasdair MacIntyre puts it thus: "Every action is the bearer and expression of more or less theory-laden beliefs and concepts; every piece of theorising and every expression of belief is a political and moral action."[2] Feminists say simply, the personal is the political.

A morality is an intermeshing set of qualities and conditions to which we attach varying degrees of value. It is not a scale or gamut; it is a context of thought and judgment. Invariably in Western societies, and perhaps in all societies, people are ambivalent about those elements that are most important to them positively and negatively—like power and sex. Moreover, terms like power and sex mean different things to different people; human beings tend to load a term or concept with symbolic or superstitious baggage, and see a quality haloed or horned. One intention of this book is to analyze the limits of what these terms *can* realistically mean, to distinguish the actual parameters of our values.

Capitalist and socialist thinkers alike generally accept the Marxist idea that the mode of production of the material means of life determines the consciousness of a society; that is, that what is fundamental to human thought is the way we produce our food, shelter, tools, and other artifacts of our material life. But humans to a large degree invent their material lives, and societies with similar modes of production have dissimilar consciousnesses. They vary in ethos, in social arrangement, and in well-being—in short, they vary in morality. The root of morality lies in the conceptual realm; what we value depends on our sense of what it means to be a human, our way of seeing ourselves.

Consider the different responses of two cultures to an unusual but not unfamiliar phenomenon, the birth of twins. The Nuer and the Mundurucu do not live identically, but very similarly, and largely by horticulture (farming done manually; agriculture is farming done mainly by machines).

The Nuer live in the upper Nile Valley, where they fish, raise cattle, and practice horticulture. They are contentious and polygynous; the men exchange bride wealth—cattle—for women. Wealthier men thus have many wives, poor men none, and women are mere articles of exchange. The Nuer regard the birth of twins as a special event. They see twins as human, and so of the earth, but also as manifestations of spiritual power, and so of the realm above the earth. The Nuer give twins the names of terrestrial birds, creatures who occupy both earth and sky.[3]

The Mundurucu live in the South American tropical forest, by horticulture, fishing, and a little hunting. They are also headhunters. Their society is rigidly segregated sexually and pervaded by intersexual discord. They see the human as living in an uneasy power relation with nature. When twins are born, they see them as a regression to animality, since animals regularly have multiple births. The Mundurucu kill twin babies.[4]

These societies conceive of themselves, of humanness, differently—with a mortal difference for infant twins. The primary ground of any definition of humanness is nature; that is, people see themselves in a particular relation to nature. The Mbuti of northeast Zaire, for instance, see themselves as part of nature, part of an immortal and perfect plan which they violated when they first hunted and killed an animal. Since that first sin, all things have been condemned to die; only if the Mbuti can find a way to survive without killing can they regain their immortality. (One consequence of their belief is that they kill as little as possible, although they are magnificent hunters.)[5] Other peoples conceive of themselves as very different from other animals—some groups therefore make sure to cook their meat, and look down on others who eat it raw as animals do.[6]

The primary determinant of a morality is the way in which a society conceives of humanness. To be able to conceive of humanness at all, it is necessary to distinguish humans from their surroundings, that is, from nature, from other creatures. Thus the very notion of humanness involves an abstraction. In the cultures that fed into and eventually became Western civilization, the notion of humanness involved a duality: humans were set in opposition to nature, rather than within it. And the primary manifestation of the relationship between humans and nature is the way a society sees men and women. For a variety of reasons, which will be discussed throughout this book, most cultures associate women with nature or that which is polluted, and men with humanness, which is seen as a condition permitting transcendence—superiority over, freedom from, control of nature or pollution.

Chapter One describes what we know about human origins: the social arrangements of other mammals, especially our close relatives the chimpanzees; and what researchers have been able to deduce about the customs of the earliest humanlike creatures (hominids). Some simple societies still remain on earth, although most have been affected by Western ideas. Nevertheless, these societies can offer hints about the social-political arrangements of ancient humans. Many anthropologists believe that hominids and early humans (*Homo sapiens*) lived in small groups centered upon the mother; that for millennia fatherhood was unknown (as it is among most mammals); and that the highest goods of the groups were the bonds among members, sharing, and a sense of participation in nature.

Over eons, intelligent humans developed more controls over nature and a new sense of what it meant to be human, which was to be distinct from nature. Human loneliness began. And, in time, that separation from nature was transformed into a sense of humanity as being not just distinct from but superior to and in control of nature. This was the first stratification, the first assertion of one thing being intrinsically superior to another. Probably simultaneously, humans created another stratification, that of gods who were transcendent. The new gods, who had different names in different cultures, were endowed with power-over; they could affect the elements, plants, creatures, and humans without being affected in return. They were male gods.

But because humans are not, were not, and cannot be in control of nature (within them or without), as the gods were imagined to be, they could attain their new status—humanness as control—only symbolically. Religious ritual and social arrangement created an appearance of—and sometimes real—control. And because of the age-old association of women with nature, the human race itself was stratified, with men taking the role of the god, the human in control, and women taking the role of nature, the human who is controlled. This process comprises the origin of patriarchy.

Chapter Two offers hypotheses about why and how this shift occurred, and discusses the morality that accompanied it. This morality, which is still with us, holds power (control) to be the highest good, and values qualities that tend to strengthen or sharpen the male image of isolation, individuality, and control. Virtue is equated with manliness; one proves one's manhood by demonstrating control over women, children, property, and other men. Many stratifications followed the first set; society was structured by fragmentation. Other elements besides sex were introduced as symbolic of, and manifestations of, superiority: skin color, wealth, religion, ethnic background, manners, dress.

Not just centuries but millennia were required before patriarchy gained domination over the minds of people in large segments of the world. But patriarchy is a militant ideology. To revere power above everything else is to be willing to sacrifice everything else to power. Many cultures accepted such a morality only with reluctance, but power worship is contagious. If a worshiper of power decides to extend his power over your society, your choices are between surrendering and mounting an equal and opposite power. In either case, the power worshiper wins—he has converted your society into a people who understand that power is the highest good. Over the millennia, patriarchy spread to all corners of the planet, and only a couple of tiny societies still exist that appear not to have been influenced by it. The full import of the morality of patriarchy cannot be conveyed in a brief statement, but requires extensive documentation. The core of this book—Chapters Two through Five—offers such documentation by showing the meaning of this morality for women, for men, and for our present situation.

Chapter Three sketches the consequences to women of living under patriarchy—in ancient Greece and Rome, through the Middle Ages, and into the present. It is a surprising story, filled with women's efforts to free themselves from patriarchal bondage, or, when that was impossible, to find ways of adapting to it that permitted some exercise of their abilities. Perhaps the most striking fact in the history of women is the way they moved out into the world and functioned expertly when patriarchal controls were lessened (temporarily); and perhaps the most striking characteristic of patriarchy is that it invariably put a stop to women's free functioning. Yet through all the ages, the old matricentric values survived, despite an increasing devaluation of them that continues into our own time.

The following chapter describes the condition of men under patriarchy, but focuses mainly on the present. Because power is so highly valued in the twentieth century, it is easy to forget that it carries a price which must be paid not just by those who sit in the seats of power, but by all who claim superiority over others or over nature. Superiority expresses itself in hierarchical forms; and such forms require that people "fit in" in precise and unvarying ways. The price for claiming "manliness" defined as control, and the rewards given to those who successfully make the claim, are discussed in Chapter Four.

Patriarchy has been the dominant morality of the West (and of the East, in a different form) for more than three thousand years. In certain areas patriarchy has probably been dominant for considerably longer. All of us, women and men, poor and rich, black, white, and people of color, have been imbued with its values, its perspective, and its taboos. We carry these into whatever we do, whether we are attempting to gain power or to ameliorate the human lot. It is our efforts, and the efforts of generations of people like us, that have produced the present situation of the world. Although many of us find it comfortable to divide the world into good and evil people, and to attribute its ills to whomever we call evil—the non-Christians, the power seekers, the educated or noneducated—in fact all of us contribute to a world situation that is without exaggeration dire. Grant me ten minutes of gloomy summary of our present prospect.

On the largest scale, the international, the picture is frightening. Weapons already in existence in the United States and the Soviet Union have for more than a decade been sufficient to annihilate all life on this planet, yet both nations continue to manufacture and stockpile more and more advanced weapons, capable of "greater" destruction. Other countries also possess nuclear weapons, as well as machines that spew napalm, which burns you alive; cluster bombs; neutron bombs, which destroy only life; lasers; small nuclear arms; and more conventional horrors. War has become more frequent as well as more deadly: between 1900 and 1941 there were twenty-four wars in the world; between 1945 and 1975 there were 119 civil and international wars involving the territory of sixty-nine states and the armed forces of eighty-one.[7] "Advanced" weapons mean that entire populations are killed in these wars, not just soldiers and a few unlucky civilians. But some of these wars are directed precisely against populations *by their own leaders*. In Cambodia, in El Salvador, and elsewhere, a comparatively small elite has been, is, responsible for exterminating their own people in huge numbers. Amnesty International has reported that half of the 154 nations belonging to the United Nations hold political prisoners of conscience, and sixty of these use torture as regular procedure.[8] In scores of countries people are arrested without due process and simply disappear; they are held in prison but their families are not notified; they are subjected to torture and are murdered with impunity.

Nineteen eighty-four has passed, and although the totalitarian world Orwell foresaw for us has not fully come into being, many people on the globe live in nations with strong central control over most dimensions of life. The strength of this centralized control, and its breadth, varies from state to state, but whether nations are socialist or capitalist, "totalitarian" or authoritarian or "democratic," no industrial state lacks such controls. The procedures of multinational corporations and their effects on national governments are leading to new forms of regulation of ordinary life, and to huge powers being held by invisible and unaccountable entities. This process is moving to encompass the entire nonsocialist world, as agribusinesses and other corporations expand their purview to Third World countries. Total control of the human race through psychological and economic means is not inconceivable now.

In addition, the planet itself is being destroyed. Pollution of air, water, and soil is not limited to Western industrial nations, and it is not containable: winds carry poisoned air, clouds carry acid rain, toxins leach into ground water. As I write, there is discussion of the danger that the drinking water of half the population of the United States is being seriously and perhaps irreversibly poisoned by this process.[9] Almost all the lakes in the beautiful and undeveloped Adirondack Mountains are now sterile, no longer able to support fish life because of acid rain.[10] In thousands of locations across the United States, lethal and explosive chemicals and compounds are simply dumped, and, as we see daily, they are making many areas of the country unlivable. Cancer and leukemia rates climb and in some cases damage is being done to the chromosomes of children, causing grave anxiety about what will become of *their* children.

Half the world's forests have vanished and they continue to disappear at the rate of eighteen to twenty million hectares a year; that is an area half the size of California. Every year fertile land about the size of Maine is eroded into desert, largely because of deforestation. Nearly two million species of plants, insects, birds, and animals have disappeared from earth, and 20 percent of those now in existence may be extinct by the year 2000.[11] Moreover, species which are saved from extinction by the careful nurturing of a small group show extreme genetic similarity, which may cause difficulties attendant on excessive inbreeding in the future. Environmental pollution and the destruction of creatures and plants are occurring everywhere, and some of the worst pollution exists in relatively undeveloped nations, which industry contaminates freely because local governments, needing the jobs industry provides, do not dare impose regulations.

Our technology has been created irresponsibly. Besides creating pollution in manufacture, and producing nonbiodegradable waste, it functions poorly and is subject to dangerous accidents. Air-conditioning systems spread contaminating viruses and even cancer-causing agents; new synthetic materials used in constructing and decorating hotels and other buildings give off lethal fumes during fires, causing deaths that might not otherwise occur. Chemicals spilled in accidents require towns to be evacuated; oil spills kill the life in the sea and on the beaches. Most dangerous of all are nuclear plants, which threaten life at every level of their existence. Exposure to plutonium is possible in the creation of nuclear power. Plutonium is deadly for 250,000 years; it settles in the food chain, in the testicles and ovaries of human beings and animals, and is passed to future generations. Operation of nuclear plants is fraught with the danger of error and deterioration; beyond that, there is irresponsible siting of the plants and the materials used to build them, and irresponsible operation, as has become evident in data from Three Mile Island.

The United States is the wealthiest nation that has ever existed; yet fully one-fifth of our people live below the poverty level. And worldwide, *one-third* of the human race do not have enough to eat: ever: not a single day of their lives.[12] Although this situation is passed over with expressions of sympathetic uninterest, and attributed to the overpopulation of many lands, overpopulation is partly a response to poverty as well as a contribution to it: people unsure whether their children will survive tend to have numerous children, hoping the law of averages will lead to the survival of a few. But worldwide lack of food is a by-product of certain policies of the industrial West, the consequence of imperialist methods of distributing and using land, dislocating local populations, land purchase by agribusiness, and a policy of requiring cash crops. The natural balance between people and land which enabled both to survive for many thousands of years has been disturbed, and no new balance provided.

Everywhere there are bitter prejudices that constrict life and in some places make it cruel or even impossible for people of particular races, sex, classes, and religions. Everything is at an extreme: our century is a period of aggrandizement and excess, of genocide of people and other species; it is a period in which all balances have been lost. The most influential political movements of our time are not Gandhi's *satyagraha* (which came to mean a loving/holding firm) or liberal democracy, but fascism and socialism, whose most conspicuous political innovations include "the unopposed single party, the party-state, political police, the politburo, revolutionary command councils, storm troops, political youth movements, cadres and gulags, propaganda machinery, and concentration camps."[13] Ours is the century of the holocaust, the first use of the atomic bomb, and massive internment of human beings.

Within our own nation alone, similar patterns of violence and excess are pervasive. Even omitting discussion of the behavior of corporations, labor unions, organized crime, various levels of police (including secret police), and corruptions of justice, of health care, the mediocrity of education, we can see all kinds of abuse in the United States government alone. Government officials of several administrations have, at the very highest ranks, been involved in petty crime; many administrations have been extremely militant, seeking occasions for war as demonstrations of their control. The years 1980–84 witnessed the use of governmental processes to mask a subversion of law—an early mark of totalitarian governments—in the areas of environmental control, equality of opportunity, and other matters of human welfare.

We all know about these and other ills, but we feel we can do nothing about them. We sigh and shrug and go about our business and try to get through our days. But the malaise of our culture penetrates daily life as well. City streets are riddled with crime; but so are city apartments; nor is the countryside free from it. Violent petty crimes concentrate on the vulnerable—the old, women, people alone. The ambience of the United States is such that it seems the entire nation is having a nervous breakdown. How else can we explain acts like the placing of cyanide capsules in bottles of headache remedy to be purchased by ordinary people at random? Or kidnaping, rape and murder of small children chosen at random? Rape and mutilation, or just shooting, of women chosen at random? What is most incomprehensible about terrorism is not that it uses violence to attain a political end, for all nations in the West have done that, but that terrorist groups secrete bombs in places where people congregate. The people killed or injured by those bombs have no necessary relation to the political question at issue: they are simply murdered randomly. There is a difference between violence directed at a particular person or kind, and violence committed without regard for its victims. The second sort shows a hate and rage and disconnection so profound that it amounts to a hatred of one's kind—that is, of human beings in general.

Finally, even our private lives are disturbed and bewildering. Old codes of marriage, divorce, sexuality, and child rearing have broken down, but the consequences of this breakdown have been mixed. People can escape from unhappy marriages, they can use their sexuality as they choose (on the whole). At the same time, men are displaying an irresponsibility about their children that is equivalent in self-hatred to terrorist murder—for are not our children expressions of ourselves? Women and children are the new poor, and a growing class.

With this background in mind, I discuss, in Chapter Five, the penetration of patriarchal morals into those disciplines founded on the belief that it is possible to ameliorate the human condition—medicine, psychiatry, education, law, and business. The best-intentioned efforts to solve human problems falter or fail because they are dyed in the same pattern of thinking that created the problems. All of us are to some extent responsible for perpetuating an inhumane way of life, and for permitting our present ominous situation. Nor will we be able to end our participation in creating hell on earth until we discover what it is we are doing wrong and what we must do to right it.

The philosophy that can offer us a new way of seeing is feminism, the subject of Chapter Six. But if feminism offers a new set of ends, human goals, new (or rather, old) ideals for humanity, it does not yet possess a clear set of means by which those ends can be attained. There are many strands of feminism, each working on slightly different assumptions and by different means, and each encountering different obstacles. Chapter Six describes these assumptions, means, and obstacles, and suggests the underlying unity of the feminist morality.

The final chapter is a further consideration of what must be done to bring a more humane morality—and thus a more felicitous society—into existence. There are, obviously, immense and serious practical obstacles to the realization of the feminist vision of social-political order. But, practical and huge as these obstacles are, they arise from a way of thinking, from the conceptual realm, from the way we *approach* things, more than from the nature of things themselves. Chapter Seven summarizes the arguments that pervade the book about the real limits of power, the reasons for human discomfort with sex, and the creation of a fully human image. The structural manifestation of patriarchal values is hierarchy; and so pervasive is this form that we can hardly imagine alternative forms. Patriarchy is founded upon duality; and so pervasive is this way of apprehending reality that most of us cannot imagine any other. Chapter Seven intimates alternative structures.

Many modern moralists believe that values are "irrational," so personal and individual as to be beyond philosophical inquiry or redaction. "Questions of ends are questions of values, and on values reason is silent." Morality can no longer encompass "essential human purposes or functions."[14] But others believe that "the idea that values are merely the result of nonrational factors is an intellectual aberration of modern civilization and a phenomenon of decay."[15]

We live in a period which prides itself on "tolerance," on a relativistic perspective toward human arrangements which masks our real and fixed values—power/control, white male superiority over a human race that is erratic, animalistic, brutal, and selfish and thus requires strict regulation. In such an age it is perilous to suggest that there are or could be universal moral principles or a universal moral good. Yet that is what this book maintains, denying the present definition of our race, denying also relativism about fundamentals. Unfashionable as such a position is, it adheres to simple common sense: we must recognize that since we are all human and share the same basic human condition, we also share the same basic needs and aversions, and what is good (in the profoundest sense) for some of us is good for all of us.

The great good upheld by this book is pleasure—redefined, as are power, structure, sex, man, woman. Such a position must be argued and demonstrated. The argument and demonstration lie before you. The great good to be worked toward is a positive one. If the discussion of patriarchy seems emphatically negative, that is because it is urgent to emphasize the ills of a way of thinking that is unthinkingly accepted by most of a society. As Nietzsche wrote, "Whoever must be a creator in good and evil . . . must first be an annihilator and break values."[16]

The intention of this book as a whole is to offer perspective on where we have been and where we are, and to suggest where we want to go. It offers not a program but a vision for the future; not only a denunciation but an understanding of the past. Above all, it is an earnest plea for reconsideration of our own image, of what we think we are and can be. With one eye on reality—whatever it may be, we know its rough configurations—and another on real human need and desire—whatever they may be, we have a sense of their qualities—we must, as a race, slowly approach a way of thinking that allows us to live, not die; and to encompass felicity.

# CHAPTER ONE

# The Long View Back: Matricentry

The earth, it is estimated, is 4500 million years old; for eighty million of these years, mammals have lived upon it. Molecular evidence suggests that the ape-human divergence occurred relatively recently, perhaps four to five million years ago; there is uncontested evidence that hominids—an early form of humans—were living in eastern Africa about three and a half million years ago.

These hominids, called Australopithecus, were chimpanzeelike creatures who walked on two feet. They had small brains but managed to survive for at least one and a half million years—something we, with our large brains, may not accomplish. Other forms of humans evolved over time, although there is contention about how. Some anthropologists, paleontologists, and molecular biologists believe that change occurred gradually, dictated by survival of the fittest. This theory presupposes no final goal to natural selection, no progress toward perfection of any kind, but only an adaptation in a given place and time to changes in environment.[1] Other theorists hold that new species appeared suddenly, rather than evolving out of old species, and coexisted with them.[2] In any case, Australopithecus appeared in two versions, a robust and a "gracile." These two kinds coexisted, on the African savanna, for at least a million years, two million years ago. For unknown reasons, the robust type, with its heavy skull, enormous teeth, and rugged face, became extinct in time, whereas the gracile species developed a larger body, larger cranial capacity, increased ratio of brain to body size, and smaller teeth, to become Homo erectus, the precursor of modern humans.[3] *

Homo erectus traveled and established themselves throughout Africa, the Middle East, and had gone as far as Java close to a million years ago. Between a million and half a million years ago, they had established themselves in northern Asia and Europe. Homo sapiens, our own species, did not appear until 100,000 to 200,000 years ago.

For only a tiny proportion of this period of human and protohuman existence—about five thousand years—do we have written records. There are architectural remains for a somewhat longer period. Before that, there is little—some bones, some stones, bits and pieces of lives caught in an eternal moment by volcanic materials. But recent technological discoveries have introduced processes which offer fascinating information about these remains. For

---

* I will refer to species of the genus Homo which preceded Homo sapiens as hominids, humanoids, or protohumans. The term human is reserved for Homo sapiens.

instance, the examination of fossil teeth under an electron microscope can reveal the kind of wear sustained by the teeth. This in turn can lead to fairly dependable hypotheses about what those teeth chewed. Examination of fossil teeth and jaws has led to new estimates about when hominids began to use tools to cut their vegetables, and even whether those vegetables were gathered or grown.[4]

The earliest hominids made use of nature in ways that did not disturb it: they used twigs, branches, leaves, bark, vines, thatch and wood for tools, containers, shelter, and bodily adornment; they used stones as tools without modifying them. The modification of stones offers the first evidence of manufacture, and this occurred very early, for with the remains of Australopithecus found at Olduvai Gorge—remains that are about two million years old—were eleven different kinds of crude stone implements.[5] Much later, close in time to our own age, there are shards of pottery, metal objects, sculptures, and in some cases the remains of buildings, from which we can gain information. But the interpretation of such material is highly subjective and a matter of considerable contention.

Another source of information about human beginnings is the animal world. Taken as a whole, this realm is richer and more varied than the human realm, showing innumerable different techniques of subsistence, survival, and sexual and social organization. Because of the enormous variations in animal behavior, and because humans are different from the animal world as a whole, it is difficult to apply knowledge of animals to the human condition. Nevertheless, observation of mammals, especially the anthropoid apes—our closest kin—can offer suggestive material about human origins. Humans are very closely related to chimpanzees and gorillas: human and chimpanzee protein molecules are more than ninety-nine percent identical, for instance.[6] As Stephen Jay Gould puts it, humans and chimpanzees are very different, but not in kind, only in degree: "Part by part, order by order, we are the same; only relative sizes and rates of growth differ.... Differences between the skulls of humans and chimpanzees are quantitative only."[7]

Over the past decades a variety of thinkers have applied information about primates to human life, claiming to find in primate life justification for human aggression, territoriality, and oppression of women. In some cases animals were studied in captivity (which alters their behavior); in others, researchers found what they wanted to find, and concentrated on species that demonstrate monogamy, male dominance rituals, or seeming male dominance of females.[8] More responsible research performed recently has modified and sometimes invalidated the conclusions reached earlier.[9] Nevertheless, it is extremely difficult to obtain an accurate picture of the life of primates. The mere presence of an observer affects their behavior. Moreover, animals are everywhere being destroyed. Game preserves protect them to some extent but the artificial environment also alters primate behavior. In areas of wilderness, the wildlife is every day being pressed back a little further as humans occupy more and more land. The animals are more crowded and have less food than they did previously; their behavior shows stress.

Finally, there remain on earth almost two hundred societies that still live in an older way, by gathering, hunting, and fishing. All of these groups have been affected by changes elsewhere in the world; all of them have changed from even a few hundred years ago, and continue to change. Some are finally giving up the ancient ways entirely, perforce: like the animals they cannot live where the game has disappeared, the rain poisons the fish, the land is so eroded that fruit trees vanish. From a proud and independent freedom maintained all these thousands of years, peoples in Australia, in Latin America, and in Africa have become and continue to become "unskilled" workers for wages, improvident and dependent on situations beyond their comprehension or control. It is no longer possible to deduce their former cultures from their present ones.

Despite the dearth of information, and the danger of direct application of much of what we have, researches into animal behavior and the life of people who still retain an earlier style of life yield richly varying results. Within the huge diversity of forms, there are certain common factors. I will consider each source in turn, and offer an interpretive portrait of our social origins.

## 1. ANIMAL EVIDENCE

In the beginning was the Mother; the Word began a later age. The single universal covering primate and ungulate (hoofed) species, indeed all mammals and much other animal life as well, is that the core of society, the center of whatever kind of social group exists, is mother and child. Such a social organization is called *matrifocal* or *matricentric*. These terms are not the same as *matriarchal*, a word formed by analogy with *patriarchal*, which denotes leadership (from the Greek root *arche*, meaning *chief*, and *archein, to be first, to rule*).* A matriarchy would thus be a society in which mothers rule in the same way fathers have ruled for the past few thousand years. There is no evidence that a matriarchy ever existed on earth. A society in which someone rules is factitious, manufactured: a person or group decides that one person shall dominate and others obey. Matricentric societies are spontaneous, organic; the mother cares for the baby until it is able to move about easily by itself, find food, and protect itself without her. The mother "rules" by greater experience, knowledge, and ability, but the intention of her "rule" is to free the child, to make it independent.

The matricentric nature of animal life has not been interesting to anthropologists until recently. Despite clear evidence to the contrary, generations of thinkers have assumed male dominance in all living forms. The Greeks believed the "ruler" of the beehive to be a male. Medieval bestiaries show the lion as king of the jungle, even though the male lion does not often kill but is depen-

---

* *Matrifocality* or *matricentrality* refer to a focus on the mother, her centrality within a family group. *Matrilocality* means dwelling where the mother dwells after marriage—that is, the groom goes to live among his wife's people. *Matrilineality* refers to reckoning of descent. Young animals know their mothers and, to the degree that they have a consciousness of identity, know themselves to be her offspring, her matrilines. They do not have any idea who their father might be, and it is probable that few animal mothers possess this information either. Among humans, matrilineality is the reckoning of descent through the female line, which was common in past ages. Both matrilineality and matrilocality still exist among some peoples.

dent upon the female. The primary interest of researchers in the past has been to find in other species affirmation of the rightness of current human arrangements. It is now known, however, that "the mother-offspring group is the universal nuclear unit of mammalian species," and that primate societies are "matrifocal almost by definition."[10] Not all adult mammals have a full society; some come together only during courtship. But even among the so-called solitary species, the mothers tend the young with great attention for prolonged periods. The mother feeds her offspring from her body, carries the infant with her, and even after it is weaned, she shares her food with it. In the process she teaches it what is good to eat and how to obtain it, teaches it about the environment, its graces and its perils, and teaches it the paths of movement through the environment that she learned from her mother.

Matricentry is essential among larger animals because they are altricial—their young are born helpless. Without the mother-child bond, the young would die. In some cases, however, the females remain together throughout life, forming a social core. This is true of elephant society, which is entirely female: males are pushed out of the group when they reach thirteen. Their mothers and aunts and sisters go on living together with extraordinary cooperation and altruism. Carnivores are solitary animals; what society there is is composed exclusively of mothers and their young. Females control and defend their territories and bequeath them to their daughters when they die or if they decide to move on. As with the elephants, the mothers expel the males during late adolescence. The core of a lion pride is a closed sisterhood of adult females who are biological sisters or at least cousins. They remain together all their lives in fixed territories passed from mother to daughter and live in great harmony and cooperation.[11]

There are a few species of animals that pair bond, that is, mate for life; among them are the gibbon, the raven, the goose, and the painted shrimp.[12] Beavers live in families in which the female is dominant and more territorial.[13] Wolves bond in pairs but hunt in packs. After hunting and eating their kill, they return to the home ground and regurgitate what they have eaten for the pups and those mothers who have remained with them.[14] Females comprise the stable core of social organization among langurs: Sarah Hrdy writes, "In all but a few species, females are permanent residents in social groups, males mere transients." Most monkeys occupy "real estate inherited by a daughter from her mother. When colonization of new habitats occurs, the role of Moses may be taken by a low-ranking older female who leads her disadvantaged lineage into the wilderness."[15] The old female has a reservoir of experience and remembered tradition on which to draw. The females in matricentric groups are the primary transmitters of group experience and memory, and the principal socializing forces.[16] Among most mammals it is the female who chooses the lair or shelter suitable for rearing her young; when a male remains as consort to the female, he accommodates himself to her choice.[17] Such arrangements are called *matrilocal*.

Because of the centrality of females in mammal species, one might conclude that mammal females are dominant. The term *dominance* is extremely murky, however, for several reasons. First, although the words are sometimes used interchangeably, *dominance* is different from *domination;* the former refers to an inherent quality which may be natural (like personality, beauty, intellect) or acquired (like rank, office, the aura of wealth) but which is part of a person for a period of time and which influences the behavior of others. Domination is the willful use of power (of whatever sort) to countervail or annul the will of others. Dominance seems to exist in certain species; the existence of domination among animals is more questionable. The behavior of hamadryas baboon "alpha" males has been interpreted as domination of females.[18] * However, that human form of domination known as *authority*—the power to control others reinforced by an assertion of a moral right to control—does not exist among primates or other animals.[19]

In the past, researchers seeking for dominance as domination found it; more recently, however, the entire idea has been questioned. Some species have rituals that appear to suggest deference among some males for another; what is questionable is what prerogatives this kind of dominance entails. M. R. A. Chance has suggested that *centrality* indicates dominance—that is, the animal the others most often watch is dominant.[20] Other researchers posit the existence of a *control animal,* one who intervenes in conflicts to end them, and of showy behavior that appears dominant, but functions as expressive greeting, play, or showing off.[21] Orders of rank do exist among some primates, and high status seems to confer certain privileges. Thus if two animals spot the same piece of food simultaneously, the lower-ranking one may back off. But often an animal's rank is determined by its mother's—rank passes in a female line. Primate females possess their highest status just after they give birth; in time it passes to the next new mother.[22] Perhaps this is an adaptation that contributes to the survival of the species. Low-status males in some species offer ritual obeisance when greeting high-ranking males. And dominant male cynocephalus baboons seem to live longer than nondominant males.[23]

Not only the form but the function of dominance is in question. The traditional view was that dominance in males guaranteed exclusive access to females (especially estrous females—females in heat) and the ability to get, keep, or usurp the better foods or a larger share of them. In other words, dominance among animals was presumed to be similar to dominance in humans.

Recent studies have shown none of these to be the case. Dominant males in general have no greater number of copulations with ovulating females than any others, and do not produce more offspring.[24] Among chimpanzees, those males who do have the best chance of reproducing themselves are those who are chosen as consort by a female. The pair bonds and goes off together for a time, during which the female copulates only with her mate.[25]

Finally, the conception of dominance is complicated by human associations with the term. Many people believe that males are more aggressive than females, larger, and stronger, and they assume that greater size and strength lead inevitably to male coercion and oppression of females. But male mammals

* Researchers have named seemingly dominant male baboons "alpha" males.

are not always larger or stronger than the female of their species; second, greater size does not necessarily lead to domination. Sexual dimorphism—a difference in form and size between the two sexes—does not lead to the dominance or domination of the larger sex in species that lack pair bonding, and that includes most ungulates and primates.[26]

Gorillas, the only dimorphic ape species that lives in groups stable enough to have leaders, have in these groups large, silver-backed males which are sometimes dominant—they may direct the troop's movements—but are otherwise mild-mannered. They have no sexual prerogatives and no preemptive rights over food, and they can protect other members of the troop only while they are within the group. Orangutan males are much larger than females, but not dominant. Cynocephalus baboons who live on plains have alpha males who are dominant; but cynocephalus baboons who live in forests do not. Among them, the old females set the direction of troop travel; there is no pattern of sexual access, and in dangerous situations the males flee first. There are some South American monkeys among whom the females are larger than the males, but so far they have not attracted ethologists. Among chimpanzees, large size has no correlation with dominance, leadership, sexual prerogatives, or special access to food.[27] Among lemurs, who show some sexual dimorphism, females are dominant.[28] Small langurs, female and male, have been observed to displace much larger monkeys when aroused.[29] Moreover, there are monomorphous species (same-sized sexes) which are monogamous, and in which the males defend the territory against male intruders and the females against females. In such species dominance is not an issue between mates, and if disagreements do occur, the female holds her own against the male or dominates him.[30]

Moreover, it increasingly appears that the element that wholly determines the dominance of male animals over other males is not superior size or strength, but the status of their mothers.[31] The macaques of Japan and the Caribbean live in multimale troops; they and some baboons are the only primates to exhibit male bonding.[32] But their troops are comprised of "ranked matrilineal clans" dependent on the support of their females matrilines.[33] Rhesus macaques have dominance orders, but rhesus mothers protect even their adult sons.[34]

Nor are size and strength directly correlated with aggressiveness. There are mammal species in which the females are larger than the males but the males are more aggressive.[35] Among some kinds of baboons, males are extremely aggressive; the female patas monkey, however, is more aggressive than the male.[36] Degree of aggression varies not only from species to species and between sexes, but according to occasion as well. Females of most species are more fierce in defending their young; whether males or females are more fierce in defending a territory varies depending on the species.

Aggressiveness in a gender or a species presumably serves the purposes of the species. If males were aggressive to infants or females carrying infants, the species would die. Yet there are recorded accounts of male primates invading a troop, dispersing any resident males, and killing the young. They then install themselves as mates to the females. Such behavior seems detrimental to the species, and some primatologists have diagnosed it as maladaptive and due to stress. Sociobiologists hold up such events as testimony to their belief that males compete and act aggressively out of a drive to pass on their personal (or group) genes, for when her infant is killed, the female primate enters estrus, and the male usurper gains a possibility of procreating.[37] But species in which such behavior was frequent *would* in time become extinct. The invading males may be driven, as the sociobiologists hold, to transmit their *individual* genes, but the chances are they are weakening, not strengthening, their species.

The animals closest genetically and structurally to human beings are chimpanzees and gorillas. Both are gentle and sociable; they live in large social communities and know each other well.[38] Much research has been conducted among these animals—especially chimpanzees—in the past few decades, and although there are differences in observations from different locations, there are some general agreements about the way these creatures live.

Chimp babies lie in the womb for eight months and are born helpless and remain so for some time. The mother carries the infant around for six months, assisted by the baby's ability to grasp her body hair with its fingers and toes. A chimpanzee mother is exceedingly protective, carrying her infant close to her body, protecting it from falling off branches or rocks and even from heavy rain, during which she hunches over the baby, cradling and covering it.[39] By the time the young one is a year and a half old, it can move rather easily along the ground or swing from branch to branch, but it is not weaned from the breast until four or five years of age. It will remain with its mother steadily for six years, traveling with her during the day, grooming her and being groomed by her, and sleeping with her in the nest she builds for herself and her young.[40]

During these years the young chimpanzee learns what plants to eat and when to eat them, what routes to take through the forest, how to build a nest, and how to make tools like the stripped twigs chimpanzee females use to gather termites. "Occasionally a mother may teach by active intervention; if an infant is seen nibbling on an unfamiliar, possibly poisonous insect, the mother might knock the bug away with her hand."[41] Females reach maturity at thirteen, males at fifteen, but neither leaves its mother for more than a few days at a time until the age of ten, and daughters may remain for a long time. They may, indeed, remain permanently.[42] It is not unusual for a mother to be helped by *her* mother in raising her offspring. For both daughter and son, the tie with the mother persists for a long time.

The young chimpanzee comes to know other creatures besides its mother; when it is an infant, other females may hold it, rock it, play with it. These females are giving affection to the young, but they are also *learning. All female primates learn to mother.*[43] Male chimpanzees do not have much to do with the young. Indeed, most primate males try to avoid the company of babies, and females sometimes physically attack males who seem to be on the verge of doing damage to infants. But those male-dominant species baboons and macaques love babies, and will hold and examine them, and sometimes even adopt them if their mothers die.[44]

The threat of death is real, and when mothers die, their infants fall into depression and often die as well, even those as old as three.[45] Females with dependent offspring suffer higher mortality rates than other females because of the increased difficulty of finding food while carrying an infant, and of finding enough food to produce milk for it.[46] Females with young spend almost 70 percent of their waking time in feeding, Nancy Tanner asserts; single females spend only 60 percent of theirs, and males, 53.1 percent.[47] Both sexes catch and kill small animals. All adults supply their own food, but males often give meat to females; females share mainly with their young.[48] Mothers continue to share food with their young long after they are weaned, spending many hours of each day feeding in the trees where most of their food grows. Although chimpanzees live in communities, they are likely to forage and travel alone or in small groups. (Gorillas forage in bisexual groups.)[49]

Chimpanzees are cooperative and gregarious; they come together in fluid groups of variable size, and use special calls to recruit others to a rich or plentiful source of food.[50] As small parties of chimps move through the jungle, they meet other parties which they greet with calls, leaps, chest pounding, and embraces. There are dominance rituals among males, but they seem to observers to be meaningless.[51] Animals rest together grooming each other for long periods; grooming is a form of conversation and affection. When troops meet, members of one—both males and females—may adopt the other troop and go off with it.[52]

Males more than females catch and kill small animals; females more than males use tools for gathering and in defense. A female may attack fiercely, with a tool, in defense of her young.[53] There is conflict among chimpanzees, but it is infrequent and not lethal. They deal with predators by scare tactics—noise, leaps, chest thumping—and by fleeing more often than not.

Sex among the chimpanzees is nonbinding. Although most observed copulations take place during estrus, when a female is not pregnant or lactating, they also occur during pregnancy and other periods when she is not estrous.[54] Females with young do not become pregnant again until their infants reach four or five.[55] Female chimpanzees sometimes simply refuse to mate, and copulation is impossible without female cooperation.[56] Male chimpanzees in the wild do not seem to fight or compete or show jealousy over estrous females, and are casual about sex in general. (The same seems to be true of gorillas.)[57] Jealousy, when it occurs, comes from infants who object to their mother's activity, or between mothers and adolescent daughters, who try to interfere with each other's copulations.[58]

It is the female who initiates sex, although on occasion males try to pressure estrous females into going off into solitude with them. Infrequently, they succeed. More often, the female chooses a consort with whom to pair off in solitude for a few days. The males they choose are social, agreeable creatures who share food and who groom the females.[59] Females avoid aggressive males, and among pygmy chimps, sex and food sharing are deeply associated.[60]

This easy, noncoercive kind of sexuality is true of most animals: aggressive or dominant behavior interferes with mating, and only when it is eliminated and the two sexes enjoy themselves and each other in mutuality can coitus occur. Rape is extremely rare in the animal world.[61] Male monkeys cannot mate unless females invite them and cooperate; female primates in estrus choose their own partners, and often many partners, one after the other.[62]

Males are marginal in chimpanzee communities as they are in most mammal communities, but they have their own pleasures. Young males play more than young females, and adult males travel over greater distances than females, ranging far from the home base searching for food.[63] Although they do not bond in all-male groups, they are very sociable and very mobile. Females are more sedentary and carry the major burdens of chimpanzee life—pregnancy, nursing, caring for the young, limiting reproduction, finding enough food for their group. But they also have the reward of a close bond with their young and with other females, especially sisters.

Research into animal behavior has, until recently, concentrated on two points that are, oddly, opposites: finding in animal life affirmation or justification for human male-dominant hierarchical organization; and finding in animal life the horizon or dividing line that distinguishes between and thus separates the human from the animal. Evidence of the first has been reported, but more objective work has modified or invalidated most of these reports. Indeed, the only absolute difference between humans and animals may well be simply male-dominant, coercive hierarchical organization of the human type. All other "dividing" traits are questionable: animals as well as humans use tools and manipulate their environment (consider bees, ants, termites, beavers), and some have social stratification as well. Animals do not have language, but they can communicate, and it is possible that whales and dolphins do have a kind of language. Birdsong varies among kinds, as does some animal vocalizing, and it has been demonstrated that some animals vocalize in dialect—a sound pattern familiar only among a local species; birds sing in dialect, and birdsong arises from both genetic programming and learning. That is, birds can learn only certain kinds of song or certain dialects at certain times in their development (a limitation that seems genetic), but they can also *learn* "foreign" dialects under particular conditions.[64]

The major dividing line between humans and animals has been thought to be incest avoidance. It has been believed that this is strictly a human characteristic enforced through taboos. However, recent research has suggested that chimpanzees and other primates also have incest-avoidance techniques.[65] Male and female siblings seem to shun each other sexually; and young females frequently leave the troop to join another, thus precluding sexual conjunction with their fathers. Information on the subject in animals is still scanty; but it may be that incest is no more common among primates than it is among humans.

## 2. HOMINIDS

The earliest hominids probably looked much like the anthropoid apes—chimpanzees and gorillas. Fossil evidence indicates that these creatures were short, walked upright on two legs, and had short legs and even shorter arms. It is possible that they could no longer use their big toes for grasping, as apes and monkeys can—although it has been hypothesized that this ability still exists in humans who practice it from birth. Humans also still possess brachiation, the ability to swing with our arms, an ability we share with the apes. But four limbs are necessary for swift tree climbing and jumping from one tree to another, and the legs of the hominids probably did not permit this. In addition, it is possible that infants could not hang onto their mothers' body hair, and had to be carried.[66]

In some ways, hominids were the stepchildren of nature: they had lost special talents and had not gained very much. Their pelvises and feet were constructed for walking in an upright position; thus they lost the speed, the ability to scurry up trees or leap from one to another, that permits apes to escape from danger. They had a reflexible thumb (a thumb that bends across the hand—not found in primates), and a small brain—about 450 cubic centimeters on the average. Gorillas often have larger brains, but Australopithecus weighed only fifty to ninety pounds, while large male gorillas may weigh six hundred or more. The effectiveness of the brain is properly measured not just by size but in proportion to body size.[67]

The image we have been given of early humans is a crude, brutal, predatory one, with extreme male dominance: "cavemen" bashing each other over the head and dragging women by their hair. But the likelihood is that the early hominids were gentle and playful, with a society that centered on a set of mothers and infants. Like chimpanzees, hominids were altricial, and mothers spent most if not all of their lives feeding, caring for, and educating their offspring. Hominid mothers probably had to carry their babies everywhere, since the babies could not hang on by themselves. Because of this, birth control of some sort was even more necessary for hominids than for ape mothers. There is argument about the method used. Hominid mothers were extremely active, walking great distances to forage for food, and while they were nursing they probably did not gain enough body weight to resume ovulation.[68] It has recently also been theorized that frequent nursing may set up a chemical reaction that impedes ovulation. Present-day !Kung mothers nurse their children an average of every thirteen minutes for the first two years of their lives.[69] The !Kung still live by gathering, in the old way, and so provide some hints about what the old ways may have been. It is estimated from the average number of children born to a present-day !Kung mother—five—that hominid mothers may have produced five or six children in their lifetimes.[70]

Like young apes, hominid infants were totally dependent upon their mothers, who fed, carried, groomed, caressed, taught, and communicated with the child. The care of hominid children involved even longer periods than the care of young apes because hominid young developed more slowly, and the bond between mother and child was just as strong as it is among apes. From their mothers, young females learned to mother and the young of both genders learned to share.[71] A mother might be carrying an infant and leading a small child by the hand, with one or two older ones hovering close by, as she taught them plant, insect, and animal lore; strategies for protection against weather and predators; modes and routes of travel.

The nucleus of hominid society was a mother and her children, often accompanied by the mother's mother and sisters, by her brothers, and by adult males who had attached themselves to the group. Alien males would have been more readily accepted into the group if they were cooperative, if they killed small animals and shared the meat, if they found twigs and branches to make tools and helped to defend the group against predators.[72] Each group was probably small, and camped every night near the same lake or river. Members of groups might shift to other groups encountered in their wanderings, but sibling ties were very important, especially after the mother died.[73]

Hypotheses of harmonious relations between the sexes are based on several factors, among them the size of canine teeth, which offers more information about behavior than body size or dimorphism. The canine teeth of early hominids are small and nondimorphic—that is, the same size in both sexes. This suggests that Australopithecus was friendly and sociable, that agreeable relations existed between the sexes and among members of each sex.[74] Thus, far from being Freud's "primal horde," an unruly and rebellious group of brothers ruled by a tyrannical father, early humans probably lived in close, affectionate groups, with a strong bond between mother and children, affection among the youngsters playing together, and friendship among all members.[75] Conflict was probably resolved (as it still is among some peoples today) by the departure of one of the antagonists to join another troop.

Possibly small clans grew from this first kin group.[76] It is unlikely that the sexual bond was permanent or exclusive.[77] The core group of adult sisters with their children provided the nucleus of a community, as adolescent males and perhaps some females drifted to other groups, attracted by playmates or sexual partners. The "dominant" member of the group was probably the mother or the oldest female—but this dominance had the character of centrality and experience, not domination.

We can hypothesize that the hominid female was economically independent, like all female animals, entering into association with males according to her desire, probably with those males who were willing to share food and the care of the young.[78] It is not known when humans discovered the male role in procreation, but it is argued that this discovery was made fairly recently, perhaps as late as ten thousand years ago. How, when, and why female hominids lost visible signs of ovulation—estrus—and developed menopause are still matters of speculation.[79] It has been argued that loss of estrus in human females was responsible for the development of pair bonding and the nuclear family. Women who could become pregnant at almost any time of the year, rather than seasonally, would require protection by a male they could control, if they were to control their procreation. Such an idea rests on the assumption that males are naturally rapists, forcing women into unwilling coitus, and that only the protection of another male or a policed society prevents such behavior. It does not seem likely that hominid or early human males acted in this way. Nor is estrus a strictly biological event even among animals: macaques have shown signs of estrus after they have conceived, and chimpanzees have been known to initiate sexual encounters when they were not in estrus.[80]

Small, mainly harmonious groups of Australopithecenes wandered from place to place foraging for food. Their diet was probably excellent, like the diets of present-day gatherers. Vegetable foods accounted for most of it (perhaps as much as 90 percent); small animals, birds, reptiles, and insects for the rest.[81] The modern !Kung Bushmen, studied by Richard Lee, gather mongongo nuts and eat about three hundred of them a day. This portion gives them 1260 calories and 56 grams of protein, which is equal in calories to two and a half pounds of cooked rice and 14 ounces of lean beef in protein. These nuts comprise 50 percent of the weight of the Bushman diet, the rest being made up of eighty-nine other species of fruits, melons, berries, roots, and bulbs. To collect this much food, the women work two to three days a week. Men gather mainly for themselves, although they also collect small animals; they work only twelve to nineteen hours a week. Children and adolescents do not work at all. People begin to work only after marriage, which occurs between fifteen and twenty years of age for girls and twenty to twenty-five for boys. Ten percent of the population is over sixty, yet all elderly and impaired people are cared for.[82]

Hominid life evolved over the millennia. Because certain tools—digging sticks, containers—decay in earth, we cannot be sure of dates or progressions, but it is probable that hominid females adopted or continued the use of the digging stick to collect ants and termites, both of which are still eaten in various places on the globe. Indeed, roasted termites are considered a great delicacy in some places. It is likely that hominids began to use sharp-edged rocks to help dig up roots, to scrape dirt from them, to pare tough outer parts, and to cut up large items for sharing. Rocks could have been used to crack open and halve nuts and large fruits with tough rinds. Since females were mainly responsible for collecting and sharing food, they may have developed these tools.[83] We do know that there were stone implements with the remains at Olduvai Gorge, fossils of Australopithecus dated at two million years old.

Containers too were probably developed early, and the first ones may have been made of strong leaves or bark. They were used to carry one's baby on one's back, to carry water during long gathering journeys, and to carry the fruits of these journeys back to the settlement. The invention of the container was a major step in human evolution. It provided the first step between humanoids and animals, because it permitted gathering rather than foraging. Animals forage—that is, they collect food, eating it as they go. Gathering is the collecting of food so one can carry it elsewhere and save it for later. The container suggests cooperation, because the food is meant to be shared; it permits movement of a troop to a new location, and even over long distances in which food supplies are unpredictable. It also permits settling into a home base, however temporary. And this step too was probably taken by females: "It was the mothers who had reason to collect, carry and share plant food; at this time, males were likely still foragers, eating available food as they went," writes Nancy Tanner.[84] Improved containers meant that gathering hominids could migrate. They did: the earliest hominid fossils outside Africa were found in Indonesia, and are approximately 1.9 million years old.[85]

The kinds of tools found throughout the Lower Pleistocene—two million or more years ago—are simple flakes and hand axes, useful in digging, scraping, and pulverizing vegetables but not in hunting large animals. Small game can be caught in the hands or trapped; it was doubtless occasionally part of the hominid diet as it is, episodically, part of the diet of chimpanzees. Every major change led in a cycle to other changes. Improvements in their tools made it possible for the women to process the vegetables they gathered. This in turn led to the gradual vanishing of large chewing teeth. Eventually meat was butchered, hacked off the bone: crude butchering tools have been discovered that seem to date back 1.7 to 1.8 million years.[86] It is unclear whether, at this point, hominids actually hunted, or whether they simply butchered animals that were already dead.

The next major step in dividing the experience of humans from that of animals is the use of fire. The control of fire allowed food to be cooked rather than eaten raw; and it permitted cave dwelling, unsafe before that because of predatory animals.[87] Until recently, fire was believed to have been harnessed only half a million years ago: a 500,000-year-old hearth was found in Zhoukoudian, China, near Peking. But in 1981 the remains of a hearth were found in Kenya, in Chesowanja near Lake Baringo, that is believed to be 1.4 million years old. Near the fire were small pieces of baked clay, tools, animal bones, and fossil remains of Australopithecenes.[88]

Projectiles do not appear until the Middle Pleistocene (about one and a half million years ago), and there is also evidence dating to that period of slain game animals at kill sites.[89] In other words, it is unlikely that humanoids began to hunt until about one and a half to two million years after they appeared. Gathering, not hunting, was the universal adaptation; and remained so even after hunting began.

Hunting, however, seems to mark a profound change in human or humanoid experience. Some thinkers believe hunting was responsible for the first diminishment of women's status, because women could not hunt. But women did and still do hunt, and cave paintings have been interpreted as showing women hunting. Nevertheless, in most modern groups hunting is a strictly male occupation. Hunting alters the relation of humans to nature: it changed our relation to other animals. We would not conceive of animals as "wild" if we had not hunted them, transforming them into victim and threat. In game preserves, when people approach them, animals sometimes remain where they are, peacefully feeding along with other species, sharing the same waterholes, the same sun, the buzzing quiet of the natural world.[90]

Each development—the use and refinement of tools, the invention of containers, the harnessing of fire, and the beginning of hunting—separated early humans a little further from their animal origins. From immersion in nature, humanoids were moving to a posture of control over nature, over their environments. Although, as I suggested earlier, many animals also exercise some form of control over their environment, early humans used a variety of means for control, each of which seemed to separate them from the animal world as a whole and to confer upon them a special identity.

Only one step remained to be taken before humans would see themselves as distinct from nature: the abstracting of reality through a conceptual capacity. When this occurred we don't know. Some thinkers believe Australopithecenes had language; some believe there was no language until *Homo sapiens*; most believe language had developed by the time of the Neanderthals.[91] Neanderthals had a limited voice box, and therefore a limited speech capacity, but keen intelligence.[92] Certain remains also suggest that the abstracting capacity necessary to language existed earlier than *Homo sapiens*.

At whatever point in the human past language began, it had to emerge from mothers communicating with their infants and children. The old notion that males on the hunt developed language to communicate is absurd: one doesn't learn to speak after one is physically developed. We know that language is learned young or not at all.[93] It is reasonable to assume that mothers cooing to, warning, and teaching their youngsters developed a symbolic system that was then built on and transmitted by the children.

There are remains of cave burials from the third ice age, 150,000 to 100,000 years ago. A burial involves ceremony and ritual—that is, an ability to conceptualize and to propound significance. Chimpanzees know each other as individuals; many animals mourn the death of a beloved one. But a formal burial suggests a ceremony that places a beloved dead person in a framework, a seeing of the dead as part of a larger scheme. The ceremony may be devoted to easing the passage of the dead one to another dimension, or to placating the guardians of another dimension, or to consoling the group for a terrible loss by ritually making the dead person part of those left behind, or simply by celebrating what the person was for the group. In any case, significant capacities for abstraction and conceptualization, imagination and scope, are required. Such capacities, if possessed in combination with necessary physical equipment, would be sufficient to permit speech.

In addition, there are rocks with line markings believed to be 100,000 years old which appear to be early calendars. Most anthropologists believe that women began these, tracing their menstrual cycles with the changes in the moon, the first deity. In some tribes women are still custodians of the lunar calendar. Yurok Indian women kept tally systems and could predict a birth within a day.[94]

The entire period under discussion, from 3.5 million years ago to about 10,000 years ago, was a peaceful period. There are no remains of weapons used by humans against humans, no signs of groups of humans being slaughtered. Thus the early forms of humanity, far from being savagely aggressive and cruel, were probably a gentle, humorous, peaceable folk, like many tribes living to this day in gentle climates. The picture previously offered of early societies—that of a patrilocal band of related males who exchanged women and treated them as commodities—is a patriarchal construct; such societies probably never existed. Most likely, early gatherer/hunters lived in fluid, flexible egalitarian groups.[95] This is not to say that these people lacked aggressiveness and did not experience conflict. But they developed social skills for dealing with negative interaction; their education focused on personal relations, cooperation, their part in a larger whole.

A group life centered in child care and sharing could not survive in a highly aggressive environment. Intense aggressiveness would have destroyed the species. And among present-day gatherer/hunters, whose customs vary from extreme male dominance to more or less equal but segregated male/female societies to integrated egalitarian societies, one factor is universal: all live by sharing. A degree of aggressiveness would seem to be a necessary and perhaps even an enjoyable characteristic; but aggressiveness is culturally induced: where it is not valued, it is not strong.[96] This "advance" was left to *Homo sapiens* and that glory, civilization.

## 3. HOMO SAPIENS

"Evolutionary success is reproductive success," according to the sociobiologists.[97] This suggests that the highest values for any species are survival and continuation. In this sense, and perhaps in others as well, Australopithecus was a success: the species lasted for over a million years and may have been the ancestor of later hominid kinds, and so of *Homo sapiens*, the last example of this lineage to appear so far. *Homo sapiens* has a large brain capacity and a body structure we recognize as human despite many variations in size, shape, and other characteristics. All people who exist on earth today, whether in simple older cultures or industrial societies, are of this kind—*Homo sapiens*. But it is not known precisely when this form appeared, and if there is general agreement that *Homo sapiens* is no older than 200,000 years, there is little assurance of its actual age: some estimates place its emergence as recently as 35,000 years ago.

Nor is there certainty about when hominids or humans made important changes in their way of living. Some groups continued for thousands of years to wander nomadically, settling only temporarily; some probably wandered circularly with the seasons, as the Lapps do today; it is hypothesized that the early settlers of Mexico and South America, for example, came originally from Asia. Other groups created permanent settlements. Modern nomads may have been settlers at one time, displaced by climatic change or social disruption.[98]

It is likely that paternity was unknown and that early humans were matrilineal. Insofar as mating was permanent or semipermanent (that is, bonded for a period), it was almost certainly matrilocal. Although people probably owned private property—a cache of containers, tools, adornments, weapons—there was no sense of possession of land or animals until the beginning of horticulture and domestication of animals. Indeed, even modern gatherer/hunters like the Australian Aborigines, who claim ownership of tracts of land, allow others to move freely upon it, to gather and even to hunt.[99]

Judging partly by primate habits and partly by some present-day groups, anthropologists have theorized about early human life. Probably social order was fluid and permissive; people moved continually from camp to camp, staying as long as they chose with kin or lovers. "Marriage" was informal, casual. Children remained with their mothers, and if the mother died, with their grandmothers or aunts. There were no chiefs, no leaders, merely fluctuating groups of people. If a quarrel between two people could not be resolved, one would leave the group to join another. Such a political-social arrangement is true anarchy; people ruling themselves without need of leaders. Among those who live this way at present are the Hadza, !Kung, Mbuti, Ik, Dogrib, Netsilik Eskimos, and Gidjingali.[100]

In the prehistoric past, foragers could gather more easily than they do today, because the world was still covered with growing things. Today, gathering people have been pushed back by cities and farms; they live only in deserts, deep tropical rain forests, hills, and the Arctic region.[101] Like the hominids, early humans lived in small kin groups formed around a mother or mothers. They walked great distances to gather fruits, nuts, and roots, in groups or alone, several times a week. Both men and women gathered and set traps for small animals. Sometimes groups of women and men went hunting or fishing; sometimes an individual would hunt alone, probably with a dog, and sometimes groups of men went hunting for a day or for several days or weeks. Fishing, especially net fishing, was a group activity, but gathering of shellfish was often done by children and old people, for whom the short walk along a coral reef or shoreline was not too strenuous. People also ate lizards, birds, and certain insects.

They took only as much food as they needed for the time and, at first, probably made no effort to manipulate the environment so as to foster the creation of more food. Thus, although early humans had excellent brains, their relation to nature, to growing things and animals, was still one of equality: they took their food from nature and lived within it, finding or making shelter from inclement weather just as other creatures do. When they decided to camp in one place for a time, the women built shelters from twigs, leaves, fronds, small logs. They made fires just outside their shelters and sat in groups talking, singing, and bantering (especially about sex: the size, smell, and functioning of other people's sexual organs is still a source of great communal humor to certain gathering peoples), and telling stories. Life was not generally hard. If an area became depleted of food or water, they moved on.

There was probably always a division of labor based on sex and age. It is important to realize, however, that this division was not like those that exist in our world. In the first place, it was arbitrary: that is, in one group men fished while women made pottery; in another group women fished and men made pottery. In some societies the demarcation between male and female activities was fluid; the two sexes could share tasks, or one could do the job of the other without serious consequences. In others the lines were rigidly drawn, and only exceptional circumstances allowed the participation of one sex in the job expected of the other. It is possible that this division arose from the fact that women, fairly universally, did the gathering *for the group*. The fact that women from the first took responsibility for the young, feeding and teaching and protecting them, probably led by analogy to their taking responsibility for feeding the entire group. Female animals take responsibility for creating and finding shelter, making nests, for their young and themselves; early women continued this activity, building shelters both temporary and permanent. In many societies women still perform this task. The first feeding of the young from women's bodies may have led by analogy to responsibility for other forms of feeding—to grinding and cooking the vegetables they had gathered. Male responsibility was far more limited: among many groups even today, men care for *themselves*— they gather for themselves, make tools for themselves—and contribute minimally to the needs of the community. It is conceivable that strict divisions of labor arose because men needed and wanted a clear function within their groups in equivalence with the women's functions.

The value placed upon work performed by the two sexes was probably very different from current evaluations of work. Almost universally today the tasks performed by women are regarded as less important than those performed by men. Some theorists posit that at one time the tasks of the two sexes were valued equally; but it is far more likely that in the distant past women's work was granted more importance than men's.

Because at present it is the males in most societies who do the hunting and fishing, the division of labor has for a long time been seen as between man the hunter and woman the nurturer and gatherer. Yet women still hunt in some societies: the Agta of the Philippines, some Aboriginals—the Shoshoni, for instance. Mbuti women go net hunting with the men; Chipewyan women hunt when the men are away; Copper Eskumi and Ainu women hunt large mammals alone, and the Agta women—superb hunters—hunt, like Tiwi women, accompanied only by a dog.[102] (The Tiwi live on Melville Island, off the coast of northern Australia.)

Fishing is even more variable. In some societies it is a communal activity, in some exclusively female, in some exclusively male. The collecting of fish— that is, gathering it along reefs and shoals—is generally the job of the very young and the very old. But in most groups men do both the hunting and the fishing.[103] They also make the weapons, and smelt and treat metals. In only one known society is the mining of ore a female job. Woodcutting is usually a male task; carrying heavy loads a female one.[104] In "primitive" societies women do most of the housebuilding. And in almost all societies women work harder than men. Among the Nsaw of Cameroon, men clear trees and heavy shrubs to open new fields, and they help in the harvest: they work about ten days of the year. The rest of the time they sit in the village drinking palm wine and chatting, while the women work the fields. The Nsaw say of a bachelor that he "has to work almost as hard as a woman."[105] The Hadza men of Tanzania spend much of their time gambling. Although they are hunters, about half of them never go hunting, and some of those who do are great failures. They retire from hunting at forty-five.[106]

The multiple uses of the grain einkorn, a wild high-protein wheat grown in the fertile crescent, were probably discovered by women about 20,000 years ago; but it is unlikely that horticulture began that early.[107] In the beginning, grain was probably gathered; the group may have returned seasonally to the site where it grew. But farming is a much more arduous way of life than gathering, and the chances are that people did not resort to it until circumstances made it necessary.

Gathering requires a large territory to feed a small group of people. Conditions of living for Neanderthal and Cro-Magnon people were very good; the comparative ease of their conditions probably led to an increase in population. No doubt the protohuman population had been increasing over millennia, but easy migration kept this from becoming a problem. Perhaps because of a steep rise in population, perhaps because people had become accustomed to living in settlements and were unwilling to migrate, by the Magdalenian period (around 12,000 B.C.E.), four times as much land was occupied as had been formerly. In addition, the supply of game was slowly dwindling.[108] Some kind of change was becoming necessary to survival. The change humans chose was to develop horticulture, a change that it is estimated occurred about 10,000 B.C.E.—although there is evidence of land cultivation in Egypt 17,000 years ago.[109]

Modern scholars distinguish between *horticulture*, farming with hand tools, and *agriculture*, farming with plows and—later—other machines. Horticulture is still practiced in many places on earth, and is done more by women than men; agriculture is done more by men than women.[110] The first raising of crops was performed with hand tools, probably by women. When crops are grown rather than gathered, a small swath of land can feed many people, but the work involved is much greater: the land must be prepared, the seed must be reserved, then sown; the crops need watering and weeding, and they must be reaped all at once.

Horticulture requires a different relation to the earth from gathering: humans were no longer patiently attendant upon what nature supplied, but were actively furthering their own needs. To grow crops one must manipulate nature: it is an activity involving control over nature. Each step taken by protohumans involved an increase in control: let us reprise. The container permitted storage (which in turn permitted more or less permanent settlements, days of leisure, travel over unknown territories with unpredictable food supplies); fire permitted cave dwelling, the cooking of food, warmth in the cold and light in the darkness. The making of clothing from animal skins permitted migration into cold areas. The powers of conception permitted a mental abstraction of reality communicable through language. Each of these developments removed humans from the state of participation in nature to one of control over it, but control itself was probably not yet a conscious idea. There are groups living today who do not exercise control over nature, who do not, for instance, leave some roots in the soil when they gather, so the plant will grow again, or leave behind part of a beehive when they gather honey so the bees will return and rebuild it.[111]

Boats were being built in the late Paleolithic age (35,000 B.C.E. to about 20,000 B.C.E.); hunting became important about thirty thousand years ago, and dogs were being domesticated and used for hunting. People were beginning to use bows and arrows. Cave paintings were made showing animals, plants, fish, birds, and people—all the riches of nature: spawning salmon, foaling horses, growing grain. Techniques were discovered for making pottery. According to at least one theorist, women began to make pottery, molding the clay on their breasts.[112] If humans still felt connected with natural processes, they also felt a degree of ability to control some of those processes, and thus some elements of their own lives.

Settlements were built, probably around land cultivated by women. There may have been as yet no sense of ownership of land itself, but only a sense of ownership of rights to land and its fruits—usufruct rights. These were passed in a female line, from mother to daughter (just as "rights" to territories are passed from mother to daughter among certain animals), partly because women worked the land and partly because paternity was probably still unrecognized. Mating or marriage would therefore have been matrilocal, the husband or lover coming to live with the wife and her family. In many matrilineal groups, the mother's brother would have been the male primarily responsible for her children. In groups where women gathered as well as farmed, or farmed for long periods, women were away from home much of the time and uncles would have been caretakers of their sisters' children.

From all evidence, the large span of hominid and human existence was peaceable and less fraught with natural peril than we tend to imagine. Cultural change occurred very slowly during the first two to three million years of proto-human and human life, but it accelerated after the transition to *Homo sapiens*. In addition, there are far more vestiges of the past dating to the past 100,000 years than for the previous time, and especially of the past ten to twenty thousand years.

## 4. VESTIGES OF THE PAST

To understand a past age is difficult even when written records exist. Documents that are preserved usually serve the interests of the preservers, and all events are reported from a personal—that is to say, biased—perspective. It is far more difficult, however, to recreate a period in which there was no writing. For evidence of early human life we must depend upon vestiges. These fall into three categories: artifacts, traces in myths, and traces in customs.

### Artifacts

There are extant metal ornaments dating back to 9500 B.C.E., although metallurgy was not widespread in Europe until 6000 B.C.E.[113] And during this period, throughout "Old Europe" (the Balkans, Adriatic, Aegean, middle Danube, the western Ukraine areas, as well as present-day Hungary) hundreds of figurines, sculptures, and pieces of jewelry were manufactured. Analyses of radiocarbon content and dendrochronology (study of the growth rings of trees) have led researchers to date these objects at 7000–6000 B.C.E.[114]

Some of these figurines are of males and some are sexless, but the overwhelming majority are of females. It has been viewed as a phenomenon that so many female figurines and sculptures are found across such a huge area of the world, dating as far back as the upper Paleolithic period, through the Mesolithic, Neolithic, into the Bronze Age, through the Classical period, and almost to the threshold of the Christian Era.[115] Such figurines have been found in Mesoamerica, China, and the Middle East, as well as all over Europe from the far north to the Mediterranean and in Middle Europe. They have many forms: some are tiny and seem designed to hold in the hand; others provide the form for a useful object, like a ewer or a cup, or part of an object; still others seem to have been parts of altars.

Many researchers believe these figurines were important in a religion worshiping a principle of regeneration and fertility, a Mother Goddess, whose symbols included eggs, butterflies, and the aurochs (the wild ox of Europe), as well as other animals whose metamorphoses or forms express rebirth, resurrection, or eternality.[116] The Goddess, or Great Mother, seems to have been the most sacred figure of prepatriarchal eons. She ruled over both life and death, and was worshiped simultaneously as Mother Goddess, mistress of the animals, and receiver of the dead.[117]

This goddess was worshiped over a huge area, under a multiplicity of names, and in myriad forms: many of these are documented by Marija Gimbutas in a study of such objects found in Old Europe. They vary in size, although most are small. As Nerthus, Cybele, Astarte, Inanna, and hundreds of other names, a Mother Goddess hovers in the background of many myths. She appears in many statues, figurines, and objects linked to natural but nonhuman forms—as a bird, for instance—or connected to such animals as dogs or pigs. Early art was symbolic, and blended naturalistic human forms with purely symbolic forms like zigzags, or with animal forms: sometimes the human and the animal are linked into a hybrid figure; sometimes an animal mask is fashioned for a human face. In the seventh and sixth millennia B.C.E. in Old Europe, most of these figures were female; in the fifth and fourth, they were both female and male and elaborately dressed.[118]

In some Old European towns, houses had altars to the goddess in each room. She often stands flanked by animals, usually male animals. The corpulent goddess of the late Paleolithic is transformed in horticultural society to a slimmer figure flanked by domesticated rather than wild animals. The animals most frequently depicted are dogs, the bull, and the he-goat. The goddess is also frequently associated with the bear. Gimbutas theorizes that the maternal devotion of the bear made a deep impression on Old European horticulturalists, so that she was adopted as a symbol of motherhood; in any case, many figurines of mother and child show the child with the head of a bear.[119] The vegetation goddess was associated with pigs. The meanings of these animal associations are not always clear. Pigs are fast-growing and associated with grain; dogs bay at the moon, the cosmic body identified with the goddess and with regeneration, waxing and waning; and dogs constituted the major sacrificial animal. Bull horns resemble the lunar crescent.[120]

The goddess of regeneration was connected with the snake, which loses its skin, and the butterfly, which is a consequence of transformations: both seem to be reborn. (The butterfly image is sometimes perceived as a double ax, but it predates the metal ax by several millennia.) Other images of regeneration are the caterpillar, the crescent of the moon, and the swift-growing bull's horns. Images of females with large chickenlike bodies holding eggs seem devoted to the power of latency. The "Lady Bird" figure—a woman's head, a bird's body with an egg in its buttocks, and a phallic neck—was ubiquitous in Old Europe until the infiltration of the area by Indo-Europeans in the fourth millennium B.C.E. After that, she vanishes, but reappears later in Greece, Minoan Crete, and the Aegean Islands.[121]

Sometimes the goddess is a musician, holding panpipes adorned with rings. Often her body bore inscriptions which Gimbutas believes are related to (undeciphered) Linear A: they include spindle whorls, perhaps a reference to the still new art of spinning, and the thread of life; chevrons, which because of their placement—near breasts—seem to indicate rain. Rain and mother's milk are considered identical in many ancient cultures. There are markings suggesting snakes, the ubiquitous emblem of resurrection, renewal, rebirth; and there are markings that resemble vulvas holding eggs or dots suggesting them.[122]

The commonest religious object found in ancient Palestine is the figurine of a bare-breasted woman. Such figures date as far back as 7000 B.C.E. and appear until roughly four hundred years after David's kingdom; they seem to have been objects of worship.[123] They are found also in Babylonia and Assyria and in Bronze Age remains in Denmark.[124] Some figures of the goddess that have been found in Denmark show her wearing neck rings and kneeling as if she were driving a chariot. Tacitus, in *Germania* 40, refers to a goddess who was carried about in a wagon from place to place to bring fertility. Only her priest could touch her or look inside at Nerthus; the little wagons are still extant.[125] The cultural shift suggested by a change from a goddess driving a chariot to one being drawn about in a little wagon by a male priest who controls it—and her—points to what happened to goddess worship everywhere, over time. In northern Europe, as well as in the Mediterranean area during some periods, the goddess is connected with a necklace or neck ring, and there still exist stories of Freyja, a goddess in the Norse pantheon, and an extraordinary necklace.[126]

There are almost identical figurines in Mesoamerica, some still preserved in the great Anthropological Museum in Mexico City. Although many cultures lived in Mesoamerica, the earliest remains from all areas are female figurines. In Tlatilco—which in Nahuatl means *the place where things are hidden*—female figurines were placed in graves. Shamans were often women. There are almost no male representations, although there are male skeletons, dating to the period from 3000 B.C.E. to 300 B.C.E. This period—known as pretheocratic—gave rise to an overwhelming number of mother/child figures but no sexual or obscene images; occasionally there is found a female figure, like some in Old Europe, with the phallus made into part of her body.[127]

Other areas of Mesoamerica have revealed very realistic ceramics depicting everyday life—pregnancy, childbirth, children at the breast, children playing, sexual situations, and caricatures. Some show exaggerated genitals. From the beginning of the Classical period (300 C.E. to 900 C.E.), however, women appear in sculptures only as goddesses or priestesses.[128] Then, in most areas, depictions of women utterly cease until about the fourteenth century, when goddess representations reappear as the huge, ugly, terrifying images we find in Aztec art.

There are other images of females in early art, in cave paintings. One

Mesolithic rock painting—in what is now Algeria—shows the goddess as "mistress of the animals." A naked female figure stands looking at a naked male who holds a bow and arrow. She raises her hands and from her vulva a force flows directly into the penis of the male as he is about to shoot at an animal. There are other paintings similar to this one.[129] In addition, many of the oldest extant buildings have been shown to have the shape of a woman's body; the megalithic temple on Malta, and buildings in England, Wales, the Hebrides, and Egypt have the same form as the goddess figurines.[130]

Arguing that interpretation of these artifacts is not simple, Sarah Pomeroy offers as a possible parallel the many images of Virgin and Child which permeate a Christian culture that is both misogynous and male supremacist.[131] Certainly images of women in various stages of dress and undress pervade our own technological, male-supremacist culture. But the Madonnas and Annunciations coexist with many crucifixions (which might well puzzle an interplanetary visitor), portraits of saints and Church Fathers, martyrdoms of various gory kinds. Secular art shows condottieres on horseback, gorgeous naked Davids, kings and ministers in ermine and gold, wizened-looking Protestant merchants with their wives and possessions spread around them. Without much knowledge about the Western world from 1500 to 1900, one could deduce from its painting and sculpture that it was not ruled by women.

Moreover, it is not necessary to see the goddess figures as indicative of matriarchy. Rather, they suggest the primary concerns of their culture, its major values: fertility of all kinds—plant, animal, and human; fruitfulness of nature and of communities. The Madonnas of Renaissance Italy indicated a similar concern; they beatify mother love and nutritiveness for sons. There are very few representations in Paleolithic or early Neolithic* times of males or of phalli, and in Anatolia (where there are Neolithic remains) these disappear after 5800 B.C.E., when hunting became rather unimportant.[132] It has been suggested that this absence means the role of the male in procreation had not yet been recognized; but it could as easily indicate the marginal role of the male in activities surrounding the major values of these cultures.[133] When men are shown, it is often as hunters.

In 10,000 B.C.E. the village of Eynan, near the sea of Galilee, had fifty houses—small stone domes around a central area holding storage pits. It was the center of a gathering culture.[34] The earliest known settlements in Europe were around the Caspian Sea. The town of Catal Huyuk, in Anatolia, was larger, covering thirty-two acres and with a population of several thousand. The remains of this town, excavated by James Mellaart, show it to have had a high culture. The rooms of the houses are painted or have clay reliefs of humans, animals, and ornamental patterns. The people had a lead and copper industry, stone and woolen textile industries; they made

---

* These terms refer to levels of culture, not geological periods. They describe, generally, periods in which tools were made of chipped stone (Paleolithic), or were more shaped and polished (Neolithic) but not yet made of metal, as they were in the Bronze Age. Thus no absolute time is implied—one area might be in a Paleolithic state while another was in a Neolithic state. Roughly, however, the Neolithic age did not begin until 12,000–8000 years B.C.E.

obsidian mirrors, jewelry, ceremonial daggers, baskets, wooden vessels, and eventually ceramics. The culture endured from about 7000 to 6000 B.C.E. Mellaart and others believe that women were dominant or central in Catal Huyuk because they were buried, with children, jewelry, and obsidian mirrors, under the large central platforms of the houses, while men were buried in small corner spaces with only Stone Age hunting weapons. Also, small as they are, females are considerably larger than males in their figurines![35]

Although the biblical town of Jericho was armed and moated in 7500 B.C.E., these Anatolian towns lacked walls, nor are there signs of violence in the remains.[136] Near Catal Huyuk is Hacilar, a small village dating from the sixth millennium; in this village there were no male statues at all.[137] Khirokkitia in Cyprus had a thousand houses in 5500 B.C.E., each large enough to hold several people. It also had stone-paved roads, workshops, roofed corridors, and ramps from the houses to the street. There may have been an administrative center but there are no signs of social stratification—of wealth and poverty, or rank and lack of rank coexisting.[138]

The great Minoan culture that flourished in Crete in the second millennium B.C.E. may be related to the culture of Catal Huyuk or other "Old European" cultures, since the markings and dress of the figurines of the two cultures are similar.[139] The Minoan culture was lavish and developed, with aqueducts, irrigation channels, harbors, and effective drainage systems. The art that remains shows women in a host of activities—as merchants, ship captains, farmers, chariot drivers, hunters, and priestesses of the goddess. This suggests equality between the sexes. Even thinkers who do not believe Minoan Crete was ruled by women or was strongly egalitarian believe that the religious life of the Aegean world from the Bronze Age into the Classical period was dominated by the "Earth Mother."[140] It is likely that goddess worship pervaded ancient Greece even in the Classical period: Emily Vermeule writes that although the power and insistence of this religion so deeply rooted in agricultural life "may have been outlawed, made unofficial, transformed, suppressed, harnessed," it never died out in Greece.[141] And Pomeroy asks why, if the goddess was not being worshiped, there should be four times as many Neolithic female figurines as male ones, and a predominance of females in Minoan frescoes.[142]

At the very least, the figurines, sculptures, and cave paintings demonstrate that for millennia, across a huge area of the earth, certain qualities were of great importance, and that these qualities were associated with women. The qualities are fertility, regeneration, and a sense of humans as integrally connected with nature, whether because they had the same qualities as certain animals or because they wished to have them. What is important to my argument is that although humans were exerting control over nature, they did not see themselves as separate from it. The goddess or principle of fertility or regeneration or vegetation was part of nature and worked from within it. The sacred was still immanent in the world and the flesh, in the creatures of earth and its plants, in human birth and death. Minoan culture lasted from about 3000 B.C.E. to about 1500 B.C.E., when it was destroyed, presumably by the consequences of a volcanic eruption on Thera (Santorin).[143]

There were no fortifications in any Minoan town, and no military scenes in Minoan frescoes until about 1400 B.C.E., probably after an invasion by the Achaeans.[144] A similar situation seems to have existed in Mesoamerica, in villages of Formative (2000 B.C.E. to 300 C.E.) cultures in the Valley of Mexico. Despite the bloody myths and history of later ages, the early villages were egalitarian and peaceable; the contents suggest only minor differences in status or wealth, and skeleton remains show no signs of death by war or sacrifice.[145] Lack of fortification may reflect a peaceable society living without fear; however, it may also reflect the safety felt by inhabitants of an island whose cities were controlled by a strong central government. For by the time of Minoan culture, war did exist in the Middle East.

What led to this violent change in human customs can only be surmised. A greater population required a change of economic system. The plow was invented in the Middle East around 3000 B.C.E.; use of the plow often involves the use of animals in (coerced) labor. Moreover, with the introduction of heavy machines like the plow, males took over a formerly female activity. The same amount of land could yield far greater crops. Agriculture transforms farming from a subsistence activity into a potential source of surplus—profit.

Population may have been increasing everywhere, and towns that had for centuries lived in peace, ruled by custom, not law, found themselves host to bands of strangers unacquainted with local mores.[146] The form of rule had to change as small autonomous kin groups gave way to expanded groups who in time lived side by side with others. It is not clear precisely why, as political form altered to give rise to the state and to war, and economic and social forms shifted, creating stratification of classes, women fell in status. This crucial question will be addressed in Chapter Two. What is clear is that it happened, and that the emergence of these new forms occurred in a period of wrenching misery. Widespread warfare, enslavement of human beings, and human sacrifice began to bloody the Middle East. Social stratification led to the emergence of classes of very rich and very poor, and people were enslaved; it appears that the first slaves were women, possibly because men were killed during and after battles.[147] For the first time, adultery was called a crime—but for women only—and made severely punishable. In Ur, "the burial of kings was accompanied by human sacrifice on a lavish scale, the bottom of the grave pit being crowded with the bodies of men and women who seemed to have been brought down . . . and butchered where they stood."[148] Invasion followed invasion in Mesopotamia, each succeeding empire becoming harsher as Sumer gave way to Babylonia, which in turn gave way to Assyria and what historians call "the cult of frightfulness." Whole populations and armies were chopped to pieces, so that the landscape was literally dyed red with blood.[149] We know that the Sumerian word for *freedom* in the early part of the third millennium B.C.E. was *amargi*, which literally means *return to the mother*, and may refer to the earlier matrilineal clan system.[150]

Yet it is precisely these characteristics that are considered marks of civilization; so an anthropologist describing a society on the northwest coast of Canada calls it "advanced" because it shows "social stratification, including a hereditary caste of slaves and ranked nobility."[151] The reasons for this way of seeing also require analysis.

## Myths

Mythic suggestions of a moral order prior to patriarchy are, if anything, more widespread than artifactual evidence: that is, there are hundreds of myths, from all over the world, referring to a previous age in which women ruled men.[152] Many of these seem to be vindications of a male takeover—some weakness, cruelty, or "sin" on the part of women that incited men to rebel. Joan Bamberger describes these as "social charter" myths, invented by men to justify their behavior toward women.[153] But the fact that men felt such myths were necessary implies that some change was occurring or had occurred in the social order. If we cannot know precisely how society was arranged before the male takeover, we can at least surmise that it was arranged differently; and the frequency of ascription of blame to women suggests that women had higher status or greater power in the prior arrangement.

Joseph Campbell divides his study of creation myths into four stages: in the first, the world is created by a goddess alone; in the second, the goddess is allied with a consort and the efforts of the pair lead to creation. Next, a male creates the world using the body of a goddess in some way; and finally, a male god alone creates it.[154] It is possible to trace several of these stages in certain mythologies.

The most widely studied myths are those of the Greeks, in which traces of an earlier time and the progressive diminishment of female power are evident.[155] The mythic cycle, which is syncretic—it organizes and blends together myths of different peoples—and which reflects a series of invasions of the Greek territories, depicts a series of usurpations. Many redactions of these myths omit altogether or relegate to insignificance the figure of Ge or Gaea, the first creator. Ge (Earth) creates the universe; she gives birth to a son, Uranus, with whom she mates and produces many children, including the Titans and the Cyclops. Uranus hates his children, however, and imprisons them in Tartarus, the underworld, until Ge rebels and gathers the Titans together to overthrow Uranus. Cronus castrates his father, takes his place as supreme being, and marries his sister Rhea. He knows his eventual overthrow is inevitable, so he swallows his children. Rhea too eventually rebels against this, and when she is about to deliver her sixth child, she goes to Crete and gives birth in a cave to Zeus, who is raised secretly. She returns and gives Cronus a stone to swallow in place of the baby.

When Zeus is grown, a goddess (sometimes Thetis, sometimes Zeus' wife, Metis) gives Cronus a potion that causes him to regurgitate his first five children—Hera, Poseidon, Demeter, Hades, and Hestia. With them Zeus wages war on Cronus and defeats him. In turn he takes his place as supreme being, marrying his sister Hera and dividing the world with his two brothers. Scholars have discovered, however, that at one time Hera was the primary goddess, and that Zeus becomes powerful by marrying her. In time Hera is transformed from a powerful being into a mere consort, a jealous wife, shrewish and scolding.[156]

The great trilogy, the *Oresteia*, of Aeschylus is a dramatic rendering of the power shift from female to male. In *Agamemnon*, Clytemnestra gains control over her husband's city, Argos, by killing him. Although in some versions of the myth Clytemnestra murders Agamemnon because he murdered their daughter Iphigenia, Aeschylus shows her to be motivated mainly by the desire to rule Argos with her lover Aigisthos. Clytemnestra is a powerful character, but the moral tone of the play condemns her and haloes Agamemnon with righteousness, despite his sacrifice of his daughter, despite his bringing back to the palace his captive slave–mistress, Kassandra. Agamemnon's death is seen as part of the working out of an old curse, but Clytemnestra and Aigisthos are reviled by the Chorus. In the second play of the trilogy, the *Choëphoroi* (Libation-Bearers), Clytemnestra's daughter Electra, who has saved her brother Orestes from murder by Aigisthos, urges him to revenge their father's death by killing their mother. He does so, to the approval of the Chorus. In the final play (*Eumenides*), Orestes, having murdered his mother, is pursued by the Erinyes (or Furies), the guardians of mother-right, who intend to punish him for his crime. He is saved by Athene, who commends Apollo's judgment that the father is the true parent of a child, the mother merely the nurse; and thus that murder of a mother—or any woman—is not as serious as the murder of a man, especially a husband. This play opens with mention of the goddess Phoebe, who has freely given her name and her dwelling place to Apollo. Thus in each segment females have considerable power, but good is seen to reside in their giving over that power to males. The Erinyes are transformed into the Eumenides, friends of Athens, and implicitly supporters, like Athene, of the patriarchy.

Over a period, the oracle at Delphi which once belonged to Ge is also taken over by Apollo; the powers of procreation shift from females to males; and the proof of this male power is Athene herself. There are many myths about Athene's birth, but the one which gained currency is that in which she is born from the head of Zeus.[157] Just as the Furies, who were associated with snakes and thus were probably later versions of the regeneration goddess, are transformed into hideous and vengeful creatures, Athene, who was also at one time associated with snakes and the Gorgon, and who is credited with the invention of spinning, weaving, the plow, the yoke, horse taming, and shipbuilding, is transformed into a representation of asexual wisdom at the service of male heroes, and a staunch supporter of everything masculine.

The Garden of Eden that appears in the Old Testament is kin to other gardens of delight, all presided over by females in other mythologies. Eve too is associated with the serpent and with knowledge, a kind of knowledge forbidden by the new patriarchal god. There is a Talmudic tradition that Yahweh must make a sin offering because he has caused the moon (associated with the goddess) to lose its importance.[158] Hera governed the Garden of the Hesperides, which is destroyed by Heracles.

In early Sumerian myth, Siduri rules in a kind of paradise, which is usurped by a sun god. Later, Siduri is diminished, and in the epic of Gilgamesh she is a mere barmaid.[159] In early Sumerian myths, goddesses were the creators of everything. As late as the third millenium, the goddess Nammu, known as "the one who gave birth to heaven and earth," appears without a consort. Eventually, however, gods appear as consorts to the goddesses; eventually male gods alone rule in the Sumerian world. Inanna, a primary Sumerian goddess of vegetation and weather, of morning and evening stars, is demoted to goddess of prostitutes![60] The Babylonian and Assyrian story of creation dates from the second millennium B.C.E., but its translator and editor, Alexander Heidel, asserts that it is not a creation story at all, that its primary purpose is to justify the promotion of Marduk to chief god of the Babylonian pantheon. This accession is accomplished by Marduk's defeat of Tiamat, the divine mother. Heidel concludes that the epic is not just a religious treatise but a political one, and that it was written in a period in which the kingship of Hammurabi and Babylonia's political supremacy were being established![61]

The Norse myths retain memory of a conflict between two sets of gods (and thus two sets of values). The Vanir, the older gods, represented fertility. They were magicians; they permitted marriage between brother and sister; and their primary deity was probably Nerthus, the Earth Mother whom Tacitus described as having been worshiped in Denmark in the first century C.E. In later days, Freyr, god of Plenty, and Freyja, who is the only major goddess left in the existing mythology, represent the Vanir. Kevin Crossley-Holland writes that Freyr "appears to have been a descendant (who somehow changed sex) of Nerthus."[162] The war between the Vanir and the Aesir, war gods, was won by the Aesir, and most memory of the Vanir was obliterated. The Aesir now claim the power of magic, but it is a maternal uncle who teaches Odin his magical songs.[163]

References to females and female representations are rare after the rise to power of a theocratic and later a militaristic-theocratic regime in Mesoamerica, especially among the Aztecs. Some myths, however, reflect an overthrow. One tells of the paradise that existed at the world's beginning, a paradise ruled over by Xochiquetzel, Earth Mother or Precious Flower. Xochiquetzel lives on Coatepec, the world mountain thrust up at the world's beginning; she bore the Huitznahua (the Titans) and the Four Hundred Southerners (the stars). While she is sweeping, a tuft of white feathers falls from heaven. She tucks them under her skirt and becomes pregnant. Her children are ashamed of her (the myth clearly emerges from a patriarchal period) and her daughter, Coyolxanhqui, goddess of the moon in pre-Aztec cultures, a deity who wears tinkling bells, leads her brothers, the Four Hundred, in an attack against Xochiquetzel. The Earth Mother has foreknowledge of this attack, but is reassured by the child in her womb. At the moment of attack, Huitzilopochtli springs from her womb fully accoutered and painted for war. He kills Coyolxanhqui by decapitating her and rolling her body down the mountain so that it breaks. He also destroys and scatters the Four Hundred.[164]

Although this myth seems to refer to a battle between two female deities, it refers, I think, to three periods in Mesoamerican culture: the time ruled by the Earth Mother, long since gone since she is relegated to sweeping; the time ruled by the moon goddess, an avatar of the Earth Mother, also long gone considering the sexual code implicit in the myth; and the present of the myth, ruled by Huitzilopochtli, the sun god to whom human sacrifices were made. A huge disc representing Coyolxanhqui was recently found during the restoration of the Aztec temple in the middle of Mexico City. Her figure is depicted in fragments adorned by bells.

In other versions the primary goddess was Coatlicue, who began time: her name date is the first in the elaborate Aztec calendar she is said to have created. (I have already mentioned the hypothesis that women created mensuration of time by correlating their menstrual periods with the phases of the moon and marking them on stone, possibly as a guide to planting.) Two gods decide to destroy Coatlicue: Quetzalcoatl, the plumed serpent, and Tezxatlipoca, the smoking mirror. After trying various methods and failing, they become snakes and thus destroy her. Her bottom half becomes the sky, her top half sinks down and becomes earth. At night, she cries, and the only thing that quiets her is to be fed human hearts.[165]

In still another version, the Earth Mother is a dreadful goddess who kills her children, but who is overpowered by a heroic son. She is killed by fire but survives as the demanding flint knife, used to cut out hearts in Aztec sacrifices. Mexico means *place of Mecitli*, the great mother. Whatever she may have meant to earlier generations, to the Aztecs she is hideous and bloodthirsty, decapitated in the year 1 Rabbit, the year of the creation of earth, the year of her calendric name. "The Mother and her many forms derived from an early level of Mesoamerican religion. . . . The masculine orientation of later and more warlike societies may then have gone on to elaborate the deathly qualities of the goddess and generally to embellish her ghastliness, perhaps because of an unconscious hostility toward her—perhaps also because of a failing allegiance," writes Burr Cartwright Brundage.[166]

Coatlicue for the later Aztecs is the huge, hideous, and threatening figure depicted in the sculpture that stands in front of the Anthropological Museum in Mexico City. She is the Filth Eater, who wears a skirt of snakes and is responsible for creation and destruction of all life. As Earth, she devours the sun at night and regurgitates it in the morning. She survives as the flint knife, hungry, demanding human sacrifice.[167]

Memories of a former eminence of women appear in myths of tribal cultures as well. In the Western Desert area and central Australia, there are myths about women who live by themselves, rejecting normal family arrangements; another "and much more widespread mythical theme . . . contends that in the creative era women owned and controlled all or some of the most secret-sacred songs, rites, myths, and objects, to the exclusion or partial exclusion of men, but that men reversed this situation through trickery, theft, or persuasion."[168] There is a multitude of such myths: women were conquered and subjugated by men's stealing of trumpets, flutes, and masks in many South American tribes; in the thinking of many African and Melanesian tribes, women invented the religious rituals and the masks but are now forbidden to use them.[169] Papuan initiation rites relate that women were once omnipotent, but men stole the powerful snake grease from them and now own all the power.[170]

The Yanomamo of Brazil and Venezuela recount a creation myth: the upmost layer of the universe is now empty, or void, but it used to contain an old woman, and was *tender*.[171] There are female knowledge/power figures in the myths of the totally male-dominated Chipewyan.[172] The Mbuti, an egalitarian people, have one ritual from which women are excluded, *molima*, a solemn ceremony performed at times of stress or after a death. Men sit around a central fire singing and blowing horns. As the ceremony nears its conclusion, the women break in and take it over. As they do so, they claim they had it first but men stole it from them.[173] A creation myth of the Hausa of northern Nigeria, Niger, and Chad relates that a woman, a black Moses, leads her people out of the wilderness into a promised land which is near water; she founds a kingdom which has a permissive cast, settles there, and establishes the traditions of her people.[174] The idea of a female founder occurs in many African legends and myths. According to the Tiwi, "Pukwi made the country the first time. The sea was all fresh water. She made the land, sea, and islands. She came out of the sky in daytime. She was big as Karslake Island. Like an alligator she was and she was black. . . . Puriti said, 'Don't kill our mother.' But Iriti went ahead and killed her. He struck her on the head. Her urine made the sea salty and her spirit went into the sky."[175] There are myths of female creators ousted by male gods among the Mbuti, in Patagonia among the Onas and the Yahgans, and among the ancient Persians.[176] A Dahomeyan myth relates that the god Mawu created men and women blind and unable to walk. The two wanted to be together, but the man was afraid to attract the attention of Mawu. The woman caught a toad and ate it; its poison sprayed in her eyes and opened them. She moistened leaves and rolled on them toward the man, telling him how to see. He rolled toward her, but forgot to moisten the leaves first, and Mawu heard him. He did not punish the man for stupidity; rather he cursed the woman, claiming that in future she would have to wait for a man to come to her.[177] (This is a typical patriarchal myth, with its demand for absolute obedience and punishment of personal will and gumption.)

Among the Kikuyu, the story runs that once women were cruel warriors, dominant, polyandrists, and jealous to boot, condemning men to death for adultery and other minor offenses. The women were physically stronger than the men, and better warriors. The men decided on a plan for rebellion. On a selected day, all the men copulated with their wives (they seem to have had the power to initiate sex): six months later, all the women were pregnant, and the men took over, established polygamy and prohibited polyandry, and dominated the tribe. The Indians of Tierra del Fuego have a similar tale: among the Ya-mana and the Selk'nam, it is told that once women ruled, and men were submissive and did the housework. The women, under the leadership of Mrs. Moon, ruled through disguises. But Mrs. Moon's husband, Mr. Sun, overheard women talking beneath the disguises and led a rebellion in which the men killed nearly all the women. After that, the men disguised themselves to frighten their future spouses into submission.[178]

In some cases, men's choice of a relation of domination over women is vindicated by claims that women previously dominated men. But many myths depict men choosing domination out of jealousy of female powers symbolized by musical instruments, through rites and ceremonies. Both kinds of "social charter" myth justify present domination of women but also rationalize domination itself as the relational mode.

There is another kind of myth, one which erases the past by transforming it, and this kind is far more insidious than the social charter myths. In transforming myths, figures representing female power are diminished, weakened, or deformed; from benevolent supporters of life they are turned into essentially unmotivated malevolent forces, forces of evil for its own sake. Thus the hideous Medusa, whose glance turned men to stone, was originally a fertility goddess. The snakes that coil around her head once symbolized regeneration but became an image of death, terror, and ugliness. So too Pandora, whose name means *giver of all gifts*, was transformed into the taker of all gifts given, the bringer of all ills. And in Mayan culture, among others, the earth goddess became identified with the jaguar, the animal that humans do not eat but that eats humans.[179]

Social charter myths implicitly ascribe power to women, if only in the past. They can be read as suggesting that the sexes were once equal, or that women once dominated men. Myths transforming or diminishing female figures like Hera elide such suggestions. Instead, they omit the past and transform the character of the female into something venomous, ugly, dark, mysteriously threatening. By erasing any reference to an earlier power or power struggle they make the hostility of these female figures appear unmotivated, a given. Social charter myths at least acknowledge intersexual conflict. Transforming myths do not: thus the evil power of females appears to be biological, natural. Such a procedure penetrates the moral realm and affects an entire society's view of women.

## Customs

The present world almost universally values men more than women; both customs and institutions subordinate women to men. In some societies men have authority over women; in some it is the male line that is remembered or recorded, the male's family that a bride joins. Although in modern industrial society many such customs have vanished, signs of them survive when, for instance, a woman gives up her name for her husband's at marriage, and a child bears only its father's family name.

But beneath the surface, female-centered practices continue, and they appear more clearly in certain cultures than in others. Such appearances were thoroughly researched by Robert Briffault in his 1927 work, *The Mothers.*[180] Using a host of ancient sources and many modern ones, Briffault found thousands of examples of matriliny, matrilocality, and what he interpreted as matriarchy (rule by women over men). He also examined etymologies, which yield information about forgotten customs: for example, the Dene of Alaska call a married man *yeraesta*, which means *he stays with her.*[181] Although some of Briffault's examples do not stand up—mainly because some of his ancient sources are no longer considered valid—and many of the customs he described have vanished, the overwhelming number of them offers persuasive evidence that patriarchal customs are not universal, and were even less so in the past.

The Mexica who gave their name to Mexico are the children of the Earth Mother Mecitli; so too, Chinese clan names are made up of the signs for *woman* and *birth*. In old China people could not marry others with the same clan name and could not leave their property to a person with a different clan name.[182] Early Chinese dynasties traced their descent from women alone, and upper-class Chinese women held high office until the eighth century C.E. Upper-class Japanese imitated the Chinese move toward male dominance, but among lower-class Japanese the wife remained dominant. There was no patrilocal marriage in Japan until the fourteenth century; the husband merely visited the wife in her mother's house. There was no real marriage, only sexual cohabitation. Korean men used to pay homage to their wives every morning.[183]

In ancient Egypt, royalty was passed in the female line, and a few sisters married their brothers. Descent was often traced matrilineally until the Arab conquest in the seventh century. All children belonged to the mother and none was considered "illegitimate." Women also owned the houses, and the word for *wife, nebt-per*, means *ruler of the house*. The Maxims of Ptah-Hotep, a book that dates to 3200 B.C.E., states that husbands must obey their wives, and as late as the Nineteenth Dynasty (1320–1200 B.C.E.), men were seen as boarders in a woman's home.[184]

Herodotus wrote that the Lycians reckoned descent matrilineally. Briffault cites Nicholas of Damascus on Lycian women, who "are more honoured than the men." In some Greek cities, descent was traced matrilineally, and women had the right to own property and to divorce. Early Greek genealogies are mainly "catalogues" of women.[185]

The Hebrew denoting a group of kinsmen is *rahem*, which means *womb*; a tribal subdivision is *batn, belly*, and the word for clan or tribe is the word for mother.[186] To this day Jewishness is inherited through the mother and the prayer for recovery from illness names only the patient and mother.[187] Before the establishment of the Kingdom under David, the Hebrews were organized into matrilineal clans. Only later did they take the names of male ancestors.[188] "The Jewish Rabbis themselves surmised and acknowledged that, originally, the 'four Matriarchs,' Sarah, Rebecca, Rachel, and Leah, had occupied a more important position than the 'three Patriarchs.' "[189] Recently, David Bakan has theorized that the original mothers were Leah, Rachel, Rebekah, Hagar, and Keturah.[190] The tribe of Levi—the priestly group—was actually named after Leah; Israel was originally the tribe of Sarah.[191]

The early Hebrews were also matrilocal, and a contest between matrilocal and patrilocal customs is described in the story of Jacob's struggle with Laban. Samson lives with his wife's people, and Joseph's children by his Egyptian wife belong to her.[192] The marriage canopy still used in Jewish wedding ceremonies is a symbolic reminder of the tent of the woman to which the husband went after marriage.

Sarah *is* Abraham's sister, as he insists when they are in Egypt, but they have been permitted to marry because they had different mothers.[193] (In many cultures, having the same father is not considered kinship.) The story of Jacob, Esau, and Rebekah also reflects a struggle over changing customs; it was Rebekah, not Isaac, who had the right to give the blessing: she had mother-right.[194]

Mongols and Tatars retain in their names signs of a foremother, and in marriage the groom pays a bride price and the bride supplies the house—evidence of an earlier matrilocality.[195] At the time of the rise of Islam, when patriarchy was fully established, Arab genealogists recognized that the ancient clans were matrilineal, even as they tried to exhibit patrilineal descent.[196] Queens were powerful for a long time in the Arab world, and a man who desires a divorce speaks the equivalent of "I will no longer drive thy flocks to pasture," words that suggest women owned the property that men tended. The Bedawi of Arabia and other Arab tribes were matrilocal into the early decades of the twentieth century.[197]

There is evidence of female descent among the Teutons and the Celts; the latter were also matrilocal. In early Scotland the Picts were matrilineal and matrilocal, and a man's property passed, on his death, to his sister's children.[198] The Eskimos of Labrador are matrilocal, and male Berings of Kodiak take their wives' names at marriage. Many American Indians are matrilineal, and some are matrilocal as well. These customs survive among various peoples in South America, Africa, Malaysia, and New Guinea.[199]

Briffault believed that the shift to patrilineality and patrilocality may have resulted from the emergence of surplus, profit, and the accumulation of property, which men desired to transmit to their own rather than their sisters' children. Thus in some places, like Dahomey and among the Tlinkits of Alaska, wealthy classes are patrilineal while poorer classes are matrilineal.[200]

Briffault also offers a wealth of evidence of women in positions of status and in activities from which they have long since been barred. Queens led armies and practiced diplomacy, women were warriors and hunters, healers and chieftains, serious scholars and artists. To say this is not to hypothesize a matriarchal period, but rather to point to a past time in which numerous women had more freedom and power than they have at the present time in many places in the world. This is partly because women of upper-class families have sometimes been able to exercise power in cultures in which family is important. As aristocratic families became less powerful over the course of Western civilization, so did women.

## 5. CONTEMPORARY GATHERERS, HUNTERS, AND HORTICULTURALISTS

Ideally, this section would offer a complete survey of the ways of life and thought of people who still live in the old way, by gathering, hunting, and horticulture. But their number, their variety, and the amount of research that has been done on them make that impossible. In 1949, G. P. Murdock identified 175 societies as living in this way; later anthropological researches have increased this number considerably.[201] Nor is it possible to draw generalized conclusions about these groups. Some have been studied rather fully; some are little known; and in every case, what we know about these societies depends upon the interests and biases of those who studied them.

In all these groups, women give birth to babies and raise them; in many, but not all, men are deeply involved with the group's children. In none of them do women rule over men; in some, men rule over women, and in many, men have higher status than women. All these groups live by sharing, although some are more cooperative and others more competitive. War is rare in these societies. All have some division of labor by sex, but this division ranges from a flexible one with fluid interchange to an extremely rigid one having the force of taboo. And in just about every group, whatever men do or produce is valued more highly than what women do or produce, even though what a man does in one society is done by a woman in another society. In most societies, it is not the thing done, nor the object produced, but the sex of the doer that confers distinction upon act or product.

Michelle Rosaldo summarizes the various ways in which the contribution made by men to a society is more highly valued than that made by women: in some groups, men grow yams and women sweet potatoes, and yams are the prestige food; in others, the food grown by women is the staple of the group's diet, but the meat occasionally contributed by the men is the valued food.[202] In other groups, behavior is enjoined upon women—they are required to defer, or are infantilized—that diminishes them in relation to men. For example, in preindustrial Europe, spinning and weaving were women's work. When the loom was improved in the High Middle Ages, making it more expensive, weaving became men's work—although many women continued to do it.[203] Tibetan nomads believe that women are incapable of managing needle and thread; among them, women weave the cloth but men do all the spinning.[204] Rosaldo concludes that the relation of a woman to her child is consuming; and that men, lacking such a relation, put their energies into broader associations which become the public realm. The relation of women to children is intimate and private; men, functioning in separateness and among peers, appear more important, at least to themselves, and sometimes to women as well.[205]

A number of studies of matrilineal and patrilineal groups have examined them for cooperation, competition, and overall ethos.[206] The consensus is that matrilineal societies are almost always "accommodating and integrative," whereas patrilineal societies are usually competitive within and without the group.[207] Under patriliny, individuals or cadres quarrel or compete with each other, and the society as a whole quarrels or competes with other societies.

Matrilineal societies are noncompetitive about land and its fruits. They flourish when the population remains stable, and they promote stability.[208] They tend to be cooperative, to work together for a common end, and to foster an ethic of assisting others toward their private ends. In matrilineal societies there are more sexually integrated activities and more sexual freedom for women. Such groups retain feminine creation symbolism in their myths and rituals and raise their children with love and nurturance given by both parents and by the mother's brother(s) as well.[209]

Patrilineal societies lack feminine creation symbolism and depict the world as created by a male god alone. Yet in many such groups fathers do not take part in rearing and socializing children but are distant, controlling, and demand complete obedience and deference from their children. They consider women fully inferior and the culture as a whole is characterized by suspicion, competition and sexual antagonism.[210] As Martin and Voorhies point out, cross-cultural studies show that patrilineal groups tend to be acquisitive and divisive.[211]

Although in matrilineal groups women are the focus of the entire social structure, women do not necessarily have public power. Relations among women determine those among men, but positions of authority are consistently assigned to elder males, and if women have influence or power, it is behind the scenes.[212] But patrilineal and patrilocal societies are more likely to be more male supremacist than matrilineal groups.

Matriliny more than patriliny leads to sexually equal or at least symmetrical systems. Elise Boulding argues that matriliny is unacceptable because it involves instability of marriage, and she offers examples showing a greater incidence of divorce or separation of partners in matrilineal groups.[213] But there is nothing sacrosanct about a sexual or marriage tie. The greater stability of marriage in patrilineal groups often arises not from choice but from coercion.

For some examples of the various sociopolitical systems, we will glance at five groups that live, or once lived, in the old way: an egalitarian one, the Mbuti; the Iroquois (and other American Indian tribes), who come as close to being matriarchal as any group known; the Chipewyan, who are male-dominated; some separatist societies; and the Australian Aborigines, about whom there is a huge mass of conflicting evidence: most Aboriginal groups are male supremacist; many are matrilineal; and yet all are in some ways egalitarian.

The Mbuti, studied by Colin Turnbull, are a generally egalitarian people. For these Pygmies who live in northeast Zaire, gender is important only at the adult stage of life. They have one word for elders, whether male or female—*tata;* one word for younger people, whether female or male—*miki;* and one word for peers—*apua'i.* Yet procreation and childraising are the centers of Mbuti life, and womanhood is equated with motherhood.[214]

The Mbuti are hunters, and all "real" males hunt—there are men who do not, but they are classified as clowns. Women hunt as well, but only with the men; women also gather. The people live and work within their permissive environment without trying to control it.[215] Arrangements are made so that as soon as young people become sexual, they may act sexual, although with certain controls exercised by the women. For some reason, it seems that no woman ever becomes pregnant before she is married.[216] When a woman gives birth, she remains sequestered for three days, then rejoins the hunt or other activities. She may take her child with her or go on a half-day hunt leaving the baby in the camp.

There is, however, a taboo on sexual intercourse between husband and wife for three years after a birth. The husband is permitted to return to the embraces of the young women, or to have an affair with a married woman (although sometimes this causes disruption); the wife seems to feel no lack. This taboo guarantees that the new baby will have a good start in life before the possibility of another pregnancy and the loss of mother's milk, but Turnbull feels it to be a source of hurt and resentment among the men.

The Mbuti have a beautiful fatherhood ceremony, however. When a baby is two years old, the mother carries it to the father, who is seated alone in the center of the compound. The father has had minimal relations with the child up to this time. He takes the child and holds it to his breast. The baby tries to suck, and begins to cry *ema!* (mother!). The father then gives the child its first solid food and teaches it to say *eba* (father). Thus, Turnbull writes, "all males are first perceived by their children as 'another kind of mother,' one who cannot give milk but does provide other kinds of food. The importance of this is inestimable."[217]

There is nothing sentimental about the Mbuti, however. They are a lively, open people who enjoy bantering with and teasing each other. They have a dramatic ritual, *ekokomea*, a transvestite dance, in which the women mock the male penis and the men mock the women's menstruation.[218] The !Kung, too, openly tease each other about their sexual organs, although males seem to come in for most of the mockery.[219]

Another society that seems to have been harmonious is that of the Iroquois. Because of the records kept by Jesuits who visited with them in the seventeenth and eighteenth centuries, considerable information about their earlier way of life has been preserved. They lived for centuries in what is now northern New York State, and were originally a horticultural people. They lived in sturdy frame longhouses shared by a few dozen families. They were matrilinear, matrifocal, and "matrimonial"—that is, the fruits of the land passed by mother-right from mother to daughter. The women farmed, foraged, and collected herbs for medicine. The men hunted. Some researchers believe that for long periods the Iroquois lived peaceably; others think the high degree of female autonomy and internal political control was a consequence of men being away, at war or trapping, much of the time. The women controlled the distribution of goods in the longhouses, and seem to have been dominant. As in all matrilineal cultures, marriages were easily dissolved when either mate was unhappy.[220]

At some point, however, warfare developed among the Iroquois, and they established a Council of Elders to treat among the clans. This council was made up entirely of men. The women elected their male representative to the council—a choice that could be vetoed by the council—and could warn and even impeach him if his actions did not please them.

Many other peoples among the American Indians have lived or live today like this—the Huron, and the Montagnais-Maskapi of Labrador and eastern Canada. These peoples live in lodges shared by several nuclear families. All the able-bodied hunt, fish, and trap or snare. All cook, but the women do the daily cooking. Children are cared for by women, but men are loving parents and there is group responsibility for children. Women make most of the decisions and do most of the work, but there is little quarreling, much bawdy talk and play, and harmony.[221]

The Chipewyan, who live in northwest Canada, provide a considerable contrast. These people live almost entirely on fish, moose, and caribou: fish and game provide 90 percent of their diet. The area they inhabit contains almost no vegetation. The women are not permitted to hunt with the men; they hunt only if the men are absent and they are hungry. Nevertheless, the women work extremely hard at unpleasant tasks: they process all the food and all the skins the men bring back to camp. This involves cutting, boning, and drying—over open fires whose smoke rises continually into their faces—of fish and game; and treating the pelts. These arduous tasks require skill, knowledge, and patience.

Despite their contribution to the life of the tribe, Chipewyan women have low status within it, both individually and symbolically. Women are excluded from all activities considered male, and from the major male pursuit, a mystical concept of knowledge that is also power. Chipewyan men believe in animate beings who reveal only to men a knowledge that is power. The revelation comes in dreams, and although there are female "deities" who confer this knowledge/power, no woman can receive it. Male knowledge/power gives them control in all important areas—hunting, healing, sorcery, and sports (races and gambling). They also receive, with the knowledge/power, a resistance to physical degeneration with aging.[222] (This belief may be the consequence of an actual difference in appearance between men and women: men have a great deal of leisure; when they do work, they exert themselves physically in the open air, hunting. The women are almost always involved in preserving food, breathing in all day for weeks at a time the smoke of drying fires; or in giving birth, suck, and care to children.)

Among the Chipewyans, as in most hunting societies, activity is intermittent, seasonal, dependent on the times the animals run. Thus in most groups it is seen as subject to magical control, and a hunter who experiences a run of bad luck may stop hunting for a month or more. Men are frequently at home in these societies. In some they care for the children; in others they visit and gossip, dance or gamble. Chipewyan men gather herbs and gamble. Chipewyan women rebel against their inferiority and blame the men for idleness or a shortage of meat. They complain and put pressure on the men to go hunting, but also blame them when they fail. And women can threaten to destroy men. Simply by touching them, a woman can ruin a man's store of medicinal plants or destroy the potency of his rifle. When she is menstruating she can, by stepping over something, destroy its power or ruin luck.

Whatever happens on the hunt, Chipewyan men attribute the results to their power. If the hunt is successful, the men's faith in their power/knowledge is reaffirmed, and the women's belief that they must pressure men is reinforced. If it is a failure, men assert that these things are mystical, impervious to women's urging and defiant of men's strong physical effort. Women are reinforced in their doubt of the men's vaunted power/knowledge.[223]

Some tribes live segregated existences. The Keresan Indians of New Mexico, descendants of the oldest settled horticulturalists in North America, are matrilineal and matrilocal; their land is passed on from mother to daughter. The women live separately in their households with the children; the girls remain there all their lives, but boys, at a certain age, undergo initiation into maleness and join the men in their Kivas, ceremonial moieties that organize ceremonial and governmental functions. Men and women copulate at will, but that's about all they do together. The men run the "public" side of things, the women run the household, arrange marriages, and raise the children.[224]

The Tchambuli of New Guinea live primarily by fishing and manufacture, and trade the products of these activities for vegetables. The women do the fishing and make the most important manufacture, plaited mosquito bags, two of which will purchase an ordinary canoe. They also raise the children and run the households, where they live with the children. The women live in an atmosphere of solidarity, friendship, and cooperation, and are, according to Margaret Mead, cheerful, industrious, and energetic.[225]

The men live together in ceremonial clan houses. They collect their own firewood and do their own cooking. Skilled artists, they make elaborate masks and personal ornaments. Now that they can buy iron tools, they make their own canoes. They live in extreme competition with each other, full of jealousy and suspicion; frequently a man who feels slighted will simply pick up and move to another clan group.[226]

The Zuni of New Mexico also have a segregated culture. The women dominate the household, living in matrilineal clan houses. The men come and go, but "in the things that count most in Zuni life, in matters of ritual, the man is an outsider in the house of his wife. His most permanent ties are with the house of his sister."[227] Men are deeply involved with their sisters' children. Divorce is simple but most marriages last.

The Zuni have been agricultural since prehistory. At some point the men gained economic independence by sheepherding and sons can inherit sheep from their fathers. These tribes are wealthy, but their wealth is fluid, and they frown on excessive concentration of wealth. They own, but often lend and share, and it is the cooperative people who are respected in the community.[228]

The men mainly occupy themselves with esoteric societies which women rarely join because of the heavy ceremonial responsibilities involved. The men must spend most of their time memorizing rituals and performing ceremonies; maintaining these responsibilities is a matter of status, keeping face. The esoteric societies are dominated by a priestly hierarchy.[229]

There is archeological evidence of continuity in Aboriginal life dating back forty thousand years.[230] Over the century or more in which they have been studied, the Australian Aborigines have received diverse interpretations. Only one judgment seems to stand unchallenged through all that time: the work of the women provides the "chief basis of the economy."[231] Early descriptions gave the impression of cruel, even sadistic treatment of women, an impression not fully borne out by later researchers. Males do try to beat up their wives, but women do not submissively accept punishment; they counterattack with their fighting sticks, owned by all wives and brandished with great skill. Moreover, if a woman finds her husband lazy or unlucky, she may initiate attack "with both tongue and tomahawk."[232]

Marriage customs are oppressive. Marriages are arranged; wives are bought by older men who have earned enough money to pay for them and who have pressed their suit with the girl's mother for years. The society is polygynous, and the older men corner the market in women, not only because of their comparative wealth but because there is a high rate of female infanticide.[233] Aborigine women seem to have freedom in their sex lives, however, and will often abort themselves in an effort to postpone motherhood because it would interfere with their sex lives.[234] Nevertheless, Aborigine society lives by reciprocity and cooperation.[235] The understanding that marriage is a mutual economic arrangement and that cooperation between husband and wife is essential to the well-being of both is of central importance in Aborigine life.[236]

Severe initiation rites for men maintain social control over young men, and males dominate the ceremonial life of the Aborigines. But women have their own secret cults and rituals (a part of which is knowledge of how to perform an abortion) and an important religious life of their own, according to Catherine Berndt, who has studied and lived among this people for many years. Still, the oppressiveness of Aborigine marriage customs is felt by men as well as women.[237]

The picture drawn by Richard Gould in his Yiwara, however, skims past the institutions and depicts the daily life of a small group of Aboriginal people.[238] Living in the isolation of a desert, these people keep themselves and their relatives alive, and derive satisfaction from having done so by their own knowledge and skill. They have "deep feelings of belonging to a harmoniously ordered universe" in which they are participants, not controllers.[239]

In the morning the women go gathering. They take their digging sticks and place large, deep wooden bowls filled with water in a loop on their heads. They put a twist of grass in the bowls to keep them from sloshing. They take the children, the dogs, and a lighted firestick which they will use to communicate with each other. They walk for many miles. They and the children gradually drink the water; then the women fill the bowls with fruits and vegetables. The children help and the women praise them generously. They work swiftly, with an eye on the weather. They understand the weather; they must get back to camp before the hot winds spring up.

If the gathering is not good, the women will go out again later in the day when the sun is cooler. But usually the gathering is good and they return laden and spend the rest of the day until dark grinding the vegetables.[240] In other environments, Aborigine women hunt with dogs they have raised and trained with great affection; they bring down small game and even kangaroos.[241] Like the !Kung women of the Kalahari, Aborigine women can discriminate among hundreds of edible and inedible species of plants at various stages of their life cycle.[242]

Aboriginal men go off hunting in their own groups, taking their spears and spear throwers. They walk only a short distance and, on the day Gould describes, come back empty-handed. They find a lizard and carry it to camp, triumphant: "This small catch has redeemed the hunting trip."[243] The men spend the rest of the day in idleness. "For all their talk about this or that kangaroo they once killed, or the pros and cons of a particular spot for hunting, the men contribute relatively little to the subsistence of the group."[244] While the women grind the vegetables, the men go off to where they store their secret cache of sacred objects, objects having to do with the hunt, with cult life, their totems. The women are not permitted to go near these objects or know anything about them. These rituals, however, are not intended to control the environment in any way, but rather to help the men to become at one with it.[245] The men are more prestigious; the women are more necessary; both, according to Gould, are content.[246]

## 6. THE BEGINNING OF THE END

Yes, there was a garden, and in it we gathered fruits and vegetables and sang to the moon and played and worked together and watched the children grow. For the most part life was good, and we made art and rituals celebrating our participation in the glorious spectacle and process of life within nature. We were bound to the goddess who was immanent in nature, in the vegetation and the moon, mistress of the animals, who fed us freely—most of the time. Death was terrible, but in it the goddess received us again, and we returned to the process of eternal recurrence, still part of the chain of life.

But the garden was not Eden. Flourishing with nature's bounty, we grew in numbers and the fruits of gathering grew thin, the game disappeared. Sometimes the river dried up and we trekked for miles in search of water. There may have been times when we did not find it, and another group embarked on the same search found our parched bodies and saw visions of their own fate. One year a frost arrived early and ruined the vegetables we thought would see us through the winter; a flood killed our kin in the valley; a storm flattened our village.

We saw and understood and remembered. We prayed to the goddess to find solutions to the precariousness of the human state, modes of lessening our terror. The goddess—or the naturally endowed imagination of human beings—responded, with ideas about ways of protecting human well-being. People polished the stones they used to cut vegetables and learned to sharpen those they used for butchering game. For reasons we can only guess, they decided to plant crops and tend them, instead of simply returning each year at the proper season for the flowering of a patch of grain. They decided to settle in a particular spot—although not all peoples did this, and some remain more or less nomadic to this day. They built houses of stone; they stored vats of oil and grain in the earth to keep them cool. Perhaps they dug wells, or dammed a stream, imitating the beavers.

With each step, as I have suggested, the relations of humans to nature altered slightly. The hunting of animals in an organized way had to transform the mind-set of humans: from a sense of full participation in a grand cosmic balance of plantation, creatures, and weather, they must have moved a little distance from the creatures they hunted. Animals hunt for food too, it is true, but their hunting is not planned, and animals hunt selectively, each kind having a limited range of diet. Humans eat everything—except jaguar: mammals, rodents, birds, fish, even insects. This distance from animals of all sorts placed enmity between humans and other creatures: seeing them as objects for acquisition, humans could no longer feel an easy fellowship with animals. Indeed, the Mbuti believe they are the children of the forest, and were immortal until one of them killed his brother antelope. They will continue to die until they can learn not to kill.[247]

Yet the Mbuti have a far closer relation with nature than other societies, especially our own. They kill animals only when they must, and they never kill each other.[248] And hunting began about two or two and a half million years ago. The separation of humans from nature that led to patriarchy was not caused by hunting.

Horticulture too must have increased the distance between humans and nature: no farmer loves the weather. Nature is more enemy than friend to those whose hard labors can be eradicated by a single storm or too long a drought. Attitudes toward nature are of course always ambivalent: nature has both benevolent and malevolent aspects, both highly subjective. People love and hate nature, but those who grow crops fear nature in a way others do not. A goddess of nature, a principle of fertility, might seem more fearsome to horticulturalists than to gatherers. The domestication of animals also reinforces the importance of control over manipulable nature.

It may be that discovery of the male role in procreation was the triggering event that brought together isolated or divergent elements into a new "philosophy," a new way of perceiving experience. For millennia men had felt marginal to the miraculous business of generation, and to the social and economic life that arose from it—the care and feeding of the group. Suddenly they were aware that in fact they were part of the process. It may even have seemed that they caused it, since no one could see the active physiological processes occurring within women's bodies. Men planted the seed: who knew that it took *two* seeds to make a baby? Women were indeed closer to nature than men; they were like the earth—rich, fertile, but empty unless a seed took root in it. Men could control procreation without the burden of carrying a fetus inside their bodies, the danger and pain of giving birth, the continual bond to a nursing infant.

However or whenever it occurred, in whatever places it did occur, over whatever span of time, humans came to see themselves in a new light, a radically different light from before. Their self-definition changed. And the new definition was the foundation stone and the *raison d'être* for patriarchy.

# CHAPTER TWO

# The Fall: Patriarchy

In the beginning was the Mother; the Word began a new era, one we have come to call patriarchy. The word, a symbol, an arbitrary and abstract entity, can give reality to something nonexistent, invented, imagined. That women have babies is a reality (although it may not always be one; experiments with DNA and ex utero conception may alter it); they also generally take care of them. We may choose to see birth and mother love as great powers—as do people in simple cultures—or as vulnerabilities, sources of weakness and dependency—as do people in complex cultures like our own. However we see them, the facts remain.

Male dominance is not a reality in this sense. It is not necessary. There are cultures and situations in which males are not dominant. Men are not always stronger than women, nor does the rule of might lead to male dominance per se, but to the domination of certain individuals, males and females (unless females are purposely excluded by consensus of the males), over all others. Rule of might overlaps with male dominance but is not identical with it. Males are not dominant *by nature*, or they would *always* be dominant, in the way females *always* have the babies. In one sense, patriarchy is an attempt to make male dominance a "natural" fact.

Patriarchy is, however, a reality in our world, so much so that many people cannot imagine any other way of organizing human life. They believe humans have *always* organized themselves as they do now in the West. To analyze patriarchy, it is necessary to look at its origin; but to do that, one must first allow the possibility that it *had* one, that some form of male superiority or supremacy has not been a permanent fixture of protohuman and human life. Chapter One presents a survey of the evidence for a different human adaptation. This chapter will offer hypotheses as to why and how patriarchy developed, and evidence of its underlying attitudes, the emotional/intellectual bases on which the structures of patriarchy are erected.

## 1. THEORIES ON THE ORIGIN OF PATRIARCHY

Toward the end of the nineteenth century and into the twentieth, various thinkers began to posit a prepatriarchal age in which women "ruled": matriarchy. J. J. Bachofen wrote on mother-right; Robert Briffault culled ancient texts for signs of either rule by women or women having control in a huge number of societies; Elizabeth Gould Davis presented a picture of an ancient world ruled almost totally by women.[1] Anthropological studies demonstrated that kinship and sexual systems varied across the world; this knowledge inspired Lewis Henry Morgan, who in turn inspired the theories of Frederick Engels.[2]

Engels shared Marx's belief that division of labor ruined primitive communism. Division of labor led to specialization, which in turn led, in certain occupations—cattle breeding, metalworking, and agriculture, for example—to production of an excess, something left over after subsistence needs had been met. This surplus, or profit, could be used for exchange, or, in a later period of centralized government, to provide for a ruling class, a class not required to work. However used, surplus gave rise to the notion of property. When descent was reckoned matrilineally, a man's property passed to his sister's children. Engels hypothesizes that the simple shift to patrilineal descent, which permitted a man to leave his property to his own children, amounted to the "world historical defeat of the female sex," and led to the degradation of women.[3]

Another argument based on the existence of an excess is that possession of a surplus led to storage of grain, oil, jewelry, metals, and that the existence of such stores aroused the greed of others. Greed coupled with aggression led to war, and thus to male supremacy.

The problem with these arguments, like Lévi-Strauss's notions about women as objects of exchange in a male system of alliances, is that they leave women out.[4] They take as a given that women were in this early period passive obedient creatures who could be decreed to. Why should property be considered a male prerogative when women also produce, when in matrilineal cultures land is passed in a female line, when, even in male-supremacist hunting cultures, the meat belongs to the male only until it is brought into the house or clearing, at which point it becomes the property of the female? Why should matrilineal descent not involve the degradation and enslavement of the male, but patrilineal descent inevitably cause the degradation and enslavement of the female? Why would the notion of patrilineal descent even occur to people, when there is certitude only about female parentage? The use of an excess to build up private property is frowned on in most simple societies, even those which exhibit male superiority. It is not clear that human greed for things was always greater than human reverence for life. It is clear that women have been great warriors: war need not *necessarily* lead to male supremacy. Nevertheless, because patriarchy has been throughout its history so connected with and centered on property, the association of the two remains vital.

Many theories associate the origin of patriarchy with hunting. The simple version of this runs: women were encumbered with babies and could not hunt; men who hunted were trained in aggression and the use of weapons; eventually they turned both against women.[5] Marvin Harris elaborates on this theory by positing meat as an absolute human need. Because of this, hunters became the most valued members of their cultures. Hunting, however, led inevitably to competition and war as populations grew and meat became scarce; and war leads inevitably to the degradation and enslavement of women.[6]

Again, these theories suffer from cultural blindness: because domination seems a good to us now (some of us anyway), we assume it seemed a good in past millennia. But if—as I believe—matricentric life was contented and rich, if men were not degraded within it, why would they wish to destroy the arrangement, to harm and inflict suffering on the mothers, sisters, mates, and children they loved, to substitute estrangement for mutuality and trust?

There are other objections to Harris's theory. His assumption that meat is an absolute human need is not supported by fact: many cultures live peaceably and contentedly with very little meat in their diets. It is true that most humans enjoy meat, however; and thus possible that hunters were highly valued. But in that case both female and male hunters should have enjoyed superior prestige, and this is not the case. Nor are extant hunting cultures notably competitive or warlike; they are far less so than large industrial states with heavy meat consumption. It may be true, as Eleanor Leacock believes, that the most egalitarian cultures are those in which both sexes contribute to food production, but it is also true that males (but not females) have higher status even in cultures in which they contribute very little to the support of the society.[7]

Nevertheless, some connection between hunting and male dominance seems likely. Strong male dominance characterizes hunting peoples whose diets are almost entirely animal, who live in far northern areas where there is little vegetable food.[8] It is widely believed that the male-god-worshiping Indo-Europeans who swept down into the Mediterranean in the fourth millennium B.C.E. and to India in later millennia came originally from such northern wastes.[9]

It is likely that all these factors had some effect on the change in social organization. I hypothesize a very gradual process of development of the social structure we now call patriarchy. Let us recapitulate some of the points made in Chapter One.

The structure of matricentry was loose: families clustered around a mother or set of mothers (sisters), who had strong bonds with their children, especially with daughters, who probably remained with the mother throughout her life. Men were marginal in the matriliny; the closest bond for men was with their mates and the children of their sisters.

Most of the work of the group was done by women, as it still is in simple societies. They took responsibility for their children and, by extension, for the entire group. They provided most of the food, built the houses, and were the primary educators of the young. Again, men were marginal. They may have helped with certain heavy tasks; they may have hunted and provided meat. Both contributions were valued, but men had far more free time than women. They devoted much of this free time to caring for their weapons and for the instruments used in their hunting cults, from which they probably excluded women.

A degree of distance had opened between humans and their environment as a result of increasing controls exercised over nature, controls that led humans to feel alien from nature. A sense of separation frequently arouses hostility, regardless of which party was responsible for the separation. Distance and strangeness arouse fear, which causes enmity. In addition, nature had always been feared as well as loved; the sun can be an enemy, and rain can be a friend.

Once people were planting their own crops, their relationship with nature became even more fraught with anxiety: a drought or a storm can wipe out weeks of labor. If the habit of wandering to gather food had been broken, bad weather could present a group with the prospect of a hungry season.

Finally, the discovery of the male role in procreation must have been of extreme importance to the attitudes of matricentric groups. The male role can be interpreted as a controlling one: a "shudder in the loins" that brought ecstasy to a man was all that was required of him to procreate: the woman bore the entire burden after that. Possibly men began to see women not as miraculous bearers of babies but as the soil, as a mere receptacle (so it may have seemed) for male seed which by itself engendered the new growth.

Over centuries, perhaps, these ideas led to the emergence of a new value: *the idea of control.* The idea of control is not the same as the exercise of control. A small child exercises control when it first walks or speaks; animals exercise control when they build nests or dams, when a chimpanzee, say, uses a digging stick. But they do not abstract control itself as a value. To value control, *power-over,* means that any form of control seems a good simply because it is a control. It is valued simply because it exists more than for what it accomplishes or creates.

Because men believed they had the controlling role in procreation, and because the gods of their hunting cults were in some sense already controlling gods, men began to worship a transcendent deity, a god who was not part of nature, like the old immanent goddess, but who had power over nature without being part of it. A transcendent god is not subject to what he creates; he controls it without participating in it. The mere idea that such a power could exist is astonishing, for early people must necessarily have been aware that any manipulation reverberates not just on the object but on the subject as well.

It seems likely therefore that the new value was established slowly and shakily; possibly a small group of men held it as their secret, a mystery/hunting-cult god of power. Adherents of the new god would have defined themselves in the god's image: that is, they would have identified themselves with their deity, as beings separate from and with control over nature. In addition, the idea of control is contagious: if a person is interested in power without reference to any other value, he or she will be able to gain power relatively easily over those who are not interested in it. For example, if two people mate, and one wants power over the other, domination, and the other wants love, the former will perceive all acts of the latter in terms of conquest or submission. Whatever the latter does will be turned into part of a contest. The person who wants love will have only two options—to abandon the relation entirely or to play the game. The same thing is true on a larger political scale: if one state desires power over other states, states which wish to live in peace and freedom will be overrun. They have to learn to value power or be eradicated.

It is likely that the new value was for a long time attached to religious cults that tried to gain adherents by demonstrating some form of superior power over the people of their group or over other deities. It is also likely that the small group of adherents became the god's priests, and attempted to convert men, rather than women, to the new religion. For it was men who had something to gain from it, or so it seemed. The priesthood may have advocated patriliny or patrilocal marriage, for instance.

Because women had for millennia been associated with nature, had been seen as having a special relation with it to which men were marginal, the new value gave men a centrality and power they had lacked. In addition, since the new god was transcendent, having power over nature without being touched by it, those who worshiped him claimed the same position: as their deity had power over the earth, men had power over creatures of the earth, animals and women.

It is not to be imagined that women accepted subordinate status peaceably. Moreover, it is difficult for any human group to prove it is transcendent. Men do not, of course, have any more control over nature than women do. If men's physiological functions are less visible than those of women, who menstruate, get pregnant, and lactate, men are equally limited by their greater vulnerability to death and disease in every decade of life, and their inability to control their own sexual organ. Indeed, the marginality of the male is biological. This unpleasant fact is the equivalent of the unpleasant fact that women bear the burden of racial continuation. Males are more fragile than females throughout life. Although more males than females are conceived—110 to 100—and more are born—104 to 100—by the second year of life the sexes are numerically equal, and men die younger than women in every subsequent decade of life. A famished woman is more likely spontaneously to abort a male than a female fetus.[10]

There are natural reasons for this imbalance. In times of hardship the purposes of the species—survival and continuation—are served by the production of more females than males. Human females carry their young for many months; they give birth to one at a time, as a rule; and they must devote themselves rather completely to the feeding, protection, and education of the young for many years before the children are capable of independent survival. The continuation of the species requires that many females survive to produce and raise the young, and that they limit their pregnancies.

However, a single male can impregnate many females: there is need—and room—for only one cock in a barnyard.[11] Matricentric social structure reflected this biological situation. The new structure, early patriarchy, was not a modification but a reversal of this arrangement and its morality. In positing that men were superior to nature and women, it was reversing traditional values. Women's generative processes, once seen as superior to men's, were degraded, diminished precisely because of their supposed closeness to nature. The marginality of men in the work life of matricentric groups was reinterpreted, seen as freedom, a life of volition. To accomplish these reversals of traditional values, it was not necessary to change anything in the life people led. Rather like women meeting in consciousness-raising groups in the 1960s, men may have spoken together secretly at cult meetings, rethinking the attitudes they inherited. Change came later. When the cults were large and strong enough to attempt to impose their attitudes on the group, men's larger musculature may have provided them with their single unanswerable argument. But before men could be willing to use their strength in this way, they must have been convinced that only by dominating women could they prove themselves "men," according to the new definition.

The period in which the first groups of people made the transition from matricentry to male superiority may have been complicated by an increase in population in the Middle East. This increase would have necessitated a new political structure, one that could encompass and harmonize many small autonomous clans or tribes living in close proximity. This period, which so far as we know preceded the invention of writing, may have been extremely contentious. Certainly the earliest written records of a patriarchal state, Sumer, refer to events of great violence. And marks of conflict are on patriarchy, implanted in its assumptions and its customs. In this chapter we will examine some of these marks.

Patriarchy is not universal, nor is male dominance. The more isolated a culture remains, the more likely it is to be egalitarian. An egalitarian group, the Tasaday, was found in the jungles of the Philippines some years ago; another recently discovered group is the Waorani, an Amazonian people in eastern Ecuador. They have lived in isolation for thousands of years, and after eight years of research among them, anthropologists report they are completely egalitarian, although they have a fixed division of labor.[12] But most societies endow men with some kind of superiority over women. There are degrees of male dominance, however. Discussion of these degrees will lead into a discussion of the reversals of value that occurred in the creation of patriarchy.

In some cultures men have greater prestige than women, in some there is male domination of women, and some are patriarchal. Often all three are lumped together as showing male dominance, but the three types exhibit great differences. Anthropologists define male dominance variously. It has been described as preferential access to prestigious activities.[13] Such a definition makes virtually all societies male-dominant, even some which are essentially egalitarian. A "male-supremacist complex" has been defined as a set of institutions showing "asymmetrical frequencies of sex-linked practices and beliefs," a set that includes all institutions or customs that favor or emphasize the male—reckoning of descent, post-marriage residence, marriage forms, occupations, and social roles.[14] This definition would encompass many simple and all complex societies without discriminating among them. Peggy Reeves Sanday offers two criteria for male dominance: the exclusion of women from political and economic decision making, and male aggression against women in any form—from cultural idealization of macho maleness, to exclusionary practices, to actual institutionalized or traditional male violence against women. This definition can serve as a standard by which to measure male dominance in a given society. However, it yields unclear results, as societies in which women possess some political or economic power may also feature considerable male aggression against women.[15]

Defining "male dominance" is complicated by two factors: first, even societies in which men are not aggressive toward women, or in which women have some worldly power, manifest what Susan Carol Rogers has called the "myth of male dominance."[16] That is, in many cultures the men and women seem to have made a bargain: women agree to call men more important, and allow them to monopolize public authority and prestige, while they, running the household, the farm, or small shop, possess most of the real power in village life. Such a bargain was probably at the root of male superiority, and is common enough even in modern households in industrial nations. It is enshrined in a joke about division of responsibility in a family: she makes the small decisions—how to spend their money, where they should live, how the children will be educated; while he makes the large ones—such as should the United States recognize Communist China.

Second, since those of us who study this problem come from male-dominant cultures in which the standard for everything (except gynecological functions) is male, we carry our standards with us in investigating other cultures. Even some feminists seem to perpetuate this standard, and judge equality as the achievement by women and minorities of what males already possess. Such a perspective is inadequate in perceiving the moral and sociopolitical structures of certain societies.

A more useful standard in describing varied societies might be an examination of the kinds and degree of controls exerted over nature. It is likely that the more highly control is valued in a given society, the greater will be its regard for males and the more intense will be its diminishment of females—even in societies in which women are associated with the tame (culture) and men with the wild (nature). (This is because in such societies, women are part of the tame only because men have confined them within it, men having taken over women's "wildness.") Moreover, there are different kinds of controls. In some societies, control is purely mystical; nature is brought into line symbolically, through rituals alone. In others, controls are physical but simple: the land is cultivated, animals are domesticated, houses are built to endure for an extended period. And in some, both physical and "spiritual" controls are exercised. In patriarchy, both are used and bolstered by institutionalization.

In what I will call "male-superior" societies, there may be considerable egalitarianism in customs and practices. Post-marriage residence may be matri- or patrilocal, descent traced through either parent, and initiation practices may differ for girls and boys; marriage customs may control women, but they confine men as well. The culture may be exclusionary or segregated, but it is one in which women maintain their own traditions, cults, and beliefs. Men have greater status, but women are not highly controlled, and may have their own ideas about male "status."

A male-supremacist society is one in which women are subject to considerable male control, including important exclusions. For example, Arapesh men and women are cooperative, but a wife is expected to act as a daughter to her husband, and on important ritual occasions she is expected to behave like an ignorant child—a process that has been named infantilization.[17] Among some African cultures, including the Yoruba, women have considerable power over food supply, money, and trade, but when approaching their husbands they must act ignorant, obedient, and servile, kneeling as they serve them.[18] The most important control in such groups, however, is exclusion from the public realm, especially from economic decision making, but also from councils and cults with political decision-making power.

Male-supremacist societies seem always to exhibit great fear of women's power—as represented by menstruation, urination, or nakedness—and strong antagonism between the sexes. Few of them, however, go as far as patriarchal societies in denying women's sexuality or forcing sex upon them. The Mundurucu, for example, who practice gang rape of women and boast, "We tame our women with the banana," know they are using rape as a punishment, and do not, like some men in industrialized societies, confuse coerced sex with love.[19] Kathleen Gough asserts that hunting societies do not exploit women's labor to control what they produce, or rob women of their children, or confine women physically. Such groups never display the kind of male possessiveness that leads to "such institutions as savage punishments or death for female adultery, the jealous guarding of female chastity and virginity," and other infringements of female bodily autonomy.[20]

Patriarchal cultures control women, exclude women, and attempt to control all those things women produce—from children to manufactures. They attempt to take over as their own the very physical functioning of women's procreation, by assigning children to men and diminishing the role of women in procreation. They do this through *the word*: that is, by decree and institutionalization—the setting up of independent hierarchical structures devoted to control in a particular field or area. Not only unequal degrees of status but also the ideas that sustain and perpetuate male control over females are institutionalized in patriarchy. Thus the fundamental nature of patriarchy is located in stratification, institutionalization, and coercion. Stratification of men above women leads in time to stratification of classes: an elite rules over people perceived as "closer to nature," savage, bestial, animalistic; it legitimizes its rule by claiming to be more in control than others and closer to "God," which essentially means less connected to nature and the flesh—which is why it is a contradiction for women to be numbered among the elite, and one reason why they have been so severely controlled within that class. Control is achieved through institutions: it is decreed that certain people may own property, or pass laws, or receive education, and institutions are created to perpetuate such decrees. An institutionalized society requires coercion because it is oppressive, and because it is factitious. If there were in fact a group of humans who were *in every way naturally superior* to other humans, they would *rule automatically*; they would not require force to maintain supremacy.

To create a male-superior culture, all that is needed is a perception that there is a difference in volition between women and men. If *it seems* that women are bound by nature to work, to take responsibility for others, and to provide; that men are not so bound but may choose to work or not, then it seems that men are in some way a privileged group. If women are willing to grant men special praise for what they do to contribute to the group—instead of simply refusing to share with those who do not contribute—that praise could easily, over time, be institutionalized into status. The "Big Man" systems that exist in the highlands of New Guinea, for instance, are devices that prevent the buildup of wealth, that perpetuate sharing and division of wealth. Under such systems women as well as men produce goods which are passed in a system of exchange as gift giving. Men derive great status and praise from giving huge feasts, and thus sharing with others; men possess political prestige. Women do not, although their labor has contributed to the feasts. In our own world and time, it is frequently seen that women offer inordinate praise, flattering the strength or cleverness of men who are in any way helpful, while the labor and helpfulness of women is often taken for granted.

A male-superior culture could become male-supremacist if hunting is important in it. Gathering is fairly dependable: the women almost always return laden with vegetables, fruits, and nuts, and provide the major sustenance of gathering peoples. As we have seen, hunting is unpredictable. It may also be dangerous—depending upon the prey—but gathering can be dangerous too when predatory animals inhabit the gathering area.[21] It is less the danger of either activity than the unreliability of hunting that makes hunting so anxious an occupation.

The unreliability of the hunt is humiliating to the hunter of good intentions, strength, skill, courage, and pride. Hunters can and often do return empty-handed. (Thus the cheese dish "Welsh rabbit," a derogation of Welshmen, who presumably came home without the real thing.) The hunters' embarrassment at failure is compounded into shame by the reliability of the women's gathering. To relieve this, male hunters devised various approaches to hunting that removed some of the responsibility for failure from their shoulders. They use narration of past successes—tales about the one that got away, or scrapes with death—to remind listeners of their competence.[22] They posit a mysterious dimension to hunting in which powers above humans govern human success. All hunting societies, Lévi-Strauss asserts, have a ritualistic attitude toward animals, and the males of such societies frequently have cults which exclude women. The purpose of these cults is to control a species.[23] Some societies have such cults for horticulture: their rites are solicitations of the god, and are intended to exercise *control* over (not beseech aid with) growing a particular vegetable.[24] Such cults worship gods, not goddesses, although there have been many vegetation goddesses; they worship a transcendent, not an immanent, principle.

As the women go about the business of subsistence—grinding vegetables or grain, tending children, making utensils—the men retreat to their sacred cave, arbor, or tree. They handle sacred objects and utter sacred words. In some groups there is a legend that the sacred objects were stolen from the women long ago. But now the men invoke a power that women cannot contact. Briffault writes that "the first step in the limitation of the primitive status of women was associated with the arrogation by the men of the monopoly of religious and magic functions."[25] The kind of power the cults invoke varies: some beseech power-over; some assert the continuity of men and nature. Through the word, the rite, the two are placed in the same realm so that men can act on nature. Totemic societies attempt to incorporate nature into the social order.[26]

There are, however, also societies with high gods, although only 35 percent of gathering-hunting societies believe in such gods.[27] The notion of a high god is more likely to be found in more complex societies, those which have fully accepted control over nature as a high value.

The shift in worship from the goddess to the god took place at various times in various places. Although once a goddess was "mistress of the hunt," most hunting cults worship male deities. The shift from one to the other parallels a shift in the value of women and men. There are, still, twinned gods, perhaps remnants of a period when men and women worshiped separate deities. The goddess, a primary figure until very late in horti- and agricultural societies, is usually immanent in nature. She is the divine principle inspiring nature, intrinsic in the moon and its phases, a principle of fertility, recreation, and regeneration. The god is usually disconnected from nature and has power over it. He controls things without being implicit in them: he is the unmoved mover. He inhabits a mysterious realm; he cannot be seen or felt but only sensed in the working out of events. Thus Australian Aborigines who are members of matrilineal clans discover their totems in flesh, while to members of patrilineal clans totems reveal themselves in dreams.[28]

With a shift (however gradual and irregular) from goddess to god worship, there probably occurred a shift in the makeup of worshipers as well. We can hypothesize that horticultural people worshiped the goddess, and that priestesses and priests were active in this worship. Invasions of warlike, god-worshiping hunting peoples from the North brought new ideas to such groups, which may have adopted the new gods while retaining the old goddesses. As gods became more important, priests took over the control of worship of both gods and goddesses. Something like this happened in Sumer, where sometime in the third millennium B.C.E. priestesses were degraded into temple prostitutes.[29]

But further alterations in attitude are necessary to turn a male-supremacist culture into a patriarchy. Recognition of paternity was hugely important, although we do not know when this occurred among which people. There are cultures which refused to acknowledge biological fatherhood as late as our own century.[30] It is reasonable to assume that this recognition occurred late, judging from the lateness of attempts to efface signs of matrilineality from Old Testament and Islamic records (to be discussed later in this chapter), and the late date of the *Enuma Elish* (second millennium B.C.E.), which celebrates the institutionalization of male supremacy in the Middle Eastern Sumerian-Babylonian area. Shifts from mother-right, matrilineality, and matrilocality probably occurred after the recognition of biological fatherhood.

As I have suggested, population growth led to the coexistence of alien peoples, not always peaceably. This coexistence required new forms of organization—the self-government of matricentry no longer sufficed. The coexistence of alien peoples may also have created a new sense of property, that is, ownership of land, which contributed to the gradual demise of the old high value of sharing. The domestication of animals (which may have begun in the Middle East as early as 9000 B.C.E.) may have altered with understanding of the male role in procreation, and become a coerced thing, like some of the savagely cruel techniques of our own period. The productiveness resulting from coercion may have given rise to the idea of coercion of people as well, as Elizabeth Fisher believed.[31]

Knowledge of paternity arrived late indeed. Consider the technique used by Jacob: Jacob made a bargain with Laban claiming as wages for tending the flocks those that were spotted, speckled, and brown. But he then put striped rods of poplar, hazel, and chestnut in the watering troughs, so that the flocks "should conceive when they came to drink" (Genesis 30:38), and bring forth speckled and spotted young. He did this, however, only with the stronger animals; thus the feebler ones remained unspotted, and Laban's flocks grew weaker as Jacob's increased in number and strength. There is a strange passage earlier in this same chapter of the Bible. The childless Rachel says to Jacob: "Give me children, or else I die"; and Jacob replies: "Am I in God's stead, who hath withheld from thee the fruit of the womb?" (Genesis 30:1–2).

Indeed, the entire Jacob cycle of stories reflects a conflict between matrilocality and patrilocality, and perhaps the shift from one to the other. You will recall that Jacob is Rebekah's favorite son, and that she urges and helps him to deceive his blind father, Isaac, when the old man, dying, wants to give his firstborn son his blessing. She prepares meat, the dish Esau usually brought his father, and covers Jacob's smooth skin with kidskin, so that he feels hairy like his brother. Isaac is deceived and gives the younger twin the blessing. This story is read by some scholars as reflecting a conflict between the old mother-right and the new father-right. Presumably the blessing could involve not only a wish for a child's future but also the passing on of property—patrimony: flocks or territory.

When Jacob marries, he remains in the house of his wives' mother (references to her have been expunged, according to biblical scholars), but later makes a stealthy escape with his wives and flocks. In the desert he struggles with an angel—possibly the spirit of matricentry—and prevails, although he is lamed (like Oedipus). He is newly named Israel, from whom his people would take their name: but the tribe of Israel was originally named for Sarah.[32]

The essential question about the origin of patriarchy is why people should have altered an ancient and revered way of life. Patriarchy did not arise after three million years of peaceful hominid and human life because men suddenly became more aggressive, or suddenly decided to oppress women. Either the new values held by the men's cults themselves changed behavior or some change in the human situation seemed to require a new adaptation, which was available in a moral change that had to have occurred earlier: the positing of control as a value superior to the old values of fertility, continuation, and sharing. The fundamental nature of this new morality is explicit in the Old Testament, in the opening of Genesis, which propounds the principles of patriarchy. The gift of the male god to man is *dominion* over nature. The old values are still present—humans are to replenish as well as subdue the earth. But man is to have dominion also over woman. The key word is dominion: power-over, control.

Once control was elevated and nature demoted in the morality of humans, forms developed to foster and transmit power. The distinction in status between men and women was institutionalized. In Greek thought the private was distinguished from the public realm. The private is the realm of animality—of nature—and of *necessity*. It is the realm of women. The public realm is created in *freedom*, is the domain of the human, and transcends the first. It is the realm of men. Although some men—indeed most men—are relegated to the private realm, the *idea* of the distinction exalts all men.[33] Aristotle distinguished between free male citizens and women, children, mechanics, and laborers, who comprised the "necessary conditions" of the state. Free males inhabited the *polis*; activities within it were defined as existing outside the realms of nature and necessity; the private realm was seen as the sphere of unfreedom.[34]

In the *Symposium*, Plato's hierarchy of virtue and rationality places women midway between men and beasts; Socrates specifically compares symbolic fatherhood—homosexual love between men, the creation of thought, poetry, and law—to biological fatherhood and asks, "Who would not prefer such fatherhood to merely human propagation?"[35] The association of women with nonvolition—necessity—and nature persists in Western thought. Both Hegel and Marx view childbearing as a nonvolitional activity and, moreover, one that precludes women from thinking about their experience.[36]

The forbidden fruit woman ate, causing the fall, is in Hebrew *jadah*—knowledge, penetration, power, possession.[37] It may well be that women took the first bite, the first set of steps into this new realm of control, but men took the second. And in time control superseded natural values; as it did, men superseded women in value. By the twentieth century we have reached the point where an anthropologist can claim "it is natural for man to be unnatural."[38]

## 2. First Steps into Patriarchy

Although I am speaking as if patriarchy were a discrete form of social organization, I do not wish to suggest that it appeared suddenly, or without preparation. Patriarchy evolved, developed, from other male-dominant social orders. And to understand the sociopolitical order of our own forms of patriarchy (for patriarchal forms vary according to religion—Islam, Judaism, Hinduism, and Christianity, for instance—and according to capitalist and socialist systems) it is helpful to see the tendencies exhibited by other male-dominant social orders. In order to come into existence, each of these had to break some of the bonds of matricentry, to reverse them. To become dominant, men had to splinter women's power in three major ways: they had to break the bond of mutual affection between women and men and substitute a bond of power; to break the bond of unity among women; and to break the bond of love between women and children, substituting a bond of power between men and children. These fractures probably did not occur in a linear way, but that is how we must analyze them. In addition, and simultaneously, men had to teach, to disseminate as widely as possible, a new definition of manhood, and to develop rituals for that purpose.

## Breaking the Bond of Love Between Women and Men

It is impossible to know how men defined themselves, or even if they did define themselves as a sex—that is, different from women—in matricentric culture. Perhaps all members of a group—a clan or a tribe—saw themselves simply as a people, as the translations of certain group names would indicate: Bantu means *human being*, for example.[39] The first step in intentionally altering matricentric culture was the creation of a new male identity, probably by leaders of the hunting cults.

Lévi-Strauss claims that a ritual attitude toward animals is universal in hunting societies.[40] Hunting is unpredictable and therefore seems to require magical control.[41] Every hunting culture I know about has a male cult and ritual that excludes women—even those in which women also hunt. These cults involve myths expressing male power over women, and sacred objects—totems or weapons or tools—which women are not supposed to touch or, sometimes, even to see. Among modern hunting peoples, the exclusion of women from solitary hunting of larger mammals is correlated with the making and using of weapons in cultic contexts.[42] The Desana of Colombia divide the world's energy—which they see as limited—into masculine and feminine forms. Masculine energy is *tulari*—force, power, impulse; feminine energy is *boga*—transformation and creation. The two together are fertilization and fecundity. Hunters are *tulari*; animals are *boga*. Thus hunting is making love to animals, and to kill is to copulate.[43] For Hadza men, meat itself is connected with rituals deemed highly serious.[44] Although many simple societies believe in the participation of humans and animals in a single natural process and have ceremonies affirming this connection, the purpose of the connection is to permit the human to act on—control—the animal.[45]

In societies in which control was abstracted from its context and became a good in its own right, local immanent gods became transcendent gods, gods of power. In a series of imitations like those involved in homeopathic magic, the leaders—now probably priests—of the cults claimed powers similar to those of the god; in time, such powers were extended to all male adherents of the cult. Maleness was redefined as ability to control, but not all men had this ability. Thus a man is not like a woman, born to her estate; a man must learn to be a man. Put another way, all females are women, but not all males are men. One must learn to be a man, be made a man of, earn the right to the name by showing control.

To teach this new way of seeing, initiation rites were devised for young boys. Common to these rites—which otherwise vary considerably—is the notion that boys must be born twice, once through the mother and the second time through the men of their group. Initiation ceremonies are most fierce in societies with traditions of polygyny, patrilineality, and a long postpartum sex taboo—thus late weaning. Among such groups little boys live almost totally with women and are identified with them until puberty, when they are "taken away to be 'made men,' often with prolonged humiliation and severe genital mutilations."[46]

In many societies, boys who have been initiated leave their mothers' huts to enter a separate men's house; in some the men's cult fulfills this function. For example, the Hopi cult, Kachina, excluded women; its rituals were designed to maintain the dual nature of men and the single nature of women. They believed women care about giving and keeping life; men must be germinators and guardians of life, but they must also be predatory warriors.[47]

Often boys are removed from their mothers' houses, instructed in practical and esoteric lore, and kept in the men's house for several months. Some initiations use varying means of purging "all that is woman-like in the boys," the defilement of having lived with the mother.[48] In some cases boys are required to call their uncles "mother."[49]

There are societies which force ordeals on boys, which wound or mutilate them. Austromelanesians inflict wounds on the penis to make it bleed in imitation of women's menstruation.[50] Wounds to other parts of the body serve the same symbolic function. Most initiations of boys symbolize rebirth as a man by men: they may involve the boy being swallowed by a symbolic crocodile and emerging newborn, or being housed in a symbolic (male) womb and tended by male "mothers."[51] Among the Gimi, for instance, the penis is a gift to the initiate, a gift created by males, and new initiates are called "new vaginas."[52]

Through such initiations boys are taught to be "women" to older men, and to be "men" to women. Punitive and sometimes cruel rites of male initiation express hostility between the older men and boys, and between men and women.[53] The rites are designed to detach the boy from natural affection and natural role, to teach him that a man does not act on feelings but rather on meeting an external societal standard of manliness that is focused on exhibiting self-control and control over others.

Such rites may be cruel or protracted, depending upon the degree of control expected of males in a given culture—that is, upon the degree to which control in itself is considered a good. It is necessary to exert great pressure on the children, because what they are learning contradicts both nature and reason. By "nature," they would act on their feelings; by reason, they would act in such a way as to achieve a desire, solve a problem, use their skills. What is required of them, however, is that they act so as to demonstrate control, whether or not they desire it, whether or not their manifestation of control contributes in any way to a given situation. It is in this way that control is a transcendental value: it is urged on grounds of some "higher" purpose, some symbolic state, and without regard to the actual context of events.

The contrast between initiations of girls and boys is instructive. Girls are initiated when they begin to menstruate: the initiation recognizes a natural, biological, nonvolitional event. Moreover, since girls reach puberty individually, each girl is initiated alone, and most initiation ceremonies isolate her even further by confining her in a particular space within the settlement, or even outside it, for a given period of time. She may be served special foods or she may be forbidden to eat at all; she is often taught rituals for purification of her body and traditional lore of motherhood. In many South American societies she is instructed about "lifelong prohibitions and restrictions" on her behavior. In such rituals, symbols of male power may be introduced to frighten her.[54] In general, girls' initiations celebrate biological maturity, fertility, potential motherhood, a stage in a natural (nonvolitional) cycle. Girls are taught their form of power: it is power to pollute. (There are societies which initiate girls and boys similarly, but they are not male-supremacist. Mbuti girls are welcomed into a girls' hut after the onset of puberty, in which they sleep together and may accept the embraces of chosen boys, but the Mbuti are nearly egalitarian.)

Boys' initiations are very different. They are not triggered by a particular biological change, and groups of boys are initiated together. The feeling, then, is not one of separation from the community, but entrance into a male community. Rites for boys are longer and more elaborate than those for girls, since boys must be taught a new estate—manhood—while girls are simply fulfilling their biological capacities. Girls are becoming what they were born to be; boys are learning to see themselves differently, as creatures in control.

The new male self-definition excluded women: men were seen as fully human, "man," whereas women were seen as mediators between the human and some other power—usually nature. But to be human is not a "natural" identity: it must be earned, learned, achieved, striven for. This division between human and semihuman existence, between men and women, pervades the thinking of many societies, both simple and complex. On the one hand, the division of the sexes on the basis of control grants men greater power than women. But since men must work to achieve that power, and women, being close to nature, have *innate* powers, men in many cultures feel jealous of women. Because the relation between the sexes is not one of equality but of domination, men cannot trust women, but believe the inferior sex is continually attempting to undermine them. Such lack of trust is inherent in any relation based upon inequality. The power of women is therefore seen as malevolent, and it is centered in menstruation. It is not just in Judaism that men are warned to shun a menstruating woman.

The Chipewyans believe that to be female is to *be* power, whereas men must acquire power. What men may—or may not—attain, women possess by nature. A Chipewyan woman can destroy all the power resident in objects belonging to a man—guns, tools, medicinal herbs—simply by stepping over them while she is menstruating.[55] But just as her menstruation itself is nonvolitional, so is the power it confers upon her. She can destroy a man's possessions unknowingly, unintentionally. The only security a man has is to control her movements. His power, on the other hand, is not just sought after, but is acquired self-consciously, fully volitionally.

The Gimi of Papua New Guinea have a horror of female menstrual fluid that extends to many other substances and objects. The vagina is feared as the site of bleeding, as is any object that in any way resembles the vagina. An object touched by a menstruating woman will crack in the hands of a man, a stone ax may turn on its holder; plants wither and die, ground loses its fertility, if stepped over by a menstruating woman. Boys recently initiated must avoid the forest, lest they unwittingly stand between the thighs of female marsupials leaping in the trees overhead. Women raise certain crops; during initiation, young men are taught ways to vomit in order to rid their bodies of female foods—"mother's" food, polluting breast milk. Women are isolated during their menstrual periods so as to avert the danger to the community. Nevertheless, it is at this time that women are found most attractive by Gimi men, who use the isolation huts as places of assignation.[56]

Despite this tremendous power of women—or perhaps because of it—Gimi society is strongly male-dominated. Women are confined within fenced gardens inside the hamlet, while men are free to enter the "wild" unfenced plots near the forest. Gimi myths tell of women who fled from men to live in the forest and acquired tremendous powers of creation until men wounded them and brought them back to live confined in the settlement. Now men are safe in the forest because women are not there; the female characteristics of the forest—plants and animals bearing symbolic resemblances to female form or functions—are the property of men when they are detached from actual women.

The Papagos of southwest North America consider women the vehicles of such a tremendous force, manifested in menstruation, that it has to be nullified. Women are therefore excluded from places where men meet—communal ceremonies, council meetings, all areas of the tribe's political and economic activity. There is also inequality based upon age; young adults of both sexes are inferior to their elders.

Although the Papagos believe that both females and males possess power, the female kind is considered negative: for a man to touch a menstruating woman can lead to his death, and even to look at her can cause weakness. Contact with her enervates his weapons and can poison his food. Thus menstruating women are segregated, and must undergo ritual purification to *nullify* their power. But all women possess this power from the time of their first menstruation; whereas a man must acquire power through the performance of a ritual act—he must kill an enemy, kill an eagle, or fetch salt from the ocean. After such an act, the man too must undergo ritual purification, but his rite nullifies only the evil part of power and transforms the power into a beneficent force.

A warrior who takes a scalp is treated like a menstruating woman—he must undergo isolation and fasting and rituals of purification. The scalp he has taken is treated like and called his "child." But female menstruation enervates the warrior and his weapons; thus a man whose wife is menstruating cannot enter battle. It is blood that binds the mature woman and the warrior, but the blood must be tamed into childbearing, whether of a real or a symbolic child.[57]

Women of the Kaulong of southwest New Britain are believed to carry contamination continuously from sometime before puberty to after menopause, although their polluting power is considered greatest during menstruation and childbirth. At these times a woman must remove herself from the central clearing of the community, from all dwellings, all drinking water sources and supplies. She may not touch anything with which a man may come in contact, and her polluting power flows outward from her in all directions. But her pollution is dangerous only to males, and, it seems, only to adult males, in whom it causes respiratory illness and death. Thus men must be careful where they walk lest they pass under a tree or bridge on which a menstruating woman has walked; houses raised from the ground are dangerous to men, who cannot enter the space beneath them for any purpose, lest a menstruating woman has sat on the floor of the house.

Kaulong men fear marriage because contact with women brings certain contamination and death. Sexual intercourse is also considered animal-like, and is relegated to the forest (rather than the clearing or the gardens). Because of male fear, Kaulong women take the initiative in courting, through gifts, flirtation, or physical attack—to which men are not permitted to retaliate but must either submit or flee. Women choose their husbands, and sometimes even kidnap them with the help of their brothers.[58]

Certain New Guinean cultures—the Káfe and the Bimin-Kuskusmin, for instance—believe all bodily secretions are potentially dangerous and in need of control. Káfe women will refuse to wash men's clothing that may have semen on it, and both men and women are forbidden to step over food or people, lest they pollute them.[59] There are long postpartum taboos among the Hagen of Papua New Guinea, who believe male semen may harm the newborn baby. Menstruating women are secluded and must follow carefully certain rules for controlling menstruation and its possible pollution.[60] Men of the Bimin-Kuskusmin find menstrual blood the most dangerous of all substances to them, and believe that they, not women, have the ritual means to control it. Male fluids are seen as sacred contributions to procreation; female fluids are seen as pollutant.[61]

Societies which are not strongly male supremacist are likely not to have strong menstrual taboos. For example, among the Ashanti of West Africa, chiefdoms are composed of matrilineal clans; although the Ashanti are ruled by men, the queen mother has the most power in choosing the king—or did until the British occupation of West Africa in 1896. It is believed that women alone contribute the blood to a child; men contribute *ntoro*, soul, spirit, or, sometimes, semen. Women's menstruation and childbirth are paralleled with men's hunting and warfare; both activities are highly valued in Ashanti society, and women have retained power and authority in Ashanti life.[62]

Many societies posit a different realm from the earthly one (in which women seem dominant), a realm for which women's very earthly abilities make them unfit. So in myths recounting creation by a female goddess, she starts within something like earth, water, or body; whereas those recounting creation by a male or an animal god show the creation as started from without—sky, another country, by magic, from wood or clay.[63] Hagen males claim special powers of fertility in a Male Spirit Cult which offers them access to the spirit world that women cannot attain.[64] The Gimi believe that men's life with women creates order in human life but pollutes the male and forces him to seek a higher, purer form of existence, one without women. This all-male higher order is attainable only in death. Just as Gimi men are safe in the forest when women are confined in the clearing, they feel the female element purified when it is "masculinized." Male rites among the Gimi aim at nullifying "the boundary between human and non-human so as to transcend mortal existence."[65]

Many tribes set up spatial limits that are essentially moral; the wild is opposed to the settled. Some have complete conceptual sets, like the Chipewyan, who associate food production, physical action, and positive power derived from transcendent sources and oppose these to food processing, verbal exhortation, and negative power derived from nature.[66] Some groups consciously perceive their myths of seizing the women's "instruments"—flutes, trumpets, or whatever—to describe male seizure of control of women's procreative powers.[67] The Gimi claim that men have the ability to give birth and possess worldly power, and believe this dual power is the secret of their dominance. Male semen alone creates the fetus, and women are defined as the barren sex. If women could procreate, they would have dual powers and males would be doomed.[68] Other tribes, unable to maintain such delusions, use initiation rites in which boys are born again, symbolically, to men. Initiation rites in general imitate and usurp the initial act of birth, as they teach that birth from a male is a higher order of experience.[69] In various groups, males periodically let blood from the penis.[70] The Fore of New Guinea say, "Women's menstruation has always been present; men's bleeding, that came later."[71] The Papagos believe all women are born powerful whereas only some Papago men achieve power.[72] Most of these groups also have myths relating an earlier time in which women dominated.

The most intense and complete male domination found in simple societies exists among peoples who live where there is little or no vegetation, like the Chipewyan or the Netsilik Eskimos. They have the "most precarious human adaptation on earth," according to Richard Lee.[73] Their economies are based almost completely on caribou, seals, salmon, reindeer, and musk ox. The women of these groups hunt, but only when the men are away.

These cultures have a strong tendency to invent male creation myths; they have strong male dominance and rigid sexual segregation with menstrual taboos. They see a special role as necessary for male but not female identity. Females are believed to have identity *naturally*; they are associated with life and fertility; men are associated with death and barrenness. Male power is seen as something that must be acquired with effort, something involving not a flowering ability but control and manipulation. These cultures have a tendency toward migration and conquest.[74]

Strong menstrual taboos are not the cause but the evidence of enmity and fear between the sexes, or, more precisely, of a male fear of retaliation from those whom men have subjugated. Dominant Mundurucu males exclude women from all political and religious activities; nevertheless their myth and ritual are dominated by fear of women and their "pollution."[75] Gimi men fear they will remain forever merged with the female and indistinguishable from her, like a phallic appendage to the mother's body.[76] Other kinds of intersexual discord are common in strongly male-dominant societies: the Mundurucu live in great discord; the Hausa of northern Nigeria were more or less equal until the Holy Wars of 1804–10, after which they became Moslems and confined women. Now memory of an earlier time remains among the women, creating a "spiritual guerrilla movement."[77] The Yanomamo oppress women through female infanticide, polygyny, and brutality. They also fight wars for possession of those women allowed to live.[78] The Netsilik Eskimos perform euthanasia on the old and invalids; they also frequently commit suicide.[79]

In short, enmity between the sexes was created by the new male self-definition, which placed an unequal value on men and women. That difference in value is reflected in sociopolitical customs or (where they exist) institutions. In some societies, men not only are more valued than women, but have authority over them—at least over wives and daughters. Any bond that grows up between partners in such a relation is permeated with power, the greatest hindrance to a love based on mutuality and trust.

The bond of love between sisters and brothers, so strong in matrilineal and non-male-supremacist systems in which brothers are responsible for their sisters' children and at home in their sisters' house, is broken by the assertion of patrilineality and male supremacy. In such systems sisters become commodities for exchange, subject to the control and power of brother as well as father. That such exchanges are seen this way by men themselves is suggested by a quotation from an Arapesh male: "What, would you like to marry your sister? What is the matter with you? Don't you want a brother-in-law? Don't you realize that if you marry another man's sister and another man marries your sister, you will have at least two brothers-in-law, while if you marry your own sister you will have none? With whom will you hunt, with whom will you garden, whom will you go visit?"[80] The bond among men supersedes the bond between men and women.

Even the bond of sexual love between women and men is broken by male supremacy. Although there is a division of labor in simple societies, this division enforces interdependence of the sexes and heterosexual marriage. Lévi-Strauss describes meeting a Bororo man of about thirty in poor condition—unclean, undernourished, and morose. Lévi-Strauss thought he was ill, but his problem was simply that he was unmarried: "In a society where labor is systematically shared between man and woman and where only the married status permits the man to benefit from the fruits of woman's work, including delousing, body painting, and hairplucking as well as vegetable food and cooked food (since the Bororo woman tills the soil and makes pots), a bachelor is really only half a human being."[81] Interdependence of this sort fosters mutual respect between the sexes, even in male-superior societies. If desire or love does not bind partners, their need for each other does.

Patriarchy distorts this interdependence. By placing all rights in the male, granting males most or all of a society's economic and political power, it transforms productive adult women into dependent minors. By devaluing women's contributions, by treating them *as if* they, like female physical processes, were nonvolitional, automatic, *natural*, patriarchy disguises interdependence, giving it the appearance of dependency. So Athenian men who spent all day with other men talking, drinking, or playing could scorn the household labor which, under the direction of their wives, sustained their lives. So the men of ancient

Israel—more respectful of women than the Greeks—exalted the woman who works continually to support her husband, who "sitteth among the elders of the land" all day in the gates of the city (Proverbs 31:10–31). This tradition continued in later Judaism in the priestly scholarly caste, whose wives supported them but were granted minimal respect, while awe attended the nonproductive work of the scholar or rabbi.

Placing all economic and political rights in the male makes the female unequal to him. Requiring sexual fidelity of women, but not men, makes women's bodies men's possession without the reverse. And unequal relations are relations of power, not love. Such relations may, in special cases, be diffused with love, but that is not and cannot be their primary character. A man may *grant* his mate equality, but it remains his to confer, not hers to require, and he can at any time withdraw his gift.

Finally, the bond of love between the sexes was broken—or deformed—by making women *morally* unequal to men, and it is this level of inequality that proves adamant even in cultures and times in which women have regained some economic and political rights. The major element in this diminishment of women was the diminishment of sex.

Sex is associated with women because of the importance of female procreative—sexual—functions. It is also associated with animals and with nature, while killing, an act also performed by animals, is not consistently associated with either. Moreover, sex is the major link between women and men; whether as sons, mates, or fathers, they must conjoin with a woman. Sex gives a woman power over a man, the power of mother, mate, or nourisher of his child. Thus sex had to be transformed into a pollution and a threat before a higher realm of action could be posited for men.

Many intelligent people are aware of the injustice of current male-female relations, yet accept it as necessary to the well-being of the entire race. Women, it is argued, can manage despite their subjugation, because they are granted the most profound experience on earth—childbearing; whereas men, without some special impetus or purpose, might very well remain appendages to their mothers, as the Gimi fear. Women's identity is, they feel, conferred by birth, whereas men's is not. Men must be dominant or they are nothing. But such thinking is based on faulty logic, like Simone de Beauvoir's statement that it is not in giving life but in risking it that man is raised above the animal, and that this is why males who kill life have been granted superiority over females who bring forth life.[82]

In fact, women can and do also kill; and giving birth entails risk to women's lives. And men contribute to creating life. The real difference between women and men in this fundamental dimension is that women take responsibility for the young almost automatically and men do not. Moral codes may be created that place the onus for economic support of the young on those who have the economic power—men. But as we have seen in the past two decades, those codes are shaky and, unless backed by law or strong social pressure, do not suffice to persuade many men to this task.

The sloppiness of our thinking allows us easily to assume that men require a transcendent identity if they are not to exist as mere appendages to women. That this is not the case cannot be proven, but it makes simple sense that a man of energy and desire will become a person in his own right without the bolstering of a factitious self-definition. Over all the centuries of oppression, women of energy and desire became full people in their own right despite laws and economic codes designed to prevent it.

A second argument that is advanced in defense of current male-female power relations is that men are stronger than women and can dominate them; therefore they do. This argument is based on the assumption that domination is a good, a desirable state. As I hope to show in this book, that assumption is false. Domination is an ill, not because of some abstract moral principle but because of a concrete moral fact: it makes people unhappy. Domination makes impossible the most essential and felicitous element in life: trusting mutual affection. Domination sets up a dynamic whereby a person or group claims superiority to another person or group. This supposed superiority is as necessary to the claimant as air to breathe: the claimant has no identity without it. To demonstrate this superiority, however, the other(s) must offer deference or be punished. The deference is granted but it conceals rebelliousness, contempt, and resentment. The two parties to such a relationship cannot under any circumstances have an honest, trusting, and loving relation even if they are husband and wife. The assertion of superiority leads to manipulative behavior on both sides, isolation and wariness on both sides, and mutual fear.

If domination had not become a high value, differences in size and musculature among humans would be inconsequential. Indeed, they are inconsequential in many ways. Although human males are generally larger and stronger than human females, many women are larger and/or stronger than many men. In most animal species females are larger than males; although among mammals males are usually larger than females, there are a substantial number of mammalian species in which the reverse is true.[83] But there is no direct correlation between such dimorphism and dominance (where dominance exists). It is highly unlikely that the dimorphism of the human race is the cause of male domination; rather it has contributed to the reinforcement of the domination.

Musculature is not a given; like a brain, muscles have to be used and trained to develop. The men of Bali were as slight as the women when they did little heavy work; however, those who worked as dock coolies developed the heavy musculature associated with males.[84] Present-day Western women are the inheritors of a tradition in which women were admired for smallness—encouraged (or forced) to eat little, and that little not especially nourishing; and if they were middle-class or above, expected to do little heavy work. Because of these standards, small women were preferred marriage partners, and were more likely than large women to pass on their genes.

In some cultures, like that of India, women are still systematically underfed, but this was true in Europe as well for centuries, and the standard is still with us in the form of an aesthetic. Women who emerge from a different tradition—Russian peasant women, black American women who demonstrate the result of the slaveowners' desire for large-bodied field workers—stand in strong contrast to women who emerge from a middle-class background. Thus among some groups sexual dimorphism has been made more extreme, for political reasons, over the past millennia, long after the triumph of male supremacy.

Third, larger size and musculature are not sufficient, whether as reasons or as means, for domination. That is, largeness and strength by themselves do not provide motivation for domination. If they did, the impulse of the tall, large-boned Scandinavians and Teutons, some American Indians, and various African groups would have been to conquer and dominate smaller people. The Japanese and Chinese, the Indians, and Africans like the Mbuti should in such a case have been made extinct, and the Finns, or someone like them, should be ruling the earth. There is no pattern of aggression by large peoples against smaller peoples; nor does such a pattern exist among individuals. Tall sons do not regularly attack their smaller fathers, nor tall or strong daughters their mothers.

Size can be seen as a drawback, as it was by the Mbuti when Colin Turnbull lived among them. Turnbull, white and six foot two, wanted to accompany the Mbuti, who are black and average four foot two, on a hunt. In all affection, they refused. His height and whiteness would make him too visible in the jungle; his weight would make him too noisy; and besides, his body smell was so strong it would scare the game away.[85]

Domination can be accomplished by many other means than physical strength. Cleverness, intelligence, is a primary means. Institutionalization of a particular dominance is very powerful: laws and systems can cow even the strongest and most courageous.

A further argument advanced to justify male domination is the greater aggressiveness of the male. Yet even the sociobiologists who maintain this argument admit that aggressiveness (like mothering) is learned.[86] Some women, even mothers, can be ferocious and predatory; it is not unknown for mothers to treat their children with cruelty and even to injure or kill them; nor did women as a sex refuse to participate in the horrors of the Nazi concentration camps. Among the Manus, men raise the children because they are more tender and loving than the women. There are cultures in which the women are more aggressive than the men. Degree of aggressiveness varies from person to person and from culture to culture, and the most aggressive cultures are—naturally—those which value aggression most. Recent researches show that males are generally more aggressive in defense of a territory, and females more aggressive in defense of their young.

Although the split between women and men described in this section is ancient, it is not necessarily "natural."[87] It is a result of two primary events: the elevation of control into a governing principle, a god, in human life; and the identification of men with that principle. Probably the great majority of men resisted such a self-definition for many centuries, but as I have suggested, power is contagious: you adopt it as a value or you are eradicated by those who do. Power swept through the ancient world, creating gods-on-earth, conquerors. At the same time it created slaves-on-earth, women (and probably most men). To accomplish this, adherents of power—priests, soldiers—had to teach men contempt for women, teach men to dominate women. In the process, they isolated men not just from women but from those values associated with women. They "made men" of men.

## Breaking the Bond Among Women

Women's early centrality and solidity was essentially familial, a connection of mother with daughters and granddaughters, sisters with each other and with nieces and grandnieces, and among cousins. Breaking this core is essential to asserting male superiority or supremacy. The first major step in this fragmenting is assertion of patrilineality and a shift to patrilocality.

In requiring a bride to move to the paternal home of her groom, patrilocality separates her from her core, the women who would nourish and sustain her and present a united opposition to any possible male abuse of her. Patrilocality removes her from this web of affection, isolating her in a home in which she is an alien. Since women's work is traditionally in or near the home in horticultural or early industrial societies, her alienation is complete. She may find a sister or cousin in her new home; in polygynous cultures she may have a friendly co-wife. But the political and moral power inherent in a unit of related women is lost.

Later, refinements on the isolation of women were developed. By excluding women from the public realm, men prevented them from forming alliances there. Some cultures confine women within the home, where they may be subject (as in China) to a mother-in-law who, oppressed in *her* youth, has been trained in the ways of oppression. Athenian women were confined in ancient times in their husbands' homes, where they had only slaves and children for company. In some sectors of Islam women are strictly confined, although they have relatives for company. *Nevertheless*, despite such arrangements, men continued to feel overwhelmed by the world of women, and victimized by it.

The final step in the fragmenting of female unity is what is called "invisibility," treating women as if they are not present. This was accomplished in Islam by requiring women to adopt purdah, and to wear garments that make all women uniform and identical—women, not individuated people. A subtler variation of this occurs in present-day Western society, in which many men treat all women as either sex objects or subordinates (secretaries, waitresses, low-level workers) and ignore utterly women who "invade" the public realm as equals—refusing to recognize their presence, their words, or their acts.

By fragmenting the family social unit of women, and denying them the opportunity to form a broader-based political unit, patriarchal societies prevented women from unifying. By treating women as invisible and inculcating a strong misogynistic strand in culture, men taught women to have contempt for themselves and each other. Nevertheless, women continued to form strong bonds with other women. As we shall see in Chapter Three, women in Italy in the sixteenth century were deprived of the right to bequeath their own property, largely because they tended to leave it to other women, rather than to the male line of the family. Recent historians are discovering diaries, letters, and documents demonstrating the importance to women of past centuries of friendships with other women. This closeness among women has been falsified by philosophers like Schopenhauer and totally ignored by centuries of poets and writers of fiction, who depict women as jealous of each other and without resources except for important male figures.

Women continued to befriend each other, to help each other, and to work together. What they were unable to do was unify in such a way as to gain power for themselves or to challenge unified male power. As women in our own time are slowly being admitted to the institutions that preserve male power, they are adapting to the fragmentation of individuals such institutions impose, and losing the old great gift of friendship.

## Breaking the Bond Between Mother and Child

The bond of love and sharing between mother and child provided the core of society in protohuman times and throughout early human existence. So ancient and satisfying a social organization could not be easily displaced. Nor has it been displaced in simple societies, despite male superiority or supremacy. In many such cultures, fathers and uncles are also deeply affectionate and attentive to children. Patriarchy, however, has displaced and deformed this bond. Even so, it survives, and stands in contemporary thought as a psychological crux.[88]

The impulses to patriarchy were, as we have seen, based in a desire to control nature, a desire of men to assert a primary relation with children (paternity), and a pressing need for a new form of sociopolitical organization. Since men were associated with control (as women were associated with nature), since the male role in procreation was probably still being assimilated, and since men took, perhaps by default, the primary responsibility for the new realm (women being so firmly in command of the private one), the new way of relating was essentially a new way for men to relate to nature, to women, and to each other. The new moral system was a male moral system.

Part of the intention behind the establishment of patriarchy may have been to carve out for men a role of responsibility and caretaking similar to women's. This intention may well have been perceived by women as beneficent and useful. But because part of the intention was also to gain control—power over nature—control and power superseded fertility and continuation—natural values—as the highest good in men's morality. In addition, men's efforts to carve out a role for themselves may have conflicted with women's traditional "rights," and it would have been difficult to overcome the objections of these traditionally powerful figures and the men—surely there would have many—who held them in reverence.

It has been believed that the dividing line between humans and animals is the incest taboo that was supposed to be universal. Ancient myths, however, portray goddesses as having sexual liaisons with sons and brothers as well as lovers and husbands; sometimes gods too have a broad spectrum of sexual relationships.[89] And many societies permit some form of incest.[90] Sister-brother incest has been and perhaps remains common enough, and sexual assault on a boy by an uncle or older male cousin is not infrequent. Sexual assault on a girl by her father, uncle, or other male relative is forbidden in our culture, but occurs frequently. The kind of incest most focused upon by literature and myth is the least frequent type—indeed, I have never heard of a case (outside fiction): mother-son.

Mother-son incest is the subject of a considerable body of myth, as Lévi-Strauss has shown. Such myth appears in segregated cultures, in which mothers live in separate huts with their female relatives and their children, while the men live together in larger houses. The women and children sleep together, and the myths suggest that this intimacy is sexual. The incest myths described by Lévi-Strauss deal with young boys' desire to remain among the women and not be forced into ritual initiation into manhood and segregated living. Almost all these myths involve the murder of a mother or surrogate mother by her son, an act viewed with approval or indifference by her husband, the boy's father.[91]

Mother-son incest seems to have been viewed differently in the far distant and distant past. In early versions of the Oedipus myth, Epicasta (later Jocasta) marries her son and makes him king: he rules in honor for many years without guilt. In a later version, Oedipus is declared guilty of having accidentally offended the gods. But in the latest version, source of classical tragedy, Oedipus' acts are seen as crimes: the murder of his father and marriage to his mother are seen as parallel acts.[92]

Prohibition of incest is tied, according to Lévi-Strauss, to the rule of exogamy—the rule requiring people to marry outside their immediate group. This rule precludes the establishment of a biological family as a closed society: "the bond of alliance with another family ensures the dominance of the social over the biological, and of the cultural over the natural."[93] The rule thus guarantees the establishment of a public realm, an arena beyond the extended family.

It seems likely that the taboo on mother-son incest was politically inspired to protect the status—and perhaps the life—of fathers. Making such incest taboo casts suspicion on mother-son intimacy. Yet this step was not sufficient to break the bond between them. (And it is mothers and sons who are primarily at issue here: fathers wanted to take control of their sons, to indoctrinate them with the new values.) At some point a new device was contrived, perhaps by a class of priests, that would affirm a stronger bond between fathers and children than the one between mothers and children. What bound mothers and their offspring was love; but to prove one's loyalty to one's god, and to affirm the greater power of a bond of control, it was decreed that the father should sacrifice the firstborn child.[94]

If a growing population was problematic, child sacrifice may have held some benefits for the society. It has also been theorized that men, unsure of the length of time between impregnation and birth, would not have been unhappy to do away with their wives' firstborn.[95] In any case, child sacrifice was widespread in ancient times in the Middle East, performed by the Carthaginians, the Babylonians, the Phoenicians, and the Canaanites. Commands to kill children are recorded mainly in male voices. Thus the Old Testament quotes

YHWH as ordering, "Sanctify unto me all the firstborn, whatsoever openeth the womb among the children of Israel . . . it is mine" (Exodus 13:2).

Patriarchy was a revolution against the power of the mother, against familial bonds of love and affection and obligation. Carol Ochs finds parallels in old patriarchal forms, in that they supersede the allegiance to children and kin found in matricentry with a primary obligation to an abstract moral principle, the voice of God. Obedience to a transcendent god—one disconnected from and in control of nature—must be proven by a willingness to destroy the greatest gift of nature: offspring. Ochs adds, "In order to prove that Abraham is not rooted in the older tradition [matricentry], god demands that he renounce the most fundamental tenet of the matriarchal religion and kill his own child."[96] Child sacrifice involves the forceful removal of an infant from its mother by a "superior" power with a "higher" claim.

Although David Bakan asserts that there is substantial evidence that human sacrifice was prevalent in ancient Palestine until at least the seventh century B.C.E., the Old Testament records a gradual abatement of this demand among the Jews, and a shift to animal sacrifice.[97] But Ezekiel complains about this YHWH who brags that he polluted men in their gifts, making them dedicate to the fire all the firstborn, "in order that I might destroy them, in order that they would know I am YHWH" (Ezekiel 20:25–26). The very wording of this claim clearly shows its values. Power is being asserted as superior to nature, killing as superior to giving birth. The story of Abraham and Isaac may represent a softening of the demand, permission to use an animal as surrogate. So too do the exhortations of prophets like Ezekiel; and according to later Hebrew tradition, the Messiah will be a new kind of king, one who will not require the murder of children. But there are other instances of child sacrifice in the Old Testament—Jephthah's, for instance.

The entire cycle of Greek myths referred to earlier is, after the ascendancy of a male (Uranus), a cycle of murder of children by their father. The Oedipus myth is recalled as the tale of a son who murders his father and marries his mother, but its first act is the attempt of Laius to murder his son. There is a legend testifying to the greatness of Pericles on the ground that he presided calmly over a public event on the day his son died. John Boswell points out that when there is a conscious effort to persuade a populace of the superiority of state or nation over family loyalty, praise is often given to men like the Roman Junius Brutus, who sacrificed close relatives, especially sons.[98] Nietzsche perceived the pattern and mocked it, writing that the god of Israel demanded that the father should sacrifice his son, but the god of Christians went him one better and sacrificed his own.[99]

With this insistence on child sacrifice, and its spread across the populous area of human settlement, the idea of human sacrifice began. The wives and slaves of a king, or the wife of an ordinary man, might be buried with him, or burned in his funeral pyre. During the Roman Empire, gladiatorial contests involving human (not child) sacrifice were dedicated to the gods.[100] Such sacrifices are rooted in a value structure that was created by breaking the matricentric bond: display of power through killing is a greater good than life.

Edmund Wilson described a conflict between the war minister and the

Prussian legislature in 1862: the legislature was willing to grant an appropriation to finance two years of army service; the minister wanted enough for three. Three were necessary to their needs, he claimed: the first two to teach the soldier to shoot the foreign enemy, the third to teach him to shoot his father and mother.[101] In a way, such pronouncements are only the just rewards of a culture that has been sacrificing its sons (and daughters), not to a god with a name, but to the state or nation, in the wars that have pervaded society since the emergence of patriarchy. The present ruler of Iran, the Ayatollah Khomeini, has frequently declared that "the martyr" [to the state] is "the essence of history."[102] One of the elements political scientists use to characterize totalitarianism is the invasion of the private sphere by the public or the blurring of the line between them. But the priority of the public sphere—as religion or state—over bonds of blood and affection was accomplished millennia ago, when patriarchy was first established.

## 3.   THE ESTABLISHMENT OF PATRIARCHY

The positive accomplishment of patriarchy—what was created rather than what was destroyed—was to make men central (and women marginal) to human life. Again I must point out that this was a factitious accomplishment: women remained and remain central. They procreate, and they nourish; they provide subsistence in most of the world and maintenance in all of the world. There is a class of women who do not work, but it is a tiny one compared to the number of women on earth. Men are central in economic and political life, from which women are largely excluded, and, because of this, women are dependent upon men.

The decreeing and enforcement of women's subordinate status through law was accompanied by the enslavement of women. In time, groups of men were also decreed subordinate and enslaved. Wars of domination—by a man, a class, or a state—followed or accompanied this process. A new political order—a state ruled by a single man and his supporters, or by a class—emerged. Feminist theorists are now analyzing the quantitative and qualitative differences in male subordination of women in states.[103] But it is clear that women refused to be silenced and to silence them a propaganda campaign began that continues to this day. This "campaign" was a dissemination of the idea that men and women represent different categories of people, an institutionalization of this division of humanity, and its enforcement through law and physical might. I call the terms of this division masculine and feminine principles. Human experience is laid on a gamut; one end is declared male and the other female. The terms that follow are drawn from twenty-five hundred years of literature, theology, philosophy, and law.

### The Masculine and Feminine Principles

The two poles defining the limits of human experience are segregated by gender. "Masculine" experience is rooted in power-in-the-world, with its epito-

mizing act: to kill. "Feminine" experience is rooted in nature, with its epito-
mizing act: to give birth. Certain qualities are androgynous or asexual—both
sexes are considered capable of, for instance, moral courage, good manners, or
generosity. But even these have masculine and feminine aspects; a code of
manners, for instance, is "masculine," whereas a "natural" grace of manner is
"feminine." I use quotation marks around these terms for several reasons. First,
I myself do not subscribe to the division of experience I am recounting: actions
or qualities cannot reasonably be assigned gender, even if they are found more
often in one sex than in another. Only the ability to give birth is absolutely
gender-related, and that is paralleled by the essential male contribution to procreation. Second, although it is necessary that we examine the associations that
underlie millennia of Western culture and continue to inform our present culture, it is also necessary that we become aware of the falseness of these associations to actual human nature and behavior. Thus, quotation marks.

"Masculine" qualities are those which demonstrate control and transcendence. Anything that fixes, makes permanent, creates structure within the
seeming flux of nature, is "masculine." So codifications of laws or prestige or
customs are "masculine": authority, rank, status, legitimacy, and right. The
right to own or do something is related to rights over and to rightness—all associated with the male. Qualities supporting the ability to kill—prowess, courage, aggressiveness, and physical skill—are also "masculine." Ownership,
possession, is "masculine" because it is a fixing of property or persons. Permanence and structure are "masculine" ideals because they "control" or seem to
control fluid experience.

This appears to be an old set of associations. Until the recent past, for example, Aboriginal women made only those tools and weapons which were temporary, which would not last: their digging sticks, bark baskets, woven dilly bags
and mats. They would prepare twine, and collect and crush clay and ochres for
body painting. Aboriginal men made the more substantial, enduring equipment, things carved or hewn. Even the secret wooden objects for women's cults
were made and consecrated by men.[104]

Permanence transcends the flux of time, structure the flux of experience,
and immortality the flux of generational life. The impulse toward immortality
and those elements which confer it are therefore also "masculine." It is "masculine" to write a book, to found an institution or a dynasty, to build a bridge, to
perform an action in hope of being remembered for it. In the time described in
the Old Testament, men desired sons to continue their names, as is still true in
many parts of the world; the ancient Greeks were immortalized in poetry that
celebrated their acts of prowess or wealth or fame, along with their male ancestors. Christianity projected immortality to an eternal sphere.

Not only those things which counter fluidity, but also those which demonstrate freedom from or transcendence over nature are associated with masculinity. So asceticism of all kinds is "masculine" (even when women manifest it)
and is associated with the "highest" form of virtue, saintliness. Repudiation of
food and drink in fasting; repudiation of the need for shelter, common to holy
men of the East; repudiation of sex; self-flagellation, wearing of hair shirts or

chains about the body; and even self-mutilations like castration are seen as virtuous because they assert superiority to natural need, and thus to nature. Humanness is identical with control, and control is opposed to nature.

Control is exercised by an individual; and humans are individuals, unlike animals, who are only members of species. The masculine principle is therefore the principle of individuality; and individuality involves competition and rivalry. The masculine principle is associated with linear time, time that has a beginning and end; linearity coupled with rivalry leads to a vision of life as a struggle, a competition, for some transcendent goal to be won within time (or, in Christianity, after it). Victory itself is more important than the content of the victory: not the card game or the contest or the battle, but the winning is what matters. The individual man involved in this struggle stands out within time, separated from its undifferentiating seasons; he has a personal name and a destiny. In contrast, Roman women before the Empire were given no personal name; they were called by their father's name in the genitive case, feminine form; after marriage they took the genitive form of their husband's name: that is, they were denoted simply Marcus's or Antonius's, like things owned.[105] Consider also all the portraits of a named man—John Doe, say—and "his wife," unnamed, an appurtenance to her husband.

Because individuality, transcendence, and control are the marks of the human and of the male, any failure in control is seen as unmanly. Since hierarchy requires obedience, however, men must give up control to others. This is resolved: men may properly cede control to superior men, but never to women. Thus sex in the masculine code can only be a controlling act—rape, ownership of women (through marriage or slavery), or rental of them (prostitution).

The feminine principle is associated with nature, and is not considered a fully human principle. It is associated with everything fluid, transient, and flexible, qualities sometimes denoted *weak;* with nature, the flesh, and procreation. It is thus the pole of sexuality and bodily pleasure, of nutritiveness, compassion, sensitivity to others, mercy, supportiveness, and all giving qualities. It is also the pole of emotion, and includes fury, raging grief, sorrow. It is associated with lack of control in every area—sensuous, sensual, emotive, and bodily.

Love is "feminine," especially the nonegoistic love associated with mothering. This love is valued, but also disdained as being undiscriminating, for mother love does not seem to discriminate in worldly ways. The feminine principle is therefore also the pole of moral flexibility (and women are often accused of being without a moral sense—a point that will be discussed in Chapter Six). All flexible and fluid experience is "feminine"—spontaneity, playfulness, creativity.

The feminine principle is the pole of life; the masculine, of civilization. And life is the highest value for "feminine" people; whereas control is the highest value for "masculine" people. "Masculine" categories are meaningless within the feminine principle, which is essentially subversive of them. The arrangement that has obtained for two to three millennia is that males are expected to demonstrate "masculine" behavior, and females "feminine" behavior. But because of the enormous power of the feminine principle and the nature it symbolizes, it was split in half, into what I call *inlaw* and *outlaw* aspects. "Inlaw" women were expected to show all the loving, maternal, giving qualities in support of the masculine world yet without becoming part of that world. They were to abjure power-in-the-world while simultaneously feeling and acting obediently to uphold it. "Outlaw" feminine qualities are seen as bestial and depraved; this aspect is the subversive pocket, the dumping ground for everything that threatens masculine control. It is rooted in sex, and contains abandonment of control, the antagonism to "masculine" structures associated with the feminine principle, and everything in life that is uncontrollable, unpredictable, and eternally dangerous. For the inlaw feminine aspect, sex is an act of submission for the sake of procreation; only in the outlaw feminine is sex a powerful drive toward another and an abandonment of control.

The feminine principle is not the realm of the human, but of nature, and therefore those associated with it are considered nonhuman. Inlaw feminine women are superhuman, the idealized paragons of poetry and morality; outlaw feminine women are beasts, animals, who deserve to be treated as subhuman and are considered to have no rights whatever. Women who move into the masculine principle and dare to attempt to hold power are considered monsters, unnatural fiends.

The terrible and terrifying aspect of nature (and by extension, women) is seen as hostile not only to civilization but to all its manifestations—legitimacy, authority, and significance. For the "feminine" mind, the only significance resides in being, and usually that mind is granted no relation with intellect. "Feminine" thinking is reflective, associative, and circular; it is found in some male poets. "Masculine" thought is of course rational—that is, logical, linear, and highly exclusionary. It always moves toward a specific goal. Even a language may be categorized as masculine or feminine: Jespersen, for instance, praised English for its virility.[106] There are gender categories within languages; and verse endings are categorized as masculine and feminine, the masculine being the standard ending in a given language, the feminine being the deviant—thus the same sound pattern can be masculine in one language and feminine in another. Renaissance thinkers discriminated between spoken and written languages in gender terms: the spoken word "is stripped of all its powers, it is merely the female part of language . . . just as its intellect is passive; writing, on the other hand, is the active intellect, the 'male principle' of language. It alone harbours the truth."[107]

These categories are translated into actions and attitudes. The men who have been most esteemed are those who controlled most—people, territory, ideas, wealth. No other qualities are required of those who control—not humanity or decency, love or respect for others, not truthfulness, principle, or scruple. A woman who behaved in this way would be seen as a demon. Women are idealized if they are, like Esther, the good women of Proverbs, or Mary, content to be handmaidens, *ancillae*, to "masculine" needs and desires; if, like Cornelia, the famous Roman matron, they find their fulfillment through giving and love. On the other hand, there are the troublemaking women, devils and temptresses, *femmes fatales*, viragoes, and sirens. Virgil's *Aeneid* focuses, on the surface, on a man's creation of a kingdom; but its secondary theme is conflict among kinds of female figures and between women and men. The furious raging female figures of the second half of the book must be vanquished if kingdom and order are to be established.[108] Christianity turned Eve, the mother of all living, into this sort of figure. A thirteenth-century writer, Jacques de Vitry, characterized her thus: "Between Adam and God in Paradise, there was but one woman; yet she had no rest until she had succeeded in banishing her husband from the garden of delights and in condemning Christ to the torment of the cross."[109]

The proper relation among these supposed aspects of human experience varies, depending upon whether a man or a woman is in question. Men are supposed to demonstrate "masculine" qualities, especially with regard to women. But in all-male groups like churches, armies, corporations, governments, and prisons, some men must be the women to the elite men. However, men who demonstrate "feminine" qualities are considered either fools, freaks, fags, *or saints*. Women are expected to demonstrate inlaw feminine qualities with regard to men, but there has been, ever since patriarchy was established, one class of women reserved to serve the needs of men for outlaw experience, namely sex and pleasure. Whether slaves, concubines, hetaerae, demimondaines, prostitutes, or "kept women," this class is extremely vulnerable because it receives no protection of law and no respect within society.

The qualities permitted an inlaw feminine woman are very wispy: the role is a narrow and spineless one. Yet women are watched very closely; they must tread a fine line or be found at fault. Outlaw feminine women are beneath regard, seen as a scandal to their sex and as responsible for all uncontrolled human sexuality. The seal, or guarantee, of a woman's submission to "masculine" requirements has traditionally been chastity—that is, virginity before marriage and fidelity after it. A woman who exhibited all the other proper inlaw qualities but had deviated in this one regard was condemned totally and without possibility of redemption. Female sexual freedom has of course varied. There are many accounts of young girls who have been raped and then killed by their families because of their dishonor; to this day girls in Islamic families are raped by men in the family, then killed to cover its shame.[110] Yet there have been highly patriarchal cultures in which women had some sexual freedom— like the last centuries of the Roman Empire, or the French or British aristocratic cultures of the eighteenth century. Almost always sexual freedom in women is blamed for a general moral "depravity" and held responsible for the demise of a class or state. The connection is unclear, but perhaps it lies in a sense that women would not have sexual freedom if men had not abandoned tight control over them, and that men's abandonment of control leads to "decadence."

Women are rarely seen as individuals, but as members of a sex and of an inlaw or an outlaw class—"good" women or "bad" women. A supposed flaw in one woman evokes damnation of all: "Women!" a man announces with contempt. Hamlet exclaims about his mother's behavior, "Frailty, thy name is woman!" So too feminine symbolism and imagery show a propensity toward polarization: "sometimes utterly exalted, sometimes utterly debased, rarely within the normal range of human possibilities."[111]

Men are generally seen as individuals, except when they are clearly inferior: thus a military commander or a prison warden speaks of "the men," and union leaders of "the rank and file." A failure in one man is never projected as a failure of the entire sex. And males may run the gamut of the principles: so a male figure like Satan or certain dethroned rulers is identified with the outlaw feminine principle; leaders like Gandhi, or servants like the loyal family retainer, are identified with the inlaw feminine principle. Within the masculine principle itself, there is room for usurpation and conflict; the test of legitimacy is success, as a sixteenth-century epigram suggests:

> Treason never prospers; what's the reason?
> For if it prosper, none dare call it treason.[112]

Nor is the masculine principle itself ever subdivided, as the feminine principle is. In its entirety, it is seen as good. But men themselves are subdivided according to their positions in the hierarchy. Full power and control are granted only to the elite group of men; the right to kill is possessed by institutions and the men who control them. The lower on the ladder a man's position, the more he is associated with the feminine principle and required to show obedience and submissiveness.

Reality, of course, constantly challenges the categorizations of patriarchy. Actual women and men possess drives toward both "masculine" and "feminine" qualities, even including their extremes. If men cannot give birth, they can be as mothering and nourishing as women; women can kill, and do. There are extremely controlling women and extremely compassionate men. Both men and women can be ardently sexual, in mutuality and abandonment, without a power element—that is, without a drive to control or be controlled. Most people, indeed, might be said to have all the qualities of the gender principles in moderate amounts.

Nevertheless, it is also true that people are likely to be judged according to their "fit" into their "proper" slot. Generally, women who take control are seen with some animosity, whereas men who do not take control are seen with some contempt. A woman who kills is considered unnatural, whereas a man who kills is considered either a hero (if his killing is performed under institutional auspices) or a criminal, but not as a person who has lost personhood. And most people feel societal pressure to conform to the expectations of the gender principles, and tend to feel guilt or rebelliousness or both when they defy or stretch them.

In addition, the written word—that source of truth—often falsifies actual behavior through omission, deformation, or outright falsehood. The written word slants our perception. So history by and large omits women from the arena of power; women who have exercised power in the past are remembered mainly with a sexual legend. Jezebel, an alien queen with her own gods and a drive to control, is recalled as a fornicatress (which, in the sense of adulteress, she was not), and the cultivated and powerful Queen of Sheba is remembered as a mistress of Solomon. Female saints are remembered mainly for their repudiation of sex. Even women of the more recent past—Emily Dickinson, say— are of interest to many readers on grounds of their personal lives more than of their work. Whether a woman had a sex life, what sort of sex life it was, whether she married, whether she was a good wife or a good mother, are questions that often dominate critical assessment of female artists, writers, and thinkers.[113]

The categorizations of human experience into gender classes have had more powerful a hold on human imagination than actuality itself. Like the masculine principle, these categories structure what we see and know and give it a shape we can understand and believe. We see what we expect to see. When what we see clearly violates our categories, we blot it out of our minds, transform it into the expected, or view the actor with horror, or at least repugnance. Actuality is opaque, fluid, diffused with emotion; it is vague and confusing compared with the certainty of our inherited categories. These categories have been reinforced in every generation and in every aspect of culture—art, philosophy, literature, law, religion, and politics. Although they may from time to time be reinterpreted, they are never seriously challenged by any culture as a whole. The complaints of those who feel demeaned or doomed to invisibility by patriarchal categories are viewed as strident hysteria. The greatest armor against categorization in the past has been illiteracy and ignorance, as is shown by the bouncy resilience of lower-class women and men in the occasional document, poem, or tale in which we can catch a glimpse of them. Universal literacy, a goal that is on the whole admirable, also guarantees universal control of mind formation by the media.

Because patriarchy is at bottom *unnatural*, it cannot survive without tradition and institutionalization. Patriarchal attitudes must be given repetitive expression over time and over the space of a culture; that is, they must be passed on through generations and replicated in every area of the society in order to be maintained. They do not arise naturally from living, as matricentric values do; they are imposed upon us and the young respond to the power world with shock and bitterness—or did, before television.

The division of experience into masculine and feminine categories was accompanied by the fostering of and dynamic interaction among other attitudes. These attitudes—still with us—are all of a piece in our heads, are integrated. But I must use a "masculine" method—breaking them down into discrete units—to discuss them. They are forms of institutionalization of the corollaries to the division of experience: diminishment of women; and diminishment of nature.

## Diminishment of Women

One of the oldest extant documentations of patriarchal ideology is the *Enuma Elish,* a Sumerian epic composed probably about 1350 B.C.E. In the mythology that preceded it, goddesses are extremely powerful; in the *Enuma Elish,* the god Marduk ascends to full power. But the condition of his assumption of power is that he must totally subjugate women: he must destroy the goddess Tiamat, the original progenitor, creator of everything, who was degraded by later myth into a principle of chaos, inertia, and anarchy. Despite her degradation, Marduk cannot defeat her by his superior strength: her strength is equal to his. He vanquishes her, finally, because of his superior *armament.*[114]

Patriarchy was probably first established by a priestly elite who determined certain rules for proper worship and proper life; in many ancient cities this caste of priests was superseded or joined by a military elite. Eventually, in most of the Western world, both gave way to an aristocratic elite; at the end of the second millennium of the Christian Era, a managerial elite has taken ascendancy. The stratification institutionalized by patriarchy is called hierarchy, the root of which is *hiero*, the term for priest. Contests among priests of different persuasions existed: for instance, that between Elijah and the priests of Ba'al, which Elijah wins, proving that his god, YHWH, has more power over nature than the priests of Ba'al (I Kings 18). The *Enuma Elish* may reflect the ascendancy of a military elite in Babylon.

Women and men ruled in early Sumerian city-states, as earthly representatives of the goddess Ninhursag and the god Enki, both children of the goddess Nammu. A class of priests were their logothetes, imperial administrators, and did the actual organizing and public administration and, at times, controlled public distribution of food.[115] When war erupted on earth, women became warriors. But they usually tried to solve conflicts peacefully, and were gradually ousted from power as a male warrior class established itself and, in some cities, usurped the priestly caste. Warriors require war, and in war, men are killed and women are enslaved. Around the same time, a slave class emerged in Sumer.

By this time, many Sumerian cities were fortified and fought each other continuously about borders. This state of war led to greater centralization of control, to the imposition of taxes, and to the corvée—forced labor to maintain the defenses. Eventually the war leaders "emerged as kings—lugals—literally, 'great men.' "[116] And in time the kings built palaces, temples, claimed land to support them, assumed priestly functions, claimed divine origin, and set up hereditary succession.[117] By the third millennium B.C.E., men alone made up the assembly of Uruk.[118] Women retained some powers: they could practice medicine, carry on trade, make contracts, run businesses; and both boys and girls were educated. Laws began to be recorded. Urukagina's Code was codified to protect the property of the ruling elite and of the temples. Urukagina led a revolution against a warrior class, and his laws also protected the rights of widows and orphans: it is noteworthy that widows and orphans *required* protection at this time. He also imposed monogamy on women, although they had customarily taken two husbands. And he passed edicts on an act never before recorded as a crime: adultery—but a crime only for women. That women were being suppressed in this period seems unquestionable; for instance, one item in Urukagina's Code held that a woman who "has sinned" by "saying something to a man that she should not have said" would have her teeth crushed with burned bricks.[119] Ruby Rohrlich concludes that the code institutionalized patrilineal inheritance and descent, patrilocal residence, and the patriarchal family.[120]

Around 2600 B.C.E., Sargon united Sumer with northern Mesopotamia; and around 1800 B.C.E., Hammurabi established a dynasty at Babylon, swallowing Sumer. By this time the repressive atmosphere for women had become even more severe. Two-thirds of Hammurabi's Code was devoted to defining and constricting women's rights—yet a twentieth-century commentator asserted that it gave women more rights than they possessed in twentieth-century

England and America.[121] Among its provisions were the punishment of ordeal by water of a wife who neglected her house; the impaling or crucifixion of a wife who caused her husband's death in order to marry another man; and the enslavement in her own house of a "worthless" wife if her husband decided to take another wife.[122]

The shift in women's status is evident in Hebrew documents as well. Julian Morgenstern first demonstrated in 1929 that biblical texts were altered to excise signs of matrilineality and to name the tribes after patriarchs.[123] Knowing this helps to make sense out of seemingly confused tales or relationships, like that of Sarah and Abraham, who were permitted to marry because they had different mothers and descent was reckoned through the mother. David Bakan asserts that the biblical editors turned the original matriarchs (see p. 55) into "mere wives or the concubines of males."[124] He concludes that the P document—the priestly strand of addition, excision, and alteration in the first books of the Old Testament—in fact comprises "an intense effort to firm up patrilineal descent and the concomitant social and political organization. Patrilineal descent is strongly associated with ownership of property. There is great emphasis on obedience." The major preoccupations of these editors were "origin, death, property, and power."[125]

When Moses takes a Cushite wife, he is violating his own laws, supposedly the laws of YHWH; and his sibs Miriam and Aaron criticize him. But it is not Moses but Miriam who is punished. "God's punishment of Miriam is in the order of a father spitting on a daughter's face ... the story implicitly acknowledges a father's right to do this ... Not only lineage, but authority as well, is ascribed to the male side." Bakan deduces that the text at this point is establishing not just patrilineality but also patriarchal control and authority.[126]

The new laws of patriarchy were also recorded, mainly in the book of Leviticus. Written by men and for men, most of its admonitions concern male behavior. A great many acts make men "unclean," in need of purification which can be offered only by the priests—naturally. The book defines these acts, stipulates the correct purification ritual, and specifies the portion of the animal sacrifice that is to be given to the priest as payment.

The things that can make a man unclean include the most basic: what he eats and with whom he copulates. Thus the intervention of the priest is required in the most ordinary events of life. (Similarly, the sacraments of the Catholic Church involve priestly intervention in the most ordinary and essential events—birth, puberty, marriage, and death.) In Leviticus, *all* sexual acts are unclean (abominations) and many forms of sex are entirely forbidden. But a most interesting fact is that the book associates sex, the female body, and disease. Chapter 11 treats of clean and unclean animals (what may and may not be eaten); Chapter 12 deals with purification rituals after childbirth (forty days of isolation for a son, eighty days for a daughter). Chapters 13 and 14 deal with purification rituals for leprosy; Chapter 15 with those for a "running issue" (ulcer?) in a man; and those for a man and a woman after sexual intercourse; and for a woman during and after menstruation.

Thus disease, sexual intercourse, and the ordinary conditions of womanhood—menstruation and childbirth—are seen as related, and equally unclean. Indeed, menstruation is called *sickness* and childbirth *infirmity*, and there is severe punishment for a couple who have intercourse while the woman is menstruating—exile. It may seem remarkable to link such items, but they do share one characteristic: all are manifestations of nature in humans. The food that enters the mouth, and the mouth (vagina) into which the male organ enters, link men with nature, animal, and woman. The diseases treated here are only visible diseases, those with emanations. The fluids—water, mother's milk, menstrual blood, semen—which were once holy have become tainted.

A similar progress occurred millennia later and continents away, in Mesoamerica. Originally a goddess-worshiping culture, peaceful, horticultural, and egalitarian, Mesoamerican communities came in time to be dominated by priests, builders of monuments (like the Sumerian kings' buildings, ziggurats). We have discussed the degradation of goddesses as gods began to take their place and the notion of state arose: "Civacoatl, goddess of earth and birth, 'she who plants root crops,' often called 'our mother' . . . became a harbinger of war, loss, and disaster, a representation of the grief of women who died in childbed and who lost their men in the frequent Aztec wars."[127] Coalicue, the huge demonic figure with the skirt of snakes, also called the Filth Eater, is a later avatar of Cihuacoatl (Civacoatl), and was the mother of the god of war, Huitzilopochtli.[128] She was retired, so to speak, when her son became dominant, but was considered to "preside over and personify the collective hunger of the gods for human victims."[129] The earth mother (who, in some versions, was killed by fire) survives as a sacrificial knife clamoring for human hearts. Burr Brundage writes that blood sacrifice was "the central concern of the Aztec state." The flint knife, legacy of the goddess Cihuacoatl, was the ultimate principle of the universe.[130] This transfer of devotion reflects a shift in loyalty from nature (life, fertility, nurturance) to power (control, killing, sacrifice, and obedience).

As Mesoamerican states became centralized, new practices arose, which were codified, for example, by Nezahualcoyotl, ruler of Texcoco, in the mid-fifteenth century. His laws provide different punishments—for the same acts— performed by people of different classes, occupations, age, and sex. Among these acts are drunkenness and adultery: men transgressed the adultery laws only if they became involved with married women. The Aztec state became centralized in the fifteenth and sixteenth centuries; as it did so, it codified a series of laws regulating women's behavior. These laws granted women some rights, but required chastity of girls and fidelity in married women. Polygyny was legalized, concubines were permitted, and men had the right to reject their wives on very slight (and unprovable) grounds.[131]

The Aztec priests, who could foresee their future no more clearly than women had when they granted men status, demanded war. They needed more captives taken in war, who were forced to mount the many narrow steps of the pyramids, who were urged not to "act like a woman," and made to lie on the altar of the sun and have their hearts cut out with the flint knife. More war meant more soldiers; and in time, a military elite took control of Aztec culture. The Aztecs "practiced human sacrifice on an unprecedented scale" and the entire culture was built around this practice.[132] Young men were pressured to become properly "masculine," to go to war and to kill. Women mocked men who had not yet made a capture; fathers killed sons who were insufficiently warlike. Many young men committed suicide.[133]

The quality of Aztec life seems to have been grim. The people were pervaded by a sense of sin and filth. Suicide was common, and not just among young men. There was self-mutilation of hideous kinds, especially on the part of the priests.[134] Long before the arrival of Cortez, the continual incursions of the Mexicas into neighboring lands, their militarism, and their warfare had made them hated by all their neighbors: which is why Cortez was able to muster other Mesoamerican societies to fight against the Mexicas, to assist the Spanish in vanquishing them.

Although the old Norse had a sense of humor and some sexual freedom, they too had a grim vision of existence. As we have seen, they too "killed" their earth mother, Nerthus, and their extant myths reflect the overthrow of the fertility deities, the Vanir, by the gods of war, the Aesir. Kevin Crossley-Holland writes, "A culture finds the gods it needs and the Norse world needed a god to justify the violence that is one of its hallmarks."[135] Odin, god of battle, was "terrible, arrogant, and capricious." He started wars among the humans living in Midgard, the middle world between the realm of the gods and the realm of chaos and death. He entertained slain warriors in his hall, Valhalla; and he demanded human and animal sacrifices.[136]

The myth of Odin was accompanied by human worship in kind: human sacrifice was part of the ritual devoted to Odin and other Germanic war gods. Adam of Bremen, an eleventh-century historian, records that he saw the bodies of many people hanging in the sacrificial grove at Uppsala near the temple containing idols of the trinity of the Norse: Odin, Thor, and Freyr; and the sagas—the prose Eddas—depict human sacrificial victims as being pierced with a spear and dedicated to Odin.[137] Among the epithets of Odin were "God of the Hanged" and "God of the Spear," and the mythology predicts that Odin will die at Ragnarok, hanging on Yggdrasill, the world tree, just as his victims did.

Compared to such grim and bloody traditions, the Greek way seems mild. We can hypothesize that the extremities of "masculine" values do lead to the extinction of the people and culture that entertains them. It was the milder Judaic and Hellenic traditions that flourished and combined to reemerge as the Christian world. (If there is a lesson in this, we have not yet learned it.)

The Greeks were never quite able to eliminate the power of women, despite strong measures. The "feminine" and the female are not as absent from Greek culture as they are from later Aztec or Norse culture. This is not, however, to say that the female element is accepted in Greek culture. Far from it. Attacks on women pervade Greek literature, and they have a strident and hysterical tone. Hesiod, in the eighth century B.C.E., associated women with nature in its uncontrollable, violent, and spontaneous forms: "Gaia sends forth both rampant vegetation and monstrous semi-human creatures" in his rendering of creation. For Hesiod, the triumph of the male deity is a triumph of order and control, the subduing of nature to useful purposes, the restraint of its destructive aspects.[138] Hesiod and other Greek writers seem obsessively focused on women's insatiable sexuality, whorish ways, insubordination to men, ignorance, sloth, and untrustworthiness. One wonders what the women could have been doing to merit such concentration and vituperation: one suspects they retained some kind of power.

Semonides of Amorgos wrote a long misogynistic diatribe against women, claiming they were mere animals; Euripides, the one Greek playwright considered sympathetic to women, wrote, "Woman is a more terrible thing than the violence of the raging sea, than the force of torrents, than the sweeping breath of fire."[139] Such attacks must be considered in the context of a culture in which women were secluded within the household or harem, excluded from all participation in city-state affairs, could not control their own property, and were little better than slaves. Sarah Pomeroy suggests that male-female tensions in Greece were extreme: they appear even in myth. The many tales of Zeus involve frequent rape; so do many tales about Apollo; and Zeus and Hera are depicted as constantly bickering, with a little battering (and even torture) of Hera as well.[140]

Hera had been a primary goddess in the Greek past, and Philip Slater believes her power was still great during the period of intense misogyny in Greek literature. He points out that in *The Iliad*, Zeus cannot save Troy even though it is his favorite city, because Paris broke laws upheld by Hera; and that Zeus courted Hera by appealing to her as a small bird which she warmed in her bosom.[141] Slater builds a theory about Greek life from the tensions and rage that appear in the misogynistic writings of Greek men and from knowledge about the condition of women.

Briefly, he explains that women were infuriated by their virtual imprisonment within the home, and by the disdain with which their husbands treated them. Athenian girls were not educated and were married very young; their husbands were much older and often educated. In response to this situation Athenian women tried to control and influence their sons; Athenian men avoided the home as much as possible. This, Slater concludes, led to women having an overwhelmingly powerful influence within their own domain, and an influence pervaded by anger. The Greek male's contempt for women could arise only from an intense fear of them and "an underlying suspicion of male inferiority. Why else would such extreme measures be necessary? Customs such as the rule that a woman should not be older than her husband, or of higher social status, or more educated, or paid the same as a male for the same work, or be in a position of authority—betray an assumption that males are incapable of competing with females on an equal basis; the cards must first be stacked, the male given a handicap."[142]

Unlike the Jews, the Greeks did not project power and control onto a deity who was a punishing (and occasionally rewarding) father; unlike the militaristic cultures—the Babylonians, Assyrians, Hittites, Medes, and others, who worshiped power in men, and envisioned it as conquest—the Greeks did not express their values through unremitting war. The Greek gods were less powers superior to humans than they were expressions of powers and impulses within humans. The Greeks could rise in a militaristic, macho way, but most of the city-states were not militaristic. They had a different vision of power, and therefore a different vision of Man.

They saw man (and here the term is not generic but specific) as a creature in control *of himself*. Reason is the chariot driver, restraining the horses of concupiscence and irascibility; the good life is a harmony of physical and intellectual achievement in a realm completely cut off from necessity, from domination by nature. (I am reminded of the Chaga culture in which men, once they are initiated, claim never again to defecate.) *Necessity* is the realm of nature, the basic, "animal" part of life, the nonvolitional. And the Greeks saw women as nonvolitional beings. "Among the classical Greeks, women were silenced in part because that which defines them and to which they are inescapably linked—sexuality, natality, the human body (images of uncleanness and taboo, visions of dependency, helplessness, vulnerability)—was omitted from political speech."[143] The theoretical discussions in the agora, the development of a political realm, the creation of a class of *hetaerae*, women who could speak and think articulately, who pleasured the men gracefully but had no claim upon them, and the prostitutes, who serviced their bodies, the much-admired life style of the Athenians that has been emulated by generations of scholars and parliamentarians, was based in a desire to escape the private realm, the emotion, intimacy, and suffering of the family, "evocations of female power."[144]

The thought of the Greeks of the Classical period has been the foundation stone of Western culture—all philosophy is a footnote to Plato, it is said. Yet that theory was based on an incomplete, even biased view of human life, on a vision of life disembodied, disconnected from the very things that sustain it. Women's bodies and blood and pregnancy; the labor of women and slaves and lower-class men; eating and excretion; emotion and bonding: these were elements in the lives of the men who created the theories that ignored such things. It is possibly because the thought of the Classical Greeks soared so high above the earth, disconnected men so totally from necessity, that they have the distinction of having written more hatefully and intensely about women than any previous culture. Women, associated with necessity (nonvolition), with nature, flesh, emotion, were emblems of what had to be rejected in order to create a transcendent world. Insofar as women had actual power or influence over the well-being or imaginations of men, they threatened to destroy men's fictions with their facts.

What is certain is that Greek literature, from Hesiod through to Euripides, demonstrates a "consistent and systematic association of the world of nature" with female power.[145] In art and poetry two themes recur continually: the battles of the Olympian gods against the Titans, and the battles of the Athenians against the Amazons. The Titans, who seem to represent unleashed human passion and force, and the Amazons, forceful women, are the enemies of the order asserted by male deities and male control.[146]

The masculine and feminine principles as descriptions of human experience divided by gender arise from Greek thought more strongly than any other source. The outlaw feminine is Hesiod's rampant, uncontrolled, sexual nature; the inlaw feminine is the tamed earth, as in Sophocles' famous "hymn to man" from *Antigone:*

> And she, the greatest of the gods, the earth—
> Ageless she is, and unwearied—he wears her away
> As the ploughs go up and down from year to year
> And his mules turn up the soil.[147]

Aeschylus' declaration that the father was the parent of the child and the mother mere vessel, like the earth in which the man plants the seed, was given theoretical, scientific validation by Aristotle, who teaches that the sperm is merely nourished by menstrual blood to create the father's progeny. This was the final step in the defeat of the ancient world of matricentry—the usurpation by men of the one talent they do not share with women, the appropriation of procreation. It is a belief still current in many parts of the East and Middle East.

Similar patterns associating women with nature and both with impurity are found in other cultures. Islam decrees six states of impurity: three are female—menstruation, birth, and afterbirth bleeding; three are male—seminal discharge, sex, and death.[148] Women's impurity has to do with natural processes; male impurity has to do with desire, connection with women, and the end of life. Presumably women do not die, but are, like animals, invisibly recycled in the life of the species. Islamic temples bear a warning against the entrance of women, dogs, and other impure animals.

The Chinese of Tsinhai believed that women are always impure and that their impurity is connected with blood, especially menstruation and afterbirth bleeding. A mother must be purified after giving birth, a purification that takes longer after the birth of a girl than that of a boy. Among certain Buddhist groups, only men can attain a pure heaven and only women are doomed to a pure hell. In pure heaven creatures are reincarnated; in pure hell, which is made up of blood, creatures must wait to be redeemed. The women of these groups lament their own impurity but hope to attain a higher reincarnation by giving birth to a boy. That gives them the right to return in their next life as a human being. A human being is a man.[149]

## Diminishment of Nature

It is remarkable that almost never, in lists of impurities or uncleannesses or abominations, is there mention of urine, vomit, sputum, or feces, all more unpleasant in odor and more potentially disease-ridden than either sperm or menstrual blood. There are no special rules for disposing of such things. What patriarchy finds appalling is that which ties men to women and thus to nature.

Both sexes may, with good reason, have desired to transcend and control the natural world. The raw state of the human in nature is not always aesthetically pleasing, comfortable, or secure. But the way the ideology of patriarchy divided responsibility and reward permitted men (more than women), and permits them still, to maintain the delusion that they are not as tied to necessity and nature as women and other animals.

Because belief that a person or a sex is not bound by nature and necessity is patently false, maintenance of such a belief depends on continual denial of actuality, and substitutions of symbolic formulas for actuality. Denial often takes the form of ignoring or toughening oneself to the needs of the body and affectionate emotions. The thought of the West ignores the fact that pride, arrogance, and an extreme drive to power are rooted in emotion. Such thinking is not logical. Thus a male may acceptably display anger, which does not *seem* to be a loss of control, but not compassion, which may not involve any loss of control at all, but seems to be a melting. Emotions or states which offer an appearance of control, and bodily needs like hunger, warmth, and excretion that do not necessarily involve intercourse of any sort with women, are by and large free from taint.

The diminishment of nature in men takes two major forms: "toughness" and asceticism. "Toughness," which has different names in different cultures, has to do with overcoming the emotions and the body. It is deeply associated with the military, and probably has been since the emergence of patriarchy. Spartan training, the discipline of Roman legions, and the basic training of American soldiers that teaches them to kill are all of a piece. Shakespeare's Antony is praised by Augustus because in a time of famine while he was being pursued by an enemy host, he was able, "though daintily brought up," to eat the bark of trees, rough berries, and to drink the stale of horses. Shakespeare's Coriolanus, a great fighting machine, is able to go on fighting after being wounded: he does not feel his wounds, he does not weaken from loss of blood. Othello claims to have slept on the "flinty and steel couch of war."

Training in toughness involves a mental and physical stoicism, a refusal to feel need and pain, bodily and emotional. The body is toughened through torture—exercises that drive the body past its endurance—continued over a long period, so that the endurance is extended. The emotions are toughened through brutalization, such as that offered in British public schools and in certain military or protomilitary boys' schools; and through indoctrination in repression, which occurs early in the life of almost every boy. It is assumed that once the body and emotions are toughened, a boy has become a man, able to control any situation. That no one is so able is ignored; the pretense is taken for reality.

More is required of the ascetic. The tough man can get involved with women—indeed, *should* get involved with them if only to prove he is not homosexual. Homosexuality is seen as tainted because in it, according to ancient lore, one partner must lower himself to become a woman. (The ancient world did not conceive of mutuality in sex but saw it as a power relation, with the man vanquishing and the "woman" surrendering.) Homosexuality is also often associated with bestiality and with animals (although same-sex copulation is rare among animals): this association betrays the fundamental need of patriarchy to dissociate men from nature and to assert that man's relation with it is one in which he has entire control. The ascetic finds all of nature repugnant, especially women. He denies all his needs, usually starting with sex and moving to food, warmth, and other bodily necessities.

So there is a tradition within Judaism of holy men living in the desert eating locusts and honey in order to concentrate upon the divine. The Essenes, an old Hebrew sect who lived near the shore of the Dead Sea and are believed to have influenced Jesus, were celibate and ascetic, so ascetic they did not allow themselves to urinate on the Sabbath.[150]

The teaching of Siddhartha, and the underlying premise of Buddhism, is that man is trapped by his own ego in a never-ending cycle of births and deaths, a continual round of reincarnations, each of which is painful. Life is lowly and miserable, and the aim of Buddhist teaching is to enable men to get beyond the self and so beyond this cycle, to reach Enlightenment, and eventually *nirvana*, a place that transcends this natural course. Hindu thinking shares this sense of things, and both religions have given rise to extreme asceticism.

Hindus following the Laws of Manu lie or sit on spikes, wear sandals lined with spikes, hold an arm in the air until it atrophies, clench a hand until the fingernails grow through the palms, hang their heads down in the smoke of fires, fix iron rings into their penises.[151] One sometimes suspects that more ingenuity has been devoted to conceiving punishments and tortures for the body than has been spent on improving its condition.

Barrington Moore, who discusses these forms of asceticism, explains that they arise from a wish to escape from the endless cycle of lives and to free the self from desire, but also from a drive to control the outside world.[152] Many ascetics believe they have a way "to conquer the powers of the universe itself, the macrocosm, by subduing completely their reflection in the microcosm," their own organic being. Heinrich Zimmer believes ascetics manifest "an extreme will for power, a desire to conjure the unlimited hidden energies that are stored in the unconscious vital part of human nature."[153] In much of Hindu legend, asceticism is presented as the most effective way to compel the will of the Supreme Being. The power drive of ascetics is extraordinary in that it is rooted in an effort to control the controlling deity it has projected. Crucifixion is seen as a device for compelling the divine will; thus, Moore suggests, to be crucified is to be aggressive against deity. The greatest fear of many ascetics is sexuality: if it were succumbed to, the ascetic could, in an hour, in a night, spill out "the whole charge of physical force that he had spent a lifetime striving to accumulate."[154]

Although Christianity did not require celibacy of its priests until the eleventh to twelfth centuries, there was always a strong antisex current in the religion. The libertine sexual climate of the Roman Empire was repulsive to many people, Christians and non-Christians. But Christianity also manifested a strain of disapproval of all emotion, in line with its background of Stoicism.

The central doctrines of Christianity focused on love and fertility, the old values, even as the Church itself became a ground of contention and rivalry in an effort to establish a patriarchal structure—hierarchical, coercive, and demanding of obedience. But within the Church there was considerable misogyny, and tracts condemning women are frequent. Katherine M. Rogers asserts that by the time of Tertullian (160–230), the Christian aversion to sex had hardened into universally accepted dogma; Tertullian's tracts increasingly excoriate sex and women.[155] Saint John Chrysostom wrote that women were to be avoided because the mere sight of them caused so much physical anguish.[156] In the Epistle to the Romans, he asserted that "the passions in fact are all dishonorable."[157]

For Augustine, "the body of a man is as superior to that of a woman as the soul is to the body."[158] Yet Augustine found the bodily state of men humiliating because of the lack of control over the penis, which is "moved and restrained not at our will, but by a certain independent autocracy." This lack of control seemed shameful to him, and he believed that the condition "was different before sin . . . because not yet did lust move those members without the will's consent."[159] Women, then, provided the stimulus to events that reminded men they were not transcendent but were still part of nature. Augustine was willing to eradicate nature even "to the point of wrecking its designs and bringing about the physical end of the human race."[160]

The desire to transcend and control nature led to the positing of a higher realm, the realm of the spirit, of a god in whose name children were sacrificed. This conception of reality is racially suicidal, but its suicidal impulses are disguised by the positing of that higher realm. As John Boswell writes, Christians believed that the New Testament "clearly and consistently taught that celibacy was the highest response to human eroticism, that not only was there no imperative to procreate, it was in fact morally better not to do so. . . . At high theological levels, 'nature' could not be accommodated in a Christian frame of reference at all."[161] Even in sex devoted to procreation—the only proper use of sex in Christian doctrine—the existence of pleasure was considered sinful by many members of the early Church; Saint Basil wrote that "he who follows nature in these matters condemns himself in that he has not yet completely conquered nature and is still ruled by the flesh."[162] Nature was the old dispensation; the new one was grace—whatever that meant.

Christianity too offers examples of severe asceticism: barefoot monks living in impoverished hardship; people (like Sir Thomas More, for instance) wearing hair shirts all their lives, or wrapping chains around their bodies. Spanish monks marched through the streets whipping themselves, and whipping of self or others is still practiced in convents. Beyond that, there are the hideous punishments—disembowelings, use of the rack, and burning alive—that Christians visited upon each other during the long struggle between Catholicism and Protestantism.

Women as well as men have been ascetic, although they seem to avoid the extremities of ascetic practices. For a woman, the prime requirement is chastity, and preferably virginity maintained throughout life. Such a state is admired, however, only if it is maintained on principle; the woman who remains virgin by chance is pitied rather than admired. Moreover, if virginity is required for holiness in women, it has also been demanded of unmarried women throughout most of Western civilization, and is still in Islam.

At present, asceticism is more common in the East than in the West;

wherever it exists, women are perceived as the enemy. There are places that no woman may enter: lamaseries, Buddhist temples, and the area around the altar in Catholic churches. More striking in our own culture is the response of certain churches to the ordination of women as Episcopalian priests. One Episcopalian church and school (for boys) picked itself up, left its home church, and joined the Greek Orthodox Church rather than countenance the ordination of women.[163] A sin considered heinous for centuries—apostasy—seemed preferable to this group to the knowledge that women served as priests within their religion. One wonders what the presence of women in this role means to these men, what kind of horror is conveyed by a female body on sacred ground. At the same time, Catholicism, which remains adamant against the ordination of women and the marriage of priests, has nevertheless agreed to receive into its bosom married priests who are defecting from Episcopalianism because of the ordination of women.[164] But paradox is implicit in patriarchy, as we shall see.

## The Median Place of Women

It is necessary once more to reprise our argument. Humans at some point in the distant past felt a need to distinguish themselves from other animals and to that end devised a high god, a god of power-over, and asserted that man had been made in the image of this god. Man was distinct from other animals because like this god he had control over them and over all of nature. This assertion cannot be demonstrated: neither men nor women, then or now, have control over nature, whether their own "human natures" or the environment. Many forms of control over both have been invented in the millennia since this assertion was first made, but each causes new problems, and the totality of these controls now threatens human survival.

It has, however, always been obvious to anyone who examined the proposition that humans lack control over their lives. What was contrived to conceal this fact was a symbolic formula: women were of a different species than men and were, by virtue of their biology, connected with the realm of the necessary. Men might need food, a bath, warm clothes, but these items were the responsibility of women. Men might sweat, fall ill, need to excrete, but these states were ignored: men's proper sphere was the use of power—of mind, of "spirit," and of body (prowess or arms).

Women, then, were a mediating link between men and necessity, men and nature, men and the intolerable other. Human vulnerability, failure in control, surrender to sensation and emotion were projected onto women alone (for the most part). Women's behavior, regardless of its character, was interpreted as displaying these "weaknesses," while men's behavior, when similar, was either ignored or interpreted differently. Women were defined by those traits men wished not to possess. This splitting of human experience into gender roles, however, made women even more necessary to men.

Some years ago Sherry Ortner wrote a highly influential essay discussing the association of women with nature and men with culture.[165] Drawing on the thinking of Lévi-Strauss, Ortner examines these associations and finds them present in much thinking of both simple and complex societies. Since the appearance of the essay, many anthropologists have considered the question further, and have modified or challenged Ortner's position.[166] In some societies there do not seem to be categories of nature versus culture; in some the acculturated are not men, but married couples, for instance. The nature-culture dichotomy is probably most prominent in societies in which control is seen as a high good; if women are not identified with nature, the reason is that men have "tamed" them, and usurped their powers of the wild. In cultures valuing control, however, women are seen as mediating links, liaisons, between men and another realm. No matter how humanness may be defined, women are not quite full humans, but semihumans with one foot in man's realm and one foot in another.

The male Bakweri of Cameroon, for instance, have a myth of beginnings in which there was a town with four inhabitants who could not live together. The four had a contest and Moto won: the others were forced into the wild. Moto is or becomes a person; the others are the ape, the rat, and the mermaid, all of which are in this mythology associated with women and children. Women are included among human beings, but they are also part of the wild, and in actual life go every day to the forest to collect firewood—a backbreaking task. The men live on enclosed farms. The women have secret rites, the *liengu*, in which they become mermaids; they have a secret language as well. The intention of the *liengu* seems to be to retain women's power over their own reproduction.[167] In this society, men are associated with personhood and women are mediators between humanness and the wild.

The Gimi of Papua New Guinea associate men with nature and "profane interactions between men and women" with culture. The men's realm is the forest; the women are expected to remain within fenced gardens. However, the Gimi have a myth that describes how woman originally fled her worldly husband to enter the forest and mate with a marsupial. She had huge powers; she raised her children and cultivated her crops in broad, open expanses. But in time the men of her husband's lineage shot her and brought her back: she lost her freedom after receiving a wound that was a mouth but also a castration. Thus women's association with culture, the enclosure, is essentially an imprisonment. And the word for the wild, the realm of men, is the word for afterlife as well—*kore*. It denotes indestructible (permanent) or spiritual (supranatural) traits, and is used in opposition to the ordinary and mundane—*dusa*.[168] Thus men have taken over the wild from women and reformed it; only men have access to the spiritual world; women, tamed, remain intermediaries. Only by controlling women can men control the wild and transcend it.

Laymi culture is centered in language. The Laymi, who live in the Bolivian Andes, are for the most part egalitarian. Women compose the music, sing, and weave important designs; men play musical instruments and knit. But all political activity and the highest religious roles are reserved for the men because, they say, women do not speak well. The Laymi have extramarital sex in the wild; marital sex occurs within the house.[169] Since it is in sex that men are most connected to and vulnerable to women, this association is based on a sense of women's natures. Men have access to a control over nature, a higher power—language. Free sexuality is associated with nature, the wild, women's realm.

The Igbo- and Ibibio-speaking women of eastern Nigeria rose in rebellion against British colonial rule in 1929. Angry about a new tax, they created assemblies of women ranging from a few hundred to more than ten thousand, and attacked the courts and headquarters of the colonial administration. They freed prisoners and looted European trading warehouses.

Their rebellion was extremely disturbing to the Europeans, partly because it was women who led the only widespread rebellion against colonial rule between 1914 and 1930, but partly because of the women's behavior, which the colonists described as "obscene, hostile, and disrespectful." The women were dressed only in fronds and leaves; they were dressed, as they themselves saw it, as the "wild." This concept had tremendous force for the men of their culture, who still remembered the traditional rights of women, associated with the wild, with nature. The men were either cowed by the women or joined them.[170]

Crow culture was matrilineal, and women had important roles in tribal ritual. Nevertheless, during menstruation women had to ride inferior horses and were not allowed to approach a wounded man or men starting out in a war party. Moreover, women were not allowed to handle the single most sacred object of the Crow, a Sun Dance doll. Ortner concludes that despite the rights and powers possessed by women, a line is drawn: "Menstruation is a threat to warfare, one of the most valued institutions of the tribe, one that is central to their self-definition; and the most sacred object of the tribe is taboo to the direct sight and touch of women."[171] Here too, despite considerable egalitarianism, women were associated with nature, which threatens men, who are connected with power and transcendence.

Lévi-Strauss cites a series of myths from South American peoples in which women are mediators between men and jaguars. The arrangement varies from myth to myth, from the Ge to the Opaye-Shavante to the Mataco, the Toba-Pilaga, and other tribes. In some cases the tale is related to the difference between men and jaguars—men eat cooked meat—but it occurs also in other contexts, such as the discovery of tobacco. In most cases the woman is dispensable and is killed once the relation between men and animals is fixed.[172] The woman may be identified as a jaguar, or as the jaguar's wife, or as a human who has married the jaguar and is gradually transformed into an animal; what seems constant is that women stand in a different relation to the wild than men, and mediate between the two. The egalitarian Mbuti see the forest as the true life giver, and women as closer to the forest than men.[173]

The Greek Pandora is comparable to Eve as temptress, and the box opened by Pandora may be a metaphor for sexuality: the sexual act thus exposes men to the ills within Pandora's box.[174] In Christianity, a witch is a woman who sleeps with the devil, and a nun is a woman who marries her god.[175] In later centuries of Christian culture, women were identified as intermediaries between men and the divine—angels in the house, agents of male redemption—and between men and the demonic—Tertullian's "the Devil's gateway," the *vagina dentata*, Munch's vampires, for example. Even when women are idealized, they remain intermediaries. In eighteenth-century France, for example, certain male thinkers reacted against their highly intellectual, abstract, and rational culture and exalted women because women were considered nonrational and sentimental, because their lustfulness was a form of love, which had become a beneficial principle, and because their weakness seemed suddenly delicacy, a virtue in a period of denigration of heroic strength. Women were newly endowed with a special form of knowledge—intuition—which they possess from birth, without effort, while men must acquire knowledge through work and experience.[176]

In nineteenth-century America, at a time when control was taking new and world-shaking forms (expansion, industrialization), *Godey's Lady's Book*, the women's bible of its time, defended and justified its female readers by claiming that they were "the connecting link between man and the inferior animals, possessing a central rank between the mysterious instinct of the latter and the [for women] unattainable energies of men."[177]

An interesting variant is found in gypsy culture. Gypsies distinguish between the clean and the unclean: the gypsy world is clean. It is also unsocialized, wild, and contains complex cleanliness rituals. One doesn't, for instance, wash one's cup and one's hands in the same bowl, and food is prepared very carefully, according to ritualized rules. But most gypsy food comes from the outside—Gorgio—world, which is polluted. It is the gypsy women who go "calling" to obtain this food; they also prepare it. Women are thus the intermediaries between the unclean, alien, socialized Gorgio world and the clean, wild world of gypsy men.[178]

Clearly, men perceive women as the Other. But women's otherness is of a particular kind: women stand between men and whatever elements of experience they disconnect themselves from, renounce, or fear. Whether it is wildness or uncleanness, the divine or the civilized, women are held responsible for men's relation with the alien realm.[179] This sense of women's not-quite-human status may be a consequence of the old notion that women were part of nature and men marginal within it. It may also be related to the fact that men are defined by their relations to females, as Gayle Rubin points out.[180] However much men may transcend necessity or the unclean, the animal or the earthly, they are related to each other through their inevitable tie to the female body—to mother or wife. Only in institutional life can men pass power directly to other men without the intervention of a woman. Institutional life therefore has great meaning to men, and is often perceived as a truer home than the familial home. Because of women's procreative capacities, men can never, they think, be more than marginal in a women's world. Patriarchy is an extreme attempt to create a man's world, but the basic dependency of men on women has still not been extirpated. What men have been able to do is to cast contempt on women and their natural functions and their allotted roles, and to place women in an intermediate position between them and an alien realm, so as to convince themselves that their own realm is purely male. Such things have been accomplished by the *word*, by the statement that these things are so. Since actuality frequently demonstrates that these things are not so, the words must be repeated over and again. And so too, patriarchy must be re-formed and reborn over the ages.

## 4. REESTABLISHMENTS OF PATRIARCHY

Certain values are fundamental to patriarchy: control is the highest good; control over nature—transcendence—is the mark of the human; men are human and women are part of nature; it is necessary for men to prove their loyalty to the transcendent by demonstrating power over nature (by extension, women, flesh, and feeling). These values are embodied in structures. Since men control women, men are superior to women; this difference in status stratifies the human race; and this first stratification allows people to invent others—of social and economic classes, of colors, and then of smaller splinter groups. In complex cultures, such stratifications involve differential access to resources and functions—that is, some people are permitted to have and do things denied others. For example, in Mbum society women may not eat chicken, while men may;[181] in other cultures, women may be barred from playing a musical instrument or approaching a certain tree that is held sacred by the men. In complex societies people of many kinds may be denied education, housing in a pleasant neighborhood, political office, the right to vote, the right to join clubs, the right to walk on the street alone at night, the right to wear a particular kind of clothing or hair style, the right to speak in public. They may be denied access to jobs that pay well, depriving them of the things that money can buy.

Differential access to resources and functions thus causes resentment, and the more extreme the differences among strata of a population, the more extreme the resentment. Because of this, coercion is necessary to maintain stratification. But coercion imposed by physical force required extensive manpower, time, and money; thus a substitute for force was developed—dissemination of a morality of fear, obedience, and a sense of personal worthlessness, on the one hand, and on the other, of awe and respect for authority, the (sometimes) bland face of physical force. In addition, patriarchal societies have regularly used a technique of setting different groups against each other—men and women, races, religions, classes, and subclasses. Stratification creates levels of superiority and inferiority—an elite that is fully human, while other groups are less so (or even more extremely, an elite that is in touch with the divine, while others are merely human and subhuman)—and the idea of superiority is sometimes fostered in fragmented groups to maintain a divided population.

Although patriarchy began with a desire to assert a "masculine" power and to gain cultural centrality for males, and was originally a campaign to gain control over women, it needed to control men in order to accomplish this. Because of other stratifications—rank, economic status, and so on—patriarchal societies have never been able to relinquish control over men by an elite which is, more subtly, also controlled by the morality of the culture. The terms used to divide populations or cast contempt on certain kinds of men are predictable:

they resemble the terms used to lay scorn upon women, and associate men with the animal (e.g., "big black buck") and with sexual depravity (e.g., "mother-fucker").

The great threat is still nature, seen as a swamp into which men slide when they forget to maintain control. As Darwin put it in *The Descent of Man*, "Man still bears *in his bodily frame* the indelible stamp of his lowly origin." That lowly origin was the animal ancestry; thus throughout European history despised groups such as Jews and gay men were continually characterized as animals.[182] Some gay men have accepted these terms in turn: a gay poem of the late Roman period states that "men under the sway of women are no better than dumb animals."[183] In the United States, blacks have been associated with animals as well as with uncontrolled sex.

The implicit denial that men (or the elite class or group of men) are rooted in nature is fraudulent. Slater asserts that there is "something fundamentally fraudulent at the core of organized social life. Certainly only a very thin line separates the major fraternal orders in our own society from Chaga men" (those who pretend they no longer defecate once they are initiated).[184] Because the ideology of patriarchy is basically factitious, it can never let go its grasp but must proclaim, disseminate, and enforce its values unremittingly, from generation to generation, across the globe. The militant expansion that has characterized patriarchal regimes and institutions from the beginning is to a large degree based in a need to insist upon its values, to make real what is false and to "prove" its reality by extracting unanimous consent.

As Peter Berger and Thomas Luckman describe this phenomenon, institutions delineate a symbolic area which they call *reality*, and define and regulate relations and actions within that area. Knowledge generated within this area "is socially objectivated *as* knowledge, that is, as a body of generally valid truths about reality." Thus any alien—deviant—kind of knowledge is seen as a "departure from reality," or as "moral depravity, mental disease, or just plain ignorance." But groups may share a deviant version of the symbolic universe, and elevate it into "a reality in its own right," thereby challenging the claim of reality made by the orthodox group. Berger and Luckman conclude that "such heretical groups posit not only a theoretical threat to the symbolic universe, but a practical one to the institutional order," and invariably lead to repressive or suppressive procedures.[185]

Because patriarchal structures are coercive, they engender rebellion against them. Sometimes this is rebellion by a fringe group declared to be and treated as subhuman. But the major revolutions of the Western world have been the sort Freud described—rebellions of sons against fathers. Since the fundamental step in establishing patriarchy—the murder of children by fathers—has remained a constant in its techniques (whether through war or the subtler means of strict indoctrination of children, extended control over them into adulthood by means of wealth, or possession of the keys to every institutional kingdom), rebellion against the fathers has been necessary and justifiable. Usually, the values espoused by "sons" are more "feminine" than those of the fathers, and constitute a loosening of rigid and oppressive codes; but just as usually, as soon as the "sons'" regime is established, it imposes its own oppressions and rigidities. Each revolution appears to be a liberation, and to carry with it a new morality; but although there have been changes in forms and ideas in the past five or six millennia, the fundamental position of patriarchy has not changed.

Judaism, with its fierce and jealous god, was revised in the sixth century B.C.E. and afterward, as a new YHWH was proclaimed by the prophets, a god of compassion. YHWH was feminized: the Hebrew word for compassion comes from the root *rehem*, the uterus.[186] Nevertheless, Judaism remained male-dominated and male-centered.

Buddhism, born around the fifth century B.C.E., spread swiftly in the East; it was originally a reformist religion, concerned with alleviating suffering. Buddhism—and Jainism, another reformist religion—decreed the outlawing of caste distinctions, abolished hereditary priesthood, made poverty a precondition of spirituality, and condemned war, cruelty, and violence. Both religions posited life as sacred.[187] The method used by Buddhism to accomplish its purpose, however, was patriarchal: it taught people to attempt to gain control over their lives through denial of feeling, to abolish desire by denigrating it, and to reduce the impact of life by imagining a transcendent realm. The process of making life more bearable was essentially a process of denying life.

In its early phases Christianity was also a reform religion. It offered "salvation" to the poor and to women, neither of whom was able to spend time or money in the temple, sacrificing small animals to placate God. It taught that the kingdom of God was within a person, thus countering traditional Judaism. It opposed the values of the Romans by regulating marriage as a form of birth control, in an attempt to alleviate the horrors of Roman customs: many children, particularly girls, born in the late Roman era were unwanted, and were abused or sold into slavery.[188] In the beginning, Christian doctrine attempted to revolutionize the moral climate of the Roman world, with its emphasis on property and power and its absolute dictators.

The values of early Christianity were the values of later Judaism: mercy, compassion, gentleness in dealing with others, responsibility toward the helpless and vulnerable, in particular the poor and women without men.[189] Jesus taught that such qualities were "higher" than power and its accessories, wealth and status. Consequently, the religion appealed to the disinherited; like any cult that unifies the disinherited, it was perceived as a threat to the establishment, which is always greatly outnumbered by the disinherited. That the cult was maintained after the state-sanctioned murder of its leader was arguably because it combined this "feminine" message of a better way to live (which countered most of the values of Roman culture as practiced if not as claimed) with a "masculine" message that fit into the overall value structure of the time yet transcended it: power was still the highest value, but it was exerted over all men, including worldly princes, by a transcendent god. The heavy dependency on miracles of some of the gospels and the kind of intellectual doctrine developed by the early Christians demonstrate the primary importance of the transcendent.

Although early Christianity desired to oppose to Roman morals something more humane, the poor and women were expendable in its thinking. Jesus was hardly a feminist, although his recorded legend suggests he was humane toward women; but Paul was demonstrably a misogynist, and it was his tradition that became dominant as the doctrines of the Church were slowly compiled. The very notion of the Trinity expresses the most complete triumph over and expulsion of women from human culture ever created until our own times. That a male god should be able to open his mouth and speak a word, which became flesh, and his son; that the father and son should, through their mutual love, be able to create a third entity, known as the holy spirit; and that, in all of this, a woman should function rather as an oven in which the bread is baked, a mere vessel for its maturation, comprises an extraordinary myth of creation. What is even more extraordinary is that millions of people have believed it, not as a symbolic truth for a patriarchal age, but as literal truth. Although the central doctrines of Christianity remained teachings of love, mercy, compassion, and charity, the expressions of those doctrines as well as the superstructure of the institution increasingly placed power and strict code in the foreground. The thinking of the early Christian patriarchs was antinature and antisex—opposed to intercourse and procreation.[190] By the time of Irenaeus (130?–202?), the primary requirements of Christians were that they should *fear* God and *obey* the priests: standard patriarchal values.[191]

Early Christianity was made up of small groups, some of whom had their own ideas about the content of the religion. These were known as the "Gnostic" sects, and many of them opposed hierarchy and would alternate leading roles in the meetings of their small cells. Some of these groups ate the meat they sacrificed to their idols, and were openly and freely sexual.[192] The Gnostics were roundly condemned by the mainstream Christian writers and by some radical Christians like Tertullian, who was upset mainly because women were participating in the rituals with equal status. Irenaeus condemned them because they were not sexually abstinent and monogamous; he claimed that young women were being exploited sexually. Even the Gnostic sects, however, taught that the flesh was evil, and their leaders were always men.[193] In time, the Gnostic sects were suppressed.

Indeed, one of the most remarkable elements in early Christianity is this suppression. Many religions flourished side by side in ancient times; many goddesses and gods attracted their own adherents. Some groups, like the Jews, maintained a fierce belief in the superiority of their own deity, and demanded adherence to the Law by Jews: yet Judaism was never proselytizing and always encouraged theological speculation. Some states superstitiously required ritual observances to placate municipal deities, and forbade disrespectful (blasphemous) references to them—as in Athens and Rome. But no religious or secular institution before the Catholic Church ever forbade speculation about the nature of deity and the universe. No earlier institution demanded utter acceptance of a single Truth, delineated orthodoxy, labeled all other hypotheses "heresy," and punished those who entertained them.[194] Perhaps early Christianity took this extraordinary step to protect its extraordinary claims about the exclusively male nature of godhead and its generation. Nor did it stop there but worked both peacefully and militantly to impose its Truth on the rest of the world. Both steps were imitated. Gautama, the Buddha, was also attributed to a virgin birth. Orthodoxy was established by the time of Irenaeus and became a common feature of Western institutions.

Islam, which developed in the sixth and seventh centuries C.E., was also an effort to ameliorate inhumane living conditions. Mohammed, whose wife supported him economically and psychologically, posited a basic equality between men and woman, although he clearly had ambivalent feelings about this. He outlined women's rights of inheritance, administration of property, and freedom to choose and to divorce a marriage partner: these rights were later denied women by urban Moslems, although some rural Moslems retained them.[195] Mohammed specifically instructed that women be allowed to worship and to go on pilgrimages to Mecca. Within a few years after his death, they were barred from both. In the early days of Islam, women were still warriors, poets, and professionals of various sorts. Naila Minai believes it was the influence of the Ottoman Empire, which overcame Arab and Byzantine civilization, that led to the most severe constrictions of women in Islamic countries.[196]

But what is clear in the study of any of these institutions is that attitudes and rules that counter patriarchal values get lost along the way, and those that endure are those that support the patriarchal vision. The terms of patriarchy are not flexible: it is an ideology committed to the eradication of matricentric values and to the erection of a transcendent world. It was established in opposition to a specific morality, and all of its terms are designed to fabricate a reality that negates the reality of nature. The Judaic vision, which was seminal in Christianity and Western thought in general, created a god who was not bound or constrained by life as it was, but who offered a promise of things to come.[197] This promise, the ultimate transcendence, is implicit in Christianity, in Eastern religions (and in the workers' utopia of Marxism). Carol Ochs, writing about Christianity, explains this sense of opposition: if "this is a world of time, Heaven is timeless; this is a world of change, Heaven is changeless; since this is a fertile world, then Heaven must be barren and infertile. So Heaven is defined not in opposition to Hades, but in opposition to life, and in most important ways, is identical to Hades. When Persephone dies and rises, her triumph is over Hades. When Christ dies and rises, his triumph is over life."[198]

Death is called "eternal life" and held as superior to life. A similar shift occurred in meanings of other words, as Ivan Illich points out. By the third century, the term "holy mother the church" had ceased to mean a volitional assembly of the faithful in love in order to engender new life, and meant instead "an invisible, mystical reality from which alone those services absolutely necessary for salvation can be obtained. . . . Access to the good graces of this mother . . . is entirely controlled by a hierarchy of ordained males."[199] The word *education* had, in its Latin root, referred to a feeding and nurturing done only by women; *alumnus* originally meant a suckling, a nursing child. The shift in meaning of these words corresponds with a symbolic usurpation by males of female functions.[200] As Christianity became more "masculine" in its values, it became more acceptable, and it was eventually (in 313) established as the official religion of the Roman Empire.

But religion and religious education were not the only propagational vehicle of patriarchal ideas; other systems of thought and value also delivered the message. One of these was science, which emerged in the seventeenth century mainly in England; its first and greatest propagandist was Francis Bacon.

There is no question that Bacon in his many writings and experiments sought knowledge for the advancement of human good—he died from a cold that developed after he buried a chicken in the snow to see what would happen to flesh that was frozen. And it is understandable that he and others would at that time believe that human good was dependent upon control over nature. Bacon wrote: "My only earthly wish is . . . to stretch the deplorably narrow limits of man's dominion over the universe to their promised bounds"; "I am come in very truth leading you to Nature with all her children to bind her to your service and make her your slave"; he justified the right of man to dominate nature by invoking the command, given in Genesis, to have dominion, to subdue. The scientist could lead man to this level of power: "the mechanical inventions of recent years do not merely exert a gentle guidance over Nature's courses, they have the power to conquer and subdue her, to shake her to her foundations." Although Bacon believed that "we cannot command Nature except by obeying her," that it was essential to understand the workings of nature in order to control them, and that this act of understanding was an act of obedience, he also saw nature as female and "rebellious." Bacon set science on a course which has not been questioned until this decade: a course of attempting to dominate rather than understand and cooperate with nature, based on a belief that dominance hierarchies exist in nature. This belief has been undermined by study of ecology and of subatomic phenomena.

Descartes was important, if not alone, in furthering the kind of thinking Bacon had advocated. Descartes posited a split between mind and matter which was extended to fragment mind and body, mind and feeling. This may not seem a new idea, since it was in some sense implicit in the Greek belief in reason as the controller of impulse, and the Catholic belief in human ability to control emotion through faith and submission of will. Yet the context of Enlightenment thought was new. In earlier Western societies, production and consumption were inevitable parts of everyday life. There was a network of obligations linking members of communities. These factors prevented people from seeing others simply as objects, or seeing objects as mere items for use.

The new mode of thought ushered in what is called instrumentality, that is, people began to view other people and things not as ends in themselves but as instruments for the furtherance of their own ends. Those ends invariably involved power, which is its own motor, since one can never have enough of it. Instrumentality is therefore limitless: it is a continuing search for an end that is precluded by the very nature of the means used. Without instrumental thought, science would not have taken the course it did.

At first the revolution of scientists against a dominant Christian ideology was a fight for concrete rights which, they believed, would lead to improvements in medical knowledge and techniques, and thus to a betterment of the human lot. It was a fight for the right to examine concrete life—the body. But the body was approached by scientists with the same attitude of conquest implicit in the general culture, and the struggle for a science of health was specifically equated with a struggle against women and nature—"female nature had been unclothed by male science."[201] Wax figures were made of men to demonstrate various physiological systems; these were usually upright and often in a position of motion. Those of women were recumbent, seductive, and sometimes even adorned: they were even labeled "Venuses." The Paris medical school of the eighteenth century contained a statue of a young woman with bared breasts and bowed head: it was inscribed, "Nature unveils herself before Science." Female figures were intended mainly to demonstrate procreative functioning, and the conclusions drawn from such research emphasized the *natural* passivity of women. Researchers performing vivisectional analyses in the seventeenth and early eighteenth centuries believed that living matter was utterly passive under their active intrusion and manipulation.[202]

The scientific advance upon nature continues into our own time, with results that we can see. Many things are possible that were not possible earlier, and in some ways life is easier; in others, it is more difficult, since the conquest of nature has led to a corruption and poisoning of the environments in which we live. Moreover, the scientific advance upon nature led to industrialization, which is also a mixed curse and blessing; and industrialization led to the expansion of capitalism. The backbone of capitalism was the middle-class family, with its objectives of "the continuity of the male line, the preservation intact of the inherited property, and the acquisition through marriage of further property or useful political alliances."[203] These values—power through property possessed by males—intensified the stratification of classes: the rich had more ease and luxury than any but an oriental despot had possessed in earlier ages, and the poor were more utterly dispossessed, vulnerable, destitute—landless, homeless, and starving—than they had been under feudal regimes.

Industrial capitalism carried to an extreme the tendencies of instrumentalism. Having lost the land they used to work, the communities in which they used to live, people were forced to sell themselves, their labor power. For the first time, masses of workers were deprived of any control over the production of what they needed: they could not choose what to make, when to make it, or how to make it. Workers became, for capitalists, merely another factor of production, along with raw materials and machinery. Moreover, if the capitalist wants to survive, he must act "rationally": that is, he must treat workers as means to his end (profit) rather than as fellow human beings.[204]

Imperialism—capitalism extended to alien peoples—developed naturally enough, and a new class of "nonhumans," indigenous populations, was added to Western consciousness. Whether they were seen as innocents in need of Western "light," or as expendable resources for exploitation, indigenous populations presented themselves to the imagination of the power-worshiping West as a "free" territory for the exercise of Western "virtues" (among which was acquisitiveness). What is extraordinary in most accounts of the colonization of Africa is the fervor of those who directed it. They were not deterred by physical impediments—mountains, deserts, climate, flood, drought, disease—nor by the resistance (whether "active" or "passive") of the inhabitants. They were not deterred even by the fact that, despite exploitation of people and resources, colonization often drained money from the colonizing nations. There is an evangelical tone to the writings of both missionary and profiteer, a wild drive to "raise" the "savages," to "civilize" that gorgeous continent, which goes far beyond the bounds of greed, desire for power, or desire to do good for others (which some missionaries and politicians seem sincerely to have believed). There is a kind of absolute need in these utterances, as if the mere existence of a huge continent and varied peoples who lived by values other than power, who lived in a different relation to nature than people of the West, was a shocking aberration that had to be brought into conformity, as if Africa constituted a profound threat and cast shadows of doubt upon the Truth of Western beliefs.

Like early industrialization, like early capitalism, imperialism was described at first in terms of expansion and liberation of the human spirit and improvement in material circumstance. But all new waves of patriarchal thought are described in this way, and are no doubt conceived of in this way by those who incite them and those who are persuaded to follow them. Even small revolutions are fought on grounds of liberation.

In its turn, socialism was a further attempt to alleviate suffering and injustice, and to create a more humane living arrangement. Yet like capitalism, socialism as it was realized in our patriarchal world was cast in a patriarchal image. Inevitably it became, in its turn, an oppressive structure. Socialism emerged from the thinking of men like Michelet, who had been inspired by Vico to a vision of human destiny, and who opened his *Universal History* with this statement: "With the world began a war which will end only with the world: the war of man against nature, of spirit against matter, of liberty against fatality. History is . . . the record of this interminable struggle."[205]

Both Marx and Engels believed in the necessity of dominating nature. Engels believed it was domination over nature that changed apes into man and separated him from "lesser" creatures: "The animal merely *uses* its environment," he writes, man "masters it." (At the same time, he insists humans are part of nature.)[206] Marx celebrated Man, who "opposes himself to Nature as one of her own forces, setting in motion arms and legs, head and hands, the natural forces of his body in order to appropriate Nature's productions in a form adapted to his own wants."[207] For Marx began with the old Greek distinction between freedom and necessity, locating man within the realm of freedom. But working men could not attain this freedom because labor is part of the realm of necessity. Marx did not consider women at all, except as part of a force of workers which would be liberated under communistic order. For workers to be liberated, work must be organized as rationally as possible, and reduced as much as possible.[208] Since this was the thrust of capitalism, Marx favored capitalism in many ways. Although he worked toward and predicted its death, he was also its sincerest advocate. He found praiseworthy the capitalist tendency to reduce nature to a mere object for use, and the advance of theoretical knowledge designed to subdue nature to men's requirements.[209] He envisioned a communistic order that would carry these tendencies even further, but applauded as a "civilizing influence" capitalism's persistent expansion of power and scope.[210]

Emphasis on transcendence and the asceticism which so often accompanies its exaltation infuses socialist thinking. Edmund Wilson traces the roots of socialism to Renan. Renan created a list of moral excellences, placing the saint at the top and the man of action at the bottom; he believed that as soon as the moral enters the realm of the practical, it becomes as corrupt as the world.[211] Trotsky was willing to give up the lives of his family and his followers, all comfort and peace of mind, the pleasure of political power in this world, and even his own life, in pursuit of his heaven.[212] He was as saintly—or as inhumane—as any Christian martyr. Marx had a highly developed sense of superiority and eliteness and viewed himself as further than other men from bestiality. In his correspondence with Engels he continually referred to their followers in the most contemptuous terms, as beasts and asses (a usage Engels soon fell in with).[213] Their correspondence is filled with "outrageously rude remarks (sexist, classist, and racist) about others in their circle."[214] There was no room in Marx's mind for love, ordinary human imperfection, charity, or self-analysis; his values were traditional patriarchal values, with the tempering of the Old Testament requirement of justice and provision for the poor. As Wilson writes, "He desired that humanity should be united and happy; but he put that off till the achievement of the *synthesis*, and for the present he did not believe in human brotherhood." His values were closely linked to those of the place and structure he most detested, imperialistic Germany.[215]

There are many ironies in the dominance of patriarchy. One is that its emphasis on power, individualism, and struggle as a way of life fosters contention among adherents of different patriarchal groups. So various religions see each other as the prime enemy. As H. R. Trevor-Roper put it, "Since the end of antiquity two great religions have competed for the soul of the world: Christianity and Islam." Both originated in Judaism, which has been a nonproselytizing religion, while Christianity and Islam have been "aggressive, missionary, imperialist. Other religions have invariably gone down before them. The state paganism of the Roman Empire, the state Zoroastrianism of the Persian Empire, were almost totally destroyed by their impact. Hinduism and Buddhism shrank at their approach, or were overlaid by them. Primitive religions were dissolved or absorbed by them. Only against each other do they seem to fail."[216]

Even sects within these religions contend against each other—the Protestants contended against the Catholics through much of Western history; the Shi'ites and Sunnis, both Moslem sects, do to this day. Capitalists vie against socialists, and each group believes the other desires to eradicate it. Adherents of such beliefs can see only the differences and not the similarities in their ideologies; nor do they see themselves as a set of embroideries on a patriarchal theme. Contention, individualism, supremacy, and power are highly valued in patriarchy; for this reason, the goal of power seems today to be monolithic power, hegemony over the entire world. Only this, it is believed, will create peace and harmony, or rather the disguises that pass for them, suppression and uniformity. But severe contention and savage war for power will continue as long as patriarchal values continue to hold sway in our imaginations.

Another irony is the place of women in the institutions under discussion. Women have in fact supported many of them, especially in their early, formative years, and have been ancillary supporters after their establishment. Women as well as men accept the division of the world into nature and human, spirit and flesh, and the transcendence of the word. Women have been martyrs and have oppressed others in the name of such causes.

It is unrealistic to expect women to live totally apart from their cultures, to have a perspective and a doctrine with which to oppose those cultures. Men have also been oppressed by patriarchal institutions, but we do not expect them to be able to see, through the veils of patriarchal ideas, precisely what it is that oppresses them. It is also true, however, that women as a group have fought, at least privately, in every regime in which they have lived, for a place of their own, a realm in which they could use some of their talents and in which they could exercise some control. Women are notable by their absence from even those presiding councils which do not specifically disallow them. If this is partly a response to the atmosphere of such councils, which if not legally exclusionary is morally so, it is also partly because women feel alienated from the concerns that motivate governments and institutions of power. To many women, the conflicts of the public world seem foolish, even insane.

The great Simone Weil, who was a committed socialist, saw the conflict between the USSR and Germany escalating, and called it a conflict "with no definable objective."[217] (She wrote this in 1937, before she perceived the Nazi campaign against Jews. But the war waged by the Allies against the Nazis was not in fact a response to the Holocaust, which was ignored. Only in hindsight and with blurred vision can we discuss World War II as a moral war. That it upheld a moral good was incidental to the purposes of those who presided over it.) And indeed, the systems developed by the Nazis and the USSR were remarkably similar. The two are presently lumped together under the rubric *totalitarianism*, just as Catholicism and Protestantism are presently lumped together as Christianity, despite many centuries of hideous, savage struggle between them.

In the end, patriarchy returns to its beginnings. Wars are waged with "no definable objective"; the thinking of the antagonists is so similar that most people shrug and choose the present evil over the unknown one—until they are fired up by propaganda to believe the enemy is demonic. There are, of course, differences in regimes, but they are differences in degree only. The fight is really over hegemony, the hegemony of a few. It is hard to find justification for war in such a situation, but as Weil pointed out, when pressed, governments urge the sacrifices already incurred as "a perpetual argument for new ones."[218] The children are still being burned to prove the fathers' right.

Hannah Arendt defined totalitarian systems as having a new and unprecedented concept of power and reality. They had, she believed, a disregard for immediate consequences and for the real and concrete, because they had "unwavering faith in an ideological fictitious world."[219] But this applies not just to totalitarian systems, but to patriarchal systems in general. Marvin Harris writes that "the rise of the state was the descent of the world from freedom to slavery."[220] It would be truer to say the rise of patriarchy created such a decline, for patriarchal thinking created the state.

Matricentry, as described in these pages, may have been a social arrangement that was inadequate to a highly populated world. Some revision was probably required to deal with the problems attendant on crowding. (Indeed matricentric values and relatively matricentric social structure endured for millennia in small communities and in isolated areas, long after patriarchal ways had taken over in cities.) But patriarchy was not an attempt to revise matricentry, but to overthrow it, to reverse its values and its organization. From a loose grouping of people who lived democratically, even anarchically, patriarchy created a tight, stratified society held in place by coercion; from a society dedicated primarily to love and bonding, fertility and continuation, patriarchy moved to dedication to power above all, although sometimes in the name of survival (which seems similar to fertility and continuation) and love—not of fellow beings, but of a higher power, a god or a state.

Many of the features of the world we live in were devised only because of this devotion to power in Western culture; and many of us would not wish to give up these features. But it is not impossible that mechanical changes would have occurred even if the human race had maintained matricentric values; if such changes had occurred, however, they would presumably be less destructive of nature and human nature than those we have developed. But this is entirely hypothetical. Patriarchy is with us and we are where we are: the question is what to do now. Before answering that question, we must fasten firmly in mind the character of patriarchal values.

Perhaps a picture *is* worth a thousand or more words. One picture that seems to me to sum up our values most beautifully is a carved ivory plaque, made in Rome in the sixth century C.E., depicting the triumph of Emperor Justinian under the banner of that compassionate deity Christ. Justinian is on horseback holding a cross; above him are heavenly figures proclaiming the blessing of Christ upon him. Beside him, only a little smaller, is a peasant man touching his lance in submission. Trampled by his horse's hooves is a woman, much smaller, offering utter submission and holding in her apron all the bounty of nature. Beneath all of these are the crouched figures and animals who represent the vanquished. The plaque is called *Defender of the Faith*. The figures are, as any art critic will remind us, symbolic: but in patriarchy, the drive is to make the symbol real. And indeed, the moral arrangement of this plaque is the actual arrangement of our world.

# CHAPTER THREE

# Women Under Patriarchy

The history of patriarchy comprises the history of the world as we have been taught it. It is a history of power. Until recently, events that were not manifestations of power held little interest for mainstream historians, and even most social history focuses on those elements of ordinary life that seem to have influenced larger events. There is little interest in studying things simply because they existed.

Because patriarchy is an ideology rooted in the denial of worldly power to women, the proportion of women who have wielded power is small. But those who did hold power are generally omitted from accounts of the history of power. William McNeill wrote a history of the world that lists only one woman in the index—Catherine the Great of Russia. A study of textbooks used in college courses in American history found that only .05 to 2 percent of their texts deal with women, although females appear in 6 percent of the illustrations.[1] One widely used text manages to discuss insane asylum reform in the first half of the nineteenth century "without mentioning Dorothea Dix, muckraking without mentioning Ida Tarbell, and the Montgomery bus-system boycott without mentioning Rosa Parks."[2] The struggle for woman suffrage, which took seventy years and the unremitting struggle of generations of women, is not even mentioned in a history of the development of American democratic thought.[3] A recent book on the emergence of a patriarchal religion from a predominantly matrifocal culture—Rastafarianism in Jamaica—does not touch at all on the position of women within the new religion.[4] The history department of the University of California at Berkeley refused to permit a course on "Women in American Politics" to be taught, claiming that women had been active in politics in only a few periods, and that their work did not engage "major themes and developments in the United States."[5]

History, a set of elements selected, arranged, recorded, and interpreted, provides the substance of what future generations will know, and consider to be the truth: the Greek word for truth, *aletheia*, means *that which is not forgotten*. The truth—in this sense—of women's past has been "declared inoperative," has been judged nontruth, not worth remembering. Only as helpless dependents or sexual lures, roles which make men central, do women figure. Yet the actuality of the past shows women as powerful, active, influential, and resilient creatures. To obliterate them has required considerable determination.

To rediscover the past of women requires going beyond historical accounts and searching original documents. For the past two decades feminist historians, women and men, have been doing this work, ferreting through dusty boxes of yellowed flaking papers in basements and back rooms of museums and libraries, spending years reading old letters, diaries, forgotten books written by women. They have resuscitated fine scholarly work dealing with women that was published and consigned to oblivion—like that of Eileen Power, the early-twentieth-century Oxford medievalist.[6] Slowly a history of women is emerging, and it is impressive. It is a record not just of women but of entire cultures that went busily on beneath the surface show of power.

There are some special problems in treating the history of women under patriarchy. Women are largely absent from the records of their time. They do appear as objects in laws governing property and morality, but sometimes it is difficult to tell precisely what gave rise to a law. The Code of Hammurabi, for example, contains a stipulation that a priestess who opens a wine shop or even enters one is to be burned.[7] It is hard to imagine precisely what could have inspired such a provision, especially since no equivalent provision exists covering the behavior of priests. Most wine sellers in Babylon were women, and it would seem that priestesses were entering this trade or no such ruling would have been necessary. Perhaps they were doing it because they were no longer able to survive economically as priestesses. But we cannot be sure of this: we cannot deduce the actual condition of women from the law alone.

Women have never been a unified group; they have been female members of social and economic classes with whom they identified their interests. The perception that women constitute a separate class regardless of their socioeconomic status is only now beginning to penetrate human consciousness. The lives of aristocratic women, women of the propertied classes, and poor women were very different; so were the lives of those who lived in cities and those who lived in the countryside. To focus on any one of these classes and claim to be discussing "women" is to falsify, but to discuss all strata of women, especially those classes on which there is little information, is almost impossible in any study. One can select a particular group for discussion, for a purpose. Mary Beard chose to examine women who exercised power, in an effort to provide examples to encourage women of the present.[8] Mary Wollstonecraft and Simone de Beauvoir concentrated on women's powerlessness and victimization, in hope of rousing women to an understanding of their condition.[9] It is possible to study "feminine" values as upheld by women.[10] I have tried to touch on all of these—power, powerlessness, and "feminine" values—to give a sense of the round.

It is commonly believed that women are better off today than they were in the past. Male myths about brutal cavemen dragging women by the hair seem intended to assure women that they are better off in a "civilized" world, civilization being seen as identical with patriarchy. Even within patriarchy, we are assured there has been "progress," and are reminded of the state of women in Classical Athens, when they were virtual prisoners within the household, or in ancient Rome, when they were viewed simply as property. The right of middle-class women to remunerated employment is seen as a gain, as was the granting of suffrage. What is forgotten is that poor women always worked; that middle-class women were enormously productive and sufficient not for themselves alone but for large extended households up to the nineteenth century; and that the granting of universal suffrage occurred only after political power (on a large scale) had already passed into the hands of monied interests, which firmly control all political parties. Both rights were good and necessary, but they do not necessarily confer upon women more power over their own lives than they possessed in past ages.

There are many forms of power. We usually think of it as power-in-the-world—political control, economic control, the force of arms—and are inclined to forget or devalue the power of connections—influence through intellect or personality, the more tenuous powers of influence through artistic, theological, or philosophical expression, all of which are at times equal in strength to other worldly powers.

There is also a form of power that mediates between the self and the world—power wielded through intellect, charm, beauty, or sheer force of will, over lovers and mates, children and parents. Personal power arises from individual personality and cannot be transmitted in that form. Unless personal power wins institutional rights for a family, sect, or group, it dies with its possessor. It is, generally, the "feminine" form of worldly power, partly because women have been excluded from public power and partly because men feel uncomfortable in this realm. But many men exercise this kind of power too.

Finally, there are fundamental powers—the power to be, to use the self, to exercise one's abilities. Abilities are innate, but the power to use them requires intercourse with the world. One must be able to acquire some sort of education, must have the freedom to move around in the world, must have some right to determine what one will do in one's life. Most basic of all is the power over one's own body—the right to be free of physical abuse, to control one's own sexuality, to marry when and whom one chooses, or not to marry; to control one's own reproduction, to have rights over one's own children, and to divorce at will. In many cultures, past and present, some men have been restricted in some of these rights; in all Western cultures, past and present, most women have been restricted in all of these rights. Without these fundamental powers, power-in-the-world is unattainable.

There have been—and are—cultures in which women of a certain class are granted education but not sexual freedom; there have been cultures in which certain aristocratic women were even able to wield power-in-the-world, while the rest of womankind was permitted no political power at all. There have been cultures like that of ancient Rome, for instance, in which the paterfamilias controlled the private as well as the public realm, but from which strong-willed women were able to wrest some autonomy, some control over their own lives.

But the confusion about power does not end here. There have been, and still are, huge numbers of women and men who were willing to cede power-in-the-world to others in return for the right to run their private worlds in their own way. Many religious men and women have renounced worldly values, preferring to nourish and care for others. Mothers have accepted subordination to their husbands in order to raise their children with love and nutritiveness. The right to cultivate one's own garden—to create a felicitous living arrangement, to offer and receive love, to provide compassion and care to others, to feel connected to the human race—offers pleasures and graces difficult or impossible for those who exercise worldly power. There are and always have been legions of people who valued the feminine principle more than the masculine, for whom power-in-the-world was not a great good.

This "feminine" morality informs a pervasive strand in literature from Horace to Spenser, from Theocritus to Voltaire, from Virgil to Mark Twain and Virginia Woolf. But often, even as these authors idealize the pastoral life, "green worlds" removed from power, they convey an emphatic warning to men about such ideals: the idyllic pockets of the world get invaded and destroyed by rampant aggression, individualism, and power seeking. The idyllic haven may be women's proper home, but a man has work to do, he must protect his domain. In actuality, women have through the ages tried to create idyllic niches, and defended them by themselves. Creation of a haven does not generally get recorded, especially if no defense of it was necessary; it does not figure in accounts of power. But it may have made women happy.

And this is the crux of the problem in recounting women's—or men's—history. In a patriarchal world, power is not just the highest but the only value. People and events are judged important or interesting according to the degree of power they possessed, their impact on their time and their influence on the future. But this single standard omits almost everything that makes up an individual life and the life of a society. In describing the past, historians do not include pleasures, only powers or lack of power. We lack information about pleasure; and there are many who would claim it to be inconsequential, subjective, without meaning. Yet to the individual, and to a society as a whole, contentment or felicity is surely supremely important.

The focus of documentation—the standard about what needs to be written down, remembered, preserved—is singular and linear, as is the focus of those who research the old documents. A proper history of the past would require an expanded focus; it would trace the course of power, the growth and solidification of "masculine" values, but also examine "feminine" values—the forms in which they survived and their gradual erosion, even extinction from the Western world. Feminist historians, tracing the well-being and (occasionally) even power women gained from their friends—today often called "support networks"—have recently begun to offer a fuller picture of the life of the past.

A few further generalizations are in order. The categories into which history is usually divided—periods like the Renaissance or the Enlightenment—hold little relevance to women's history. Although shifts in power arrangements or in attitudes do affect women, their condition is most vulnerable to changes in social structures, such as transitions from aristocratic to middle-class or from feudal to bourgeois rule. Most important has been the shift from production in the home to factory labor—the Industrial Revolution.[11]

Poor women are for the most part missing from this account, just as they are missing (along with poor men) from history, but it should be remembered throughout that poor women were personally freer than women of the propertied classes. The latter, seen as property themselves, have been jealously guarded and transferred like property. They had greater ease but less freedom than poor women, who could walk around in the world at will if not in safety, who controlled their own sexuality and their children more than propertied women, and who sometimes controlled even their own little businesses. Poor women were also, of course, freer to starve, to work like beasts of burden, and to suffer from random male abuse and violence. For an example of this, consider Juliet and her nurse in Shakespeare's *Romeo and Juliet*; the nurse is Juliet's social inferior, but she can go out freely and so can deliver messages for her mistress. As she does so, early in the play, she is verbally assaulted by two young "gentlemen," even though she is accompanied by her manservant. Being neither clever nor tough, the nurse is affronted. An actual street woman would probably be both, but there is no guarantee that assaults aimed at her would remain purely verbal. Women of the propertied classes were protected from random abuse, but they probably suffered as much as poor women from violence, imprisonment, and murder by men of their own households.

In general, the women of the past were indeed victimized by their cultures. They suffered, as men did, from particular cultural constraints, but they also suffered from men, who on the whole had more rights and power than women regardless of class. When women rose up in rebellion, it was often because they were unable to feed their families, and not because they wanted power-in-the-world. It is easy to have impatient contempt for women on these grounds, but invidious comparisons are unwarranted. Men also have been and continue to be victimized in similar ways without rising up in rebellion. In approaching women's history, therefore, it is useful to begin by considering colonization and slavery, institutions that victimized men as well as women. The accounts of these institutions are for the most part written by men, and are as misogynistic as anything else in our culture. Nevertheless, by considering the terms of male subjugation of males, we may gain insight into subjugation in general.

## 1. THE CHARACTERISTICS OF COLONIZATION

An important figure in the literature of colonization, Frantz Fanon, claims that the first step in colonization is to divide the world physically in half. Before such an act can be performed, however, the world must be divided in half *conceptually*, into human beings (the colonizers) and the colonized, who are seen as subhuman or sometimes as nonhuman, as animals possessed by a kind of viciousness nonhuman animals do not exhibit. Because of the differences between these two groups, the physical world is divided into "compartments" which are "inhabited by two different species."[12] The territory so appropriated and divided was previously the homeland of the colonized, who may have had no sense of possession of land, who, like the old matricentric societies, only used it. Once the territory is appropriated by the colonizers, however, parts of it may be declared off-limits to the colonized, who must have special permission to enter. These "European" or "white" quarters have broad avenues and stately buildings, while the "native" quarter is crowded, unsanitary, and foul-smelling. The unpleasant nature of this part of town is attributed to its inhabitants.

When colonization takes the form of enslavement, slaves may be required to wear distinctive dress or hair styles, or may be marked or mutilated in some way so they may be distinguished from the master class. In the United States, where only blacks became permanent slaves, other distinctions than color were not necessary, although the lack of them caused considerable difficulty for freed slaves. Unlike the colonized, slaves are not penned in a separate part of the city, but in a separate part of the farm, factory, or house. Both groups, however, spend most of their time in the spaces belonging to the master class, laboring and serving. They may have great responsibility for those spaces, but no rights over them. The colonized or slave class is not made up of individuals, but is an "anonymous collectivity," a Them.[13] The character of this mass is animalistic but vicious; colonizers may have more affection and respect for their animals than for these people. "The terms the settler uses when he mentions the native are zoological. . . . He speaks of the yellow man's reptilian motions, of the stink of the native quarter, of breeding swarms, of foulness, of spawn, of gesticulations."[14] Bestial and subhuman, the "native is declared insensible to ethics; he represents not only the absence of values, but also the negation of values. He is . . . the enemy of values, and in this sense he is the absolute evil. He is the corrosive element, destroying all who come near him."[15]

In the late eighteenth century, many American slaveowners were freeing their slaves; in 1806, the state of Virginia restricted manumission, preventing this emancipation. An expanding net was cast about freed slaves: first they had to leave the state within two months, and masters were forbidden to provide slaves with the thing they most needed—land; then surrounding states forbade blacks to enter to take up residence. Thus a slave was emancipated only to have nowhere to go and no way to live. Winthrop Jordan shows that this series of acts went counter to the prevailing moral thought of the period, and investigates why they were passed.[16]

His conclusion is that for the Virginians, blackness was symbolic of all those things they condemned within themselves, human qualities they were ashamed of or feared. To free black people meant to free those impulses. Blacks were seen as "dangerous incendiaries" who would incite enslaved blacks to run away. The slaveowners' sense of blacks was as a raging impulse of evil and rebellion. In actuality some freed or escaped blacks did heroically help others to escape, but they were unusual. Most freed people wanted simply a decent life for themselves. Nevertheless, the Virginians were "intent" on regarding freed blacks as threats.[17] The threat of insurrection always accompanies domination; one of the reasons control is so unsatisfying is that it begets not a sense of power but a sense of fear. Suppressed people seem always to be lying, plotting, and deviously seeking their own good, a good that is counter to the good of the dominators. Thus the dominators hate those they oppress.[18]

Yet at the same time the master class cries out in nightmare with Kurtz,

"Exterminate the brutes!" it does not wish to do anything of the sort. For "the brutes" must multiply or "the cost of labor will rise."[19] Moreover, the colonist knows that without the colonized his own life would have no meaning, and this "intolerable contradiction fills him with a rage, a loathing, always ready to be loosed on the colonized, the innocent yet inevitable reason for his drama."[20] For the character of the enslaved or colonized defines that of the colonizer, who projects onto his inferior those qualities he disdains in himself; he, the dominator, can then define himself as not being what the inferior is.

This is especially true in the area of sexuality. The dominant male treats the body of the subjugated male as mere matter for labor; he treats the body of the subjugated female as matter for labor and for sex. Having a corps of always available sexual partners, the dominant male views his promiscuity as licit and of no consequence to his family, the "most vital institution of cultural integrity" of white slaveholders. "If the white man's sexual license" had not been "prudently defined and circumscribed," Jordan suggests, he might have discovered it was he and not the black who was licentious, who threatened the "integrity" of the family, who was "bestial" and without restraint.[21] The delusion that sexual use of slaves was of no consequence, that it did not threaten the family nor affect the virtuous character of the white male, would not have been possible, however, without the collusion of white women, who sacificed their own integrity and outrage to their fear of men and male institutions. Slavery (and colonization) thus corrupts everyone involved in it; it is not a single relation between colonizer and colonized, master and slave, but an entire network.

The treatment offered the colonized (or enslaved) brutalizes them; the conditions under which they are forced to live in time permeate their sense of self; and in time the oppressed come to be or to appear "more and more like what they would have to be like to deserve their fate."[22] The argument that those who can be enslaved deserve their slavery is as old as Aristotle. The oppressed are seen as animals in need of masters who provide restraint and guidance; or as children in need of parents. So the historian Ulrich B. Phillips, writing about slavery in 1918, reassured his readers by explaining that blacks were "by racial quality" submissive, lighthearted, amiable, ingratiating, and imitative.[23] Like animals or children, oppressed people are expected to identify their interests entirely with those of their masters (parents). Using moral teaching "to induce the slave to assimilate with the master and his vocation has been and is the great desideratum."[24] That the desires or needs of the oppressed are singular and different from those of the oppressor is inconceivable; the thinking of dominators in such situations is obsessively narcissistic—that is, the oppressor refers every act of the oppressed to himself. Albert Memmi explains that if a colonized servant fails to appear at work, it will not occur to the master that she might be ill, or needed by her family, or in some trouble. He will say only, "You can't count on them."[25] He will see himself as the target of all her acts. In the United States, when slaves ran away their masters were incredulous. For the most part, slaves ran away only after severe punishment; yet their attempts to escape were seen as illustrating the "ingratitude and especial depravity of the African race."[26] "Kindly" masters were even more outraged by attempts at escape or assistance to runaway slaves. "There is no gratitude among them," wrote a Mississippi planter about a slave, Nancy, who had been caught carrying food to some hidden runaways.[27]

In time, then, the oppressed group takes on the image impressed upon it by the master class; worse, in time the oppressed group comes to accept that image as its actuality. Kurt Lewin, writing about Jewish experience, reminds us that "constant reiteration of one's inferiority" can often lead to "its acceptance as a fact."[28] Oppression thus leads to contempt for the self and for those who are like the self, a phenomenon Florynce Kennedy has labeled "horizontal hostility." This condition leads to hatred, competition, and contempt among members of an oppressed class, as they exalt the qualities of the master class. Gandhi, for instance, was as a young man pleased that his sons were being trained in a good English school to be good English gentlemen. The irony of this is compounded: true Englishmen of the time would have seen the Indians as a couple of wogs regardless of their dress and manners. American blacks burn down their own neighborhoods in a frenzy of despair, unable to turn their rage against whites. Even in the Nazi death camps there were examples of people who identified themselves with the values of the master class. This internalization of the standards of the oppressor is the most serious affliction from which oppressed people suffer, and the most difficult to eliminate.

For Memmi, a man writing for men, the most serious blow suffered by oppressed people is "being removed from history and from the community." The institutions of colonization preclude the colonized from taking any role whatever in their own culture, from participating in social, economic, cultural, and political decisions that may deeply affect their own lives, and that always affect their environment.[29] In some cases even the language of the oppressed people is despised or repressed: during the partition of Poland, for instance, it was forbidden to teach in Polish; and Olive Schreiner recounts receiving severe punishment as a child in Africa for using the Afrikaans word "Ach," the language of the despised Dutch, rather than English, the language of the gentility.[30] Black slaves in the United States and colonized people in Africa and Asia experienced an obliteration of their native tongues. The colonized must learn to chart their way through their own countries by means of a foreign language.[31] In every way, then, the colonized are forced to live "isolated from [their] age."[32]

If we transpose the descriptions of colonized and colonizer to women and men, they fit at almost every point. Women are seen as different from men in kind, as members of a different species. Perhaps Aristotle put it most succinctly: "Wherever possible and so far as possible the male is separate from the female, since [he] is something *better* and more divine in that [he] is the principle of movement for generated things, while the female serves as their matter . . . We should look upon the female state as being as it were a deformity, though one which occurs in the ordinary course of nature."[33] As we have seen, women are considered subhuman (or superhuman) as a sex; women are "them," not individuals. All cats are gray at night, and all women are the same, whether they be perceived as loving, giving nourishers or as troublemaking furies. "They" are poor drivers, poor at math, cry easily, but excel at sewing on buttons and cooking meals. When a woman seems to fail a man, he is likely to damn all women and to see her failure as an expression of female malevolence directed at him.

We have noticed too that women are identified with animals; their bestiality makes them lustful and voracious, from the time of the Athenians, through the Roman Juvenal, through the early Christian Church, to the satirists of Renaissance England, to the poets and painters of the late nineteenth century, to satirists like James Thurber and sociologists like Philip Wylie. Cato warned in the second century B.C.E. that women must be strictly controlled or they would rise up and dominate men; so did John Knox in the sixteenth century C.E. Writers as different as Ovid, Shakespeare, Dickens, and Conrad often portrayed women as frail and foolish.

The territory of earth, once shared by all people, was carved up and appropriated by an elite group of men. They turned the earth's goods, including women, into property at their disposal. Just as colonizers deny such rights to colonized people or slaves, men have denied women the right to property. Like slavemasters and colonizers they have expected women to identify their interests with their oppressors'. When women have attempted to gain something the oppressors themselves needed or wanted, they have been seen as wily, calculating, and deceitful; when they have insisted on their own needs and desires, they have been seen as willful bitches, selfish monsters, and demonic castrators of men. Women who have attempted to escape from brutal husbands have been punished for their *rebellion*; in the sixteenth century in England, sexual interest in a man other than one's husband was considered *revolt*. The most frequent attack on women throughout the Middle Ages was on grounds of insubordination. The proper behavior of women was depicted in many tales of "patient Griselda," who accepts her husband's verbal and physical abuse with love and fortitude and thereby wins his love. The politics are clear even if the psychology is flawed. Even today, a woman's desire for a life of her own is interpreted by many men as an assault against them.

Women are not always segregated spatially, compartmentalized, although this is not uncommon. From the time of the Classical Athenians to the present in the middle-class Moslem world in the Middle East and in tribal cultures in Turkey, Afghanistan, and Pakistan, women have been required to occupy certain quarters of the house. They are responsible for maintaining all of the habitation, and may spend considerable time in men's quarters, serving and laboring. But they have no rights in these places.

Some women are not permitted to walk about in the world alone, or even with other women. They must be accompanied by a male family member. Only well-to-do families can maintain such customs, since they entail the loss of women's labor in the fields, but all women can be (and are) prevented from entering certain "public" spaces, like mosques. It is not necessary, however, to pass laws excluding women from particular places. Exclusion can be achieved simply by abusive behavior by men toward any women who enter. In Turkey, women are in peril if they take a train alone, or enter a male preserve; in Saudi Arabia, women are forbidden to drive cars.

But all cultures segregate women to some degree. There are jokes about men's discomfort in lingerie shops, in kitchens and nurseries, kindergartens and day-care centers. There are no jokes that I know of dealing with the severe discomfort of women in men's bars, or standing in the outer rooms of male-only clubs, or in expensive restaurants frequented by men. Women may enter certain male enclaves in a subordinate position—waitress, secretary, or cleaning woman—but if they attempt to enter as equals, women tend to feel discomfort in most board rooms, legislatures, the Pentagon, the supreme command of any government.

There is little problem in distinguishing men from women; indeed, the first thing we perceive about another adult is their sex. But the outcry that developed when women first began to adopt male dress, short hair, and shoes in which they can really walk shows that such distinctions are desirable to many men, and some would even like them to be heightened. The wedding ring, once worn only by women, was a form of shackle; high heels, once worn only by men of the French court, are a terrible impediment, almost as painful and hindering as bound feet. Elaborate coiffures and dress require not just money but great time and energy which then cannot be spent on more productive work. Such adornments serve profound functions. Just as the veil makes women invisible, removes their obscene presence from observation, an elaborate toilet places women in a class and removes them from consideration as individuals. (That a related tendency is occurring among men in the twentieth century will be discussed in Chapter Four.)

The various restrictions on women's behavior, freedom, and property rights have kept women in slavery for millennia. Although some people object to this term as extreme, what other term can one use to describe a state in which people do not have rights over their own bodies, their own sexuality, marriage, reproduction or divorce, in which they may not receive education or practice a trade or profession, or move about freely in the world? Many women (both past and present) work laboriously all their lives without receiving any payment for their work.

We have discussed at length the symbolic nature of female and male roles and the associations made between women, regardless of their characters or abilities, and nature, body, emotion, and sex. The independence of women has, from the time of Aristotle to the Moral Majority, been seen as a threat to "the family." This is true even of philosophers who assert human equality.

Hobbes, for instance, based his political philosophy on the argument that human beings are equal in nature. Inequality of rights, privileges, and authority is a result of a bargain made between the governed and the governors; it is grounded in mutual consent. In keeping with this belief in equality, Hobbes denied that dominion over children belonged to the father because he is "of the more excellent Sex," and claimed the mother is the true parent. But when he shifts his focus from the state to the family, he completely ignores his earlier statements and assumes that the father is dominant by nature.[34]

Even John Stuart Mill, the great supporter of women's independence and rights, assumes that the interests of the paterfamilias are identical with the interests of the mother and children, according to Susan Moller Okin. Mill never questions the strict separation of the family from the public realm and from economic life, which results in the swallowing up of the mother's identity and requires her unpaid labor.[35]

For Hegel too, "the unity of the family is founded on the refusal to cede to women any independent existence at all. One of the Additions to the section on the family asserts that, whereas men are like animals, women are like plants. Since women are not perceived as having any distinct life or interests at all, it is not difficult for Hegel to perceive the family as a place from which all discord and conflict of interest is absent, and where love and altruism reign supreme. The loving unity of Hegel's family is founded on the denial of a personality to its wife and mother."[36]

The assimilation of the oppressed into the identity of the oppressor was far more successful with women than with other oppressed peoples because children born to the union of wife and husband are in fact a common interest. The welfare of families was not equally shared: in general, men ate better and lived more freely than women. But women accepted such discrepancies more or less gracefully for the sake of their children, whose economic survival was dependent upon having a father.

The most serious problem, one that is residual even in cultures in which women have gained some rights, is the internalization of the standards of the oppressor and the image of unworthiness patriarchy has painted of women. The horror and scorn with which many classical writers regarded women have been described and will be again in this book. The early Christian Church taught that all souls were equal before God; nevertheless, women were viewed as morally frail, rebellious, and inclined to lead men into sin. (That women lack a high moral sense is asserted in our own time by Lawrence Kohlberg and will be discussed in Chapter Six.) The Protestant revolution reasserted human equality and denied the authority of the Church hierarchy. Nevertheless, women were relegated to secondary roles in Protestantism too.

Even science, with all its authority, has supported this view of women. The female body was considered to be illness incarnate; Aristotle found the female mind defective.[37] The Greeks held the father to be parent to the child, the mother mere vessel, a view of things Catholicism apotheosized. Much later, biologists declared male sperm to be active and energetic, while females were passive preservers of nutritive substance.[38] Darwinist doctors claimed that the female brain had diminished in the course of evolution while the male brain had enlarged.[39] It has been theorized by highly respected doctors that the essence of women lies in her ovaries; that children inherit intelligence from their fathers only; that women are closer to the "lower races" because their feet incline to be flat.[40]

Schopenhauer held that women were suited to raise children because they were themselves childish; the anthropologist Paul Albrecht demonstrated that women were closer than men to beasts because they had more hair.[41] Phrenologists measured the skulls of women and blacks to prove the inferiority of their intelligence. The German neurologist P. J. Möbius referred to the female as *it*;

he was relieved that women were bodily and spiritually weak, which made them less dangerous than they would be otherwise. He fought against education for women because it caused them to seek power over men and to produce sickly children deprived of mother's milk.[42] A former professor at the Harvard Medical School published a book in 1872 in which he used clinical evidence to show that women who went to college would suffer mental and physical breakdowns and possibly even become sterile.[43]

In the late nineteenth and early twentieth centuries, a time when women in England and the United States had in some ways fewer rights than women in Classical Athens, when doctors were performing clitoridectomies on women who showed signs of possessing a sexual nature, and when the majority of women were struggling on the verge of starvation but trying to keep their children alive, an entire artistic "school"—the Symbolists—began to depict women as demons, sirens, and vampires whose very existence threatened the lives of men; the German physician Max Nordau proclaimed that women's deepest instincts were toward "promiscuous sexual intercourse and prostitution"; and the psychologist Otto Weininger asserted that women lacked the ability for ethical and rational thought, intellect, a soul, individual personality, and an ego. Woman is only sexuality and sensuality; she demands coitus from men who wish only to be chaste and pure because she has a lust for a child or for mastery over a man.[44]

This sense of women as threatening and voraciously sexual is not uncommon in our own period: consider the paintings of women by Willem de Kooning, and James Thurber's drawings of women. Recently a circuit court judge in Wisconsin labeled a five-year-old girl the "aggressor" in a case of sexual assault by a twenty-four-year-old man whom he exonerated.[45] Even motherhood has been attacked in our century, first by Philip Wylie, who claimed the true nature of mothers was cunning, ruthless, and power-hungry; then by the more serious psychoanalyst Erik Erikson, who accepted Wylie's terms and discussed "Momism."[46]

Memmi's accusation that colonization denies the colonized a voice in their own culture and their own destiny has been true also for most women in most cultures. Indeed, women have not been deprived just of a cultural voice, but even a personal one. Women too are regularly spoken of collectively; they are the girls, the broads, the ladies, the bitches, women, Woman. They speak a language to which men do not listen and for which men have contempt; and they find, when they try to enter the public world, that men speak a language they do not understand. Women suffer deeply from horizontal hostility. Some of the worst attacks on women are made by women, and women frequently betray deep contempt for their own sex. In a poll taken in 1946, over a quarter of the women responding revealed they wished they had been born men.[47]

There are, then, many parallels between slaves, colonized peoples, and women, but there are also some important differences. Although there may occasionally be love between a slave and master, a colonized person and a colonizer, in general love does not complicate their power struggle with each other. A woman, however, finds her oppressors to be father, brother, husband, and son. It is easier to have an enemy one can clearly identify as enemy. Although children are born in unions of oppressed and oppressor, those children are usually cast out into the mother's class. But children create a deep bond between wife and husband, a common ground of interest. Finally and devastatingly, women often share in the economic and cultural goods of their male relatives. They may be given some education or training; they may partake of wealth; or if they are poor, they identify themselves with the oppression of their fathers and husbands. For these reasons, it has been even more difficult for women to rebel against patriarchal rule than for enslaved and colonized peoples. Women are caught in the strange bind of being part of a group their husbands, the men they sleep and eat with, would not admit to their clubs.[48]

We must question why the domination of classes of people exists at all. Memmi, speaking of colonized people, and Kenneth Stampp, speaking of black slaves in the United States, agree that the purpose of domination is to offer "a systematic method of controlling and exploiting labor."[49] Although colonization does sometimes allow short-term profits for a small group, its full economic costs—not to speak of its human costs—are never reckoned up. To support colonization, a nation must pay for a huge corps of colonial administrators and overseers, for armies and police, and the price of Europeanizing unsettled jungle, desert, and veldt. It remains a matter of contention whether slavery was profitable in the narrow sense. People could of course send slaves into disease-ridden swamps to labor and die instead of going themselves; but some of the masters, or master surrogates, had to accompany the slaves and take the same risks. Masters frequently caused the death of their slaves even though such deaths produced financial losses for them.

The methods used to intimidate and coerce colonized peoples and slaves conflict with the ostensible goals of such oppression. To whip severely enough to maim is to eliminate a healthy body from the work force. Leopold of Belgium ordered the hands of rebellious colonized Congolese to be cut off, and Mark Twain saw the pile of human hands higher than his head. Did this increase the tractability of the remainder of the slaves? Were Angolans motivated to work harder by seeing the lips of their fellows who complained pierced and fixed shut with padlocks? (This practice was abandoned only recently.)[50] When pregnant slave women were forced to work for twenty-two hours a day in planting or reaping season, so that they lost their babies and sometimes their lives, was this good for business? The Nazis spent enormous sums of money and considerable manpower planning, gathering, transporting, and interning Jews and other despised groups in concentration camps, some of which were intended as work camps. Arrangements had been made with I. G. Farben and other companies to provide slave labor and so assist the war effort. Yet the internees were fed almost nothing, deprived of sleep by overcrowding of bunks, given almost no clothing, and forced to work for long hours. Naturally, they died. Considering the resources spent on maintaining millions of people in such camps, did this help the war effort? White slaveowners had to pay high prices for their slaves, yet many kept their slaves on starvation diets and flogged them when they were caught stealing food: does this make business sense?

In a world in which power is the highest good, and economic power the most desirable sort, economic gain is seen as the motivation for most behavior, especially that which is cruel and oppressive. Although I have been discussing their similarities, slavery in the United States and colonization in various African and Asian states were not identical phenomena. In some cases slavery or colonization was profitable to a group of men. An econometric analysis of American slavery attempted to prove that slaveholders earned, on an average, 10 percent on the market price of their slaves, a rate of return equal to investment in nonagricultural enterprises.[51] This analysis aroused considerable contention, and the question of whether slaveholding was profitable is still at issue. If slaveholding and colonialism were not profitable to some, it is unlikely that people would have continued in it—although even this is not certain. (Companies today are persisting in building nuclear power plants, although most evidence points to their unprofitability.)

My point is not that no one made a profit on such kinds of oppression, but that the society as a whole did not. We are not used to thinking about profit in a large context. But if one considers, with regard to slavery, the costs of lawmakers who justified it and codified guidelines for it, the hiring of police, the expense of their time and their weaponry, even quite apart from the costs of the Civil War, it is doubtful that society as a whole profited from the institution. The costs of colonization are staggering. It requires transport of large numbers of people, the expense of creating housing and institutional headquarters for them, their wages and maintenance; it may also require—and frequently does—hosts of soldiers, weapons, vehicles or animals, fortresses, outposts, spies, communications networks, the bureaucracy to back these up, and, sometimes, gunboats. The cost is often war, with all the losses that entails. It also involves considerable loss of life in war, or from disease, of colonizers as well as the colonized.

The price is high also in personal terms. Stampp cites many cases of slaveowners who were made miserable by their state. The wives of slaveowners were equally miserable. One woman, hearing about the Emancipation Proclamation, cried out, "Free at last!" She added that she would prefer poverty to "the cares and perplexities of ownership." Another commented, "Our burden of work and responsibility was simply staggering . . . I was glad and thankful on my own account when slavery ended, and I ceased to belong body and soul to my negroes."[52] It is an obvious fact, yet one which our society ignores, that the dominator always belongs to the dominated, that he must spend his life devising controls, silencing mechanisms, and motivations to keep the dominated in line, that he is never free from the demand of the dark murmuring oppressed mass he controls.

Yet a principal reason for owning slaves is that they are status symbols, "badges of honor, prestige, and power."[53] So too, in some places, men of power use eunuchs as mediators between them and their subjects. The eunuch is considered not to be a man, and is associated with filth and pollution; as the gypsies use their women, semidivine rulers use eunuchs.[54] Possession of such beings brings status to the owner.

The moral price of such oppression is overwhelming. I do not speak here of the oppressed, who are of course deformed, corrupted or destroyed by such a system, but of the oppressors. Not just the person in immediate control of an oppressed group, but all those involved in such a system are deformed, corrupted, or destroyed by it. They must live day by day in fear and suspicion. Some of them sleep, like the inhabitants of a beautiful house I visited in Kenya, behind barred gates that slide down at night outside their bedroom doors. Ever watchful for the slightest sign of insubordination, which might signal the onset of rebellion, they cannot trust or love those around them. Fear leads to hate, which corrupts. But perhaps most important, the character of the dominator is defined by the oppressed. All that the oppressed is, the dominator can deny being: this is symbolic truth, contradicted by reality. British colonists in Kenya's Rift Valley flogged their servants for laziness or incompetence, yet themselves lived lives of incredible idleness, drinking all day, taking drugs, and spending their days and nights partying.[55] Yet it is the native who is seen as lascivious and unrestrained.

I believe that this kind of projection is at the root of colonization and enslavement: economics play a part, but the principal gain is symbolic—the ability to look down at a set of human beings and attribute to them all that one has been taught to despise in the self. The dynamic of colonization and slavery is identical to that of male supremacy. The relationship is destructive because it is based on deceit: neither the oppressor nor the oppressed is, by nature, what the oppressor claims.

Yet domination creates an unbreakable bond of unfreedom between dominator and oppressed; they are connected in an ecstatic hell (like that of sado-masochistic sex), in which each confers meaning on the other's life. The oppressed have no responsibility; the dominator has no freedom. In his control of others, he is always controlled by them. Yet so blindly insane has patriarchy made us that for many of us even the illusion of control is preferable to the pleasure of being. To maintain that illusion people sacrifice ease and relatedness, trust and well-being, honesty, and sometimes even life itself. Domination is a hysterical attempt to emulate God, to be in complete control of nature, others, and self: it is not possible to human beings. It always fails in its purpose, yet, like the drunk driver, takes down with it those who do not accept its terms, those who live by other values.

## 2. ANCIENT FRAGMENTS

It is 1650 B.C.E. The nomad Sarah and her band are setting our for Palestine from the edge of Arabia. Sumer has been swallowed up by the Semitic kingdom of Sargon of Agade; its fragmented city-states already entertain patriarchal values. Nomadic tribes from the north—Hittites, Scythians, and Hurrians—who have spent the last two millennia in the Danube and Don regions, are overflowing into Asia Minor.[56]

Four centuries later, Miriam, with her brothers Moses and Aaron, will lead Israel out of Egypt, and two centuries after that, Deborah will lead Israel into war against Canaan, against Sisera, the head of King Jabin's armies. Deborah and her general, Barak, will upset Sisera's armies, and Sisera will seek help from a woman, Jael, who offers him drink and food and sleep in her tent, and then will hammer a nail through his temple. Then Deborah will sing in celebration, creating a poem, a fragment of which constitutes the oldest portion of the Bible. Part of her song is: "The inhabitants of the villages ceased, they ceased in Israel, until that I Deborah arose, that I arose a mother in Israel" (Judges 5:7). Women may have participated in war in Old Testament times; they also built cities—Sherah built Beth-Haran the nether, the upper, and Uzzen-Sherah.[57]

We possess tantalizing bits of information on ancient worlds, like the foregoing biblical material. I will mention only two other civilizations, that of Egypt and that of Minoan Crete, both of which offer us some knowledge about women of the distant past.

Egypt was already an ancient civilization by 2000 B.C.E. In preliterate, prehistoric times, it seems that Egypt was matrilineal and that women were prominent in its culture, perhaps even dominant. Royalty and property passed in the female line, and tombs show equality between men and women, although there appears to have been stratification of classes.[58] Women had full competence and rights in law and business even much later; they could sell and administer property, execute wills, sue at law, and officiate as witnesses of records.[59]

In the beginning, the Egyptians worshiped goddesses and gods separately; later they were paired; and eventually a god, Amon-Ra, became supreme. The male priestly class attempted to consolidate its position, but the Mother Goddess, in some places called Neith, continued to dominate the imaginations of the people. Neith was served by priestesses only during the epoch of the Old Kingdom. Although the royal couple were brother and sister, the males ruled. Later pharaohs built enormous tombs for themselves, the pyramids; each in turn effaced the monuments of previous pharaohs and tried to outdo them in size and number of statues. By this time the burial places of queens were scanted, but Egyptian women still worked as professionals—as estate managers, as physicians, architects, soldiers, musicians, and scribes. They were poets and priestesses; wealthy women were merchants and long-distance traders. A woman was a military commander. Working-class women and men were paid equally and worked side by side in temples, running taverns and inns, weaving, and as domestic servants. Marriage was a matter of choice; divorce was easily obtained. Men and women dressed alike and used the same eye paint, jewelry, and perfume.[60]

The Hyksos invaded Egypt and ruled it for some time. It was a queen, Ahotep (c. 1550 B.C.E.), who led the movement to overthrow them. The struggle occupied several generations, and when it was successful, Hatshepsut ruled as pharaoh. She turned the country away from war and began large-scale domestic reconstruction. But she ruled for twenty years, and her resentful and impatient son-in-law, Thutmose III, suppressed women when he acceded to the throne. He also halted the reconstruction and reverted to militarism.[61]

At some point, separatism developed in the court and temples, and a women's court, or *harem*, was set up. This was not a place of sequestration or polygamy: it was a school and court, parallel to male institutions, a training place for female diplomats, where women could learn foreign languages, music, dancing, and business practices. It was an agency handling affairs that were governed by the women's courts, affairs that touched both men and women. Gradually, however, women were edged out of politics and trade, the arts and science. In the tenth century B.C.E., when Cush ruled Egypt, Egyptian women were sent as slaves to work in Cushite temples.[62]

Nevertheless, in the seventh century C.E., before the Arab conquest, there was still no such thing as an illegitimate child; all children belonged to their mothers, as did the house and property. The word for wife—*nebt-per*—meant *ruler of the house*. Men were considered boarders or visitors in the places owned by women, and if a man built a house it became his wife's property. Women drew up and dictated the marriage contracts and cared for their parents in their old age. Documents show that sometimes men managed to exploit women, taking all their possessions.[63]

The Maxims of Ptah-Hotep, probably the oldest known book (c.2400 B.C.E.), directed that men should obey their wives. Although it is unlikely that this state of things continued over the millennia, as late as the first century B.C.E., Diodorus Siculus visited the country and wrote that men did obey their wives and that the arrangement led to the happiest results.[64] The trend, however, was toward continued diminishment of women. After the XIIth Dynasty, there were no priestesses; after Ptolemy Philopater, the word *husband* appears for the first time. This Ptolemy, whose name means father lover, was a vicious and dissolute ruler who murdered his mother, brother, and wife. He also decreed that women required their husbands' authorization to dispose of property.[65]

Still, Cleopatra could rule in the first century B.C.E., brilliantly and bravely—although she needed Caesar to rid her of her husband/brother, Ptolemy XII. Her legend has been falsified and diminished, for it was transmitted by the Romans, who hated her. Sir William Tarn wrote: "Rome, who never condescended to fear any nation or people, did in her time fear two human beings: one was Hannibal, and the other was a woman."[66]

There is disagreement over the beautiful civilization of Minoan Crete, discovered by Sir Arthur Evans and named for a man who ruled the island after the "Minoan" period. Evans himself found Crete to have a "matriarchal" cast, but some of his proofs have been questioned. One can understand why he believed as he did, though: the palace at Knossos, on a hill under the clear Mediterranean sky, surrounded by green hills, unwalled and peaceful, its rooms covered with drawings of beautiful women elegantly adorned, *feels* female. There are no huge ramparts, no monolithic towers, no signs of self-aggrandizement. Like Pompeii, it seems to testify to an ideal way of life. Of course, so does the Moslem Alhambra in Granada.

Although Crete lay in the center of trade routes, it was not for a long time invaded or conquered. Its people lived in matricentric clans, trading peacefully, making high art. Towns grew from settlements scattered around the harbors, each having a marketplace that served as a center for trade, religion, and social activity. The Cretans produced pottery, textiles, and metalwork, which they traded for luxurious materials like gold, ivory, and lapis lazuli. They also sold timber.[67]

There was stratification but no segregation of classes—the rich and the not-so-rich lived side by side.[68] It was the clan that owned the land, and burial was communal throughout most of Minoan history. Although there was a royal class, it does not seem to have exerted strong centralized control.[69] Within this society women had high status. They are very prominent in Minoan art, standing or sitting in the foreground of frescoes depicting public scenes. They seem to have carried on long-distance trade: a woman steering a ship is depicted on the Ring of Minos, and a woman disembarking from a ship and carrying a tree is depicted on a gold signet ring found in a grave in Mochlos.[70] Pictures on seals, rings, and sarcophagi, as well as statues and frescoes, portray women farming, tending orchards, healing, dancing, and functioning as priestesses. They are shown driving chariots, and hunting with bows and arrows. They hunt the wild bull with the men, and play the dangerous game of leaping over the bull. Men's and women's clothing is differentiated not by sex but by the activity in which they are engaged. The daily attire of women and men was extremely sexual. The goddess with the "double ax"—the immortal butterfly—appears frequently.[71]

This civilization vanished, devastated by the aftermath of a tremendous volcanic eruption on Thera (Santorin) in the fifteenth century B.C.E., and Crete was then invaded by Achaeans, Greek-speaking people from Mycenae, who took over its ruined palaces before 1400 B.C.E. It is hypothesized that they enslaved those Minoans who did not escape. That many did escape is suggested by the many tales that arose in this period about Amazons along the coast of Asia Minor, tribes known for their powerful women and egalitarian customs—the Lycians, the Carians, the Lydians, and the Mysians, all Cretan-related people.[72]

Mycenae was the wealthiest and strongest kingdom on the Greek mainland, and had long been influenced by Minoan economic activities and Minoan culture. The Achaeans, who later conquered Troy, were a militaristic people who spoke Greek and kept records in Linear B, a form of Greek. Linear B records and artifacts from this later period show that the Achaeans continued to worship the Minoan goddess figure along with male gods. There is a reference to an offering to Posidaeja, the feminine form of Poseidon, one of the three major gods of the Greek pantheon, but no reference to the name in its masculine form.[73] There are records of religious offices that must be held by women, but also lists of people doing menial tasks—servants or refugees—most of whom seem to be women.[74] Linear B tablets from Pylos show both women and men in serving capacities, and list the tasks of women as fetching water, providing baths, spinning, weaving, reaping, and grinding corn.[75] Their love of weapons and military scenes, demonstrated by their artifacts, may have led the Achaeans to invade Troy in 1250 B.C.E. and raze it to the ground, but it did not prevent the same fate from overtaking them when the Dorians invaded and overcame them fifty years later. In such a world, the values of Minoan Crete were barely a memory.

## 3. The Glory and the Grandeur: Greece and Rome

Many separate groups comprised the people we now call the Greeks, who lived in independent city-states during the period of their dominance. Ancient Greek history is divided into three periods: the Archaic, from the eighth to the sixth centuries B.C.E., the Classical, from the sixth to the fourth, and the Hellenistic, which extends to the Roman takeover of Egypt after the death of Cleopatra in 30 B.C.E. Although each of the Greek city-states had its own customs and laws, most of what we know about ancient Greece concerns only Athens in the fifth century B.C.E., the "golden age." It was not so golden for women, however.

Some historians believe that Greece had a matricentric past. Briffault asserts that early Greek genealogies are essentially catalogues of women, and that "matriarchy" is apparent in the structure of Greek speech and legal customs.[76] Charles Seltmen points to coinage in Magna Graecia and Sicily, which as late as the sixth century B.C.E. bore depictions of female deities.[77] The strongest evidence for a tradition of powerful women, however, seems to me a negative proof—the extreme rage and vituperation directed at women by generations of Greek writers. Even though by the time of the Classical age Athenian women were completely subjugated, misogynistic tirades do not cease.

The situation for women in this period was probably worst in Athens. In Sparta, for example, girls were educated as well as boys, if differently: they raced, threw discus and javelin, but did not wrestle.[78] Exceptional women appeared in cities other than Athens, which suggests some form of education was open to them.[79] Dorian women had more freedom than Ionian women, and among the Dorians, Spartan women had the most rights. Adult freewomen in Sparta managed the home and the property; they also raised the children, did gymnastics, and made music. Household work was left to slaves or servants. The women of Sparta managed to become quite rich by the fourth century B.C.E., owning two-fifths of the land and property of the city-state.[80]

The freemen of Sparta lived in all-male groups. They ate and slept together and spent their time training for war; homosexuality among them was not discouraged, although Sarah Pomeroy comments that in fact they liked the young, and either sex would do.[81] In most Greek city-states, men and women were separated because the men went off to military service, because of culturally accepted male homosexuality, and because of the scorn in which women as a group were held. These attitudes tended to hold down the population. In addition, there was widespread infanticide, especially of girls. Families might choose to raise more than one son to guarantee a male heir, but it was unnecessary to have more than one daughter. Extra males were not a problem: men had to do military service—in Athens, ten years was required—and many were killed. Athenian girls were married at fourteen to men of thirty who might be dead by forty-five. The woman could then be passed on to another man while she was still in her childbearing years. In the Hellenistic period, many families had only one child, a son, almost never more than one daughter.[82] Some girls may have been discarded, to be picked up as slaves or prostitutes; some may have been turned into servants in their parents' houses.[83]

Despite war losses, the longevity for adult males in Classical Greece was forty-five; for women it was 36.2.[84] Women's short life span was probably a result of an inadequate diet and of giving birth before their bodies were completely grown. According to Xenophon, Greek girls, with the exception of Spartans, were brought up on a sparse diet with little protein, almost no meat, and watered wine, if indeed they were given wine at all.[85] In fifth century Persepolis, the "mother's rations" granted to those who had given birth to a boy were twice the amount of wine, beer, and grain given to those who bore a girl.[86] Thus in Classical Greece, as in the period in which Leviticus was written, boys were worth twice what girls were worth.

Relations between spouses were poor. The values of the culture exalted men, demeaned women. There was a huge disparity in age, education, and experience between a middle-aged man who had moved freely in the world and an adolescent girl who had been sequestered. These differences led to male condescension for their wives, or worse—scorn, contempt. Women were largely confined to the house, quarters that were dark, squalid, and unsanitary. Men were mocked if they spent their days at home rather than in the broad spaces and impressive, graceful, light-filled public buildings where men gathered.[87] Athenian law held that sufficient causes to invalidate a man's legal acts were senility, drugs, disease, constraint, or being under the influence of a woman.[88]

To have legal existence, a family required at least one male descendant, since a family was considered to be made up of males only. Certain family rituals could be performed only by men. Nevertheless, men were extremely reluctant to marry, and Sparta was forced to deny the rights of citizenship to unmarried men; in Athens, a magistrate had to be charged with the duty of preventing any family from becoming extinct—that is, lacking a male descendant.[89]

Women were expected to be extremely hard-working. In the Homeric epics, even aristocratic women and goddesses are shown constantly spinning, weaving, doing laundry, bathing guests and making up beds for them, and preparing and serving food.[90] In the actual life of later ages, women were completely responsible for running a household that was essentially a small factory, supervising production, slaves, and children.[91] In The Laws, Plato complains that "we huddle all our goods together . . . within four walls, and then hand over the dispensing of them to the women."

It is impossible to know how women themselves felt about their lives. Silenced by lack of education and no right to appear or speak in public forums, oppressed by being unesteemed, married off when they were still children, and immediately made responsible for running complex households and raising children, they are silent for eternity. Perhaps some of them were the furious manipulative mothers postulated by Slater, training their sons to avenge them.

Perhaps some of them found pleasure in their work, their usefulness, laughing together at male illusions, knowing how dependent upon them the men really were. They may even have had an entire life of their own, a subculture of affection and pleasure, as Amy Swerdlow deduces from depictions of women in vase paintings, which show women working wool together in dignity, harmony, and grace, or in affectionate companionship at the baths.[92] Perhaps some women even managed some personal freedom, as suggested by a spoof called "The Laws of Zaleucus." One order of this mock code decrees that "a free woman may not have more than one girl escorting her unless she is drunk, may not leave the city at night except for adultery."[93]

It was women of the propertied classes who were regulated. That is, in general, the women attached to the men with the most rights had the least rights. Propertied Athenian women did have economic security; their dowries were their own in law, if not to use. If a woman left her husband, he had to return her property or pay interest on it; if she remained with him, he had to support her.[94] And the state guaranteed her right to life (if not liberty); her husband or father could not kill her with impunity except in infancy. Nevertheless, citizen women were perpetually under the guardianship of a man—father, uncle, husband, or even son. And laws institutionalized by Solon, the sixth-century lawgiver, drew a distinction between "good women" and "whores." Citizen women were the good women, whose lives were completely prescribed by Solon, who laid down rules for their "walks, the feasts, the mourning, the trousseaux, and the food and drink."[95]

Conditions for the "whores" were a different matter. Solon set up state-owned brothels staffed by slave women who may well have been the daughters of citizen men, exposed as infants and picked up by slave dealers. Slaves and poor women were not confined within the house. Like poor women everywhere and in every time, they went out to work. They sold goods in the marketplace, ran inns and cafes, and worked with wool. They were vulnerable to charges of prostitution, as are women alone today. Many of them were entertainers, courtesans, and prostitutes who worked the all-male dinner-party and orgy circuit.[96] Some of these women became rich and were able to buy their freedom (if they were slaves, as many were) or to establish themselves in business.[97] Indeed, prostitutes were "the only women in Athens who exercised independent control over considerable amounts of money."[98]

In spite of the severe restraints, some women in Classical Greece managed to distinguish themselves in the arts or in intellectual pursuits. Many of these lived in Athens, but none, it seems, were born there. Women poets had a tradition, or perhaps more than one tradition. The great Sappho had students, at least one of whom, Erinna, wrote poetry that her male contemporaries considered as good as Homer's. A group of women poets called the "nine Earthly Muses" were viewed as the best poets of their age. Their work, Pomeroy writes, offers "the happiest picture of women in Greek literature."[99] One of them, Myrtis, was the teacher of Pindar and Corinna of Tanagro, who was thought second only to Sappho.

It is significant that the work of such women has not survived at all, or remains only in fragments, while the work of Pindar endured. So too we have only the name of Cresilas, who placed third behind Polyclitus and Phidias in a sculpture competition for the Temple of Artemis at Ephesus. The names of many other women artists and musicians survive only because they are mentioned in works by males.

For instance, Socrates claimed Diotima was his teacher. Philosophy instructors, however, used to scoff at this: Diotima was a symbol, they claimed, for certain kinds of wisdom. But in fact there is no reason to doubt his statement. She was probably one of many female Pythagoreans—for Pythagoras, like Epicurus, admitted women to his school on the same terms as men.[100] Another of these was Theano, a mathematician and expert in medicine, physics, and early psychology, who first articulated the theory of the "golden mean" with which Pythagoras has been credited, and who succeeded him as head of his philosophic institute.[101] Some women disguised themselves as men in order to gain education. Axiothea, for instance, studied with Plato, who called her (although it is unclear whether he knew she was female) "the mind bright enough to grasp" his ideas.[102] Plato—and doubtless other Greeks—were aware that women had capacities denied them in Athens. Plato had known both Athenian and Spartan women, and wrote in a dialogue that beside Spartan women Sarmatian women seemed like men.[103] There was much resentment in male-supremacist Athens of the late fifth century B.C.E. over the fact that a woman, Artemisia, commanded one of the ships that fought against that city in the Battle of Salamis.[104]

The status of women became a political issue in the fourth century B.C.E., when repression of women had reached a peak.[105] This was a period of great change in Greek political organizations, as the Macedonian kings Philip and Alexander tried to unify the Greek city-states by war and conquest. It was a time of increased centralization of state power simultaneously with loosened control of localities and of nonmilitary, nongovernment affairs. Consequently Greek women were able to find more room for action. From the middle of the fourth century, Greek girls went to school with their brothers. Although they still required the aegis of a man, Greek women could participate more in economic affairs, making contracts, buying and selling, receiving inheritances and making legacies. Marriage became more of a partnership, and occasionally a woman would be appointed to a political office that had previously been filled only by males.[106]

There is evidence that women proposed and supported candidates for municipal elections in Pompeii, and that women controlled certain social and religious matters in Ephesus. In Phrygia women were appointed to the important post of monetary magistrate.[107] A first-century inscription from Asia Minor names a woman, Phyle, as holding the highest state office and as building a reservoir and aqueducts for her city; a woman was *archon* (high magistrate) of Histria; a woman harpist was rewarded with the right to own land in her city, Delphi.[108] Women taught in the academies at Alexandria.[109] They were granted honorary citizenship for outstanding service in some cities which had not previously granted citizenship to women.[110]

However, what was extended to women in this period was the right to participate in a shrunken power. By the time women were permitted to own property, property ownership no longer led to citizenship; women were occasionally made officials of the *polis,* but the *polis* was no longer the seat of governmental power.[111] The gap between the rich and the poor was widening, and the poor were losing their land. Women's sexuality was more open and accepted in this time, and education was somewhat available to them; yet the pursuit of education and admission of sexuality still brought criticism to women who displayed such aberrant behavior.[112] The changes in women's rights no doubt required struggle and determination on the part of individual women; these changes occurred over a period of several hundred years, longer than the struggle of women in our own period (which began in 1848).

But there was little change in the condition of women in Athens; indeed, the situation there became even more repressive for women, largely because legislation governing them derived from the influence of Aristotle, who believed that "the deliberative part of woman's soul was impotent and needed supervision." Regulators censored women's conduct and even controlled the lavishness of dinner parties.[113] The Stoics joined the Peripatetics—Aristotle's school—in narrowly confining women within the household, and in perceiving women as defective intellectually and physically. And Stoicism was adopted by the Romans.[114] It was thus the Athenian rather than the Hellenistic tradition that was perpetuated. The status of women in Greece and Asia Minor later declined even further.

There are important points to be deduced from this material. We must emphasize the fact that the moment local controls were relaxed, women moved out into the world, tried to gain training and education and some control over their lives. They knew what they wanted, and some of them got it. They were able to do so because local controls were lessened as centralized control increased. The situation may be compared to what happened in the United States when the federal government began to legislate matters that had previously been in the hands of municipalities: local authorities lost some of their powers. Yet a central government may not concern itself with all local matters, and people previously repressed may have more room to maneuver. They may even run for political office, although that office no longer holds the same powers. An example nearer home may be the American publishing industry. As women began to be hired for top editorial jobs, a level from which they had previously been barred, publishing firms were consolidating and being bought by huge conglomerates. The centralization at the top means that whereas formerly such editors were empowered to buy the books their companies publish, now they have to have purchases approved by the "money men" at the top. Women are admitted—but the power is diminished. This was the case also with Greek women: the power available to them was less than it had been to men in the same positions a century or two earlier. As we shall see, admission to a diminished power is a constant in the acquisition of control by women; it is something to remember when we consider our own period.

But what is perhaps even more important is that Athenian men were not isolated from the larger world. They saw what women were doing in other parts of Greece and Asia Minor. Indeed, they had always had before them the example of distinguished women raised in other parts of Greece and Asia Minor who came to Athens to work. They knew, in other words, that living women refuted Aristotle's descriptions of women, that women as a class and sex had the capacity to be competent human beings, and that extraordinary women existed. They could not maintain out of ignorance the belief that women as a class and sex were in fact and by nature what Athens had made its women into. That they nevertheless maintained that belief was therefore a political and moral act, a choice that contradicted what they knew to be true.

The question is why they did this. It can be given, like so many questions, an economic answer: by keeping women virtually enslaved, men profited from their labor and did not have to reward them. But again, this answer takes a narrow view of profit. If women had been educated, allowed a little freedom, they would have done a better job of organization, administration, and production: profits would have increased. Of course, if women had been educated and allowed some freedom, many of them might have refused to oversee their home factories; they might have rebelled, and men might have had to do this work themselves.

Yet many men might have enjoyed it: men today enjoy managerial tasks. That, however, was an unthinkable proposition for the Greeks. For male self-definition rested on freedom and volition, on control over the realm of the necessary. To maintain that self-definition, it was necessary to coerce others to provide a contrast with it. For example, suppose someone declares himself intelligent who is not especially intelligent. To create an illusion of great intelligence, however, he surrounds himself with people who are far less so than he. He refuses to educate his children, and scolds them when they speak or ask questions. He treats them with scorn, as stupid. In time, he will appear not just to himself, but to those around him as well, to be highly intelligent. The denial of any capacity other than childbearing, child rearing, and for "menial" tasks to women, the thwarting of all native ability by a whole set of institutionalized repressions, creates a race of child-women who will, by comparison, make men, who have not been so thwarted, look *actually*—by nature—superior. The costs of this, not just to women but to men, are never considered, but are very high. (This will be discussed further in Chapter Four.)

The Romans derived from the Etruscans, about whom little is known. According to Athenaeus, Etruscan women were sexually free and reared all children born to them equally. They were also athletic, good-looking, and heavy drinkers.[115] Inscriptions frequently record the name of the mother of their dedicators, but not that of the father.[116] Briffault writes that the Etruscans were matriarchal and matronymous, and that women had the more highly ornamented tombs. They had, he asserts, no word for father and perhaps no words for husband or wife.[117] Rigorous feminist scholars question the bases of such claims, but whether or not they were true, Etruscan mores did not survive. The Romans seem from their earliest literature to have been a solemn, even pompous, people with a righteousness that masks strong aggressiveness.

Rome was supposed by one tradition to have been founded by Aeneas after his flight from Troy in what Alexandrian scholars fixed as 1184 B.C.E.; and by another tradition to have been founded in 753 B.C.E. by Romulus and Remus, who were symbolically motherless and suckled by a she-wolf. Another legend has it that their mother was Rhea Sylvia, the last member of the family of Aeneas. She was a Vestal Virgin, and although she claimed she did not break her vow of chastity because Mars was the father of the children, she was executed. Livy remarks that *she-wolf* was a common word for prostitute (much as the word *bitch* is used today for women generally).[118]

At first a monarchy, Rome became a republic ruled by aristocrats (similar to the early republic of the United States, in which only property-owning white males had a voice) around 500 B.C.E. After 27 B.C.E., it became an empire. It was never ruled by a woman and, unlike other cultures we have discussed, did not even have a myth of being founded or ruled by a goddess. On the contrary, the myth of the settling of Rome was the story of the rape of the Sabine women. This story describes the settling of Rome by a group of male marauders from Alba, who attacked a neighboring tribe, seized their women, and held them under the rule of *confarreatio*. This word means *marriage* in later Latin, but derives from *far*, which means *spelt* or *grain*; the word thus means a *sharing of the spelt*. Under this form of marriage, the wife is in the absolute power of the husband and cannot divorce him. If she is drunken or unfaithful, she can be punished by her husband or her own family; if she is properly obedient, she remains mistress of the house in her husband's lifetime and inherits a share of his property, together with the children if there are any, when he dies—unless he has stipulated otherwise.[119]

In the Roman family the paterfamilias had the right to inflict physical punishment on or even to kill his children. A husband had similar rights over his wife, except that he could not kill her without conferring with her relatives. Thus Roman women did not have the right to life that Athenian women had. On the other hand, they were not forced to live in seclusion like Athenian women. A Roman wife shared familial religious responsibilities with her husband and went out with him in public—something Greek wives never did. She was the hostess at all social events within the house.[120] In law, however, women had the status of *imbecillitas*.[121]

The laws of Rome changed greatly over its history, and there is strong evidence that Roman women continually found ways to get around the constrictions placed upon them. But whatever freedoms they won, they *never* won the right to a political voice. From the beginning the doctrines of *infirmitas sexus* and *levitas animi* were applied to them, and they required the guardianship of a male. All children were under the absolute rule of their father; if he died, prepubescent boys and all girls came into the possession of their oldest uncle or brother, who could kill them or sell them into slavery. Boys came into their freedom when their father died or—according to the earliest Roman law, the Twelve Tables—after their father manumitted them or sold them into slavery three times! Females never obtained freedom, except for those who qualified after Augustus decreed that freeborn women who bore three children and freedwomen who bore four were to be released from male guardianship.[122]

Augustus, anxious to repopulate Rome and its armies, determined the proper age of marriage for girls at twelve, but Roman girls had always been married young. They had the legal right to refuse a proposed husband only if they could prove he was morally unfit, something a twelve- or thirteen-year-old might find difficult to do. The marriage laws of the early centuries prescribed marriage *in manu*, under the hand of the husband, which gave him the same kind of power over her that her father had possessed.

The position of women in Rome was intricately connected with attitudes toward property. As we saw in Chapter Two, under patriarchy women became links between men and another realm—the wild, nature, culture, the polluted Gorgio world—or, as Lévi-Strauss postulates, between alien men. In Rome, women became links between men and property. When marriage laws were eased, the reason was not concern for the well-being of women but the fact that fathers wished to retain control of their daughters' often substantial dowries. Marriage *in manu* was modified so that if a woman spent three nights a year in her father's house, he could retain control of her property. As time went on, mature women found ways to evade guardianship; they named their own guardians and chose men they could control, who would rubber-stamp their decisions. They found ways to will their property to their children rather than their uncles, and to inherit from their children. Although in law most women remained forever in male control, the tendency over the centuries was a gain in control over property, marriage, and divorce.[123]

As women's rights and powers changed, so did the attitudes of Roman men toward them. In early histories of the city recounted by the historian Livy, women are described as examples of ideal nobility, devotion, courage, and even heroism. Cornelia, the mother of the Gracchi,* was a woman of considerable accomplishment but devoted herself utterly to her sons and the state. Octavia, the sister of Augustus, was completely supportive of the male establishment, her brother, and the state; she also raised, with dignity and affection, it seems, Antony's children by Fulvia even after he deserted her for Cleopatra. Lucretia killed herself after she was raped; Brutus's wife, Portia, swallowed hot coals in a kind of suttee after he died.

As time went on, the brave and heroic image of women was softened; the ideal Roman matron was chaste, maternal, and devoted to the family and state—there was nothing heroic about her. In the later days of the empire, when some women gained considerable behind-the-scenes power, the sex was vilified. The Romans were the first people in history to heap praise on the *univira*, the woman who had had sexual relations with only one man (usually because she had died young or committed suicide at her husband's death).[124]

By 200 B.C.E., some aristocratic girls were being educated along with boys.[125] By the new millennium, marriage contracts were mutual and voluntary. When Augustus came to power in 19 B.C.E., he attempted to transform

---

* Tiberius Sempronius and Gaius Sempronius Gracchus were active in military, diplomatic, and political affairs in Rome in the second century B.C.E. Both were democrats who attempted to restore the land of small independent farmers, which was being absorbed by rich owners of great estates who used slave labor to cultivate their land. The Gracchi were unsuccessful, and both died violently in civil disturbances in the city.

the aristocratic republic into an empire ruled by one man, in part by undermining the aristocracy and building himself a power base among the new class of bourgeoisie. He thus altered laws having to do with debt, allowing family property to be sold and transferred to creditors. In an effort to strengthen the hold of the state, he proclaimed acts that had previously been civil offenses to be crimes against the state. One such act was adultery, although not until the time of Constantine could a wife prosecute her husband for this "crime." The lex Julia of 18 B.C.E. and the lex Poppaea of C.E. 9 made marriage virtually compulsory and gave rewards to parents: Caesar needed fodder for his legions.[126]

The nation was suffering (just as Greece had in the Hellenistic period) from depletion of population. Thousands of men were killed in Rome's nearly continuous wars. In Rome as in Greece, baby girls were exposed or murdered. Male homosexuality was widespread.[127] Augustus began a campaign to force people to marry and women to bear children. Men were required to marry by age twenty-five, but they could betroth themselves to a girl of ten and fulfill the requirements of the law without actually marrying: women could not do the same, and were forced to marry after puberty.[128]

Some egalitarian reforms occurred during the period of the late republic. Public-assistance programs were instituted, although these benefited only freemen and boys.[129] The daughters of plebeians could attend school in the Forum, but they were removed before their marriages at twelve or thirteen.[130] Women from wealthy families who managed to gain some autonomy involved themselves in law, politics, and literature; they hunted, fenced, and wrestled; they registered as prostitutes so as to control their own sexual lives; they married and divorced serially, getting richer with each change.[131] One historian, writing in the 1930s, claimed that Roman women of the first and second centuries C.E. "enjoyed a dignity and an independence at least equal if not superior to those claimed by contemporary feminists."[132]

But no matter what wealth or liberty they possessed, they were never able to achieve political power. They were never allowed to vote, to run for public office, to sit on juries or plead in court. Before Justinian—in the sixth century C.E.—they could not even be legal guardians of their own children. Except for those who, after Augustus' rule, claimed the rewards of the law of three or four children (see p. 147), women never obtained the right to administer their own affairs.[133] Even the ambitious, calculating, and politically savvy aristocratic women of the later empire operated by influence, not by law.

That women had few legal rights and could not directly affect the course of the state did not prevent men from blaming them for its disasters and deterioration. When the Romans were defeated at Cannae in 216 B.C.E., it was suspected that misconduct by the Vestal Virgins might be responsible, and they were prosecuted. Juvenal blamed the sickness of Roman society of the late first and early second centuries on the rottenness of its women, and Tacitus did the same thing more obliquely.[134] Later historians have followed suit.[135] They are in an ancient tradition: Aristotle blamed Spartan women for the deterioration of Sparta, and Livy and Theopompus claimed that Etruscan women's love of luxury contributed to the decay of Etruria.[136] Such thinking is so illogical that it provokes inquiry: how could intelligent men blame political failures on the very group who lacked a political voice? It seems that in men's minds, women stand between them and whatever they fear. If disaster or decay occurs, it is because women have not been rigidly maintaining the roles men set for them, roles it is believed protect and "save" men.

In the background, of course, were the poor women, who worked, as always. Along with men, they did laundry. They also worked at grain mills, were butchers, and hawked clothing. Fisherwomen sold their catch in town at the end of the day. Some women and men were fullers and weavers. Freedwomen sold exotic items like purple dye and perfume. They were dealers in beans, sellers of nails, commercial entrepreneurs and physicians. They owned brickworks and stonecutting works; they constructed buildings and made pipe.[137]

And one hopes they played too. The happiest picture of Rome that I can conjure is of plebeians threading narrow cobblestoned Roman streets, crowded together, laughing, talking, arguing; large-bodied, lusty Roman women hawking their wares, bantering, bargaining, drinking, enjoying sex, having children—*living*. I know I idealize: I omit hunger, violence, fear, disease. But to me, the life of poor women seems only slightly more dangerous and considerably more vivid than that of their pale protected regulated and civilized upper-class sisters, leashed by money to men's will.

## 4. THE CHRISTIAN AGE

At its inception, Christianity, like most other religions, was a revolution against patriarchy. Like other reform movements within late Judaism, it protested social and economic injustice, stratification, the concept of legitimacy, and the oppression of inhumane laws. Like Buddhism and Jainism, it postulated another realm that was superior to the realm of worldly power in both might and morality. Best of all, God was to be found within the self, and thus was under the control of the individual.

Judaism had become a religion of law and ritual, one in which the "letter" bore more weight than the spirit. Those who could afford to spend their days in the temple, praying and sacrificing small birds and animals that were on sale just outside, were considered holy. Thus holiness was limited to those well-to-do men whose wives ran productive homes, farms, and enterprises, overseeing servants, slaves, and children. Jesus, who knew "the Law," rebelled against it, teaching that fulfillments of its requirements such as animal sacrifice were not necessary to reach God, that, indeed, wealth was an impediment. His values harked back to matricentric culture. He and his followers were rootless wanderers, confident that food and shelter would be found wherever they went, committed to sharing and a community of equals, men and women.[138] They believed that a life devoted to acquisition of wealth and power was a life given over to the gods of this world, who offer no nourishment to the soul and no contentment to the heart.

In many ways, the period in which Jesus lived resembled our own. It was a time of expanding hegemony, of breakdown and violence, of moral questioning

and moral bankruptcy. Ordinary people were dispossessed by the power establishment as Rome dug its tentacles into the entire known world. Jesus' doctrines attempted to deal with this situation and to counter Roman values with
old Judaic values. He taught that one must render to Caesar that which Caesar
demands—tax money, deference, trappings of power—but that life and truth
were not to be found in those things but in the quality of life, in love and sharing, compassion and mercy, and the renunciation of power. Such a morality
does not seem to threaten any establishment, but it is precisely the morality
that patriarchal institutions most fear. A philosophy that focuses on the moment, on feeling and experience, rather than on a linear vision of life and long-
term acquisition of power by a few, subverts the very foundations of patriarchy.
The elite demands acquiescence to its values by the many, in the form of obedience, deferred gratification (necessary to the nonwealthy who wish to acquire
wealth), denial of body and emotion, and acceptance of one's inferiority to all
above one in the cultural hierarchy. Only such deference can maintain order in
a society of inequality. Thus in Jesus' time as well as in the twentieth century,
moralities that seek to turn people away from patriarchal values even peaceably
and in good will are first diminished and then persecuted.

Jesus' doctrines were truly revolutionary. At first the establishment treated
them with scorn and derision (much as the love children of the sixties were
treated). But when his doctrines began to achieve widespread appeal, prosecu-
tion was initiated in an effort to curtail the contagion. The mouth of this great
Hebrew prophet and moralist was silenced.

But followers continued to sing his song because for them it was a joyful
song, an announcement of liberation. They went on meeting in the back rooms
of synagogues, and they were all equal—women and men, Jews and Greeks,
slaves, tax collectors, publicans, freed people. Their sect was not yet called
Christianity, and no one then could foresee that it would evolve into a Church
that would persecute the very people from whom the prophet and his Church
sprang. Cells were created by evangelists, men and women, who traveled the
coast of Asia, Greece, and Italy, building small bands of dedicated Christians in
Corinth, Ephesus, Galatia, Philippi, Colossae, Thessalonica, Macedonia,
Rome, and Athens.

As people everywhere were quickened by the affirmation of values their
culture despised, the religion grew and Rome took further action against it. It
was Paul, a Jew in the service of Rome, who, converted in a bolt of light on the
road to Damascus, actually laid the foundations for the Church that was to become Christianity. Paul and other leaders were indefatigable in their efforts to
create a coherent body of doctrine and regulations that would bind an anarchic,
dispersed set of independent cells. But to create a structure from spirit is to
"masculinize" it, to codify is always in some sense to kill feeling. To oppose the
power of Rome, the new religion required power. In the process of institutiona-
lizing the new religion, giving it rules in place of a way of seeing, form rather
than freedom, Paul and those who followed him altered the prophet's message
beyond recognition.

The major change concerned power. Insofar as we know the actual teachings of Jesus, he repudiated power entirely, suggesting that the truth of life lay in another realm. It was because of this repudiation and the difficulty of using language to describe the emotional (sometimes called the spiritual) life that he spoke in parables, expanded metaphors. His remarks about his father's kingdom were taken literally, however, and what was made of them was a realm apart from and above life, a realm of transcendent power. As hierarchical as earthly kingdoms, as rule- and law-bound as any state, requiring the same fear, obedience, and sense of unworthiness any earthly ruler demands, the properly named *kingdom* of heaven was a realm of superhuman, superworldly control. The power of God was like that of earthly rulers, only greater; and the keys to this kingdom were in the possession of a set of self-proclaimed hierarchs who by virtue of their office alone were superior to other humans, even earthly rulers. The new religion was disseminated by emphasis on "miracles," superhuman acts, and the prophet—like many heroes before him, both male and female—was apotheosized.

These developments took centuries, during which adherents of the sect suffered from Rome's persecution and from conflict among themselves. But inevitably those involved in the battle to dominate the religion, to dictate dogma and the structure of the Church were those interested in worldly power. Those who were not went on quietly living and believing, dying too, but in silence.

The postulation of a realm that synthesized the "masculine" qualities of structure and permanence (it was eternal) and the "feminine" qualities of love, forgiveness, and compassion, a realm that blended justice and mercy, satisfied the profound human need for an integrated world. But because it existed not on earth and not during life but afterward and elsewhere, it cast a shadow upon earthly life. It was transcendent, superior to this world, this life, and thus constituted a magnificent symbol for the patriarchal tendency to demean necessity and those things associated with it. It diminished not just flesh, emotion, sex, and nonvolitional labor (labor for subsistence), but kings and emperors, power and worldly glory as well. It offered an avenue of vengeance in the afterlife for every oppressed and miserable being. The idea of heaven is thus antilife and essentially suicidal.

This suicidal tendency within the religion was manifest in its early years and, indeed, was given force by the action of its moral founder, who chose crucifixion just as Socrates chose the hemlock. Early Christians being charged by Rome "refused to make the token gestures toward established religion that would save their lives, or failing that, refused to avail themselves of the convenient pause between judgment and execution in which to escape."[139] Roman magistrates were exasperated by the obstinacy with which Christians insisted on martyrdom and their provocation in the face of clemency. They were eager to die for their creed because they believed that martyrdom eradicated all sin and offered certain redemption. Tertullian forbade good Christians to attempt to escape persecution, promising that they would be avenged, would peer down from paradise and be able to exult at the spectacle of their tormentors tortured in hell for eternity.[140] The desire of certain sects for martyrdom was so extreme that the Church was forced to declare them heretical; revulsion against their behavior and the strong argument of Augustine resulted eventually in a pronouncement that suicide was a sin, but not until the sixth century—in 562 the Council of Braga denied funeral rites to suicides and in 693 the Council of Toledo ordained excommunication for attempted suicide.[141]

Any philosophy that aims at transcendence of this world invariably entertains the greatest contempt for things of nature, for blood, bodily emanations, flesh, and sex—and for the people associated, identified with those things, women. Hatred of sex in a man is tied to hatred of body, feeling, nonvolition, and women. What is perhaps less evident is that hatred of sex in a woman has precisely the same associations. Hatred of sex is rooted in disgust and contempt for the natural processes of life, which are in every culture associated with only half the human race. Women as well as men maintained celibacy, lived ascetically, sought or accepted martyrdom, valued virginity more than life and clutched it to them as they faced the fire or the lions.

Hatred of sex is manifest in Christianity from the time of Paul. Jesus' recorded and remembered speeches make little reference to the subject beyond suggesting that men not throw stones at women for doing what they do themselves, and that there is little distinction between lust felt and lust acted upon. But Paul had strong feelings on the subject. In his famous letter to the church at Corinth, he asserts that it is better for a man never to touch a woman. Married people care about each other, whereas the unattached are free to care only about God. (It is unclear what "caring about God" consists of. If the phrase means continual work to disseminate a religion, it means devotion to power; if it means repudiation of the world in favor of continual prayer, it is essentially an insistence on the volitional nature of humanness, and a concern for another level of power, the power to "save souls." Only when "caring about God" issues in nourishing, healing, and teaching the poor, the sick, and children does it seem a blessed activity.) Marriage is preferable to fornication or the pains of desire. Paul's position reverses traditional Judaic morality, which requires men to marry and procreate, and sees procreation, especially of males, as a good.

Throughout the writings of Paul runs an inner argument, a vacillation between a profound, almost "instinctive" contempt for sex and women, a revulsion against being dragged into "trouble in the flesh" (I Corinthians 7:28), and his understanding that a major religion could not be built on a discipline that most people felt to be a deprivation. He understood that all men are not "even as I myself" and that some people feel strong desire: "it is better to marry than to burn" (I Corinthians 7:7, 9).

At the same time, he promised that the new religion made no distinction between Jew and Greek, slave and free, male and female, "for ye are all one in Christ Jesus" (Galatians 3:28). The thinking of women who swarmed to the new sect is, like the thinking of women through much of history, lost to us. But there is considerable evidence of great activity by women in the early Church.[142] They had to be aware of Paul's proclamation that God is above Christ, Christ above man, and man above woman, of his injunction against women speaking in church—often the very churches they had founded or maintained—and his rule that they must cover their heads in church, a sign of humility. His notion of the proper behavior of women was sketched in a letter to Titus, who was establishing a church in Crete; they were to be "discreet, chaste, keepers at home [housebound], good, obedient to their own husbands" (Titus 2:5). And the doctrine of the Trinity, implicit from the earliest days of Christianity, became more important as time went on; in its teaching of a godhead shared and transmitted entirely among masculine figures, it assumes the exclusion of women from divinity. The question, then, is why did women flock to the new religion?

This question must be considered in the light of the rest of the culture of the period, dominated by Rome. The new religion postulated an ultimate if not a worldly equality of women and men; such a claim was to be found nowhere else in the Roman Empire. Women were permitted to take active roles in the new Church, both while Jesus was alive and after his death; thus they had a scope for their energies that was hard to find elsewhere. And the core values of Christianity have always been "feminine," whatever the morality of the Church structure. Finally, Christianity offered women a kind of freedom not found in traditional Judaism, in Hellenistic or Roman culture—the right to remain virgin or celibate.

JoAnn McNamara asserts that virginal women were a disturbing element to their contemporaries, and that the virginal life for women was not sanctioned by the orthodox Church until after women had made it a reality.[143] Celibate women were essentially nonexistent in ancient culture. In the Judaic as well as the Greek and Roman traditions, girls were married young and required to remarry upon widowhood. Thus they were always under the power of men. A celibate life freed women not only from the burden of domesticity and childbearing but from subjection to men. To many of us renunciation of sex seems a sacrifice, but it is questionable whether it seemed so to women of that time, married not by their own choice, while they were still children, to much older men who were strangers and expected them to be fertile, hard-working, and obedient. Under such circumstances marital sex is a form of rape. That many women felt this is demonstrated by the many communities of consecrated women that grew and thrived under the Christian aegis. If it is true that "only before the lions, confronting the terrors of the public executioner, could early Christian women remain the full and equal partners of Christian men," it is also true that virginity (or celibacy after widowhood) represented a responsible and respectable way to achieve, not equality, but a measure of independence.[144]

The early Church was a loosely knit association of small independent units, many of which maintained their own ideas and customs as the religion became more centralized and defined. As orthodoxy was established, women drifted to sects which did not follow the orthodox line and which sometimes permitted them leeway to speak and act. Among these groups were the Gnostic sects which flourished in the first three centuries C.E. Many of these were democratic, antihierarchal, and on occasion, celebratory of sensual pleasures. Services in some of these groups were run on democratic lines, the members throwing lots at each meeting to determine who would take the roles of priest, bishop, and prophet.[145] Some had a bisexual conception of deity, although that conception did not challenge traditional associations with the sexes, the gender principles. In one Gnostic writing, the world is said to be governed by "a great power, the Mind of the Universe, which manages all things and is a male," and "a great Intelligence . . . a female which produces all things."[146] Such a notion perpetuates the division of experience into male control and female giving. In another writing, the Lord is male and the Church—traditionally—female, but also suffering, in pain.[147] In the *Apocryphon of John,* Sophia (wisdom) desires to bring forth, without the approval of her consort, the great Spirit, and gives birth to a monster-god who creates man. Man shares both the light and the dark aspects of his mother. That dark side, subject to evil powers, imprisons man in a material body, and creates woman and sex.[148] In the Gospel of Thomas, Simon Peter is quoted as saying, "Let Mary leave us, for women are not worthy of Life," to which Jesus responds, "I myself shall lead her in order to make her male, so that she too may become a living spirit resembling you males. For every woman who will make herself male will enter the Kingdom of Heaven."[149]

Although the Gnostic sects are not free from the misogyny of more hierarchical and authoritarian thinkers, they were attractive to women because, unlike orthodox Christianity, they mentioned women and included femaleness in their theology. Yet underneath the mystical cosmology lies the same old set of associations: woman is she who labors and produces without volition and is tied to necessity; man is he who controls woman and thereby transcends nature and necessity. For example, *The Dialogue of the Savior* teaches that only in death are the "works of femaleness" dissolved, so that light and life can rule. Men are ordered to pray in the place where there is no woman and to destroy the works of femaleness "so that they will cease."[150] The "works of femaleness" are essentially the human being in body, feeling, and sex, from which mind (or spirit) is extracted, made alien to its "prison," and equated with transcendence, purity, holiness, and God. This thinking resembles the thinking that lies behind many "primitive" male initiations.

Because Gnosticism was relatively more open to women than orthodoxy, allowing them to hold positions of importance, many women followed these sects. Their presence furnished one ground for orthodox theologians to declare the sects heretical.[151] Tertullian (160–230 C.E.) especially protested the participation of "those women among the heretics."[152] Irenaeus (130?–202?) condemned one group for eating meat sacrificed to idols, attending pagan festivals, and violating his "strict warnings concerning sexual abstinence and monogamy."[153] He demanded they adopt the correct attitudes: to fear God and obey the priests.[154] So swiftly had the joyous good news turned into the old patriarchal injunction to misery: fear, obedience, and unworthiness.

In 395, with the Theodosian Code, Christianity became the official religion of the Roman Empire. By this time, its structure and many of its values were indistinguishable from those of that empire. Only the core remained, like a small underground spring around which is erected a monumental edifice, reminding those who peer up in awe of the reason the structure was built in the first place. It was partly that core and partly the freedom to live a religious life (read: lives less subject to men, childbearing, and endless labor) that continued to draw women, some of whom chose to live as solitaries in desert caves, sometimes disguised as men![55]

In the fourth century, small communities of women were formed, usually by a noble or wealthy woman, to study, work, and live together. Later, monastic orders were founded and nuns and monks made the trek north and undertook missions in wild country. They converted Germanic tribes, built monastic houses, and came in time to control vast tracts of land. During this period abbesses became very powerful, and remained so until the ninth century, when Charlemagne attempted to centralize control over a territory that would be called the Holy Roman Empire.

Charlemagne, king of the Franks, wished to be an emperor; he also wanted to impose centralized control on a diverse set of peoples. Historians usually praise efforts at centralization and consolidation, as if they were inherently beneficial to the human race. Such efforts are almost always, however, rooted in one man's desire for power, and seem positive to those who worship power. One argument advanced in favor of centralization is that it lessens the local feuding of petty nobles and the confusion of multiform cultural, legal, and moral standards. That large-scale battles must often be fought to impose central control on petty nobles, and that imposition of uniform standards violates those who possess their own, is not weighed in the scale against centralization. Centralization advances power: and those who profit by it are those who value power and are permitted to hold it.

Autonomous local groups, idiosyncratic customs, and the power of women are eradicated by moves toward centralization. Often, centralization is urged in the name of "reform" or "purification," and one element that must be purged to achieve "purification" is any power, influence, or competence on the part of women.

The reforms of Charlemagne showed this tendency. He wished to bring *purity* to the Church: and purity means the segregation of the sexes and the exclusion of women from certain roles. So he segregated men and women and forbade nuns and canonesses from assisting priests at mass; he placed abbesses under the control of bishops; and he reinstituted Paul's rule and forbade the nuns to teach boys. Explaining that it was not fitting that a woman educate men because of "the weakness of her sex and the instability of her mind," he removed boys from the care of the nuns, intending to educate them in palace schools. However, the Carolingian Empire fell, and with it the palace schools; the monastery schools endured. The ironic consequence of Charlemagne's action was that girls continued to be educated and boys were left illiterate.[156]

From the ruins of the Carolingian Empire in the late ninth century, the family again emerged as the most stable and effective institution. Women regained power. Abbesses were often responsible for overseeing not only the nuns and monks of their houses, but also the welfare of the thousands of people who lived on and worked their land. They were educated to the limits of contemporary learning; "they ruled over large domains, held their own judicial courts, and raised armies for their kings."[157] They established schools and, despite the dictum of Paul that women might not teach men, taught both boys and girls. The great convents of Germany became centers of learning—a rarity in that period. Their power was (as always with women) actual, practical, rather than episcopal: they did not act with legitimated authority. But it was "equal to that of abbots and sometimes even bishops."[158] They served as representatives of the king or pope and participated fully in political assemblies like the Imperial Diet in Germany. This situation lasted for roughly five hundred years, from the seventh to the twelfth century.

So active and competent were women that in the tenth and eleventh centuries there were "no effective barriers to the exercise of power by women. They appear as military leaders, judges, chatelaines, and controllers of property."[159] They helped to keep culture alive in a time of violence and cruelty. The ninth and tenth centuries witnessed new waves of invasions from the Scandinavian territories, and convents, with their wealth and their women, were favored targets. Women were raped, tortured, and killed, and many nuns displayed courage and heroism in the face of these attacks. One such group, in a nunnery at Coldingham, in Scotland, faced certain rape by an army of Danes in 870. Their leader, Ebba, gathered the nuns together; they followed her in slashing off their noses and upper lips, then turning to face their would-be rapists. "The horrified Danes burned the convent, and the sisters victoriously achieved the status of martyrs," still virgins.[160] A tenth-century nun, Hroswitha of Gandersheim, celebrated the heroism of Christian women like these, placing it, however, in the distant past. Negatively inspired by Terence, she challenged his depiction of female promiscuity with one of female chastity. She wrote histories, religious short stories, saints' lives, poetry, and dramas, "making her the only European dramatist for nearly five centuries."[161]

The people of the early Middle Ages lived in scattered settlements across the countryside. The nobility, constantly at war over land, lived in fortified burgs or castles or behind moats and drawbridges. Within these confines lived entire villages of people, and like those in monasteries, they had to be entirely self-sufficient. The women of these establishments, especially the ladies of the manor, had to be skilled in every agricultural and domestic activity; they had to know how to raise raw materials and process them into the food, clothing, medicine, and armament needed by the hundreds of people who lived within. The men were frequently away attacking other such establishments, or (later) at the Crusades or on pilgrimages. The women had not only to run the establishment but to defend it against frequent attack. Margaret Paston, chatelaine of Caistor Castle, was defending her house against armed attack as late as the fifteenth century.[162] In Frankish and Carolingian royal households, the queen had responsibility for overseeing the entire administration and also the royal treasury; the royal treasurer reported to her and she paid the knights their yearly wage.[163]

Women were essential at every level. When, in a wave of reform in the late tenth century, priests were ordered to put away their wives, they protested that without their wives' support they would go hungry and naked.[164] Nevertheless, there was widespread infanticide, especially of girls. The Icelandic Saga of "Gunnlaug Serpent-Tongue" tells of a lord's declaration that if his wife gave birth to a girl, the child must be killed, but a boy might live. Male babies were nursed twice as long as girls.[165]

Anglo-Saxon Britain was also patriarchal. In the sixth century Aethelbert promulgated a code of law by which women could be sold and bought as wives—a custom that persisted in England into the nineteenth century.[166] Men could have several wives, but women could take half the household goods with them if they decided to leave their husbands. The arrival of Christianity in England did not really disturb the easy divorce laws or end "unlawful" marriages, but by the mid-seventh century women were governing monasteries. In the tenth century, Queen Aethelflaed commanded armies and built and repaired fortresses; in the eleventh century, Cnut of Denmark (ruling England) decreed that no woman could be sold or forced into marriage, and that women could inherit and bequeath property.[167]

With the arrival of the Normans in 1066, Britain shifted to a feudal organization. Native language and customs were suppressed and superseded by Norman French language and customs. Most native inhabitants were made unfree, except for those few noblemen left alive. Widows and daughters of dead noblemen were married as often as possible to Normans.

Feudalism was a system based in land and organized hierarchically for war. Feudal lords did not own much, since their land was held as a fief from the king. Noblewomen, who were not expected to go to war, were disregarded. They were placed in guardianship, in absolute subjection to their husbands, and considered to own *nothing* while they were married. A woman's husband controlled the revenues of her land. But widows could come into control of huge complexes of estates, and some realized the independence of their position.[168] Studies of chronicles of the period before the Norman Conquest demonstrate that vigor, ambition, daring, and intelligence in women were remarked and praised; after it, such behavior was regarded as "unwomanly."[169]

Whatever the law, lower-class people were more egalitarian. No farmer could survive without a wife, and mutual dependence meant greater equality. Whether the members of the household were free or unfree, the women set the standard for its life. Lower-class women could own, bequeath, or inherit property. Some women farmed independently, or were brewsters; some engaged in litigation; some were highway robbers. The penalty for adultery or bearing an "illegitimate" child was a fine. And when a wife had higher social standing than her husband, the children took her name. (This was customary especially among Anglo-Scandinavians.)[170]

Europe became more settled toward the middle of the eleventh century, and the Church again attempted reform. With regard to the status of women, "the Middle Ages can appropriately be bisected by the Gregorian reform movement of the late eleventh century. This reform demolished the double monasteries of the earlier era and quite effectively walled women's houses off from the institutional hierarchy of the Church. The great medieval churchwomen, Hild [Hilde] at Whitby, Leoba, Hildegard of Bingen, Roswitha [Hroswitha] of Gandersheim, all belong to the earlier period. As the influence of churchwomen waned, Church writings showed a greater tendency to regard women as the 'other,' the basis for a growing misogyny and a violation of the orthodox Christian belief that all souls, without distinction of age, class, or sex, are equal in the eyes of God."[171]

Again the Church tried to impose celibacy on the clergy and it eliminated lay control of Church offices. Noblewomen who had been deeply involved in the disposition and protection of ecclesiastical positions lost their influence at a stroke. Ironically, it was three powerful women—the Empress Agnes, Beatrice of Tuscany, and her daughter Matilda—whose help enabled Peter Damian and Pope Gregory VII to accomplish these reforms.

Peter Damian was the thirteenth child of a woman of the Italian lower nobility who, weakened by excessive childbearing, did not wish to suckle him. He lived only because the wife of the local priest intervened and put pressure on the worn-out mother. Nevertheless, when he was grown, Damian led a hysterical, virulent campaign urging celibacy on priests in hostile, misogynistic terms. At the same time he carried on a romantic correspondence with the Empress Agnes, whose powerful support was a factor in the success of his movement.[172] Beatrice and Matilda contributed both military and financial assistance to Pope Gregory VII in his struggle to subdue Emperor Henry IV; and the castle to which Henry was forced to walk barefoot in the snow to do obeisance to Gregory was Matilda's castle at Canossa. After Gregory's death, Matilda secured his victory on the battlefield, and at her own death, she left her Tuscan land to the papacy, giving it a strong power base. Yet the achievement of the Gregorian reforms excluded women like Matilda from any future influence whatever.[173]

All leadership roles for women in the Church were precluded, as the center of policy making shifted from the monastic system to Rome and the papacy. At this time the great cathedral schools were being established; they quickly became centers of an explosion of learning and debate. Women were completely excluded from these schools, and not even the priest's wife, once a familiar figure in religious institutions, appeared in them. Both the students and the staff were required to be celibate males.[174]

Only in Spain and Italy, where there was an ancient tradition of women scholars, could women study alongside men. In Italy, Moslem and Christian women studied in the universities, became professors and medical doctors. Anna Comnena founded a medical school in Constantinople in 1083, taught and practiced medicine, and wrote history. A Persian princess built a medical school and hospital in the thirteenth century; a woman was court astronomer in the Seljuk court.[175] Trotula wrote treatises on gynecology and obstetrics that remained the major medical reference works on the subjects for centuries afterward. But she is remembered only as Dame Trot, author of children's stories, and Renaissance commentators tried to change *Trotula* to *Trotus*, and assign authorship of her books to a man.[176] There were many women physicians in Salerno, women lawyers in Bologna.

In time, however, they too were pushed out. The Church, male doctors, and universities united to disqualify and penalize women physicians at every opportunity. By the fourteenth century, women were forbidden to practice surgery in France, and many Jewish women physicians in France and Italy practiced under a double penalty, since Jews as well as women were under proscription. Women who continued to work did so under the aegis of a man, who also took the credit. Tycho Brahe's sister was also an astronomer, but only he is remembered. The sister of the Van Eyck brothers, Margaretha, worked on the family pictures, but she is never mentioned.[177]

Parallel with reforms in education and medical licensing, government was reforming itself and becoming more bureaucratic. A professional class was emerging in which education was required for membership—and women were excluded from education. "The single most prominent aspect of the period from the later twelfth to the fourteenth century was a sedulous quest for intellectual and institutional uniformity and corporatism throughout Europe."[178] Civil and ecclesiastic power and bureaucracy were strengthened and consolidated; theology was made systematic, and the Inquisition was established to stamp out any possible divergences of opinion. Even secular knowledge was being made uniform through the assembling of encyclopedias.

As I mentioned earlier, historians tend to exalt such movements; the "twelfth-century renaissance" has been seen as benefiting European civilization. But centralization and uniformity are not inherently beneficial to the human race. What is centralized is power: a single administrative core reserves to itself the right to transmit power through a hierarchy to those who fulfill its requirements. One of those requirements is uniformity. There are arguments to be made for a degree of uniformity in knowledge; it is convenient and presumably efficient to have everyone in a given culture fluent in a shared language; communication is easier when everyone in a given culture is familiar with the same set of "great books," for instance. But such uniformities do not necessarily enrich that culture. A rigid, uniform curriculum creates a shared, communal perspective, an approach to learning and thus to experience; but it inevitably omits far more than it can include. It trains those given access to it in a single way of thinking; and separates them greatly from all others, who are not given access to the training. The twelfth-century renaissance in education shaped European education for many centuries to come. Although it was modified in later centuries, the division of the curriculum into the *trivium*, the basic studies of grammar, rhetoric, and logic, and the *quadrivium*, advanced studies in arithmetic, geometry, astronomy, and music, defined what was important, of value, for men of intellect. All these subjects are abstract, involving an approach to experience that is distant, quantitative, and manipulative. There is no history, no study of human relations, no study of the arts for the sake of pleasure: the study of music was a mathematical exercise.

By so defining what mattered, this kind of education also taught men what they were expected to be, how they were to approach life. It separated men from all women (for no women were permitted to enter the universities) and from uneducated men, and made them a new elite dedicated to knowledge as a form of power. All other kinds of and approaches to knowledge became illegitimate, insignificant. And simultaneously with this move to institutionalize knowledge, to centralize and institutionalize government (by establishing bureaucracies), laws were passed further constricting women and the poor, both of whom experienced a profound loss of freedom and power. For the first time groups became "minorities," and "the poor, who rarely appeared in documents before the thirteenth century except as abstract objects of ethical concern, increasingly troubled the authorities."[179] They were blamed for causing social unrest—and they may indeed have done so. Suppressive legislation regarding them was passed in many countries.

Except for their work in the Church, the schools, and the courts, women went on as always. They lived on farms, where they did everything except the plowing: men too did domestic work and gave time and care to their children.[180] Women thatched roofs, sheared sheep, reaped, made butter and cheese, beer and candles, cloth and linen. There is a little book, written in 1392–94 by an elderly man, the Menagier of Paris, for his child wife, who has asked him to teach her her duties. It is a kindly book, written by a man who claims he is an exception in this regard: he warns his wife her next husband will in all likelihood not be as kindly as he. He deals first with the lady's moral and religious duties, her deportment, and her duty toward her husband. He emphasizes that the last is the most important. He then lists her tasks in the household, which are extensive and require knowledge of a host of different areas—managing servants, agriculture, husbandry, medicine, manufacture of a great many domestic necessities—and require, even with servants, labor from dawn until night, almost without rest.

But the most telling passage in the book is a metaphor he uses to describe the correct relation of wife to husband. The wife, he says, should be like a little dog who remains near its master always and avoids other people, who thinks of nothing but its master even when the master is away, who waits at home for his return and follows him whenever it is permitted. If the master whips the dog or throws stones at it, the dog wags its tail, lies down before him, licks his hand and attempts to mollify him.[181]


## 5. STRUGGLE FOR A ROOM OF THEIR OWN

The exclusion of women from the learned professions, government, and active life in the Church left aristocratic and educated women with few avenues in which to use their energy and talents. But they did not accept this exclusion without protest.[182] Some aristocratic women devoted themselves to a new intellectual pastime, the courts of love; great numbers of women joined the heretical movements that were sweeping through Europe in the twelfth and thirteenth centuries: both the heretical sects and courtly love were in some ways "subversive of the religious and social foundations of medieval society."[183]

The literature of courtly love—and it is only through literature that we have any knowledge of this phenomenon—will be discussed later in this chapter. The attitudes found in the poetry of courtly love, which placed women on pedestals from which they ruled over and trained men in *courtoisie*, did not filter into life, and had no perceivable effect on the daily life of women of the time. The heretical sects were eventually suppressed, and one branch of the Cathari, the Albigensians, was exterminated. The female *perfectae*, who preached and administered sacraments among the Cathari, and the women who supported them with money and shelter during the Albigensian Crusade were courageous in the face of martyrdom.[184] In the thirteenth century, the Catholic Church instituted Inquisitorial Courts intended to maintain the narrow categories and uniformity of its doctrine and practices; the operations of these courts completed the extermination of the Albigensians.

The attitudes toward women that had filled men's heads since the inception of Christianity—woman was Eve the temptress or Mary the unsexual handmaiden—were becoming even more rigid. In religion, both views flourished: the cult of the Virgin, which spread like a song across Europe in the early Middle Ages, had its roots in the old rich memory of the Mother Goddess, a more nourishing deity than the Christian God, and therefore often more popular; and, like a *basso continuo*, the work of monastic writers on women, which in this time grew even more contemptuous in its vituperation of the bestial, lustful, vicious, mindless sex.

In literature too there is the aristocratic strain of courtly love, the *dolce stil nuovo*, and romance, but there are also the *fabliaux*, folk tales of the bourgeoisie which center on two major themes—the outwitting of an aristocrat or wealthy man by a plebeian, and the power struggle between men and women. In the latter, women triumph over men through cleverness and men subdue women by physical force. Shakespeare's *Taming of the Shrew* is a mild, late version of such *fabliaux*. The law specifically permitted the corporal chastisement of wives, and ingenious forms of punishment were apparently a source of continuing interest.[185] Even the author of the aristocratic guide to the art of courtly love, Andreas Capellanus, reserved artful lovemaking for ladies only, advising men attracted by lower-class women not to dally long but to rape with impunity.[186]

At the same time, more and more women lacked the protection of a male. Women outnumbered men in most towns and villages in Europe, partly because of losses of men between the eleventh and thirteenth centuries in the Crusades, and partly because the large numbers of men in the clergy and monastic orders were now required to be celibate. In addition, guild rules forbade members who had not reached the status of master to marry. There were population increases during the thirteenth century (and again in the sixteenth), which led to a situation in which journeymen increased in number but were unable to move up to master status, and thus could not marry. Men who were employed by large manufacturers in early capitalist factories were paid too little to marry, living close to starvation themselves.[187] Thus many women remained single. Yet women without men were suspect, especially those who were able to create for themselves a decent life, a life with self-respect. They did this in various ways.

Poor women carried on a wide variety of trades and in some places had a monopoly on certain ones—usually brewing and spinning. Women could be members in their own right of some guilds; others admitted them under the auspices of their living or deceased husbands; some excluded women entirely. Women in England were shipwrights, tailors, makers of spurs, water bearers, barbers, and barber-surgeons who practiced surgery along with surgeons proper, and later joined with them to found the Royal College of Surgeons—from which the females were then barred. They were mercers, grocers, and drapers; they baked, sold poultry and fish, made silk. But in every trade, whenever they worked for wages, they were paid less than men. In the rural workshops of France, women received three-quarters of a man's wages in the fourteenth century, one-half in the fifteenth, and less in the sixteenth. Within guilds and wherever work was regulated, women were confined to the lower-status, lower-paying jobs. But some women ran their own businesses: in England women supplied horses, jousting equipment, wheels, and armor for the king. Here even a married woman could do business on her own, under the legal denomination of *femme sole*, which gave her legal and trade powers independently.[188]

There was another class of women, related perhaps to the Wife of Bath, who loved to go on pilgrimages. Pilgrimage, a journey to a sanctified place for devotional purposes, was for many people a euphemism for pleasure and adventure through travel. Chronicles of the period give the impression that "ships and overland trails were clogged with passengers of both sexes, and they supply attractive anecdotes about the physical and moral agility of women."[189] There were female vagabonds who traveled together in troops—hearty, hard-working, fun-loving women who moved from fair to fair picking up pennies as they could. They entertained, ran soup kitchens, contracted for trading voyages. They were part of the crews that built the great cathedrals. Bands of such women went to war together with men, fought beside them, fetched and carried, and ran first-aid stations.[190]

Indeed, everywhere women were the healers. A small group of men were trained as physicians, but women were healers, apothecaries, and surgeons. The great lady, the nun, and the country housewife all had to care for the many people in the household when they fell ill or had accidents.[191] From our perspective, we might think the trained physicians gave better care, but medical training then consisted of education in the four temperaments, the "humours," and physicians used incantations and rituals in their treatment, and based diagnoses and medication on astrological charts. Descriptions of their practice sound barbaric today (as one hopes ours will too, one day) and it killed the patient more often than it helped. Many people went from male physicians back to their local wise woman, who, whatever her limitations, knew the family and its medical history, knew the chemical functioning of herbs and drugs. She also had knowledge about bones and muscles, childbirth, prevention of conception, and abortion, and her knowledge was passed down through generations. In 1527, Paracelsus, the "father" of modern medicine, burned his text on pharmacy in the middle of the witch hunts because he had "learned from the Sorceress all he knew."[192]

Women healers used their skill for the benefit of others. Most gave treatment simply as a matter of course, as they would provide a meal. Those who were "professional" made a living but did not get rich. Even the celebrated Italian women physicians did not try to turn their expertness into a power base. Nevertheless, their talent was to prove lethal to them.

Women are excluded from the ranks of the legitimate in all institutions; if they are permitted any participation, it is on the lowest level. They join new sects that spring up in rebellion against the narrowness of legitimate institutions, and are persecuted and killed as heretics. Women who work for wages are forced to survive on lower pay than men. It is reasonable to assume that women as a caste might be angry and resentful, especially the poorer ones; and that men as a caste might feel guilty, and look for arguments to justify the situation. Such arguments invariably rely on denigration of women's characters and abilities. Thomas Aquinas, in his great *Summa Theologica,* written in the thirteenth century, found it necessary to open his discussion of women by asking why they exist at all. His justification for God's creation of women is that they are necessary to procreation. Women were, to the intellectuals of the period, merely a necessary evil.

Paranoia is an inherent element in the process of centralizing unification. Whatever is not included under the canopy of orthodoxy, or under the umbrellas protecting those who offer deference to it, is automatically a challenge. One can see the logic in this chain of reasoning. It is true to its premises even though it may entirely falsify the motivation and nature of aliens. So logic often fails. For those who erect orthodox structures believe deeply that they possess the Truth, the Right, and that they can incarnate clear, articulate moral/political truth in the institution. The institution is therefore Right, and those who do not bow to it are clearly Wrong. Since all institutions exclude far more than they include, those in command of them, no matter how grand their pretensions, feel surrounded by enemies. Anyone who dares to ignore, evade, or oppose such a clear moral Right must by nature be evil and subversive, and thus threatening to the institution. Refusal to submit becomes a hostile act that justifies any retribution, no matter how cruel. Such thinking recurs in history, and is not limited to medieval Europe; it is rampant in our own time, in parties and nations of all political persuasions. It is this kind of thinking that punishes victims.

An institution declares certain elements to be unorthodox. These elements may be particular political or religious ideas, a dislike of authority, or simple lack of interest in structures. Those who hold to such positions will often be punished. But the qualities declared unorthodox may also be inherent and unchangeable. So people are persecuted for being what they are, for qualities they cannot alter, escape, repudiate, vindicate, or compensate for, like sex, ethnic origin, color, age, or poverty. Such people are victims to begin with, being members of groups considered unacceptable to a society. Punishment of them nevertheless makes perfect sense to those with a passion for uniform but embracing structure. They push unwanted groups to the fringes of society and then punish them for being there.

Women were such a group in the medieval period, unless they lived according to a stipulated pattern of marriage (and remarriage), possession of some wealth (by their husbands), obedience, and submission. For the first time in Christian Europe, a fixed role for women was emerging, one that defined women in complete opposition to men, and as subversive unless they accepted that fixed role. Treatises on witches referred to their sabbath as *synagogue*, suggesting that in the orthodox imagination witches were linked with heretics and Jews, people considered not just alien but threatening.[193] (The denigration of one of these groups is almost always attended by the denigration of the others. It is questionable whether it is mere coincidence that the two primary centers of witch trials and executions were also the two primary centers of genocidal practices toward Jews in our own century.)

We know, for instance, that the charges against Joan of Arc, who was condemned to death by burning in 1431 for heresy and witchcraft, were politically motivated. Joan, a mere woman, had vanquished the British, who labeled her a whore and a witch, although even the English chroniclers admit she seemed to be a virgin and pious. What outraged her captors most, according to Holinshed, and made her death mandatory, was that despite repeated warnings and promises of mercy if she would reform, she insisted on wearing "men's" clothes.[194]

In this section we will look at two kinds of women whose efforts to gain a little independence were crushed by the growing institutional machine.

## Beguines

Unable to find husbands, deprived of their former occupations, and endangered by living alone, women shifted for a way to live safely, independently, and in decent conditions. In Belgium in the early thirteenth century, a few well-to-do women began a movement that soon spread to the Netherlands and the Rhineland: beguinage. Beguines were women who chose to live together in semiseclusion in small communities. (Beguinages still exist. There is a charming one in Amsterdam, a group of houses set in a park and isolated, although it is just off a main street. The women there wear nunlike clothes, make lace and sell it.) The beguines supported themselves by weaving, lacemaking, embroidery, and nursing. They taught children and did manual labor; they helped the poor and the sick.[195] Beguinage offered women a secure life, companionship, pleasant if austere living conditions, and the ability to earn an independent livelihood.[196]

The beguines were pious, but they took no special vows. They were assigned confessors, but often they managed their own spiritual lives, conducting their own prayers and rituals, hearing each other's confessions, writing their own psalters and listening to women preachers. They acknowledged the authority of bishops, who protected them but did not control them, which made Pope John XXII uneasy.[197] Ever since the Council of Mainz in 1223, the Church had been trying to bring under the control of priests women who took private vows of chastity without entering a convent.[198]

In addition, the beguines were well organized and hard-working. They set up industries and formed corporations; they bargained with the city for tax relief and for the right to practice certain occupations, and won those rights.[199] Eventually the guilds protested.

Ernest McDonnell, who has studied the beguines in depth, asserts that in their actual poverty, actual service to the community, simple communist ideas about sharing, and their autonomy, they constituted a real threat to the "sacramental-hierarchical" organizations of Church and commerce. The Church offered mainly an appearance of service to the poor and sick, and John XXII was suspicious of spiritual Franciscanism—real poverty, service, and sharing.[200] The guilds were interested in profit and could not tolerate being undersold by women who desired only bare subsistence and enough to help the poor and the sick. The Church began to put pressure on the beguines to place themselves under its control by joining convents. The guilds lobbied the state to act against them. Statutes reflect that even accusations of sorcery were brought against them. The state did persecute them, seizing their property.[201] Once more, those who actually lived by the ideals mouthed by Western culture were perceived as constituting the greatest threat to it and were eliminated.

The beguines did not all go gentle into that oblivion. Many defied the Church and a number were burned at the stake. A few continued to follow their own version of Christianity, writing their own scriptures and preaching in public, which was forbidden to women. Some were canonized much later, because of their goodness and their martyrdom. Some were free spirits, believing a god of love removed the taint of sin even from sexual passion, believing themselves in joyful harmony with God. If there was no sin, there was no need for Church control.

By the fifteenth century, the unified persecution of Church and state had succeeded in suppressing most beguine orders. Beguinages remained; they were no longer religious houses, but shelters run by women for poor women and children. Whenever these groups again tried to be self-sustaining, to set up an industry or gain immunity from taxes, they were again persecuted under guild pressure.[202] Female autonomy was not to be permitted.

Women continued to join other dissenting sects, however, sects like the Catholic Brethren and Sisters of the Common Life, and the Lollards. The Catholic Brethren and Sisters of the Common Life lived and believed much as the beguines did, but they managed to escape persecution, possibly because the Church believed that the Sisters were properly controlled and regulated by the Brethren. They were not, but the Brethren did defend them intellectually.

The Lollards were followers of the great John Wycliffe. Wycliffe attacked papal supremacy, advocated clerical marriage, attacked monasticism, and, above all, wanted the Scriptures translated into the vernacular, so that ordinary people could read them.[203] For this last heresy especially, he was hounded throughout his life and finally burned at the stake. When the Bible was Englished, about two centuries later, many of Wycliffe's translations were used as bases for the King James version.

Wycliffe was burned in 1384; the Lollards were threatened with death and went underground after 1401. The movement lost most of its intellectual content, but it continued to draw to it people who were dissatisfied with the organized Church: at least a third of its members were women.[204] Lollards encouraged women to read the Bible, recite Scripture, and preach at meetings; some even held that women—*perfect* women—were capable of priesthood.[205]

These movements were suppressed, but they did not die. They arose again in the sixteenth century, when Martin Luther, John Calvin, Huldreich Zwingli, and John Knox all took up the protest, reiterating many of Wycliffe's demands.

## The Witch Trials

The words *witch* and *wise woman* were interchangeable in sixteenth-century Scotland, according to Reginald Scot.[206] In that age, Scotland executed four thousand of its wise women. "Wise women" were healers, herbalists, midwives, and surgeons, and were sometimes called "blessing witches."[207] As early as the twelfth century, a new motif appeared in accusations of heresy, a charge that the accused had made a pact with the devil. (This charge was also used against Jews and Templars in the thirteenth century, and against Joan of Arc in the fifteenth.[208])

By the fifteenth century many serious and intelligent men viewed witchcraft as "the single greatest threat to Christian European civilization."[209] Perhaps by this time the anger of displaced women and the guilt of the men who were displacing them had mounted to create a paranoiac fear of any woman who deviated from the single accepted pattern.

The first fully articulated theory of witchcraft and the start of massive persecution did not appear until the end of the fifteenth century with the publication of the *Malleus Maleficarum*, written by two Dominican Inquisitors who explicitly identified witchcraft with women. Among the statements made or quoted in this book are: "There are three things in nature, the Tongue, an Ecclesiastic, and a Woman, which know no moderation in goodness or vice"; "When a woman thinks alone, she thinks evil"; "I have found a woman more bitter than death and a good woman subject to carnal lust."[210]

The authors claim that women are witches because they are more subject to the wiles of the devil than men; this is because they are more impressionable, credulous, feebler in mind and body, and more carnal. Their intellect is of a different nature from men's. They have slippery tongues and can't keep silent; they are formed from a bent rib and so are defective; they always deceive. The Inquisitors conclude: "Blessed be the Most High who has so far preserved the male sex from so great a crime." They even offer a derivation of the Latin word for woman—*femina*—as *fe-minus, of lesser faith.*[211]

Witches were accused of making men impotent, devouring newborn babies, turning their neighbors' milk sour or keeping their butter from setting, causing their cattle to die or their children to fall ill.[212] They were also charged with offering contraceptive measures to women, performing abortions, and giving women in labor ergot to ease their pain.[213] Both midwives and the women who needed their services were open to charges of violating the laws of the Church.

Charges of witchcraft were being brought against women healers even before the publication of the *Malleus Maleficarum*. Male physicians attempting to exclude women from the colleges were urging fines and imprisonment for women physicians—although not in obstetrics—and as early as 1460, when the University of Paris initiated a medical curriculum open only to male students, aspersions of witchcraft were being made against women.[214] Women were being excluded from the practice of medicine, and the witchcraft trials of women healers eliminated most of those who remained. However, the trials also functioned to draw a strong distinction between male physicians and female healers, placing the males on a high moral and intellectual plane, allied with God and the Law, and on a professional par with lawyers and theologians, while degrading women to subhuman status, allying them with the devil, darkness, evil, and magic.[215]

Not only female healers were accused of witchcraft, nor only women. But 85 percent of those who perished were women, most of them also poor and alone.[216] An overwhelming proportion were old. William Monter theorizes that the trials were projections of social fears onto "atypical" women, those who did not fit the increasingly constricted mold.[217] But many factors coincided to create this phenomenon. The expulsion of a traditionally peasant class from the land had led to a new class, the itinerant—beggars, landless, homeless, and utterly subject to those who might hire them. In such conditions, women are hired less often and for lower wages than men. After the Reformation, many convents were closed and their wealth confiscated by the state; in many cases the nuns were simply turned out on the street as it were. It was in the sixteenth century, after the Reformation, that the witch trials reached their peak. Women then as now were the poorest members of the poorest class, and among women those without men—widows and spinsters—were the poorest of all.

Such women had few options, and had to depend on communal help. They might come to a neighbor's door and ask for help, or food, and be turned away with scorn, curses, or a blow. In helpless despair, summoning what pride she possessed, a woman might curse the neighbor. If, later, misfortune occurred to the neighbor's property or family, both the neighbor and the poor woman believed the curse to have been effective. "The important point is that, paradoxically, it tended to be the witch who was morally in the right and the victim who was in the wrong," writes Keith Thomas, who adds that charges were usually brought against a "witch" when the accuser felt not only that she bore a grudge against him but that she was justified in doing so.[218]

Sometimes a male relative who coveted a woman's bit of land brought charges against her; more often charges were brought against old women "who had come to the door to beg or borrow some food or drink or the loan of some household utensil" and had been turned away empty-handed.[219] Often the old woman herself believed she had been led by the devil and, under torture, many confessed to this sin. In an age in which most strong emotions were considered temptations from the devil, impoverished women might well have believed that it was the devil who induced them to steal, to curse, to hate, to attempt suicide, or to kill one child so that the others might have more food.[220]

The rage of the indigent against those who seemed to have enough is understandable. They muttered and shouted, wishing ill to those who harmed or
did not help them. To control a "troublesome and angry woman who, by her
brawling and wrangling amongst her neighbours, doth break the public peace,
and beget, cherish and increase public discord," communities used the ducking
stool, a chair in which the woman would be strapped, to be jeered at or pelted
with missiles, or sometimes ducked head first into water; or put the woman in a
cage, or led her around the streets by a metal bridle.[221] The next step in ridding
a community of its victims was to accuse them of witchcraft.

For witches were accused by their neighbors, not by high-level authorities.
They were, however, tried by state or Inquisitorial courts; the number of executions seems to have depended on whether a nation permitted the use of torture
to extract "confessions." Thus England, which prohibited torture, executed
fewer than a thousand "witches," while smaller Scotland, which allowed torture, executed four times as many. Inquisitorial courts, which searched for heresy rather than witchcraft per se, executed far fewer people, and in Spain and
Italy, where these courts functioned, the number killed was smaller.

The primary epicenter of executions for witchcraft was the Holy Roman
Empire, especially southern Germany (Baden-Württemberg), Bavaria, Switzerland, and Austria. Indeed, the witch trials began in Austria. The southwestern
corner of Germany and Bavaria were each responsible for the deaths of thirty-
five hundred people. In Poland, the second most heavily afflicted area, large
numbers of "witches" were killed between 1675 and 1720, long after the witch
craze had ended in Europe.[222] In some German cities, six hundred "witches"
were executed in a year; in the Würzburg area, nine hundred in a year; in
Como, a thousand. In Toulouse, four hundred were killed in one day. In the
bishopric of Trier in 1585, *two villages were left with only one female inhabi-
tant each.*[223] Even little girls were accused and burned at the stake. In London,
a Scotsman confessed that he was responsible for the deaths of over 220
women, for each of which he had been paid twenty-one shillings.[224] That he too
was burned is little consolation. Estimates of the number of people burned at
the stake range as high as nine million, as low as a hundred thousand.[225]

Some of the women who were accused and possibly executed were members of "heretical" sects like the Albigensians, or small, unnamed prayer circles.
All of these were offered a choice between the stake and submission to the
Catholic Church, and many chose the latter. The Inquisitorial courts had fewer
victims than state courts partly because they offered such an alternative. Indeed, although the mania was begun by two Dominican Inquisitors and at first
intensified by this group, it reached its height in Protestant countries. But "in
the sixteenth and seventeenth centuries absolutely no part of Europe escaped
the witch mania altogether; executions varied from country to country and
from province to province, but witch trials happened everywhere."[226]

The hysteria and paranoia implicit in the witch trials resemble the terror
of males in some simple cultures of the malevolent powers of menstruating
women: even Aristotle believed that the glance of a menstruating woman could
tarnish a mirror.[227] The trials are symbolic of what was occurring to human

qualities in this period, as "masculine" qualities slowly but unremittingly moved forward, dominating the minds and imaginations of educated Europeans, in the process eradicating "feminine" qualities or treating them with contempt. Old women, most respected in the matricentric culture, were now not only the most despised of humans but were deemed worthy of death. The trials also must have affected those women who were left, reminding them of what could happen to them too if they were not properly submissive and conforming. It appears that Europe had to go through a huge bloodletting, ridding itself of a female element, before it could proceed on its course of erecting the masculine principle into the most elaborate machine the world had known.

In the seventeenth century, the witch trials stopped as suddenly as they had begun. Christine Faure writes, "What had hitherto been attributed solely to the action of the devil was now attributed to a sickness."[228] They stopped in Europe, but they crossed the Atlantic with the Puritans and ravaged many New England villages.

During the centuries when the literature of *courtoisie* with its worship of women dominated the artistic imagination of Europe, female witchcraft and demonism dominated its moral imagination. Monter concludes, "The sad truth is that, in women's 'real' social history, the pedestal is almost impossible to find, but the stake is everywhere."[229]

## 6. OTHER DOORS CLOSING

The institutional consolidation that began in the twelfth century slowly transformed the character of European society. In feudal society, on the whole, everyone had a place by birth. It may not have been a comfortable place, but it was ready-made and recognized. Serfs were subject to overlords and bound to the land, but they had that land to live on and work. Freed people worked or owned small farms or lived in villages with commons, communally shared grazing land for the one cow belonging to each household. The economy was based in barter more than cash, and even aristocrats were likely to pay for services at least partly in vats of wine or bushels of grain. Servants in a mansion or castle might receive clothing or wine, and almost no money, but they were guaranteed food, something to wear, and a place to sleep. Most people were poor but only a small class was destitute. However, that class began to grow with centralization and enclosure movements, in which communally owned lands were sold to owners of large herds of cattle and fenced off. This dispossessed many women whose one cow had provided them with a hedge against starvation. Destitution became suddenly noticeable in Tudor England when Catholic charitable institutions and monasteries were dissolved. More people were indigent, and more impoverished than they had been before. Since women always comprise a large percentage of the poor, they were profoundly affected by these changes.

But even women from propertied families were experiencing constriction.

In Italy, middle-class and noble women were usually kept from any knowledge of life. Italian girls were considered to have reached majority at twelve (it was raised to fourteen in the fifteenth century) and were immediately married. In law, however, they remained minors throughout their lives. They were not permitted to travel or engage in business, something men of the lower-middle classes did, thus gaining some form of education.

Although Italy was one of the few places in Europe where women could obtain advanced education, it is understandable that under these conditions few did so. But of those who did, many attained distinction. Italy produced both women scholars and such poets as Veronica Gambara and Vittoria Colonna, who is credited by some modern scholars with genius. It also produced the first feminist writer, Christine de Pisan, although she was raised in France.

Nevertheless, in some Italian states, women were not permitted to enter a court, and their depositions had to be taken at home or in a church. In 1330 the daughter of a jurisconsult replaced her father in the lecture room at Bologna and taught—from *behind a curtain*.[230] A widow could not remarry without the assent of her family. A father could, by a provision in his will, condemn his daughters to life sentences in a cloister.[231]

Women had some privileges. They were rarely punished by law, and were not held responsible for their fathers' debts. In Siena, in the last half of the thirteenth century, a special law court was established for hearing suits brought by women against men. An "adulteress" who left her husband forfeited her dower but regained it if he took her back. Sometimes a widow would be granted the usufruct rights to her husband's property, at least for as long as "she remained single and chaste."[232]

Lower-class women lived in wretched poverty, limited to the most poorly paid tasks. They were domestic servants, charwomen, water carriers, and washerwomen; barbers, innkeepers, hawkers; shoemakers, dressmakers, milliners, embroiderers, and chefs. Some ran brothels; some women weavers formed guilds; in Venice women were rowers.[233]

What most affected Italian women during the late Middle Ages was changes in property laws. As they became systematized, women were restricted in the personal dispositions of their dowries and in their right to make a will. Women tended to be less concerned than men with maintaining the patrimony of the lineage, that is, keeping the family fortune in the hands of family males. Rather than bequeathing their money to their male kinsmen, they were leaving it to the people they loved, usually distant female relatives, often elderly widows. They bequeathed their property overwhelmingly to other women, something that men considered a betrayal and dispersal of family property.[234] By the sixteenth century most Italian cities had decreed that women could inherit nothing from a father or husband if he died intestate, despite the relationship.[235]

In France, women were barred from succession to the throne at the end of the fourteenth century, and a new code of law promulgated in the sixteenth century turned women into servants.[236] Toward the end of feudalism in France, women had all the rights of men—they administered justice, signed treaties, decreed laws, commanded troops, and entered combat. Simone de Beauvoir writes that "there were female soldiers before Joan of Arc."[237] Countrywomen in France were treated like servants, not eating at the table with their husbands and sons, and working considerably harder than the men. But because they were absolutely necessary to the men, they were respected and exercised great authority within the home.[238] This tradition of combined low status and high respect continued among the peasant class. It was the women of the propertied class who were suffering from suppressions; only a few aristocratic women retained access to power or education.

In Germany too, women had for a long period exercised great powers of the kind attached to the land—levying troops, holding courts of justice, coining money, and participating in legal assemblies. But with centralization and consolidation, they were deprived of these rights, and in 1356 a law was passed allowing only males to inherit.[239]

In sixteenth-century England, monopolies were granted to early capitalists which enriched the royal treasuries but further impoverished the poor, who had to pay a higher price for the goods covered by them. English kings who wished to enlist the bourgeoisie—a growing class of merchants and entrepreneurs—in an alliance against the lesser nobility passed laws giving fathers broad controls over property and their families. The bourgeoisie began to amass large fortunes and, in turn, supported the king, offering obedience to him as the father of his people. A flood of official propaganda emphasized the need for authority and obedience to the king, and parallel with that, the need for obedience to the power of husband/father; this created a chain of power that affected people from birth.[240] Authoritarian rule of husband/father over wife and children was especially strengthened by the Reformation, when Protestants rejected canon law and rediscovered the Old Testament.

Indeed, the Reformation was the major political movement of this period. It can be dated to 1517, the year Martin Luther nailed his ninety-five theses to the door of Wittenberg Cathedral. Luther's drive to purify and reform the Catholic Church was joined by others, and the movement led to two centuries of bloody, fiery conflict in Europe and England, and to the mounting of a Counter-Reformation by the Church.

## The Reformation

The Reformation was another revolt against the fathers; like the Christian revolt, it attempted to free the sons from the rigid, overweening, and corrupt law. The Renaissance affected an intellectual elite; the Reformation was a widespread popular revolution. Like all such revolutions, it accepted women in its early stages and expelled them when the revolution was complete. To the people of this period, religion was as embedded in the state as economic system—capitalism, socialism, or a mixed economy—is in our own. Religious struggle meant severe conflict, even war, within nations and between them.

It has been argued that the Reformation benefited women, the proof being that women in Catholic and Greek Orthodox countries have fewer rights than those in Protestant countries. If Protestantism had such an effect, it was inadvertent. Protestantism is linked with capitalism, as Max Weber and R. H.

Tawney long ago demonstrated. Protestantism emphasized the individual and gave rise to the Calvinist theory of predestination, according to which only some are chosen. The only clear sign of chosenness was worldly wealth: thus to be rich was also to be virtuous. Protestantism repudiated medieval Catholic dogmas that barred men from certain activities—notably in science. In other words, Calvinism in particular and Protestantism in general made possible the attitudes that led to capitalist exploitation of nature and people, the amassing of wealth, and the rise of science which gave industry its foundation. In the process of exploitation and technical discovery, however, capitalism diminished women and "feminine" values more profoundly than any previous system; it will be argued later in this book that that devaluation is at least partly responsible for the rise of feminism. As we shall see, whatever rights women possess today they owe to one thing alone: the feminist movement. It is possible that women in Catholic and Greek Orthodox countries did not rebel because, although they were restricted, they were not utterly degraded, they continued to be central in the family, and felt that the old religion offered support and validation of the values they upheld. This was not the case in Protestant industrial nations.

In any case, the Reformation began, much as Christianity had, by offering all people autonomy before God. Challenging the rule of the pope and the Church hierarchy, it proclaimed the authority of Scripture and named each man—and each woman—their own rabbi. Women flocked to these sects as they had to the early Christian cells. Antiauthoritarian, antihierarchical groups always contain a high percentage of women.

But none of the protesting leaders was interested in changing women's role in society. Protesting men took positions on issues that concerned women only because they wished to reform the Church and general "morality." For instance, they opposed clerical concubinage, the system whereby priests paid a tax to the Church for their traditional right to maintain concubines and prostitutes. The reformers opposed the double standard on fornication and adultery, and wished to permit divorce under certain circumstances. But what seems to have most appealed to women was that the new movements offered a personal, nonhierarchic, lay-dominated religion using Scripture alone as its authority.[241]

Protestantism put great emphasis on faith as the condition of salvation, and, like early Christianity, preached the equality before God of men and women. That equality was spiritual only, however. Luther, Calvin, and (above all) Knox insisted that in this world women were to be obedient to their husbands, keep silent in public, and busy themselves with their households.[242] The Puritans had an exalted conception of the family and denounced wife beating, but they continued to demand bodily and civil obedience from women.[243] Homilies read in churches reaffirmed male authority.[244] The Virgin, the only female figure intimate with the Christian pantheon, was demoted, as were female saints. Pictures of sacred mother and child were denounced for implying the Divine Son might ever have been under the influence of a woman. Convents were abolished and no educational or spiritual institutions for women replaced them. No avenue of activity was permitted women that might conflict with control by their husbands.[245] The "insistent theme," the "epitome," of Protestantism is the word *Father*.[246]

However, the Protestant fathers did believe in education for women. This was especially important in a time when economic and political rights were approaching a nadir for women: married women could not own property, inheritance rights were nil or minimal, women were increasingly restricted to unpaid work within the home and did not even have a voice in village affairs.[247] Although early in the Reformation proposals were made for divorce on grounds of adultery, desertion, prolonged absence, and extreme incompatibility, by the end of the sixteenth century in England divorce was difficult and remarriage after divorce required a special act of Parliament for each case.[248]

Some historians believe that the long-range effect of Protestantism on women was beneficial, because its leaders insisted that girls should be taught to read and write so that they would be able to read the Bible for themselves and later for their children. Comparisons of literacy rates of Protestant and Catholic women (outside convents) show the Protestant rate to be higher, which may have helped women in Protestant countries to organize feminist movements in the nineteenth century.[249] Some think otherwise, claiming that Luther and Calvin set back the progress made in education of women by demanding the abolition of convents and monasteries. What was substituted for convent education, which had always included some classical learning, was "a narrow vocational education that would fit women for their household duties" and reading of the Bible.[250]

Because women were now confined to the home and to domestic tasks as they had not been since the days of Athens, they were forced to gain their identity solely from their domestic roles. With guidance from a literature of domesticity, they created a new profession—motherhood. In the process, childhood was discovered, at least for boys.

Before the thirteenth century, all children were enclosed in swaddling clothes. Swaddling clothes bound the baby completely so it could not move its limbs; they offered an early and ineradicable experience in constriction. This lesson never ended for women. Boys went from swaddling clothes to a little dress and long hair until they were shorn and breeched at seven—the age of reason—but girls went directly into adult clothes.[251] Their tiny bodies were imprisoned in bodices and corsets reinforced with iron and whalebone that molded them into the prevailing female fashion. They were expected to maintain a dignified posture, a slow and graceful walk, and generally to conform to the standards of adult females. "The contraptions used to achieve these ends often frustrated them, leading instead to the distortion or displacement of the organs, and sometimes even death."[252] Boys, however, were left free to play. "They were the first specialized children." They played with dolls; adults played with children.[253]

At the same time that childhood became a distinct category (as all things had begun to be categorized), it became a category to fear. Like women, children were part of nature. To tame the nature within them, parents began to whip them. Whipping of children—the same severe whippings the Puritans imposed on their children, which so shocked the American Indians—became mandatory. "More children were being beaten in the sixteenth and early seventeenth century, over a longer age span, than ever before," writes Lawrence Stone.[254] Even at school boys were whipped and spied upon by their masters, sometimes until the students were past twenty.[255]

The socialization of girls was different. "The three objectives of family planning were the continuity of the male line, preservation intact of the inherited property, and the acquisition through marriage of further property or useful political alliances."[256] (Until the eighteenth century, "family" meant the line, and not a single generation.) Daughters were often disruptive of such goals. To give them dowries, the father had to break pieces off the property, which then, like the women themselves, became the property of another family to use if not to keep. Unless money was brought *into* the family by a daughter's marriage—which it sometimes was—girls caused dispersal rather than concentration of the family's wealth. And there is no question that despite the new sense of children and family, to the well-to-do property remained more important than persons. The chastity of girls was strictly guarded because it was essential to their market value. Only female chastity could guarantee that a man's succession was his own (legitimate).

The closing of convents, suppression of beguinages, and exclusion of women from most guilds left single women without means to support themselves. There was great pressure on everyone—male and female—to marry.[257] The main Protestant churches—Lutheran, Calvinist, and Presbyterian—were completely male-dominated. Women unhappy with their lives or with male-supremacist religion were drawn to the Protestant sects. There were many of these—Brownists, Independents, Baptists, Millenarians, Familists, Quakers, Seekers, Ranters, and the radical Levellers and Anabaptists. All believed in a pure Church and in spiritual regeneration—what is now known as being "born again"—as a condition of membership. Women were as likely as men to achieve this state, and might do so even if their husbands did not. Thus women joined these sects independently. Once admitted, women could participate in church government.[258]

"Women were numerically extremely prominent among the separatists. . . . In the episcopal returns and indulgence documents of the reign of Charles II conventiclers are frequently described as being 'chiefly women'; 'more women than men,' 'most silly women,' and so on. During the [English] Civil War period it was a favourite gibe against the sectaries that their audience consisted chiefly of the weaker sex. . . . In Norwich in 1645, for example, the congregation contained thirty-one men and eighty-three women."[259] Women were also important in larger religious bodies, the Scottish Presbyterians and the outlawed Roman Catholics in England. More women than men were among the large body of English separatists in London in 1568, and many left their husbands to go overseas to the Netherlands with groups seeking religious liberty.[260]

Women helped to form new independent congregations—as Anne

Hutchinson did in Massachusetts, for which she was banished. They preached with enthusiasm in groups that permitted it—the Baptists in Holland, the Puritans in New England. Among the Quakers, the right of women to speak in public assembly was explicit in the doctrines of its founder, George Fox, but remained a matter of contention.[261]

Women used their regeneration and their husbands' failure as justification for leaving them. (It seems men were correct in believing that any loosening of the leash would lose them not only command over their wives, but the wife herself. In eighteenth-century Geneva, there was no barrier to a wife leaving her husband—since this had been unanticipated—and women deserted their husbands "in record numbers," walking across the border to France.[262]) Women of the sects also took new husbands from among the regenerate.[263]

Many women, insisting upon their faith, were martyred for it, persecuted by Anglicans, Lutherans, and Catholics. In Spain, dissidents were persecuted by the Catholic Inquisition, and many women were executed or exiled. One of these, Isabel de la Cruz, was "interrogated" (tortured) for five years without recanting, and was finally killed.[264] In England, Catholics were persecuted by the Anglican Church; among them was Margaret Clitherow of York, a young mother of several children, who was crushed to death for refusing to attend services of the Church of England.[265]

Although it is likely that there were long-term effects of the Protestant willingness to educate women, the immediate effects were minimal. The major Protestant churches were adamant in denying that the "priesthood of believers" included women, and even the more radical sects changed as soon as they took institutional form, becoming conservative, especially about the organization and discipline of the family. "The Quakers were notoriously patriarchal and the Baptist churches continued to punish rebellious wives and servants."[266] From the standpoint of possibilities for women, "the progressive elements," writes Sherrin Wyntjes, "were expunged."[267] As everywhere new conceptions of class, of family, of gender, of dress, of education became rigid, they manifested "the same intolerance towards variety, the same insistence on uniformity."[268] Again a revolution had occurred with the assistance of women and had left them out at the end.


## 7. LEARNING AND LITERATURE

Although this section breaks the chronological sequence of this chapter, there are good reasons for discussing education and literature separately. Women's learning and writing, and writing inspired by women, were, like women themselves, cut off from active influence on their own culture. This is not to say such literature did not influence later periods: some of it did. But to discuss it in the same section with its actual period might cause confusion. Some of the writing we will allude to was read relatively widely in the period in which it was written (although only a small percentage of people were at any time literate). Some of it was read by a tiny group, and is being rediscovered only now. Whether or not women's writing was read or praised in its own time, it had no effect on the society for which it was written. It comprises a kind of underground literature, subversive, and likely to be omitted from literary surveys.

Throughout the Middle Ages boys acquired primary education at home or in an apprenticeship. Outside of Italy there was no higher education in letters or the sciences until universities began to grow from cathedral schools in the twelfth century. Some colleges, founded as homes for poor male students in the twelfth century, developed into teaching institutions by the fifteenth. But by the sixteenth century boys were being sent to school as early as eight or nine years of age.[269]

Girls could attend convent schools, where they existed, and at times had a higher literacy rate than boys. But institutionalized education completely excluded them. Yet at no time in the Christian Era were all women deprived of education: there were always fathers who wished to educate their daughters and had the means to accomplish this. Women from propertied families were educated at home, by tutors, and many wealthy or aristocratic women became noted for their learning. After being excluded from all institutional exercise of their abilities, from the twelfth century on, many such women turned to literature. They acted as patrons of male writers, or wrote themselves, or both.

The first "school" of literature to be dominated by learned women was the literature of courtly love. "Courtly love" is the name given to a set of attitudes that informed European aristocratic literature during the twelfth century but are familiar to students of literature to this day. In the poetry of the French troubadours, a male singer pours out his love for a highborn woman and pleads for reciprocation. The ladies are alternately benevolent and withdrawing; the poet is alternately ardent and angry, hopeful and despairing. There is always a difference in rank between them. In later courtly love poetry, this difference is maintained even when the lover is an aristocrat like the lady he woos: the lover woos on his knees, regardless of his class. Moreover, although quite a number of the troubadours were women, including aristocratic women, the point of view is usually male.[270]

Courtly love is outside marriage, and aims at physical consummation. Some troubadour work may have been religious in nature, hymns of love to the Virgin.[271] It is often opaque, even hermetic, which suggests that some of it may have been the songs of a heretical sect like the Cathari. Its opacity directs the reader to read allegorically, to look for hidden meanings. The conventions of courtly love, the tendency to allegorical interpretation, and the literary forms of the *lai* and the romance combined to create late-medieval secular literature.

The situation out of which this literature is presumed to have sprung is composed of arranged marriage in which affection was unimportant, a tolerance for extramarital love, and the existence of a great number of powerful women running their own courts. The theory is that poor male troubadours sang of their love for such women to praise them and win reward; aristocratic female troubadours presumably sang simply for the love of singing. Such songs led in time to a great literature: *chansons*; the *lais* of Marie de France, a princess and the abbess of Shaftesbury, who wrote to entertain the court of Eleanor of Aquitaine (1122–1204); the tales of Chrétien de Troyes, court poet of Eleanor's daughter Marie de Champagne, who gave him the plot of his most famous story, *The Knight in the Cart.* Eleanor and Marie de Champagne were said actually to have held courts of love. Andreas Capellanus, author of *The Art of Courtly Love*, was probably chaplain to the court of Marie. Apart from the passages on courtly love itself, which were probably written—dictated—by Marie, this manual is somewhat cynical and quite sexist.[272] As a whole, the book reinforces strongly the notion of love as a competitive game, a power struggle.

Historians are firm in agreeing that courtly love exerted no influence on women's actual lives or their legal or economic status in this period. Literary scholars find courtly love important because its ideas and conventions influenced later literature; C. S. Lewis believed that the revolutionary elements of courtly love literature formed the background of European literature for the eight hundred years that followed, and that "compared with this revolution, the Renaissance is a mere ripple on the surface of literature."[273] But literary historians do not suggest that the literature of courtly love changed conditions for actual women.

I do not believe, however, that an important artistic movement emerges from nowhere, or exists without ties to actual life, or that what is thought and felt and imagined is without influence on what is done and lived. However, one must probe beneath the surface of both literature and life to find that influence.

The period we are discussing is one in which women's sphere of action was being severely curtailed, in which they were being relegated to frivolity and adornment, obedience and hard work. The curtailments occurred over generations, and women forgot the greater liberties their sex had earlier possessed. There was no open revolution by women. What they did, as they usually do, was to seek out avenues in which they could influence the world in which they lived. Aristocratic women found in the ideas of courtly love, which some of them helped to create, a literary vehicle with which to propagate a new morality, a morality of *courtoisie*. In this morality, women are treated with respect and admiration, and through their efforts the knight-hero learns a new way to approach experience, one that includes *gentilesse* and *courtoisie* and respect for women along with prowess and control and hardiness. Thus "feminine" values are added to the repertoire of the ideal man; he learns that he must sometimes give up control, especially to female figures, and that kindness and gentility and gratitude and respect for women are as important in his quest (whatever it may be) as the more brutal excellences of medieval warriors. The literature of *courtoisie* "feminized" European ideals and led in time to the notion of the gentleman.

A most important element in this literature is that it posits women as the moral superiors of men. It is sometimes suggested that the nineteenth-century idealization of the Victorian "lady" constitutes the first suggestion of Western civilization that women were morally superior to men, and not the moral inferiors posited by centuries of Christian patriarchs. On the contrary, female moral superiority is explicit in courtly love literature and medieval romance, even though in some works it coexists with or counters satirical misogyny. This strain, women as morally superior to men, is one of the many devices in women's campaign to feminize, humanize culture that backfired. For in most courtly love poetry and in the romances, women are exalted and knowing, but they are also utterly static, that is, they exist as moral poles in the human experience of a man, as archetypes of good and evil. Men are still the standard of humanness. Narrative centering on a woman's moral experience, with the necessary failures and errors required for learning, was not yet thinkable. Although archetypal figures may in some way exalt femaleness, they cannot function as literary-moral examples for actual women, and in the end they serve to perpetuate and fortify the imprisonment of women within images of static perfection.

Women fostered and created such works, but they are works designed for men, who still held the power to shape culture and plan the future. The literature of *courtoisie* is intended for the moral enlightenment of men. Female figures are important in the works as teachers and moral guides to men. They are almost always images of beauty, desired and pursued. But their main purpose is to incarnate moral poles, good and evil absolutes among whom the hero-knight must choose. Groups of beautiful ladies appear in an empty castle and miraculously spread a banquet on a white cloth before the famished and exhausted hero: then they vanish. Or they appear before him and sing and dance, refreshing his spirit and courage, providing nourishment to lead him on. Part of the drama lies in the fact that the knight (and the reader) does not know how to interpret these women. For readers accustomed to Christian allegory and pilgrimage in literature, the images suggest sin and error, the wrong path, a fleshly goal. They are female and sensual: they allure. But they are usually beneficent, bringing nourishment to the body, spirit, and emotion of a hero-wanderer tired and homeless and bruised by brutality and fear. They teach him *gentilesse*.

The new morality inherent in such works did have an effect, although it may be difficult to trace. It subverts Christianity as it had become—a hierarchy of fear and obedience, absolute, with overtones of asceticism and puritanism— by reminding readers of the mercy and compassion, the beauty and joy, of early Christianity. It also revises the Christian attitude toward femaleness, replacing connotations of lust, vice, vanity, and temptation with connotations of beauty, grace, and nourishment.

The affirmation of gentle qualities as part of the makeup of a good man becomes an important theme, quite apart from courtly love, in works like *Piers Plowman* and *The Pearl*, and remains in English literature right up to the twentieth century. This strand in literature operates to counter the increasing "masculinization" of culture that occurs in the same period, although at no time does it dominate, or even deflect the masculinizing process. The new morality, then, did not alter this march; what it may have done was to sweeten the imagination or the lives of some people.

One theme of the literature of *courtoisie* and the literature that followed it—the romances of Ariosto and Boiardo in Italy, of Sidney, Spenser, and

Shakespeare in England—was to define love. It is portrayed as a power relation, which certainly was the nature of aristocratic marriage, but the positions are reversed: the male lover begs favors from his proud lady. In addition, especially when the lady is "virtuous," sometimes called *cold*, her beauty and his desire lead the lover not to her bed, but to God. This is a new conception of the emotion—new in literature and perhaps in human experience. Love had often enough been seen as pure eros, as slavery to the flesh, or as madness. There was also sacred or spiritual love, reserved for God. But not until the poets of the *dolce stil nuovo* and Dante in the thirteenth century and the Neoplatonists of the fourteenth and fifteenth centuries had it been seen as both at once, with physical desire feeding into, giving substance to, a transcendent ideal passion that, unconsummated, is sublimated into religious fervor, a passion for God. Despite the decline of religion in the eighteenth and nineteenth centuries, this notion of love endured, becoming a vaporous—or noxious—romanticism in which unconsummated desire led to the artificial maintenance of ecstatic longing, no longer for God, but essentially for death.

On the one hand, then, sexual desire is forbidden consummation, and becomes a vague but intense yearning for an ecstatic union with something transcendent. On the other, the power relation between the sexes—differences in status, economics, and political rights—is charged with erotic energy. In literature from the eighteenth century onward, difference in powers, of whatever sort, becomes a source of sexual excitement. For the Marquis de Sade, the difference usually lies in physical and emotional force possessed by the sadist "hero," and used against the masochistic "heroine." The high rank and economic power of the young master is used against a poor servant girl in Richardson's *Pamela*, titillating both of them. In Richardson's *Clarissa*, the difference is moral: the wealthy Lovelace is inferior morally to the wealthy Clarissa, and is willing to use physical force and drugs against her—again with considerable titillation. A more unequal situation arouses passion in the lowborn heroine for the wealthy "master" in Charlotte Brontë's *Jane Eyre*. And the tie between a slave and a master is charged with sexual desire in Thomas Pynchon's *V*. In all these cases, and in many others of the same sort, the sexual relation between men and women is seen essentially as male conquering and female surrender. Even in erotic literature aimed at male homosexual readers, the victim is female. This infusion of power by sexuality, or sexuality by power, characterizes most of our present-day pornography, especially in its more violent manifestations. As one of America's elder statesmen has said, power is the greatest aphrodisiac. But such a statement can be made only in a society that worships power and that sees sex as one more area for the exercise of power.

Thus the literature of *courtoisie*, which was intended as a softening, humanizing influence, led instead to the opposite. This is not the fault of the literature. What characterizes the Western world over the past millennium is its brilliance in absorbing countermovements and shaping them to patriarchal ends. The notion of romantic love was turned toward the transcendent (in Romantic literature), and toward a vision of sex as power (in sadomasochistic literature).

The actual literature of courtly love was not long-lived, although long narrative poems, called romances, continued to be written after the twelfth century. The next important European literary event was the Renaissance, a movement within the arts and letters. Inspired by the rediscovery of Greek art and some Greek literature, especially Platonic thought and tradition, the Renaissance began in Italy in the fourteenth century and spread north, generating a huge body of art, literature, and philosophy. It reached England in the sixteenth century, where, in the time of Henry VIII, it stimulated education and, in the time of Elizabeth I, literature.

The effect of the Renaissance, however, was limited to educational matters and to propertied people. There was a new emphasis on education for the sons of the rich and middle classes, and occasionally education was also extended to their daughters. A few schools for girls as well as boys opened in the fifteenth century, and more parents allowed their daughters to study with their sons and the family tutor.[274] Wealthy men, princes, and kings hired humanist scholars to teach their children, girls as well as boys. That this education did not have more effect is understandable if one considers what it consisted of. After a millennium of ages "darkened" by illiteracy and continual conflict, of loosely held power in autonomous regions, in which women had simply taken advantage of their natural abilities—intelligence, force, energy, and talent—and risen to positions that allowed the exercise of those abilities, they were now being taught the literature and thought of Athens and Rome. Consider the attitudes of that literature toward women, and you will understand the confusion of women to whom it was taught as great enduring wisdom.

The aim of the new education was to develop the whole being—the entire person, the well-rounded, universal, Renaissance *man*. To his abilities to ride, hunt, joust, and fight, and to administer principalities, was added a knowledge of the classics, Greek and Latin poetry and philosophy, the avant-garde thinking of Neoplatonic writers. He needed an audience to watch, to draw him out, to witness to his talents, to applaud. Scholars like Vives (1492–1540), the Spanish philosopher who was tutor to Mary Tudor, taught the next British queen to defer, submit, and offer the Renaissance man a "splendid silence." Alberti, sculptor, artist, musician, architect, and founder of Renaissance art theory, also wrote a treatise on education and the ethics of domestic life. He taught that the perfect housewife controlled her staff and family without raising her voice.[275] Cardinal Bembo claimed that girls should learn Latin because that would charm men, and Antonio Galateo advised Princess Bona of Savoy "to please men, being born to command them."[276] The education of women, then, although derived from the same texts men studied, conveyed a different message. The new ideal was engraved on women's brains, and Ruth Kelso, who has studied in depth all known manuals and guides for "ladies," writes that "the first law of woman . . . was submission and obedience."[277]

Nevertheless, "even at the height of the Renaissance, there were women who passed their lives over embroidery and were left under guardianship and espionage. No dame, not even the most highly instructed, ever neglected her domestic duties."[278] William Boulting tells the story of Isabella Morra, a highly educated and cultivated young woman whose brothers considered her learning improper for a woman. When her father was on a journey, they cut off her correspondence and imprisoned her. She smuggled out a plea for help, and the governor of Taranto came with guards to release her. But the brothers murdered him and his men, and cut their sister's throat. Her rather mournful verses were published after her death.[279]

Not every literate woman suffered the melodramatic fate of Isabella Morra (it is a wonder no composer ever wrote an opera about her); and many rebelled against the terms of their education and the concepts and values of their culture. The first of these to write about women's experience was Christine de Pisan, who lived at the end of the fourteenth century (1364–1430?) and initiated the woman's side of the *querelle des femmes.*

From the time of the founding of Christendom there had been a literary (as well as a theological) debate on the vices and virtues of women, but it had been conducted entirely by men. Some men wrote in vituperation of women, scorning the entire sex and diminishing it ribaldly. Women's defenders took the position there had been some "good" women in history, some who were able to rule and go to war. Their defenses of good women were usually lists of such women, often ambivalent. Boccaccio, for instance, wrote about illustrious women, and lamented their poor female bodies, forced to incarnate "magnificent virile spirit."[280]

Kelso writes: "Vituperation of women seems always, as far back as we have any record, to have been a manly sport. Nor was it ever confined to any one region or class. Folk tales notoriously make women the butt of their satire, and Scheherazade's bedtime stories are one long penance for women's infidelity. But it took the Middle Ages to produce the phenomenon called the war of the sexes."[281] This war, however, was "a controversy waged entirely by men."[282] Until Christine.

Christine de Pisan was a poet and novelist who also wrote history and political commentary. Thrust suddenly into widowhood and impoverishment, with three children and a mother to support, she became almost overnight "the most popular literary figure in France."[283] She began by writing ballads and romances, but her major interests were political. She focused on the problems of women and the literary depiction of women; the political problems of France, military strategy and international law, and the idea of a historical destiny.[284] She is the first female writer to address head-on men's literary attacks on women, and to deal with them *not* by enumerating certain women who escaped the general rotten mold, but by discussing women in terms of their own lives— their needs, their constriction, their institutionalized deprivations. She retorted to the misogynistic *Roman de la Rose* in 1399, and wrote *City of Women* to attack a clerk's lamentation.[285] This book was translated into English in 1531, but fell into oblivion and was not republished until 1982.

After Christine, women in Italy, France, and England joined the battle. Joan Kelly, who has studied the documents of the *querelle*, writes that all of these women were extremely conscious of the political constriction of women. They knew that gender—the role we are taught to play—was different from sex—the body we are born with; they understood that authors' social positions dictated their values and ideas: they exposed the prejudices of patriarchy. Lucretia Marinella wrote in full awareness that men would not read what she wrote, and would brag about that; Mary Astell wrote ironically, agreeing with male writers that strength of mind accompanies strength of body, and added: "'Tis only for some odd accidents, which philosophers have not yet thought worth while to enquire into, that the sturdiest porter is not the wisest man."[286]

The battle reached fierce heights as men rebutted. Joseph Swetnam's *The Arraignment of Lewd, Idle, Froward and Unconstant Women*, "a savage anti-feminist piece of polemic, went through no less than ten editions between its first publication in 1616 and 1634." It generated "fierce rebuttals."[287] The Swetnam debate continued throughout the seventeenth century. In the eighteenth, the historian Catherine Macaulay wrote sadly of the "censure and ridicule" women suffer from writers of all kinds. The notion was hardening that women, *as women*, were devoid of authority and power; Kelly points out that this one subject was able to unify men of otherwise opposed classes and parties: they joined ranks in conviction about woman's "natural subjection to man."[288] The *querelle* thus served men's purposes and those of patriarchy, whatever women felt.

Toward the turn of the eighteenth century, another shift occurred in European thinking, a shift described in books dealing with a variety of areas of thought (or discourse) by Michel Foucault. In general, this shift was in the direction of "modern" ways of thought; like earlier shifts, it involved greater institutionalization, further narrowing of disciplines, and the encompassing by prescriptive modes of thought of greater areas of human experience. It was, in short, a move toward greater human (male) control over nature and life itself. One of its methods was an increased compartmentalization of knowledge.

The compartmentalization of knowledge within strict disciplines meant the banishing of not just certain kinds of knowledge but certain approaches to experience. Whereas in the Middle Ages the task of knowledge had been "to dig out the ancient word from the unknown places where it might be hidden," by the seventeenth century its job was "to fabricate a language" that permitted analysis and calculation.[289] Before this shift in consciousness, thinking was both linear (logical) and circular (associative). After it was complete, only linear thought was respected, associative and meditative thought being left to poetry. It is misleading to speak of completion, perhaps, since the process continues and intensifies still; linear logical thought made possible modern science and modern industry which in turn built the technological world. It is important to remember, however, that a statement can be logical and have no connection with reality; and that although linear thinking carries one faster than circular thinking, there is no guarantee of the desirability of the goal it carries one toward.

The shift in thinking reflects a change in the way thinking and knowledge were conceived of. In the ancient world, power had been seen as conquest, authority, and wealth; only a handful of philosophers would have considered knowledge power in a worldly sense. But in the period between the fourteenth and seventeenth centuries, knowledge became a form of power; it was valued not for its own sake, as a tool of understanding, but as a means to an end, a tool for control of nature. This function of knowledge may have been an element earlier: knowledge of God, for instance, was desirable because it enabled man to control the supernatural (or so it seemed). But people did not consciously think about knowledge as power, did not view it as separate from themselves, a commodity that enabled the purchaser to control elements of this world.

From the late sixteenth century, with the experiments of small coteries of "scientists" in various areas, and with the enormous influence of Francis Bacon, science had begun to develop as a pursuit in itself. The Royal Society was established after the Restoration in England to foster scientific thought; the discoveries of Isaac Newton revolutionized it. Social scientists in France, the *philosophes* of the eighteenth century, were animated by the desire to apply scientific methods and attitudes to all of life, using Newton as their example. Newton had rejected authority, relying on his own reason, and had reduced the mechanism of the cosmos to three simple mathematical laws. It seemed to the *philosophes* that scientific reasoning could equally simplify human social life.[290] By subjecting all ideas to tests of prejudice, as Bacon demanded, and outlawing superstition; by analyzing the structures of society according to precise criteria, they would discover the laws that governed human life in the same way Newton had discovered those of the cosmos. Behind the thinking of scientists and social scientists lay Bacon's dream of the mastery of nature by men— the dominion promised in Genesis. Each discovery, each new neat encasement of experience within a category, must have seemed a step on a golden staircase to the paradise of total control.

As science too was institutionalized, women were barred from knowledge of it. Indeed, after Descartes, who is credited—or blamed—with articulating a kind of final split between mind and matter in the seventeenth century, women were associated with the inert matter upon which the mind of man experimented. The language of science, as we saw in Chapter Two, was explicitly a language of domination of women and nature. In a parallel movement, women were diminished even further than they had been in the fifteenth and sixteenth centuries, by the thinkers of the late seventeenth and eighteenth centuries.

The Enlightenment, a period of great intellectual activity centered in eighteenth-century France, is considered a progressive and rational period, an age of light and reason. It gave birth to stirring assertions of the equality and brotherhood of man, to Rousseau's powerful proclamation that although man is everywhere in chains, he is born free. The *philosophes* set out to achieve "objectivity," to carry the light of reason to every social problem. They wished to overcome prejudice. One prejudice, however, they did not consider. When they mentioned women at all, it was only to argue why women were and should be subordinate. Rousseau fed his ideal fictional woman only milk and sweets and made her a child, a doll, even as he offered a plan for a rich and complex education for his ideal fictional man. The *philosophes* spoke of human rights: but women were not included in the term *human*.

It is important to understand how institutionalization functions to transmit power along strictly male lines, as a parallel to female procreation. That is, females give birth to females who give birth to females: the power of conception is transmitted along the female line alone. Although females also give birth to males, males do not inherit this power. Institutions, set up in a similar linear way, provide for the transmission of power from male to male, excluding women entirely. In addition, the power contained in institutions is declared superior to the mere "animal" power of conception.

Exclusion from institutionalized education had important effects on women and the general culture. Much of the education of the late Middle Ages and later periods—in some cases, up to the early nineteenth century—required knowledge of Latin or Greek. Girls barred from schools but taught to read at home would learn the vernacular, but not Latin or Greek. But if a girl was taught the classical languages, she still could not enter a school for advanced training. If her father was trained, and taught her at home, she still could not practice her training. There was no avenue in the world where women could use their talents.

In earlier ages, the family had provided the power base for most men and women: family wealth, name, and honor were primary concerns and allowed some men and women to exercise influence over a larger sphere. The institutionalization of most public activities relegated the family, and especially women, to a diminished realm of necessity, to a private world. Women of the middle class and above were confined to the home. Because they were inactive they became pregnant easily and often had huge families. Babies were sometimes sent to baby farms, ostensibly for wet nursing but actually to be killed. Upper-class women were satirized in the eighteenth century as being vain, frivolous, shallow, extravagant, and promiscuous—all of which many of them, and their men, may have been. Unlike the Athenian household, the middle-class home of the eighteenth century did not produce most of its own needs, but obtained them from specialized, even professionalized compartments of the culture; thus the middle-class housewife did not produce very much.

Within the domestic sphere, she was entirely a link. She mediated between men and nature, as a man's mother and the mother of a man's children; between men and culture, as a civilizing agent; and among men, as an object of exchange. In all these functions, what was important was a woman's body—her sexual organs in particular. She lived completely for others, if (ideally) on many planes. For her husband she was (ideally) a friend and intelligent companion, intent on pleasing him in every way, and an upper servant, linking him with the household and children while making sure their troubles did not trouble him. In the household she was the administrator, but she lacked the authority that accrues to people who do one's own work better than one can do it—who know how to spin and make butter and weave and concoct medicine. She was rather an overseer, supervising a thousand details, including the servants' work, behavior, demeanor, and morals. For the children, she was mother, a new profession, but one which was thought to require neither education nor experience and which earned no payment. She saw to their physical care, education, manners, and morals. In many countries her sons were removed from her when they were seven; her daughters remained longer. For them she was a link to their father, to the world of adulthood, to the world itself: but her usefulness was limited.

In England girls attended petty schools from the time of the early Reformation. They did not attend grammar school (which taught boys Latin and Greek), and were taught to read and write in the vernacular only. But this led to the creation of a whole new class of readers—middle-class women, increasingly idle, increasingly bored. Tracts were written condemning the freedom of girls to choose their own reading material, urging that they be limited to the Bible, sermons, devotional works, and household reference books. Women did read these things, but they also read for entertainment. By the end of the sixteenth century a new mode of literature had arisen that aimed at this audience—the sentimental romance.[291] The rising middle class also read books about manners, as it attempted to pass into gentility, and in its literature a new set of social ideals appears—a gospel of hard work, discipline, and sexual repression leading to the new goals of life—wealth and social distinction.[292]

By the eighteenth century, the curriculum of girls' schools included history, geography, literature, and current affairs. Stone quotes one woman as writing, "Boys at grammar school are taught Latin and Greek, despise the simpler paths of learning, and are generally ignorant of useful matters of fact, about which a girl is much better informed." And in 1791 the *Gentleman's Magazine* admitted that "the fair sex has asserted its rank, and challenged that natural equality of intellect which nothing but the influence of human institutions could have concealed for a moment."[293] Nevertheless, girls' education in the eighteenth century lacked the classical linguistic skills taught to sixteenth-century women, and thus precluded access to untranslated works.[294]

In Geneva there were almost no schools for girls, and there was a tremendous difference in male and female literacy. Monter relates the shock of three sophisticated Genevan men who traveled to Italy in 1751 and heard Laura Bassi's lecture on physics in Milan: "Nothing in their culture had prepared them for a genuine *femme savante*."[295]

In France, which had remained a Catholic country, girls were still educated in convent schools. The famous school of Madame de Maintenon, Saint-Cyr, founded in 1686, took girls between the ages of seven and twelve and kept them until they were twenty; it taught them to be obedient housewives, a true brainwashing School for Wives.[296]

Whether because of or in spite of the education they received, women of brilliance and talent continued to appear. In England some brilliant feminists emerged at the end of the seventeenth century, among them Aphra Behn and Mary Astell; Astell wrote (in 1706), "If absolute sovereignty be not necessary in a state, how comes it to be so in a family? Or if in a family, why not in a state? ... Is it not then partial in men to the last degree to contend for and practise that arbitrary dominion in their families which they abhor and exclaim against in the state? ... If all men are born free, how is it that all women are born slaves?"[297] In 1770 women founded an exclusive club, the Female Coterie, to which men could come only as guests. It was the first purely female club, and was subjected to considerable ridicule.[298] The Female Coterie was not an intellectual group, but its very existence was a feminist statement. It reflected a climate created partly by the feminists still engaged in the old *querelle des femmes*, a climate which would give birth, at the end of the century, to the work of Mary Wollstonecraft.

In France women ran salons. These were meetings, in the graceful surroundings of women's homes, of the talented, the distinguished, and the famous. They functioned to introduce people to each other, generate intellectual conversation, advance careers, and publicize people and ideas. "They were the focal point of literary, political, and artistic criticism. Philosophy, religion—every subject had its own coterie, and every subject was discussed at some time in someone's drawing room."[299] People wandered from one salon to another, and certain salons had regular schedules: thus "Pascal and La Rochefoucauld were to be found at the salon of Madame de Sable, Montesquieu at the salon of Madame de Tencin, Voltaire at the salon of Madame du Deffand, and d'Alembert at the salon of Mademoiselle de Lespinasse."[300]

Some of the women associated with these salons were themselves distinguished thinkers, although they did not receive the same veneration as the men. Madame de La Fayette and Mademoiselle de Scudéry wrote novels in the seventeenth century; Madame de Sévigné's letters are literary masterpieces; Madame du Châtelet was a mathematician and astronomer; and Madame de Staël was one of the greatest literary figures of her time.[301] But the brilliant men they fostered and stimulated wished them to be merely comforters of men. The writings of the *philosophes* treat women as inferior to men intellectually, physically, and emotionally.

Moreover, the science of this age verified what the Athenians had believed and the Christians had institutionalized: women were inferior to men. Facts seemed to bear them out. The sparse diets still fed to girls and women, the terrible stays and corsets and back straighteners they wore, had induced frail health in many women of the upper and middle class. "By a strange twist of cultural fate, the sex which is the toughest and most resilient of the two became identified with both physical and psychological delicacy and debility."[302] The blind and prejudiced medical "knowledge" of the physicians bore out this idea: in every way, women were inferior by nature.

But just as in England there were women working against the prevailing current—one that was by now so strong it swept most women before it—so were there in France, and in the very salons frequented by the *philosophes*. Carolyn Lougee has shown how the French salons in the seventeenth and eighteenth centuries continued the *querelle* in another dimension.[303] In the sixteenth century, the *querelle* had centered on the moral worth of women; in the seventeenth, it centered on the influence exerted by women on French social structure. People argued about whether or not women should have salons, basing their arguments on the most profound question—were women fully human? It was stated (as in Islam) that women did not have souls, were not created in the image of God, who was male, and were part of a subhuman species—a link between man and the animals. But this debate was the mask for a political argument. Women were fostering the careers of artists and intellectuals or merely rich men, attempting to advance them into the higher reaches of the social hierarchy. Men who wished the nobility to remain a small, exclusive club opposed women's salons because they opposed this goal. Moreover, women were deeply committed to this goal, since they included themselves among those who should be advanced. By defending women as human, lucid, and possessed of souls, they also defended the right of those who had not been born to the aristocracy to equal distinction by virtue of talent. What the women stressed was the fundamental equality of all people.[304]

The "opposition was vehement for the same reason that feminists were ardent: because the place of women had ramifications for all sectors of politics and the economy."[305] Both the women and their opponents agreed that women holding positions of public influence would change value systems, social structures, and economic practices: as in the battle in the United States and Britain over woman suffrage, both sides agreed on the consequences but disagreed on the desirability of those consequences.

The women "won" that battle, but not for themselves. The social elite of France was transformed by new ennoblements and the assimilation of new-rich families. The salons were still necessary, however, for the *bourgeois gentilhomme* was a ludicrous figure and had to be taught manners by women, as in the medieval courts of love. The women won little for themselves, but their thinking would erupt again, during the revolution for which they helped to prepare the ground.

## 8. REVOLUTION

Before plunging into the complex history of the more recent past, we may pause for a few generalizations about the many cultures we have glanced at. First, women gain the use of power—not the right to it—in periods of loose control. In conditions of severe hardship, like famine or war, women and men struggle together for survival; in periods of tight control, men exclude women. Women can use their talents only marginally in times that have margins.

Just as striking is the unending and profound need of men to control and degrade women, a need so urgent that one can believe men's argument that they cannot be men without such control. This argument is based on a definition of manhood as a state of volition and freedom from necessity (nature). Because no human is actually in such a state, as long as this definition is entertained men will require an inferior class whose degradation offers a standard by which they can measure themselves and offer self-congratulations for their good fortune. Feminists are appalled at the irrationality of men who persist in regarding women as inferior despite the example of strong, intelligent women functioning with competence. But no example can carry weight sufficient to offset men's need to maintain their culturally inherited image, and that need is self-justifying: if women (or blacks, or any class seen as inferior) are not *really* any more tied to necessity and nonvolition than men, men will make sure that they are, through laws, exclusions, and prejudices.

There are those who, in the face of all evidence to the contrary, continue to believe that women are by nature inferior to men. If this were the case, however, there would have been no need for the creation of laws and institutions constricting women's rights and freedom, excluding them from the public world. If any class is actually inferior to any other class in all ways—physically, emotionally, and intellectually—it is not necessary to subjugate the inferior class. As Aldous Huxley implicitly suggested in *Brave New World*, the only way to keep a class in servitude is to see to it that the group is *born* inferior: in his novel, fetuses are slotted into lower classes by their treatment from the moment of conception. Men have had to manipulate women into inferiority.

Finally, in the eras we have been examining, women have tended not to fight for themselves as a distinct class. When Roman women protested, they claimed the rights of the patrician class to which they belonged. Women fought, suffered, and died as Christians in the Roman Empire, as Gnostics or "heretics" in the Christian world, as Protestants or dissidents in Catholic states and as Catholics in Protestant states. But they did not struggle and die as women for women. The first recorded example of their doing so was during the French Revolution.

## Women, Work, and the French Revolution

The intellectual and cultural currents we have discussed had little effect on people who lived on the land. Mostly illiterate, isolated, and absorbed in work, they had a tradition that was unaltered for centuries and probably seemed unalterable. Those who owned enough land to provide for the wants of a family were the fortunate ones.

As always, the women worked harder than the men and were the backbones of such families. They reaped, threshed, collected and spread dung, and plowed. The wife always did the work of the kitchen garden and dairy—milking, making butter and cheese, caring for the poultry, making up medicinal potions from the herbs in the kitchen garden. She also supervised the children and servants, if there were any. She rose at dawn. She baked bread daily, brewed beer for the house, made sure the soap was boiled, the candles molded, and the meat smoked or salted for the long winter. She preserved fruits and vegetables and made jellies; she also cooked the daily meals, did the washing, made the cloth the family used, and sewed its clothing.[306]

However, not all farms could support a family, and often one or more members had to seek income elsewhere. In the country, women hired themselves out for mowing, reaping, and sheep shearing, although they were paid less than half of what men received for such work. They wove, or sometimes they did the spinning—the most tedious and time-consuming step in cloth production—while their husbands wove. Women had less to eat than men; they gave birth frequently. It is not surprising then that their life expectancies were lower than men's. But for both sexes the life expectancy was under thirty years and few people lived beyond forty.[307]

Yet such lives were the most secure of all lower-class lives. Those who owned no land, who lived in towns, had a more precarious existence. Unless they had a highly specialized skill, even men who worked for wages earned little more than enough to keep themselves alive. Women were always paid less and often had children to support. Domestic service was recompensed mainly by grim and scanty room and board, with enough left to purchase over some years the sheets and household linen which constituted a working girl's dowry. Married women spun wool or cotton and made lace. Lace making was "the most flourishing female industry in France even if the lace-maker only received a pittance for labours which would ultimately take her sight."[308] Excluded from the new commercial organizations that had superseded the guilds, women still made up the bulk of workers in the female garment trades: they were seamstresses, milliners, corset makers, embroiderers, ribbon makers, and glove makers.[309] The only work available to middle-class women of some education was as governesses or ladies-in-waiting to gentlewomen; such work paid paltry wages, but it did provide a place to live and food to sustain life.[310]

Poor women occupied the lowest rung of the employment ladder. They performed the heavy, distasteful, menial tasks, especially load carrying. They carried soil, heavy vegetables for market, water, wood—anything. In cities they worked as rag sorters, cinder sifters, refuse collectors, and assistants to masons and bricklayers.[311]

Under the pressure of poverty, many men abandoned the families they could not feed, "not able to bear the cries which they could not relieve."[312] In Metz, after the Revolution had begun and it was possible, 268 working women sought divorce for desertions that had occurred five or nine years earlier, during periods of severe dearth (in 1785 and 1789).[313] The curé of Bort wrote that he was overwhelmed with the laments of women who came to him to beg bread but also to report that their husbands threatened to leave them if they did not let the youngest children die; a curé in Tours described a "hierarchy of hunger": women, he said, are not the first to die of hunger, but they are the first to feel its pangs because they deprive themselves to feed husband and children. He compared mothers to the symbolic pelican who gives her blood to feed her young. Olwen Hufton adds, "This is not to say that women did not drink, thieve, lie, prostitute themselves, indulge in every criminal practice one can think of, but that in general they clung more devotedly to their families."[314] The importance of this devoted and self-sacrificing figure was "immense"; if she died or became incapacitated, the family was likely "to cross the narrow but extremely meaningful barrier between poverty and destitution."[315]

It was the masses of people of this large, ignored, and despised class, the poor, who propelled the social protest of late-eighteenth-century France into a revolution, and it was often poor women who protested independently, or led a protest, badgering men into joining them. Women had protested before on economic matters, during the British Civil War, for instance. But in the French Revolution, women also protested against exclusionary laws and practices.

Women were excluded from all political forums, including the assembly, the Estates General. But they had the right of petition to the king. Early in 1789, poor illiterate women dictated a list of their complaints to a scribe and submitted them in a set of unofficial *cahiers*, notebooks. They complained of poverty, tax collectors, the grim speculators who caused the price of bread to rise. They charged that their sick children were jammed four to a bed in city hospitals, with no measures taken against the spread of communicable diseases. Middle-class women demanded equal laws for men and women, access to education, and protection against their husbands' abuse of their bodies and their dowries. Working women wanted work. The *cahiers* were full of hope. They had no effect.[316]

Alerted to the king's plan to starve Paris into submission, Parisians stormed the Bastille on July 14, and violence broke out in city and countryside. A new parliamentary body was formed, to express the will of the nation: the National Assembly. It was charged with framing a new constitution, and in August of 1789 it issued the Declaration of the Rights of Man and the Citizen. It made no mention of women. When, on October 5, the market women discovered there was no bread in Paris, six thousand of them marched the twelve miles to Versailles to protest to the king personally. He promised to help them, and they marched triumphantly back to Paris with the royal family in tow. But nothing changed, and six months later, Reine Audu, a market woman, was sentenced to a year in prison for helping to lead the October march. Nevertheless, the women's march reinforced the the National Assembly's pressure on the king to sanction the Declaration of Rights.[317]

In the years that followed, women were extremely active, both in trying to assist the National Assembly in creating a new constitution, and in their own behalf. Prosperous women donated their jewels to the Assembly; actresses, singers, and demimondaines, along with respectable matrons, gave money and politicked. A playwright, Olympe de Gouges, wrote political tracts praising the Revolution—*and* the king. Women began to produce their own newspapers, and demanded rights to education, to serve on juries, to take part in electoral assemblies; they called for reform of marriage laws and for the right to divorce. They founded clubs for women, hundreds of clubs, even in the countryside. They marched in processions, some carrying arms.[318]

In 1791 the king attempted to escape from France, and the people became aware that foreign powers might intervene on his behalf. There was another political crisis, and although the Assembly was not at that moment concerned with women's rights, women participated in and led demonstrations against the monarchy, and were among those fired on by the National Guards under Lafayette's direction. The king finally took an oath to support the new constitution. Olympe de Gouges, in protest against its failure to mention women's rights, published a Declaration of the Rights of Woman and the Citizen, in which she proposed freedom of thought for women, equal rights in property, government employment, and better education for women. She also listed reform of marriage laws and a "social contract" between husbands and wives. She argued that if women had the right to mount the platform to the guillotine, they deserved the right to mount political platforms. This was sadly prophetic, as she herself was later beheaded by the republicans for her royalist sympathies.[319]

In April 1792, France declared war on Prussia and Austria, and later that year foreign troops invading France met little resistance from the French Army; the people began to suspect the king of treachery. Throughout the military phase of the Revolution, women acted with strong national loyalty. Even before the outbreak of war, they asked for the right to bear arms and to train with the men; they demonstrated and organized. Women fought in the insurrection at the Tuileries that resulted in the overthrow of the monarchy. France was declared a Republic in September of 1792, and the king was executed in January 1793. The events in France threatened the monarchies of Europe (much as socialist victories threaten capitalist nations), and by the spring of 1793 the French were fighting a coalition of five countries. Women participated as fully as they were permitted in the defense of France: they rolled bandages, were *tricoteuses*, knitting clothing for soldiers, and went to battle with their men. Some disguised themselves as men and were recognized as women only because they were singled out for special praise for bravery.[320]

So in 1792 and 1793, the new Republic rewarded women by granting them rights to divorce, custody of infants and daughters, equal inheritance rights, and the rights of wives to share family property. In 1794 and 1795, it decreed the founding of free primary schools for all children, compulsory and segregated by gender. (These schools were never actually established.) Political rights were not forthcoming, however, and women founded political clubs. The leaders of the Revolution believed deeply that they were furthering the natural rights of man; among those rights, it seems, was the right to an inferior mate. They were not at all sympathetic to women's demands for a public voice; they considered such demands subversive. As the ruling elite broke into two distinct factions—the conservative, professional, ambitious Girondins, and the more democratic, more tolerant Jacobins—and struggle between them mounted, both were suspicious of, and actively impeded, all political activity by women: women were publicly whipped, imprisoned, and guillotined. Some women formed a group to support the Terror; they patrolled the streets in trousers with pistols in their belts; other women attacked them. Charlotte Corday assassinated Jean Paul Marat, a Jacobin who had accused Mme. Roland, the wife of a Girondin minister, of being an influence upon her husband (Mme. Roland later ended in prison for this sin). Women were active on every side, and the National Convention, which had become the governing body of France, turned against women entirely: first women's political clubs were suppressed, then all political action by women. Eventually women were forbidden to attend popular assemblies.[321]

After Robespierre fell, the Terror was ended but so were price controls. Inflation leaped and the poor of Paris starved. Whole families, unable to bear their hunger, jumped together into the Seine and drowned. The daily bread ration fell from six to four to two ounces. Again women rioted and organized marches. In May of 1795, poor women gathered in the streets; they called men away from their work, forced shops to close, persuaded other women to join them, and beat drums calling men to arms. They surged into the hall of the Convention demanding "Bread and the Constitution of 1793!" The next day they marched again, many thousands strong, and received promises; the following day the Convention ordered the army to surround Saint-Antoine, a rebellious poor neighborhood, and starve it into submission; the day after that, the Convention decreed that women were disturbers of the peace and must remain inside their homes. Gatherings of more than five women were to be dispersed by force.[322]

Women won no political rights as a consequence of the Revolution, but they did win laws protecting their rights in property, marriage, and education. They became a revolutionary force unprecedented in history, a living memory and an example for women during the uprising of the Paris Commune in 1871. But they had no time to consolidate their gains and build upon them. In 1804, Napoleon Bonaparte became emperor and wrote a code of law depriving women of all rights, requiring their unconditional obedience to father and husband, denying girls and married women citizenship, forbidding women to practice law or act as guardians. He forbade investigation of paternity and prescribed harsh treatment of unmarried mothers and their children. He took away, in fact, all rights except that of divorce, but that too was removed after the 1815 restoration of the Bourbon monarchy. The laws of the Republic lasted a little less than a decade; the rule of the Napoleonic Code lasted for a century.[323]

## Women, Work, and the Industrial Revolution

Between the fourteenth and sixteenth centuries, a series of laws regulating labor were passed in England. These laws had the inadvertent consequence of forcing all poor, unemployed countrywomen over twelve into farm labor at extremely low wages, while men, who were more mobile, were able to evade the regulations. In the late fifteenth century in Metz an ordinance was passed decreeing that "all married women living apart from their husbands, and girls of evil life, shall go to the brothels."[324] Any woman living alone and poor women who worked were treated as prostitutes. (This is still true in much of the world, even in "advanced" countries like Italy.)

Everywhere women were being squeezed out of the guilds. Increasingly they were confined to a few specialties—dressmaking, street vending of food, brewing, and domestic service. A quarter of the adult female population of Coventry in 1523 were maidservants.[325] When brewing became a factory operation, women lost control of one of their traditional monopolies.[326] Despite their increasing circumscription, however, working women offered no organized protest.

Part of the reason for their silence was a sense of illegitimacy: women were not supposed to speak in public. However, in the seventeenth century the Protestant movement, especially some of the radical sects, offered women a new sense of legitimacy, and one of the most startling manifestations of women's new confidence was their behavior during the English Civil War. In 1642, "women, operating without help from fathers, husbands, or other males, took independent political action on the national level as women, for the first time in

English history." More than four hundred working-class women made destitute by the war petitioned Parliament for a change in public policy. "When the outraged Duke of Richmond cried, 'Away with these women, we were best have a Parliament of women,' the petitioners attacked him physically and broke his staff of office." In 1643, thousands of women mobbed Parliament demanding peace and work.[327] They were told to go home, but about five hundred remained, and were shot, stabbed, and killed by the sword. But again in 1647, maids petitioned Parliament complaining about unreasonable working conditions.[328]

In the spring of 1649, masses of women assembled at Westminster; again they protested the economic crisis, but they also demanded the release of the leaders of the Levellers, who had been imprisoned. The House told them they were dealing "with matters above their heads, that Parliament had given an answer to their husbands, who legally represented them, and that they should 'go home and look after your own business and meddle with your housewifery.'" They retorted that they had a right to an equal share in the ordering of the Church, "because in the free enjoying of Christ in his own laws, and a flourishing estate in the Church . . . consisteth the happiness of women as well as men." If this was so, they had also a right to a share in the state: "We have an equal share and interest with men in the Commonwealth." Their protest, however, came to nothing, and Stone comments that "even the Leveller leaders always excluded women from their proposals for a greatly enlarged suffrage."[329]

These protests emerged in a period of upheaval, when women always become more vocal and active because authority that would normally control and punish them has broken down. In the British Civil War, upper-class women became warriors, defending their manor houses against attacks from both sides. At the Restoration, with the reestablishment of traditional authority, women were again silenced.

And as the West moved inexorably toward greater "masculinization" of life, women's condition continued to deteriorate, in terms of legal rights, freedom of action, and economically. By the late eighteenth century, when in France poor women were rising in protest, the English jurist Sir William Blackstone could write that "the husband and wife are one, and the husband is that one." Wives could own nothing. Not only all property but the children too belonged solely to the husband. Even after his death a widow had no rights over her own children unless he had made her their guardian in his will. Regardless of the provocation, a woman who deserted her husband could take nothing with her—not money or children—and her husband could compel her to return. If she earned money, or someone gave her financial assistance, her husband had the right to seize it from her at any time. The 1857 Divorce Act permitted a man to divorce his wife for adultery; she could not divorce him for the same deed unless it was accompanied by cruelty, desertion, bigamy, rape, sodomy, or bestiality.[330]

The position of working women in England, like that of working women in France, had been precarious since the seventeenth century. Earlier, men of all classes gave time and care to their children and young men did domestic work. There were some women capitalists running coal mines, keeping tennis courts, assaying gold and silver, leasing land, recovering penalty debts, transporting goods, getting patents and monopolies, acting as merchants and shipping agents. Some of these were widows, but many ran businesses in their own right.[331] Women worked in all three classes of industry—skilled trades, retail trades, and provision trades. But by the seventeenth century they could work in these only as their husbands' partners or assistants: the medieval right of *femme sole* was gone. As guild rules changed, and craft guilds became trade organizations, women were driven into either dependence on men or work in one of the "sweated" industries—those which did not provide their workers with the means for keeping themselves and their families alive.[332]

At first men and women wove cloth together. When a heavy loom came into use, women were excluded on the ground they had insufficient strength to work it. Men who owned their own looms hired women to work them, however, which led men who worked for wages to complain, and formal orders were passed forbidding women from weaving. Still, they went on, weaving the less lucrative items—tape, ribbon, strip gartering—right into the nineteenth century. They worked very hard at home doing piecework to get threepence or threepence farthing a day—enough to feed only one person. The result was the pauperization of large numbers of women and lowered physical efficiency of both them and their children.[333]

The Industrial Revolution was not a sudden event. There were capitalists—men who bought cheap and sold at a profit—as early as the tenth century (see Chapter Five, pp. 397–398). By the fourteenth century some merchants had become entrepreneurs; instead of buying a product from an artisan and re-selling it, they hired workers to make the product, paying them low wages and controlling the process of production and merchandising. Such an enterprise required an initial outlay of money—capital. Gradually, as science led to the invention of technology, heavy machinery was introduced. The first major change for workers of the eighteenth and nineteenth centuries was that they had to leave their homes to do their work, and that they had to work at hours set by others. This made it difficult for parents to tend small children while the family worked, and to perform the chores necessary to maintain a small farm if the family owned or leased one.

Early capitalists hired the entire family as a unit, but men were preferred for work with heavy machinery. As work was shifted more and more from the home, women with small children were under increasing disadvantage. The Industrial Revolution did create many new jobs, but most of them were restricted to men or to single women. The new organization was a hardship for men too. They were unused to long hours of work, and now were required to put in ten-, twelve-, or even sixteen-hour days. By the early nineteenth century, Marvin Harris writes, "Factory hands and miners were putting in twelve hours a day under conditions that no self-respecting Bushman . . . or Iroquois would have tolerated. At the day's end, after contending with the continuous whine and chatter of wheels and shafts, dust, smoke, and foul odors, the operators of the new labor-saving devices retired to their dingy hovels full of lice and fleas . . .

Only the wealthy could afford meat. Rickets, a new crippling disease of the bones caused by lack of sunshine and dietary sources of vitamin D, became endemic in the cities and factory districts. The incidence of tuberculosis and other diseases . . . also increased. . . . In 1810 the workers in the factory districts of England were chanting 'Bread or blood.' More and more the impoverished masses had to steal in order to eat. Annual convictions for larceny in England rose 540 percent between 1805 and 1833; 26,500 people were hanged between 1806 and 1833, mostly for thefts of minor sums of money."[334]

Workers' protests eventually led to the work week being reduced to six, then five and a half days, but conditions remained terrible, and as always women suffered more than men. First, they continued to be paid half of what men earned for the same work and to be excluded from better-paying jobs on grounds of physical ineptitude. It was the men of their own class, not the owners, who protested against the hiring of women. Often owners would fire men from jobs men claimed exclusive rights to and hire women (despite their "physical ineptitude") because they could pay them less. But men were successful at keeping women out of jobs that required long apprenticeship; they also formed unions and fought to keep women out of them. Some jobs required special technical training for which women were considered inadequate—until they were needed during World War I.

Second, women were subject to physical harassment in the workplace. In the days of home workshops, men had beaten their wives, maids, and children; they continued to do so in the early days of the factories, when the family went to work together.[335] However, the family unit was soon broken up, and women were placed under male supervisors who were strangers but who took over the paternal prerogatives.

The experience of women was similar throughout western and central Europe and in Russia: wherever the Industrial Revolution occurred. In the textile industry, women worked a fifteen-to-eighteen-hour day in factories with no toilets, no place to eat or sit down, and little time to do either. The heat was excessive and they were exposed to chemicals and fibers; there was considerable brown lung disease. Children began to work at the age of five or six. "To stop workers from rebelling against the low wages and inhuman working conditions, factory owners maintained a brutal system of control which included punishments in the form of instant dismissal, transfer to the worst jobs, and . . . fines for the slightest infractions. . . . Women were also sexually abused . . . and faced punishments or dismissal if they resisted."[336]

Shopgirls in France worked from 8:15 in the morning until nine or ten at night. They had to walk up and down six flights of stairs to fetch merchandise, and were sent on errands that had them climbing as many as forty flights of stairs a day. In such a job they had to spend money to maintain a decent appearance, but they were paid one franc a day and a commission of between three and twelve francs.[337] In Lille in the 1830s, women in the spinning mills earned between seventy-five centimes and one franc seventy-five centimes a day; in Paris in 1860, seventeen thousand working women (17 percent) earned less than or only one franc twenty-five centimes a day. A woman could not feed and house herself, let alone children, on this amount.[338] In 1873, 200,000 Frenchwomen earned less than five centimes a day; between 1889 and 1893, they received half the pay of a man for the same day's work.[339] In the United States in 1918, factory women received half the pay of men; in German mines in 1920, women got 25 percent less than men for the same amount of coal dug.[340]

Tuberculosis was the great killer of the period, but more women died of it than men. In Oldham, England, a mill town, in the early 1850s, deaths from tuberculosis were double the national average, and triple among women twenty-five to thirty-five. Every year fifteen out of every thousand mill workers were killed or mutilated by the machines. In the 1860s working mothers in Bradford, England, lost 68.8 percent of their children, and even in the twentieth century, mothers working in small London trades lost 55.5 percent of theirs.[341]

A report on conditions for women in Russian factories written in 1914 describes millions of female workers, nearly half a million in textiles alone. They also did bookbinding, and made cardboard, shoes, rubber, bricks, earthenware, and china; they were in printing and stamping. In all these trades they did the heaviest and hardest labor. In wood depots and sawmills they had to carry tree trunks and boards. Thousands of these women were less than fourteen years old. The government decreed a minimum of twenty-one rubles a month for men, seventeen for women. The women lived on tea and bread, with a bottle of milk twice a month. They were fined for laughing, feeling unwell, or sitting down. If they were ill, they were discharged. They were physically punished. Although the usual day was ten to eleven and a half hours, sometimes they were required to work sixteen to eighteen hours, and physical force—such as tying them to the machines to keep them standing up—was used on children too tired to work overtime. When the women went on strike, the owners fired them all and hired younger girls. Women were raped, sexually harassed, and punished for resistance to sexual abuse.[342]

Married women fared very poorly under the new system. Owners did not want to hire them, believing they would be unreliable, and male workers did not want their competition. They could do piecework at home, but such work paid less, sometimes only half as much as factory wages. It was the only alternative, however, for mothers who had children under five, too young to work themselves. Nevertheless, these women were often the main breadwinners, since men were frequently out of work, or abandoned their families. Married women were also under a disadvantage because they could not travel to places where more lucrative work was found but were bound to remain near where their husbands worked. In addition to the burden of caring for home and children, and working long hours, they regularly walked much further every day than men to and from their jobs.[343]

Outside the home, women labored in textile mills or peddled goods in the streets; inside it, they took in boarders, or laundry, or did piecework for garment manufacturers. Inside or outside the home, they also marketed, cooked, and did the washing up; they did laundry, sewing, and cleaning; they raised and educated the children. Although our image of the Victorian family, created by novels, includes a staff of servants, most families were too poor to have servants and too poor to send their children to school. Even middle-class families could not afford such things: in 1803, 32,000 English families had incomes under a hundred pounds a year; by 1867, nearly 800,000 had incomes under a hundred pounds a year. Since the average yearly wage of female servants was about twenty pounds a year, and the average price of boarding school 130 pounds, such families were unable to afford household help or education for their children.[344]

In poor families, the lot of the mother was dire. She had worse food than her husband, and often lived on bread, drippings, and tea. The little meat that was bought usually went to the father. Surveys of the period 1860 to 1950 in England reveal that seven to eight pence a day was spent on men's food, while the entire remainder of the family lived on threepence a day or less. Large expenses, like another childbirth, were paid for by cutting back on the food of the women and children, while men, as a rule, had pocket money for smoking and drinking, sometimes as much as a quarter to a half of their wages.[345]

Such a financial arrangement was not (necessarily) caused by male abuse. Women themselves fostered it, denying themselves food even when they were pregnant to give it to the men. They did this not because they were self-sacrificing or because they believed their husbands more deserving than themselves, but as a matter of practicality: they and their children were dependent upon the man. A woman was reluctant to complain about a man spending his free hours in the pub with his mates, smoking and drinking up money that could have fed the children. A man discontented with his treatment at home could take himself and his wages off, leaving the family to starve entirely: and many did. Better to have the portion of his wages that he did not drink up, even though his presence brought the risk of further pregnancies, more mouths to feed. This situation made women promising recruits for the temperance movement when it began in the mid-nineteenth-century United States.

In nineteenth-century England, 42 percent of women between twenty and forty were without husbands, and the number was equally high in western Europe. By 1850 or so there were thousands of prostitutes in major cities like London and Paris and around military bases.[346] People without resources were sent to the workhouse, where they were separated from their children and spouses.[347] In one of the best of these, women were required to work from seven in the morning until seven at night and to go to bed at nine. Silence was enforced in the workrooms, and the women needed permission to go out during their free hours.[348]

As most married women were dropped from the labor force, the status of married women also fell. Yet during this period, women were bombarded by propaganda idealizing motherhood and women's domestic role. This propaganda held up a standard that only a tiny percentage of women could attain, a life of idleness. The irony of the situation was probably lost on women totally occupied with a grim struggle for mere survival. A French writer summed up the case of women: "Pet or beast of burden: such is woman almost exclusively today."[349]

The Industrial Revolution unquestionably made life easier in some ways, and perhaps more interesting as well. Life expectancy rises in industrial societies, and for women, who are the hardest workers in every society, certain advances have been boons.[350] At the same time, the Industrial Revolution thrust millions of people into a level of misery, enslavement, and destitution lower than had been seen before; this process continues in our own era, although obliquely, as the methods of agribusiness and multinational corporations thrust into starvation people on distant continents who once were self-sustaining, out of sight of the industrial societies for whose sake they are being exploited.

Michel Foucault describes industrialism as a new mechanism of power which is "more dependent upon bodies and what they do than upon the Earth and its products." It extracts time and labor, rather than wealth and commodities, from bodies. In its old forms, power manifested itself periodically; the lords of earth maintained themselves and their projects by taxes, levies, or corvées collected from people discontinuously, on certain occasions, allowing people time to feel free, and perhaps to find ways to cheat. In its new form, power manifests itself constantly, "by means of surveillance."[351]

Before the Industrial Revolution, most men were to some degree their own bosses, as farmers, artisans, or entrepreneurs. Often they began life under the eye of a master to whom they were apprenticed, or of a father or other relative. Such training involved punishment as well as surveillance, but the surveillance was necessarily intermittent, and they could look forward to a time when they would work unsupervised. Men's hours were not long, and there were frequent holidays. Farmers worked long hours at certain times of the year, but for months they were relatively idle.

This is not true under the factory system. Required to appear at a stipulated time and place and to work a certain number of hours a day and a number of days a week, men were watched continuously by overseers, supervisors, and managers. Not a moment of idleness was tolerated. Demands made of humans were based not on human need but on the machine, which could run on and on untiringly until it fell apart, and even then could often be repaired. At the beginning of the industrial era, employers expected workers to labor seven days a week, from ten to twelve—or more—hours a day. The many holidays that broke up medieval life vanished. So did any sense of autonomy.

But those who oversaw were themselves overseen. Foucault discusses Jeremy Bentham's Panopticon, a plan for a prison in which guards situated in a central glass tower have continual surveillance of all prisoners locked in cells or working in a surrounding glass-walled structure. This plan was the model for many nineteenth-century buildings. The unexpected irony of it is that the guards are as subject as the prisoners to surveillance. "It's a machine in which everyone is caught, those who exercise power just as much as those over whom it is exercised . . . There is no need for arms, physical violence, material constraints. Just a gaze."[352]

In fact, there *is* a need for arms, violence, and constraints to keep prisoners or other coerced people in line, but in the modern form of enslavement, which we may not call enslavement, the threat of physical coercion lies at a distance like the threat of starvation, which seems absurd in the face of one after another high-heaped supermarket. The "gaze" does not substitute for harsher methods of coercion; it is their bland representative, a symbol. Middle-class people may walk securely, complacent that "their" governments would never use violence on *them*, good citizens and upholders of the state, but history has shown that it would and has and does so today in scores of nations. Most poor people are fully aware of their precarious condition. The function of the gaze, then, is not to maintain order cheaply but rather to remind the overseen and the overseers that stronger methods of coercion are available.

The gaze has another function, however, one that goes to the moral core of the industrial age. There are many reasons for work. One, which applies to a minority, is that it is fun—it challenges, engages, exercises one's faculties, and brings rewards of various sorts, even though it is inevitably tedious and wearing at times. Another reason is survival: the pleasure may be minimal, but it offers workers the satisfaction of independence, of sustaining themselves and perhaps others. When work of this sort does not reward the worker enough to sustain life, it engenders despair and desperate thoughts. And finally, there is work that is utterly coerced, performed under the threat of some sort of punishment. The line between this kind of work and work for survival is very tenuous.

One can say *all* work is coerced, since most people work to survive (according to their definition of what constitutes survival—whether bread, drippings, tea, a hovel, some heat, and a pair of shoes, two cars, membership in a country club, trips abroad). But some people work not primarily for economic survival but for the well-being of the entire self, for their integrity, their ability to use their intellect, imagination, creativity, aggressiveness, skills, whatever. Even such people, however, fall into situations of coercion that can poison their activity. The "gaze," surveillance, can poison *any* work because it creates the illusion or reminds one of the fact that one is working *because one is watched*. It turns all work into coerced labor, into a power struggle between the watcher and the watched, even when the worker is willing to do the task at hand. It negates personal will, overrides it, gives the work the feeling of enslavement even if that is not the worker's attitude toward it. Surveillance separates will from act.

Peasants of the Middle Ages labored in the face of nature to bring in crops, to make the butter set, to spin and weave, to preserve food for the winter; their work was arduous, their standard of living generally very low, and they no doubt cursed the lord's agents who came round demanding a share. But they had clear distinctions between their needs and the demands of their oppressors. When the very gestures of one's hands and feet, one's speech or silence, laughter, faint, illness, seem controlled and judged by a watcher, personal freedom ceases to exist, all actions seem responses—whether of deference or rebellion—to an onlooker who controls. One does excellent work perhaps because one prizes excellence, but it is interpreted as a desire to please the controller. One who is capable of good work may produce sloppy work out of resentment at the controller. Time seized for idleness seems a victory, and indifference toward the product or the people serviced seems the only independent stance.

Certainly some workers lived under such conditions before the Industrial Revolution; what changed was that after it *most* workers lived in this way. Not just those who worked for wages at machines or at desks, but their overseers, and their supervisors, and the managers themselves were caught in an ascending coercive scale. Indeed, almost no one was free from this sense of being controlled, of having no will of one's own.

This was the state in which most women had lived since the onset of patriarchy. Laws and customs in many of the cultures we have talked about deprived women of exercising will over their bodies, their minds, their relationships, their children, their own lives. The Industrial Revolution, that great triumph of human control over nature, in fact had the effect of depriving men of a sense of control and placing them in a position similar to women's.

It is understandable, then, that during this period of the nineteenth century, certain attitudes toward women, not in themselves new, were carried to an extreme that *was* new with an intensity that gave them a different character. If in the face of the loss of any illusion of volition and autonomy men were to maintain a "manhood" that was defined as volition and freedom from necessity, they had to degrade even further women and other groups considered inferior. This was the age of the many imperialist ventures in Africa and the savage treatment of Africans by Europeans, of blacks by whites. Similar ventures occurred in Asia. Out there, far from the machine, a man could still feel like a man. In the cities, controlled, regulated, bought and sold—like women—men outside the small, privileged, and shrinking upper class abandoned the image of sensitivity, social grace, and emotionality that had been popular in the previous two centuries, abandoned the notion of the "gentleman" who did not soil his hands with work, and adopted an image, still popular today, of hardheaded hardheartedness, of harshness and brutality, toughness, *realism*.

Women were cast into the roles that most contrasted with this one. They were "exalted" as pure, virginal, frail maidens out of touch with reality and unable to bear its pressures; they needed men to intervene between them and the world, men to guide and control them. Men were not primarily links, however; they were firmly set within reality, and the fragile girl was the link between a man and something divinely pure, free from the taint of this new, dirty, completely male reality. The maidens grew up (or didn't) to be housewives who might still be exalted in literature and in their men's boasts, as angels, madonnas, sweet smiling agents of morality and divinity, but who were also treated with peremptory contempt and authoritarian cruelty by men who required inferiors. As Barbara Bodichon, a nineteenth-century feminist, put it, "A woman is courted and wedded as an angel, and yet denied the dignity of a rational and moral being ever after."[353] It was in this period, the latter half of the nineteenth century, that sexuality reached a nadir of respect, and efforts to control it expanded. To this day, Victorianism is synonymous in most imaginations with extreme sexual repression. In the last third of the century, the *femme fatale* emerged in art, literature, and psychology, the vampire woman who was utterly irresistible and who dragged men down into sex and emotion conceived of as insatiable, devouring, and destructive.

There were revolts against the inhuman treatment of workers by those who felt it most directly—not by the managers, who could still maintain an illusion of control because there were so many they could look down on. Sporadic worker uprisings had some success: the work week was shortened; the work day was shortened; in some factories, women overseers were appointed to eliminate sexual harassment of women. But the elimination of severe abuses took a long time because of the difficulty of communal action. The policies of employers set men against women, more highly paid men against lower paid men, and in some places one ethnic group against another.

Industrialization was divisive in many ways. People were divided within themselves: their wills were separated from their acts, their acts separated from the products of those acts, and the products separated from the profits they earned. The family was divided: the husband/father was separated from his children and from the wife/mother. Women, whether they worked inside or outside the home, did not separate themselves from their children. Like the institutionalization of the fourteenth century, the Industrial Revolution "masculinized" society; it fostered "masculine" values and it expanded the male realm. At the same time it isolated men, separating them from the land, from the work of their hands, and from their families. This made them extremely vulnerable, since it deprived them of any identity except their work function. It is still possible to meet a woman for the first time and take her simply as a person, not completely determined by her work; it is not possible to address a man in the same way—he *is* what he does. Thus employers gained the power almost to determine whether or not a man existed. His work is not what a man has, but what he is, and being only that, he fights frantically to maintain his position, in the process further alienating himself from those he loves and from other men. Competition became the primary law of the new reality.

"Feminine" qualities were further degraded; men who demonstrated compassion, sensitivity, or indifference to acquisitiveness were deemed unfit. These qualities, urged upon women by various kinds of literature and by religion, became an absolute requirement for women: what men might not possess women must. But women, constricted within an image of sweetness and docility, complaisance and gentleness, chastity and even nonsexuality, could maintain such qualities only by willfully blinding themselves to what was occurring in the outer world. Women who knew their own misery and resentment maintained brittle smiles, uttering pious phrases that masked rage and resentment; many fell ill—women's health was generally poor in nineteenth-century America.[354] And they taught their children precepts that prepared them for no place on earth.

## Women, Work, and Revolution Within the System

Women had been politically powerless before the Industrial Revolution; they had been deprived of property rights before; and they had long been treated as the second sex. But never before had they been treated as extraneous to the entire business of life, as the ornamental frame around the picture.

Athenian women who were secluded in the home had the knowledge that the well-being, even the survival, of the household depended on their management. This was true also of peasant and bourgeois women throughout the period before the Industrial Revolution. But now, "pet or beast of burden," women had no human standing whatever.

Poor women, the beasts of burden, were entirely absorbed with the survival of their families; although some of them did organize and protest, their rebellions were easily quashed—at first. Middle-class women, part of a new class, the bourgeoisie, which had grown increasingly over the past six centuries, had a different problem. What they faced could be called a schizophrenogenic situation, one that induces insanity: a culture that exalted them and made them impotent with the same stroke.

As we have seen, men's self-image changed with increasing industrialization, and with it, men's behavior. Heightened aggressiveness and competitiveness, a frantic racing toward a goal that suggested power, and a shrugging off of scruples or sensitivities that might impede their race characterized the new breed of men. This class emerged in all industrially developing nations, but nowhere was it more dominant than in raw America. Europe still possessed an entrenched leisure class with a tradition of gentility; the tea table and the salon fostered social intercourse between men and women and a habit of polite and sometimes witty discourse. Both Henry James and Edith Wharton commented on the lack of such a social common ground in the United States, where, except during dances, men and women segregated themselves, the men to talk business, the women to follow what were considered more trivial pursuits.[355]

America's new "aristocracy" was made up of men lacking social background—steel and railroads lords, speculators and bankers—who bought culture and wives who could provide it. Narrow in interest, driven only by the race for money power, they quickly came to dominate America's economic and political life. Even pleasure—felicity—lost its primary value: consumption was valued for its conspicuousness, as Thorstein Veblen pointed out.

Women were primary among the conspicuous elements of well-to-do life. Women of the wealthy wore the jewels and furs and gowns that advertised their husbands' achievements; the well-to-do emulated them. In contrast with the beasts of burden who comprised the majority of women, these women were conspicuously idle, their soft white hands and elaborate dress and coiffures testimony to their freedom from the need to work. In the moral dichotomy of the time, home was heaven and woman was God's emissary on earth, quietly waiting for her man to come back, wearied by the brutal "real" world; woman would then lay a cool hand on a brow, whisper a soft word into an ear, creating an atmosphere of felicity and grace cut off from the roughness and cruelty of the outer world. Even men who were not well-to-do encouraged their wives not to work outside the home, and to be "as beautiful, as delicate, and as cultured as money, good fortune, and application allowed."[356] The ideal of the graceful, cultivated, leisured woman became an ideal for all women in society, even those who had no hope of realizing it.[357] The function of the lady was "to appropriate and preserve both the values and the commodities which her competitive husband, father, and son had little time to honor and enjoy; she was to provide an antidote and a purpose for their labor."[358]

Although they might turn a blind eye to what was happening in the outer world, women were not blind. Caught in utter economic and political impotence, they tried, like the women of the thirteenth and fourteenth centuries, to turn their disadvantage into advantage. With the blessing and assistance of men, women mounted a campaign to exalt "feminine" values and their own role, to give importance to the one task they were still permitted to perform: they founded the "cult of domesticity." The roots of this campaign can be traced back to Rousseau's *Émile*, to the image of woman fostered by the Protestant reformers, and to the fictions of writers who had been influenced by the chivalric tradition and romance. It idealized the mother and wife as "the angel in the house," as Coventry Patmore called her, a ministering semideity who never raised her voice, who was sweet, gentle, submissive, and happy in self-sacrifice. Indeed, self-sacrifice was the core of her nature, the fate she was born for. The woman responsible for the creation of felicity had herself *become* that felicity.

The cult of domesticity had ramifications that cannot be entirely traced. It seems certain that the inhuman standards it upheld were a source of dejection and anxiety for many women who found they could not maintain them, but its wide-scale effects remain a matter of contention.[359]

One result of the new female ethos was a fostering and supporting of the new male ethos. Remaining outside the "real" world in a haven of peace and healing, women provided men with the sustenance they needed to continue in their brutally competitive endeavors. The moral message of the period was an effort to reconcile traditional Christian ethics with an isolating and corrosive individualism by searching for the communal good within autonomous achievement and by warning against the baser nature of man.[360] In his struggle with this baseness, a man had an ally, a better half, his wife, who upheld religion and charities and organized social and cultural events to benefit the community. She thus provided both respite from and justification for his avarice and striving.

The cult of domesticity caught fire; it offered thousands of women a purpose in life. Magazines and manuals taught make-work, something that had not before been necessary on a wide scale—handicrafts and household tasks designed to decorate the person or the home, and to take up time. Many women—and many men—wrote articles, manuals, and books extolling motherhood, domesticity, and the feminine principle. The work of writers and religious leaders in this vein is not found admirable today: none of it reached the status of art or important thought. It could not—no work can that blinks the unpleasant realities of life, casting a rosy glow over the blood on the wall. It is easy enough to despise the efforts of these people, and most critics do. Ann Douglas has blamed the sentimental "feminization" of culture for our present debased culture with its Pollyannaish comedies, its emphasis on consumerism, and its advertising slanted toward the perfect housewife.[361]

But no event has uncomplicated consequences. Men happily concurred in

the assertion that women were morally superior to men, since it left them free
to pursue their own purposes, and cast upon them the image of strong, self-
willed—read volitional—driving heroes superior to the common run of people,
creating a new era of control. But that assertion also offered women a slot, a
role, a function in society, and challenged the notion of women as passive.[362]
Indeed, in the interest of this aloof, nonparticipatory moral superiority, women
strove for higher education. Sophia Smith, who founded Smith College, established it with the hope that "the higher and more thoroughly Christian education of women" would enable them to remove "the evils of society," especially
"the filth" in literature.[363]

The apotheosis of motherhood seems an irony in a period in which prosperous people were having fewer children, and those few were leaving home
sooner because of the spread of public education.[364] But it led to a deeper concentration on the few children a mother had, a greater involvement with children as people—which in turn has had mixed consequences: rich nurturing but
also overprotection, a heightened sense of individuality in children but also a
feeling of great pressure from the family.

The situation is pervaded by ironies. A campaign designed to counter the
dominating thrust of an aggressive and acquisitive society partly reinforces and
furthers it; an effort to exalt the qualities of the feminine principle in fact debases and trivializes them; assertions of women's moral superiority and aloof-
ness from practical affairs help to establish higher education for women which
in its turn leads women to involvement in those affairs; and charitable activities
undertaken in some condescension, out of boredom and women's sense of
themselves as gracious ministering angels, in fact lead to improvement of society.

For this was the result of many charitable activities. Middle-class women
were deeply engaged in several struggles over the course of the nineteenth and
early twentieth centuries. Three strands can be isolated: the struggle for the abolition of slavery; the struggle to improve social welfare; and the struggle for
women's rights. Black women were also deeply involved in the struggle for abolition, sometimes in conjunction with white women and sometimes on their
own. Working-class women and women in the labor movement were also involved in the fight to improve the living conditions of the poor, especially immigrants. At times in these movements, women were able to transcend class
and color differences to fight together as women; at times they fell sadly below
that standard.

There is considerable documentation on these movements. But they are so
complex, involving so many important characters and events, that it is impossible to describe all of them in detail here. Yet this is preeminently *our* history:
what the women of the last century and the beginning of this one did and
thought and changed affects all of us, blacks and whites, women and men. For
this reason I urge the reader to several general accounts of this period of
women's history that are cited in the notes.[365] They are fascinating to read and
moving as well. I find these accounts awesome, and not simply because I am a
woman. They describe arduous and frustrating work performed with good

humor and courage, unremittingly, indefatigably, by generations of women. For me their heroism is more staggering and inspiring than any tale of violence. This section will trace the work of some of these women and the changes they were responsible for.

Unlike violent revolutions, the changes these women brought about did not create a new tyranny in their wake. They were assimilated by the culture, and although some of them have been annulled since, and some need rethinking now, they have endured and they have benefited those they were intended to benefit. Often the names of the women who helped to create new institutions have been erased; few people today remember that Crystal Eastman founded the American Civil Liberties Union but attribute its founding to a man.[366] All of us, but especially women, should know more about our own history.

Because of the enormous complexity of this material, I have concentrated mainly on events in the United States. This is because I am most familiar with this material; because there seems to have been the most agitation here; and because in this raw nation which at the opening of the nineteenth century lacked a fixed aristocracy (or so we are told), there was more freedom for women to move and prejudices stand out strikingly, undisguised by the masks so common in more "civilized" countries.

In the centuries since Europeans settled here, women in the United States had gone through experiences similar to those of the women of Europe. In the early Puritan settlements in New England, women worked in traditional ways on farms or in trade. Unattached women were expected to support themselves, and Puritan town councils sometimes provided parcels of land to needy spinsters. Women produced most of what families needed—all of its cloth and clothing, and much of the shoemaking of the settlers. As the settlements expanded into towns, women expanded their skills, becoming butchers, silversmiths, gunsmiths, and upholsterers. "They ran mills, plantations, tan yards, shipyards, and every kind of shop, tavern, and boarding home. They were gate keepers, jail keepers, sextons, journalists, printers, 'doctoresses,' apothecaries, midwives, nurses, and teachers."[367] They learned their skills just as men did, through apprenticeships. Colonial authorities were more lenient about women's property rights in America than British common law allowed. Women needed no dowry, so marriage and remarriage were freer and easier.[368]

European visitors remarked on the freedom of American women and the esteem in which they were held. Nevertheless, American women saw themselves and were seen by men as auxiliaries to men, supportive of male, not female status, as contributors to the welfare of a whole—the family. Both education and politics were discriminatory. Still, after the Revolution, many localities allowed women to vote. The culture and standards that new waves of immigrants brought from Europe, however, emphasized the propriety of women's position being subordinate and inferior to that of men. The Revolution had created an egalitarian atmosphere in the new country, but that egalitarianism did not extend to women. Women's work outside the home began to be frowned upon, and many businesses and occupations women had formerly pursued were closed to them. Increasingly they were deprived of the right to vote, beginning with New York in 1788 and ending with New Jersey in 1844.[369]

After 1840, the ideal of the genteel lady began to capture the American imagination, and more doors shut. Both black and white women had previously been physicians—one was even an army surgeon; but as medicine became "professionalized," women were excluded from it. Education was also professionalized, again excluding women. Women, who like men had acted as their own attorneys, were excluded from law once it was professionalized. As early as the 1830s women ran shops only in businesses that served strictly women.[370]

At the same time, the franchise was being extended to more and more men, and the professionalization of certain occupations, and entrepreneurship, both open to men, led to upward mobility for great numbers of males. Men gained in wealth and status as women lost it. Gerda Lerner believes it was this sense of deprivation in the white middle class that led to the emergence of the women's movement.[371] Richard Vann believes the tradition of Quakerism was also a factor in this emergence, since the Quakers permitted women to speak at public meetings—the Grimké sisters, Lucretia Mott, and Susan Anthony were all Quakers.[372]

However, the feminist movement in America is deeply rooted in the struggle for abolition. The Grimkés, Angelina and Sarah, were among the first people to speak out publicly against slavery. Daughters of a South Carolina slaveholding family, they left home as young women and went North in 1836 to campaign against slavery. They were attacked—continually and savagely, and sometimes physically; but the grounds of attack were, more often than not, that they as women dared to speak in public forums. They responded by expanding their protest, addressing the issues of slavery and women's rights from the same platform. Lucy Stone also gave her first public lecture for women's rights in 1836. Male abolitionists were uneasy about the merging of the two issues, fearful of losing those sympathetic to abolition by the interjection of a subject few men had sympathy for.[373]

Black women founded the first female antislavery society in the United States, in Salem, Massachusetts, in 1832.[374] In 1833, Lucretia Mott founded the Philadelphia Female Anti-Slavery Society separately from the already existing American (sic) Anti-Slavery Society, because the latter did not permit women to speak at its meetings, though it did permit them to listen. Lucretia Mott managed also to address the men. She made her home a station on the underground railway, and in the face of an armed guard she once helped a black woman escape in her carriage.[375]

In London, in 1840, a World (sic) Anti-Slavery Convention was held; many women attended, including Mott and Elizabeth Cady Stanton. The presence of women delegates outraged the men, who relegated them to galleries where they had to sit behind a curtain. Three men joined them there: Charles Redmond, the black leader of the abolition movement; William Lloyd Garrison; and Nathaniel Rogers.[376] Mott and Stanton were so outraged by this segregation that they determined on their return home to agitate for women's rights, and they held the first Women's Rights Convention in Seneca Falls, New York, in 1848.

The abolition movement continued largely because of women's work. Female antislavery societies outnumbered male groups; women abolitionists largely financed the movement with fund-raising activities, and did much of the work of writing propaganda and distributing magazines and newspapers.[377] They described the lives of slaves.

Seven out of eight slaves, women and men, were field workers.[378] They performed extremely heavy tasks in textile, hemp, and tobacco companies, in sugar refining and rice milling, in transportation and lumbering. Women slaves worked in coal mines and iron foundries, were lumberjacks and ditchdiggers, worked to build levees, railroads, and canals. They were treated like beasts of burden, pulling trams in the mines.[379] Black women were used instead of horses to haul canal boats.[380] The women also had to watch their young children being pressed into the same service.

Many black women fought back: they poisoned their masters, committed sabotage, fled North, joined maroon communities (groups of fugitive blacks). To this day the heroic Harriet Tubman remains the only woman in the United States ever to have led troops into battle.[381] But the master usually had the victory. Accounts of appallingly savage treatment of female slaves are plentiful.[382] In addition to physical mistreatments, the master could tear parents and children apart and sell any of them where he pleased. Although extant letters and personal accounts demonstrate deep bonds of affection among all members of black slave families, no doubt mothers were more agonized by the loss of their children and the knowledge that they would almost certainly never see them again.[383]

Physical conditions for many black people were not improved after the Civil War and the abolition of slavery. They had no money, owned no land, and were resented by many whites. No longer legally slaves, they remained a colonized people, and to some degree remain so to this day. Throughout the nineteenth century many women continued to work toward equality for blacks as well as women's rights, but their support of black equality was undermined by the divisive tactics of white male lawmakers and politicians who at every step set women's and blacks' rights in opposition to each other. To understand this we must retrace our steps somewhat and discuss the beginnings of the women's rights movement.

At the time of the Seneca Falls convention, women in the United States (and, with variations, in England and throughout Europe) did not have the same access to divorce as men, did not have the right to custody of their children in cases of divorce, and did not even have the right to keep their own wages. They were denied most forms of education and employment, were not equal to men at law, had no access to a political voice, and were subject to their husbands' physical abuse. The Seneca Falls Convention passed eleven resolutions calling for redress of these wrongs. The women who attended were white and middle class, and for the most part ignorant of and unconcerned with the plight of lower-class white women, if not of slaves. The single exception was

Susan Anthony, who remained dedicated to the improvement of the lot of all women throughout her career.[384] The convention was concerned more with political than with economic goals; among these political goals was abolition.

The women, helped by some sympathetic men, embarked on a feminist campaign. They held meetings (perhaps early versions of consciousness-raising meetings); they wrote pamphlets, spoke wherever they could. Between 1850 and 1860 they had yearly conventions (except for 1857). They published their own newspapers and journals. The established press and the churches were overtly hostile to them. They had no money of their own, no vote, no access to institutional forums; single women were expected to be as silent as married ones, not to travel, and not to create disturbances. Like British women of a later date, they had to rely on those men they could persuade to help them in political arenas.[385]

In 1854, Susan Anthony suggested the women obtain thousands of signatures on a petition and submit it to state legislatures, which were expected to grant suffrage (while the federal government was expected to abolish slavery). Her first petition was directed at the New York legislature and asked for three reforms: the right of women to vote, to control their own earnings, and to the guardianship of their children in case of divorce.[386] The petition did not produce change, but the process gave heart and direction to the movement.

For the next sixty-six years, women would trudge from door to door to get signatures, enduring hostile responses and ridicule. Although it was considered improper, they traveled alone across the country, living from hand to mouth because they had no money. They slept in carriages, there being no hotels—and they could not have afforded them anyway. Anthony was frostbitten. Black women like Sojourner Truth, Frances Harper, and Sarah Redmond traveled on foot, and by stagecoach, train, and steamboat, to tiny villages in Ohio and upper New York State, to Vermont and Maine and Wisconsin and down the Missouri River to Kansas City. Black and white women persuaded, lobbied, politicked; they wrote and spoke. They won and celebrated a few victories in a few states—the right to vote in some local elections, a Married Women's Property Bill in Massachusetts.

They were wary of Lincoln, and when he was elected they toured the country with mottoes like "No Compromise with Slave Holders" and "Immediate and Unconditional Emancipation." Mobs wielding guns and knives threatened the women, and the police refused to help them.[387] When the Civil War began, women for the most part put their own desires aside and dedicated themselves to emancipation and winning the war. Because men were in the army, women were again acceptable on the labor market, and many took jobs. Some women tried, despite great hostility on the part of the army, to serve as nurses. Among them were Louisa May Alcott, Clara Barton, and Dorothea Dix, who assisted the Sanitary Commission, an early form of the Red Cross.[388]

When the war ended, women expected to receive the right to vote. Instead, their problems mounted, as did those of black people. Although they were legally free, blacks in the South were arrested on the slightest pretext. Punished with fines they could not pay, they were imprisoned. The state then "leased" them to planters to "work out" their fines. Chained together in gangs, abused more severely than they had been as slaves because they were no longer some farmer's walking investment, they did slave labor to work out long sentences. Women and men were housed together at night and chained together by day.[389]

In the North, many male abolitionists were now campaigning for suffrage for black males only, and opposing women's suffrage. This strategy was deviously clever, and succeeded in splitting the women's movement. Lucy Stone and Julia Ward Howe conceded it the "Negro's hour" and gave up the fight for suffrage to work for other legal and political rights for women; Stanton and Anthony took over the radical National Woman Suffrage Association, which demanded suffrage and a complete change in women's status. Later, this radical branch of the movement was destroyed by the crisis over Victoria Woodhull's advocacy of "free love."[390]

The position of the dominant white male class set white against black. Had women and black men unified, they would have far outnumbered the white males. But white men urged women to support the "superiority" of "white civilization," and some women took the bait. The Fourteenth Amendment was passed, granting political representation on the basis of the number of male voters, white or black; and the Fifteenth, which granted suffrage to black males, although it would take a century to get the Fifteenth enforced in the South.

The years following the Civil War were bitter for all southerners, all blacks, and political women. But women continued to agitate, black and white women together. Black and white women together led the struggle for education in the South, trying to open and maintain schools for black children against great odds and persecution.[391]

There were women like Ida Wells, who was licensed to teach at the age of fourteen after most of her family had died of yellow fever, leaving her the sole support of four younger children. Wells taught school for seven years, wrote articles for small newspapers, then bought a share in a newspaper, became its editor, and mounted a campaign against the lynching of black men, pointing to the economic basis that underlay many such acts. She was driven out of the South, but started women's clubs throughout the country and continued to campaign against lynching.[392]

Black women organized their own societies, first on a local and later on a national level, for educational, philanthropic, and welfare activities. In 1896 they formed the National Association of Colored Women, uniting over a hundred local women's groups.[393] Such groups provided kindergartens, nursery schools, and day-care centers for black children; they founded orphanages, homes for the aged, and other welfare programs.[394] Sadly, when black women's clubs tried to merge with white women's clubs—feminist or nonfeminist—they were rebuffed.

The scandals attendant on Victoria Woodhull's free love program were a terrible blow to the National Woman Suffrage Association, which was already under suspicion because its principles threatened "marriage and the family."[395]

This phrase was then as now code for *the proper place of women;* what it insinuates is that if women had any social freedom at all, marriage would be endangered and the family would disappear. Because such a notion was widespread, women were prevented from broadening their criticism of society to include social and economic institutions. With the exception of the great Charlotte Perkins Gilman, who continued to write broad social critiques, suffragists turned all their energies to obtaining the vote.[396] They continued to travel across the country, to make speeches, lobby, start newspapers, petition, and demonstrate. Sometimes they voted illicitly; Anthony was tried for this offense.

But other women were exploring different avenues. Under the direction of Frances Willard, the Women's Christian Temperance Union became a formidable organization; in the 1870s it was the largest women's organization in the country, with 200,000 members in every state in the union.[397] Women wanted prohibition because drunken husbands were physically abusive to them and their children, and frequently drank up most of their—and sometimes their wives'—wages. But the organization fought for other projects besides prohibition: Willard had a broad program of social welfare reforms, prison reforms, work for the shut-in sick, aid to prostitutes, the teaching of hygiene, the establishment of kindergartens, and also suffrage.[398]

At the turn of the century a new alliance emerged between middle-class and working women. In Chicago, Jane Addams founded Hull-House and recruited affluent young women to help to improve the lot of poor and working women.[399] She and Lillian Wald, founder of the Henry Street Settlement in New York, came to the conclusion that the problem was not so much ignorance as intolerable poverty, and began to foster the establishment of labor unions for women.[400] Settlement houses were opened in other cities as well, and middle-class women tried to help poor, mainly immigrant, women and children to speak English, to read and write. They taught hygiene and sanitation, and helped women to market frugally in a foreign food market. Many well-to-do women came to dabble in charity and stayed to become devoted welfare workers. Jane Addams and Lillian Wald are only the most famous of American women who lightened the burden of life for hundreds of poor women.

Dorothea Dix single-handedly campaigned for reform of prisons and mental institutions. Elizabeth Blackwell, with help from male sympathizers, opened her own hospital when she could not find work as a physician anywhere else. She staffed the hospital entirely with women and dedicated it to helping the poor. Many institutions of higher education for women were founded, and everywhere women fought for entrance to professional schools. Margaret Sanger, the woman who brought birth control to the poor, began her career as a visiting nurse among the poverty-stricken people of the Lower East Side of New York; she was also a socialist and a supporter of the Industrial Workers of the World.[401]

In England, Mary Carpenter dedicated her life to the establishment of separate penal institutions for children; Louisa Twining led a movement of women urging reform of the poorhouse, a movement that was successful in its time; Olivia Hill built decent dwellings for the poor and trained a corps of young women rent collectors who visited the tenants with an eye to helping them.[402] Florence Nightingale single-handedly transformed nursing in England from filthy, distasteful work performed by drunks and aged prostitutes into a profession with qualifications and standards. She improved hospital and health conditions in England immensely.[403]

Throughout this period women worked in many ways for different goals, all of which can be gathered under one rubric: the feminization of society. Women wanted to change the character of everyday life, and they realized that to do this they needed political, social, and economic power. The "angel in the house" and the cult of domesticity didn't work: it constricted women, and it had little effect on the policies and manners of the nation. A movement directed at morality which ignored or blinded itself to the highest moral value of its culture—power—could not possibly change that culture.

The women who worked in the many social movements mentioned here did not disregard power. But unlike men in social and political movements, they did not aim for personal power or even power for their particular group; they wanted to improve life for themselves and others, to ameliorate poverty and deprivation and ignorance and disease, to make life more pleasant. Had they urged an elite class to use particular services or products to achieve beauty, health, or power, as do those who merchandise such things, they would have been successful more quickly. Had they been men, urging change but maintaining a sharp lookout for their own status and power, their personal success would have been greater. As it is, they achieved their goals slowly and with difficulty, paying for every success with labor, endurance, and every ounce of courage they could muster; yet in the end, most of their work was swallowed up by males, in male-headed institutions.

In the West, some states were quietly granting women suffrage. In 1870 women in Wyoming began to serve on juries although their husbands threatened to leave them if they did. Other states followed. The suffrage movement was becoming more respectable and was drawing less revolutionary women. Radical women were swelling the ranks of the labor movement, which was at its most incendiary during the 1890s. Split first by the issue of black male suffrage, the women's movement was split again over the question of whether to support unions. The conservative middle-class nature of their rank-and-file members led women's groups to hedge; like middle-class America in general, the suffragist movement was silent as business inflicted terrible retributions upon protesting or striking workers.[404]

Feminists watched their small victories accrue, expecting that soon they would obtain the basket into which they had put all their eggs—national suffrage—but it was not forthcoming. World War I broke out, the war that was to desolate the leisure class of Europe, to murder an entire generation of young men, and to toss the world like a prize into the laps of the technicians and managers. Remembering the experience of women during the Civil War, some feminists refused to give up their struggle: they picketed, gave speeches, were arrested, imprisoned, went on hunger strikes, were hideously force-fed and sometimes martyred. Other women entered the labor market, which once again welcomed them; they worked in blast furnaces, foundries, and plants manufacturing steel plate, high explosives, armaments, machine tools, agricultural implements, electrical, railway, automobile, and airplane parts. They also worked in the smelting and refining of brass and copper, in the refining of oil, and in the production of chemicals, fertilizers, and leather goods.[405] Gone were their frailty, their incompetence, their mental weakness; above all, gone was their position of competition with men.

In January 1917, North Dakota granted its women the right to vote in presidential elections; soon afterward, Ohio, Indiana, Rhode Island, and Nebraska followed. New York City politicians voted in favor of a referendum on suffrage. The National American Woman Suffrage Association threatened that if the Sixty-fifth Congress failed to submit the Amendment for Woman Suffrage to the states, the Association would throw its considerable opposition against the reelection of those who voted against it. On January 10, 1918, the amendment passed the Congress.[406]

But it still had to be ratified, and that took another fourteen months of lobbying, speechmaking, petitioning, traveling. None of the women who had initiated the movement lived to see woman suffrage become law: Lucretia Mott, whom Eleanor Flexner calls the "moral force" of the movement; Lucy Stone, "its most gifted orator"; Elizabeth Cady Stanton, "its outstanding philosopher"; and the magnificent Susan Anthony, the "incomparable organizer, who gave it force and direction for half a century."[407]

After the amendment was passed, one of the leaders of the movement, Carrie Chapman Catt, wrote:

> To get the word "male" in effect out of the Constitution cost the women of the country fifty-two years of pauseless campaign. . . . During that time they were forced to conduct fifty-six campaigns of referenda to male voters; 480 campaigns to get Legislatures to submit suffrage amendments to voters; 47 campaigns to get State constitutional conventions to write women suffrage into State constitutions; 277 campaigns to get State party conventions to include woman suffrage planks; 30 campaigns to get presidential party conventions to adopt woman suffrage planks in party platforms, and 19 campaigns with 19 successive Congresses.[408]

In 1919, after decades of work by the Women's Christian Temperance Union, the Eighteenth Amendment was passed; the Nineteenth Amendment, guaranteeing woman suffrage, became effective in August 1920. Under the prodding of Alice Paul, the Equal Rights Amendment was submitted to the Congress in 1923, and women were determined to see it passed even if it took a decade. From the beginning of the battle in 1848, woman suffrage took seventy-two years to be achieved. It may take the same amount of time for women to get inserted into the Constitution a statement declaring them equal to men.

In Continental Europe and in Britain, as in the United States, middle-class women did charitable work; like their American counterparts they became increasingly concerned with helping poor women and their children. Their work with the poor led many of these women to realize their underlying kinship with women of other classes. Just as white female abolitionists saw that they shared sexual subordination and nonfreedom with black female slaves, and middle-class American woman saw that the social and political deprivation of poor women was the image of their own, European women began to realize that despite some privilege and wealth, "they too were subordinated and oppressed by men and man-made laws."[409]

They perceived that "feminine" values could eliminate a host of problems, social and economic, as well as their own sense of oppression. This perception led to the emergence of a middle-class feminist movement that spread across Europe from the middle decades of the nineteenth century. And like American women, women in this movement believed that suffrage was an essential step. During their fight for suffrage they also participated in local government, became members of school boards, poor-law guardians, and factory and prison inspectors. They joined working-class socialist groups. They wrote about and agitated for social welfare reform, the improvement of women's legal rights, and middle-class women's education.

In England, the history of woman suffrage centers mainly on one name—Pankhurst. Emmeline Pankhurst was concerned with helping poor women before she became involved in the fight for suffrage. In 1874, Emma Paterson had founded the Women's Protective and Provident League, a union for working women. To placate male unionists, she and her colleagues avoided the term *union* in their title, but in 1890 they changed the name to the Women's Trade Union League. The league tried to organize locals of women in a particular trade and then get the appropriate national union to accept them.[410] Thus there was a climate of female protest in England at the time Emmeline Pankhurst became involved in the Women's Suffrage Society in the 1880s. In an attempt to disrupt the suffrage movement, Gladstone, the Liberal prime minister, set up a competitive group and promised women that if they joined and supported men in party politics, they might "earn" the right to vote. The women who followed him were, of course, betrayed: Emmeline Pankhurst did not. The Liberal Party also urged women to serve in municipal offices to "prove" their fitness for the vote. Many women did this, including Pankhurst, who served on the Board of Poor Law Guardians and therefore came into close contact with poor people and people in the workhouses. She became convinced that only women's voting could change conditions for them.[411] In 1903, she and her daughters Christabel and Sylvia founded the Women's Social and Political Union, which became the strongest women's organization in England and included many working-class women.[412] Its motto was "Deeds, Not Words."[413]

The dramatic years that followed included mass meetings, heckling of male politicians, imprisonment, promises and betrayals by the government.[414] In 1908 suffragists chained themselves to the fence around the house where the British cabinet was meeting, and gave speeches. The government threatened more severe punishments, and the women began to throw rocks and break windows in Parliament Square. Again and again Emmeline Pankhurst was sent to prison—and many other brave women with her. By 1909 these women were refusing to eat while imprisoned, and King Edward VII demanded they be force-fed. Although the public protested, this procedure was used extensively thereafter.[415]

The class-conscious British would not have abused a member of the aristocracy. Only because Lady Constance Lytton gave a false name when she was arrested was she imprisoned, abused, and force-fed with the other women. Her brother, Lord Lytton, aghast at what had happened to her, formed a Conciliation Committee for Woman Suffrage, which presented a bill to enfranchise the one million women in England who were heads of household. Although it passed, the prime minister, Asquith, deferred putting it into effect. Women protesting his delay were met by police and brutally repulsed.

Afterward public statements were made asserting that women were not really committed to suffrage, that men would have fought harder. So the women began to smash streetlamps, cut up golf courses, blow up fuse boxes, break windows, burn empty houses, and damage objets d'art. In return they were sentenced to hard labor. To draw attention to the suffrage movement, one woman committed suicide by stepping into the path of the king's horses. There was more violence, more imprisonment, more hunger strikes, more force-feeding, more police brutality, more arrests. . . .[416]

One wonders how long this struggle would have gone on if the war had not begun. The war split the women, the Pankhurst family among them. Emmeline and Christabel committed the WSPU to help the country and encouraged women to work in munitions factories and essential services, partly because of patriotism and partly because they believed women's efforts would be rewarded by the vote when the war ended. Sylvia Pankhurst, more deeply involved with poor women than her mother and sister, saw the war as a patriarchal and class struggle, and attacked the government for going to war. She continued her work with poor people.

Emmeline Pankhurst traveled through England rallying women, and the government gave her a two-thousand-pound grant to finance her campaign. Sylvia's group claimed that the government was exploiting women as a source of cheap labor; she demanded equal pay and decent working conditions with safeguards in the hazardous munitions and airplane factories. Her agitation caused some improvements, but Sylvia was publicly repudiated by her mother.[417]

When the war was over, Parliament decided to grant the vote to all soldiers, including those men who did not own property or could not meet residency requirements. A moderate women's group insisted that women be included in this bill, and some were: the vote was granted to unmarried women on the Local Government Register and to wives of men on the Register—if they were over thirty. The age limit prevented women from becoming a majority of British voters. Eight million British women were enfranchised on January 10, 1918.[418] During the 1920s the vote was granted to women of other European countries, although in Switzerland women did not win national franchise until 1971, and do not even now have the right to vote in certain local elections.[419]

The opposition of men, especially those of the dominant class, is the primary reason why women's struggles take so long. But the suffrage movement in Britain and in the United States was also impeded by its narrowness. It was a movement of educated women who wanted to use their skills, wanted to change things. These women were often extremely class-conscious and separated themselves from working-class women and, in the United States, from black women as well. White women sometimes discouraged black women from participating in the suffrage movement so as not to antagonize politically powerful white-supremacist males.[420] This is particularly ironic since the American suffrage movement grew out of the movement for abolition.

Nevertheless, a heavily financed and widespread campaign by males provided the greatest barrier to the attainment of suffrage in the United States.[421] As in the later fight over the Equal Rights Amendment, men placed women in the foreground of the opposition campaign: the wives of wealthy businessmen, mere puppets for male interests. There were two main grounds of opposition, one moral/political and the other economic. Catholic clergymen, machine politicians, and industrial leaders united against woman suffrage on the ground that it would be dangerous for "the country." The Texas Businessmen's Association, Gulf Oil, Swift Meatpackers, the Santa Fe Railroad, the American Express Company, and the Southeastern States Portland Cement company agreed with Tammany Hall that if women had the vote they would force reform of child-labor laws; investigate grants to railroads, franchises, and rate schedules; improve the conditions of working women; and support a graduated income tax.

The most powerful identifiable lobby against woman suffrage was the liquor industry, which feared the passage of laws prohibiting the sale of its product. Certain businesses, and the Catholic Church, worked against suffrage groups less openly. Although the surface stance of opposition was papered with moral arguments, including their assurance that God was against it, their real opposition to woman suffrage was economic.[422]

Indeed, all the things these men feared did occur, but business has proven adequate to the challenge. Child-labor laws have been instituted, factory conditions improved for both women and men, a graduated income tax was established and grants to railroads were investigated. Nevertheless, businessmen were able to dump the railroads on government when they were no longer profitable, keep their taxes at a minimum, and keep women earning little more than half the wage of men. And they again combined to prevent passage of the Equal Rights Amendment—for similar reasons.

Protests of United States working women began even earlier than those of middle-class white women and black women of all classes. Industry began in New England early in the nineteenth century, and the unmarried daughters of New England farm families provided its first labor pool. The factory owners assured these families of their common moral purpose: the owners promised to establish supervised boarding houses for the girls to live in, and to teach them hard work and discipline.[423] They kept their promise with a vengeance. The young women were herded into crowded dormitories, watched and regulated strictly. They worked between twelve and sixteen hours a day in factories with no fresh air, no running water, and no toilets. Given half an hour for dinner, they had to run to the boarding house, eat, and run back within that time or pay a fine for lateness. They developed high rates of dysentery and tuberculosis.[424]

Driven by the desire for higher profits, employers began to cut wages, and in 1824 women workers in Pawtucket, Rhode Island, joined a strike against a wage cut and longer hours. Employers had begun "speedups" and "stretchouts": they brought in larger and noisier machines that would produce more swiftly, and they demanded that workers tend more machines for less money. In 1828, in Dover, New Hampshire, women struck alone; in 1834, women had an important "turn-out" (strike) in Lowell, Massachusetts, in which they made ardent speeches.[425]

The women lost their battles, conditions in the mills continued to worsen, and in 1845 the women founded the Lowell Female Labor Reform Association. Again they struck; again they lost: but this time they publicized their plight in a labor newspaper and pressured the Massachusetts legislature to hold hearings on factory conditions. The main effort of the women at this time was to shorten the work day from fourteen to ten hours.[426]

The factory owners swiftly abandoned their stance of common purpose with the farm community. They got rid of native-born women and hired immigrants, who were more easily cowed since they were often unable to speak English, illiterate, and frightened of the unfamiliar country.[427] But protests continued. At this time working women were earning only a quarter of what men earned, and men were poorly paid. From the 1820s on, other women's labor organizations were formed, like the United Tailoresses Society of New York, and the Lady Shoe Binders of Lynn, Massachusetts. The women's unions were unsuccessful, as a rule, mainly because the women were isolated and inexperienced; they received almost no support from men's unions in their trades, and often were actively impeded by their male relatives.[428]

New York tailors organized and tried to shame employers by publicly naming those who paid women ten to eighteen cents a day. The Female Industry Association was founded, but the women still did not have the numbers, force, or skill to deal with employers, and their meetings "drew men who circulated among them with offers of an easier life through prostitution."[429] Laundry workers struck in Troy, New York, but were starved out. To get their jobs back they had to pledge to renounce the union, which collapsed in 1869 after six years of existence.

The first national union of women workers was that of women shoe binders from Lynn to San Francisco. At its height it had more than forty lodges, but it too was short-lived. Black laundresses started Mississippi's first labor organization, the Washerwomen of Jackson, in 1866. After the Civil War a few male unions allowed women to join. The National Union of Cigar Makers took in women and blacks in 1867. Later the Women's Typographical Union was founded by women alone; when it disbanded nine years later, women were allowed to be members of the national union on equal terms with men, but no further women's locals were chartered.[430]

Although women were not supported by male unionists or the men of their families, they supported male strikes. During the railroad strike of 1877, a hundred thousand men and women confronted police, militia, and federal troops. It was a bitter fight and the press remarked particularly on the behavior of the women on the lines, describing them as "enraged female rioters," an "unsexed mob of female incendiaries," an "Amazonian army."[431]

By 1880 two and a half million women were working for wages; in 1890 there were nearly five million. In 1896 the top 1 percent of American families had more wealth than the bottom 50 percent: the top 1 percent received almost a quarter of the national income, the bottom 50 percent received less than a fifth. Relations between employers and labor were warlike. When Andrew Carnegie's steelworkers struck, he brought in immigrant scab laborers, transporting them to the workplace in sealed boxcars so that even if they could speak English, they could not find out what was going on. Once there, they were locked inside the factories and forced to work at gunpoint.[432]

In 1881 the Noble Order of the Knights of Labor gave a charter to the Working Women's Union. At that time there were several other female unions in Chicago, organized by trade, and 120 in the country as a whole.[433] The Knights accepted blacks and demanded equal pay for equal work. In 1885 women members of the Knights went on strike in Yonkers; twenty-five hundred women formed a mass picket line around a mill. Police violence aroused public support for the women, and they held out for six months. When they finally won, what they won was the *rescinding of a pay cut.* At its peak, the Knights of Labor had a membership of 700,000 people, of whom 50,000 were women.[434]

As the Knights declined, the American Federation of Labor arose. New jobs were opening to women in retail sales, telephone switchboard operation, and clerical and secretarial work, as well as in the garment trades. The official policy of the AFL was to organize women and urge equal pay; in practice, it did neither. Only 5 percent of its members were female, although in 1888, under pressure, it gave women a charter for the Ladies' Federal Labor Union Local No. 2703.[435]

In 1889 the Women's Alliance in Chicago campaigned for compulsory education for children. Fifty thousand children in that city went neither to work nor to school; at least ten thousand of them slept nightly on the city streets. Many of these children worked for pittances in the sweated industries. (There are photographs of such children in New York in Jacob Riis's *How the Other Half Lives.*[436]) The alliance forced passage of a bill ordering a twelve-to-twenty-four-week school year for children between seven and fourteen, with time off half of each day to go to work.[437] *

By 1903 the Chicago women's labor movement included the overwhelming majority of workers in twenty-six trades: 35,000 of them marched down Michigan Avenue in the Chicago Labor Day parade that year.[438] In that year too the National Women's Trade Union League was founded (in imitation of the British League), with the backing of rank-and-file workers and the expertise

---

* Such arrangements still existed in New York City as late as 1918, when my mother split her day between school and the box-making factory.

and money of middle-class women, who were beginning to assist their working sisters. Organizing progressed slowly until the September 1909 strike of the International Ladies' Garment Workers Union shops in New York and Philadelphia. Between twenty and thirty thousand women joined and picketed throughout a cold winter, near starvation and frequently arrested and sent to the workhouse. Most of them were between sixteen and thirty years old; they held mass meetings and built a strong union, with as many as a thousand women joining each day.[439]

Despite the heroism of these women, who held out for thirteen weeks, immediate gains were small. Settlements were made separately, shop by shop, and one of the two largest shirtwaist makers, Triangle, continued to refuse to recognize the union. Three hundred and thirty-nine shops did, however; a foundation had been laid. About two years later, there was a terrible fire in the New York loft building that housed the Triangle Shirtwaist Company. The doors to the fire escapes were locked to keep women from stepping outside for a little air. One hundred and forty-six women, mostly young girls, burned to death. Some, their clothing in flames, leaped out the windows to death in the street. The two partners in the firm were tried and acquitted; later, one was fined twenty dollars. But legislation to increase fire safety in factory buildings was subsequently passed.[440]

In 1910 almost eight million women were working outside the home. Many of them worked in factories where their pay, ranging from two to six dollars a week, was one-third that of men doing comparable work. They worked late into the night in filthy, airless fire traps, without overtime pay, continually on their feet, their evening meal some bread gulped in a stairwell.[441] Many of these women were organized—over 37,000 in Chicago alone in the early years of the century—but a depression in 1907–09 devastated the unions and drove women—marginal workers, the lowest paid—out of work or into jobs taken on the employers' terms. By 1909 the Chicago unions had only ten thousand women members and there was not a single all-female local left.[442] The support of middle-class women was not reliable. For instance, a mixed-class suffrage organization in San Francisco fell apart in 1909 because the middle-class women refused to support a strike of streetcar conductors; working women felt betrayed and abandoned the group.[443]

Still, women provided important support to male clothing workers in their Chicago strike of 1910. In IWW agitation women were more militant strikers than men: women workers and wives of workers in the front ranks were beaten, fire-hosed, and arrested all across the country.[444] Women led the Lawrence textile workers' strike of 1912, which was caused by a pay cut of thirty cents in wages of a few dollars a week. This was the cost of five loaves of bread a week, quite literally the difference between life and death. The lowest-paid women in the mills earned nine and a half cents an hour. The strike went on for eight weeks before the owners would even meet with the strike committee. They finally agreed to a 25 percent increase for the lowest-paid women, less for the higher-paid, and overtime of time and a quarter after fifty-four hours a week.[445] The Lawrence success led to a wave of strikes across New England, and by

1913 the owners had shut down many of the Lawrence mills in an effort to break the union by unemployment. And later on the corporations began moving textile mills from New England to the South, where there were no unions.

The Women's Trade Union League remained important; eventually it merged with the Amalgamated Clothing Workers of America, a union with 75 percent female membership but in which no woman has ever held top office at the international level, and in which women are still a small minority of the executive board. The IWW was important in Lawrence, and it encouraged women to join as organizers. Some of these, like Elizabeth Gurley Flynn, attained national prominence, but no woman ever held a key leadership position in that union either.[446]

Thus we come to a second phase of oppression of twentieth-century working women: like men, women first had to fight employers for a decent wage and decent working conditions; like men, they struck and starved, endured abuse, and persisted. But once the victory was won against industry, and unions were legitimate, men excluded women from policy-making positions.

In 1944 Rose Pesotta complained that the ILGWU, with a membership that was 85 percent women, had regularly limited women to one seat on its executive board. As of mid-1984, the ILGWU has never had more than two women among the twenty to twenty-three members of that board. As of 1974, only two small unions of the AFL had women presidents, and no woman sat on the AFL-CIO Executive Council. In 1984, there were no women union presidents, two female members of the Executive Council, and not one woman among its twenty-three regional directors. The only woman to head a department in the federation is the librarian.[447] Many unions, especially those of higher-paid skilled workers, still exclude women from their membership; and the trades in which women predominate—the lowest-paid ones, such as domestic, agricultural, retail, and office work—are not organized on an effective national scale, nor are the large unions interested in basic organizing in these areas.

In Europe, women began to form protective societies in the late eighteenth and early nineteenth centuries; their strikes increased after the 1870s. The first European women's trade union was formed in England in 1874, among bookbinders. Unions in other trades followed: dressmakers, milliners, mantlemakers, upholstresses. Louise Otto-Peters, a feminist and novelist who had been active in the unsuccessful liberal revolutions of 1848, became president of the General German Women's Association, founded in 1865, and strove for equality for women in every sphere, including suffrage.[448]

The German political system and ethos was authoritarian; within that context the Women's Educational Association of Leipzig was democratic, although it was middle-class and class-conscious. The group fought for women to be hired by the civil service; in 1873 some were. But those who were hired were never promoted, were paid very low day wages, and received no vacations, although men got two weeks. And after that year no more women were hired.[449]

Many German unions barred women, and in those which did not, men were hostile to the women. German textile workers had especially bad conditions. They worked from six in the morning to seven at night in temperatures as high as 126 degrees, breathing in chemical fumes. For this they were paid between one and one and a half kroner a day. Amalie Seidl, an Austrian textile worker, in 1892 began to organize the women in her factory. She was dismissed from her job, but she continued and persuaded seven hundred Viennese women to strike in 1893. They won a ten-hour day for eight kroner a week, and one holiday a year, May First. Afterward Seidl was imprisoned.[450]

In 1905 a school for social work admitting women was established in Germany, and by 1911 over a quarter of a million German women were union members; they were bakers, butchers, glaziers, woodworkers, leather workers, lithographers, metalworkers, and saddlers, among other occupations. Teachers' unions were also important in Germany.[451] Agitation in France led to permission in 1891 for women to be dentists, chemical workers, and pharmacists.[452]

European women fought for suffrage and participated in local government as members of school boards, poor-law guardians, and factory and prison inspectors. They worked for reform and social welfare programs. And they had considerable success. They improved women's opportunities for education and employment. They ended state-regulated prostitution and white slavery; they aided dependent children and single mothers, and changed marriage, divorce, and custody laws. They helped establish compulsory education for children, although that education was only half-time for children who had to work. As mentioned before, they won suffrage in many European states.[453]

With these gains won, the women's movement was proclaimed victorious—and over. Further agitation was declared unnecessary, and male politicians and businessmen were no longer willing to listen to women's demands. Even the sensitive British novelist E. M. Forster could not understand why Virginia Woolf—a friend of his—had written Three Guineas in 1938; in Two Cheers for Democracy he called Woolf's great and gracious essay "cantankerous"; he could not understand why she was fussing about such an "old-fashioned" thing as feminism when everyone knew the battle was over and women had won it.

Many women felt the same way. The middle-class feminist movement in Europe and the United States essentially collapsed after suffrage had been achieved. Women believed that the franchise would automatically lead to the eradication of other barriers to their entrance into the public world, and would allow them to influence that world in humane ways. It did not. Discrimination against women hardened and was fixed into policy. In 1920, only 40 out of 482 hospitals would accept women interns; from 1925 to 1945, medical schools (not then complaining about quotas) maintained a quota of 5 percent on admissions of women, and elite law schools refused to accept women students at all. The New York City Bar Association excluded women until 1937. Some farsighted women—mainly the National Women's Party—lobbied for passage of the Equal Rights Amendment. The League of Women Voters and other women's groups were founded; they urged women's rights and sat on presidential commissions on women. Occasionally a woman was appointed or elected to a high-level position in government. Voting gradually lost its violent aura, as schools replaced saloons as polling places, reducing the drunkenness, fraud, and violence that had characterized American elections.[454] The nominating process was, however, still firmly in the hands of men, and took place in private "smoke-filled rooms." Things changed little in industry and commerce, and the Great Depression of the 1930s set women back from whatever small gains they had made in the twenties.

Women still constituted the majority of the marginal labor force, that body which is exploited in times of need and expelled in times of cutbacks. During the Depression, laws were passed denying employment to married women; women were fired before men. The jobs still open to women were mainly the very lowest paid, jobs men would not take.

In 1941, with the outbreak of World War II, things changed immediately. It took Congress only *two weeks* then to pass the Lanham Act, providing federal financing for day-care centers. Special crash training programs were established to teach women skills which, a few months earlier, they had been considered incapable of learning. Women instantly assumed positions of responsibility and authority, earning good wages.[455]

But when the war ended in 1945, the prewar status quo promptly reasserted itself. Men were reinstated in their jobs and granted the benefits of the G.I. Bill; women were fired, the child-care centers dismantled, and the training programs ended. Some women managed to remain in the labor force, but at lower rank. The old cult of domesticity also reappeared—for women, but for men too. Although men still bore the responsibility of supporting their families, there was widespread disenchantment with the regimentation and conformity demanded of men in their gray flannel suits, and during the 1950s both sexes were implicitly urged to find their satisfactions in the domestic realm.

The postwar period, from the mid-forties to the mid-sixties, stands as the terminating point of the vivid, turbulent, many-faceted women's movement that had begun almost precisely a century earlier. The "second wave" of the women's movement, which began in the mid-sixties, will be discussed in Chapter Six. To conclude this section, however, it may be instructive to examine the long-term effects of this century of struggle in the United States. For the sad fact is that women's struggle has been ignored or diminished by male historians; many of its effects have been eroded by the government; and even feminist historians tend to criticize the works of their feminist predecessors.

Male historians like to claim that women voted conservatively, against social change, even though there are absolutely no statistics broken down by sex for several decades after women gained suffrage.[456] Only recently have women's voting patterns become matters of interest: and these statistics indicate that women vote for candidates who claim to desire peace and social welfare.[457] That candidates do not always act upon such claims once they are elected has nothing to do with women and much to do with the fact that the franchise was not extended to women until long after power interests had firm control over both political parties. Business interests controlled government to a great degree from the mid-nineteenth century on; by the turn of the century they dominated government.[458] Over the next fifty years "big business" lost some of its control, but other powers—unions, and what a Republican president, Dwight Eisenhower, termed the "military-industrial complex"—joined businessmen in control of government. Occasionally on the local level, but almost invariably on state and national levels, voting is a choice between candidates who are more bound to power interests than to the electorate.

Feminist historians have criticized the women who worked in settlement houses, who taught immigrant women the basic skills of homemaking in America and child-raising techniques, for fostering the image of woman as domestic worker only and perpetuating the ideal of woman as wife and mother.[459] (They have also disparaged upper-class women in England and France who taught lower-class girls to become good servants and dressmakers, because such women perpetuated an unjust economic structure and taught the poor merely "to survive *within* their status."[460])

There is ground for such criticism. Many ostensible solutions to problems perpetuate the real causes of those problems. But it is unrealistic to imagine that anyone, no matter how farseeing or aware, can accomplish anything in a society without perpetuating some of the values of that society. People are not, and cannot be, completely free of the prejudices and preconceptions of their age. Although it is useful to point to the ways in which people unconsciously support structures and values they may not respect, it is unfair to blame them for behavior we in our turn are not able to avoid. Indeed, disparaging women of the past for not being more aware of or committed to change of the political structure, while ignoring or diminishing their actual contributions, is in itself a perpetuation of patriarchal values. Such a posture betrays an acceptance of the patriarchal idea that power is the only important value, and gaining power the only important accomplishment. This attitude disregards the fact that many women improved the quality of life for thousands of other women, children, and men. Few of the changes women created or contributed to have had the effect those women intended; but many of them added some felicity to the daily lives of generations of people.

The efforts of settlement-house women and those working for social reform led to welfare programs and laws that are still in existence. Women provided facilities for school lunches, playgrounds, and parks for poor children, as well as laws to assist the poor. If the former are being dismantled by a reactionary government, and the latter being found inadequate to the present condition of our cities, that does not change the fact that they have served a purpose, that they have made life a little better for generations of families. Welfare seems inadequate to the needs of the poor at the same time that it locks them into poverty by its restrictions; it is oppressive and humiliating. But it would have meant the difference between a life of daily anguish and mere hardship to women like my maternal grandmother. *

The consequences of the tireless and dedicated work of generations of women during the past century and the early years of this one have been real

* She was widowed in 1913 and unable to earn enough to support her four children, with the result that all of them except my mother were taken away from her and placed in orphanages.

and almost invariably beneficial. Women are able to receive education on every level; they have access to far more forms of employment than they had a century ago. The lives of poor people have been made a little easier than they were a century ago, and working people have many protections that did not then exist. If such reforms do not go far enough, and if some of them need revision, that does not lessen their worth. If welfare constitutes a new form of regulation of women, that is inevitable in a society obsessed with control. Legislation and professionalization of services transformed what settlement women did free into paid social work. Women did enter the "helping" professions as nurses, social workers, and teachers. But as the institutions of education and social services grew into powerful agencies, men took them over. Men were named as executives within them, and "women became subordinate in the work they in large part had initiated."[461]

Prohibition, decreed in 1919, was repealed in 1933; this chapter in women's history is little discussed and perhaps viewed as an embarrassment. But we must recognize its success: it broke the hold of a destructive pattern on workingmen—the ritual after-work drinking in pub or saloon that led thousands of families into destitution. When the first temperance society was formed in the 1820s, per capita consumption of hard liquor in America was more than three times what it is today. Despite bootlegging and bathtub gin, the years of prohibition cut liquor consumption to its lowest point in American history.[462] It inculcated new habits and injected some freedom into men's habits—it had been almost compulsory for men to drink in this way; as in Joyce's Dublin, men who did not were viewed askance. Without approving of enforced protection of people against themselves, we can understand that women and children who were forced into dependence upon men needed protection against this male abuse and the battering that often followed it.

The passage of the Prohibition Amendment is an indication of what women can do when they are even moderately united. Such unity was not, unfortunately, characteristic of the women's movement as a whole. Within the labor movement, for example, there was a faction in favor of protective legislation. This group urged provision of a legal base for demanding decent and respectful treatment of women by men in workplaces, sanitary facilities, a limit to the number of hours women could be forced to work or the weight of loads they could be forced to lift or carry. The situation was most severe for black women, as Fanny Barrier Williams (who founded the first training school for black nurses) reminded women's conventions: "I do not wish to disturb the serenity of this conference by suggesting why this protection is needed and the kind of men against whom it is needed."[463]

Other working women's groups feared that such legislation would backfire against women. This dispute led to a split among various women's groups and especially between the Women's Trade Union League and the National Women's Party, which spent considerable energy fighting each other rather than addressing the roots of their problems.[464] In time, protective legislation was passed, and it did backfire. Employers reluctant to hire women, or eager to hire them at the lowest possible wages, used the excuse of the cost of "protections" to justify their discriminatory practices.

That the women of a century or more ago did not recognize the profundity of male prejudice and need to subordinate women can hardly be held against them. Women of our own time, and men too, are equally myopic. Men of our time can be heard to lament, "What do women want?" and to assert that this twenty-year-old second wave of the feminist movement has now accomplished what it set out to do. Women of our time are bewildered to find that even when they demonstrate their ability, male prejudice does not disappear. But patterns remain constant: in the labor movement, in the movement for social welfare, just as in the movement to establish Christianity, Protestantism, and (as we will see) socialism, women were accepted by men during the struggle for establishment, but rejected after establishment of the institution.

Moreover, male competition with women remains fierce. Some people accept discrimination against women on grounds of competition to be understandable, "natural"; and in a sense, of course, a competitive world breeds competition in everyone against everyone. There has been extreme rivalry and resentment between whites and blacks, and among various ethnic groups: this contention is fostered by our society. But one must ask why it is that the weakest sense of competition and rivalry lies in middle-level men against upper-level men, whom they are likely to respect, revere, or be awed by; whereas the strongest sense of competition in every class is found in male feelings about females who appear to be intruding on what men consider their turf, their prerogatives, their preserve. The women for whom men entertain such feelings are often of their own class, ethnic group, and religion, and sometimes of their own family. To exclude them, especially from remunerative work, is to harm the family or group of which the men are members. Yet they do so almost without thinking. Clearly, no discrimination is as important to men as that of sex. This reinforces the argument that female inferiority is essential to male self-definition.

Nevertheless, throughout the difficult and painful period from 1850 to 1950, women helped to keep alive values that were being crushed. Today the cult of domesticity is considered ludicrous; at the same time, many of its elements are being reevaluated. The raising of children, once a secondary task (they just grew, after all), then an affectionate, anxious, and responsible one, then a divine mission of women, is seen today as a deeply rewarding occupation for men as well as women, despite its difficulty. Preparing food, decorating a home, and entertaining, once trivialized as women's tasks, have become satisfying and pleasant parts of a stylish life. The cult of domesticity may have been compelling, as one historian describes it, because in a world given over to power struggle and abstraction, it offers sensuous satisfaction, nutritive values, and relief.[465]

Finally, everything women did in this hundred-year period required organization. Women have always had bonds of friendship, have been part of groups Carroll Smith-Rosenberg calls homosocial (or same-sex) networks that supported them emotionally and intellectually. Such bonds provided the bases for many reform groups, like the New York Female Moral Reform Society, which tried to help prostitutes and which attacked men for their sexual behavior.[466] In many cases, women transformed their bonds of friendship into formal organizations, and created models for the "second wave" of the women's movement. In agitating for abolition, temperance, unions, and reforms, as well as suffrage, women heightened their political consciousness and learned organizational skills. They came to understand that leadership was not limited to males.[467] This is just one of the legacies of women's revolutions within the system.

## Nationalist and Socialist Revolutions

Women were participants in every revolutionary uprising in the first part of this century. Even earlier, in the 1880s and 1890s, Italian women joined an anarchist-communist movement known as the *fasci*, against the orders of the Church.[468] Spanish women participated in the anarchist movement before the Civil War of 1936–39.[469] Indian women were deeply involved in Gandhi's passive resistance movement, and some were not passive at all but became terrorists and assassins. When Gandhi was sent to prison in 1939, a woman, Sarojini Naidu, took over temporary leadership of the movement.[470]

Women participated actively in partisan and underground movements during World War II. A hundred thousand women took part in the Yugoslavian Partisan movement; of these, a quarter were killed, and 40 percent more were wounded. Twenty-five thousand Italian women comprised part of that country's Partisan movement; nearly five thousand of these were captured, arrested, tortured, and killed; 625 were killed in action or wounded, 2,750 were deported by the Nazis, and 15 were awarded Italy's Gold Medal.[471] Women parachuted into France to work with the Maquis; women participated importantly in the French Resistance.

Emerging from strict Islamic seclusion, Algerian women were very active in the war of independence from France. Until 1955, combat was waged exclusively by men. Women helped to nurse wounds and shelter revolutionaries, but most were kept in "absolute ignorance" of what their men were doing.[472] The men began to include women because they needed them enough to overcome the weight of tradition for both sexes. At first only married women were used, because the virginity of the younger women had to be strictly guarded. But married women had children, who were left motherless when the women were killed; thus single women were permitted to act. Women functioned as messengers, terrorists, and the carriers and planters of bombs. Many of them were captured, imprisoned, and raped repeatedly by the "civilized" French; they were also hideously tortured. Two women—Djamila Boubired and Djamila Boupacha—became heroines because they held firm under torture.[473] Women's apparel became a political issue. At first, working within the Kasbah carrying tracts and acting as liaison agents, the women wore veils. Later, when they ventured into European sections of cities, they wore Western dress. After 1957, when the authorities became more alert to women's involvement, they resumed the veil in order to carry bombs, grenades, and machine-gun clips strapped to their bodies. The French then began a campaign of forcible unveiling of women, and in response women who had repudiated the veil took it up again.[474]

Nevertheless, when the war was over, women were not consulted about their preferences, but were "sent back to the couscous," required to live under purdah. Liberal proposals for women's personal status and position in the family, drafted in 1966, were never passed.[475] Algerian women who wanted to live freer lives were charged with aping Frenchwomen and betraying their Moslem and Algerian heritage. "Traditional consciousness has combined with Marxist ideology to stifle liberating changes in male-female relations."[476]

The major world movements in the first half of the twentieth century, however, were the National Socialist movement in Germany and the socialist revolutions in the USSR and China. Women were involved in all of these.

Germany had an authoritarian tradition which had constricted women for centuries; it is notable that much of the worst misogynist writing of the nineteenth and early twentieth centuries appeared in Germany and Austria, by men like Schopenhauer, Nietzsche, Weininger, Max Nordau, and P. J. Möbius. Yet Germany also had a Socialist Party which incorporated woman suffrage into its demands long before any major party in other Western European nations, or in the United States. In the upheaval that followed Germany's defeat in World War I, the Socialists were temporarily entrusted with government power, and they enfranchised women and decreed equal rights. But when the 1918–19 crisis subsided, so did loyalty to all Weimar reforms. Germans, including women, were unfamiliar with the idea of "rights"; for centuries German political philosophers had viewed rights as contingent upon "responsibilities," and not as inalienable.[477]

Socialist ideology since the 1870s had espoused women's emancipation, and the party had always recruited women; it opposed autonomous women's organizations. In practice, however, this "integration" of women into the party was a submersion of them: the socialists (then as now in nonsocialist countries) expected women to place their own demands far below the overthrow of capitalism and the organizing of the working class; and they "redefined" the "woman question," narrowing it into a demand for protective legislation. To attract women, party propaganda stressed education and improved conditions for women workers.[478] But at the same time women workers were blamed for "unfair competition" because they worked for lower wages than men. Although the Weimar Republic established many committees dedicated to women's concerns—domestic work, servants, venereal disease, for instance—and despite the official guarantee of equal rights in the 1920s, women did not receive equal pay, were barred from many occupations, and were rarely allowed to hold positions of leadership even within the socialist parties.[479]

After 1918, German liberal and conservative parties also incorporated women, but their appeal stressed antisocialism, nationalism, and the restoration of a national pride deeply wounded by defeat. They called upon women to lead a spiritual revolution to revitalize the nation through their traditional functions with *kinder, küche, kirche*. Because the idea of rights was foreign to them, and because they perceived the fraudulence of the "equality" that was mouthed by the socialists, women followed the bourgeois parties—especially the Catholic parties—in great numbers. Some women within all the political parties pressed for women's rights, but they were blocked by the parties themselves.[480]

The question of why women would support Hitler and the Nazi Party cannot be answered simply. The Nazis were thorough misogynists: Hitler did not address himself to women's concerns at all until 1932; he almost never mentioned women; the party never ran a woman candidate. Hitler told Goebbels privately that "man is the organizer of life, woman is his organ for carrying out plans."[481] One could ask the same question today about American women who support political groups and candidates who oppose women's emancipation. Many women were mustered to oppose the Equal Rights Amendment; women are in the forefront of the campaign against legal abortion; and women continue to support candidates who favor the dismantling of civil rights legislation, that is, who follow racist policies. On the whole, these American women, like the women who supported the Nazis, are seduced by a rhetoric that urges "family values." The women conceive of "family values" as dedicated to the well-being and economic security of children and women, and to the fostering of "feminine" values. They seem unaware of the fact that groups that claim to support "family values" in fact support the continued primacy of power, especially military power, the continued supremacy of white males, and the continued subordination of women and other groups held to be inferior.

Many German women did oppose Hitler, and paid the price for that opposition. But here we will concentrate on those who supported him, those who imagined the revolution he led would improve their lives and those of their children.

Nazi women adored Hitler. They found in him "a genuine German hero—honest, God-fearing, and righteous." They thronged to the Nazi Party and in the early 1920s made up 20 percent of its membership; as time went on, however, more men than women joined, and women's participation dropped to less than 5 percent in 1933.[482] At no time did women have any role in policy making for the Nazis, and of more than fourteen hundred Nazi leaders in 1944, only nine were women.[483]

Nazi women believed the propaganda that told them they were the equals of men but filled complementary roles. This propaganda was highly racist, claiming that among "inferior races" (like Mediterranean peoples) women might be inferior to men, but German women had always been equal to theirs. In time, a superior race would be bred and society would be stratified by race, with the "Aryans" on top. Women accepted this, believing their "Aryan" blood would count for more than their femaleness. They also believed that the creation of their own separate hierarchy within the system would give them greater access to power than assimilation in the male hierarchy. And for a time the situation did seem to justify their expectations.[484]

The story of Nazi women is dishearteningly like that of women in the Protestant sects: they saw themselves as revolutionaries, attempting to "purify" the sexual mores of Weimar Germany, and, as participants in power, having a voice. In the end they were silenced, and men arranged sexual mores to their own liking. In the midst of a desperate economic situation—34 percent unemployment and incredible inflation—they cried out for the restoration of some "natural" order, which seemed to reside in "more masculine men and more feminine women" (whatever that means). Angry, rebellious, and credulous, they had an almost religious faith in the *Führer*, and worked to exhaustion, at times in danger, putting up Nazi posters after dark, smuggling campaign literature through regions of Germany where the party was illegal, and caring for fugitive and wounded SA men, the party's storm troopers. Wearing Nazi armbands, they were harassed in the streets. They were proud of their solidarity and endurance, and, ironically, of their engagement in "unfeminine" acts to restore traditional female roles.[485]

But most of their activities were "feminine" enough—conducting door-to-door campaigns, handing out leaflets, collecting food and clothing for poor party members, sewing clothes for unemployed SA men. The party was uninterested in them and generally ignored them; thus they had considerable autonomy and took this for a sign of trust and respect. They founded clubs and by the late twenties one organization claimed 200,000 members. Elizabeth Zander formed the Red Swastika (later renamed the Order of German Women) and proclaimed herself Hitler's right-hand woman. She and her group published a newspaper, collected large sums of money, arranged charity for Nazi families and homes for SA men. The primary emphasis of her propaganda was motherhood.[486]

By 1931 the Nazi leaders realized they could not seize power by coup or revolution and redirected their efforts toward electoral activities. Hitler knew he needed the women's vote, and in 1932 he introduced two new themes into his speeches: he declared Bolshevism to be a destroyer of the family, and he promised, if elected, to find jobs for all husbands and husbands for all unmarried women. (Two million German men had been killed in World War I, and many women lacked husbands; unemployment was the worst in Europe.) The female vote for the Nazi Party soared, and on the eve of the Nazi takeover, the party attempted to control the women's groups. When the Nazis came to power in January 1933, they announced their policy: "There is no place for the political woman in the ideological world of National Socialism . . . The intellectual attitude of the movement on this score is opposed to the political woman . . . The German resurrection is a male event."[487]

Once in power, Hitler tightened his authority over the party and began a move to "purification"—elimination of political dissidents and "racial undesirables": Jews. Every important woman leader lost her position; some SA and Democratic Labor Front dissidents were purged. Zander was replaced by a man; Gertrud Scholtz-Klink, a woman with no record of achievement or independence, was put in charge of the Women's Bureau, and imposed strict discipline upon it. Yet after four years in office she complained that "while she had marched with Hitler and often appeared on the same speakers' platform, never once had she been allowed to discuss any aspect of his policy on women." In 1942, Hitler wrote, "In no local section of the Party has a woman ever had the right to hold even the smallest post."[488]

The Nazi revolution began as a protest movement, appealing to those who felt alienated by industrialization, threatened by economic depression and socialism, and who yearned for the stability, community, and clarity of a mythical past. But very early the Nazis revealed their intention to possess total power—power to imprison and murder, to control the press and education, and, finally, to eradicate entirely the private realm. Many protest movements erect an "enemy" group, a focus for hatred and revenge, but the intensity of Nazi racism was extraordinary. The formulation of the "final solution"—the determination to murder every member of a people, the Jews, in all of Europe—was shocking enough, but Nazi racism did not end even there. It also aimed to eradicate Poles, gypsies, and others seen as "inferior," as well as people deemed physically, morally, or politically undesirable, some of whom were German.

The Nazi program amounted to an inexorable campaign against everything human except for a narrowly defined standard of humanity, those who were to produce a master race. Thus it aimed straight at the heart, at breeding. Promising to support men in small businesses, artisans, farmers, and housewives, it moved into the private realm and destroyed it. The party took control of marriage, offering state loans to couples who were non-Jewish and who promised the wife would not work outside the home. The loan was reduced by a quarter for each child born, and special awards were given to couples who had nine children—or seven sons. It instituted a series of laws outlawing birth control and making abortion a more severe offense than it had been. At the same time, it asserted that all children belonged to the state and pressured them into joining youth groups—although the party was concerned mainly with the activities of boys. Illegitimate children were declared legitimate, and divorce was made easy for men. The Nazis sterilized women for prostitution, psychological disorders, and genetic defects; they also killed the old, feeble, or impaired. The ideal held up for women was motherhood: Hitler needed men for his armies. Women whose husbands worked for the government had already (in 1932, pre-Hitler) been dismissed from their jobs with the concurrence of all parties except the Communists. But now women under thirty-five were denied permanent jobs, quotas were imposed on women with higher education, and women physicians were forbidden to practice except jointly with their husbands. Women's church organizations were deprived of even the semblance of autonomy.[489]

After 1936, as Hitler began to think more concretely about war, the Nazis reversed their employment policy and began to recruit women for jobs. Quotas and restrictions were silently dropped. Women's wages remained unequal—75 percent of men's—and when women complained, the Ministry of Labor declared, "There can be no basic equality with the man." Propaganda offered a new image, woman as eternal mother and fighting comrade of man; at the same time, the Nazis in private memos referred to women as "geese" and "dumb prattlers" and blamed women for poor morale because they cluttered up the streets standing in line to buy food.[490]

But when war began in 1939, many women, occupied with their large families, resisted outside employment, and in 1943 the Nazis forced women to register with the employment bureau. They were then sent into previously all-male jobs in construction, munitions factories, shipyards, and foundries. Listed as "social workers," they were sent along with the armies to defeated countries. Through it all they were expected to continue to bear children and to indoctrinate them with Nazism, and children were pressured to report parents who did not do this. In 1939, special camps were set up for young unmarried women; men visited them there, and after they had filled their function, the women were taken to special homes for unwed mothers. Even as Allied bombers were destroying Berlin, and Hitler was living in a bunker, he was planning breeding practices for after the war, a polygamous society in which every decorated soldier would be permitted more than one wife. As the country fell to pieces, Hitler informed women they were now equal: he pressed them into service in the military as scouts, saboteurs, medics, communications aides, and messengers, although they were given neither uniforms nor weapons.[491]

Thus the Nazi revolution was a disaster for those who supported it as well as those who opposed it and those who were its prey. Socialist and Communist women delegates to the Reichstag during the Weimar Republic, and women who opposed Nazi rule, were executed along with their male counterparts, or sent to one of the five concentration camps built especially for women. Some women played up to male Nazis by behaving maternally or flirtatiously while they transported forged documents or harbored Jewish refugees. Their names have passed into oblivion, although there is evidence of their actions.[492]

To concentrate on the oppression of women during a period of such horror to another group of people may seem an evasion of moral judgment, especially since I have focused on those women who supported the Nazis. But it is precisely such women whose experience is instructive, for Nazi policies toward women were at root imbued with the same values as their policies toward Jews. When sorrow is put aside, what can we learn from Auschwitz? Aghast, we are forced to accept the depths of hate and cruelty of which human beings are capable. But if we want to understand how such events can occur, how the human mind can adopt Nazi attitudes, Nazi values, how the heart can be turned to allow one to perform such actions, we can learn from the experience of Nazi women, victims who colluded in their victimization. Believing ultimately in the innate superiority of one kind over others, believing that society should be purified of elements seen as polluting, as if it were water passing through a filter, believing that obedience and dedication to "feminine" values could win them respect and admiration, they are easy to scorn in hindsight. Unless we are willing to call such attitudes *evil*, we cannot call Nazi women evil; yet such attitudes are found today, everywhere, among people who consider themselves most virtuous.

In no other revolution did women play so significant a part as the Russian. Even before the Boleshevik uprising, women had agitated on political issues. They took the lead during the Cossack Revolt of 1819, and participated in the uprising at Sevastopol in 1830. After the latter 375 women were condemned to death.[493]

There is evidence of egalitarianism and independence of women in the pre-Christian period of Russian history; the notion of mother-right persisted longer among Slavs than among other Europeans. Consanguinity was determined by the maternal side, and household management, cultivation of the soil, and productive industry was in the hands of women. They appeared for themselves in courts, and undertook ordeal by battle; they acted as judges, law-givers, and rulers. In the nineteenth century a Russian historian claimed that Slavic civilization was created by women.[494]

After Russia converted to the Greek Orthodox Church around 1000, oriental customs developed, which were fostered during the period of the Tatar invasion (1238 to about 1450). Women came to be seen as tainted and sinful, and were virtually imprisoned for life in the private parts of the homes of their fathers or husbands. Liberalizing reforms occurred under Peter the Great in the seventeenth century, Catherine II in the eighteenth, and Alexander I in the early nineteenth, but in the mid-nineteenth century Russian women still lived in oppression, and often in extreme degradation.[495] As in Germany, the system was authoritarian; those granted authority had the legal right and the weight of tradition behind them whether they bought and sold and brutalized their serfs or practiced verbal abuse and physical punishment on their wives and children. Male serfs abused by their owners in turn abused their families.

Authoritarian patriarchal behavior oppresses sons as well as daughters, but bourgeois sons can escape from the home eventually and can gain education. As in other revolutions, it was Russian sons who first rebelled and who argued for the liberation of women. The writings of these men inflamed bourgeois women in the 1850s and 1860s, and some of them devised means to leave home, while others banded together in women's groups to discuss their needs and raise their consciousness. They tried to rid themselves of stereotypic "feminine" characteristics; they wanted education, employment, and the right to leave their fathers' houses.[496]

After the serfs were emancipated in 1861, many families of the gentry faced financial disaster and could not support their unmarried daughters. The young women fled from their families but found they could not support themselves. In 1862 three middle-class women formed the first organization for women run by women, intending to provide housing and, later, jobs for poor but genteel women without men. They called it the Society for Inexpensive Quarters. They wished to function, however, within the limits set by the existing government and the prevailing ethos. Their hierarchical, elitist methods alienated young, politically aware women. These women experimented with communal living and collective workshops, but neither proved successful.[497]

Political repression forced women and men into political activity and sometimes radicalism. Male revolutionaries courted women, who joined their groups eagerly, but the men excluded them from decision making and leadership positions, used the women casually for sex, and at least in one group went so far as to ask the women to support them through prostitution.[498] In the 1870s, university classes—but not degrees—were opened to women and they flocked to the cities. Most of them were feminists, but many were socialists also, and they were torn by the conflict that actually (if not in principle) existed between the two. A group of Russian women studying in Zurich formed the first female radical organization; they debated about the proper relation between intellectuals and the peasantry. Michael Bakunin and Paul Lavrov were also in Zurich, and it was their theories that formed the matter of the debate. Lavrov believed intellectuals should educate themselves as fully as possible and then use their knowledge to benefit the peasants; Bakunin believed that education increased the distance between the two classes, and that intellectuals should abandon education and go to work among the peasants to persuade them to the revolution and to learn from them. Peasants were illiterate, and comprised more than three-quarters of the population.

Most of the Zurich group became Bakuninists, and on their return to Russia in 1874 joined with men of similar views to form the Pan-Russian Social Revolutionary Organization. This organization's aim was to go to the country and work in factories, converting the peasants to socialism. Only the women actually carried out this task, taking jobs that involved thirteen to fourteen hours a day of hard labor, sleeping on narrow boards in filthy, infested dormitories, locked inside the factory except on holidays. After work, taking great risks, they tried to talk and read to the exhausted, uninterested workers. They were not very successful at first, and just as their labors were about to bear fruit, they were arrested. The state held them in solitary confinement for three years before they were tried.[499]

Governmental surveillance and oppression was extreme, which made peaceful efforts at education and propaganda impossible. In 1878, Vera Zasulich, a revolutionary, shot the governor general of St. Petersburg for ordering the beating of a political prisoner who had not removed his cap in the governor's presence. Her act triggered a split in the major populist organization, Land and Liberty: one group chose to continue to work through education and propaganda; the other, calling itself the People's Will, became a terrorist organization. Women were important in both, but made up a third of the People's Will, which stressed total commitment and self-sacrifice for the cause. Its members, women and men, set type and ran illegal printing presses together; prepared bombs, forged documents, and planned and executed six assassination attempts against Alexander II. One member of the group, Sofia Perovskaia, directed the actual assassination of the czar. She was hanged, becoming the first woman in Russia to suffer capital punishment for a political crime.[500] But other women were suffering as well: of the more than 2500 people arrested for political crimes between 1873 and 1879, about 15 percent were women;[501] of the forty-three sentences to hard labor—probably for terrorist acts—handed down between 1880 and 1890, half were to women.[502]

Vera Zasulich, who was acquitted at her trial, remained active and founded a Marxist party in 1898, but women were less prominent in Marxist groups than in terrorist groups like the Socialist Revolutionaries.[503] Zasulich's party, the Social Democratic Workers, split into Bolshevik (revolutionist) and Menshevik (gradualist) factions. Revolutionary fervor was fueled by an oppressive government and by the fact that life was terrible for the poor, who comprised the overwhelming majority of the population. Marxists—both Bolsheviks and Mensheviks—accepted the idea of the equality of women, but had no specific plans for achieving it and little energy to spare for working on it. It was largely because of pressure from Nadezhda Krupskaia (Lenin's wife) and the feminists Alexandra Kollontai and Inessa Armand that the Bolsheviks eventually formulated programs designed to assimilate women into the public sphere.

Russia had begun to industrialize in the 1890s, but in 1897 women still made up only a tiny percentage of the industrial labor force. By 1913 they comprised 26 percent, but they were earning only 47 percent of what men earned. By 1917 they made up 43 percent of this force, partly because so many men were in the armed forces or had been killed in World War I. By then, all major parties were in favor of equality for women, and the czarists promised them suffrage because of their sacrifices during the war. Because so many men—nearly four million—had been killed, wounded, taken prisoner, or were missing, many women were the sole support of their families. Educated women were highly conscious of feminist issues, and working women were aware of them. Women revived the militance of earlier years and began to demonstrate again. It was women who triggered the February Revolution of 1917, when, against the advice of all parties, they decided to call a general strike on International Women's Day. They exhorted women workers to join them; they called out to housewives standing on bread lines; they went to the Putilov works and asked the metalworkers to follow them. Reluctantly, and only after it was clear that the army would not fire on them, the men joined.[504] An article in *Pravda* described it thus: "The women were the first in the streets of Petrograd on their Women's Day. The women of Moscow in many cases decided the destiny of the troops: they went to the barracks, spoke to the soldiers, and the latter joined the revolution."[505]

The struggle continued, and in March the czar was forced to abdicate. A provisional government was formed to rule until an assembly could be elected. It granted women the vote, making Russia the first major power to so so. But the provisional government was not adequate to its task, and struggle among the various parties continued until November, when the Bolsheviks took over. During the struggle, women acted as soldiers and scouts, cavalry, machine-gunners, commanders, and drove armored trains.[506] The poor women of Petrograd swarmed into the streets along with boys and men armed only with shovels. The women were physically deformed from overwork, malnutrition, and abuse; they lacked weapons; they did not even have decent clothing.[507] Louise Bryant wrote, "Women ran straight into the fire without any weapons at all. It was terrifying to see them. . . . The Cossacks seemed superstitious about it. They began to retreat."[508] On November 7, 1917, the Bolsheviks began to rule Russia.

Almost immediately their government began to pass laws freeing women from male domination. It mandated equal pay for equal work, an idea as yet unthinkable to the rest of the world. It established prohibitions against women doing certain kinds of hot, heavy, or hazardous work, as well as against overtime and night work. It set up protections for pregnant and nursing women. The revolutionary Family Code of 1918 abolished distinctions between children born within or outside marriage; granted each person—female as well as male—control of their own earnings; and granted women the right to retain their own names after marriage, live where they chose, have their own passports, and obtain divorce easily. Alimony was abolished; all women were expected to work outside the home. Under Alexandra Kollontai, the first commissar of social welfare (and later the first—and last—female ambassador from Russia), nurseries and prenatal care facilities were created.[509] In 1919 a set of women's bureaus—the Zhenotdely—were established; they began campaigns for literacy and special education for women.[510]

But even as such legislation was being prepared, and before new customs and institutions could be fully established, civil war erupted, in June 1918. It was an especially cruel war for everyone, but particularly for women, who were savaged by men on both sides, Bolsheviks (Reds) and anti-Bolsheviks (Whites), who raped women with impunity. One city declared it a crime for a woman to "refuse a Communist," and another declared all women state property, along with any children born of such unions. Women and men were conscripted for "labor armies" and forced to work under military discipline in hideous conditions.[511]

The Civil War ended in 1921, having killed almost 10 percent of the population and leaving seven million homeless children roaming the countryside. The country and the economy were a shambles. In the ruined nation, protective legislation was an impediment: there was no money for the compulsory education the government had decreed, or for child-care centers, nurseries, and laundries. Although laws against women working at night and in mines had been repealed, other protective laws remained, making employers reluctant to hire women. Men objected to paid maternity leave, and managers did not want to pay it.[512] Lowest paid, last hired, first fired, consigned to the most menial work, women who could retreated back to the home. By 1928 women comprised less than a quarter of the labor force; most of these were widows, divorcees, and unmarried girls. However, compulsory primary education had lowered female illiteracy from 90 or 95 percent (in 1919) to 70 percent.[513]

The story of women throughout the period of agitation, revolutionary activity, and the aftermath of the revolution in Russia is particularly poignant, because there (as in China) some real effort was made to improve the condition of women, yet it improved little and perhaps even deteriorated. Some might say, with those who opposed the civil rights movement in the United States in the 1950s, that morality cannot be legislated. Certainly men's abuse of women during the Civil War was a cruel and stupid response to notions of women's emancipation, and such responses continued. Men were in short supply and women were grateful to find one: this tended to make them defer to the male. Easy divorce enabled men to walk away from marriages, leaving behind a woman who could not find work and who often had more children to care for than she had before. Men accused women who refused them sexually of "bourgeois prudery." The grievance most frequently brought before Zhenotdely was that male plant managers used women workers as a harem. In the country, some peasants married women and used their labor in the fields for a season, then divorced them after the harvest, having had free labor, owing the women nothing. By 1926 the number of destitute women and children alarmed the government and forced another revision of family law.[514]

The government decreed that cohabitation meant marriage, and that alimony could be granted for a year to women who could not find work. All children were to be supported by their fathers, and if a woman was not sure of the identity of the father, all possibilities had to take partial responsibility for the child. The law also instituted "postcard divorce." After passage of this law, the divorce rate rose 450 percent in Petrograd and 300 percent in Moscow; most were initiated by women who hoped to obtain some support. The courts usually allotted a third of a man's wages for support, but when men had two or three or more former wives, the situation became impossible. Moreover, in cities men simply disappeared.[515]

Some problems women faced in this period were shared by men—an economy struggling to become sufficient, primitive living conditions, harsh work conditions, illiteracy. But women had special problems, as they always do. They are seen as inferior and as sexual prey; they have the babies; and, by and large, they are the ones to take responsibility for those babies. These problems are not limited to Russia, nor to socialist countries, and they will recur in this study. They were severe in Russia because the condition of the country at large was dire.

When Stalin came to power, he instituted a totally planned economy of massive industrialization. He abolished Zhenotdely and pressed for employment of women in assembly-line factory work, training for the entire labor force, and the eradication of illiteracy. He created female quotas in technical schools and recruited women for party membership and positions of some prominence. Because juggling work and child care was so difficult, young women began to choose not to marry or have children. The birth rate began to fall off.

So Stalin ordered a return to conventional family structure, a pronatalist policy, and puritanical sexual morality. Abortion was restricted and in some places abolished; divorce was made more difficult and costly. Anticipating frequent pregnancies, managers hesitated to train or promote women; Stalin annulled female quotas in technical schools and the number of women accepted dropped by half. Propaganda offered a new female image, the superwoman who worked all day, had several children, yet made a "serene" home for her husband. In 1936, Stalin began the purges of the "great terror." Only 10 percent of those purged were women, but they included almost all women who had attained any position of authority.[516]

The Germans invaded the USSR in 1941, forcing mobilization, and policies regarding women were again changed, as they were in Nazi Germany—and elsewhere. Again women were recruited for industrial work; by 1945 they comprised 56 percent of the labor force, a majority of miners, and a third of the workers in the Baku oil fields. They worked fourteen to eighteen hours a day without complaint. They took part in combat as guerrillas, machine-gunners, and snipers. Several air regiments were composed entirely of women and many women worked in the medical and signal corps.[517] The nation was fighting for survival and, as a nation, it was heroic, men and women. But when the war was over, women were again restricted.

So many people had been killed—twenty million men alone—that the government became even more strictly pronatalist. It removed women from jobs to give them to men, and to keep men in the family it granted them de facto head-of-household status and preference in inheritance. Illegitimate children were deprived of inheritance and stigmatized, and women lost the right to file paternity suits. Abortion was now illegal, and women were rewarded for having many children. But women still had to work: and many of them were without men—there were 150 women to 100 men in Russia after the war. A small percentage became professionals—doctors, engineers, and scientists. But most did the most poorly paid work: they dug ditches, shoveled snow, built roads, worked in construction and, as always, in the fields. In the 1950s women comprised four-fifths of the unskilled laborers.[518] It is an appalling statement on the condition of women before the Russian Revolution that their condition afterward—and after two more wars—was in fact improved. We will return to Russian women in the next section.

The condition of women in China before the 1949 revolution was so terrible that women frequently chose death over life. The national literature is full of stories of women who, finding their lives intolerable, threw themselves down the family well or hanged themselves from the marriage bed still dressed in their wedding clothes.[519] Young women might be sold into slavery, or beaten by their parents to force them into marriage.

In 1919, Chao Wu-chieh of Nanyang Street, Changsha, was prepared for a wedding over her objections. She had met the man she was to marry only briefly, but had disliked him intensely and refused to marry him. Her parents compelled her. Dressed in the wedding costume, seated in the ceremonial chair in which the bride is carried to the home of the groom's family, where she will be isolated and abused for most of the rest of her life, Miss Chao Wu-chieh was lifted aloft. She slid out from behind the cushion the dagger she had hidden there and slit her throat. The event was unremarkable; it was a common occurrence. It is remembered only because it was the occasion of protest of a young man from Changsha, who wrote nine impassioned articles about it, using it as his base for discussion of women and the family in China. His name was Mao Tse-tung, and he was not yet a Marxist.[520]

Some scholars believe that ancient China was matrilineal. It had a tradition of shamanesses and powerful empresses in the first millennium C.E., Western time. Like Greece, China has a literature replete with female figures of great power and dignity and a history in which women are diminished and degraded, isolated within the home, without rights. Footbinding was established at some time between the T'ang (618 C.E.) and the Sung (969–1257) dynasties, as a symbol of class and for aesthetic reasons, small feet being seen as beautiful.[521] But aesthetic reasons often mask political ones. Footbinding is quite literally torture that begins when a little girl is seven and ends when she is fully grown, in adolescence. Once her bones have stopped growing and the foot bones are completely curved in on themselves, the pain ends. If she has not died of gangrene, the girl is crippled. Until then she is freed from the bindings only for brief times during the day, when they are removed and her feet bathed.

When the bindings are removed permanently, she has presumably learned what she needs to know about being a woman. Occasionally a family that expected its daughter to marry into a higher class would bind her feet but then be unable to find her a higher-class husband. She would then have to do the work appropriate to her class—laboring in the fields, pulling canal barges, carrying water—on crippled stumps of feet.[522]

But footbinding was only the most obvious torment girls suffered. They were not considered members of their natal families and had no position within them. The only position women possessed was through their husbands' lineage. If a girl died before being married, there was no place in the ancestral temple of her own family for her soul.[523] Even after she was married, a woman was not accepted by her husband's family until she gave birth to a son. It was forbidden for a man to show affection to his wife in public, and even in private he was expected to ally himself with his family against his wife. Whipping of wives was common, and a Chinese proverb runs, "A wife married is like a pony bought; I'll ride her and whip her as I like."[524] A wife was not permitted to "go out into society," that is, to mingle with people outside the household group. She was expected to be a serving drudge within the family.

Often families would purchase girl children as wives for their young sons, so as to get several years of work out of them before the marriage could be consummated and childbearing began. A girl was subject to physical abuse by her own family before she married and by her husband's family afterward; she could be locked up, beaten, and even tortured or killed.

For most women there were no alternatives to marriage except slavery.[525] If a man had no son, he would adopt one and leave him his entire estate, which included any natural daughters; the adopted son could dispose of them as he wished. A widow became the property of her late husband's family, which could sell her as a wife, a concubine, or a slave. If she remarried, the first family could keep her dowry and any property she brought into the marriage—thus there was often pressure on a widow to remarry so the dead husband's kinsmen could obtain her property. At the same time there was social pressure for women to remain "chaste widows," like the Roman *univirae*. Women were caught between the contradictory pressures.[526] The only women with any power at all were mothers-in-law, who were granted the right to inflict on their sons' wives the cruelty they had endured. Chinese fiction offers many female figures of great power—mothers-in-law, shrewd wives, and clever concubines— who were able to exert great influence on the family through their intelligence, their understanding of family politics, or their great age, but in all cases these women's power was personal, a consequence of their own characters. It never amounted to authority, to institutionalized rights.[527]

Mao Tse-tung perceived early the injustice of the family order. His mother was loving and nutritive, his father tyrannical. The father bought an older woman as a bride for his son when Mao was still a boy, in order to exploit her labor until Mao matured. When it was time for them to be married, Mao ran away from home in protest. He was brought back, but was able to contest his father's will. However, he never forgot the incident, and the suicide of Chao Wu-chieh apparently touched a deep chord of sympathy in him.[528]

There were two main currents in Chinese thinking: Taoism and Confucianism, with its three bonds *(san kang)*: those binding ruler and subject, father and son, and husband and wife.[529] (Women were bound by the "three obediences": to father, then to husband, and, as a widow, to son.[530]) Thus Chinese men also suffered from oppression, and China has a long history of peasant revolts, outlaw uprisings, and local rebellions. In the early twentieth century young men began to agitate for moral and political change to free them from their fathers. Certain intellectuals and revolutionaries were convinced that the oppression of men was connected to the oppression of women and that freedom could not be obtained for one without the other. Marriage after all was unfree for both sexes; obedience was enjoined on both. The original membership of the Peking Alliance for the Women's Rights Movement was two-thirds male; for a long time in China men were the major supporters of women's rights.[531]

Young men were also agitating for revolt against the domination of China by European powers and in some cases against the domination of China by the Han, the large majority among various Chinese ethnic groups. There was great frustration in China throughout the nineteenth century because of the extreme rigidity of the culture, overpopulation, and oppression by white—European and American—societies. It was Han culture which was the most rigid and demanded most subordination of sons and women.

Not all women were utterly constricted. Some wealthy fathers educated their daughters and treated them gently; at times they permitted their daughters considerable latitude. Peasant women were not secluded, nor were their feet usually bound. They were needed to work in the house and fields, and consequently had some access to the outside world of the village. Because of this groups of village women were able to speak together and could often influence the behavior of cruel mothers-in-law and men. Chinese men had an almost superstitious fear of a furious woman, and a woman who could rouse herself to rage and maintain it might be beaten but might also have an effect on family matters.[532] Daughters of "Boxers" who belonged to the Taoist cults received training in the martial arts, and minority (non-Han) generals trained their daughters as well as their sons in soldiery. These women often entered the political arena as rebels or bandits.[533] Lower-class women from families with similar traditions might become nuns or shamans, herbalists or midwives.[534] It was women such as these who participated in the Taiping Rebellion, which lasted from 1850 to 1864 and was one of the world's worst civil wars.[535]

The rebellion arose in the southern provinces of China, which were suffering from agrarian distress, unemployment, and inflation. The rebels had a revolutionary program that included redistribution of land, the establishment of communal property, and equality of the sexes. Some of the founding members of the revolutionary force were Hakka women, who had a freer and less subordinate tradition than Han women. They influenced the Taiping platforms, which included an edict against footbinding and the right of women to take Taiping examinations—a kind of local civil service examination—and function in official positions. They demanded complete equality of women and men, communal property, abolition of prostitution, and monogamy based on mutual love. They organized their own fighting corps, and their mere presence, it was said, defeated the morale of the imperial armies facing them.[536] The Taipings were defeated in their civil war, but their women had already been defeated—betrayed—by their own men, whose attitudes toward women's rights had been at best ambivalent throughout the struggle.[537] Still, the Taiping program remained to serve as a model and inspiration for the Chinese Communist Party (CCP).[538]

Agitation continued, and in 1904, Sun Yat-sen created the Nationalist Party, the Kuomintang (KMT); it accepted women as well as men as members. The first woman to join was Ch'iu Chin, a revolutionary who had been educated but then forced into an unhappy marriage. She fled it to become a schoolteacher in Shanghai and tried to organize her pupils to start an uprising. She established the first feminist newspaper, the *Chinese Women's Journal;* she also wore Western dress, which provoked a riot. For her participation in an assassination attempt, she was captured, was subjected to terrible torture, and finally confessed. Her confession was a poem: "Autumn rain and autumn wind sadden us." She was beheaded at the age of thirty-three.[539]

A major rebellion occurred in 1911, and among the fighters were battalions of women demanding women's rights. After the empire fell, Sun Yat-sen became president and a new constitution was drafted. Although it made provision for education of girls and denominated women as citizens—for the first time—it did not guarantee equal rights. Women in the cities rioted, smashed windows, and trampled the military guard, but they were too few to force change. Their behavior provided an example for women in the provinces, however, who began to submit demands to legislative bodies. Women's groups organized to fight for equality and suffrage around the country.[540]

The new government was shaky; in 1912, Sun abdicated to a military man, Yuan Shih-k'ai, who tried unsuccessfully to make himself emperor and died in 1916. During this period Chinese society became militarized; shady deals were made with the imperialist countries, especially Japan, which were given financial rights in China in return for loans; and the ideals of full democracy were crushed.[541] Women members of the revolutionary party were expelled or forced to submit to the new government. Deprived of legal political expression, women again resorted to military action, and joined the National Army or the Assassination Corps. As they had in the previous revolution, they dressed and equipped themselves like men.[542]

On May 4, 1919, there were massive student demonstrations against China's humiliating treatment by the Western powers at the Versailles Conference. The students organized to fight for nationalism and feminism, and against Confucianism and imperialism. Among other demands they listed equality of the sexes, freedom of marriage and association.[543] It was during this period that Mao wrote his feminist articles; at this point he had continually to remind his readers that women were part of *jen*—roughly, the human race.

The May Fourth Movement was China's first modern cultural revolution, and, in a sense, it had no end. It continued and continues to attack Confucianism and its three bonds; it was led by men who were deeply feminist, like Li Ta-chao, Ch'en Tu-hsiu, Hu Shih, and Mao Tse-min, the younger brother of

Mao Tse-tung.[544] There were also female feminists. One of these was Hsiang Ching-yu, who, like Mao, came from Hunan. She attended Changsha's most progressive school for women and later established a coeducational primary school in which she tried to create an environment that was sexually equal, antihierarchical, and that inculcated missionary zeal. She went to France with a group of students in a work-study program and, like her contemporary, Simone Weil, supported herself there by working part-time in a rubber plant and a textile mill. She came to understand profoundly the conditions of proletarian life. She began to study anarchist, Marxist, and social-democratic thought, and she concluded that the May Fourth Movement was "a bourgeois fight of women against men," and that the emancipation of women could occur only within a socialist revolution.

Others were coming to a similar conclusion, and the Chinese Communist Party was organized in Shanghai in 1921. Hsiang and her husband, with others in their work-study group, joined the CCP from France. The party was small at first; when Hsiang returned to China in 1922, she was appointed the first woman member of the Central Committee, and head of the Women's Department. At this time the CCP worked within the KMT, although the Communists took their direction from Moscow. Hsiang went to Moscow to study Marxism-Leninism, and returned to China in 1927 to organize male and female contingents of the labor movement in and around Shanghai.[545]

The KMT accepted Communist participation in the laborious ongoing conflict with various warlords, who had to be subdued one by one. But Sun died in 1925, and Chiang Kai-shek, a young general, took command. He subdued warlords and ousted foreign powers. Flushed by victories, he marched toward Shanghai in 1927, demanding that Communists rid themselves of their weapons and give the city over to KMT forces. Uneasily the CCP obeyed Moscow's orders to obey Chiang. The events that followed are recounted vividly and movingly in André Malraux's *Man's Fate*, although that novel deals only with men.

Chiang took the city with no opposition, but immediately began to round up all CCP leaders, members of Communist-controlled labor unions, and people simply suspected of being opposed to Chiang. He unleashed the "white terror" which killed thousands of people in Shanghai and other cities. Women were killed simply for having bobbed hair.[546] A young woman who had freely chosen her fiancé was tortured, then shot seventeen times; women's noses and breasts were cut off. Before beheading young women, KMT soldiers shouted at them: "You have your free love now!" The Women's Department was destroyed and its organizers imprisoned and tortured. Hsiang went underground but was later captured and publicly executed. She defended herself by citing the revolutionary goals of *liberté, égalité, et fraternité*.[547] After 1927, women were no longer an important political entity within the KMT.

The Communists retreated and regrouped in 1929 in Kiangsi, where they organized peasants, reaching out to women as much as to men. Peasant women, whose lives were unrelievedly hard and bleak, were very responsive to the Communist message. The CCP tested and developed various social and economic policies in their base areas. In 1931 they announced a new marriage policy; they prohibited infanticide, footbinding, prostitution, as well as tyrannical mothers-in-law. Property rights were to be held equally; marriage and divorce were to be by mutual consent and to cost nothing.[548]

Because marriages and divorces had to be registered, the Communists planned state involvement in the marriage system for the first time in China.[549] Centralization and bureaucratization superseded hierarchy and tradition. KMT attacks were constant, and women were organized in defense forces, nursing units, and intelligence and sabotage work. "Large-feet," women whose feet had not been bound, worked in the fields. In Kiangsi, women were extremely active politically, making up 30 percent of the district congresses in 1930, 62 percent in 1931, and 64 percent in 1932.[550] But the political order set up in Kiangsi proved to be a short-lived experiment. Although they were threatened by the Japanese, who after the Versailles Treaty had intensified their encroachment upon China, the KMT directed their energies to pursuing the Communists with fervor, and in 1934 drove them out of Kiangsi. The CCP armies headed north, hoping to link up with other Communist units: a hundred thousand men went on the Long March; with them were perhaps thirty to fifty women.[551] Women whose feet had been bound could not march; the women stayed with the land. A great many of those who remained were killed.

For several years the CCP had been urging Chiang to form a united front with them against the Japanese, but Chiang was backed by monied interests and preferred to fight Communists. Japan's massive invasion of China in 1937 forced Chiang into a united front, but after the first year it was an uneasy match and continued shakily until the end of the Sino-Japanese War in 1945. And the moment that war ended, the War of Liberation, between KMT and CCP forces, began. As in Russia, there was no respite.

During the war years women entered production in great numbers—but you have heard that story before in these pages. In addition to their usual role of household drudge, they worked making vegetable oil, curing leather, making paper. The Japanese occupation and the KMT blockade had cut off sources of cloth, and Mao urged women to spin, weave, and sew: by 1947, areas under CCP control were self-sufficient in cloth. As the women did this work, however, they gathered in groups. This was a novelty for women who had been forbidden to mingle with people outside the household. They spoke to each other; they compared notes; they politicized each other. Eventually they organized and began to speak out in public. The Women's Association became a vital part of village life. It trained its members to do sabotage and repair bridges and roads, to gather intelligence and carry messages, to prepare food for soldiers and nurse the wounded.[552]

As soon as the Japanese had been expelled, the CCP instituted land reform in the areas it controlled. It took land from the landlords and gave it to people—not to families, but to men and women. For the first time in at least a millennium, Chinese women had something of their own. Women who had never before worked in the fields began to do so; they also began to leave oppressive and abusive husbands. In CCP-controlled areas of northern China between January and June of 1948, 64 percent of all civil cases were petitions for divorce, most brought by women. On the other hand, in 464 cases in which a woman's death was investigated, 40 percent had involved women who had wanted divorces but had been unable to get them. Some of these deaths were suicides; others were murders.[553]

The War of Liberation took four years—or forty years, depending on how you count. The People's Republic of China was established in 1949; women were among those on the presidium, among those who wrote the new constitution. When the People's Congress met in 1954, women comprised 14 percent of the membership elected by popular vote. They made up as much as 40 percent of elected officials in certain districts, and some were heads of town governments. The All-China Democratic Women's Federation formed in the spring of 1949 was "possibly the largest single mass organization and the most active one ever formed in the history of mankind." In 1956 it had 76 million members; the CCP had only 11 million.[554] It worked to support, unify, and offer direction to the thousands of Women's Associations throughout the country, and to help millions of women learn economic self-reliance.

The Chinese Revolution seemed a wonderful anomaly—the only revolution in history to remain faithful to the feminist principles with which it began and to the women who participated in it. But so was the Russian: at first.

## 9. UP TO THE PRESENT

"Up to the Present" is somewhat misleading, because broad, general tendencies cannot be perceived until time has elapsed. Collections of data are always obsolete by the time they appear. In addition, statistical data must be culled and interpreted by researchers, which sometimes takes years; this is especially true for countries like the USSR and China. This section will bring accounts as close to the moment as possible, but by the time you read this, the moment will be long gone.

The age of terrible class revolutions is not over. They continue in Africa, Southeast Asia, Central and South America. Some are directed at ousting imperialist powers; some begin that way and continue as civil wars. These revolutions are terrible because they are usually wars in which a small elite class—backed usually by a Western power, not infrequently the United States—is granted arms and sometimes men to help them fight against the poor or lower-middle classes, the majority of their populations. The cruelty and savagery of these struggles is reflected in Amnesty International's figures on political prisoners, arrest without trial, and torture in dozens of countries around the globe. If one's sympathies are generally with the poor majority, one still must recognize that often those who claim to represent them impose restrictions as oppressive as those of the ousted elite; that indeed, a new elite is formed.

In this process of power seeking, women are discarded. Women were extremely active in the Sandinist revolution against the dictatorship of the Somozas in Nicaragua. They were organizers, soldiers, guerrillas; they also offered traditional kinds of female support, providing nursing, food, clothing. When the revolution was won, however, conflict broke out between male and female Sandinistas: the men wanted the women to go back home, and the women, having helped to direct the revolution, wanted to help direct the new establishment. But at present there is no woman among the five members of the governing junta or the nine members of the Sandinist National Directorate, although there is one woman in the cabinet, the minister of health, and the Nicaraguan ambassador to the United States in 1981 was a woman. Moreover, the new government is now engaged in persecution of a minority group, the Miskitos, in Nicaragua—that is, if the information we receive is accurate.

The women of western Europe also continue to struggle against great odds. Greek women comprise 78 percent of the illiterates in Greece, and earn only 68 percent as much as men—the lowest ratio in Europe, although it is higher than the 59 percent of the United States. Like Italian women, they have had to struggle for the right to divorce, for legal abortion and other rights over their own bodies. Until the Ayatollah Khomeini's forces took control of the revolution in Iran, Iranian women were active both in the struggle to overthrow the shah and in furthering their own rights.

The discussion in this section, however, concentrates on those nations which have made the greatest effort to incorporate women as full members of the human race—China and the USSR—and those which have made the greatest effort to keep women in dependent seclusion—the Islamic nations. The recent reemergence of the women's movement in the United States will be discussed in Chapter Six.

## China

Traveling down the east coast of China you see broad fields watery and light green with rice shoots. The water evaporates in the sun, sending a shimmering haze from the land. Each parcel of land is carefully banked and dammed, in squares or wonderful crazy patterns, all the way to the mountains. There are always mountains, and in summer there is always sun. The baked adobe houses with red tile roofs abut each other along hillsides, so old and weathered that they look part of earth itself, like the cave dwellings of ancient tribes. Everywhere something is growing. There are trees around the houses, the willows you'd expect from Chinese paintings, and in the little ponds, some mere muddy puddles, there are always ducks. Boys laugh, pulling at a water buffalo who is bathing itself in a stream; children throng before small clusters of houses, so many that you can't believe the government's natal policy is working in the countryside. In the rice fields people walk slowly, forty or fifty in a line; some carry umbrellas or waxed-paper parasols; some hold hands. As they walk through the ankle- or calf-high water, they weed the rice fields with their toes. In middle age, they develop arthritis.

The change in China in only thirty years is astonishing. Major diseases are under control. The population is fed. (There are rumors of local famines; like other disasters, these are concealed by the government.) Medical care is good, even excellent, and almost all children receive education.

There are few roads, and most of those are primitive. There are comparatively few motorized vehicles, but still the roads are clogged with them, trailing behind a hundred stubborn bicyclers who will not give way no matter how often the trucks honk their horns. Horn honking is the only form of traffic control in China, and in the cities it is constant. Many vehicles are horse-drawn carts—small ones carrying faggots or logs or vegetables, always overloaded and shaky-looking; and large ones carrying hay. Adolescent boys and girls lie sleeping on the hay piled high in the truck; it is only two in the afternoon, but they probably started work at five or six. Smiling boys and girls carry buckets on yokes across their shoulders. Often the buckets contain highly aromatic night soil, human excrement that is collected and saved and used to fertilize the fields. Infants, everywhere, are held and treated gently, as often by a man as by a woman, and usually by the old. Children shine with joy and pride as they demonstrate Tai Chi, or dance, or perform on musical instruments, girls and boys together. (But there are only girls in the embroidery classes of the Children's Palaces.)

Everyone works who can. A woman of sixty who lives in a commune in Shanghai tells you of her terrible childhood in the ravaged city, homeless, orphaned, and starving. She smiles with great pride at her neat two-room apartment, home for four people. They share a kitchen with three other families; it too is spotless. There is no refrigerator, so no quarrels about whose food is whose. There is no stored food to speak of. Our hostess keeps her tea and rice in a cupboard in her apartment. She does not work because of a serious unemployment problem in China. Women are forced to retire (with a pension) at age fifty-five, to make way for the young. Her husband still works, however. The commune's factories, small workshops making children's clothes for export—American-style T-shirts—are filled with young women and men at sewing machines.

On a tiny balcony outside the communal kitchen are a metal tub, a washboard—also metal, and only about eight by eleven inches—and a clothesline. The clotheslines of China are always full, especially those of Shanghai, which is damp. There is no hot running water. Men and women wash clothes: whoever has time. At dinner hour millions of Chinese head home from work on their bicycles. It is as likely to be a man as a woman who has stopped at a street vendor's and has tied a huge bundle of greens to the back of the bike. Everyone is fed, but everyone is thin. (Do I imagine that the girls in the Children's Palace are spectral, while the boys are only thin?)

Everyone works different shifts, so that husband and wife may take turns with child care. (But it is only men who sit together in the commune courtyards, smoking, drinking, and playing cards.) It is considered shameful for a Chinese woman to smoke or drink. People live in incredible closeness: four or five or more, sometimes, in a room no bigger than a middle-class New York apartment kitchen. But the people have inviolable circles of privacy around them: China has always been crowded. Even when they are excited, people do not usually push or bump each other as they do in the West. Affection is not displayed publicly; only in Shanghai does one sometimes see two lovers holding hands, and in Peking a boy sleeps on a park bench, his head in his brother's lap, and the older boy caresses his hair.

Out in the country you have the sense that a glass dome was placed over the land thousands of years ago, and that nothing has changed since. The mountains, the trees, the fields, the people—all look much as they do in old brush paintings. In the cities, China has entered the twentieth century. Life is hard in both places, but harder in the country. The reward there is the sheer beauty of it. The cities are not beautiful: they are gray, undistinguished. The newer buildings are all the same, high-rise concrete with flaking rusting balconies (the balconies are not for pleasure but for laundry). Like the buildings in many parts of Russia and Siberia, they are all made in the same mold; poorly built, they are already falling apart. But they provide homes for millions of people who would otherwise be homeless.

The changes in China required huge effort. Mao attempted to follow Stalin's policy of Five-Year plans for centrally controlled, unified programs of development. The difference between the two countries is that the Chinese put a greater emphasis on feeding, housing, educating, and giving medical care to its population of nearly a billion people than on industrialization and the building up of military forces. Both countries have attempted to accomplish both tasks, but the USSR, closer to the West and more threatened, possessed of an immense border to be guarded, has placed a greater priority on guns. Moreover, whereas the Soviet Union deserted its feminist programs when they proved difficult, China never has, although it has downplayed them in certain periods.

After the establishment of the new government, there were efforts to increase agricultural production and to sell the new marriage laws to the peasants. Peasant women were shy about speaking in public; men were opposed to change. Meetings were convened in every village to "speak bitterness" against those who oppressed others, and model couples were singled out for praise. Women's anger was crystallized through these meetings, and they gained confidence. But this kind of effort did not further economic development, and during the years of the first Five-Year Plan (1953–57), women's issues were deemphasized; it was claimed that women were now liberated. Discriminatory laws giving men higher wages and preeminence in family matters had been abolished, and talented women were being given education and an opportunity to rise in the hierarchy.

During the "Hundred Flowers" period of 1957, women were able to register their complaints formally with the government. However, there were still few day nurseries and not many jobs in newly established industry, and many women remained dependent upon men. In the Great Leap Forward (1958–59), rural People's communes were formed in which all members were paid according to their labor, and women were urged to participate in agriculture, experimental agriculture, construction, heavy industry like iron smelting, and the invention or improvement of tools. Elisabeth Croll cites an estimate of nearly a hundred million women added to the labor force through such organizations.[555] Intense pressure was also placed on women to work in small-scale handicraft enterprises. Throughout this period male-supremacist behavior in homes and workplaces was ignored by government instruments like media and institutions.[556]

The Cultural Revolution, which began in 1966, revived interest in newly hardened power structures and attempted to shake these up. Women were directed to unite politically to oppose authoritarian bureaucracies and the rule of men in the home. They were encouraged to study, organize, and criticize their families. They were instructed thus:

> Over thousands of years our family relations have been that son obeys what his father says and wife obeys what her husband says. Now we must rebel against this idea ... We should make a complete change in this. ... It should no longer be a matter of who is supposed to speak and who is supposed to obey in a family, but a matter of whose words are in line with Mao Tse-Tung's thoughts.[557]

Authoritarianism had not disappeared, but had only changed form.

Figures dating from about 1972 show that women comprise about half the workers in light industry. They work in heavy industry as well; they mend high-tension wires with the current on, weld steel plates onto ship hulls, and operate huge cranes. They comprise about a third of the workers in heavy industries like petroleum refineries, iron and steel complexes—but often their work lies in support services like clinics, day-care centers, and canteens.[558] China specialists in 1984 estimated that the proportion of women in industry has dropped to about 33 percent, but that figure was not documented.

In the countryside, the wage pattern has been slanted against women, since it assigned work points for tasks, with the highest number of points being to the heaviest labor. Able-bodied men were able to earn nine or ten a day, and there were teams of "iron girls" who could earn as much. But most women could manage no more than seven or eight, and women who must take off hours from work for chores in the household could earn only six or seven. Women therefore earned less than men. (This system has recently been somewhat changed.) There are no day-care centers or soup kitchens for pregnant women, and they get no paid leave. Although they are assigned light work during the later months of their pregnancies, this brings a drop in work points, and so a drop in earnings. After childbirth, women frequently work only part-time, which lowers their income even further.[559] In many areas women are excused or even barred from doing agricultural work during menstruation. The reason given is that it would be detrimental to their health, but the unspoken reason is that old superstitions about menstruation as pollution still exist. These factors combine to guarantee that women earn less than men: on a typical commune, yearly income for women is between 280 and 360 yuan, and for men between 480 and 520 yuan.[561] (The official rate of exchange in 1984 was 2.56 to the U.S. dollar.)

Thus in China, as elsewhere, work that women do which is essential to their families, and childbirth and childraising, which are essential to any culture, are utterly without respect and are unrewarded. Housework is officially defined as "nonwork" along with the work of students. There is no recompense for time spent preparing meals, caring for children, washing clothes or mending them, *unless it is done outside the home in a workshop*.[562] Work done for one's family is seen as nonvolitional and thereby not deserving of acknowledgment.

Furthermore, women do not have many positions of leadership in the rural collectives. It is claimed that they make up between 10 and 37 percent of the cadres—the leadership personnel—but this figure includes women in charge of crèche and nursery groups, and leaders of small all-female work groups within the team or brigade. Although women are 51 percent of the work force, thus holding up more than the half of the sky Mao granted them, they remain only 27 percent of the cadres at brigade and commune levels, and only 40 percent at the small work-team levels.[563]

Working women in the cities often have access to excellent day care, and most urban women get fifty-six days paid maternity leave.[564] Life in city communes—now called work units—is comparatively easy. These communes are made up of blocks of apartment buildings arranged in squares around treed walks and lawns. Most work units are self-sufficient: they have their own "factories," small workshops in which the members work and which house the only showers. They have a clinic, schools, theaters, and shops. An effort is made in education and in culture to counter male-supremacist ideas; heroic women are the subjects of many Chinese theater pieces.

For many Chinese, this way of life seems satisfactory. It is utterly controlled and regulated; there is essentially no privacy—everyone knows what everyone else is doing. This lack of privacy has some beneficial ramifications. There is little battering of wives or children, because neighbors interfere to prevent it. Women on street or block committees intervene not just to prevent violence but also to pressure men to help with housework and child care. Criminals can be singled out fairly easily, and methods of reassimilation into communal standards can be discussed by the community together. Although there is unhappiness at the government's present policy of permitting families to have only one child, it is clear that people understand the reasons for this action. The reasons are respectable: China is the size of the United States, but only about 15 percent of it is arable; its present population is about one billion. Yet the government's pressure on citizens in this area constitutes an intrusion on the most private of private affairs. Moreover, since they are limited to one child, many Chinese families are using modern technical means for predicting the sex of a fetus, and aborting girls; in some cases they are even resorting to infanticide.[565]

Sexual mores in China are extremely puritanical. Even depiction of nude bodies in painting is frowned upon.[566] Married couples are often separated for years at a time by assignments in different parts of the country; they see each other only during the single travel time permitted each year. But many of these conditions existed before the present regime. The Chinese were extremely regulated by Confucian morality; they have been crowded for a long time. They are used to repression of sex as well as anger.

The Chinese people as a whole are better off now than they were. Wages are low but so are expenses. In cities the government subsidizes all housing and social services are free; in the countryside peasants build their own houses and must pay for low-cost medical care. Medical treatment in the clinics is personal, peaceful, and pleasant; and 76.5 percent of Chinese are literate.

And women too are better off than they were. Many receive professional training; they marry and divorce (if rarely) by choice. But women comprise 70 percent of those who are illiterate. In addition, there are few women in top decision-making positions in China; those who have appeared in the top ranks have been wives of leaders, or figureheads, or were limited to cultural affairs. Even at middle levels women are not given leadership positions in proportion to their numbers and are shunted into areas dealing only with women. In the most progressive communes women held only about a third of the leadership positions in 1971.[567] Of the twenty-six members of the Politburo elected by the eleventh Party Congress in 1977, 85 percent were males over sixty years of age, with an average age of sixty-five, and only one was a woman.[568] As of 1983, there was still only one woman (and one woman alternate) in the Politburo, and eleven female members and thirteen female alternates out of a total membership of 348 in the Party Central Committee: 210 full and 138 alternate members. There is one woman out of thirteen members of the State Council, and four out of forty ministers. In addition, since most women hold more than one title at a time, the actual number in high government posts is even smaller than these figures suggest.[569] Like other countries, China is ruled by men.

## The Soviet Union

The Soviet Union never developed a tradition of obedience like that of the Chinese; its people are more rebellious, and therefore repression is more severe, more palpable. To the question of whether women are better off now than they were before 1917 the answer must be *yes*; so are most men. Almost everyone is educated; illiteracy among those aged nine to forty-nine is nonexistent. Women as well as men are encouraged to go on to university, to which entrance is earned by passage of competitive examinations. As of 1981–82, women comprised 52.2 percent of all university students. But once at the university, women are slotted, as they are in the United States, into areas that lead to lower-paid work. Child care is widely available and is free or low-cost; birth-control devices and information are supposed to be legally disseminated and abortion is supposed to be legal and available. There is a policy of equal pay for equal work, equality before the law, and an acceptance of women in all professions.[570] In principle.

The actuality is a little less rosy. Ninety percent of Soviet women are employed and they constituted 51 percent of the work force as of 1980, but they earned only about three-quarters as much as men.[571] They comprise 49 percent of factory workers and 46 percent of those holding manual jobs, but they make up less than a third of those who use mechanical lifting equipment. Men lift by machine, women lift by hand.[572] And women comprise only 6 percent of workers in skilled mechanical trades.[573] Men dominate the more mechanized, less strenuous labor that offers higher status and income. Rural men are twice as likely as rural women to have some higher education, and they virtually monopolize administrative positions on the collective farms: as of 1961, women comprised about half the agricultural labor force but held less than 2 percent of the directorships of farms. Propaganda teaches that work is the only true source of individual pride and accomplishment, but for most women in factories and farms, work is arduous physical labor with little chance of advancement.[574]

In many areas, however, the number of women exceeds the number to be found in such occupations in the West. There are women managers in industry, agriculture, lumbering, transportation, and communications; as of 1959, they made up 12 percent of this class, and data from the 1970 census show relatively little change in occupational gender differences. As of 1970 they were 40 percent of the agriculturalists, livestock experts, veterinary surgeons, and technicians. Scientific occupations are categorized by degree of physical hardship involved: the first is space flight, and the Russians have had a woman space pilot; second is permafrost scientists, in which there is a high proportion of women.[575] Women comprise 73 percent of doctors, 35.4 percent of lawyers, a third of the engineers, well over a third of the scientists, and over half of the technicians and certified specialists. Some of the USSR's top mathematicians are women.[576] A table comparing percentages of women in various professions in the USSR and the United States as of 1975–76 shows the far greater advancement of women in the Soviet Union (see p. 251).

But doctors are poorly paid: a good mechanic can earn more. Of all doctors, the most highly paid are surgeons—a field dominated by men. Law pays poorly also, except for judges and prosecutors—most of whom are men. Among teachers the lower grades are taught mainly by women; higher-paid administrative positions are held mainly by men.[577] Professions like medicine and teaching, in which women predominate, pay less than engineering, where men predominate.[578]

Administrative posts in the government bureaucracy, as well as in the Communist Party apparatus itself, are largely closed to women.[579] As of 1970 only one of the fifteen constituent republics of the USSR had a woman as chair, with thirteen vice-chairs, ten vice-prime ministers, and twenty-seven ministers. Of the fifteen lower-ranking autonomous republics, women chaired five.[580] In 1981, 26.6 percent of 5002 delegates to the Party Congress and 3.1 percent of the Party Central Committee were women. Although party membership is nearly a quarter women, there are no female ambassadors or ministers, and only one woman, E. A. Furtseva, has ever served (1957–61) in the Politburo.[581]

Before and after work, the life of Soviet women is hard. Mechanical devices that make housework easier are still not easily procured. There has been little change in this situation since 1970 when only 38 percent of apartments in the comparatively luxurious Moscow-Leningrad area had refrigerators—and the refrigerators are small; washing machines are primitive, requiring considerable manual labor for their operation.[582] Whether because of lack of refrigeration or shortages in the shops, it seems that marketing must be done every day. The queues are long, and since different items are sold in different shops, one must stand for hours in one queue after another. Meat and fish are hard to find. In areas distant from the warm southern states, fresh vegetables and fruit are also rare. Lake Baikal is the largest fresh-water lake in the world, and in Irkutsk, the

# WOMEN IN THE PROFESSIONS, US AND USSR

*(Proportion of Females in Selected Professions, 1975–76)*

| PROFESSION | USSR    *(in percent)* | US |
|---|---|---|
| Doctors (M.D.) | 69 | 9[a] |
| Lawyers | over half | 6[b] |
| Judges | one third | 2 |
| Accountants *(ekonomist)* | 76 | 21.6[c] |
| Engineers | 40[d] | 1.6 |
| High school teachers | 71 | 49.5 |
| Elementary school teachers | 79 | 84.5 |
| Scientists | 42[e] | 10.2[f] |
| Factory directors | 13 | 1 |
| Middle-level industrial managers | 24 | 5–6 |
| Collective farm directors | 22 | —— |
| Ph.D.s *(kandidat)* | 31 | 16 |
| Full professors *(doktor nauk)* | 13.8 | 9[g] |
| Associate professors | 22.9 | 15.2[g] |
| B.A.s | over half | 40 |

[a] Women now account for 15 percent of the medical students in the US.
[b] Women now account for 16 percent of the law students in the US.
[c] Includes nondegree-holding accountants.
[d] This amounts to one million women. There are more Soviet *women* engineers than US male engineers. The reason there are so many more engineers in the USSR is that engineering there plays a role similar to business and law as well as engineering training in the US, in that this is the profession from which industrial managers and leading politicians are recruited.
[e] This amounts to 500,000 women, whose employment is ensured by a quota system that is strictly enforced by the Communist Party.
[f] Includes lab technicians.
[g] Women actually account for 27.1 percent of teachers in higher education in the US, but most of them are employed in part-time, nonpermanent instructor positions.

*Compiled by Roberta T. Manning.*

Siberian city near the lake, one would expect to see piles of the fish for which the lake is noted. There are none. Either pollution has killed all the fish, or it is shipped abroad to get foreign currency. You can get canned fish in Irkutsk, if you can afford it, as well as canned vegetables and canned fruit juice.

Paucity of fresh food does not seem to be a feminist issue: it results from the inadequacy of the road system, and a shortage of trucks and railways to haul food. But that inadequacy is a direct result of the emphasis placed on military buildup and industrialization. The military entrenchment along the endless border from East Germany through to Mongolia is huge even to the casual reporter's eye, which is not permitted to penetrate the surface. The question is whether Soviet fears are justified by the behavior of the Western nations. However one answers that question, it is evident that the policies of nations affect deeply such seemingly trivial issues as how we feed our children—an issue that is not trivial at all to any mother. In fact, all issues are feminist issues.

Most people in the USSR do their laundry in the bathtub and cook on a one-burner stove; 25 percent of city dwellers share kitchen and bath, and some have no hot running water.[583] This is not ground for disdain; to pull such a huge country as the Soviet Union into a twentieth-century technological culture in the face of its earlier poverty and of almost continual—and devastating—war has required great energy, direction, and unremitting work. The point is that women suffer more from the difficulties of this culture than men. A Soviet report states that women average nineteen hours a week more housework than men. In Poland, which has a similar structure of work and mores, it is said that women work "in two shifts," one their job, the other the housework, and the women themselves say their heaviest work is done at home.[584] However, this problem is now being openly addressed in the Soviet press.[585]

There are many men—but more women—in the ubiquitous queues in both countries. While more men, especially younger ones, are spending time with their children, many simply sit in front of the television set, or get drunk, while the women queue up for food, cook, clean, care for the children, and do other chores. Women get less relaxation and less sleep; they tend to be less productive at their jobs, and this tendency is used to justify their lower pay. Many women are reluctant to vie for higher-ranking jobs, knowing they have no more time or energy to give.[586]

Although there are a few good child-care centers, there are not nearly enough and many have a bad reputation with women. It has been claimed that children fall ill in the centers because they accept too many children for the number of staff, and do not feed them enough, and open windows in the cold hoping the children will get sick. The staffs, it is said, steal the better food for themselves.[587] But some arrangements are good. I observed one program in Poland, for instance, in which city children are taken by their teachers out to the country for a month in the summer, to live on a farm; and country children are taken to the city to go to ballets, operas, and plays.

Soviet laws protecting women from physical abuse are better than those in the United States, but there is a very high rate of alcoholism among Russian men, and much wife beating. There are no shelters for battered women or rape victims, and most women do not report such events. There is a Russian saying, "She whom I beat, that's whom I love."[588] Rape victims are blamed for their own victimization. Divorce rates are very high. Many divorces are initiated by women, but there is considerable abandonment of families by men. Twenty percent of each year's live births occur to women without men, and family units made up of mother and child—or children—sometimes with a grandmother, comprise a large minority within the population.[589] I have no explicit information on this, but I would imagine that this situation resembles the situation in the United States at present, in which poorly paid or unemployed women try to care for their families and have come to comprise an entire class of the new poor.

Birth control and abortion are supposed to be legal and available in the Soviet Union, but in actuality the government has at present a racist pronatalist policy. The Union is made up of many different ethnic groups, some of whom live in republics (like Uzbek, Azerbaidzhan, or Kazakh) far from Russia proper (the old "Great Russia," centered in Moscow), and who maintain their own customs. Fearing the prolific growth of these populations, the government wants Russian women to have more children. Consequently contraception is hard to find: diaphragms are seldom available, there are no IUDs, and the pill is not manufactured in the USSR. Vaginal suppositories (for whatever they are worth) exist but are also hard to find; there are condoms, but men don't like to use them. Thus Soviet women often resort to abortion.

The state abortion clinics are, according to a Russian feminist, "butcheries" where women are made to feel immoral. Women do not receive sick pay for abortions. Abortion by a private doctor, with anesthetics and antiseptics, is *illegal*, very expensive, and difficult to find. There are midwives who will perform simple curettage at an early stage, or full abortion later—but they do this with no anesthetics and whatever means are handy. Some pour vodka into the uterus, which brings on a hemorrhage and disinfects, but burns the uterus. One method that is widely used (as it used to be in the United States) is for women to drink dangerous liquids—solutions of soap and manganese, or saffron and tobacco elixir. Some women get intravenous injections of Synestrol to contract the uterus. Usually these methods entail severe complications, often blood poisoning. Hospitals refuse to treat women for such complications until they inform on their abortionist. Many die.[590]

Despite its desire for Russian women to have children, the government does not assist women who have small children and are without men. A woman cannot stay at home with her children, but must find work and get care for them somehow. A woman without a man is vulnerable in many ways. If she has contact with men, she is considered a prostitute and can be arrested for "vagrancy."[591]

Such information on the actual condition of women in the Soviet Union cannot be procured through official channels. My data come from interviews by Robin Morgan for *Ms.* magazine with a group of exiled Russian feminists in Vienna. These women committed the crime of publishing a feminist magazine. All thoughtful, educated women, they had various experiences which brought them into conflict with the system. They wanted to reach out to other women, to share their experiences, offer sisterhood, and perhaps create a nucleus of a group to work for change in women's lot.

It is illegal for individuals to possess copying devices, so they had to type each copy of their journal individually: they produced ten. They were terrorized by KGB men, who attack women and threaten rape but finally allow them to escape.[592] Then they were imprisoned, interrogated, and the four leaders finally exiled. Some of these women had spent time in the camps and wrote about their experiences, but their work cannot be published in the USSR. Even dissident men reject feminism, calling it frivolous (with the exception of Andrei Sakharov); the government considers it treason.[593] The Russian women who produced *Women and Russia*, the first feminist *samizdat*—underground publication—knew absolutely nothing about feminism in other parts of the world. They wrote and tried to distribute their journal because of their own hunger, and the hunger of other women they knew, for a voice.

So where are they, the wonderful ideals of the first revolutionaries? Gone with the ideals—or promises—of the first Christians, the first Protestants, the avant-garde revolutionaries of any age. Women in Russia are better off than they were because all Russians are better off than they were. The degree of abuse of women permitted is lessened but the pecking order remains the same.

## Islam

On the other hand, there is Islam, where the continued subjection of women is part of both practice and principle. Like Christianity, Islam is monotheistic and proselytizing: it has a history of persecutions of "heretics" and unbelievers, and of forceful conversion. It posits a realm higher than life, but, unlike Buddhism and Hinduism, does not believe earthly life to be an illusion. Also like Christianity, it concerns itself with the events of ordinary life, and attempts to regulate small details of living. Unlike Christianity, however, it is fully totalitarian: it does not believe in separation of church and state, insisting the two should be merged in a theocracy. Everything, it is claimed, has been prescribed by the Prophet.

Because I do not want to give the impression that other world religions devoted to high gods are not patriarchal, I will glance at Hinduism and Buddhism. Like Islam, Hinduism teaches close supervision of women and promulgates a special ideal for womanhood. It has created a hierarchy of humans in which all Hindus are relegated to castes; this hierarchy is based upon notions of pollution, with the lowest caste literally "untouchable" lest it contaminate. But Hindus—and Buddhists also—believe this world to be an illusion. Nothing that happens here is real; therefore Hinduism does not regulate the daily lives of its adherents with the strictness of Catholicism, Moslemism, and, to a lesser degree, Protestantism and Judaism. Consequently Hindus have not erected a monolithic church to administer such regulation.

Buddhism is fully otherworldly; it holds that true religious life can be lived only in complete isolation from the world. It shares with Hinduism the belief that women are an inferior species, but has a more humane and liberal view of them than Hinduism. It even permits women to be nuns—the lowest rank in its religious hierarchy, but a position of autonomy, independent of males.[594]

The Hindu ideal of womanhood is realizable only in well-to-do families, in which women are completely submerged; they have more status and actual power in poor Hindu families. Because of the otherworldly nature of Buddhism, little attention is paid to mundane events, and the structure of the Buddhist family is simple and roughly egalitarian. There is no child marriage, no forced marriage, and divorce is open to both partners; inheritance is equal and there is joint ownership of property. But only boys are educated and have political rights. Both Hindu and Buddhist countries have passed laws and made reforms tending to improve education for women and stipulating equal rights. Thus in Southeast Asia and in India, women have equal rights by law; the impediments to realization of this law are poverty, illiteracy, and old custom: most people are not even aware such laws exist.[595]

In the laws of Islamic countries women have few rights and freedoms. The Arabian and Persian nations had powerful women even within recorded history: queens, warriors, and poets whose verse comprises a large part of Arab pre-Islamic poetry. Women owned property: a man who wanted a divorce said to his wife, "I will no longer drive thy flocks to pasture." Mohammed himself was able to spend his time founding a religion because he was supported by his first wife, Khadija, a wealthy businesswoman.[596] In its early days Islam welcomed women and many of them fought to establish it. The long list of women warriors includes Mohammed's seventy-year-old aunt, Safiya, who clubbed down an enemy intruder.[597]

After Mohammed's death, and despite the Prophet's specific instructions to the contrary, women were forbidden to worship in Moslem mosques and to go by themselves on the annual pilgrimage to Mecca. And after the Ottoman takeover of Arab and Byzantine civilization, rigid sexual segregation was established.[598]

Under Islam, women are secluded within a back section of a house and may not come into public rooms if there are male visitors. For many years women below the upper classes were given no education at all. Laws are inequitable: a daughter is entitled to only half the inheritance of her brother; a woman's testimony is worth half as much as a man's on the witness stand. Female but not male adultery is punishable by death. But probably the worst suffering undergone by Moslem women is clitoridectomy and infibulation.[599]

Clitoridectomy is practiced today on thirty million women in twenty-six countries. Usually a little girl of six or seven is seized from sleep in the middle of the night and hauled into a room where a woman, using no anesthetic and a crude knife, cuts out the child's clitoris, while her mother and other family members watch approvingly. This was the experience of Nawal el Saadawi, who has spent her adult life as a physician campaigning against this practice, and being persecuted by Islamic governments as a result. Clitoridectomy makes sexual pleasure and orgasm impossible for the girl; the operation and the way it is performed also engrave upon her mind her impotence and isolation within the culture. It does her no good to cry out: there before her, smiling, are the very people she would have counted on to help her.[600]

Even worse than clitoridectomy is infibulation. All external genital organs are cut away: the clitoris, the two major outer lips of the vagina (labia majora) and the two minor inner lips (labia minora). Then the wound is sewn up. The only portion left intact is the outer opening of the vagina, but even this is narrowed during suturing, by a few extra stitches. On the marriage night the vaginal opening is slit open with a sharp scalpel or razor. If the woman is divorced, her vagina is again sewn up.[601]

The operation is both dangerous and agonizing, done as it is without anesthetics. It also makes childbirth agonizing, for the normal function of the labia is to assist that process. It is practiced in Somalia, Ethiopia, Djibouti, the Sudan, Kenya, Egypt, Nigeria, Mali, and the Arabian peninsula. It produces "a chastity belt of flesh."[602] Both operations are performed to guarantee a woman's virginity at marriage and her fidelity within it—for she has no pleasure in sex and therefore presumably is not tempted to search for it with other men. But, like footbinding, it carries another message: impotence, pain, and victimization.

Middle-class girls and women are maintained in seclusion; some live in the harem system. According to Naila Minai, this system is not as degrading and demoralizing as it sounds. The presence of many women allows those of well-to-do families leisure, which many use to gain education. In the past, before strict segregation, wealthier women became patrons of artists and scientists; they subsidized the education of both slave girls and princesses, and gathered scholars and artists in their salons, thus contributing to the blossoming of Arab civilization during the Middle Ages. These women tried to attract caliphs to their salons, and some became so powerful they could make or break caliphs. They studied medicine and law; some taught in colleges; many were religious instructors and judges in Islamic law.[603]

The main advantage of the harem system today is that women live in a separate but parallel society and do not have to deal with men in their work life. Some women live happily in such arrangements. They are taught by women and healed by women. Minai asserts that life in an Algerian harem is full of fun. The harem is also a center of power: the women make marriages, make decisions that affect the whole family, decide how to assist those in need. They unify to put pressure on oppressive husbands and mothers-in-law. Men who ignore harem power risk "their domestic tranquility and public dignity."[604]

After 1453, when Arab territories were absorbed by the Ottoman Empire, there were centuries of restrictive laws for women and abandonment to luxury by men. New vitality came from the West, with its new ideas of abolition of slavery and concubinage, universal suffrage, and equality of the sexes. Reforms in Islamic countries began in the mid-nineteenth century. The first middle school for girls was founded in 1858, the first teachers' college in 1870; and in 1914, for the first time, women were allowed to enter universities.[605] Kemal Ataturk instituted many reforms in Turkey. In 1923 he abolished polygamy and established a minimum age for the marriage of girls, equal rights in divorce and child custody, and equal rights in inheritance. By 1934 he had granted women suffrage, the right to hold office, and the right to *appear in public*. (In 1920 a woman had been arrested for acting on a Turkish stage.) Ataturk also enlisted women in his revolutionary forces as soldiers, ammunition carriers, and nurses.

Despite the uprisings of Egyptian women during 1919–22, when they demonstrated, organized strikes and boycotts, and performed sabotage, they were not granted the right to education until 1924 and even then were allowed only to teach or be midwives. However, they were able to establish a Feminist Union that today runs clinics, child-care centers, orphanages, and vaccination programs for young children.[606] Nevertheless, the old ways persist. In Egypt, one survey showed that girls are still subjected to clitoridectomy in 97.5 percent of uneducated families and in 66.3 percent of educated families.[607]

Most Moslem countries have raised the minimum age for marriage to eighteen for boys and between fifteen and seventeen for girls, but in Algeria, 16 percent of girls are married between the ages of eight and sixteen, and girls are also married very young in Tunisia.[608] This is the case despite the work of Habib Bourguiba, who in 1957 passed a set of laws granting Tunisian women many rights to equality with men. Since then Tunisia has granted women the right of abortion within the first three months of pregnancy, and the right to be judges. Although girls may be sent to school in Moslem countries, they are removed before puberty to guard their chastity. In Tunisia as of 1975, 63 percent of girls aged six to eleven are in school, but only 24 percent of those between twelve and seventeen. The figures are similar in Algeria. In Morocco, 30 percent of younger girls, 20 percent of older ones, are allowed education.[609] The illiteracy rate for women in some Moslem countries is staggering: 98 percent of Afghani women are illiterate; 95 percent of Saudi Arabian women, and between 70 and 95 percent of Iranian women cannot read or write.[610]

In Turkey, Kuwait, Algeria, and Libya women are an established minority in professional schools, occupying about a quarter of the places in law, business administration, medicine, chemistry, and pharmacy; Turkey and Egypt have been admitting women to universities since the 1930s, but they still comprise only 30 percent of students. Algeria had no women in university in 1954, and has a female-student enrollment of about 20 percent now. In Kuwait and Libya there were no female students at university level in 1964, but they comprised 60 percent of Kuwaiti student bodies in 1975 and 18 percent of Libyan student bodies in 1976.[611]

The courts in most Moslem countries are male-dominated and unconcerned with women's rights. Men's "crimes of honor" are punished lightly and female adultery is still punishable by death. In cases of divorce, the law is interpreted in men's favor and they get custody of the children. In some of these countries, women can now instigate divorce in specific circumstances. In Tunisia and Algeria women can divorce with no grounds given if they pay their husbands off; in Egypt a woman can divorce on grounds of cruelty if her husband treats her in a way that is intolerable to one of her social status. Divorce is possible for women whose marriage contracts contain a divorce clause, but usually requires that the husband keep the dowry. A woman can seek divorce on grounds of nonmaintenance, abuse, desertion, impotence, disease, or insanity. This has always been legally possible, but it is very difficult to carry out: many women are ignorant of their rights, and male family members often impede them. Men can still divorce their wives simply by saying three talaqs, talaq albida: I repudiate you.[612]

The highest divorce rate, oddly, is among the poor. Liberalized divorce laws have had in Islamic countries the same effect they had in the Soviet Union, the same effect they are having in the United States. Regardless of who seeks the divorce, men can walk away, paying little or nothing toward the support of their children. In Islamic states, women are often illiterate, ill-trained, and poor; they can find only menial work and must support their children. Divorcees and widows constitute the majority of the female labor force in unregulated low-level jobs. They are "the newest proletarian underdogs." In Morocco, for instance, between 1960 and 1971, single households headed by women increased by 33 percent, and most of these women were divorced or widowed.[613] Understandably, many women oppose liberalization of divorce laws.

Some changes are positive, however, especially for middle-class women with some education. Working women in the Middle East tend to congregate in elite occupations, and a high percentage of them are engineers, physicists, physicians, accountants, teachers, nurses, and skilled technicians. They are entering fields like aviation and television. They have begun to open boutiques. This is important because until recently men did the shopping for their women since women could not go out unaccompanied by a man. The new boutiques do not permit men to enter; so, wonder of wonders, women can now go to such shops and buy their own clothes.

But there are no women prime ministers or presidents in Islamic countries, and the few women who attain ministerial rank are relegated to women's departments. In some countries women must have their husbands' written permission to work or travel abroad; in 1982 Iraqi women were denied travel rights regardless of husbands' permission. Some women in politics have experienced grave humiliations: although a woman may be a governmental minister or ambassador, she is still required to have her husband's written permission to go on an ambassadorial mission. If she forgets to obtain this her husband can have her arrested. Younger men seem not to object to their wives' working, but they do not share in domestic responsibilities.[614]

Moslem women participate in their own constriction. The power of passivity and submission are well known, and many secluded mothers chain their sons to them by insisting on the old traditions. This will continue, no doubt, and not just in Islamic countries, until men fully share the responsibility for their children. The veil is a subject as fraught with contradiction as any other. When I was in Paris some years ago, a beautiful young Iraqi woman was taking a course in French, and in class discussion announced that at home she wore the veil. In reply to the horrified exclamations of the European women around her, she said, "Look at me, I am attractive. If you knew Iraqi men, you'd wear the veil too." If the veil obliterates women as human beings, it also protects them.

Moreover, the veil has become a strong political issue: wearing it can be taken as a sign of submission to an oppressive system, but it can also be taken as a sign of Moslem nationalism, antagonism to Western values. For instance, the USSR has long had severe problems in assimilating Moslems in central Asia. In 1923 the Soviets launched a campaign to liberate women, seeing that as the best method for breaking up traditional Islamic arrangements and bringing the people under party control. Among the laws they promulgated was a command for the unveiling of women. Many men, however, killed their own wives for removing the veil, and local courts refused to punish them for it. In 1927 the Moslem men began an assault of terror against independent—unveiled—women: two hundred of them were kidnaped, raped, and sometimes murdered, in Uzbekistan alone. Stalin eventually ended the campaign of liberation because he needed the support of local men in his Five-Year Plan.[615] (Yet some change is occurring: William Mandel reported in 1970 that women in Uzbekistan, refusing to be seen by or to mix with men, had established cooperative shops for women. They also began an Artisans' Cooperative for women only and kept their own earnings, rather than giving them to their husbands as they had formerly.[616]) The Soviet effort to assimilate Afghanistan has encountered similar problems. One cause of the current rebellion was the Russian demand that women be permitted to attend village meetings and learn to read and write. The Afghanis objected—strenuously. It was to this war, and to defend the male Afghani position, that President Carter wanted to send female soldiers.[617]

Wearing or not wearing the veil was a political issue during and after the Algerian revolution, and again, more recently, during the Iranian. Many middle-class Iranian women were obtaining education abroad during the reign of the late shah, and had adopted certain Western values. They were extremely active in the long struggle against the shah, and a substantial number of women were imprisoned and tortured by his secret police, SAVAK. They welcomed Khomeini happily, marching unveiled. One wonders if they knew their own history. "It is not too much to say that without the powerful moral force of these so-called chattels of the oriental lords òf creation . . . the revolutionary movement, however well conducted by the Persian men, would have early paled into a mere disorganized protest." This was written about the deposition of the old shah in 1909. When that revolution was over, women were sent back to the harem. They were not granted the right to go out unveiled until 1935, to suffrage until 1963, or to sue for divorce until 1975.[618] The recent revolution, unhappily, has had the same consequences for women—indeed, those rights that had been granted are being rescinded, and among the demonstrations and attacks that occurred in the early weeks of the Iranian revolution were attacks upon women demonstrators, upon Iranian women by Iranian men.[619] Having subdued the women, they took the revolution over for themselves: after the first weeks of the revolution, no women at all appear in photographs of demonstrations.

A concise summary of the present condition of women is provided by the statistics in an International Labor Organization study presented at the United Nations Conference on Women in Copenhagen in 1980:

Women provide two-thirds of the world's work hours.

Women produce 44 percent of the world's food supply.

Women receive 10 percent of the world's income.

Women own 1 percent of the world's property. (And much of that ownership is on paper only, for tax purposes.)

## 10. CONCLUSIONS, OUTLOOKS

Although the history of women is rich, diverse, and as chaotic as life itself, certain patterns can be traced. What is perhaps most extraordinary about women's history is our ignorance of it. Most people are hardly aware that women have *had* a history, that they have not been, since the emergence of the first hominids, merely the servants and sex objects of men. Even feminists are unaware of important periods in women's history. And with the exception of feminist historians, none of us, women or men, are as familiar with notable female figures of the past as we are with notable males. Because of this nearly universal ignorance, I have tried to give my account a broad time span.

The geographical span is more limited, centering mainly on what is called Western civilization. The glimpses of other civilizations that recorded data offer demonstrate that women are oppressed in them much as they are in the West. But non-Western societies have not gone so far in "masculinizing" culture as the West, and therefore do not present as great a threat to the continuation of life on the planet. The West is the most important area of concentration in a study of the morality of power because it has carried that morality to the greatest extreme.

The account presented here is intended to demonstrate the enormous resilience, vitality, and endurance of women, and their eagerness to pursue personal freedom and public effectiveness through any passage that is open to them. Hosts of women have achieved one or both. But men as a class have never chosen to infer from the example of the few the potential of the many. Men as a class have chosen to see women with expertise in government, the military, in intellectual, scientific, or artistic endeavors, as aberrations; in some societies, even women who displayed "virtue" (chastity, fidelity, and submission) have been considered unusual in a sex seen as vicious, depraved, foolish, lustful, and, in general, defective, not full members of the human race. Over and over again women—and those men who supported them—have had to remind their society that women are human.

Because women who were able to achieve in the public sphere were seen as aberrations, men could with impunity obliterate their words and deeds from the record of history. Thus they were forgotten. Moreover, a woman who struggled alone to free herself from the barriers of her culture gained power for herself alone. She could not transmit her personal power to her daughters, real or spiritual. Her power, unlike institutionalized male power, died with her.

At times, however, groups of women were able to exercise their power in the public sphere, and were able to transmit it to women who followed them. Such was the case in the great monasteries of the eighth to twelfth centuries, and in certain guilds in medieval Europe. But this power is always marginal: it was taken because male control was loose enough that no one specifically denied it to women or had the authority to enforce a denial. As soon as male control was centralized and solidified, men removed women from their positions and specifically excluded them from the institutions within which they had acted.

Sometimes women worked to establish a sect or party. Men tolerated women as partners in the struggle for establishment, but once the sect became a religion, or the party a political order, men excluded women from partnership within it. Although women have struggled and died, contributing greatly to the success of every major political and religious revolution that has occurred in the

West (and in Islam) in the past millennium, you would
from the present leadership of such political or religious
books—unless you read feminist history.

But not until the French Revolution did women
class. On this occasion they did succeed in institutio
pressuring men to include them in the laws of the Re
rights guaranteed to women were rescinded by Napoleon—and only
decade later. The abrogation of legally held rights of women has occurred elsewhere, too: in Islam, after Mohammed died, and again when Khomeini took
over in Iran; in Germany under Hitler; in the Soviet Union, several times; and
to some degree in the United States.

Thus whatever women do, they continue to face the same obstacles, century after century. And although, as feminist and nonfeminist critics suggest,
women often impede their own causes, they do so because the price of struggle
is so high, and the victory so uncertain and insecure. Women are as capable of
heroism as men; but they are never equally rewarded. We must face the fact
that the greatest impediment to the acceptance of women as full members of
the human race comes from men. I do not state this provocatively, nor with ani-
mus. If we put aside subjectivity, if we stop insisting that we, or our spouses or
relatives, are not like that, and look quietly at the account of women's past, the
facts are clear.

On every level, men block women's use of their abilities outside the private sphere. Eminent women are treated as aberrations; they are prevented
from transmitting their power, and are obliterated from history. Groups of
women who are able, in a marginal period, to exercise their abilities and transmit their powers are denied both once the margins have been brought within
male control. They too are excised from history. Women who work to establish
an institution are afterward barred from leadership within it, and left out of its
history. And even when women's rights are institutionalized, a new male government sometimes annuls them. There can be no question that men as a class
have made a continuous, unremitting effort to keep women under male control.
Laying aside our dislike for this unpleasant fact, we must seriously ask why it
should be.

The first level of control imposed upon women is the physical. Almost all
extant cultures regulate women's procreation, through regulating marriage, or
women's sexuality, or both. Until the present period, women in fully patriarchal
societies could escape the brutal control of men only by being possessed of
great wealth and status and great force of personality, or by renouncing marriage and childbearing entirely. And not all cultures permit such renunciation.
Most of the societies we have looked at precluded any sexual independence for
women by marrying them off early and decreeing them legally subject to their
husbands. Many feminists have emphasized the link between women's sexual-
generative powers and their subjugation.[620]

The connection between male fear of women and women's sexual powers
is clearer in simple cultures, in which male subjugation of women is balanced
by male fear of female menstruation, than in complex cultures like our own. In

...tern civilization, fear of or repulsion toward menstruation is not universal; ...men's generative powers are viewed condescendingly; and many men are unconcerned with having children, with continuing their "line." Patriarchy's success in teaching people to disdain the "animal" parts of life is responsible for obscuring the connection between those parts and the drive to power.

Yet the basis for the male drive to power is precisely female generative abilities. Prevented from possessing such powers, males, once they understood their part in procreation, set about controlling them. Unable to claim the powers of nature, they asserted a power that was superior to nature, transcendent. Males defined themselves as the controllers, and continue to do so. But an identity based in control can be demonstrated only by creating a class of people forbidden to control. By depriving women (and other degraded classes) of the means of control—money, status, legal rights, education—and placing women under male control, men have been able to create an appearance of possessing power by nature, as women possess their powers by nature. But because all men, I would hazard to guess, at some time in their lives recognize the fatuity of this claim, yet believe the flaw to be in them and not in the claim, many men turn against women in fear and hatred, anticipating rebellion against their rule and, worse, a challenge to their right to control.

Since men's very identity is (or seems to be) at stake in their relations with both inferiors and peers, men are often willing to sacrifice the possibility of affectionate, trusting relations with each other and with women. Substituting a relation of power for a relation of love, they, in effect, declare war on all others—for to define oneself (or one's class) as the controller is effectually to declare war on all others, who make up the material that must be controlled.

This nearly universal obsession (in the West) with maintaining a controlling identity taints men's personal relations and deprives them of most forms of human fellowship and affection. This is a serious problem, for women as well as men. But the reflection of this problem in the public sphere is grave. For the male drive to transcend is not merely a drive to subjugate women and men not of one's immediate group; it is at root a drive to demonstrate that men are not bound to nature and necessity. Male permanence defeats nature's transiency; male volition and freedom soar above women's constriction; male power challenges the power of the cosmos.

And there is no question that the "masculine" drive to power has achieved great power. Through intellectual structures, patriarchal ideas have come to dominate the Western mind so totally that many of us do not comprehend that there are other ways of thinking; through mechanical structures, patriarchal methods have been able to dominate most of the globe. But the morality that lies beneath patriarchy is reflected directly in the present state of the globe. On the one hand there are machines of conquest so powerful that they threaten human extinction; on the other, nature lies defeated, its air polluted, water poisoned, trees, plants, fish and animals dying everywhere.

The course of history, as traced here, is characterized not just by increasing constriction of women by men, but also by increasing degradation and destruction of nature, outside and inside us. Control of our emotions, bodies, and attitudes is urged or imposed upon us by society in general, by commercial advertisers, political agencies, and many learned professions. On every level control is the greatest good.

No diplomacy, no politicking, no victory in any war can alter the present world situation, and no legislation can alter the basic situation of women, unless there is a change in human morality, a profound alteration in what we value. In the United States, especially, so universal is the value of control, and so pervasive, that what is necessary is an analysis of control itself, a realistic appraisal of what it can bring us and what it costs us. The following chapter surveys the costs and rewards to men of control and hierarchy; and Chapter Five surveys the consequences to some of our institutions of worshiping control.

# CHAPTER FOUR

# Men Under Patriarchy

The last chapter opened with the statement that history as we know it is not the history of the human race but the history of patriarchy, of power. This statement may seem to suggest that traditional history is an account of men: it is not. If it were, it would focus on all classes and kinds of men, the powerless as well as those who have wielded power or influence. Nor is traditional history entirely focused on power: if it were, it would pay full attention to the women (many in number if small in proportion) who have exercised power, and it does not. Traditional history has an extremely narrow perspective: it focuses on power wielded by men. Its true subject is male potency.

Like other disciplines, history has concentrated on creating and maintaining an image of man as the controlling agent of his own transcendent destiny. Greatness in the "judgment of history" so frequently invoked by politicians rests mainly on two quantitative elements—the degree of change imposed upon a culture by a man or a movement; and the relative permanence of that change. Such changes are measured in numbers—the size of the boundaries, their expansion or diminution; the number of people affected; the proliferation or dwindling, the relative strengthening or weakening of institutions, and the amount of time a change endured. Historians seem to conceive of cultures as chaotic and morally neutral swamps from which "great men" carve out plantations; great men are those whose quantitative effect was largest.

Qualitative elements are considered less important, and are limited mainly to considerations of the degree (again, a quantitative matter) of influence or impact of a man or a movement on the future, or on other areas, dimensions, or movements. There is little interest in whether the changes wrought by a "great man" improved or worsened the lot of ordinary people; whether a class or group of humans was sacrificed in a trend toward conformity and centralization; or whether a given change in the long run increased or lessened the felicities formerly available. Traditional historians tend to concentrate on strategies, political maneuvers, or on the huge figure of a strong man striding across a landscape he barely regards, intent upon his destiny. When moral judgment figures in an account—and it often does—whatever its perspective, it melts away before the fascination, obsession, with the raw fact of power in a man.

Both men and women have been denied knowledge of their past, but *for different reasons*: women's history has been expunged in order to obliterate the record of female *power*; men's history has been censored in order to cloud the record of male *powerlessness*. The elimination of women from history was a complement to the elimination of women from public life, and was paralleled by the promulgation of exclusionary laws and codes. The omission of ordinary men from history had a more complex purpose.

History has identified men with power just as women have been identified with nature. It has created an image of man with which all men can feel some kinship, and in which all men can take some pride. But the identification has not been intended to imbue all men with a sense of their *own* power except vis-à-vis women. Lower-caste men heartened by a sense of their own power might make demands or start rebellions. No: the myth shaped for men taught them to shine with reflected glory in their village streets, to walk with bravado in their neighborhoods, but to approach other men, men of more power, with humility, obedience, and subservience.

Over the past decades feminists have written considerably about the many double binds in which women are placed: for example, they are expected to surrender themselves and their wills entirely to men and yet have enough will, self-respect, and pride to work hard, raise children, and maintain households; they are expected to remain chaste throughout their lives, and yet offer warm sexuality to their husbands. Male writers, however, have rarely remarked on the similar double binds laid on men, who are expected to be in total control of their immediate surroundings and especially their women, but to surrender control to "superior men" while maintaining self-respect; they are expected to find identity and a satisfying life in pursuit of power, and to scorn and deny the very elements that could bring them felicity and contentment. On the rare occasions when this double bind is noticed, it is usually blamed upon women— the myth is that men sacrifice themselves in unsatisfying or dehumanizing work for the sake of a demanding wife and family.

Although women may contribute to it, they are not responsible for men's condition. Responsibility rests with the male myth itself, the identification of men with power and associated qualities. This myth has been devised by generations of thinkers, rulers, conquerors, millionaires, poets, and artists. We must pass beyond questions of blame to analyze the components of this myth.

It would be easiest to delineate the male myth by using examples from literature, which often simultaneously provides a critique of it. For this study, however, I will use mainly philosophical statements about the nature of "man" (it is often unclear in philosophy whether this term is being used generically or specifically, but for the most part, philosophy ignores the existence of women); and analysis of the structure of male institutions, in which the myth is incorporated. Many readers should find the description of institutions fitting and familiar, but will disclaim the quotations about the nature of man: "I am not like that" is a frequent response to general discussions of male behavior, although the very men who demur may describe other men in the same ways. But the image of man offered here is a *cultural* standard, informing all Western institutions. It is most evident in television, movies, novels, history, philosophy, biography, and male conversation. It is not a universal personal standard, but all men are in some way affected by it.

## 1. The Image of Man

The Bible is more literature than philosophy, but it is a major starting place for Western culture, both philosophical and artistic. We will glance only at a few images and tales, to examine their assumptions. These assumptions are implicit rather than explicit. In Marxist thinking, culture (in the narrow sense of the word) is a mystification of the real sources of oppression and exploitation, and is a justification of the status quo. Although I believe that art often attacks and challenges the very notions it upholds and perpetuates, the Marxist description seems to me apt. To the degree that it is accurate, we must look beneath the surface of a work to discover what is being mystified and why.

In the first account of creation in Genesis (Genesis 1:1–31), which was written later than the second (Genesis 2:4–3:24), by a group of authors believed to be priests, humans are created together in the image of deity, and given dominion over nature. The second but older account is a tale that was repeated and probably altered over generations before it was written down. It focuses on a male who is subject to a woman and is *therefore* disobedient to "God," his creator and master. Thus woman and God are placed in opposition from the start: fidelity to one means infidelity to the other. Man is forced to choose between them, and in the beginning, we are told, he chooses wrong.

In analyzing anything that has a moral dimension, we can often discover more about cultural attitudes from those acts called wrong, or sinful, than those considered right or good. Heroes, male and female, tend to be bland amalgams of pieties (except in tragedy, in which in a sense the hero is also the villain, his or her own destroyer), and when they are not, they are simply happy accidents, incarnations of attitudes acceptable in a particular culture. One learns little from them. The real attitudes of a culture are most easily discerned in those things it considers sinful. This is particularly true in the Bible, which rarely informs us *why* a particular figure is "good" or finds favor with God, or even why a particular person or place is evil. We must deduce these from context.

So we must question why God and woman are set in opposition to each other, why obedience to God is so necessary, and why eating the fruit of the tree of knowledge of good and evil is a sin. Why God and woman are opposed should be clear from the first two chapters of this study; moreover, the creature allied with woman is the serpent, a major religious symbol in matricentry because its shedding of its skin was a form of rejuvenation, and thus symbolic of regeneration. Like the butterfly, it was important in a religion that seems to have emphasized regeneration through transformation.

Opposed to woman—and therefore in some sense her enemy—is God. God here is seen as the creator of the universe and of man—and later, woman. Since it presents a male as progenitor, this tale does seem, as Bakan suggests, to represent an effort to digest new knowledge of the male power of insemination. But there is no hint that creation or procreation is a mutual act requiring two progenitors of different sexes. It is rather an assertion of unilateral power, all the more remarkable because infants grow inside women, not men. It seems, then, to be an attempt to usurp for men a power traditionally associated with women only; to take over what women had in the same way women had it. Bakan also suggests that patriarchy may have been an attempt to "effeminize" men, to engage them in the act of fatherhood and force them to take some responsibility for children.[1] But men probably already cared for children; they needed something different to embody their new role; what they found was power over children. God is less concerned about Adam's welfare and happiness than with Adam's obedience, which has no other function than to testify to God's power-over.

Obedience is the prime virtue in stratified cultures, cultures in which one class rules other classes. It has been a prime virtue of women throughout history, sometimes under the rubric *submissiveness*. When it is held up as a prime virtue of man vis-à-vis God, we know we are observing the work of a priestly class, since only such a class presumes knowledge of God's demands and taboos. These include prohibition of acts that seem "naturally" wrong, that would make one unhappy to perform regardless of one's cultural background: murder, for instance, or the injuring of another; wastefulness of nature's—or humanity's—fruits; and cruelty. But many acts considered sinful in various cultures are really what the great Anglican theologian Richard Hooker called "things indifferent," acts that offend because of their associations rather than because of their inherent nature. Eating, for instance, can be dangerous if one ingests poisonous berries or mushrooms, or large quantities of certain medicinal but also toxic herbs. Some things do not taste very good; some things are also unpleasant to eat—thistles, say. But to surround the act of eating with ritualistic regulations is to declare eating itself a perilous enterprise. Since it is in eating and in sex that the body of man is in deepest contact with nature and women, the alignment of woman (as opposite to deity) with eating, and with the serpent that symbolizes an ancient religion of regeneration, underscores an association among them.

The little story might be read then as a description of the growth of morality. Women first engaged with nature—the serpent, food—and from this engagement learned that some acts were naturally wrong. But the priests repudiated "natural" wrong and right, matricentric morality, insisting on a morality decreed by the Word, supposedly God's Word. Man learned the distinction between good and evil from woman; but at the moment he learned it, biting the apple, he became disobedient to God; ignoring God's Word. But in relation to a divine male progenitor, man is always wrong.[2]

Man's wrongness earns him hardship in life; the old gathering/hunting days of ease are gone; he must sweat to eat. But he maintains his relation with deity; he also occupies a position of superiority toward women, and animals are doomed to be trod upon in hate. This structure, imposed as punishment for unclear "sins," is the essence of patriarchy.

The next human act is murder, and murder of a brother. The meat eater kills the vegetarian. Cain's act is punished by exile from his community—which may reflect an actual practice of driving away from a group a person who commits violence within it, a practice that still exists among some peoples. It is a very different kind of punishment from, say, Hammurabi's "eye for an eye," or our modern custom of locking people up. It expresses, or subsumes, an idea of the community as a desirable, nourishing, and comforting home, and of exile and isolation as frightening and cruel: it suggests that rejection is the worst punishment thinkable.

Cain becomes a fugitive vagabond but he is consecrated by a special mark decreeing that he shall not be harmed. Thus the act of murder is encompassed, assimilated to the human image. Cain goes to the land of Nod (wandering), marries, and builds a city. His descendant Lamech continues his tradition of murder; his descendants Jabal, Jubal, and Tubal-cain create culture—cattle raising, music, and metalworking. Cain, not Adam or Abraham or Noah, is the true forefather of Western man.

Very quickly God sees the race he has created as evil: "the wickedness of man was great in the earth" (Genesis 6:5); "the imagination of man's heart is evil from his youth" (Genesis 8:21). We are not told in what this wickedness consists, only that it exists. (Man is wrong before God.) God destroys the earth "for man's sake," all except Noah and those he has saved. Noah is a good man, he has found grace in God's eyes: but we do not know why. We are told that he is just, and perfect in his generations, and that he walked with God: but precisely what these phrases mean we cannot tell. God makes a covenant with Noah not again to destroy the earth, and renews the promise made earlier in Genesis, that man shall have dominion over plants and animals. He also decrees that murder will be repaid by murder, and that all men will die. Since it is likely that matricentric morality focused on regeneration rather than death, and had a less severe penalty for murder, these statements may be repudiations of matricentric customs and beliefs. God here forbids only one thing—the eating of "flesh with the life thereof, which is the blood" (Genesis 9:4). This injunction is reflected in the processing of kosher meat but in its time may have been a prohibition against eating creatures alive, or perhaps raw. If the latter, it resembles the Chipewyan taboo against eating raw meat. The Chipewyans disdain the Eskimos, who do eat uncooked meat, as if they were another species, and subhuman (see Chapter Two, note 172). This distinction between raw and cooked, as Lévi-Strauss has developed it, is a symbolic distinction between animals (who eat raw meat) and humans. The important point is not whether or not people ate raw meat; it is that humans found it important to make a distinction between themselves and other animals. It seems that such a distinction was made in Israelite culture in very ancient times; the symbolism of eating remained important—even into the present.

Although not much is known about what portions of the Torah (the Pentateuch, the first five books of the Bible), especially the tales in Genesis, were composed first, or from what period they emerge, it is likely that the earlier parts of Genesis date to a very early period in Israelite history. But it is patriarchal throughout. In a brief passage preceding the story of Noah, we are told that the "sons of God" married "the daughters of men" (Genesis 6:1-2), suggesting that at the time the passage was composed, men were seen as being of a different order from women. Not only were they bound to a transcendent principle; they had already taken on the aura and status of being of a different race. Distinctions were already being made between men and animals, men and women, and groups of men: witness the story of the tower of Babel, in which human unity is seen as a threat to deity.

Certain events suggest a different world order. True, Abraham, who is promised a nation to grow from "his" seed, seems to have to plant that seed in Sarah, for some unexplained reason. His son Ishmael, conceived through Hagar, will not do. The story of the destruction of Sodom and Gomorrah suggests that the matricentric value of sharing persisted into early patriarchal times. The "wickedness" involved here is noncompliance with traditional laws of hospitality, essential in any nomadic culture. Abraham and Sarah receive their angelic guests properly and are rewarded; the men of Sodom do not, and they are punished (along with the women, children, and all inhabitants of Gomorrah as well). Later interpretations of this tale put sexual connotations foremost (as for the story of Adam and Eve), but the story itself does not. True, the men of Sodom want to rape Lot's guests—and perhaps rob them; but it is also true that Lot, that good man, offers them his daughters as substitutes (and that those daughters later conceive by their father to continue his line, an act that is not punished). Sex as sin probably emerged from a period later than that in which this story was conceived.

Over the millennia many tales have been told around late-night fires. But only some were repeated over generations; only some were saved to be written down. And those that were saved upheld the attitudes of the caste in charge of writing down; although in some cases—say, the Song of Songs—literary value might be given priority over a suspect moral value. What we can discover in these few opening tales in Genesis is a morality developed and elaborated by later stories.

Man is different from all other animals, and is given power over them. He is different fundamentally from woman also, and has dominion over her as well. He must carefully guard his sexual life and eating habits, those things that involve close interconnection with nature or woman. Man, not woman, is connected to a transcendent principle of power and knowledge which extends over the entire cosmos. Man (but not woman) can participate in this power/knowledge to the degree that he finds favor in the eyes of the deity. The quality which obtains this favor is not primarily the offering of gifts—sacrifice of the tasty innards of animals, of grain, or wine—or a special personal quality that wins the heart of Athene or Zeus, or intense concentration on the divine, which helps Chipewyan man attain knowledge/power. No, the special requirement of this deity is obedience.

Some major patterns stand out vividly when we consider the material of the Old Testament generally, as well as the few tales mentioned here. One pattern shows the new way of thinking (patriarchy) as insistent upon defining itself in opposition to the old way of thinking (matricentry). Another shows early patriarchy as deeply subject to a priestly caste, which perhaps even invented it.

Whenever there is a struggle between opposing forces, elements which under other circumstances might seem burdensome or even noxious may become valuable. For instance, Iranian women educated abroad, "Westernized" in customs and attitudes, refused to wear the *chador* at home. But at the time of the revolution many adopted it again, to show their opposition to the shah and their solidarity with the aims of the revolution. Poles who may in fact be hostile to religion throng to the Catholic Church when it stands against governmental oppression because it is the only institution that can provide expression of opposition. In the 1960s many young people in the United States who preferred comfort and luxury adopted austere or even grimly impoverished styles of living to protest their elders' values. In periods of struggle, what is normally considered an ill can become a good.

Patriarchy defined itself in opposition to matricentry, and those elements valued by the mothers became either ills or lesser goods in the new ideology. This is clear enough in the story of Adam and Eve, which places God/man and woman/nature in opposition; many other biblical tales reflect a power struggle between men and women that is conceived of as a struggle between God and "feminine" values, father- and mother-right. The story of Abraham and Isaac implies that love of one's children should properly be secondary to obedience to God. But many other qualities are involved. I mentioned before Carol Ochs's set of oppositions between an earthly realm of time, change, and fertility and a transcendent realm of timelessness, changelessness, and barrenness. Ochs also contrasts the primary devotion of matricentric cultures—to one's offspring and, by extension, to blood relatives—with the primary obligation of patriarchal cultures to an "abstract moral principle, the voice of God."[3] In addition, the "feminine" goods of home, settlement, and community were degraded in favor of a set of ills—homelessness, wandering, and isolation. These were ennobled and made emblematic of the highest masculinity.[4] Indeed, all mythic and epic heroes from Gilgamesh to Shane go through ordeal by loneliness, hardship, and exile.[5]

The patriarchal image of man was created in direct opposition to the prevailing image of woman, and designed to overreach, surpass it. And the patriarchal ideology itself reversed the ideology of matricentry, with the design of transcending it. The matricentric world was a world of time; patriarchy values timelessness in various forms. Time can be transcended by the creation of a structure that is designed to outlast it, like a dynasty, an institution, or a nation; it is transcended by the idea of heaven, which is eternal, or by the idea of the nation-state which will endure eternally.

The matricentric world was one of change; the patriarchal world reveres permanence, and thus reveres writing, the building of a tradition or an institution, the erection of monuments to a man's fame—anything that seems to confer permanence on transitory human lives and affairs. The highest matricentric value was fertility, of plants and animals, but especially of humans: giving birth was the miraculous ability that made women sacred in the old order. The patriarchists could not but concede this to be a great power; but men had a greater—the ability to kill. Murder transcends birth by annulling it and is more permanent. The ability to kill soon became the distinguishing mark of the heroic man. (A woman who kills is rarely seen as heroic; she is considered *unnatural*.)

The matricentric world was one of sharing, of community bound by friendship and love, of emotional centeredness in home and people, all of which led to happiness. The patriarchal world gave higher regard to the individual than to community, to ownership of property than to sharing, to competition and rivalry than to friendship, to wandering and isolation than to the centrality of home; and it held power rather than love to be the greatest good. But property, competition, homelessness, and isolation cannot lead to happiness. Patriarchal myths almost forbid happiness to men, attributing to it a failure of heroism. The greatest heroes, those who achieve a kind of holiness, repudiate forever the comforts of domesticity, and remain lonely wanderers seeking Truth or God or the Good—or dying in the search. They repudiate ordinary human needs for food and drink, warmth and security (rest, sleep), community and affection. Bakan concludes from his study of the Old Testament that its primary concerns are to establish the role of the male in conception, patrilineality, and patriarchy; that war was a major factor in this establishment; and that the major concerns of the "P" strand (revisions and additions by the priestly caste) are ownership of property and obedience.[6] Ownership and warfare both involve competition among men, competition which hinders friendship. Ownership is a form of control—over land, artifacts, animals, women, and other men. Both repudiate sharing, acceptance, and communality: matricentric goods. Only by such repudiation can men attain the higher knowledge/power available to those who serve the transcendent principle. It is ironically inevitable that the creators of the ideology that reveres power-over also invented servitude.

The second emphatic theme embodied in the biblical material centers on this servitude. It is rooted in a single statement: the imagination of man's heart is evil from his youth. Man is evil by nature. Thus to find favor with deity he must search continually for ways to overcome *himself*, his own tainted nature. He can find such ways only with the assistance of those who have somehow evaded or transcended the taint, who can speak more or less directly with God—the priests, who can teach him to set aside his evil ways and align his will with God's will. Obedience, that central concern of the Old Testament, is the answer.

Stephan Chorover points out that the Christian doctrine of original sin means that all creatures born need priestly intervention from the moment of birth if they are not to spend eternity in hell or purgatory. One of the great ideological conflicts of Christianity was that between Augustine and Pelagius, the fifth-century theologian, on this issue. Pelagius insisted that humans are endowed with the capacity to choose between good and evil; Augustine, who in his own life did choose what he considered good (religion) over what he considered evil (youthful sexual libertinism), insisted that all of mankind was cankered at the root and lacked free will. Augustine won; the very survival of the Church "depended upon the idea that man was sinful by nature." A victory by Pelagius would have made the Church and "institutionally authorized redemption" unnecessary.[7]

Centuries earlier, the Israelite priestly caste also made itself indispensable by declaring man evil and obedience to God necessary. Devoted to a god of power, they taught men to kneel, to give up their will to another called God who was actually a priest.

The double bind knotted around men is already apparent in this discussion. The pinnacle of creation, man is nevertheless utterly dependent and isolated: he requires women to mediate for him with nature and priests to mediate for him with the divine. Required to dominate in the first relation, he must accept domination in the second. Man, the fully human creature, the one identified with power, is governed by requirements over which he has no control. He must learn to negate his natural needs and desires and to find his satisfaction in that negation alone. He must dominate those (women) with whom he might prefer to rest in affection, and scorn the very elements that give him comfort. He must learn to call good ill and ill good. Beyond that, he must even hate himself, find himself worthless and evil, especially if he discovers in himself a tendency to enjoy those things he is supposed to disdain. He must isolate himself, seek to be alone with God, before whom he must repent and atone. He must seek power rather than happiness. And power is obtained by acceptance of utter powerlessness in the face of a dominant god or male caste. The continuing influence of this myth of male supremacy and its double binds should not be underestimated.

Another powerful element in patriarchy is the idea of purpose. Because this ideology shifted humans' vision of life from a cyclical to a linear shape, life was endowed with an end, which was both a terminating point and a *telos*. Most simple cultures—and, we may hypothesize, matricentric cultures—envision human life as part of the eternal recurrence of nature. Just as the seasons change, the moon alters its shape, animals are born, grow, and die, so each returns again, as winter moves back into spring, the moon returns to its fullness, and new young animals reappear. Worship of the goddess, with its emphasis on regeneration—on the snake, the butterfly, and other symbols of transformation—seems to have envisioned human life in a similar fashion, as cyclical, offering a rebirth through transformation. A cyclical vision of life precludes end, for circles have no end. (Eastern religions combine cyclical and linear visions, positing cycles that do eventually reach an end.)

People in most simple cultures are concerned with the present, with the quotidian, with their own well-being. Their gods function to increase present well-being, to bring people more in touch with nature, and sometimes as guides to regeneration. Patriarchy entertains a linear vision of life, and gods who transcend life. Patriarchal gods demand obedience to a set of rules; implicitly, they keep watch on people's behavior, punishing violations of the rules and rewarding obedience. Because they are superior to life and themselves immortal, patriarchal gods provide as it were a frame for life, a beginning and an end: they encompass humanity and in that very act provide it with a purpose. People exist in order to please God. If rewards and punishments are not meted out here on earth, they will be, presumably, after life.

The idea of purpose is paradoxical. First, purpose is believed to increase the dignity of life. Scores of late-nineteenth-century writers whose faith was faltering lamented the loss not of a god, but of life with purpose. Purposelessness seemed terrifyingly *free*, like a flabby body extricated from a corset. Yet it is a loss of dignity to define humanity as a race designed to please a higher being, rather than as a race whose only end is to please itself. Second, the reason the idea of purpose was fostered was to compensate for the sacrifices entailed in obedience to God's law. If one cannot do on earth as one desires because it is forbidden by some rule, one needs the promise of some reward (or the threat of some punishment) as motivation. The "gift" of purpose to the human race is thus very expensive; one can fulfill one's God-given purpose only by sacrificing felicity while one is alive.

Moreover, the idea of divine purpose was extended to everyday life. It may be enough for animals merely to live, to have pleasure, to work to obtain food, to procreate, but it is not enough for godly human beings. It is enough for a woman to produce a son who will carry on the patriliny or be dedicated to God. But a fully transcendent man must accomplish a higher purpose. He may wish to establish a people in his name, something Abraham was promised. He may wish to establish a nation, like Aeneas and scores of conquerors, real and fictional, since.[8] He may wish to found a business, a dynasty, or to perform something that will engrave his name in history. This motive did not disappear after Christianity offered the promise of eternal life in bliss to the virtuous; if anything, it increased, and probably most people in the West today feel failed if they have not achieved some linear goal in their lives.

One of the most important functions of the idea of purpose is to rationalize suffering. Because a transcendent god encompasses one, one does not suffer alone, or in vain. God is witness to one's pain, and will award one points in a heavenly account book. Perhaps God will also remember to punish those who cause one's suffering, although often enough it is God himself who is responsible. Nevertheless, suffering purifies the soul seeking sanctity; it redeems sin. Suffering becomes a vehicle of redemption—as it is in the addended book of Job (the book as it presently stands), in Deutero-Isaiah, in Christianity, and other religions—rather than an end in itself, a mere wretched part of experience. Suffering becomes a means to an end and thus, as Nietzsche wrote, pain was robbed of its innocence.[9] The idea that suffering is a means to redemption also functions politically. In both East and West, passive acceptance of suffering helps to keep the natives—that is, the poor and powerless—quiet.

The idea of purpose was most fully developed by Christianity, which will be discussed later in this chapter. But the idea that man should strive to be right with God and that good men are rewarded by God is very strong in early (Old Testament) Judaism. Judaism and Hellenism, the two sources of Western culture, are very different, yet equally patriarchal.

The idea that mankind was evil never violated the Greek mind; nor, as Nietzsche pointed out, did the idea of God as master.[10] Zeus, though powerful, cannot even save Troy, the city he loves most, from the ill will of his wife, Hera. The existence of a pantheon, many powers at odds with each other, protected the Greeks from monolithic religion. Nor were the Greeks priest-ridden. Mindless power inheres in nature; rational power in men. The second is matter for negotiation; the first is not, despite ritual supplication of the gods described in the poetry. Only a slave bends to a master, and the Greek notion of man emphatically excluded servitude. Because priests did not rule the culture, obedience was less stressed than in Judaic culture. Consequently no purpose was suggested for life, for "purpose" is the reward promised for obedience. Although heroes wished to achieve renown and be remembered in poetry, to live a good life was enough.

This difference between Judaic and Greek culture is paradoxical. For the Greeks, who disdained servitude, created a culture that rested on the backs of that majority of the population that is excluded from discussions of "man"— women, children, slaves, and laboring men. The first three had to obey; free laborers were as subject to the well-to-do then as they are now. Man, a creature with freedom, volition, and dignity, was thus defined in opposition to the rest of his culture; his characteristics separated him from other people. Yet man means human: thus the rest of the culture must have been seen as something less than human.

The ancient Israelites also had obedient wives and slaves, and there were poor people in Israel too. And in Israel, priests and prophets were objects of respect, or at least fear. Yet the prophets' constant exhortation to obedience, their castigation of the populace as stiff-necked and backsliding, suggests that people in general were not at all obedient. Since women as well as men are castigated—if anything even more than men—we can surmise that in actuality Israelite culture was more democratic, more anarchic, and more tolerant than Greek culture.

The prophets who exhorted the Jews to obedience were asking deference to a principle of power and morality from a proud and independent people. The Greeks, who defined men as living in freedom, with volition, and refusing servitude, actually coerced men into obedience to the state, through law and social pressure. Many Greek city-states demanded long military service from male citizens. Socrates died to show his fidelity to the state. By calling men's enforced service to the state by some name other than obedience, the Greeks disguised the actuality. The gods of Greek and Judaic culture were different, but at bottom they made the same demand.

In other areas, there is considerable similarity between Greek and Judaic images of man. Like the Judaic, Greek images were caught in tales that were collected and refined and revised much later. The two epic poems, *The Iliad* and *The Odyssey*, were to the Greeks what the Torah was to the Israelites. And, like the various books of the Torah, the two differ slightly in perspective.

In *The Iliad*, man is predominately a killer. Both the Achaeans and the Trojans are warriors, full of prowess and courage, but the two groups represent different moral worlds. The Achaeans are camped on the shore outside Troy, and when the epic opens they have been there for nearly ten years. The Achaeans are fighting ostensibly for a woman, Helen; but in reality they are defending the honor of the husband she deserted, and fulfilling an obligation to his brother, the most powerful of the Greek chieftains. They are fighting, in other words, for "masculine" reasons, in recognition of men's codes of honor and obligation. Some of the warriors are primarily motivated by the desire to win fame and glory.

The Trojans, on the other hand, are fighting to defend their beautiful city, their home. They too are bound by the masculine code of honor which precludes the surrender of Helen to the Greeks, but at the point at which the epic opens, they know they are defending their civilization itself. The moral difference between the two forces presages the outcome: in the period in which the poem was probably composed, one after another felicitous homeland was falling before the swords of invading conquerors. Power is the central value of *The Iliad*, but it is an utterly destructive value, corroding beauty, pleasure, and love. The poet still sees men as part of nature, as being in some sense kin to plants and animals. He compares the fall of a young warrior to the fall of a young tree, and laments both; he remarks the flights of birds as well as the flights of men. Possibly men can be related to nature because women are not very important in the poem. They provide symbolic occasions for men's battles, and they represent felicity and emotion—love, sorrow, and anxiety—but men represent both sides of the conflict: Hector, Priam, and Paris the "feminine" Troy; Agamemnon, Achilles, Ajax, and Odysseus the "masculine" Achaeans.

The Achaeans are a barbarous group. Camped on the beach, they get food, women, and slaves by marauding villages along the coast of Asia Minor. They are essentially homeless, in exile, and their lives in their tents lack the luxury and grace of life in a Trojan palace. They compete with each other and are almost murderously jealous of each other's privileges or prizes: indeed, the action begins with an argument of rivalry between Achilles and Agamemnon which leads Achilles to withdraw from the battle. Achilles' beloved Patroclus is goaded into returning to the fight; when he goes, Achilles asks Patroclus to win for him, but not to win the war single-handedly, because that would diminish Achilles' honor. Finally, he prays that not one of the Trojans *or* the Greeks survive the war except Patroclus and himself.[11]

In fact, few do. Agamemnon survives only to learn that you can't go home again, and Odysseus spends another ten years trying to return to Ithaca. This is the subject of *The Odyssey*, a tale of exile and wandering. The Achaeans, in destroying Troy, also destroyed their own homes, their own felicity. Odysseus remains a powerful warrior, but in his second ordeal he needs guile and cunning more than prowess. Nature is the enemy in this poem, which significantly has a substantial female cast. Winds blow the hero off-course; he is threatened by whirlpool and strait; a storm destroys his ship and kills all his men; sirens lure the sailors toward foundering rocks. Beautiful and powerful semigoddesses attempt to keep the hero with them; so does a young and beautiful princess, fully human. The hero's task in this poem is to outwit, evade, or escape from the "feminine" world to return to a home which is a place of power, and where he fights his most perilous battle.

Odysseus is protected by Athene, who, unlike Zeus in *The Iliad*, is powerful enough to save him. His home is protected by his faithful wife Penelope, who is besieged with suitors who want to marry her and her land; clearly Ithaca belongs to Penelope, not Odysseus, and her wealth goes to her husband. (So important is the female presence in this poem that Samuel Butler theorized it was written by a woman.) At the same time, what threatens the hero consists of "feminine" elements, and home, Ithaca, is transformed from a place of grace and felicity into a slaughterhouse. Still, the ending of *The Odyssey*—Odysseus' settling down happily with Penelope—felt so wrong, so unheroic, to later readers that a new legend was started and poems written about Odysseus' setting forth again on wandering adventures in his old age.

In the writings of Greeks of later ages, man is identified with power and freedom. Aristotle distinguished between free male citizens and the rest of the population—women, children, mechanics and laborers, slaves. The latter are part of the "necessary conditions" of the state; they function nonvolitionally.[12] We discussed this distinction in Chapter Three: as Slater points out, the Greek male rejection and derogation of women was also a rejection and derogation of domesticity—of home, family life, and child rearing.[13] Life proper to a man was war against other men or intellectual adventure. Nobility adhered to him who was "brave, skillful, and successful in war and in peace."[14] *Arete*, virtue, accrues to the man who has courage, prowess, leadership, and intelligence; the only *arete* of which women are capable is beauty.[15]

Aristotle believed that all relationships were negotiations of power, and saw this as natural and right. The Greeks were exceedingly competitive: from competitions testing physical prowess they moved to competitions in the "realm of the intellect, to feats of poetry and dramatic composition."[16] They staged contests in anything that offered the bare possibility of a fight—from male beauty, singing, riddle-solving, and drinking, to the ability to stay awake.[17] Slater comments, "Nothing seemed to have meaning to the Greek unless it included the defeat of another."[18] This competitive sense extended to the relations among the various city-states, and the wars fought among them fatally eroded them. For fame and glory, those seemingly permanent monuments to an impermanent human life, the Greeks in a sense destroyed their own culture. The poet of *The Iliad* may have been blind, but he had foresight.

There are, of course, many other images of men in both the Old Testament and Greek literature and philosophy. Even women, who are shown in a far more limited range, are given images that deviate from or stretch any categorical description. Men are granted a broad range of characters and moralities. They may be a bit simple-minded, like Samson, full of guile, like Jacob and Odysseus, sullen, stubborn, or arrogant, and still remain heroes. They may rebel against the Father, like David against Saul or Job against God, or Oedipus, blindly; or they may avenge the Father, like Orestes. They may be wise and no warrior, poetic, brilliant, intellectually dense but strong, saints or sinners, rich or poor (although it is always better to be rich): they may be almost anything and be considered heroes. It is with the male image above all that we must examine the negative: what cannot a man be and still be a hero?

A man cannot be under the power of a woman; he cannot be like a woman (effeminate: this has no connection with homosexuality). Usually he cannot be passive, but one of the most popular heroes of the West, Hamlet, is passive and indecisive through most of the play. A man runs a risk if he is gentle and sensitive, unless he becomes Saint Francis of Assisi. What a man cannot be is too close in character to what women are presumed to be. In a sense, then, the definition of woman dictates the definition of man. Women, associated with the body—flesh and feeling—become the incarnations of what no real man is; men

can be anything, everything else, but to prove themselves men, they must eschew "feminine" characteristics. This division of human capacities is most important in the area of control: for men to appear to be always in control, women
must be denied any control whatever.

Thus the single power granted to women in simple male-supremacist cultures—the power of procreation with its related power to pollute through menstruation—is denied to women in patriarchal societies. Although it is clearly
women who carry fetuses in their bodies and nurse them after birth, patriarchal
societies have claimed that the mother is only a vessel, and the father the true
parent. God promised Abraham he would make "his" seed a people; Aeschylus
asserted the father is the true parent, the mother merely a container; and Aristotle put the whole thing on a "scientific" basis. He taught that male semen
was the vital force that gave form to the inert matter of female menstrual blood,
and that the sex of a baby was determined by the direction of the winds at the
time of impregnation. The first became established fact; there continued to be
argument about the second. This is how women come to drop out of culture:
how could a mere woman, uneducated and unworldly, argue against Aristotle?
(If, indeed, she ever heard of him.) But she probably knew her child was supposed to be an incarnation of her husband alone. Yet what did she think when
she watched her child and saw in it her own eyes, or mouth, heard a voice like
her own, saw coloring like her own? She thought what she thought, and held
her peace, and felt a bit like an outlaw.

For centuries men continued to believe they were the true parent; this did
not, however, impede them from blaming their wives for not giving birth to
boys, and sometimes, in the case of royalty, from divorcing them for this failure.
The female's contribution to the child (beyond the house room she gave it and
the nutrients her body fed it), the mammalian egg, was not observed until
1827, under microscopy: it had never been hypothesized, although ancient
prehistorical images showed woman/birds bearing eggs. And no new theory
of sex determination appeared until 1902, with the discovery of sex chromosomes.[19]

Men were then forced to acknowledge what anyone could have guessed
and what in many cases anyone could have seen: both parents transmit their
qualities to a child. Despite visual evidence, and despite the claim of the philosopher Hobbes that the mother was the true parent, law continued to regard the
father as the true parent until the late nineteenth century, and in some nations
this is still the case. Fathers gained custody of the children in cases of divorce;
and if a father died, his family took precedence over the mother in controlling
the child. (Such things were invoked, of course, only when money was at issue;
no one wants the children of the poor.)

Although patriarchy denied women the power of procreation, it granted
them the power of sexuality. Indeed, Christian literature of the Middle Ages
gives the impression that men were utterly helpless in the sexual area, completely subject to women's behavior and appearance. And when sexual affairs
appear in early codes of law or morals, they generally take the form of restrictions on women, not men. Leviticus is unusual in this regard, since it attempts
to regulate the sexuality of men. As we have seen, in Leviticus all sex is regarded

as contamination: any mingling of a man's body with a woman's is pollution, requiring priestly intervention and supervision. Various forms of sex—with a menstruating woman, with a mother-in-law, with a mother and daughter, or with another man, for instance—are abominations subject to severe punishment, including exile and death.

Yet the biblical stories and histories show little sign of sexual guilt or fear in men. Priests married and had families; Samson, consecrated a Nazarite from birth, is forbidden to cut his hair and is subject to dietary restrictions but is permitted to marry. Kings and rich men have many wives and concubines, and prostitution seems not to have been uncommon. The major admonition to kings was not to take foreign wives because they worshiped foreign deities and led Israel away from YHWH. When accusations of fornication are leveled, they are for this sin—worshiping foreign gods—rather than for sexuality.

The Greeks saw sex with women as natural enough, if a kind of slumming. Sex with wives was obligatory, at least until the desired son was produced. There were banquets for men to which prostitutes were brought; and the *hetaerae* provided felicities for mind and body. But the form of sex that was exalted in Athens and most common in Sparta was male homosexuality: only men were worthy of a man's love, whether or not that love issued in physical sex.

The Catholic Church placed sex very high on its list of behaviors to be regulated in almost every detail. What was exalted by the Church was virginity, or at least chastity (after widowhood, for instance). Most sexual arrangements were proscribed *for both sexes*. This was remarkable, but it had little effect on the majority of men; the effect on women was probably also minimal. Women of propertied families were guarded and restrained as they had been in Rome and Athens, and lower-class women were probably relatively free sexually, as they had always been.

The attitude of the Church did, however, lead to the emergence of a new male type: the man who exemplifies the feminine principle. The Jews and early Christians were familiar with all-male religious sects that were ascetic in every way, but not especially "feminine" in their values. The new type was a man who was nutritive and compassionate, in touch with nature perhaps, gentle and charitable. He was permitted to demonstrate such qualities because (it was understood) he had no physical contact with women. Such figures may have appeared more in literature than in life, but there were a few saints of this complexion. So too, Gandhi fostered a legend of sexual asceticism (which was quite contrary to his actual behavior), a trait exalted in the East. Men who have no contact with women, or who have their women under strict control, can be freer in their behavior, can show "feminine" qualities, can even display affection for each other (as do Islamic men).

Church reforms that led to the rule forbidding priests to marry were directed more by a hatred of women and a desire to exclude them from the corridors of Church power than by a wish to regulate male sexuality. Priests continued to resort to prostitutes and to keep concubines after the rule against marriage was enforced. The same is true of the requirement of celibacy of men in universities: it was not sex but marriage which was forbidden. Marriage assimilates women into institutions; this was especially true in small towns in which institutions were closely knit with the community that provided them with basic services. Marriage permits women the possibility of influence over a man, and, through him, over the institution. It was this integration that anti-marriage laws sought to prevent.

Male sexuality was not regulated in the West until the eighteenth century, when the "masculinization" of culture had progressed to a high degree and body, emotion, and any element deemed subversive of male control began to be despised by a large part of the literate population, not just a handful of ascetics. In the beginning, this regulation was directed mainly against boys, whose masturbation was newly proclaimed diseased. It proceeded by categorizing sexual proclivities and declaring some of them "sick." By the mid-nineteenth century, sexuality itself was somehow suspect.[20]

In early Western patriarchy, man was not sexual, but he was a killer. Although in actuality men killed for territory and booty, in literature for millennia the purpose of killing in war or hand-to-hand combat was fame and glory. But there is always the strong possibility that fame and glory, if achieved, will be bestowed posthumously. Killing is dangerous, frightening, and, it would seem, unpleasant. There is no question, given the descriptions of combat in ancient and not-so-ancient writers, that some men relish hacking up or making holes in another's body. There is a question about whether they would do so if they had not been trained to. Killing seems the most unpleasant of the ills renamed good by patriarchy.

Possibly because this is so, killing became the mark of the truest man, of manhood itself. The willingness to kill does delineate humans from most animals, who generally do not kill their own kind; but killing also offers a prime instance of control. This control is somewhat self-defeating—if you kill all of those you wish to control, there is no one left to control. But in Western thinking, murderousness and manliness have often been equated. Shakespeare made ironic use of this equation in *Macbeth* and *Coriolanus* and in *King Lear*, when Edmund orders a soldier to murder Cordelia and Lear in their prison cells and he replies, "I cannot draw a cart nor eat dried oats; / If it be man's work, I'll do it."

The emphasis on competition as a proper way of life for a man means that murderousness is at its most fierce between brothers, whether biological or spiritual. Florynce Kennedy's description of horizontal hostility, attacking those on one's own level rather than those above, has been applied to blacks and women who fail to support their own kind, or who perhaps even prey on their own kind. But this phenomenon is most pronounced in the lives of men, who turn fury against their *semblances* more often than on those who govern them. Civil wars are the cruelest kind, and people hate their close neighbors with an intensity lacking in their hatred for their society's devils. So there is animosity between North and South in this country and many others; or among cities, as in Italy; or between ethnic or racial groups sharing the same purlieu.

As with women, the one who is the same but different is the one who must be subjugated or annihilated: the brother, the secret sharer, men who are alike in most ways, complements. Literature is rife with examples, from Abel/Cain, Achilles/Hector, Aeneas/Turnus, Coriolanus/Aufidius, to Norman Mailer's white Rojack/black Shago Martin. But we hardly need to go to literature for our proof: men in business, government, or any other institution are apt to find their worst rival in the man who could be their closest friend. This inevitable competitiveness between men who are similar (both of whom are striving, symbolically, to gain the attention of the Father) enforces the solitude enjoined on the hero, and, by extension, on all men. If a man cannot befriend those who are like him, he has no place to go. To go home is to submit the self to the realm of women; camping out means other men and the temptation, like that between Mailer's D.J. and Tex *(Why Are We in Vietnam)*, to make love. (Mailer is our most acute poet of the male myth.) Beyond that, there are only animals, God, and the void, the hero's true companions.

Yet it is obvious, if one cares to look, that man is not a killer by nature. If he were, it would not be necessary to train him in competition, mistrust, and murder. It would never have been necessary to remove boys from home (the realm of women) and send them to schools "to make a man of" them. Schools and athletics, today's equivalents of ancient *gymnasia*, field training of boys in feudal societies, Britain's "public" schools, and other such institutions, are training grounds that practice systematic brutality, both physical and emotional. Boys are taught not to show emotion and, if possible, not to feel it; they are taught to hate those who abuse them and to turn that hatred horizontally, at "the enemy," who may be a brother. The point of military discipline is to teach men to obey without hesitation and to hate: psychological training sessions, such as those conducted during the Vietnam War, rouse men to a hysterical pitch, teaching them to "hate Charlie."

Just as it would not have been necessary to decree and impose inferiority on women if they were really inferior, it would not have been necessary to do more than train men in the use of weapons and the body if they were really dangerously aggressive. The situation has become extreme in our own time because of movies and television. While all Western cultures have purveyed an image of murderousness in men and have fostered competition and hatred among them, training in these qualities has been local and limited. When reading was the main avenue of culture, only a small literate class could be inflamed with the values of *The Iliad* or *The Aeneid*, could relish the righteous murders of the Old Testament. Religious art, so full of violence, concentrates on the suffering, martyred aspect of that violence, not on the perpetration of it.

But movies and television can and do reach everyone, whether literate or not. And the presentation of American life offered in movies and television is overwhelmingly violent. Films and series focusing on women are not generally violent: they are often comic and the men who appear in them are often shown as foolish or ludicrous, reinforcing the notion of the female realm as one in which men are "unmanned." But films and series focusing on men portray a male world of exuberant violence; moreover, it is a violence that costs nothing. That is, the male hero is unlikely to be killed or maimed, and if he is, he has died for "justice," the new name for the old fame and glory. Hideous forms of bodily harm are shown without remorse or compunction in the characters responsible for them, without any suggestion that it might hurt to kill, that killing or harming another also kills or harms something in the self. Football, the most popular television sport, is a national pastime for watchers who sit safe and comfortable in front of an electronic box viewing cruelty and violence. It is said that watching brutal competition like football sublimates violence. Perhaps. But recent researchers affirm a connection between American television's widespread dissemination of a violent vision of life and the fact that the United States has a homicide rate eight to nine times higher than that of any other major industrial country.[21]

Like women, men over the millennia have been molded into images they might not choose for themselves. They have been taught to value lonely and unsatisfying power (for it is both, as I will try to show in Chapter Seven), and little enough power at that, and to despise the qualities that could provide them with contentment. Many men do choose lives of contentment—but most, I would guess, feel less like "men" as a result. We must ask the same question we asked about women: Why did men not revolt? Why didn't they cast off the oppression of this way of thinking?

Actually, men have rebelled against Fathers many times in the course of history. But they have rebelled against the form of power exercised, not against power itself as the primary value. Thus their solution has been to seize power themselves and re-form it to their liking; so they in turn become oppressive Fathers to new generations of sons. Men have been aware that they were unhappy; but they have not often been able to see through patriarchal terms to the underlying premises.

But some men have tried to do this, and have succeeded in stretching the male role a bit. Montaigne, in the sixteenth century, emphasized the loneliness of the thinking/feeling man, his homelessness of soul if not of body. He named cruelty the primary sin, the worst sin, regardless of the end it was imputed to serve. He considered Europeans' contempt for their bodies and physical nature a sign of imbecility, and asserted that animals were superior to men in every way.[22] In play after play Shakespeare dramatized the consequences for individual men and for society as a whole of placing "masculine" values above "feminine" values, or of extirpating the "feminine" entirely. His comedies and his tragedies concentrate on the necessity for men to embrace the full spectrum of human qualities and to learn that love, forgiveness, nutritiveness, and compassion are in actuality more important to a life than power and its trappings.[23] Both of these men had an important effect on subsequent cultures, but for the most part the import of their work was distorted and pressed into the service of "masculine" values.

Francis Bacon, who emulated Montaigne, also believed himself to be rebelling against an oppressive tradition. Deriding the orderly categories of medieval thought as unrealistic, he offered the possibility of a new approach to experience. In the early seventeenth century he pronounced a "Great Instauration," a renewal and restoration of man's fallen state. The instrument of renewal was a *novum organum*, a new method of approaching reality. What he was advocating was the sort of approach that we now call the scientific method. Use of this method would restore man to his primal state: "For man by the Fall fell at the same time from the state of innocency and from his dominion over creation."[24] Nevertheless, "after the Fall of man some dominion over rebellious nature still remained—to the extent at least that it could be subdued and controlled by true and solid arts."[25] Science could restore man's dominion over nature, although Bacon insisted that "man is the helper and interpreter of nature. He can only act and understand in so far as by working upon her or observing her he has come to observe her order. Beyond this he has neither knowledge nor power."[26] (If we include *woman* with *nature* as the referent of *her*, we have the basic patriarchal belief.)

Bacon's work was the herald of a new era which did overwhelm completely the medieval approach to knowledge; and since scientific research did in time lead to the mechanical and technical revolution of the past two centuries, it conferred upon man a dominion over nature that was unimaginable earlier. This rebellion against an oppressive fatherhood, then, furthered and strengthened the masculine principle: it was a rebellion against a form of patriarchy, not against patriarchy itself. Unlike Montaigne and Shakespeare, Bacon had no quarrel with the notion of power as the highest value.

A generation later, Thomas Hobbes, who had studied Bacon's work, expanded certain strands of his master's thought. He too rebelled against sentimental or rigid orthodoxies. He was a materialist and saw man as a bundle of appetites and desires. He saw the life of man in nature as "solitary, poor, nasty, brutish, and short."[27] He terrified his own age by decrying the Christian notion of a moral purpose to life, insisting there was no *summum bonum*, no *finis ultimus*. He denied "masculine" notions of linear goal and ultimate reward for obedience, but had nothing to put in their place. Unlike Shakespeare, he could not envision experience itself as its own end. "I put for a general inclination of all mankind a perpetual and restless desire of power after power that ceaseth only in death."[28]

All thinkers of this period, even the sweeter-minded of them, like Richard Hooker (sixteenth century) or Jeremy Taylor (seventeenth), believed in the innate depravity of the human race. Man was steeped in sin, and so perhaps it was understandable that his life was benighted: "As our life is very short, so it is very miserable; and therefore it is well it is short," wrote Taylor.[29] Hobbes believed the nature of man was dominated by competition, distrust (his term was *diffidence*), and ambition (which he called *glory*).

Lawrence Stone believes that ordinary life in England during the Elizabethan and early Stuart periods was violent and pervaded by suspicion and competition. He summarizes a letter written in 1607 by a nobleman to his son: "The basic assumption is that no one is to be trusted, since . . . everyone—wife, servants, children, friends, neighbours, or patrons—are only kept loyal by self-interest, and may, therefore, at any moment turn out to be enemies."[30] With the gradual increased hegemony of "masculine" values through increased centralization of control, uniformity, and institutionalization, the influence of "feminine" values was waning. Previously, such values had been upheld through religion; through localized pockets of semiautonomy (farms, villages, towns) in which women had some voice, and in which they, children, and land remained important; and through the presence of women in councils of church and state. Hobbes and others believed themselves to be exploding pious myths about the nature of man, clearing the air. And so they were—but the import of their work too was pressed into service, and by the end of the seventeenth century, men were beginning to accept the description of themselves as egocentric and power-seeking, but were also asserting that egocentric pursuit of self-interest contributed to the public welfare.[31]

Despite many references to God's existence, for men of intellect or business he was dead long before Nietzsche announced the fact. If life had no ultimate moral purpose, God had no function. He created the universe but then absconded. A new deity was needed, and men returned to Greek thought and made reason God, a god that resided within men (some men, but not all; and not within women). Descartes located existence itself in the mind alone, announcing that being meant the ability to think. This idea had broad ramifications, for it separated the mind from the rest of the being. If the original need of patriarchy had been to split the human from nature (using women as the link between them), Cartesian splitting of the mind from the body refined and reinforced the original division. For men were mind, women body. Man was now a mind disconnected from his body, abstracted and presumably without desire or will. He was an impartial, objective observer of the rest of creation, notably matter. Nature is matter without spirit, as is body—and woman. Man could observe matter, tinker with it, mutilate it, experiment with it, and himself remain untouched and untouchable. Inert matter could not reciprocate or revenge man's depredations. Nor did man have to fear harming matter as he mutilated and destroyed it: for matter is eternal.

Descartes asserted that matter was inert and passive, and that bodies remained in their given state, at rest or in motion, unless acted upon by another body. Newton complicated this relation by positing a set of passive forces, although he continued to maintain that matter was passive and could not move itself. There were three of these passive forces: the *vis insita* or innate force caused bodies to remain in their given state (rest or uniform motion); the *vis inertiae*, force of inertia, caused bodies to resist external forces; and the innate *vis conservans*, conserving force, maintained bodies' forward direction by successive impulses. Change occurred as a result of the *vis impressa*, or impressed force, which acted upon matter from the outside. Gravitational force acted on bodies at a distance, drawing particles of matter together on the earth's surface.[32]

In this new mechanistic universe, all things were isolated, separate, distinct from one another. Even space and time were seen as dimensions separate from each other and detached from life. What linked things was power—the dominance of one force over another. The cosmos was activated by material and efficient causes only, by matter and force. Leibniz took this theory further by arguing that corporeal bodies were not, as Descartes had claimed, substances, but collections of confused minds (monads), perceived as extended bodies, and that this extension and motion were mere attributes of bodies, while force was real.[33] The god of power euhemerized into a force of nature, but power remained supreme.

The consequences of this mechanistic view of the universe were extraordinary. As Carolyn Merchant describes it, "Between 1500 and 1700 an incredible transformation took place. A 'natural' point of view about the world in which bodies did not move unless activated, either by an inherent organic mover or a 'contrary to nature' superimposed 'force,' was replaced by a non-natural non-experiential 'law' that bodies move uniformly unless hindered. The 'natural' perception of a geocentric earth in a finite cosmos was superseded by the 'non-natural' commonsense 'fact' of a heliocentric infinite universe."[34]

The medieval mind saw connections everywhere, among the elements of the cosmos and of the earth, and within human life. The world was bound by associations, symbolic resemblances, and the great chain of being, which linked the lowliest to the highest in an admittedly hierarchical universe. So a cat may look at a queen, and the clod and the pebble show the configurations of God. If some of the resemblances and associations drawn by medieval thinkers seem quirky or amusing to us now, they offered humans of the period a sense of being part of and at home in a huge extended family embracing all creation. At the same time, people maintained a largely subsistence economy, trading what they had for what they needed.

This cohesion was banished in favor of a sense of things as fragmented, and of a new kind of categorization drawn up by Linnaeus and others, which emphasized distinctions rather than similarities, underscored discrete units rather than a unified related whole.[35] In economic matters, subsistence was gradually replaced by a drive to accumulate profit (more than one needs) in an open-ended way (one never has enough). The old sense of nature as animate and alive gave way to a sense of nature as dead and inert, while money, a truly inert substance, was endowed with life.[36]

Domination became the underlying principle of life, and the planet became an inert, passive, dead globe in which only the mind of man can soar free to attain perfect control through perfect objectivity. We (or some of us) have since realized that objectivity is not a human possibility: humans cannot gaze at any object, person, or event without feeling, preconception, or bias, whether conscious or unconscious. What people can do is turn persons, objects, and events into mere objects without value. That is, one can choose to see not an old ceramic bowl fired and painted by one's grandmother, bequeathed to one, and associated with memories of family events, but merely a ceramic bowl of certain dimensions, with worn painting, somewhat brittle from age, and of no value on the market. One can choose to see other people not as fellow beings, ends in themselves, but as contacts or noncontacts, useful to some project outside themselves, or useless. This is not objectivity but objectivization, and it permits what is called an instrumental view of experience. Nothing exists for its own sake; nothing has value in and of itself unless it is instrumental in achieving some variety of power—control, profit, influence.

Instrumentality permitted experimentation and manipulation that could not have occurred in earlier ages, and is responsible for most of the scientific discoveries of the past few centuries; it is also responsible for most of our pollution and all of our weaponry. Beyond that, however, it gave birth to the modern psyche, the alienation of people from their planet, from each other, and of the mind from the body, senses, and emotions. Alienation as Marx used the term referred to the detachment of humans from the things they produced, a detachment that resulted from their lack of control over their own labor and the things they made. But it is a general malaise, covering much of our experience. Instrumental thinking degrades objects, people, animals, and the entirety of nature, turns them into means, rather than ends in themselves. At the same time, it isolates the manipulator, the thinking mind, which is alone in its own artificial kingdom, separated even from its body and senses. The qualities of experience are secondary to its use as a means to an end that can never be realized, for power (as we shall see in Chapter Seven) is an illusory end, a goal that can never be reached.

This general alienation is thus the most desperate condition humankind has experienced. Life is seen as struggle for domination, but no satisfying level of domination can ever be attained; thus life is a constant pursuit of the tantalizing. Alienation is responsible for the fragmentation of communal life, the desperate isolation of urban life, and for a belief that seems nearly universal among Western men (and many Western women) that only by the exercise of control over their environment can they claim to exist at all.

There were, in the centuries in which the instrumental view of life was growing, thinkers who offered seemingly opposite views. One of these was Rousseau, who asserted that nature was the seat of basic human virtue. In a society in which legitimacy is presumed to emanate from God through his agents the monarch and the church, it was revolutionary to posit nature as the original—and therefore superior—source of right and morality. In the place of a world view in which nature (with all the associations we have discussed) is despised, savage, and polluting, and requires the saving grace of God and civilization to restrain and harness it, Rousseau offered a vision of nature as simple and clean, and man in the state of nature as inherently virtuous. Here culture becomes the polluting agent, distorting what should have grown straight, deforming instincts and senses.

Nevertheless, Rousseau's "natural man" is in some ways very like the ideal man of the burgeoning middle-class industrialist—he is above all self-sufficient and independent of others. Like mind freed of body, he is man freed of bonds to community. And Rousseau's description of man did not extend to women. Women were still considered especially close to nature, but *their* closeness was seen as a drawback. Rousseau and other Enlightenment figures used the ostensible connection between women and nature as a reason for continuing to exclude women from the political realm and as an explanation of women's inferiority. Rousseau, accepting nature, rejected the idea of original sin—but he held the female sex responsible for the ills of the human race, "ills of which it is the cause."[37] If eighteenth-century thinkers on the one hand saw nature as something to be conquered and mastered, and on the other hand debated about how much value to grant to bodily processes, instincts, and senses, they displayed little disagreement about women.[38]

As men of the educated class continued to rebel against their intellectual fathers, revising the images of man, life, and nature, the majority of men plodded on in much the same way from era to era. Subjugated economically, politically, socially, and intellectually, powerless and knowing their powerlessness, they took part in large revolutions—the establishment of Christianity, the establishment of Protestantism, and many uprisings over the centuries. But like women, they did not rebel as a class. For one thing, many still possessed deep connection with land, with women and children, with their bodies; for another, however miserable they might be, they had more autonomy and were less miserable than women. And each wave of revolution, reform, institutionalization, left a larger number of men slightly better off. Education became accessible to greater numbers, and men of low (nonnoble) origin could gain prestige as priests, or part of the growing professional class. A middle class developed; for some men, upward mobility was possible. As the economic state of men improved, so did the economic state of women. But the exercise of talent and energy, independence of body or mind that men were achieving was increasingly denied to women. The division between the sexes grew wider as the status of ordinary men improved and the status of ordinary women diminished, and men had even more to thank their creator for.

Concomitantly, the gap between even modest prosperity and poverty widened, and in times of dearth or in postwar recessions, the poor (then as now) were not only the first to feel pinched, but also were often (then as now) punished for it. Such a condition was the reason the poor *as a class* rose up in the French Revolution. After the violence ceased and the country returned to stability, having starved to death enough of the poor to silence the rest, again men were slightly better off—they won the vote. Women did not. Always there was this class, women, to remind men that they were not so badly off after all. Until the Industrial Revolution.

This is not to say that men did not go on earning more than women, little as it was; or that they did not still possess rights over women and rights women were denied. What men lost was their edge in autonomy, their sense of being relatively free. In the factories, they were subjugated like women, made wage slaves and placed under surveillance without the right to set their own hours, move about at will, or set aside one task in favor of another. It was then that the massive revolts of the poor began, and theories of anarchy, socialism, and unification of workers arose. And it was in this period of class war that the image of man lost whatever refinements and endowments of nobility it had possessed in previous incarnations. It was also in this period, when men felt no better than women, that racism (and imperialism) became widespread.

The Rousseauian notions that man was born free but was everywhere in chains, and that he should be permitted by culture to grow unfettered, were interpreted as arguing that all restraints should be removed from men who wished to accumulate property, enter into contracts at will, and to treat other humans as inert matter, more disposable than the machines at which they worked.

Hobbes, Rousseau, and other contract theorists had second thoughts about "natural" man. He is an ideal only as long as he is alone in nature. When there are two men, they are inevitably in competition to wrest what they need or think they need from a nature seen as limited and exhaustible. This conception appears throughout Western thought after the seventeenth century. From Hegel on, life was seen as struggle, as if it had no other components. The struggle against nature is referred to as *scarcity*, and treated as if it were a universal fact of life. In the mid-nineteenth century Marx wrote, "Just as the savage must wrestle with Nature to satisfy his wants, to maintain and reproduce life, so must civilized man."[39] Yet as we know, people in simple societies tend to work far fewer hours than those in complex societies, and they do not, on the whole, suffer from scarcity. Simple societies may experience drought, flood, or severe storm, but so do people in complex societies. The idea of scarcity, like the idea of life as struggle, is based on a conception of nature as withholding, an enemy, and allows for no modification, no suggestion that the infant experiences as much acceptance and affection as thwarting, or that sharing, a basic value in simple societies, modifies whatever scarcities may occur. In other words, the assumption that life is struggle against scarcity (of love, of recognition, of food, of other goods) is narrow and partial, obliterating other visions. It functions, however, to justify an image of man as alone, in conflict, and therefore necessarily aggressive.

Hobbes and Rousseau vacillate in their view of nature, finding it sometimes idyllic and sometimes hellish; it is hellish when other men are in it. If the "natural" in man is admirable, the "natural" in society is not.[40] For the defining traits of man are selfishness and the drive to conquer and dominate. These are useful traits when man is alone in nature, but destructive when two men fill the same stage. That man is selfish and driven to dominate is asserted by every liberal philosopher since Locke, writes Mihailo Markovic.[41] Such a view of man is not found only in philosophers. As Erich Heller points out, the Romantic poets insisted that the world must become imagination and poetry, even as Hegel insisted the world must become rational consciousness, but they meant the same thing. They show "above all the ambition of the human mind to dominate the real world to the point of usurping its place."[42] Freud, and especially his followers, find a central fact of life to be power as symbolized by the penis. The profound fear of the boy child is castration by the powerful father; the profound grief of the girl child is recognition she lacks a penis. The boy submerges his fear and anger at the father and molds himself to resemble him and thus gain power—a large penis; the girl sublimates her envy and disappointment in the compensatory hope of having a child—or, as Juliet Mitchell sees it, she develops bitter hostility to the mother who failed to make her a boy.[43] Freud too saw human nature as essentially selfish and aggressive; and "what we criticize in ourselves, we attribute to our animal past," writes Stephen Jay Gould, commenting on this Freudian attitude. We see our brutality, aggressiveness, and selfishness as "the shackles of our apish ancestry."[44]

The description of man as selfish and aggressive served several purposes. It was a transposition of the old heroic values into the economic and political realm: men who doubted they would have had the courage to face an armed opponent with only a shield and sword could nevertheless feel like heroes on the battlefield of political and economic manipulation. Further, if egocentric greed and competition were "natural" human traits, a man was not "sinful" for pursuing them. Everything in nature had a purpose; if human nature (manly version) was aggressive, aggressiveness must have been necessary to keep the human race alive. In erecting this structure of thought, men used any materials that came to hand, either oblivious of or indifferent to the fact that they were distorting them.

For example, Darwin's theories of evolution and natural selection were specifically intended to describe local adaptation to changing environments. Evolution and natural selection occurred at particular moments in response to particular circumstances: they had no ultimate end. Indeed, most species become extinct in time. Darwin had no notion of *progress* in nature; adaptive changes were not stages in a process of perfecting a creature; they did not bear on improvement, but only on survival in a given situation.[45]

But Darwin's ideas were picked up and used in precisely the opposite sense to the one he specified. Biological evolution was seized on as a metaphor, and applied in ways that offered support for extreme competition, free enterprise, and a capitalistic system, as well as imperialism (colonization). A set of writers took up the task of applying to human societies ranked categories like those applied to nature. But the human categories were not neutral; they had a moral overtone. So the social orders of the world were placed in an ascending series, from "savagery" to "barbarism" to "civilization"; the various races were also placed in a hierarchical ladder. Thomas Huxley described warfare in nature; the social Darwinists extended this to warfare in the marketplace, giving the "burgeoning industrial world of the time a 'scientific' sanction for free, unregulated, and often quite ruthless competition."[46] The idea of the "survival of the fittest" offered those who were scraping to become richer a "natural" justification for their behavior. They called the consequences of industrialization "progress," without glancing at its effects on people; they expected and generally received social approval of the personal qualities that created the industrial explosion—"personal ambition, greed, self-aggrandisement, competitiveness, exploitation of others and indifference to their plights."[47] In nineteenth-century America, the major image of man was as self-made, industrious, disciplined, and strong-willed.[48]

Darwin's work suggested the unity of all living matter and the continuity of all species; it could have provided a biological base for philosophical theories emphasizing context, continuity, and impermanence—indeed, it is doing so now in the work of dialectical biologists and of ecologists.[49] Darwin's work could have led to a repudiation of Cartesian and other dualistic theories of humankind and nature, to a repudiation of the notion of subject and object as alienated from each other, and to a focus on the interpenetration and interconnection of life processes and living matter. Instead, it was used as proof of an absolute distinction between biological and cultural evolution, in which culture became the new dividing line between man and animal. It was preeminently racism that barred men from seeking a more integrated view.[50] But if racism had not been available, sexism would have filled the gap. Without a group to look down on, men would lose their special place, they would become merely humans: and for men raised in an elite, that is an intolerable status.

The vision of men as driving, aggressive, selfish, and brutal creatures is a false one, despite the examples we may know. It is false not just because it excludes a great many men, but because it fails to take account of the whole of any man. It is a partial view, of society and of individuals. Entire areas of life and functioning are omitted from its purview. Robert Paul Wolff, discussing Hobbes, Rousseau, Kant, and Bentham, points out that none of them "considered the facts of the human condition to be philosophically fundamental to an understanding of man as a political actor." At least half of our time in life is spent sleeping, eating, cleaning our bodies—insides and outside—dressing them, in conversational or affectionate exchange, and in play. Philosophers do not regard these areas—the supposed nonvolitional areas of life—as having any effect on what we think. Wolff adds that even death "is treated as accidental to man's nature as a moral and political being. It terminates life, but . . . does not infiltrate it, as it were."[51]

Indeed, Lawrence A. Blum remarks that Kant and Hegel specify that rationality, self-control, strength of will, consistency, adherence to duty and obligation, and acting on "universal" principles comprise moral behavior; they specifically exclude from the makeup of moral man qualities like sympathy, compassion, kindness, nurturance, and concern for the community, which are associated with women.[52]

Western philosophers adopted the Greek exclusion of the realm of the "necessary" (the nonvolitional) from political and philosophical thought. "This systematic setting to one side of the fundamental facts of birth, childhood, parenthood, old age, and death results in an image of the public or political world as a timeless or static community of [male] adults."[53] Even relationships among people are regarded as extrinsic rather than intrinsic, accidental rather than essential.[54]

This image of man functions to justify and explain the behavior of men in the world. In its presumption that most of experience is irrelevant to intellectual (political or economic or military) matters, it justifies the behavior of men who are consumed with strategies and manipulations focusing on power seeking, and who show little concern with the everyday conditions of their own lives. Such men do not seem to see a connection between their acts—polluting air or water, say—and the fact that they and their children breathe that air and drink that water. They do not seem to consider that the weapons they order or build have a strong probability of killing them and their children. Not just the domestic realm, but what we think of as the *human* realm—the realm of experience rather than theory—is extraneous to the thinking of such people. But of what use is a political or any other sort of philosophy that is not firmly rooted in human experience?

The person who first noticed this phenomenon was Nietzsche. He wrote (in the late nineteenth century): "We [German philosophers] never make . . .

everyday matters (such as eating, housing, clothes, and intercourse) the object of a constant unprejudiced and *universal* reflection and revision." From the failure to attend to the everyday is "derived *nearly all the bodily and spiritual infirmities* of the individual. Ignorance of what is good and bad for us, in the arrangement of our mode of life, the division of our day, the selection of our friends and the time we devote to them, in business and leisure, commanding and obeying, our feeling for nature and for art, our eating, sleeping, and meditation, ignorance and lack of keen perceptions *in the smallest and most ordinary details*—this it is that makes the world 'a vale of tears' for so many. . . . [We] still inherit in our blood some taint of this contempt for everyday matters."[55]

In *The Will to Power*, Nietzsche writes of the "artful and blind hostility of philosophers to the *senses*," and speaks of the leitmotifs, the dominating thrust of all of philosophy, as being "a sort of revenge upon reality, a malicious destruction of the valuations by which men live." Surely he was writing, as we all do, of himself and the sources of his own misery: but he had the courage to let himself see. "The history of philosophy is the story of a secret raging against the conditions of life, against the feelings of life, against partisanship in favor of life. . . . Philosophers have never hesitated to affirm a world, provided it contradicted this world, and furnished them with a pretext for speaking ill of this world."[56] Misogynist that he was, Nietzsche could probably never have named those "real values of life" the feminine principle.

It was left to a female thinker, Simone de Beauvoir, to depict in detail the grounds of male disdain for the everyday realm, the permeating and constant elements of everyday life that provide much of its texture. The smell of sweat, excrement, urine, farts, baby spit-up, and semen must be banished, and therefore so must all smells. De Beauvoir locates degradation in the condition of femaleness itself, with its nonvolition, victimization, and filth. Females are in a state of immanence, mere being, as opposed to male transcendence.[57] De Beauvoir would agree with the passage in the Gospel of Thomas in which Jesus declares that women who make themselves male shall be able to enter the kingdom of heaven. And that kingdom must transcend the everyday, for everyday life is a morass, a bog, not civilization but swampy nature. For de Beauvoir, as (one suspects) for many men, the fetus is a tenant, a parasite on the mother; menstruation is horrific and disgusting; and nursing is merely exhausting.[58]

However men see themselves—as transcendent mind/spirit without body, as mechanically efficient emotionless executors, as brawn and body without sentiment—the ground of their pride is always that which is *missing*. Men see themselves as superior (to other men, to women, to other races or ethnic groups) because they lack what the Other has. Men are men because they don't cry, don't feel, don't need. Like Henry Moore's sculptures, much of their greatness consists of a hole. And in general, what is missing in them is whatever they conceive women to be. Often the lack centers on what Nietzsche called the "value feelings" of life, its quality and color. William Gass describes an actual campaign waged by philosophers from Aristotle on: "Aristotle insisted that qualities were accidents and could not be part of essence."[59] Only relationship—form—was essential and could be known. This idea limits legitimate knowledge to perception of relations among things, structure, patterns of dominance; it invalidates the kinds of knowing that emerge from the senses, the emotions, or what is called intuition. It makes quantity more important than quality.

The narrowness of the male conception of self was alleviated somewhat in actual life by attributing to women those elements not permitted to men. Hegel, for instance, sees men as in possession of independent personal self-sufficiency and "knowing and willing of free universality." Thus men are capable of "the self-consciousness of the conceiving thought, and the willing of the objective final cause." Men possess mind, volition, and self-consciousness, their relation to the world is one of "power and mastery," and their essential life is lived in the state, the sciences, in battle, in *struggle*—with the world and with the self. Women also have a spiritual dimension, according to Hegel, but show it in their desire for unity and concord; women's relation to the world is "subjective and passive." Yet the "self-sufficient" man cannot attain concord except in the family.[60]

The Industrial Revolution brought greater segregation of sexes because the two no longer had much in common—they did not together run the farm, the shop, the manor. Men went away from home to work and women were constricted within home and the social realm. There was less chance for the woman to fill what was "missing" in a man. As the technological revolution succeeded the industrial, men at all levels began to feel a loss of autonomy. No longer just the workers and overseers and supervisors, but managers and even owners lost the sense of being free agents. In the mid-nineteenth century, the women's movement began, threatening the very bases of men's dignity: the women whose inferior position guaranteed that they would provide men not just with felicity but also with reinforcement of their manhood (superiority) were standing upright, showing their stature. Women became suspect, and for some men they became the enemy. Speaking of the wave of mother hatred in the mid-twentieth century, Ehrenreich and English write, "Behind the hatred and fear of the mother was a growing sense that men had somehow lost power—that they were no longer 'real men.' "[61]

In fact, more and more parts of experience were considered off-limits to "real men." If, for a long time, men had not been supposed to weep, they were permitted a wide range of other emotions; they were open to sensation, to passion, to emotional display, to rich and gaudy clothing, elaborate manners, excellence in dancing, singing, playing the lute, and guiltless (or comparatively guiltless) "wenching." As the world became more and more "masculinized," such expressiveness was increasingly deplored.

The constriction of men has continued into the twentieth century, as institutions increasingly narrow the range of expression men are permitted. At the same time, advanced technology has permitted more centralized control, and men are increasingly losing control over the daily events of their lives. Christopher Lasch asserts that loss of almost all autonomy has led to widespread feelings of powerlessness and victimization, has weakened the party system in America and undermined local institutions of government. He adds, "The invasion of culture and personal life by the modern industrial system produces the same effects that it produces in the social and political realm—a loss of autonomy and control, a tendency to mistake the exercise of consumer choices for self-determination, a growing ascendance of elites, the replacement of practical skills with organized expertise."[62]

Thinkers who wished to expand and enrich the human image and human life strengthened old values instead, or, like Darwin, were distorted by later generations. Marx and Engels clearly desired the betterment of the human condition. But they thought this had to be achieved through "masculine" modes. Both believed deeply that man must dominate nature; neither considered that emphasizing this fundamental hierarchical division might constitute an impediment to the eradication of hierarchical divisions among humans. They did not expect the complete elimination of class distinctions until some future date; nor would they have welcomed them, these men who indulged in contempt for the mass of humankind, and even for their closest associates and supporters. Edmund Wilson, writing of the correspondence between Marx and Engels, comments that "as the years go on, the word *Esel* [ass] seems almost to become synonymous with *human being*."[63]

Regardless of the alterations it has made in Marxism, the twentieth-century Marxist movement is bound to Marx's basic beliefs—that nature has no value whatever in itself, that relations between humans and nature lack any moral dimension, that work is the mode in which man appropriates nature to his own purposes and thereby aggrandizes himself, and that power and power struggle are the central facts of existence.[64]

Trotsky lived like a religious ascetic, sacrificing comfort, peace of mind, and even life itself—his own as well as those of his followers and friends. He was willing to give up even "that enjoyment of political power itself which is the only worldly satisfaction that Marxism allows to its true priesthood," wrote Edmund Wilson. He also attained "a perfection of revolutionary form and standards of revolutionary honor that seem almost intended to rival that of the Tsar's dueling officers." But Wilson acclaims Trotsky by citing Ibsen: "The strongest man is he who stands most alone."[65]

More recent thinkers show the same tendencies. Sartre's existentialism focuses on freeing man from his past, unshackling him from oppressive traditions and customs. Although such a liberation is in many ways desirable, freedom from is not the same as freedom to, and the question is what new form can encompass humans felicitously. Sartre offers mainly the void; for him, "freedom is an ultimate; exercising it, man constantly stands on the brink of the unknown, of the unnamable. His is a life of anguish. He and he alone makes himself, whatever that self turns out to be."[66] Sartre defines freedom as total responsibility in total solitude. This is an extreme vision of life, an extreme definition of man as a being isolated and in exile. It is depicted in Sartre's play *No Exit*, in which hell is the presence of other people; this is the complete realization of the Enlightenment notion that two men in the same space inevitably means conflict. When hell is other people and man is responsible for creating himself in "dreadful freedom," man's struggle is finally with *himself*. Vacillating between being and nothingness to realize his "essence," he makes a permanent rupture with the world in an effort to find the divine, which is now located within himself. The Christian hell has not disappeared, but has shrunk from Dante's populated hierarchy to the obsessed individual self, as in the work of Samuel Beckett.

Bertram Morris describes Sartre's world as "a heroic one, in which only man is responsible for his condition—not science, not technology, not impersonal forces, not even the subjectivities of emotional life."[67] This way of thinking derives from the Cartesian world view, in which fully rational human beings are distinguished from inert matter and no other life forms exist.[68] Like Ernst Cassirer, Sartre envisions life (manly life; for no one, I think, suggests that such freedom is possible to those with female anatomies) as created wholly by the self. This philosophy assumes that life is lived entirely in the mind, and that, moreover, the mind remains imperturbable, impregnable to what is occurring to the body, to other people, to the world around one. Supremely elitist, this philosophy takes "man" to be a handful of the fortunate. The patriarchal bias is clear: since the world and life will not conform to will and the idea, will and idea shall be declared the only true reality—the rest is dross, inessential, discardable.

Sartre was a political man, and the "freedom" he admired implied the courage to stand against tyranny and injustice. Nevertheless, the solipsism of his philosophy offers justification for turning one's back on power, refusing to be engaged by the large-scale movements of one's time and choosing to cultivate one's own flower box. Indeed, by insisting that choices must be made in isolation, disconnection, Sartre removes the ground from which most choices really emerge—our emotional ties to people and principles, our sense of our bodies and the physical context of our life. We may disguise, even from ourselves, the fact that we make choices with our entire selves; we may try to make choices with only our intellects—although how that can be accomplished is not clear. The exaltation of mind that pervades philosophical thinking perpetuates the human obsession with ridding humans of all of what seems to tie them to nature.

But even to stand superior to nature is not humanly possible. Not only is mind tied to, affected by, emergent from body, senses, and emotion; it is also dependent upon the air the body breathes and the food it eats, the comfort or discomfort of its situation, the emotional context of its life. Moreover, mind itself emerges from nature, is a natural endowment. The notion that man is separate from and superior to nature is so patently false that it requires one who accepts it to lie to himself not occasionally but perpetually, about almost every event of life. At every turn the truth of human connection with nature threatens to pierce through the veil of lies and illusions that "civilization" has woven. "Civilization," indeed, is largely a symbolic system, a carefully erected artificial world for which is claimed all sanity, courtesy, art, and knowledge, while the real is called *animal*, inconsequential, or evil. Civilization is founded on the Word, and the Word is a lie. Patriarchy is based on a distortion of language, so it is no wonder that throughout the ages, thinkers have complained about the degradation of language, albeit always that of their own period.

The primary symbolic act incarnating human dominion over nature is the division of the human race into sex classes that represent the two supposedly opposed entities. Any ideology that begins with a division of the human from nature (and concomitantly a division between the sexes) will inevitably, necessarily, have to continue to draw such distinctions. If an ideology posits a divine, supreme being made in the image of the human, but with more power, it will inevitably create an elite class that is more in contact with that "being" than other men. If it makes a human capacity—reason, the mind, work—the grounds, the symbol of human superiority over nature, it will inevitably create an elite class that is more possessed of that capacity than other men. Because such ideologies simultaneously deny a real relationship and manufacture a human identity that incarnates the grounds of that denial, patriarchy is not just rooted in a lie but is made up entirely of the factitious, so that all of life becomes a game of "let's pretend." And since any elite can be only a small percentage of an entire population, leaving the majority in either the subhuman class or a kind of limbo between human and subhuman, patriarchy can never, whatever its form, improve the human condition for the majority of humankind. And often it makes the elite the sickest and most unhappy class—like the Aztec priests or the faceless suits who rule much of today's world.

Thus when philosophers define "man," they are defining an invented being, a cultural ideal; it is doubly remarkable, then, that the ideal creature should be so destructive, aggressive, inhumane. But because he is denied bodily pleasures and needs, sensory pleasure for its own sake, emotion, and a sense of himself as part of a community, ideal Western man must find other ways to experience his existence and to prove that he exists, and these ways must be forms of control. Obsessed with finding such forms, Western man and the philosophy that formed him disdain those who do not fit this sort of "manliness"—women, minority and lower-class men. Western man plows over ordinary life with tanks, concrete, and space stations; Western philosophy dismisses ordinary people and ordinary life with a sweep of a pen.

Over and over we can see in philosophers the insistence Nietzsche pointed to on creating an image of man that omits most of man's—and woman's—experience. The major characteristic of this invented man is his control over his life; even when a deity is involved, man is assured that through proper behavior and obedience to the religious institution, he may control that deity as well. The strange thing is that as humans have in fact achieved more control over nature, hatred and contempt for nature have increased. Although the body and emotions have been seen as tainted in some past patriarchal cultures, they have never been as submerged and concealed as they are at present. The old need to dominate nature has become a need to eradicate that persistent presence in man as well as outside him. It is not, I think, an overstatement to claim that our period's incredible wave of massacres of different peoples (sometimes by rulers of the same people), of terrorism, torture, and indiscriminate murder are related to this powerful hatred for those elements in humans that are not transcendent, for the human itself. Carl Friedrich writes of Hitler that he was not "an 'incomprehensible accident' but was possessed by something—a hatred for the human in man. His victims died as 'deputies in the most desperate assault ever made upon the human being.' "[69]

Such attitudes toward humankind may be most concisely encapsulated by philosophers, but obviously are not limited to them. Although there are writers who will not allow us to forget the importance of the human dimension—and who thereby, like Joyce and Woolf, earn our enduring love—writers and artists too share patriarchal values. So do critics and readers. Two relatively recent articles demonstrate such values in more-or-less popular culture.

Sidney Bremer contrasts a group of novels about Chicago written between 1890 and 1915 by men and women.[70] Bremer asserts that overall these novels are equally good. Yet the names of the male novelists are almost all remembered—Theodore Dreiser, Frank Norris, Upton Sinclair, Hamlin Garland, and, less known, Robert Herrick and Henry Blake Fuller. The names of most of the females are forgotten: Ella Peattie, Clara Burnham, Edith Wyatt, Susan Glaspell, Clara Laughlin, Alice Gerstenberg. Only Willa Cather is known, and she is clearly the greatest of all these writers. Bremer believes Edith Wyatt's *True Love* to be a neglected masterpiece, and Clara Laughlin's *Just Folks* to be excellent.

In discussing differences in the reception of works written by women and by men, we must look at several interwoven factors. First, people in general approach men's work with greater respect than women's, and often the work of the two sexes is judged in separate categories. Lists of the best writers of a period are likely to include only men's names, whereas women writers of excellence are referred to as the best *women* writers. (Only with the latest rise of feminism in the United States have compilers of bests-lists begun to tack on one or two women's names, and those names may not refer to the most accomplished writers but to those most acceptable to the male literary establishment.) Critics show the same proclivities as people in general, and treat men's work with greater seriousness than women's. Second, what is acceptable in a male writer may not be acceptable in a female. Emily Brontë's *Wuthering Heights* was applauded when it was thought to be written by a man, and condemned when the author's identity was discovered. But beyond prejudice against persons of a sex, there is a subtler sort. Male critics (and female critics educated in male values) prefer work that contributes to the dominant definition of *man* and frequently find incomprehensible work that emerges from a different sensibility. Without going so far as to posit such a thing as a female sentence, one can see general differences between male and female visions of life.

Bremer postulates precisely this. The men's Chicago novels, she believes, gave utterance to the dominant vision of America, and so found acceptance and remembrance. In this vision the male hero is a lone newcomer who must pit himself against a huge and terrifying city that is socially fragmented, a profiteering machine and an economic battleground. The city "embodies a perverse substitute for nature"; it dwarfs human beings; it is a burned-out wasteland "without a sign of life." Its tentacles invade the surrounding countryside, threatening all organic life. The country is idyllic, an idealized paradise. The city is a form of hell. The society that exists within the city is alienated, divided rich versus poor, class versus class. The hero struggles with this "colossus that resists all efforts at control," and may succeed or fail; but the author succeeds in controlling the city through language, by depicting and symbolizing it.[71]

The vision of the women is totally different. Their heroines are women who grew up within the city; they are journalists, workers at Hull-House, participants in city life who also go to the country on occasion. In both the urban and the rural worlds they find or possess a network of family and friends, people loved and trusted. The city and nature "interpenetrate"; the female writers do not demonize the city or idealize the countryside. For them, society is organic and continuous, interconnected at every level. The women's is "a modest vision, not one that promotes control . . . In place of masculine individualism, women's novels present urban interdependence."[72]

Bremer concludes, "The differences between the known and unknown novels simply do not amount to difference between better and worse novels." To readers guided by a largely male literary establishment, the male novels seemed to depict "the real thing," whereas the women's novels seemed to sweeten existence.[73] But for many people, men as well as women, life *is* lived in interconnection, in a largely harmonious network of friends and loved people, and contains considerable felicity as well as sorrow and struggle. It is not that the male vision is truer to *reality* than the female vision; both individual struggle and harmonious interconnection exist in life. But we emphasize the patriarchal image of reality: life is struggle, life is hell. Such a vision fosters the image of man in control, or, supremely heroic, failing or dying in the effort to control.

Ann-Janine Morey-Gaines writes about the American frontier as metaphor.[74] In her description the West has two zones, one wild and one agrarian, and two heroes, the gunfighter and the farmer. But the agrarian realm is associated with women—it is home, the settlement, the realm of felicity. Its men, tainted by their association with these despised elements, are dwarfed in comparison with the huge image of the gunfighter, who is shown by the camera in profile against endless barren hills. (Morey-Gaines writes about novels, but her analysis can be applied to Western films just as well.) Nature is presented as an impersonal force both beautiful and terrible, but above all powerful. Women are idealized, suppressed, "and finally vilified": the gunfighter may battle ostensibly to defend a woman, but "in actuality every gun battle is as much a defense against her as for her." Sexuality is rare in such works because the "consummated sexual act is performed between men, with guns."[75]

Commenting upon Frank Norris, Hamlin Garland, Max Brand, John Steinbeck, and Jack Schaefer (the author of *Shane*), she explains that every gun battle secures for the hero a physical and moral territory that is the visible symbol of his manhood and his rightness.[76] Woman is a theme in such male literature mainly because the basic problem of men is what distance to maintain between themselves and women, or perhaps—I think of works that feature no women to speak of—themselves and the feminine principle.

The same metaphors appear in works set in different purlieus: Morey-

Gaines mentions Hemingway's "The Short Happy Life of Francis Macomber," in which "the once-adoring, waiting woman has become the biggest enemy the American male faces in the new frontier," and Ken Kesey's *One Flew Over the Cuckoo's Nest*, in which male potency is embodied in freedom of mind, and the mechanical bestiality of the world is embodied in a woman, Nurse Ratched. A symbolic rape humbles the nurse and liberates the man.[77]

Placing on women the responsibility for miseries caused mainly by the "masculinization" of culture by an elite, mainly male group is part of an ancient technique. This is not horizontal hostility, but blaming the victim, for it is women who are most deprived of freedom of mind and body in all cultures. This tendency is found everywhere; when men are mocked in cartoons or on television, it is usually because they are doing "women's work" or are under the control of women.[78] Maintaining enmity in men for women (but definitely not the reverse) is essential to maintaining patriarchal values.

In the past few decades we have been witnessing the bankruptcy of old images of man, and attempts to stretch these images to include more "feminine" qualities. But some men strongly resist such stretching; and the stretching can go only so far with any man who finds his identity synonymous with control over others. The greatest temptations are to love (really love, not desire; love annuls power differences and is destroyed by power struggle), and to participate democratically in a community. But the felicities offered in such situations are believed to cause men to lose their manhood—as if it were something that could be lost. On the one hand, there is felicity to be found in participation, in communal pleasures of the parlor, kitchen, and nursery; on the other hand, to create with a stroke the image of a diminished man, one need only draw him with a dish towel tucked into his pants as an apron. It is not accidental that nuns live in *convents*, from the Latin *conventus*, living together; while monks live in *monasteries*, from the Greek *monos*, alone, solitary. Saint Theresa, founder of a Carmelite order, often said, "Our Lord is also to be found among the pots and pans."[79] But not for men, who do not seem to recognize that the image of themselves they have been taught dooms them to a life of dissatisfaction.

If the traditional patriarchal image of women has constricted them greatly, depriving them of most of life's activities and pleasures, the traditional patriarchal image of men has deprived them greatly, of the core of life, its central "purposes" and values: pleasure, love, intimacy, sharing, and community. Women have been imprisoned in the core, and men on the fringe; and the two areas have been renamed. People can see through the veils of deceitful language, however; women know that their "fringe" area is actually central, and men sense that they have been exiled from real satisfaction. Efforts to stretch either realm can be successful only minimally as long as we continue to define Man, men, in opposition to an Other (nature, femaleness, blackness), rather than as an embracing of every quality in the universe. Lévi-Strauss has suggested that the contrast between nature and culture is an artificial creation of culture, or even merely a methodological device.[80] But for many structuralists after Lévi-Strauss, the eighteenth-century discovery of the opposition of nature and culture is a "fundamental matrix of human thought."[81] It is, of course, fundamental not to human, but to patriarchal thought.

## 2. MALE STRUCTURES

That men are distinct from nature is a mental concept only, an idea. But mental concepts that are treated as basic truths need some concretization, some physical demonstration. The *idea* that men are different from and superior to nature is always accompanied by the division of a culture into sex classes: the division demonstrates the idea. And, in turn, such a division encourages the establishment of two separate cultures, sometimes in the area of work alone. Segregated labor occurs frequently in both simple and peasant cultures: men and women work the same territory but perform different tasks within it: the men hunt, the women fish; or the men fish and the women grow crops. In peasant cultures the men plow by machine, the women do most manual tasks. In such cultures, however, despite this segregation, almost every concern is shared; the well-being of the group, the food supply, the weather matter to all members equally. Although there may also be some segregation in other areas—religious rituals, play, bodily adornment—much is shared in these areas too.

In cultures in which women and men do very different work in different places, and in which the work of each is also sex-specific (done only by one sex), they share little. When women are consigned to the home and men to work away from home, when land, weather, and crops are irrelevant, the only common areas are sex, money, and children. Play may be shared, but often play is sexually segregated as well; the women go to teas or bridge games, the men to golf or squash. Or the women have coffee with each other and visit their mothers; the men hang out in bars and pubs. Because little is shared there is only a small common ground of concern: often the few shared areas become a battleground for two different perspectives. In the United States, where this split in culture appeared early, it was frequently remarked upon. Even before Henry James and Edith Wharton made their telling comments, the British novelist Mrs. Trollope, visiting in the 1820s, wrote, "In America, with the exception of dancing, which is almost wholly confined to the unmarried of both sexes, all the enjoyments of the men are found in the absence of women. They dine, they play cards, they have musical meetings, they have suppers, all in large parties, but all without women."[82] Ann Douglas, writing about Margaret Fuller and Herman Melville, makes the real point: "Fuller was a feminist, Melville was not; yet both saw the tragic segregation of the sexes in America as evidence of a deeper and even more troubling bifurcation in their culture: that between . . . 'the intellect' and 'the feeling.' "[83]

Segregation of the sexes has been practiced to some degree in every patriarchal culture. It permeates least those members of the culture who live on small farms or run small shops; it is most in evidence among the elite of any culture. It is often accomplished by simply excluding women from certain purlieus, as it was in Athens and Rome, as it is in Islam, in the Catholic Church, and in most governmental and military bureaus. Sometimes women are granted the right to set up "auxiliary" organizations that imitate and support the male organizations but lack any power. Sometimes these arrangements are seemingly accidental and informal: in modern suburbs the letter carrier may be the only man seen all day; at American parties the sexes may segregate themselves in different rooms or even the same room, and speak different languages—the men talk instrumentally about objects, or competitively about competition; while the women talk affectively about people and feelings.

Such segregation creates a deep sense of kinship among women, who often, although strangers, smile at each other in city streets, on buses, in supermarkets. They fall into conversation with each other easily and sometimes make instantaneous friendships. Their kinship is based on only two things: that they have generally similar reproductive systems, and that they share the experience of being women in a male-dominated society.

Segregation creates a sense of kinship among men as well, but it has different bases. Sexual prowess is one area of male competition; another is success in male-dominated society. What men share is distance from women and an intuitive understanding that their identification as males rests on this distance. Men also share the myth of male supremacy, which in "democratic" cultures suggests that all men possess equal access to power structures: all men were boys who could have grown up to be president.

But in fact men possess highly differential access to power structures, which are closely tied to economic, social, and educational class. Men are enormously different from each other. Nevertheless all male structures are similar. Whatever function they fill, and in whatever kind of society, they have similar forms and purposes. Whether they are governmental or industrial, whether they call themselves the military, the church, labor, crime, or punishment, they have almost identical forms. They are alike in capitalist, socialist, and mixed economies; in theocracies and oligarchies and monarchies.

## Form

First of all, male structures are hierarchical. A hierarchy is a series of ascending steps, a ladder or pyramid maintained by coercion and incarnating power and authority. On the whole, the larger the institution, the less connection it fosters among its members; even in small institutions, however, there is little dialogue across status barriers within or outside of work. The main exception to this is the spousal relationship—often the wife of an executive or professor or administrator works as a secretary or in another nonmanagement job, in the same institution as her husband, but is permitted to socialize with him and his colleagues nevertheless.

There are organizations that are not hierarchical. They are always small, and usually include mainly young people. A doctor's office, a small shop, or a small service may be centered on one man—the doctor, the owner, the servicer—who is assisted by others. In these organizations there is sometimes a kind of democracy in which each member feels free to offer opinions, suggestions, and perhaps even mild criticism of procedures, environment, personal treatment, or the substance of the work. The unit may manifest strong cross-lines of power: the grocer's stock boy may be more intelligent than he, the nurse may be more intelligent than the doctor, the secretary may be married to a man who has more money than her boss, the boy assistant's father may be rich. It is more difficult to ignore such cross-lines in a small organization than in a large one.

Democratic procedures are not permitted in large organizations, even within their small internal units. Hierarchy incarnates superiority, and the superiority of any superior is absolute. An inferior may not question it. Dialogue cannot exist in a hierarchy; there is only monologue with a supporting echo. Speech that comes from below is not part of a conversation but a report to a superior.

Most large hierarchies are pyramidal in arrangement, with the majority of people clustered at the bottom. This order is justified as encouraging mobility, efficiency, and the rise of excellence: it is supposed to be *just*. Newcomers are slotted in at the bottom of whatever rank their education and experience entitles them to, and may slowly move upward. In fact, most pyramids are made up of a series of rectangles, self-contained and containing units. Once inside such a unit, a worker is likely never to leave it. Unskilled workers are likely to remain unskilled workers; at most they may rise to supervisory status. Skilled workers may move into supervisory status and lower management but, usually, not further. Within some of these rectangles there is an invisible dotted line (it is in the mind of those who are part of the organization and does not require being made visible). Beneath it are women. In whatever capacity they are hired, they remain, and remain the lowest paid in that category. Salesmen may become managers, but secretaries do not. Some rectangles are for women only. Some structures do not now or have not up to the very recent past permitted women at all, but relegate them to auxiliary organizations: the military, the Church, and the penal system, for instance.

There are higher rectangles for those whose entering status does admit of rise, and a small top triangle for those who are in charge of the organization. In these small triangles it is highly unusual to find a woman or (except in black nations) a black. The small governing body usually consists entirely of white (or black) males, and these are all a certain kind of white (or black) male—Protestants, Catholics, Jews, Moslems, or members of a political party. Although in recent decades, these governing bodies have begun to allow entrance to a somewhat wider diversity of men, they remain quite narrow.

The interior of the pyramid can be designed in different ways, which generate different procedural methods. Structures may be designed for surveillance at every level. In such cases every department or larger subunit contains one person who has access to a secret avenue to the top. In such organizations, there is a line of espionage on the workers at every level. In structures designed at least partly to guard the personification of ultimate power—the American presidency or the papacy—all lines end at a set of Palace Guards who alone can open the door to supreme authority. In some institutions, certain levels of command are permitted a degree of autonomy—the military in the field, for instance, or teachers in the classroom, or priests and ministers at the parish level. Such institutions tolerate a police or army sergeant, a parish priest or professor who is incompetent, ignorant, or cruel. What it will not tolerate, at any level, is less than complete loyalty to the organization.

Institutions themselves are ranked in a huge embracing national or international hierarchy whose leaders are sometimes hard to identify. The military, industry, and government dominate institutions of labor, crime, and the technocracy, which in turn are more important than academia, the Church, the medical establishment, which dominate educational, penal, and social welfare institutions. The lower the rank of an institution, the more middle-level women and minority members it will contain.

Hierarchical channels provide for the transmission of power in two ways. Lower-level workers generate power; that is, their work contributes to making a product, teaching children, overseeing prisoners, keeping records, "manning" weapons or other systems. The people involved in such things have low or middling status, low or middling wages, and little or no autonomy; they are, in another form, the matter upon which the mind of management works. Higher-level workers apply the power provided from below; they make policy, determine procedures from the most minute to the grandest, and oversee all lesser ranks of overseers. They have comparatively high status, comparatively high wages, but even they frequently have little autonomy. They are, however, *perceived* as possessing this highly valued quality and are envied for it.

Hierarchies are permanent. They allow for no shifting or alternating of command, no "taking turns." Command lies in a set of chairs; men come and go but the chairs remain. This is true even in cases of complete overhaul in a company, or revolutionary overthrow of governments. One or two chairs may be removed; but one or two others will be substituted. Often what occurs is simply a renaming of the old chair. Despite its different philosophy, the new management or government will establish structures identical in principle and often even in details to those that existed before. So the labor movement, for instance, was created by people at the bottom, by the courage and idealism of working men and women; once established, it made itself an elite governed by an elite. If the governors of the labor movement are not as oppressive and greedy as management was (and this is questionable), they are not free from such traits. They transformed the labor movement from a movement of working people into a contained unit of well-paid workers, contributing to the creation of a new class of poor, those not welcome in the unions. Revolutions that are caused at least partly by the excesses of a corps of secret police immediately set up a new corps of secret police. Organized crime, set up as an alternate structure to provide access for the illegitimate to avenues to power used secretly by the legitimate, at some level cooperates with the legitimate and oppresses those in its lower levels.

Institutional process is known as "the system," and the system is always *right*. Designated procedures remove responsibility from the people required to follow them, and create a feeling of utterly secure boredom. Even when a system is patently unworkable, when it creates gross injustices, information clogs, and inefficiency, suggestions of change meet with great resistance. For the system becomes a primary truth, a fact of life, a "purpose" larger than the individual. Even when human lives are ground up by the machine, people defend it. It becomes, like patriarchy itself, a substitute world: and, like nature itself, an absolute that must be adjusted to. (For although men pretend to be superior to nature, they in actuality must adjust to their bodies, emotions, and the external world.) The system creates finity. It is considered beyond justification, like the seasons' difference, like snow or fever heat. People sometimes break down in response to real changes in a system: they retire or quit because they cannot adapt.

The hierarchical chain of command is a visible representation of power of the sort we call authority. Some people who function within hierarchies also possess personal power, a talent, a special sensitivity, a skill at organizing, administering, or inspiring others, or for dealing with the materials which are the institution's domain. Personal power is extremely valuable in such a system, because people feel less resentment about deferring to authority when it is reinforced with real skill or knowledge. Just as in private life we attend to those who have knowledge in an area in which we are troubled, even though they have no authority over us—our physicians, psychologists, teachers, automobile mechanics, repairmen, and so forth—people in hierarchies are more likely to attend to those whose ability as well as position they can respect. If, however, the person in authority seems lacking in the particular skill necessary for that position, he must nevertheless be obeyed and attended to, for his authority resides in his position and not in himself.

A position or office confers upon its holder certain rights, prerogatives, and responsibilities; but more important than these, the office symbolizes superiority. In principle, that superiority rests on the greater responsibility and greater skill demanded of the officeholder; in actuality it is an instrument of coercion.

All personal power and all authority are limited. The physicist must be led like a child around a foreign city with an unrecognizable language; the surgeon does not know how to care for his or her automobile; the college president has no understanding of the humanities; the person who understands relationships among people does not understand chemistry. Even within their own fields, people are bewildered and incompetent when faced with the unfamiliar. When we speak of superiority, then, we speak of a particular kind of excellence, and it is often a narrow one.

When we say people are created equal, we are referring to a particular kind of equality—*human* equality. What this term means and implies is that all humans are equally bound to the human condition, regardless of attempts to pretend otherwise, and equally bound to uphold a universal moral standard; that all humans are equally deserving of sharing in nature's resources, of respectful treatment, and of equal treatment in law. Human equality remains an unfulfilled ideal in each of these areas. In principle, superiority is a category subordinate to human equality; one *can* be superior to others, but only in certain ways. In male structures, however, authority is an enshrinement of *human* superiority.

Now, there is no such thing. It is not possible. Even if we say of someone that she is a better human being than others, we cannot claim human superiority for her. Possession of wealth or status, talent or knowledge, beauty or strength certainly makes people superior to others in those areas, but it also makes them inferior to others in other areas. The wealthy man does not know as much about how to survive in poverty as the welfare mother; nor can we determine which quality—wealth or knowledge, strength or beauty, for instance—is fundamentally more essential or important.

In hierarchies, however, one's superior *is* superior in every way. The "boss" not only understands your job better than you do and the workings of your department better than anyone else in it, but is also its resident expert on the best restaurants, the proper way to dress one's body and hair, manners and morals; he may even be its cultural guru. The opinions of the boss are deferred to, and so is the boss's person. His utterances are law, his caprices rules of nature. Nor does his superiority terminate at five o'clock: it extends to the departmental cocktail party, the personal as well as the business dinner. Not just you but your spouse must defer to this god on earth. The cardinal rule is not to offend him.

This enshrinement of authority and the system it is designed to uphold lead to gross violations of common sense and efficiency as well as of humane interaction. The boss may be severely neurotic or severely stupid; he may be morally defective; he may have defective knowledge about the area he is supposed to oversee. Yet you must obey him and fear him; you must defer to him if you do not wish to ruin your own possibilities. Because of this contradiction—and examples of it are rife in any structure of any size—all hierarchies operate by coercion. They must coerce a complaisance they cannot earn.

Coercion varies in kind and degree. In some structures the threat may be a bad report, no raise this year, dismissal; it may also mean the guillotine, a note from the emperor commanding you to commit suicide, shooting by the imam's executioners, incarceration in a gulag, exile, dishonor, a court-martial. In its subtler forms it may be a weak smile informing you of the displeasure of someone whose respect you value, or sighs, or raised eyebrows, all of which are really warnings; or it may be emotional exile, terrible to undergo but innocuous on the surface. Whatever its forms, techniques of coercion essentially threaten expulsion from the institution (and sometimes from life). Even in positions with tenure, like those of some academies, coercive techniques can be applied that isolate an individual from the academic community and from a voice in the structure, so that although the body is present in the structure, the person is effectively removed. *Every hierarchy maintains itself by the inculcation of fear.*

The most subversive acts in any institution are to deny or ignore this fear, to refuse to defer, to reject the idea of human superiority. Those who break rules of an institution are more readily forgiven than those who maintain an attitude of independent judgment, even if this attitude issues in no definable disobedience. To "go over the head" of your boss, even to a superior who is aware of the boss's inadequacies, is unforgivable because it implies a lack of proper subordination. To assume an attitude of human equality with one's superiors is to subvert the organization more profoundly than to betray it by espionage or to attempt to leapfrog to success by jumping from one company to another to another. For such acts, dismaying as they may be, demonstrate that the actor entertains the same basic values as others in the institution.

Lack of deference is subversive in a way that manipulation and even betrayal are not because the primary purpose of any institution is to control men and to confer upon some men the illusion of having control. In furthering this end, institutions have foundered, since their governors put the maintaining of control before the maintaining of the specific institutional purpose. Whatever area the institution is designed to function within, whatever function of a society it is intended to fill, *the true end of male institutions is to maintain at any cost the appearance of male control.* Thus even subordinate managers who know they possess in fact very little autonomy will not admit this or complain of it publicly. Some of the conflict that occurs in institutions arises over the trappings of power (office size, windows, carpets, secretaries, use of locked toilets, company planes, and apartments), emblems and symbols of a power that in fact may be slight.

The difference between actual and illusory control is less important to many men than the appearance of control—status. Men are not so blind as not to know they are being manipulated by "status symbols." But they are trapped in this system, held there by ties as essential to them as the lines to life-support equipment for victims of serious disease. Indeed, that metaphor is fully appropriate.

We remember the first theorem of patriarchal ideology: that man (the human male) is distinct from nature—not a unique species within it, but a species separate from it. The second theorem is: what makes man separate is his kinship with a higher power (God, rationality, systems of control) that grants him control over the rest of creation. And the third is that if man ceases to control the rest of nature, he loses his transcendent position and slides back to the status of intermediate beings like women, workers, blacks, and other despised kinds, or even below them, under *their* control.

We have seen that the first theorem is false: men are bound to nature as other humans are; separation between men and nature is impossible to achieve. Therefore it has been realized *symbolically*, through the creation of a self-image supported by law, theology, and philosophy, and through the creation of lower classes: women, workers, and scorned races or ethnic populations, who mediate between chosen men (the fully human) and the beast. The symbolic nature of this distinction is equivalent to an *appearance*, a public persona. Law, custom, and manners were devised that allowed the chosen few to appear to be in control not only of other humans but of natural functions and phenomena. This control is a mark of divinity which, like the mark of Cain, decrees that men may murder or perform other normally antisocial acts but remain beyond human punishment, for they are God's surrogates on earth.

As men's actual control over nature increased (partly because of this mode of thinking), the potential power of individual men also increased. To keep this from erupting into full democracy (or anarchy, as some would see it), small cliques of men devised systems to keep the masses of men in continued control.

Control over nature became control over *human* nature. This control has several foci: systems of all kinds to control groups of humans; control over emotion; and control over the body. But all forms of control are delusory; that is, we do not really control, we simply lay concrete over grass. We create an appearance. So control over nature has harnessed nature's powers in many ways—through the mining of metals, the creation of electricity, the use of natural sources to provide energy. But nature does not meekly submit: it dies, it becomes diseased, or (as with insects, for instance) it adapts to controls and confounds them.

Human nature, found in smaller units of being, shows its disruption more quickly. Emotion may be controlled on the surface—suppressed or repressed—but it erupts in hives, heart attacks, nervous breakdowns; bodies may be trained or ignored, but they go on functioning as bodies, and we can create an appearance of control only by molding form—by using brassieres, corsets, or surgery; cosmetics; and deodorants for all parts of the body, and even for the toilets, sinks, and rooms in which bodies are most bestially themselves.

In all its manifestations, control is more appearance than reality. But the appearance is all we have, it is our single claim to power. Loss of the appearance is loss of the power, because it is the appearance that makes others defer or bow to us, appearance that makes them fear to rebel. So a terrified dictator regularly mounts displays of weaponry in public parades, a frightened director regularly enforces his will on humiliated underlings, and a frightened manager fights tooth and nail for the carpet, the window, the personal secretary which function for him like a dictator's tanks: symbols of the power you are up against when you confront him.

It may be argued that the symbols are nevertheless real enough, and so they are. But they can disappear as swiftly as a cobweb, given the right broom: witness the evanescence of the power of President Nixon once he had lost "credibility," although he still sat in the symbolic Oval Office; or of the Shah of Iran, who "controlled" the most powerful military establishment in the Middle East; or of any executive just fired.

Men are aware, although they may not think about this consciously, that everything lies in the appearance, and so will fight for appearances and forget or ignore realities. Obviously this can lead to severe problems. Consider the present situation in El Salvador, about which a recent reporter, Joan Didion, wrote: "It was not until late in the lunch [with Deane Hinton, United States ambassador to El Salvador] . . . that it occurred to me that we were talking exclusively about the appearance of things, about how the situation might be made to look better, about trying to get the Salvadoran Government to 'appear' to do what the American Government needed done in order to make it 'appear' that the American aid was justified."[84]

It is not just the disparity between realities and appearances that disheartens moralists of whatever persuasion, but men's willingness to spend all their energies in maintaining the latter while ignoring the former. This situation is endemic in all patriarchal institutions. Of course it always was, and the world has not always been in such an ominous condition as it is now. The symbols of human power are real, if not quite as clearly in human control as is claimed, and they are greater now than at any past time. The search for power has led to power; but the search for control has not led to control.

## Purposes, Rewards, and Requirements

Because they have defined themselves in opposition to women, men do not have the option of regarding themselves simply as *beings: women* are beings. Having eliminated from the qualifications for male identity those elements that are associated with the feminine, men cannot define themselves by bodily fruitfulness or beauty, sexuality, emotionality, or bonds to parents, children, and friends. They have defined themselves as possessing the main quality forbidden to women—strength, whether of body, mind, spirit, or will. Renouncing the realm of being, they are restricted to the realm of doing, whether intellectually or physically. If a woman is what she looks like, a man is what he does. And most of what men do (indeed, most of what most people do) is work.

A woman is simple being; a man is something more. But what more is there beyond being? In the human imagination, there is control. To keep women in the class of beings, women's work must be seen as nonvolitional—not in their own control; a man's work *is* a form of control. A man is identified with control, and with his work. Work is essential to most men, and they often break down if deprived of it. But it is necessary that this work at least appear to be volitional. Men assigned tasks as members of chain gangs, military units, or prison rosters do not identify themselves with their daily work but as soldiers or prisoners, even though men in the outside world who may not be much freer from coercion (economic rather than of force) and who do the same daily work as prisoners or soldiers do identify themselves with their work.

Just as man is identified with control, male structures exist to embody control and the appearance of control. As a mother transmits to her daughter the power to conceive and procreate in a natural "tradition," men transmit to younger men the power to conceive and generate elements in an intellectual tradition. The exclusion of women from the earliest institutions was therefore essential; institutions were to be the male answer to female power. And the need to exclude women from institutions remains despite recent attempts to coerce institutions to accept them. Even men who easily recognize the "brightness" (never brilliance) and competence of particular women are deeply uncomfortable at their presence within "male" institutions. Men who like women and who consider both women and themselves rational creatures feel uneasy about their own uneasiness. But all the fundamental qualities of institutions point to their origin, which lies precisely in their ability to exclude women, because all the reproduction that occurs within institutions is symbolic: women and their bodies are utterly unnecessary.

What is transmitted by the institutional structure is basically power, regardless of the function of the particular institution: the institution therefore exists primarily as an embodiment of power, to foster the reality or illusion of male control. Consider: a town could do very well without institutions, and many did and still do. If the residents wanted their children to read and write, they could appoint as teacher the most literate resident. The same is true of healing, ministering to the spirit or psyche, and other functions. If such a mode of functioning sometimes means less than excellent performance, the professionalization of skills, the imposition of uniform standards, and the requirement for licenses have not at all guaranteed excellence. Licensing could exist without institutions—it does in the important area of driving a car. Lack of general institutionalization would give both localities and individuals a greater sense of autonomy. But the control inherent in autonomy (of whatever degree) is antipathetic to control as a principle.

Institutions are created to centralize, harness, and manifest power over others, whereas general autonomy requires tolerance of the powers of all. Institutions try to appeal to people's desire for autonomy by suggesting that one's personal power will increase by association with the institution. But while it is true that institutionalization can sometimes help individuals get some of what they want—more money, status, and legitimacy—it never increases a person's sense of or real autonomy.

If the structure of the institution is designed to overweigh the female transmission of power, the purpose of the institution is to overweigh the female realm, nature. The ostensible purpose—to provide spiritual guidance, to teach, to heal, to govern, to counsel on law, to represent workers in the face of management, to punish, to reform—is subsidiary to the need to stoke the manufactured, abstract body itself, to keep the institution powerful and to confer upon those within it the appearance of wielding power. But at the same time that institutions create an appearance of power, they deprive individuals of power. They transform separate people into ranked members of an association dedicated to controlling them. So a student of industrial organization states that hierarchy in a factory system exists not for the sake of efficiency but for more effective control of the labor force by employers.[85] Another student of corporations claims that controls on management are even more constricting than those on lower-level workers, because managers are not permitted to adopt an adversary relation with the institution and have no union to represent them.[86] Yet workers often bear justified resentment toward their unions as well; the real difference between the two may be expressed in the joke popular in eastern Europe a few years back: Which is better off, an East German or a Polish dog? Answer: Well, one dog is well fed, but the other is able to bark.

If the purpose of institutions is control—power—the purpose of those who join them emerges from the same values. People throng to work for institutions for two reasons: one is economic power—better wages and more job security than they might obtain outside an institution; the other is legitimacy. The halo of power that surrounds the institutional name reflects upon the individuals it employs, and the more prestigious that institutional name, the more glory it reflects on its members. The system works: as long as one's goals are its goals. The exclusivity of institutions creates in another form the old discriminations. If (now) blacks are able to get education, institutional policies still promote superiority of an elite. For example, in 1979, when the poverty line in the United States was $8,414 for a family of four, the median income for men (black and white) was $12,530; the median income for women (black and white) was $10,168; and the median income for white men alone was $17,427.[87]

But legitimacy is not, even in a highly money-oriented culture, purely a matter of money. Legitimacy has aspects of authority, knowledgeable power, and acceptance within the dominant structure of a culture. Institutionalization is able to confer legitimacy on millions of men who without institutions would be merely men; it confers legitimacy even on its lower-level members—down to a point.

It is essential to realize that legitimacy is a totally artificial quality. Like manhood, which at present is defined in opposition to and postulated upon womanhood, legitimacy is stipulated upon illegitimacy, and could not exist without it. Legitimacy is an invisible but palpable if sometimes unclear line between those who are considered part of the elite or potential elite, and those who are not and seemingly never can be. As "democracy" has broadened, legitimacy has been extended in descending degrees to men below the monied, educated class. A truck driver who works for a large company has legitimacy in comparison to a waitress in the diner he frequents, to the stock clerk with whom he drinks, and to his wife. But he does not have legitimacy in a room full of his superiors unless he becomes a high official in a labor union.

Exclusivity confers legitimacy on those hired. Not everyone can join the club, whatever club it may be. Until recently most institutions in the United States had fairly restricted membership: Jews, Catholics, Italians, Irish, and other groups have all faced such policies. Blacks still do. Women of all groups can often find employment in institutions, however, because they constitute a subclass—the clerks, secretaries, and more menial workers who have no access to promotion; thus they do not become part of the "legitimate" class. The movement of women into jobs with access to promotional tracks has been slow and is still stubbornly resisted.

Above all, the embracing institutional structure provides men with a purpose, an end in life. (Many women find their purpose and their central concern to be their children; often they are neither as ambitious nor as devoted to institutions as most men. Some women are ambitious, of course, but they suffer from the general diminishment of their sex.) To be accepted, to be approved, and to rise in the institution is similar to being welcomed into the company of the blessed, being praised, and coming into the sight of God. Certain promises are implicit in the act of full acceptance into an institution (full acceptance usually occurs after a probationary period, of course). People are told that the major concern of the institution is performance, that those who do good work will be rewarded or preferred, and those who do not will not. This sounds simple, rational, and just. People believe it. They are told that their welfare is important to the institution, and are implicitly promised security in their jobs barring abuse or gross incompetence. They are told that their salaries are determined by a fixed scale, which implies there is justice in this as well. Salaries in different kinds of institutions vary greatly—in the more prestigious institutions, like industry, they are generally high; they are generally lowest in teaching and social welfare organizations. Some institutions pay very poor wages to their lower-level employees—soldiers, church workers—but offer higher-level workers enough perks and money to confer an aura of wealth on them.

In return for the rewards of legitimacy, money, security, and the potential for success, institutions require a variety of forms of obedience which may be called membership dues. (The following argument applies in lesser degree or with variants to those admitted only to the lower, self-contained rectangles of the structure.)

The first and most important has already been discussed: it is that insubstantial but utterly unmistakable quality called *attitude*. The correct attitude is a delicate balance between servility and pride; servility alone may keep a job, but it will not advance a man very far; pride alone leads to expulsion except in extraordinary cases. The attitude required must be concealed under a surface of self-control, yet must, through small gestures, tone of voice, and facial expression, demonstrate that underneath the self-control there is fear of the superior and a willingness to obey him. Before the superior, as before God, man is always wrong. This subtle mix of self-respect, fear and obedience is *deference*, without which few men go far in male structures. Mediocre or even poor work is far more tolerable in institutions than insubordination or lack of deference.

The second form of obedience is loyalty to the institution: this may be a party, a company, an incorporated entity, or a leader. Hitler considered personal loyalty to him sufficient ground for membership in the early Nazi Party, and Luther considered faith in (his interpretation of) God sufficient ground for membership in his sect. Political parties demand that a man identify himself with them and abide by their rules. But we must ask what loyalty really means in such cases.

Personal loyalty means fixed affection and respect for a friend or loved one. It claims to be permanent, although it is not always. Above all, it means that you try in all circumstances to see the point of view of your friends, to find the rightness in whatever position they find themselves, and to go on loving and supporting them no matter their conditions. It is, I think, uncommon but not unheard-of in the male world: it is very common in the female world.

But loyalty to an institution or the leader of an institution has a different character. It means placing that entity above yourself, adopting a position of subordination to it. The institution is larger, greater, more important than the self. On these grounds it is also always *right*, and men are expected to accept its rightness even when they themselves are being punished by it, diminished or expelled from it. Thus in some socialist countries people about to be punished or expelled from a job or party are required to "confess," to admit their own wrongness before the rightness of the institution, and thus to accept or even welcome their punishment. Lack of sufficient loyalty to an institution is grounds for expulsion from it in all capitalist enterprises as well. Institutional rightness is exemplified in a movie cliché: an older military man, hard, cruel, inhumane, castigates for disobedience a younger one who is a trifle arrogant, or who has a soft side, or who dislikes disciplining his subordinates. An old hand, inferior in rank to both, an NCO who is not in competition with either, watches wisely. Afterward, he approaches the younger man kindly and says, "Yeah, the old man's tough but he's *good*." And indeed, the lesson the movie will teach is that the old man *is* good, that he is above all *right* (like the army or navy itself); his harsh ways are right and necessary in a violent world. So men are taught to love their oppressors. Moreover, only the special man, the chosen man, is permitted to question at all. The one who questions and is answered is the one who is slotted to rise to the top. The rest are expected to offer blind obedience and loyalty.[88]

The third requirement is conformity, a tired word and perhaps a tired concept, but extremely important and budding with ramifications. It is not called conformity by those who demand or offer it; it is called "fitting in." A person who doesn't "fit in" requires no other fault to be expelled. The qualities that make one fit in are rarely itemized and probably almost never explicitly stipulated. One must simply apprehend them tacitly—indeed, asking about them openly is tantamount to defying them. No one wants to admit that such requirements exist.

First, one must be male. (The inclusion of women in administrative and managerial levels is too recent for us to be able to perceive its effects. So far it seems the old dictum is in force: she who makes herself male will be permitted to enter the Life.) Many institutions also have further restrictions as to skin color, religion, or ethnic background; there are all-black, all-Native American, all-Chinese, all-Moslem (or all-Sunni, or all-Shi'ite), all-Catholic, all-Protestant, all-Jewish organizations. But in American institutions not defined by kind, the most important ground of exclusion after sex is skin color, and the presence of a black male is likely to make the "boys" almost as uncomfortable as the presence of a woman.

The chief complaint against those who do not "fit in" is merely this kind of discomfort. Men say they would have to be careful of what they said, for instance. But they would not have to be careful of what they said if what they said was not opprobrious to women or nonwhites—if their self-definition was not premised upon superiority to these groups. The presence of a woman or a black suggests that in fact the white men are not superior to other groups, and are not different from them. It is the intolerability of this idea that creates the hostility and resentment toward them.

Although intelligence is valued in male structures, it is also suspect. It is most easily tolerated in fringe personnel who work mainly in isolation: the resident engineering genius, the professor who sits in silence at departmental meetings and does not attend faculty meetings, the lawyer who starts his own firm. Men who work in groups distrust brilliance, especially if it comes (as in men it often does) with sharp edges. A recent article on one of New York's major law firms cites one of its founding partners as saying, "Brilliant intellectual powers are not essential." Imagination, wit, and cleverness tend to intimidate "the best clients."[89] (Arrogance to one's inferiors or acquaintances or family is not relevant; moreover, it occurs in people with less than brilliant minds.) But brilliance itself makes others uncomfortable: again, it suggests that they are not the elite they need to believe they are. Solid, hard-working mediocrity is far more valued in most institutions; it is easier to live with and far easier to intimidate. This is not to say that brilliant and arrogant young men do not sometimes succeed in institutions. But they are generally subjected to some humbling along the way: fathers do not like to gaze at sons who believe themselves their equals.

The insistence on conformity extends beyond such qualities, however, to far more personal elements such as dress, hair style, and personal life. Most institutions insist that their members wear a uniform. Some, like the military, the clergy, and repair servicemen, have actual uniforms; others quietly expect their members to show up in three- or two-piece suit and tie; or slacks and shirts; or blue jeans and work shirts. Showing up in the wrong clothes can be quite literally a sin, and punishable accordingly.[90]

Uniformity of dress has a number of origins. Most immediate is the trend toward democratization that began with the English Civil War and the French Revolution. Clothes, used as signs of class and as competitive manifestations of wealth or power, were declared sinful and vain, and plain dress was decreed. Gone were the silks and satins, lace and ruffs, brocades and velvet, ermine and mink, gold chains and rings, flowing capes, high-heeled shoes and boots worn by the aristocracy of Europe. (Elaborate and expensive clothing is still permitted to lords of the Church and to academics in procession, as well as to some military classes.) In its place, sober garments concealed power or wealth, made all men appear the same, and thus, presumably, equal.

But at the same time this shift to sober dress was occurring, European culture was being masculinized, institutionalized. Because women were subjected to increased limitations, their boundaries were clearer, and the qualities they were assigned were made increasingly off-limits to men. Women were permitted emotionality and self-expression, and thus expressive clothes as well. Some women, of course, also wear uniforms—those in the military, nurses, and corporation wives, for example. But women who want to express themselves as individuals rather than as members of institutions may continue to wear extravagant, fanciful clothing. Men's abjuring of such dress is a further sign of their unlikeness to women, their transcendence of body and feeling. Women who want to join institutions are urged to adopt inexpressive dress.

The cultural revolution of the sixties in America created a new uniform—blue jeans. Adopted by both sexes, they announce equality even more strongly than suit-and-tie, which in its more expensive manifestations had come to symbolize exactly what satin, brocade, ermine, and velvet once symbolized, if less expressively. Blue jeans also announce that their wearers labor, use their bodies in work. Since this is not always true, blue jeans are likely to undergo the same process of heightened valuation and subtle discrimination that suit-and-tie underwent—indeed, since this study was begun, they have, as designer jeans. However, blue jeans still announce an attitude toward the world more than one's status within it, and thus remain expressive.

The importance of hair styles might have escaped our notice had we not lived through a period in which the style of hair on head and face became symbolic of political stance. The connotations of hair styles have remained, although they are less clear now. Still, it is impossible to regard a man with a crew cut today without imputing to him a particular set of political and moral attitudes. The more "rebellious" styles, on the other hand, Afros, Isros, long hair, pony tails, and beards, have been adopted by men personally, without regard to institutional affiliation or political stance. They thus represent a trend toward expressiveness. But there also remain, in various institutions, implicit or explicit rules regarding length of hair and the form in which facial hair is (or is not) allowed to grow. Generally, the greater the pressure against personal expressiveness in an institution, the more likely it is to have such regulations. But personal expressiveness is a profound need, and it always finds some way to manifest itself. When all individuality and dissidence is forbidden, some men will still wear their hair an inch longer, adopt sideburns, prefer gaudy ties. In conformist, unisex China, a young woman will daringly don a cheap flowered cotton skirt.

Gestures, manners, and above all language are also subject to scrutiny by institutions. The standard for these things is not gracefulness (beauty) or any Victorian notion of propriety, but rather avoidance of expressiveness and emotion. Indeed, gestures and manners must avoid grace lest they seem "effeminate": they should be forceful but not too forceful. They should not call attention to themselves.

Language must not be expressive of any emotion except perhaps forcefulness (and that only in top officers); affect must be moderated. Not only the delivery but the content of speech and writing must avoid any sign of emotion; thus jargon is really preferred, despite all the complaints about it. Language that is used nowhere else but in a particular discipline or area, words that have no human meaning, are pure, free from any possibility of attribution to emotion. Where jargon is not available, institutions prefer language to be abstract. Abstraction in language emphasizes the transcendent nature of the institution's purpose and its discontinuity from ordinary life and ordinary concerns.

What *is* permitted is a category we might expect to be censored—slurs on "inferior" groups. Depending on the makeup of the immediate group of men, one can asperse Jews or Christians, blacks or whites, and ethnic subgroups. Misogyny is always permitted and is a dependable source of humor and relief: like women themselves, language that debases or diminishes women provides men with an old secure ground for easy superiority. There is little language that diminishes men. Terms of reprobation can be taken as matters for pride—like *stud* or *prick*. The worst terms applicable to men make women of them—if once they were *pansies* or *fairies*, now they are called *cunts*.

The approach to experience that is expressed in language should be instrumental rather than affective. Instrumental language not only has the virtue of removing the discussion from the domain of ordinary human affairs; it also lends itself to heavy use of the passive mode and subjectless sentences, as if tools and weapons were manipulating themselves, as if changes in procedure affected procedures, not people, as if by calling a thing "medical delivery services" rather than "healing and tending," one could eliminate the people involved entirely. (See Chapter Six, pp. 449–451, for further discussion of this sort of language.) Not just institutions but life itself can thereby be transformed into a set of channels of power/powerlessness without regard to any cries or whispers that may hang faintly in the wings of the new human drama. In the military, such language is advanced: one need not quail at the thought that one is about to burn people to death, but can manlike stride into a plane to drop antipersonnel bombs. So too the astronauts who landed on the moon were not mere men in an unfamiliar environment, struggling with shovels and a cart, but exalted creatures wielding strange, complicated-looking tools with new, unfamiliar names.

If in certain institutions room is granted for a degree of personal difference, that is because those institutions—academia, say, or the Church—are among the less important in the culture. In cultures in which teaching is considered important (in the Catholic Church or in socialist cultures, for example), it may not be well paid but it is closely supervised, and uniformity is required in those who indoctrinate the young. In the more important institutions in American culture—industry above all, the government and the military—introspection is discouraged, and personal relationships within the institution are strongly shunted toward a superficial friendliness that provides a thin cushion for the real relationships, which are based entirely on institutional business. Difficult or controversial subjects are avoided; differences and anger are almost impossible to express; the atmosphere is kept determinedly bland and easy-going.[91]

It is extremely difficult to sort out the complexities of institutional intrusion into men's private lives. Governments have often in the past decreed the marriage age for men as well as women; at times they have put pressure on men as well as women to procreate or (as in today's China and India) not to procreate. They have codified male authority within the domestic sphere. This did not seem at the time a tampering with private life, since it granted men power over wives and children; but it does seem one now, to some men at least, as government is denying men those powers.

Religions have also intruded themselves into the private realm, demanding that people receive instruction and ritual purification at important thresholds of their lives. Marriage among many people is still simply a choice to live together, but churches as well as governments demand consecration before they grant such unions legitimacy, and laws over a wide spectrum enforce this demand by making life difficult for those who lack that legitimacy.

Some cultures have suffered extreme intrusion by church or government: Nazi Germany, for instance, attempted to eradicate the private realm entirely by regulating breeding and ordering sterilizations and euthanasia. This eradication of the private was also Plato's suggestion in The Republic, because it remains impossible to rationalize life completely as long as we consider our individual identities, our relations with others, and our particular histories to be essential.[92]

A major force in regulating private life has been public opinion, which may be affected by but is not an institution. European villages in centuries past, and American small towns more recently, have been able to wield considerable control over individual behavior, male and female. This is less possible in large towns and urban areas, even in cultures with heavy surveillance, like the Russian. It remains possible in China, however, despite its huge population and crowded cities, mainly because people continue to live together in small enclaves within large cities.

In general, in America today the intrusive paternalism of companies like IBM or Hershey is disappearing, and changed mores have led to greater acceptance of male adultery (when conducted discreetly or with a group of men who are roughly equal in status or within certain institutions, when men are away from home) and divorce—although it is said that Mayor Daley of Chicago used to dismiss any man suspected of marital infidelity. That seems to have been *the* crime for the machine politician. Other elements in life style are also tolerated by institutions as long as they do not interfere with a man's work—alcoholism or drug addiction, for instance. In fact, almost anything is acceptable as long as it is performed *secretly,* furtively. The secretiveness of behavior is an admission of fear; refusal to be discreet is taken as open defiance of the institution and is punished swiftly. There remain some acts, however, which are unacceptable even if performed "discreetly": homosexuality (especially in government and the military), and marriage to a woman who is openly not in her husband's control, openly not deferential to his superiors.

The "dues" I have listed here are general, and vary from one to another institution. But they all fall into two basic categories: attitude, loyalty, and conformity are forms of obedience; and conformity of all kinds falls also under the heading uniformity. Obedience, as we know, is the cardinal requirement of patriarchy; but uniformity is a relatively new requirement, one that grows more stringent with each passing decade. A demand for uniformity suggests a negative root: that is, it is not uniformity itself that is so greatly valued, but the fact that it demonstrates the absence of other values. Like men's self-definition, institutional self-definition is based on what is absent, missing.

What is absent is personal expressiveness. This characteristic, a quality so valuable that it can be equated with humanness itself, has provided most of the color, humor, and vividness of life and literature throughout history. It is, alas, vanishing in men, especially those higher on the male-superiority ladder, and institutionalization is primarily responsible for its disappearance.

The modern idea of rationality is itself irrational: from Plato's notion of rationality as a power balancing emotion and knowledge, Western minds moved to a Cartesian notion that split reason off from feeling. There are times in life when "reason" and "feeling" seem to be in opposition; when, for instance, the prudent thing to do is not the thing you want to do. But beneath the prudence is feeling (fear, say), and beneath the desire is thought: at no time do thinking and feeling not coexist, even if feeling is rigidly repressed. The false conception of reason, however, led to a belief that processes and life itself could be "rationalized," made reasonable. Based on the idea that passion (emotion generally) was the root of both evil and error, just as nature (the "beast") was the root of ugly human behavior, this belief strove to realize forms that would eradicate passion or minimize its force.

The structure of modern—post-eighteenth-century—institutions was tailored to this end. By constant surveillance, by a series of controls over men at every level, managers imagined they could negate emotion, body, passion, expressiveness itself. These elements were deemed to undermine the efficiency of the whole; "the very design of organizations . . . was oriented toward and assumed to be capable of suppressing irrationality, personality, and emotionality."[93] Naturally enough, however, managers in patriarchal organizations believed the "irrational" elements were to be found only in lower-level workers.

In time, though, similar controls were imposed upon upper-level men. What has happened is that personal expressiveness has been sacrificed by men at all levels. Uniformity is embraced almost gratefully, as if the uniform could protect men from the line of fire. The uniform speaks: it proclaims to the world that its wearer is not a person given to passion, body, or even eccentricity; that when its wearer pushes the button that releases the missiles, he is feeling nothing at all.

Rosabeth Kanter maintains that conformity of kind—keeping the power in the hands of a single group—provides a base of reality for managers' belief that their kind rules because it deserves to rule—"homosocial and homosexual reproduction" makes the factitious appear actual. She also says that men themselves choose uniformity in life style. Because evaluation of work is utterly without real standards, is capricious to an extreme, men feel uncertain, and adopt whatever measures they think may win them a point over their rival: so they imitate, more modestly, the life style of the boss, who has imitated his, and so on.[94]

Such are the purposes, rewards, and dues for membership in male structures. We must next address ourselves to the question of how well these structures work, for society as a whole and for individual men.

## The Actuality: Contradictions, Deceptions, and Betrayals

For some men, institutional life is fulfilling within its boundaries. In many organizations life is comparatively easy and safe if a man makes no major blunders. In a bland, easygoing atmosphere, men who desire emotional distance from others and a smooth social surface dedicated to "getting along" find precisely the environment they need and want.[95] They are able to exercise their talents and expand their scope. Such men are likely to see the institution as their true home, and some even refer to it as "mother."

But this is not always the case. Critics of male structures focus on three main areas of betrayal, promises that are or seem to be made but are not kept. These promises are that good work is the major criterion for advancement; that performance will be rewarded; and that the institution rewards the workers' loyalty in kind—is loyal to them in turn and offers job security to all who do not seriously transgress. (These are similar to the promises made by institutionalized religions—obedience and loyalty are the major criteria of desert and will be rewarded by a deity who "loves" his adherents in return for their "love" and faith, and who in some versions even loves them regardless of their attitude.)

More often than not, however, job performance is irrelevant to promotion or monetary reward. One analyst writes of corporations that "in most instances, the cause of reward is not performance, but some other circumstance or combination of circumstances." Sometimes reward is given to those whose attitude of deference is sufficiently humble to please superiors; sometimes it is given to men who know how to give the appearance that they are responsible for good work done by others. The commission system rewards those who happen to be assigned to a good territory.[96]

It is generally known that in institutional life it is often wise not to do one's best, since one's best might threaten or challenge one's superior. This has been observed at least since the Renaissance, when Shakespeare put these words into the mouth of one of Antony's lieutenants who had just won an important battle: "I could do more to do Antonius good,/ But 'twould offend him; and in his offence/ Should my performance perish." Punishment, on the other hand, does not necessarily reflect poor performance—it may be a result of bad luck, personal caprice, dislike, or scapegoating. The latter is especially common in government, in which an official may be forced to resign, taking with him the blame for a decision made in conjunction with or by a higher official.

Thus men who enter a system hoping to succeed within it by following the stated rules will often be disappointed. What seems to be a rational and orderly structure is in fact a maze. "A man who heeds the lesson of the maze will learn that his choices are constant fear or complete obedience," as Earl Shorris puts it, and he goes on to describe "bewildering corridors," "devastating pitfalls," and destruction for no reason.[97] Such situations are more common, I believe, in institutions most intensely geared for profit, and in jobs that are connected with sales and administration; that is, in the areas most vulnerable to economic tides and human response. But even in supposedly nonprofit organizations—the government, education, the Church, labor unions, the penal system—the corridors are filled with men disappointed over lack of advancement, men resigned to half-hearted, half-minded work that seems to be all that is wanted from them. Energetic efforts to improve a procedure or alter an unwieldy system are as often as not met with downright disapproval and suspicion.

In certain organizations rule is not by caprice but by actual terror. Anthony Sampson describes the workings of ITT in a book published in 1980. In this conglomerate, the highest executives, ultimate authorities in their own companies, were controlled, constricted, and terrorized by the chief executive, Harold Geneen. Geneen kept lines of access into each of his companies which were essentially espionage lines, secret from those who were officially responsible. Each line of products was covertly surveyed by managers based in Brussels, who were apart from and not responsible to the actual executives of the various companies. Once a month all the official executives were flown to Brussels for a brutal group interrogation. According to the executives, these meetings were terrifying ordeals. Geneen supervised them using a strategy of confrontation, humiliation, and exposure: "You have to be prepared to have your balls screwed off in public and then joke afterward as if nothing had happened," said one executive.[98] Geneen was hardly the only administrator to use such tactics, nor are they always considered opprobrious. Articles about such men may hint at the terror they stimulate but at the same time refer admiringly to them as men who "get things done."

Although the institution demands loyalty as a primary requirement, it may in fact not value loyalty at all, but grant its greatest admiration to men who hop from one organization to another in an effort to advance themselves. Such men may have their real expertise in understanding how to use a system that is basically political to their own advantage, and may be less knowledgeable about their jobs than more stable, less adventurous souls. But they often glean more respect from the executive level than their solider counterparts, who are likely to be passed over for promotion. More time on a job, more knowledge about a company are seemingly advantages that could be used to the benefit of the company. Seniority, in other words, should earn employees a greater voice in institutional policy, more autonomy, or more control over their own functions. It does not. The institution loses an important source of internal criticism and reform, which could lead to greater efficiency and higher morale among the workers, by refusing to listen to those of its staff who *are* loyal.[99] In keeping with the patriarchal penchant for renaming things, people are often "promoted" into less important jobs, are praised in equivocal language, or are given top jobs in distant places—in what amounts to an exile.

Wages and salaries are also supposed to be assigned in a just, fair manner, according to the job slot, the experience, and the education of the worker. But they are randomly assigned in most corporations, Kanter discovered, and information regarding wages is not available even to heads of departments, who are sometimes unaware that one of their subordinates is earning more than they themselves.[100]

The loyalty of institutions is something the wise do not count on. If you recall, we discussed the promises made by early textile mills in New England to the families of the young girls first hired to work in them, promises assuring the families that their interests would be fulfilled by the interests of the companies. This happy agreement lasted until the first strikes, after which the companies hired immigrant women. When even these women began to unionize, the companies moved South, where there were no unions. In recent decades, despite a propaganda campaign by some American companies urging people to "buy American" products, hundreds of them had already shifted their production units to Southeast Asia, Taiwan, and Hong Kong, where labor is cheap.

Companies frequently dismiss men only months before they are due to retire, thus denying them their pensions. Labor unions have been known to steal funds from the pension plans of their own members, plans they fought management to obtain. This lack of loyalty in institutions to their members extends even to the largest institutions—governments and religions—as we will see in some detail later on.

In short, the "promises" offered by institutions are mere appearances designed to elicit obedience. When they are kept, it is an event as random and capricious as when they are not kept. The promises of institutions are part of the fiction upon which the organization itself is based—that its primary function is its real purpose, that is, that the purpose of corporations is to provide products or services of a stated kind: of educational institutions, to educate; of military institutions, to maintain a nation's defenses; of religious institutions, to minister to the spirit. In actuality, the primary purpose of the men who manage institutions, and therefore of the institutions themselves, is to maintain and extend power in the world, to maintain and extend control over their members.

It follows that to guard the power of one department or one man, certain data are kept secret. This can lead to failures in ordering or delivering products or services, to duplication of effort, and to mystification of line workers. For example, there are information clogs; these are reported in just about every book on institutional workings. They are caused by the particular system used, and they hinder efficiency. Yet they are not removed. For they serve the purposes of control, as do random, capricious decisions. Some organizations purposely obliterate clarity from their procedures.[101] It is far easier to arouse and maintain fear when one behaves inconsistently, erratically, than when one is consistent: consistency in a superior means one needs to fear only when one has broken a rule. Erratic rage tyrannizes many a household, and many an institution. Consistency can lead to strict obedience in stipulated areas but the exercise of a degree of autonomy in other areas. Inconsistency of reward or punishment leads to fear of acting in any area at all, to a dread of responsibility and a relieved ceding of it to superiors. This is precisely the condition reported to exist in many institutions.

A recent analysis of the American defense establishment by David C. Jones, former chairman of the Joint Chiefs of Staff, points to such difficulties in "the largest organization in the free world." Jones writes that the defense system *appears* rational and orderly, but that the appearance breaks down because what is planned is not possible. Among the faults he finds is that leaders within the establishment must spend most of their energies obtaining resources in competition with the other services (thus they spend themselves on getting and keeping power for their organizations, rather than improving the organization); that people avoid making difficult decisions and there is little accountability for decisions made; and, finally, that the real business of the establishment, the "combat effectiveness of the fighting force," the supposed end of this organization, receives little attention.[102]

The tendency to create a surface appearance that is praised for its "rationality" and order, while beneath it seethe rampant caprice and cruelty, is intrinsic to patriarchy and has been since its inception. This tendency has been raised to a fine art by modern institutions, which claim to be embodiments of rationality. For example, management manuals teach men how to think in a patriarchal mode. Among their precepts is the basic one: a successful manager is a man who can control his emotions, whereas workers cannot. One such manual describes the leader: "He knows that the master of men has physical energies and skills and intellectual abilities, vision and integrity, and he knows that, above all, the leader must have emotional balance and control. The great leader is even-tempered when others rage, brave when others fear, calm when others are excited, self-controlled when others indulge."[103]

Writers on management practice and organization theory distinguish between "the managers' logic of efficiency" and "the workers' logic of sentiment."
Studies of the informal organization of institutions focus on expression of emotion and sentiment, and of political attitudes, among *lower-ranking* personnel
only. What is suggested is that only lower-ranking personnel are subject to such
things.[104] Although executive personnel committees issue descriptions of those
who are prime executive material, the characteristics listed are so vague as to be
meaningless.[105] The same is true of published lists of criteria for promotion:
they are not only vague but utterly manipulable.

In short, patriarchal divisions never cease. Like one-celled animals that reproduce by fission, patriarchy thrives by applying the initial division of
human/nature, man/woman, into every realm. Qualities associated with nature and women—emotion, the body, personal relations and community as significant defining boundaries—are attributed to lower-, not upper-level workers.
Higher-level workers define themselves by their difference from lower-level
workers. For example, a corporate lawyer informed that workers were buying a
large share of a failing company commented, "My God, the monkeys are going
to run the zoo."[106]

Douglas McGregor asserts that the way an institution is managed has less
to do with its formal structure than with the attitudes of its managers or administrators toward their jobs and toward their subordinates. He points out that
the literature offering instruction in organizational and management practice
invariably posits authority as an absolute, and adds that the most troublesome
problems in administration are the result of that assumption. Those in authority, despite their own feelings (perhaps subconscious) toward control from
above, attempt to control the behavior of their subordinates in inappropriate
ways.[107]

Such strategies, McGregor says, resemble those taken by adults toward
children, and thus they infantilize workers. Those in control view workers as if
the latter disliked work and would avoid it if possible; thus they must be
coerced; the managers claim that workers appreciate coercion because they do
not want responsibility.[108] He concludes that if the practices of "scientific management" were "deliberately calculated to thwart human needs for respect and
appreciation," they could hardly succeed better than they do.[109]

But indeed, they *are* deliberately calculated to thwart human needs for respect and appreciation in that they are calculated to cause men and women to
kneel, to create the illusion that those in control have control. Although they
may not be conscious of this, all members of institutions who do not live with a
sense of active rebellion, and even some who do, worship control as the highest
human good.

But control is illusory in many ways. Hegel defined the relation of the
subject of a sentence to the object of a sentence as a relation between master
and slave. And there is a great difference between these two formulations: *he
fucked her* and *they, fucking*. The syntax of most Western languages embodies
power struggle, just as the preceding sentence attributes a power relation to the
act of love. There is no question that the idea of power as the highest good has

permeated every element of life in the West; what is questionable is what it means to be master or slave.

Many years ago I went to a conference in Tennessee, and while I was there I took a tour of some of the facilities at the Oak Ridge Atomic Plant. It offered the fascination of the abomination. One of the sights was a long room with one wall composed of a series of leaded but transparent glass windows, each about twelve feet long. The windows looked on small enclosed rooms whose floors were level with the window base. Inside these rooms were seemingly random sets of objects—containers of different shapes and sizes, objects with no clear purpose which had been exposed to radiation. Each room also had in its solid wall a small door like the doors people install for their pets, which open with a push. Connecting these doors was a moving belt, like an assembly line.

Outside the windows, in the room where we walked, were a series of high stools, fixed into the floor and mechanically adjustable like the chairs in a dentist's office. Each stool faced one window, and just beyond it, within easy reach, was a long handle that rose to the ceiling. The handle had controls attached to it, and its arm ran into the ceiling and through, into the glass-walled room beyond. Here the arm hung down five or six feet, and ended in a metal claw. The controls on the handle manipulated this claw and the arm, so that the mechanism could pick up radiated materials and move them about, sometimes to the assembly line that would transport them to another "room," presumably for different experiments. Men sat on the stools in postures of great intensity, concentrating on their work. I do not know what would be the consequences of a spill inside one of the rooms, if one of the containers tipped over and its radiated contents washed the air, but I assume it was at least not a desirable event. The crane operators—for that is really what they were—worked under severe tension. As I watched one of them slowly move a small container from a base in the room to the assembly line at its rear, I glanced at the label on the machine. It read: Master-Slave Machine. I laughed nervously as the man finished his operation, and he glanced at me. "Who's the master and who's the slave?" I asked. He glared at me.

It was not just a challenge, it was a real question. We examined earlier some of the costs of slavery to the masters. No worker, no matter how low on the ladder, is more oppressed, more subject to pressure, more filled with fear than those who run institutions. Living walled in from the world for fear of assassination, walled in from people for fear of confrontation, distrustful even of close associates who might want to usurp his position, the controller of men is the most controlled of men, the least personally free. It is well known that Stalin lived in constant fear of assassination, and also in "panic that the whole ramshackle edifice of Soviet power would collapse under the onslaught of a wild, anarchical rising of the millions of camp inmates and national minorities."[110] But lesser controllers are no freer: the pleasures of relaxed anonymous movement through the world, of easy conversation with others, of trust and love as part of a community, are impossible for them.

But the betrayals made by institutions are not limited to exploitive treatment of individuals or to failure to fulfill their promises to individuals and groups. Institutions and the men who govern them betray even themselves and their own reason for being. Political and religious groups, and even states, all claiming to exist for the sake of the people who are their adherents, often betray their entire following. Men destroy the nations they have ruled for the sake of personal safety (or that of a small group) and well-being; or for the sake of a cause or belief; or in an irrational obsession with control, or vengeance, or paranoia. Consider a few examples.

As early as 1920, Lenin proposed sacrificing or injuring Communist parties in other nations if that seemed to benefit the Russian Communist movement. He thus condemned to imprisonment or death many people who had worked devotedly for the cause he also espoused. Inspired by visions of a more humane world, and by promises of approval for success, these people became expendable in a period when strengthening the Soviet Union and making it secure took primacy over the declared purpose of spreading the socialist ideology throughout the world.[111]

On a mere suspicion that Polish army officers who had supported Soviet rule in Poland could at some future date act as leaders in a revolt of the Poles, Stalin had them all murdered by the NKVD.[112] He forced collectivization on Russian peasants, choosing a stategy of compulsion that was irrational and irrelevant and based on figures he knew to be false, rather than adopt the more gradualist policy urged by Bukharin. The result was disaster for millions of people. Stalin killed twenty million people in his purges, among them almost everyone who had attained any position of power.[113] The majority of these people were committed both to the Soviet Union and to socialism.

The socialist government of Cambodia "purified" Cambodia of a large percentage of its population and almost all of its educated people. The Chinese Cultural Revolution, if less extreme, did considerable damage in its longer reign. But we do not have to look at socialist nations to discover controllers obsessed by control and driven by their obsession to subvert their own principles and harm or destroy their own "kind."

The ancient Greeks continually overreached themselves; Slater gives the example of the Sicilian Expedition. Athens was already at war with Sparta and the city under siege, yet the Athenians chose to risk everything to send forces to "the largest and most expensive military expedition ever fielded by a Greek city," directed against "the most remote and irrelevant enemy Athens had ever attacked."[114] Athens never recovered from the disaster, which marked the beginning of its decline. Similar statements can be made about United States involvement in Vietnam, and about the economic disaster it caused, from which we still suffer.

Hitler demanded utter loyalty to himself, and identified himself with Germany's good. He ran a shadow government—that is, the official, public government had little real power, and a set of secret bureaus run by the SS made the decisions. Hitler's obsession with "purifying" Germany and the rest of Europe of those elements he considered subhuman caused him to divert men, weapons, and other resources from the war he had begun. He enlisted and coerced support from the entire German population in the war to make Germany supreme, a Reich that would last for a thousand years. Yet he was even in the beginning planning, after ridding Europe of Jews, gypsies, Poles, and other "inferior" people, to rid Germany of its "defective" citizens (the grounds of defectiveness were never very clear). Finally, when defeat was imminent, he ordered Albert Speer to turn Germany into a desert afterward.

Anastasio Somoza Debayle, the tyrant who ruled Nicaragua until the rise of the Sandinistas, punished the nation for rejecting him by seriously damaging industry and commerce, and leaving behind him a $1.6 billion foreign debt. He himself left the country a millionaire. So did the shah, when he left Iran.

The Islamic revolution in Iran was founded in the promise to set up a reformed nation cleansed of Western and non-Islamic influence—strict in its regulation of women within the family and of morality in general. It claimed to defend old virtue and reinstitute Islamic family life. Yet the chief justice of Iran proclaimed in September 1981 that any dissident would be put to death upon the testimony of two witnesses; that the parents of those put to death had no right to "complain even mentally to the authorities." Parents, he decreed, must denounce their children to the revolutionary guards if they could not control them, and informers would be protected by the state.[115]

In the United States, we have watched as the highest executive in the country condoned and concealed crime, and have understood his bitterness—he, after all, was merely one of the few who were caught. Automobile companies produce cars that are defective, and when the defect is brought to their attention, they haul in their legal experts and attempt to decide whether it would be cheaper to recall and repair the car, or to handle the lawsuits brought by people whose family members were killed because of the defect. We see companies pollute the air, water, and land that must sustain the men who work for these companies, even the men who make these decisions, as well as their families and friends.

Men in high office are hounded and harried; presidents age swiftly in office; power brings terror. Institutions that proclaim themselves devoted to the public good are in fact devoted only to their own survival; and the men who are currently in charge of those institutions do not care even about that, but only about their own personal survival. What are we to think when we discover that American FBI or CIA agents helped to safe and secure lives men who were high officials in the Nazi hierarchy, who had murdered Jews and others, who were part of the enemy whose defeat took thousands of American lives? Klaus Barbie, "the Butcher of Lyons," allegedly responsible for murdering hundreds of Jews, was paid $1700 a month by the CIA for information—after the war was over.[116]

To whom do institutions actually give loyalty, and who actually controls them? It has been suggested many times, almost as metaphor, that no one controls the system, that it is a machine running on its own, and out of control. But it is the *idea of control* that rules the world. While the cast of characters sitting in the highest chairs changes frequently, it is an interchangeable cast, all of them devoted in the deepest way to the delusion that sufficient power can bring safety, can impose one's personal image upon the world, and can somehow, some day, bring a sense of well-being. This utterly irrational idea is called rationality.

## The Actuality: Costs

The "dues" of male structures are not all of the actual cost that must be paid. What one must be on the job has an effect on what one is off the job. Young people who enter large institutions may at first find them intimidating, oppressive, and even immoral. They may try to behave as they must on the job, and be themselves—"let it all hang out"—in their private lives. But to keep this up they must become either hypocrites or schizophrenic. Although the hypocrite has for centuries been a figure of ridicule in literature, in actuality very few people are hypocrites; indeed, sustained hypocrisy would seem to lead to madness. People who find their work role too dehumanizing leave the workplace; others eventually embrace the values and the role, and persuade themselves that both are worthwhile.

It is impossible to condemn people for doing this. The values of the workplace are the values of the public world, and most people are neither arrogant nor foolhardy enough to try to oppose that world single-handedly. To continue to challenge it even privately comes to seem "sinful," willful and self-indulgent. The higher one rises in the structure, the less possible it becomes to entertain a separate standard, especially for men who identify themselves with their work.

And so, sooner or later, most managerial-level men and women and many below adopt the values of the institution. Those values are not unfamiliar: boys are exposed to them young, in reading material, on television, on the streets, and often in their own homes. Many schools teach such values. But they also have extreme personal reverberations.

A person who values control over anything else is incapable of any relation that might weaken or penetrate that surface of control; thus such a person becomes almost incapable of intimacy, equality, or trust, each of which requires the abdication of control. Needing to hold oneself apart and above so that the appearance of control may not be shattered—or conversely, needing to hold oneself apart and below (subordinate) so that one's self-respect may not be shattered—one is terrified at the nakedness and vulnerability that seem to hover beyond the carefully maintained wall of control.

In addition, the values of the workplace demand the suppression and if possible repression of emotion, for emotion is considered out of place, a sign of instability, "not cool," naïve, childish, not manly. A man who spends most of his waking hours in the workplace, repressing his feelings, is not easily able, especially after some years, to come home and unlock the forbidden hoard. This repression of emotion, reinforced by the need for control, often creates a zombielike creature who comes alive only in discussions of work.

Finally, the extreme competitiveness of the masculine world teaches all men to fear and mistrust each other. Although many men have "buddies," with whom they play or drink or compete in sports, the relationship between them is rarely permitted to dip below surface bantering, rivalry, and bravado. The competition of the workplace carries over into the private sphere; most all-male activities involve other forms of competition or almost ritualistic discussions of competition—conversation about football, baseball, tennis, politics, or about comparative values of cars, cameras, or lawnmowers. "Buddyship" is a particular kind of relation, not to be confused with friendship. Most men do not have friends and are not capable of friendship because they are afraid to let down their guard.

The effect of maintaining these three qualities—control or its appearance in every situation; suppression or repression of emotion; and extreme competitiveness engendered by fear and mistrust—is to isolate men in a solitary confinement of the emotions. Moreover, because males begin to repress emotions and mistrust others when they are very young, their emotional awareness and expressiveness do not grow and develop. They remain adolescent in many men, who, when they do give vent to anger, sound like fourteen-year-old boys in a tantrum. Some men become emotionally paralyzed, their emotional awareness having atrophied to the point where they can no longer feel their feelings. The activities that would enable them to grow emotionally are forbidden to them—intimacy, friendship, and caring for others, especially children.

As a result, the personal lives of many men are empty, lonely, bleak. They fulfill the patriarchal prophecy of lonely exile as the "heroic life." Men who have done everything their culture has insisted they should are left bewildered, wondering where the reward is for their good behavior, the love, glamor, power, and popularity promised for achieving success. There are few "heroic" qualities in most men's lives. Peggy Sanday describes "male-supremacist" societies among simple cultures: men are distant from their children and completely controlling; they expect utter obedience. They see all women as inferior and thus unworthy of trust. They feel competitive with other men. The entire society is characterized by hostility, power struggle, suspicion, competition, and sexual antagonism.[117] Simpler and "primitive" such groups may be, but they resemble our own "sophisticated" society.

Much has been made of male bonding, but it "is not a vehicle for male-male emotional relationships, but rather a substitute for them."[118] There are a number of studies that show that men have much greater difficulty than women in achieving same-sex identification, that they show less affect, and are less empathic, and that they have deficits in emotional behavior and relationships.[119] It is one thing to point this out, however, and another to suggest the richness and interest and joy of what is lost. Many men have had friends, and know what lack of them means. Still, especially as men go higher on the institutional ladder, it is extremely difficult for them to overcome the fear and mistrust of other men enough to become friends, and sometimes even harder, especially as they age, to find another man with whom they have that special rapport necessary to friendship. Men also fear the imputation of homosexuality that might be made if they allowed themselves to love another man. Yet they do not really examine why it is that women can love other women without such imputations, and they cannot.

Many men, then, depend on a woman with whom they have some intimacy to provide all of their emotional nourishment. If power struggle does not poison the relationship over the years, the single relation of marriage (or living together) can sustain men. They can pour their fears and humiliations, their longings and dreams into the ear of this one woman, who usually—or even un-failingly—offers sympathy, understanding, and support. They believe they have intimacy. But in fact, many such men do not, for they are not equally available for sympathy, understanding, and support when their wives or lovers need it. They do not hear the woman's pleas, they do not respect her fears: trained to control, they answer every lament and sorrow with a promise to "take care of" a situation that, it may be, cannot be taken care of. When women are seriously ill, when they lose a child or a parent, or even when they are feeling wretched for lesser reasons, they turn to other women. They have to; they do not get from their men what they give them. One result of this is disenchantment with a man, and divorce; another is that men whose wives die are likely to die them-selves soon afterward, while the reverse is not true.[120]

The most serious consequence of men's emotional stunting is the stunting of their relations with their children. Although there are signs that this is changing, it remains true that most men are not good fathers. The history of fatherhood is a history of tyranny and often of violence. The emphasis on con-trol, obedience, and fear as the "proper" relation between fathers and children can debilitate even fathers who would prefer a closer and more affectionate and supportive relation. They fear they will ruin their children if they do not follow the "tried and true" method. That the "tried and true" method of raising chil-dren may bear some relation to the tyranny and violence of the world is not no-ticed. Sons who grow up in houses watching their fathers beat their mothers as well as the children learn early to hate. One ten-year-old boy who was inter-viewed promised, "When I grow up, I'm going to kill Dad."[121]

Sons are usually punished more often or beaten more severely than daugh-ters, but they are also allowed more latitude. Daughters are more often mo-lested or raped by fathers or other male relatives. The frequency of such acts is staggering. Freud was appalled that "perverted acts against children were so general," and he added, "I find it's the closest relatives, fathers or brothers, who are the guilty men." He suggested that even his own father had engaged in such acts.[122] Sandor Ferenczi declared that many of his patients in analysis disclosed that they had been assaulted as children.[123] Karl Menninger of the Menninger Foundation in Topeka, Kansas, wrote in 1981 that 75 percent of the "way-ward" girls his foundation assists had been molested as children by an adult.[124] Such assaults on young girls are not at all limited to the uneducated and the unmonied.

If many adult males molest or rape children, if many fathers use extreme physical violence on their children, the majority do not. Yet some fathers are extremely verbally violent to their children, which clinical experience suggests can be equally damaging psychologically. Other fathers simply retreat from fa-therhood entirely, by physical or emotional absence. Yet at the same time fa-thers more than mothers insist that children learn "proper" sex role behavior, and are more likely to enforce it.[125]

Society at large does not consider men's treatment of their children a significant part of their characters. Men are called "great men" despite abusive treatment of their families. Feminists need to investigate the effect on a man's work of his actual morality: How did Tolstoy's or Marx's conception of his own family affect the terms of his work? Dr. William Shockley, the Nobel-Prize-winning physicist who supports genetic determination of intelligence by race (that is, he believes whites are genetically superior to blacks), was interviewed after donating his sperm to a sperm bank for withdrawal by women who want superior children. Asked whether his own children were superior, he had no compunction in announcing for publication that they constituted "a very significant regression." His daughter was graduated from Radcliffe, one son had a Ph.D. in physics from Stanford—but with academic distinction only of the second rank, Shockley said—and another son was a drop-out. The flaw, he said, was in their mother, who "had not as high an academic-achievement standing" as he.[126] One only hopes she loved them better.

In past decades, indeed, ever since the workplace was removed from the home, it has been considered normal that fathers have little to do with their children, especially when they are infants. But it is in the period of infancy that the bond between adults and children is formed. Fathers who ignore their infants never form the same bond that most mothers do. This bond, contrary to general belief, does not arise from the act of giving birth. It occurs regularly between mothers and adopted children, and some natural mothers never develop it. The bond between children and adults arises from caring, nourishing, entwining one's emotional life with that of the child so that its needs, pains, joys, and accomplishments become one's own.[127] Fathers who fail to forge this bond tend to see small children as rivals for attention from the mother/wife and their grown sons as rivals and daughters as sex objects. When divorce occurs, such fathers often neglect to see their children again. In 90 percent of cases mothers get custody of children, largely because fathers do not want them and mothers do. In the United States, less than 20 percent of fathers continue to help support their children after divorce.[128]

Even when there is no divorce, many children grow up hardly knowing their fathers, who avoid the domestic sphere, or at least involvement in it, almost as much as the ancient Greeks. Their work may take them away from home for long stretches; they may work late frequently, out of choice as much as necessity. They may spend their evenings with other men, watching a competition on television or bantering competitively. On weekends, many men prefer the golf course or tennis court to time with their children. And men who do spend time with their children often use it to teach competition, aggression, and the importance of winning.

Since the relation of parent and child is the most profound relation on earth, and one of the richest parts of life, we must question why men in general continue to neglect it. One major reason is that the workplace is set up to accomplish this separation of men from the private sphere. Employers assume that the pace of work should be rapid, that men should spend most of their waking hours on the job. They assume that men have wives who will maintain the private sphere and raise the children. These assumptions reflect employers' unconscious assimilation of patriarchal principles—that men properly pursue power, and leave the "necessary" to women; that women and the domestic realm threaten men, manhood; and that it is in this separation that the superiority of men over women is rooted.

But men in general have also assimilated these principles and understand that they remain men by virtue of avoiding the realm, the tasks, and the concerns of women. It is heartening that new generations of young men are refusing to accept such limitations on their lives, but millions of men continue to do so. It is also true that women in general have not been eager to share the raising of children with men. This rich, challenging, difficult, and painful task has been women's major work since production was removed from the home; it is *their* job, the major element that is in their control, and they have tended to derogate men's efforts in this work. But as women increasingly work out of the home as well as inside it, shared childraising becomes more desirable to women.

The hollowness of so much male behavior, like the brittleness of so much female behavior, emerges from an attempt to form the self in line with patriarchal dictates, from mistrust of the self and one's emotions. In Chapter Three I suggested the cost to women of patriarchal principles; they are precluded not just from power, wealth, and legitimacy, but even from the exercise of ability, a sense of selfhood, control of any sort over their own lives. There is a cost to men as well, however, for enforcing inferiority on women and denying themselves the use of those qualities deemed "feminine." These costs are primarily psychological—they involve the loss of sensitive, vivid life rather than of wealth or power. But the costs extend beyond emotionally stunted lives. In an essay on corporate men, John Kenneth Galbraith sums up the costs paid for membership in an affluent class. They include the "extremely severe sacrifice of the right to personal thought and expression," as well as "a wide range of personal enjoyments," any contribution to the arts, learning, or politics, and even a sense of personal recognition. For regardless of a man's eminence in his work, Galbraith writes, "the organization has taken over; the head is unknown." When men leave even the highest offices, they fall into "an oblivion that continues until the few touching lines appear in the obituary column."[129]

The promises implicit in Genesis have been kept for men: they have achieved considerable control over nature and women; they have on the whole remained faithful to the god of power, and have been rewarded by sharing in power. They remain heroes, wandering in lonely exile forever homeless; and they remain willing to sacrifice their Isaac. In regal isolation they contemplate their dominions. They make up 47 percent of the world's population, yet earn 90 percent of its wages and own 99 percent of its wealth. They are also far more likely than women to be alcoholic or violent; they are more subject to a number of stress-related diseases; they have shorter lives and a higher suicide rate. It is remarkable that the highest suicide rate in the United States is precisely among those who have reached fullest success—white males over sixty-five.[130]

The picture is not so bleak for all men, of course, but no man is entirely free from the constrictions placed on men in our society, just as no woman is.

For an elite class of men, work is really satisfying and may even provide some sense of autonomy. More and more men are making an effort to have true intimacy with their lovers, wives, and children. A few men are working at learning friendship.

But men as a class are as impoverished as women as a class, and for the same reason: the exclusive division and categorization of both. Caught between the demands of a dehumanizing public life and an overwhelming (or so it seems) private life, men, like women, try to walk a fine line, try to be *right*, good. Erving Goffman writes that there is a set of qualities considered ideal for American men: they must be white, young, urban, northern, married, heterosexual, Protestant, college educated, fathers, employed, with a good complexion, weight, and height, and with a recent record in sports! He comments, "Any male who fails to qualify in any one of these . . . is likely to view himself—during moments at least—as unworthy, incomplete, and inferior."[131] Another commentator concludes that "the birthright of every American male is a chronic sense of inadequacy."[132]

It is true that one can place one's trust and love in someone and be betrayed; that years of loving nutritiveness cannot guarantee that a child will grow into a decent human being; that the demands of community and interconnection sometimes cost more than they return. For centuries, poets have lamented the transiency of love; Bacon saw wife and children as "hostages to fortune," bonds holding men back from the free exercise of their powers, impediments to men's resiliency. And Freud concurred, finding emotional ties the least dependable connections.[133] Freud urged work, a recommendation many of us, male and female, have adopted.

Yet for most of us, work is no more dependable than love and bonding. Many people are prevented from doing work up to their abilities and spend their years performing tedious tasks by rote. In some cases our best work is not received as we believe it should be, and may even be castigated, while lesser performances are rewarded. But the situation is particularly acute for men, who, Myron Brenton writes, dedicate themselves utterly to their jobs in the hope that will bring them love, but discover that their effort has destroyed the affection they crave.[134] Anthony Sampson describes the price paid by high executives—they suffer from personal tension and anxiety, and are not permitted creativity, imagination, the use of hunches, or emotional involvement with what they are doing. One executive hung a plaque on his office wall that read: "For at least another hundred years we must pretend to ourselves and to everyone that fair is foul and foul is fair, for foul is useful and fair is not. Avarice and usury and precaution must be our gods for a little longer still."[135]

Work can fail a man's needs; it can also disappear. An article describing stress among automobile executives facing dismissal points out that because they have always perceived themselves as superior and invulnerable to currents that push and drown men of lesser status, they are devastated by their loss. An interviewer of such men writes, "They are people who, up until now, have always felt in control of things." They are suddenly experiencing what the reporter calls an "impostor phenomenon," the suspicion that they are not as good as they thought they were. It may not occur to white men blessed by fortune that it was their birthright, their whiteness and maleness and, often, background, that put them in line for the blessing; that their talents or intelligence may not in fact be better than those of people who were not on the same line. Because such men found their entire notion of themselves on a set of invented beliefs, they lose that notion when the beliefs are challenged or fail. So, "once their job is gone, they have no identity."[136] The effort to make oneself or one's class invulnerable invariably also makes one vulnerable—to different things. For man, a creature born for death, invulnerability is not a possibility.

## 3. MALE REVOLT

Certainly, over the ages, men have perceived their oppression and tried to lighten it. It is fully comprehensible that people would have found nature responsible for much of their wretchedness, because living in nature is hard for humans, and its miseries blind us to its felicities. Not until human domination of nature had produced enough miseries of its own could we perceive those felicities clearly, or the limitations of our method.

Men have also rebelled against other men as the source of their oppression. As we have seen, however, every successful revolution generates oppression of its own and thus makes further revolution inevitable. In addition, revolutions often create power vacuums into which steps an oppressor as bad as or worse than the former one. A result of the French Revolution was Napoleon; of the struggle that brought Allende to power, Pinochet; of the Russian Revolution, Stalin. Although these men too fell or will fall, that is little consolation for the millions who suffer or die while they are in power.

Men's revolutions have not affected basic oppression because the sources of oppression have been mystified. People in general—for women participate in men's revolutions—have not perceived the actual source of those miseries the human race has created for itself. People kept in servitude have rebelled against that servitude—yet almost unfailingly have insisted that others remain in servitude. No revolution has ever challenged the notion of superiority itself, although some have claimed to. For whatever class benefited from a given revolution, women have always been returned, at its end, to a position of inferiority. This reaffirmation of inferiority has affected other classes as well, in particular cases—blacks were restored to inferiority, *de facto* slavery, after the Civil War; and minority ethnic groups have suffered after revolutions in China, the Soviet Union, and Central America, among others. But the restoration of women's inferiority is universal, basic, the root.

Revolutions decry certain distinctions as matters of rights: the rebelling class claims it has a *right* to a certain form of worship, to worship of a particular deity, to a greater share in the profits of its labor, to a different economic organization. *Rights*, however, are arguable matters: Who or what confers them? can guarantee them? Arguments about rights are legalistic, tendentious, and temporizing. No revolution has ever insisted that distinctions between superiors and inferiors are false to *fact*: the fact that no human is humanly superior to any other; that standards of superiority/inferiority are culture-bound, transient, and self-perpetuating, as well as self-serving. No revolution has ever protested patriarchy itself.

Patriarchal culture is, after all, all we know. The signs and hints of another way of being have been lost or obliterated; and those signs that exist are not absolutely clear. The history that has been preserved, those artifacts that remain, for the most part tell a patriarchal story. Patriarchy's values have been with us for so long, and there is so little suggestion of any others, that it is hard to imagine one could live by others. Beyond that, language has been so demoralized by the patriarchal insistence on calling foul fair and fair foul that it is hard to think straight. Meanings of basic words like *power* and *sex* and *love* are clouded and cluttered by falsehoods; and the symbolic nature of our associations defies logic and obliterates the real.

Still, men keep trying to rebel against oppression. There are three major categories of rebels: those who oppose a system and wish to replace it with another; those who feel exiled from the system and decide to prey upon it; and those who feel alienated from the system and decide to live outside it. The first are political activists; the second are criminals; and the third may be called *marginal men*.

Political activists are generally men of high ideals and vision, sometimes men who have been severely damaged and can find no purpose in life beyond retaliation—often understandably. It is rare, however, for a man of high ideals or vision actually to rule once the revolution has been accomplished; like Moses, he glimpses Zion only from a distance. Although some revolutions—the American, for instance—establish governments that are less oppressive than the former one, many do not. But there is no way to measure this completely. The present Cuban regime, for instance, may well be less oppressive than Batista's regime—*for most people*, if not for all. The same is true of the Russian and Chinese revolutions. So many factors are involved, and information is so sparse and so biased, that measurement is difficult for such places as Zimbabwe or Algeria. Discussions of results usually focus on one class of people—males only, either middle- or lower-class—and the sample determines the conclusion.

Criminals are of two general kinds: petty, more or less independent criminals, and organized criminals. Organized crime is not at all a revolution against the system but an imitation of it. It worships the same values, creates the same kinds of structures, and demands the same qualities from its workers. It may even require the same amount of work, if not of the same sort, as "legitimate" enterprises. Devoted to power in the form of money and influence, and of control over its own echelons, it requires fear and obedience, and some conformity in manner and appearance and life style, just as "legitimate" institutions do.

Nor are petty criminals really different. They are freer, as the poor, the outcast, the marginal are always freer. They do not have to conform as rigidly to a class or group standard. They are also freer to want, to need, to lack; and they also live in fear. They too are devoted to power in the form of money and force, and since they have little power themselves, they tend to prey on those with even less. The extreme youth of many of our petty criminals suggests that there is little or no cultural hindrance—no attractive alternative message—to their learning the message our culture teaches so loudly and clearly: power is the greatest good. Power may lie only in possessing a large portable radio (a "boom box"), or in a surge of excitement as one pummels a blind old woman to get her purse and its meager contents, but it is all there is. There is no other strong value; no community of loving adults and no modifications of violence intervene between the child and the value he perceives to be dominant. The oedipal promise—that if a boy or young man sublimates his anger, fear, and envy, he can grow up to be daddy—seems to have dwindled. The world of adults is not enviable: stilted, dead in many ways, lacking in autonomy, and as pressured by fear as the world of children, it lacks rewards sufficient to its costs. Without suggesting that such young people be regarded as anything but moral monsters, we must also see that they are the most complete victims of our values, an entire class of sacrificed sons (and daughters): they act out the dreams of "legitimate" military and police strategists, espionage bureaus, and makers of fiction—comic books, television programs, and movies. The rage and hate of our culture flames across pages and screens, as its artifacts, so dearly bought, so cherished, explode one after the other in a great triumphal rite of destruction.

Criminals of whatever kind are not rebels against the system but inevitable components of it. "The system," after all, refers to the institutionalization of all activities; and institutionalization, as we know, offers prestige and legitimacy *because* it excludes certain classes of people from its walls, palings, its cathedral close. It *decrees* people illegitimate to confer a sense of superiority on those accepted. The criminal class is a manufactured class.

It is not always easy to distinguish between legitimate and illegitimate structures, for there is no real difference between them except the declaration of their status. Organized crime in the United States behaves on the whole much better than the legally constituted government of Hitler's Germany. And as we have seen in recent years, the ties between organized crime and "legitimate" business and government and labor unions are intricately interwoven. Government and labor figures who are accused of wrongdoing often seem shocked at the accusation, not because they are innocent of such acts but because such acts are common practice, and they have merely been unlucky enough to be selected from the commonality as examples.

If the hiring of known criminals to commit crimes against leaders of foreign nations is "legitimated" under the heading of *intelligence,* as necessary for the "national security," then why should not a corporation whose well-being is threatened by revelations of one of its employees also eliminate her? It cannot be proven that Karen Silkwood was murdered by the Kerr-McGee company when she attempted to demonstrate that the plant was contaminated with uranium and that control records for plutonium fuel rods were being falsified, any more than it can be proven that the government was implicated in the fact that every major Black Panther leader was either killed or imprisoned within a few years of the inception of the movement.[137] But strong cases have been made that FBI infiltrators in various dissident groups taught those groups how to make bombs and suggested using them—something that might not have happened without the infiltrators; that an FBI infiltrator among groups opposed to black civil rights shot and killed a woman marcher; that members of government were involved in break-ins, robberies, and drug testing of unknowing subjects; that the CIA under pressure from ITT helped to overthrow Salvador Allende's government in Chile. Even when such things are proven, nothing really changes. Even when there is advance warning, nothing happens: Who believed Martha Mitchell's revelations except a handful of women? A few scapegoats go to jail; a few may disappear or be murdered (whatever happened to Dita Beard? Jimmy Hoffa?); but the system goes on as before.

It goes on as before because the goals of all our institutions, legitimate or illegitimate, are the same. All want to get, keep, and expand power; all accept as basic that power is the greatest good; all accept coercion as a natural and right method of maintaining themselves. Institutions for the illegitimate imitate those for the legitimate. In prisons, not just the guards but the inmates are ranked in hierarchical progression; in some cases a powerful criminal has more control over the institution than its legitimate administrators. Coercion is used by administrators and guards upon inmates, but also by inmates upon inmates, to uphold the rules they set up. There is even a "female" contingent, men at the bottom, who are sexually used and scorned like women.

If one believes in the innate depravity of the human race, such knowledge is received with a shrug: What do you expect from man, a being whose imagination is evil from his youth? From a being whose first act was one of disobedience? But the idea that man is innately depraved is at the heart of patriarchy, and is asserted and maintained by patriarchal documents. In those documents obedience to God alone can redeem man from this inherent evil. And those who accept religious teachings about the inherent evil of man and the necessity to obey Allah, or Jahweh, or God the Father, are precisely those who perpetuate the God of power. Holding up the rightness of violent and destructive behavior "in the name of God," they have helped to foster the present coercive, oppressive organization of Western institutions.

In fact, of course, power always wins. That is the great stumbling block to idealists who have urged more humane modes of interaction. There is no way to oppose power except by power. For example, if a small nation wishes to continue to live in a simple way, organized by clan or tribe, devoted to sharing and pleasure, concerned with continuation and well-being, it has no defense against another nation that wishes, for its greater prestige or profit, to add this territory to its domains. The small nation can either surrender or repel the invader; in either case it will learn the ways of power. This is true in personal relations as well. If one partner in a relationship feels love, desires to share, trust, and enjoy intimacy, but the other perceives all relations as power struggles, the relationship will inevitably become a power struggle. The second partner will interpret every statement and act of the other as a power move, will respond to counter or outweigh it, and this will preclude intimacy, trust, and love. Power seeking is contagious. It cannot be resisted. One can retreat from a relationship, or learn to play the game. The small nation, which cannot change its geography, will in time learn to play the game. Thus a philosophy of power as the highest good continues to spread itself over the globe.

It is this message that our political leaders keep offering us: that we must have sufficient power to offset the power of the Enemy. This message is comprehensible in the present condition of the world. But given the ominous situation the world presently confronts, it is time to penetrate a bit further into the meaning of power: What do you win when you win? You win power. You may also win many unhappy conditions that accompany power-over, and, in the process of winning, lose everything that makes life more than a grim wearing-down to the grave.

Because we have not, as a race, considered the real costs or rewards of power, we have never been able sufficiently to challenge patriarchy. This ignorance of the truths of power constitutes the major problem of marginal men, those who attempt to build a life for themselves outside the corridors of power, beyond the public buildings, camped out as it were in isolation from the public world. Marginal men do really try to rebel; they try to substitute other values for power, and to live in ways not dictated by institutions. Yet they carry within themselves the values they have tried to leave behind. Limiting themselves to the private sphere, they act negatively, not positively, opposing themselves to everything that suggests power; and in the process they strip themselves of positive forms of power—sometimes even of selfhood. Or they may abdicate power in the public realm but insist upon power over their women, or over small groups of other marginal men.

Attempts to live a marginal life may perpetuate patriarchal attitudes even as they challenge them. Jesus, who argued that worldly power was not a primary value, perpetuated the idea that men are homeless wanderers who scorn the contentment and materialism of "home"; his apostles are fishers of men, dedicated to a transcendent good. Gandhi, besides fostering a legend of nonsexuality, also taught people to scorn earthly goods. Whether through their intention or through later interpretation of their lives, these men offered a path of transcendence of both nature and a felicitous life.

There were many experiments in alternative modes of life in nineteenth-century America—the Oneida Movement, Hopewell, and Brook Farm, among others. One critic, T. J. Jackson Lears, discusses the impulses behind such movements, and condemns them because all were devoted to personal experience and individual salvation in the form of "authenticity" rather than to political action and the welfare of the larger community.[138] Most experiments in alternative modes of life do not last long—not in the nineteenth century, and not in the twentieth either. Few of the communes founded in the 1960s in America still exist. In part this is because it is difficult to live "against the current," to maintain values not widely held in a society. But in part these experiments failed because they insisted upon a mode of life that was predicated on an untrue notion of human nature. They might insist, like the Shakers, on denial of sexuality; or on denial of aggression; or on obedience to a single dominant figure. Their failure cannot be attributed simply to their focus on the personal, the private sphere; nor is there necessarily an indication of inherent inadequacy in dedication to personal experience and individual salvation. It is far more likely that the way salvation has been defined is inadequate to human desires and needs, which include sex, aggression, and participation in the public world.

What is necessary is a revaluation of the value of power itself, an examination of what one wins when one wins, and a revaluation of other, less respected qualities. Only a fundamental moral revolution can provide what is needed for real change in human institutions and behavior. This too many thinkers have attempted to supply. But they all encounter a basic stumbling block: to get to the meaning of power as a value, and to put it into a more realistic perspective, it is necessary to reexamine the traditional relations between men and women, the traditional notion of the female and her association with nature, and to confront the fact that the entire establishment of patriarchy is founded on the ambition to usurp the "natural" position of women. Male thinkers have been unwilling or unable to do this.

The one subject that can unite men across lines of class, color, or other background is women; although different kinds of men might use different kinds of language to describe it, and although there are varying degrees of desiderated subjection, almost all men want, need, and believe in the subordination of women. The two forms of discourse that occupy all-male groups and unite them are discussions of competition and derogation of the female. Through diminishment, objectification, or hostility, the latter topic provides one of only two bases for male bonding. Derogation of women thus serves two major purposes in perpetuating patriarchy: it is so pervasive and accepted that it becomes a fact of life, like the weather; thus in trying to probe human structures, men cannot challenge or doubt female inferiority. Second, despite the irrationality and absurdity of such behavior, so ingrained is it that men do not perceive the absurdity of blaming women, rather than male structure itself, for their miseries. Women have been blamed for male wretchedness for millennia—at least since the story of Eve and the apple was devised.

This blaming of women can be profound or ridiculous. The Greeks and Romans who blamed women for defeats in war or indulgent luxuriousness in their culture at times when women had no legal standing and no voice in national policy have their counterparts in our own time. An important, indeed founding, work on sex typing appeared during the Great Depression, a period which caused "the single greatest crisis in the traditional institutional basis of the male role . . . of family provider."[139] This work, *Sex and Personality*, gave rise to the MSRI (Male Sex Role Identity) paradigm which has been used in psychological testing ever since.[140] The MSRI paradigm grew out of psychoanalysis, although neither Freud nor his immediate followers developed sex typing. Freudian psychology did, however, offer a framework for American psychologists obsessed with defining masculinity. "What Freud left out, they filled in, and with a vengeance. Indeed, they made their preoccupation with the maintenance of masculinity the dominant feature of Freudian thought as it came to be understood and popularized in American culture," writes Joseph Pleck. The male was, by nature, aggressive and driven, always in control. These standards were invoked again with particular intensity at the end of World War II, when men, "validated by war, returned to find women economically and psychologically self-sufficient."[141] At this time the "feminine mystique" was developed to accompany the MSRI, and "castrating" mothers and wives became the focus of cultural blame. This was a profound kind of blame because people believed it and tried to alter their behavior; it caused a good deal of unhappiness.

But there are lighter sorts. For instance, a member of Nixon's cabinet blamed the energy crisis on women with all their household appliances; and more recently, Ronald Reagan blamed the high unemployment rate on working wives. The blaming of women reaches grotesque lengths, however, in killers who choose their victims because of their sex, like one man who kidnaped a young woman, a stranger to him, forced her into the trunk of her car, and later shot her. He confessed to the murder and urged the jury to give him the death penalty; he warned that he might do it again and he explained why: "I'm just motivated by women."[142]

There are times when women have the power to ruin men, but the power is *given* to them by men. Stanley Brandes studied the men in a small town in Andalusia, San Blas.[143] It is a fairly typical Spanish town; the men have a macho mentality, although they do not use that word, or any word, to describe it. They are much freer than the women; they can move about in the world singly or in groups, can lounge in taverns, sit around the plazas any time of day or night. Women are severely criticized if they walk alone in the streets: they may walk only with a male relative or another woman, and may go only to the market or to church. During the past decade, they have begun to enter bars, but lower-class women must be accompanied there by their husbands, and upper-class women by relatives or friends. Men are not expected to spend much time at home: they say, "the home is for eating and sleeping; otherwise a man belongs out with his friends."[144]

Young girls are given duties to perform; young boys are not. Girls have strict curfews and their behavior is constricted: they are trained to show no spontaneity or demonstrativeness. If they do not adhere to this training, they limit their chances of finding a husband and will eventually be ostracized from the community. Boys are free in body and mind; they may initiate conversations; girls may not.

Brandes asserts that women on the whole abide by their restrictions: they work very hard in the home, are almost never unfaithful, and seem devoted to their families. Nevertheless, the men feel seriously threatened by them, and they have generated a mythology that completely reverses the actual situation. "Women are portrayed as dangerous and potent, while men suffer the consequences of female whims and passions." Male imagery for women pervades their conversation, Brandes reports; it depicts women as of the devil, and men as inherently more virtuous and closer to God. Women, they say, dress like serpents; and they blame women for perpetuating the San Blas class system, for being elitist snobs. Men are associated with God and with sheep, women with the devil and with goats.[145]

The San Blas men claim to be terrified of female sexuality, which, they say, will rob them of their maleness and make women of them. Women's insatiable desire drives men to premature death, or leads them to commit adultery and thereby give other men the horns of the cuckold. Men believe that women wish for their husbands' death, that they want men only as temporary security or in order to legitimate their children. They think the women are happier as widows, and they announce, "All women are whores! *Todas!*" They have notions about sexual organs and anuses which are found elsewhere in the world as well. They believe men are driven by and conquer with the prick *(polla)* or balls *(cojones, huevos)*, and that even ideas and opinions emanate from these organs. Anal penetration is a threat so grave that it is not wished lightly upon another man. Men will not even use anal suppositories.[146]

They complain about being tied down to one wife and to family obligations; it is perhaps an understandable projection that they believe women constantly crave after men, even though, Brandes observes, there is very little sign of this. The women are obedient to the mores of their environment, and are harder-working than the men.

Nevertheless, women admit they are happier after their husbands die. The men spend a large proportion of the family income treating their friends in bars, and one cannot doubt that in such an environment there is considerable wife battering. For women do, Brandes asserts, have a great power: they *can* commit adultery. It doesn't matter that they don't, nor do the men consider what consequences such an act would have on the woman herself. They only know that she has the power to perform an act men have forbidden, and can by that stroke ruin her husband's dignity, her daughter's chance of marriage, and the family honor.[147]

Here, men blame women for their constriction and their anxiety and suspicion, when it is the moral system itself that constricts both sexes. They not only blame, but punish women for a situation beyond women's control. And the San Blas moral/social arrangement is hardly unusual: it appears even in sophisticated cultures. A few years ago, for example, a feminist-inspired television program was begun in Brazil. The program reaches mainly the urban population, not the televisionless villages and jungle settlements. Brazilian women have few civil rights, and live in a tradition of submissiveness. Although some women work outside the home as well as within it, women are economically dependent on men. It is still shocking for a middle-class woman to take a job, and only recently have women been permitted to serve on juries. The image of women in the culture is that they remain inside the house, that they are sweet, fragile, dreamy, and friendly, but that above all they are submissive to the whims of their men.

Nevertheless, the women's television program, watched by thousands of women, has, since its inception, been receiving a huge amount of mail on a single subject: wife beating. Among its offerings is a segment dealing with law, run by a male lawyer who tries to counsel women about their rights. He receives 125 letters a day, and of these, ninety complain of battering.[148] Despite the fact that women are essentially powerless economically and politically in this Catholic country, despite a strong tradition of male control and female submissiveness, men blame women for whatever they suffer and punish them accordingly.

Quite apart from the matter of women's suffering in physical pain, humiliation, and constriction, blaming and punishing women cannot solve men's problems. It is not even a satisfying outlet for male outrage and pain, because it must affect profoundly a woman's regard and love for her husband, and he must look at his handiwork when he gazes at her bruises. Whatever satisfaction he derives from his control over this disenfranchised creature is undermined by recognition of her powerlessness, and thus the unworthiness of his behavior. But for men even more than for women, it seems unthinkable to look upward with hostility.

Perhaps the Freudians are right, and the figure of Father has been made invulnerable and utterly Right by childhood psychological processes. Or perhaps centuries of propaganda have made this figure sacrosanct. Our myths offer us some truths. The Hebrew creation myth posits the beginning of civilization with a fall from harmony with nature; the Norse myths suggest that what we know as civilization began with a usurpation by the Aesir, a warlike, male-dominated set of gods, and predict the end of civilization and the world in a terrible war that will destroy the Aesir along with everyone else. To avert such a conclusion we must put aside the belief that God is power, power God. The ironic truth is that a religion of power is a religion of fear, and that those who worship power most are the most terrified creatures on the earth.

# CHAPTER FIVE

# The Present Perspective

For the first time in history, humankind must gaze directly into the face of a Gorgon that is not female at all, nor wreathed with snakes, but is shaped like a penis and bears the message *power*. God the destroyer is alive and well and living (this time) in silos clear across the planet, but this time, humans cannot evade the truth that destructive power destroys the self as well as the other. This has always been true: the crushing of any life diminishes us all, as John Donne told us long ago, because we are involved in humankind, and none of us is an island, entire in ourselves. But so imaginative are we, erecting devils along with gods, that it has been easy to forget that those people over there, even they whom we now bomb, are no more "evil" than we, and no better, but semblances, and that when we kill them in the name of ridding the earth of some hated quality, we kill ourselves and our potential.

For the self-hatred engendered by patriarchal thinking is grave, and threatening, and when—if—the world is destroyed by atomic cataclysm, the destruction will occur not in the name of justice or self-defense or fame or glory or even power, but as testament to a profound abhorrence of self, a protest at the fact of humanness that *cannot* be *trans*cended and so must be ended. The philosophy we live by, willy-nilly, only partly comprehending it, cries out for a universal Jonestown.

But perhaps—only perhaps—this present situation can lead us to stop for a moment and think what we are doing. Perhaps this terrible power humans have learned to use can teach us to sit still so that we may consider the costs of power and the limits of our control. If we understood these realistically, we would never have erected power into our god, but would have used it with pleasure, as a means to the improvement of life. In order to do that, however, we would have had to have some fairly substantive notion of what really improves life. Operating with the patriarchal assumption that those things are desirable which prove or create the appearance that humans are distinct from and superior to nature, we have turned an impossibility into our greatest desideratum, and thus decreed unending pursuit.

The present perspective is not reassuring. Everywhere cruelty intensifies, hatred breeds, the willingness to die in order to kill becomes a universal counsel of despair. The systems are all in place that will carry us to the relief of termination, extermination of a race that could not rest because it could not be what it desired to be, and never imagined there might be other modes of being: there is heaven, the full transcendence, and there is hell, the subsidence into matter. Still, here and there are people working dimly toward a different end, working at least partly with different values. But good intentions, intelligence, and dedication do not guarantee that the goal will be reached, or even that the goal, if reached, will deliver what is desired. We need, above all, clarity about what we have been doing, what we are doing now, and what we want.

At present, the masculine principle is in full sway in the Western world and, increasingly, in the East. Problems are diagnosed in accordance with its assumptions and solutions devised in accordance with its values. The tendency in the West during the past five hundred years has been in a single direction: toward greater centralization of control (with its concomitant, greater reliance on appearances); greater institutionalization (with its concomitant, greater numbers and kinds of illegitimacy); and increased instrumentality (with its concomitant, greater disdain for qualitative and affective elements).

To my mind, these trends amount to a single trend: a movement toward totalitarianism.

## 1. TOTALITARIANISM AND PATRIARCHY

There is no single definition of totalitarianism on which all political theorists agree. Most concentrate on form—the structures of a society that make it totalitarian rather than authoritarian or democratic, or elements present in the former that are lacking in the latter two. But this is a problematic approach: as Benjamin Barber points out, few elements in totalitarianism as defined by most modern theorists cannot be found in "all modern developed political systems."[1] Governments not classified as totalitarian contain structures identical or similar to those that are; and different "contents"—fascism and socialism, for instance—may take strikingly similar forms. Moreover, a society with a two-party system may have an ability equal to one with a one-party system to stifle real dissent and render real opposition innocuous. A two- or multiple-party system may, in other words, be able to create an *appearance* of dialectic if all parties argue about surface issues and ignore the basic problems churning beneath, inchoate because they lack words, terms, framing. Populations can be silenced by terror—or by tranquilization.

The definition of totalitarianism that has the greatest currency is probably that of C. J. Friedrich, who lists the following characteristics: 1) a totalist ideology, 2) a single party committed to this ideology and usually led by one man, the dictator, 3) a fully developed secret police, 4) monopolistic control of mass communications, operational weapons, and all organizations including economic ones.[2] Other thinkers insist that an essential point is the obliteration of the separation of public and private realms, that is, institutional control over marriage and family life.[3]

Hannah Arendt, who was one of the first theorists to attempt to define totalitarianism, and who remains the most profound, saw it as *qualitatively* different from other kinds of government, different in spirit as well as form.[4] Karl

Popper believes it to be merely an extension of a tradition that is as old as our civilization itself.[5] Friedrich and Z. K. Brzezinski also find totalitarian societies logical exaggerations of "the technological state of modern society."[6] Although Arendt found totalitarianism unique, she also rooted it in certain traditional tendencies, namely anti-Semitism and imperialism. All these thinkers, while finding totalitarianism unique, a new form, at the same time assert its kinship with other governmental forms.

Recently, however, Jeane Kirkpatrick asserted that there were great differences between totalitarian and authoritarian regimes, differences great enough to dictate an acceptance of the one, but not the other, by the government of the United States.[7] Kirkpatrick claims that "revolutionary autocracies" are more repressive than traditional ones. This is probably true, but the difference is one of degree, not kind. "Traditional" autocracies were violent and repressive when they were founded; having long ago silenced opposition, they have seen to it that institutions of press, church, and education conform carefully to the policies of the regime.

Authoritarian regimes permit freedom of speech (or press) no more than totalitarian regimes; they are also intrusive into private life (although they may leave such intrusions to their religious institutions); they control communications, weapons, and most organizations, and they all have extensive secret police. They are capricious and secretive about arrests and imprisonment without due process, and are more likely than the stabler socialist regimes to murder suspected dissidents. Authoritarian states, like totalitarian states, forbid debate; in neither kind of society do people have a voice. Both forms of government exercise surveillance over the population and coercion in most areas of life; both operate through terror.

Kirkpatrick did not mention the real distinction between authoritarian and totalitarian regimes: totalitarian states entertain as a goal the remaking of humankind. Because of this, they cannot tolerate the existence of institutions that are not under their direct control. Authoritarian regimes permit the Catholic Church, for instance, to flourish; and accept fully capitalist enterprises. Both of these tend to support authoritarianism. "Traditional autocracies" permit egress to their populations; those who wish to leave are mainly intellectual dissidents and the poor. The former cannot find refuges that permit them to be effective; and the latter are unwelcome everywhere, and voiceless everywhere.

Authoritarian regimes are cynical, worship only power, and believe every human being is corruptible; totalitarian regimes are idealistic and attempt to transcend the worship of power, rule by a self-interested elite. It is a major irony that totalitarian states, dedicated to a humane ideal of community, should have raised oppression, dedication to power, and rule by an elite to the greatest level ever reached on earth.

Yet it is inevitable, given the mode of thought that created totalitarian states, that this should be so. For totalitarian revolutions, seeking to remake humankind in a new image, are treading in the same path as authoritarian governments, although going further on that path. They can go further because they link an idealistic goal with high technology and industry; Christianity, in its day, was also an attempt to remake humankind. In sum, totalitarianism is rooted in the same ideals as authoritarianism, the same ideals that inform all Western institutions—the ideals of patriarchy.

As we have seen, patriarchy is an ideology founded on the assumption that man is distinct from the animal and superior to it. The basis for this superiority is man's contact with a higher power/knowledge called god, reason, or control. The reason for man's existence is to shed all animal residue and realize fully his "divine" nature, the part that *seems* unlike any part owned by animals—mind, spirit, or control. In the process of achieving this, man has attempted to subdue nature both outside and inside himself; he has created a substitute environment in which he appears to be no longer dependent upon nature. The aim of the most influential human minds has been to create an entirely factitious world, a world dominated by man, the one creature in control of his own destiny. This world, if complete, would be *entirely* in man's control (even weather, disease, and death), and man himself would have eradicated or concealed his basic bodily and emotional bonds to nature. (Only rarely in post-Renaissance thinking is it suggested that mind—reason—too emerges from nature.)

The stratification of man and nature led to further stratifications: If man was superior to nature and distinct from it, how could he explain his clear bonds with it? Those bonds arise from woman, who taints all her offspring with the imprint of the beast. Woman's ties with nature are ineradicable—she menstruates, conceives, and lactates, and passes her fallen nature on to all her children. But male children are freer than female children from the taint that dooms one to enslavement to the body, and through strict discipline and dedication to the principle of power, men can eradicate the "woman" in them and the "womanly" from life. Only when this is accomplished will man be truly divine, truly free.

Many forms have been contrived over the millennia to realize this goal, and they have become increasingly ambitious. At first the major form was religious: priests taught methods of reaching the divine principle that offered control over animals (in the hunt), over women (early patriarchy), and over the self (as in early Judaism). Military conquest offered another avenue of control, as power over others became symbolic of control over self and defeat of an enemy was seen as defeat of the feminine principle (as indeed it was). Such conquest appeared to offer transcendence over time and mortality, as it spread the fame of the conqueror over large stretches of land, and established his dynasty. In terms of time and space, the greatest of these attempts in the West was the Roman Empire. The subsequent reign of the Catholic Church lasted longer because it was subtler: it used not only military force and economic regulation, but indoctrination—and it also coerced the internalization of a morality.

The Industrial Revolution completely altered forms and kinds of control. It made possible forms of control over nature and over people not imagined before. It controlled people by two main methods: one used on the many and one on the few. For the many, it first pauperized millions: pauperism as a mass phenomenon was virtually nonexistent in the preindustrial world.[8] Pauperization made the majority of the population of Europe dependent on those with capital, reducing the humble and the poor to full servitude. The mode of work introduced by the Industrial Revolution alienated people from their work by breaking the connection between producer and product. It introduced specialization, which, as Theodore Lowi points out, made families which had previously been relatively autonomous and independent dependent upon both an employer and a host of systems to supply their daily needs.[9]

The Industrial Revolution separated people, especially families, from each other; people from the land; and the home from the workplace. Since men blamed their diminished autonomy on women, it created an even wider gap between the sexes; since men's work and interests set them apart from their children, who were no longer from childhood on helpers in the shop or farm, but were for many years mere consumers of the father's labors, it created a wider gap between men and their children. The effect was felt by men, women, and children: it fragmented community, and rang the death knell for old matri-centric values of cooperation, sharing, and the primacy of bonds of blood. What was created was a pervasive sense of isolation and impotence, the loneliness of the totalitarian mass that Arendt writes about.[10]

For the few, the Industrial Revolution established a new language of values, one suited to the power-seeking men who were suited to thrive in such an atmosphere. It is difficult to describe this new vision without offering a bookful of biographies, because it subtly infiltrates most of our culture. It is a vision of control without end, control for its own sake, boundless ambition; home is superseded by a state of permanent exile, the pursuit of power; the excitement of the chase is substituted for the affections of the heart. The vision has been made into an image of "modernity" and glamour, of a man who controls technology and is invulnerable to emotional need. Power, in many manifestations, is not just the greatest but the *only* good.

In a revulsion against these values, in moral abhorrence of the materialist excess on the surface (like the weights used to press religious dissidents to death) that conceals widespread and life-threatening poverty, people sought for another moral/economic arrangement, one that would aspire to social justice and human equality: socialism. But the men who were able to triumph in a world given over to power were men given over to power: the actuality of socialism is not a dream but a nightmare.

All regimes we would call totalitarian have had an encompassing vision of human possibility. The nature of this vision varies: it may be the creation of a fully transcendent master race; it may be the creation of a state offering full justice and equality; it may be the creation of a state that realizes to the letter the writings of the prophet. Because the vision is or sounds admirable, it draws the most idealistic people; it appeals, for a time at least, to the most aspiring in us.

Democratic and authoritarian societies are not free from this kind of vision; but they accept visions of the past, see man as aggressive, selfish, competitive, and greedy, struggling for power. This state of things being considered inevitable, the ambitious ride with the current: to domination or death. Totalitarian societies do not accept this vision, although they may in many ways demonstrate it. They propose to realize a vision they see as morally higher than the view of man as depraved, but in a traditional way—through coercion.

The traditional view has never been universal, nor has it been imposed on all members of society: it is enough if an elite corps accepts it. Visionary societies demand that all citizens submit to their vision, do so ardently and without question. It is in this sense that they are totalist. Such societies feel threatened by other ways of seeing, especially those closest to them—like Catholicism and Protestantism, Sunni and Shi'ite Moslemism, or Moslemism and Christianity, two aggressive, monolithic, and proselytizing religions; like Soviet and Chinese socialism. Intent on the realization of the vision, fearful of its corruption by a corrupt world, totalitarian states lock their people in.

This is extraordinary. For the first time in history, nations are walled, huge nations, not to keep an enemy out, but to keep citizens in. There is only one parallel, and that is laws preventing women from traveling, or from traveling without their fathers or husbands. Such laws currently exist in Iraq, for instance. Women have often in history been locked in—in the house, the town, or the state—an imprisonment possible because men enforced it. Technological advance has now made possible the imprisonment of entire populations by a few.

*Why* do totalitarian societies want to imprison their populations? The Soviet Union could allow those Jews and dissidents who wish it to emigrate, as could the Ayatollah Khomeini and rulers of other totalitarian states. Permitting emigration would seem to solve the problem of dissidence. But totalitarian regimes are absolute; they insist that the vision be realized at home, but aim at universal acceptance. Hitler's goal was not the elimination of Jews from Germany or even Europe, but from the face of the earth. Socialists want worldwide socialism; capitalists want worldwide capitalism.

People are locked in, dissent is stifled, discontent concealed: all to create an appearance that the vision is in fact a reality. Chips cut in the walled state showing glimmers of discontent or dissent are deeply embarrassing to totalitarian regimes; as are uprisings, riots, and protest movements to the rulers of authoritarian or democratic states. All want to present an appearance of harmony achieved because their vision is true.

Freedoms are curtailed to keep intact the surface appearance of an achieved vision. Regimes lie, claiming success, and they demand that the people lie with them. Refusal to lie is dissidence or treason. Expressive behavior is also dangerous, for expressiveness is always individual, and therefore possibly deviant. Not just a single institution, but all institutions, in the embrace of the state itself, have been totally rationalized and emancipated from traditional bonds; "rationalization and emancipation, however, tend to collide, especially since the state increasingly becomes the most important rationalizing agency and thus the most important institution *from which* individual emancipation must be wrested." This collision is most crushing in totalitarian states, which see themselves as epitomes of rational control, and in the name of emancipation suppress the individual entirely.[11]

As Arendt pointed out, "Authority, no matter in what form, always is meant to restrict or limit freedom, but never to abolish it. Totalitarian domination, however, aims at abolishing freedom, even at eliminating human spontaneity."[12] She asserts that totalitarian regimes are difficult to understand, not because "they play power politics in an especially ruthless way, but that behind their *Realpolitik* lies an entirely new and unprecedented concept of reality . . . an ideological fictitious world."[13] The declaration, the Word, cannot alter reality beyond a certain point. It can create the machine, which alters our world; and the tranquilizer, which alters our mood; but it cannot do away with our participation in nature—our emotions, bodies, needs, and aspirations. "Because ideologies cannot really transform reality, they achieve an emancipation of thought from experience by ordering facts into an absolutely logical procedure which starts from an axiomatically accepted premise and deduces everything else from it."[14]

Totalitarian states are, as Popper suggested, the extension of a tradition "as old as our civilization"—that is, patriarchy; they are, as Friedrich and Brzezinski claim, an exaggeration of the situation found in all modern technological states: totalitarianism is unique only in the degree to which it has carried its insistence on realization of a vision. Beside totalitarian states, authoritarian and democratic states preen themselves complacently, proud of the "freedoms" they offer, unashamed of their own falsehoods.

Authoritarian states may claim good will toward the people, but in fact they are run for the benefit largely of one man and the class that supports him, the monied class. This may not be fully apparent until a regime is shaken: the Somoza family had a fortune stowed away in a safe place, and Somoza intentionally ruined the Nicaraguan economy before he fled. Others have also seen to it that their fortunes were safe—King Farouk of Egypt, the Shah of Iran—and we may be sure that authoritarians in power today are equally prudent. Their amassing of wealth is hardly new—Aristotle called such regimes tyranny. What is new is the escape plan. In the old tyrannies, kings usually remained; they were killed with or by their people. They did not have safe houses in Switzerland, Paris, or the United States, and Swiss bank accounts shored against ruin. Perhaps this is because there were no luxurious, safe refuges in ancient times, and no jet planes to carry them swiftly away; or perhaps the new image of man as individualistic, isolated, unbonded to community, extends even to those who claim to rule in the name of a people.

What is also new is the tendency of rulers to slaughter their own people—like Idi Amin, the Duvaliers, Pinochet, Pol Pot, Stalin, and, to a lesser degree, Mao. Arendt points out that Hitler's plan included not only the extermination of the Jews, the Poles, the Ukrainians, 170 million Russians, and the intelligentsia of Europe such as the Dutch and the people of Alsace and Lorraine, but also "all those Germans who would be disqualified under the prospective Reich Health Bill of the planned 'community alien law.' "[15] She adds that "a totalitarian movement seizes power in much the same sense as a foreign conqueror may occupy a country he governs not for its own sake but for the benefit of something or somebody else. The Nazis behaved like foreign conquerors in Germany when, against all national interests, they tried and half succeeded in converting their defeat into a final catastrophe for the whole German people; similarly in victory, they intended to extend their extermination politics into the ranks of 'racially unfit' Germans."[16] But it is not only totalitarian dictators who "occupy" their own countries; authoritarian dictators behave the same way.

Authoritarian regimes permit more "freedom" than totalitarian states in two major areas: they give a free hand to business interests (which is why they are acceptable to the United States) and they allow emigration. But they lack even the semblance of concern for social justice and equality that does exist in many socialist totalitarian states. They have no concern whatever about the poor, the homeless, the starving, those whose land has been appropriated; indeed, when the poor organize co-ops to try to improve their ability to deal with large corporations, they are often murdered.[17]

Democratic regimes are qualitatively different from either authoritarian or totalitarian regimes. They allow for a relatively wide participation in political process and material goods, and thus they tend to be stable. They claim concern for social justice and a sharing of the national wealth and make some efforts to realize that claim. The ideal in most democratic states, certainly in the United States, is purely material—"the good life" means increased wealth and comfort for a fairly large percentage of the population although that entails almost total dispossession for the rest. Dissidence is permitted as long as it remains limited to a small percentage of the people—thus scholarly books on Marxism or feminism can be published, small groups are permitted to meet even when their interest is in radical change, and a wide range of opinion may be disseminated. Only when a group desiring radical change becomes large does the government show its true colors. The Black Panthers were almost completely wiped out within a few years of their establishment; the antiwar movement of the 1960s and 1970s was accused of treason by government officials, and tear gas and bullets were used on student protesters. In the latter case the government drew back from the sternest measures against the children of the middle class. There was a measure of accountability to the people.

Yet democratic regimes are, like authoritarian and totalitarian states, dedicated to power above all: power vis-à-vis other nations, power over their own populations, and power over nature. Power lies in the hands of a small elite class of men who, as in socialist states, are nearly invisible to the populace. And what drives these men is the maintenance and extension of their own power.

Without denying that democratic states permit citizens a wider range of action than authoritarian or totalitarian states, we must also be aware that the actual degree of autonomy is far smaller than it appears. The right to choose between two or more candidates in an election has less meaning than it might if monied interests did not control all major parties. The right to start one's own business—to engage in free enterprise—is an empty right if a small business cannot compete with large businesses which have the advantage of size and resources, as well as government connections that produce favorable legislation, loans, and subsidies. The right to choose among a variety of newspapers, magazines, and television channels means less than it might if almost all of them did not avoid taking strong positions on most issues, and stand as if embattled a few

inches to the right or left of center in a culture in which center means patriarchy, capitalism, and domination.

Indeed, in the United States, right and left are blurred. That is, both conservative and liberal administrations adopt policies that contradict their basic
philosophies. For example, the conservative Reagan Administration has
claimed to favor diminished centralization of the federal government and an
increase in states' rights. Yet the Reagan Administration firmly supported federal regulation in three important matters—the right of states to legislate
against banks and money-lending institutions, the right of states to legislate
standards for the building of nuclear plants, and the right of states to regulate
corporate take-overs. In all three areas, a conservative administration favored
the interests of big business over their own alleged interests.[18] Reagan also
called for a radical increase in his control of the budget and for extended CIA
activity inside the country—with less congressional surveillance; both would
increase centralized power.[19] Liberals who wish to protect the rights of certain
individuals—women or members of minority groups, say—call for federal control of state institutions; but federal control leads inevitably to bureaucracy, in
which there is no room for individuals. Conservatives who wish to abrogate
certain federal controls, especially over business, and return to a more laissez
faire attitude, also support the enforcing of a narrow sexual standard.

Such contradictions between announced policy and actual behavior are
not really due to hypocrisy. They are caused by blindness. Certainly people on
either side of the political center have certain ideals, imagined ways of being,
that they would like to realize. But both sides can see only one way to realize
them—through increased control, which inevitably means greater centralization of power. Any other approach seems fanciful, risky, dangerous, to the
minds of people who do not recognize their own worship of power as a worship
of a false and destructive ideal.

This blindness to any value other than power is not limited to the United
States. The tendency in all of the West and much of the East in the past few
decades has been toward increasing diminishment of autonomy in individuals,
localities, states, and nations; toward increased centralization of power—greater
power over a wider scope of activities, held by a smaller central cadre. This is
one of the elements shared by democratic, authoritarian, and totalitarian states.

Frithjof Bergmann writes that history is the story of a gradual increase of
ever more centralized control over larger territories.[20] Centralization of power is
a primary requirement for any tyrannical form of government, whether of nations or of institutions. Yet it is also true that centralization (to some degree)
increases efficiency; that by creating uniform practices it can simplify life by
preventing the confusion that results from confronting a host of different regulations in each new area one enters. In some cases, centralization contributes to
social justice. Despite a civil war and several constitutional amendments, only
government intervention in voting regulations finally gave black Americans a
voice at the polls, one which they are using effectively at local levels.

The tendency of Western culture for hundreds of years has been toward
centralization for good and ill. Ivan Illich, for instance, persuasively demon-

strates that adoption of a standardized national tongue is the first step in gaining control over a nation.[21] A standard orthography, free compulsory education, and a standard curriculum all seem at first glance improvements because they simplify communication or encourage the spread of literacy and learning. It is argued that we will understand each other better if we all spell the same way, if we can all read, write, and figure; and that we will understand each other's allusions if we have all read the same hundred great books. But such "improvements" endow an elite caste with great power, since it selects the "great books," determines the curriculum, and sets the standards of instruction. Selection of what constitutes legitimate knowledge in a culture has never been nor can it ever be free from political bias.

Centralization always means rule by an elite class, and the greater the centralization, the smaller (proportionately) and tighter that class will be. Yet there is no guarantee that greater personal freedom and more social justice exist in relatively uncentralized domains. For example, there are pockets within the Soviet Union that are less in the control of central government because they are geographically isolated and difficult of access, and because they have strong traditions of their own and resist being impressed under socialist rules. However, these pockets are mainly Islamic, and severely oppressive of women.

Centralization, then, is ambiguous; it is not inherently an ill or automatically a good, although it has been treated as an absolute good by most progressive institutions in past decades. It is a quality which must be weighed in a balance, seen as part of a larger context. We must ask what it will offer, and what it will cost. It has been accepted as a good mainly because it seems to offer greater control over people, and when this is the case, the long-term costs—a pervasive sense of impotence, refusal to accept responsibility, general indifference, and malaise—outweigh the questionable benefits of "control." And it is rejected as a good reactively, by people so overwhelmed by its bad effects that they are blinded to its occasional usefulness.

Centralization is assisted by industrialization, and some degree of industrialization seems to be necessary in creating totalitarian control. This is partly because industrialization forces masses of people into isolated servitude—it breaks the bonds among people, between people and land, people and tradition—and creates a vacuum into which a totalitarian government can step as the single moral, political, and intellectual guide.

There are totalitarian and authoritarian states that are not highly industrialized—Cambodia under Pol Pot, Vietnam, and Cuba; the Philippines, Chile, and Uganda under Idi Amin, for instance—but these dictatorships could not have been imposed without sophisticated communications equipment, techniques of surveillance, advanced methods of transport, and weapons capable of inflicting multiple deaths at a blow—all of which, obviously, allow the few more easily to rule the many. Moreover, such regimes are not at all stable (some have already collapsed); they encounter the kind of resistance that comes from people with living traditions and customs, and they find it necessary to use a considerable amount of terror.

The third shared element is a fully developed secret police, something that exists in every major nation. Foucault claims the police were invented in Louis XV's France—the late eighteenth century.[22] There were, of course, sheriffs and constables long before that. Surveillance in some form is as old as patriarchy, although in ancient times it was performed by the family itself, with wives, children, and servants reporting to the father on each other and on slaves. Stone discusses the effort of institutions to strengthen the power of the father in sixteenth-century England because he could require that younger family members be kept under close scrutiny. "In a society almost entirely without a police force, it [the family] was a most valuable institution for social control at the village level."[23] A similar system operates at the village and commune level in China today.[24]

But police as an institutionalized body exist to uphold the written law; as states have been forced by social pressure to adopt an appearance of democratic legality, they have increasingly developed a body of unwritten law. It is to enforce this that secret police were created. Unwritten law guards the power of the elite—who are not fully visible either—in democratic or totalitarian regimes. It is indefensible *as law* in nations supposedly committed to justice and equality, since it curtails citizens' rights of speech, press, and association. Unwritten law in totalitarian regimes concerns itself with what citizens say and read and write, with whom they talk, what they wear, their hair styles, manners, and sexual habits. Democratic governments do not scrutinize such things among the general public (although they do with government employees), but leave the surveillance to institutions. Businesses, academia, churches, unions, all keep an eye on their members' behavior. Although they are independent—unlike their counterparts in totalitarian states, they are not directly under state control—they share the concerns and standards of the government. Nor do democratic governments go quite so far in their tacit requirements. They do not automatically suspect those who speak to foreigners, do not oversee most people's reading material or mail, and sometimes tolerate unorthodox life styles. Indeed, it is only recently that democratic states began to use their secret agents to police their own citizenry.

The secret police in authoritarian states are used as much to terrorize the citizenry as to enforce unwritten law; this is true also in totalitarian nations. Michael Curtis points out that all nondemocratic regimes impose political controls over expression, use secret police widely, and incarcerate political prisoners, but not all are equally terror-ridden. The difference, he believes, lies in the personality of the dictator: when the ruler is paranoiac, the regime will be terror-ridden.[25] This possibility exists in institutions as well as states. As I suggested earlier, there is no *inherent* difference in patriarchal institutions; differences emerge from the character of their personnel and their functions rather than from articulable criteria of legitimacy or illegitimacy, morality or immorality. Generally, however, the more power is centralized in one man, the more fear he will feel, and the more likely he is to behave paranoiacally.

Secret police are one part of a secret government, something that exists in all totalitarian and authoritarian states and most democratic ones. But a secret set of laws also exists in totalitarian regimes. Arendt discusses duplication of structures as a mark of totalitarianism.[26] She refers primarily to Nazi Germany: Hitler, you will recall, was *elected* to office, he did not seize power. The Weimar Constitution was still in force in Germany. Hitler left the constitution in place and at first operated through it, using existing agencies and departments. But gradually he found these methods unsatisfactory, and created Nazi Party agencies that duplicated the functions of the Weimar bureaus; the old bureaus remained, giving an appearance of normalcy, but had no power. The real power, centered in Hitler himself and the SS, was disseminated by the party bureaus. A similar situation occurred after the Bolshevik take-over in the Soviet Union; the original revolutionary constitution was left undisturbed and the government bureaucracy functioned on the surface, while more and more power devolved to Communist Party agencies. Arendt calls this "invisible government."[27]

Invisible government can take another form, however, when a ruler ignores or weakens governing agencies created to regulate or guarantee activities decreed by law. We have seen a number of examples of such weakening in recent years. Civil rights matters were ignored because the Justice Department under the Reagan Administration reinterpreted statutes requiring integration and equality of opportunity; the Equal Employment Opportunity Commission and other civil rights guardians were allowed to languish, receiving minimal funding and being subject to delay in appointments. Under Reagan too, the Environmental Protection Agency was gutted. Personnel dedicated to environmental improvement were removed and replaced with people loyal to and under the influence of an antienvironmentalist, the beer tycoon Adolph Coors, as well as other businessmen of similar inclination. The actual function of the agency, to control pollution by demanding cleanups and enforcing pollution laws, was subverted by a staff loyal to the polluters. Similar suggestions were made about the Department of the Interior when James Watt headed it. Such manipulations could not occur without the approval of the President. They constitute an invisible law, for they permit a change in what is done in the country without any necessity for changing the nation's laws.

Monopolistic control over mass communications can also be disguised in nontotalitarian societies, where there seem to be many different centers of communication but all offer essentially the same moral vision. To allow only one approach to life to be published or otherwise disseminated is censorship, and censorship exists even in democratic countries.

Many organs practice censorship: newspapers, magazines, learned journals, publishers, radio and television networks, film makers, all select material they will disseminate, and reject material that does not fit into their usual approach. This form of censorship is unavoidable, but it is more widespread in some countries than in others. Although it is probable that in every nation there are particular subjects that are ignored or dismissed, countries that are less involved in a serious power struggle within or without the state are more likely to tolerate dissemination of a wide range of opinions, opinions that are radically different from each other. The Scandinavian countries, the United Kingdom, the Netherlands and Belgium, for instance, permit respectful treatment of subjects like Marxism and, to some degree, feminism, on their mass media, even though in some of these countries television is state controlled.

Totalitarian and authoritarian states keep firm control of all media of communication: it is illegal even to own a mimeograph machine in the Soviet Union, Poland, and other socialist countries. Censorship is open, admitted; it is recognized by the populace, who learn to read signs and silences and to probe between the lines to find truth. But democratic states that claim to permit freedom in communication can nevertheless influence what appears in mass media. There are ties between government and news magazines, government and newspapers. Business interests to a large degree control television and radio. And the tendency in the United States in recent years has been toward the dissolution of small independent organs, especially newspapers, and the assimilation of newspaper, magazine, and book publishers by conglomerates which derive their major profits from such industries as steel, oil, and telephone equipment. The influence of their control is to warn communications media away from anything that might be disturbing, and toward a bland, best-of-all-possible-worlds point of view. Although people have a wide range of reading and viewing material to choose from, the majority of it offers the same kinds of distraction—fads and fashions, surface glitter—or tranquilization: all problems are solvable, no serious injustice or evil is permitted to continue.

The last outpost of real intellectual freedom in the United States is the book-publishing business, which still occasionally offers readers approaches and opinions that vary radically from mass-media pap. Small literary and learned journals also sometimes offer new and different ideas. The class that controls America is not seriously bothered by this—as yet—probably because such a small proportion of Americans read such material.

A similar situation exists in the economic sphere. Government does not dictatorially control economic institutions in democratic and authoritarian states as it does in totalitarian states. But, as with Franco and the Catholic Church, it does not have to. Indeed, the situation is almost the reverse—large economic interests have considerable control over government, and intermesh with it.

Political theorists emphasize the monolithic structure of totalitarian regimes, which have control over all aspects of political, social, economic, and cultural life, and admit of no limits to governmental interference, no political opposition, no independent organization.[28] The state controls not only all organizations but the very means of organization.[29] Such arrangements often involve a dictator to whom absolute loyalty is required. Neither Hitler nor Stalin, for instance, used his cabinet much; both had a personal coterie of faithful lieutenants whose professional and technical skill or proficiency was less important than their loyalty.[30] Personal loyalty is the major requirement today of certain African dictators.[31] But loyalty is also a major requirement of rulers in democratic nations, especially in the United States.

Two- or multiple-party systems are supposed to guard against the excesses of authoritarian and totalitarian regimes, and to some degree they do. But the suspicion of many people that the actual governing of democratic nations is

performed by an invisible group of people who remain essentially the same
from one administration to another is not mere paranoia. The "invisible hand"
that is imagined to guide economic matters to a realistic path does not exist;
but invisible government does. Thus in the United States Barry Goldwater
campaigned for the presidency in 1964 on a platform that advocated intensifi-
cation of the war in Vietnam, and was defeated at least partly on that ground;
but Lyndon Johnson, who defeated him, proceeded to adopt precisely such a
policy. François Mitterand campaigned in France on a platform opposed to nuclear power, yet a few months after he became president he was approving its
use. The pressures that coerce leaders to take positions they themselves have
renounced come from behind-the-scenes groups of powerful interests, groups
that are not elected and therefore are not responsible to the public, and that
pursue their own interests single-mindedly.

In the United States, legislation that has been shown many times to be
desired by a majority of the population does not get passed because of the
opposition of a powerful lobby or invisible pressure group: gun control is
one example; another is the lamented Equal Rights Amendment. Environmental controls on pollution are supported by an overwhelming majority of
the population, yet conservative administrations have actively worked against
them.

Again I must emphasize that there are important differences in the quality
of life in a democratic state compared with that in an authoritarian or totalitarian state. What I am talking about is tyranny, regardless of the name we give it,
and tyranny means directing the course of a society so as to heighten the real or
apparent power of one man or group of men, without regard for the needs and
well-being of the society as a whole. The antinuclear movement, one of the
most profoundly grassroots movements of our time, has been labeled subversive
in the United States and elsewhere, and certainly would be in totalitarian states
if it were allowed to flourish there. What is called subversive is whatever opposes the rule of the faceless, nameless elite of our time. If tyranny has been the
true name of government in most places at most times in the history of the
world, and if tyranny has been responsible for the demise of culture after culture, never before has tyranny coupled with the shortsightedness that is its
major characteristic (for it is concerned above all and often only with maintaining its own power) threatened the continued existence of the entire planet, its
fruits and vegetables and insects and animals and trees and mountains and
lakes and air and clouds, as well as all people. The traditional ways of dealing
with tyranny have been for people who understand and can function in its
terms to use it for their own purposes, and for others to find a corner of the
earth they can make secure, only bowing to the tyrant as he passes. This latter
response is deeply ingrained in us, and we continue to seek that refuge, even
though the present situation does not admit of secure corners of earth.

The characteristics that tilt a tyrannical form of government (of whatever
degree) into the full constriction we call totalitarianism are two: profound interference with human sex, breeding, and family life; and an impulse toward
"purification."

Purification is a movement to eliminate not just those who oppose a regime, or who might possibly rise against it, but those whom the regime declares impediments to the realization of its vision. These impediments are always "feminine," and the condemned are always assigned the taint and pollution attributed to body, feeling, and fluidity by the patriarchal mind. They are considered contaminated with bestiality, with "degeneracy," or with lack of absolute unwavering obedience. The drive to purification is a symbolic attempt to exorcise elements disdained and feared by the dominant cultural morality.

Purification is different from terror, although the two overlap. Hitler consciously used terror as an instrument of control to silence the population and smother dissent. His example has been followed by countless regimes since—in the Soviet Union, Cambodia, Argentina, Chile, Haiti, South Africa, and El Salvador, among others. Swift, unjustified, capricious murder, arrest, torture, disappearance can reduce a population to submission (although it cannot, ever, eliminate entirely the rage that will some day rise). Enslavement or colonization can provide seemingly cheap labor (cheap if one does not consider all its costs), profit in the short term for a few.

But purification is another matter. It is aimed at a particular group of people; it is transcendent, and likely to be talked about in the highest, noblest patriarchal terms; it is seen as an act of vengeance (god-style) or cleansing (priest-style) that will leave the remainder of the population free from the taint of deviation. Purification lies in a direct line with other basic premises of patriarchy: by eliminating from humankind despised elements connected with nature, men imagine they can turn humans into gods.

To those not caught up in the fiction, the mythology, purification movements seem insane: unfortunately, millions do get caught up in the mythology. There was little international protest at the treatment of Jews by the Nazis, who maintained they were "purifying" Europe, and claimed the Jews were being "purified" by work—as if they had not worked before. Even in the face of their treatment in the camps, the world did not rise in horror. Few people remember, although it did not happen that long ago, that the most terrible massacres in history occurred in Africa.[32] The Boers massacred Hottentot society, Carl Peters murdered wildly in German East Africa, and Leopold II of Belgium reduced the peaceful Congo population of twenty to forty million to eight and a half million between 1890 and 1911.[33] Many thousands more were mutilated in this move to free white Europeans of "black" qualities. The effort was supremely successful: the Congo is no longer noted for its peaceful population—it has been "civilized," Westernized.

But purification movements are no more insane than other parts of patriarchal ideology: they are of a piece with it, one more symbolic element designed to create the appearance of a man who controls the world and his fate. Jews, blacks, and women have been its victims for millennia; other minority groups occasionally fall into a scorned category, although when these same groups are a majority, they persecute others. *All despised groups practice the same kinds of symbolic moral stratification,* within their own groups and on alien groups. All groups suppress women on grounds of men's moral superiority and contempt for the "feminine"; and the line between suppression and extermination is not as clear as we believe it to be. All that was necessary to shift the European tendency toward suppression of Jews (which involved prejudicial laws and customs, double standards of behavior and punishment, and isolation) into extermination was technological instrumentation—more powerful weapons, transport, and communications devices like radio, telephones, and telegraph—plus the will. The will to eliminate despised groups is stronger when a population is pervaded with a sense of self-hatred and impressed with a notion of a "higher" way of being—with the repression consequent to these—and provided with an avenue of "proving" (giving an appearance of) its transcendence. But almost every population is so indoctrinated. Given the right leader and the right message, what nation could not be swayed to extermination of a group in its midst?

Public interference in personal sexual and family arrangements is, like censorship, unavoidable. In simple societies, sexual and family matters are dictated by custom and religious beliefs that have arisen over decades (or longer) as solutions to practical or symbolic problems. These arrangements can be as oppressive and misery-producing as any in more sophisticated cultures. The difference between the two kinds is that the people of simple societies *believe* in the necessity of their arrangement. This does not make their customs less unhappy, but it does make them feel less oppressive.

Neither the Church nor the state was able, through several millennia, to alter profoundly the sexual and domestic arrangements of those in power—men of property. It was this elite group of men who imposed oppressive constraints on their women; and the constraints could be enforced because of pervasive surveillance of women. But all totalitarian forms have set out at first to gain control of the sexual life of the community, men as well as women—"Reich and Marcuse and Fromm all observed that authoritarian and militaristic regimes always base themselves on severe sexual repression."[34]

Although many thinkers associate sexual repression, along with awesome authority, strict discipline, and the power of the father, with strong, healthy cultures, these characteristics may in fact be signs of decline. John Boswell points to the changes that preceded the fall of Rome: increasing centralization of political power, a tendency toward absolutism, increased dependency of people on the state, the extension of government control into minor personal aspects of people's lives, and an emphasis on self-denial and repression in sexual matters.[35]

The Catholic Church established itself by extending, not diminishing these tendencies, especially the last two: "At bottom, only a single point was dealt with, abstinence from sexual relationships," wrote Adolf von Harnack. Every other regimen was secondary because "he who had renounced these found nothing hard." An extraordinary unanimity prevailed as to the meaning of sin, "whether we turn to the Coptic porter, or the learned Greek teacher, to the Bishop of Hippo, or Jerome the Roman presbyter, or the biographer of Saint Martin. Virginity was the specifically Christian virtue, and the essence of all virtues."[36] Protestantism did not place the same emphasis on virginity, but it strictly regulated sexuality, and because it eliminated Catholic confession/penance/forgiveness, it made unsacramentalized sex even more guilt inducing.

One of the first steps taken in establishing a totalitarian regime is regulation of sexuality and family arrangements. The exclusion of women from the work force may not seem to be an element in the regulation of sexuality, but it is: enforced dependence of women on men affects sexual relations between them. Pressure or coercion to marry and produce children is usually exerted more on women than men, but Athens and Rome, at various periods in their histories, extended such pressures to men as well. Hitler and the Bolsheviks both pronounced upon these matters; Stalin rescinded most of the freedoms earlier granted women. Ironically, even as Hitler was selectively murdering and sterilizing German women, he was urging them to have babies; so too Stalin, urging a repopulation of Russia after World War II, was imprisoning and killing millions in his purges.

This contradiction lies only on the surface. Although both Hitler and Stalin doubtless really desired the birth of more baby boys who could grow up into soldiers (as did Augustus, at the beginning of the Christian Era), this desire coexisted with a drive to "purify" the population. The basic ground of purification is nature, the "animal"; and sex is the major area of nature that humans have seized upon as symbolic. Regulation of sex equals regulation of nature, which is tantamount to control over nature. It is not necessary to forbid sexuality in order to control it. What must be precluded is freedom, for sexual freedom leads to mutuality, affection, and satisfaction, all of which threaten repressiveness. Mutuality means that men are as moved and bonded to women as women are to them; they thus come under feminine influence. Regulation of sex usually places the onus of blame and responsibility upon women. Women's consequent fear and reluctance about sexuality make them less willing partners; men's lesser fear makes them more aggressive partners. Sex is "masculinized": rape or possession are nonmutual forms of sex; they reinforce masculine control, transform a mutual experience into a conquering, and imply a lack of feminine influence over the male. (In fact, that influence can be felt regardless of the form. But it is not admitted to.) Hitler's arrangements institutionalized "masculine" sex. Any movement to prevent women from exercising freedom in the sexual area—forbidding of contraceptives, abortion, or unwed motherhood; requiring women to marry or procreate; or arranging society in such a way that a woman cannot support herself and raise her children at the same time: all operate to transform sex as mutuality into sex as a power relation.

All Western nations and many in the East promulgate codes and arrangements that foster such a vision of sex. Under the rubric of coercing a "wholesome moral code," they insert their values into the deepest part of the human psyche. It is less the content of the message than the control inherent in it that must be registered. In China, for instance, the government discourages sexuality, early marriage, and childbearing, and penalizes the couple who disobey: but in actuality the woman is made to suffer more for disobedience or for producing a baby of the "wrong" sex.

One element that functions both to denigrate sex and to "purify" is propa-

ganda urging a particular sort of "manliness" and emphasizing aggressive sports
and activities, male solidarity, and, often, racial divisiveness. Lears discusses the
campaign waged in the United States in the early twentieth century by Theodore Roosevelt, Henry Cabot Lodge, and others who were terrified by the influx
of Latin and Slavic immmigrants, by the rise of the urions and socialist ideas,
all of which were seen as threats to capitalism. They thus proposed eugenic
codes involving sterilization of certain groups and propagation by Nordic white
groups, and held up an ideal of "manliness," (white) racial solidarity, and a
warrior ethic.[37] America was threatened, they said, by "effeminacy" and decadence.

Hitler haloed a mythic past of German *Volk* and *Bruderschaft*, male solidarity, militarism, aggressiveness, and violence to oppose the "effeminate" and
decadent (read: Jewish) currents in German society. But as we have seen, similar if less extreme associations exist in many cultures, even in little Spanish
towns. They are part of the fabric of our thought and have been for millennia.
Yet any clear-eyed examination could reveal the falseness of the associations,
and the destructiveness of the method used to combat an invented "enemy."

Arendt discusses the "Great Game," the use of groups or nations of people as "pawns or stepping stones to riches and rule in an unending process of
power expansion and accumulation," and Kipling's dictum in *Kim*, "When everyone is dead the Great Game is finished. Not before."[38] To see life as a
"Great Game," however, is to deny that life has any meaning or purpose of its
own and to say it must be given one by man's imagination. Games are invented: spaces are artificially divided, rules devised, winning and losing defined.
None of what occurs in a game has any significance or relevance to the experience of living unless playing the game brings pleasure. What patriarchy has
done is turn many parts of life into games which interlock with each other (just
as gambling, say, interlocks with certain sports) and declared *winners* those who
achieve great wealth and/or power.

Yet beneath this artifice, patriarchy is essentially religious, that is, it has its
eye on another world. Patriarchy is symbolic and imaginative, driven to transcend mere humanness through some sort of control deemed divine. The drive
to wealth and power is undertaken less for the sake of the wealth (how much
does one need to live in felicity?) and the power (for power is oppressive, a burden) than for their symbolic significance; a man of wealth or power is considered a "great" man, a man who has transcended, a man who has achieved
control that all the world can see.

Arendt believed that "the totalitarian form of government has very little to
do with lust for power or even the desire for a power-generating machine, with
the game of power for power's sake which has been characteristic of the last
stages of imperialist rule."[39] She distinguishes between patriarchal "contempt
for factuality," which contains the "proud assumption of human mastery over
the world," and totalitarian desire to "transform human nature itself."[40] But
what more ambitious aim can men have? What degree of power is necessary to
transform human nature?

Totalitarianism is a natural outgrowth of the "masculinizing" tendencies of the past three centuries, but its roots are set in patriarchal soil. Two millennia ago, Christianity attempted to build a religion that would transform human nature, or at least "redeem" a humanity seen as depraved, tainted at birth by original sin. To its own not dissimilar message modern totalitarianism can add industrialization and technology that make possible central control over huge populations in diverse and minute details of their lives.

Those of us who live in democratic states may feel complacent at our good fortune. But there is little to protect any industrial society against sliding into totalitarianism. Even nonindustrial nations can become totalitarian, if they contain an elite with strong faith in control and in possession of weapons, transport, and communications systems devised by modern technology. Pluralistic forms guard us only against visible, serious abuses of government; indeed, Marcuse insisted that contemporary industrial society is on the whole totalitarian despite pluralistic forms.[41] Totalitarian control—that is, control over every manifestation of collective life, which involves interference with private life as well, may well be "an artifact of modern life."[42]

What is most threatening in the modern world is the unending pursuit of power in the form of wealth (which leads to poisoning of the environment, impoverishment of entire nations, and exploitation of the majority of every nation) and might (which is leading to nuclear war). In the face of these threats, other constrictions seem minor; yet it is precisely the minor constrictions that carry the larger message; it is the values we are taught from every organ of our culture that make it possible for a small group of men to poison our wells and threaten our planet without a huge outcry from populations across the world. It is therefore important to examine the ways in which our institutions perpetuate the patriarchal morality, and press us on toward Armageddon, the end of the Great Game and everything else. It is most important of all that we realize the ways in which we ourselves contribute to this tendency, even we, the pillars of society.

## 2. PILLARS OF SOCIETY I: THE HELPING PROFESSIONS

In a remarkable series of books, Michel Foucault has demonstrated that areas of intellectual discipline—fields of discourse—are not just structures of thought, but structures of power. "Images of madness, theories of pedagogy, definitions of sexuality, medical routines, military disciplines, literary styles, research methods, views of language, or procedures for the organization of work": all are conceptual systems defining the pattern of domination of a given period.[43]

What is included and what excluded in a field is as important as the way the field is organized; and although the relation between those who organize a system and those who find themselves trapped in others' categories may seem to be one of dominator and dominated, mind and matter, in fact everyone in a given culture is formed and dominated by the values underlying the structures.

Let us examine several disciplines and try to point to what underlies their structure.

## Medicine

The practice of medicine seems to be an expression of compassion and love, of a desire to alleviate pain and to heal—and most practitioners have probably held such a vision of the discipline at some time. But whatever their personal visions, these feelings have little place in the modern practice of medicine in Western industrial society. Critics of contemporary medical procedures focus not only on the way medicine is practiced but also on how medical care, health, and illness are defined: in general, medicine is seen as primarily curative rather than preventive, and as a commodity—something for which one pays, largely unavailable to those unable to pay; sickness is defined as a condition preventing one from carrying out normal activities. People suffering from depression, anxiety, migraine, insomnia, or chronic indigestion, who can nevertheless perform their given work, are not considered really ill.[44] Health is defined as "fitness" rather than as well-being. To put it another way, medicine is seen as a response to incapacitating illness, and focuses on sickness, not on health.

Most people do not conceive of medicine as an instrument of social control and a disseminator of patriarchal values. Yet it is both, and has been since its first institutionalization. Before institutionalization, healers were organic parts of any community and, usually, the women in one's own family. They were not paid at all, or, if they were not family members, they were perhaps repaid with a gift of food or handiwork.

The professionalization of medicine changed it into a commodity, something offered for money. In addition, it became exclusive, as women (and often Jews) were barred from medical study and licenses. The practice of medicine in this period was crude, indeed murderous; some of its "cures" were horrifying.[45] Local healers probably did far less damage with their herbal brews. But doctors of this early period did consider the whole patient, diagnosing their disease in accordance with their astrological chart and their "humour," or personality type.

After the seventeenth century, however, the mechanistic view of the cosmos was applied to the human body, which came to be seen as a set of mechanical parts rather than an organically integrated system. The "scientific method" involved discovering and explaining patterns of events so as to predict them and thus control them. To control events is to have power over them. Understanding, which had been good in itself heretofore, now became an instrument of power. And the way doctors saw, interpreted, events was influenced by their value structure, their morality. They consequently saw women differently from men.

The mechanical approach to medicine was responsible for those aspects of medicine which have been successful in curing or preventing disease—vaccination, antisepsis, anesthesia, and antibiotics. If it fails with other aspects, that is partly because it has kept medicine inside the boundaries of a curative, individualistic, and interventionist task, in which patients are objectified.[46] In addition, medicine has acted as one of the many forces aimed at keeping women inside *their* boundaries.

The sparse diets and deforming apparel of women led to general fragility and ill health among middle- and upper-class women; by the late eighteenth century, frail health was associated with "the weaker sex."[47] By the nineteenth century it was generally believed that to be a woman was to be sick: the entire female procreative system, especially the uterus, was seen as a debility, and women were seen as mere extensions of their procreative systems. (Indeed, as late as the 1937 edition of Roget's Thesaurus, one set of synonyms for *weakness* centered on femaleness.) A New Haven professor announced in 1870 that it seemed "the Almighty, in creating the female sex, had taken the uterus and built up a woman around it."[48] Doctors considered the uterus "a highly perilous possession" that exerted a "paramount power" over women; it was magically potent but madly capricious, and caused women to be subject to twice the number of illnesses that affect men.[49]

In other words, female functions were seen as *inherently pathological:* Ehrenreich and English point out that this conception was "not advanced as an empirical observation, but as physiological fact." Menstruation and the lack of it were equally serious threats to life.[50] Puberty changed a girl entirely; she became tremulous, rosy, rounded (and titillating, although this word is never used); she also became "moody, depressed, petulant, capricious, and even sexually promiscuous," writes Carroll Smith-Rosenberg, who quotes a nineteenth-century physician describing puberty in men and women: in a man, it leads to the development of all parts of the body; "the principles of life superabound in his constitution, and he vigorously performs all the noble pursuits assigned him by nature. Women, on the contrary, delicate and tender, always preserve some of the infantile constitution."[51] Only a strict regimen could get a young woman safely through this difficult time, and the regimen advocated by physicians was a "routine of domestic tasks, such as bed-making, cooking, cleaning, and child-tending."[52]

Menopause was equally dangerous, and though the state was different, the cure was the same. Illness at this time of life would result from continuing to engage in sexual intercourse, too much gaiety and socializing, and refusing to give in to "old age." Menopausal women were supposed to retire in quiet dignity from life itself, dedicating their "old age" to the purposes and aims of others in the family. They were supposed especially to avoid any mental activity. The medical literature on menopausal women describes them in a hostile way, as if their very existence threatened the physicians. They are seen as physically repulsive, stupid, dull, and jealously piqued at being no longer young.[53]

If women's normal reproductive functioning was seen as sickness, all sickness in women was seen as a result of normal reproductive functioning. Diseases of the stomach, liver, kidneys, heart, and lungs were tied to the uterus; tuberculosis *in men* was blamed on environmental factors; in women it was considered a result of reproductive malfunction.[54] "One of the earliest uses of the developing field of gynecology was the overt social control of women through surgical removal of various of her sexual organs"—the clitoris, its fore-skin, or the ovaries. Operations like clitoridectomy were performed in England as early as 1858, to cure women's "mental disorders" such as "sexual desire or sexual behavior," things "deemed pathological in women." Circumcision (re-moval of the foreskin of the clitoris) was performed "on women of all ages to stop masturbation up until at least 1937." Paradoxically, the ovaries were very often removed as a cure for women who were too "masculine"—too assertive, aggressive, or unruly.[55] In France at the end of the nineteenth century, "great surgical operations are performed on girls, veritable tortures: cauterization of the clitoris with red-hot irons was, if not habitual, at least fairly frequent."[56] Al-though clitoridectomy was rarely performed in England, it was common in the United States from the 1860s on into the twentieth century, the last well-known case occurring in 1948 on a five-year-old girl, to keep her from mastur-bating.[57] After the 1940s lobotomies were used instead to keep women in line.[58] But the male desire to tinker with female reproduction continued as un-necessary hysterectomies were widely performed.

However, middle-class women in America in the nineteenth century did suffer from general ill health of a kind we might label "unhappiness." Head-aches, weakness, and depression might well be the response of women sub-jected by their husbands to callous or even brutal sex, expected to spend their lives in an unending round of tedious, laborious domestic tasks, precluded from most of the interesting and pleasant physical, mental, and sexual activities available to men. Some physicians were able to see women's illnesses as re-sponses to the tedium and lack of satisfaction of their lives, and attributed the high level of "insanity" of middle-class women to the monotony of their exis-tences, the "ennui, disgust, and misery" that led to "speedy or protracted sui-cide."[59] But these doctors considered women morally reprehensible as well as ill; the illness was a sign of women's moral depravity. They suffered from hys-teria (caused by the womb et al.), which changed a woman, made her irritable, indecisive, lacking in will power, morose, and jealous; such women were guarded and cunning, with a "deceitful and perverted consciousness." They ne-glected their proper duty and sometimes even committed "acts of a depraved and indecent nature."[60]

At the same time, it was held that involvement in worldly activities made women ill: "unfeminine" pursuits like intellectual exercise, sexual desire, and ambition to achieve were deemed to cause breakdown, and lack of submissive-ness and selflessness were symptoms of that breakdown. An argument fre-quently used against education for women was that it would lead to nervous collapse; on the other hand, so would reading "lascivious" books, or frequent "indulgence in sexual intercourse."[61]

Sexism was not the only form of social control to which medicine lent its halo of authority. At the same time that middle-class women were being diag-nosed as basically, fundamentally inadequate because of their sex, lower-class women were being diagnosed as poor mothers, responsible for their children's high mortality rates and incidence of disease. Government policies were de-signed to educate working-class mothers to look after their children better; doctors and other health-care workers asserted their superior knowledge and authority and laid down moral sanctions. Few people paid attention to the facts that these women had to work to survive, had to live in crowded unsanitary housing, received wages inadequate to subsistence, and starved themselves—with the result that they gave birth to undernourished babies suffering a gamut of complaints.[62] Illness, like poverty, was a sign of poor morals.

During the industrialization of the Western world the medical profession as a group has rarely protested about what industrialization does to people. It is frequently noted that industrialization has raised life expectancy. But this is a simplification and distortion of the truth. In the early years, industrialization caused a deterioration in the material welfare of most rural and all urban poor. In the years 1831–39, in Great Britain, the mortality rate in the country was 18.2 per thousand people; in the cities, 26.2 per thousand.[63] A different breakdown during roughly the same period showed that in Manchester the average age of death in the middle class was thirty-eight years, in the working class seventeen; in Liverpool the averages were thirty-five for the upper, fifteen for the lower classes.[64] One doctor wrote in 1832, "Not ten percent of the inhabitants of large towns enjoy full health."[65]

The health of the British working class in the early nineteenth century was so poor that it interfered with production. Because of that, not because of concerted protests by doctors, public health legislation was passed. It provided for a supply of clean water and for sewage disposal, with some slum clearance.[66] Unions were formed and demanded shorter working days, better working conditions, and better pay. With these two kinds of change the adult mortality rate began to fall: but not until the 1870s. And as it fell in the industrialized West, colonialization was creating similar, often worse conditions for Third World people.

Nor have doctors as a group protested dire working conditions that cause a variety of illnesses as well as industrial accidents; indeed, many doctors have sided with corporations in denying any responsibility for such problems. It is clear from every statistical survey that working-class people die earlier than middle-class people and that they suffer more ill health. In capitalist countries, the distribution of ill health follows the distribution of income.[67] In the United States, black and white neighborhoods contiguous to each other—as in the Boston area—show greatly different figures for both infant and adult mortality (see p. 366).

The medical establishment supported the dominant caste in suppressing women and justifying their suppression on "scientific" grounds. It has supported the exploitation of millions of people by keeping silence in the face of disease caused by malnutrition and unsanitary living conditions, dangerous working conditions, and the poisoning of the environment. It has also supported other forms of discriminatory behavior. In the United States, black slaves were considered diseased or morally depraved if they tried to rest or rebel. A famous Louisiana doctor, Samuel Cartwright, described a disease he called Drapetomania, a mental disorder found for some reason only in black slaves. Its primary symptom was a sulky and dissatisfied attitude; treatment consisted of questioning. If clear answers to the questions were not forthcoming, the disease was treated by whipping. Another disease, Dysaesthesia Aethiopica, led its victim to be careless and clumsy; when punished, or forcefully coerced to work, slaves suffering from this disease tended to ruin their tools or wreck the crops. Cartwright explained that such behavior was due to the "stupidness of mind and insensibility of the nerves induced by the disease."[68] He also "proved" scientifically that blacks lack red blood to the brain except when they are under the control of the white man.[69]

Nineteenth-century physicians "proved" the inferiority of Jews, blacks, and women through phrenology, the study of the bumps on the skull. They explained that larger brains mean greater intelligence, that larger brains require more room and the skull bulges a little to accommodate them: therefore brighter people have more bumps. When they discovered that their expectations were not supported by the evidence—white males did not have more bumps than others—they falsified their experiments and announced their assumptions as proven truth.[70] College psychology textbooks used up to the 1950s claimed there was a category of feeble-minded people who were breeding wildly and would soon ruin the entire human race with their defective genes.

The invention of feeble-mindedness permitted the development of the "science" of eugenics, fostered in the United States from 1904 on by the Carnegie Foundation. It began a drive to persuade or compel the "feeble-minded," most of whom were non-Nordic immigrants and blacks, to be sterilized. Feeble-mindedness was diagnosed through IQ tests administered *in English* to new arrivals at Ellis Island: among their results were the conclusions that 83 percent of Jews, 80 percent of Hungarians, 79 percent of Italians, and 87 percent of Russians seeking entry were feeble-minded. Legislators were convinced by these terrifying statistics, and "the United States became the first nation in modern times to enact and enforce laws providing for eugenic sterilization in the name of purifying the race."[71]

Eugenics was actually a legitimation of forced sterilization and birth control to "prevent the American people from being replaced by alien or Negro stock, whether it be by immigration or by overly high birth rates."[72] Over a period of about forty years, nearly 8,000 sterilizations were performed in North Carolina, five thousand on black women; between 1964 and the early 1970s, 65 percent of the women sterilized in North Carolina were black.[73]

Sterilizations could be performed by physicians at their personal inclination, but were supported by state and federal agencies. It is revealing that during a campaign exposing sterilization abuse, the Department of Health, Education, and Welfare issued a set of false figures claiming that in 1972 about 16,000 women and 8,000 men had been sterilized under federal auspices. Carl Schultz, former director of HEW's Population Affairs Office, later revealed that in 1972 alone somewhere between 100,000 and 200,000 people had been sterilized with federal funding. (Hitler managed to sterilize only 250,000 during his entire regime.) Not only blacks and immigrants but Native Americans and Hispanics have been the targets of sterilization campaigns. By the 1970s more than 35 percent of women of childbearing age on the island of Puerto Rico had been sterilized; by 1976, 24 percent of Native American women of childbearing age had been subjected to the same mutilation.[74]

Children have also been the objects of the ministrations of the medical establishment. It was clergymen and doctors who led a drastic campaign against childhood masturbation in the latter nineteenth century.[75] Remedies were scanty diet, little sleep, vigorous exercise, regular bowel movements including frequent enemas, cold showers, and indoctrination with intense guilt. Apart from inflicting physical and emotional misery on children, these attitudes and policies heightened the lure of sexuality. As Foucault has shown, the concentration on the sexuality of children by doctors, clergymen, and parents eroticized *for them* the very bodies they were attempting to control.[76]

Ronald Hayman has described the misery suffered by Nietzsche as a young boy living under a similar regimen in a boarding school.[77] In Nietzsche's youth, much of Germany was under the sway of the Dr. Spock of the period, Daniel Schreber (1801–61). Schreber's approach was quite different from Spock's, however. He taught that the will of children must be broken entirely from the moment of birth. A baby was not to be picked up and comforted when it cried, but rather to be punished corporally. He invented a set of devices to force a child to lie, sit, and walk straight. An iron crossbar pressed against the collar bones and shoulders prevented a child from leaning forward at table; a vertical bar attached to it prevented a child from crossing its legs; a belt with ring-shaped shoulder straps fastened to the child's bed and running across its body kept it from turning in sleep; a head holder prevented the child from turning its head sideways or allowing it to fall forward; a chin band held to the head by a helmetlike device ensured the "proper growth" of jaw and teeth.[78]

Schreber was almost apotheosized; Schreber Associations, societies for calisthenics, gardening, and fresh-air activities, had over two million members in Germany as late as 1958.[79] After his death he was praised for opposing the "degenerate decadence" of the age, and a 1936 biography lauded him as the spiritual precursor of Hitler.[80] Indeed, Schreber wanted his child-rearing system to have "macro-social effects"; he found his age "soft," decadent, and he urged governments to take children's training in hand seriously.[81] Schreber used his ideas and his machines on his own sons, both of whom went mad, one of whom committed suicide. The other wrote a memoir of his madness which Freud analyzed.

If some extremes of the past have been modified, the values of the medical establishment (if not of all doctors) remain the same. Manipulations are more sophisticated, and in a world of fragmentation, isolation, and disconnection, they do not stand out. But the medical establishment is no more effective in increasing human well-being today than it was a hundred or so years ago.

For the modern doctor, the causes of illness are primarily two: microorganisms commonly called germs or viruses; and inherent degenerative processes. It is claimed that because people now live longer than they did in the past, they are subject to a host of ailments found almost exclusively in advanced industrial nations: arteriosclerosis, diabetes, hypertension, cancer, chronic bronchitis, dental caries, duodenal ulcers, appendicitis, diverticulitis, and varicose veins.

These diseases are often "blamed" on their victims, whose diets, lack of exercise, and emotional stress—as well as smoking and drinking—are found responsible for causing them. But those diets, drinking, and smoking are parts of a commercial system, and are strongly urged by advertising without government interference. In England alone a million pounds a week are spent persuading people to smoke. The government does not interfere because what its National Health Service would gain from not having to treat as many heart and cancer patients would be more than offset by lost revenue from taxation and the need to pay old-age pensions to more people. Jobs would be lost, newspapers would lose advertisements, and sporting events would lose sponsors.[82] The unhealthful refined wheat and sugar products now being peddled in the Third World have long since won their markets in industrial nations.

Most serious of all is the fact that 80 percent of cancers are environmental in origin, and that doctors know this. Philippe Shubik of the United States National Cancer Advisory Board asserts that most cancers are caused by the environment and are therefore largely preventable.[83] Doctors should be insisting on cleanup of the air, water, and land to *prevent* the disease. But to do this would be to confront the profit structure of the country—industry—and government as well, to the degree that it is in league with industry. Instead of this; cancer patients are blamed for their own illness—as Susan Sontag has pointed out—and are subjected to the hideous torture of chemotherapy.[84] Meanwhile, government is as staunch as industry in denying its responsibility for leukemias and cancers that have flourished in areas where atomic testing occurred, where Agent Orange was used, where murderous gases and bacteria were accidentally or experimentally released.

Environment itself is our greatest killer, despite the spate of articles blaming people for their bad habits. People's bad habits do of course take a toll also; but companies do not cease to advertise cigarettes, drugs, and foods with little or no nutritional value. The pressure group in the United States which has the greatest power to affect governmental or corporate policy on these matters is the medical establishment. But it remains largely silent.

Although the nature of disease is different in Third World countries, its causes are rooted in the same values. It is suggested that overpopulation is the cause of Third World famine, but the major cause of famine is the agricultural and, before that, colonial policies of imperialist countries in Asia and Africa. Infectious diseases kill many Third World people, but these diseases are able to kill because half of the children in these countries are undernourished, and because imperialist policies ruined indigenous methods of disease control. These policies will be discussed in the next section, but for now it is necessary to point out that medical problems in nonindustrial countries are, like medical problems in industrial countries, to a large degree consequences of the policy of placing profit and power not just first but alone in one's value structure—a policy maintained by governments as well as industry.

It is, unfortunately, a policy followed by the medical establishment itself. Although many doctors are not caught up in the politics of the American Medical Association, or any establishment, their disconnection permits the medical establishment to continue unimpeded in its traditional ways. Even in Britain, which has a somewhat better medical system than this country, the system is dominated by an establishment which is committed to high-technology medicine, to bigger and better machines which grant status to inventor, users, and hospitals that possess them. Many of these machines are not worth what they cost.

For example, cardiac intensive-care units, so glamorized on television, require three times the equipment and five times the staff needed for normal patient care: *but they show no evidence of lower mortality*. Patients prefer to remain at home; the higher mortality of those given mechanical care in the hospital is ascribed to fright.[85] EMI body scanners are extremely expensive and confer status on owners and users, but they have only limited usefulness.[86] We export sophisticated technology to nonindustrial nations where, for a variety of reasons, they are of little use. People there die of diseases like cholera or dysentery while awaiting transport to a hospital; but these diseases could be treated locally with a simple sugar–fruit juice solution.[87] Ivan Illich cites figures showing that on the whole, the more expensive a treatment, the less its value in terms of life expectancy, especially for the terminally ill, whose dying is prolonged by early initiation of painful and expensive treatments.[88]

Doctors are taught to favor such an approach to medicine. The emphasis in medical schools is on specialization and the application of complex technological devices, by men who put no value on human relations or the relief of suffering.[89] In England, a medical report urging the placing of "people before buildings," and practical expressions of help for old and handicapped people, was labeled "sentimental" by an editorial in the *British Medical Journal*, which argued instead for the expansion of acute services like kidney dialysis and transplantation, increased use of EMI scanners, and *more acute intervention in obstetrics*.[90] Great publicity and huge amounts of money are given to high-technology experiments like an artificial heart connected to a compressor so heavy—375 pounds—that a person cannot move with it, and to high-technology experiments on heart replacements that have so far cost about two hundred million dollars, yet the United States ranks *sixteenth* in infant mortality, a form of death that is overwhelmingly caused by undernourished mothers living in unhealthy environments.[91] In some urban areas an extremely large number of children die before their first birthday—for example, in parts of Detroit thirty-three out of every thousand, in the Avalon Park section of Chicago fifty-five out of every thousand children die in their first year. About two-thirds of all infant deaths are associated with low birth weight, which in turn is connected with malnourished, impoverished mothers.[92] Among fifty-three countries reporting such data, the United States ranks twenty-third in death rates and sixteenth in life expectancy.[93]

A recent study designed to demonstrate the usefulness of autopsies inadvertently demonstrated something else—that one in four diagnoses were wrong at a major Boston hospital. New technology—ultrasound, radioactive tracers, and CAT scans—sometimes "contributed directly to a missed diagnosis."[94]

In the United States, the medical establishment is imitating big business and forming conglomerates devoted to the pursuit of profit. These medical conglomerates own chains of hospitals, nursing homes, kidney dialysis centers, diagnostic laboratories, pharmacies, medical office buildings, and small local surgical and emergency centers. These new medical corporations prefer not to serve the poor or those with high rates of illness, for neither group yields maximum profits. H. Jack Geiger comments that doctors first created cultural authority for medicine, and so increased demand; they then controlled supply by ending sectarian quarrels within the field (in religion this is called establishing dogma), restricting entry to medical schools, regulating licensing, and establishing their authority over medication as well.[95]

Pharmaceutical companies constitute one of the greatest affronts to the ideals of medicine ever known. Careless about testing, they sell "cures" that result in ruined lives—Thalidomide babies, for example. They operate with extremely high profit margins and exploit nonindustrial countries scandalously. They charge extremely high prices for medicines that are cheaper closer to home; they ship to nonindustrial countries drugs that have been declared dangerous in the industrial nations; and they send drugs that have little or no efficacy in local conditions for local diseases, with claims that they do. For example, the drug dipyrone is extremely risky—it kills one person out of every two hundred who take it. It is sold in the United States only for patients with terminal malignant disease whose fever cannot be reduced by other means. But it is sold over the counter in Brazil, with promises to alleviate a number of everyday complaints, from toothache to rheumatism.[96]

Ivan Illich discusses "iatrogenesis"—damage caused by the medical system itself—and defines three types: damage done by doctors in the course of treatment; the medically created adulation of doctors, seen as authoritative and all-knowing, which results in patients' addiction to medical care as a solution for all problems; and the destruction of patients' autonomy as a result of the structure of the medical relationship.[97] He describes medical techniques that are not just ineffective but downright harmful, and medical involvement in techniques designed primarily for social control, such as lobotomies and various forms of sedation, tranquilizers, and mood-altering drugs.

The application of these techniques of social control is based upon precisely the same value structure that has governed such application since medicine was professionalized. The first wave of lobotomies performed in the United States was aimed mainly at females—by two out of three. Fifty thousand people were lobotomized before 1964, with very little evidence that it helped and considerable evidence that it harmed them.[98] Doctors have developed new methods of mind control through the destruction of parts of the brain by ultrasonic waves, electric coagulation, and the implantation of radium seeds.[99] The elderly are sedated in institutions, to keep them quiet until they are quiet for good; "hyperactive" children are drugged to calm their behavior.[100] The use of psychosurgery and drugs is also urged for prisoners, who as we know are overwhelmingly from the poorest class.

In the United States at least, the poor, indeed, continue to be objects of little medical concern. They are humiliated in hospitals by being forced to wait hours for treatment, by being given perfunctory or even contemptuous care, and by being used as organic guinea pigs or teaching aids for medical students. The poor in rural areas may lack physicians entirely. And most important, death rates in poor areas remain much higher than those in well-to-do neighborhoods. That this is true in England, which has a National Health Service, as well as in the United States, strengthens the indictment of environment as the major cause of ill health—the poor cannot escape from poisoned environments. In 1973, black infant mortality rates in the United States were 26.2 per thousand as opposed to 15.8 for whites; black life expectancy was 65.9 years, white life expectancy 72.2. Such figures are even more striking if they are drawn from an urban area: the infant mortality rate in central Harlem in New York City is 49.5 per thousand; whereas the infant mortality rate in the more well-to-do and white areas of Kips Bay and Yorkville is 14.7 per thousand. Poor families in the United States suffer from disabling heart disease three times more often than middle-class families; and from visual impairment seven times as often. William Ryan writes, "Affluent white America is as healthy as Sweden. The health of the black poor American nation is comparable to such nations as Venezuela, Romania, and South Viet Nam."[101]

Women also suffer in special ways from medical treatment. The treatment of women in childbirth, an experience appropriated from women by doctors, and arranged for the comfort of the physician rather than the woman in labor, has been thoroughly treated by Adrienne Rich, among others.[102] Female patients are treated with less seriousness than men by male physicians; their complaints are frequently dismissed as "mental," and even then not referred for counseling, but silenced or smothered with psychoactive drugs—tranquilizers or mood elevators. Sixty-seven percent of such drugs prescribed in the United States are prescribed for women, and a third of all American women over thirty are given a prescription for a psychoactive drug each year.[103] The association between women and a vague malaise that can be "cured" by drugs is insisted upon by pharmaceutical companies, who show women *fifteen* times more than men in ads for mood-changing drugs.[104] In England, twice as many women as men receive prescriptions for mood-altering drugs.[105]

The male-dominated medical educational establishment does not even bother to keep abreast of new knowledge in some areas that affect women. It took a campaign led by a laywoman to bring physicians to question their automatic use of radical mastectomy in breast cancer. Although there is strong medical evidence that nausea during pregnancy, labor pains, and dysmenorrhea have physical causes, doctors continue to attribute them to the neurotic nature of women and girls who do not want to accept their "femininity."[106] Alfred Kinsey in 1953, and Johnson and Masters in 1966, presented scientific information on female sexuality that refuted both Freud's theory that mature women had vaginal orgasms and the tradition of female frigidity. Perhaps because this evidence did nothing to exalt the male penis, or even the male role in female sexuality, it has been almost completely ignored by medical textbooks. In a 1973 study of gynecological textbooks used from 1943 to 1972, Diane Scully and Pauline Bart found little trace of the work of either group of researchers. Two-thirds of the texts failed to discuss clitoral versus vaginal orgasm at all; eight continued to state that the male sex drive was stronger than the female; half claimed that procreation was the major function of sex for women. Two declared that most women are frigid, and one said that a third of all women are sexually unresponsive. Two continued to assert that vaginal orgasm was the only mature response in sex.[107]

The elitist stratifications of medical practice are reflected in the structure of medical institutions as well. They are dominated by white males. Although women have won the right to a medical education and licensing, they continue to suffer in medical school and afterward. Women remain a major source of humor and contempt in medical school lectures, where they are characterized as overemotional, incapable of rational or analytic thought, scheming, opportunistic, and, as patients, not worth the doctor's time and care.[108] In England, women are better medical students than men, qualify with honors more often, and more often have no failures in final exams. But once qualified, they less often gain higher degrees, and obtain fewer consultant and senior posts.[109] This is partly because British medicine continues to function as an old-boy network, and because women continue to be given primary responsibility for raising children—not cooperative but hierarchical responsibility—in a country that, like the United States, makes little provision for child care.

In America as well, women are less likely to be in the top reaches of the medical establishment, more likely to be doing community medicine—which may be a matter of choice—and less likely to be in the highest-paid specialties, like surgery. Women, on the other hand, make up the overwhelming majority of nurses, here and abroad, and the gap between nurses and doctors, in status and income, is enormous. The most exploited group in medicine is the ancillary workers, practical nurses and hospital workers, who in England are 75 percent women, and in the United States are largely women and male and female members of minority groups.[110] These people receive extremely low wages and have little status. The category of nurse-practitioner, long suggested, is on the whole opposed by doctors jealous of their prerogatives and eager to maintain a godlike authority within the hierarchy. Although nurse-practitioners would improve medical care for large numbers of people by working in poor rural areas with few doctors and by handling less serious cases in doctors' offices, thus reducing patients' waiting time, doctors' power is more important to them in this area (as in others) than the supposed true end of medicine—nourishment and healing of people. United States medical schools and the hospital structure are also racist, not just against blacks but against non-northern-European foreigners in general.

The emphasis here on women, children, and the Third World may suggest that white middle-class males are treated well within the medical establishment. But this is not true if they are patients. They are treated with more respect and concern than any other group, but that means little. Even doctors, hospitalized for the first time, find their treatment appalling. They, like the rest of us, are treated as people with no knowledge, children who must obey, objects, bodies, to be manipulated—and often they, like other patients, are given the wrong medication, and subjected to courses of treatment that are unnecessary or harmful. This incompetence is the most outrageous factor in the entire process. That the medical establishment is hierarchical, devoted to power, exclusive, and wealthy we might be able to accept if these qualities were necessary—as it is claimed they are necessary—to "maintain excellence." But medical care in the United States is mediocre at best and poor more often than the establishment cares to acknowledge. The medical profession has the right to set its own educational and professional standards, but it fails to maintain a standard of competence. Abuses of patients are "overwhelming," according to the New York State Commissioner of Health,[111] and the spate of malpractice suits is testimony to more than human greed. Although no human can be expected never to make a mistake, malpractice suits were not common against small-town doctors who maintained humane relations with their patients and showed concern for the whole person, the whole family, the whole community.

The qualities earlier named as tendencies in our time that can lead us to tyranny are found in the "benevolent" institution of medicine—increasing centralization, through medical corporations and through centering practices near large hospitals; and industrialization, through high-technology instruments and procedures. Although some doctors choose to practice in poor areas or Third World countries, doctors as a class are more devoted to their own power (wealth) and the political power of the medical institution than to the well-being of the population. To further their own profit and power, physicians have limited the spread of free dispensaries and prevented the development of public health centers. Their powerful lobby was able to prohibit public health programs from offering curative medical care and thus impinging on their private practices.[112] For this reason they do not as a group strongly oppose the sickening world being created by industry and government; they do not devise (they leave this to the politicians) ways of distributing better health care to the poor and the isolated. They do not share their knowledge with their patients, bringing the patient into the treatment process as an equal, as a person to be advised rather than a body to be manipulated. Fragmented in mind, they apply themselves to sickness as a problem to be solved, rather than to health as an ideal to be reached by everyone, wholly—in mind, body, and emotion.

Such a goal may seem idealistic: but consider the example of China, a nation with far less wealth and far fewer resources of communication, transportation, technological medical aids, and education than the United States. In only a few decades this nation, which had one of the poorest health systems in the world, has managed, according to an American physician, Roy E. Brown, to provide adequate medical care for all its citizens. It has reduced its rate of infectious diseases to equal that of Europe. Even in huge cities Chinese people can go to small, clean, pleasant local clinics where they are treated as friends; curative and preventive measures are seen as one and applied together. Dr. Brown writes that what China lacks—and this is its great advantage—is "an antiquated system of a hierarchy of health professionals."[113] Medical knowledge is inclusive, not exclusive; it is spread as widely as possible instead of being jealously clutched, like secret lore.

Illich suggests the participation of all people in their own health care, the spreading of medical knowledge as widely as possible. Thomas Szasz suggests a consumer bureau for evaluating medical knowledge and granting licenses.[114] Although both suggestions point in a desirable direction, they are insufficient. Technology may be overemphasized, but it is with us and is sometimes useful. The danger is that technical advances will serve to increase the control over our lives that the medical establishment already possesses. For example, new methods of birth control have given women more freedom in choosing the kinds of life they want. Doctors had little to do with the development of these new methods, but they—and through them the state—have taken control over their dispersement. Doctors and the state, in both capitalist and socialist countries, decide whether a woman may have contraceptive devices or abortion, and how she will give birth. Thus at the same time women's autonomy has increased, so has the capacity of others to control their lives.[115]

The future of medicine contains the possibility of huge powers. Present experimentation with genetic elements, among humans and animals, has gone much further than most of us are fully aware. The overwhelming majority of dairy cattle in this country, for instance, are produced through artificial insemination of a superior cow by the sperm of a superior bull and the replanting of this transcendent fetus in a quite ordinary cow mother.[116] One supposes that those performing these manipulations are sure just what constitutes a superior cow or bull; no doubt they give more or richer milk, or have a greater proportion of meat. It is not impossible that someone will suggest a similar process for humans.

Already the medical establishment has the power of genetic screening. Genetic screening permits the determination, before birth, of the sex and health of a fetus. It is an instrument of enormous potential power and can be used in racist, sexist, or other discriminatory ways.[117] Next there is DNA. It seems likely that the medical establishment will try to retain control over experiments with DNA and applications of their results; and in view of its record, we can also be sure that the medical establishment will be compliantly cooperative with the values of those who rule. Vicente Navarro claims that "the primary controllers and managers of medicine are not the professionals, but rather the controllers and managers of Capital."[118] This is true; but who are the controllers and managers of medicine in socialist states? If American physicians employed by government and corporations are willing to declare that black lung disease, for instance, is not a result of working in a textile mill or a mine, and Soviet psychiatrists are willing to declare insane someone who dissents, what is the difference between them? R. C. Lewontin writes that "there is no evidence that scientists are falsifying nature any less in the twentieth century than they did in the nineteenth."[119]

Decent medical care would begin at the root: the world we live in, the diet we eat, the noise we hear, air we breathe, water we drink, and use we make of body and mind. It would be available to all people easily. And such care would not require highly specialized technicians. They are required only in a small percentage of cases. Decent medical care would begin with values: the value of life and well-being would be primary, for people as individuals and for the community as a whole. It would not be staffed by people driven for power and wealth, would not be cowed by power and wealth, and would not treat those with power-wealth better than those without them.

What makes it practicable is the large number of physicians—we all know one, probably—who do concern themselves with their patients' overall well-being, and who oppose industrial and governmental actions that will undermine general health. But it is not enough that they exist individually: they must band together. Physicians have joined scientists in the move to ban further development of nuclear weapons; physicians support organizations dedicated to environmental cleansing. But the medical establishment does not. What is necessary is altering the values of those who run medical schools, medical corporations, and medical lobbies. Physicians themselves could do this.

## Psychology

Psychology is connected with medicine, and in the United States medical doctors control the psychological establishment. Both fields are founded on theories about what human beings are: medicine, as we saw, is still largely based on a mechanistic interpretation of life, in which people are made up of separate parts, which presumably can be treated without affecting the other parts. Medicine is concerned with how the human body functions. Psychology, however, is concerned with the functioning of the entire person—mind, emotion, and body—and a person's interactions with others. Whereas physicians can study the healthy functioning of a "normal" human body, psychology has no such model. To determine the "mental health" of a person is essentially to make a judgment about the nature of humanness itself.

Thus psychology is rooted in philosophy, in a vision of what humanity is or ought to be; it is moral. For this reason the discipline is filled with contradictions, vagueness, and sectarian quarrels. In discussing it we need to distinguish three strands which are not always easily separable: cultural definitions of madness (the "abnormal"), the philosophy underlying modern psychology, and the psychological establishment.

"Madness," however we define it, has always been a term applied to those whose behavior deviated from the ordinary behavior expected or demanded from a person in a particular class or role. Although there have probably always been people who expressed kinds or degrees of unhappiness or disturbance that puzzled others, much behavior that has been labeled *mad* is actually behavior that is inappropriate to one's caste or status rather than to the condition of humanness itself. Thus the rich man is "eccentric," the poor man is "lunatic"; sexual desire is normal in a man, but has frequently been seen as insane in women.

Madness does not seem to be a category in simple societies, which perhaps are more tolerant of a wide range of behaviors, or perhaps lack the extreme constrictions and stresses of more complex societies that may produce what we call madness. In some cultures a wildly deviant person is considered inspired, in contact with forces beyond the ken of ordinary people. Some cultures have ready-made roles for certain kinds of deviance—like the clown figure among the Bushmen and the *nadle* among the Navajo: categories for males who are uncomfortable in traditional male roles. History is replete with tales of insane Roman emperors, French aristocrats, and German patresfamilias, and noble eccentrics of other cultures who went on functioning in their given capacities. (No one, for example, considered Dr. Schreber insane; instead he was much admired.) But madness has on the whole been treated differently in different classes. Periodic madness in rulers, for instance, has been permitted to dominate the realm, as it did in some of the Roman lunatic emperors like Elagabalus, Caligula, and Nero; or the ruler may be withdrawn for a time and a surrogate put in his place (as with Henry VI of England). England's George III ruled in the latter way, although he was also "treated" in keeping with the techniques of his time—incarcerated in machines, chained to a stake, beaten, starved, threatened, blistered, bled, and given poisons and emetics to drink.[120] But from the time of the later Middle Ages deviance among the poor was "treated" by locking them up in cages. Then as now, madness was seen as a moral failure, as a religious rather than a psychic disorder; often it was conceived of as possession by devils and was treated by exorcism.

People who felt ill consulted healers who treated both mind and body without distinguishing between them, and who found in grief or distress of mind ample cause for physical ill-being. The casebooks of one of these healers, the Reverend Richard Napier, an Englishman who lived in the early seventeenth century, have recently been discovered and analyzed by Michael MacDonald. Napier was an educated theologian but also an astrologer, alchemist, and conjurer. His fees were low enough that all but the very poor could consult him.[121] Of the sixty thousand consultations recorded, only a small number of patients—less than 5 percent—would today be classified as suffering from psychological disorders: however, of this 5 percent more than two-thirds were women.[122] And almost half of these women were upset by two things—the oppression of cruel or drunken fathers or husbands, and "searing grief" over the loss of their children. Almost as many men as women were worried about economic problems; a substantial number were upset by troubled courtships. But the number of distressed women soars in the areas of domestic oppression and bereavement. Women, more than men, suffered from the "hatred, fear and violence" that MacDonald believes were endemic in rural England in Napier's period.[123]

Only extreme and violent behavior was categorized as "madness" in the Middle Ages. Foucault theorizes that for the medieval mind the insane stood as symbols of the basic animality of humans, incarnations of human vice (rooted in animality). Thus the treatment of the mad was to lock them up in cages, with no heat or clothing and little food, and to beat and purge them: as animals, it was presumed, they did not require "civilized" comforts. They were even exhibited as major tourist attractions in some places. In England, the mad incarcerated in Bethlehem (Bedlam) Hospital were displayed for a penny, and earned the hospital an annual revenue of around four hundred pounds. They were also shown at Bicêtre, in France, and sometimes forced to dance under an overseer's whip.[124]

By the time of the Renaissance, Foucault asserts, the vision of animals as symbolic of human traits was reversed into an image of the beast stalking man, revealing a truth about him that had been concealed and imprisoned in darkness. Images of impossible animals escape from a "demented" human imagination, illuminating a secret reality: "Animality has escaped domestication by human symbols and values; and it is animality that reveals the dark rage, the sterile madness that lie in men's hearts." The insane who were confined in asylums were treated with incredible brutality—left lying in water, sometimes water mixed with sewage and floating with rats who bit the incarcerated people; they were chained, leashed, whipped. "When practices reach this degree of violent intensity, it becomes clear that they are no longer inspired by the desire to punish nor by the duty to correct."[125] The mad, emblems of the animality resident in humanity, were to be extirpated, or reduced to pure animal with no discomfiting vestige of humanness.

At the beginning of what Foucault calls "the great confinement," the mad were not segregated from others who were rounded up and imprisoned in the many burgeoning institutions of the mid-seventeenth century. The mad were simply another variety of the poor, the idle, those who refused (or so it was claimed) to work. The seventeenth century contained economic crises of its own, but it also reaped the full fruit of the dislocations and disinheritances of the centuries preceding, as feudal economy gave way to capitalism. At times a third of the population of Paris, for instance, was made up of beggars and the poor—peasants driven from the land, disbanded and disabled soldiers, the sick, people unable to find work. The government of France commanded a literal hunt for these people, who were placed in a series of institutions—most of them were children and women.[126] Only after a time were the "mad" kept separately from other indigents. The point of the exercise was to rid the streets and towns of those who might protest, riot, or otherwise disturb, and, secondarily, to enforce upon the poor the discipline of work.

In the eighteenth century, a period of simultaneous humanitarian reform and passion for control, the medical profession took control of the insane and initiated gentler methods of treatment. Bigger and better asylums were built for a larger percentage of the population. It was a simple matter for people of any authority to have someone incarcerated in a madhouse; Lawrence Stone remarks that "nothing was more common in the eighteenth century in a marital quarrel than for a husband to threaten to lock his wife up in a madhouse."[127] In this period the drive to classify became important to scientists of all sorts.

In the eighteenth century, then, the definition of madness underwent a change. Originally, in medieval Europe, only the extreme and violent had been segregated and called "mad." These people were treated very badly, but they were a small proportion of the population, mainly drawn from the poor. Later, violently antisocial people were incarcerated along with sick and poor people to be treated badly but without special punishment. Then the "mad" were segregated from the sick and poor. But in the eighteenth century those lacking political power, even women from the middle class, could be incarcerated as mad if they were not as obedient or submissive as their husbands desired. It was no longer *madness*—extremely violent antisocial behavior—but nonconformity that provided the basis for incarceration on grounds of insanity. And that nonconformity could be judged by the standards of a single man. At the same time, theorists began to classify behavior and categorize it narrowly; this did not lead to more sophisticated definitions of kinds of madness, but rather to rigid definitions of what constitutes *normality*.

This shift of focus involves a tremendous alteration in world view. Instead of defining madness, and classifying as insane a tiny proportion of the population, doctors were defining normality with definitions that probably fit no one, but which could be applied punitively and selectively to those whom wealthy and middle-class men wished to control—women, children, and the poor. By the twentieth century, normality was defined as adjustment; those who were unhappy were by definition maladjusted. Since no one can avoid being unhappy sometimes, everyone is maladjusted, and everyone can on this ground be made subject to social control if those around them collude. In place of the medieval notion of segregating and abusing those who could not live in society, twentieth-century physicians provided a criterion of madness so vague and general that it could be used to incarcerate and abuse anyone who lacked power to fight the incarceration. These doctors provided a legal means of control over anyone who disrupted society, for whatever reason.

There are two primary visions of humanity, two "philosophies" governing modern psychological practice. One harks back to the medieval tradition of punishing or coercing those who were mad—or in our time, who refuse to adjust; the other is based upon the work of Freud, who created a revolutionary disturbance in that tradition. Rebel that he was, however, Freud too perpetuated and gave new force to ancient patriarchal ideas.

Freud's theories of the Oedipus complex and of penis envy were essentially encapsulations of the basic myths of patriarchy. These theories not only locate male superiority in biology but assert a mental/emotional set that reflects patriarchal categories as a universal experience. They tell us that, regardless of the culture in which they live, all men develop the same psychological set, and that all women develop the same psychological set, but one that differs from men's. The major difference between women and men lies in the construction of their genital and procreative systems; under patriarchy, the penis and penile forms have been exalted. Freud's theory of penis envy makes the penis the most important object of *all* human experience, male and female. "Oedipal desires and castration anxiety are closely connected: castration anxiety contributes to the abandonment of Oedipal strivings."[128] The presence of a penis offers the possibility of eventual power and possession of the mother; its absence is equivalent to a life sentence to subjection.

These central Freudian theories are essentially a theory of power, legitimating on psychological grounds a political reality. Power is: and people shift to accommodate themselves to it; just so, the penis is: and boys and girls and women shift to accommodate themselves to it as a symbol of power. Although

Freud deduced his theories from the revelations of his patients, many of whom were women, in the end he discounted women profoundly; like Aristotle, he conceived of them as deficient or deformed men. He dismissed women's unhappiness and pain in a scrawled note of disgust: What do women want? Indeed, one can say that he even betrayed his female patients by using against them their own traumatic suffering.

In his many analyses of young women, Freud had become aware of the enormous evidence of male abuse of young girls, and in 1895 he wrote his friend Fliess that hysteria (a woman's disease) was the consequence of a "presexual sexual shock."[129] Two years later, he declared that he had found that sexual assaults on girls were made by "the closest relatives, fathers or brothers."[130] With regard to some of his most famous analyses, he knew that "Dora's" mother was engaged in an affair with a neighbor, and had given her husband carte blanche to seduce the fourteen-year-old girl; he could have known—if he chose—the treatment Daniel Schreber had received from his eminent father, but he disregarded the father's writings.[131] He intimated to Fliess that his own father had performed some act of "perversion" against someone in his family.[132] He confessed to feeling desire for his own daughter, Mathilde, in a dream.[133]

Yet in September of 1897, he reversed completely his interpretation of what he knew. He decided that accounts of incestuous acts were projections of *infantile* desire: "it was hardly credible that perverted acts against children were so general," he wrote, in the same letter in which he admitted the possibility of his own father's culpability.[134] Yet the accounts of incest that he had heard were not cast in a light of desire fulfilled but of fear and suffering. Whatever else incest and child molestation may imply, they are primarily political acts—that is, they come about because of the power of one person over another, they are sexual manifestations of a power relation. They are not expressions of mutual sexuality, but of coercion of a being too young to feel sexual volition and too dependent to oppose another's. By evading the political implications of incest, Freud avoided confronting the fact that domination by the father leads to abuse. By evading even the metaphorical implications of incest—his female patients *felt* raped by intimate older males who represented the power establishment—he could blame the victim and turn his eyes away from the victimizer. He followed the advice given him in a dream that occurred the night after his father's funeral: "You are requested to close the eyes." (The phrase appeared on a notice posted in his barber's shop.)[135] This dream occurred in November 1896, before his realization that fathers were inevitably the guilty ones, before his dream about Mathilde, and before his reversal of his interpretation.

This dream suggests the meaning of castration to Freud. To challenge father-right, the power and dominance of the father, is to undermine one's own power if one is a male. For the prerogatives of the power will some day be one's own, if one simply "closes the eyes" to their abusiveness. This process of thought, whether conscious or unconscious, allowed a thinker as subtle and deep as Freud to close his eyes generally to women's point of view, to declare, for instance, without bothering to investigate physiological reality, that mature

women had vaginal, not clitoral orgasms. This single point, so potent and re-
verberant, so much a source of contention, derives its importance less from
women's attitudes toward it (for women, in masturbation, know perfectly well
how they attain orgasm) than from men's. It is the vagina, not the clitoris, that
accommodates the penis; vaginal orgasm posits female dependency on the male
organ and thus on the male, and permits men to go on believing that what satisfies them also satisfies women. It maintains the male illusion of control.

It would not do to go on attacking Freud, who was in so many ways on the
side of the angels, were it not for his tremendous influence and the invocation
of his name by generations of psychologists who have both applied and misap-
plied his theories, who have modified, added to, and perhaps laundered them.
Some therapists still try to educate women patients to accept their secondary
role in the world because that is decreed by nature and Freud; physicians as
well as psychologists continue to discuss "vaginal" orgasms.

The exculpation of the father reinforced the absolute nature of his role,
and of power as a value. As nature was once, so is power now: the absolute
which must be adjusted to, which is beyond reproach or question. The exculpation of the father in a psychology that located the formation of character in
childhood led directly to the inculpation of the mother. Generations of psychologists have laid the blame for almost all our unhappiness at her tired feet.
Mothers are too loving (smothering) or too distant and cold; or they give mixed
signals. If the father is abusive, she is to blame for not stopping him; if he is
absent, she is to blame for not managing to keep him at home; if he is ineffectual, she is to blame for managing too much. In any case, she chose him. Upon
her weary back she bears, like Pandora or Eve, the ills of the race—responsibility for almost all forms of neurosis, hostility, rebelliousness, criminal behavior,
and depression. She has been found guilty of being the single direct cause of
schizophrenia (the schizophrenogenic mother), homosexuality (Momism), and
anorexia nervosa.[136] One wonders how long it will take for recent studies to
penetrate, if indeed they ever do, the minds of the psychiatric establishment—
studies indicating that male homosexuality has no clear relation to parental behavior, that schizophrenia may be inherited, and that most anorectics come
from families in which both parents have dominating personalities.

This blaming of the mother is not just scapegoating; it serves a more profound purpose: it allows us to avoid looking directly at the consequences of our
own morality of power. By identifying ill (in whatever area) with the relatively
powerless in a culture—women, the poor, blacks—we avert our eyes from the
father, the principle of power, and retreat from confrontation with our own
values. This habit of mind is utterly illogical, for it both refuses to perceive the
real source of much of our misery and also endows with great power for ill people who are simultaneously denied any power at all. Attributions to women,
especially mothers, of the power to harm are made even as women themselves
are systematically ignored by psychological thinkers. Female experience is
disregarded as insignificant, as deviation from the normal—male—standard. So
Ernest Becker could write a book linking behavior with the fear of death—a
fairly universal emotion—from an exclusively male point of view, referring to

women as, for example, "failing *our* . . . needs."[137] And Abraham Maslow, claiming the authority of one who had spent a lifetime providing therapy and writing about people's most profound needs and desires, stated in the deceptively titled *The Farther Reaches of Human Nature* that none of his points applied to women and that he did not know what did.[138]

On the other hand, there are Freudian doctrines and practices that were not picked up by the psychological establishment—although many individual practitioners use them. Predictably, these are precisely those practices and beliefs that do not reinforce the basic premises of patriarchy. Freud urged the study of psychoanalysis, "not as therapy but rather because of what it reveals to us about what concerns man most closely: his own essence; and because of the connections it uncovers between the widest variety of his actions." He hoped that analysis would free people from repressions and anxieties *that were unnecessary* (not from all), and reveal the symbolic nature of hatreds and fears; in time, he hoped that the spread of psychoanalytic ideas would reform the raising of children.[139] He was utterly unconcerned with "adjustment," and was thoroughly opposed to the assimilation of psychoanalysis by medicine. He wrote to a friend that he wished "to protect analysis from physicians and . . . priests."[140] Nevertheless, in the United States the physicians took it over, and in 1926 in New York State, for example, the legislature decreed psychoanalysis the sole prerogative of physicians, declaring any other analysis illegal.[141] Although this is no longer the case, physicians still dominate the profession.

Freud's work was also profoundly altered by his British translators, as Bruno Bettelheim has recently shown. The English translation makes "Freud's direct and always deeply personal appeals to our common humanity appear . . . abstract, depersonalized, highly theoretical, erudite, and mechanized"—in short, "scientific."[142] The translation, like the emphasis on a non-Freudian "adjustment," reshapes Freudian ideas so that they are acceptable to the "masculine" values of the English-speaking world. It does this by eliminating the passion and human concern of Freud's language, by replacing simple terms with abstruse ones, and by shifting the approach.[143]

The depersonalization that results from this translation functions, as do other alterations in Freud's texts, to create a distance between the speaker and the referent. This does not change the focus of psychoanalysis itself, does not broaden it from the individual to a society. Rather, it distances the person from the self; if one uses the terms to refer to oneself, one seems to stand outside oneself. If a therapist uses the English terms to refer to the patient, he or she appears to be discussing something external, something in the patient which the therapist does not share.

Without these alterations, it is questionable whether psychoanalysis would have become so widely popular in the United States. With them, it is subtly transformed from a humane and artful study of common human feelings/thoughts/states into an abstract, abstruse discipline available to an elite who can use it to manipulate others whose condition (their language suggests) is not shared by that elite. And it is in this way that psychoanalytic ideas have been used by many practitioners. In a sense they have totally "masculinized"

Freud: for he studied the passions and the symbolic level of human life, and much modern psychology has concentrated on attempting to control the passions almost out of existence.

Freud's postulation of an unconscious realm challenged Western notions of control, for the unconscious cannot be controlled. We can learn to hear it, feel it, become aware of it, and through this process we can learn to discriminate between emotions aroused by real events and emotions aroused by symbolic representations of past pains and satisfactions. At best, we can increase control of our behavior through learning to listen to the unconscious; its very nature precludes controlling it. Indeed, much of what has happened in psychology since Freud can be interpreted as a frantic revision asserting the possibility of finding methods of control of this unruly dimension of self.

One of the most important parts of Freud's legacy is the notion of psychoanalysis as a listening. This idea was revolutionary, breaking with Cartesian objectification, with the idea of a dominant mind dealing with subordinate matter, with the formula of a manipulator objectifying his material. Freud substituted for what Foucault calls the "gaze"—the distant, controlling, manipulating approach that has come to dominate Western life—a listening, heeding, sensitively attendant eye and ear. Freud said he listened with "hovering attention." Because he did this, his lack of sympathy with a female point of view is even more notable. Even when a brilliant colleague like Karen Horney attempted to revise his formulas about women, he reacted hostilely—as he did to male colleagues also, unless they accepted his ideas unquestioningly. On the other hand, his technique, used widely by psychotherapists, has been dismissed by many of those who manage the psychological establishment.

Finally, Freud was keenly aware and concerned that by focusing on individuals as the source of their own pain and self-destructiveness, psychoanalysis deflects attention from larger outside pressure from the culture itself. It thus obviates institutional change.[144] Locating illness entirely within the context of an individual life isolates people and their pain; it teaches therapists to have myopic vision, impedes them from seeing large cultural patterns. Such an approach, as Dorothy Tennov points out, gives psychological sanction to the status quo and reduces the likelihood of generating enough pressure to change those social and environmental sources of stress. Thus, she writes, the "latent purpose of psychotherapy is social control."[145]

This is the major charge brought against the American psychological establishment. It is a complicated charge, since it is brought by both the right and the left, and on different grounds.[146] As I suggested at the beginning of this section, such charges are consequences of the fact that psychology is almost entirely a moral science (or art): it begins and ends with an interpretation of what it means to be human. Here, however, we will focus on those elements within psychology that follow the major cultural tendency toward increased centralization of power and an increase in the value of control.

The field of psychology is fragmented, containing thousands of independent practitioners who are not deeply attached to institutions. Yet there is a psychological establishment, and it resembles the medical establishment: it is centralized, dominated by white male doctors (psychiatrists), and its hierarchy is reinforced by medical insurance companies, who will pay for psychotherapy only with psychiatrists or psychologists with Ph.D.s in clinical psychology. And this establishment functions with rigid standards, not of madness in the old sense, but of normality. It bases its diagnoses primarily on the categories found in one book, the Bible of the therapeutic establishment: *The Diagnostic and Statistical Manual,* Third Edition, or DSM III.

The DSM III contains rigid categorizations of behavior, giving them scientific-sounding names which convey imputations of serious illness. The book wields great power because it is accepted by the state, insurance companies, and other institutions. Even practitioners who do not accept its categories are forced to use them to get reimbursement or otherwise deal with institutions. It is used by state mental hospitals, prisons, and schools. It provides an official language by which patients are labeled, in records that follow them ever after. And to be placed in the classification of having mental illness is to be illegitimated throughout one's future life.

Institutional mental health in the United States is dominated by a small elite who impose the standards of the DSM III. According to reports of psychologists who have worked in mental institutions, the elite is authoritarian and rarely listens to those beneath them in the hierarchy, who have more day-to-day contact with patients than the psychiatrists. Yet a single man, or group of elite men, makes the decisions for the entire institution, dictating every aspect of the work life of the staff and the entire life of inmates without sympathy or knowledge of the needs of either group.[147] They are, like the dominant people in most institutions, concerned above all with their own power or illusion of power, and with the power of the institution. "At the apex stands the psychiatrist, often in isolated and self-isolating splendor." Beneath him in orderly rank stand the clinical psychologist, the psychiatric social worker, the "generic" social worker, the probation officer, the child-care worker. Only those at the bottom levels actually know the community, live in it, understand its culture; they are more active and knowledgeable than those at the top. Yet they have almost no influence on decisions made within the structure that is designed to help the community.[148]

Absurd or destructive orders are sent down to a staff whose members are increasingly silent and resentful, fearing to protest and lose their jobs. The orders are realized and the patients, feeling like manipulated puppets, fall into hopeless apathy. The institution subsides into a custodial prison: psychiatrists, like gods, appear and disappear; custodians do the daily tasks on the wards for infantilized patients who must increasingly be drugged to keep them tractable. As the situation worsens, a consultant is sent in to advise and to train the staff. Most consultants, however, do not try to share their knowledge but hug it to themselves and try to attract a personal following who will be "forever dependent upon the forever superior wisdom of the consultant."[149]

On occasion a person of rank will descend to the floor and try to talk to the patients. But the patients, especially if they are black or very young, speak a different language from the psychiatrist, who, in keeping with the patriarchal prejudices we are all taught, does not recognize a different culture and language and try to bridge the gap, but dismisses the patients as incompetent and retarded.[150] Barbara Lerner concludes sadly that "systems and institutions with authoritarian structures cannot effectively mobilize the therapeutic potential of any community."[151]

Once inside therapeutic institutions, patients become total subjects. Although there are laws designed to protect them, they have few means to enforce those laws, and therapeutic institutions vary in their adherence to them. Depending on the policy of the institution, patients can be drugged, locked up, put in strait jackets, and there is not much they can do about it. Although in most states the patient or a guardian must consent to treatments like electric shock or psychosurgery, it is not a difficult matter to obtain such consent from an angry spouse or a drugged, unhappy patient.

The psychiatrists who manage the mental health establishment are as fascinated as other doctors with technological approaches to cure, with instrumental rather than affective forms of treatment: psychosurgery, electric shock treatments, and drugs. However, although it is claimed that lobotomies and shock treatments are performed to help the patient, there is little evidence that they do, and considerable evidence that they damage or mutilate: Stephan Chorover presents evidence of psychosurgery being performed on patients who were not seriously disruptive to begin with.[152] In the face of this, one must question the motives of those who continue to perform such treatments. The procedures are essentially punitive; they tame patients, subdue them. It would appear that the motivation behind them is not healing but social control. Drugs too, which can be extremely effective and help patients live outside of institutions, can sometimes be used to control patients instead of to help patients control themselves. Drug treatment by itself can be irresponsible: thorazine, for example, is known to cause jaundice, liver and kidney damage, and Parkinsonian effects (tremors); if used long enough, it can lower the immune system, affect vision, and cause great weight gain.

The accusation that mental health institutions are dedicated to social control rather than healing has been brought by many critics, who perceive an expansion in control of a vulnerable and potentially unruly part of the population. Since denial of civil rights has become a valid ground for legal action, the dominant class, which can no longer with impunity abuse and punish the helpless, has resorted increasingly to incarceration and "treatment" as a method of control in the areas of mental health, alcoholism, drug addiction, and recalcitrant children. Despite the Community Mental Health Act, which led to the release of many people from institutions, more and more people are being institutionalized in special centers or wards for drug therapy, alcoholism, and juvenile offenses. "Those incarcerated under the state's *parens patriae* powers already far outnumber those imprisoned under the state's criminal sanctions," writes Nicholas Kittrie, who adds that for every criminal sent to prison, more than four people are subjected to noncriminal incarceration.[153]

The problem is that psychology provides a legitimate ground for imposing treatment upon people who are in some way defenseless, and yet the institution has no clearly defined responsibility to those people.[154] Since many patients in mental hospitals have alienated their families, or are old and unwanted, they sometimes lack support from outside the institution.

Judge Justine Wise Polier points out that by law people are held responsible for violent crime as long as they retain the barest vestige of rationality, but can be deprived of the management of their persons or their property for "far less serious mental impairment."[155] People incarcerated on psychiatric grounds can be held in detention for indeterminate periods while awaiting trial—nor are they left alone in this detention, but are subjected to a variety of manipulations that are dehumanizing or worse.[156]

Such procedures are not widely practiced on middle-class men in the United States; they are reserved for the poor, the criminal, those who have slid out of class through alcohol or drugs, and for middle-class women who cannot "adjust." As Chorover writes, "behavior control always guides human behavior toward the achievement of *socially defined* standards of success. And socially defined standards are always based on the value judgment which reflects the interests of socially dominant individuals and groups."[157]

Far more women than men seek psychotherapy and enter mental hospitals.[158] Emotional disorders and detention in mental hospitals are also far more common among the poor than the rich.[159] The lowest economic class in the United States comprises less than a fifth of the population (18.4 percent) but almost 40 percent of those who need some form of psychiatric help. The highest economic class comprises only 3 percent of the population and 1 percent of those who need psychotherapy.[160] Yet such help is far less available to the poor than to the rich.

Psychiatric experts claim that the poor cannot properly use education, or medicine—they are too ignorant, dirty, illiterate, or immoral; the same claim is made about psychotherapy.[161] Such claims provide justification for a social arrangement that purposely creates an illegitimate class and maintains it for exploitation: the democratic revolutions of the past century have impeded that exploitation, but have partly transformed the illegitimate class from an easily exploitable labor pool into a dependent, locked-in community. The poor, who suffer more stress, sense of impotence, and alienation than others, cannot pay enough for good psychotherapy, and therefore cannot find it. In the rare cases—nowadays—in which public mental health clinics exist, they are likely to be impersonal and alien. Lerner writes that most proponents of community health projects see the poor as "objects of social manipulation to be planned for, not with."[162] Procedures are imposed from above, in accordance with what the planners—who generally come from a different class—deem proper for dependents, rather than emerging from the actual situation.

The poor are often lacking in confidence; sometimes they speak a different language or dialect from those supposed to help them. Above all, they speak in concrete images and metaphors (like poets) and do not understand or trust the abstractions of the learned class. They see and feel the repugnance or disdain for them and their ways that is intrinsic in the manner of the staff and in the procedures of the clinic. Naturally, such an ambience cannot contribute to their well-being.

During the 1960s and 1970s, when the Community Mental Health Act gave strong federal support to community mental health centers, many small local clinics were founded and maintained by personnel full of excitement at the project, and willing to experiment. The boards of these clinics often included members of the community, who helped to plan their programs and even the physical layout of the clinic. The intention was to maintain and support people in a small community: those who were chronically ill could enter the inpatient section for a time, and then, after release, attend sessions at the outpatient section. If they had to return to the hospital, they returned to a friendly place where they felt somewhat at home. Such an arrangement curtailed the time of incarceration, since trust and acceptance and familiarity already existed between patients and their healers.

Revolutionary practices began: patients were allowed to have a clock on their ward, so they would know what time it was; were allowed to serve themselves on real plates instead of being served predivided meals in segmented baby dishes. In some clinics patients ran their own ward, assigning cleanup and serving tasks, voting on rules for self-government. The staff was also run democratically, in what is known as a "therapeutic community": all staff members consulted together and all decisions were made by consensus. Although the physician (psychiatrist) was still legally responsible for admitting or discharging patients, in fact admissions and discharges were decided upon by the group in democratic sessions. In those sessions, all members—the psychiatrist(s), clinical psychologist, psychiatric social worker, psychiatric nurse, mental health assistant (a paraprofessional), recreational therapist, and occupational therapist—had equal voices. Each was assigned as the primary therapist for a set of patients, and had the responsibility for overseeing their day-to-day functioning.

Lerner describes such an experimental clinic for the poor in a large city, arranged in what she calls a "participatory democracy." The staff listened to the patients, had real conversations with them, and made decisions together after consultation with patients. Lerner's clinic and others like it were highly successful: the patients' sense of well-being and their ability to live in the world improved considerably. The rate of recidivism decreased. The staff experienced an increased felicity too; they felt they had some autonomy, and could use their talents to improve both their own lives and that of their community.

The effectiveness of such projects did not prevent their being dismantled—and this raises serious political questions. They were expensive, no doubt, but probably cheaper than the police, weapons, and maintenance of present mental hospitals, residences for the homeless, and prisons that are necessary to keep the poor under control. They were dismantled under Nixon, and Reagan totally eradicated such programs. The mental health establishment has returned to its old ways.

Moreover, the most rigid and stereotypical norms offered in psychology have been adopted by other institutions. Psychological tests devised in a mechanical and narrow-minded way are used by educational and business organizations. Tests based on such notions of "masculinity" are given to prospective employees, who are not hired unless they meet certain standards of aggressiveness; such tests also function to inform new employees about the attitudes they are expected to adopt on the job. The Femininity Scale on the widely used Minnesota Multiphasic Personality Inventory was originally "validated" on thirteen gay men.[163] IQ tests (which will be discussed further in the next section) are used to categorize people, though they are not reliable guides. Psychologists themselves show sexist attitudes in studies attempting to measure sexism.[164]

There are several encouraging factors in the present perspective on psychology, however. The most severe criticism of the psychological establishment comes from members of the profession themselves. Many of these people object to coercive practices, and to psychologists who try to influence people to accept "totalitarian methods of government, the dingy culture of an urban slum, the contemporary . . . law of marriage, or . . . the standards of an acquisitive, competitive, hierarchical, envious society."[165]

Psychologists are not just self-critical; they also make continuous efforts to expand the vision of their discipline to include the personal *and* the political, the uniquely individual and the socially pervasive. Social psychiatry, family therapy, network therapy, and other approaches are expressions of the belief that there is no healing of heart and mind except by personal, engaged recognition of patterns of pain and love; and no healing of a society excruciated by pain and self-hatred except by recognition, acknowledgment, and an attempt to alter large-scale patterns of behavior. What is necessary is that the psychological establishment sever itself from the idea of power as the highest good. Until it does so, psychology, like other institutions, will continue to try to produce humans fit for this world rather than a world fit for humans.

## Education

It cannot be expected that values dominant in other "helping" professions, and indeed in the culture at large, will be lacking in education. The educational establishment in the United States is huge, encompassing the public school system, private schools, colleges and universities, libraries, teachers' unions, textbook publishers, and governmental agencies at all levels. The public school and higher education systems show with special clarity the values implicit in all these areas.

American schooling through the eighteenth and nineteenth centuries was unsystematic and informal: schools were part of the community, stamped with its particular character, under its control, expressive of its values. The fact that schools were local, communally run, does not mean they were necessarily humane, just, or of high quality, but it does mean they had a personal quality. The idea of compulsory public education had been discussed as early as 1642, in Massachusetts; throughout the nineteenth century a debate was waged about it. Women's and mothers' groups, organized labor, and schoolmen supported educational legislation; organized business opposed it—especially the United States Chamber of Commerce, the National Association of Manufacturers, the Southern States Industrial Council, and the Investment Bankers Association of America.[166] Such groups wanted to maintain a large corps of unskilled workers who could justifiably be paid low wages. In many states, poor children were not educated at all.

The nineteenth century was a period of explosive violence in the United States, as labor fought for unionization, mobs rioted in economic despair, and groups fought each other in spasms of ethnic or religious horizontal hostility. Schoolmen founded their arguments for public education on such outbreaks and on the middle class's fears of mobs, immigration, socialism, and anarchism. They claimed schooling would, like the poorhouse, remove the young from "corrupt homes and neighborhoods" and teach them "order, regularity, industry, and temperance"; above all, they would be taught to "obey and respect" their superiors.[167] From the beginning, systems of public education, including compulsory schooling, were urged as a method of socializing the poor, and the intention was less to train poor children intellectually or cognitively than to indoctrinate them morally.[168]

American schoolmen watched as Condorcet in France and Frederick the Great of Prussia developed national systems of education with two key elements—regulation of curricula and articulation among different levels of accomplishment.[169] But not until 1852, in Massachusetts, did any American state pass compulsory school attendance laws. After this, throughout the latter half of the century one after another state did so. By 1900 thirty states and Hawaii had such laws, and by 1918 all states had them. The laws required attendance through eighth grade only, and often allowed for part-time attendance by children who had to work. Moreover, the laws were often disregarded.[170]

The public was aroused to demand fulfillment of the laws by the results of tests administered to army recruits during World War I, which showed a quarter of them as illiterate, a far larger percentage with limited literacy, and 35 percent to be suffering from physical debilities that could have been prevented with diagnosis and treatment in childhood.[171] After 1920 compulsory attendance was enforced, although even then only about a third of the nation's fourteen- to seventeen-year-olds were in high school.[172] It was the pressures of urban life, above all, that led to the building of school systems—standardized, rationalized, and unified arrangements. The cities, with their crowds, their unrest, their poverty, their homeless youngsters, demanded disciplined procedures.[173]

The fundamental intentions of public education—its true ends—created its character. As early as 1818 legislators were being told that "the system operates with the same efficiency in education as labor-saving machinery does in the useful arts."[174] To persuade business of the advantages of education—its potential for curbing social unrest, and for being the "foundation stone of the Republic, an insurance policy against Bolshevism, sedition, and any attempt to tear down government"—the schoolmen increasingly spoke in the language of the corporation.[175] They argued that public education was "the most humane form of social control and the safest method of social renewal."[176] Business felt a need for greater control of workers: the methods of the factory system were in direct conflict with the values of many immigrants. Those who came from preindustrial cultures were used to some sense of personal autonomy in both production and product. They expected to complete a task they had begun, not work on a small part of it; they were used to deciding themselves which task to take up at a given time, and how long to spend on it.[177] Public education would train the next generation of workers in temperance, industry, and obedience to the bells and buzzers that divide the day in coercive institutions. Thus urban education in America "did more to industrialize humanity than to humanize industry."[178]

In addition, standardization and centralization of control could and did serve to eliminate cultural distinctions, and to indoctrinate all children into "aggressive Protestantism, temperance, and English-language chauvinism." A movement that in its time appeared humanitarian, progressive, and democratic concealed at its heart "racism, a yearning for social control, and a desire to make the world safe for the corporation."[179] The schools produced workers who would take their generational place in a class of obedient workers in a hierarchically structured labor force.[180] Textbooks taught children they must be of service and accept their place in a perfect America.[181]

And the educational system itself was built on corporate lines, with centralized control administered through a bureaucracy: the "one best system," which, it was believed, could work for everyone.[182] The organization of the system contains and reflects its purpose—the control of the many by the few, with control of all layers of workers as well. There was a large gap between the upper and lower castes, the upper being mainly white and male, the lower mainly white and female. The upper caste dealt with decisions and finances; the lower (like all lower castes) dealt with the real clientele, the students. And the students themselves, those who were supposed to be served by this system, were treated—like patients and welfare recipients—as objects to be manipulated with disregard for their needs and desires. There was much difference in status and income between administrators and teachers and, at first, between male and female teachers. Only in states in which women were permitted to vote on school matters were women promoted to administrative jobs, and they remain to this day a small percentage of administrators. Equal pay for women teachers was won after a struggle waged by feminists for a decade after women were nationally enfranchised.[183]

Teachers were—and still are—required to conform to a uniform curriculum and had little autonomy. Curricula and teaching methods could be vetoed by school boards, which, as the system became more centralized and bureaucratic, were made up increasingly of business and professional men. Not only the students but the teachers were required to conform obediently and prevented above all from teaching in freedom. Under the guise of avoiding contention about subjective matters like religion, sex, politics, and morality, schools avoided tests and methods that might trigger independent thought, which in turn might challenge the dominant values. Except in areas like mathematics and science, in which thinking is abstract, students were not encouraged to think at all.

Moreover, a policy of racism pervaded American public education. Segregated schools existed in both North and South, and far less was spent on education of blacks than whites, far more on well-to-do children than poor children. In 1939–40, a small percentage of American children (fewer than twenty thousand) attended schools that cost six thousand dollars per classroom while twice that many attended schools that cost less than a hundred dollars per classroom.[184] Mere numbers cannot convey the difference between bright rooms with plants, animals, a variety of books, enough pencils, crayons, paints, paper, a good library, and such special resources as film projectors, record players, pianos, and lab equipment, and ancient soot-covered buildings that look like prisons, with dark, creaky halls, textbooks so old their paper crumbles in the hand, scarcity of all supplies, a paltry library, and an atmosphere of deprivation and fear. Such inequities continue to pervade public school systems across the country: the more affluent a neighborhood, the more its financial allocation for education. In addition, inner-city schools are assigned teachers with less experience and lower verbal ability than others.[185]

A major instrument in maintaining racism in schools has been the IQ test. The first Stanford-Binet IQ test was published in 1916 by Lewis H. Terman. When it was administered to the student population, it showed females at all levels outscoring males of the same ages by 2 to 4 percent. So Terman and his colleagues *changed* the test, removing the questions on which girls did especially well; they thus created boys and girls equal.[186] One wonders what would have been done if the first results had shown boys outstripping girls: Would the test have been changed? Would it have been used as proof that boys were more intelligent than girls?[187]

It is obvious that IQ tests are manipulable, that they can be geared to produce a desired result. That their results correlate with degree of success in white middle-class schools is hardly surprising; the children who do best on IQ tests are those to whom the tests are geared; moreover, they are those for whom the wheels are oiled throughout society. One does not need IQ tests to predict they will do well, nor is such prediction their function.

The IQ test developed from a mass experiment conducted during World War I by leading American psychologists, who worked for a little over a month to create an examination to be given to army recruits. The Alpha and Beta tests proved useful mainly in slotting men into particular jobs, but they were also felt to demonstrate that the United States was a true meritocracy: the "fittest" usually occupied the highest positions. They were interpreted as demonstrating that Alpine and Mediterranean races were intellectually inferior to Nordic races, and that blacks were across the board inferior to whites in intelligence. Although such "proofs" were later discredited, when it was shown that predominantly "Nordic" soldiers from the South made the lowest scores of any white soldiers in America, and that black soldiers from the North scored well above southern whites, these results had less impact than the racist interpretation.[188] Racism of all sorts, not just against blacks, was pervasive: thus the results at Ellis Island, showing the largest percentage of most immigrants to be "feeble-minded"; thus eugenics; and thus the adoption of IQ tests by educational, civil service, and business institutions, as a measure of what these areas considered acceptable abilities.[189] The IQ test and the pseudoscience behind it enabled institutions to label people inferior without the appearance of prejudice: "Testing legitimized segregation within American education."[190]

Segregation in schools was decreed illegal by the *Brown* decision of the

Supreme Court in 1954; sections of government itself—the states—opposed the decision. Nevertheless, desegregation has been fairly successful in precisely those southern states where separate facilities were formerly required by law. It has been far less successful in the North, where segregation occurred because blacks and whites lived in different neighborhoods. In all but a few cities the percentage of black students in schools with 90 to 100 percent black enrollment has *increased* markedly since the *Brown* decision.[191]

Efforts to integrate education have failed for several reasons. Private schools spring up; people move out of cities; busing has been stubbornly opposed by whites and even some blacks, and is being dismantled by the Reagan Administration. But the failure to integrate schools is part of a larger failure, for which schools alone are not responsible. Few people, of any color, would *choose* to send their children to an inner-city public school. Those who can avoid such a situation because they can afford private schools for their children, or because they can move to an all-white neighborhood, on the whole do so. Inner-city schools, almost entirely black or Hispanic, are old, poor, and dangerous: in 1983 in New York City nearly 1700 weapons—guns, knives—were found on students, and there were almost three thousand attacks on teachers by students.[192]

Two major processes seem to be at work here. One is the nature of black culture itself, the other the fact that every institution in our society functions to keep blacks a separate, slave class. Despite proclamations and amendments, emancipation has not occurred, nor will it until the patriarchal assumption of superiority over those who are different is eradicated from our consciousness.

If blacks could move, as other ethnic groups have, into integrated neighborhoods without the panic, the blockbusting of realtors, and wholesale flight of whites that usually ensue, blacks would be assimilated into schools of varied hue (surely more interesting places) without legislation. If blacks were able to get and keep better jobs (and residential integration were achieved), they could afford to leave the ghetto. To attempt to integrate schools when blacks are squeezed at both ends of this course of assimilation is like trying to draw to an inside straight: success is the exception.

Moreover, education does not work for blacks the way it does for whites. Inner-city whites who gain education increase their earnings substantially and decrease their possibility of unemployment. This is not the case for inner-city blacks. Bennett Harrison studied ten urban ghettos: in none of them did education reduce unemployment by even 2 percent per year of schooling, and in many cases more education led to greater chance of unemployment.[193] Job development programs for the urban poor place them in "horizontal" (jobs on the same level previously occupied) rather than "vertical" (jobs leading upward on a ladder) positions.[194] Often, more educated blacks earn only a little more than they earned before, and they are systematically underemployed; they also face almost the same expectation of unemployment that they did before.[195] Contrary to the belief of some people, black youths are eager to work and remain at their jobs longer than white youths.[196]

Although many blacks have "passed"—entered society as white—for most, blackness is as unchangeable as one's sex. It is partly this unalterability that makes women and people of color such dependable sources of gratification for male supremacists. Moreover, blacks, like women, have been locked out of white male culture and, in their isolation, have created their own culture—a culture in some ways like that of women. Intermeshed, communal, and flexible, black culture is bound by bonds of love and friendship; it is a "feminine" culture in this sense. In keeping with its priorities, the white middle class requires blacks who wish to move out of poverty to move also out of their own culture into the more "masculine" white culture, adopting white mores, language, and styles. Unemployment programs foster such moves, implicitly judging indigenous culture inferior.[197]

But "feminine" cultures do not work like "masculine" cultures. "Masculine" cultures aim at success (power, control), are concerned with rules and techniques and instrumentality. "Feminine" cultures are concerned with affection, bonding, cooperation, with being and being-together. (Differences in "masculine" and "feminine" attitudes will be discussed further in Chapter Six, pp. 475–484.) When job training programs or schools treat black dialect as an improper tongue, and black mores and styles as vulgar and crass, they are doing more than asserting an elite style: they are forcing repudiation of one way of life in favor of another. They are teaching blacks that to escape poverty in the United States, they must adapt to the prevailing morality and thus accept power as their highest good.

Although whites suffer from losing a chance to enrich white culture by exposure to black, and by carrying around hatred and fear of blacks, the black community unquestionably suffers more, and none more than the children. The victimization of blacks in American education has been systematic, the consequence of a structure "erected carefully and painstakingly."[198] The values implicit in the American educational establishment have caused suffering to all children *and* teachers.

For the values of the culture necessarily pervade the classroom. Teachers may not digress, but must teach a narrow linear view of subjects, with an eye to helping students to pass standardized tests; the students' performance on these tests fixes them in a rank on a ladder, a rank that is likely to be immutable throughout their educational careers and afterward. Only extraordinary education is concerned with learning; most is concerned with *achieving:* and for young minds these two are very nearly opposites. One is dedicated to experience, the other to control. Schools are boring and sterile for pupil and teacher as they bend wearily over one more excruciatingly boring workbook. Students are not encouraged to read full works, or to discuss them or write about them. Rather, they are handed short passages and asked to fill in short answers on exams. The passages are carefully selected to "offend" no one, a euphemism meaning they are sure not to touch on anything that is emotionally or intellectually significant to children. Teachers do not have the freedom or the time to use innovative methods of teaching, such as John Dewey's progressive ideas about learning from experience as well as from books, or deemphasizing competition and authoritarianism and allowing students to initiate their own work.

Such approaches cannot be realized within a rigid hierarchical bureaucracy. Teachers "run a serious risk of censure" for experimenting,[199] and many "progressive" experiments end up entailing more supervision, more red tape, more filling out of forms, and more committee attendance for teachers.[200]

Suspicion of progressive programs extends, these days, to parents as well, who fear in a period of economic cutback that their children will lack the credentials that could place them on the assembly line directed to economic prosperity.[201] But in spite of all obstacles a few new programs seem to be working well—Head Start, magnet schools, and the City High School Recognition program, which rewards schools that have improved themselves under adverse conditions, and others.[202]

Two generations ago, Robert and Helen Lynd pointed out that in the contention between those who uphold qualitative goals for education and those who focus on quantitative efficiency of administration, "the big guns are all on the side of the heavily concentrated controls" of the managers.[203] One generation ago, money was poured into programs intended to remedy the "cultural deprivation" claimed by psychologists as the problem of the poor. So little of this money actually reached the ghetto schools that one observer described pouring funds in at the top of school bureaucracies intending to help the students as "like feeding a horse in order to feed the sparrows."[204]

Curricula and procedures are still mandated from above and imposed on teachers (and students) despite studies showing this to be an ineffective process.[205] As usual in the "helping" professions, the people with status who make the decisions are those cut off from contact with the actual situation and the people involved in it. The focus of the institution is thus aimed outward, at enlarging or maintaining the power-in-the-world of the institution or its chief managers, rather than inward, at the people it claims to serve.

The educational establishment is thus a hierarchy primarily concerned with power, with maintaining its own power, and with teaching students to adapt, in whatever way, to power as the highest good of our society. But within the larger hierarchy that is this nation, the educational establishment occupies a low rank. To judge rank one need only inspect the federal budget and the influence of a lobby on the Congress. The United States spends very little on education: during one year of World War II, the United States spent more for military purposes than it had spent on public education over its entire span of existence. In 1955, a year of peace, the federal government spent over forty billion dollars on the military, almost four times the amount spent on public education from its inception.[206]

The world of colleges and universities is also pervaded by problems of hierarchy, concern above all with control and power, and lack of concern with those low in the hierarchy—again, teachers and students. Racism and sexism pervade the academy, and excellence is less important than "fitting in," despite academic proclamations of the opposite. Open admissions policies designed to compensate for the utter failure of lower schools to teach poor youngsters have all but disappeared. College education is again being restricted to a small percentage of the population. In academia as well as in lower education, the student, the person for whom the entire structure is intended, has the least significance and power. Shuffled around in a bureaucratic procedure, students are treated, as Lionel Lewis puts it, like welfare "clients."[207] The general direction in which they are thrust in their university education is toward technical expertise, abstract forms of knowledge, and logical, "rational" thought. Frances FitzGerald's study of textbooks shows a shift in their emphasis that has occurred in the past few decades: they now teach that knowledge is power, and that the ability to think means ability to control.[208] Both the rebellion and the apathy encountered on college campuses in recent decades are two faces of the same response to intense pressure in every area of life to fit into a single mold, the narrow and inflexible demands of the new corporate state.

The major criticism of academia by academics themselves is that it disregards the dimension of life they label *imagination, feeling, the will,* or *intuitive insight.*[209] The humanities shrink in esteem as its values are declared invalid and antiquated, and even those most dedicated to them tend to be impressed by the latest pseudoscientific literary or artistic approach. Above all, as students themselves will tell you, a training in the humanities does not get you a good job—or any job at all.

The situation is most extreme in universities, especially the more prestigious. Since their founding, American universities have been deeply involved with government; in this century that has meant corporate research, weapons research, shared personnel, and, most serious, shared values. Thorstein Veblen showed half a century ago that the norms and conduct of the business world had permeated academia, from its governing boards through the administration and into the classroom.[210] Now the ideology of business has almost entirely superseded the religious ideology that used to dominate American higher education.

Philip Rieff believes that academia is "even further advanced" than the corporate world in acceptance of goals of technological domination: "the knowledge managers are sophisticated enough and the scientists tolerant enough to share their dividends with the gurus; this joint enterprise is part of the feed, back and forth, between 'multiversity' and corporate technology."[211] The multiversity to which he refers was the inspiration of Clark Kerr (chancellor, 1952–58, and president, 1958–67, of the University of California at Berkeley), who wished to shape a servant institution to corporate society, a place that would teach superior technology and the values that foster it. Howard Perlmutter of the Wharton School even devised a plan for a University of the World, a college that would be supranational, technical, and practical. Students would be given on-the-job training in police work and other forms of social supervision and surveillance, and no arts or humanities whatever were to be taught.[212]

Attitudes of the corporate state permeate the university at every level. College and university teaching remain among the most autonomous jobs available today. The college teacher offers a course in an area that must be approved by a department head or a curriculum committee, but once it is approved, the teacher has complete control over texts, approach, and emphasis.

Although extreme unpopularity or great eccentricity of approach can cause difficulties—criticism or even dismissal (if the teacher is untenured)—most teachers have considerable freedom. Because of this, controls are exercised before the teacher enters the classroom, at the time of hiring.

Universities claim to reward excellence in teaching, publication, and on occasion in such fringe areas as service to the community. They claim to function as a meritocracy that advances the most intelligent and competent fairly, rationally, and thoughtfully. But Lionel Lewis, who has studied the actuality of university practice versus its claims, finds those claims hollow.

Excellence in teaching should be a real standard in a college—or any school. But teaching is the least of the administrator's concerns. Indeed, prestigious positions in major universities often involve relief from most teaching chores, which are assigned to inexperienced graduate students. Teaching is considered the housekeeping of the academy; no professor of status wants to teach freshmen, for instance, the most exciting of all college students.

Research and publication are supposed to be the real test of whether a candidate is granted tenure. But in actuality the huge majority of male faculty have published little or nothing. A study of a large university published in 1967 showed that 71 percent of the faculty had never published an article and 90 percent had never published a book. In the top twelve academic institutions (including Harvard, California, Columbia, and Yale) only twelve out of every hundred faculty members published articles in major learned journals in 1958; of the next ten (including Pennsylvania, Minnesota, Stanford, and UCLA) the figure was 5.5 out of a hundred. A 1970 survey showed that 30 percent of university faculty had published nothing, and another 30 percent had published between one and four papers.[213]

Neither publication nor teaching excellence showed any correlation with salary. The single factor of significance in determining higher salary or promotion (in a 1969–70 study) was administrative work. The factors which led to having the lowest salaries were, in order: being female; teaching in the humanities; and having attended an unprestigious undergraduate institution.[214] Lewis concludes that the dictum of publish or perish, which at best seems to operate in only a handful of major universities, is mostly a fiction used to justify actual hiring and promotional practices. In the university, as in the corporation, the "rationality" is all on the surface. Those who engage in what is broadly called community service and those who take on administrative duties have academic careers as successful as or more successful than those who are occupied with scholarship. Lewis believes that this policy has resulted in the furtherance of mediocrity and incompetence, as less intelligent or able people rise to the highest academic rank and "more and more peripheral tasks and positions" are created to "justify their existence."[215]

The most important element in hiring and promotion of faculty, according to Lewis, is "fitting in." A candidate should be like the already existing faculty, which is mainly or entirely male, white, middle-class, and relatively tractable. The Puritan work ethic is admired; the faculty can accept those from poor backgrounds if they work hard and have "raised" themselves, as long as they have remained deferential to superiors, have pleasant personalities, and are compliant. Possession of a gracious wife is an important factor, writes Lewis.[216]

*Fitting in* clearly excludes women, blacks, and other people of color. And this discrimination about candidates for the faculty is also applied to students. Even liberals these days huff and puff at the mention of quotas in admissions or hiring. Yet colleges have always operated on quotas. College admissions officers are required to achieve a balance in the student body among athletes, scholars, people with special talents, people with rich parents. To add another category to the list—women, blacks, chicanos—would be "in no way a deviation from the ordinary process of decision making in admissions offices."[217] Moreover, there have long been quotas for the *exclusion* of certain groups: Jews, for instance. Administrations determine upon a mix of 2:5 or 1:3 women to men in admissions, and protest, if challenged, that if they simply took the top students the school would be mainly female. Many Jews fear quotas because quotas have so often been used to exclude them, and the proportion of Jews in college is greater than their proportion in the population. But as far as I know, affirmative-action quotas are not based on population proportions; they are not intended to exclude, but to include formerly slighted groups. And if admission to college were granted on basis of grades and SAT scores alone, neither women nor Jewish students would be excluded. There is no reason why, with actual good will, a college could not balance fairly its proportion of a variety of student types.

Once they are admitted, female students in particular continue to experience discrimination. They are slotted toward the humanities and away from "hard" science (the most prestigious area); they are judged by appearance and behavior far more than male students; they are subject to sexual harassment; and they must deal with a general pressure (within as well as outside them) against distinction in their work. Black students feel isolated and deviant; beyond that they are keenly aware of the difference between "black" culture and the abstract, disconnected world of the university, and torn between loyalty to past influences and ambition for their futures. Few blacks survive the system with any desire to remain in it.

Many females want jobs in academia. But the same standards applied to them as students continue to be applied. Their letters of recommendation are biased, their interviews are followed by remarks about personal appearance and dress, and they are never granted the same weight as serious scholars as men.[218] "Women scholars are not taken seriously and cannot look forward to a normal professional career . . . [They] tend to be discriminated against in the academic profession, not because they have low prestige but because they are outside the prestige system entirely."[219] Like the women of New Guinea societies, they are outside the prestige system; their work helps to produce the food, but the men give the feasts that gain the status.

Consequently the greatest numbers of women are found in the lowest rank or in "off-ladder" positions—jobs that are usually part-time, offer no fringe benefits, no possibility of tenure or promotion, and are usually very poorly paid. The situation of women in academia is particularly cruel because young women are promised something that is not delivered. Many young women finish college with distinction, many enter graduate schools and get their advanced degrees. But the paltry figures representing women in the top two academic ranks—professor and associate professor—offer another picture. Moreover, the situation has worsened for women in academia: by 1920 the suffrage movement and opening of colleges to women had led to women's receiving about 15 percent of all Ph.D.s; in 1970, in the midst of the feminist revolution, they were receiving only about 10 percent.[220]

The prejudice against women and blacks in academia is not entirely rooted in their sex or color. Whether deservedly or not, women and blacks are associated in the minds of white males (and sometimes in their own as well) with what we have been calling "feminine" qualities—nature, the body, emotion, sex, community, expressiveness. We have seen that these values are increasingly being edged out of any claim to legitimacy as the world moves toward domination by technical, abstract, logical, and "rational" procedures, which often mask extreme irrationality. The most prestigious areas of learning are the hard sciences, followed by the soft sciences; the humanities, with their murky ambiguities and their moral questions, are extremely discomfiting to "masculine" minds. Indeed, the progress of the technological world depends upon the obliteration of moral questions—the advancement of "value-free" judgments. But of course "value-free" judgments are impossible: the term is a euphemism for tacit acceptance of prevailing values. Technical universities have moved increasingly since the 1970s to decrease the size and importance of their humanities programs. Institutions focusing on technological studies do not want their students to ask moral questions, and they do not want faculty that will encourage them to do so. This is part of the reason why so many colleges are reluctant to establish women's studies or black studies programs: programs of study that focus on the deviant (nonwhite, non-power-focused, female) aspects of culture suggest there are other ways of being, other ways of seeing the past, and therefore other ways of seeing the future.

Academia may be the last remaining institution with any vestige of independence: it was, after all, the center of the antiwar movement during the Vietnamese atrocity, and a center too of anticorporate agitation. Nevertheless, the ties between academia, government, and corporations are increasing, often in nearly invisible ways. In closed sessions, sometimes secret even from affected departments, administrators of large universities and managers from industry are making questionable alliances. Since some of these universities are funded by taxpayers (the University of California, for example), the barring of press and community leaders from discussions of such alliances is irresponsible.

The nature of these alliances threatens traditional university prerogatives: academic freedom; research as an educational instrument; publication and free exchange of scientific information; and the right of the faculty to determine its own makeup. These are, essentially, being traded for a share of the profits anticipated from research that is geared to the desires of a private corporation, kept secret, and used for profit. Alliances between corporations and universities are very widespread: for example, Carnegie Mellon is cooperating with Westinghouse in robotics research; Honeywell, Sperry Univac, GE, and Minnesota Mining and Manufacturing are cooperating with the University of Minnesota in microelectronics research; MIT is involved in various forms of research with ITT, General Motors, Exxon, and ten other firms; Rensselaer is involved with IBM, GE, Grumman, Lockheed, Prime Computer, Bethlehem Steel and others; and in genetic research, Harvard works with Monsanto, Washington University with Mallinckrodt, Cornell with several agribusinesses; and Harvard Medical School with Du Pont.[221] This is far from an exhaustive list.

In 1981, MIT made an unprecedented agreement with a private firm, Whitehead Institute for Biomedical Research, according to which the firm establishes a separate organization adjoining the MIT campus, to do research in molecular genetics and developmental biology. For a minimal amount of payment to MIT, the firm will have access to all MIT facilities, faculty, and staff, and the right to initiate appointments of faculty members. The major loser in this agreement is the present biology faculty at the university; since they were too "timid and 'clubby' " to take a strong stance against it, one could dismiss the entire situation as one in which people got what they deserved.[222] But it has ramifications far beyond its immediate effects.

Lucy Benson, Under Secretary of State for Security Assistance, Science, and Technology in the Carter Administration, has pointed to a new, important interaction between science, technology, and foreign affairs.[223] Multinational corporations see science and technology as the area that will dominate power thinking in the future. They believe that technical knowledge is a commodity (like everything else), and can be bartered for natural resources and political power. Thus "control over scientific knowledge has become a central goal in the strategies of multinational corporations, strategies which, to a large extent, will determine national policies and prospects." Since universities are the major source of scientific knowledge, the multinationals are invading them, "seeking to acquire privileged access to and control over the form and flow of scientific research."[224] In the process, corporations take control not merely over information but over the course of research itself, from institutions that are supported by taxpayers and the public, and use it for their private profit.[225]

The dangers of this process, especially in the powerful area of biological and genetic research, are that a small group of men concerned with power and profit alone will gain possession of techniques and formulas that can affect all our lives profoundly. Some universities, aware of the rising protest at such policies, are adopting guidelines limiting the powers of the corporations in such alliances. Harvard, for instance, has produced a code that would prevent faculty members from becoming creatures of a single corporation; that requires public access to basic research, whether federally or privately financed; and that renounces responsibility for secret information possessed by corporations. Some corporations have responded that Harvard's guidelines would "make it virtually impossible to sponsor some research on the campus."[226]

There is little question who will win in such a conflict, however. As is true in government as well, university officials are also corporate directors. Paul Gray, president of MIT, is a director of the Cabot Corporation; Howard Johnson, chairman of the MIT Corporation, sits on the boards of many other corporations as well; even faculty members are directors of corporations.[227] Without any need for conspiracy, academic interests converge with corporate interests. Clearly, such men intend to dominate the future and have the means to do so—if there is a future.

The three fields just discussed—medicine, psychology, and education—are known as "helping" professions, disciplines devoted to the well-being of humans. Yet each of them proves on examination to constitute an oppressive force in this country. Almost every study of these professions is pervaded with accusations of "social control." At the same time, each of us knows members of these professions who are indeed dedicated, competent, humane people. The question that stares out from this seeming contradiction is: How does it happen that good people with good intentions end up as participants in an inhumane power structure that is leading the country toward a kind of totalitarianism?

There seem to be three major reasons for this inexorable tide in our affairs, and all three involve not just members of the professions I have discussed, but all of us. They have to do with the way we think and what we value; they are, that is, moral.

First, the drive to control is deeply rooted in us, so deeply that we do not recognize it as one drive among many, one method among many, but see it as the only method for achieving desired ends. Those who claim to wish for the improvement of the human lot, who may even themselves believe they desire this improvement, tend to attempt to achieve it by imposing rules, by coercion. Like Dostoievski's Grand Inquisitor, they believe humans fear freedom and cannot handle it. They think people must be forced into doing "what is good for them."

Michel Foucault describes the program of a doctor who lived during the French Revolution, Sabarot de l'Avernière. He was an idealist who considered priests and doctors people who should be selflessly dedicated to the consolation of souls and the alleviation of pain. He devised a scheme by which the enormous wealth of the Church would be used to pay priests and doctors, who would then be able to work for nothing among all who needed their help. He believed the first task of the doctor was political: to struggle against disease, one must first struggle against bad government, because bad government fosters extreme richness, which leads to bad diet and bad habits, and extreme poverty, which leads to insufficient diet and unhealthful living conditions. Wealth generates greed and idleness. In his period it was not yet evident that it also generates a polluted environment, although it did for the poor.

De l'Avernière believed medicine must begin not with the idea of curing ills, but of creating the *model man*; its first knowledge should be the knowledge of "the healthy man." To this end physicians must carefully supervise culture: they must insist the work period be broken up with festivals; must examine cultural artifacts like books and plays to be sure no bad habits are encouraged by them; must oversee the bases of marriage, which can be happy, he claimed, only when it contributes to the "benefit of the state."[228]

The distance is not great between this benevolent doctor with his oppressive plan and Hitler and his plans for supervising breeding, marriage, culture, economics, and other areas in the interest of the state. A question that occurs frequently in post–World War II literature is how "good" people could have lent themselves to Hitler's policies. Yet those policies constitute merely an extension of tendencies in the West for the past three or four millennia—to have faith in control as the means to transcendence; to believe in the existence of an elite which is truly humanly superior to other classes; and to have contempt for those other classes, seeing them as essentially subhuman. If these beliefs were true, the tyranny of a benevolent elite would indeed be the best method of improving the lot of ordinary humankind. But they are not true, and have led to millennia of incredible cruelty, as well as continual disruption and rebellion.

People who are in the "helping" professions are not immune to the idea that patients or students, underlings on the staff, clerical and maintenance workers need to be coerced. We convince ourselves that what we demand of the student and the patient is what they need, partly because we lack any alternative method of approaching our work. Permissiveness, as practiced in some universities in the late 1960s and early 1970s, has proven inadequate. Despite encouraging experiments in mental health clinics and hospitals in that same period, the mental health establishment returned to hierarchical, coercive methods, claiming the experiments were too expensive, ignoring the huge expense of maintaining large hierarchical institutions. Medical doctors who prefer to maintain small personal practices find themselves worked to death, while others, secure in huge hospitals full of exorbitantly expensive equipment, and devoting minimal attention to patients, live more easily. In resignation, people give in to prevailing mores, which *work*: not for the patient or the student, but for the practitioner.

Second, as industrialism has expanded and intensified, we—all of us—have come to depend primarily on science and technology to solve our problems. Knowing our society is sick—as people have known for several centuries now—we have accepted as the best methods to cure it more advanced machinery, drugs, and manufactures; greater institutional efficiency and rationalization; and greater central control. In areas in which philosophical and moral debate is utterly essential, we have abdicated to the scientific experts, and accepted the possibility of "value-free" diagnoses.[229]

Finally, we all, in varying degrees, even those of us who rebel against it, share the dominant values of our culture. Power and wealth seem the highest goods even to those of us who do not actively pursue them. There is no escape from this, for they *are* the highest goods in the society, and people who eschew them feel defensive, apologetic, or resentful at not having them; people who are prevented from reaching them—those locked into poverty—see themselves as fenced out of a world of joy and ease. It would be comic if it were not so sad.

Some programs have operated to improve the material welfare of certain people. People are more highly educated now than they have ever been in America.[230] Schooling intended to train the children of immigrants to be more docile workers in fact opened doors to them. They learned to read newspapers, to speak the language of the dominant class; they learned the proper ways to channel their considerable intelligence and energy. They also learned the values of their new society. When they grew up, they *were* tractable, they worked hard, lived frugally, maintained temperance and cleanliness and improved their economic condition and thus the potential of their children. They transmitted to those children the values they had learned, and the children, despite rebellion, basically accepted them: money was the goal, and money required hard work, discipline, education, the sacrifice of other values, and—for males, at least—aggression. The immigrant poor were assimilated to the dominant culture, and it was the dominant culture that triumphed.

Alvin Gouldner discusses a group he calls the New Class, many of whom are descendants of the immigrant waves. This class is made up of professionals and high-level technicians, managers in the new corporate world. Gouldner believes the New Class is in conflict with the old monied class (the owners), since it depends not on traditional privilege and affluence but on its own expertise and belief in efficiency, technology, and "logical" thought. Gouldner suggests that this class has better moral values than the old monied class, although it is elitist, exclusive, and technologically oriented.[231]

This is doubtful, since elitism could not exist at all if people did not entertain other attitudes—a belief in human domination of nature, which ramifies into male domination of women, white domination of blacks and other people of color, domination of the general population by a small group, ethnic and religious stratification, and stratification by wealth, class, or education. Moreover, this New Class, according to Gouldner, speaks its own language, which he calls CCD, careful and critical discourse. This language is disciplined, reflexive, and leaves itself open for criticism and discussion—but only on its own level. It is free from contaminating dimensions like emotion and expressiveness.[232] Gouldner's New Class is thus simply the avant garde of the latest version of patriarchy—technology minded, corporate minded, speaking a tongue that omits persons and feelings and that uses logic to conceal illogic.

Cultural disdain for emotion and expressiveness is pervasive, being the other face of the coin of control and power. Even those who believe they oppose the dominant culture participate in this contempt, and attempt to eradicate feeling. The director of the New York City drug prevention program in 1981 ascribes widespread drug taking among youngsters to a desire not to feel and a trust in chemical control: "All their lives they've been raised on it: progress through chemistry. The message is don't ever feel anything."[233] More sophisticated cocaine users appreciate the drug because it dulls emotion while swelling the ego: it is a metaphor for our time. Christopher Lasch points out that the major message of the counterculture of the sixties was "emotional detachment"—being laid back—as a method of "emotional liberation."[234]

Because we are not aware of our actual morality, because we blind ourselves to both our true values and the nature of those values, we cannot find solutions to our malaise. At their very best, all our institutions can do is enable us to live in our world. They cannot further the changing of our world because the entire nature of institutions is "masculine"—they preserve, make permanent, create an exclusive body of knowledge and maintain it. We would criticize a system of education, for instance, that did not help youngsters to establish themselves in the world as it is, that tried to form them for some ideal vision. At its best, then, education can produce youngsters who are geared for entrance into an unworthy society. The structure of institutions alone guarantees continuation of that unworthy society: it embodies total control by a few male superiors over descending levels of male administrators with lesser control; at the bottom is a huge corps of mainly female caretaking personnel who are involved with the supposed subjects of the institution—patients, clients, students—and who have a clearer understanding of the situation, but whose voices are totally ignored. At the very lowest level are those for whom the structure was created: utterly powerless, inconsiderable, insignificant, mere matter.

Difficult as it will be to alter the structure of institutions, it will be less difficult than altering a morality so malignant and so pervasive. Institutions can be changed so that those directly in contact with the human situation can use their knowledge and engagement in potent ways; so that responsibility and a degree of autonomy are accorded in a coordinate, rather than subordinate, way. But to restore emotion to value, to put control and power in realistic perspective, will require nothing less than a moral revolution.

## 3. PILLARS OF SOCIETY II: LAW

Simple cultures have unwritten customs which bind the community through general consent. This is true even in societies we would not call "primitive": J. M. Synge described how twentieth-century Aran fishermen, if they had done wrong, would take the boat over to Galway alone and put themselves in jail.[235] Simple communities "cannot be said to have 'law,' because there is no way to distinguish . . . legal . . . from other social rules."[236] Law emerges with centralization, stratification, and the ownership of private property. Most early codes of law are concerned with property rights. Even the very early Mosaic code warns against coveting the property—wives and animals—of others. Although most of us think about laws as guardians of life and limb, modern law is overwhelmingly concerned with property. And no profession is more bound up with the expansion of control, and the gradual shift toward totalitarianism, than law.

Modern law is the creation of the bourgeoisie; ironically, for several centuries it based its claims on liberty, justice, and natural rights. Now lawyers are placing their skills at the service of those who wish to centralize control in ways that erode the very rights law once fought for. But then, as Michael Tigar and Madeleine Levy point out, "lawyers have always been in the service of those who could pay—the lords, the princes, the Church, the bourgeoisie."[237]

The bourgeoisie evolved from a merchant class that traveled in Europe from about 1000 C.E. Merchants were called *pieds poudreux*, "dusty feet," in derision at their traveling from town to town on foot or horseback, carrying all their goods with them. They were objects of scorn because they sold at a profit, something considered dishonorable in feudal society.[238] People bartered, exchanged: they gave that of which they had a surplus and took that which they needed. To buy at one price and sell at another was considered usury, a sin.

Despite the hostility of the noble class, which saw them as a revolutionary force, and despite the unfriendliness of feudal law, the merchant class persevered and prospered, if in constant conflict. Trade on any scale required some degree of guaranteed physical safety, credit, insurance, and systems for transmission of funds. To obtain these the merchants had to modify, add to, alter existing law. They "embodied their demands and later their victories in the form of charters and treaties": thus they created a place for themselves within feudal law.[239]

By the thirteenth and fourteenth centuries, rich merchants had created an alliance with newly powerful monarchs (always in need of money) and with the legal profession. The lawyer–civil servant emerged, and law became the creature of the economically powerful.[240] By 1600 the main principles of bourgeois law had replaced those of feudal law: feudal law was concerned with personal, but fixed, relationships that governed property ownership and exchange; the new law was concerned only with contracts, property, and trade.[241] The feudal system, which guaranteed everyone a place (lowly as it might be), was superseded by a system that gradually ousted large segments of the population from those places, and from the land. The medieval town had been the common possession of its inhabitants and their descendants, its common lands open to all. Incorporation of towns led to the installation of the most powerful, richest men as town officials; they did not hesitate to treat the town's property as their own, selling it to men rich enough to buy and keeping the proceeds. Fields had to be enclosed and guild privileges overridden; land laws were revised. Such changes required a strong central government, and the bourgeoisie were early champions of a powerful centralized state.[242]

More new legislation was necessary to protect the growth of manufacture, as merchants realized their profits would be greater if, instead of buying from an artisan and reselling at a higher price, they hired artisans for wages and controlled production at every step. Such a project required an initial outlay of large sums, however: and capital was born. "Having achieved a redistribution of land and having profited from the breakup of village life," the bourgeoisie sought help in restraining the Crown from interference in trade and manufacture. "The common lawyers proved ready to join such an alliance."[243]

The conflict between this central power the bourgeoisie had helped to instate and the growing ambitions of the merchant class led to continual struggle, even revolution, as the bourgeoisie demanded fairness, equality, justice, and liberty, rights they (and their philosophers) declared were "natural" and inalienable. Certainly people who fought for such standards, and philosophers and poets who enunciated them, believed in their cause. Behind them, however, providing the money and the legal arguments were the merchants and their lawyers, and the freedom they desired was the freedom to organize systems of production and exchange. In bourgeois legal ideology, work is a matter of private choice; this was called a liberation from feudal legal ideology, in which labor was an obligation performed in return for a grant of land or payment, and in which the kind of labor was stipulated in detailed rules of law. The merchant class claimed that no one *had* to work; that labor was sold to an employer by contracts made by free choice. This claim is, of course, a fiction: people do have to work to eat, and people displaced from their land and their villages, lacking money and transport to travel, were forced to hire themselves out for whatever wages an employer was willing to pay in a given area. Indeed, a central doctrine of the bourgeoisie—the notion that property is merely a relationship between a person and a thing, without further ramifications of dominance—is a fiction. When property consists of the means of production, it becomes an instrument of control over people.[244]

Thus the law as we know it is concerned above all with property; concern for human rights, or even civil rights, is relatively new in law, and does not exist in many societies. To obtain these property rights, the bourgeoisie had to erect other rights as parts of law—rights to life, liberty, and equality. Once the bourgeoisie was firmly in control of most Western societies, however, it lost interest in these rights, and began to use the legal façade of free choice and fairness to conceal the reality of coercion and social control. It increasingly depended upon public-law institutions to protect its interests and to foster increasing concentration of capital and power. It controls governments yet pretends the state is a neutral arbiter among equal forces.[245] The lawyer's role in this system is, according to one lawyer and teacher of law, "to make it look good, to provide at least the appearance of justice."[246]

Philip Green writes, "It may not be a coincidence that the closer the issue of equality came to being on the agenda of practical political action, the more social scientists began to provide arguments supporting existing elites and the maintenance of gross inequalities."[247] In other words, the mottoes of liberty, equality, and justice were for a certain class merely catchwords used to gain power. Once that power had been consolidated, the elite class lost interest in those concepts and promulgated new ones: efficiency, rationality, law and order—the latter a euphemism for broad social control. The social scientists of whom Green writes are part of the new learned elite, Gouldner's New Class, which has come into prominence in America in the last fifty years. It has found acceptance precisely because it has lent itself to the intentions of the ruling monied interests. Lawyers have been serving the interests of the wealthy from their first emergence.

The word *law* covers an elaborate, many-faceted structure. There is written law, a set of guidelines and strictures which embody the values of a given culture. In the West, this has meant, since the late Athenian age, that law crystallizes power relations among varied groups in society.[248] Beneath the apparent trivialities of actual laws lie the principles upon which a society is built, a set of traditional beliefs and values. These constitute a legal ideology which stands above and outside society and seems to have an independent existence. These principles are never shared absolutely. Law functions to move contention over the principles from field and street into tribunals that pretend to exist, as it were, outside life; that make the implicit claim of determining adherence to a legal ideology seen as absolutely right. Warring factions must in these tribunals translate their actual argument into differing interpretations of legal ideology.[249] In turn, these arguments, whatever their outcome, affect future arguments, affect the law and the ideology upon which it rests. Thus legal ideology may be the most stable and enduring part of law, but it is constantly in process, not static and immutable.

Law has two parts: first, it offers a norm, or order; second, it is an instrument of force, might, for securing that order.[250] The legal ideology of a society is often at odds with the ideology of its government, even when governments are elected. When power is seized, new rulers may discard the old ideology and produce a new one. Elected governments, however (even when election is mere appearance), prefer to legitimate themselves by appearing to honor the old ideology. They leave the traditional code in place and subvert it by removing its power, that is, by obliterating the second part of its functions, as Hitler did with the Weimar Constitution. Governmental agencies can also be subverted by denying them the money they need to operate, and thus limiting their ability to place force behind laws. This has been occurring in the United States in the past few years. Both kinds of subversion produce invisible government, rule without responsibility to an electorate. Rules are determined by a ruler and his cronies and enforced according to their caprice.

Lawyers in the United States, who helped to erect a system based on ideals of liberty, equality, and justice—whatever its practice—are now helping to dismantle that system. The ruling class and "their servants in the judicial system, be they prosecutors or judges, are turning upon their own system, are abandoning their own stated rules, designed once in a bygone age to embody the then revolutionary principles of fairness, equality, justice, and liberty."[251] The present economic system is unable to sustain itself without severe exploitation of labor: when prevented from exploiting labor domestically, it exploits the labor of less fortunate nations, leaving American workers to starve. It cannot reap the profits it wants without having labor on its knees, something it has accomplished ruthlessly in Third World countries and is attempting to reestablish in industrial nations. As multinational corporations come to dominate the economics of the West, national laws can rarely touch them: and even when they can, the monied interests have great influence over the law and the state.

The executive branch of government, made up partly of lawyers, has for some decades been undermining existing law. Government wages war without declaring war, illegally, and sometimes does so secretly: this was the case in Chile, in Vietnam, and in Nicaragua. Lawyers have assisted in the undermining of various governmental agencies, and have lately helped in efforts to overturn the exclusionary rule, which reinforces rights guaranteed by the Fourth Amendment to the Constitution by prohibiting prosecutors from using evidence that has been seized illegally.[252] Overturning of this rule would mean that police or secret police could with impunity break into people's houses, stop them on the streets, and search them without warrant. In actuality this rule is broken regularly in police dealings with the poor, especially with blacks. Because in our culture it is considered legitimate to suspect the poor and blacks of crime, such abuses are usually papered over, even though they sometimes explode into murder. If the exclusionary rule is annulled entirely, capricious and dictatorial surveillance by police and secret police (FBI, CIA) could be extended to classes that are not now culturally suspect.

Many of the initiatives emanating from government since the late 1970s have been in the direction of more control by a central power and less individual autonomy. Censorship of various sorts has been established.[253] Attempts have been made to increase the control of the administration over the budget, to expand the powers of the secret police while reducing congressional surveillance over the CIA, and to annul (without changing the law) equal rights laws.[254] None of these initiatives could have been launched without the assistance of lawyers. Yet what these lawyers, who are sworn to uphold law, are trying to accomplish for their governmental masters is an installation of invisible government, a subversion of law. The new practice in the United States is one of circumvention. The old laws are not rescinded, not addended, not superseded; they remain in place while lawyers, and the Justice Department itself, seek for ways to nullify them by limited funding, hostile agency administrators, and outright impediment of the sort that in the army is called goldbricking. Such practices can gut a set of laws without even touching them.

The Justice Department, the legal arm of the executive branch of government, has for decades supported invisible government, with the cooperation of the secret police, the enforcing arm. During the late 1960s, FBI infiltration into civil rights and antiwar organizations was widely recognized. The involvement of an FBI informer in the murder of a civil rights marcher, Viola Liuzzo, is a matter of record, but legal procedures against him and against the government have been unsuccessful.[255] Revelations of associations of secret police agencies with organized crime and their use, or intended use, of criminals to carry out some of their projects should give the entire nation pause.

Since such actions occur with the cooperation or tolerance of members of the American legal system, Tigar and Levy are correct in pointing out that this system is being subverted from within. The American Constitution is not a perfect document—it lacks, as we know all too well, a guarantee of sexual equality—but it is as just and humane a set of laws as can be found in a large industrial country. It is less the Constitution than the reams of law built upon it that grant special privileges to large industry, the wealthy, and to clandestine, surreptitious actions mounted by privileged groups. That laws favoring such groups have been passed is testimony to the control they maintain over government. The issue confronting us now is how far the American public will allow a ruling class made up of industrialists, administrators, and their lawyers to go in grasping control over every element of our lives, whether de jure or de facto.

Often the argument used in proposals of centralizing control is a devious and deceitful appeal to terror. The argument runs: we need these powers to counteract subversion by foreign powers and their instruments here in the United States; we need these powers to guarantee the safety of "the American Way." Yet these powers would totally erode the "American Way" if that way is founded in the Constitution, especially the Bill of Rights. The real argument is this: the United States is dealing with totalitarian nations; to maintain the prosperity of its major industries and corporations, it is necessary to adopt totalitarian methods here as well. And it is possible that, unless we are alert, this move to totalitarianism will be made.

The legal profession shows its devotion to power as the highest good, to dominance and stratification, and to increased control of low-status groups, in other ways besides its support for governmental initiatives toward greater centralization of power over broader areas. In this it follows the thinking of the class that created the Constitution, which saw itself as a group of outsiders and wished to guarantee its own rights. One consequence of this wish is the adversarial system.

Like the emphasis on competition, individuality, and aggressiveness that has pervaded Western thinking for several centuries, the idea that justice is best obtained through competition is basic to most Western systems of law. So good government is somehow supposed to result from pluralistic pulling and hauling among competing interests—one of the most dangerous and false assumptions of contemporary liberalism, according to Theodore Lowi.[256] Conflicts among huge powers—business interests, military branches, well-financed lobbies—rarely benefit the nation as a whole. And when conflict occurs between individuals or citizens' groups and large institutions, the body possessed of the greater wealth inevitably wins. Our present legal system operates on a false assumption. Just as capitalists claim justice and fairness for the capitalist system because work is based on a contract made freely between worker and employer, and that property is a relationship between a person and a thing, legal doctrine holds that adversarial conflict leads to justice, and assumes that such conflicts concern only the parties to them. Workers do not have the resources to make free choices about their employment, and ownership of property confers dominance on the owner: these arrangements *create* inequality, and have broad reverberations for communities and states. Adversarial relations could be said to promote fairness and justice only if both parties to the conflict were indeed equal, and if their conflict did not affect communities and states. This is not the case.

The adversarial system is notoriously unfair in the realm of criminal justice. It redefines *justice* as victory, and transforms judicial process into a game which one wins or loses. It arises from the old patriarchal assurance that God grants the victory to the good, even as those who led wars fought with this claim knew that might makes right, victory accrues to the more powerful, and the powerful decree what is good. Like the old ordeals by fire or water, the test is made to discover some miraculous intervention that indicates innocence.

In the present-day version of adversarial trial, the rich, the well connected, and the prestigious are rarely accused of crimes, are even more rarely found guilty, and if they are, are imprisoned in relatively luxurious institutions. Such people can afford to hire batteries of clever, aggressive lawyers who do not hesitate to bribe or threaten (or even arrange for the murder of) witnesses or jurors, who manage, despite laws forbidding such things, to suborn perjury, manufacture or destroy documents, who can influence judges by buddyship or veiled promises of advancement. Money and power are the only real values operating in the American legal system, and everyone caught up in it learns this if they did not know it before. Those lacking money and power are ground up by the system, whether they are innocent or guilty of the charged acts. American prisons are filled with the poor.

Foucault points out that the prison system was always designed not for punishment but for social control. In the early nineteenth century, people in power intended to create and segregate a criminal class which could be of use to them. It was this criminal class that in France supervised the huge prostitution industry, provided surveillance of citizens, was hired to break strikes, to infiltrate organizations, and sometimes assisted those who, like Napoleon III, aimed to seize power.[257] But the widespread development of the penitentiary and the use of imprisonment as a common punishment evolved along with industrialization and the disinheritance of the masses. Poor people without work, or demoralized factory workers, often lashed out against their situation by rioting. The invention of the professional, full-time, urban police force in the early nineteenth century was a response to the bourgeoisie's fear of these spontaneous, disruptive groups.[258]

In the United States the dispossessed are largely black: almost nine times as many blacks are imprisoned as whites. They are also largely poor, and the poor receive much harsher sentences than people from higher income levels accused of the same crimes. A profile of jail inmates compiled by the Federal Bureau of Justice Statistics shows that the median income of male prisoners before incarceration was about $3,800 a year, one-third of that of the general population. Those accused of "white-collar" crime and drunken driving, "which involve more money and more deaths, respectively, than any other categories of crime," are punished far less severely than other offenders because they are often from the middle class.[259]

The poor are often inadequately defended by neophytes or by overworked or half-hearted attorneys appointed by the court; they lack resources to pay lawyers, much less to mount their own investigation of the crime if they are not guilty. They are sent to swell the numbers of an incarcerated subclass—nearly four hundred thousand adults (384,316) were imprisoned as of March 1982.[260] Only two nations in the world—the Soviet Union and South Africa—imprison a larger percentage of their population than the United States.[261] Of these four hundred thousand only about a third have been convicted of violent crimes; more than 90 percent of the offenses in all categories recorded by the Federal Bureau of Investigation's 1980 crime report were crimes against property.[262] The adversary system on the one hand, and the invariable resort to incarceration of the poor on the other, combine to keep the poor oppressed; neither one, however, serves to reduce crime or recidivism.

The United States spends more than six billion dollars on correction each year, almost 90 percent of which goes for incarceration. It costs far more—$75,000—to build a medium-security cell than to build a classroom or assist a poor family with welfare; it costs $17,000 to maintain that cell each year.[263] We must question the priorities of a nation that chooses to spend its money in this way. Why would people prefer to spend large sums of money to incarcerate an already victimized group rather than attempt to ameliorate their victimization?

The favored solution to the problem of crime in the United States is clearly more and more control: more police, more weapons, more prisons—that is, more money spent on attempts at domination of those who commit ordinary (not white-collar) crime. Yet we have already seen that such methods are minimally successful. To change our attitude toward crime would require changing the thinking and the values of the entire legal system—not just lawyers, legislators, and judges, but the entire enforcement apparatus: police, secret police, militia, armed forces; the penal system; and those who service such systems, psychologists, sociologists, teachers of law. To change the way we handle crime, we have to change our morality.

In China, where the community is very strong and tight, lawbreakers are tried by the community as a whole. The offender is defended by those who sympathize, attacked by others, and ideally the goal of the trial is to find a solution whereby a person who performs antisocial acts may best be reassimilated into the community. This may involve incarceration for "reeducation"—which, of course, we might call brainwashing. But is it less a brainwashing to send a young man who has committed a petty theft to a prison in which he will be demoralized, humiliated, raped, and brutalized?

The Chinese cannot provide us with a model. Their ancient culture has not been fully industrialized, and they have not experienced the fragmentation of community that pervades the United States. Beyond that, Chinese society is totalitarian, and community pressure has force partly because it is backed up by a monolithic structure that makes escape difficult. There are few holes for an offender to slip through. In addition, the community system has at times permitted extreme abuses. Nevertheless, the Chinese system of handling petty crime can offer us some light. Justice, which must be more than the rule of the powerful, can better be approached by considering all people individuals within a context, whose acts affect not just a few people but the larger context of their community. The aim of judicial process should be to help an offender reenter the community in a more rewarding role. Our aim should not be to punish, because punishment does not reform. We may wish to exile serious offenders from the ordinary human community by imprisoning them. But a society that regarded the welfare of the whole, human felicity, and bonds among people as supremely important would seek to find ways to integrate, rather than further fragment, that society.

Trotsky suggested that there should be two standards of moral judgment, that different criteria should be applied to a "slaveowner who through cunning and violence shackles a slave in chains and a slave who through cunning and violence breaks the chains."[264] Actually, most Western societies do precisely this—rewarding the slaveowners and punishing the slaves. But if the image is applicable in one sense—most of those called criminals are part of a victimized class—it does not hold in the other. Few American criminals are attempting to liberate themselves. Most criminal acts performed by the poor are not acts of self-liberation or even revenge on the oppressors. They are desperate, mindless acts of violence, expressive of rage, the only emotion that is still viewed with respect (or fear, which Machiavelli suggested is better than respect). The poor prey, for the most part, on the poor. Violence consists largely of indiscriminate vengeance on those seen as more helpless than the criminal—the old, women, gay men.

Although our institutions of law and penology are largely responsible for methods and approaches to "justice," all of us carry some responsibility for the use of legal systems in social control. We may blame factors external to us for our lack of a sense of autonomy, communal responsibility, and personal responsibility: at some point it stops mattering what is to blame. We do abrogate our own responsibility and thereby our own powers; we are getting the kind of society we deserve, one in which we have little voice. And as we cede our powers, we ask, consciously or not, for greater centralized control.

We cannot control our children, and so we haul them into family courts. One family court judge has demanded that the courts be empowered to order whatever is necessary for the overall treatment of troubled juveniles whether or not they have committed any crime. "Everyone says he hasn't committed any crime," one judge protested, speaking of a young boy brought to court because he was uncontrollable. "Are you going to let him live out there on the street until he does?"[265] It is true that sometimes we cannot manage our children: because we live in such isolated ways, because there is no community to turn to for help, because we have lost memory of a sense of context, interdependence, living together.

We demand to be protected against all eventualities, yet do little to contribute to that protection. We do not recognize that all protection is oppression; sometimes—as in raising a small child, for instance—the price of oppression is worth paying. To fence in a small child is better than having it killed in the street. But those protections that are worthwhile are a small percentage of those we demand from government. And the burden of protecting us has been placed largely on the legal-judicial system.

Judge Polier points out that "both law and psychiatry are caught up in the demand that they should prevent persons from behaving in such a way as to disturb the peace of the community," and should "control and rehabilitate them." This demand is more than the law can handle. The social courts, Polier asserts, act as mere lids to contain problems, to conceal them from public scrutiny. Those problems largely emerge from poverty and dehumanized living conditions.[266]

"Primitive" societies do not have laws, according to legal theorists, but only customs which bind because of communal acceptance. Laws arise out of self-conscious awareness of the process of making them. Yet in a sense there is no law without the communal acceptance of custom that orders "primitive" or simple societies. In the past few decades American courts have been asked to provide controls and norms for such things as air pollution, nurse training, student loans, water resources, maternal and child health, mental retardation, vaccination, community health centers, library services, youth offenses and delinquency, foster care for dependent children; and to enforce laws dealing with the treatment of delinquent children and youths, the mentally defective and ill, deprived preschool children, and children not motivated to learn— among others.[267]

The picture this suggests is of a desperate society, one that lacks any moral standard and any sense of community, lacks the sense that it has the right to demand adherence to any particular level of behavior, and that hopelessly asks the legal system, the psychiatric establishment, or the state to provide standards and enforce them. In the past few years people have begun to demand that the legal system solve their marital or divorce disputes as well.

Such a cession of responsibility grants even more power to an already too powerful state; it weakens the community even further; and it adds the final fillip to the transformation of people into helpless infantile "matter." But the process is twofold: the state, with its huge corps of experts in institutions that work together with the state, willingly steps into the moral vacuum and, under the guise of benevolence, extends its control over the entire population; the population, demoralized by the inhumanity of religious moral attitudes, by loss of tradition and cohesive communality, by the undermining of authority through relativistic and progressive movements of thought, gives up in despair and cedes its small remaining purlieu to the state.

Iredell Jenkins criticizes contemporary schools of legal thought for being so caught up in the "legal apparatus as a mode of social control" that they have forgotten that law can exist only within a social context.[268] No amount of police, laws, courts, judges, prisons, mental hospitals, psychiatrists, and social workers can *create* a society with relative harmony. The most institutions can do is to *impose* the appearance of relative harmony, something that has happened in socialist countries, and which many of the most fiercely antisocialist corporate leaders would like to emulate here.

Legal process, as it currently exists in this country, is an enormous, interwoven bureaucracy that vainly attempts to handle the moral breakdown of our culture, and in its attempts uses the very methods—broader and more centralized control, and an instrumental view of people—that have led to the moral breakdown. Lawyers and others in the legal establishment are not singularly to blame for this. Yet lawyers are now and have long been—Chaucer mocked them in the fourteenth century—first among those who foster extreme individualism, contentiousness, and struggle for profit. Attorneys are not ashamed of winning freedom for murderers and members of organized crime. Attributing bad faith to judges, prosecutors, and police who are willing to distort or conceal evidence, lawyers feel that any strategy is legitimate in defending a client (who can pay for such defense).[269] Lawyers who represent corporations are among the highest paid in the nation; they are not ashamed of winning victories for exploiters, and submerge any shame they might feel in the luxury of hottubs or Caribbean waters. Attorneys are ashamed of only one thing: poverty.

As with doctors, psychologists, and educators, there are exceptions among lawyers. Lawyers have participated in social movements even when they had no expectation of remuneration for their work: in the labor movement, the campaign against anti-Semitism, the black civil rights movement, and the feminist movement (although it was almost entirely female lawyers who helped feminist campaigns in the early years). Others try to concentrate on helping despised classes—people of color and the poor. Many young law students start out with humane values, and some manage to maintain them despite the brainwashing called law school. Over the past few decades there have been numerous projects directed at helping the poor gain control over their own lives. Store-front legal services such as the MFY Legal Services in New York help the poor, the illiterate, and the non-English-speaking weave their way through the complexities of welfare red tape, evictions, veterans' and Social Security disability programs, consumer fraud, immigration difficulties, and family programs.[270] Because they are helping the poor, such lawyers themselves need financial help, and it is to government that they turn. But government is extremely busy helping the rich, and federal aid in all services designed to help the poor is vanishing. Government has been attempting in underhanded ways to abolish the Legal Services Corporation, which provides lawyers for the poor. Because the program cannot legally be abolished, the executive branch cuts back on funding, refuses to appoint directors, or appoints directors who are opposed to the service they are supposed to administer.[271]

In defense of lawyers, it must be repeated that power is contagious: one can fight it only with equal power. Even lawyers dedicated to humane causes try to create a power base, knowing that without one any cause is lost. Those most knowledgeable about law have long insisted it has nothing to do with justice. To suggest that it should is to risk sounding sentimental and visionary, unrealistic. Marxists and capitalists agree on more than they disagree about: both see economic concerns as primary. Power is the highest good; law is an embodiment of power relations in a society; those power relations are created by economics. To be realistic in our age is to cast aside any other concern but these. To be hardheaded is to impugn any motive but the desire for power—as wealth, influence, or might.

But we must see where our values—our aims, priorities, and methods—are carrying us. It is one more absurdity that the very people in the United States who are most militantly antisocialist, and who regard socialist nations as a threat to very life, are devoting themselves to producing in this country a political and social system that contains the monolithic structure, the totalist philosophy, and the totalitarian control that are the features of socialism which even those of us sympathetic to other socialist aims fear and deplore. It is absurd as well to imagine that broader and more centralized control can cure the diseases it has partly caused. It is necessary to begin to think creatively, morally, about our problems. But a great force opposes such thinking; instead it tells us we have the best of all possible worlds and urges that we adopt a more totalitarian system, to keep the world safe from socialism and keep the corporations (euphemistically called *democracy*) alive. Democracy—true democracy, participatory democracy—is indeed the best system of government ever devised; it was probably the system, or mode, used in matricentric cultures. The greatest impediment to true democracy in the West is not socialism but the corporate world.

## 4. PILLARS OF SOCIETY III: CORPORATIONS

Simone Weil, that brilliant analyst who died too soon, wrote in 1933: "Up to the present mankind has known two principal forms of oppression, the one (slavery or serfdom) exercised in the name of armed force, the other in the name of wealth transformed into capital; what we have to determine is whether these are not now being succeeded by a new species of oppression, oppression exercised in the name of management."[272] Feudalism fell because of "the substitution of trade for war as the principal means of domination." She concludes, "Every human group that exercises power does so, not in such a way as to bring happiness to those who are subject to it, but in such a way as to increase that power."[273]

No one who is attuned to current events in this nation should require proof that not just our lives, but the lives of people clear across the globe are being formed and deformed by the operations of American corporations.

If we exclude agricultural workers, 20 percent of the American labor force work for some level of government (which is structured like corporations); 30 percent work for large business enterprises (those with more than five hundred employees); and a large proportion of the remainder work for private institutions like hospitals or universities. Thus considerably more than half our population is in the direct control of large corporate institutions. Twelve million people work for firms that employ more than ten thousand people.[274] Centralized control has increased in recent decades: in 1955, 44.5 percent of Americans who worked in manufacture and mining worked for the top five hundred corporations; by 1970 the figure was 72 percent and the share of the market controlled by those five hundred corporations went from 40 percent to 70 percent.[275]

As John Kenneth Galbraith has shown in a number of works, the number of corporations shrinks as their share of the market increases.[276] One thousand corporations produce half of all the goods and services not provided by the state, and the 333 largest industrial corporations possess 70 percent of all manufacturing assets. In 1968, the two hundred largest corporations in the United States controlled the same percentage—around 65 percent—of all manufacturing assets as the *one thousand* largest firms had owned in 1941.[277] This shrinkage in the number of firms that control assets and employees has significance for our lives: that fewer companies are in control means less competition and less variety in what they do and what they demand; it also makes more possible a consensus among them that can in some instances be called collusion.

These corporations have power over every dimension of our lives: they produce what they (not we) want produced, of whatever quality they determine; they fix prices and costs; they decide on the future of each of their employees and sometimes on the future of entire towns and localities. They can determine "where people live, what work, if any, they will do, what they will eat, drink, and wear, what sorts of knowledge schools and universities will encourage, and what kind of society our children will inherit."[278] They also affect all of us in their treatment of our natural resources, in how they decide to deal with their own garbage. They influence our elections, our foreign policy, and even our image of ourselves, both through what they produce and how they advertise it.

Our economic system is sold to us under the name of "free enterprise," but as almost every economist and political scientist points out, free enterprise no longer exists, if indeed it ever did. Free enterprise is a system in which buyers and sellers meet in a neutral marketplace, possess equal power and equal information, and make their exchange without leaving any litter behind, any "spillover" nuisance effects, without, that is, altering the space in which the exchange occurs.[279] But a market is not neutral when government passes legislation that rigs markets, gives certain groups investment tax credits, incentives, depletion and depreciation allowances, subsidies, rebates, research and development funding, demonstration grant programs, and price supports. Government gives subsidies to the energy industries alone of 134 billion dollars a year (yet these industries argue against the extension of such subsidies to solar and renewable energy industry on the ground that these companies should compete in the "free" market).[280] Regulated industries, such as power companies, airlines, radio, television, railroads, and telephone companies—companies that provide the essential services of society—are heavily subsidized by government.[281]

There remain a few genuinely competitive markets in the United States: retailing, and some older industries like clothing, textiles, and commercial printing. But most sectors of the economy are dominated by some concentrated market power—Pentagon defense contracts, for example, price leadership by General Motors in the automobile industry, alliances between corporate farmers and the Department of Agriculture, "tidy arrangements between public utilities and the public service commissions that 'regulate' them," and control of interest rates by the combined pressure of the Federal Reserve and major money market banks.[282]

Government primes the pump of business through the military budget: in the early 1970s the Department of Defense was financing half of all research and development costs in the country, including 90 *percent* of that done in the aviation and space industries.[283] Many of the multinational corporations, like IBM and ITT, grew to their present size because of substantial help from the Pentagon.[284] Although oil companies like to present an appearance of permanence, stability, and a "lofty superiority to all governments," as they treat national governments cavalierly and announce themselves as the guardians of the security of the West and the peace of the world, in fact they fly to the government whenever they are in trouble.[285]

Thus in our system neither small and big businesses nor buyers and sellers are equal in any way. It is a system that guarantees the continued dominance of the dominant. Behind the imposing façades of large corporations stands the government as a prop; the government runs on taxes: thus we pay not only for what we buy but for the operations of corporations whose products we may have no use for. Barber sums up the situation: "Business may parrot the rhetoric of entrepreneurial capitalism from time to time, but there is little doubt that our multinational corporations look to government to buy their goods, prop up their prices, subsidize their inefficiencies, protect their monopolies, minimize their competition, guarantee their credit, cover their losses, and absorb their bankruptcies."[286]

The idea of free enterprise also connotes the existence of many sellers in competition with one another; this is supposed to be an automatic, invisible control guaranteeing a fair purchase price. But "up to the 1880s, most businessmen competed with one another. After the 1880s, smart businessmen combined with one another."[287] Those small firms that continued to compete with one another have disappeared by the thousands; what remains is "oligopolistic competition," in which a few large companies compete according to stipulated rules—never on prices, as little as possible on new technology. This policy sometimes leads to difficulties, when foreign industry outstrips American industry with new technology, greater efficiency, or lower prices. At such times industry in America turns to government for tariffs or assistance. Little change is made in its procedures, and large corporations continue to adhere to the "mutually protective rules of the game," channeling their rivalry into forms that do not involve cutting prices.[288] Most businesses find that a dollar spent on advertising brings quicker return than a dollar invested in a product.[289]

Business has changed its form somewhat in the past century and a half. Originally a relatively free-enterprise system involving many individual entrepreneurs, business was already highly concentrated by 1900, with wealth in the hands of a few. At that time American business totally dominated our government. Over the past eighty years control became diffused as rich families lost control of their companies, as banker-based interest groups weakened. From this diffusion and shift emerged a few large corporations which had absorbed other industries. Some observers believed this shift was "as momentous as the shift from feudalism to capitalism," because the new ruling class was a group of managers who own little stock and work on salary, and whose family name and integrity are not tied to the company. Political scientists hypothesized that these managers would be less greedy and acquisitive, more efficient and more responsible to the general public good—very much as Gouldner believes his New Class will behave. But Edward Herman concludes there has been no change of that sort whatever: the profit motive "has suffered no discernible eclipse as a result of the rise of management control."[290]

During the period of transition, however, business lost its exclusive control over government, and has since worked to regain it. It has mounted a strong campaign to reduce the size or rate of growth of government, and to eliminate some of its functions. In particular business wants to eliminate regulatory agencies overseeing business; and social welfare programs. It wishes to eliminate government assistance to the lower fifth of the population, the very poor; but when it is in need, it demands strong government protection. Herman calls this a "whipsaw" treatment of government that discredits it and diminishes its authority.[291] The reverse—governmental attempts to control business—has been largely ineffectual. Antitrust laws do not really cover conglomerates, and in any case, "the history of anti-trust in America is a history of evasions and compromises, and repeatedly the biggest corporations have shown themselves stronger than governments."[292]

From another perspective, however, business and government are not separable entities. Richard Barnet and Ronald Muller point out that business interests dominate both major political parties and certain key members of Congress through their financial holdings; they own or influence much of the mass media; and they participate in government itself at times, through appointments to cabinet posts and regulatory agencies. For example, in 1983 Pentagon auditors accused the Defense Science Board of conflicts of interest and cronyism. The board, which advises the armed forces on future weapons programs, and which has a "major impact" on decisions about weapons, included executives of the weapons industry, who could vote for programs that would benefit their companies.[293] Through their control of both communications media and institutions seemingly separate from government or business, such interests propagate the ideology of "salvation through profits and growth" that prevails throughout our society. This explains, Barnet and Muller conclude, "why the government of the world's mightiest nation musters so little power to protect the interests of its people."[294]

Ralph Miliband asserts the existence in America of a single economically dominant class, rather than interconnected government and business groups. This class controls both wealth and major institutions—government, police, industry—and influences communications, using ideology to gain popular consent to its policies.[295]

Business has been able to turn to its advantage even those events that seem to counter its influence. For example, Proposition 13 in California sprang from local concerns: ordinary people felt overburdened by taxes. The results of its passage were curtailment of local police, firefighting, and sanitation services. Most of the tax relief, however—65 percent of it—went to business and real estate investors. Hazel Henderson points out that the proposition left intact high-level administration costs and bureaucratic featherbedding in state government, cost-plus contracts, cost overruns, and "the largest segment, special tax subsidies to business, including shipping, oil, nuclear energy, trucking, and construction."[296]

Large corporations and combined business interests have enormous power in this country. But multinational or global corporations have even more power over a wider area. As corporations are absorbed by multinationals, centralization intensifies. The multinationals arose as formal colonialism was phased out; it was no longer legitimate for one country to "own" another, and to impose by force a European culture on a Third World state. Colonialism did not disappear, however; it was transformed into economic domination of Third World states by companies known as multinationals because they operate in many areas of production and work in many countries: the vast majority of them, however, are American.[297]

These companies are huge. Even in the mid-nineteenth century Rockefeller and Standard Oil were bigger than any state in the Union; by the mid-twentieth, many conglomerates were bigger than most national governments.[298] In 1973 the revenues of General Motors were greater than the gross national products of Switzerland, Pakistan, and South Africa combined; Royal Dutch Shell is larger than Iran, Venezuela, and Turkey; Goodyear Tire is bigger than Saudi Arabia. The average rate of growth of most successful global corporations is two to three times greater than that of the most advanced industrial countries, including the United States, and they control over 200 billion dollars' worth of physical assets.[299] The oil companies are the largest global organizations in the world: they command entire fleets, pipelines, refineries, and chains of filling stations. They control not only oil but petrochemicals, coal, and nuclear power.[300]

Most multinationals are involved in many different lines of business. Thus they centralize control while extending their power over many areas. Their production is based on advanced technology, which requires basic research and product development, which in turn requires long-term investment on a huge scale. So great is the investment that companies ensure the sale of their products by any means that come to hand—market research, marketing, advertising, and sometimes corruption.[301] This is not to say that there is anything wrong with doing marketing research or using marketing techniques to sell a product; what is reprehensible is using such techniques to stimulate desire for something that is not otherwise desirable or to stimulate desire for a shoddy product. The idea of deriving profit from an exchange that seemed sinful to people of the Middle Ages does not seem so sinful today. To add a surcharge to an item to pay for one's time and labor in finding and buying it (or overseeing its manufacture) and perhaps transporting it seems well within the limits of fairness. But to manufacture something simply because one imagines one can sell it, and to expend more energy on methods of selling it than on making it well, or making something useful, is to transform the process of exchange into a con game.

The multinationals are not managed by owners, shareholders, but by a consortium or association of men with varied technical knowledge and experience.[302] The characteristics of global corporations are strange, even paradoxical. The managers are less interested in reaping huge profits for the shareholders than in expanding the company to their own benefit; they often invest in automated equipment not to reduce costs but to increase their own power and security by reducing a potentially troublesome labor force.[303] This behavior exemplifies the mindlessness of our present world; if insanity is acting inappropriately to actual circumstances to one's own detriment, such a way of doing business is insane. It does not improve the world but clutters it up with junk; and it does not increase security for managers because it increases the number of unemployed, who can no longer buy industry's products and who comprise a potentially rebellious force.

Like all patriarchal institutions, multinationals involve huge bureaucratic structures and a labor force to which they preach loyalty, obedience, conformity, and a gospel of shared interest, but they have no loyalty either to that labor force or to any of the nations in which they operate. Sometimes a global corporation builds duplicate facilities in a distant place, to which it can shift in the event of labor (or other) trouble in the home plant. Sometimes this involves shifting from one nation to another with more tractable labor. When it suits them the multinationals abandon entire localities without compunction, leaving behind entire towns—people and their houses, shops, schools, and churches—and a haze of pollution.[304] Richard Gerstacker, president of Dow Chemical in 1972, promised that some day Dow would be able to elude all government controls and laws, in the United States and elsewhere, by relocating itself on an island in the middle of an ocean, beyond the reach of any nation-state.[305]

Although global corporations offer little loyalty to workers or nation, they depend upon national government to support them, and infiltrate governments by means of money and influence. Thus government and global business have come to have "interlocking directorates and representatives," and represent identical interests.[306] As was mentioned earlier, many of the people who went to work for the Environmental Protection Agency in 1980–81 had previously been connected in one way or another with companies opposed to pollution controls, like Chemical Waste Management Inc. and the Adolph Coors Brewing Company.[307] Three executives of Boeing were given severance pay totaling $400,000 when they left Boeing for high-level posts in the Department of Defense.[308]

Beyond this, the activities of large corporations require large governmental infrastructures to coordinate and foster them: the automobile industry alone has generated the building of highways and bridges, licensing of drivers and vehicles, and systems of traffic police—all paid for by taxpayers.[309] Sometimes the behavior of global companies is so blatantly outrageous that government is forced to intervene; but whether the companies use government or abuse their power to the point of requiring government intervention, they enlarge it, willy-nilly.[310]

Thus multinational corporations are primarily responsible for the movement toward totalitarian rule in the United States and in other Western nations. They centralize huge powers—wealth, ownership of property in many nations (and therefore control over people who live or work on that property, and those who sell products or services to those who work on the property), and influence over governments. They cause the enlargement of government. The area within the control of these corporations is also huge and diverse, ranging over continents, including many kinds of businesses and diverse forms of work. In the United States and in some European countries, the directorate of these corporations is interlocked with government members to comprise a group that is truly the elite of the world, managing so many elements that none of us is unaffected by their actions.

But their primary interest is not in creating world harmony or benefiting the world—which may be an advantage. If this elite were to decide what was good for us, we would not be able to escape the consequences of that decision. Their primary interest is not even in making profit, although that is important. They are concerned above all with extending their power and increasing their security—through gaining greater control. Their goal is therefore limitless: it cannot have an end, there is no degree of control that can be enough.

It is these people we mean when we refer, vaguely, to a *They* that represents an enemy to us. But these people could not function as they do if we did not abet them. We work for them—more than half of us; we believe their advertising; we buy their products. We do not, as a group, sit on our hands, demanding better quality, more responsible and responsive reactions to the real needs and desires of the human community. We vote for officials we know to be interlocked with such corporate institutions. We have accepted a state of little autonomy, accepted that power is the highest good, and when power proves empty, we imagine, as the corporations do, that more will be better.

Although multinational corporations are interlocked with government, and depend upon it to assist them when they are in difficulties, they are no more loyal to nations than they are to localities or communities of employees. Indeed, the degree to which global corporations are indifferent to national origin can be appalling. Anthony Sampson has traced the career of ITT under two different heads—Sosthenes Behn and Harold Geneen—both of whom offered apparent loyalty to a number of countries. Through ITT subsidiaries in Germany and South America, the company helped to build the Nazi war machine and sent Hitler information on ship sailings and cargoes. Even after Pearl Harbor ITT continued to cooperate with the Axis powers through its companies in Switzerland and Spain. The Swiss rival of ITT, Halser, refused to make equipment for Germany, but ITT did not demur: throughout the war it manufactured army equipment for the Nazis and sent them such raw materials as zinc sulphate and mercury.[311]

At the same time, however, ITT helped the Allies, and after the war its head was awarded the Medal of Merit, the highest civilian honor, for providing the American Army with land-line facilities. "While ITT Focke-Wulf planes were bombing Allied ships and ITT lines were passing information to German submarines, ITT direction-finders were saving other [Allied] ships from torpedoes."[312] When the war was over, ITT presented itself as an innocent victim and requested reparations—and was granted them. It received 27 million dollars for war damage to its factories in Europe, including 5 million for damage to Focke-Wulf plants bombed by Allied planes. "If the Nazis had won, ITT in Germany would have appeared impeccably Nazi; as they lost, it reemerged as impeccably American."[313]

In 1926, Standard Oil made a deal with the large German firm I. G. Farben, agreeing to cease research for synthetic rubber. The oil company maintained its agreement even after Germany invaded Poland.[314] In 1953 it put pressure on the government to have the CIA overthrow the Iranian government of Mossadegh; this cost the taxpayers $700,000, and perhaps cost some American as well as many Iranian lives then and since. Sampson believes the success of this coup encouraged the CIA to intervene in Guatemala later.[315] In 1956 the oil companies took advantage of the political crisis that occurred after the conflict at Suez to raise oil prices in their home nations.[316] Under pressure from the United Fruit Company, President Eisenhower in 1954 authorized the CIA to "destabilize" the government of Guatemala. Since that time Guatemala has suffered under a series of brutal right-wing military regimes.[317] In 1973 Saudi

Arabia ordered Aramco, an American-British oil company, to cease oil deliveries to the American military, and Aramco followed those orders. During the boycott of that year, American companies were reluctant to favor the United States at the expense of other nations, and the States lost a greater proportion of its oil supply than other nations.[318] The country suffered but the companies did not: in the shortage that followed, oil company profits rose staggeringly: Exxon's went up 80 percent, Gulf's 91 percent. The companies justified these profits by claiming they needed funds to pay for new exploration and development, but in the months that followed, they tried to buy expensive nonenergy businesses like Montgomery Ward and Ringling Brothers–Barnum and Bailey.[319] Since 1973 oil companies have invested heavily in other industries: Gulf bought chemicals, Atlantic Richfield bought copper (Anaconda, the second-largest copper company in the United States), Exxon bought electronics. Mobil merely stepped up publicity and patronage activities.[320]

Beyond this indifference to national well-being, corporations sometimes foster wars in which Americans, as well as other people, are killed. During the Nixon Administration ITT plotted with the CIA to prevent the election of Allende, a reformer, in Chile; after he was elected, they worked together to create economic chaos in that country, and eventually encouraged a coup to overthrow him. To this end Harold Geneen offered a contribution of a million dollars to the Nixon White House.[321] Allende was killed and replaced by a dictator who scourged the country and even fomented violence in the United States, but who remains in power.

If global corporations are short on global and national loyalty, domestic corporations are often indifferent to their own localities, communities, the places where many of their workers and managers live and raise families. In outrageous indifference to general well-being, the New Jersey corporation Ray Miller Inc. sold substandard steel components to nuclear plants throughout the country. These components were fraudulently marked, and could in the future cause trouble in primary cooling systems or emergency core-cooling systems.[322] Recent revelations show that Dow Chemical executives were aware of the possible dangers of dioxin dumping as early as 1965, when they held a closed meeting with their counterparts in other chemical companies to discuss the disastrous toxic effects of the substance on animals and humans. But Dow's public stance, despite the knowledge displayed at this meeting, has been steadfast denial of serious damage caused by dioxin (which is presently considered the deadliest chemical made by man). Even in the face of memoranda from this meeting, Dow's current president, Paul F. Oreffice, insists the only damage caused by dioxin was a rash called chloracne.[323] Critics claim that Dow has systematically resisted federal and state efforts to learn about and regulate dioxin, a charge that is given considerable substance by evidence that Dow put pressure on the Reagan Administration to force the EPA to suppress references to Dow's responsibility for contaminating the area around its plant in Midland, Michigan, with dioxin.[324]

The behavior of Kerr-McGee Corporation involves grave matters apart from the death of Karen Silkwood and others involved in trying to show the company negligent in its handling of plutonium, another utterly lethal substance. There is clear evidence that the company did allow the escape of plutonium from its plant, probably caused Silkwood to be contaminated, and lied about its amount of reserves.[325] Silkwood worked at Kerr-McGee, and became a union organizer. She saw increasing inefficiency and sloppiness in handling the dangerous substance—a bag of plutonium "the size of a softball is enough to give cancer to every child, woman, and man on earth."[326] As she tried to garner evidence of the company's abuse of workers and her suspicions that they were falsifying their quality control records for plutonium fuel rods, she found herself contaminated several times, the last time *internally*. An inspection team went to her apartment and found the entire dwelling "hot," with the highest levels of plutonium on the toilet seat and in the cheese and bologna in the refrigerator. Silkwood claimed she had gathered the necessary evidence; she was killed before she could deliver it. Several other sudden deaths have occurred among people working in the same movement with her.[327]

By 1974, seventy-three workers at the Kerr-McGee plant had been contaminated internally by plutonium. Between 1973 and 1974, the company had amassed 3,333 violations but was penalized by the Atomic Energy Commission for only eight. Kerr-McGee owns real estate, coal, natural gas; it processes helium, phosphates, asphalt, pesticides, potash, and boron. It is the nation's largest producer of uranium, and controls oil firms and drilling rigs. In Kerr-McGee's Mesa mines in Arizona, Navaho workers were exposed to radon gas; of the one hundred original miners, eighteen were dead of lung cancer by June 1974, and twenty-one more were dying. The company disclaimed responsibility.[328]

Such stories are, of course, only a tiny sample of actual abuses of people's bodies, neighborhoods, and—because of the flow of air and water, because of seepage—the entire North American continent. It is understandable that companies, like the general public, were not aware twenty or thirty years ago of the consequences of their methods of dumping waste products, or sending toxic elements into the air through smoke. They did not know, perhaps, that they were befouling their own nests—and ours. But since they have been made aware, their response has been to deny and conceal, to refuse to take steps to end pollution, and to shrug off any responsibility for what has already occurred. Yet it is precisely the people who manage such companies who express contempt for minorities and welfare pensioners for *their* "lack of responsibility."

Large corporations rarely take moral responsibility for the consequences of their operations for communities or workers. Nor are there many ways to hold them legally accountable. Governments are at least subject to public scrutiny. They can be voted in or out; they go up or down in polls; scandal can force changes in personnel. But companies operate in secrecy; they are not accountable to any constituency except shareholders (generally concerned only with profit); and global corporations are often more powerful than, and so invulnerable to, national governments. The United States government cannot even discover the true profits of the oil industry, the destination of oil supplies, or the amounts of oil on reserve: oil companies do not like "informed government," an oil official has said.[329]

Large corporations can dominate entire small nations, dislocate national economies, and upset the flow of world currency as they speculate on the currency market, switching from pounds to marks to yen for maximum profits. Large corporations were probably the prime force behind the currency crisis of 1971, when they sold U.S. dollars; it is suspected that ITT started the run on sterling in 1972 that resulted in the floating of the pound, and that it also precipitated the 1973 monetary crisis in the United States.[330]

Such actions affect all of us deeply, since they change the value of our money. In 1945, Paul Porter, then chairman of the Federal Communications Commission, warned that international communications companies were in a position to shape the international communications policy of the United States and might potentially serve interests opposed to those of their home country.[331] In 1980, Sampson wrote that despite the scandals that shook ITT in the early 1970s, it still regards itself as above government controls: "It presents itself still as an American company in America, British in Britain, German in Germany; but it owes loyalty to none of them and regards each government as an unnecessary obstruction."[332] John DeLorean, who was for many years an executive at General Motors (before he got caught up in macho fun and games), admitted in 1979 that "the system has a different morality as a group than the people do as individuals, which permits it to willfully produce ineffective or dangerous products, deal dictatorially and often unfairly with suppliers, pay bribes for business, abrogate the rights of employees by demanding blind loyalty to management, or tamper with the democratic process of government through illegal political contributions."[333] Sampson writes bitterly that although oil companies speak the language of statesmen and sovereigns and proclaim their dedication to the "American" (or British, in the case of BP) philosophy, in actuality they are simply committees of engineers and accountants preoccupied with profit margins, safeguarding investments, and avoiding taxes.[334]

The values of multinational corporations carry patriarchal priorities to such an extreme that it is inconceivable they could be carried further. Power and control are literally the *only* values; contempt for nature, and for those people seen as subordinate, is as limitless as the drive for control. The managers are not loyal to any nation—they do not contribute fairly to taxes; they work with any nation, regardless of its policies; they feel no responsibility to the people of the communities in which they own factories, and no responsibility to the world's people to keep nature's resources clean.

One can imagine, given their lack of loyalty to community, state, and nation, how global corporations treat the smaller, poorer countries in which they operate. Even rich small countries are utterly victimized by these corporations, which can on any given day change their marketing strategy and thereby completely alter national economies. A company may decide that in the future Germany, rather than France, should supply a certain product to Switzerland, or the reverse; it may determine that henceforth "all refrigerators will be made in Italy and all radios in Germany."[335]

The havoc that can be wreaked by unilateral decisions of global corporations in poor small nations is even more devastating. More than half of the 160 largest companies in pre-Allende Chile were owned or controlled by multinationals: the situation is similar clear across South America. The multinationals own half of the fifty largest companies in Argentina, 68 percent of Mexico's metal industry, and all of its tobacco industry; they glean 70 percent of the net profits in major sectors of the Brazilian economy.[336] It is largely because of this foreign ownership of local assets that the economies of these countries have been so subject to vacillation, trapping the entire population in their fluctuations.

Global firms justify their manipulations in these countries by pointing to an increased per capita income and a higher GNP, but the human reality that lies beneath these statistics reflects the human reality in the United States and Africa alike: the rich are getting richer, and the poor are becoming unbelievably poorer. The increased income in these South American countries goes to the top 5 percent of the population, while the lowest 40 percent have experienced a striking decrease. The majority of the people in South America have less food, poorer clothing, and worse housing than their parents had; indeed, worldwide, the diet of the lowest *40 to 60 percent* of the people is steadily becoming worse.[337] In 1900, people in poor countries had a per capita income half that of people in rich countries; by 1970 they had one-twentieth (measured in 1900 dollars) or one-fortieth (measured in 1970 dollars).[338]

The maneuvers of multinational companies further impoverish countries that are already poor in a number of ways. First, the multinationals put pressure on the governments of poor countries to grant them loans. The loans are granted because the investment seems secure, and the government hopes for an influx of dollars. But the money it lends the globals is therefore not available to local businesses. However, the profits earned by the globals are often—Barnet and Muller suspect *always*—removed from the host country and placed elsewhere. In the samples they cite, between 78 and 83 percent of the financing comes from the poor nation, and 79 percent of the profits are removed from it.[339]

An example of how this process works on the poor of the poor countries comes from Guatemala. The United States is promoting a "free-enterprise" venture in the Caribbean Basin; it subsidizes agribusiness projects by offering tariff and tax incentives for corporate investment in nontraditional agriculture, in crops like cucumbers, pineapples, tomatoes, and cut flowers. Alcosa, the Guatemalan subsidiary of an American corporation, Hanover Brands, receives financing from the Latin American Agribusiness Development Corporation, a consortium of big banks and agribusiness firms supported by the Agency for International Development. In 1975, Alcosa began contracting with Guatemalan peasants in seventeen villages to plant cauliflower and broccoli instead of their traditional corn, beans, and cabbage. The broccoli and cauliflower were processed and shipped frozen to North American supermarkets.

At first the income of the peasants increased; but under Alcosa's direction it began to decrease substantially. The peasants could survive only by going into debt to Alcosa for hybrid seeds and expensive insecticides. When crops were reaped, Alcosa paid itself back its loan before it paid anything to the peasants, so that farm families went as long as three months without income. When

Alcosa stopped buying vegetables in one village, it was devastated: cauliflower and broccoli will not fill a belly as corn, beans, and cabbage will. The people starved; their children had to leave school and leave home, tramping from town to town to find menial labor in other villages simply to be able to eat.

One of the villages, however, established an informed co-op. It negotiated a better contract with Alcosa, and it advised farmers (against Alcosa's advice) to plant corn among the cauliflowers and to use smaller doses of a cheaper insecticide. This village was the only successful one in the venture. But the strange thinking that pervades global corporations and their relations with host countries does not seem hospitable to this success. The organizers of peasant co-ops are being assassinated by Guatemalan government forces, and peasants who participate in them are being murdered by the hundreds.[340] Why? Whom does the modest prosperity of peasants threaten? Why is not cooperation that works well for both sides encouraged?

To suggest that global corporations and forces within the governments of a number of countries, but especially within the United States, are actively working to eliminate those people—millions of them—who do not assimilate themselves to power as the highest value and a "masculine" view of life perhaps sounds extreme. Yet the policies of large institutions in the United States and abroad suggest a double bind on the lower half of the population (lower only in the sense of income) that can result only in their extermination. Concentration camps and gas ovens are not necessary: starvation and disease do the job as well, and government bullets complete it. People who have lived for centuries in comparative harmony, in economies only slightly above the subsistence level, who have taken care of themselves and their children and aged better than we do in industrial economies, are being wiped off the face of the globe.

The multinationals are acquiring more and more of the world's arable land, which they own and whose use they can therefore dictate. What they dictate to peasants who once farmed for themselves is the growing of cash crops, crops that bring a profit on the world market—tea, coffee, carnations. If the world market drops, the peasants cannot eat these crops, as they could eat their old rice and beans. Peasants are turned into wage slaves, just as European peasants were under industrialization, and must plant what they are told. The country can no longer feed its own population and poor countries must use their limited foreign exchange to import food. The luxury crops are supplied to the rich of the West, but the people in poor countries cannot afford to buy even fruit or vegetables, much less meat or fish.[341] As we all know, millions of them are starving to death.

The stories we receive about these poor do not suggest a "final" cause for their plight, but only an "efficient" one: local famine, drought, flood, disease. But these people have lived for millennia in far more decent conditions. Yes, there are droughts, famines, floods; there is disease; but cultural traditions taught methods of dealing with such catastrophes. Those traditions have been eradicated first by colonialism and second by the policies of multinationals.

In the precolonial ages, the indigenous agriculture of Africa (and South America) was highly productive. Most cultures had more than a simple subsistence economy; many grew a wide variety of crops and had a well-balanced diet. They had forms of exchange and barter, they had food storage techniques. Many societies had rituals that allowed for balancing the surplus earned by a few—the communal feasts that still occur in parts of New Guinea, for instance, or the beer parties of Africa.

During the colonization of Africa, European nations established areas stipulated for the growth of sisal and other cash crops—cotton, coffee, and tobacco. Their second priority was areas designated to grow crops to feed the Europeans and their labor force. The remaining regions—outlying territories and less productive land—were the reservoirs for migrant labor who could plant for the Africans themselves. As the population grew, the land designated for the people's use did not; the people were forced to reduce fallow periods; they exhausted the soil, and it gave lower yields.

The African labor force was paid too little to cover the cost of food, or given rations too meager to sustain health; they were granted cheap bulky diets, sometimes of such poor quality that parasites in the food caused intestinal illness. (An interesting work, the autobiography of Andrée Blouin, a woman of half-African, half-European parentage who was dumped in a Catholic orphanage by her white father, describes the diet of the little girls in the same way—it was gruel full of bugs. Andrée refused at some point to eat it, and ate instead the chalky surface of the walls of the building in which she was incarcerated.[342]) The workers, of course, became ill on such a diet, but this was not of concern to the colonialists; they sent sick workers home, counting on an endless supply. Disruption of village life and practices made people dependent upon what the colonialists supplied. Men were pressed into labor, women into prostitution. Venereal disease spread through Africa. The only alternative for women in settlements (where they no longer owned communal land) was to brew and sell beer.[343]

When the colonists left, the multinationals were already in place. They moved right in on a labor force used to low wages and without substantial trade unions and continued the process of directing Third World agriculture to the whims of the rich in industrial nations. The consequence has been massive malnutrition of the native populations, particularly in Africa. Decades of agricultural and nutritional depletion are now being lumped together and discussed in the West as a "food crisis" blamed on population growth. It is true that the most threatened people have the most children: they continue to do so because five out of six of their children die before the age of three.[344]

Western efforts to aid Third World countries issue from Western convenience. The West unloads surpluses on them for payment or as aid; this increases the dependency of once-independent nations. Attempts to improve their agriculture fail because Western technicians see technology rather than socioeconomic change as the solution. Anxiety caused by increasing famines, poverty, and urban migration in these nations led to the "Green Revolution," in which the West used high-yield seeds to try to increase agricultural production. But the program's methods of administration intensified structural inequalities. Poor farmers working poor land could not afford the machines and fertilizer necessary for participation; the program concentrated on cereal crops, rather than the nutritious peas, beans, and lentils that had been traditional staples. Fertilizers had to be imported regularly—from multinational companies who dictated the terms of purchase.[345]

Global companies place special prices on products sold in poor countries: prices higher than those in the United States. In Colombia, Chile, Peru, Ecuador, Iran, Pakistan, and the Philippines, among others, drugs are sold at prices 155 percent higher than in the United States; rubber costs 40 percent more, electronics anywhere from 16 to 60 percent more. In addition, the companies frequently sell meretricious products in poor countries. Marketing surveys find ways to persuade a population to buy a product they do not need and have never before wanted, and which may not be beneficial to them. The companies want people worldwide to adopt the same tastes and consumption habits. As the chairman of the National Biscuit Company said during an advertising campaign for Ritz crackers, companies are not selling a product: "We are selling a concept."[346]

Although the people in Third World countries have as much intelligence and ability as people anywhere, their culture has not trained them (as ours has) in cynicism, incredulity, and sophistication in judging advertising. They are subject to the globals' marketing strategies and buy the products they push—the worst possible products for hungry people: white bread, polished rice, refined sugar, snacks, sweets, and sodas. Such products have high cachet and are advertised with images of glittery, sophisticated white culture. Underfed girls starve themselves further to buy a lipstick; people suffering from malnutrition buy Ritz crackers or imitation milk, soups, noodles. Companies convince mothers that infant formulas are better for their children than mother's milk; the women buy the formula, having neither the knowledge nor the means to use it properly. The result of these policies is a heavy incidence of deformity and brain damage in babies because of malnutrition.[347] As such products damage the bodies of already poor and underfed people, the message that accompanies them damages their minds. The message is that white is beautiful, that the foreign culture is better than theirs, that their traditional values—spirituality, politeness, relaxed good humor—are old-fashioned in the face of the new imports: the thrill of success, the thrill of violence, the thrill of consumption.[348]

The multinationals pollute at home, and are beginning to poison the environment of distant places as well. Poor countries welcome their factories, hoping for jobs and an influx of money. But there is evidence of increasing serious ill health from urban industrial process and from pesticides banned in industrial nations, especially, for example, in Brazil.[349] Illich offers an example of another kind of pollution. For a long time western Brazilians bought tin buckets made of scrap by the local tinsmith. But plastic buckets from São Paulo are lighter and cheaper than the tin ones: people therefore buy the plastic buckets. This puts the tinsmith out of business and in time his age-old trade will be forgotten. The scrap he used remains unused, to clutter the landscape. But worst of all, the fumes that emanate from the process of making the plastic "leave a special trace on the environment—a new kind of ghost." They are inevitable byproducts of the process, "and will resist all exorcisms for a long time. . . . In economic jargon, the 'external costs' exceed not only the profit made from plastic bucket production, but also the very salaries paid in the manufacturing process."[350]

Governments of Third World countries see what is happening and are torn. They feel if they don't welcome the global companies, other nations will and they will lose some potential for economic growth. Managers of local branches often understand the effects of the policy of these companies on their populations, but operate with the same reasoning.[351] Herman believes Third World countries have only two options: to redistribute land and develop social programs to aid the rural population; or to buy arms and create a strong military force to coerce the rural population. The governments and financial institutions of industrial nations, partly at the prodding of the global corporations, pressure Third World governments to do the latter.[352]

The latter policy supports what is actually occurring on the economic level, even in countries that have supposed "economic miracles." Mexico, for instance, had an extremely top-heavy distribution of wealth in the 1950s, when the richest 20 percent of the population had ten times the income of the poorest 20 percent; by the mid-1960s, however, the top 20 percent had *seventeen* times the income of the poorest. Over the decade 1960–70, Brazil's "Decade of Development," the income of the forty million people at the bottom of Brazil's economic ladder went from 10.6 percent of the whole to 8.1 percent; the income of the richest five percent went from 27.8 percent of the whole to 36.8 percent. During the 1960s, beef production increased worldwide, but consumption of beef in the countries where it is grown decreased or increased only slightly: the beef went to American fast-food chains. The average American eats 314 eggs a year now; the average Indian eats eight.[353] It is the consequences of these tendencies, in which those who are already poor are being literally starved out even as the pot gets bigger and the rich get fatter, that is causing much of the unrest in the Central American nations at present. The governments of many of these nations and the government of the United States are following or urging a policy of armed coercion of the peasant class; those who offer other solutions are unhesitatingly named *communists*. For this situation the multinational corporations are largely responsible.

The multinational corporations do operate to the advantage of their home countries unless there is a conflict among the several homes they possess, in which case their loyalty is placed opportunistically. They have no basic loyalty to countries because they see nations—national boundaries and policies—as archaic. They manufacture products wherever they please, move goods where they please, and ignore or evade national restrictions, tariffs, and quotas. They move their plants from country to country to increase profits, and export items from one subsidiary to another at will. Because of this, countries become dependent on the companies for balance of payments. But because these transactions involve global firms, and the buyer and the seller are the same company, it is impossible to discuss fair market prices.[354]

In such a climate the corporation appears the most stable and contained entity: Geneen believes companies are more important than governments because they alone can make jobs, provide security, incentives, and "independence" to their employees.[355] Barnet and Muller demonstrate that the goal of corporate diplomacy is to replace national loyalty with corporate loyalty: corporations see themselves and try to build "faith" in themselves as the "principal engine of peace and progress."[356] And indeed, "the global corporation is the first institution in human history dedicated to centralized planning on a world scale."[357] The global corporation could be the instrument for achieving total control over the nonsocialist world.

The multinationals justify their existence, their size, and their methods by pointing to higher GNP rates (omitting reference to their distribution of profits), to their philanthropic contributions, to their contributions to taxes in many nations, and above all to their efficiency, which, they claim, makes possible better lives for more people for less money.

We must examine these claims. Corporate charitable contributions have hovered around 1 percent since 1944, although the tax deductible limit is 5 percent.[358] Nor are contributions urged within these companies for their own sake, for the assistance of worthy educational, charitable, or public service causes. Executives urge rather that a contribution will advance profits through positive publicity. Dow, for example, received so much adverse publicity for manufacturing napalm that its profits on napalm were lost through lowered sales of other products and difficulties in recruitment of personnel.[359] This may be one reason why Dow was one of the few corporations in the country that made a surface show of cleaning up some of its own pollution—although not dioxin.[360]

Nor is the record of the globals in tax paying admirable. In fact, they spend considerable energy and money avoiding taxes, and pay, on the whole, much less than you and I. In 1969 and 1970, when the earnings of ITT increased, it managed to pay less tax than it had previously.[361] In 1972 the percentage of profits paid in taxes by the oil companies ranged from 1.2 percent paid by Gulf to 6.5 percent by Exxon. Over ten million dollars in bribes have been paid by the oil companies in Venezuela, Bolivia, Ecuador, South Korea, Canada, Italy, and other countries, and to Nixon's presidential campaigns.[362]

Almost everyone who writes about corporations points to their inefficiency. As mentioned earlier, this inefficiency has two primary causes—policies of secrecy and competitive practices among rivals. These lead to information clogs, to fear of making decisions, to lowered morale, and to reduced productivity.[363] Sampson believes that corporations are inefficient because their executives have limited vision and imagination.[364] The secrecy of corporations allows them to exercise imagination in one realm, anyway—bookkeeping. They can turn losses into profits on paper; they can sell off assets secretly, or shift moneys from one country to another to create the appearance of efficiency and profitability. Barnet and Muller conclude that although optimal plant size varies from industry to industry, in almost all it is smaller than that which presently exists. A study of thirty industries showed that increased size led to increased profits in less than a quarter of them.[365]

The global corporations have brought the world closer together and have forced governments to lay aside their narrow concerns and take broader perspectives.[366] They have also always supported right-wing dictators, and have condemned policies urging a fairer distribution of wealth as communistic. There is some truth to their message of progress through technology—at least life is easier for some of us because of technology. But because of technology life is also harder—dirtier, noisier, more polluted. Felicity is harder to come by. The effect of these companies on their own employees is often damaging as well. Let us glance at the effect of the policies and structure of these companies on their employees, on the population in general, and on the environment.

Many observers assert that the growth of companies beyond a certain point stunts the growth of those who work for them by increased coerciveness, secrecy, and the caprice behind high-level decisions. Moreover, the goals of large corporations are increasingly in conflict with the needs and values of the people they employ. A former vice president of ITT claims that more and more managers cannot accept the goals of their companies.[367] The head of strategic planning for General Electric's international group admitted that the modern corporation is a "virtual dictatorship."[368] After Geneen took over ITT, he not only built up a complex system of control and surveillance but taught executives to think only of profits and not about products, because in his philosophy it is not good for business to think about products. He conceived of the corporation as a self-contained world ruled by one man, himself: and only he was aware of all that was going on in it.[369]

The high degree of centralization and technology, the absolute loyalty to the director that is required, the rigid coercive hierarchy, and the fear and sometimes even (directed) impotence of middle management to make decisions or initiate action lead to inertia and inefficiency in the organization, depression or illness in the "managers."[370] Good work, if it is done, belongs to the organization, which assigns punishment or reward arbitrarily; superiors may even praise mediocrity and criticize success, putting their underlings in a state of complete intellectual disequilibrium.[371] Managers who do rise to the top often suffer from a sense of personal insignificance, believing themselves to have little personal worth and their success to be due entirely to the corporation. On Rorschach tests, many see themselves as worms or mice.[372] Given the priorities of the corporation, they may have been promoted because of their agility at deference, paralysis, and willingness to have their own abilities, originality, decisiveness, and knowledge ground into grist for the corporate mill. They know—because most people who rise high enough in corporations to see their goals do know—that the goals of the corporation are inhumane and destructive to people and the environment; yet they have been willing to profit from participating in those goals. It is true that these people are also victims; but about one thing at least Catholicism is right: sin is first of all violation of *self*.

High-level corporate executives live in fear of their superiors and their inferiors (either of whom might take their jobs away), but also of people in general, the population they are helping to exploit. They frequently speak of their offices high in skyscrapers as if they were besieged citadels.[373] Why not? The President of the United States said the White House would "stonewall."

And the tendencies among the exploited population are grim. Twenty million Americans are hungry, yet are sold food with *lower nutritional value* than dog food.[374] Despite social programs 21.3 percent of our people were living below the poverty line in 1965, and 21 percent in 1976.[375] In 1960 the richest 20 percent of the population had 43 percent of total income; by 1969 it had 45 percent. Their gains came from the middle 40 percent of the population.[376] Social welfare programs helped somewhat: the position of the very poor has not been as dire as it was early in this century, and food stamps have helped to alleviate starvation, if not malnutrition and hunger. But these programs, including the essential food stamps, were cut back severely between 1980 and 1984.

Welfare programs for the poor are utterly necessary in an industrial capitalistic world. In simple societies, everyone works and contributes to subsistence—even the aged, the impaired, women late in pregnancy or nursing their babies contribute to the well-being of the group in various ways. The very few who might be unable to contribute anything at all are generally cared for lovingly in these societies. Industrial capitalistic societies, however, operate cyclically, and because of the conditions of work, it is extremely difficult for aged or impaired people or new mothers to work gainfully. Capitalism depends on continuing expansion of markets for its survival. It requires a corps of workers for periods of expansion, a corps that is expendable during periods of contraction. Some observers believe that periods of retrenchment and contraction are contrived by the business establishment to lessen the bargaining power of labor. In any case, during low fluctuations a huge mass of people hit the streets, jobless and without resources. As Frances Fox Piven and Richard A. Cloward have demonstrated, welfare arrangements are initiated or expanded during times of dearth when the number of unemployed is great enough that the government fears civil unrest or disorder. These arrangements are abolished or curtailed when political stability is restored. Some people remain on the relief rolls, of course—the aged, disabled, disturbed, and mothers of small children. These are granted aid, but under conditions so degrading and punitive as to "instill in the laboring masses a fear of the fate that awaits them should they relax into beggary and pauperism. To demean and punish those who do not work is to exalt by contrast even the meanest labor at the meanest wages."[377] Thus the intentions behind welfare programs are not at all humanitarian; the programs function as thresholds against penury so severe as to cause death, not because of concern about these deaths but because of fear of the protest of the living. They are, once again, social controls, not a public recognition of unfairness in our society and of the need for temporary assistance to people of pride and independence.

Moreover, in the United States government intervention in housing, health care, and education, even as it increased, did little to help the poor. Often it hurt them further, as when New Deal agricultural subsidies caused the displacement of many tenant farmers and sharecroppers, or when urban renewal schemes displaced poor blacks from familiar urban neighborhoods.[378] The welfare policies of government have functioned to lock the poor into their poverty; instead of acting as a prop to help people find a way to get beyond poverty, welfare is removed when a person finds work at a certain minimum income. Such a policy makes no sense: Why not continue to help people until they no longer need help? But it makes perfect sense if one recognizes that these policies are dictated by corporations and their needs. If a large body of the poor are on their knees, labor is less likely to cause difficulties; if corporations want to expand, a labor pool of the very poor is available. Meanwhile, the corporations have much invested in keeping them precisely where they are.

The people who pay to maintain the poor in poverty are taxpayers, not the corporations at whose behest the class has been created and penned. Corporations frequently whine that they produce wealth which is then siphoned off by government (through taxes) to pay for social welfare programs introduced by government and benefiting the lazy and incompetent. The situation is precisely the opposite; it is what Michael Harrington describes as "the state as milch cow." Corporations act in considerable freedom to make profits, sometimes huge ones, while the government (which includes all taxpayers) stands there patiently giving milk—underwriting corporate investment risks, paying for the social destruction corporations wreak, and having no voice whatever in decisions about those investments, and no share in the profits.[379]

The effects of corporations on people and their environment are incalculable, primarily because the companies are so large. They move in, they create an ugly environment of factories, and they hire. People flock from all over to find work; they put up houses, sanitation systems, roads. They need schools, shops, churches, town hall, and police. Transportation lines are brought in to move raw materials, products, and personnel. Most companies take little or no responsibility for these things; they consider they are doing an area a great favor merely to put the workplace in its midst. Like no creature in nature, corporations dump their waste products in their own nests, their own localities, ruining whatever felicities there may have been—brooks, ponds, rivers, lakes, forests. They send filth into the air or bury it in the earth.

The quality of life of its employees does not much concern corporations, although there is usually a green suburb for its executives. The work they do often exposes workers to hazardous substances, injury, or psychosomatic disturbance, and the environment in which they live—also dominated by the workplace—increases this hazard. This is one reason why working-class people die earlier and generally suffer more ill health than the middle class, and why in capitalist societies the distribution of ill health broadly follows the distribution of income.[380] If workers demand higher wages or agitate for pollution controls, the corporation may close down the factory and move to a poorer state with a more humble work force, or to a Third World country where people are happy to earn enough to eat, even if it is not enough to eat properly.

And if it closes down and abandons the town, the transport system, schools, shops, and the people who depended upon it, the corporation may leave them a final bequest—poisoned water, soil, animals, and plants. Between 1946 and 1971, pollution levels in the United States rose between 200 and 2000 percent: production rose 126 percent.[381] Companies use pollution-prone technologies because they increase the output per unit of labor and therefore increase profits. In 1947 the profit on laundry soap was 30 percent; in 1970 the profit on laundry detergents (which pollute) was 52 percent.[382] *Large corporations are the principal agents of pollution in the world.*[383] And the United States has produced more hardware and created more entropy in a shorter period than any other culture in the history of the planet. As of 1981, military machinery and military expenditures were consuming forty-three cents out of every dollar spent by the government. Military pursuits are the most entropic activity of humans because they use up intensive energy and convert it and materials directly into waste material without any intervening use of benefit to human beings.[384] In other words, it takes labor, energy, and material to build a bomb; but once it is built, that bomb has no other use except to destroy itself and everything around it. Nothing on the planet benefits from the manufacture of military equipment except the arms industry itself, which works closely with the state, both in the United States and elsewhere. The arms trade is enormously profitable, and industrial nations are selling arms to Third World nations so they may subdue their poor. America controls half the world arms market, but neutral countries like Sweden and Switzerland are also large exporters of arms, and therefore engaged in polluting military research and production.[385]

But even the most benign activity can pollute when it is pursued on a large scale. One of the most comic forms of pollution—it is, of course, not comic for those who suffer from it—is the tide of acidic sludge, 400,000 gallons of it, made of flour, tomato paste, cheese, vegetables, and pepperoni, that has clogged the industrial sewage system of Wellston, Ohio, since Jeno's opened a frozen pizza plant there. The plant was welcomed happily—it employed a thousand people in a town with nearly 20 percent unemployment. Now a half-million-dollar conveyor system is needed to dry and biologically decompose the sewage. Jeno's, naturally, expects Wellston—a town of just over six thousand people—to arrange for the correction. The town, naturally, looks to the federal government. If the problem is solved, it will be solved by tax payments from you and me, not by Jeno's.[386]

Barnet and Muller write, "Whether one believes the more alarmist projections or the less alarmist projections, there is a point at which the earth's ecosystem will tolerate no more gases, sludge, radioactive wastes, or excessive heat." It is difficult to comprehend the continuation of policies of waste, pollution, and planned obsolescence by men who are intelligent, who must know that these things are ruining the world around them for them, for their families, and for future generations. True, the worst pollution seems to occur in areas where the poor live; and those who run the global corporations have clearly not only no concern for the poor but a disdainful sense of their expendability. Yet the employees of large companies are among the people who will have to pay taxes to assist children brain damaged by lead, cancerous from dioxin, dying of lung diseases. And the spread of polluted elements into the Canadian forests and the Appalachian lakes constricts life for everyone as fish and bird species disappear.

It is cheaper to spend money on a campaign to fight pollution controls than to spend it on research into ways to control pollution.[387] But again the real question is: What do you win when you win? The modern industrial system unthinkingly consumes the very basis on which it has built itself, by treating as income irreplaceable capital—fossil fuels, coal and oil.[388]

Corporations bring great resources to oppose even small steps that could be taken to conserve energy. As two examples among many:

One-way containers and bottles require 3.11 times more energy to produce than returnables. Maine and Michigan have saved 5.5 trillion BTUs a year by ordering the use of returnables: this equals forty million gallons of gasoline. The litter created by one-way containers has been reduced by 82 percent; total solid wastes are down 4.5 percent; and four thousand new jobs have been created. The taxpayers have saved fifteen million dollars.[389] Yet in every municipality in which the issue is raised, corporations spend huge amounts of money fighting against the use of returnable containers.

City rapid-transit systems save energy, but in many cases corporations have literally destroyed such systems. In the 1920s, General Motors, in collaboration with the local oil company, Socal, and Firestone Tires, bought the entire rapid-transit system of the city of Los Angeles and tore it up to increase the sale of automobiles. General Motors made similar deals with oil companies, forcing people to dependence on cars while the railroads decayed.[390]

As Barry Commoner has shown, it is not that Americans live so much better than they used to, but that the same life style now requires more energy because of the current technology and materials used. There was little substantial change in the basic needs of Americans in the years 1940–70. We eat about the same number of calories, proteins, and other foods, although we take in somewhat fewer vitamins. We use about the same amount of clothing and cleaners; occupy about the same amount of new housing; require about as much freight; and even drink about the same amount of beer. But our food is grown on less land and uses more fertilizer and pesticide; our clothes are made of synthetic fibers rather than natural ones, and are washed in synthetic detergents rather than soap. We live and work in buildings made of aluminum, concrete, and plastic rather than steel or lumber. (Lumber burns more easily than concrete, but plastic kills people by its fumes alone, even if the fire itself is at a distance. This is why so many people have died in recent hotel/motel fires.) Goods are more often shipped by truck than rail now, and drinks come in disposable containers. Many people have air-conditioning at home, most have it at work, and it is common in cars. Cars are driven twice as far as in the past and use synthetic rather than rubber tires, more gasoline per mile, and the gasoline often contains lead, which is poisonous, especially to children.[391] More people live more interestingly now than in the 1930s, if not the 1920s; but we also live under more stress of various sorts, much of it caused by our environments. If cancer is the lethal disease of our age, allergies are the nonlethal but unpleasant and pervasive disease.

For even the environment has been turned into money, as cash value is placed on "air, water, space, and even human life itself, as well as loving, caring relationships among humans."[392] The euphemistically named Environmental Protection Agency has expanded the ability of companies to buy, sell, or trade *the right to pollute the air*. It quantifies and contains emissions of pollutants from a factory in the way a comic strip places the characters' words in a bubble above their heads. A single source of pollution is thus treated as if it were a containable mass and as if it constituted the only source in an area. As long as the degree of pollution within a given bubble meets the health standards of the Clean Air Act—which allows certain bubbles to pollute on a grand scale if they are balanced by other bubbles without pollution—all sources of emission within that bubble are regarded as in compliance with the law. If a company that owns one bubble reduces its polluting emissions, it can sell part of its right to pollute to another company.[393] If a company moves from an area, it can sell its total right to pollute to another company.[394]

But pollution, as grave a problem as it is, is not the only serious one caused by the scale of operations of large corporations. Since secrecy, caprice, and lack of loyalty to areas lead firms to move about, cities cannot plan balanced growth. Corporation headquarters sometimes appear in desolate areas which must then be built up; highways are insufficient and become jammed; neighborhoods suddenly spring up or decay; public services in some metropolitan centers barely function. Giant corporations create noise, filth, ugliness; their policies cause inflation, recession, unemployment; all of these lead to crime, alienation, and misery.[395]

But corporations are not interested in trying to solve these social problems. "Providing ever more sophisticated products for an affluent minority is highly profitable. Providing for the basic sanitation, nutrition, health, transportation, and communication needs of the majority is not." Barnet and Muller discuss demonstrated plans by which a vehicle can be produced for a hundred and fifty dollars, a radio receiver for nine cents, and a one-channel television set for nine dollars (these figures were cited in 1974).[396] Such things are not produced because they do not lead to high profits.

There is opposition to the policies of large corporations. Organized labor is aware that conglomerates use cheap labor in sweatshop conditions, moving to other places as necessary to deny labor its power of opposition. But union officials fear open discussion of the reasons for workers' unhappiness because open discussion might lead to suggestions for radical change in the conditions of work, which might involve change in the organization of unions as well. About the same proportion of workers dissatisfied with their jobs are dissatisfied with union leadership and policies.[397]

Other groups advocate zero growth and insist that the goals of corporations are irrelevant to human well-being. But it is not necessary to insist on no-growth policies. Many commentators have suggested a return to some degree of autonomy—from the extreme of small-town living, using barter, self-help, and mutual aid to achieve relative self-sufficiency, to insistence on smaller business, neighborhood and community enterprises, and industries owned and managed by workers themselves. Henderson points out that between 1969 and 1976 the one thousand largest United States companies used 80 percent of the investment tax credits and 50 percent of the industrial energy, and created seventy-five thousand new jobs. In the same period six million new small businesses created nine million new jobs.[398]

It seems unlikely that such suggestions will be able to alter the present economic structure of the West, or shift the course of corporate/government policy. As Herman reminds us, corporations are adaptable and devious, and "it is not possible to alter the structure of power without the mobilization of equivalent or greater power."[399] Neither appeals nor pressures by moral constituencies have had much effect on corporate behavior, which is also supported either tacitly or overtly by government.[400] Howard Perlmutter estimated some years ago that within the near future 80 percent of the productive assets of the nonsocialist world would be owned by two to three hundred global corporations.[401] It is hard to point to the most dangerous area of this situation. Is it the unconcerned poisoning of the earth; the increase in control over people across the globe as their small businesses or farms are absorbed by giant corporations and they are transformed from somewhat independent entrepreneurs to wage laborers; or the fact that giant corporations constitute a shadow government in many nations, a force behind elected and appointed officials which is unaccountable to and uncontrollable by the public although it makes "decisions daily with more impact on the lives of ordinary people than most generals or politicians"?[402]

The gradual loss of autonomy that has occurred over the past two to three centuries since industrialization has demoralized the populations of industrialized states. When protest does occur, it takes one of two forms—wild destructive rioting that induces further control by government; or workers' demands for more money, fewer hours, more job security—the very sorts of things managers want for themselves. Very rarely is there a protest against the way the system works, against the shoddiness of products, or even against inhumane working conditions. Many people in the United States feel that something is radically wrong with the way we live, but we are so brainwashed with the idea that power is the highest good that we cannot imagine how to improve our lives. We continue to believe that more power (or money) will make things better.

Yet it should be obvious that corporations and government could not function as they do without our tacit assent and even our willing assistance. It may be true that a power structure cannot be changed without mobilization of an equivalent opposing power. But there are many kinds of power. The kind mobilized by Gandhi in India was *satyagraha*, firm, loving resistance: it did not depend upon weapons or money. The tendency toward totalitarianism in this country can be resisted—but before we can do that, we must know what values we want to put in the place of power.

## 5. THE JOURNEY TOWARD TOTALITARIANISM

This chapter opened with the suggestion that the United States, if not the West as a whole, is moving swiftly toward a condition of total control that resembles totalitarianism. Friedrich's list of the characteristics of totalitarian states, described at the beginning of the chapter, included: 1) a totalist ideology, 2) a single party committed to this ideology, and usually led by one man, the dictator, 3) a fully developed secret police, 4) monopolistic control of mass communications, operational weapons, and all organizations including economic ones.[403] Other characteristics of totalitarianism include the use of a shadow government, the obliteration of the private realm, and a racist or imperialist ethos. The situation in the United States does not conform specifically to some of these characteristics, but it does reflect them in a general way. For example, we do not possess a single-party system, nor at present or in the foreseeable future is it likely we will have a dictator. However, what we do have is two parties committed to only slightly different approaches and controlled by the same set of people. This situation permits the *appearance* of choice without its substance. Our government has a fully developed secret police, and substantive control of operational weapons. Although individuals may possess weapons, and some even possess private armies, the difference in equipment between these groups and the government's resources is so extreme as to resemble private corps of archers facing machine-guns. Again there is an appearance of diffusion of weapons without much substance. Finally, economic affairs are moving swiftly into the condition predicted by Howard Perlmutter, in which large corporations control 80 percent of all assets worldwide (excepting socialist nations). As things are going, within a decade or two we may all be wage slaves, controlled by large corporations rather than by nature or markets.

The present state of affairs somewhat resembles a training period, in which we are taught to occupy our given slots without complaining. Corporations are "inherently undemocratic" in structure, and their policies of secrecy, collusion, and influence on government provide a shadow government that is unaccountable to the public.[404] The form alone of giant companies—centralized power, bureaucracy, hierarchy, lack of autonomy—provides a structural example for totalitarianism, and teaches us the qualities we need to submit to it: fear of responsibility, fear of making decisions, fear in general; obedience, subservience, and conformism. Corporations are not of course the only institutions built this way, only the most powerful and widest reaching. As they spread their tentacles across the globe, they propagate themselves, for simple governments cannot deal with them and must imitate their form. The managers of corporations, heirs of the bourgeoisie that created "democratic" processes so they might gain a voice, are now in a position of such power that they feel they can do away with those processes: no group, not even a group of nations, can threaten their supremacy. They have almost all the voice there is.

Moreover, as they and other institutions centralize themselves, they replicate the fragmentation that began with industrial capitalism. People may be "part" of the corporation; the corporation may be the most secure "home" they know, and the stablest element in their environment. But their participation in this environment is nothing at all like being a member of a relatively contented family, community, or network of friends. The corporation (or other institution) is not concerned with a whole person, not interested in individual eccentricities or personal brilliances: it wants conformity, passivity, and work according to its own values. Communities and families are fragmented as a result, and the individual is broken into parts.

The corporate structure itself is broken into small components, partly to assure secrecy, partly (supposedly) for efficiency, but mainly to guarantee greater control by top executives. But executives themselves are controlled in turn, by the demands of their position, by peer pressure, and by superiors. There are few people on earth who do not have "superiors." Because of the fragmentation of their form, corporations cannot approach any problem holistically despite their size. Galbraith points out that "nearly all the consequences of technology and much of the shape of modern industry derive from this need to divide and subdivide tasks."[405] No one in the structure stands above, looks at the surroundings, considers things with any perspective: there is no god in the corporation, only emperors without clothes.

The fragmentation that results from corporate structure has many effects. It guarantees that no group within the institution will cohere sufficiently to challenge the top administrators. It impedes the formation of groups outside the institution that might challenge the entire structure. Such effects contribute to political security—of managers (administrators) and of the system itself. But fragmentation also impedes the formation of social, communal groups and the division of work from private life impedes cohesion in families. What existed in the past, and could exist again with a different structure—smallish communities with permanence and cohesion, places where people were known and tolerated, even accepted—has given way to total individuality, separateness, isolation in the midst of crowds, alienation of the most complete sort. That this way of living is not satisfying for most people can be shown by statistics on crime, alcoholism, drug abuse, and divorce; loneliness and rootlessness do not offer us statistics, but they are apparent in any large city.

In our society, such factors are not weighed against the alleged benefits that accrue to the present organization of most work, or against the values that drive those who control the society. The alienated faceless mass that Arendt found a condition of totalitarianism is us.

As we have seen, most of the conditions political scientists believe are necessary to the establishment of totalitarian governments now exist in the United States and other Western nations. There are two others, however: a totalist ideology, and monopolistic control of mass communications. To what degree do these also exist here?

The United States government is continually extending its control over the dissemination of information. I mentioned earlier the steep increase in classification of materials not bearing in any way on "national security" (which by itself can cover a multitude of extraneous elements). In early 1983 the editors of the New York Times summed up steps taken since 1980:

Secrecy rules eradicated specific grounds for declaring a document classified and ordered doubtful officials to decide in favor of secrecy.

A directive on national security information extended strict rules used by the CIA to tens of thousands of non-CIA public employees.

Administration officials urged a new criminal law to punish disclosure of anything marked "Secret."

Not content with a bill protecting the identities of American agents from international disclosure, the Reagan White House lobbied for and won a law punishing the naming of CIA agents if there was "reason to believe" such disclosure would harm foreign intelligence.

William Casey, director of the CIA, worked to get rid of the Freedom of Information Act. "Other officials, more subtle, seek to 'reform' it out of existence," and use delay and quibbling over fees to thwart use of the act.

The administration of 1980–84 refused to try to pass legislation regulating FBI infiltration of citizens' groups, but attempted to broaden such infiltration by softening existing regulations.

The same administration excluded foreign visitors not because they might *do* anything untoward, but out of fear of what they might *say*: one visitor to be so treated was Hortensia Allende, widow of the assassinated president of Chile.[406]

In the past few years the government has attempted to restrict information that is not classified. For example, it is using the powers of the Trading with the Enemy Act to place an embargo on magazines or newspapers from Cuba, North Vietnam, and Albania (but not China or the Soviet Union). These materials are easily available abroad; they are not embargoed because they threaten American secrets but because they might contain information the government does not want Americans to know. This development carries us perilously near to an established system of official censorship. Recently, officials confiscated Iranian books purchased by television journalists while they were abroad; the only reason for such confiscation is to prevent the dissemination in this country of information that is available abroad.[407] This amounts to a "protection" of citizens similar to that existing in socialist countries.

The administration of 1980–84 pushed for broader use of lie detector tests on government employees; such use by corporations has also greatly increased in recent years.[408] Three films made in Canada were forced to announce themselves as political propaganda emanating from a foreign country. The films are two documentaries that explore all sides of the problem of acid rain, and one that surveys the dangers and improbability of survival of nuclear war.[409] The center of opposition to such films would be companies that burn or provide coal (the cause of acid rain) and the nuclear industry. But it was the Department of Justice that required the labeling.

The most potent medium of communications, however, is television, which reaches the young, the illiterate, those who do not read newspapers or books, and people in foreign countries, including the Third World. Television is the essential means for selling products in nations with high illiteracy rates; the technical, practical, surveillance-oriented University of the World designed by Howard Perlmutter and associates was to disseminate its "curriculum" through television.[410] American networks play a dominant role in Third World countries, especially in Latin America, which is saturated with broadcasting that serves the interests of multinational corporations: as of 1974, CBS distributed its programs to one hundred nations.[411]

Television networks are controlled by large corporations and used to sell their products. When cable television was first promoted in the United States, it was depicted as a force for pluralism that would provide balance in programming and more democratic, widespread control of the medium. But in spite of the profusion of cable and satellite networks that has emerged in the last decade, the industry is still dominated by a "handful of corporate behemoths" like AT&T, Warner Communications, Time, Inc., CBS, ABC, and RCA.[412] Moreover, the form television has been given reflects centralization: nine hundred separate channels have been effectively reduced to four centralized networks. This reduction helps to ensure a uniformity of message.[413]

Because the values of these corporations are identical, they naturally do not offer a balance of attitudes to the viewer. Even when large corporations do not own a communications arm, they influence network thinking because they refuse to sponsor programs of whose contents or attitude they disapprove. This kind of censorship is understandable: we all surely have the right not to support what we find reprehensible. But this situation is dangerous because almost all of television is controlled by people who think alike, and because of the character of what they do approve and support.

What appears on television is, in the words of a successful television writer, David Rintels, "one long lie." He adds, "The networks get bombarded with thoughtful, reality-oriented scripts. They simply won't do them."[414] When a relatively probing or realistic program does get through, it is intercalated with commercials that undermine its vision by pounding home the alternative vision so familiar to viewers from both commercials and most programming: life is beautiful in America; if yours isn't, it can be if you will buy X. Actually, the vision offered on television is more complex than that, if difficult to describe discursively because it is almost entirely imagistic. But it is the vision, more than any product, that the medium exists to sell. Indeed, Barnet and Muller write that the most important product of multinational corporations is ideology itself, and its most important medium here and abroad is television.[415] One of the major corporate struggles of the last decade or two has been the attempt to dominate communication facilities in Europe and the Third World in order to dominate the ideology presented by those facilities.[416]

It should not come as a surprise that the cornerstone of the ideology sold by mass media is traditional sex roles, the division of experience that is fundamental to patriarchy itself. Television is obsessed with gender roles, according to an anthropologist studying North America.[417] The primary image offered is that of man as controller, even when a female is the protagonist of a piece. Occasionally a female is shown as wiser or more knowing than the men around her, but she handles situations and offers her knowledge or wisdom in traditional "feminine" ways—through compassion, nutritiveness, or peacemaking. Women who act on their own, who do not accept the control of males, are generally villains. Moreover, men far outnumber women in television: there are three times more males than females in its programs, and the males generally have more important roles, more camera time. Males in serious drama are shown as in control: independent, solitary, cut off from intimacy and community—the lone hero. Only in comedy are males shown as lacking in control, but they are always restored by their women to the illusion that they are in control.

The primary emphasis of mass media is on sex role, but its next priority is to offer an image of America. The image purveyed is far from America's reality. There is extreme underrepresentation of older people, blacks and other minorities, and the working class. When old people are shown, they tend to appear feeble, silly, ill, and sexless. Most television blacks are either middle-class whites with darker skin or subservient, occupying the role of sidekick to a white. There is little depiction of the actual lives of older people, whether middle class or the old poor; and almost none of actual black culture with its rich interconnections. Although about 60 percent of the American population hold blue-collar or service jobs, only 6 to 10 percent of television characters are similarly engaged.[418] And even when working-class people are shown, their living conditions are usually made more spacious and pleasant than they are in reality.

Such omissions are not a result of "the market." Although television executives talk as if only popularity (profitability) guided their choice of what to present, programs that have shown the circumstances of working-class lives have been extremely popular—consider *All in the Family,* and Jackie Gleason's portrayal of the bus driver Ralph Kramden. The omission of realistic portrayals of life from television is a result of censorship, whether conscious or not.

The reality of the texture and events of everyday life is censored: yet violence is not. Murder is two hundred times more prevalent on television than in life, and crime is twelve times more violent on television than in actuality.[419] After ten years of research, the National Institute of Mental Health has concluded that television violence increases aggressive behavior among teen-agers who watch television. It estimates that young people will have witnessed *eighteen thousand* murders by the time they are sixteen.[420] The vision of life offered by television is a "grossly distorted picture of the real world that [viewers] tend to accept more readily than reality itself."[421] Those who watch television frequently believe the world to be more dangerous, violent, and untrustworthy than those who watch it infrequently.[422] Viewers accept the distortion more readily than they do reality because they have been taught by their culture that the distortion *is* the reality—and television is not alone in responsibility for this education.

The "message" offered by mass media is that humans are in control of themselves and the world, that they can and do create themselves, and that humans are utterly disconnected from nature and the animal. Nature is a backdrop—idyllic for romantic scenes, violent for dramatic scenes; it is never the element in which humans live and with which they interact. Gender roles are important because they teach us how to "create" ourselves; on that foundation, we go on to invent the world. Violence is permitted for several reasons. Rage and destructiveness are emotions permitted to men, emotions that appear to show men in control. But violent programs reflect the real rage that exists under the surface in many people, television writers and directors included. Violence is individual; it isolates; it carries competition to its ultimate. Beyond that, violence on television and in movies often involves the blowing up of *things*—cars, boats, weapons, houses—the very things our society tells us will make us happy, the things which provide the concrete manifestation of our supposed superiority. Watching these things explode seems to stimulate glee; at least that is what one gathers in movie houses. The depiction of the destruction of the very things we are being urged, during commercial breaks, to purchase shows ambivalence at the very least.

Nevertheless, the only alternatives are to own things or to destroy them. And the conclusion of most television and movie fare piously asserts that justice exists, that all is right with the world, especially in America. Bill Nichols analyzes the subtle means by which this overt message is reinforced—camera angles, lighting, and backdrop, for instance. He discusses how such things are used to confer authority on newscasters yet disconnect them from responsibility for the usually terrible events they report, and to emphasize the concluding assurance that all is nevertheless well with the world, and getting better.[423]

Many elements contribute to the total complex image offered by television. Both the content of commercials and their arrangement within a given program affect the overall contrapuntal tension that is created. Much of what is pleasant (as opposed to violent) on television comes in the commercials. It is necessary to examine what constitutes pleasantness. When there is community, what holds it together besides the breakfast cereal? Why are these people laughing?

Todd Gitlin analyzes television as the propagator of an ideology "camouflaged as value-neutral" but essentially economic: the forces behind television want only to sell products, but to do so they first manufacture the consumer.[424] He quotes a motivational analyst: "In a free enterprise economy, we have to develop the need for new products. And to do that we have to liberate women to desire these new products. We help them rediscover that homemaking is more creative than to compete with men. This can be manipulated."[425]

Gitlin thinks the aim of television programs of whatever sort is to "flatten consciousness—to tailor everyman's world view to the consumer mentality, to placate political discontent, to manage what cannot be placated, to render social pathologies personal, to level class-consciousness."[426] This is essentially the same criticism made against medicine, psychology, and education; against the widespread use of tranquilizers and drugs; it could easily be made against the performing and fine arts, literature, and much of our thought.

Such analysis goes further than most, but not far enough. One can accept that the ideology sold in mass media would aim at assuaging or deflecting protest against the way our society is structured; one can also accept that a major priority of those who control the mass media is to sell their products to an audience massaged into wanting them. But to answer the question of why the images chosen are chosen, we must go further, must uncover the powerful, unconscious desire of the controllers to realize a fictitious world in which humans are finally liberated from nature, necessity, and the human condition, by the corporations of America.

In a museum in Prague, in 1975, there hung an exhibition of photographs showing Nazi concentration camps in Czechoslovakia and their liberation by the Soviet Army. Each photograph was captioned in several languages, including English. Under the final picture, showing inmates being freed from the camp by Russian soldiers, the caption read: "The Red Army liberates the inmates and eradicates unhappiness from the earth."

The drive to totalitarianism is a drive to eradicate unhappiness from the earth. Many patriarchal institutions have been motivated by this desire. Yet each has brought waves of misery and oppression that increased human unhappiness, because beneath the drive lies the false belief that unhappiness is caused by bonds to nature, by necessity, by lack of the ability to transcend. Television and other mass media offer transcendence: it is as cheap and easy as a flick of the dial—or pressure on a hypodermic needle. Or it may require the discipline of prayer leading to nirvana. The only way to happiness, for patriarchal minds, is to blot out the real.

The most serious problem with television—and I am speaking in general; there are programs on both commercial and public television which stand outside this critique—is its denial of what we all know and call reality. It is this denial which makes so much programming vacuous; and it is this denial which undermines youngsters. There is nothing wrong, after all, with depictions of human violence: what could be more violent than *Titus Andronicus*, for instance, or *Hamlet?* Although we are right to call into question the quantity of violence on television, quantity is only one factor in its devastating effect. The other is its *unreality*. It must be a deeply disturbing experience to see someone violently killed, to see human blood pouring out into the earth, to see pain and mutilation; it is necessarily even more disturbing to cause death. But television heroes show little remorse or distress—a shake of the head, a sigh of relief, a sober face, and in the next scene they are striding along, beautifully dressed, to meet a beautiful girl on a patio overlooking the sea for cocktails.

Violent behavior has no lasting repercussions in the television world. Whereas in life, to kill is a profound act, one that must change the killer as well as the victims, in television few acts have serious consequences. Like sadistic acts in pornographic literature, which arouse but leave no trace—welts are creamed away, the punisher can do anything to the victim without leaving permanent scarring or maiming—television violence offers thrill without consequence. This is a serious matter for the young, who become inured to the violence and do not perceive the falseness of its portrayal. Some become inured to even the visual consequences and are able to harden themselves when they try their hand at such actions, so that they feel nothing, just like the heroes they admire. In a sense there is no death on television, because the heroes of series cannot be killed, and all viewers know it.

When problems that exist in reality are portrayed on television they are merely glanced at; in short order a solution is arranged, a solution that makes no one suffer, that leaves no one with serious loss. Indeed, a major message of television is *there is no need*. The elderly can find pleasure; poverty and disease are curable. All around us are dedicated professionals waiting to help us, to make us happy. The import of television as a whole is contradictory, because part of its programming and almost all its commercials depict a life beyond serious need, and suggest that humans can live without continuing pain, sorrow, or injustice; and part of it offers gratuitous violence and sadism toward women, both of which have real social consequences.[427] But somewhere the sitcoms and the dramas come together. *To free oneself from the abject*: that is the great goal. Whether through saccharine comedy or thrilling fantasy (for crime dramas are nothing more than they are fantasy), to lock out the real is, like locking out nature, the major desideratum. Television accomplishes this by transforming experience itself into a commodity: and commodities are replaceable.[428]

Great drama was a communal ritual; I doubt if this is true today, even when the great dramas of the past are presented. Our culture has few shared values, and thus little sense of community. However, great drama, like poor drama, reflects and enforces the values of a culture. What is striking about ours is its poverty: we are the heirs of a long tradition of transcendence who discover in our triumph the emptiness of airless height. Television is the epitome of noncommunal art. As predicted in science fiction and prophetic novels, we sit alone in our cubicles fixed on images of delusion. The introduction of cable television has exacerbated this tendency, for the profusion of channels is being used to fragment an already fragmented populace by offering "discrete, specialized, one-issue or one-interest" programming: channels for sport lovers, movie lovers, for pornography, business, religion. Blacks, Hispanics, and Christians watch different channels: but the message is the same on all.[429] All is well and getting better.

This is the message transmitted by communications media in socialist countries as well—along with exhortations to personal effort for the general good. There is little of even this kind of communal appeal on American television: exhortations usually urge personal reform for one's own sake—we are told to stop smoking, to call AA, to exercise. I do not know enough about the shape of propaganda in socialist nations to offer substantial comparison, but I do know there is considerable appeal to the welfare of the population as a whole, to the glory of the state.

American television and other communications media reinforce fragmentation of people and groups, setting them against each other. Herman describes the practice of corporations as "careful stoking of social polarization and foreign threats."[430] Stuart and Elizabeth Ewen discuss the ways consumerism engenders passivity and conformity.[431] They point out that to create a consumptionist ideology it is necessary to posit people and nature as at odds with each other; nature being inhospitable, industry now claims for itself the rights and powers of creation.[432] Both the Ewens and Lasch complain about the modern presentation of "promiscuity" as an ideal; I interpret these complaints, which sound unpleasantly like arguments for monogamy, to mean rather that our culture approves of sexual relationships with no core of feeling, physical acts performed not out of real desire for another but out of desire to act out a role. That one should not feel love or desire is necessary if one is not also to feel pain, loss, and yearning. In short, one should not feel.

The media are not monopolistically controlled in the United States. Television news retains some independence.[433] Newspapers, magazines, and books that offer alternative visions on the whole reach too small a population in this country for government to worry about them. Publishers in general aim for the large audience, which means that serious works dealing with issues of concern to minorities or feminists, or dealing with real social change, must often seek publication by small houses with poor distribution systems or small organs with an audience of the already converted.

Almost every American critic of our system points to the profit motive as the villain. Such thinking is short-sighted. The goal is control (wealth in capitalist countries): to make the dream *seem* true. As Henderson points out, the problem of industrial nations is not who owns the means of production, but the untenability of human values in the face the present means of industrial production.[434] In socialist countries *everything* is centrally planned, and the centralization and bureaucratization of all processes impede the smallest motions of life, overwhelming simple daily living with their requirements. There too industrialization has led to alienation, the disease socialism was supposed to cure; there too people are disconnected from traditional communities, from their work, and from each other. They too lack any sense of autonomy, and are in terror of making independent decisions. There too people suffer from doubt about whether the structure and values of their society are in harmony with human need and desire, or even with announced values.

Hierarchy, coercion, uniformity, and secrecy exist in socialist institutions as well as capitalist ones. Socialist nations too are experiencing a depletion of natural resources, and the USSR has a high level of pollution. In socialist nations too, leaders are willing to sacrifice people and the environment to accumulate more goods more cheaply, to maintain social order.[435] "The fierce and supposedly fundamental debate between Marxism and capitalism . . . has turned out to be a surface argument."[436]

"The Russian kind of conformism is overtly authoritarian and dogmatically rigid; the American kind of conformism is covertly compelling—as by a natural process—and technically flexible. But conformism it is, here and there. Under both systems a person is forced to sell himself. The Russian way leads to mental enslavement and ideological stultification, the American way leads to all-pervading functionalization and commercialization."[437] Erich Kahler's comment avoids describing the effect of conformism on the American public; just as The Stepford Wives omitted showing the brainwashing of husbands along with (or even prior to) that of wives. American conformism leads to robotization, violence, and malaise. Placing all the blame for our situation on the profit motive allows us to pretend there is an economic solution to our problems. The phrase gives us a screen against despair.

But both capitalist and socialist systems are dedicated to control above all. This is not to exculpate the profit motive from criticism; it is rather to suggest that the profit motive is a symptom, not the cause, of our disease. Critics who lay all blame for twentieth-century horrors on the profit motive are freed from looking more deeply into themselves and the culture. Profit is not inherently evil, despite centuries of Christianity and a century of Marx.

And the socialist system has accomplished miracles of improvement in Russia and China, just as the capitalist system accomplished miracles in the industrial West. Both miracles exacted a terrible price in human terms. But it would be foolish now to suggest that everyone return to village living (which can be as cruel, narrow, and deprived as urban living), or give up cars and use only bicycles, or abjure all products of global corporations. Such solutions partake of the same values as the disease they aim to cure: they are based on an either-or vision of life, on a notion of virtue as sacrifice and hardship, and on a conviction of moral superiority. A more just distribution of the goods of life is essential; but those goods include not just money and consumer goods, but community, security, and well-being. Neither the socialist systems in existence nor any capitalist systems in existence can offer this kind of justice.

Meanwhile, corporations and governments, especially the American variety, are impelling us headlong toward a system that resembles the most totalitarian socialist systems under a surface appearance of multiple choice, while spouting the words *peace* and *freedom*. As Marcuse reminds us, "Free choice of masters does not abolish the masters or the slaves. Free choice among a wide variety of goods and services does not signify if these goods and services sustain social controls over a life of toil and fear."[438] One of the best comments on American freedom emerges from the corporate world itself: a recent commercial on television showed a political orator booming hollow phrases and words—like *freedom*—at a bored audience. A young, attractive member of the audience leaps up at the mention of freedom and runs off, swiftly followed by the rest of the audience, to his local convenience store, which is proclaimed to be the real conferrer of freedom, since one can buy all its (mostly nonnutritious, overpriced) foods twenty-four hours a day.

All that is lacking is a "totalist ideology": but I am not sure it is lacking. Patriarchy itself provides the ideology: a transcendent philosophy that holds power to be the highest good, that holds the masculine principle to be of more value than the feminine, and that has faith that "masculinization" of the world will lead to salvation. Even air has been "masculinized": quantified, treated as a commodity. So has food, the basic good of life, now called a "weapon" by a secretary of agriculture, John R. Block.[439] For their leaders, control of the globe by huge corporations represents the triumph of a "transcendental unity," a wave of the future, unstoppable because "nothing can stop an idea whose time has come."[440] Such exalted phrases are intended to describe a system of merchandising of meretricious products in meretricious ways for the great goal of money, money, money: socialists, who proclaim the ideals of human justice and equality, could not find more noble language.

My own sense of what tilts a controlled society over into the hell of insane totalitarianism is a drive for "purification" like that which characterized the Nazis and devastated the Russians and Chinese during Stalin's and Mao's purges. Russian society remains anti-Semitic and racist (the Russians are the dominant group); Chinese society is also racist (the Han are the dominant group). Racism characterizes American society more than any other except the South African, however; and there is a strong prejudice against the poor and those who live by "feminine" values—which has no name but an American face.

Beyond that, a strong and vocal minority is making a drive to a kind of "purification" in the United States: the "Christianization of America." Groups like the Moral Majority are well organized, well financed, and prepared to stay in the fight for a long time. One group of millionaires, led by Nelson Bunker Hunt among others, is trying to raise a billion dollars to bring the gospel of Christianity to everyone in the world within the next decade. (This was precisely the gospel preached to Africans as they were enslaved, their land appropriated, and both exploited for European profit.) According to the members of this group who spoke at a "Financial Success Seminar," 210 millionaires have already pledged a million dollars or more apiece for the crusade. Hunt articulated the goal: "The most important thing is to have a spiritual environment in this country that will mean we can keep the money we make."[441]

So that's what *spiritual* means!

The first step in "purification" drives is often the regulation of women's work, sexuality, and reproduction. Such regulation is certainly high among the priorities of those presently attempting Christian-capitalist reform in America. They have been waging a strong fight to forbid women to control their own bodies through abortion and through birth control; they have been attempting to introduce a "family protection act," which would eliminate help to raped and battered women and deny federal aid to states or cities in which police aided such women (who in the family is being protected by this act?). They are trying to hinder young girls from getting birth control information or abortions. And they are trying unremittingly to force public schools to introduce prayer. This last is seemingly comic: a moment of prayer in school will not guarantee better behavior of children, nor even make children more religious. It has no function whatever except as a symbol of control—"Christian" control—over public education.

We remember that the first step in the deification of patriarchy was also the suppression of women to a level at which they could be regulated. Over and again, structures that seem to have nothing to do with women find it necessary to raise themselves by debasing women. This oddity, this seeming irrelevance, is explained if we understand the symbolic nature of much of what we do, say, think, and believe, and the associations that pervade much of human symbology.

Feminists of whatever period, whatever class, whatever nation, have always grasped this element in culture. But so deeply is it implanted, and so complex are its expressions, that we have had difficulty in attacking the problem at its source. Yet feminism is the only philosophy that is seeking real alternatives to patriarchy, that is attempting to build a fully humane yet practical and realistic ideology. It has, naturally, problems of its own as well as problems with the culture. But feminist thinking, to which we will now turn, offers a train of ideas that can provide the basis for a different sort of society.

# CHAPTER SIX

# Feminism

Feminism is the only serious, coherent, and universal philosophy that offers an alternative to patriarchal thinking and structures. Feminists believe in a few simple tenets. They believe that women are human beings, that the two sexes are (at least) equal in all significant ways, and that this equality must be publicly recognized. They believe that qualities traditionally associated with women—the feminine principle—are (at least) equal in value to those traditionally associated with men—the masculine principle—and that this equality must be publicly recognized. (I modify these statements with *at least* because some feminists believe in the superiority of women and "feminine" qualities. Indeed, it is difficult not to stress the value of the "feminine" in our culture because it is so pervasively debased and diminished.) Finally, feminists believe the personal is the political—that is, that the value structure of a culture is identical in both public and private areas, that what happens in the bedroom has everything to do with what happens in the boardroom, and vice versa, and that, mythology notwithstanding, at present the same sex is in control in both places.

These tenets may compel agreement from people who do not consider themselves feminists but would find it easy enough to agree that men and women are or ought to be equal, or that love, nutritiveness, and compassion are or ought to be as important as power and possession. Many nonfeminists would ardently confess their adoration of "feminine" virtues—*in women*, or in heaven. Most religions claim the feminine principle as their core. But this has not prevented them from creating hierarchical structures and exercising multiple standards of judgment (according to the sex and rank of the person judged), from betraying their principles by bowing to worldly power, or from using anathema, torture, imprisonment, murder, and war as instruments of policy. Such a split between pronounced value and actual value, between what is said and what is done, is not acceptable to feminists.

For talk is cheap. The same man whose eyes glaze with tears when he mentions his sainted mother (long dead) may abuse his wife and exploit his secretary without perceiving any contradiction. Patriarchy, a transcendent ideology willing to trade the real for the symbolic, can juggle language with equanimity: so lethal weapons are named *peacekeepers*, and an invading force backed by elite monied interests can be called *freedom fighters*. Acceptance of the equality of women and of "feminine" values is not enough: it is necessary to work for the public recognition of this equality, in both public and private worlds. This is extremely difficult to manage, in an individual life or in the culture as a whole, but this is the feminist goal. To reintegrate humanity requires not just treating women as human beings, but valuing in one's own life and actions love and compassion and sharing and nutritiveness equally with control and structure, possession and status.

There are also those who believe they consider women equal to men, but see women as fettered by their traditional socialization and by the expectations of the larger world. These people see women as large children who have talent and energy, but who need training in male modes, male language, and an area of expertise in order to "fit in" in the male world. One philosopher, for example, has commented that women are *not yet ready* for top government posts. This is not just patronizing; it shows a lack of comprehension of feminism. For although feminists do indeed want women to become part of the structure, participants in public institutions; although they want access for women to decision-making posts, and a voice in how society is managed, *they do not want women to assimilate to society as it presently exists but to change it.* Feminism is not yet one more of a series of political movements demanding for their adherents access to existing structures and their rewards. This is how many people see it, however: as a strictly political movement through which women demand entry into the "male" world, a share of male prerogatives, and the chance to be like men. This perception of feminism alienates many nonfeminist women.

Feminism *is* a political movement demanding access to the rewards and responsibilities of the "male" world, but it is more: it is a revolutionary moral movement, intending to use political power to transform society, to "feminize" it. For such a movement, assimilation is death. The assimilation of women to society as it presently exists would lead simply to the inclusion of certain women (not all, because society as it presently exists is highly stratified) along with certain men in its higher echelons. It would mean continued stratification and continued contempt for "feminine" values. Assimilation would be the cooption of feminism. Yet it must be admitted that the major success of the movement in the past twenty years has been to increase the assimilation of women into the existing structure. This is not to be deplored, but it is only a necessary first step.

There have been many revolutions against various patriarchal forms over the past three or four thousand years, but in each case, what has succeeded an oppressive structure is another oppressive structure. This is inevitable because, regardless of the initial ideas and ideals of rebellious groups, they come to worship power above all: only power, they believe, can overwhelm power; only their greater power can bring them victory over an "enemy" that is the Father. But each victory has increased the power of the *idea* of power; thus each victory has increased human oppression.

It is impossible to realize humane goals and create humane structures in a society that values power above all else. Well-meaning people tinker with the machinery, but the factory keeps turning out oppression. The benevolent are appalled at discovering themselves somehow coopted; or at realizing, after a life dedicated to instituting a "humane" reform, that the reform is more constricting than the ill it was designed to alleviate. Those who are perhaps more penetrating declaim bitterly that the world of Realpolitik is the only truth, that power is all that matters, that all other values are placebos for the sentimental. Power is not just the highest good, but the only reality—another irony, for power is of all things the least real, or at least the most delusive.

The only true revolution against patriarchy is one which removes the idea of power from its central position, and replaces it with the idea of pleasure. Despite the contempt in which this quality has been held for several millennia, pleasure, felicity—in its largest and deepest sense—is actually the highest human good. Restoring it to centrality in human concern would permit us to make discriminations that are now difficult or impossible and to revest experience with innocence. For example, it is frequently difficult to distinguish between power-to and power-over, since the latter is often seen as a means to the former. But power-to primarily increases pleasure, and power-over primarily increases pain. Power-to involves expressiveness and a degree of autonomy; whereas power-over involves structure, coercion, fear, and sometimes violent cruelty.

To restore pleasure to centrality requires restoring the body, and therefore nature, to value. Although it should be clear that experience of any sort is rooted in a continuum of mind/body, the split made in this continuum is so old and respectable as to stand as truth. Pleasure is disdained because it appears to be rooted in the body alone, and body is disdained. Sensory pleasure and sexuality are little valued in our time unless they can be quantified as parts of some larger linear goal—good health, sexual conquest, fulfillment of a regimen or life plan. Because of our requirement of transcendence, experience has no value of its own, is not treasured for its own sake, but only if it provides a means to some "higher" end.

The restoration of body and nature to value would preclude the treatment of both bodies and nature that pervades our world—the torture and deprivation of the one, the erosion and pollution of the other. Cooperation with nature would replace exploitation of it, which is the model for other forms of exploitation; exploitation of any sort would become illegitimate. Lacking transcendent goals, we would have no reason to sacrifice well-being, harmony, sharing, cooperation, and pleasure to symbolic superiority; the very notion of superiority of one kind over another would disappear, although differences among kinds would remain.

If women and men were seen as equal, if male self-definition no longer depended upon an inferior group, other stratifications would also become unnecessary. Legitimacy (which has no meaning without the idea of illegitimacy) would no longer be a useful concept, and its disappearance from human minds would lead to the establishment of new structures for social organization. These structures would blur the distinction between public and private spheres, a distinction that was originally created not only to exclude women from a male (public) arena, but to permit discourse which ignored and effectively eliminated from existence the parts of all lives that are bound to nature, that are necessary and nonvolitional. If public and private life were integrated, it would no longer seem incongruous to discuss procreation and weapons systems in the same paragraph. Since pleasure would be the primary value of both personal

and public life, harmony (which produces pleasure) would be a universal societal goal, and would no longer have to be manufactured in the ersatz form of
coerced uniformity, conformity. Love too would regain its innocence, since it
would not be coerced into playing a role within a power structure and thus
functioning as an oppression—as it often does in our world.

The foregoing is a sketch of feminist beliefs. It is difficult at present to
provide more than a sketch, for to create truly feminist programs we must rid
our heads of the power notions that fill them, and that cannot be done in a
generation, or even several generations. The sketch may sound utopian: I think
it is not. That is, I believe such a world is possible for humans to maintain, to
live within, once it is achieved. What may be utopian is the idea that we can
achieve it. For to displace power as the highest human value means to supersede patriarchal modes while eschewing traditional power maneuvers as a
means. But it is impossible to function in the public world without using power
maneuvers; and revolution does imply overthrow of current systems.

Two elements cast a friendly light on feminist goals. One is that the movement is not aimed at overthrow of any particular government or structure, but
at the displacement of one way of thinking by another. The other is that feminism offers desirable goals. The first means that the tools of feminism are naturally nonviolent: it moves and will continue to move by influencing people, by
offering a vision, by providing an alternative to the cul-de-sacs of patriarchy.
The second means that feminism is in a state I call blessed: its ends and its
means are identical. Feminism increases the well-being of its adherents, and so
can appeal to others on grounds of the possibility of greater felicity. Integration
of the self, which means using the full range of one's gifts, increases one's sense
of well-being; if integration of one's entire life is not always possible because of
the nature of the public world, it is a desirable goal. Patriarchy, which in all its
forms requires some kind of self-sacrifice, denial, or repression in the name of
some higher good which is rarely (if ever) achieved on earth, stresses nobility,
superiority, and victory, the satisfaction of a final triumph. Feminism requires
use of the entire self in the name of present well-being, and stresses integrity,
community, and the *jouissance* of present experience.

The world at large offers severe impediments to the realization of a feminist vision in one's personal and public life. But feminism is not a disconnected
moral stance—as, say, religion is for many people. It is not a set of words and
ideas in which one claims belief while acting in ways that contradict those
words and ideas, and then ritually atones for the "sin." It is necessarily activist,
and thus necessarily political—it involves public expression of personal ideals.
Feminism must be lived. The great question is *how*.

## 1. MODES OF APPROACH
## TO REALIZING THE FEMINIST VISION

All of us, women and men throughout the world, live under patriarchal
structures. This means we learn to speak languages formed and weighted by patriarchal values, that the culture we absorb is pervaded by patriarchal images

and ideas, and that we learn to approach problems—and indeed living itself—in "masculine" modes. Although the equality of women and men is not widely accepted, many of the ideas of feminism are: they constitute, in fact, a running commentary on the dominant culture, offered by religions, philosophies, and art. But in each form in which they appear, "feminine" values are likely to be embedded in forms and ideas of male supremacy. They are posited as the ends which power and the masculine principle must serve, and, as such, are themselves cut off from power and force. They must remain "pure"; founded in renunciation of power, they are deemed polluted if they reach out for it, as if mercy or compassion or nutritiveness or communal values would no longer be themselves if they were expressed assertively, defended with forcefulness, or allowed to interfere with a structure. This splitting off of virtue from power has less to do with any "purity" required for "virtue" than with the suspicion and fear with which empowered "virtue"—associated with motherhood—is regarded in a patriarchal world.

To create a feminist world, we need to perceive the factitious nature of patriarchal ideas and structures and to develop a voice of our own. But the development of a feminist voice has to begin with repudiation and rebellion against patriarchal ideas: we must say *no* to patriarchal alternatives before we can begin to find more felicitous forms. To remain in a negative posture, however, dooms us to infertility, and even worse—to the building of a new world on a set of "thou shalt nots," as we forbid ourselves and others use of patriarchal modes and manners. This is precisely how patriarchy began; its desire to eradicate matricentric modes and manners is responsible for much of its ugliness and cruelty. We do not want to recapitulate such a development.

Nevertheless, we must deal, every day of our lives, and in every dimension of them, with patriarchy and its ideas, called by some feminists "the master's toolshed." Although some feminists question this, it is quite literally impossible not to use some of the "master's" tools to dismantle that toolshed. The major divisions among different groups of feminists today lie in this area: not what we must do, but how. There is general agreement about basic principles, premises, as well as about the vision of a feminist future, but there is considerable controversy about how to go about creating that future—and living the present. Much as we may dislike the fact, feminism is still partly at least a response to patriarchy. The great body of work done by feminists of the more distant past and of the last two decades is a foundation, but we do not yet have structures to work with, and there is even disagreement about whether we should.

In this section, we will look at some approaches taken by feminists.

## Feminist Separatism

Separatism is less a movement than a stance; although there are separatist organizations, they are for the most part informal, communal, and without institutional structure. Separatists believe that men are either genetically inclined or socialized to "masculine" values like competitiveness, aggressiveness, illusory independence, and excessive rationality—narrow, linear thinking. They believe that women are either genetically inclined or socialized to "feminine" values like cooperativeness, emotionality, and associative thought. But because the world is dominated by "masculine" values, and women must live in the world, women but not men learn to value both "masculine" and "feminine" qualities; thus women are more fully human than men.

Partly because of their fuller integrity, women can easily be absorbed into "masculine" structures and thinking; indeed, survival often requires just this. The assimilation of women into a world dominated by "masculine" values leads to a weakening of women's values, a loss of ability to act on those values, and amounts to a use of those values in support of destructive and ugly societies pervaded by racism, sexism, exploitation, war, competition that destroys community, and isolated independence that destroys communal effort and nature.[1]

For women to participate in such a world is equivalent to their consorting with the enemy: for some separatists, transactions with men are invariably tainted, and pollute women—much as gypsies believe intercourse with "Gorgios" is polluting, and leave it to their women. There are degrees in the separatist position, but generally it advocates that women maintain a separate culture, dealing as much as possible only with women, living only with women, and living by "feminine" values. There is a tendency toward sainthood in the separatist position; I have even heard the phrase "ideological purity" used, although not by American but by German separatists. Since *purity* seems to me a dangerous term when applied to anything more abstract than butter or cream, it is possible that there is also a tendency toward totalitarianism in some separatists, a tendency consonant with sainthood.

Some separatists draw the line at intimate dealings with men, some prefer to have no dealings of any sort with men, and some refuse to deal with women who are involved with men. These choices are personal and political and, although they may be eloquently urged, are rarely imposed on others. Some separatists live in small communes; some are involved in large networks which allow them to earn money and spend it within an all-female context. There are separatist bookstores, for instance, which do not permit men to enter; there are separatist restaurants, which either do not permit men or allow them entrance only if they are accompanied by women. There are separatist shelters for battered women, women's clubs or houses, all across Europe and in this country. Separatist women are rarely aggressive and do not spend much energy trying to affect the male world. What they try to do is provide a warm, nourishing, gentle, supportive haven for women, whether in their own homes or in a larger and more public space: there is often a pot of soup on the stove in women's havens, a couch to rest on, coffee, some books.

The obvious objection to such a way of life is that it is marginal, and therefore does not influence society, does not advance change. This is not necessarily true. Separatists write books and poetry, they influence other women, and above all, they demonstrate by their own way of life that "feminine" values can be sufficient to sustain life. Perhaps the cultivation of one's own garden is the best way to realize feminist values; and perhaps the walled garden, the turned back are seductive to those outside.

It is arguable that separatism emerges from weakness, from women's fear of losing their values if they immerse themselves in the male world, and fear of emotional strain from the abrasions of dealing with it. On the other hand, what better way to test "feminine" values than to try to live them out? And although some separatists may not be actively fighting against the policies of the patriarchal world, and cannot, if the bomb falls, demand immunity, they do enjoy felicity here and now.

Separatism is a target for those who believe feminism must engage the women of the mainstream if it is to realize its goals, and think that mainstream women are offended by the principles of the separatists, and fearful of their sexual choice. The issue of lesbianism has been a source of conflict and division among various feminist groups and associations, and some contention remains. But many mainstream women live essentially homosocial lives—they see almost only women, deal with almost only women in their work and leisure; and over the past two decades, especially in the United States, many mainstream women have adopted lesbianism. There are lesbians who believe that lesbianism is quintessential feminism, and that one cannot really be a feminist without repudiating the male world. But feminism is a human movement; the future of all of us—girls, women, boys, and men—depends upon our all comprehending and realizing feminist principles. Repudiation of the male world may be a principled and felicitous position for the short term, but it is not enough for the long term.

It may also be argued that separatism contradicts basic feminist principles, which are invoked when women attempt to integrate a private men's club or society, or demand representation on an exclusive (exclusive of women, that is) board or committee. The two positions are not similar, however. Feminists do not attempt to integrate male associations simply because they exist. Feminists try to integrate associations which consolidate power, in which policy is made, in which the decisions taken affect the entire population, not just men. Separatist associations make policy only for themselves; indeed, they largely reject the pursuit of power. It is not exclusivity of sex that feminists oppose, but sexual exclusivity of power.

## Revalorization of "Feminine" Qualities

Connected with the separatist movement both by occasionally overlapping membership and by shared values, the women whose primary dedication is the revalorization of "feminine" qualities are writers and artists. They focus mainly on the symbolic realm—on myths, images, and language. They are attempting to uncover a female tradition from the past, and to create one anew. Like those historians who seek to retrieve a specifically female history, and those scholars and researchers who seek to consider the female when they look at reality—whether of animal life, archeological remains, or present psychological, social, or political life—they begin from a new premise: that the female part of experience—in past and present ignored, erased, or viewed as illegitimate, irrelevant—is legitimate, valuable, and interesting. The revalorists are attempting to create a women's art and a women's language.

The question of language is basic. Some feminist writers, following Virginia Woolf's suggestion that a woman's sentence is different in nature from a man's, project, with Adrienne Rich, the "dream of a common [female] language." It is perhaps not accidental that such projections of a woman's language arise at a time when the most fashionable literary theory, deconstruction, is dominated by notions of the phallus as "transcendental signifier," and the pen as penis, inscribing, enrapturing, or raping a passive hymenesque ear. Even in less rarified—but just as transcendental—airs (those of industry, the military, and government) language has taken on a new character in our time. In medieval Europe, the common folk were distinguished from clerics by their vernacular speech and (usually) inability to read. Clerics formed a universal elite: they could read and speak a common language—medieval Latin—that transcended national boundaries and class of birth. Something similar is occurring today. Although the language of the technological world is based on the vernacular of any given nation, and uses the same pronouns and articles, and some of the same nouns and verbs, in its larger manifestations—sentences, paragraphs—it is all but incomprehensible to the untrained.

> Congruent command paradigms explicitly represent the semantic oppositions in the definitions of the commands to which they refer.

This language relies heavily on the passive mode and impersonal constructions, which create the effect that there is no actor, that no one is doing anything to anything or anyone else, that things are happening within some superhuman machine that runs apart from human will:

> To provide equal outside awareness opportunities to all employees, and minimize energy consumption, a perimeter corridor system is used.

It is a curt language, and admits neologisms to save time: some people now say "we accessed them," rather than "we saw that they were introduced." Brevity and high seriousness without gracefulness prove the solid business values of the speakers or writers. At the same time, unnecessary words are used simply out of awkwardness:

> There is also the requirement to remote the control units away from within the computer room.

Nouns become verbs, nouns become adjectives:

> This implementation is necessary in order to size the impact on reliability and could potentially provide a prime component to the tool buy decision.

At the same time, the language uses convoluted and lengthy phrasing to avoid two primary areas of taboo: a strong sense of person(s), whether acting or acted upon, and any expressiveness. Consider the following way of saying, "People should talk together before anyone makes a decision on what to do."

It is anticipated that relevant discussion and coordination between
concerned parties . . . is to take place before any decision is made for
specific action on individual problem resolution.[2]

Consider the violence concealed behind the phrasing of these directions in
the *Handbook for Shelter Management* provided in the late 1960s by the Department of Defense:

> The first step in preparing the shelter for occupancy is to selectively
> recruit, train, and assign shelter management personnel to key man-
> agement positions. . . . Although pre-emergency selection and assign-
> ment of a management cadre is desirable, it may be necessary to
> recruit most of the management staff from the shelter population
> after the shelter is put to use (p. 3).
>     Disturbances, conflicts and disorders may be prevented or mini-
> mized by: Immediate and forceful corrective action, particularly in
> the case of serious violations such as assault, revolt against authority,
> and so on (pp. 21–22).[3]

Language has probably always been used to conceal; thus we have a term
for such use, *euphemistic*. Perhaps what is different in our age is that people
feel required to conceal everything that is alive and human, as if those things in
themselves are shameful; or perhaps acts of violence have reached an intensity
and degree of ubiquity that drenches bland statements with bloody irony.[4]

Even when it is dealing with emotions, the new language is instrumental.
This passage is part of a discussion of what Harry Stack Sullivan called "malevolent transformation," a psychological mechanism in which someone who desires tenderness attacks another rather than ask for it:

> Malevolence is then given the status of an appearance concealing the
> reality of thwarted utility and is thus in some contorted sense itself
> rendered useful. It supports a secular theodicy and a psychotherapy
> which dares not under any circumstances be moralist.[5]

Technological language is a tongue from which emotion has been obliterated, and is therefore appropriate to institutions that aim to obliterate emotion in their workers, especially those at the upper levels. It is also pretentious,
not to say pompous; its very awkwardness testifies to the seriousness with which
the speakers take themselves. Lack of a sense of the personal and of feeling
demonstrates the speaker's transcendence of such elements. This language con-
veys a sense of the world that is overwhelmingly mechanical, of a system that is
cosmic in scope, as absolute as nature itself, and in which people are unfeeling
instruments of a "divine" purpose.

This is primarily a male language, although not all men speak it or can
understand it. It is one trademark of a new elite whose approach to the world is
entirely instrumental—"masculine" things exist not to be experienced, but to
be used as tools in achieving some linear goal. Their language has many dialects, depending on the discipline in which it appears, and speakers of one dialect do not necessarily understand those of another. But the same tendencies
appear in all.

Not only those who are likely to write directives—executives and managers—but those workers who read them speak this language, if in less polished form. They understand words that refer to the instruments discussed, and they come to understand the odd syntax. Men who work on machines refer to the manipulated objects as "she"—just as people continue to refer to nature as "she"—a terminology that shows original attitudes far more rawly than the new male language.

But most women, excluded from the kind of work and workplace where such language is taught, cannot speak or read it, and, along with many men, dislike it when they encounter it. For feminists, the claim of objectivity (symbolized by impersonality) is false and dangerous.[6] Nevertheless, it is impossible for women to work in government, industry, or the sciences, hard or soft, or to write discourse and expect to be read by colleagues, to gain respect and get promoted, without learning and using the abstract, impersonal, inexpressive discourse that is equated with professionalism in our time.

It is inconceivable that any religious leader in our world could exclaim, as Luther did, that he could "cut wind" in Germany and Rome would "smell" it.[7] Such language is entirely too bodily, sensuous, vivid, and expressive for us. Quite apart from the dangerous and inhuman delusions that are fostered by the new abstract technological language, it presents a major threat to feminists. To learn a language is to learn to think in its terms, which requires assimilation of its implicit values at a profound level of the self. People who use a language that pretends to objectivity and authority, that masks its biases with these qualities, and that ignores or disdains expressivity, must, willy-nilly, come to share its biases, both surface and underlying.

Some feminists have countered this language—and male discourse in general, with its absence of women, body, and feeling—by creating a different kind of language, one that is extremely expressive, is based in the personal, uses female imagery extensively, and refers even to large-scale public and cultural conditions in terms of personal experience. A body of criticism has sprung up around this writing, mainly in France. Marguerite Duras, for example, has defined "feminine literature" as organic, "translated from blackness, from darkness." She demands that women "reverse everything: make darkness the point of departure in judging what men call light, make obscurity the point of departure in judging what men call clarity." She writes: "I think the future belongs to women. Men have been completely dethroned. Their rhetoric is stale, used up. We must move on to the rhetoric of women, one that is anchored in the organism, in the body."[8] Hélène Cixous writes, "Woman must write her self: must write about women and bring women to writing, from which they have been driven away as violently as from their bodies—and for the same reasons, by the same law, with the same fatal goal. . . . Now women return from afar, from always: from 'without,' from the heath where witches are kept alive; from below, from beyond 'culture.' . . . Here they are, returning, arriving over and again, because the unconscious is impregnable. They have wandered around in circles, confined to the narrow room in which they've been given a deadly brainwashing."[9]

The subject matter of most of the new women's writing is women's bodies, their bodily processes, their feelings, their relations with each other, their attitudes toward the male world, and men's attitudes toward women. The intention is to revalorize the "feminine" elements, even to exalt them. Monique Wittig's prose poem about sex war, *Les Guerrillères*, opens thus:

> When it rains the women stay in the summer-house. They hear the water beating on the tiles and streaming down the slopes of the roof. Fringes of rain surround the summer-house, the water that runs down at its angles flows more strongly, it is as if springs hollow out the pebbles at the places where it reaches the ground. At last someone says it is like the sound of micturition, that she cannot wait any longer, and squats down. Then some of them form a circle around her to watch the labia expel the urine.[10]

All bodily processes are accepted as parts of experience that are legitimate subject matter for literature—a position first taken by Joyce, in *Ulysses*. Wittig handles it very differently, but like Joyce insists on the unpleasant and disgusting as well as the pleasant:

> Some of the women swim letting themselves drift toward the last splashes of sunlight on the sea. At the most luminous spot when, dazzled, they try to move away, they say that they are assailed by an unbearable stench. Later they are seized with vomiting. Then they begin to moan as they strain with their arms, swimming as fast as they can. At a certain point they collide with the floating decaying carcase of an ass, at times the swell of the sea reveals sticky shapeless gleaming lumps of indescribable colour. They say that they shouted with all their might, shedding many tears, complaining that no sea-breeze got up to drive away the smell, supporting under the arms and groin one of them who has fainted, while the vomit accumulates around them on the surface of the water.[11]

Body parts are not treated in accordance with stereotypes: "Some laugh out loud and manifest their aggressiveness by thrusting their bare breasts forward."[12] Motherhood is seen as important, and the mother-daughter relation as central, but neither is sentimentalized.[13]

The revalorists stretch or play with various elements of language—punctuation, syntax, and word forms, as well as sentence and paragraph structure. Here is a passage from Susan Griffin, *Woman and Nature*:

> The spiraling descent. The legend of endless circling. The labyrinth from which none return. She falls into this labyrinth. Into the room of the dressing where the walls are covered with mirrors. Where mirrors are like eyes of men, and the women reflect the judgments of mirrors. . . . The room of the dressing where the women are afraid to touch. Where the women are not close. Where the women keep themselves at a distance. . . . Where all her words are dressed.[14]

Women of color frequently use individualistic punctuation and capitalization in their writing, in an effort to avoid as much as possible the rules of the language of domination and the dominant class. Chrystos begins "I Don't Understand Those Who Have Turned Away from Me":

> 5:23 A.M.—May 1980
>     I am afraid of white people     Never admitted that before     deep secret
>     I think about all the white women I knew in San Francisco     Women with Master's degrees from Stanford University & cars that daddy bought, women with straight white teeth     clear skins from thousands of years of proper nutrition     They chose to be poor     They were quite convincing in the role of oppressed victim     I want to tell them to go down to Fillmore & Haight & tell somebody about it[15]

Elements of this kind of writing appear in works written with more traditional syntax, like Audre Lorde's *Zami*:

> Madivine. Friending. Zami. How Carriacou women love each other is legend in Grenada, and so is their strength and their beauty. In the hills of Carriacou between L'Esterre and Harvey Vale my mother was born, a Belmar woman. Summered in Aunt Anni's house, picked limes with the women. And she grew up dreaming of Carriacou as someday I was to dream of Grenada.[16]

Independence of traditional rules appears even in theoretical works, like Griffin's and those of Mary Daly. Griffin uses poetic techniques to express personal/political experience and ideas; Daly uses a brilliant, quirky language of her own, full of neologisms and hyphenations that sharply underline the patriarchal bias within language. Daly adopts Gertrude Stein's ideas on capitalization: "Sometimes one feels that Italians should be with a capital and sometimes with a small letter, one can feel like that about almost anything."[17]

This paragraph appears in a section in which Daly refers to possession by devils as being the feeding by males, especially the Father, on female energy; and to patriarchal culture as a maze/haze of deception from which women must free themselves:

> As a creative crystallizing of the movement beyond the State of Patriarchal Paralysis, this book is an act of Dis-possession; and hence, in a sense beyond the limitations of the label *anti-male*, it is absolutely Anti-androcrat, A-mazingly Anti-male, Furiously and Finally Female.[18]

She concludes *Gyn/Ecology* thus:

> In the beginning was not the word. In the beginning is the hearing. Spinsters spin deeper into the listening deep. We can spin only what we hear, because we hear, and as well as we hear. We can weave and unweave, knot and unknot, only because we hear, what we hear, and as well as we hear. Spinning is celebration/cerebration. Spinsters Spin all ways, always. Gyn/Ecology is UnCreation; Gyn/Ecology is Creation.[19]

Sandra Gilbert and Susan Gubar call such writing "vulvalogocentric" in analogy with the "phallologocentric" vision of the deconstructionists.[20]

The language of the "vulvalogocentrists" tries to accomplish many things at once. By using in praise and pride images that have long been tossed at women in scorn, the writer makes the negative positive. She gives them new value, revalorizes them. By stretching the "rules" of discourse—semantic, syntactical, and typographical rules—the writer carves out an avenue of experience that can no longer be reached through traditional forms. She symbolizes experience of and through the body and senses, of and through emotion charged with thought (rather than thought charged with emotion). She is attempting, as Julia Kristeva points out, to alter the symbolic dimension of women's position, and the "sociosymbolic contract" imposed upon them. She wants "to break the code, to shatter language, to find a specific discourse closer to the body and emotions."[21] She wants to restore the magic and mystery, the wonder of the unstructured, all lost in what Max Weber called the "Disenchantment of the World."

Syntactical experimentation in particular attempts to represent experience in a nonlinear, non-"masculine" way. Syntax in most Western languages is representative of a power relation: a doer does to a done-to. Syntax (along with the pronoun) is the part of language most resistant to change. Yet there have been periods in history in which reflective, meditative, associative writing was popular, writing that did not so much narrate as convey experience.[22] There are languages less aggressive than English and other Western tongues, languages in which it is impossible to say "he fucked her." Even in dialects drawn from English, one might more likely say "they lovin'."

The absence of expressiveness in twentieth-century public language parallels a debasement not just of personal expressiveness, but of all affective elements in our thinking and perhaps in our lives. One cannot refer to certain states and expect to be taken seriously. It is risky, for example, to write about love: the word is sloppy, has too many meanings, and besides is sentimental. Sentimentality is a cardinal sin in writing, and discredits the writer's position: recall the editorial in the *British Medical Journal* quoted in Chapter Five on a statement by a member of the government health service: "By putting 'people before buildings' and by giving practical expression to public sympathy for the old and handicapped, Mrs Castle has perhaps allowed sentiment to overrule intellect."[23] Yet similar complaints are not made against the use of the word *power*, which also has many meanings, and which arouses passion in many hearts. Terms like *tenderness, compassion, nurturance, giving, touching* bring sneers to many lips: only *babies* and *motherhood* are more disdained.[24]

The denial of the importance of "feminine" elements is directly involved with their increasing absence in more and more areas of life. Absence of reference to them in serious discourse not only mars that discourse but in the long run mars life. Elshtain urges feminists to create a language that is bold and firm yet at the same time shows awareness of "fragile and vulnerable human existence": but that is precisely what "masculine" thinkers want to forget.[25]

Elshtain complains that intellectual discourse, with its claims of objectivity and value-free statements, is actually a language deprived "of a grammar of moral discourse," that forces "all of life under a set of terms denuded of a critical edge."[26] As Catharine MacKinnon, among others, has shown, the apparent lack of a point of view (a personal bias, subjectivity) is possible only because the actual (patriarchal) point of view is so universal, so widely shared. Bias is obscured, no personal exhortation is necessary, when an attitude is assumed to be truth.[27]

Some feminists oppose the feminologists, those who attempt to revalorize the female and "feminine" qualities through language. Julia Kristeva suggests that when women deny existing culture, reject theory, and exalt the body, they may be crossing the cultural borderline into hysteria, which is potentially liberating but also limiting.[28] Others assert that to use imagery which has been degraded is to lay claim only to those metaphors and parts of experience that have already been ceded to women. And clearly, writing that is pervaded by emotion, that refers to labia and vulvas, blood, breasts, milk, weeping, bleeding, leaking, that concentrates only on women, is not likely to be read by many men, and certainly not by those who manage society.

On the other hand, such men rarely read anything women write anyway, even in traditional modes. There is no hope of influencing such men: only revolution or death can change them, and revolution puts others like them in place. We simply do not know whether we can change a society by standing outside it and creating a culture of our own: but it is as worth trying as any other course. In the meantime, revalorist writing is important to women themselves, for the first time in history (if not in the span of human existence) praising and speaking of their own breasts, their own pudenda (whose root is *shame*: and the first meaning of which refers only to the female). For women, as for society at large, it is necessary now to reach out both to the dishonored body, discredited emotion, to blood and milk; and to self-control, power-to, assertive being in the world. Only by incorporating both can we attain integrity.

## Feminist Socialism

Socialist feminism grounds itself in an analysis of oppression different from that offered in this book. Socialism is as dedicated as any other patriarchal form to the domination of nature; it has been able to absorb feminist ideas by rhetorically breaking the association of women with nature, and enlisting women in the struggle against it.[29] That this severance has remained a matter of rhetoric is demonstrated by the continued second-class status of women in socialist countries, by their continuing difficulty in regulating such matters as sex, marriage, procreation, and divorce so that women do not bear the onus of sexual transactions and the entire responsibility for continuation of the race.

The socialist diagnosis of society rests primarily on economics, and holds that cultural and moral change derive from changes in economic structure. The oppression of women arose with the concept of private property: mainly because women could reproduce, they, like animals, were defined as property. Because capitalism is founded on the idea of private property, the oppression of women is inherent within it and necessary for its perpetuation. Sexism is functional for capitalism because it allows employers to get two workers for the price of one: the man is paid wages; his wife performs the services necessary for him to live even though he spends most of his hours at work, but she is not paid. Women also provide a cheap reserve labor force, which keeps wages down and profits up.[30]

Marxist theory has traditionally tried to comprehend social differences as class difference, and many Marxists have been unable to consider issues of sex or race as having the same weight or importance as class differences. Because women are seen as workers, the particular conditions of women's socialization and responsibility are not taken into consideration at all. It is assumed that with the creation of socialist structures, sexism, like the state, will simply wither away.[31]

Many feminists are also socialists. They find socialist ideals to be feminist ideals as well, while capitalism can hardly be said even to possess ideals. Socialist revolutions have led to immediate institution of feminist reforms: in Russia and China, women were admitted to suffrage, to education at every level, and to paid employment at almost every level. The law recognized women as full human beings, something it does not do even today in some capitalist countries, and socialist governments have made at least intermittent efforts to eradicate oppressive sexist attitudes and customs. The present conflict in Afghanistan arose partly because of Soviet efforts to educate Moslem Afghani women, and to permit them a voice in the community. Women did not have to wage separate struggles for equality in socialist nations, because equality is a basic socialist principle.

However, because socialism adopts the patriarchal stance of necessary domination with regard to nature, and because socialists, like other men, profoundly associate women with nature (regardless of their enlistment in the struggle to control it), socialist theory cannot take account of certain functions—procreation and child rearing in particular—with which women are charged. In socialist as in capitalist states, almost the entire responsibility for producing and maintaining the single most important "product" on earth—children—lies almost entirely with women. As Catharine MacKinnon puts it, under socialism, "women become as free as men to work outside the home while men remain free from work within it."[32] Crowded living conditions are not intrinsic to socialism, but they exacerbate the problems of raising children, divorcing, or marrying, and as we saw earlier, it is the women who usually end up with the children and without means for caring for them. In the 1970s a study of twelve countries, both capitalist and socialist, showed that gainfully employed men devoted half as much time to the care of their children as gainfully employed women; and that unemployed men did even less than they had when they were employed.[33] Not only children but the necessities and felicities of life are left to women in socialist countries as well as in the West: a USSR study recorded that women spent an average of nineteen hours more than men on housework every week.[34] And in Poland it is said that women work "in two shifts"—on their jobs and in the home.[35] In China women are actually penalized for the energy and time they spend in pregnancy and raising children, since they lose income.

It is a patriarchal, not a capitalist idea that procreation and childraising are nonvolitional and therefore can be expected or compelled and require no reward. Indeed, childbearing and childraising *would* require no reward beyond themselves in a culture in which they were not made impediments to survival but were embraced by all as essential to the larger survival of the group. The idea that producing and raising children does not contribute significantly to society—childraising is not included in the gross national product—emerges neither from capitalism nor socialism, but from modern industrial society.

It is true that there is a difference for women in various economic and political structures, that it does not mean the same thing "to be on the bottom in a feudal regime, a capitalist regime, and a socialist regime," but it is also true that "bottom is bottom."[36] The situation of women workers in socialist states is in some ways better than in capitalist states—day care is available, most medical and educational services are free or low-cost—and is unquestionably better than it was in those states before socialism. Nevertheless, in socialist as well as capitalist nations, women as a caste earn less than men, are relegated to more menial, low-paying kinds of work, and are absent from the highest reaches of power. As in capitalist states, the presence of large numbers of women in an occupation functions to downgrade the occupation. In the Soviet Union, for instance, women comprise a majority of the physicians, but physicians are not highly respected or well paid. Women as a group have no greater voice in the destiny of their nations in socialist countries than in capitalist countries.

Women continue to espouse socialism despite its failures. Barbara Ehrenreich, for instance, has written that "there is a difference between a society in which sexism is expressed in the form of female infanticide and a society in which sexism takes the form of unequal representation on the Central Committee. And the difference is worth dying for."[37] But in today's China there is both female infanticide *and* unequal representation on the Central Committee; in most capitalist nations there is unequal representation, but little female infanticide. Moreover, it is patriarchy that erects ideals "worth dying for"; the entire thrust of feminism is to create a revolution worth living for.

There is a difference in treatment of women in socialist and capitalist nations: as we have seen, socialism has done far better by women in the areas of access to education, medical care, and child care. On the other hand, the Soviet Union persecutes through imprisonment or exile those feminists who dare to speak openly on women's issues.[38] Socialists conceive of powerlessness as entirely an extrinsic affair. They see feminism as bourgeois, individualistic, and idealistic and do not perceive either the special socialization of women which leads them to internalize certain repressions, or the larger concerns of feminism which have to do with the community of humans as much as with the individual.[39]

At the same time, the ideas characterizing capitalism are inherently antagonistic to feminist principles: if all patriarchal forms worship power, capitalism worships power primarily in the form of property which can be amassed only through exploitive use of people and resources. Capitalism is designed to create stratifications and maintain them so that there will always be both a superior (elite, transcendent) class, and classes whose inferiority functions as a seal, a guarantee of the elite's superiority. Any political-social structure that worships power necessarily involves such stratification, but socialist *theory*, at least, is intended to eliminate it.

Socialist theory, with its emphasis on social and economic justice, equality of opportunity, and respect for the dignity of work, functions amicably with feminist theory. Yet thus far, attempts to create a synthesis of socialist and feminist theory have not been notably successful. Socialist women ruefully admit the necessity of forming separate women's groups if any discussion of "women's issues" is to occur, and acknowledge a lack of intellectual, emotional, and economic support from male socialists. Recent socialist revolutions—like that in Nicaragua, for example—have imitated the pattern of earlier ones in their wide use of women during the period of conflict and exclusion of them afterward.

Feminist and socialist theory cannot be synthesized because of their different attitudes toward nature and power. In fact, socialist ideals cannot be realized through existing socialist theory because no really profound sense of human equality can ever emerge from a philosophy rooted in a stance of human superiority over nature. Because of the falseness and irrelevance to human actuality of that belief, it must continually be "proven" by demonstrations of power, and cannot be proven except symbolically. Until we understand this basic fact, and until feminists convince nonfeminist socialists that "women's issues" are not a small back room in the world's house but are intrinsic to its entire structure, we will not be able to create the kind of synthesis we need.

## Feminism Under Capitalism

The Western world has been capitalistic for roughly the past five hundred years. The capitalist system generated a new ruling class and eradicated, displaced, or assimilated the old feudal aristocracy. The feudal nobles had earned their status largely by might—that is, they had wrested land from others—and kept it by the income from that land and the people (serfs) who came with it, by marriage, and by continued use of might. The new elite owned land, but also, and more important, banks and investments in the means of production.

The end of this form of capitalism occurred in the twentieth century. Its date of death is not certain; many people cite World War I as the termination point of "Western civilization," because that war killed almost the entire generation of scions of the elite class in Europe, those who had been trained for war and leadership. World War I also marked the end of the security of that elite class, and of the life style it followed. The elite, the leisure class, included many people who did not work at all. Possessed of secure wealth and status, they did not seek money and power and considered it vulgar to do so: only through marriage did they openly attempt to increase their fortunes. They followed pleasure, grace, and style, cut off from lower classes and callously unaware of their parasitism upon them. But they did give a small return to their "inferiors": an image of life as leisurely, graceful, beautiful, pleasant, courteous. Although some people continued to live in this way after 1918, it became more difficult: new money had taken over, the old family-owned factories were old-fashioned and inefficient, and their paternalistic form of management had lost its charm for workers who had also been forced to join the aristocrats' war, who had watched their fellows die in the trenches or lost their sons or husbands.

If the death throes of the old Western civilization began during the First War, the birth of a new form of it was apparent only to a few—like Simone Weil—until after World War II. That war hastened the triumph of technology and those who managed it by demonstrating the effectiveness of massive planning, deployment, disposition, and regimentation of people and a wide array of things—food, clothing, equipment, weapons of all sorts—initiated and coordinated by a central power cadre. Only the United States, of all the Allied powers, fought two different wars at opposite ends of the earth; emerged from a state of unpreparedness to victory; and created the most lethal weapon ever devised. The procedures used to accomplish these acts were immediately applied to the affairs of ordinary life.

The resurgence of the cult of domesticity which accompanied this shift in values was a necessary component of it. Before the war, most people worked fairly close to home—on farms, in factories, offices, and shops that were within walking distance, or a bus ride away, from their communities and families. After the war, the tools that had turned out weapons were turned to peaceful uses, like automobile manufacture. Highways were carved out so people could drive to work. Large industries sought to become larger, and technological "advance" became a priority. At the same time the regimentation and conformism that had helped win the war were applied more widely to win a war of economic domination.

The ideals of the old leisure class faded from memory, visible now only in an occasional painting, poem, or novel; but the new elite had no image to confer upon the masses. For the most part uncultivated, without class or ethnic tradition (for they were Americans), passionate only about power—money and technology—the new managers were also faceless, without definition. The new life style was dominated by speed, noise, swift change, by fortunes made and lost overnight, by steady mediocrity leading to the trust of superiors, and so to power. There was little pleasure or beauty in these lives or images of them.

Beyond this, the men and women involved in World War II ended sick at heart, exhausted and disgusted with mass murder, with the terrible machines of war, with killing, deprivation, and sacrifice. They craved peaceful order, pleasure, affection; they needed to create new life after the devastation. The cult of domesticity was a manifestation of this natural need; but it was picked up and pressed into service by the new managerial elite. For the elite too had been in the war, and felt their own cravings, their own hollowness.

The pleasures of small community life, of interaction and interconnection in one's domestic and work life, became increasingly unavailable to masses of people. As transport improved, businesses grew, small businesses failed. Yet without some joys, some promise at least of felicity, it is difficult to motivate people. The new form of the cult of domesticity had several aims: through commoditization it offered glittering images of sensuous beauty and pleasure, and it located the implied felicity in the domestic realm—in love, marriage, children, and a home. It locked women firmly into the domestic realm by making them responsible for the creation and physical maintenance of this felicity—thus they would not protest their renewed exclusion from the workplace; and it locked men firmly into their work, necessary for the economic maintenance of this felicity—thus guaranteeing their obedience, acquiescence, and availability to whatever projects management decreed. Control by the power elite was thus extended not only over family structure and morals (all power elites have attempted to control these), but over the most private aspects of family and personal life. Pleasure itself became subject to control; the quality of life was gathered up in the machine, and packaged and sold as a commodity. Domestic pleasures were packaged and sold as washing machines and refrigerators, ranch houses, lawn mowers, backyard wading pools. The joys of parenthood, of intimacy and sensuous pleasures, were substantiated in advertising images of golden-toned children and trees, radiant young women in aprons, and handsome, arrogant men in business suits, tawny cowboys puffing Marlboros.

The odd consequence of this commoditization of experience was that it diminished not packaging but reality. Packaging and the creation of images continues to be successful, continues to exert influence over people so that they will spend money on an item because of the imagery with which it is sold; while the experience itself, which invariably fails to live up to the golden haze of the image, is blamed for failing. "Feminine" qualities, already held in contempt by a high-power, high-tech world, suffered even further degradation, as the sophisticated cast their cynicism on the "feminine" parts of experience, which did not live up to the images purveyed. The high-power world was also commoditized and sold—in ads for men's suits, cars, airlines, cigarettes: men were depicted with a cold, controlling arrogance; their major characteristic was imperviousness—untouchability, transcendence, invulnerability to the undertow of emotion, the anxieties of actual experience, any kind of hurt.

Thus control became the primary good not merely for a class but for entire populations; even the illiterate could comprehend the images of advertising. Groups which had not generally thought in terms of worldly control began to do so. In the 1950s Jews waged a campaign against anti-Semitism with considerable success; and in the 1960s the black civil rights movement inspired the national imagination. The idea that men can control their lives was not lost on men: from the late fifties they began to rebel against regimentation and conformity, above all against what they saw as slavery to a wife, children, a house, a mortgage. The "hippie" movement became a metaphor for the restlessness of American men. As Barbara Ehrenreich has shown, they began to leave their families, seeking the excitement of new sex, new romance; in time they began to leave even their jobs, looking for more autonomy in their work lives.[40] Throughout their rebellion, however, they were concerned only with themselves, shrugging off economic as well as emotional and physical responsibilities to their children and former wives.

The situation of women during this period—from the mid-forties, when they were economically and psychologically coerced into adopting domesticity wholeheartedly, to the mid-sixties—was unhappy. In 1953 Simone de Beauvoir's *The Second Sex* shattered whatever pride thinking women retained in their femaleness, but suggested no alternative except denying ("transcending") that femaleness. There was no economic avenue by which women could escape the role they had been cast in, and as men began increasingly to leave their wives and children, women's economic situation became increasingly dire. The birth control pill, marketed for the first time in 1960, offered women the possibility of control over their bodies: but this benefited mainly younger women.

It was probably Betty Friedan's *The Feminine Mystique*, published in 1963, that first galvanized American women into action. Women legislators had seen to it that laws passed to redress wrongs done to blacks were expanded to include women. The Equal Pay Act was passed in 1963; the Civil Rights Act in 1964. Title VII of the latter prohibited discrimination on grounds of sex, race, color, religion, or national origin. The word *sex* was included as a result of maneuvers by Representative Martha Griffiths, Senator Margaret Chase Smith, and a reporter, Mae Craig. In 1965 the Supreme Court held that laws banning contraceptives were unconstitutional, and in 1966 a federal court declared that an Alabama law barring women from juries violated the Fourteenth Amendment (guaranteeing equal protection under the law). In that year too, the National Organization for Women was founded.

Agitation and lobbying under such laws as were available to them erupted from women's groups across the country, especially from chapters of NOW. At the same time, younger women active in the anti–Vietnam War movement were becoming disenchanted at discovering that young men shouting "morality" through foghorns on college campuses displayed toward women the very exploitive and degrading treatment the men complained about from the government. These women formed their own groups, which sprang up independently in many cities in the United States and Canada in 1967 and 1968. Through imaginative demonstration they captured national attention, and consciousness-raising groups flourished everywhere.

The decade that followed was enormously fertile; the seeds planted then are still bearing fruit. Women scholars began to delve into women's history, to break away from male interpretations and lay the groundwork for an alternative view of anthropology, psychology, sociology, philosophy, and language. Politically oriented groups pressed for legislation granting women equality in education, housing, credit, and promotion and hiring. Other women established feminist magazines, journals, publishing houses, and bookstores. Some strove for political office; some entered the newly open "male" world of business and industry. In the exhilaration of that period, women who had felt crippled found limbs, women who had felt marginal found a center, women who had felt alone found sisters.

It is now less than twenty years since the rising of the "second wave." The difference is astonishing. Women are now working in hundreds of jobs that were closed to them in the past. Women can sign leases, buy cars and houses, obtain credit; they cannot be denied telephone service because they are divorced. They can be seated in restaurants although they are dining without a man. Although some women's fashions still inhibit mobility, they are no longer *de rigueur*. Women are no longer expected to produce elaborate entertainments: life can be easier, more leisurely, for both sexes.

Most important of all, women now possess reproductive freedom. Although men have long had access to condoms, which were and are sold over the counter in every drugstore, women needed doctors' prescriptions to purchase diaphragms and, later, the birth control pill. This is still true, but such prescriptions are widely available now, and women do not have to be married to obtain them. (In France, where men can also obtain condoms easily, women could not purchase contraceptive devices in drugstores until 1967, and such purchases still require the authorization of the minister of social affairs.[41]) Clearly, it is not birth control—or, more accurately, the prevention of conception—per se that is offensive to patriarchal culture, but the placing of that control in the hands of women. Despite continuing attempts to wrest it from them, American women are likely to hold on to this right over their own bodies. But in some Western nations—Ireland, for example—they still do not possess it.

The difference is great for a huge number of women, and because the difference permeates their lives, change may seem complete. But in the scale of things, the change is minimal. Capitalism, under great pressure for almost a hundred and fifty years, has yielded women about what socialism yielded them immediately. But it has managed—as has socialism—to retain its essential character. Capitalism has assimilated women, it has not broadened itself; it has swallowed women rather than alter itself. And it has done this in accordance with its traditional structures. Thus the women who have benefited most from the changes are well-educated, white, middle-class women, often without children. Thus the divisiveness of racism has pervaded the women's movement itself. Thus women have by and large been kept out of the most sensitive and powerful areas of business and government, so that they have not achieved a voice in the running of our society. And thus women who have not managed to live like men, or with them, have been condemned to the lowest rank in our society: women are the new poor. It is not an exaggeration to say that although feminism in capitalist states has freed many women and improved the lives of others, it has had little effect on the patriarchy, which has simply absorbed a few women who appear acceptable to its purposes, and barred the door for the rest.

The issue of race divides women for several reasons: women as well as men have been infected with the racism that is a disease of our culture, and which thrives among people of all colors. Since they themselves are similarly categorized, one might think that women would be immune to a way of thought that categorizes people by a physical attribute, and that ascribes to them qualities seen as close to nature—animalism, lack of rationality, lack of a moral sense. But women are no more immune than any other underclass. It is a sad human fact that people diminished by a master culture reconcile themselves to their inferior status by ascribing an even greater inferiority to other groups.

Accounts by black feminists demonstrate the racism of some white feminists, who treat blacks as tokens, who do not listen to black women to understand the problems particular to feminists of color, yet who presume to speak for all feminists.[42] White feminists often assume postures of condescension toward Latino culture, which they consider profoundly macho, as if their own were not. White feminists write books analyzing patriarchal culture, attempting to establish feminist theory, or examining a dimension of women's condition without mentioning women of color at all—women of color are as invisible in these works as women as a sex are in the work of many men.[43] And indeed it sometimes seems that the gap between colored * culture and white culture is as profound as the gap between white male and white female culture. It is also of the same nature.

Possibly the most anguishing problem for women of color is the necessity many of them feel to break away from their traditions. They and their mothers often emerge from African, Latin, or Asian traditions rich in emotion, art, expressiveness, bonding, and "feminine" values—nutritiveness, compassion, intimacy, spontaneity, playfulness. To break away from such a tradition is a serious deprivation; yet to remain within it means not assimilating in any way to white culture, and in our society nonassimilation to white culture leads to poverty at best, and often serious deprivation or death. In addition, these traditions often contain a strong and offensive element of male supremacy. To repudiate that requires denying the men of one's own culture, which is painful and which leaves women of color in a limbo of isolation. They must to some degree detach themselves both from their women—mothers, female relatives, and friends—and from their men—fathers, brothers, lovers—if they are to realize their own principles and desires.

Some women of color believe that race solidarity is more important than sex solidarity, that the women and men of any particular group must place their interests together. In practice, this means that the problems of men are seen as primary to those of women. Many people believe that men of color, especially black men, have been "castrated" by white culture—that is, they have been treated like women, and denied that special quality of male identity that is necessary for men to function within this society. As we have seen, however, that special quality is an illusion of control: superiority at being what women are not, or power to force women not to be whatever men think they themselves are. It is rooted in a sense of difference from and superiority over women. If indeed black men lack this sense of identity, they would seem to be prime candidates for working with women to create a broader human identity that does not rest on superiority over nature (or other people) but on cooperation, community with both. We all recall Stokely Carmichael's answer to the question about the proper position of women within SNCC: supine. Such a remark demonstrates that a portion of the black movement shares principles identical to those of any white patriarchy. Yet the treatment of black men by our society is so

* I am using this word as it is used in *This Bridge Called My Back: Writings by Radical Women of Color*, eds. Cherrie Moraga and Gloria Anzaldua, to refer to all Third World peoples and peoples of color.

threatening and humiliating that it is difficult for black women not to feel a need to defend and support them. In this area too, women of color feel torn, divided in loyalty regardless of their choices.

On the other hand, black women and other women of color never underwent the "shrinkage into vapidity" that afflicted middle-class white women in America.[44] They are less likely to suffer from feelings of fragility, dependency, and fear of action, from the lack of a sense of moral right in assertion of self. Black women *always* worked: even the women of the black gentry of the late nineteenth and early twentieth centuries were deeply involved in volunteer community action. Black women have lived in a culture in which they could be personally independent, often acting as the support and mainstay of their own families and extended "families," yet remained interdependent with others in the bonded network that characterizes black culture. These benefits, however, are offset by the poverty to which blacks have been consigned and by the degrading treatment offered black women in our society, which treats all black women as if they were either whores or servants. This treatment, a daily matter, perforce arouses rage and hate; but no one wants to live in such a boiling state, and such emotions hinder attempts to bridge the gap between feminists of different subcultures. Indeed, women of color frequently suffer from prejudices against each other.[45]

Encompassing everything else, however, is the economic situation of black women and other women of color. Partly because of this situation, black women have an 80 percent fatality rate from breast cancer, and three times as many unnecessary hysterectomies and sterilizations as white women. Black women are three times more likely than white women to be raped, assaulted, or murdered.[46] Women of color remain the lowest-paid group in the nation, and nearly half of America's black children live in poverty.[47] The gains reaped by the black civil rights movement benefited mainly men.

In 1947 black men earned only half as much as white men; by 1975 they were earning three-fourths as much. The latest census figures show the average annual income of white males as $17,427, of black males $12,738 (73 cents of a white male dollar), and of Hispanic males $12,658 (73 cents of a white male dollar). In 1947 black women earned only one-third as much as white women, and worked primarily as domestic servants; in 1978 they nearly equaled the earnings of white women.[48] *But* the gap between male and female earnings has increased. According to the last census, the mean income of white females was $10,244 (59 cents of a white male dollar), of black females $9,476 (54 cents of a white male dollar), and of Hispanic females $8,466 (49 cents of a white male dollar).[49] Despite differences in the concerns and approaches of women of color and white women, in the realm of economics, women as a caste comprise a lower class.

The poor of America are women: the poor of the world are women. In 1980, in America, the median adjusted income for men was $12,530; for women, it was $4920. In 1980 the poverty level was $8414 for a nonfarm family of four, and nearly thirty million Americans live beneath it.[50] Seventy percent of these are white, 30 percent black—and we may note that only 12 percent of the population is black—two-thirds of them women and children.[51] If we limit these figures to adults, two out of every three poor adults are female. If present trends continue, by the year 2000 the poor of America will be entirely its women.[52]

There are a number of reasons for this. A presidential report published in 1981 claims that women are "systematically underpaid," that "women's work" pays about four thousand dollars a year less than men's work, and that occupational segregation is more pronounced by sex than by race: 70 percent of men and 54 percent of women are concentrated in jobs done only by those of their own sex.[53]

Because women are still held responsible—by themselves and by men— for raising the children, they are forced to take jobs that are close to home, that offer flexible hours (like waitressing), or are part-time; jobs that do not require extended traveling or long hours. They are not able to "compete" in a job market that demands single-minded devotion to work, fast running on a narrow track. For some this is a tolerable situation: some women are not notably ambitious, prefer a balanced life, and have working husbands. But this is not the case for all, or even most, women.

More women than ever in the period covered by American record keeping on this point are living without men: they are single mothers, divorced mothers, and widows, as well as single working women. The reasons for this are complex. Two major reasons, however, are the movement for "sexual liberation" and the feminist movement.

The movement for "sexual liberation" begun in the 1950s was a male campaign, rooted in ideas that seem for the most part honest and beneficial: that sex was good, the body was good; that trading sexual access for financial support degraded sex and the body; that virginity was a questionable good in women and not at all necessary in men; and that the requirement of sexual fidelity in marriage was an oppression. However, the campaign was also extremely self-serving: it was not based on a philosophy that saw a joyous sex life as one element in a life concerned with the pleasure and the good of self and others. It was not a responsible movement: in fact it "masculinized" sex by making it a commodity and by isolating sex from other elements intrinsic to it—affection, connection, and the potential for procreation. To speak lightly, what the sexual revolution accomplished was to change the price of sexual access to a woman from marriage to a dinner.

At the same time, the ties of marriage lost their force—for men. As of 1963, almost all divorces sought in America were initiated (whether openly or not) by men.[54] Divorce—like marriage—is morally neutral. Insofar as it ends a relationship of misery, it is a good; insofar as it ends a long-term intimacy, it is to be lamented. Even when a marriage involves children, it cannot be prejudged: divorce may be better for the children than the marriage was. It seems reasonable to assume that if one party to a marriage wants a divorce, divorce should occur. But marriage and divorce are both tied to responsibility, and it was this tie that was broken by the "sexual liberation" movement.

If a man—and society in general—requires a woman to set aside ideas of an individual life, and to accept the role of functionary—wife, mother, housekeeper—without payment, then that role must be structured to guarantee that woman a secure life despite her unpaid labor. In cognizance of this contract, traditional divorce laws stipulated alimony. Laws did not, of course, prevent men from abandoning their families completely, or failing in alimony payments. But the new sexual morality was growing in the sixties, a period when feminists were struggling to gain the right to paid employment above the menial level, and when many women who had gained such work were initiating divorce themselves. The thinking of legislators and judges underwent an amazingly swift change. The new assumption was that women worked, that they earned as much as men, and thus that they did not require alimony—which is rarely granted now, and even more rarely paid. In 1979, only 14 percent of all divorced or separated women were granted alimony *or* child support, and of those at least 30 percent did not receive what they were awarded.[55]

This situation is unjust to women who have accepted lesser jobs to help their husbands through school, or given up fellowships or promotions to accompany a husband to his new job. It is appallingly unjust to women who have neglected their own potential careers to care for husbands and children. But it becomes outrageous when we consider the statistics (if we need statistics; many women are too well acquainted with the reality behind them) on men's support of their children after divorce.

Although some very rich men use the power of their wealth to take the children away from their mothers after divorce, most men who divorce leave not just a marriage but a family.[56] Men father children; although the degree to which they participate in childraising varies, it seems likely that they have some love and concern for those children. Nevertheless, after divorce they often disappear: they contribute neither emotion, time, nor money to the care of their own children. More than 90 percent of children who live with one parent live with their mothers; in 1978 there were 7.1 million single mothers with custody of their children in the United States.[57] The number of men raising children on their own declined in the decade of the seventies. "The result of divorce, in an overwhelming number of cases, is that men become singles and women become single mothers."[58] Women's incomes decline by 73 percent in the first year after divorce; men's incomes *increase* by 42 percent.[59] The father is better off: the children are often hungry.

In recent years judges have tended not to award child support to mothers with custody; they have denied it to 41 percent of such mothers. Studies of the amounts awarded vary, ranging from as low as an average of $539 per year to an average of $2110.[60] But over 50 percent of custodial mothers never receive the amounts due them.[61] Lenore Weitzman's research in California shows that only 13 percent of women with custody of preschool children receive alimony: child support payments (even when they are made) are almost never enough to cover the cost of raising small children.[62]

The low value placed on children by divorced fathers is unfortunately not an aberration in our society. People who complain about taxes rarely direct their complaints to the huge amounts spent on a massive weapons system, on manufacturing and maintaining instruments of murder and suicide. Rather, they complain about the paltry percentage spent on assistance to poor people, especially "welfare mothers." Budget cuts made during the Reagan Administration of 1980–84 were aimed at this class: services to the elderly (two-thirds women), victims of domestic violence (almost all women), recipients of food stamps (69 percent are households headed by women), and CETA programs, in which women constitute a large element.[63] Moral and political values are clearly perceptible in the Reagan Administration's plan to count school lunches given to poor children as income, while not demanding that expensive business lunches be counted the same way; and to deny food stamps to poor women who flee brutal husbands and take haven in shelters for battered women.[64] A 1984 budget study shows that women and children are bearing the brunt of three years of federal budget cuts.[65]

Yet even before the 1980–84 budget cutbacks, in no state were the combined benefits of Aid to Families with Dependent Children (the major form of public assistance) and food stamps enough to bring a family *up to* the official poverty level. For women supporting families on their own, unemployment means destitution, and employment at minimum wage is not much better.[66]

This situation is not limited to the United States. An International Labor Organization report on eighty nations counts 600 million women in the work force of the world—one-third of the entire force. It also shows clearly that women are treated poorly in work: they are restricted to less desirable work, are underpaid even when their jobs require high qualifications, and are the first to be dismissed in times of retrenchment.[67] I repeat the statistics mentioned earlier: women do two-thirds of the world's work, provide 45 percent of its food, earn 10 percent of its income, and own 1 percent of its property.[68]

Women suffer wherever male supremacy exists. It is male supremacy first and foremost, not capitalism, socialism, or industrialization, that exploits women. There are many simple societies like that of the Kotha, who live in the southern Indian state of Tamil Nadu, in which women do everything—all the work, productive and reproductive—while the men paint and ornament themselves and dance around the temples.[69] There are many villages in Greece and Africa in which the men sit idle while the women do all the work.[70] Many societies are arranged so that women are required to be economically dependent on men, but men are not required to support them. Nearly 30 percent of the women in western Asia and nearly 50 percent of the women of North America do not have men to provide for them.[71]

Women are receiving the message sent them by capitalist society: they must live *like* men or *with* men to survive. Women in capitalist society have three major options: poverty with marginality, undependable dependency on men, or attempting to assimilate, to live like men. Ambitious women, women with strong talents, education, and a drive to use them, are now able to assimilate within capitalism. They are more and more likely not to marry, but to dedicate themselves to their careers as men do: a 1982 survey of women who are officers in America's largest corporations show that less than half of them are married and 70 percent are childless.[72] The birth rate in the United States and other industrial nations is dropping: a survey of seventeen countries in the East and West shows that in all but four, women are not reproducing at a rate sufficient to maintain the current population; in the remaining four, the rate of reproduction is expected to drop below the replacement level in this decade.[73]

At present, a drop in population is not worrisome, but if current arrangements do not change, if childbearing becomes even more identified with helpless poverty, we may reach the point finally in which childbearing and childraising are recognized for the essential and valuable acts they are, and we may have to pay women to perform them. The notion that women have a profound, innate need to bear children has been demonstrated to be false: even physiological, hormonal bases for women's desire to mother children they have given birth to seem to be lacking.[74] Women may ardently desire children—especially sons—in cultures in which their own identity or well-being depends on it. They may wish to have children simply because they have the physical capacity to do so, or because they see childbearing as a rich experience. But that wish is in many cases not great enough to counter the lack of esteem for reproduction that pervades our society. The most unhappy group in our own country is young women with young children, especially those with low-paying jobs.[75]

At the moment, the policies of government and industry are working smoothly. Large institutions have adjusted to political pressure brought by feminists, have learned to hire a certain kind of woman for a certain level of job: women are given high visibility but little chance at decision making. There are no women at all at the "highest" reaches of power. Feminism is an annoyance to men, but not much more. Institutions draw lines everywhere, forcing women to fight one protracted battle after another simply to maintain control over their own bodies, to gain promotion or raises, to rebut sexual harassment, to be hired, to be accepted in a union. Above all, millions of women must struggle just to survive. As long as the mass of women is struggling on this basic level, corporate America does not have to worry about a women's movement that intrudes into large-scale policy, about a strong women's voice in affairs that affect all of us—war, weaponry, nuclear energy, and pollution. The old advice about how to keep a woman quiet and submissive—keep her barefoot in winter and pregnant in summer—has been adapted to the twentieth-century industrial capitalistic world—keep her poor.

The women's movement under capitalism has worked almost unbelievably hard and made large gains. Those gains are changes in law and custom, and they affect all women, although they have their greatest effect on middle-class educated women. But feminism has not been able to budge an intransigent establishment bent on destroying the globe; it has not moved us one inch closer to the feminization of society. Indeed, it seems to lose ground with every decade, as the nourishing, procreative, communal, emotional dimensions of experience are increasingly ground into dust, as high technology and more intense pursuit of power are increasingly exalted.

This situation constitutes a quandary for feminists. Only by bringing great numbers of women with feminist values into the institutional structure of the nation can women achieve a voice in the way this country is run. Only by unified political action can women influence the course of the future. But at present, and for the foreseeable future, women are carefully screened, hired in small numbers, and watched for deviance. Women hired by institutions are far more likely to be coopted by institutional policy than to change it; they will assimi-

late or be fired or quit. Some feminist groups oppose women's efforts to enter
the establishment on the ground that women should not contribute to a structure that is sexist, racist, and dedicated to profit and power. On the other hand,
to refuse to enter the establishment is to refuse even to try to change it from
within and thus to accept the marginal position women have traditionally held.
To refuse to enter American institutions may also be to doom oneself to poverty, and poverty is silent and invisible. It has no voice and no face.

For this problem, as for so many others, there is no clear right answer.


## 2. THE CARYATIDS: ANTIFEMINISTS?

That women are not just entering the work force in unprecedented numbers, but fighting for decent wages and positions within it; that they possess the
right and the means to reproductive freedom and, in many cases, choose to
have children as single parents, or not to have children at all, is extremely
threatening to many men, especially those of the American Christian right.
These men, especially those of the Mormon and Catholic churches, organized
and funded the movement that placed women in the foreground of a battle to
defeat the ERA. There is also a women's movement against legal abortion, the
right-to-life movement; this seems largely to be led by women, although it too
has the backing of the Catholic Church. But whoever originated or funded
these groups, many women are deeply committed to the principles they
uphold; and although the two groups are not identical, they share many
principles.

These women may be called the caryatids. Even when women occupy
professional and community positions of great solidity and centrality, they are
not called pillars of society: pillars, it seems, are male. Yet no society could
continue to function for even a day without the support of women, as the
Greeks seemed to recognize when they used fully draped female figures as col-
umns or pilasters supporting the entablatures of their buildings. Caryatids hold
the entire roof on their heads. Whether or not women approve of or enjoy the
way our society is managed, they hold up, to paraphrase Mao, more than half
(53 percent) of the sky.

The women who can be characterized as caryatids are those dedicated to
the feminine principle but opposed to feminism. Many of them are members of
patriarchal churches and accept the traditional division of experience as a manifestation of natural law and God's will. They are proud and do not consider
themselves a second sex; they see their role as complementary to men's. They
consider procreation and childraising a sacred and essential task; and they are
devoted to the qualities of nutritiveness, compassion, and community.

They also deeply suspect men. Seeing themselves locked into an unchangeable system in which women have the babies and take care of them, always have and always will, they look to ways of safeguarding themselves and
their cherished burden. They believe that the qualities they feel themselves to

represent—the "inlaw" qualities of the feminine principle—are necessary to life, but also vulnerable, incapable of sustaining them in the face of the power world. The caryatids do not imagine that compassion or nutritiveness, caring for children and the community, can be synthesized with worldly force, assertiveness, or independence. In order for these qualities to flourish, they must be encompassed by a strong "masculine" guardianship. These women are willing to give up the potential for equality and the opportunity for a life in the world, in exchange for male economic protection of them and their children.[76]

The caryatids are not blind: they see how things are going. They understand that the freedom to work outside the home means essentially the freedom to be doubly a slave—to work outside *and* inside the home. They see the impoverishment of women without men, and some feel they too lack refined skills and experience, and would be similarly impoverished if their men left them. Although some may admire the high-powered world of technology and money, and others may shrink from it, most of them know they would not be comfortable within it; they feel they "do not belong" there. They believe that only strong family laws can protect them from exposure to poverty, the crude, exploitive male world, and the cruel struggle of trying to survive on their own with their children.

The caryatids appraise realistically the social and economic vulnerability of women, especially mothers. But they do not have a realistic appraisal of protective legislation. Even when divorce was socially scandalous, men left their wives. Even if strong "family protection" legislation should be passed, making abortion illegal again, limiting women's (but not men's) access to birth control, and preventing any level of government from assisting rape crisis centers or battered wives' shelters, it is most unlikely that laws modifying or rescinding men's freedom to divorce, abandon their families, or abuse them will be part of the package: the "family" protected by such legislation consists only of men. However, divorce is still infrequent among certain groups. The caryatids would like to keep things that way, and perhaps they can for decade or two. But they are fighting a tide.

Acquiescence and submission do not guarantee male fidelity; if anything, they ease the path of male infidelity. Nor do a degree of independence and autonomy automatically guarantee male abandonment. The idea that they do is part of the gospel of sexism, but the gospel is false. If many feminists are without men, that is in large part because of the heightened sensitivity of feminists to male diminishment and oppressive habits, and women's new economic power, which allows some of them to live comfortably without men. The caryatids are not unaware of the way men in general treat women; some of them think worse of men than feminists do.

What the caryatids are really saying is more antimale than any feminist statement. They are claiming that things are as they are, you can't beat the system, and men run the system. Women can't win, they can't even break even. Men are destructive children and you cannot expect them to care for the real children, to offer nutritiveness, tenderness, and love. You have to *force* them to do their part in the essential task of raising the young, by locking them out of sex without marriage, by forcing married men to support their families, by making divorce difficult and holding men responsible for their families even if they are divorced. Women's only bargaining chip is sex. Access to legal abortion is anathema because it gives men the freedom of promiscuity; if pregnancy results, the woman can have an abortion: men take no responsibility, run no risk. Although the fact that abortion kills a fetus is featured in the pro-life campaign, those same campaigners have not been prominent among groups opposed to war and nuclear proliferation, which have no function other than to kill. The pro-life campaign, I fear, is less cherishing of life than opposed to sexual freedom.

The caryatids are among the most desperate of women, and the most furious, as is evident in antifeminist gatherings, which have an outraged, hysterical tone. These women are like a colonized people who continue to believe the colonizers will protect them better than those who are rebelling against colonization. They may be correct for the short haul, but not the long. They can provide a façade for the defeat of the ERA, but that cannot gain for them what they want—security for themselves and their children. Their fear of forces hostile to their values perpetuates the power of those forces; indeed, support for such forces is what they offer in exchange for protection by them. The New Right believes married women have entered the labor force because of high taxes and inflation caused by the growth of the welfare state. But the welfare state is a response to, not a cause of, the new morality with its high divorce rate, repudiation of responsibility by males, and willingness of women to have children alone.[77] To dismantle the welfare state is to destroy the only existing—albeit inadequate—attempt to solve social problems which are rooted in deep cultural devaluation of "feminine" elements and exaltation of "masculine" ones; it is like trying to rid society of cancer by throwing away aspirin.

Men who support the antifeminist position and oppose equal rights for women have their own motivations. Many of the men and women on the right have a strong suspicion of sex, in keeping with the repressive religions in which they have been raised. Some consider all feminists lesbians, and homosexuality to be quite literally evil, a perversion, but nevertheless a lure so strong that one glimpse of it is enough to seduce. The freedom to exercise one's own sexuality is equivalent to a license to murder, and perhaps even worse; oblique allusions to depraved corrupting of innocent little girls and boys rise around the edges of antifeminist rhetoric like smoke smelling of burning brimstone.

The motivations of the men who fund antifeminist movements, however, are not so personal. Connie Paige has described the ways money is raised and funneled into campaigns to prevent passage of the Equal Rights Amendment and to oppose legal abortion, among other measures. Such campaigns are waged by the New Right, which, according to Zillah Eisenstein, "developed in large part in order to counter the gains made by the women's movement."[78] Paige lists corporations that contribute to these New Right campaigns; among them are Ford, General Motors, Coca-Cola, Pepsico, Hershey, the *Reader's Digest*, Pizza Hut, Citibank, IBM, Exxon, and Consolidated Foods. She also lists as donors personal or family foundations, such as the Adolph Coors Foundation, the Bechtel Foundation, and the Lilly Foundation, and fundamentalist groups like H. L. Hunt's Christian Crusade.[79] It is forces like these, with their money and influence, that defeated the ERA, not the women of America, who in poll after poll have shown themselves to favor its passage.

The majority of American women, like the majority of women everywhere, are opposed to war, are dedicated to programs that foster "the welfare of people in general regardless of one's own personal financial situation." They are deeply concerned with the plight of the poor, and with the environment.[80] And most women, whether or not they have children, are committed to values favorable to the raising of children and to personal and communal well-being. Caryatids and feminists are allied in this attitude, although the caryatids do not realize that; they see feminism strictly as a move to force women to live like men, to either abandon their "female duty" or to go out to work, raise the children, and take care of the house besides.

The caryatids of our time are related to the nineteenth-century women who formed and maintained the cults of domesticity that long dominated female literature. They have inherited the moral mantle of the women who exalted motherhood; home as a haven of peace, order, and sweetness; and women as above politics. This exaltation involved considerable sentimentalization, a laundering of life of its blood, pain, and conflict. That such an ideal was felt to be necessary is a sign of how diminished women felt, and how inhospitable the public world was to "feminine" values. Whatever their intentions, the women who maintained the cult of domesticity functioned to support the existing public world with all its ugliness and dehumanization; but also to lead some women into political action on behalf of the principles they upheld. The caryatids are trying to revalorize "feminine" qualities in their own way. In the distant future, they may be seen more as part of the feminist struggle for a more felicitous world than as antagonists to it.

In the face of the obstacles, no mode, no approach can be denominated totally correct, effective, or morally good. No single way, no *tao* is available to us. Every way has its drawbacks, its costs, its limits; every way, like life itself, compromises us in some way. The caryatids have chosen a thankless path, however; defending a beleaguered ground by giving up their weapons and trying to bind their soldiers to them with unbreakable links, they are forced to focus continually on the strength of the links, the demeanor of their men, and possible threats to their alliance. They cannot afford to consider the price they are paying for the protection they are purchasing; thus they cannot afford to think about themselves and their own well-being.

There is considerable evidence that feminism has improved women's well-being, that "the mental health of women has improved with the women's movement. Feminism leads to equality and equality to mental health." One long-term study has shown that even older women are happier since the inception of the women's movement: almost never, these days, does one see or hear of a woman collapsing into mental or physical illness because of menopause, as so many did in the past, according to the whispered explanations of our mothers.[81]

No transcendence except that of death is around the corner for any patriarchal institution: the millennium keeps arriving, empty-handed. The only transcendence possible for humans occurs through continuity, through the procession of generations and culture, through the creation of new generations and the maintenance of a decent world for them to live in, a decent intellectual and artistic tradition for them to delight in. And continuity is a feminist ideal—earthbound, female, rooted in body, but no less able to soar for all that. Often it is an ideal for antifeminist women too.

### 3. THE IDEAL OF EQUALITY

Some of the earliest feminists—the brilliant Mary Wollstonecraft, for example, or some of the suffragists—did not suggest that they wanted equality with men.

But equality has been a major demand of second-wave feminists, who realized that the right to vote, the right to go to school, and even the right to hold a job above the menial level did not give women a voice—as individuals, as a caste, or as a moral constituency. They thus began a movement for equality based on the black civil rights movement. Using the principles of the foundations of the state—enunciated in the Declaration of Independence, the Constitution and the Bill of Rights that is its heart—blacks and women began what seemed a campaign for assimilation. Unlike other social protest movements—the labor movement, the campaign against anti-Semitism—the civil rights movements of blacks and women have been only moderately successful. Because blacks and women are symbolic of elements patriarchy was designed to transcend, they cannot be assimilated into society as it stands. For members of these groups to be absorbed into society, they would have to transform themselves into white males. They would have to enunciate the values and standards of the white male world, adopt its modes of behavior, dress, and life style, and prove their devotion to the principle of stratified power, to hierarchy. Women and blacks who have been able to do this are treated as almost equal by the white male world. It is the best status they will ever achieve, since they cannot change their sex or their skin color.

Equality continues to be the goal of many women's and black groups, however. Because of the unbridgeable gap between white and black, male and female, every gain made in the name of the latter groups is rescinded the next day and must be earned again and again. The resistance to receiving women and blacks as equals of white males is so profound, so undying, and so implanted in the culture, that the example of one woman or black doing a good job is not enough to ease the lot of the next; and assimilative acts performed under political (or moral, or social) pressure are often undone as soon as the pressure is removed. It is impossible to rely on the endurance of improvements in hiring practices, promotion, or pay, in assimilated dwelling, education, or work (for blacks), in ownership of rights over one's own body and reproduction, assimilated work, or political representation (for women). Only warily can blacks or women attempt to use past accomplishments as foundation stones to build on, because so often, in a month, or a year, or three, these advances are annulled, the struggle must be refought against an opponent whose resources are so much greater, whose life is so much more comfortable, that it can afford to sit back and litigate: for years.

There are those who, seeing this immovability, this intransigence, and perceiving the rigidity of the society, advocate violent overthrow of the present system and the creation of a new one from the ground up. The problem with this idea (quite apart from the fact that it is unlikely to succeed) is that the new society would be created only from the ground up, with the old roots still in place. Those who hold such a position, however, scorn the fight for equality, finding equality in an unworthy society an unworthy goal.

Nevertheless, given the intransigence of our institutions, their rigidity toward symbolic entities that are actual people, the struggle for equality continues to be necessary, both for its potential to improve life for some people, and because it provides a course of action and thus a cause for pride (if also frustration and despair) to those engaged in it and those who benefit from it.

At the same time it is essential to keep in mind the kind of equality we desire. Assimilation in an unworthy society *is* an unworthy goal. The white male world offers an unhappy and unworthy standard. The equality we must fight for is political and economic sufficiency: a position strong and broad enough to give us a voice in the large decisions affecting our culture, a position rich and admirable enough to allow alteration of that culture through example and influence.

There has been, and remains, a tendency within feminism to hold the white male world up for emulation, to compare white male and general female modes and find the latter lacking. I doubt if there is a feminist alive who has not sat up late for nights in conflict over what to do in a given situation. For example, a woman may suspect that a male colleague has done something unprofessional which has harmed her, perhaps run her down to an important customer. Her first thought may be: What would a man do? She may decide that a man would first obtain clear evidence of the colleague's act and then complain to their superior. But she feels reluctant to do that; what she wants to do is confront the colleague and ask him why he tried to harm her. She knows, however, that he will be evasive. She also knows that for her, a woman, to use a man's mode of handling the situation may turn the superior officer against her. She also has deep emotional reservations about using this method. She wants revenge—it would satisfy her; but she does not want to be the kind of person who acts in vengeance, partly because she has been socialized not to be aggressive. The method she wants to use is typical of a woman and is almost guaranteed to fail; and it may violate her feminist principles, which require her to assert herself. There is no adequate model for this woman within the white male world; nor is there any possibility that her action, whatever it may be, will be interpreted as it would be if a white male performed it.

Equality is not possible in a world that worships power and transcendence. Women's dilemmas in functioning in a misogynistic world are insoluble; if women make decisions using equality as a standard, they violate principles they have learned to cherish and frequently fail anyway. At best, they become pseudo-men. What is necessary is the development of a set of moral standards that women feel comfortable with, that express their value structure, and that are generally disseminated. Women must build a morality that can stand in the world despite its difference from male morality. And the first step in the creation of such a morality is broadening or even altering present standards of evaluation.

In the past two decades, considerable research comparing men and women has been done in three major areas of experience: in the area of motivation (success or success avoidance); in language; and in morality. The initial research showed women to be in some way different and *therefore* less adequate than men in these areas. Later research was based on a broader perspective and opened up questions that men as well as women need to confront; it challenged current (male) standards.

The earliest work on achievement motivation was done by David McClelland and associates. Their book, based on studies done in 1953, was nine hundred pages long and discussed achievement motivation as if the authors' theory applied to everyone. Only one footnote informs the careful reader that data on females do not fit into the theory.[82]

In the late 1960s, Matina Horner published the first studies of women's attitudes toward success.[83] She and her coworkers presented college students with the opening of a story and asked them to finish it. The opening described a young woman aiming for a career in medicine, a traditional success ladder. Most of the women who took the test gave the story an ambiguous or unhappy conclusion, showing that they had unpleasant associations with success. Horner interpreted this response as expressing a fear that success would lead a woman to be socially rejected and to lose her "femininity."

Horner's interpretation was based on a male standard: that is, men show a desire for success; if women do not, they demonstrate an inadequacy. Such an interpretation offers those who wish to use it a pseudoscientific basis for the fact that women are so rarely successful, and for continued male exclusion of them. Although Horner herself did not foster such ideas, her work was widely cited in support of them. After it was published other researchers studied the subject; most attempted to challenge Horner's results rather than her interpretation. Success avoidance remained strong among white college women, but—during an era of doubt and hostility toward institutions—also appeared in an increasing number of white college men.[84] Other studies showed that black women had less avoidance of success, and that the higher a young woman's socioeconomic class, the greater her fear of succeeding.[85]

Little was made of tests showing that men who desired success believed it would bring them not only money and status but love and intimacy as well, whereas the behavior required of a successful man impedes his capacity for love and intimacy. Not until 1976 was there a suggestion that the women in Horner's experiment were less afraid of success than of the negative consequences for those who deviate from traditional sex-role expectations, and that Horner's subjects displayed not a deep-seated psychological condition but a realistic appraisal of the ways of the world.[86] In addition, John Condry and

Sharon Dyer suggested that to describe success in terms of doing well in school or having career goals is to limit that term unduly. Other recent researchers have found that women do express the desire to achieve in areas designated as feminine, especially those of affiliation and affective ties.[87] No one seems to have given such tests to older women.

But Martha Mednick, Sandra Tangri, and Lois Hoffman conclude that to judge female motivation by male standards is ultimately destructive. Both men and women must give up important parts of themselves to succeed in prestigious careers like medicine. They hypothesize that the reluctance of young women to do this testifies to their possession of more integrated personalities, a conception of what a life should be that is wider and richer than "success." That young women from the higher socioeconomic class—that class whose members have achieved worldly success—are most likely to wish to avoid that kind of success is an implicit criticism of their families, probably especially their fathers. Young women may be saying they do not want lives like those lived by their parents.

Horner's work was important because she bothered to test women at all and to take her results seriously. Her use of a male standard in judging women was inevitable at the time. But researchers have lately been opening their minds to new positions: that female standards are not identical to men's; that the difference may not indicate inferiority; and, although this suggestion usually remains implicit, that men might be better off with female standards.

Considering the great stress many men live with, their shorter life spans, greater loneliness, and relative incapacity for intimacy, community, and love, it is possible that women's values are superior to men's. Perhaps we should not be asking why women do not on the whole want to be president of General Motors, and ask why men do. It is conceivable that success in our world is not a desirable goal for anyone, that any enterprise requiring the sacrifice of expressiveness, interrelatedness, compassion, and (often) humane standards is not worth what it costs. Men are socialized to believe that worldly success will automatically bring them love, interrelatedness, and acceptance, as well as money and status: women know better, for themselves at least. A more useful guide to attitudes and motivation might be a question about what people believe constitutes a successful life, rather than a question about motivation to success in current worldly terms.

Early work on women and language began with the same bias. This complex area of study involves at least three subareas: gender in language; comparative study of how men and women are described by language; and comparative study of how women and men use language.[88] The third category has been the subject of considerable research in the past decade, and at first both male and female researchers tended to hold up male use of language as a standard that demonstrated the "weakness" shown in female deviations from it.[89]

An early (1972) article on the dialect of Norwich, England, discusses the more grammatical language of the local women, the cruder, rougher language of the men.[90] The data stand: but the interpretation put upon them belongs to the researcher, Peter Trudgill, who implicitly accepts the male dialect as basic and realistic, the language of real men, and considers the women's more correct and refined language pretentious, an attempt by status-conscious people to raise their status. Since male language is equally status-conscious (although a different kind of status is involved), this interpretation is biased.

In 1973 Robin Lakoff published what was probably the most influential early article (later expanded into a book) on female language behavior.[91] The article concentrated on three instances of difference in female (as opposed to male) speech, and its stance is condescending to women: Lakoff believes their speech illegitimates them, deprives them of male authority and force. Her strong male standard was probably responsible for the wide dissemination of her conclusions in popular organs—again, her work seemed to justify women's inferior status; it was also responsible for a host of follow-up studies by female researchers.

The first characteristic that Lakoff discusses is women's use of tag questions. Women, she writes, are far more likely than men to attach a question to a statement, as in, "This war in Vietnam is terrible, isn't it?" A man might say, "This war in Vietnam is an atrocity!" Lakoff thinks tag questions display unsureness about the self, a fear of assertiveness and a need for reassurance from others, whereas male utterances display authority and confidence.

Second, women, but not men, use a questioning tone in answering questions. Thus if one asks a woman, "What time will dinner be ready?" she may reply, "Oh . . . around six o'clock?" To Lakoff this shows the speaker's lack of confidence, a lack so profound as to require confirmation and support even in a situation she ostensibly controls.

Finally, women avoid strong statements; here Lakoff's examples compare commands to questions. A man is more likely to order, "Close the door!" or "Do close the door." A woman is more likely to request, "Will you close the door?" or "Please close the door?" or even, in the negative phrasing that invites rebellion, "Won't you close the door?" Again Lakoff concludes that such locutions reinforce women's lack of authority.

Later researchers have questioned some of Lakoff's results. One study demonstrates male use of tag questions either as veiled threat ("You agree with me, don't you?") or to make a real question sound like an assertion, so that the man appears to be in control of a situation ("That is the case, isn't it?").[92] But a larger issue than the accuracy of Lakoff's data is the implicit bias of her interpretation. The question we should be asking is not why women are different from men, or how women's behavior or attitudes perpetuate inferiority; but, as Susanne Langer asked about each art form, *What does it create?* Let us assume that Lakoff's report on women's language is correct: I, at least, see no reason to doubt it. We are facing two different ways of using language: What does each create?

Men's statements, unmodified by questions, tend to be pronouncements: these silence discussion, shut people out, intimidate them, and thus impoverish conversation. Men's statements could easily be interpreted as a sign of fear rather than confidence: they brook no contradiction, risk no argument, admit no equality. The use of tag questions could be seen as a sign of grace, generosity, and sociability, since they invite discussion, include others, and provide opening instead of closure. Similar comments apply to Lakoff's other points. No one, not even the most insecure woman, would respond, "Oh . . . about six o'clock?" if the question were "What time does the plane leave?" Responding to a question with a question in the way Lakoff describes is a shorthand way of making a statement. The woman is saying, "Well, I thought we'd eat around six, but if that's inconvenient, if you need to go out early, or if you're not hungry, we could make it a little earlier or later." Responding with a question to a question is a tacit way of suggesting that an item is negotiable, that the speaker is not rigidly committed to one plan, that she is open to the needs and desires of others. This device too opens up a situation, shows a will toward harmony and mutual satisfaction in a matter that *is* adjustable. The flexibility implicit in such an answer is another sign of grace.

And anyone, anyone at all, would prefer to be asked to close a door, or open a window, walk the dog, whatever, than to be ordered to do so. Orders are *always* humiliating; humiliation may be lessened or removed when orders are the ritual form of communication, as in military services, or when orders are shorthand requests made of intimates. But a request shows respect for others and sensitivity to them, both of which require some degree of personal strength and self-assurance. Command shows neither and requires of the commander nothing internal whatever, only external status, the right to command.

It is, of course, possible that women's language shows timidity and lack of confidence; many women feel these things (so do many men), and express them not just in the words they use and their tonality, but in voicing, facial aspect, and general demeanor. But it is also true that in general women's language aims for harmony with others rather than an expression of control over them, and that the former seems preferable to the latter as a societal standard. Speech patterns vary from place to place, suggesting a difference in the conception of conversation. For example, in Australia (and to a lesser degree in New Zealand and Britain), there is a pattern of intonation in which an entire set of statements rise at the end as if they were questions, so: "I went downtown . . . ? And there in the window were these lovely jumpers . . . ? So I went in and asked the price . . . ? And they were a hundred pounds, can you imagine!" I have heard such intonations from both men and women, although more often in women's speech. They remind me of patterns in the speech of children who ask, "You know?" after every few sentences, in an attempt to engage the listener, to receive a response, to be assured of attention. Like the child's, the Australian pattern can be either engaging and endearing or annoying, probably depending on one's feeling for the speaker and how interesting or boring the content is. Such intonations can be seen as a sign of weakness, since they emanate from a wish to seduce, rather than a belief that one is strong enough to dictate attention. But here too appearances and realities, weakness and strength, are paradoxical. It may take a greater sense of personal worth to ask for attention than to command it.

There are many other areas of life in which males are seen as providing the standard and women the deviation, but perhaps none is more dismaying than the area of morality. Despite the daily evidence of eye and ear, it remains a by-word of patriarchy that women as a sex are by nature deficient in moral sense and character. This belief has been "proven" anew by each new wave of patriar-chal thought: in recent times, its primary exponent was Freud, who believed that because women maintain a pre-oedipal attachment to their mothers, and do not experience anxiety about castration, they do not achieve a clear-cut oedi-pal resolution, and thus do not attain fully formed superegos:

> I cannot evade the notion (though I hesitate to give it expression) that for women the level of what is ethically normal is different from what it is in men. Their superego is never so inexorable, so imper-sonal, so independent of its emotional origins as we require it to be in men. Character-traits which critics of every epoch have brought up against women—that they show less sense of justice than men, that they are less ready to submit to the great exigencies of life, that they are more often influenced in their judgements by their feelings of af-fection or hostility—all these would be amply accounted for in the modification of the formation of their superego. . . . We must not allow ourselves to be deflected from such conclusions by the denial of the feminists, who are anxious to force us to regard the two sexes as completely equal in position and worth.[93]

Jean Piaget follows in this tradition. Although he seems to think all chil-dren are boys, making few references to girls, he does compare the two sexes morally. He roots moral development in childhood games in which boys dem-onstrate a fascination with rules and procedures, and girls show a "pragmatic" attitude toward rules, accepting those that forward their game and rejecting those that do not. Girls do not regard rules as sacrosanct, and are more innova-tive about them. This Piaget interprets as showing that girls are deficient in the legal sense he considers essential to moral development.[94]

The most recent of such theories is that of Lawrence Kohlberg, who de-vised several tests of sex-role behavior, among them a test of moral develop-ment. Upon giving the test to men and women, he found that few if any women developed very far. Kohlberg's scale has three ascending levels, each with two stages, a lower and a higher.

Level I, the lowest, is concerned with morality as act. In Stage 1, the lower stage of this level, a person behaves as he does because he fears punishment or desires approval from others. (I use *he* throughout this discussion because Kohlberg's published results refer only to males.) Stage 2, the upper stage of this level, includes behavior based on what will satisfy the self. To consider the self in isolation seems to Kohlberg a higher state of morality than to consider the self in relation to others.

As a boy matures, he reaches Level II and becomes concerned with moral-ity as role. At Stage 3 he has a "good-boy orientation," and tries to gain ap-proval by helping others. He learns to conform to stereotypical images of his sex and age, and begins to judge others less by deeds than by intentions. It is at this stage that Kohlberg locates most women: they want to win affection and acceptance from others, and do not progress beyond this posture. The next Stage, 4, is similar, but more public: at this level people defer to patterns of authority and convention: they do their duty to win respect, rather than affection. Both these stages focus on how one is viewed from the outside.

Level III, the highest and most rarely attained, is described thus: "Moral right resides in conformity by the self to shared or shareable standards, rights, and duties." That is, it involves a morality based on principle. Its lower stage is legalistic: people who reach it act according to contract or agreement; they accept the "rules of the game," whatever they may be or however arbitrary. Relationships with other people are based on mutual distance, on "avoidance of violation of the rights of others." Stage 6, the highest of all, the level of saints, is reached when people act according to universal principle. The rather opaque description of this stage is, "Orientation not only to actually ordained social rules but to principles of choice involving appeal to logical universality and consistency." One's own conscience functions as one's guide and points toward "mutual respect and trust."[95] It is hard to know where that *trust* came from, since there is nothing in the earlier stages suggesting that other people may be trustworthy, or are anything but hindrances to self-development.

Indeed, it is hard to know how Kohlberg's saints become apprised of "universality," since all his stages focus on the person separated from others. Whether a boy acts in a particular way because he fears punishment or desires approval from others, or because he wants approval and so learns to help others, he is utterly divided from those others, who are merely instruments manipulated to satisfy his desires. At the highest level of moral development, according to Kohlberg, a man detaches himself from others totally, in order to act according to contract (Stage 5), or principles of choice (Stage 6), which involve universality. Kohlberg's scale is actually a scale of power: in the early stages the person must defer to others to gain a sense of rightness and identity; in the late stages the person transcends other people entirely, and guides his behavior by legal or moral codes. At the very highest level, achieved by only a few humans, according to Kohlberg, the moral relation between the person and the world is characterized by distance, formality, and judgment. Kohlberg's vision of the self in the world is antisocial, rooted in traditional male values—independence, isolation, and disconnectedness.

What is conspicuously lacking in many male versions of human relations is any connection apart from power exchanges. Nancy Hartsock describes exchange theorists in sociology who depict human relations as power trade-offs, assuming that people are fundamentally isolated from each other and that encounters between people emerge from opposing interests. She comments that such a view of society is unrealistic: people are born helpless and survive only because of the dedication to them of their mothers or mother figures, a relation that cannot be described as a power exchange.[96] But male accounts of life omit the feminine: females and "feminine" qualities. Thus Erik Erikson asserts that interdependence, intimacy, and care are necessary parts of adult life, yet offers no suggestion about how these qualities are learned or developed beyond infancy. After the initial period in which an infant learns to trust its parent(s), the child's experience consists entirely of steps toward greater independence, according to Erikson, who sees the separation of child from parent(s) as an absolute good, "the model and measure of growth."[97] Yet children who did not develop trust, expressiveness of feeling, and intimacy in their growing years would not be capable of the interdependence, intimacy, and care Erikson posits as essential to mature life. In other words, the "feminine" side of experience is simply assumed by such theorists; like the nature of the female, it is a given, endowed by nature, and requires no exercise or learning to be developed.

Kohlberg shares this mental frame. One test he devised demonstrated that boys with higher IQs shifted their preference from adult females to adult males by about four years of age, while duller boys took an additional two years.[98] He asserts flatly that family influence is irrelevant to children's moral development, yet this assertion directly contradicts findings he himself reports: that children who show "moral arrest and moral pathology" often come from disrupted, unhappy families; that physical punishment and rejection seem to impede moral growth; that there is no relation whatever between the moral developmental level (according to his scale) of fathers and their children, but a clear correlation between the level of mothers and their children.[99]

Kohlberg not only envisions people as isolated units pitted against an outside world from which approval must be wrested; he also implicitly regards obedience to codes and principles as morally superior to bonds of affection and cooperation. Although no doubt he would demur at such an example, his levels and stages seem to confer higher morality on a man who obeys a code of rules than on a woman who refuses to judge harshly a friend accused of a violent act, because she understands why her friend acted, how she felt. Rules and principles, whether ordained by others or by the self, are poor substitutes for sensitive, flexible adjustments of a basic set of humane guidelines. Principles of right can be and have been used to defend the most immoral acts imaginable. Victorian fathers used them to justify casting out into destitution or death their pregnant unmarried daughters; they have been used in every war, massacre, slaughter performed on earth. Kohlberg might argue that such principles are not of *right*: but in any given time, how can anyone be sure? Only a sense of the sanctity and vulnerability of human life, a sense of the dignity and selfhood of others can guide us in periods when "our" people—British Protestants, say—are describing the pope as the anti-Christ, and the Catholic Church as the whore of Babylon; or when "our" people—German colonizers—are justifying the slaughter of East Africans on grounds that they are lazy, worthless, savage animals. Only a standard of shared humanity, a deep knowledge of fellowship in yearning, pain, and death, can provide us with a dependable guide to behavior.

Kohlberg's work has been challenged, primarily by Carol Gilligan, who does not overtly criticize his standards or his results but suggests that women have a different mode of experience, and thus a different set of values.[100] Her work shows a clear perception of the omissions in his: for instance, she asks people to invent stories about a set of illustrations showing people in varying degrees of closeness. Men's stories increased in violence as the figures moved closer together: a picture of a couple sitting together on a bench near a river, with a low bridge in the background, elicited stories of violence—homicide, suicide, stabbing, kidnaping, or rape—from 21 percent of male respondents. Women's stories increased in violence as the figures moved farther apart, and they projected the greatest violence onto a picture of a man sitting alone at a desk.[101]

Gilligan discusses studies that show that boys learn primarily through game, in which rules dominate; and girls learn primarily through play, which has no winners or losers, and in which rules may be changed or thrown out. The end of game is victory, which automatically requires a loser; the end of play is experience. Such studies seem to suggest a genetic difference between the sexes in this regard. Yet Colin Turnbull's study of Mbuti children, boys and girls together, describes their play as geared to teach cooperation and sharing, to avoid the shame of either victory or defeat, and to be highly noncompetitive. Such work suggests that the difference is cultural rather than genetic.[102]

American studies show that when quarrels occur among girls, they end their play rather than pursue the quarrel; they find something else to do. This is not true of boys. But Mbuti girls and boys learn early to avoid conflict by removing themselves from a site; in extreme cases, as adults, they may even move away from the settlement. Female morality thus seems related to the morality of cooperative cultures, cultures that have retained ancient matricentric values. According to Gilligan, female morality is more concerned with the web of relations than a hierarchy of rules. For women, morality lies not in rights but in recognizing connection and taking responsibility for it. Women's ethic evolves around a central insight: that the self and the other are interdependent. Thus violence destroys both; care nourishes both.[103]

Kohlberg's example of a perfect "Stage 6" is Mohandas Gandhi, a man who upheld both autonomy and nonviolence, *satyagraha*. Yet in his personal life Gandhi psychologically violated his family and the children of the ashram by bullying them and negating their feelings. Erikson, who was writing a book about Gandhi, at one point felt unable to continue because of "the presence of a kind of untruth in the very protestation of truth; of something unclean when all the words spelled out an unreal purity."[104] The saintliness or virtuousness of many men is equally compromised: a man often reserves his charity and magnanimity for public dealings, while his treatment of intimates may be tinged with cruelty. Gilligan comments that "the blind willingness to sacrifice people to truth . . . has always been the danger of an ethics abstracted from life." She connects Gandhi with Abraham, that Abraham in whom we located the principles at the root of patriarchy. Abraham, Gilligan asserts, was willing even to sacrifice his son to demonstrate the integrity and supremacy of his faith. She contrasts him with the woman who comes before Solomon "and verifies her motherhood by relinquishing truth in order to save the life of her child."[105]

Women and men—in general—have different moralities because they have different goals. Male morals are designed to permit male transcendence. Life—that mass of breathing flesh, sweating pores, darting sensation, uncontrollable being—is rooted in nature, in the fetid swamp, the foul murk into which manufactured nature—cities—seems always about to sink. Above these, stark, pure, beyond the pull of heart or genitals, soar a rigid set of principles, rules, taboos. To prove his full manhood (which is sainthood) a man must cleave to these and abandon the other, which is the realm of woman. Since actual transcendence is not possible, transcendence is postulated in a beyond which is death. That even in death one cannot transcend, but is transformed into the very materials of the murk and swamp, the minerals that feed plants and animals, thus becoming nourishment for the very element one despises, is ignored, for this material part is despised, and the spirit, it is presumed, will rise into the ethereal.

Female morals are designed to permit survival. Life *is* the highest good (*pace* Hannah Arendt): not necessarily one's personal life, but life itself, of plants and animals and humans, the community, the tribe, the family, the children. Violence has been committed in an effort to save the child, the relative, the friend; but such violence is minuscule compared to that committed in the effort to prove the rightness or truth of some transcendent doctrine, or to gain power over others.

Female morals foster survival: which means they foster those elements, both material and immaterial, that are necessary to life. Women grow much of the world's food, and everywhere women prepare food for those they live with. They do this because they are expected to, because they expect to, because they want to: so that the act is seen as nonvolitional and unnecessary to reward. It is rewarded by the well-being of those fed. This is true. What kind of morality teaches us to see this as contemptible?

But women everywhere provide food for the soul as well as the body, offering compassion and support, touching, praising, loving. Germaine Tillion has written of her experience in the Ravensbrück concentration camp, an environment sufficient to kill every shred of the dignity necessary to sustain life. Tillion writes of the bonds that formed among the women, sometimes between a mother and daughter, sometimes women from the same town who had been seized at the same time, sometimes between sisters. "This tenuous web of friendship was . . . almost submerged by the stark brutality of selfishness and the struggle for survival, but somehow everyone in the camp was invisibly woven into it."[106] This caring connectedness allowed many women to survive, emotionally and physically, through sharing of resources. Another survivor of the camps recalls a moment when women, in a railroad car stopped en route to Bergen-Belsen, saw men in a car across the tracks. Although the women and men were both "skeletons, in identical stripes . . . the men's bodies reflected so much more pessimism than did ours. . . . We reached for our little morsels of bread and threw them to the men."[107] A group of female survivors report that relationships with other women were critical to survival: "Bonding with other women was of supreme importance," asserts a woman who was interned in Theresienstadt, Auschwitz, and Ravensbrück. There were no rules: although the survival of children was linked to their mothers, for some children it was the physical connection with the mother that meant salvation and for others it was separation. Some mothers kept their children, others gave them away: both sets of mothers acted as they did in the hope that the children could survive.[108]

In a world in which transcendence means power, in which there is contention among nations that wish to demonstrate their possession of the greatest, the superior, the supreme power, and in which the only way to do this is to use that power to destroy, we might consider the benefits of a morality of survival and well-being, rather than one of transcendence and superiority. A similar position can be taken toward other dimensions in which men and women are compared and males are seen as the standard.

Equality is an abstract notion that can never be substantiated. It is a principle intended to guide attitude, so that different people can receive, not identical human treatment, but identical consideration by rule and law. Equality is a principle necessary only in societies dominated by rule and law rather than by affection and bonding.

Equality is not similarity or identity. To be equal to men does not mean to be like them. It is essential that women confront the pervasive attitude that what men do and how they do it represents a *human* standard with the question: What do these actions create? And what is created by women's behavior in this situation? Doing so, women—and men—might discover their own unarticulated moralities, and perhaps even the nature of their real desires, for power, for love.

## 4. THE DILEMMA OF FEMINISM

The major problem facing feminists can be easily summed up: there is no clear right way to move. Accustomed to patriarchal notions of purity, and forgetful of its real duplicity (which allows an appearance to stand for a reality), some feminists imagine the existence of a course of action that avoids all compromise, any participation whatever with people, acts, or ideas that are inimical to their principles. There is no such course, and has never been one for any political or philosophical movement. Christians may have died before the lions rather than retract their faith, but the Church made peace with Rome and has fed lions aplenty itself. To encounter, daily, situations that feel corrosive, that are corrosive, and still to maintain belief in feminist principles and a sense of fidelity in acting upon them is difficult, but it can be done, is done, by many feminists. Nothing is ever pure: even in the days when women were not allowed to approach the high altar in Catholic churches, the nuns who baked the wafers given in communion were allowed to replace in the altar the store of "the host," and cleaning women swept and washed the space. Rigid and misogynistic as patriarchy is, it has never been able to act fully on its principles. Nor has any particular form of it. This is partly because its principles are so inhumane: but it is likely that any human enterprise suffers from the impossibility of fully realizing its theory in practice, and this may in fact be a humanizing phenomenon.

Feminists who enter male institutions in hope of influencing them may have some success. Most often, however, they feel thwarted or even abused: they are treated like outsiders and their ideas or values cannot be heard even when they are uttered. The work in such institutions may be interesting, may be deemed important, may offer better pay than other jobs: but these pleasures may be offset by daily abrasions so severe that women leave the institutions and accept lower-paying jobs that offer more satisfaction, greater ability to nourish other people.

Women may retreat entirely from the male public world and create small communities of their own. But no one on earth can avoid dealing in some way with the male world. Like the priests who shunned women but needed them for servants, women can shun men but inevitably use or buy land, houses, or products in which men have had a hand. Separatism should exist for the pleasure of the thing, although it means renouncing most forms of influencing the larger world. Purity is a dangerous concept.

The appeal of socialism varies from place to place. In countries with extremely rigid socioeconomic systems, like many of those in Central America, in which a tiny percentage of the population owns almost all the assets and resources of the country and is entrenched in all the corridors of power, revolution seems the only course offering any possibility of change, and it is likely to come only from the left. The more extreme, unyielding, and entrenched the forces of the right in a given state, the more extreme and desperately violent will be the forces of the left. The most militant feminist groups I have encountered were German and Spanish, women from nations with deeply entrenched fascist populations.

Countries that offer more than lip service to ideals of justice and equality—the Scandinavian countries in particular—have active socialist parties that are integrated into the political life of the nation. But in the United States a strange phenomenon persists. There is a strong and productive left, a strong and productive feminism. These groups live in a ferment of discussion, argument, writing, theorizing. Between them they produce a huge number of books every year, a wide variety of journals and magazines. Yet they live in a ghetto. For the most part they are not impeded in their writing and discussion; they are not visibly censored. But the true nature of their thought—their basic principles—never penetrates the gauze curtain, the media wall: it never makes its way, undistorted, into widely read magazines or newspapers, television, popular radio programs, movies. These ideas remain the primary focus for a substantial number of people (who nevertheless constitute a small percentage of the population), but are almost unknown to the general population except in wildly deformed shape. It is hard to decide on the best course in the face of this subtle covert censorship and containment.

There is no clear right way to realize feminist ideals; every way in some measure participates in, and therefore upholds, this society. That is inescapable: we live in this society; our work is part of its production, our procreation part of its continuation, our well-being part of its pleasures, our sorrow part of its failure. Even those who fight militantly against it stop at their local convenience store for something to eat. There is a moral and psychological difference between willing and reluctant or partial participation; among being silent, silenced, and coopted; among ignoring injustices and cruelties, observing them, pointing them out, and committing them.

Ellen Willis has deplored the creation of women's organizations for reasons other than fighting sexism: women's groups formed to fight consumer fraud, to improve schools, to work for peace or a healthy ecology seem to her to reinforce female segregation and the stereotype of the feminine principle.[109] They may do both, and at the same time constitute women's only way of being heard in these areas. Feminism is broad enough to contain them. Any movement that works in whatever way for realization of the feminist vision is validly feminist. People should not be coerced to work in single file: their passions may lie outside that file, and passionately motivated work is the most effective and the most pleasant. The shape of feminism is not a "masculine" line but a "feminine" circle, approaching problems within contexts, in a round, giving equal legitimacy to a variety of concerns.

What sustains feminists in their struggle, which is often lonely, is other women. Many of us feel we could not have survived without our friends, without the nourishment, support, acceptance, love, and wild humor of a group of feminist women to whom we can go, in need or momentarily out of it, to whom everything does not have to be explained, with whom arguments occur on the ground of what we all believe. Sometimes this group includes family members, lovers and mates. This context makes life bearable and sometimes better than that—pleasant—despite the daily abrasions of the workplace, the overall culture—the sexist daily newspaper, the sexist morass of television, the power-seeking rhetoric and actions of political figures, the terrifying buildup of pollution and of arms.

Male opposition to feminism is rigid, deep, and broad, and functions on many levels. One is personal: the equality of women means the eradication of a servant caste. If a caste of people is not born subhuman, is not designed by nature to serve—not programmed, as it were, to perform nonvolitionally—then men must take its grumbling and resentment seriously, must reward services or share them, must credit the responsibility and love that underlie the behavior of those people. This few men are prepared to do.

Another level is political. Women in general do not share the attitudes toward power and control of men in general. Since many men blindly, unthinkingly, worship control, especially power-over, they find women's thinking timid, opaque, and irrelevant. They do not wish to be dissuaded from their exciting, driven ways of life; they shun conversion to a new belief that would call into question their previous values and experience. To change one's life from its bases up is difficult, as millions of women have discovered. Few men are willing to do so when the changes they would have to make lie in a direction they have been taught to despise—emotion, the body, and "feminine" nurturing qualities. It was easier for women to adopt the wearing of pants than it would be for men to adopt the wearing of skirts, even on hot days, and despite the example of noble Scotsmen and macho Arabs. It is easier to change one's life so as to include qualities and states valued by a culture. This is not to diminish women's courage and thoughtfulness in changing their lives, for their change often involves giving up decent income, a life style of status, and sometimes even confidence in the survival of oneself and one's children.

But the primary level of men's opposition to feminism is religious and psychological. Having been taught that male identity essentially rests on female identity, that men are what women are not, or men are not what women are, they dread moving into a state of nothingness, of being women to themselves. One can touch the depths of male contempt for femaleness by suggesting that a man act like a woman, or consider himself one. Male identity rests not only on *not* being a woman, but also on being in control of all the women in one's immediate life, and preferably in one's work life as well. In patriarchal faiths women exist to be controlled by men and thus to certify the superior and transcendent nature of the male. For this purpose it is not sufficient that a man possess one woman—wife, secretary, lover—who is acquiescent and subservient. One, or a dozen, or even a thousand subordinate women will not serve this purpose. *All* women except a chosen few, *women as a caste*, must be subordinate to men if maleness itself is to be a sign of freedom from bondage to nature, for the phallus to be a "transcendental signifier." And by extension, in racist societies all members of the despised race—again with a few token exceptions—must occupy a lower place in the hierarchy of transcendence.

Men as a caste therefore have a huge investment in keeping women subordinate. To accept women as fully human means to accept "feminine" values as human values appropriate to both sexes. To accept women politically means admitting their point of view to the halls of power and opening one's mind to sharing it. This would be a truly revolutionary change, one that would alter all our institutions and the international pursuit of power. To accept women personally would involve more than doing the dishes occasionally. To accept them religiously would mean accepting the actual limitations of the human condition, the equality of human fellowship, and a stance of respect toward nature.

In the face of widespread opposition from a sex that possesses all the power (not all men have power, but only men have power), feminists must shift and parry, demonstrate imagination, spontaneity, opportunism, and joy in the quick jab. Feminist policy must be flexible enough to pursue a course only as long as it is effective, and shift position when necessary. A feminist world will not come into existence in a linear way, as the result of a single-minded drive, but in a cyclic, circular way, working in all dimensions of a culture, moving from one position to another, not in reaction but in interaction with other forces. Feminism abjures the self-sacrifice, self-abasement, and self-diminishment patriarchy demands from women, offering instead an ideal of personal integrity and pleasure; it condemns the pursuit of power, stratification, and the repudiation of body and feeling that patriarchy instills in the public world, offering instead an ideal of felicity and human integration at every level—self with other (intimacy), self with others (community), and the private self, in body and mind, emotion and thought, sensation and vision. Because the highest value of feminism is pleasure, not power, feminists, female and male, perform a service by living their own lives with an eye to integration, fullness of experience, and pleasure. The word *pleasure* has been degraded by patriarchal thinking to denote trivial, frivolous, selfish pursuits, but the things in life which give us the greatest pleasure are never trivial or frivolous. We need also to rethink the meaning of *selfish*. Sometimes the greatest gift we can give others is our own happiness, our own sense of well-being. Feminists can convert by example as well as precept: there are men who deeply envy women's expressiveness, the richness of their experience, and their intimacy with other women—community. Feminists can make their values central by living them as well as by teaching them.

The teaching, however, remains essential. Already, in only two decades, a huge body of feminist scholarship has been built. There is solid, brilliant, unimpeachable work by feminist historians, anthropologists and ethnologists, psychologists, ecologists, and sociologists. There is a small, endangered body of law decreeing equality that can stand as foundation for future action. There is feminist art, not enough perhaps to be called a tradition, but the start of one. Feminist ideas and values have permeated women's writing for over a century, constituting a history if not a tradition.

Only recently have women taken on the overwhelming task of evaluating male-supremacist philosophy, political theory, economics, and science, fields in which the inadequacy of "masculine" values is not always immediately apparent. This, it seems to me, is a primary area for development now. To attempt to create a feminist political theory, an economic theory that includes all of what has been omitted by male theories, to write philosophy from a perspective that includes the body and emotions, despised castes, labor, childbirth and child rearing, that addresses itself to the complex and unclear matter of reproductive rights, responsibilities, and purposes, to love and need, is to tackle problems at their most profound level.

We do not need a program: a program is a grid that is lowered upon a population and kills those who fall under its bars. It makes uniform, it regulates, it forbids. We need theory and feeling as rough guides on which to build a next step and only a next step; flexible, responsive emotional theory capable of adjusting to human needs and desires when these create contradictions. No set of values can call itself a human morality unless it begins with the actuality of the human condition; no political system can contribute to felicity unless it begins with a humane morality.

The feminist vision of the world will not be realized in our lifetime, our century, or this millennium. But it is still possible, in pockets of one's life, to build "a Heaven in Hell's despair."

CHAPTER SEVEN

# The Long View Forward: Humanity

Although some feminist groups consciously work toward immediate political goals, feminism as a philosophy does not include a political program for the construction of a more humane world. However gratifying such a program might be in some ways, it would contradict feminist principles, for programs require uniformity and rigidity. In addition, any program devised in the present would be inadequate for future generations, because the minds of all of us currently alive are permeated with patriarchal values, categories, and methods. We may be able to integrate parts of our lives, but no one in our culture can avoid occasional participation in patriarchal modes of thought. For good or ill, we have been nourished and deprived by patriarchal culture since infancy.

Because patriarchal values and perspectives are so pervasive and seem to be universal, many people believe them to be inevitable. Such thinkers discount the existence of cultures which entertain different values and live in ways far removed from those of the West. They may argue that such cultures are becoming extinct because of the superiority or the invincibility of Western patriarchy. They may also remain unpersuaded by the projection of a matricentric world based on fragmentary evidence, or hold that if such a world existed, it perished in the face of a morality that was necessary to the development of "civilization."

Yet no one can deny that the world has changed greatly over the millennia, or that humans created the changes; and that, therefore, humans are capable of altering their ways of thinking and living. Thus to call patriarchy inevitable is essentially to choose it, to choose not to attempt to alter the human course. In this section we will consider the foreseeable consequences of continuing to live by patriarchal values and methods.

## 1. The Probable Future of a Patriarchal World

"Civilized" life—that is, human life under patriarchal control—has always been miserable, in contrast to what we consider less advanced cultures. Colin Turnbull, who has spent much of his life among "primitive" peoples, insists their life is not "nasty, brutish, and short": "On the whole, anthropologists have found otherwise, and . . . have accumulated an enormous mass of data to support their view." He adds that if we value above all else longevity, sophisticated technology, and material comforts, then we would find such cultures wanting. But if we value "a conscious dedication to human relationships that are both affective and effective, the primitive is ahead of us all the way." "Primitive" people work at feeling, being, and interacting in all their occupations; all members of such groups are imbued with social consciousness from their infancy, and because of that sense, all of them feel they are people of "worth and value and importance to society . . . from the day of birth to the day of death."[1]

Moreover, the very means by which we try to ameliorate our lot work to increase our misery. Freud wrote, "What we call our civilization is largely responsible for our misery, and . . . we should be much happier if we gave it up and returned to primitive conditions. . . . In whatever way we may define the concept of civilization, it is a certain fact that all the things with which we seek to protect ourselves against the threats that emanate from the sources of suffering are part of that very civilization."[2]

Patriarchal ideas of dominance over nature, of power as the highest good, and of life as secondary to a system designed to transcend, have led us to the kinds of knowledge we possess. They have inspired and made possible discoveries and inventions that demonstrate tremendous power over nature, and even power within the cosmos, which we are beginning to penetrate. It is possible that without such a stance, we would still be living like Turnbull's Mbuti: but ours is a questionable gain.

But even if we decide that patriarchal values are self-destructive, and must be changed, we find ourselves blocked. The institutions of any society function almost automatically to maintain that society as it is; and the ideology of any society functions to justify that status quo as being both necessary and beneficial. In capitalist and socialist states alike, enormous sums of money and great numbers of people are dependent upon the production of weapons. In each kind of state this situation is "justified" by ideology that emphasizes the threat posed by the other kind of state; the moral argument is that amassing arms is necessary to protect a beneficial way of life. The ideology heightens the sense of conflict and fear, which in turn stimulates greater emphasis on defense, offense, and weaponry. This vicious cycle guarantees its own continuation: it is inconceivable that either side will stop or slow production of weaponry without some massive worldwide intervention by citizens.

Yet the arms race increases the frequency of what Henry Kissinger long ago dubbed "limited" war. Those who order or manufacture arms want to see them used, and require markets for them. Governments find it easier and more profitable to sell weapons to small states than to urge other modes of handling conflict. Beyond this, the continuation of the arms "race" increases the likelihood of global nuclear war. Between them, the United States and the Soviet Union have achieved, in numbers of nuclear weapons and means of delivery and destructive capacity, "levels of redundancy of such grotesque dimensions as to defy rational understanding," writes George F. Kennan.[3] Roy and Zhores Medvedev argue that of the two, the United States is more likely to initiate a nuclear war. They assert that in neither country are arms subject to democratic control, and that the fluctuating leadership of the United States, always new

and untested, always trying to prove itself, is more erratic than that of the Soviet Union, whose leaders may be rigid and wary but are stable. Beyond that,
American policy makers have long believed that a nuclear war can be limited to
Europe, which for a generation has been the "primary military operational the-
atre for the United States."[4]

The thinking of American leaders is not unique to them, nor more ugly
than other examples of patriarchal thought over the millennia: but the stakes
are higher now. Everyone knows, or should know, the cost of nuclear war.[5] Yet
our leaders discuss "protracted" nuclear war and survival percentages, and
order evacuation plans to be drawn up. They call themselves "realists" with regard to nuclear war and the character of the Soviet Union.[6] They cannot, will
not, renounce a power greater than any other devised on earth, greater than
most of nature's powers. They imply that those opposed to nuclear energy or a
hard line on nuclear war are either dreamers or traitors. Indeed, those so opposed *are* traitors—to the patriarchal god. Insisting that limits are necessary in
human endeavors, that restraint of power is required, they deny the driving
force of patriarchy and show themselves "women," holding to the earth, not to
the deity, the god of power. The leaders of the 1980s say anything is possible to
heroes who dare, who risk all. Anachronisms, they cling to the morality of a
time when heroes fought each other hand to hand, and paralyze whatever
chance we have—we, and the Soviet Union—to come to terms with the
present.

Just as threatening, if on a somewhat smaller scale, is the proliferation of
nuclear plants. As fossil fuels became increasingly depleted, so that their exhaustion was foreseeable, nuclear energy was hailed as a savior. Even governments elected or supported because of opposition to its use end by advancing
it—as in France and Norway, for example. Yet it is well documented that nuclear energy costs more than it is worth: nuclear power stations cost more to
build and run than conventional generators, even ignoring the incalculable
costs of their wastes, of actual and potential accidents and the anxiety they
cause. In 1980, nuclear energy cost 50 percent more than coal; it cannot substitute for oil. Nuclear plants produce only electricity and plutonium wastes
which can be used as material for bombs. Plutonium wastes remain lethal for
thousands of years, settle in the food chain, in the testicles and ovaries of
humans and animals, and are passed to future generations. And nuclear plants
are short-lived—their metal cracks, becomes brittle, or corrodes; the tubes in
their steam generators dent, crack, and corrode. Few are built with a capacity to
withstand earthquakes.[7]

Given the huge expense of erecting, running, and maintaining nuclear
plants, given the enormous danger they present, and the minimal revenues they
produce, the marketplace itself—if we really had a free enterprise system—
would long ago have abandoned nuclear power. But we do not have a free enterprise system: twenty-four multinational corporations dominate the nuclear
industry in America and, as the *New York Times* puts it, constitute "what may
be the single most powerful business enterprise in history." Nineteen of these
companies rank among the 150 largest in the United States, and are closely as-

sociated with eight of the country's nine largest banks, its seven largest insurance companies, and many of its most important investment and law firms. These companies exert tremendous influence over both political parties and our political system. "It is the public investment decisions, made in Washington by Democrats and Republicans alike, and presently overseen by a supposedly free-enterprise President, that keep nuclear power alive and squelch such alternatives as solar energy." Yet a Harvard Business School energy project—among many others—has shown that a national policy of conservation and solar energy would produce more jobs, greater economic growth, and greater national security than nuclear energy.[8]

Yet even without Armageddon, or a "local" nuclear catastrophe, the future of the planet and of the creatures who depend upon it is endangered. So complicated and far-reaching are the effects of pollution that no one knows what the condition of our planet will be in a decade, much less in fifty years. If the greenhouse effect melts the polar icecaps; if forests disappear; if more species of animals and plants become extinct—life on earth could become tenuous for those which are left. It is not inconceivable that humans could in time make their planet uninhabitable.

The political situation is even more ominous. Although cruelty against populations is not new, only in the twentieth century have leaders begun to massacre their own people. What Hitler and Stalin began has been imitated by governments in Cambodia, El Salvador, Argentina, and other nations. Massacres and terror are used as tools to bring populations under the control of a single leader or party. Dishearteningly, most emerging nations are moving toward totalitarian control and one-party systems; yet even states with multiparty systems move toward totalitarianism when the same set of money interests controls all the major parties. And however idealistic the initial reasons for expanding government control over a population, the intended benevolence inevitably and quickly is transformed into a desire to remain in power, with all the disenfranchisement that entails.

In a world of amazing wealth, fully one-third of the human beings on this planet do not, ever in their lives, have enough to eat.[9] The United States is the wealthiest nation that has ever existed, yet more than one-fifth of its people live below the poverty level. Statistics and formulas like "poverty level," however, cannot convey the human suffering involved. People have for millennia lived simply at the subsistence level; some have died of hunger or drought in past times. But the processes of the modern world have heightened and broadened such misery, and in a period of great prosperity for large numbers.

Stratifications, insistence on conformity, obedience, and the unworthiness, the depravity of "man" have always characterized patriarchy; but now leaders are empowered by technology and industrialization, so patriarchal systems can reach clear across the globe and affect every creature on it. In this new and threatening ambience, few people can maintain complacency; fear and mistrust color the lives even of the fortunate, the peaceable, the relatively secure. A recent study has shown that Americans are increasingly perceiving the public realm with skepticism if not contempt. Even traditionally raised, conservative people have lost faith in the claims, the workings, and the values of institutions—of government, business, unions, the press, and churches. They no longer believe institutions serve anything but their own power, or preserve anything but the elite class.[10]

But it is not just Americans who are questioning their institutions, and turning inward, seeking significance in the private realm. The uses and purposes of power itself have become suspect. As Foucault reminds us, monarchs always had the power to kill, and society always had the right to manage itself (albeit by principles of which the monarch would approve).[11] But monarchs gave the people something: an image of luxury and pleasure. Their palaces and powers created an image of delight, desire, delectation. Monarchs themselves might be living in fear and suspicion, but their luxuries and splendors offered food for the imagination.

All this has changed. Governments now claim to take responsibility for the welfare of populations. At one or another level, governments help to support the poor, suppress crime, provide education, medical care, legal aid. They also possess a formidable power to kill not just malefactors, or citizens of foreign nations, but, with caprice and malice, their own citizenry. Thus the stature of a human has shrunk since prehistoric times, from a condition of personal autonomy within nature to a condition of almost complete subordination to an engulfing manufactured structure.

At the same time, the face of power has changed into a bland uniformity; definition and expressiveness have been eliminated. Power is exercised by committees of interchangeable faceless men, some of whom are also anonymous, both in the United States and in socialist countries. Little delight or pleasure is permitted to contaminate the absolute pursuit of power. Once upon a time peasants complained to each other about the monarch's taxes, and cynically raised their eyebrows at the luxurious use made of them; now people are forced to march in line by governors who also march in line. Power used to purchase pleasure is not just, but it is comprehensible in a way that power is not when exercised by depersonalized men in business suits for no reason but to aggrandize the impersonal "state."

Moreover, power exercised over almost the entire personal life and the entire public life of huge societies is unwieldy, and it may just be, despite technological devices, impossible to manage. Inflation, unemployment, "stagflation" exist in all mature industrial societies. Many socialist societies—the centrally planned societies of eastern Europe and the USSR—are experiencing similar cycles and states.[12]

It is impossible to review the present state of the world and not perceive in the actions of humans the self-hatred, hatred of humanity itself, that is implicit in the origin of patriarchy. The need to transcend arises from hatred of that which must be transcended: for millennia that has been called "nature," as if our bodies created cruelty. By defining man as something man can never be, patriarchists betray a powerful impulse toward suicide, a drive to kill the real human in order to manufacture a "better."

There are, however, certain rewards for living in patriarchal society, although these are less universal and dependable than they were in the past. In past centuries many men could feel complacent about their superiority over women and lower-class men; few can feel so today. In the past, many men possessed a degree of autonomy in their lives; few do today. In more religious periods, entire populations could assuage their sufferings with the certitudes of a just God imposing just laws. It can be argued that the insanity which characterizes many current patriarchal manipulations is related to patriarchy's loss of moral legitimacy, its sense of rightness.

The primary reward offered those who live in industrial patriarchal societies is commodities: this is true in the East, where commodities are not easily available, as well as in the West. Commodities, things, are what people are allowed to want, taught to want, and do want. In the West, commodities are quite cynically touted and sold as substitutes for true felicity. (Yet at the same time a major characteristic of movies and television films is the violent destruction of cars, boats, radios, houses—the very things that we call goods.)

One popular form of commodity is diversion—fads, games, resorts, entertainments that shift our concern from our realities to the symbolic. Television programs clearly function to dull the throb of actual concerns; sports like jogging accomplish the same end. It may be that humans, with their huge capacity for suffering, require some opiate to dull it, but at some point dulling of pain becomes an inability to feel. And a life unfelt is a life unlived.

Important among diversions is competition, a major value in patriarchy. Competition heightens our individualism and our sense of accomplishment; it also undermines our sense of fellowship with others, increases our isolation, and trains us to be incapable of trust. In addition, competition is linear and quantitative: one can compete only on specific grounds, grounds which permit measurement. Competitive thinking has penetrated areas that were once relatively free—like play and sex—but are now discussed in terms of performance, technique, and achievement.[13] We do not play for pleasure but to measure our laps, miles, master points. If we have no one handy to compete against, we compete against ourselves, our past "record."

A final reward offered by our technological world is convenience. This is also problematical, for while it *is* more convenient to have running water, a washing machine, an automobile or a plane, than to have to go to the well, scrub clothes by hand, and walk long distances, the subsidiary inconveniences of these conveniences are deeply oppressive. Traffic jams, late planes, the noise of cities, the poor air and water quality are only a few of the payments required for our conveniences. The stressful quality of our lives arises mainly from our "conveniences," as we become aware when we spend time away from urban centers, in more "primitive" environments. We are not willing to give up our "conveniences," yet we cannot find a way to live with them in relative peacefulness.

Just as our present morality offers us no imaginable alternative to the domination of power, to power as the highest good, so our present social and political situation provides us with no imaginable alternative to the three "worst" scenarios: global nuclear war; global totalitarianism; or desiccation of the planet. We cannot spread our minds into a distant future; like alcoholics, we take life one day at a time, plodding on, hoping the worst can be averted until we ourselves are dead. We choose the status quo, not in freedom but in despair; we fear action, since any act may entail something worse than the present situation.

But if we decide actively to oppose patriarchal values, and try to create a new system, we find no clear direction. For our system incarnates patriarchal values; our institutions are invariably hierarchical. Hierarchy is a structure designed to retain and transmit power; thus as long as our institutions are hierarchical, power remains supreme. Yet, because power is indeed supreme, no alternative structure is as successful in our world. Experiments with more democratic arrangements, conducted in classrooms, businesses, and editorial offices during the 1970s, ended in rancor and nonproductiveness. Again we confront a closed and vicious circle.

New structures can emerge successfully only in response to a new or different set of ends. When we value pleasure—human well-being—as much as profit (power), new structures will seem to generate themselves. And indeed, examples of forms other than hierarchy abound in the scientific disciplines at present, available to serve as metaphors for social and political arrangements. Many thinkers have suggested that our models of the universe are essentially metaphors, images that make concrete our vision of the relationships among forces in our world.[14] Important shifts in scientific thinking are always followed by shifts in sociopolitical structures, whether because a shift in thought in one discipline eventually permeates a culture as a whole, or because a shift in cultural attitudes is most easily perceptible in its most rigorous thinking—scientific thinking. In any case, although we may have difficulty imagining a business, say, structured other than hierarchically, we can stretch our imaginations by considering the new metaphors that have arisen in astronomy and subatomic theory, in human portrayal of the macro- and microcosm—and in biology and ecology.

## 2. NONHIERARCHICAL STRUCTURE

Classical astronomers developed a cosmology that culminated, in the second century C.E., in the Ptolemaic system. According to this system—or metaphor—earth rested immovable at the center of the cosmos. Beyond it was a sphere of air, then fire, and around earth the planets traveled in perfect and concentric circles. Beyond the finite universe was God, the Prime Mover, who made and controlled all. In the Christian version of this system, each star and planet had its own resident angel, as unchangeable and incorruptible as the planet itself, who sang as the cosmic bodies moved majestically in their orbits, creating the music of the spheres.

This image of the universe dominated Western thinking for fourteen centuries, and influenced moral and political conceptions. The Church was central in the spiritual realm, the Prince in the worldly, and around these still centers of Church and state (there were those who believed there should be only one center, a Church-dominated state, or a state-dominated Church) moved circles of men in their various estates. The fixed, unalterable structure of the universe was imitated on earth in a rigid hierarchy of estates, "the great chain of being." Everything that existed had a place within this structure, from the lowliest pebble or plant to the lion, who was "king" of the forest, to men, who occupied an intermediary position between animals and angels. Men were also ranked by class and ruled by a surrogate god. The females of every species, including human females, were considered subordinate to the male. Everything reflected the divine order; consequently, everything had a significance beyond itself, beyond mere being: everything reflected the nature of God's Law.

Because it posited a clear distinction between what was corruptible (changeable) and what was eternal (permanent), this vision fostered contempt for the world. The dividing line between what was mutable and what eternal was the moon: sublunary existence was seen as miserable because it suffered change. Only those things which did not change—that were above the moon—were worthwhile. Matter was corruptible but the soul was eternal; thus the body was despicable while the soul rose to God. In addition, this metaphor posited domination as the principle of the universe. What stood in the center dominated those things which circled around it and each estate was superior to those below it. Since domination was natural and inevitable in the heavens, so it was on earth. Obedience to the "lord"—of whatever sort—was therefore necessary.

In the sixteenth century, the Polish astronomer Nicholas Copernicus, working from other models of the universe (especially that of Aristarchus), developed a new image. Copernicus believed the earth traveled around the sun, and that the sun was the center of the universe, the earth merely one planet among the five other visible planets. The universe, he claimed, was immense and seemingly infinite. Copernicus' ideas shocked the Europe of his time, which repelled them. Nevertheless, slowly, other astronomers found the new view fruitful and developed it. One of them, Giordano Bruno, was burned at the stake by the Church for positing an infinite universe in which even our sun was only one of many such stars. Bernardino Telesio conceived of, and coined the name, space. Tycho Brahe asserted that the planets and their movements were *not* immutable, that change could occur in space, and that even the universe was transient. Johannes Kepler claimed the planets moved in elliptical circuits, not in a perfect—and holy—circle. And Galileo Galilei (who managed to escape burning by recanting after torture) reaffirmed the Copernican system, concluding that the moon's light was a reflection of the sun's, through the agency of earth; and that even the sun moved, rotating on an axis.

The Copernican universe was not fully incorporated until the Newtonian synthesis of the late seventeenth and early eighteenth centuries. With the hypothesis that an invisible world existed under the surface of the visible natural world, modern physics was born. This invisible world was believed to be comprised of a set of mechanisms, absolute laws governing the motion of falling bodies, of projectiles, the tides, the moon, and the stars. According to Newton, matter was solid, eternal (always conserved), and discontinuous; it moved within continuous time and space. Motion was comprised of the force of inertia, a passive principle, and of active principles like gravity, which impress themselves upon particles of matter. Space was not a void but filled with an airlike substance that was unchanging and immovable. The universe remained a beautifully orderly arrangement of spheres moving in an infinite expanse of absolute space, and events occurred in sequence in a realm of absolute time.

As Newton and others devised new metaphors for the workings of the universe, new structures arose in the political and social realm. The new physics envisioned a dynamic universe rather than a static one (like the Ptolemaic cosmos); and new methods of trade and exchange developed which were also dynamic. The invisible world was an abstraction; and the visible world was a consequence of transactions among abstract forces. Money, an abstraction, superseded barter as a primary means of exchange, in imitation of the interaction of abstract forces.[15] Human labor was now quantified as being worth a certain amount of money, and human beings "became merely hands capable of so many hours of work a day, needing to be stoked with a given quantity of food so that the maximal surplus value could be extracted from their labor."[16]

Feudalism, a political and religious structure in which everyone had a place and the dignity (at least) of an immortal soul, gave way to capitalism, in which people were only bodies whose place was changeable. The long series of revolutions based on ideas of *rights* that continue into our own time began in the seventeenth century, when Copernican thought was being assimilated. The sun still dominated the earth, whether or not it moved or was unique; and domination continued to be a major element in human thinking. But no longer were the privileges and position of aristocracy deemed divinely endowed: and the people of England, and later the people of France, executed their kings. God also moved. Instead of ruling from the outer sphere of a finite universe, he "absconded" after creation, set things in motion and then drifted away to distant realms, to the infinite, as it were. The powers of God were transferred to the forces he had set in motion, physical forces that were comprehensible and possibly manipulable by divinely endowed man. Political powers were also fragmented. If political power had always been to some degree shared—a matter of balances and adjustments among classes—it had not been conceived of in that way, but rather as absolute and centered in a single sovereign. In the seventeenth and eighteenth centuries, people began to think differently about it. Earlier, wars, conflicts, and usurpations aimed to *seize* power; now, revolutions and uprisings were designed to *arrange power differently*, with checks and balances within nations and between them. What Foucault calls a new form of discourse entered human thinking about nature and human interactions, as the old chain of being was broken and new categories, divisions, and definitions developed.[17] And massive displacements of people and classes began, as human thinking abandoned the idea of fixed place, fixed obligation, fixed responsibility.

In a *Discourse* of 1637, Descartes compared the world to a machine; his model was adopted not as a metaphor but as an actual description of human life, in which human functions that were similar to animal functions were reduced to mechanical explanation. But since humans also had consciousness, mind, the old dualism was reintroduced: matter was inert, passive, dead, subject to the laws of the universe; but mind, the new version of soul, was still immortal. The two were bound like the earth by gravity: by domination. So it was legitimate for a man's mind to observe, manipulate, and disdain the material world. Matter could be treated any way at all, for it was eternal; it could not be killed or destroyed but merely transformed. The animate principle was intellect, which was a dominating force. And mind, of course, was seen as male, while matter remained female; the eternal female earth groaning under man's plow was now to be manipulated for a new form of power—knowledge.

The mechanistic metaphor of the cosmos was subjected to many qualifications and modifications over the years. Faraday and Maxwell replaced the Newtonian idea that physical forces were rigidly connected to the bodies they acted upon with the image of a field of force, an area of influence not necessarily connected to any material body. (And slavery or serfdom as a relation between owner and owned was superseded by the idea of hegemony.) But the mechanical model was fully displaced (at least in thinking about the universe) when Einstein enunciated the theory of relativity. According to it, all measurements involving space and time lack absolute significance; they have significance only relative to other observers. Space and time are a four-dimensional continuum, and the structure of space-time depends upon the distribution of matter in the universe. Mass has nothing to do with any material substance, but is a form of energy. Astronomers are now convinced that the sun does not govern space, and "neither does anything else; the cosmos is a lawful anarchy." The galaxies are simply clusters of stars, dust, and gas, and are homogenous in property with everything else in the universe.[18] Nothing rules, yet there is peace, as each segment follows its own course and exists in cooperative relation with everything else.

A similar lack of domination appears to characterize subatomic phenomena. Fritjof Capra writes, "At the subatomic level, matter does not exist with certainty at definite places, but rather shows 'tendencies to exist,' and atomic events do not occur with certainty at definite times and in definite ways, but rather show 'tendencies to occur.' "[19] These tendencies are called *probabilities*. At the subatomic level of existence, solid material objects dissolve into wavelike patterns of probabilities; the patterns they form represent probabilities not of things but of *interconnections*. Thus nature is a complicated web of relations which include the observer, who is not separate, distinct from what is observed, but whose position and perspective affect what is observed. "The human observer constitutes the final link in the chain of observational processes, and the properties of any atomic object can be understood only in terms of the object's interaction with the observer. . . . In atomic physics, we can never speak about nature without, at the same time, speaking about ourselves."[20]

Through electric attraction, the positively charged atomic nucleus exerts force on the negatively charged electrons. The interaction of this force with electron waves generates all structures and phenomena. Neither one thing nor another dominates: the interplay among them provides the basis for all solids, liquids, gases, organisms, and biological processes. The nucleus of the atom is comprised of an electrically charged proton and a neutron which is two thousand times bigger than the electron but has no electrical charge.[21]

Subatomic particles are simultaneously destructible and indestructible; thus matter is both continuous and discontinuous. Force and matter are different aspects of the same phenomenon, as are space and time. There is an oscillation between poles, a circular movement; matter can appear as discontinuous particles or a continuous field. In the common language available to us now, particles can neither be said to exist nor said not to exist. "All the concepts we use to describe nature are limited. . . . they are not features of reality . . . but creations of the mind."[22]

Space-time is really timeless; all events are interconnected but not causally, and can be interpreted as part of a process of cause and effect only when they are read in a single direction.[23] Thus the world of subatomic phenomena, that which underlies everything in the universe, is "feminine"—nonhierarchical, fluid, transient, many-sided, and eternal.

If we apply the metaphor of subatomic phenomena to human existence, we discover an exciting new model. Interconnection, interplay, is the cause of everything that exists. Power is neither substance nor force precisely, but the coming together of particular things in a certain way, at a certain moment. Mass and energy are two aspects of the same phenomenon and all subatomic existence has the capacity to take different forms. Nothing is dominant. Things work by attraction, and even what is negative has a place. The large neutron has no charge. And even the detached observer is connected with what is observed: no observation can be made without causing both some disturbance to the system being observed and some alteration in the being of the observer.[24] No one can be an unmoved mover, a controller unaffected by what he or she controls.

A similar condition obtains in the human body, which Lewis Thomas describes as a continent made up of small elements, all interconnected and all— regardless of their nature, whether they are islands of parasites, sustainers, or utterly separate foreign colonies seemingly independent of their context—all are necessary for the survival of the body as a whole. Nothing dominates—not mind, heart, liver, gut, or genitals; everything participates and is involved in what occurs in other parts.[25]

Each organism within the body is a living system, and thus has flexibility and plasticity; each is self-organizing yet connected with everything else in a nonlinear and complex way. Breakdown, when it occurs, cannot be attributed to a single element. Living organisms have a dynamic stability; they change continually, yet maintain the same structure. For instance, all the cells in the human body (except those in the brain) replace themselves every few years, yet remain the same.

These systems reach outside themselves to their environments. Systems within the body reach out to other systems in the body; the organism that is the body reaches out to the natural environment for food, air, and water. And the larger environment itself is an organic system, an ecosystem containing a host of small ecosystems. Every subsystem is both relatively autonomous and a component of a larger organism: many are symbiotic, their various members utterly interdependent. Capra discusses recent research indicating that the planet earth is related to its biosphere in precisely the same way the body is related to the planet. The biosphere regulates the chemical composition of air, the temperature of the earth's surface, and other aspects of the planetary environment.[26]

We know that within any ecosystem—meadow, sea, or mountain—all elements, even predation, are necessary to maintain the balance of the whole. The removal or eradication of even one species of plant or animal can do serious damage, can lead in time to the destruction of that system. Remove the termites from it, for example, and an entire wetland can begin to die. It makes sense that such meshing interconnections would function at every level, even into the cosmos. The Renaissance thinkers were right about interconnection, if not about hierarchy; and what better way to describe the marvelous plan than as reflecting the glory of God? Even if that word has little meaning for you.

These images reverse totally the way we conceive of power, matter, and the necessity for dominance and hierarchy. They offer us a metaphorical basis for planning human structures. Power is an interaction rather than a substance; anarchy—order without dominance—may be a possible form for human life as well as subatomic phenomena. The metaphors created by scientific thought comprise a new image of the universe and intimate a new moral vision. In this image, energy is everything, as Blake knew, but it can take myriad shapes and can seem shapeless. Anarchy is not the absence of order, but a delicate interaction. Entities exist in their self-organization yet are necessarily connected to other entities; thus our new metaphor for nature involves considerable autonomy along with interdependence, maintenance of structure with continual regeneration.

These new perceptions of the way things work undermine the idea that hierarchy is the only available form for large associations of people; they also challenge a traditional problematic philosophical notion—the either/or.


## 3. BEYOND THE EITHER/OR

Western thought is profoundly dual, which is to say that in the West difference is more important than similarity. Put another way, distinction is more important than equivalence, division than solidarity. Such a valorization is a necessary component of a morality that exists to confer superiority on one group or caste of humans; their superiority rests upon their difference from other humans. The philosophical problem of the Either/Or, as Kierkegaard referred to it, is therefore largely a factitious problem, in which philosophers attempt to synthesize or reconcile oppositions that are created primarily by their own categorizations. We are told that a thing is either A or not-A, and logically these categories are exclusive. But such division is not intrinsic in reality, in which elements flow into each other and possess similar properties.

We speak of oppositions like black/white, red/green, yet all colors reflect light waves of varying lengths along a spectrum, and there are hundreds of shades of black, white, red, or green. Oppositions like good/evil are too broad, and based too subjectively, even to allow discussion. Dichotomous thought does not arise from an honest effort to comprehend experience but from a hubristic effort to reshape it. By excluding most of experience, and limiting discourse to a set of opposed constructs, men have been able to create the *appearance* of comprehension of experience and to attribute superiority and inferiority to its elements. Thus the claim that man is very different from woman, that the two are opposites, as are man and nature, white and black. Ignoring the far greater similarities than differences among humans, patriarchy divides and conquers.

Even so seemingly innocuous an element as laterality has been categorized and used for invidious comparisons; parents still sometimes attempt to force left-handed children to use their right hands. Since the time of Classical Greece, however, right/left opposition has involved an opposition of the sexes. This may be, as some people think, because women invariably carry their babies on the left arm, where they will lie closer to the mother's heartbeat. But the association of women with the left and men with the right has been, like all other such dualities, developed to the disparagement of women.

In Pythagorean numerology, the number *one* is associated with God, unity, light, order, the sun, religion, reason, and the right-hand side—with the attendant notions of right and rights. Jesus sits at the right hand of God, just as the favored guest sits at the right of the host. A right-hand man works on one's behalf, and rights accrue to those who win them, who are said to be in the right. *One* is also the number of the male. The number *two* is associated with qualities antipathetic to those just listed; with mystery, divisiveness, darkness, chaos, the moon, magic, irrationality, and the left-hand side, the *sinister* in Latin. It is also the number of the female.

Early hypotheses about sex determination manifest these associations of sex with laterality. In the second century C.E., Galen taught that semen from the right testicle produced males, from the left, females. Simultaneous ejaculation from both testicles resulted in hermaphrodites. Nine centuries later, in the eleventh century C.E., Avicenna proposed that semen deposited in the right side of the female uterus produced males, in the left side, females, and in the middle, hermaphrodites. These ideas were not laid to rest until the mid-eighteenth century, after demonstrations that a man with only one testicle, and a woman with no right uterine tube, had both parented children of both sexes.[27]

Although the meanings of right, rights, and sinister remain, we do not really recall these associations with left and right. So we wonder how it happens that the buttons on women's shirts and jackets are on the left side, and men's on the right; or that during a marriage service the friends of the groom sit on the right side of the place of worship (facing the altar), while friends of the bride sit on the left. Yet many a man would be humiliated at being discovered in a "woman's" shirt, and guests at a formal wedding dismayed at "improper" seating.

Early research on the brain attributed different capacities to the left and right lobes; this research still appears to be correct. But the qualities ascribed to the two sides are in many ways precisely the opposite of those ascribed in old associations. The left hemisphere, which, according to traditional association, should be the realm of the mystical, irrational, chaotic, and feminine, is logical, analytical, and sequential; it is the source of orderly, reasoned thinking, and controls language and speech. The right hemisphere, which should be analytical and logical, looks at things holistically, is intuitive and creative, and provides us with pictures and images. It controls drawing.

The left brain can be pushed, coerced to work; the right brain cannot. It functions best when we relax, when we give up the attempt to control. This is probably why so many artists feel they are not in control but transmitters for a power beyond themselves, an inspirational "muse."

But to complicate the matter even further, the right lobe governs the left-hand side of the body and the left lobe the right. Further, it is now believed that testosterone produced by the testes of male fetuses may sometimes inhibit growth of the left hemisphere of the brain and result in left-handedness, certain disabilities in learning language, and certain immune-system diseases. Most left-handed people do not, of course, have autoimmune diseases, and they may even be at a lower risk for others, such as infectious diseases and cancer.[28] There is neither clear advantage nor disadvantage to either left- or right-handedness. What is important, so far as the brain is concerned, is to be able to use both lobes, to exercise all one's capacities.

The emphasis of Western culture, especially its most recent technological phase, however, has been on abilities within the purview of the left lobe. Right-lobe thinking, inaccessible to coercion and control, inclined to viewing contextually, and expressive of what is called intuition—which is really an extremely subtle form of perception—has been increasingly disdained and disparaged over the past centuries. But just as alpha (domineering, emotionless) and beta (cooperative, sympathetic) styles of management are being studied by managers searching for more effective techniques, right-lobe thinking is also being scrutinized and advanced. Techniques for calling upon the right lobe are being devised, and managers are beginning to exhort others to see things in context rather than separately, and to seek "intuitive" and creative solutions. Right-lobe thinking is clearly about to be commoditized.[29] What is perhaps most shocking to students of the two ways of thinking is that women seem better able than men to switch back and forth between the two lobes. They may therefore be better equipped to handle complexity.[30]

Although such conclusions may refer not to a physiological difference between the sexes but to differences in habit and training—men are trained to think narrowly, to act within rigid categories, and to block out sensitivity; women have been permitted to retain flexibility—they offer one more reason for men to include women at the highest reaches of power. Until men can develop flexibility themselves, the thinking of women may prevent them from carrying us to the apocalypse.

In any case, left and right are not opposites, but interconnected; and surely much of our thinking draws on the capacities of both lobes. Other seeming oppositions also vanish under scrutiny. Consider the opposition of active and passive. In actuality they are adopted styles, modes of behavior rather than innate characteristics. But even as styles, neither is exclusive to either sex, as our mythology claims. Nor is activity necessarily productive or good: it can be play—undirected, diffuse, purposeless; it can be directed at destructive ends; and we can also use constant activity merely to scatter energy, as a substitute for directed action. On the other hand, passivity can be intensely directed: it can be a demand, a powerful and frustrating form of aggression. Because passivity is a style that implicitly repudiates action, it permits no confrontation or reprisal; it is a prime weapon against anyone with a sense of guilt.

Aggressiveness can be a mode of expressing timidity or fear; timid passivity can be a mode of expressing anger. Women who easily shrug off their husbands' or bosses' bluster and tantrums understand that these men are really expressing frustration or anger at being made afraid; men subjected to the timid passivity of mothers and wives understand that these surfaces entail demands that *cannot* be refused.

Strength and weakness are often two aspects of the same quality. They are not simply balances, as when someone strong in a certain direction or dimension is weak in another: certain strengths are simultaneously weaknesses. For example, the quick strength called upon by short-distance runners disables them in long-distance endurance running, and a capacity for the latter often· means weakness in the former. People with highly developed ears, sensitive to nuance in sound, to tonality, rhythm, and timbre, often lack strong vision, eyes that take in an entire scene, that see sharp edges, colorations, spatial relationships. Intellectual strength in a particular direction often entails a corresponding weakness, for strong focus involves side-blindness, a partial or complete unawareness of peripheries. As all form is also deprivation, all strength is also weakness.

A person who has strong self-control gives an impression of strength and independence yet may be as helpless as a child in expressing feeling, precisely because of that self-control. Like many other descriptive terms, "strong" and "weak" properly refer only to an area or field, not to an entire person.

Nor do dependence and independence make much sense. The most domineering or dominating people are among the most dependent; and dependency in one area—say, the financial—does not equal dependency in others—say, the emotional. Both "dependence" and "independence" are merely momentary appearances of interdependence, appearances which can shift from moment to moment.

Ice burns and poisons cure; mass and energy are two ways of seeing or two ways of being the same thing. Love contains hate and hate love, and both exist in any strong bond. Moreover, self-love, a quality condemned by most patriarchal moralities, is necessary for any other kind of love. "One ceases to love oneself *properly* when one *ceases* to exercise one's capacity for love towards other people."[31] Love is different from possession, although it shares some of its exclusivity.

And at every level self is part of group, group part of self. Alasdair MacIntyre points to the absurdity of the modern notion that extrication from group—family, tribe, village, community, society—means freedom, when in fact one's group identity is intrinsic to one's personal identity, whether we like that or not, whether we admit it or not.[32] Our insistence on individuality, independence, freedom defined as freedom from bonds to others, has fostered competitiveness and rivalry; together, these values have made modern life a battleground, a noisy, dangerous, filthy, urban nightmare, from which the only relief *is* isolation and retreat. As Iredell Jenkins reminds us, only with a sense of our identity with others, of our participation in family, community, or society, can we create a harmonious home, a community in which laws are assented to rather than enforced, in which concord rather than discord predominates.[33]

The oppositions upon which we lay so much weight are false to reality; worse, they impede us from finding solutions that require integration of qualities. But we cling to oppositions, because only through them can we exalt part of the human race, part of experience. Only by distinguishing sharply between man and nature, man and woman, can men maintain their superior status. It is evident that nature exists within men and men within nature; it should be evident that men and women are more alike than different, physiologically, emotionally, and intellectually.

A further impediment remains to the realization of the feminist vision: our present morality itself. It was a nonfeminist, indeed a misogynist, Friedrich Nietzsche, who insisted that a more honest and bearable world required better philosophers—moral philosophers like himself. He offered a list of "innovations" which he considered fundamental to the building of a truer and more humane philosophy; all of these involved rethinking values.[34] This list includes a rethinking of the value of power ("domination") and of emotion ("affects"); it suggests that culture be regarded as a complex—that is, as an integrated environment which forms those who live in it. Nietzsche also urged a "naturalization of morality," which I read as the creation of a morality based in nature rather than on transcendence of it; and the replacement of metaphysics and religion by "the theory of eternal recurrence." Although Nietzsche links this to "breeding and selection," the subtext intimates the replacement of belief in transcendence by an acceptance of continuity.

Nietzsche believed the articulation of a new morality to be basic to the construction of a society more responsive to actual human need and desire; and it is in the area of morality that some of the most important feminist work has been done, especially in examinations of power, sex, and gender roles. Patriarchy is founded in the desire to refute, minimize, or disguise natural realities, and to assert symbolic structures that "transcend" those realities. Thus examination of our moral values requires extricating what is real from a mass of symbols—images, preconceptions, associations. This book is an attempt at such extrication. The next four sections of this chapter summarize the arguments about power, aggression, sex, and gender roles that inform this work.

## 4. POWER

Few people would deny that power is the primary value in the political world; yet many would deny that it is the primary value in their personal worlds. This latter denial would vanish, however, if instead of power we used the word *control*. *Power* and *control* are often used synonymously, so that we read that a nation controls another nation, or a corporation controls a market; but there is a difference in thrust between them. *Power* suggests large size, and has connotations of moving outward, like an armed fist; *control* suggests tightness, detailed instrumentation, and has connotations of moving inward, pressing together or down—repressing, suppressing, oppressing, depressing. Power connotes ability and energy; control connotes restraint, regulation, a harnessing of energy. The two may be related as the political and the moral are related: at some point they are identical, but one faces outward to the public world and the other faces inward to personal and private life.

Most theorists, however, do not distinguish between power and control, and tend to discuss power alone. Bertrand Russell defined power as the ability to compel obedience.[35] Talcott Parsons considered power something possessed, a property possessed by an actor that enables him to alter the will or actions of others so that they conform to his will.[36] In other words, power is usually defined as domination, yet our uses of the term encompass a broader meaning. In addition, domination is usually seen as admirable: it is the goal of most states, businesses, churches, and military establishments, among other institutions. Yet it is not considered admirable when practiced by "inferiors"—women, children, servants—upon "superiors"—men, adults, employers.

Thus even when power is defined as domination, the term is murky and dependent on personal prejudice. By limiting their thinking to categories, political theorists have narrowed all relations to a series of power relations, and transformed experience into Realpolitik. Some feminist thinkers, however, have begun to reconsider the meaning of power.

To begin with, there are different sorts of power: there is power-to, which refers to ability, capacity, and connotes a kind of freedom, and there is power-over, which refers to domination. Both forms are highly esteemed in our society.

Power-to is considered a personal attribute, based in innate ability and developed through self-discipline. But in fact, power-to is achieved not by individuals but by communities or networks supporting individuals. First, an ability must be perceived by others; then the talented person must have the good fortune to live in circumstances which permit the talent to be fostered (through education or training) and in a society which permits that person to practice that talent. Every society values—rewards—certain talents and not others.

Thus children born to a poor uneducated family are unlikely to have their talents perceived or fostered; a child of the "wrong" gender or color may not be permitted to develop certain talents; and adults of the "wrong" color or gender may not be permitted to practice their skill in the world even if they have managed to receive training. Finally, a society that values one kind of talent will encourage it above others. Although these facts are self-evident, our society tends to forget them.

Our society claims, often, to be a meritocracy. The very word conceals layers of falsehood: it implies that all members of society have equal access to all doors of development and all avenues of practice; and that those who are most excellent rise to the top. It implies that the unskilled and unsuccessful deserve their fate, that they are less able *by nature*. In addition, our society praises those with power-to as gifted *individuals*—when, in fact, no one develops and uses a talent without assistance from others at every step: from family, friends, and educators; from trainers and coaches; and from a larger community, which accepts a person's exercise of an ability. An ability, like a person, requires nourishment and scope if it is to grow. It reflects not just individuality, independence, and a drive to excellence, but also dependency, interconnection, and the acceptance of society.

Power-to overlaps with power-over, domination. Insofar as the practice of a skill is competitive, the practitioner must "defeat" other practitioners to be "successful." And some abilities involve managing or persuading other people. When a talent involves influencing others, it becomes what we call authority. There are two forms of authority: noncoercive authority and authority that masks might or force. Noncoercive authority exists when someone possesses a special skill or knowledge which is useful to others. People consult the authority but are not required to comply with his/her advice. Yet often enough those with special knowledge—physicians, say—convey such godlike superiority and omniscience that they compel compliance from their patients. Teachers possess noncoercive authority but are transformed into coercive figures when they administer grades. And managers and administrators, who in the ideal act as guides and advisers to those "beneath" them, in fact practice coercion more than not. There is coercion in the most benevolent management—even in the raising of children.

Coercion—domination—is not eradicable. It is impossible to envision a world in which some form or degree of domination is lacking. At the same time, the urge to dominate is responsible for most of the ills humans impose on themselves. Political theorists discuss the problem of how to construct a society in which domination is not possible, but the solutions devised invariably involve a set of checks and balances which in fact create a new level of dominators.

Although its psychological roots may be complex, the urge to dominate is based in self-aggrandizement; it may also, however, emerge from a strong idea about the common good. A person possessed of special skill or knowledge convinces himself that he can organize a group, community, state, in such a way as to advance human well-being. This may not always have been the character of dominators: it is doubtful whether Alexander and Tamburlaine entertained any ideal but their own fame when they set out to conquer the world. There are probably many dominators in the world who lack a moral ideal, but for the past century all have acted in the name of an ideal.

Whatever the political content of these ideals, the actual content is always the same: control. And since in our age control is seen as a good in its own right, for its own sake, those with the greatest power are considered the "greatest" men. Because of this blind adulation of power, we rarely consider its costs, its consequences, or its limits.

Yet striving for power is extremely costly. It requires the direction of almost all a person's energy and attention toward the immediate step of power he
or she seeks; it therefore requires the sacrifice of almost everything in life that
does not advance power. Yet because most of life's felicities lie in another
realm, the pursuit of power requires the sacrifice of most pleasures other than
those attendant on a momentary victory. And as anyone is aware just from
reading about presidential campaigns, the savor of victory is short-lived; it must
yield to the necessity for planning the next one. When a person achieves the
pinnacle of power—becomes president, or executive officer, or prime minister—the perquisites of power, pleasurable as they may be, are far outweighed by
its problems. Power is personally costly; it narrows the experience of life into a
linear progress toward a goal that cannot be achieved—for no one ever has
enough power-over.

The pursuit of power is sometimes celebrated simply because it requires
the sacrifice of personal pleasure: populations are exhorted to adore the chairman precisely because he has given up personal pleasure in order to manage the
state. Few inquire what kind of person would be willing to sacrifice pleasure to
such an ideal, what distortion of character is necessary to make such a choice.
But the personal cost of power seeking involves more than the sacrifice of pleasure. For the exercise of domination has consequences that are invariably unpleasant.

There are only two ways to control living beings: eradication and domestication. Eradication means, simply, murdering people, a tactic which has become extremely popular in our century. It is the easiest, fastest way to gain
control, but it has drawbacks. The murder of people arouses enmity; the murder of large numbers of people arouses the enmity of proportionally larger numbers of those who suffer from the loss. It is a tactic that lays the ground for
rebellion and guarantees the continued embattlement of the dominator and his
supporters. He seeks to secure his power by extending it. "Every human group
that exercises power does so, not in such a way as to bring happiness to those
who are subject to it, but in such a way as to increase that power," wrote Simone Weil.[37] Amos Perlmutter asserts that totalitarian states are governed by
men who are anxious, who are most concerned about legitimacy, political survival and sustenance. Because of this anxiety, they create control groups, police,
and purges, which do not alleviate their fear but expose them to double insecurity—challenges from inside and outside the palace, fear of their own instruments of terror.[38] The only way to avoid this perpetual warfare is to kill
everyone: but then there would be no one to control, which would presumably
be a loss even to dominators whose concern is only for themselves. "Every victory over men contains within itself the germ of a possible [future] defeat, unless it goes as far as extermination. But extermination abolishes power by
abolishing its object."[39]

Domestication requires more time and patience but is a more effective
means of control, since in time it brings the will of the populace into line with
that of the dominator. Domestication has many forms: imprisonment, punishment, intimidation, religious or moral education. Patriarchy has, since its in-

ception, used both eradication and domestication to teach people the rightness of its ways and the truth of its vision of God. When a patriarchal form—a religion or a political arrangement—accomplishes its goals through education (of whatever sort), it achieves stability. The people internalize the morality of the institution, and support it without coercion. Only then can the dominator begin to rest. But even then he must be eternally vigilant against any force that might undermine the dogma of his regime. In this struggle the importance of ideology cannot be overestimated. Those who believe morals are not highly significant in our age ignore the weight placed upon ideology by the dominators of our world, who understand that unless the values of a regime are widely assented to, the regime is threatened.

But in fact there has never been a regime on earth which was not troubled by dissent. Dissent is inevitable in any controlled situation, and when it is throttled, it may subside for a time but often merely goes underground to reappear as rebellion. Thus the dominator is continually besieged. The personal cost of ordering eradication and domestication is higher than we can estimate: cruel or even callous actions cannot be performed without cost to the actor, who becomes numbed by his own acts. Not just sensitivity but trust, fellowship, and ease are destroyed; and without trust, fellowship, and ease, love is impossible. And although the power seeker may entertain the dream that some day he will be able to rest, that day does not occur until he is ousted from power or dies.

The cost of domination to a populace cannot be measured, nor have historians on the whole focused upon it. The suffering of populations, the spilled blood, the tortures of body and mind, the human price paid for human worship of power are far less popular subjects than the "greatness" of dominators. Despite the price paid by both ordinary people and those who seek power, power retains its ability to dazzle, its supremacy in our moral scales.

Yet as much of the discussion in this book suggests, power is not what we think it is. Power is not substantial; not even when it takes substantive form. The money you hold in your hand can be devalued overnight; the gold you store up would be worthless, not tradeable for a cabbage, if there were a nuclear war. A title can be removed at the next board or departmental meeting; rank can be a burden to be maintained without resources. A huge military establishment, like that of the Shah of Iran, can disintegrate in a few days; a huge, economic structure can collapse in a few weeks, as happened in the depression of 1929, which affected every industrial nation. In 1983 a group of former heads of government met in Vail, Colorado, to discuss the fragile and transient nature of political power. Their remarks suggested that they were surprised to find themselves mere citizens: "I had to pinch myself last night and almost punch the rest of them to remind ourselves that we were no longer in power," said Malcolm Fraser.[40]

"All power is unstable.... There is never power, but only a race for power.... Power is, by definition, only a means ... but power-seeking, owing to its essential incapacity to seize hold of its object, rules out all consideration of an end, and finally comes ... to take the place of all ends," wrote Simone Weil.[41]

Power is a process, a dynamic interaction. *To have power* really means to have entry to a network of relationships in which one can influence, persuade, threaten, or cajole others to do what one wants or needs them to do. Although no other syntax is available to us, it is in fact false to speak of "having power." One does not possess power: it is granted to the dominator by hosts of other people, and that grant is not unretractable, despite elections to presidencies for life. When the actions of dominators violate public morality too greatly, the grant of power is removed. This happened to Richard Nixon, who retained the trappings of office but could no longer preside effectively, could no longer wield power. His resignation was simply recognition of a situation. This happened to Khrushchev, King Farouk, Batista, the Shah of Iran, and the rulers of Argentina after the war over the Malvinas (Falkland) Islands.

It is therefore extremely ironic that patriarchy has upheld power as a good that is permanent and dependable, opposing it to the fluid, transitory goods of matricentry. Power has been exalted as the bulwark against pain, against the ephemerality of pleasure, but it is no bulwark, and is as ephemeral as any other part of life. Coercion seems a simpler, less time-consuming method of creating order than any other; yet it is just as time-consuming and tedious and far more expensive than personal encounter, persuasion, listening, and participating in bringing a group into harmony. None of this is unknown, unfamiliar, unperceived. Yet so strong is the mythology of power that we continue to believe, in the face of all evidence to the contrary, that it is substantial, that if we possessed enough of it we could be happy, that if some "great man" possessed enough of it, he could make the world come right.

Power-to is one of the greatest pleasures available to humans; power-over is one of the greatest pains. It is always true that those whom we control control us. Insofar as a sense of freedom, autonomy, is a basic human good, dominators, pressured and threatened on all sides, have less personal freedom than an itinerant laborer, and some dominators, chafing under this oppression, impose equal oppression on others. To keep a slave in a ditch, one must stay there oneself, or appoint an overseer to guarantee the slave's obedience. But then it is necessary to appoint a supervisor who will make sure that the slave and the overseer do not collude; then a governor who will make sure that all three do not collude . . . and so on. There is no place of safety for a dominator, ever; there is no security, peace, or ease. The urge to control others backfires: it cannot be satisfied and it entraps the controller. "It's a machine in which everyone is caught, those who exercise power just as much as those over whom it is exercised."[42] The prison guard experiences imprisonment just as the prisoner does; the guard can look forward only to his day off. The dominators of the world never have a day off.

"Power contains a sort of fatality which weighs as pitilessly on those who command as on those who obey; nay more, it is in so far as it enslaves the former that, through their agency, it presses down on the latter."[43]

Although juridical theory views power as a right one can possess like a commodity, and which one can transfer to others, Michel Foucault too asserts that it is actually a relationship, the "name given to a complex strategic relation in a given society."[44] Power is "never localised here or there," it is "never in anybody's hands," it cannot be appropriated like a commodity. Rather it "circulates," functions like energy moving through a chain. Those who exert power "are always in the position of simultaneously undergoing and exercising" power.[45] Power-over is costly to those who exercise it as well as to those over whom it is exercised. It is not pleasant, requiring the sacrifice of most felicities and unremitting tedious effort to maintain it. And at its peak, it does not bring the rewards it is believed to convey.

Power is limited. Contrary to the image of power fostered by thinkers who believe in transcendence of the human condition, which suggests that certain people rest utterly secure in luxury, invulnerable to the currents and climates in which the majority of the human race is caught, power does not create invulnerability. It may cushion its "possessors" against financial worry, may permit a high level of comfort in living and create an enviable appearance. But the joys of power lie mainly in appearance and the ability to torment underlings—a questionable joy. Maintaining power requires full-time dedication to manipulations of all sorts; and because a power status is enviable, it is threatened by other ambitious people. It also seduces, and a person in a power seat can never be sure whether it is the seat or himself that is attractive to others. Occupying a seat of power creates vulnerabilities and fears that the majority of people do not suffer.

A major problem for executives in business and industry is that they do not understand the real limitations of power: they have accepted the myth and failed to understand the less exalted reality. Douglas McGregor asserts that the most troublesome problems of administrators arise from their belief that authority is an absolute; they attempt to control their "inferiors" in ways that are "inappropriate."[46] The truth about business and industry, about government and politics, about finance, and even about some aspects of scientific disciplines, is that they are subject to emotion, require delicate, unremitting personal manipulation, and are not logical, rational processes at all. McGregor, along with many other students of the corporate world, affirms that all the efforts made during recent centuries to bring business under rational controls have accomplished only the creation of an appearance of rational control, "a skillful dramatic imitation."[47]

The dream underlying the drive to power is transcendence: the accomplishment by humans of a godlike invulnerability, impregnability, untouchableness, the ability to affect others without being affected ourselves. Dominators crave an unimpeded ability to transform social and political structures, or even human nature itself. Every innovation in procedure or technique is touted for its capacity to bring men closer to this goal. The Industrial Revolution, which created so many conveniences and so much misery, was hailed as a progress toward the overcoming of human fragility and vulnerability.[48] People superstitiously clutch the myth that power is a good because surrendering the superstition would mean recognizing that the human race is limited, that it cannot attain invulnerability, that neither the race nor any member of it, no matter how "heroic," can transcend the human condition.

Such recognition is difficult because faith in transcendence is implanted in many of our structures and artifacts; we breathe it in from infancy. The religious have faith in an afterlife of transcendence; socialists have faith in an eventual workers' utopia on earth; power-seekers have faith in their own ability to reach an impregnable and secure position. Some still claim to believe that technical progress can bring the human race into a paradise of ease and comfort. As long as we continue to hold to these dreams, superstitions, delusions, we will be unable to find ways to construct a world that is humane and non-transcendent. Until we see the limits of power more realistically, we will not be able to leave off worship of the idol, power, and begin to worship those elements that foster life on this planet.

The conditions of human life have changed drastically over the past few centuries, largely because of the potency of the idea of power. We continue to worship the principle that has brought us to this pass, without considering the nature of the pass. We seek solutions in the very mode of thinking/acting that has caused the problems. We must remember, as Stephen Jay Gould reminds us, that failure to adapt to changed conditions is the main cause of extinction of species.[49] Two stunning changes dwarf all others that have occurred: the ability to prevent conception or birth with minimal danger to the mother; and the ability to eradicate in a few hours most or all of the world: the pill and the bomb. The pill, affecting the most personal areas of life, seems to most of us a good; it eases the human condition. The bomb, affecting the most public areas of life, seems to most of us an evil; it threatens all humans and all life. Yet both powers are powers to destroy. We do not have equivalent powers to create.

In truth, it is easier to destroy than to create: destruction requires less thought, energy, patience, endurance, and moral/spiritual strength than creation. Possibly, possessed of such powers, we can now stop and think about the actual costs and rewards of power. Power has turned: it is biting its own tail. Power must now become its own keeper. No guards, no United Nations, no series of international police can accomplish what needs to be done. War no longer serves any human purposes—if indeed it ever did. Even conventional wars are now wars of attrition; one can hold back certain tides in human affairs for only so long. Thus it is a possibility, at least, that the invention of nuclear weapons could in time prove to be a boon. The bomb could become the symbol of the insanity and impossibility of life conceived as power struggle, of continuing delusive, sacrificial power seeking. It may force us—all of us, the human race—to stand still for a moment and think: If we can no longer channel our energies and miseries in aggressive action, what shall we do with ourselves? That we can go no further in our obsession for power without destroying ourselves could force us to confront that obsession, to inquire into its nature, its costs, its rewards, and to ask ourselves, perhaps for the first time as a race: What do we want to be that we *can* be?

*Domination does not increase well-being*; it does not even, in the long run, increase security. For example, the United States has declined from its position of domination of the world at large, a position it had secured at the end of World War II. At that time America accounted for 50 percent of the world's military expenditure, produced 60 percent of the world's manufactured goods, and had the highest per capita income of any nation in the world. In 1975, America accounted for only 25 percent of the world's military expenditure, produced 30 percent of the world's goods, and was seventh worldwide in per capita income. Yet this decline from dominant status has not meant a national decline (what decline has occurred is largely a result of the huge cost of the Vietnam War); most people in the West are living better now than they did in 1950, and the well-being of other nations contributes to and enriches our own.[50]

Domination is not eradicable, but we can lessen its attraction for humans if we can learn to see it for what it is—a desperate shift, made in the belief that humans are predators and incapable of felicity. The need to dominate is a substitute for faith in affection and other satisfactions. It is true that pleasure cannot be guaranteed to endure—but neither can power.

## 5. AGGRESSION

It is not power worship or power seeking that have been blamed for the miseries of civilization, however, but aggression and sexuality. Many thinkers have believed with Freud that repression is necessary in order to regulate and control these two aspects of human behavior. Freud called aggressiveness "the greatest hindrance to civilization."[51]

Biological determinists (sociobiologists) hold that aggressiveness is innate in human males, and develop elaborate theories about genes and hormones to justify this claim.[52] There are hormonal differences between women and men; there are also differences in structure and hormonal interactions between the male and female brain. But no one has any knowledge about what those differences mean, or whether they lead to gender-differentiated behavior.[53] Claims that differences in men's and women's behavior are rooted in biology cannot be substantiated at our present state of knowledge. Nevertheless, scientists have been making them for centuries, and continue to do so.

Yet simple logical thinking demonstrates that such claims provide ideological positions with a scientific mask. Biological determinists consider aggressiveness one of the traits that were selected in the ancient past because it contributed to the "survival of the fittest." Yet some biological determinists also assert that the aggressiveness of blacks and other subordinate classes is "excessive" and "deviant," and urge treatment of it by drugs or brain surgery.[54] If aggressiveness is of value for survival, why is it not valuable in blacks? If aggressiveness is innate, how does it happen that in general men are more aggressive than women? If male hormones (which women also possess) are responsible for this difference, how does it happen that there exist some extremely aggressive women and some nonaggressive men? If these variations comprise deviations that are the consequence of individual mutation, how does it happen that all the men in the world are not equally aggressive? There are striking differences in aggressiveness from one to another culture.[55] As Lenore Weitzman has pointed out, if hormones were responsible for aggressiveness and passivity, people from different cultures would have to have different hormonal structures.[56] The great differences in male and female aggressive level and behavior cannot, however, be attributed to genetic or hormonal structure: genes by themselves do not directly create instincts that develop differently in the two sexes, and there is no substantial experimental evidence that sex hormones are directly responsible for behavioral differences in the two sexes in the areas of aggression, assertion, or dominance.[57] Prenatal hormones do seem to establish levels of tolerance; that is, both females and males are endowed physiologically with similar capacities, but these capacities manifest themselves at different thresholds. John Money asserts that aggressiveness is in general more readily elicited in males than in females in situations involving predators and territory; and in females more than in males in defense of the young.[58] But this conclusion is tentative, and is based mainly on study of monkeys.

Edward O. Wilson, perhaps the best-known American sociobiologist, who believes humans (especially males) are innately aggressive and driven to dominate, asserts that humans are less aggressive than some animals; but animals do not make war, and only a few species fight their own kind to the death. Other researchers, who claim to be able to measure aggressiveness, perform experiments such as placing a rat and a mouse in the same cage and clocking the time it takes the rat to kill the mouse.[59] Carnivorous animals kill to eat: humans kill real people for symbolic reasons, most cultures making a point of not eating their human victims. There is considerable evidence of hormonal factors causing aggressiveness in some male animals, but comparable evidence for aggressiveness in human males is much weaker and less consistent.[60] Nevertheless, human males in our culture demonstrate greater aggressiveness than females as early as two or two and a half years of age.[61]

But even if the biological determinists turned out to be right—if aggressiveness were found to be innate in humans, and in a greater degree in men— what would that mean? What is aggressiveness? Despite all the discussion, it is used as vaguely as the term *power*. R. C. Lewontin, Steven Rose, and Leon Kamin point out that the same term, *aggression*, can be applied to a man beating his wife, a melee among sporting fans, political struggles against domination, and military actions involving nuclear weapons.[62] If we define it as hostile impulses directed outward, the term can cover an angry look or murder; it can describe the driving energy of a strong argument, exhortations to some action, anger of any degree, and physical or emotional violence. Sometimes aggressive expressions are useful, on occasion necessary, and sometimes they are fun—as in a tennis match, or a good argument. Even if one believes that aggressiveness is a part of basic human biological equipment that does not mean that human society must be contentious, violent, and unremittingly embattled. Wilson also asserts that violent aggression is culturally induced; it is a learned realization of a potential. He reminds us that during wars, other forms of violent action increase.[63]

We cannot discuss aggressiveness in a vacuum, as a known quality. Differences in degree and kind of aggressive expression are enormous; the importance of context in a moral consideration of aggressiveness cannot be overestimated;

and finally, aggressiveness is perceived differently depending on who is expressing it. Even the form of the word connotes a difference in meaning. In our society, the noun *aggression* is almost always an expression of disapproval. No
state ever admits to being guilty of aggression; only enemies "aggress." But the
adjective or adverb is frequently a term of praise when applied to businessmen,
sports figures, politicians, or corporate policies. A corporation may aggressively
pursue policies that lead to the starvation of great numbers of people, yet be
considered praiseworthy because it aggressively increases profits. But to call a
woman *aggressive* is to denigrate her, and to call a black *aggressive* is to paint
him or her as menacing.

In the area of "aggression"—whatever we mean by it—the same act performed by a young black man, a middle-aged white woman, and a middle-class
white man does not appear to be the same act. Extremely angry verbal expression by a woman is usually interpreted as a sign that she is hysterical or irrational, and in need of psychiatric care; in a black, such expression is usually
perceived as terrifying, a threat to life, requiring imprisonment. In young white
males, such expression is also found threatening, but only to order; unruly
white boys are believed to require discipline. When adult white males express
extreme anger verbally, however, as often as not they cow their listeners, who
try to appease them, who defer to them, who in short accept anger as a white
man's prerogative.

Indeed, aggressive qualities are associated with "manliness" in the West.
To be a man in patriarchal society means to appear to be in control. Self-asser-
tiveness is an expression of a strong sense of individuality (permissible only to
men, because "found in nature" only in men); the same is true of violence. Although most emotional expressions are not permitted to men—a tear can lose a
man an election, guilt and fear are intolerable in a leader, and affection for a
person who is not strictly within a man's control diminishes him, makes him
seem a fool—anger is not merely permitted but expected. Although it can be as
irrational (inappropriately directed) as any other emotion, anger is permitted to
men because it *appears* to be an instrument of control. Anger may emerge from
fear, as it does in bullies; it may emerge from a loss of control; but because it
can function to intimidate others, it is part of "manliness."

The questions we should be asking about aggressiveness are not whether
or not it is innate, or whether it is found only in males and a few deviant females, but what we mean when we use the term; what human (rather than personal) purposes aggressiveness serves; and why cultures foster violent
aggression. Many societies do and have done so—the world of Homer's
Achaeans, of imperial Rome, imperial Great Britain, Hitler's Germany, and the
United States since the nineteenth century. In the past, however, when class
lines were clearer and stricter, aggressiveness was instilled in those who were
expected to lead a state during war: it was taught through *The Iliad* and *The
Aeneid*, on the playing fields of Eton and in the gymnasia, in the ethos of
upper-class male society.

Aggression constitutes a major problem in all industrial nations, yet any
survey of popular culture will reveal that it is encouraged and exalted in the

"myths" we are taught. States instill and encourage aggressiveness as a general practice, in order to tap it for war. Aggressiveness is regulated by law not because societies disapprove of it but to make it the property, the right, of the state. Societies which are not deeply involved in the struggle for world hegemony are less likely to foster aggressiveness in their populations; and those societies which are most power-seeking, most driven to dominate, will foster the greatest degree of aggressiveness in their populations. Violence is taught because it *must* be taught: it is not so "innate" that people resort to it unthinkingly. And it is taught sub rosa, through ideological channels, because the official line is that the state wants peace. Violence is the prerogative of the state, which reserves aggressive action to itself. States usually prohibit the establishment of armed forces under private control, so that there is no challenge to the state's ability to put down insurrections. The very creation of a centralized state is bound up with the desire, seen as a need, to make war. As Weil wrote, "What a country calls its vital economic interests are not the things which enable its citizens to live, but the things which enable it to make war ... Thus when war is waged it is for the purpose of safeguarding or increasing one's capacity to make war."[64]

But educating a populace in violence and aggression backfires. In Julius Caesar's Rome, it was dangerous to walk on the street at night without bodyguards carrying torches. Areas of London were too dangerous even for the police in the nineteenth century, as we know from Dickens; and most large cities in the West are unsafe today. If a leadership wants to foster violence in a population yet retain social order, it must utterly intimidate the entire population— as the colonels did in Greece (from 1967 to 1974), as Hitler did in Germany, as the Soviet government does. And this extreme measure is urged by some people in the United States today. If a state fosters aggressiveness without brutal intimidation of its population, that aggressiveness will spill out in unwanted and unexpected forms.

Of all Western nations, the United States is the most violent. In 1977, ten American men died by violence for every Japanese, Austrian, West German, or Swedish male.[65] More people are killed weekly in some American cities than in a year of violence in Northern Ireland, in a state of civil war. American culture is violent, from television films to cinema, from football to a secretary of defense who talks about nuclear war as if Americans (but not their "enemies") could survive it.

We would not have such a violent culture if we did not want a violent culture. Whatever its biological root, aggressiveness is learned. One need not even exalt violence (as our movies and television films in fact do) to foster it: one need only create a culture that worships power, individuality, disconnection from others, and competition; and disparages the satisfactions of life devoted to affection, fellowship, and harmony. Since aggressiveness is learned, it is a moral rather than a biological quality. We can thus choose to esteem it or not. We should also realize that cultures that exalt aggression and the qualities that foster it are invariably militaristic, and, in the past, have destroyed themselves through war.

On the other hand, it will not do to declare aggression, wrath, a "deadly sin" and demand its extirpation. We can no more preclude aggressiveness than we can domination: there is no way to eliminate these qualities from human life. What we can do is esteem it less. Some assertiveness, even a degree of aggressiveness, is beneficial; lively contest helps people to form themselves and grow. Remembering that societies foster aggressiveness in males in order to prepare them for use as soldiers, remembering also that exalting the individualistic, isolated, violent "hero" is a major means of such fostering, we must reconsider and recreate our culture, not by attempting to eliminate aggressiveness but by attempting to subordinate it to, make it a means to, pleasure.

Aggression is often linked with sex: the two "drives" have frequently been seen as the source of all human disorder, and Freud claimed that aggression is the foundation of all relations of affection "with the single exception, perhaps, of the mother's relation to her male child."[66] In Western culture there does exist a strong aggressive component in sex, and, for some people, a sexual component in aggression. The motivation of rape is not sexual pleasure but a desire to degrade and humiliate another, and to demonstrate control and domination: many rapists are unable to reach orgasm or even to maintain erection in the act.[67] Some male killers select only women, and usually a particular kind of woman—blondes or brunettes, prostitutes, young women or old women, girls—as their victims, while others select only young boys whom they rape before they kill. Men who fight each other physically often feel affection or even love for each other after their contact. Even tender lovemaking may involve acts that cause pain—pinching, biting, anal penetration. Violence between spouses constitutes 57 percent of all family violence, and 91 percent of that consists of attacks upon women by their husbands or former husbands.[68]

Again we are confronted with the question of whether this linkage is biological or cultural: and behind the argument that any quality is rooted in biology lies the assumption that if it biological it is unchangeable. And again we must recognize that if a quality is biologically rooted it will be utterly, totally universal. It is utterly universal that we eat, excrete, require sleep, warmth, and shelter. It is utterly universal that we have emotions. But the sources of our emotional expressions differ, as do the expressions themselves.

With regard to sex, it seems universally true that all cultures regulate sexuality in some way. I know of no studies of the linkage of sex and aggression in simple societies, but it is clear that not all cultures link sex and aggression as Western patriarchy does. So again we must consider what such a linkage provides, what end it serves.

## 6. SEX

It is generally believed that repression and regulation are necessary to control the two major sources of human disruption, aggression and sex. In the West, this notion can be traced at least as far back as Plato, who taught that reason must be the chariot driver controlling the two horses, concupiscence and irascibility. Yet the two threats are not perceived as equal. Sexuality is as heightened and fostered as aggression by books, television, films, and an entire subculture of pornography and illicit sex, but it is also more often blamed for the "corruption" of humans than aggression is. This has been true through most, perhaps all, of Western civilization. No rendering of aggression, no matter how ugly and violent, mechanical and inhuman, pathetic and terrifying its depiction in Shakespeare, Goya, or the reminiscences of prisoners in concentration camps, for example, possesses the profound horror, the sense of filth and taint, demoralization or fatality, the hate and abhorrence of depictions of sex in Shakespeare (consider Hamlet's excoriation of his mother, Claudio's of Hero, *Troilus and Cressida* and *Measure for Measure* in their entirety), *fin-de-siècle* painting (Aubrey Beardsley's "Salome" is only one version of this subject, popular in the late nineteenth century; Edvard Munch's "Vampires" and "Jealousy" are other examples), or meetings of ERA opponents, for instance.

Aggression per se is often unambiguously admired in our society. Sex may also be admired, in an image, say, of Marilyn Monroe, but never without the revealing giggle. Literature describing aggression is not removed from the shelves of libraries or magazine shops, and almost never is any art form censored for aggressive content. Books, magazines, films, and plays about sex *are* censored in the West, and even more rigorously in authoritarian states—in Brazil and South Africa, Poland and the Soviet Union, China and Iran. At the same time there has been an increase in Western commoditization of sex involving degrading images of women and considerable pornographic depiction of violence toward women.[69]

To glimpse the difference in how these areas are regarded, imagine that you have young children who are playing in a garden behind your house. You glance out a back window and see them fighting. Your decision whether to run out and stop the fight will depend on who is fighting and how. You glance out and see them in sexual play: there is no question about what most people would do, regardless of which children were involved or the degree of gentleness of the play.

True, many books and even organizations teach that sex is a natural, healthy activity, but the existence of such an argument testifies to the existence of an opposed view. The position taken in this chapter is that despite individual variation, despite the existence of a huge sex industry, patriarchal morality considers sex the greatest evil. Why this should be is a question that has been addressed in various ways throughout this book. Here let us try to summarize the answers.

Sexual desire is one of the most powerful impulses in the human makeup. It can, on occasion, be stronger than the need for food or drink, warmth or rest, safety or other bonds. However, it is not often so strong. It can be put aside in a way that need for food cannot. One can go without sex for long periods, and one will not die from lack of sex even if it is eschewed lifelong. The sexual urge therefore appears to be subject to volition in a way other basic needs are not.

Judith Ochshorn has studied attitudes toward sex in ancient manuscripts of polytheistic cultures in Sumer, Egypt, Babylonia, and Crete, among others, dating to periods in which patriarchy was not yet fully developed. She reports that in these documents, sexual distinctions were less important than social or individual differences; that the exercise of divine power was not seen as the exclusive prerogative of either sex; and that rarely was ascription of power to a deity of one sex connected with ascription of inferiority to the other. Perhaps most important, fear of female biology and sexuality is entirely lacking in this literature. All kinds of sexual liaisons occur, both goddesses and gods are depicted as sexually active, and no dichotomy is drawn between body and spirit, nor does sex or body carry any taint of "sin."[70] Although we cannot automatically project actual sexual customs from the literature of any culture, Ochshorn documents cases in which literature depicted female sexuality as linked to the benefit of the human community, in cultures which held liberal attitudes toward women's sexuality.[71]

However sex was viewed in matricentric eons or in early patriarchy, the view of sex that has endured and permeated Western culture emerged from a monotheistic religion in which deity was male. Almost our entire cultural inheritance regarding sex was created by men, and since many, perhaps most, men experience desire as desire for women, women have been the objects, the receptacles, and the antagonists of male desire. In addition, because of the association of women and sex with procreation, sex has been seen as a quality *inhering* in women. That is, it has not been seen as a human characteristic but as a female one. Male sexuality is acknowledged, recognized, yet at the same time disavowed. Just as Adam says to God, "The woman whom thou gavest to be with me, she gave me of the tree, and I did eat" (Genesis 3:12), patriarchal culture sees sex as a temptation offered men by women—an assault, as it were, on men's weakest point. Men's surrender to women's temptation has been seen as a sin; if it is sometimes a forgivable one, it is also a source of guilt.

Yet there is nothing inherent in sex that necessarily arouses guilt. The sexual lives of those animals closest to humans in makeup appear to be volitional, free, and without moral consequence. Some might say that animals do not have a moral life, yet the fact that they choose certain patterns over others, accept certain behaviors and not others, is indicative of a kind of choice which in humans we call moral. But animals live so as to facilitate their basic activities—the getting of food and rest, procreation, and the rearing of the young. In contrast, for several millennia much of what we call civilized life has been organized in a way that makes procreation and child rearing difficult to combine with obtaining food and rest. Insofar as sex is procreative, it has consequences for the economic survival of child rearers. Sometimes these consequences have entailed moral sanctions.

We have seen that patriarchy established itself with the idea of sacrifice: only sacrifice of something precious could prove men's fidelity to a transcendent being who demanded obedience. The sacrifices required were of those relationships most dear to men, which could undermine their commitment to the transcendent deity—relationships with their children and their women. Men were taught to view these connections as secondary, even contaminated, since they involved men in nature, body, and emotion, the very elements that were to be transcended. A major area of men's attachment to women is sex.

The earliest extant patriarchal literature suggests that sex is contaminating for men. The Levites, the priestly group, laid down for men of Israel a set of rules and regulations governing social and political relations. They devoted one book, Leviticus, primarily to men's relations with their own bodies—in disease, in relation to food, and in relation to women. In all three, men's contact with nature is described as extremely perilous, requiring regulation, taboo, and purification either after or before such contacts. Certain animals (notably the pig, sacred to Demeter, a manifestation of the Great Goddess) and particular parts of animals—usually the nether half—were perceived as more abominable than others, and were taboo. So were certain sexual acts—having intercourse with a mother and her daughter, or with one's father's wife, with a menstruating woman, or with another man, for instance. But *all* forms of sexual intercourse were unclean and required purification, cleansing. Even wet dreams (and presumably masturbation, which is condemned by analogy in Genesis) make a man unclean. However, there is no suggestion in Leviticus that because of this uncleanness, men should avoid sexual intercourse: that idea remained to Christianity. In fact, in Judaism intercourse was required; a man had an obligation to beget sons, and Deuteronomy decreed the levirate, ruling that if a man died without begetting a son, his brother must marry his widow to provide him with male issue posthumously.

Although the original prohibitions in Leviticus probably arose from a strong sense of the power of nature (associated with women), what remained vivid for later ages was the sense of taint and uncleanness, of human pollution not caused by food or disease but through women, by sex. The sense of woman as tainted entered Western civilization not just through the Hebraic strain but also through the Greek, or Hellenistic. As mentioned before, one of the earliest Greek writers, Hesiod, spent considerable space in vituperation against women. Plato asserted that the body was lower than the reason, and that unconsummated sexual desire was in some way "higher," nobler, than consummation of desire between men. For the Greeks of the Golden Age, sex with women had only one purpose—to produce sons. Aristotle saw women as defective men—as a separate species from men, inferior to them, lacking full human equipment. Yet at the same time, men of these ancient periods attributed great (albeit negative) powers to women. If this power is not mentioned by the Greek philosophers of the Golden Age, it does appear in Greek drama of the period. Even the Romans showed evidence of this feeling, in *The Aeneid*, for example, and in Catullus' brilliant poems castigating the unworthy Lesbia, who has the power to paralyze and enslave him. When women are seen with contempt (for their inferiority) and fear (of their power, their ability to pollute), sex with women is inevitably fraught with the same emotions.

Christianity posited an afterlife, a realm superior to earth; ineluctably this provided a judgment upon and contrast with the actual world and actual life. Life became a miserable period of probation, not an end in itself but a means to eternal felicity or damnation. The world was contemptible because it was made up of matter, which rots, becomes corrupt, and of experiences which are transient, in contrast to the (hypothetical) eternal realm. Earlier dichotomies had diminished nature and flesh as inferior to man and reason; and earlier cultures had depicted women as threatening and/or contemptible. But Christianity added another dimension to this duality: nature and flesh and women constituted a threat to man's eternal soul.

We know little about the sex lives of most people through the Middle Ages. Illuminations on manuscripts are rife with images of animals symbolic of sexuality (rabbits, for example), or depictions of large-stomached men playing bagpipes: the bagpipe, which inflates and deflates, was a metaphor for the responsive penis. Some folk tales suggest a bouncy lighthearted lust in both women and men, a delight in conniving to evade sexual regulation; so does some of Chaucer's work. But most documents preserved, especially from the earlier Middle Ages, were written by the clergy, and often by monks. Although we know priests married during much of this period, and later, with unofficial sanction by the Church, kept concubines, sex was a sin for monks, and it is as a sin that it appears in their writing. Here too, however, and even while women are being castigated as sinks of evil and sewers of sin, there is a recurrent and simultaneous assumption that women have great power. As late as Milton, Adam is portrayed as so meltingly adoring of Eve that he chooses damnation with her rather than salvation (through obedience to God) without her.

Medieval saints' tales always involve repudiation of sex, and when the saint is female, this repudiation is her central—and often entire—claim to virtue. Medieval romance shows different attitudes toward sex. In some desire is called love, is heightened by continual if intermittent thwarting, and is resolved with a joyful unification of the lovers. In those romances that became most influential, however, like the legend of Tristan and Isolde, consummation is taboo, and passion is heightened by that taboo: coming together is equivalent to death, just as throughout the Renaissance orgasm was called dying. These two strands permeate the literature of Europe through the nineteenth century.

The patriarchal campaign against sex mounted in the eighteenth century. Ariès describes the openness with which bodily functions were discussed and performed in France up to then: children slept with servants, who played with them sexually; brothers and sisters slept together. But from the late seventeenth century onward, there was an increasing insistence by authorities—in this case, medical doctors and religious advisers—that "modesty" should be enforced upon children lest they lose their "purity."[72] From the eighteenth to the nineteenth century, many sexual acts were labeled *perversions*: "sexual irregularity was annexed to mental illness."[73] Sexual inclinations were given names: inversion, gerontophilia, fetishism, sadism, masochism. Foucault asserts that the Victorian obsession with "perversions" was not a result of a refinement of the moral sense, or a new scrupulousness, but rather the manifestation of a drive to control the last bastion of nature, "bodies and their pleasures."[74]

Doctors in Europe and America set themselves up as experts on the body, promising that those who obeyed their prescriptions would achieve physical vigor and moral cleanliness; eugenicists planned to eliminate the defective and degenerate—whatever those words signified.[75] Everything would be controlled, regulated, planned by an elite; a society would be manufactured that was orderly, clean, healthy, and, presumably, happy. Lucien Febvre discusses how, in this period, all emotional activities and expression were "held in check and increasingly repressed" by an ever-growing, "ever-spreading system of intellectual activities which conquered, dominated, and increasingly pushed back the emotions to the very edge, one might say, to the outskirts of life, relegated to a secondary, contemptible role."[76] Among the emotions subjected to control, desire was primary: Foucault comments that the organizing and regulating of sex had the intention of "proliferating, innovating, annexing, creating, and penetrating bodies in an increasingly detailed way, and in controlling populations in an increasingly comprehensive way." Like other parts of nature the body was exploited "as an object of knowledge and an element in relations of power."[77] It was in this period that the penis came to be the symbol of power in literature.

One effect of this "advance" in the power of power was that in the human imagination sex was penetrated by and merged with power. But when sex is power, it is excised from the domain of freedom and becomes a form of domination. Power had for millennia been an element in sexual transactions, but the two dimensions were not seen as identical. Once sex had been "tamed," brought into line with patriarchal values, it could be packaged and sold like anything else. But the permeation of sex by power has had ramifications beyond the commercial world.

It was not until the late seventeenth century that references to sadomasochistic sexual pleasure began to appear. Apparently stimulated by widespread flogging of boys at school, it was labeled *le vice Anglais*, and by the eighteenth century was well established among both genders.[78] In the eighteenth century sadomasochistic erotic literature began to appear in France—Choderlos de Laclos's *Les Liaisons Dangereuses*, for instance, and the work of the Marquis de Sade.

In these works sex is primarily a power relation. Deriving perhaps from the poetry of the Languedoc, sonnets addressed by lowly poets to high-placed ladies, a tradition that continued through the sixteenth century in England; or from folk tales in which, for instance, Aristotle is tamed, ridden like a horse, and whipped by his mistress, or wives are tamed through beating and other punishments—the tradition of power as an element in sex was given an entirely new form of expression in the eighteenth century. The folk tales carried no suggestion that the taming of a wife was in itself titillating; and the love poetry concentrated on the martyrdom of the male poet. The new expression merged sexual power and domination into a single consuming and ecstatic experience. Moreover, although *Les Liaisons* depicts both a man and a woman as manipulating others into sexual submission, the objects of both are women—Madame de Merteuil acts on women out of desire for revenge against men, or out of envy; Valmont acts on women out of desire to seduce them, or to avenge himself on Madame, or on a man. In the work of de Sade too, the victim of manipulation and punishment is always female.

In this literature, the main source of sexual pleasure is humiliation with pain: the pain is necessary to create the humiliation, which is the abject surrender of the victim. This surrender of the victim's will to the will of another, the controller, is equivalent to the "surrender" of orgasm. The victim is always female, the controller always male, although the perspective of such works is usually the female's. In other words, both men and women who read sadomasochistic pornography identify with the victim. This is extremely important, not just because it challenges the notion that women are by nature masochistic and men are not, or because it shows both sexes as masochistic, but because it offers insight into our symbolic experience of sex. It is the female, or those qualities associated with the female *in us*, that feels; it is the "female" part that abandons control; and that, no longer legitimate in its own right, must be coerced into its greatest pleasure.

Whatever the supposedly dominant partner actually feels, he must seem not only in control but unfeeling. Susan Griffin suggests that "what makes the Don Juan and the femme fatale of pornographic culture both cruel and victorious is that they are in control of nature, particularly the nature of their own bodies. *They are unfeeling.*"[79] And Gilles Deleuze argues that the apathy, the unmoved disinterest of de Sade's heroes depends upon "denying nature within the self and outside the self, and denying the self itself."[80]

This is important, too. In Christian literature, males as well as females underwent the pains of martyrdom: the prime Christian figure, after all, is Jesus nailed to the cross. Most love poetry focuses on the sufferings of males, not females, sufferings imposed by proud, hardhearted women. But by the eighteenth century, a period in which control over nature had become the primary pursuit of an industrializing society and its intellectual establishment, women become the invariable victims of men who are supremely, arrogantly, always in control.

Sadomasochistic literature did not reach a wide audience, nor did it create a major tradition at the time. But toward the end of the nineteenth century, a new spate of vituperation against women arose in Europe (and especially in Germany) and Decadent painting and literature again presents the powerful, seductive, but horrifying female seducing and undermining a "pure," resistant, good but vulnerable male. The female figure is merged with the animal and the demon. This sense of things continues in the work of early twentieth-century writers and painters; some, like Hemingway and Henry Miller, showed men wreaking just revenge on bitchy women. Many men may fall victim to such a woman's wiles, but the real man puts her in her place, which is beneath his feet.

With regard to sex, nonpornographic male literature of the later twentieth century falls into three major categories: sex is absent for the most part (in such work, women are also insignificant figures); the work portrays women as bitches, and relations between the sexes as an unremitting war; or it portrays sex as a violent, fragmented event. Consider, for example, the writings of Norman Mailer, Philip Roth, Thomas Pynchon, John Hawkes, Anthony Burgess, John Osborn, among innumerable others. The trend in literature, then, parallels the dominant trend in Western society in this century: the value of control has heightened dizzily, irrationally; there is increasing contempt for the "feminine" elements of life; and there is an increasing awareness that the relations between the sexes are rooted in power, domination.

The nature of sadomasochism in pornographic literature has changed in recent years. The titillating humiliation and pain that leave no scars and do not

harm organs have given way to severe pain and·degradation. The controller uri-
nates in the victim's face, smears her with semen or feces. Sometimes the victim is mutilated; sometimes she is killed. Some pornographic films, called
"snuff" films after the title of the first one, are said to have recorded the actual
torture, mutilation, and murder of their "lead actress."[81]

The significance of this shift is frightening. Many feminists believe that
the increase in rape and wife battering is connected with increased violence in
pornography, and studies have shown a correlation between early exposure to
violent pornography and these kinds of violence toward women.[82] In addition,
the punishments of the older pornography were ritual, symbolic: they served as
imaginative motivations in the process of excitation. Nonsadomasochistic pornography of the past is full of boring repetitions that function only as motivations to masturbation, like the repetitious motions of intercourse. The old
sadomasochistic pornography depicts sex as a power relation; the new sadomasochistic pornography suggests that sex and death are indeed identical, that allowing oneself to abandon control enough to feel sexual excitation is an act
equivalent to mutilating or murdering the "feminine" qualities within the self.
Like the Aztecs, who, when they began to worship death, renamed their
Mother Goddess the "Filth Eater"—finding in "feminine" values only the
loathsome and destructive, the inexorable and slimy earth—our culture, which
worships above all else the power to kill, has reached the point of wishing to
annihilate all that is "feminine" in our world.

There are people in our culture who do not just read about but practice
sadomasochistic eroticism, and who insist that the sexuality embodied in whippings and torture is the truest, most profound sex. Such ideas were first expressed publicly—as far as I know—by a group of articulate, cultivated,
intelligent gay men. Shops selling sadomasochistic accouterments—whips,
chains, leather, breast rings, manacles—cater mainly to gay males. Edmund
White describes the "masculinization" of the gay life style: gay men now disdain the old "butterfly" image, he asserts, and want partners who are "macho,"
"butch," "masculine," with a "straight appearance." Personal advertisements
for partners may include the stricture "no femmes need apply." "So extreme is
this masculinization," he writes, "that it has been termed 'macho fascism' by
its critics."[83]

But even gay males not given to sadomasochism and its chains-and-leather
bars have moved increasingly toward a conception of sex as power, and sexual
pleasure as humiliation. Men who shun such milieus as pool halls and motor-
cycle clubs may be found in baths or the back rooms of bars, where men sit in
the dark and arouse themselves to erection while others walk through groping
for the anonymous penis that pleases them with its size; or insert their penises
through holes in a wall, on the other side of which men pass, stopping to give a
blow job to those that appeal. Such a sexuality may coexist with a peaceful relationship between a man and his lover; or it may provide a man's only sex. But
this form of sex, anonymous, totally cut off from other parts of the person and
from any emotion except a limited sort of desire, is necessarily humiliating and
fragmenting. Those who choose it presumably find it more exciting than other

forms of sex—perhaps precisely because it is isolated and concealed, and can be blotted out from the rest of one's life.

Gay men who believe sadomasochism to be the truest and most exquisite form of sex tend to sneer at lesbian sex as being "mock pro." They see lesbian sex as being gentle and tender, deeply interwoven with intimacy and the daily events of life, with true knowing of and affection for the other. In calling it "mock pro," gay men are accusing it of resembling procreative, heterosexual sex. Their contempt is shared by those lesbians who prefer sadomasochism and exalt it as the "quintessence of nonreproductive sex."[84] Those who mock "procreative" sex are exalting themselves for enjoying a form of sex that deviates from what they consider the gentle, tedious path of ordinary people; but in fact, sadomasochism is the paradigm of heterosexual sex in the Western world.

People who would be horrified at the thought of whips and chains, bondage, the infliction or reception of pain, who would never enter a chains-and-leather bar, or attend a whipping party, or walk together to a party with the male dragging the female by a chain attached to a fetter around her neck, she in chains, he in leather; men who do not slap or spank their female partners, who do not humiliate them physically during sex—still enact the same drama more mildly, less consciously. Men hold women's wrists during intercourse, so they cannot move their arms; they bite or suck breasts to the point of pain; they refuse to allow their women to be in control at any point in any way, including taking the top ("dominant") position. Some men rape their wives or lovers. Men who do none of these things may fail to arouse their wives, and simply leap on them, front or back, and hump them as if they were animals, but animals who are not in heat, who feel little. Some men rape strangers. Nor are such men aberrant, deviations from the norm of maleness in our culture. As Susan Brownmiller suggested, and later studies have affirmed, imprisoned rapists test "normal" in personality, appearance, intelligence, behavior, and sexual drive, although they are somewhat quicker to show rage. Other studies characterize rapists as meek and mild-mannered.[85]

But even men who do not defend violent sex insist that a relation of domination is necessary for male sexual excitation. Cultural patterns seem to support this position. Respectable, conforming couples often show a relation of dominance and subservience. Insistence that a husband should be older than his wife—or taller, richer, more intelligent, better educated, of higher social status—comes from a belief that men should dominate women. Insistence that men should be paid more than women, that they are more worthy of regard and respect, or are legitimate in ways women are not: all such ideas imply a vision of relations between the sexes that is based on power, and the sexual relation that follows from such a vision is equally charged with power.

Indeed, many men assert that males cannot function without female subordination. Friedan discusses writers like Steven Goldberg and Lionel Tiger, who believe that feminism is attacking the "natural, inexorable, predestined superiority of the male" and is creating a backlash as increasing numbers of men find themselves impotent. They claim this impotence will destroy reproduction and the "aggressive thrust of civilization."[86] Abraham Maslow asserted that "normal" sexual happiness can occur in our society only when the male plays the dominant role.[87] George Gilder asserts that men are savage and predatory by sexual nature, in a continual state of heat.[88]

What such writers are essentially claiming, and what our cultural arrangements suggest, is that sadomasochistic sex is not an alternative path taken by a few, but the very main street; it is not a challenge to the culture but a realization of its underlying principles. Robert Stoller, perhaps following Freud's comment that affection is rooted in aggression, asserts that aside from direct stimulation of body parts, sexual excitement is "hostility—the desire, overt or hidden, to harm another person," and believes that the components of sexual excitement are triumph, rage, revenge, fear, anxiety, and risk.[89] Georges Bataille claims that "sexual activity is a form of violence," that the male assails, despoils, and lays open the female, who is his victim.[90]

For these writers sadomasochism is the core of sexuality, its truest form. Indeed, Stoller concludes that sadomasochism is the central feature of most sexual excitement—sexual desire is a desire to hurt others in revenge for having been hurt.[91] If, for Bataille, it is the male who utterly destroys the female, for Stoller, females triumph over men through their masochism; as Andrea Dworkin puts it, the woman ultimately controls the man because she is the provocation to which he responds.[92]

Yet reports of actual s/m relations reveal that both males and females prefer to play "bottom," the submissive partner, the "masochist."[93] Indeed, sadomasochism takes its name from two men: the Marquis de Sade, the first explicit writer of this sort of pornography, and Leopold von Sacher-Masoch, who wrote similar works in a later period. Moreover, it is significant that sadomasochistic literature did not appear until the eighteenth century, the age in which the drive to power-over, toward control of all human experience, was given new impetus by science and industrialization. It is entirely possible that sadomasochism is the sexuality appropriate to an age in which it has become impossible to abandon oneself, in which the maintenance of control has become mandatory, and in which the experience of coercion is universal. Sadomasochism is a symbolic and ritual mode of gaining pleasure through coercion, and an expression of inability to give up control freely, volitionally. It is an acting out of the belief that loss of control in sex is a loss of control *to* another. Yet it is the "masochistic" partner, the "bottom," who retains control of sadomasochistic events.[94]

If the one who is abused is actually in control, the one who abuses, who seems to triumph, is actually submissive. The sadomasochistic vision of sex is as a power relation, love as war, in which the "male" figure triumphs but surrenders, and the "female" figure surrenders but triumphs. The "male" must triumph or collapse, like Simone Weil's slavemaster, who "cannot conceive of any other mode of action than that of commanding," and who, when slaves simply refuse to obey, "passes all of a sudden from the feeling of absolute power to that of utter impotence."[95]

Not all humans demonstrate such a sexual psychology, and it is extremely unlikely that such attitudes are implanted in our genes. It is true that we know little about sexuality beyond its physiological workings—indeed, what we know about those workings has been mainly discovered in the past few decades. But we must suspect any argument based on genetic tendency that functions as pseudoscientific support for an ideology. Claims that men are by nature predatory and violent, or aggressive, or sexual dominators, or anti-Semitic, or hierarchical—all claims that have been made by biological determinists—support various kinds of patriarchal status quo, but have utterly no basis in biology so far as we know now.

Human sexuality has been differently perceived in different periods, and is viewed variously in cultures existing simultaneously. In the West it has been seen as corrupt and tainted, but necessary; or as a drive that could be controlled and even extirpated by the virtuous; or as natural but unnaturally limited, since all humans are bisexual by nature.[96] At present, sexual violence is pervasive and part of men's normal functioning, as Allan Griswold Johnson observes (after studying sexually abused girls).[97] Since the idea of domination pervades every other area of our society, it is not surprising that it has also infiltrated our thinking about sex. Sex is not a fixed unalterable drive, with fixed, "instinctive" modes of expression. In the Middle Ages, when virginity was exalted, many people chose that; during the Victorian Age, when sex was expected to be repressed, many people repressed it; in cultures which reward prostitution more highly than other semiskilled labor, many people become prostitutes. Although we cannot determine the relation between our "natural" biological sexuality and our sexual enculturation, we can state with assurance that sexual enculturation is highly significant. And that means that the way we think and feel affects our sexuality, which in turn means that we can alter our sexual expressions. Michael Ignatieff suggests that it may be impossible to distinguish among a set of " 'true needs' of the body against the 'false needs' of a culture of sexual violence," that there may indeed be no true, essential sexual self. He suggests we can alter our sexuality by the application of reason.[98]

To alter our thinking about sex, however, we must understand how our thinking has been directed in the past, and what purposes that direction has served.

There is a passage in James Joyce's A Portrait of the Artist as a Young Man that expresses vividly the attitude toward sex held by many people in Joyce's time, before it, and even now. The hero, Stephen Dedalus, driven by fierce adolescent desire, has visited prostitutes. Heavy with a sense of his own "bestiality," he is subjected to a retreat, a period of religious devotion, during which he listens for three days to powerful sermons on sin and punishment, threatening vividly the torments of hell, and urging purification. In blind panic he stumbles through the streets of Dublin, searching for a church where he is not known so as to confess to a priest to whom he is unfamiliar. He knows his sin is "too grievous to be atoned for in whole or in part by a false homage to the Allseeing and Allknowing"; it is one of those "unspeakable sins by which degraded man outrages and defiles the temple of the Holy Ghost, defiles and pollutes himself." He finds a church and enters the confessional, but is still impelled to flee; at the moment the priest slides open the window, he thinks that he "could still escape from the shame. Had it been any terrible crime but that one sin! Had it been murder!"[99]

This is a staggering set of priorities, as Joyce was suggesting. We may understand that the establishment of patriarchy required educating men to fear and loathe sex in order to extricate them from their bonds to women. We know that when women were turned into property, sex became a commercial exchange, which is essentially a power relation. Women were not only literally sold and bought as slaves, they were part of exchanges of property, appurtenances in men's attempts to increase their wealth. At the same time, women's sexuality was straitly guarded to ensure "legitimate" heirs to men's property. In the eighteenth century, sex was one area focused on by those who wished to increase men's power of knowledge, and it was in this period that "normal" sex was differentiated from "deviations." Although these attitudes remain forceful in certain parts of the world, and remnants exist in all Western societies, the reasons these attitudes came into existence have faded in much of the urban industrial world.

Nevertheless, the urban industrial world has taken these attitudes a step further, and turned sex into mere commodity. Sexual bodily appeal is used to sell everything from hardware to liquor; the ideology of sex for males fostered by magazines, films, and television is that it is a purely sensual experience, without regard for persons or feelings—not just love, but even affection, even personal rapport are shown to be extraneous to the new athletic sex. Only in this form, as a merchandising tool, or as a purchasable experience (like a vibrator, say), has sex finally become tamed enough to be acceptable to capitalistic patriarchy. Sex as commodity is not a matter of bodies and integrated pleasure, but of body image and pleasure image.

Yet sex is essentially a joyful and harmless activity; by itself it is incapable of harm. When it is mutually shared, it is an act of innocence, one that has the potential for arousing the greatest sensuous pleasure of which we are capable, and that satisfies mind and emotion as well. Sex is an act of simple pleasure when it is unmixed with aggression, power, or the possibility of transmission of disease (something that can happen without sex as well). But sex has never been forbidden or regulated because it can transmit disease; sex alone of bodily functions is warned against as bestial, expressive of "mere animal lust," degrading and polluted. Ernest Becker claims that sexual guilt arises because, "Sex is of the body and the body is of death."[100] Yet other functions that are "of the body," like eating, have not since ancient Judaic times been seen as dangerous or lethal. Norman O. Brown's more complex analysis moves to a similar conclusion. He sees the "universal" denial of sex as rooted in a "universal" denial of death. Since we reject death, we reject bodily pleasure, which reminds us of death.[101] But none of these "explanations" suggests why death should be of the body and not the mind; why rejection of the body should mean denial of sex rather than any other bodily process; or why diminishment of sex should automatically involve diminishment of women.

Sex lies under some cloud of taint in all patriarchal cultures; it is not acceptable except when it becomes an instrument or expression of control; that is, when it is merely a part of power, and not a separate and unrelated element. Ernest Becker wrote that sex threatens men because it represents "the defeat of individuality, of personality."[102] In the dualistic thinking of the Western world, one does not simply give up control, one gives it up *to* someone else. Since most past writing about sex comes from men, the someone else to whom control is surrendered is usually female. This sense of things has been turned around and projected onto women from the late Middle Ages to the present, in verbal formulations in which sex was characterized not as affection but as the vanquishing, conquering, or winning of women. Today, a man "lays" a woman, or "scores." That the moment of orgasm is experienced as a giving up of control by both sexes is irrelevant to such formulations. The individuality, personality, that Becker sees as "defeated" in sex is only male.

There are some realistic grounds for men to feel that they give up control to a woman in sex. Women can fake a pleasure they do not feel; their arousal is not visible. And women who are owned or rented frequently do fake pleasure, for excellent reasons. Some women lie passively inert during sex, refusing to pretend a pleasure they do not feel. Some men feel desire for women they despise; this inevitably arouses repugnance after intercourse, and men's tendency is to avoid self-contempt by casting that repugnance on the woman alone. In such cases a man gives up control (experiences orgasm) unilaterally, alone; or derives pleasure from someone he disdains. Both lead men to feel vulnerable, subject to others they cannot control.

But such feelings result from a notion of sex as a controlling act, one among many expressions of domination, a function within a power relation. It is this vision of sex that lies behind men's lascivious gazes as they visually appropriate women's bodies; men's whistles at women on the street, reminding women that they are not free, cannot be unselfconscious; and men's freedom in touching the bodies of unfamiliar women as they stand back like gentlemen to allow women to precede them. Women's awareness of this causes them to resent such behavior.

The form of sex that has been given least emphasis in patriarchal societies is mutual sex. This is not for lack of examples. There exist many love poems of delight and joy in mutual sex; novels in which sexual love is integrated into families, communities; paintings and sculptures which express mutuality. Mutual sex exists in a different dimension from sex as a form of domination; it exists in the realm of pleasure, to which power is irrelevant. Sex continues to be diminished or deformed in patriarchal societies because volitional mutual sex offers the most desirable and accessible path to a morality truly opposed to power worship, a morality of pleasure and freedom.

Even Freud, who insisted that we recognize the existence of infant sexuality, and who in 1929 lamented that civilization "does not like sexuality as a source of pleasure in its own right and is only prepared to tolerate it because there is so far no substitute for it as a means of propagating the human race," accepted the proscription of manifestations of sexuality in children, "for there would be no prospect of curbing the sexual lusts of adults if the ground had not been prepared for it in childhood."[103] He wrote that it was impossible to support conventional sexual morality or approve of the means used to regulate sexuality, adding that "what the world calls its code of morals demands more sacrifice than it is worth," and that this code was "neither dictated by honesty [nor] instituted with wisdom."[104] At the same time, however, he believed that pleasure, especially sexual pleasure, must be devalued, set aside, if the work of maintaining civilization was to continue. He found love a value far inferior to work because "we are never so defenceless against suffering as when we love, never so helplessly unhappy as when we have lost our loved object or its love."[105]

For power to remain society's highest value requires vigilant maintenance of coercive structures. It requires teaching people to conform, to take their place in the hierarchy and bow their heads to the "truth," the brute fact of power. The greatest threat—indeed, the only threat—to this vision of life is a morality in which something matters more than power, in which a more positive value replaces power. Patriarchy cannot continue, it cannot survive, if people turn away from power and move toward pleasure. And of all elements on earth, pleasure is the one that is least able to be coerced.

People with power can compel behavior, by physical force or threats of punishment of other kinds. People can constrain our speech, our writing, our art, our manners, the totality of the way we live. They can coerce us to think as they want us to think, through education and controlled culture, through censorship of many sorts. When other methods fail, eradication of certain people can terrify the rest into submission. Authorities can force people to do, to write, to paint, to work a machine. But they cannot force people to feel pleasure. Authorities can coerce people to act as if they felt pleasure; or to assert that obedience (to God, to the state, to the Highness) confers the greatest pleasure upon humans; they can teach a society to seek pleasure in one activity rather than in others. In these ways they can influence the experience of pleasure. But they cannot coerce the experience.

And of all pleasures, sex is the most intense. Sex is the core of pleasure, which is the realm in which freedom lives. Freedom is the state in which the greatest possible harmony and sense of rightness obtains among body, emotions, and mind. Freedom and pleasure are among the values that feminism upholds. Many people deplore the unhappy consequences of an age they see as sexually "free": but sexual freedom does not exist now and has never existed as a cultural standard in history. (It may have existed in prehistory.) To achieve it, we must get beyond the worship of power, a sense that hierarchy is the only possible structure, and our sense of sex as tainted. To get to freedom of any sort, we must get beyond gender roles and the definition of man as the controller, woman as the controlled.

## 7. GENDER ROLES

Although many people believe it is women who work harder to maintain gender roles, to teach their daughters to be "ladies," and their sons to be "gentlemen," studies have revealed that in late twentieth-century America, men are more concerned than women that their children adopt "proper"—that is, dictated, traditional sex-role behavior.[106] Other studies show that boys have more difficulty accepting their appropriate sex role. David Lynn, who has conducted a number of these studies, attributes boys' difficulties to three sources: lack of male models, the rigidity and harshness of masculine roles, and the negative nature of the requirements.[107] Boys especially appear to suffer from the fact that fathers are absent, whether emotionally or physically, and from the lack of other significant males in their young lives. And the male role in patriarchal society consists, as we have seen, largely of sacrifices—men must give up the hope of happiness, the ideal of home, emotional expressiveness and spontaneity, in order to become members of an elite that values power, wandering isolation, individuality, and discipline (order in obedience).

The fact that the male role does not gratify a boy, does not arise from primary desire but from the secondary desire of wanting to be like other boys or wanting to be a man like others he sees (on television, in films, in comic books, in history books), may account for the rigid, almost ritualistic way in which many adult men "play" their roles. Lynn discovered that boys who lack fathers entirely are more likely to entertain exaggerated and stereotypical images of masculinity than boys who have fathers, no matter how absent or violent.[108]

What Westerners mean when they say they want to make a man out of a boy is that they want a boy to learn that the sacrifices mentioned above are essential, are *the* characteristics of men. And the schools, or gymnasia, or army training camps to which people send boys to "make men of them" specialize in brutalization: rigid discipline, emphasis on physical hardness and strength, and contempt for sensitivity, delicacy, and emotion. Fortunately, not all boys are subjected to such treatment, but no boy escapes knowledge of the severities of "manliness" in our society, and those who feel they have not achieved it live with lingering self-doubt, self-diminishment. On the other hand, those men who score highest on tests of "masculinity" refuse to restrain their aggressiveness even when by expressing it they lose the approval of their community.[109]

"Manliness," as defined by patriarchy, means to be or appear to be in control at all times. But remaining in control prevents a person from ever achieving intimacy with another, from ever letting down his guard; it thus precludes easy friendship, fellowship, community. Men may have "buddies," acquaintances with whom they can engage in the ritual competition of banter, sport, or game, but they rarely possess intimate friends. I mentioned before that on tests administered by Carol Gilligan, in which a set of pictures was submitted to male and female subjects, men offered the most violent and threatening narratives as explanations of the photographs showing people close to each other, and the least threatening stories to explain photographs of men in isolation.[110] Shut out from the most nourishing parts of life, men seek what they need in the channels they have been told are "theirs": work, achievement, success. They imagine that success, or the demonstration of "manliness," will bring them love; instead, it often alienates those they love.[111] They feel cheated: and they blame women.

And men have, through patriarchal forms, achieved power-in-the-world.

Men own 99 percent of the world's property and earn 90 percent of its wages, while producing only 55 percent of the world's food and performing only one-third of the world's work.[112] Men rather exclusively direct the course not just of states and corporations but of culture: religion, arts, education. Despite the assaults of various waves of feminism, men have been able to retain their control over the people, creatures, plants, and even some of the elements of this planet. Many men wish to retain these powers.

Yet psychological, sociological, and philosophical studies describe men as deeply unhappy. Writers like Philip Slater, R. D. Laing, Theodore Roszak, for instance, have described men of our time as alienated, fragmented, suffering from anomie, conflict over role, or identity crises.[113] In projective tests like the Rorschach, men from a number of different cultures showed more insecurity and anxiety than women.[114] Men seem to fall ill more frequently than women—at least they lose more work days through illness than women do; they are more vulnerable than women to diseases that are associated with stress; and they die younger.[115] These statistics do not necessarily reflect *only* biological differences: when more women died in childbirth, men lived longer than women. Part of the reason why men are physically vulnerable is the stress they live with. And some of that stress is caused by attempting to live up to a definition of manliness that is unattainable for any human.

Sex-role behavior is learned. Whatever qualities we possess "by nature," from our genes, sex role is not among them. If it were, men could not feel and act as differently as they do from culture to culture, and especially from patriarchal society to societies that are not fully patriarchal. The range of behavior within one sex is as great as that between the two sexes; nondeterminist scientists point out that we have no substantive knowledge about the meaning of genetic and hormonal differences between the sexes.[116] The research of John Money and of Hampson and Hampson shows that hermaphrodites who are chromosomally and hormonally of one sex but are raised as if they were the opposite sex lead normal lives, including sex lives, as members of the sex in which they have been reared.[117]

Most men in Western societies work in some form of institution. Institutions breed competitiveness and inculcate an instrumental relation to everything, even personal relationships. One has contacts, not friends. One chooses to cultivate people not (as many women do) because of a sense of rapport with them, but because they might be useful. It also inculcates a focus upward, implicitly teaching men to see life as a power struggle directed at dominance. Men thus tend to see their bosses as masters not only over their working lives but over all of life. Such structures impose dependency, making people feel helpless, powerless; and this in turn arouses rigid, rule-bound behavior, making people act like petty tyrants in the realms which they control. Moreover, the structure is absorbing, and tends to make people regard the other parts of life as secondary. Rosabeth Kanter, who has observed this style in depth, believes it is not a male style but a corporate one; that it is not related to maleness itself, but is a response to the order imposed and the values implicit in large hierarchical organizations.[118]

What is learned can be learned differently. Because men overwhelmingly sit in seats of access to power, there is little possibility of altering the morality of our world unless men are willing to contribute to that alteration, unless men adopt a new set of values. Many men have been reaching toward such a change—witness the many books published in the past two decades offering self-help for men, suggesting broader ways of thinking adapted from Eastern religions, or recounting a personal change toward greater integration of self and of self with world. Whether men desire to change their lives depends upon two major factors: the degree to which they are conscious of misery in their present condition; and the degree of contempt they feel for women. Many enlightened men will be offended by the suggestion that they feel contempt for women at all: but no one in patriarchal society, woman or man, is free from that feeling. If you imagine you are, imagine how you would feel if someone told you you were "womanly," or asked you to dress and act as a woman for a day. You are a rare creature if you are male and do not react with horror.

The grounds of this pervasive contempt for women have been suggested throughout this book. Basically, they lie in women's reproductive functioning, in menstruation, conception and pregnancy, and lactation, none of which men experience, and all of which men have been taught to see as disgusting or worse. But only creatures who have been taught to despise the body would see such things as disgusting; and beings who urinate, excrete, vomit, exude pus and other issue cannot justify disgust at menstruation, the production of nourishing milk, and the wondrous process of pregnancy and birth.

If men's disgust with women's reproductive functioning is the basis on which patriarchy taught contempt, it is women's mothering that allowed patriarchy to diminish women. For power is irrelevant to mothering, and vice versa. It is received wisdom that women's capacity for mothering is innate: this alone makes them unfit to participate as full partners in patriarchal society. Fatherhood, on the other hand, is seen as hardly biological at all, but as a "cultural phenomenon."[119] This contrasts conveniently with women's capacity for motherhood, considered as nonvolitional, making women "naturally" subject to coercion into other nonvolitional labors.

Yet studies show that there is no evidence of an instinctual or biological basis for mothering: there is no harm to infants, or to their mothers, if the infants are not reared by their biological mothers. There is nothing in the physiology of the parturient woman that makes her particularly suited to later child care, nor any instinctual basis for the ability to perform it. There is no biological or hormonal element differentiating a male "substitute" mother from a female one.[120] Nor is there any evidence that exclusive mothering is necessarily better for children than mothering by a group.[121]

Mothering is learned, just as aggression is learned. We often see among women that those who lacked mothers in their childhood cannot mother in turn, and are distant or abusive to their children. Among animals this has been shown frequently. Female animals who were deprived of their own mothers do not mother their babies but abuse and sometimes even kill them.[122] If a female baby rat is removed from her mother just after birth, before the mother has licked the offspring clean, that baby will not, as a new mother, lick her own offspring clean. Education in mothering occurs so early that we confuse it with "instinct," genetically programmed knowledge. But as Erving Goffman pointed out in another context, "there is no appreciable quid pro quo" between parents and children; "what is received in one generation is given in the next."[123] This is true of deprivations as well as of gifts.

Although women care for children in all cultures, men actively participate in child care in nonpatriarchal societies. Even in patriarchal ones, men are involved in rearing children in communities that live on the land, that work in or near the home. Our present notion of motherhood is quite recent, having been institutionalized only in the past couple of centuries—that is, separated from other dimensions of life, conceived of as an occupation, named, circumscribed, and prescribed as women's work, and to some degree regulated.

Exclusive mothering tends to produce more achievement-oriented men, and people with psychologically monogamic tendencies. Dorothy Dinnerstein and Nancy Chodorow, among others, believe it also creates men's dread and resentment of women, and their search as adults for nonthreatening, undemanding, dependent, even infantile women. Dinnerstein hypothesizes that men's pervasive fear of women—a fear she believes is shared by women—arises from the fact that women do most of the early mothering, that we emerge into consciousness facing a woman who appears huge, all-powerful, and awe-ful, in control of all our pleasures, all our pains. Although as we grow, we bury this sense of her and, indeed, belittle her, the sense is triggered when we encounter a mature woman in a position of authority or control. Such a woman arouses a symbolic dread and fear, preconscious emotions.[124] "Psychologists have demonstrated unequivocally that the very fact of being mothered by a woman generates in men conflicts over masculinity, a psychology of male dominance, and a need to be superior to women." As they reject the control of a woman because it seems overpowering, they also come to reject and devalue "feminine" qualities in general.[125] Sidney Bolkowsky suggests that societies that reject mothers may create their own misery, may be "unnatural," and that "precivilized" societies in which a child is raised by a series of "mothers," all offering extended loving contact, display low incidence of the psychological disorders found in "civilized" societies.[126]

A study of Russian and American children demonstrated that the Russian children were better socialized, having been cared for in group centers since infancy; there was more companionship between parents and children, and parents spent more time with their children than the American parents.[127] Collective child-rearing situations—on kibbutzim, in China, in Cuba—seem to produce children who have a greater sense of commitment to and solidarity with a group, less individualism and competitiveness, and who are less likely to form possessive, exclusive adult relationships.[128]

If we want a society that learns early to live together in harmony, collective child rearing is essential. To participate in child rearing would enlarge and enrich men's experience. It would also enlarge and enrich women's by allowing them to participate in both private and public life. Exclusive gender identity is not an expression of natural differences between the sexes but a suppression of natural similarities.[129] The unhappiness of many women would be eliminated or modified if their men provided them with the same nurturance they offer men, if their children had loving fathers, and if they were able to use their other talents in the world. It is even possible, as Gayle Rubin suggests, that if children were raised by people of both sexes, human social and sexual arrangements would be far richer, sexual power would disappear, and with it the Oedipus complex: she believes feminism must call for a revolution in kinship.[130] We cannot now predict what kind of people would result from such an integration, but it is only reasonable to assume that since they would be more integrated within themselves, people would be more content; and since they would be in greater harmony with each other, people would be more peaceful. To assume that contentment and peaceability would produce less brilliance, less art, less uniqueness than our own society possesses is unwarranted: what we would lose is the brilliance, uniqueness, and art that arises from utter isolation, self-hate, and the atrophy of personal qualities. The world as a whole has to be better off with greater integration and harmony.

Power has for too long gone unmodified and in defiant disregard of basic human feelings and needs. The exclusion of women from the public world is at once symbolic of its character and a reason for its character. Women are trained for private virtue, men for public power; and the severance between the sexes and the two realms is responsible for much of our irrational thinking and behavior, as Elshtain has shown.[131] In each realm, one is requested to close the eyes to what the other realm is doing and signifies and to connections between the two. *To disconnect virtue from power is to ensure that virtue will be powerless, and licenses power to be without virtue.* Yet there is no position of virtue for anyone who lives in a world as cruel and ugly as our own; nor any position of power for people who do not even know how to live with themselves. As Dietrich Bonhoeffer wrote, "Here and there people flee from public altercation into the sanctuary of private *virtuousness*. But anyone who does this must shut his mouth and his eyes to the injustice around him. Only at the cost of self-deception can he keep himself pure from the contamination arising from *responsible* action."[132] Bonhoeffer, a Catholic priest who persisted in opposing the Nazis, and died while imprisoned by them, was living his morality, not talking it. Those who closet themselves in a fugitive and cloistered virtue must remain adamantly ignorant or confess themselves participants in evil; those who stand only in the world and never gaze at the inner life, at connections among people, at the sharing and bonding that make all life possible, stride off and become the evil. For millennia, men have possessed fairly total worldly control over women. They have owned women, bought and sold them, forbidden them any form of independence at a cost of death. They have enslaved women, treated them as minors, defectives. In some cultures fathers had the right to kill their daughters, husbands their wives. Women's bodies have been imprisoned, removed from their own control, beaten, tortured, destroyed; women's minds have been constrained and deprived of nourishment by morality and enforced ignorance.

Yet despite all this control, men have remined anxious. As we have seen, some of the worst vituperation against women occurred in periods in which men had the greatest control over them. Wife beating does not cease in societies in which law gives men almost total control over women. It is claimed by some that feminism creates a male backlash against women; but no one can point to a culture in which women are subordinate yet are treated well. It seems that women have a choice between having some power over their lives and being hated and feared by men—and being hated and feared and having no power whatever. Whatever position women occupy in a society, men experience them as threatening; however great men's control, they do not feel in control.

Men do not attempt to establish control over women because they hate and fear them; rather, men hate and fear women because they *must* control them, because control over women is essential to their self-definition. Forced to demonstrate superiority, they can do so only by cheating, stacking the deck, by imposing on women deprivations which imprison them in a condition seen as inferior by the male culture.[133]

In hubris, bravado, and self-aggrandizement, men have declared themselves superior to other creatures. So they necessarily hate and fear the one creature who could disprove their claim, and attempt to put her in a position of such dependency that she will fear to do so. There are men who acknowledge this, yet cannot change. Their entire *human* identity rests on a manhood that is defined as control. Such men are in the deepest sense deprived, dehumanized: for they cannot find significance within nature, within their bodies and emotions, as part of a human-natural context. For them, significance is located only in that which transcends the natural context and offers something more enduring than life. Deluded by the notion that power offers what endures, they ignore the fact that nothing endures, not even art, except culture itself—the children we make, and the world each generation in turn makes. Searching for meaning in what is superhuman, men have ignored their humanity, the only possible ground for human meaning.

## 8. VALUES FOR A NEW WORLD

Beneath every sociopolitical organization lies a more or less flexible morality, an interwoven set of values in which certain qualities are central: in patriarchy, power was at one time central, but during the past few centuries it has come to dominate all other values to the extent that one can call it the single major value in Western public life and much of Western private life. Beneath any morality, however, lies a vision of "the way things are"—a vision of reality and of human nature. For patriarchy, reality is antagonistic, whether as Nature, which undermines and corrupts, or Culture or Realpolitik, in which men endlessly compete for a limited supply of resources; and human nature is depraved, wicked, greedy, selfish, and predatory. Without denying that such elements exist in humans, or that the outside world is occasionally antagonistic to human life, we must insist that these terms do not characterize either humanity or reality (however ineffable we may find ultimate reality, we have some shared sense of what is real). Feminism does not offer a fixed program or dogma, a new Law for the future, but it does offer a new vision of human nature, reality, and sociopolitical arrangement.

The vision entertained by many feminists, and the vision that informs this book, is of a humanity whose first experience—even before birth as well as immediately after it—is of being shared with, nurtured, cared for.[134] We can, in a kind of shorthand, call this experience love, and for some infants the experience may be one of absolute love. For many it is a sharing and devotion mixed with resentment and hostility; nevertheless, the sharing is more important, for those who are not given to do not survive. Thus, those of us who do survive were shared with and nurtured sufficiently.

This early experience of being fed, held, warmed, protected, is one of ecstasy; if the counterelements (resentment, hostility) are not too deforming, we seek out such experiences in our later life. In addition, experiencing nurturing teaches us all, men as well as women, how to nurture others in turn. Part of nurturing, however, is setting limits; thus opposition or frustration is included in a child's early experience. This opposition/frustration may intimidate a child or stimulate growth. In either case, it is formative. A morality—and its extension, a culture (sociopolitical organization)—that is based on human experience and need, rather than on the denial of human experience and need, would reflect this order. Nurturing qualities would be central, primary; education in limitation would be secondary in time and importance.

This may seem paradoxical, for the feminist view emphasizes human limitations in a way the patriarchal view does not. The feminist view denies the possibility of human transcendence; it denies the power of power to make men secure, eternal, fully controlling. But patriarchy, in order to teach its vision to new generations, thwarts, diminishes, or prevents the development of nurturant qualities in men, and the development of assertive and aspirant qualities in women, thus limiting both sexes in profound ways.

To urge the creation of a new morality, a new "world," does not imply that we will invent new values. There are no new values. Human values have remained constant since the beginning of human life: what changes is the way we arrange, order them. A new morality is a new ordering of an eternal set of elements. Patriarchy was also a rearrangement of values that already existed, one that made nurturing qualities ancillary, marginal, to the "real" business of human life—achieving some form of power.

This exhortation to create a new morality does not arise from mere dissatisfaction with the status quo. Although we speak of the status quo, there is no such thing: the reality around us is constantly changing. And, as I hope I have shown, the direction of change at present is ominous. It is urgent for the future of this race that we attempt to alter that direction.

Many moral treatises urge a return to the values of our "forefathers"—to strict regulation of sexuality, strict discipline of children, private enterprise, hard work, sacrifice, and strong patriotism. Such arguments ignore the fact that even if it were possible to return to such a morality (assuming that such a morality actually existed in any universal way), it would only lead to what it led to the first time—our present. In any case, we cannot go back, to the morality of a mythical eighteenth century, or to the morality of a hypothetical matricentric era. The values of both periods will and must remain: but in a different form and in a different relation to each other.

Procreation, the central good of matricentry, is no longer an absolute good. It is necessary for the continuation of the human race, and it is a source of pleasure and fulfillment for individual people, but it is not necessary or desirable that everyone procreate and it is essential that family size be limited. Limitation of family size invariably accompanies improved living conditions. Because procreation is not mandatory, not even desirable in great numbers, and because of technological advances, procreation can be a volitional act, which should restore the joyfulness of giving birth.

Matricentric cultures and simple societies today (regardless of their moral tendencies) value family bonds above others; in some societies family bonds comprise *the* principle of social organization. Although family bonds may be extremely important in complex societies, they do not limit the connections that are possible. It is probably true that we all need a "family," but we do not all enjoy our biological families, and many of us wish for a wider network. The *principle* of family—a network of intimate people devoted to each other's good—will surely remain; but kinship may arise from friendship as well as blood relationship. Nor is the value of sharing as it exists in simple societies translatable into complex society without some change of form. Most people still share among themselves, among the small family or intimate unit. This is not an adequate form for the new morality.

But we must begin to perceive that power, too, is a limited good, that it does not bring us invulnerability, but a heightened vulnerability, that it is not sufficient as a purpose for existence, but only as a means to pleasure. Power-to is often such a means; power-over, domination, brings misery more than joy. But domination is necessary; it is inherent in the human condition since it is inherent in rearing children. But if domination were seen as a necessary (and temporary) evil, if it were not seen as a good in its own right, it would not be pursued and clutched as it presently is.

Patriarchal structures will alter as human ends change, and it is impossible to predict what new forms will supersede them. Perhaps hierarchical form, a mechanistic and instrumental approach, and dualistic thinking will continue to inform certain disciplines, but they will not stand as the true and only way to see. They will be one approach among several. The broad perspective on society that patriarchy made possible is now necessary; as is the use of institutions in some form for transmission of knowledge. As morality changes, new forms will appear and more democratic structures which are not possible now will become so. Change will occur gradually, although not without conflict; the key to working through conflict must be a goal of the greatest possible harmony, of an expansiveness that permits not just a hundred flowers to grow and flourish, but a hundred different species of plants.

So too, competition will endure, if only because it can be fun, but it will be one element within a broadly shared sense of cooperation and community.

There are simple societies that foster both cooperation and competition.[135] It is impossible to guess how important competition will be to future generations; but it is clear that if we want to create a world that *can* live together without utter uniformity and totalitarianism, we must gear ourselves to cooperate, must teach our young the pleasures of working/playing together, and thinking about nature and the planet in a cooperative spirit.

The patriarchal faith in permanence must also be modified, or redefined. Personal immortality is useless to the dead and, as Hamlet reminds us, "the noble dust of Alexander" may serve to stop a bunghole. Property is no hedge against war, the desiccation of the planet, or totalitarian government; dynasties fade. Yet the human need for a feeling of permanence seems profound, and indeed there is a medium for expression of such feelings—a sense of continuation. Whether we procreate children or create art, help our communities, assist others, we are contributing to the well-being of a culture that will continue. Continuation differs from permanence in that it does not imply domination— that is, we are contributing to an ongoing reality but not attempting to *control* it (give it our name, dictate its form or content, establish a structure in accordance with our own will).

But if we are to build a new morality, it is not enough to modify the value we place on power and other "masculine" qualities. We must replace the old ideal with a new one. And in the process of creating a new moral arrangement, we must avoid proceeding by rejection. Patriarchy began by asserting a new primary value—power—to supersede the old primary value of procreation. But it moved largely through negation. Demanding fidelity to an invisible deity, it tried to suppress the matricentric order by teaching men to sacrifice children, to fear and disdain women, and to scorn the earth as a satisfying home. Thus patriarchy is characterized, early and late, by negativity, exclusions, taboos—by rigidity and harshness. The question that should provide our standard as we make the choices that will lead us to a new vision is what kinds of human behavior bring us delight.

For it is not enough either to devise a morality that will allow the human race simply to survive. Survival is an evil when it entails existing in a state of wretchedness. Intrinsic to survival and continuation is felicity, pleasure. Pleasure has been much maligned, diminished by philosophers and conquerors as a value for the timid, the small-minded, the self-indulgent. "Virtue" involves the renunciation of pleasure in the name of some higher purpose, a purpose that involves power (for men) or sacrifice (for women). Pleasure is described as shallow and frivolous in a world of high-minded, serious purpose. But pleasure does not exclude serious pursuits or intentions; indeed, it is found in them; and it is the only real reason for staying alive.

Pleasure is a response, not a commodity; an experience, an end in itself. It can arise from a myriad of sources: from being with others, from work, from cultural entertainments and activities; from sensory and intellectual stimulation; from food, drink, sleep, warmth, closeness. There is pleasure in solitude and in company; in independence and individuality. There can be pleasure merely in walking, breathing, looking, feeling the air on one's face. Many things give pleasure only or mainly because they are shared.[136]

Intrinsic in pleasure is quality: it is the quality more than the quantity of things—air, water, color, scent, friendship—that arouses pleasure. Our world, however, is devoted to quantity, to that which can be enumerated on a balance sheet or a poll. William Gass claims that quality has been banished from the twentieth-century world, and traces its diminishment back to Aristotle, who considered it accidental, nonessential.[137] Quality can be discussed, but not really measured; we can prefer one or another quality, but we cannot *prove* the superiority of one over another. Because it does not lend itself to instrumental, mechanistic argument, quality has increasingly been treated as unimportant. Like pleasure itself, it is viewed as a frill, of concern to aesthetes but not to real men.

Pleasure—a gratified response to quality—is rooted in the senses, and for pleasure to be revalorized, the body and the senses must be revalorized too. In Classical Greece the senses were considered inferior to reason (as if they were not connected with it); in Christianity they were doorways to sin; and in the modern period they are are seen as inaccurate guides to external reality. Nietzsche writes of "the artful and blind hostility of philosophers towards the senses"; he believes that this hostility emerges from philosophers' desire for "a sort of revenge upon reality, a malicious destruction of the valuations by which men live. . . . The history of philosophy is a secret raging against the preconditions of life, of the value feelings of life. . . . Philosophers have never hesitated to affirm a world, provided it contradicted this world, and furnished them with a pretext for speaking ill of this world."[138]

Many thinkers have perceived the wretchedness that results from eschewing pleasure, and choosing "duty." Simone Weil wrote, "The common run of moralists complain that man is moved by his private interests: would to heaven it were so!"[139] And Frithjof Bergmann agrees: "The general perspective which thinks of man as 'egoistic,' and as naturally satisfying his own instinctual appetites and which looks to education (and particularly to morality) primarily for the taming of this selfishness [is false]: A truer starting point . . . is . . . that all too many at some midpoint in their lives feel that they have not once done anything they really wanted."[140]

To act against one's impulses to pleasure is to act against one's best self, and makes all subsequent actions wretched. To deny one's own desires and needs is the first step into loss of self, into adoption of the image urged by patriarchy, a self devoted to creating an appearance of power (if male) or submission (if female). Nothing in patriarchy is more demoralizing in the true sense of that word than a morality that calls pleasure and selfhood *vice* and *selfishness*, and miserable submission to imposed identity and goals *duty* and *virtue*. As Nietzsche wrote, "to have to fight the instincts . . . that is the formula for decadence . . . happiness equals instinct."[141] We act for our best selves when we strive for pleasure; we also give others the gift of those best selves as example, as encounter, and a source of pleasure to them.

We commonly think of pleasure as the opposite of pain, but this is inadequate thinking. For nothing eliminates pain—neither pleasure nor power. Pleasure requires the self to be open to the external world and to other people, to one's emotions and sensations; when one is open, one is open to pain too. The opposite of pleasure is power, which requires the self to be closed off from people and events in the outside world that do not relate to one's particular power pursuit. Yet no amount of closing off of self from self can eliminate pain. Like death, pain is a constant in human experience.

Nor is pleasure the opposite of work, as it is commonly presented—a compartmentalized, bracketed time called leisure which is supposed to be as drenched with pleasure as work is permeated with displeasure. But many people enjoy their work, even people who are not among the most highly paid. Work that gives people a sense that they matter to others, that they help, are necessary, is deeply satisfying, and people cling to it under quite appalling conditions. People who make things they are proud of, who feel responsible for the things they make, enjoy their work. People who are indolent, who seem to want to do nothing, who treat their work as an annoying intrusion on their daydreams, are not lazy but deprived. They have never tapped into their energies, never found an avenue of expression for them.

There is one argument against pleasure as a primary good that seems to me to require consideration, and that is that there are people who take pleasure in cruelty. It is tempting to say—with Maslow, for instance—that satisfaction derived from cruelty is not a true pleasure.[142] Cruelty is, after all, a manifestation of the drive to power-over, and arises from something maimed within the self. It is connection made with another to arouse feeling—but the feeling desiderated is pain. Only the pain of another can testify to the power-over, the significance, perhaps even the existence, of the one who inflicts it. Cruelty is inappropriately directed revenge, revenge for a sense of worthlessness inculcated in early life. Since no morality can ever eradicate all human ills and sufferings, not even in a world devoted more to pleasure than power, cruelty will no doubt persist. But in a world which valued pleasure it is only reasonable to assume that it would be less prevalent and less acceptable than in a world which values power above all.

A final objection to pleasure as the goal of life is that the pursuit of pleasure is self-centered and self-indulgent. This objection arises from a conception of pleasure as a kind of masturbation: of the self as separate, disconnected from others; and of material goods as a limited common pot from which the strong seize most, leaving little for others. But in a world that was not devoted to power for its own sake, wealth would not be valued for its own sake; not only would the present disposition of wealth change, but our attitudes toward it would be greatly altered. Moreover, pleasure is not necessarily dependent upon material goods; we derive enjoyment from our work, from nourishing others, from play, and simple nature—a walk in the country, say—activities that do not require great prosperity. And finally, our deepest pleasures involve the company of others. The self disconnected and separate from others is a self bordering on disease; to become a person means to become a person in relationship to others, acting in social contexts.[143] Other people are essential in themselves, and to our own sense of self; and when we feel delight, joy, we are more able to be generous to others. Pleasure enlarges the spirit and, like power, it is contagious.

The very core of pleasure is mutuality. Pleasure begins in the mother's womb, in warmth, closeness, satisfaction of needs, the comforting maternal heartbeat. And women who have chosen pregnancy share that joy with the fetus. The joy of such lucky pairs continues after birth; the pleasure of being held and holding, being fed and feeding, being warmed against a body, is a pleasure given and received mutually. Mutual pleasures are the sacred core of life: food, body warmth, love, and sex. These things are sacred because they are necessary, because they confer pleasure in the giving and the receiving so that it is impossible to say who is giving and who is receiving. They satisfy the profoundest needs, and in their satisfying, satisfy two.

Mutuality is the core of pleasure because it recalls our earliest sensations of pleasure, being part of our mothers' bodies. Mutual acts satisfy the profound need to be-with-another or others. But there is another nucleus of pleasure, also profound, that originates in the moment of birth: breathing for ourselves— freedom, the sense of being a self.

Like other terms we have examined, freedom is variously defined. As it is most commonly used, it means lack of dependence upon others, exemption from constraint and domination. In other words, freedom is most often defined as a lack. But to aim at a lack is to aim at emptiness, as Thomas Mann pointed out in "Mario and the Magician": "freedom exists, and also the will exists; but freedom of the will does not exist." E. J. Hobsbawm comments that the reason most political revolutions lead to tyranny is that they have aimed at freedom conceived as a lack.[144]

Freedom is seen not just as a lack but as a kind of isolation. C. B. MacPherson asserts that "what makes a man human is ... freedom from dependence on the will of others; ... freedom from dependence on others means freedom from any relations with others except those relations which the individual enters voluntarily with a view of his own interest."[145] Such a definition arises from a view of humans as utterly separate from each other, related to each other only by exploitiveness. There is no suggestion of bonds among people that involve ambivalent emotions (as the most profound bonds do) or of pleasure derived from giving, doing for another. Such definitions of freedom are the inevitable consequence of a morality of independence, competition, and power as the greatest good.

If freedom means the absence of constraints, then freedom does not exist. Nothing on this earth lacks constraints. Plants and creatures are bound by the rising and setting of the sun, by gravity or universal physical force.[146] Human beings are constrained by the need to breathe air of a certain quality, to eat and excrete, to drink, rest, sleep, move, to feel sensations and emotions, to think. Because humans are social animals, they also experience constraints imposed by the group. As infants, we are placed in enclosures for our own protection—but those enclosures prevent our free movement. As adults, we are constrained to earn our bread; and also, because we desire and need the company of others, to abide by certain rules that make society possible, and to perform certain acts to retain the affection of others. In addition, we have an internal need for expression of feeling and thought.

Freedom defined as the absence of constraint requires absolute isolation from others.[147] Such a definition suggests that our true nature can be expressed only in an emotional desert which we leave only when we see something we want in another person. But such isolation is, for humans, a form of insanity. It does not exist. Even schizophrenics, bound inside their own minds, dissociated from others, are tied to others by necessity. Even the person who lives by a code of independence and imagines himself or herself utterly independent is bound to assistants and associates, and often suffers guilt about old bonds to parents, spouses, or children who have been emotionally abandoned.

We are bound by bodily and intellectual-emotional need to the earth and to each other. Nor can we choose all of our own bonds. Engels defined freedom as the recognition of necessity: but that is only half the story. There is no certainty that such a thing as "free will" exists; we do not know and cannot determine to what extent we are formed involuntarily, through genetic inheritance, training, and culture. But insofar as we experience an emotion or sensation or mental state called *freedom*, it is in finding a coherence, a meshing correlation between external and internal necessity.[148] Freedom is the sense that we are choosing our own bonds. It is not a lack or absence, but the presence of harmonious relations between us and our condition, our acts, our relationships. Freedom includes duty, responsibility, and bonds as well as our relatively independent states and acts; it is the sense that we are using well those parts of the self we want to use, enjoy using, in acts and states we wish to be immersed in.

The great end is pleasure, which unlike power is truly an end, an experience that is not simply a step to a further end. It includes all the values we presently entertain; it excludes nothing. While there are parts of human experience we would like to exclude—cruelty, death—we cannot accomplish this. To pretend we can, to create symbols that suggest that some people live forever, is to implant in human experience a falsehood so profound as to distort it utterly. Life carries sorrows for all creatures; sorrow and deprivation are not escapable. But it is possible to live with an eye to delight rather than to domination. And this is the feminist morality.

## 9. THE LONG VIEW FORWARD

In a fascinating book published in 1949, Martin Foss divides people into two types, sensationalist and rationalist; these types are really approaches to experience, and correspond somewhat with my categories of "feminine" and "masculine." Foss's description of the rationalist approach is the more interesting and useful for our discussion. The rationalist *trains himself* to obliterate— Foss's word is *overcome*; I would say *transcend*—the sensuous world. * He accomplishes this by inventing a closed system that excludes "the disturbing world," the world of endless flux. The system he invents "receives its final

---

* I retain Foss's use of the masculine pronoun throughout, as it seems appropriate.

meaning from something which it cannot symbolize: it has its final end in a purpose for which all symbols are means." Like a mathematical system, a religious system, or systematized industry, closed systems confer meaning on the events that occur within them, even when there is no relation between that meaning and the world outside the system. This meaning compensates for the loss of integration, continuity with reality, which is necessarily abandoned along with the perception of flux. And within the system, everything becomes a means—there are no ends. But means without ends are not means any more, but "facts."

Whatever does not fit into the rationalist's categories is "stigmatized as mere confusion." The system conceals whatever is disturbing, calling it superfluous, feeling it to be "the unspeakable." Because the system has no describable end, the rationalist transforms the means into ends, and finds his end in technique inself. "In this way the task of man will be reduced to the perfection of technique, to the systematization of interconnected means, i.e., to a machinery which runs for its own sake."[149]

There is, however, a real end to these activities, an unspoken, unacknowledged goal: it is to conceal the disturbing, "the unspeakable." But "the unspeakable" is simply the eternal recurrence of nature, the fact of meaninglessness in the face of nature. Although human beings found their "meaning" within nature for several millions of years, at some point that "meaning" became insufficient, and "man" began to define himself, to find signification in opposition and superiority to nature. The unspeakable truth, the Gorgon's head upon which patriarchy is built, is the condition of creaturedom itself.

Some may see this effort to create significance as noble, and perhaps it is. But it is also deluded, and worse, is carrying our race to the edge of extinction. But our race also carries an ancient wisdom, a subversive understanding of what matters and what does not. It simply makes sense to live in certain ways and not others, and all of us would perceive this if we were not blindered by our world's obsession with power and control.

The future, if there is to be a future, is already being planned for us in the think tanks of government and corporations; the people who inhabit these insular and insulated quarters know only more and more control, more and more centralization, more and more technology with consequent wastes and increased powerlessness on the part of most people. If we want a different future, we will have to create it. No one will do this for us.

The starting place is within the self, in an investigation of our needs and desires, a reconsideration of what gives us pleasure, what makes living seem desirable; and of our pursuit of power or control. The goal, as I have suggested, is not to eschew domination, aggression, or conflict, but to find ways to thread such drives through our lives so that they produce pleasure rather than misery, disconnection, and the ill will of others. The goal is not the impossible but the possible, for the end is not transcendence but felicity.

Essential to felicity are an integrated self, used to the fullest possible extent; and integration of the self and the world. Integration of the self means using all one's capacities—talents and abilities valued in the public and the private domains. All of us possess, to different degrees, the ability to nourish and heal, to teach and learn, to act purposively and to play. These are *human*, not male or female capacities. Integration of the self and the world means involving oneself in a community of some sort—whether a set of friends, neighbors, colleagues, or family—and participating in the public world.

If we come to understand the fragile nature of power, to see that power is insubstantial, we will realize that one cannot say some people have power and some do not. We all have power—the capacity to influence, alter, affect the lives of those around us. And until all of us use our power in the public world, it will continue to be dominated by those who are driven to domination, rather than by those who wish to use power as a means to noncontrolling well-being. We must actively forward the moral revolution, a revolution that can occur in one person but must include the entire globe. This cannot be a Grand Revolution: we will not be swept into power, cheering and waving at the crowds around us as we sit on the now quiet noses of the tanks, averting our eyes from those missing an arm or an eye. We will not be able to speechify, claiming a New Order in elation, then turn to the back rooms, the tables, to grim days of punishment and retribution, tests of ideological purity, conflict over spoils. No one now living will see the end of this struggle, nor will there be an "end," Utopia proclaimed, the New Jerusalem. We are part of a process that must continue as long as the world endures. Leaderless, deprived of the use of military might, holding to a morality of human felicity rather than one of power, we may seem a fragile and transient force.

But I am heartened by the thought of the early followers of Jesus' ideas: slaves, women, publicans, poor Jews, Greeks, and Roman soldiers, prostitutes, respectable housewives, intellectuals: people who craved a new and more loving, communal, tolerant way of life; people who were sickened by the ways of power. Of course, if their success stands as an example, the subsequent fate of their religion, which was swallowed whole by patriarchy, stands as a warning. It is necessary to be alert and "hard" in one's softness, to act with *satyagraha*. I cannot prove that we have the power to alter our society; we must simply believe that we can. There is an Ethiopian proverb reminding us that "when spider webs unite, they can halt a lion."[150]

The idea that we can transform the world may seem utopian, idealistic, or just simple-minded. But I repeat what I have said before: the world will change anyway. It is not inconceivable that humans themselves can participate in forming the direction of that change. Over history various groups have tried to create communities with values different from those of the larger society; and many thinkers have drawn up plans for organic communities.[151] But organic communities were not part of the dominant vision of the West, which defines community as a set of interactions by antagonistic or occasionally complementary interest groups—as a mere by-product of the "rational" search for gain.[152] And most experimental communities have worked on a principle of exclusion, a patriarchal value, and have tried to outlaw certain kinds of behavior, methods, or qualities. What is forbidden varies—it may be sex, or volitional sex; or possession; or anger; or use of electrical appliances and machines; or the eating of meat. But all such communities attempt to find "salvation" by transcendence, just as the outside world does; they are based in a belief that denying the self can lead to harmony and virtue.

The separation of goodness from power made goodness powerless and licensed power to be evil. Many of us, whatever our behavior in the world, think about goodness and power in this way, so that when we are good we feel powerless and when we exercise power we feel evil and defend ourselves against guilt by claiming that's the way the world is, dog eat dog. But that is not the whole truth about the world, where we find nourishment and love as well as contest; and the exercise of power is not intrinsically evil: it becomes an ill only when it has no end beyond itself, beyond the pursuit of greater power. Nor are acts normally considered good necessarily good; those who give and do not request or take harm those around them; those who identify goodness with powerlessness tend to inflict guilt on those around them.

No movement has ever been more than an accumulation of small motions of people acting within their own spheres. In rearranging our lives, we participate in rearranging the life of society. The qualities on which we have depended for several millennia, which we have imagined kept us afloat—power-in-the-world, possession, status, hierarchy, tradition—are in fact sweeping us to ruin; what is necessary to prevent that ruin are the very qualities we have feared to trust—the flexible, fluid, transient elements of affection and communality.

The past had its moment; we have ours. After a moment all life dies and is transformed, transubstantiated. The end of life is the continuation of life; the means we use to attain that end is the mode in which we live it. All of us, victors and victims, and we are all both, are transitory. Like the world, we are passing. We are like soldier ants, moving from a depleted area to seek food beyond, in an unexplored terrain. We have encountered a river that separates us from sight of the future; we have a choice only to die where we stand, or to enter it. The ants always enter: and drown. They drown by the millions, and in their death add their bodies to a bridge on which the survivors can cross over to what they hope will be richer ground, as the devoured terrain behind them regenerates itself.

All of us, members of transitory generations, help to create the bridge by which the past continues into the future. But if our lives are filled with self-denial, self-punishment, empty rewards, illusory goals, and the mutilations of power and obedience, then neither our lives nor our legacy is worth the pain. Only pleasure in the journey can make the journey worthwhile; and our pleasure in our journey is also a legacy to those who follow.

And if we fail? We fail: to turn the words of wicked Lady Macbeth to good purpose. The goal—feminizing the world—is also the means—feminizing our worlds. The end is the process: integrating ourselves and carrying integration as far into the world as we can. There is no final end; there is only the doing well, being what we want to be, doing what we want to do, living in delight. The choice lies between a life lived through and a life lived; between fragmentation and wholeness; between leaving behind us, as generations before us have done, a legacy of bitterness, sacrifice, and fear, and leaving behind us, if nothing more than this, a memory of our own being and doing with pleasure, an image of a life our young will want to emulate rather than avoid. The choice lies between servitude and freedom, fragmentation and integration. The choice may be between death and life.

There is no choice.

# Notes

INTRODUCTION

1. There are fascinating visions in some feminist depictions of a possible future. See Charlotte Perkins Gilman, *Herland* (reprint, New York, 1979); Dorothy Bryant, *The Kin of Ata Are Waiting for You* (New York, 1971); Marge Piercy, *Woman on the Edge of Time* (New York, 1976); and Doris Lessing's *Canopus in Argos* series, of which five volumes have been published.

2. Alasdair MacIntyre, *After Virtue* (Notre Dame, Ind., 1981), p. 58.

3. Claude Lévi-Strauss, *Totemism* (Boston, 1963), pp. 78–79; E. E. Evans-Pritchard, *Nuer Religion* (Oxford, England, 1956), pp. 80–90.

4. Peggy Reeves Sanday, *Female Power and Male Dominance* (New York, 1981), p. 64.

5. Colin Turnbull, *The Human Cycle* (New York, 1983), p. 180.

6. See Claude Lévi-Strauss, *The Raw and the Cooked*, trans. John and Doreen Weightman (New York, 1975).

7. Ronald Higgins, *The Seventh Enemy* (London, 1978), p. 53.

8. *New York Times*, May 27, 1981.

9. Philip Shabecoff, "U.S. Efforts Grow to Protect Water," *New York Times*, July 26, 1983.

10. *New York Times*, November 3, 1981.

11. *Global 2000*, Report of the President's Council on Environmental Quality, July 1980.

12. Ivan Illich, *Medical Nemesis* (New York, 1976), p. 20. Marshall Sahlins writes: "One third to one half of humanity are said to be going to bed hungry every night. In the Stone Age the fraction must have been much smaller. This is the era of unprecedented hunger. Now, in the time of the greatest technical power, starvation is an institution." *Stone Age Economics* (Chicago, 1972), p. 23.

13. Amos Perlmutter, *Modern Authoritarianism* (New Haven, Conn., 1981), p. xi.

14. MacIntyre, *After Virtue*, pp. 25, 57.

15. Walter Weisskopf, *Alienation and Economics* (New York, 1971), p. 45.

16. Friedrich Nietzsche, "On Self-Overcoming," *Thus Spake Zarathustra*, II (New York, 1966).


CHAPTER ONE

THE LONG VIEW BACK: MATRICENTRY

1. For discussion of misinterpretations of Darwin's theories of natural selection and survival of the fittest, see Stephen Jay Gould, *Ever Since Darwin* (New York, 1977), and *The Panda's Thumb* (New York, 1980), pp. 85–86.

2. For discussion of the punctuational mode, see Steven M. Stanley, *Fossils, Genes, and the Origin of Species* (New York, 1982), and Gould, *Panda*, Chapter 17.

3. Adrienne Zihlman, "Women in Evolution, II: Subsistence and Social Organization Among Early Hominids," *Signs* 4, 1 (Autumn 1978):4–20.

4. Nancy Tanner, *On Becoming Human* (New York, 1981), p. 250ff.

5. See John E. Pfeiffer, *The Emergence of Man* (New York, 1969), pp. 72–92; Tanner, *Human*, p. 237ff.; Elise Boulding, *The Underside of History* (Boulder, Colo., 1976), pp. 69–70.

6. Mary-Claire King and A. C. Wilson, "Evolution at Two Levels in Humans and Chimpanzees," *Science* 188 (1975):107–116; Tanner, *Human*, pp. 36–43. This similarity indicates both a common ancestry and a fairly recent divergence—that is, within the past two million years. For a different calendar see Gould, *Panda*, p. 137. Biochemical evidence suggests that the divergence between apes and humans occurred only between four and five million years ago. The meta-

phor used by Jeremy Cherfas and John Gribbin, in "Updating Man's Ancestry," *New York Times Magazine*, August 29, 1982, is that if, in an encyclopedia of DNA that describes a human, we changed only one specific letter out of every hundred, we would have the description of an ape.

7.   Gould, *Darwin*, p. 51.

8.   For analysis of some prejudicial "scientific" research, see Donna Haraway, "Animal Sociology and a Natural Economy of the Body Politic," Parts I and II, *Signs* 4, 1 (Autumn 1978):21–60.

9.   For fascinating and readable accounts for nonspecialists of animal life as related to human behavior, see Mariette Nowak, *Eve's Rib* (New York, 1980); Elizabeth Fisher, *Woman's Creation* (Garden City, N.Y., 1979); Gould, *Darwin* and *Panda*; and, on chimps and humans, Tanner, *Human*; and Sarah Blaffer Hrdy, *The Woman That Never Evolved* (Cambridge, Mass., 1981). Some researchers concentrate on primates less closely related to humans than chimpanzees or gorillas, such as rhesus macaques or hamadryas baboons, partly because these species show characteristics of male dominance that appealed to the researchers. For comment on this see M. Kay Martin and Barbara Voorhies, *Female of the Species* (New York, 1975), Chapter 5; Nowak, *Eve's Rib*, Chapter 4; Tanner, *Human*, pp. 19–28; Gould, *Darwin*, pp. 237–240.

10.   Edward O. Wilson, *Sociobiology* (Cambridge, Mass., 1980), p. 220; Jessie Bernard, *The Female World* (New York, 1981), p. 7.

11.   Wilson, *Sociobiology*, pp. 230–243.

12.   Elaine Morgan, *The Descent of Woman* (New York, 1972), p. 165.

13.   Robert Briffault, *The Mothers*, abridged and with an introduction by Gordon Rattray Taylor (New York, 1977), p. 46; Morgan, *Descent*, p. 175.

14.   Wilson, *Sociobiology*, p. 246.

15.   Hrdy, *Woman*, p. 17.

16.   Hrdy, *Woman*, p. 18; Wilson, *Sociobiology*, p. 251.

17.   Briffault, *Mothers*, abridged, p. 306.

18.   The hamadryas baboons are beloved of Edward O. Wilson (among others), who refers to them a disproportionate number of times. They are described as keeping harems—kidnaping young females and herding, guarding, and punishing them, biting them if they wander off from the group. But the hamadryas may not be a species at all but rather local adaptations of the cynocephalus baboons, who live in sexual equality. If this is the case, hamadryas behavior may be a response to the stress of isolation from their kind. See Leila Leibowitz, "Perspectives on the Evolution of Sex Differences," *Toward an Anthropology of Women*, ed. Rayna Reiter (New York, 1975), pp. 30–31.

19.   Hrdy, *Woman*, p. 9; see also Morgan, *Descent*, p. 209.

20.   M. R. A. Chance, "Sex Differences in the Structure of Attention," *Female Hierarchies*, ed. Lionel Tiger and Heather Fowler (Chicago, 1978); M. R. A. Chance and Clifford Jolly, *Social Groups of Monkeys, Apes, and Men* (New York, 1970), pp. 171ff.

21.   Both approaches are discussed in Wilson, *Sociobiology*, pp. 165, 282.

22.   Virginia Abernethy, "Female Hierarchy: An Evolutionary Perspective," Tiger and Fowler, *Hierarchies*, p. 127.

23.   Susan W. Duvall, J. S. Bernstein, and J. P. Gordon, "Paternity and Status in a Rhesus Monkey Group," Tiger/Fowler, *Hierarchies*.

24.   Wilson, *Sociobiology*, p. 546, writes that among chimpanzees, who have male dominance systems, dominance does not offer greater access to females; J. Hausfater, "Dominance and Reproduction in Baboons (Papio Cynocephalus): A Quantitative Analysis," Tiger and Fowler, *Hierarchies*, p. 3, assert that dominant male baboons have no greater number of copulations with ovulating females (females in estrus) than nondominant males; and Duvall et al., "Paternity," Tiger and Fowler, *Hierarchies*, p. 31, write that their research demonstrates that dominant male rhesus monkeys do not produce more offspring than any other males in any given year.

25.   W. C. McGrew, "The Female Chimpanzee as a Human Evolutionary Prototype," *Woman the Gatherer*, ed. Frances Dahlberg (New Haven, 1981), p. 54; Caroline E. G. Tutin, "Exceptions to Promiscuity in a Feral Chimpanzee Community," *Contemporary Primatology*, ed. S. Kondo, M. Kawai, and A. Ehara (Basel, 1975), pp. 447–448.

26.   Leibowitz, "Perspectives," Reiter, *Anthropology*, p. 27.

27.   Ibid., pp. 28–30; Ernst W. Caspari, "The Biological Basis of Female Hierarchies," Tiger and Fowler, *Hierarchies*, pp. 100–101.

28.   Hrdy, *Woman*, p. 59.

29.   Sarah Blaffer Hrdy, *The Langurs of Abu* (Cambridge, Mass., 1977).

30.   Hrdy, *Woman*, pp. 38–39.

31.   Caspari, "Biological Basis," Tiger and Fowler, *Hierarchies*, suggests that dominance as influence or centrality or privilege shifts from animal to animal in different contexts.

32. Morgan, *Descent*, p. 191.

33. Hrdy, *Woman*, p. 110.

34. Morgan, *Descent*, pp. 169ff.

35. Katherine Ralls, "Mammals in Which Females Are Larger Than Males," *Quarterly Review of Biology* 51 (1976):245–276.

36. Fisher, *Creation*, p. 18.

37. Hrdy, *Woman*, pp. 80–95; 215 n.12, n.13.

38. Birute M. F. Galdikas and Geza Teleki, "Variations in Subsistence Activities of Female and Male Pongids: New Perspectives on the Origins of Hominid Labor Division," *Current Anthropology* 22, 3 (June 1981):241–256.

39. Chance and Jolly, *Social Groups*, p. 136.

40. Hrdy, *Woman*, p. 29; Tanner, *Human*, p. 90.

41. Hrdy, *Woman*, p. 29.

42. Galdikas and Teleki, "Variations."

43. Wilson, *Sociobiology*, p. 175.

44. Morgan, *Descent*, p. 168.

45. Geza Teleki, E. E. Hunt, Jr., and J. H. Pfifferling, "Demographic Observations (1963–1973) on the Chimpanzees of Gombe National Park, Tanzania," *Journal of Human Evolution* 5 (1976):559–598.

46. Hrdy, *Woman*, p. 30.

47. Tanner, *Human*, p. 90.

48. W. C. McGrew, "Female Chimpanzees," Dahlberg, *Gatherer*, p. 47.

49. Galdikas and Teleki, "Variations."

50. Wilson, *Sociobiology*, pp. 71–72.

51. Wilson, *Sociobiology*, p. 539; Leibowitz, "Perspectives," Reiter, *Anthropology*, p. 28.

52. Tanner, *Human*, p. 88; Wilson, *Sociobiology*, p. 539.

53. Tanner, *Human*, p. 75.

54. Tanner, *Human*, p. 94.

55. Cathleen B. Clark, "A Preliminary Report on Weaning Among Chimpanzees of the Gombe National Park, Tanzania," *Primate Bio-Social Development*, ed. Suzanne Chevalier-Skolnikoff and Frank E. Poirier (New York, 1977), p. 237.

56. Jane Goodall, "The Behavior of Free-Living Chimpanzees in the Gombe Stream Reserve," *Animal Behavior Monographs* 1 (1968):161–311.

57. Martin and Voorhies, *Female*, p. 167; Tanner, *Human*, p. 94.

58. Tanner, *Human*, p. 95.

59. Adrienne L. Zihlman, "Women as Shapers of the Human Adaptation," Dahlberg, *Gatherer*, p. 102; McGrew, "Female Chimpanzees," Dahlberg, *Gatherer*, p. 54.

60. Zihlman, "Shapers," Dahlberg, *Gatherer*, p. 107.

61. Nowak, *Eve's Rib*, pp. 73, 77, 78, describes many species for whom mating is impossible when the female feels hostile to the male, among them spiders, tigers, rams, stags, bucks, and monkeys, and quotes Leonard Williams (*Man and Monkey*): "In monkey society, there is no such thing as rape."

62. Tanner, *Human*, p. 95.

63. Galdikas and Teliki, "Variations"; Leibowitz, "Perspectives," Reiter, *Anthropology*, p. 31.

64. Peter C. Reynolds, *On the Evolution of Human Behavior* (Berkeley, 1981), pp. 22–23; Wilson, *Sociobiology*, pp. 80, 87.

65. See, for example, Anne E. Pusey, "Inbreeding Avoidance in Chimpanzees," *Animal Behavior* 28 (1980):543–552.

66. Zihlman, "Shapers," Dahlberg, *Gatherer*, p. 86; Tanner, *Human*, p. 143.

67. Gould, *Darwin*, p. 183. Brain size doubled during ensuing ages. Wilson, *Sociobiology*, p. 271, estimates the cranial capacity of *Homo erectus* at 1000 cubic centimeters, of Neanderthalensis at 1400–1700 cubic centimeters, and of *Homo sapiens* at 900–2000 cubic centimeters. Beyond absolute and relative size, however, a reorganization of areas seems to be involved in the evolution of the brain. See Tanner, *Human*, pp. 206–207.

68. The argument about body weight and menstruation is developed by Rose Frisch, "Critical Weights, a Critical Body Composition, Menarche and the Maintenance of Menstrual Cycles," *Biosocial Interrelations in Population Adaptation*, ed. Elizabeth Watts, F. Johnston, and G. Lasker (The Hague, 1975):309–318; and by Rose Frisch and J. McArthur, "Menstrual Cycles: Fatness as a Determinant of Minimum Weight for Height Necessary for Their Maintenance or Onset," *Science* 185 (1974):949–951.

69. Prolactin appears to impede ovarian follicular development, necessary to conception,

and women who are breast feeding have high levels of prolactin in their bodies. Prolactin seems to be released at the initiation of suckling, and thus to be highest in women who suckle their infants often, regardless of the duration of each feeding. See Peter Anderson, "Reproductive Role of the Human Breast," Current Anthropology 24, 1 (Feb. 1983):25–43. See also Gina Bari Kolata, "!Kung Hunter-Gatherers: Feminism, Diet, and Birth Control," Science 185 (Sept. 13, 1974):932–934; Richard B. Lee, "Population Growth and the Beginnings of Sedentary Life Among the !Kung Bushmen," Population Growth: Anthropological Implications, ed. Brian Spooner (Cambridge, Mass., 1972); Melvin J. Konner, "Maternal Care, Infant Behavior and Development Among the !Kung," Kalahari Hunter Gatherers, ed. Richard B. Lee and Irven DeVore (Cambridge, Mass., 1976).

70.   Zihlman, "Shapers," Dahlberg, Gatherer, p. 90.

71.   For a brief survey of demonstrations of this fact, see Nancy Chodorow, The Reproduction of Mothering (Berkeley and Los Angeles, 1978), pp. 11–39.

72.   Tanner, Human, p. 219.

73.   Tanner, Human, p. 148.

74.   Zihlman, "Shapers," Dahlberg, Gatherer, p. 102. Tanner, Human, pp. 178–190, has an extended and fascinating discussion on the interpretation of tooth fossils.

75.   S. L. Washburn and R. Moore, Ape Into Man: A Study of Human Evolution (Boston, 1974), pp. 142–143.

76.   "The material out of which all human society has been constructed is the bond of those sentiments [the mother-child bond]. The origin of all social bonds, the only one which exists among the higher animals and in most primitive groups, is that created by mother-love." Briffault, Mothers, abridged, p. 44.

77.   "The hominid bond does not have the exclusivity of truly pair-bonded species. . . . Adultery and divorce give every indication of being as venerable as marriage." Reynolds, Evolution, p. 245.

78.   McGrew, "Female Chimpanzees," Dahlberg, Gatherer, p. 64; Zihlman, "Shapers," Dahlberg, Gatherer, p. 96; Tanner, Human, p. 210.

79.   W. C. McGrew believes that hominid females developed menopause as a safety mechanism, to preclude giving birth to babies at a time when the mother might die before the children were mature. "Female Chimpanzees," Dahlberg, Gatherer, p. 65.

80.   Reynolds, Evolution, p. 246.

81.   Tanner, Human, pp. 143–144, postulates a diet 80–90 percent vegetable for hominids as an intermediate figure between modern Bushmen, with a diet 70 percent vegetable, and chimpanzees, with a diet 90–99 percent vegetable.

82.   Richard B. Lee, "What Hunters Do for a Living," Man the Hunter, ed. Richard B. Lee and Irven DeVore (Chicago, 1968), pp. 31–33, 36. See also Fisher, Creation, p. 182, and Marvin Harris, Cannibals and Kings (New York, 1977), p. 10.

83.   Tanner, Human, p. 144.

84.   Tanner, Human, pp. 139–141.

85.   Tanner, Human, p. 205.

86.   Tanner, Human, p. 240.

87.   Kathleen Gough, "The Origin of the Family," Women: A Feminist Perspective, ed. Jo Freeman (Palo Alto, Calif., 1979), p. 93.

88.   Harold M. Schmeck, Jr., New York Times, Nov. 14, 1981.

89.   Martin and Voorhies, Female, p. 173.

90.   Sherwood L. Washburn and C. S. Lancaster, "The Evolution of Hunting," Lee and DeVore, Hunter, p. 299.

91.   Gough, "Origin," Freeman, Women, p. 93.

92.   Boulding, Underside, p. 85.

93.   "The problem of language and speech origins is clarified from another direction by the ontogenetic nature of the language capacity. If, at any point in the evolutionary process, 'language' or proto-language was to be learned, it would not have been in the context of the hunt. It would have been learned young." Alexander Marshack, "Some Implications of the Paleolithic Symbolic Evidence for the Origin of Language," Origins and Evolution of Language and Speech, ed. S. R. Harnand, H. D. Steklis, and J. Lancaster (New York, 1976). New York Academy of Sciences, Conference Proceedings, Sept. 22–25, 1975, vol. 280, p. 309.

94.   Alexander Marshack, The Roots of Civilization (New York, 1972), pp. 84–90; Boulding, Underside, pp. 83, 91–92.

95.   Lee and DeVore, Hunter, pp. 7–12, reject the picture drawn by Elman Service in 1962, and suggest rather a general egalitarianism.

96. Edward O. Wilson, *On Human Nature* (New York, 1979), pp. 101–107; Martin and Voorhies, *Female*, p. 53.

97. Zihlman, "Shapers," Dahlberg, *Gatherer*, p. 75.

98. This is the theory of Jane Jacobs, *The Economy of Cities* (New York, 1970).

99. L. R. Hiatt, "Ownership and Use of Land Among the Australian Aborigines," Lee and DeVore, *Hunter*, p. 101.

100. James Woodburn, "Stability and Flexibility in Hadza Residential Groupings"; June Helm, "The Nature of Dogrib Socioterritorial Groups"; Colin Turnbull, "The Importance of Flux in Two Hunting Societies"; all in Lee and DeVore, *Hunter*, pp. 104–110, 121, 132–136.

101. Dahlberg, *Gatherer*, p. 8.

102. Hitoshi Watanabe, "Subsistence and Ecology of Northern Food Gatherers with Special Reference to the Ainu," Lee and DeVore, *Hunter*, p. 74; Agnes Estioko-Griffin and P. Bion Griffin, "Woman the Hunter: The Agta," Dahlberg, *Gatherer*, pp. 126ff.; Martin and Voorhies, *Female*, pp. 197–198. William Irwin Thompson, *The Time Falling Bodies Take to Light* (New York, 1981), p. 132, believes women gave up hunting when game became scarce, and instead devoted themselves to horticulture and domestication of animals.

103. Kathleen Gough writes, "In 97 percent of the 175 societies classified by G. P. Murdock, hunting is confined to men; in the other 3 percent it is chiefly a male pursuit. Gathering . . . is women's work. In 60 percent of societies, only women gather, while in another 32 percent gathering is mainly feminine. Fishing is solely or mainly men's work in 93 percent of the hunting societies where it occurs." "Origin," Freeman, *Women*, p. 94.

104. Marielouise Janssen-Jurreit, *Sexism: The Male Monopoly on History and Thought* (New York, 1982), pp. 154–55.

105. Janssen-Jurreit, *Sexism*, p. 156.

106. James Woodburn, "An Introduction to Hadza Ecology," Lee and DeVore, *Hunter*, p. 53.

107. Boulding, *Underside*, p. 114.

108. Boulding, *Underside*, pp. 97, 101.

109. Thompson, *Falling Bodies*, p. 263 n.18. Recent excavation in the Egyptian desert has shown that deliberate horticulture was practiced there between 17,000 and 18,500 years ago. See Fred Wendorf, Romuald Schild, and Angela E. Close, "An Ancient Harvest on the Nile," *Science* (Nov. 1982):68–73.

110. Martin and Voorhies, *Female*, p. 283, write, "Agricultural societies are tremendously consistent in their assignment of cultivative tasks. Some 81 percent delegate males for farming as compared to only 17 percent of our horticultural sample. Female cultivation, so central to societies employing hand tools, shrivels in importance to a mere 16 percent in agricultural cases."

111. The Hadza, for instance. See Woodburn, "Hadza Ecology," Lee and DeVore, *Hunter*, p. 50.

112. Thompson, *Falling Bodies*, p. 132.

113. Boulding, *Underside*, pp. 169–70.

114. Marija Gimbutas, *The Gods and Goddesses of Old Europe* (Berkeley, 1974), p. 163.

115. Gough, "Origin," Freeman, *Women*, p. 73; Boulding, *Underside*, p. 149; Charles Seltman, *Women in Antiquity* (London, 1956), pp. 33–34.

116. Gimbutas, *Gods and Goddesses*, passim.

117. Judith Ochshorn, *The Female Experience and the Nature of the Divine* (Bloomington, Ind., 1981), p. 31.

118. Gimbutas, *Gods and Goddesses*, pp. 15, 38, 55.

119. Gimbutas, *Gods and Goddesses*, pp. 171, 195.

120. Gimbutas, *Gods and Goddesses*, pp. 171, 211–214.

121. Gimbutas, *Gods and Goddesses*, pp. 91–102, 135–145, 186–195.

122. Gimbutas, *Gods and Goddesses*, pp. 85–102, 116–132, 163.

123. Raphael Patai, *The Hebrew Goddess* (New York, 1967), pp. 58–61; David Bakan, *And They Took Themselves Wives* (San Francisco, 1979), p. 77.

124. H. R. Ellis Davidson, *Gods and Myths of Northern Europe* (Baltimore, Md., 1964), p. 116.

125. Davidson, *Gods and Myths*, p. 94.

126. Kevin Crossley-Holland, *The Norse Myths* (New York, 1973), p. 203.

127. Ferdinand Anton, *Woman in Pre-Columbian America* (New York, 1973), pp. 13–14.

128. Anton, *Pre-Columbian*, pp. 15–16.

129. For a sketch of this painting and discussion, see Thompson, *Falling Bodies*, p. 121.

130. Thompson, *Falling Bodies*, pp. 263–266 n.30.

131. Sarah B. Pomeroy, *Goddesses, Whores, Wives and Slaves* (New York, 1975), p. 15.

132. Ruby Rohrlich-Leavitt, "Women in Transition: Crete and Sumer," *Becoming Visible: Women in European History,* ed. Renate Bridenthal and Claudia Koonz (Boston, 1977), p. 40.

133. V. Gordon Childe, *Social Evolution* (Cleveland, 1963), pp. 64–65, believes the lack of male and phallic images means paternity was not recognized in Paleolithic and Neolithic cultures.

134. Boulding, *Underside,* p. 115.

135. James Mellaart, *Catal Huyuk* (London, 1967), passim.

136. Harris, *Cannibals,* p. 34; Rohrlich-Leavitt, "Transition," Bridenthal and Koonz, *Visible,* p. 43.

137. Thompson, *Falling Bodies,* p. 147.

138. Boulding, *Underside,* p. 127.

139. Gimbutas, *Gods and Goddesses,* p. 55.

140. Like John Chadwick, *The Mycenaean World* (New York, 1976), who expresses surprise at an inscription (in a Linear B record) to Posidaeja, a female form of Poseidon, and no mention of the male form; and at a child being named Alexandra, which means *she who repels men.* But he does not doubt the dominance of worship of the Earth Mother (pp. 61, 93, 94).

141. Emily Vermeule, *Greece in the Bronze Age* (Chicago, 1964); Charles Seltman, *Antiquity,* p. 119, also offers evidence of the importance of goddess worship in Classical Athens.

142. Pomeroy, *Goddesses,* p. 15.

143. Rohrlich-Leavitt, "Transition," Bridenthal and Koonz, *Visible,* pp. 42, 46, 49–50.

144. Chadwick, *Mycenaean,* p. 159.

145. G. G. Vaillant, *Aztecs of Mexico* (Garden City, N.Y., 1950), pp. 28–39.

146. Thompson, *Falling Bodies,* p. 150, offers an example of the rule of custom in the twentieth century cited by J. M. Synge, *The Aran Islands and Other Writings* (New York, 1962), p. 61, describing how a twentieth-century Aran fisherman, if he had done wrong, would take the boat over to Galway alone and put himself in jail.

147. The sign for *slavegirl* appears in protoliterate tablets as early as 3500 B.C.E. The sign for male slaves appears later and in fewer numbers: Rohrlich-Leavitt, "Transition," Bridenthal and Koonz, *Visible,* p. 54. Chadwick, *Mycenaean,* pp. 78–79, believes that only women were slaves in Achaean Mycenae.

148. Sir Leonard Woolley, *The Sumerians* (New York, 1965), p. 39.

149. Boulding, *Underside,* p. 223.

150. Rohrlich-Leavitt, "Transition," Bridenthal and Koonz, *Visible,* p. 55.

151. Wayne Suttles, "Coping with Abundance: Subsistence on the Northwest Coast," Lee and DeVore, *Hunter,* p. 56.

152. Harry Levin, *The Myth of the Golden Age in the Renaissance* (Bloomington, Ind., 1969), Chapter 1, offers an interesting discussion of various features of early versions of this myth.

153. Joan Bamberger, "The Myth of Matriarchy: Why Men Rule in Primitive Society," *Woman, Culture, and Society,* ed. Michelle Rosaldo and Louise Lamphere (Stanford, Calif., 1974), pp. 263–280.

154. Joseph Campbell, *The Masks of God: Occidental Mythology* (New York, 1970), p. 86.

155. See Robert Graves, *The Greek Myths* (Baltimore, Md., 1966); Jane Harrison, *Themis: A Study of the Social Origins of Greek Religion* (New York, 1962), p. 41.

156. Gilbert Murray, *Five Stages of Greek Religion* (Garden City, N.Y., 1955), pp. 49, 55.

157. See Graves, *Myths,* pp. 44–47, and Gimbutas, *Gods and Goddesses,* pp. 148–150, on origins of Athene and Hera.

158. Briffault, *Mothers,* abridged, p. 367.

159. Eva Figes, *Patriarchal Attitudes* (New York, 1970), p. 35.

160. Merlin Stone, private communication, 10/7/85. Ruby Rohrlich and June Nash, "Patriarchal Puzzle: State Formation in Mesopotamia and Mesoamerica," *Heresies* 4, 1, Issue 13 (1981):60–65.

161. Alexander Heidel, *The Babylonian Genesis* (Chicago, 1951), pp. 10–14.

162. Crossley-Holland, *Norse Myths,* p. xxvii.

163. Crossley-Holland, *Norse Myths,* pp. 184, 188, 195.

164. Burr Cartwright Brundage, *The Fifth Sun* (Austin, Texas, 1979), pp. 46, 76, 137–139.

165. Anton, *Pre-Columbian,* p. 58.

166. Brundage, *Sun,* pp. 139, 166, 173, 175.

167. Anton, *Pre-Columbian,* p. 58.

168. Catherine H. Berndt, "Interpretations and 'Facts' in Aboriginal Australia," Dahlberg, *Gatherer,* p. 196.

169. Peggy Reeves Sanday writes about a Mundurucu myth describing a time when women ruled and were sexually aggressive, but men hunted. The women controlled sacred trumpets which

demanded meat. The men took the trumpets by force, symbolically seizing ownership and control of female generative capacities. *Female Power and Male Dominance* (New York, 1981), pp. 37–40. See also Leslee Nadelson, "Pigs, Women, and the Men's House in Amazonia," *Sexual Meanings: The Cultural Construction of Gender and Sexuality*, ed. Sherry B. Ortner and Harriet Whitehead (Cambridge, England, 1981); Joan Bamberger, "Myth," Rosaldo and Lamphere, *Woman*, pp. 269–275, offers versions of women's subjugation by men told in the Tierra del Fuego and societies of the northwest Amazon and central Brazil; see also Claude Lévi-Strauss, *From Honey to Ashes*, trans. John and Doreen Weightman (New York, 1973), pp. 271ff.

170. Janssen-Jurreit, *Sexism*, p. 96.

171. Sanday, *Female Power*, p. 48.

172. Henry S. Sharp, "The Null Case: The Chipewyan," Dahlberg, *Gatherer*, p. 225.

173. Colin Turnbull, "Mbuti Womanhood," Dahlberg, *Gatherer*, p. 218.

174. Joyce A. Ladner, "Racism and Tradition: Black Womanhood in Historical Perspective," *Liberating Women's History*, ed. Berenice A. Carroll (Urbana, Ill., 1976), p. 182.

175. Jane C. Goodale, *Tiwi Wives* (Seattle, Wash., 1971), pp. 3–4.

176. Fisher, *Creation*, p. 123.

177. Janssen-Jurreit, *Sexism*, p. 95.

178. Janssen-Jurreit, *Sexism*, p. 94.

179. Lévi-Strauss, *The Raw and the Cooked*, pp. 83–99.

180. Robert Briffault, *The Mothers*, I (New York, 1927). Page numbers from here on refer exclusively to the original three-volume edition.

181. Briffault, *Mothers*, I, p. 271.

182. Briffault, *Mothers*, I, pp. 362–363.

183. Briffault, *Mothers*, I, pp. 368–369.

184. Briffault, *Mothers*, I, pp. 377–387. Briffault cites Gaston Maspero and Diodorous Siculus.

185. Briffault, *Mothers*, I, pp. 388–390.

186. Briffault, *Mothers*, I, p. 370.

187. For other signs of matrilineality and matricentry in ancient Judaism, see Naomi Goodman, "Eve, Child Bride of Adam," *Psychosexual Imperatives: Their Role in Identity Formation*, ed. Marie Coleman Nelson and Jean Ikenberry (New York and London, 1979), p. 43.

188. Julian Morgenstern, "*Beena* Marriage (Matriarchat) in Ancient Israel and Its Historical Implications," *Zeitschrift für die Altestamentische Wissenschaft* 47 (1929), pp. 47, 91–110.

189. Briffault, *Mothers*, I, p. 371.

190. Bakan, *Wives*, p. 71.

191. Briffault, *Mothers*, I, p. 371.

192. Briffault, *Mothers*, I, p. 372.

193. Bakan, *Wives*, p. 67.

194. Bakan, *Wives*, p. 84.

195. Briffault, *Mothers*, I, p. 363.

196. Briffault, *Mothers*, I, p. 371.

197. Briffault, *Mothers*, I, pp. 375–376.

198. Briffault, *Mothers*, I, pp. 415–420.

199. Briffault, *Mothers*, I, pp. 268–273.

200. Briffault, *Mothers*, I, p. 427.

201. G. P. Murdock, *Social Structure* (New York, 1949).

202. Michelle Rosaldo, "Woman, Culture, and Society: An Overview," Rosaldo and Lamphere, *Woman*, pp. 19–20.

203. JoAnn McNamara, personal communication, November 1982.

204. Janssen-Jurreit, *Sexism*, p. 160.

205. Rosaldo, "Overview," Rosaldo and Lamphere, *Woman*, p. 27.

206. For instance, *Cooperation and Competition Among Primitive Peoples*, ed. Margaret Mead (New York, 1937); Martin and Voorhies, *Female*; Sanday, *Female Power*.

207. Martin and Voorhies, *Female*, p. 233. Margaret Mead, "Interpretive Statement," Mead, *Cooperation*, p. 461, discovered only two groups that deviated from this description—the Dobrians, who are matrilineal but also competitive, and the Apache, who are matrilocal but individualistic.

208. Martin and Voorhies, *Female*, pp. 232–233.

209. Sanday, *Female Power*, pp. 60–61, 84; Martin and Voorhies, *Female*, p. 247.

210. Sanday, *Female Power*, pp. 62–63.

211. Martin and Voorhies, *Female*, p. 233.

212. Martin and Voorhies, *Female*, p. 225.

213. Boulding, *Underside*, p. 143.

214. Turnbull, "Mbuti," Dahlberg, *Gatherer*, p. 205.

215. Turnbull, "Flux," Lee and DeVore, *Hunter*, p. 136.

216. Turnbull, "Mbuti," Dahlberg, *Gatherer*, p. 209.

217. Turnbull, "Mbuti," Dahlberg, *Gatherer*, p. 212.

218. Turnbull, "Mbuti," Dahlberg, *Gatherer*, p. 216.

219. Margerie Shostak, *Nisa* (Cambridge, Mass., 1981), pp. 265–266.

220. Information on the Iroquois is derived mainly from B. H. Quain, "The Iroquois," in Mead, *Cooperation*, pp. 240–281; Judith K. Brown, "Iroquois Women: An Ethnohistoric Note," in Reiter, *Anthropology*, pp. 235–251; Eleanor Leacock, "Women in Egalitarian Societies," Bridenthal and Koonz, *Visible*, pp. 11–35. The impact of fur trading on Iroquois social structures is questioned by Louise Lamphere, "Anthropology," *Signs* 2, 3 (Spring 1977):612–627.

221. Leacock, "Egalitarian," Bridenthal and Koonz, *Visible*, p. 20.

222. Information on the Chipewyan from Sharp, "Null Case," Dahlberg, *Gatherer*, pp. 221–244.

223. Sharp, "Null Case," Dahlberg, *Gatherer*, p. 236.

224. Robin Fox, *The Red Lamp of Incest* (New York, 1980), pp. 199–200.

225. Margaret Mead, *Sex and Temperament in Three Primitive Societies* (New York, 1963), pp. 237–253.

226. Ibid.

227. Irving Goldman, "The Zuni Indians of New Mexico," Mead, *Cooperation*, p. 322.

228. Goldman, "Zuni," Mead, *Cooperation*, pp. 314–328.

229. Goldman, "Zuni," Mead, *Cooperation*, pp. 313, 333ff.

230. Berndt, "Australia," Dahlberg, *Gatherer*, p. 153.

231. Bronislaw Malinowski, *The Family Among the Australian Aborigines* (London, 1913), p. 288.

232. Phyllis Kaberry, *Aboriginal Woman: Sacred and Profane* (London, 1939), pp. 25–26.

233. Berndt, "Australia," Dahlberg, *Gatherer*, pp. 182–188; Frederick G. G. Rose, "Australian Marriage, Land-Owning Groups, and Initiations," Lee and DeVore, *Hunter*, p. 200.

234. Ruby Rohrlich-Leavitt, Barbara Sykes, and Elizabeth Weatherford, "Aboriginal Woman: Male and Female Anthropological Perspectives," Reiter, *Anthropology*, p. 120.

235. Rose, "Australian Marriage," Lee and DeVore, *Hunter*, pp. 200–208.

236. Kaberry, *Aboriginal*, p. 27.

237. Berndt, "Australia," Dahlberg, *Gatherer*, passim.

238. Richard A. Gould, *Yiwara* (New York, 1969).

239. Gould, *Yiwara*, p. 76.

240. Gould, *Yiwara*, pp. 8, 14, 19.

241. Rohrlich-Leavitt, Sykes, and Weatherford, "Aboriginal," Reiter, *Anthropology*, pp. 114–115.

242. Patricia Draper, "!Kung Women: Contrasts in Sexual Egalitarianism in Foraging and Sedentary Contexts," Reiter, *Anthropology*, p. 83.

243. Gould, *Yiwara*, pp. 9–11.

244. Gould, *Yiwara*, p. 18.

245. Gould, *Yiwara*, p. 128.

246. Gould, *Yiwara*, p. 192.

247. Turnbull, *Human Cycle*, pp. 51–52.

248. Turnbull, *Human Cycle*, p. 180.

CHAPTER TWO

THE FALL: PATRIARCHY

1. J. J. Bachofen, *Das Mutterrecht* (1861): an abridged English translation by Ralph Manheim entitled *Myth, Religion, and Mother-Right* was published in 1967 in Princeton, N.J.; Briffault, *Mothers*; Elizabeth Gould Davis, *The First Sex* (New York, 1972).

2. Lewis Henry Morgan, *Ancient Society* (New York, 1877); Frederick Engels, *The Origin of the Family, Private Property, and the State* (New York, 1978), was originally published in Germany in 1884.

3. Engels, *Origin*, pp. 117–121.

4. Gayle Rubin analyzes these ideas from the perspective of sex and gender in "The Traffic in Women," Reiter, *Anthropology*, pp. 157–210.

5.    One of the first to articulate this theory was perhaps Briffault, *Mothers*, abridged, p. 97, but see also Lee and DeVore, *Hunter*; Lionel Tiger, *Men in Groups* (New York, 1969); Alice Rossi, "A Biosocial Perspective on Parenting," *Daedalus* 106, 2 (1977):1–31; Roy d'Andrade, "Sex Differences and Cultural Institutions," *The Development of Sex Differences*, ed. Eleanor E. Maccoby (Stanford, Calif., 1966), pp. 173–204; and Ernestine Friedl, *Women and Men: An Anthropologist's View* (New York, 1975).

6.    Harris, *Cannibals*.

7.    Eleanor Leacock, "Women's Status in Egalitarian Society: Implications for Social Evolution," *Current Anthropology* 19 (1978):247–255. The women of the Yanomamo in Venezuela, and of the Somali of East Africa, for instance, do the heaviest labor. Among the Tsambigula of New Guinea, only little boys are allowed to play; little girls have to work. Nevertheless, among these peoples men's activities are more prestigious, and to help a woman would cause a man to lose face. Janssen-Jurreit, *Sexism*, p. 157.

8.    Sanday, *Female Power*, pp. 69, 171.

9.    Gimbutas, *Gods and Goddesses*, p. 145.

10.    Wilson, *Human*, pp. 40ff., describes this phenomenon: "Females in the best physical condition produce the healthiest infants, and these offspring usually grow up to be the largest, most vigorous adults. . . . According to the theory of natural selection females should be expected to give birth to a higher proportion of males when they are healthiest, because these offspring will be largest in size, mate most successfully, and produce the maximum number of offspring. As the condition of the female deteriorates, they should shift progressively to the production of daughters, since female offspring will now represent the safer investment. According to natural-selection theory, genes that induce this reproductive strategy will spread through the population at the expense of genes that promote alternative strategies. It works. In deer and human beings, two of the species investigated with reference to this particular question, environmental conditions adverse for pregnant females are associated with a disproportionate increase in the birth of daughters. Data from mink, pigs, sheep, and seals also appear to be consistent. . . . The most likely direct mechanism is the selectively greater mortality of male fetuses under adversity, a phenomenon that has been documented in numerous species of mammals." What Wilson is saying is that males are more fragile than females, although this statement is considerably disguised.

11.    It is this fact that lies at the root of sociobiological theory: no matter how complex it may become, it is basically a vision of nature as a competition among males to become the one cock who makes it to the barnyard while all the others are on their way to the butcher shop. By excluding most of experience, by ignoring the female half of mammal species, male sociobiologists narrow all of life down to a contest for domination which is supposed to guarantee a male creature a better chance of passing on his genes. Such a vision of nature is probably false to most animal experience—dominance orders among most primates do not seem to work this way—although it may apply somewhat more to human males. But its falseness lies as much in what it omits as in what it includes, since it omits most of what creatures do and experience and reduces all of life to a struggle for procreation.

12.    Glenn Collins, "Tribe Where Harmony Rules," *New York Times*, Sept. 19, 1983. They are also extremely harmonious within their "family" unit, although fiercely hostile to those outside it. But as yet little has been published about them.

13.    Friedl, *Women and Men*, p. 7.

14.    William Divale and Marvin Harris, "Population, Warfare, and the Male Supremacist Complex," *American Anthropologist* 78 (1976):521–538.

15.    Sanday, *Female Power*, pp. 163–170.

16.    Susan Carol Rogers, "Female Forms of Power and the Myth of Male Dominance: A Model of Female/Male Interaction in Peasant Society," *American Ethnologist* 2 (1975):727–756.

17.    Margaret Mead, *Sex and Temperament*; and *The Mountain Arapesh* (1938; reprint, New York, 1971).

18.    P. C. Lloyd, "The Yoruba of Nigeria," *Peoples of Africa*, ed. James L. Gibbs (New York, 1965), pp. 547–582.

19.    Rubin, "Traffic," Reiter, *Anthropology*, p. 163.

20.    Gough, "Origin," Freeman, *Women*, pp. 99–100.

21.    Many women do gather in dangerous terrain; for example, !Kung women: see Patricia Draper, "!Kung Women," Reiter, *Anthropology*, p. 83; and Abipon women: see Sanday, *Female Power*, p. 122.

22.    This is the behavior of the Aboriginal hunters studied by Gould, *Yiwara*, pp. 17–18.

23.    Lévi-Strauss, *Totemism*, p. 57.

24.    Lévi-Strauss, *Totemism*, p. 25.

25. Briffault, *Mothers*, I, p. 387.

26. Lévi-Strauss, *Totemism*, pp. 57, 61.

27. Wilson, *Sociobiology*, p. 285.

28. A. P. Elkin, "Studies in Australian Totemism: Sub-section, Section, and Moiety Totemism," *Oceania* 4, 2 (1933–34):65–90; "Studies in Australian Totemism: The Nature of Australian Totemism," *Oceania* 4, 2 (1933–34):113–131.

29. Rohrlich-Leavitt, "Transition," Bridenthal and Koonz, *Visible*, pp. 55–56.

30. According to Bronislaw Malinowski, *The Sexual Life of Savages in Northwestern Melanesia* (New York, 1929), the Trobriand Islanders had no word for father.

31. Male animals may have iron rings affixed to their penises to prevent them from masturbating before they are to be mated; female animals are sometimes hung, tied by all four legs, with the vagina facing out, easily available to the male. But the major form of breeding control is castration of males. In some cases the techniques for accomplishing this are unbelievably cruel. Sometimes the animal's scrotum is tied up with cord so that the testicles will atrophy; some tribes pound the testicles with stones to destroy them. See B. A. L. Cranstone, "Animal Husbandry: The Evidence from Ethnography," ed. Peter J. Ucko and G. W. Dimbleby, *The Domestication and Exploitation of Plants and Animals* (Chicago, 1969), pp. 255, 256, 257, 258. Fisher's discussion of the subject appears in *Creation*, pp. 193–199.

32. Bakan, *Wives*, p. 95.

33. Mary O'Brien, "Feminist Theory and Dialectical Logic," *Signs* 7, 1 (Autumn 1981):144–157.

34. Jean Bethke Elshtain, *Public Man, Private Woman* (Princeton, N.J., 1981), pp. 12, 46.

35. Citation from *Symposium*, 209 C, discussed by Susan Moller Okin, *Women in Western Political Thought* (Princeton, N.J., 1979), pp. 25, 26.

36. O'Brien, "Theory and Logic," *Signs*, 1 (Autumn 1981):151.

37. Ivan Illich, *Shadow Work* (Boston, 1981), p. 83.

38. Robin Fox, *Encounter with Anthropology* (New York, 1973), p. 47.

39. Gerard M. Dalgish, A *Dictionary of Africanisms* (Westport, Conn., 1982), p. 18.

40. Lévi-Strauss, *Totemism*, p. 60.

41. Lee, "Living," Lee and DeVore, *Hunter*, p. 37.

42. Watanabe, "Northern Food Gatherers," Lee and DeVore, *Hunter*, p. 74.

43. Gerardo Reichel-Dolmatoff, *Amazonian Cosmos* (Chicago, 1971), p. 54.

44. Woodburn, "Hadza Ecology," Lee and DeVore, *Hunter*, p. 52.

45. A. P. Elkin, "Studies in Australian Totemism," *Oceania* 4, 1 (1933–34):65–90; Lévi-Strauss, *Totemism*, p. 57.

46. Fox, *Incest*, p. 75.

47. Alice Schlegel, "Male:Female in Hopi Thought and Action," *Sexual Stratification*, ed. A. Schlegel (New York, 1977), p. 261.

48. Quotation from Bridget O'Laughlin, "Mediation of Contradiction: Why Mbum Women Do not Eat Chicken," Rosaldo and Lamphere, *Woman*, p. 311. See also Sherry Ortner, "Is Female to Male as Nature Is to Culture?" Rosaldo and Lamphere, *Woman*, p. 78.

49. Gillian Gillison, "Images of Nature in Gimi Thought," *Nature, Culture and Gender*, ed. Carol P. MacCormack and Marilyn Strathern (New York, 1980), p. 146.

50. Among these are the Fore (see Shirley Lindenbaum, "A Wife Is the Hand of Man", *Man and Woman in the New Guinea Highlands*, ed. P. Brown and G. Buchbinder, American Anthropological Association Special Publication No. 8 (1976), pp. 56–58; and the Wogeo (see Ian Hogbin, *The Island of Menstruating Men* [San Francisco, 1970], pp. 88ff.).

51. Fisher, *Creation*, p. 156.

52. Gillison, "Gimi," MacCormack and Strathern, *Nature*, p. 164.

53. Mead, *Cooperation*, p. 38.

54. Bamberger, "Myth," Rosaldo and Lamphere, *Woman*, pp. 277–278.

55. Sharp, "Null Case," Dahlberg, *Gatherer*, p. 227ff.

56. Gillison, "Gimi," MacCormack and Strathern, *Nature*, pp. 149–153.

57. Sanday, *Female Power*, pp. 41–45.

58. Jane C. Goodale, "Gender, Sexuality and Marriage: A Kaulong Model of Nature and Culture," MacCormack and Strathern, *Nature*, pp. 119–142.

59. Elizabeth Faithorn, "The Concept of Pollution Among the Káfe of the Papua New Guinea Highlands," Reiter, *Anthropology*, pp. 127–140.

60. Marilyn Strathern, "No Nature, No Culture: The Hagen Case," MacCormack and Strathern, *Nature*, pp. 174–222.

61. FitzJohn Porter Poole, "Transforming 'Natural' Woman: Female Ritual Leaders and

Gender Ideology Among Bimin-Kuskusmin," Ortner and Whitehead, *Sexual Meanings*, p. 128.

62. Sanday, *Female Power*, pp. 30–34.

63. Sanday, *Female Power*, p. 206.

64. Strathern, "Hagen Case," MacCormack and Strathern, *Nature*, p. 206.

65. Gillison, "Gimi," MacCormack and Strathern, *Nature*, pp. 147, 171.

66. Sharp, "Null Case," Dahlberg, *Gatherer*, p. 227.

67. The Mundurucu, for instance. See Sanday, *Female Power*, p. 39.

68. Gillison, "Gimi," MacCormack and Strathern, *Nature*, p. 171.

69. Fisher, *Creation*, pp. 156–157.

70. According to Fisher, *Creation*, p. 156. The Aborigines do this; and some New Guineans as well: see Eleanor Leacock, Introduction to Frederick Engels, *The Origin of the Family, Private Property, and the State*, ed. Eleanor Leacock (New York, 1978), pp. 39–40; and Hogbin, *Menstruating Men*.

71. Lindenbaum, "Wife," *New Guinea*, pp. 57–58.

72. Sanday, *Female Power*, p. 43.

73. Lee, "Living," Lee and DeVore, *Hunter*, p. 40.

74. Asen Balikci, "The Netsilik Eskimos: Adaptive Process," Lee and DeVore, *Hunter*, p. 78ff.; Sanday, *Female Power*, pp. 65, 69, 76, 78, 171–172.

75. Sanday, *Female Power*, p. 37; Nadelson, "Pigs," Ortner and Whitehead, *Sexual Meanings*, p. 241.

76. Gillison, "Gimi," MacCormack and Strathern, *Nature*, p. 170.

77. Sharp, "Null Case," Dahlberg, *Gatherer*, p. 227; Sanday, *Female Power*, pp. 35–40.

78. Sanday, *Female Power*, pp. 45–47.

79. Balikci, "Netsilik," Lee and DeVore, *Hunter*.

80. Mead, *Sex and Temperament*, p. 84.

81. Claude Lévi-Strauss, "The Family," *Man, Culture, and Society*, ed. Harry Shapiro (London, 1956), p. 269.

82. Simone de Beauvoir, *The Second Sex* (New York, 1974), p. 72.

83. Most animal species are insects, and female insects are usually larger than males. Twelve of twenty orders of mammals and twenty of 122 families of mammals contain species with larger females. Among certain large mammal groups, females are almost always bigger than males—rabbits, hares, certain bats, baleen whales, seals, and antelopes. Katherine Ralls points out that blue whales are the largest animals that have ever lived, and because female baleen whales are larger than males, the largest animal that exists is female. Female hyenas are larger than male hyenas generally, and they are dominant: but they are dominant even over males who are larger than they. See Stephen Jay Gould, *Hens' Teeth and Horses' Toes* (New York, 1983), pp. 21–22, 149–150; Katherine Ralls, "Mammals in Which Females Are Larger Than Males," *Quarterly Review of Biology* 51 (1976):245–276; and H. Kruuk, *The Spotted Hyena* (Chicago, 1972).

84. Figes, *Patriarchal*, p. 9.

85. Turnbull, "Mbuti," Dahlberg, *Gatherer*, p. 210.

86. Wilson, *Human*, pp. 101–108; Martin and Voorhies, *Female*, p. 53.

87. The question whether divided roles and inequality are "natural" is probably impossible to discuss fairly. Peter Reynolds, *Evolution*, pp. 258–259, attempts to answer the question of inequality with reference to primates. He finds social hierarchy among animals, but the currency of exchange is grooming, not aggression. There is a sense of family, but it is matricentric; mating is less important than kinship.

88. For recent psychoanalytically oriented interpretations of the potent bond between mother and child, see Dorothy Dinnerstein, *The Mermaid and the Minotaur* (New York, 1977); and Chodorow, *Mothering*.

89. Ochshorn, *Female Experience*, p. 34.

90. Fox, *Red Lamp*, p. 6, claims that at "last count," there were at least ninety-six societies which permitted forms of incest.

91. Lévi-Strauss, *Raw and Cooked*, especially pp. 1–81.

92. Jonathan Gathorne-Hardy, *Marriage, Love, Sex and Divorce* (New York, 1981), p. 308.

93. Claude Lévi-Strauss, *The Elementary Structures of Kinship*, trans. J. H. Bell and J. R. von Sturmer (Boston, 1969), p. 479.

94. In some cases sacrifices may have been made to a goddess, as they were in Carthage to the goddess Tanit. But Carthage was a priest-ridden state at that time (Boulding, *Underside*, pp. 241–242). In Mesoamerica it was a goddess who "wept" for human hearts, but she had long since been deposed.

95. By Bakan, *Wives*, p. 15.

96. Carol Ochs, *Behind the Sex of God* (Boston, 1977), p. 45.

97. Bakan, *Wives*, p. 148.

98. John Boswell, *Christianity, Social Tolerance, and Homosexuality* (Chicago, 1980), p. 34.

99. Friedrich Nietzsche, *Nachgelassene Fragmente* (Sept. 1870–Jan. 1871), Abteilung III, III.

100. JoAnn McNamara, personal communication, May 1978.

101. Edmund Wilson, *To the Finland Station* (Garden City, N.Y., 1953), p. 245.

102. R. W. Apple, *New York Times*, November 9, 1982.

103. See Karen Sacks, "State Bias and Women's Status," *American Anthropologist* 78, 2 (Sept. 1976):565–569; and Sherry Ortner, "The Virgin and the State," *Feminist Studies* 4, 3 (Oct. 1978):19–35.

104. Berndt, "Australia," Dahlberg, *Gatherer*, p. 194.

105. J. P. V. D. Balsdon, *Roman Women* (Westport, Conn., 1962), p. 17. Sisters were distinguished from each other by the addition of "elder," "younger," or "first," "second," and "third." After marriage, a woman's husband's name was added to the father's, also in the genitive (possessive) case. Men on the other hand had two or three names.

106. Otto Jespersen, *The Growth and Structure of the English Language* (New York, 1923), p. 1.

107. Michel Foucault, *The Order of Things* (New York, 1973), p. 39.

108. The Volsci are ruled by Camilla, although her brother is alive, and Amata claims "mother-right" to marry her daughter to Turnus. Opposed to them and to Juno are the pious Aeneas, the pious Latinus, and Zeus.

109. Jacques De Vitry (d. 1240), cited by Eileen Power, "The Position of Women," *The Legacy of the Middle Ages*, ed. C. G. Crump and E. F. Jacob (Oxford, 1962), p. 402.

110. Nawal el Saadawi, *The Hidden Face of Eve: Women in the Arab World* (Boston, 1982), pp. 14–19.

111. Ortner, "Female to Male," Rosaldo and Lamphere, *Woman*, p. 86.

112. Epigram by Sir John Harington (1561–1612).

113. Consider, for instance, Cynthia Ozick, "Justice (Again) to Edith Wharton," *Commentary* 62, 4 (Oct. 1976):48–57, in which Wharton is condemned not for her work but for her treatment of her husband.

114. Rohrlich and Nash, "Patriarchal Puzzle," *Heresies*, pp. 60–65.

115. JoAnn McNamara, personal communication, May, 1978.

116. Rohrlich-Leavitt, "Transition," Bridenthal and Koonz, *Visible*, p. 51.

117. Rohrlich-Leavitt, "Transition," Bridenthal and Koonz, *Visible*, p. 52.

118. Rohrlich and Nash, "Patriarchal Puzzle," *Heresies*, p. 63.

119. Samuel Noah Kramer, *The Sumerians* (Chicago, 1963), p. 322.

120. Rohrlich and Nash, "Patriarchal Puzzle," *Heresies*, p. 64.

121. George Dorsey, *Man's Own Show: Civilization*, cited by Mary R. Beard, *Woman as Force in History* (1946; reprint, New York, 1971), p. 77.

122. *Ancient Near Eastern Texts*, ed. James B. Pritchard (Princeton, N.J., 1958), pp. 154 (item 143), 155 (item 153), 153–154 (item 141). See also J. B. Bury, S. A. Cook, and F. E. Adcock, "The Law of Ancient Babylonia," *Man in Adaptation: The Institutional Framework*, ed. Y. A. Cohen (Chicago, 1971), pp. 154–157.

123. Morgenstern, "*Beena* Marriage (Matriarchat) in Ancient Israel," pp. 91–110; "Additional Notes on *Beena* Marriage (Matriarchat) in Ancient Israel," *Zeitschrift für die Altatestamentische Wissenschaft* 49 (1929):46–58.

124. Bakan, *Wives*, pp. 71, 73.

125. Bakan, *Wives*, pp. 25–26, 140.

126. Bakan, *Wives*, pp. 78ff, 147.

127. Rohrlich and Nash, "Patriarchal Puzzle," *Heresies*, p. 62.

128. Anton, *Pre-Columbian*, p. 58.

129. Brundage, *Sun*, p. 169.

130. Brundage, *Sun*, pp. 33, 35–36.

131. Vaillant, *Aztecs*, pp. 112–113.

132. Rohrlich and Nash, "Patriarchal Puzzle," *Heresies*, pp. 63–64.

133. Brundage, *Sun*, p. 196.

134. Brundage, *Sun*, p. 178ff, 205–214.

135. Crossley-Holland, *Norse Myths*, p. xxv.

136. Ibid.

137. Crossley-Holland, *Norse Myths*, p. 187.

138. Marylin Arthur, " 'Liberated' Women: The Classical Era," Bridenthal and Koonz, *Visible*, p. 63.

139. Except for authorship, the fragment is unidentified. See Arthur, "Liberated," Bridenthal and Koonz, *Visible*, pp. 65, 73.

140. Pomeroy, *Goddesses*, p. 13.

141. Slater, *Hera*, pp. 130–131.

142. Slater, *Hera*, p. 8.

143. Elshtain, *Private*, p. 15.

144. Elshtain, *Private*, p. 16.

145. Arthur, "Liberated," Bridenthal and Koonz, *Visible*, p. 65.

146. Arthur, "Liberated," Bridenthal and Koonz, *Visible*, p. 63.

147. Sophocles, *Antigone*, trans. Elizabeth Wyckoff, *Sophocles, I, The Complete Greek Tragedies*, ed. D. Grene and R. Lattimore (Chicago, 1954), p. 170, ll. 338–341.

148. Janssen-Jurreit, *Sexism*, p. 310.

149. Janssen-Jurreit, *Sexism*, pp. 314–315.

150. See William E. Farrell, *New York Times*, November 13, 1977.

151. Barrington Moore, Jr., *Injustice: The Social Bases of Obedience and Revolt* (White Plains, N.Y., 1978), p. 51.

152. Moore, *Injustice*, p. 52.

153. Heinrich Zimmer, *Philosophies of India*, ed. Joseph Campbell (New York, 1956), p. 400 n.102.

154. Moore, *Injustice*, p. 53.

155. Katharine M. Rogers, *The Troublesome Helpmate: A History of Misogyny in Literature* (Seattle, Wash., 1966), pp. 14–15. It is Tertullian who wrote, to women, "You are the devil's gateway," in an effort to persuade women to dress meanly, in penitence for Eve's sin, and to wear veils: "On the Apparel of Women," and "On the Veiling of Virgins," in *The Ante-Nicene Fathers*, ed. A. C. Coxe (New York, 1925), Vol. IV.

156. Rogers, *Troublesome*, p. 17.

157. Chrysostom, *In Epistolam ad Romanos*, homily 4, *Patrologiae Graeca* 60:415ff.

158. Augustine, *Contra Mendacium* 7.10, *Patrologiae Latina* 40:496.

159. Augustine, *The City of God*, trans. Marcus Dods (New York, 1950), p. 465.

160. Boswell, *Homosexuality*, p. 164, discussing Augustine, *De Bono Conjugale* 10, *Patrologiae Latina* 40:381.

161. Boswell, *Homosexuality*, pp. 148–150.

162. Basil, *Sermo* 2.235 E, *Patrologiae Graeca* 31:885, cited by Boswell, *Homosexuality*, p. 149.

163. Kenneth A. Briggs, *New York Times*, August 7, 1977.

164. *New York Times*, August 21, 1980.

165. Ortner, "Female to Male," Rosaldo and Lamphere, *Woman*. Lévi-Strauss, however, suggests that the nature-culture contrast is an artificial creation—see *Elementary Structures*, p. xxxix—or a mere methodological device—see *The Savage Mind* (Chicago, 1966), p. 247.

166. See, for instance, MacCormack and Strathern, *Nature*.

167. Edwin Ardener, "Belief and the Problem of Women," *Perceiving Women*, ed. Shirley Ardener (London, 1975).

168. Gillison, "Gimi," MacCormack and Strathern, *Nature*, pp. 145–146.

169. Olivia Harris, "The Power of Signs: Gender, Culture and the Wild in the Bolivian Andes," MacCormack and Strathern, *Nature*.

170. Caroline Ifeka-Moller, "Female Militancy and Colonial Revolt," Ardener, *Perceiving*, p. 132.

171. Ortner, "Female to Male," Rosaldo and Lamphere, *Woman*, p. 70.

172. Lévi-Strauss, *Raw and Cooked*, pp. 66–118. The distinction between raw meat, eaten by animals, and cooked meat, eaten by men, is made also by the Chipewyans, who include the Eskimo (who eat raw food) among the animals. Chipewyan society is strongly male-supremacist; men hunt the game and thus produce the food, which women process. Possibly the Chipewyans see nature—as environment—as male, its femaleness tamed by the transcendent spirits who give men knowledge-power. See Sharp, "Null Case," Dahlberg, *Gatherer*, p. 230.

173. Turnbull, "Flux," Lee and DeVore, *Hunter*, p. 210.

174. Pomeroy, *Goddesses*, p. 4.

175. Rosaldo, "Overview," Rosaldo and Lamphere, *Woman*, p. 31.

176. Carolyn C. Lougee, *Le Paradis des Femmes: Women, Salons, and Social Stratifications in Seventeenth-Century France* (Princeton, N.J., 1976), p. 31.

177. *Godey's Lady's Book* 20 (1840), p. 273, cited by Ann Douglas, *The Feminization of American Culture* (New York, 1977), p. 58.

178. Judith Okely, "Gypsy Women," Ardener, *Perceiving*, p. 61.

179. Barbara Welter, "The Feminization of American Religion," *Clio's Consciousness Raised: New Perspectives on the History of Women*, ed. Mary S. Hartman and Lois Banner (New York, 1974), p. 151, points out that in some cultures, such as middle-class American culture of the nineteenth century, women translate "nature to man and man to himself" by transforming the bold and bitter into the bland.

180. Rubin, "Traffic," Reiter, *Anthropology*, p. 192n.

181. Bridget O'Laughlin, "Mediations of Contradiction: Why Mbum Women Do Not Eat Chicken," Rosaldo and Lamphere, *Woman*.

182. Boswell, *Homosexuality*, pp. 15–16.

183. Boswell, *Homosexuality*, p. 153.

184. Slater, *Hera*, p. 79.

185. Peter L. Berger and Thomas Luckman, *The Social Construction of Reality: A Treatise in the Sociology of Knowledge* (Garden City, N.Y., 1967), pp. 65–66, 106–107.

186. Phyllis Trible, *God and the Rhetoric of Sexuality* (Philadelphia, 1978), p. 33.

187. Harris, *Cannibals*, pp. 143–144.

188. Boswell, *Homosexuality*, p. 162.

189. Elshtain, *Private*, p. 56, writes that Christianity "ushered a moral revolution into the world which dramatically, and for the better, transformed the prevailing images of male and female, public and private."

190. Elaine Pagels, *The Gnostic Gospels* (New York, 1979), p. 66.

191. Pagels, *Gnostic*, p. 45.

192. Pagels, *Gnostic*, pp. 41–43.

193. JoAnn McNamara, personal communication, December 1981.

194. Elisabeth Schussler Fiorenza, *In Memory of Her: A Feminist Theological Reconstruction of Christian Origins* (New York, 1984), ch. 2, see esp. pp. 53–55; the uniqueness, at the time, of the idea of orthodoxy was pointed out to me by JoAnn McNamara, personal communication, October 1984.

195. Boulding, *Underside*, p. 385.

196. Minai, *Islam*, pp. 17–21, 44.

197. Max Stackhouse, *Ethics and the Urban Ethos* (Boston, 1972), p. 94.

198. Ochs, *Sex of God*, pp. 25, 154.

199. Illich, *Shadow*, p. 46.

200. Illich, *Shadow*, p. 59.

201. L. J. Jordanova, "Natural Facts: A Historical Perspective on Science and Sexuality," MacCormack and Strathern, *Nature*, p. 54.

202. Jordanova, "Natural Facts," MacCormack and Strathern, *Nature*, pp. 54, 58.

203. Laurence Stone, *The Family, Sex and Marriage in England 1500–1800* (New York, 1977), p. 42.

204. Isaac D. Balbus, *Marxism and Domination* (Princeton, N.J., 1982), p. 40.

205. Wilson, *Finland*, p. 6.

206. Engels, *Origin*, pp. 251–264, esp. pp. 260–261.

207. Marx, *Capital*, Vol. I (New York, 1967), p. 177.

208. Balbus, *Marxism*, p. 253.

209. Balbus, *Marxism*, p. 260.

210. Karl Marx, *Gundrisse: Foundations of the Critique of Political Economy* (Harmondsworth, England, 1973), p. 409. Cited by Balbus, *Marxism*, p. 41.

211. Wilson, *Finland*, p. 40.

212. Wilson, *Finland*, p. 428.

213. Wilson, *Finland*, p. 173.

214. Ann Oakley, *New York Times Book Review*, May 2, 1982.

215. Wilson, *Finland*, p. 197.

216. H. R. Trevor-Roper, "Born Again," *New York Review of Books*, November 5, 1981.

217. Simone Weil, "The Power of Words" (1937), *The Simone Weil Reader*, ed. George A. Panichas (New York, 1977), p. 268.

218. Ibid.

219.  Hannah Arendt, *The Origins of Totalitarianism* (New York, 1968), Vol. III, p. 115.
220.  Harris, *Cannibals*, p. 70.


CHAPTER THREE
WOMEN UNDER PATRIARCHY

1.    The study was conducted by E. R. Schmidt and reported in Dolores Barracano Schmidt and Earl Robert Schmidt, "The Invisible Woman: The Historian as Professional Magician," Carroll, *Liberating Women's History*, pp. 43–44. The textbooks examined were used in 99 percent of American history courses in United States colleges.
2.    Schmidt and Schmidt, "Invisible," Carroll, *Liberating Women's History*, p. 50. The text described is Leland D. Baldwin and Robert Kelley, *American History*, published not in a dark age but in 1967.
3.    Aileen Kraditor points this out in *Up from the Pedestal* (New York, 1968), discussing Ralph Gabriel, *The Course of American Democratic Thought*.
4.    This is discussed by Angela Carter, "The Language of Sisterhood," *The State of the Language*, ed. Leonard Michaels and Christopher Ricks (Berkeley, Calif., 1980), pp. 226–234. The study to which she refers is Leonard E. Barrett, *The Rastafarians* (London, 1977).
5.    *National NOW Times*, March 1982.
6.    See Eileen Power, "The Position of Women," *The Legacy of the Middle Ages*, ed. C. G. Crump and E. F. Jacob (Oxford, England, 1962); *Medieval English Nunneries* (Cambridge, England, 1922); *Medieval People* (London and New York, 1966, new rev. ed.).
7.    Article 110. See Pritchard, *Ancient Near Eastern Texts*, p. 150.
8.    Mary R. Beard, *Woman as Force in History*.
9.    Mary Wollstonecraft, *A Vindication of the Rights of Woman*, ed. Carol H. Poston (New York, 1975), and De Beauvoir, *Second Sex*.
10.   Ann Douglas does so with mixed sympathy and scorn in *Feminization*. The theoretical problems of women's historiography are discussed in Carroll, *Liberating Women's History*, Part I; see also Juliet Mitchell, *Women: The Longest Revolution* (Boston, 1966), and Gerda Lerner, *The Majority Finds Its Past* (New York, 1979), esp. pp. xxii–xxxii, 3–14.
11.   Bridenthal and Koonz, *Visible*, p. 255.
12.   Frantz Fanon, *The Wretched of the Earth*, trans. Constance Farrington (New York, 1963), pp. 38–40.
13.   Albert Memmi, *The Colonizer and the Colonized* (Boston, 1965) p. 85.
14.   Fanon, *Wretched*, p. 42.
15.   Fanon, *Wretched*, p. 41.
16.   Winthrop D. Jordan, *White Over Black* (Chapel Hill, N.C., 1968), p. 51.
17.   Jordan, *White*, p. 577.
18.   Jean-Paul Sartre, Introduction to Memmi, *Colonizer*, p. xxvii.
19.   Sartre, Introduction to Memmi, *Colonizer*, p. xxviii.
20.   Memmi, *Colonizer*, pp. 66–67.
21.   Jordan, *White*, p. 578.
22.   Sartre, Introduction to Memmi, *Colonizer*, p. xxvii.
23.   Ulrich B. Phillips, *American Negro Slavery* (New York, 1918), pp. 291–292.
24.   Kenneth M. Stampp, *The Peculiar Institution* (New York, 1956), p. 89.
25.   Memmi, *Colonizer*, p. 85.
26.   Stampp, *Peculiar*, p. 111.
27.   Stampp, *Peculiar*, p. 116.
28.   Kurt Lewin, "Self-Hatred Among Jews," *Contemporary Jewish Record* 4 (1941):219–232. See also Memmi, *Colonizer*, pp. 121–123.
29.   Memmi, *Colonizer*, p. 91.
30.   Ruth First and Ann Scott, *Olive Schreiner* (London, 1980), p. 48.
31.   Memmi, *Colonizer*, pp. 106ff.
32.   Memmi, *Colonizer*, p. 102.
33.   Aristotle, *Generation of Animals*, trans. A. L. Peck (Cambridge, Mass., 1943), pp. 133, 406.
34.   Okin, *Thought*, p. 197.
35.   Okin, *Thought*, pp. 201–202, 280.
36.   Okin, *Thought*, p. 285.
37.   Aristotle, *Politics*, trans. T. A. Sinclair (New York, 1981, rev. ed.), I, xiii, p. 96.
38.   For instance, Patrick Geddes, *The Evolution of Sex* (1889).

39. See Janssen-Jurreit, *Sexism*, p. 4.

40. These theories were advanced by Rudolf Virchow, Theodosius Dobzhansky, and Rose Mayreder, cited in Janssen-Jurreit, *Sexism*, p. 187.

41. Janssen-Jurreit, *Sexism*, p. 193.

42. P. J. Mobius, *Ueber den physiologischen Schwachsinn des Weibes*, 3rd ed. (Halle, 1901), p. 53. Cited in Reinhold Heller, *The Earthly Chimera and the Femme Fatale: Fear of Woman in Nineteenth-Century Art*, Catalogue of exhibit in the David and Alfred Smart Gallery, University of Chicago, May 20–June 21, 1981, p. 10.

43. The doctor, Edward H. Clarke, published his views in *Sex in Education* (1872). It is cited by Adele Simmons, "Education and Ideology in Nineteenth-Century America," Carroll, *Liberating Women's History*, p. 118.

44. Max Nordau, *Degeneration* (New York, 1895), p. 412; Otto Weininger, *Geschlecht und Charakter* (Vienna, 1903), p. 331; both cited in Heller, *Earthly Chimera*, pp. 9–10.

45. *National NOW Times*, Jan./Feb. 1982. The judge was Wiliam Reinecke, circuit court judge in Lancaster, Wisconsin.

46. Philip Wylie, *Generation of Vipers* (New York, 1955); Erik Erikson, *Childhood and Society* (New York, 1950), pp. 288–296.

47. Helen Mayer Hacker, "Women as a Minority Group," *Masculine/Feminine*, ed. Betty and Theodore Roszak (New York, 1969), p. 134.

48. Hacker, "Minority," Roszak and Roszak, *Masculine/Feminine*, p. 139.

49. Stampp, *Peculiar*, p. 73.

50. Sartre, Introduction to Fanon, *Wretched*, p. 15.

51. Robert William Fogel and Stanley L. Engerman, *Time on the Cross: The Economics of American Negro Slavery* (Boston, 1974), p. 70.

52. Erlene Stetson, "Studying Slavery," *But Some of Us Are Brave*, ed. Gloria T. Hull, Patricia Bell Scott, and Barbara Smith (Old Westbury, N.Y., 1982), p. 77.

53. Eugene Genovese, *The Political Economy of Slavery* (New York, 1967), p. 26.

54. See Orlando Patterson, *Slavery and Social Death* (Cambridge, Mass., 1982).

55. James Fox, *White Mischief* (New York, 1983).

56. Boulding, *Underside*, p. 205. JoAnn McNamara, personal communication, June 1983.

57. Bakan, *Wives*, believes women were soldiers in ancient biblical times; see p. 155. See also Briffault, *Mothers*, I, p. 372.

58. Seltman, *Antiquity*, pp. 46–47; Briffault, *Mothers*, I, p. 377.

59. Steffan Wenig, *Women in Egyptian Art* (New York, 1970), p. 12.

60. Boulding, *Underside*, p. 222; De Beauvoir, *Second Sex*, p. 97; Briffault, *Mothers*, I, p. 387; Judy Chicago, *The Dinner Party* (Garden City, N.Y., 1979), p. 116.

61. Boulding, *Underside*, p. 229.

62. Boulding, *Underside*, pp. 230–231, 234.

63. Briffault, *Mothers*, I, pp. 380–384.

64. Diodorus Siculus, *Bibliotheca Historia* (Bepouli, 1793), 187, ii27; F. Chabas, *Les Maximes du Scribe Ani*, cited by Briffault, *Mothers*, I, pp. 385–386.

65. De Beauvoir, *Second Sex*, p. 97.

66. William Tarn, *Cambridge Ancient History*, X, p. 110.

67. Rohrlich-Leavitt, "Transition," Bridenthal and Koonz, *Visible*, pp. 42–43.

68. George Thomson, *The Prehistoric Aegean* (New York, 1965), p. 28.

69. Rohrlich-Leavitt, "Transition," Bridenthal and Koonz, *Visible*, p. 44.

70. Rohrlich-Leavitt, "Transition," Bridenthal and Koonz, *Visible*, p. 47.

71. Rohrlich-Leavitt, "Transition," Bridenthal and Koonz, *Visible*, pp. 48–50; Sarah Pomeroy, "A Classical Scholar's Perspective on Matriarchy," Carroll, *Liberating Women's History*, p. 221; on the double ax, see Gimbutas, *Gods and Goddesses*, pp. 91, 186.

72. Boulding, *Underside*, pp. 246–247.

73. Chadwick, *Mycenaean*, p. 94.

74. Chadwick, *Mycenaean*, pp. 74, 78–79, seems to believe the women were slaves, and that there are no male slaves because men are too spirited and strong, and their status too high for them to be enslaved. More recent researches lead to the conclusion that the women were either refugees or émigrés drawn to Pylos because it was a center of textile making. See Jon-Christian Billigmeier and Judy A. Turner, "The Socio-Economic Roles of Women in Mycenaean Greece: A Brief Survey from Evidence of the Linear B Tablets," *Women's Studies* 8 (1981):3–20.

75. Pomeroy, *Goddesses*, p. 30.

76. Briffault, *Mothers*, abridged, p. 88.

77. Seltman, *Antiquity*, p. 175.

78. Sarah Pomeroy, personal communication, October 1982.
79. Boulding, *Underside*, p. 251.
80. Pomeroy, *Goddesses*, pp. 36, 38–39.
81. Pomeroy, *Goddesses*, pp. 38–39 and personal communication.
82. Pomeroy, *Goddesses*, pp. 46, 64, 69, 140.
83. JoAnn McNamara, personal communication, March 1982.
84. Pomeroy, *Goddesses*, p. 63. Pomeroy derives her figures on longevity from J. Lawrence Angel's studies of skeletal remains.
85. W. K. Lacey, *The Family in Classical Greece* (Ithaca, N.Y., 1968), p. 167.
86. Pomeroy, *Goddesses*, p. 85.
87. Lacey, *Family*, pp. 168–169; Pomeroy, *Goddesses*, p. 79.
88. Lacey, *Family*, p. 173.
89. Slater, *Hera*, p. 26.
90. M. I. Finley, *The World of Odysseus* (London, 1956), p. 83.
91. Slater, *Hera*, p. 26.
92. Amy Swerdlow, "The Greek Woman in Attic Vase Painting," *Women's Studies* 5 (1978):267–284.
93. Lacey, *Family*, p. 228.
94. Pomeroy, *Goddesses*, p. 62.
95. Pomeroy, *Goddesses*, p. 57.
96. Lacey, *Family*, p. 171.
97. Lacey, *Family* p. 172.
98. Pomeroy, *Goddesses*, p. 91.
99. Pomeroy, *Goddesses*, p. 52.
100. Pomeroy, *Goddesses*, p. 136.
101. Pomeroy, *Goddesses*, p. 98; Boulding, *Underside*, p. 258.
102. Chicago, *Dinner Party*, p. 123.
103. Okin, *Thought*, pp. 68–69.
104. Slater, *Hera*, p. 10.
105. Okin, *Thought*, p. 21.
106. Arthur, "Liberated," Bridenthal and Koonz, *Visible*, p. 75.
107. Seltman, *Antiquity*, p. 179.
108. Arthur, "Liberated," Bridenthal and Koonz, *Visible*, pp. 75–76.
109. Seltman, *Antiquity*, p. 180.
110. Arthur, "Liberated," Bridenthal and Koonz, *Visible*, p. 75.
111. Pomeroy, *Goddesses*, p. 133; Arthur, "Liberated," Bridenthal and Koonz, *Visible*, p. 74.
112. Arthur, "Liberated," Bridenthal and Koonz, *Visible*, p. 76.
113. Pomeroy, *Goddesses*, pp. 130–131.
114. Pomeroy, *Goddesses*, p. 132.
115. Athenaeus, *The Deipnosophistae*, V, trans. Charles Burton Gulick (Cambridge, 1932), pp. 331–332.
116. Raymond Block, *The Etruscans* (New York, 1958), p. 58.
117. Briffault, *Mothers*, I, pp. 425–426.
118. JoAnn McNamara, personal communication.
119. Balsdon, *Roman Women*, pp. 24–25.
120. Balsdon, *Roman Women*, pp. 45, 201.
121. Seltman, *Antiquity*, p. 172.
122. Pomeroy, *Goddesses*, pp. 150–151.
123. Pomeroy, *Goddesses*, p. 163. David Herlihy, "Land, Family, and Women in Continental Europe, 701–1200," *Women in Medieval Society*, ed. Susan Mosher Stuard (Philadelphia, 1976), p. 13.
124. Pomeroy, *Goddesses*, p. 161.
125. Pagels, *Gnostic*, p. 62.
126. Arthur, "Liberated," Bridenthal and Koonz, *Visible*, pp. 82–83.
127. Boswell, *Homosexuality*, pp. 120ff.
128. Pomeroy, *Goddesses*, p. 166; Balsdon, *Roman Women*, p. 173.
129. Pomeroy, *Goddesses*, p. 202.
130. Pomeroy, *Goddesses*, p. 170.
131. Jerome Carcopino, *Daily Life in Ancient Rome*, trans. E. O. Lorimer (New Haven, 1940), pp. 93–100.

132. Carcopino, *Daily Life*, p. 85.

133. Balsdon, *Roman Women*, p. 282.

134. Pomeroy, *Goddesses*, pp. 211–212.

135. See, for instance, Carcopino, *Daily Life*, "Feminism and Demoralization," pp. 90–100.

136. Pomeroy, *Goddesses*, pp. 211–212.

137. Pomeroy, *Goddesses*, p. 200.

138. On Jesus' female followers, see JoAnn McNamara, *A New Song* (New York, 1983), Chapter 1.

139. A. Alvarez, "The Background," *Suicide: The Philosophical Issues*, ed. M. Pabst Battin and David Mayo (New York, 1980), p. 24.

140. Alvarez, "Background," Battin and Mayo, *Suicide*, p. 25.

141. Alvarez, "Background," Battin and Mayo, *Suicide*, p. 28.

142. McNamara, *New Song*, Chapters 2 and 3.

143. McNamara, *New Song*, Introduction.

144. JoAnn McNamara and Suzanne F. Wemple, "Sanctity and Power: The Dual Pursuit of Medieval Women," Bridenthal and Koonz, *Visible*, p. 93.

145. Pagels, *Gnostic*, p. 41.

146. "The Great Announcement," quoted by Hippolytus, "Refutation of all Heresies," quoted by Pagels, *Gnostic*, p. 50.

147. *The Tripartite Tractate*, Nag Hammadi Library, ed. James M. Robinson, p. 90.

148. *The Apocryphon of John*, Nag Hammadi, p. 98.

149. *The Gospel of Thomas*, Nag Hammadi, p. 130.

150. *The Dialogue of the Savior*, Nag Hammadi, pp. 229, 237.

151. Pagels, *Gnostic*, p. 60.

152. Pagels, *Gnostic*, p. 41.

153. Pagels, *Gnostic*, pp. 42–43.

154. Pagels, *Gnostic*, p. 45.

155. Boulding, *Underside*, p. 370.

156. McNamara and Wemple, "Sanctity," Bridenthal and Koonz, *Visible*, p. 100.

157. Susan Groag Bell, ed., *Women from the Greeks to the French Revolution* (Stanford, Calif., 1973), pp. 96–97.

158. McNamara and Wemple, "Sanctity," Bridenthal and Koonz, *Visible*, p. 96.

159. McNamara and Wemple, "Sanctity," Bridenthal and Koonz, *Visible*, pp. 104–109; JoAnn McNamara and Suzanne F. Wemple, "The Power of Women through the Family in Medieval Europe: 500–1100," Hartman and Banner, *Clio*, pp. 111–112.

160. McNamara and Wemple, "Sanctity," Bridenthal and Koonz, *Visible*, pp. 102–103.

161. McNamara and Wemple, "Sanctity," Bridenthal and Koonz, *Visible*, p. 101.

162. Bell, *Women from the Greeks*, p. 120.

163. Herlihy, "Land," Stuard, *Medieval*, pp. 24–25.

164. Herlihy, "Land," Stuard, *Medieval*, p. 25.

165. Emily Coleman, "Infanticide in the Early Middle Ages," Stuard, *Medieval*, pp. 57–60.

166. Viola Klein, "The Historical Background," Freeman, *Women*, p. 524, reports that in England husbands had the right to sell their wives as late as 1856. Thomas Hardy's *The Mayor of Casterbridge*, published in 1886, opens with an account of a wife being sold to settle a gambling debt. The novel is set in the first third of the century and is based, Hardy explains, on an actual case.

167. Doris Mary Stenton, *The English Woman in History* (1957; reprint, New York, 1977), pp. 1–24.

168. Stenton, *English Woman*, pp. 29–54.

169. Betty Bandel, "The English Chroniclers' Attitudes Toward Women," *Journal of the History of Ideas* 16 (1955):113–118.

170. Stenton, *English Woman*, pp. 76–85, 95.

171. Stuard, *Medieval*, p. 8.

172. McNamara and Wemple, "Sanctity," Bridenthal and Koonz, *Visible*, p. 110.

173. McNamara and Wemple, "Sanctity," Bridenthal and Koonz, *Visible*, p. 111.

174. Ibid.

175. Boulding, *Underside*, pp. 417, 472.

176. JoAnn McNamara, personal communication, March 1982.

177. Boulding, *Underside*, pp. 473–475.

178. Boswell, *Homosexuality*, p. 270.

179. Boswell, *Homosexuality*, p. 271.

180. Alice Clark, *Working Life of Woman in the Seventeenth Century* (1919; reprint, New York, 1968), p. 5.

181. Power, *Medieval People*, pp. 101–104.

182. McNamara and Wemple, "Sanctity," Bridenthal and Koonz, *Visible*, p. 114.

183. McNamara and Wemple, "Sanctity," Bridenthal and Koonz, *Visible*, p. 116.

184. McNamara and Wemple, "Sanctity," Bridenthal and Koonz, *Visible*, p. 115.

185. Julia O'Faolain and Lauro Martines, *Not in God's Image* (New York, 1973), pp. 175–178.

186. Andreas Capellanus, *The Art of Courtly Love*, trans. John J. Parry (1941; reprint, New York, 1964), p. 150.

187. Mary Nelson, "Why Witches Were Women," Freeman, *Women*, p. 461.

188. Power, "Position," Crump and Jacob, *Legacy*, pp. 410–412; A. Abram, "Women Traders in Medieval London," *Economic Journal* (London) 26, (June 1916):276–285; Kathleen Casey, "The Cheshire Cat: Reconstructing the Experience of Medieval Woman," Carroll, *Liberating Women's History*, p. 229.

189. Casey, "Cheshire Cat," Carroll, *Liberating Women's History*, p. 244.

190. Boulding, *Underside*, pp. 109, 494.

191. Power, "Position," Crump and Jacob, *Legacy*, p. 421.

192. Ehrenreich and English, *For Her Own Good*, pp. 35–38.

193. E. William Monter, "The Pedestal and the Stake: Courtly Love and Witchcraft," Bridenthal and Koonz, *Visible*, p. 129.

194. See Holinshed's Chronicles [604/1/55], *Narrative and Dramatic Sources of Shakespeare, III*, ed. Geoffrey Bullough (New York, 1960), pp. 76–77.

195. Ernest W. McDonnell, *Beguines and Beghards in Medieval Culture* (New Brunswick, N.J., 1954), pp. ix, 4–5, 140; Sherrin Marshall Wyntjes, "Women in the Reformation Era," Bridenthal and Koonz, *Visible*, p. 168.

196. McDonnell, *Beguines*, p. 83.

197. Boulding, *Underside*, p. 445.

198. McDonnell, *Beguines*, pp. 490–492, 507. Boulding, *Underside*, pp. 448–453, offers a brief but vivid picture of some beguines.

199. Beguinages in Mexico City during the seventeenth and eighteenth centuries became great banking institutions offering mortages and loans at 5 percent interest and investing in property. Bernard, *Female World*, p. 55.

200. For a fascinating fictionalized account of the persecution of sects that chose poverty, see Umberto Eco, *The Name of the Rose* (New York, 1983).

201. McDonnell, *Beguines*, p. 442.

202. McDonnell, *Beguines*, p. 573.

203. Wyntjes, "Reformation," Bridenthal and Koonz, *Visible*, pp. 168–169.

204. Wyntjes, "Reformation," Bridenthal and Koonz, *Visible*, p. 169.

205. Keith Thomas, "Women and the Civil War Sects," *Crisis in Europe: 1560–1660*, ed. Trevor Aston (New York, 1965), p. 322.

206. Reginald Scot, *Discoverie*, V, ix (1584), cited by Keith Thomas, *Religion and the Decline of Magic* (New York, 1971), p. 436.

207. Ehrenreich and English, *For Her Own Good*, p. 35.

208. JoAnn McNamara, personal communication, March 1982.

209. Alan C. Kors and Edward Peters, *Witchcraft in Europe: 1100–1700: A Documentary History* (Philadelphia, 1972), p. 5.

210. The entire text of the *Malleus* is available in Kors and Peters, *Witchcraft*, pp. 113–189.

211. *Malleus*, Kors and Peters, *Witchcraft*, pp. 114–127.

212. Thomas, *Religion*, p. 460.

213. Ehrenreich and English, *For Her Own Good*, p. 35.

214. Ehrenreich and English, *For Her Own Good*, p. 38; Boulding, *Underside*, p. 427.

215. Ehrenreich and English, *For Her Own Good*, p. 39.

216. Ehrenreich and English, *For Her Own Good*, p. 35; Monter, "Pedestal," Bridenthal and Koonz, *Visible*, pp. 132–133, offers a statistical breakdown of men and women put on trial in six regions of Europe which yields an average of 82.5 percent women. Thomas, *Religion*, p. 520, writes that the confessions suggest that most of the accused "lived in a state of impotence and desperation," largely because of "grinding poverty."

217. Monter, "Pedestal," Bridenthal and Koonz, *Visible*, p. 133.

218. Thomas, *Religion*, pp. 552–553.

219. Thomas, *Religion*, p. 553.

220. Thomas, *Religion*, p. 521.

221. Thomas, *Religion*, pp. 528–529.

222. Monter, "Pedestal," Bridenthal and Koonz, *Visible*, p. 130.

223. Ehrenreich and English, *For Her Own Good*, p. 35.

224. O'Faolain and Martines, *Not in God's Image*, p. 217.

225. The estimate of nine million appears in Mary Daly, *Gyn/Ecology* (Boston, 1978), p. 183, and is based on the figure given by Matilda Joslyn Gage, *Church and State* (1893; reprint, New York, 1972), p. 247. Ehrenreich and English, *For Her Own Good*, p. 35, simply say "millions" were killed. Monter, "Pedestal," Bridenthal and Koonz, *Visible*, p. 130, estimates less than a hundred thousand.

226. Monter, "Pedestal," Bridenthal and Koonz, *Visible*, p. 130.

227. Thomas, *Religion*, p. 438.

228. Christine Faure, "Absent from History," trans. Lillian S. Robinson, *Signs* 7, 1 (Autumn 1981):71–86.

229. Monter, "Pedestal," Bridenthal and Koonz, *Visible*, p. 135.

230. William Boulting, *Women in Italy* (London, 1910), p. 319.

231. Boulting, *Italy*, p. 314.

232. Boulting, *Italy*, p. 315.

233. Boulting, *Italy*, pp. 336–337.

234. Stanley Chojnacki, "Dowries and Kinsmen in Early Renaissance Venice," Stuard, *Medieval*, pp. 189–191.

235. Casey, "Cheshire Cat," Carroll, *Liberating Women's History*, p. 249 n.15.

236. De Beauvoir, *Second Sex*, p. 115; Casey, "Cheshire Cat," Carroll, *Liberating Women's History*, p. 235.

237. De Beauvoir, *Second Sex*, p. 113.

238. De Beauvoir, *Second Sex*, p. 122.

239. Mosei Ostrogarski, *The Rights of Women* (New York, 1893), p. 2.

240. Stone, *Family*, pp. 134–135.

241. Wyntjes, "Reformation," Bridenthal and Koonz, *Visible*, pp. 172–173.

242. Bell, *Women from the Greeks*, p. 199.

243. Thomas, "Civil War Sects," Aston, *Europe*, pp. 318, 334.

244. Stenton, *English Woman*, p. 105.

245. A. Clark, *Working Life*, p. 238.

246. Thomas, "Civil War Sects," Aston, *Europe*, p. 319.

247. Thomas, "Civil War Sects," Aston, *Europe*, p. 318.

248. Wyntjes, "Reformation," Bridenthal and Koonz, *Visible*, p. 186.

249. Bell, *Women from the Greeks*, p. 199.

250. Boulding, *Underside*, p. 527.

251. Philipe Ariès, *Centuries of Childhood* (New York, 1962), p. 53; JoAnn McNamara, personal communication, March 1982.

252. Stone, *Family*, p. 162.

253. Ariès, *Childhood*, p. 58.

254. Stone, *Family*, pp. 163–164.

255. Ariès, *Childhood*, p. 261.

256. Stone, *Family*, p. 42.

257. Thomas, "Civil War Sects," Aston, *Europe*, p. 317.

258. Thomas, "Civil War Sects," Aston, *Europe*, p. 320.

259. Thomas, "Civil War Sects," Aston, *Europe*, p. 321.

260. Ibid.

261. Thomas, "Civil War Sects," Aston, *Europe*, p. 323.

262. E. William Monter, "Women in Calvinist Geneva (1550–1800)," *Signs* 6, 2 (Winter 1980):189–209.

263. Thomas, "Civil War Sects," Aston, *Europe*, pp. 328–329.

264. Roland H. Bainton, *Women of the Reformation* (Minneapolis, Minn., 1977), pp. 5–17.

265. Boulding, *Underside*, p. 548.

266. Thomas, "Civil War Sects," Aston, *Europe*, p. 340.

267. Wyntjes, "Reformation," Bridenthal and Koonz, *Visible*, p. 187.

268. Ariès, *Childhood*, p. 415.

269. Ariès, *Childhood*, pp. 155–175.

270. Monter, "Pedestal," Bridenthal and Koonz, *Visible*, p. 124, claims that out of a hundred known troubadours active from 1150–1250, about twenty were women.

271. This is the theory of Denis de Rougemont, *Love in the Western World* (1940; reprint, New York, 1956).

272. See John Jay Parry, introduction to Capellanus, *Courtly Love*, pp. 19–20.

273. C. S. Lewis, *The Allegory of Love* (Oxford, 1936), p. 4.

274. Boulting, *Italy*, p. 46.

275. Casey, "Cheshire Cat," Carroll, *Liberating Women's History*, p. 249 n.30.

276. Boulting, *Italy*, p. 318.

277. Ruth Kelso, *Doctrine for the Lady of the Renaissance* (1956; reprint, Urbana, Ill., 1978), p. 3.

278. Boulting, *Italy*, p. 317.

279. Boulting, *Italy*, pp. 326–327.

280. See Joan Kelly, "Early Feminist Theory and the *Querelle des Femmes*, 1400–1789," *Signs* 8, 1 (Autumn 1982):4–28.

281. Kelso, *Renaissance*, pp. 5–6.

282. Louis B. Wright, *Middle-Class Culture in Elizabethan England* (Ithaca, N.Y., 1963), contains a chapter, "The Popular Controversy Over Woman," that offers a fairly complete survey of the main English documents in this *querelle*.

283. Boulding, *Underside*, p. 478.

284. Boulding, *Underside*, p. 479.

285. Kelly, "*Querelle*," *Signs* (Autumn 1982), pp. 8–9.

286. Mary Astell, *Some Reflections Upon Marriage, with Additions* (London, 1730), 4th ed., p. 120; cited by Kelly, "*Querelle*," *Signs* (Autumn 1982).

287. Stone, *Family*, p. 197.

288. Kelly, "*Querelle*," *Signs* (Autumn 1982), p. 23.

289. Foucault, *Order*, pp. 62–63.

290. Abby R. Kleinbaum, "Women in the Age of Light," Bridenthal and Koonz, *Visible*, p. 219.

291. Wright, *Elizabethan*, pp. 103–114.

292. Wright, *Elizabethan*, p. 656.

293. Stone, *Family*, pp. 358–359.

294. Stone, *Family*, p. 353.

295. Monter, "Women in Geneva," *Signs* (Summer 1980), p. 207.

296. Lougee, *Paradis*, devotes a chapter to this school, pp. 173–195.

297. Mary Astell, *Reflections on Marriage*, pp. 106–107, quoted in Stone, *Family*, p. 240.

298. Stone, *Family*, p. 341.

299. Bell, *Women from the Greeks*, p. 234.

300. Bell, *Women from the Greeks*, p. 235.

301. Ibid.

302. Stone, *Family*, p. 446.

303. Lougee, *Paradis*.

304. Lougee, *Paradis*, pp. 5–42.

305. Lougee, *Paradis*, p. 59.

306. Richard T. Vann, "Toward a New Lifestyle: Women in Preindustrial Capitalism," Bridenthal and Koonz, *Visible*, p. 202.

307. Olwen Hufton, "Women in Revolution 1789–1796," *Past and Present* 53 (Nov. 1971):90–91; Vann, "Lifestyle," Bridenthal and Koonz, *Visible*, p. 195.

308. Hufton, "Revolution," *Past and Present* (Nov. 1971), p. 91.

309. Ibid.

310. Vann, "Lifestyle," Bridenthal and Koonz, *Visible*, p. 203.

311. Hufton, "Revolution," *Past and Present* (Nov. 1971), p. 93.

312. Clark, *Working Life*, p. 118.

313. Hufton, "Revolution," *Past and Present* (Nov. 1971), p. 93.

314. Ibid. The curés wrote of situations in 1740 and 1770–74, but conditions were similar in the 1790s.

315. Hufton, "Revolution," *Past and Present* (Nov. 1971), p. 92.

316. Ruth Graham, "Loaves and Liberty: Women in the French Revolution," Bridenthal and Koonz, *Visible*, pp. 239–240.

317. Graham, "Loaves," Bridenthal and Koonz, *Visible*, p. 241.

318. Graham, "Loaves," Bridenthal and Koonz, *Visible*, pp. 242–243.

319. Graham, "Loaves," Bridenthal and Koonz, *Visible*, p. 243.

320. Graham, "Loaves," Bridenthal and Koonz, *Visible*, p. 244.

321. Graham, "Loaves," Bridenthal and Koonz, *Visible*, pp. 245–249.

322. Graham, "Loaves," Bridenthal and Koonz, *Visible*, pp. 250–251.

323. De Beauvoir, *Second Sex*, p. 123; Graham, "Loaves," Bridenthal and Koonz, *Visible*, p. 253.

324. Paul Lacroix, *History of Prostitution*, trans. Samuel Putnam (New York, 1926), p. 861.

325. Stone, *Family*, p. 28.

326. A. Clark, *Working Life*, pp. 223–228.

327. Stone, *Family*, p. 338.

328. Boulding, *Underside*, p. 560.

329. Stone, *Family*, pp. 339–340.

330. Stone, *Family*, pp. 331–332, 503.

331. A. Clark, *Working Life*, pp. 5, 25.

332. A. Clark, *Working Life*, pp. 146, 150–151, 154.

333. A. Clark, *Working Life*, pp. 102–103, 114, 147.

334. M. Harris, *Cannibals*, pp. 183–185. JoAnn McNamara, personal communication, December 1982, points out that cottages in industrial towns were less infested with vermin than those in the country, and that it is difficult to determine whether there was more crime, because the cities had more and better-trained police and so more accurate crime records.

335. Mary Lynn McDougall, "Working-Class Women During the Industrial Revolution, 1780–1914," Bridenthal and Koonz, *Visible*, p. 260.

336. *European Women: A Documentary History, 1789–1945*, eds. Eleanor S. Riemer and John C. Fout (New York, 1980), pp. xvi, 4.

337. Riemer and Fout, *European Women*, pp. 11–12.

338. McDougall, "Working-Class," Bridenthal and Koonz, *Visible*, pp. 263–264.

339. De Beauvoir, *Second Sex*, p. 127.

340. De Beauvoir, *Second Sex*, p. 130.

341. Margaret Hewitt, *Wives and Mothers in Victorian Industry* (London, 1958), p. 109; C. Black, *Married Women's Work* (London, 1915), pp. 276–280.

342. Dr. M. I. Pokzovskaia, "Report on Working Conditions for Women in Russian Factories, 1914," Riemer and Fout, *European Women*, pp. 13–17.

343. McDougall, "Working-Class," Bridenthal and Koonz, *Visible*, p. 266.

344. Patricia Branca, "Image and Reality: The Myth of the Idle Victorian Woman," Hartman and Banner, *Clio*, pp. 183–186.

345. Laura Oren, "The Welfare of Women in Laboring Families: England, 1860–1950," Hartman and Banner, *Clio*, pp. 227–231.

346. Janet Murray, *Strong-Minded Women* (New York, 1982), p. 387; see also the fascinating essay by Judith Walkowitz, "The Making of an Outcast Group," *A Widening Sphere*, ed. Martha Vicinus (Bloomington, Ind., 1977), pp. 72–93.

347. Janet Murray, personal communication, October 1981.

348. Riemer, *European Women*, p. 8.

349. G. Derville, quoted by De Beauvoir, *Second Sex*, p. 127.

350. This is a much-debated subject; for discussion see Sheila Ryan Johannsson, "Sex and Death in Victorian England: An Examination of Age- and Sex-Specific Death Rates, 1840–1910," Vicinus, *Widening Sphere*, pp. 163–181.

351. Michel Foucault, *Power/Knowledge*, ed. Colin Gordon (New York, 1980), pp. 104–105.

352. Foucault, *Power/Knowledge*, pp. 155–156.

353. Barbara Leigh Smith Bodichon, quoted by J. Murray, *Strong-Minded Women*, p. 119.

354. Ann Douglas Wood, "The Fashionable Diseases: Women's Complaints and Their Treatment in Nineteenth-Century America," Hartman and Banner, *Clio*, pp. 1–2.

355. Blake Nevius, *Edith Wharton: A Study of Her Fiction* (Berkeley, Calif., 1953), pp. 3–4.

356. Barbara Corrado Pope, "Angels in the Devil's Workshop: Leisured and Charitable Women in Nineteenth-Century England and France," Bridenthal and Koonz, *Visible*, pp. 298–299.

357. Ann D. Gordon and Mari Jo Buhle, "Sex and Class in Colonial and Nineteenth-Century America," Carroll, *Liberating Women's History*, p. 284.

358. Douglas, *Feminization*, p. 60.

359. For seminal analysis of this phenomenon, see Barbara Welter, *Dimity Convictions* (Athens, Ohio, 1976).

360. T. J. Jackson Lears, *No Place of Grace* (New York, 1981), p. 20.

361. Douglas, *Feminization*.

362. Gordon and Buhle, "Sex and Class," Carroll, *Liberating Women's History*, p. 287.

363. Simmons, "Education and Ideology," Carroll, *Liberating Women's History*, p. 118.

364. Theresa M. McBride, "The Long Road Home: Women's Work and Industrialization," Bridenthal and Koonz, *Visible*, pp. 292–293.

365. These are some recent general accounts: *America's Working Women: A Documentary History, 1600 to the Present*, eds. Rosalyn Baxandall, Linda Gordon, Susan Reverby (New York, 1976); Eleanor Flexner, *Century of Struggle: The Women's Rights Movement in the United States* (1959; reprint, Cambridge, Mass., 1975 rev. ed.); Alice Kessler-Harris, *Women and Work* (Oxford, England, 1981); Aileen Kraditor, *Ideas of the Woman Suffrage Movement* (New York, 1965); *Black Women in White America: A Documentary History*, ed. Gerda Lerner (New York, 1972); Gerda Lerner, *The Grimké Sisters from South Carolina* (Boston, 1967); Gerda Lerner, *The Majority Finds Its Past* (New York, 1979); Midge MacKenzie, *Shoulder to Shoulder* (New York, 1975); *European Women: A Documentary History, 1789–1945*, eds. Eleanor S. Riemer and John C. Fout (New York, 1980); and Meredith Tax, *The Rising of the Women: Feminist Solidarity and Class Conflict, 1880–1917* (New York, 1980).

366. See Blanche Wiesen Cook, *Women and Support Networks* (New York, 1979), pp. 4, 14; and "Feminism, Socialism, and Sexual Freedom: The Work and Legacy of Crystal Eastman and Alexandra Kollontai," forthcoming in *Stratégies Féminines/Stratégies Féministes*, eds. Françoise Basch et al. (Paris), English ed., ed. Judith Friedlander et al. (Bloomington, Ind.).

367. G. Lerner, *Majority*, pp. 16–17.

368. Ibid.

369. Alice Kessler-Harris, "Women, Work, and the Social Order," Carroll, *Liberating Women's History*, p. 332; G. Lerner, *Majority*, p. 18.

370. G. Lerner, *Majority*, pp. 18–23.

371. G. Lerner, *Majority*, pp. 51–52.

372. Vann, "Lifestyle," Bridenthal and Koonz, *Visible*, p. 211.

373. Judith Hale and Ellen Levine, "The First Feminists," Freeman, *Women*, p. 545.

374. Angela Y. Davis, *Women, Race, and Class* (New York, 1981), p. 34.

375. Davis, *Women, Race, and Class*, pp. 34–37.

376. Davis, *Women, Race, and Class*, p. 46. Nathaniel Rogers was editor of the *Journal* of the American Anti-Slavery Society.

377. G. Lerner, *Majority*, p. 153.

378. Stampp, *Peculiar*, pp. 31–32.

379. Robert S. Starobin, *Industrial Slavery in the Old South* (New York, 1970), pp. 164–166.

380. In England, "free" women were used in the same way. See Karl Marx, *Capital*, I (reprint, New York, 1968), p. 391.

381. Davis, *Women, Race, and Class*, p. 23.

382. See Stampp, *Peculiar*, passim; and Herbert Aptheker, *American Negro Slave Revolts* (New York, 1970).

383. See Herbert Gutman, *The Black Family in Slavery and Freedom, 1750–1925* (New York, 1976).

384. Lerner, *Majority*, p. 27.

385. Flexner, *Century of Struggle*, pp. 71–102.

386. Flexner, *Century of Struggle*, p. 86.

387. Flexner, *Century of Struggle*, pp. 108–109.

388. Flexner, *Century of Struggle*, pp. 105–107.

389. Davis, *Women, Race, and Class*, pp. 88–89.

390. Vickie Pollard and Donna Keck, "They Almost Seized the Time!" *Women's Liberation*, ed. Sookie Stambler (New York, 1970), p. 266; Flexner, *Century of Struggle*, pp. 145–148.

391. Davis, *Women, Race and Class*, p. 109.

392. Flexner, *Century of Struggle*, pp. 192–193; Lerner, *Majority*, pp. 84–90.

393. Lerner, *Majority*, p. 83.

394. Lerner, *Majority*, p. 84.

395. Pollard and Keck, "Seized," Stambler, *Women's Liberation*, p. 267.

396. Pollard and Keck, "Seized," Stambler, *Women's Liberation*, p. 267. See also Charlotte Perkins Gilman, *The Home: Its Work and Influence* (1903; reprint, New York, 1970); and *The Man-Made World of Our Androcentric Culture* (1911; reprint, New York, 1970).

397. Flexner, *Century of Struggle*, pp. 186–189.

398. Flexner, *Century of Struggle*, pp. 182–189.

399. Pollard and Keck, "Seized," Stambler, *Women's Liberation*, p. 271; B. Cook, *Women and Support Networks*, passim.

400. Flexner, *Century of Struggle*, pp. 214–216.

401. Sanger originally saw contraception as a way to help working women. Her later support of eugenic theories is an ugly aberration in an otherwise heroic career. See A. Davis, *Women, Race, and Class*, pp. 203ff.

402. Pope, "Angels," Bridenthal and Koonz, *Visible*, pp. 316–317.

403. Pope, "Angels," Bridenthal and Koonz, *Visible*, pp. 314–316.

404. Flexner, *Century of Struggle*, pp. 222–223.

405. Flexner, *Century of Struggle*, p. 298.

406. Flexner, *Century of Struggle*, pp. 300–301.

407. Flexner, *Century of Struggle*, p. 85.

408. Carrie Chapman Catt and Nettie Rogers Shuler, *Woman Suffrage and Politics* (New York, 1923), p. 107.

409. Riemer and Fout, *European Women*, p. 60.

410. Robin Miller Jacoby, "Feminism and Class Consciousness in the British and American Women's Trade Union Leagues, 1890–1925," Carroll, *Liberating Women's History*, pp. 140–141.

411. Mackenzie, *Shoulder to Shoulder*, pp. 8–9.

412. Connie Brown and Jane Seitz, " 'You've Come a Long Way, Baby': Historical Perspectives," *Sisterhood Is Powerful*, ed. Robin Morgan (New York, 1970), p. 21.

413. Mackenzie, *Shoulder to Shoulder*, p. 22.

414. The drama of this story was brilliantly depicted by Midge Mackenzie in her television series *Shoulder to Shoulder*.

415. Mackenzie, *Shoulder to Shoulder*, pp. 20–125.

416. Mackenzie, *Shoulder to Shoulder*, pp. 186–274.

417. Mackenzie, *Shoulder to Shoulder*, pp. 280–317.

418. Mackenzie, *Shoulder to Shoulder*, pp. 321–326.

419. Riemer and Fout, *European Women*, p. 60.

420. Jacoby, "Feminism and Class Consciousness," Carroll, *Liberating Women's History*, pp. 146–147.

421. Flexner's account of this opposition is fascinating; see *Century of Struggle*, pp. 304–318.

422. Flexner, *Century of Struggle*, pp. 307–308.

423. Kessler-Harris, "Social Order," Carroll, *Liberating Women's History*, p. 332.

424. Davis, *Women, Race, and Class*, p. 54.

425. Barbara Wertheimer, " 'Union is Power': Sketches from Women's Labor History," Freeman, *Women*, p. 340; Kessler-Harris, "Social Order," Carroll, *Liberating Women's History*, p. 332; Flexner, *Century of Struggle*, p. 55.

426. Wertheimer, "Union," Freeman, *Women*, p. 341.

427. *America's Working Women: A Documentary History, 1600 to the Present*, ed. Rosalyn Baxandall, Linda Gordon, Susan Reverby (New York, 1976), p. 46.

428. Brown and Seitz, "Long Way," Morgan, *Sisterhood Is Powerful*, p. 7. The source of the one-quarter figure is a *Boston Courier* account of 1829.

429. Wertheimer, "Union," Freeman, *Women*, p. 342.

430. Tax, *Rising*, pp. 27–29; Flexner, *Century of Struggle*, pp. 134–144.

431. Tax, *Rising*, p. 38

432. Tax, *Rising*, p. 27.

433. Tax, *Rising*, p. 46.

434. Wertheimer, "Union," Freeman, *Women*, p. 348.

435. Wertheimer, "Union," Freeman, *Women*, p. 349; Tax, *Rising*, p. 54.

436. Jacob Riis, *How the Other Half Lives* (1890; reprint, New York, 1971).

437. Tax, *Rising*, p. 71.

438. Tax, *Rising*, pp. 38, 91.

439. Flexner, *Century of Struggle*, pp. 248–251; Wertheimer, "Union," Freeman, *Women*, pp. 349–350.

440. Flexner, *Century of Struggle*, pp. 251–252; Wertheimer, "Union," Freeman, *Women*, pp. 350–351.

441. Brown and Seitz, "Long Way," Morgan, *Sisterhood Is Powerful*, p. 21.

442. Tax, *Rising*, p. 91.

443. Jacoby, "Feminism and Class Consciousness," Carroll, *Liberating Women's History*, p. 148.

444. Pollard and Keck, "Seized," Stambler, *Women's Liberation*, p. 273.

445. Tax, *Rising*, pp. 241–263.

446. Wertheimer, "Union," Freeman, *Women*, p. 351.

447. Flexner, *Century of Struggle*, pp. 342–343; Wertheimer, "Union," Freeman, *Women*, p. 355.

448. Richard J. Evans, *The Feminist Movement in Germany: 1894–1933* (London, 1976), p. 24.

449. Riemer and Fout, *European Women*, pp. 37–40.

450. Riemer and Fout, *European Women*, pp. 18–23.

451. Riemer and Fout, *European Women*, pp. 20, 47.

452. Riemer and Fout, *European Women*, p. 44.

453. Riemer and Fout, *European Women*, pp. 58–60.

454. William L. O'Neill, "Women in Politics," Tiger and Fowler, *Hierarchies*, p. 218.

455. Jo Freeman, "The Women's Liberation Movement: Its Origins, Organizations, Activities, and Ideas," Freeman, *Women*, p. 57.

456. See, for example, O'Neill, "Politics," Tiger and Fowler, *Hierarchies*, p. 211.

457. O'Neill, "Politics," Tiger and Fowler, *Hierarchies*, grants this. See also Adam Clymer, "Gap Between Sexes," *New York Times*, November 18, 1982; and Judith Nies, "Women's New Issue," *New York Times*, June 9, 1983.

458. Edward S. Herman, *Corporate Control, Corporate Power* (Cambridge, England, 1981), p. 244.

459. Kessler-Harris, "Social Order," Carroll, *Liberating Women's History*, p. 337.

460. Pope, "Angels," Bridenthal and Koonz, *Visible*, p. 321.

461. Pope, "Angels," Bridenthal and Koonz, *Visible*, p. 322.

462. Mark Edward Lender and James Kirby Martin, *Drinking in America: A History* (New York, 1982).

463. Flexner, *Century of Struggle*, p. 374 n.14. For Fanny Williams's views, see *The Present Status and Intellectual Progress of Colored Women* (Chicago, 1893).

464. Jacoby, "Feminism and Class Consciousness," Carroll, *Liberating Women's History*, pp. 142–143.

465. Pope, "Angels," Bridenthal and Koonz, *Visible*, p. 312.

466. Carroll Smith-Rosenberg, "The Female World of Love and Ritual: Relations Between Women in Nineteenth-Century America," *Signs* 1, 1 (Autumn 1975):1–29; "Beauty, the Beast and the Militant Woman: A Case Study in Sex Roles and Social Stress in Jacksonian America," *American Quarterly* xxiii, 4 (Oct. 1971):562–584.

467. Gordon and Buhle, "Sex and Class," Carroll, *Liberating Women's History*, p. 287.

468. Boulding, *Underside*, p. 637.

469. See Temma Kaplan, "Other Scenarios: Women and Spanish Anarchism," Bridenthal and Koonz, *Visible*, pp. 400–421.

470. Boulding, *Underside*, p. 723.

471. Helen Rogan, *Mixed Company: Women in the Modern Army* (New York, 1981), p. 85.

472. Frantz Fanon, *A Dying Colonialism* (New York, 1967), p. 48.

473. Boulding, *Underside*, p. 717; Minai, *Islam*, p. 63.

474. Fanon, *Dying Colonialism*, pp. 51, 57, 61–62.

475. Minai, *Islam*, p. 76.

476. Kay Boals, "The Politics of Cultural Liberation: Male-Female Relations in Algeria," Carroll, *Liberating Women's History*, p. 208.

477. Amy Hackett, "Feminism and Liberalism in Wilhelmine Germany, 1890–1918," Carroll, *Liberating Women's History*, p. 131.

478. See Renate Bridenthal and Claudia Koonz, "Beyond *Kinder, Küche, Kirche*: Weimar Women in Politics and Work," Carroll, *Liberating Women's History*, pp. 303–304.

479. The relations between feminism and socialism in Germany in this period were extremely complex; so was the position of middle-class women toward each of them. See Richard J. Evans, *The Feminist Movement in Germany: 1894–1933* (London, 1976); Jean H. Quataert, *Reluctant Feminists in German Social Democracy, 1885–1917* (Princeton, N.J., 1979).

480. Bridenthal and Koonz, "Weimar," Carroll, *Liberating Women's History*, pp. 305–309.

481. Beard, *Woman as Force*, pp. 17–20. The quotation comes from Goebbels' diary entry for March 29, 1932.

482. Claudia Koonz, "Mothers in the Fatherland: Women in Nazi Germany," Bridenthal and Koonz, *Visible*, p. 448; and Koonz, personal communication, June 1982.

483. Koonz, "Fatherland," Bridenthal and Koonz, *Visible*, p. 470.

484. Koonz, "Fatherland," Bridenthal and Koonz, *Visible*, p. 450.

485. Koonz, "Fatherland," Bridenthal and Koonz, *Visible*, pp. 450–453.

486. Koonz, "Fatherland," Bridenthal and Koonz, *Visible*, pp. 453–454.

487. Koonz, "Fatherland," Bridenthal and Koonz, *Visible*, p. 471 n.4.

488. Koonz, "Fatherland," Bridenthal and Koonz, *Visible*, p. 459.

489. Claudia Koonz, personal communication, June 1982.

490. Koonz, "Fatherland," Bridenthal and Koonz, *Visible*, pp. 466–467.

491. Koonz, "Fatherland," Bridenthal and Koonz, *Visible*, pp. 467–470.

492. For descriptions of some women who fought against Nazism see Clifford Kirkpatrick, *Nazi Germany* (Indianapolis, 1938), "The Conquest of Women by National Socialism," pp. 40–68.

493. Fannina W. Halle, *Women in Soviet Russia* (New York, 1935). See pp. 46–74 for detailed accounts of these events.

494. Halle, *Women in Soviet Russia*, pp. 1–4. The historian was Shashkov, *History of Russian Women* (1898).

495. Halle, *Women in Soviet Russia*, pp. 22–27. N. A. Dobroliubov, *Russkie klassiki* (Moscow, 1970), pp. 174–176, discusses women's degradation: cited by Barbara Engel, "Women as Revolutionaries: The Case of the Russian Populists," Bridenthal and Koonz, *Visible*, p. 349.

496. Engel, "Russian Populists," Bridenthal and Koonz, *Visible*, pp. 349–351.

497. Engel, "Russian Populists," Bridenthal and Koonz, *Visible*, pp. 351–352.

498. Engel, "Russian Populists," Bridenthal and Koonz, *Visible*, pp. 353–358.

499. Engel, "Russian Populists," Bridenthal and Koonz, *Visible*, pp. 361–365.

500. Engel, "Russian Populists," Bridenthal and Koonz, *Visible*, pp. 348, 365–366.

501. Engel, "Russian Populists," Bridenthal and Koonz, *Visible*, p. 348.

502. O'Neill, "Politics," Tiger and Fowler, *Hierarchies*, p. 203.

503. Bernice Glatzer Rosenthal, "Love on the Tractor: Women in the Russian Revolution and After," Bridenthal and Koonz, *Visible*, p. 375.

504. Rosenthal, "Love on the Tractor," Bridenthal and Koonz, *Visible*, pp. 373, 377.

505. Y. Bochkaryova and S. Lyubimova, *Women of a New World* (Moscow, 1969), pp. 57–58.

506. Halle, *Women in Soviet Russia*, p. 98.

507. Janet Salaff and Judith Merkle, "Women and Revolution: The Lessons of the Soviet Union and China," *Women in China: Studies in Social Change and Feminism*, ed. Marilyn B. Young (Ann Arbor, Mich., 1973), p. 153.

508. Louise Bryant, *Six Months in Russia* (New York, 1918), p. 178.

509. Rosenthal, "Love on the Tractor," Bridenthal and Koonz, *Visible*, p. 378.

510. Salaff and Merkle, "Women and Revolution," Young, *China*, pp. 155–157.

511. Rosenthal, "Love on the Tractor," Bridenthal and Koonz, *Visible*, pp. 379–380.

512. Ibid.; Salaff and Merkle, "Women and Revolution," Young, *China*, p. 157.

513. Rosenthal, "Love on the Tractor," Bridenthal and Koonz, *Visible*, p. 380.

514. Rosenthal, "Love on the Tractor," Bridenthal and Koonz, *Visible*, pp. 381–384.

515. Rosenthal, "Love on the Tractor," Bridenthal and Koonz, *Visible*, pp. 383–384.

516. Rosenthal, "Love on the Tractor," Bridenthal and Koonz, *Visible*, pp. 385–390.

517. Rosenthal, "Love on the Tractor," Bridenthal and Koonz, *Visible*, p. 390. Rogan, *Mixed Company*, p. 88, gives the following figures: 100,000 rifle sharpshooters, 15,000 submachine gunners, nearly 8000 automatic riflemen, over 6000 mortarmen, 4500 machine-gunners, and nearly 50,000 signalers.

518. Martin and Voorhies, *Female*, p. 378; Rosenthal, "Love on the Tractor," Bridenthal and Koonz, *Visible*, pp. 390–391.

519. Nancy Milton, "A Response to 'Women and Revolution,' " Young, *China*, p. 182.

520. Roxanne Witke, "Mao Tse-tung, Women and Suicide," Young, *China*, p. 7. These articles were suppressed after the revolution.

521. Daly, *Gyn/Ecology*, p. 139. See also Ida Pruitt, *A Daughter of Han: The Autobiography of a Chinese Working Woman* (Stanford, Calif., 1967), p. 22, for a brief but first-person account of the process.

522. Boulding, *Underside*, p. 728.

523. See Arthur P. Wolf, "Gods, Ghosts and Ancestors," *Studies in Chinese Society*, ed. Arthur P. Wolf (Stanford, Calif., 1978), pp. 148–155.

524. Elisabeth Croll, *Feminism and Socialism in China* (New York, 1980), p. 32.

525. Margery Topley has written about one exception to this fact—a group of silk workers in the Canton delta in the early nineteenth to twentieth centuries who resisted marriage. Because

they earned good wages outside the home and sent their earnings to their natal families, their refusal to marry was tolerated. See Topley, "Marriage Resistance in Rural Kwangtung," Wolf, *Chinese Society*, pp. 247–269.

526. Karen Gottschang, personal communication, April 1983.

527. Ibid.

528. Witke, "Mao," Young, *China*.

529. Hsiao Kung-chuan, *A History of Chinese Political Thought*, trans. F. W. Mote (Princeton, N.J., 1979), I, p. 386.

530. Margery Wolf, "Chinese Women: Old Skills in a New Context," Rosaldo and Lamphere, *Woman*, p. 159.

531. Roxanne Witke, "Woman as Politician in China of the 1920s," Young, *China*, pp. 159–162.

532. M. Wolf, "Chinese Women," Rosaldo and Lamphere, *Woman*, pp. 159–162.

533. Salaff and Merkle, "Women and Revolution," Young, *China*, pp. 159–160.

534. Boulding, *Underside*, p. 729.

535. Boulding, *Underside*, p. 731; Charlotte Bonny Cohen, " 'Chung-kuo Fu nu': Women of China," Morgan, *Sisterhood Is Powerful*, p. 390.

536. Croll, *Feminism and Socialism*, p. 39

537. Croll, *Feminism and Socialism*, pp. 40–41; Salaff and Merkle, "Women and Revolution," Young, *China*, p. 160.

538. Cohen, "Women of China," Morgan, *Sisterhood Is Powerful*, p. 390.

539. Boulding, *Underside*, pp. 729–730; Salaff and Merkle, "Women and Revolution," Young, *China*, pp. 160–161.

540. Witke, "Politician," Young, *China*, pp. 34–36.

541. Karen Gottschang, personal communication, April 1983.

542. Witke, "Politician," Young, *China*, p. 36.

543. Cohen, "Women of China," Morgan, *Sisterhood Is Powerful*, p. 391.

544. Ibid.

545. Witke, "Politician," Young, *China*, pp. 41–42; Cohen, "Women of China," Morgan, *Sisterhood Is Powerful*, p. 392.

546. Suzette Leith, "Chinese Women in the Early Communist Movement," Young, *China*, p. 60.

547. Cohen, "Women of China," Morgan, *Sisterhood Is Powerful*, p. 393; Witke, "Politician," Young, *China*, p. 42.

548. Cohen, "Women of China," Morgan, *Sisterhood Is Powerful*, p. 395.

549. Delia Davin, "Women in the Liberated Areas," Young, *China*, p. 74.

550. Davin, "Liberated Areas," Young, *China*, p. 75.

551. Helen Snow, *Women of Modern China* (The Hague, 1967), p. 225, says thirty women went on the Long March; Croll's figure is fifty, *Feminism and Socialism*, p. 127.

552. Davin, "Liberated Areas," Young, *China*, pp. 78–82.

553. Davin, "Liberated Areas," Young, *China*, pp. 82–86.

554. Snow, *Women of Modern China*, p. 230.

555. Croll, *Feminism and Socialism*, pp. 260–263.

556. Salaff and Merkle, "Women and Revolution," Young, *China*, pp. 166–169.

557. Newspaper article quoted by Salaff and Merkle, "Women and Revolution," Young, *China*, pp. 171–172.

558. Jane Barrett, "Women Hold Up Half the Sky," Young, *China*, p. 194.

559. Barrett, "Half the Sky," Young, *China*, p. 195; William Parish and Martin Whyte, *Village and Family in Contemporary China* (Chicago, 1978), pp. 62–63, offer a slightly different breakdown of work points: able-bodied men, 9–10 per day; able-bodied women without children, 7–8 per day; and women who must take time off each day for household chores, 6–7 per day. A new "system of responsibility" has been established in the countryside, whereby families contract with their brigade to perform specific tasks and can keep the profits from any work done beyond those tasks. Since these arrangements are made by families rather than individuals, they may work to the detriment of women, unless women maintain a sideline occupation of their own. I have not been able to find any material published on the effects of these changes.

560. Norma Diamond, "Collectivization, Kinship, and Status of Women in Rural China," Reiter, *Anthropology*, p. 385.

561. Diamond, "Collectivization," Reiter, *Anthropology*, p. 388.

562. Diamond, "Collectivization," Reiter, *Anthropology*, pp. 381, 385.

563. Diamond, "Collectivization," Reiter, *Anthropology*, p. 389.

564. Karen Gottschang, personal communication, December 1982, asserts that day care is not always available or adequate, and that many urban women send their children to their grandparents in the country. See also Ruth Sidel, *Women and Child Care in China* (New York, 1972).

565. In some cases husbands are divorcing wives who give birth to girls. Such women are sometimes beaten and abused; in April 1982 one of them killed herself by drinking seven bottles of insecticide. See Christopher S. Wren, *International Herald Tribune*, August 6, 1982. In addition, many girl babies are being murdered. See *Beijing Review* 26, 5 (Jan. 31, 1983):4.

566. See, for instance, Fox Butterfield, *New York Times*, July 6, 1980.

567. Leith, "Early Communist Movement," Young, *China*, p. 47.

568. Karen Gottschang, personal communication, April 1983.

569. *Beijing Review* 25, 42 (Oct. 18, 1982): 4; *Sisterhood Is Global*, ed. Robin Morgan (Garden City, N.Y., 1984), pp. 142–143.

570. William M. Mandel, *Soviet Women and Their Self-Image*, paper delivered May 1970 at Western Slavic Conference, University of Southern California, p. 20.

571. See *Women, Work, and Family in the Soviet Union*, ed. Gail Warshofsky Lapidus (White Plains, N.Y., 1982); Morgan, *Sisterhood Is Global*, p. 677.

572. Martin and Voorhies, *Female*, p. 378; Mandel, *Soviet Women*, p. 36.

573. Mandel, *Soviet Women*, p. 36. This figure dates from 1959.

574. Morgan, *Sisterhood Is Global*, p. 677; Martin and Voorhies, *Female*, p. 380.

575. Michael Paul Sacks, *Work and Equality in Soviet Society* (New York, 1982); Mandel, *Soviet Women*, p. 37.

576. Rosenthal, "Love on the Tractor," Bridenthal and Koonz, *Visible*, p. 392.

577. Martin and Voorhies, *Female*, p. 379

578. Mandel, *Soviet Women*, p. 22.

579. Martin and Voorhies, *Female*, p. 380.

580. Mandel, *Soviet Women*, p. 15.

581. Morgan, *Sisterhood Is Global*, p. 676.

582. Rosenthal, "Love on the Tractor," Bridenthal and Koonz, *Visible*, p. 394. Tatyana Mamonova, "The USSR: It's Time We Began with Ourselves," Morgan, *Sisterhood Is Global*, p. 684.

583. Rosenthal, "Love on the Tractor," Bridenthal and Koonz, *Visible*, p. 394; Mamonova, "The USSR," Morgan, *Sisterhood Is Global*, p. 684.

584. The Soviet report was done for the Institute for Economy in Siberia; the Polish study was done by Polish social scientist Magdalena Sokolowska. Both are cited in Janssen-Jurreit, *Sexism*, pp. 171, 175.

585. *Current Digest of the Soviet Press* 36, 23 (July 4, 1984):5, 24.

586. Rosenthal, "Love on the Tractor," Bridenthal and Koonz, *Visible*, p. 394.

587. Natalya Malakhovskaya, one of four exiled Russian feminists, makes these claims in an interview with Robin Morgan, *MS*, Nov. 1980, p. 80. The four are Yulija Vosnesenskaya, Natalya Malakhovskaya, Tatyana Mamonova, and Tatajana Garicheva.

588. Malakhovskaya, R. Morgan, *MS*, Nov. 1980, p. 81.

589. Mandel, *Soviet Women*, p. 43.

590. R. Morgan, *MS*, Nov. 1980, p. 56; Mamonova, "The USSR," Morgan, *Sisterhood is Global*, pp. 684–685.

591. Tatyana Mamonova, R. Morgan, *MS*, Nov. 1980, p. 102.

592. Yuliya Vosnesenskaya, R. Morgan, *MS*, Nov. 1980, p. 108.

593. Mamonova, R. Morgan, *MS*, Nov. 1980, pp. 107ff.

594. Barbara Ward, "Men, Women and Change," *Women in the New Asia*, ed. Barbara Ward (Paris, 1963), p. 67; Romila Tharpar, "The History of Female Emancipation in Southern Asia," Ward, *New Asia*, p. 479.

595. Tharpar, "Emancipation," Ward, *New Asia*, pp. 480–492; Ward, "Change," Ward, *New Asia*, p. 78.

596. The ancient history of this part of the world includes Sammurat—legendary as Semiramis—of the late ninth century B.C.E., who expanded the monarchal power, led her own armies, and built monuments; Arab warrior queens who fought against the Assyrians; Naqi'a, who rebuilt Babylon after Sennacherib destroyed it by diverting the Euphrates River through it; Queen Atossa, who promoted Zoroastrianism in Persia and was the mother of Cyrus' successor, Darius. Cyrus was killed in battle by Queen Tomyris of the Massagetae; and Queen Artemesia of Halicarnassus fought against Athens for Persia. As late as the time of Rashid, Caliph of Baghdad 786–809, women commanded troops and were cavalry fighters; princesses in mail fought under Mansur in the eighth century against the Byzantines. See Boulding, *Underside*, pp. 225–226; Syed Ameer Ali, *A Short History of the Saracens* (London, 1900), p. 455; Briffault, *Mothers*, I, p. 375.

597. Minai, *Islam*, p. 17.

598. Minai, *Islam*, pp. 21, 44.

599. Minai, *Islam*, pp. 85, 115.

600. Saadawi, *Hidden*.

601. Saadawi, *Hidden*, p. 9.

602. Minai, *Islam*, pp. 97ff.

603. Minai, *Islam*, pp. 34–38.

604. Minai, *Islam*, p. 114.

605. Minai, *Islam*, p. 47.

606. Minai, *Islam*, pp. 62–70.

607. Saadawi, *Hidden*, p. 34.

608. Jane Idleman Smith, "Women in Islam," *Connecticut Humanities Council News*, April 1982, p. 8.

609. Minai, *Islam*, p. 126. The percentages in other countries of girls in school aged six to eleven and twelve to seventeen are as follows: Libya, 72%/22%; Jordan, 71%/45%; Iraq, 54%/28%; Oman and Pakistan, 26%/6%; Egypt, 52%/27%; Lebanon, 85%/55%; Turkey, 66%/34%.

610. J. Smith, "Women in Islam," *Connecticut Humanities Council News*, April 1982, p. 10.

611. Minai, *Islam*, pp. 127–129.

612. J. Smith, "Women in Islam," *Connecticut Humanities Council News*, April 1982, p. 9.

613. Minai, *Islam*, p. 201.

614. Minai, *Islam*, pp. 206–214.

615. Rosenthal, "Love on the Tractor," Bridenthal and Koonz, *Visible*, p. 382.

616. Mandel, *Soviet Women*, pp. 13–14.

617. *Ms.*, May 1980, p. 83.

618. Quotation from Morgan Fairchild, in Minai, *Islam*, p. 214.

619. These attacks are vividly described by Kate Millett, *Going to Iran* (New York, 1982).

620. For a magnetic, articulate account of this linkage see Adrienne Rich, *Of Woman Born* (New York, 1976).

CHAPTER FOUR

## Men Under Patriarchy

1.   Bakan, *Wives*, p. 163.

2.   The theme of man's wrongness before God is important in the work of Kierkegaard, and in Lutheranism generally.

3.   Ochs, *Sex of God*, pp. 25, 45.

4.   Ochs, *Sex of God*, pp. 55–57.

5.   See, for example, Joseph Campbell, *The Hero with a Thousand Faces* (1949; reprint, New York, 1953), and Lord Raglan (Richard Somerset FitzRoy), *The Hero: A Study in Tradition, Myth and Drama* (New York, 1956).

6.   Bakan, *Wives*, pp. 26, 140, 154.

7.   Stephan Chorover, *From Genesis to Genocide* (Cambridge, Mass., 1979), pp. 17–19.

8.   Aeneas' goal was not really to *found* a kingdom, since he usurps Latium; he could have established a dynasty by remaining with Dido and fathering children with her. Dido's city belongs to her and will pass in a female line, but the same is true of Lavinia. The real war in *The Aeneid* is against the forces of mother-right.

9.   Friedrich Nietzsche, *The Will to Power*, ed. Walter Kaufmann, trans. Walter Kaufmann and R. J. Hollingdale (New York, 1967), II, ii, 296, p. 166.

10.   Friedrich Nietzsche, *Human-All-Too-Human*, trans. Helen Zimmern (New York, 1974), I, S.114.

11.   Slater, *Hera*, p. 36.

12.   Elshtain, *Private*, p. 46.

13.   Slater, *Hera*, p. 7.

14.   A. W. H. Adkins, *Merit and Responsibility: A Study in Greek Values* (Oxford, 1960), pp. 32–33.

15.   Werner Jaeger, *Paideia: The Ideals of Greek Culture* (New York, 1944), I, pp. 5–14, 22.

16.   M. I. Finley, *The World of Odysseus* (New York, 1959), pp. 128–129.

17.   Johan Huizinga, *Homo Ludens* (Boston, 1955), p. 73.

18.   Slater, *Hera*, p. 36.

19. Biological information from John Money, *Love and Love Sickness* (Baltimore, 1980), pp. 1–2.

20. Michel Foucault discusses this process in *The History of Sexuality*, trans. Robert Hurley (New York, 1978).

21. The National Institute of Mental Health's 1982 report on "Television and Behavior" prompted a congressional hearing reported in Frank Prial, "Congressmen Hear Renewal of Debate Over TV Violence," *New York Times*, April 16, 1983. Statistics on crime from Lester Thurow, "How to Rescue a Drowning Economy," *New York Review of Books*, April 1, 1982, pp. 3–4.

22. See Judith N. Shklar, "Putting Cruelty First," *Daedalus* III, 3 (Summer 1982):17–27.

23. See Marilyn French, *Shakespeare's Division of Experience* (New York, 1981).

24. Francis Bacon, "Instances of the Gate," *Novum Organum*, Book II.

25. Francis Bacon, *Preface to the History of the Winds*, 1623.

26. Francis Bacon, "The Great Instauration," Pt. VI, *Novum Organum*, Book I.

27. Thomas Hobbes, "Of the Natural Condition of Mankind as Concerning their Felicity and Misery," *Leviathan*, Chapter 12.

28. Hobbes, "On Man," *Leviathan*.

29. Jeremy Taylor, "Consideration of the Miseries of Man's Life," *The Rule and Exercises of Holy Dying*, Chapters 1, 4.

30. Stone, *Family*, pp. 95–96. The letter was written by Sir William Wentworth to the future Earl of Strafford.

31. Stone, *Family*, p. 267.

32. Carolyn Merchant, *The Death of Nature: Women, Ecology, and the Scientific Revolution* (New York, 1983), pp. 276–277.

33. Merchant, *Death of Nature*, pp. 279–280.

34. Merchant, *Death of Nature*, p. 288.

35. See Foucault, *The Order of Things*.

36. Merchant, *Death of Nature*, p. 288.

37. "*Des maux qu'il nouse a causés*," *Pleiade IV*, p. 709, cited in Maurice Block and Jean H. Block, "Women and the Dialectics of Nature in 18th-Century French Thought," MacCormack and Strathern, *Nature*, pp. 29–31, 35–36.

38. Block and Block, "Women," MacCormack and Strathern, *Nature*, pp. 31–33.

39. Marx, *Capital*, III, p. 320.

40. Bertram Morris, *Philosophical Aspects of Culture* (Yellow Springs, Ohio, 1961), pp. 74–75, 148.

41. Mihailo Markovic, "Women's Liberation and Human Emancipation," Gould and Wartofsky, *Women and Philosophy*, p. 146.

42. Erich Heller, *The Artist's Journey into the Interior* (New York, 1976), p. 94.

43. Juliet Mitchell, *Psychoanalysis and Feminism* (New York, 1975), p. 96.

44. S. J. Gould, *Darwin*, p. 260.

45. S. J. Gould, *Darwin*, p. 45.

46. Tanner, *Human*, p. 5.

47. Ashley Montagu, *The Nature of Human Aggression* (New York, 1976), p. 46.

48. T. J. Jackson Lears, *No Place of Grace* (New York, 1981), p. 18.

49. See, for example, Steven Rose, *Against Biological Determinism* (London and New York, 1982); and *Towards a Liberatory Biology* (London and New York, 1982).

50. Reynolds, *Evolution*, pp. 13–15.

51. Robert Paul Wolff, "There's Nobody Here But Us Persons," Gould and Wartofsky, *Women and Philosophy*, pp. 130–131.

52. Lawrence A. Blum, "Kant and Hegel's Moral Rationalism: A Feminist Perspective," *Canadian Journal of Philosophy* 12 (June 1982):287–288.

53. Wolff, "Persons," Gould and Wartofsky, *Women and Philosophy*, p. 133.

54. Wolff, "Persons," Gould and Wartofsky, *Women and Philosophy*, p. 131.

55. Friedrich Nietzsche, *The Wanderer and His Shadow*, ed. Oscar Levy, trans. Paul V. Cohn (New York, 1964), Sections 5, 6, and 16, pp. 185–187. The emphasis is Nietzsche's.

56. Nietzsche, *Will to Power*, II, 461, p. 253.

57. De Beauvoir, *Second Sex*.

58. Elshtain, *Private*, pp. 306–309, discusses De Beauvoir's attitudes and language.

59. William Gass, *On Being Blue* (Boston, 1976), p. 64.

60. Georg Wilhelm Friedrich Hegel, "On the Assertion of the Will to Live," *The World as Will and Idea*, Vol. 3.

61. Ehrenreich and English, *For Her Own Good*, p. 237.

62. Christopher Lasch, "The Great American Variety Show," *New York Review of Books*, Feb. 2, 1984.

63. Wilson, *Finland*, p. 173.

64. Balbus, *Marxism and Domination*, pp. 271–272; Hilde Hein, "Philosophy from a Woman's Perspective," in manuscript, pp. 26, 35.

65. Wilson, *Finland*, pp. 428, 437.

66. Morris, *Philosophical Aspects*, p. 143.

67. Ibid.

68. Mary Midgely, *Beast and Man: The Roots of Human Nature* (Ithaca, N.Y., 1978), p. 18.

69. Friedrich, *Totalitarianism*, p. 140. He is commenting upon and quoting Ernst Nolt, *Three Faces of Fascism* (New York, 1966), p. 430. It is useful to recall that many German writers developed elaborate theories on the differences in the nature of man and woman, and compared women to Jews. Eva Figes describes attempts made in the camps to prove inferiority by comparing the sizes of female and Jewish brains. Figes, *Patriarchal*, p. 121.

70. Sidney Bremer, "Lost Continuities: Alternative Urban Visions in Chicago Novels, 1890–1915," *Soundings* LXIV, 1 (Spring 1981):29–51.

71. Bremer, "Lost Continuities," *Soundings* LXIV, 1 (Spring 1981):31–34.

72. Bremer, "Lost Continuities," *Soundings* LXIV, 1 (Spring 1981):35–39.

73. Bremer, "Lost Continuities," *Soundings* LXIV, 1 (Spring 1981):41.

74. Ann-Janine Morey-Gaines, "Of Menace and Men: The Sexual Tensions of the American Frontier Metaphor," *Soundings* LXIV, 2 (Summer 1981):132–149.

75. Morey-Gaines, "Menace and Men," *Soundings* LXIV, 2 (Summer 1981):133–141.

76. Morey-Gaines, "Menace and Men," *Soundings* LXIV, 2 (Summer 1981):141.

77. Morey-Gaines, "Menace and Men," *Soundings* LXIV, 2 (Summer 1981):142.

78. Farrell, *Liberated*, pp. 49–50.

79. Pointed out by Drid Williams, "The Brides of Christ," Ardener, *Perceiving*, pp. 106, 110–111.

80. Lévi-Strauss, *Elementary Structures; Savage Mind*, p. 247.

81. Block and Block, "Women," MacCormack and Strathern, *Nature*, p. 39.

82. Quoted by Brown and Seitz, "Long Way," Morgan, *Sisterhood Is Powerful*, p. 11.

83. Douglas, *Feminization*, p. 290.

84. Joan Didion, *Salvador* (New York, 1983), p. 93.

85. Stephen Marglin, "What Do Bosses Do?" *Review of Radical Political Economics* 6 (1974), 7 (1975).

86. Earl Shorris, *The Oppressed Middle* (New York, 1981), p. 34; see also passim.

87. "ERA and the 59-Cent Wage Gap" (National Organization for Women, 1981). The information was collected from the Bureau of Labor Statistics, U.S. Department of Labor, and the Census Bureau of the U.S. Department of Commerce and is based on 1979 data of the annual P-60 series, No. 125.

88. Rosabeth Moss Kanter, *Men and Women of the Corporation* (New York, 1977), p. 48, writes that corporations demand "that newcomers be loyal, that they accept authority, and that they conform to a prescribed pattern of behavior."

89. David M. Margolick quotes Paul Cravath of Cravath, Swaine, and Moore, *New York Times*, Jan. 18, 1982.

90. Kanter, *Corporation*, p. 47, reports that managers have to look their part, and that despite lack of a dress code, most look alike: they are white, male, shiny, clean-cut, beardless, and have short hair.

91. Kanter, *Corporation*, p. 41.

92. Elshtain, *Private*, pp. 40–41. She writes that Plato's vision of the perfect state is one "in which the traditional web of social ties and relations has been cast aside . . . [and] human bodies are not fundamental to the identity of self; in which relationship between child and parents is eroded to promote political ends; in which those embracing a different way of seeing are silenced or banished." Okin, *Thought*, p. 36, remarks that what has horrified some Platonic commentators is that Plato, in *The Republic*, "extends to men the control and state disposal already exercised on women."

93. Kanter, *Corporation*, p. 22.

94. Kanter, *Corporation*, pp. 62–63.

95. Kanter, *Corporation*, p. 41.

96. Shorris, *Oppressed*, pp. 297–298.

97. Shorris, *Oppressed*, p. 171.

98. Anthony Sampson, *The Sovereign State of ITT* (New York, 1980), pp. 96, 110–111.

99. Kanter, *Corporation*, p. 130.

100. Kanter, *Corporation*, p. 60.

101. Shorris, *Oppressed*, p. 327.

102. David C. Jones, "What's Wrong with Our Defense Establishment," *New York Times Magazine*, Nov. 7, 1982.

103. The passage is from a 1947 management manual, quoted by Reinhard Bendix, *Work and Authority in Industry* (1956; reprint, New York, 1963), p. 332.

104. Kanter, *Corporation*, p. 24.

105. Kanter, *Corporation*, p. 61.

106. John Simmons and William Mares, *Working Together* (New York, 1983),

107. Douglas McGregor, *The Human Side of Enterprise* (New York, 1960), pp. vi, 21.

108. McGregor, *Enterprise*, pp. 33–35, 43.

109. McGregor, *Enterprise*, p. 38.

110. Leonard Schapiro, "Under the Volcano," review of Nikolai Tolstoy, *Stalin's Secret War*, *New York Review of Books*, Jan. 20, 1983.

111. Curtis, "Retreat from Totalitarianism," Friedrich, Curtis, and Barber, *Totalitarianism*, p. 57.

112. Schapiro, "Under the Volcano," *New York Review of Books*, Jan. 20, 1983.

113. Curtis, "Retreat from Totalitarianism," Friedrich, Curtis, and Barber, *Totalitarianism*, pp. 78, 86. Stalin executed one million people; twelve million more died in labor camps between 1936 and 1950. All told twenty million Russians were killed during his rule. Less than 2 percent of the Communist Party delegates in 1934 reappeared in 1939. Fifty-five of seventy-one members of the Central Committee were eliminated. Between 1936 and 1939 half of the two and a half million Communist Party members were arrested; only fifty thousand regained freedom. Almost every regimental commander in the Soviet Army was purged.

114. Slater, *Hera*, p. 38.

115. *New York Times*, Sept. 19, 1981.

116. *New York Times*, Feb. 16, 1983, and Feb. 20, 1983.

117. Sanday, *Female Power*, p. 63.

118. Joseph H. Pleck, *The Myth of Masculinity* (Cambridge, Mass., 1981), p. 150.

119. Pleck, *Myth*, pp. 20, 148–149; Bernard, *Female World*, p. 381.

120. Johns Hopkins study described in *New York Times*, July 31, 1981.

121. Georgia Dullea, *New York Times*, Sept. 16, 1980.

122. Sigmund Freud, "Letters to Wilhelm Fliess, Drafts and Notes: 1887–1902," *The Origins of Psycho-Analysis*, ed. Marie Bonaparte, Anna Freud, and Ernst Kris, trans. Eric Mosbacher and James Strachey (New York, 1954), letters of April 28, 1897, and Sept. 21, 1897, pp. 195, 215–216.

123. Sandor Ferenczi, "Confusion of Tongues Between Adults and the Child," 1932.

124. Karl Menninger, letter to Milton Klein, quoted in *New York Times*, August 25, 1981.

125. Evelyn Goodenough, "Interests in Persons as an Aspect of Sex Differences in the Early Years," *Genetic Psychological Monograph* 55 (1957):287–323.

126. *New York Times*, June 26, 1980.

127. Chodorow, *Mothering*, pp. 11–39.

128. "Divorce American Style," *Newsweek*, Jan. 10, 1983, pp. 44, 46. Bernard, *Female World*, p. 172, reports that 62 percent of husbands do not comply fully with court-ordered child-support payments in the first year after the order; 41 percent do not make a single payment. By the tenth year, 79 percent are in total noncompliance—and these figures refer only to reported cases.

129. John Kenneth Galbraith, "About Men: Corporate Man," *New York Times Magazine*, Jan. 22, 1984.

130. Joseph Williams, *New York Times*, Feb. 19, 1982. After sixty-five, white men commit 40.8 suicides per 100,000; blacks and other nonwhite men, 12.1; white women, 7.9; and nonwhite women, 3.1.

131. Erving Goffman, *Stigma: Notes on the Management of Spoiled Identity* (Englewood Cliffs, N.J., 1963), p. 128.

132. R. Woolfolk and F. Richardson, *Sanity, Stress, and Survival* (New York, 1978), p. 57.

133. Freud, *Civilization and Its Discontents* (New York, 1961), pp. 24–25.

134. Myron Brenton, *The American Male* (New York, 1966), p. 22.

135. Sampson, *ITT*, pp. 127–128. The quotation is from Maynard Keynes, "Economic Possibilities for our Grandchildren."

136. William Serrin, *New York Times*, Jan. 18, 1982.

137. On the Silkwood affair, see Howard Kohn, *Who Killed Karen Silkwood?* (New York, 1981).

138. Lears, *No Place of Grace,* pp. 64, 302–303.

139. Pleck, *Myth,* p. 159.

140. L. Terman and C. Miles, *Sex and Personality* (New York, 1936).

141. Pleck, *Myth,* p. 159.

142. *Chicago Tribune,* March 28, 1980.

143. Stanley Brandes, "Like Wounded Stags," Ortner and Whitehead, *Sexual Meanings.*

144. Brandes, "Stags," Ortner and Whitehead, *Sexual Meanings,* pp. 217–218.

145. Brandes, "Stags," Ortner and Whitehead, *Sexual Meanings,* pp. 218–219.

146. Brandes, "Stags," Ortner and Whitehead, *Sexual Meanings,* pp. 224–232.

147. Brandes, "Stags," Ortner and Whitehead, *Sexual Meanings,* pp. 234–235.

148. Warren Hoge, "In Brazil, Mornings Belong to Feminist TV," *New York Times,* Jan. 3, 1980.

CHAPTER FIVE
## THE PRESENT PERSPECTIVE

1. Benjamin Barber, "The Conceptual Foundations of Totalitarianism," Friedrich, Curtis, and Barber, *Totalitarianism,* p. 12.

2. Carl J. Friedrich, "The Evolving Theory and Practice of Totalitarianism," Friedrich, Curtis, and Barber, *Totalitarianism,* p. 126.

3. Michael Curtis, "Retreat from Totalitarianism," Friedrich, Curtis, and Barber, *Totalitarianism,* p. 59. Barber, "Foundations," Friedrich, Curtis, and Barber, *Totalitarianism,* p. 8, cites other thinkers who include this characteristic.

4. Hannah Arendt, "Totalitarianism," *Origins.*

5. Karl Popper, quoted by Barber, "Foundations," Friedrich, Curtis, and Barber, *Totalitarianism,* p. 10.

6. C. J. Friedrich and Z. K. Brzezinski, *Totalitarian Dictatorship and Autocracy* (New York, 1967), p. 24.

7. Jeane Kirkpatrick, "Dictatorships and Double Standards," *Commentary* 68, 5 (Nov. 1979):34–45.

8. Lowi, *Liberalism,* p. 10.

9. Lowi, *Liberalism,* p. 18.

10. Arendt, "Totalitarianism," *Origins,* passim, but see especially pp. 173–175. See also Stan Spyros Draenos, "Thinking Without a Ground: Hannah Arendt and the Contemporary Situation of Understanding," *Hannah Arendt: The Recovery of the Public World,* ed. Melvyn A. Hill (New York, 1979), p. 211.

11. Peter Berger, "Is History the Enemy of Progress?" review of Edward Shils, *Tradition, New York Times Book Review,* Feb. 14, 1982.

12. Arendt, "Totalitarianism," *Origins,* p. 103.

13. Arendt, "Totalitarianism," *Origins,* p. 115.

14. Arendt, "Totalitarianism," *Origins,* p. 169.

15. Arendt, "Totalitarianism," *Origins,* p. 109.

16. Arendt, "Totalitarianism," *Origins,* p. 114.

17. See for example Frances Moore Lappé and Nick Allen, "Central American Victims," *New York Times,* May 28, 1982.

18. Alan B. Morrison, "N w Fed ral sm Holes," *New York Times,* Sept. 20, 1982.

19. Tom J. Farer, "The Making of Reaganism," *New York Review of Books,* Jan. 21, 1982.

20. Frithjof Bergmann, *On Being Free,* (Notre Dame, Ind., 1977), p. 194.

21. Illich, *Shadow,* p. 40.

22. Michel Foucault, *Power/Knowledge,* ed. Colin Gordon (New York, 1980), p. 72.

23. Stone, *Family,* p. 27.

24. Friedrich, "Evolving," Friedrich, Curtis, and Barber, *Totalitarianism,* p. 142.

25. Curtis, "Retreat," Friedrich, Curtis, and Barber, *Totalitarianism,* pp. 75–76.

26. Arendt, "Totalitarianism," *Origins,* pp. 62–63. Perlmutter, *Authoritarianism,* also discusses this phenomenon, pp. 13ff.

27. Arendt, "Imperialism," *Origins,* p. viii.

28. Curtis, "Retreat," Friedrich, Curtis, and Barber, *Totalitarianism,* p. 59.

29. Perlmutter, *Authoritarianism,* p. 5.

30. Perlmutter, *Authoritarianism,* p. 34.

31. Richard Millet, *Guardians of the Dynasty* (Maryknoll, N.Y., 1977), pp. 251–261.
32. Arendt, "Imperialism," *Origins*, p. vi.
33. Selwyn James, *South of the Congo* (New York, 1943), p. 305.
34. Fisher, *Creation*, p. 309.
35. Boswell, *Homosexuality*, p. 120.
36. Adolf von Harnack, *The History of Dogma* (London, 1894–99), III, p. 128.
37. Lears, *No Place of Grace*, pp. 30ff, 98–124.
38. Quoted by Arendt, "Imperialism," *Origins*, p. vi.
39. Arendt, "Totalitarianism," *Origins*, p. 105.
40. Arendt, "Totalitarianism," *Origins*, p. 156.
41. Herbert Marcuse, *One-Dimensional Man* (Boston, 1964), p. 3.
42. Barber, "Foundations," Friedrich, Curtis, and Barber, *Totalitarianism*, p. 12.
43. Clifford Geertz, "Stir Crazy," review of Michel Foucault's *Discipline and Punish, New York Review of Books*, Jan. 26, 1978, p. 3.
44. Lesley Doyal, *The Political Economy of Health* (Boston, 1979), pp. 34–35.
45. For discussion of some of them, see Ehrenreich and English, *For Her Own Good*, pp. 40–50; and Regina Morantz, "The Lady and Her Physician," Hartman and Banner, *Clio*, pp. 38–53.
46. Doyal, *Health*, p. 29.
47. Stone, *Family*, p. 446.
48. Ann Douglas Wood, "The Fashionable Diseases," Hartman and Banner, *Clio*, p. 3.
49. Ibid.
50. Ehrenreich and English, *For Her Own Good*, p. 110.
51. Carroll Smith-Rosenberg, "Puberty to Menopause," Hartman and Banner, *Clio*, p. 26.
52. Smith-Rosenberg, "Puberty," Hartman and Banner, *Clio*, p. 27.
53. Smith-Rosenberg, "Puberty," Hartman and Banner, *Clio*, p. 31.
54. Ehrenreich and English, *For Her Own Good*, p. 122.
55. Barbara Katz Rothman, "Women, Health, and Medicine," Freeman, *Women*, pp. 31–32.
56. Foucault, *Power/Knowledge*, p. 217.
57. Ehrenreich and English, *For Her Own Good*, p. 123.
58. Rothman, "Health," Freeman, *Women*, p. 32.
59. Quotation from W. A. Alcott, "Female Attendances on the Sick," *Ladies' Magazine* 7 (1834):302, cited by Wood, "Fashionable Diseases," Hartman and Banner, *Clio*, p. 7.
60. The doctor quoted was William H. Byford, *A Treatise on the Chronic Inflammation and Displacements of the Unimpregnated Uterus* (Philadelphia, 1864), pp. 22–41, cited by Wood, "Fashionable Diseases," Hartman and Banner, *Clio*, p. 7.
61. Wood, "Fashionable Diseases," Hartman and Banner, *Clio*, p. 8.
62. Doyal, *Health*, pp. 164–165.
63. Statistics from William Farr in *Third Annual Report of the Registrar General, 1839–40*, cited by Doyal, *Health*, p. 50.
64. Karl Marx, *Capital* (reprint, Harmondsworth, England, 1976), I, p. 795.
65. The doctor was Turner Thackrah, who practiced in Leeds. Cited by E. P. Thompson, *The Making of the English Working Class* (New York, 1964), p. 359.
66. Doyal, *Health*, p. 141.
67. Doyal, *Health*, pp. 25–26.
68. Stampp, *Peculiar*, pp. 102–109.
69. Chorover, *Genesis*, p. 64.
70. Steven Jay Gould, *The Mismeasure of Man* (New York, 1981), p. 15.
71. Chorover, *Genesis*, pp. 40ff., 65.
72. Guy Irving Birch, director of the American Eugenics Society, quoted by Davis, *Women, Race, and Class*, p. 214.
73. Davis, *Women, Race, and Class*, pp. 217–218.
74. Davis, *Women, Race, and Class*, pp. 218–219. The Puerto Rican situation is of long standing. See Linda Gordon, *Woman's Body, Woman's Right: Birth Control in America* (New York, 1976), pp. 338, 401; and Bonnie Mass, *Population Target: The Political Economy of Population Control in Latin America* (Toronto, 1972), pp. 91, 92, 108.
75. Stone, *Family*, pp. 514–515.
76. Foucault, *Power/Knowledge*, p. 120.
77. Ronald Hayman, *Nietzsche: A Critical Life* (New York, 1980), pp. 27–33.

78. Morton Schatzman, *Soul Murder* (New York, 1973), pp. 21–22, 31–32, 44–49.

79. Schatzman, *Soul Murder*, p. 16.

80. The biography was by Alfons Ritter, *Schreber, das Bildungssystem eines Arztes,* a doctoral dissertation for Erlangen University, 1936. Cited by Schatzman, *Soul Murder.*

81. Schatzman, *Soul Murder*, p. 168.

82. Doyal, *Health*, pp. 81–83.

83. Quoted in R. Lewin, "Cancer Hazards in the Environment," *New Scientist,* Jan. 22, 1976, pp. 168–169. See also J. Cairns, "The Cancer Problem," *Scientific American* 233, 5 (1975), and discussion in Doyal, *Health*, pp. 60–80.

84. Susan Sontag, *Illness as Metaphor* (New York, 1978).

85. H. G. Mather et al., "Acute Myocardial Infarction: Home and Hospital Treatment," *British Medical Journal* 3 (1971):334–338.

86. B. Stocking and S. L. Morrison, *The Image and the Reality: A Case Study of the Impact of Medical Technology,* Oxford Univ. Press for Nuffield Provincial Hospitals Trust, 1978.

87. Illich, *Medical*, p. 105.

88. Illich, *Medical*, p. 98n.

89. William G. Blair, "Scientific Detail Overwhelms Regard for Human Needs at Medical Schools, Panel Says," *New York Times,* Oct. 21, 1982.

90. *British Medical Journal:* 7, April 3, 1976, p. 787; cited by Doyal, *Health*, p. 213.

91. Harry Schwartz, "Toward the Conquest of Heart Disease," *New York Times Magazine,* March 27, 1983; Robert Pear, "U.S. Reports Decline in Infant Mortality Rate," *New York Times,* March 16, 1983.

92. "Poorer, Hungrier," *New York Times,* April 10, 1983.

93. William Ryan, *Blaming the Victim* (New York, 1976), p. 323.

94. Walter Sullivan, "Boston Autopsies Find 1 in 4 Diagnoses Wrong," *New York Times,* April 28, 1983.

95. H. Jack Geiger, "An Overdose of Power and Money," review of Paul Starr, *The Social Transformation of American Medicine, New York Times Book Review,* Jan. 9, 1983.

96. Doyal, *Health*, p. 268.

97. Illich, *Medical,* passim.

98. Illich, *Medical,* p. 40; Chorover, *Genesis,* pp. 172ff.

99. Peter E. Breggin, "The Return of Lobotomy and Psycho-Surgery," *Congressional Record* 118 (Feb. 1972):5567–5577.

100. For discussion of this "disease" see Chorover, *Genesis,* pp. 128ff.; Kenneth D. Gadow, *Children on Medication,* 1979, ERIC Clearing House on Handicapped and Gifted Children; *The Psychologist, the School, and the Child with MBD/LD,* ed. Leon Oettinger, Jr. (New York, 1978); and Lewontin, Rose, and Kamin, *Not in Our Genes,* pp. 178–187.

101. Ryan, *Blaming*, pp. 162–163, 324.

102. Rich, *Of Woman Born.*

103. Ehrenreich and English, *For Her Own Good,* p. 282.

104. J. Prather and L. S. Fidell, "Sex Differences in the Content and Style of Medical Advertisements," *Social Science and Medicine* 9, 1 (1975):23–26; M. C. Smith and L. Griffin, "Rationality of Appeals Used in the Promotion of Psychotropic Drugs: A Comparison of Male and Female Models," *Social Science and Medicine* 11, 6, 7 (1977):409–414.

105. K. Dunnell and A. Cartwright, *Medicine Takers, Prescribers and Hoarders* (London, 1972), pp. 111–112.

106. K. J. Lennane and R. J. Lennane, "Alleged Psychogenic Disorders in Women: A Possible Manifestation of Sexual Prejudice," *New England Journal of Medicine* 288 (1973):288–292.

107. Diane Scully and Pauline Bart, "A Funny Thing Happened on the Way to the Orifice: Women in Gynaecology Textbooks," *American Journal of Sociology* 78, 4 (Jan. 1973):1045–1050.

108. Doyal, *Health*, p. 221.

109. Doyal, *Health*, p. 202.

110. Doyal, *Health*, p. 205.

111. Ronald Sullivan, "Health Chief for N.Y. to Act Against Misconduct by Physicians," *New York Times,* April 3, 1983.

112. Geiger, "Overdose," review, *New York Times Book Review,* Jan. 9, 1983.

113. Roy E. Brown, M.D., "China's Approach to Total Health Care," *Holy Cross Quarterly* 7, 1–4 (1975):138–147.

114. Thomas S. Szasz, *The Theology of Medicine* (Baton Rouge, La., 1977), p. 152.

115. Doyal, *Health*, pp. 228–229.

116. Wayne King, "Microscopic Techniques Have a Gigantic Effect on Cattle Breeding Industry," *New York Times*, Dec. 6, 1982.

117. Philip M. Boffey, "Panel Urges Preparations to Meet Big Demand for Genetic Screening," *New York Times*, Feb. 28, 1983.

118. Vicente Navarro, *Class Struggle, the State, and Medicine* (London, 1978), pp. 86–87. But doctors also control capital and use it politically: 87 percent of all senators and 84 percent of all representatives received money from the AMA in the years 1977–83. AMA PAC contributions to congressional candidates during the 1978, 1980, and 1982 elections totaled more than six million dollars. "Medical Moola," *Common Cause Magazine*, July/August 1983 p. 35.

119. R. C. Lewontin, "The Inferiority Complex," review of S. J. Gould, *The Mismeasure of Man*, *New York Review of Books*, Oct. 22, 1981.

120. Laurence Stone, "Madness," review article, *New York Review of Books*, Dec. 16, 1982.

121. Michael MacDonald, *Mystical Bedlam* (Cambridge, England, 1981), p. 51.

122. MacDonald, *Bedlam*, pp. 31, 36.

123. MacDonald, *Bedlam*, pp. 73–82, 109.

124. Michel Foucault, *Madness and Civilization*, trans. Richard Howard (New York, 1965), pp. 21, 68–69.

125. Foucault, *Madness and Civilization*, pp. 21, 72.

126. Foucault, *Madness and Civilization*, pp. 45–58.

127. Stone, "Madness," *New York Review of Books*, Dec. 16, 1982.

128. Bettelheim, *Freud*, p. 27.

129. Freud, "Letters to Fliess," ed. Bonaparte, Freud, and Kris, *Origins of Psycho-Analysis*, Letter of October 15, 1895, p. 127.

130. Freud, "Letters to Fliess," ed. Bonaparte, Freud, and Kris, *Origins of Psycho-Analysis*, Letter of April 28, 1897, p. 195.

131. See Schatzman, *Soul Murder*.

132. This has been expurgated from Freud, "Letters to Fliess," ed. Bonaparte, Freud, and Kris, *Origins of Psycho-Analysis*, Letter of September 21, 1897, pp. 215–216. See Ralph Blumenthal, *New York Times*, Aug. 25, 1981. This matter has been widely discussed as a result of Jeffrey Moussaieff Masson, *The Assault on Truth: Freud's Suppression of the Seduction Theory* (New York, 1984). See also Janet Malcolm, *In the Freud Archives* (New York, 1984).

133. Freud, "Letters to Fliess," ed. Bonaparte, Freud, and Kris, *Origins of Psycho-Analysis*, Letter of May 31, 1897, p. 206.

134. Freud, "Letters to Fliess," ed. Bonaparte, Freud, and Kris, *Origins of Psycho-Analysis*, Letter of Sept. 21, 1897, pp. 215–216.

135. Freud, "Letters to Fliess," ed. Bonaparte, Freud, and Kris, *Origins of Psycho-Analysis*, Letter of Nov. 2, 1896, p. 171.

136. Tennov, *Psychotherapy*, pp. 229–245.

137. Becker, *Denial of Death*, p. 167. Emphasis added.

138. Abraham Maslow, *The Farther Reaches of Human Nature* (New York, 1971), p. 292.

139. Bruno Bettelheim, *Freud and Man's Soul* (New York, 1983), pp. 32–33.

140. Quoted by Bettelheim, *Freud*, p. 34.

141. Bettelheim, *Freud*, pp. 34–35.

142. Bettelheim, *Freud*, p. 5.

143. For example, Freud frequently uses the word *Seele*, soul, by which he means the entire psychic life—mind, emotions, unconscious, and the impact of body on these things. This word in all its manifestations *(of the soul, aspects of the life of the soul, the unconscious of the soul)* was removed and replaced by *mind, mental, the unconscious mind*. Such a substitution clearly eliminates a category of experience—emotion—with which the learned classes in Britain and America were uncomfortable, and which they tended to scorn. In *Civilization and Its Discontents* (in German, The Uneasiness [or Discomfort] of Culture: *Das Unbehagen in Unbehagen in der Kultur*) Freud referred to a cultural condition found especially in the United States: *das psychologische Elend der Masse* (the psychological misery of the masses). This was rendered as "the psychological poverty of groups." In one fell swoop, the existence of masses of people was eliminated, and misery attributed to material lack.

As the emotional dimension of life is removed from the text, it is "raised," given an appearance of scientific precision it does not possess, by a terminology available only to an elite. So from *besetzen*, which Freud used to suggest "to charge with energy," or "to invest a person or thing with psychic force," he derived *Besetzung*, the occupation, or filling, or fixing of such energy on a thing; this was translated as *cathexis*, an invented word taken from a Greek root. *Schaulust*, which means simply lust in looking, or sexual pleasure in looking, becomes *scopophilia*, which sounds like a disease; *fehlleistung*, an oxymoron which means a real accomplishment achieved through failure—that is, the kind of error that fulfills an unconscious purpose—is translated as *parapraxis*. There are several other examples of similar pretentiousness.

The translation of Freud's *das Ich und das Es und das Über-ich* as the Ego, Id, and Super-Ego has the effect of depersonalizing the terms, something which, interestingly, was not done in French, in which the *Ich* is more properly rendered as *le moi*, the *Es* as *le ça* or *le soi*, and the *Über-ich* as *sur-moi*; or in Spanish, in which *das Ich* is *el yo*. The I—or the *me*—the *it*, and the *over-me* would have been perfectly acceptable in English. Bettelheim, *Freud*, pp. 53–60, 70–78, 80, 86–91, 99.

144. Sigmund Freud, "The Claims of Psycho-Analysis to Scientific Interest" (1913) S.E., Vol. XIII, pp. 186–187, quoted in Mitchell, *Psychoanalysis*, p. 330.

145. Dorothy Tennov, *Psychotherapy, the Hazardous Cure* (New York, 1975), pp. 63–64.

146. Some critics accuse the mental-health establishment of being devoted to maintaining the status quo; others accuse it of forcing change, fostering feminism, and invading the sanctum of family privacy. Ivan Illich and Thomas Szasz believe there is no such thing as mental illness. Szasz claims that what is called mental illness is merely problems in living, and that the term conceals conflict as illness and justifies coercion as treatment. (Thomas S. Szasz, *The Theology of Medicine* [Baton Rouge, La., 1977], p. 137.) At different times, in different places, very different acts and attitudes are taken as signs of illness. (Thomas S. Szasz, *Law, Liberty and Psychiatry* [New York, 1963], pp. 11, 14.) At times, masturbation and divorce have each been seen as symptoms of pathology. Fifteen years ago in Catholic mental hospitals, young women who had performed some unsanctioned sexual act were punished by shock treatments; in the Soviet Union today, dissidence is deemed pathological self-destructiveness, and punished by incarceration and drug treatments.

Nicholas Kittrie claims the "therapeutic state" is a "subterfuge for effecting social controls without guaranteeing constitutionally protected rights"; Szasz claims that the substitution of judgments about mental health for judgments of morality is "moral Fascism." Such critics believe the state as therapist denominates that behavior healthy and mature which tends to permit its control. (Kittrie, *Different*, pp. 384, 401; Szasz, *Law*, p. 248.)

On the other hand, Christopher Lasch, among others, scathingly attacks psychologists for promoting a "democratic" conception of domestic life, permissive child rearing, the rights of women, and greater emotional intimacy among family members. In opposing sexual repression and censorship, he suggests, psychologists have fostered a sexual revolution that is undermining the family. Lasch also attacks a psychiatrist who urged his colleagues to enter the field of preventive medicine and fight against bad social conditions, bad schools, and bad families, claiming that in these lay the roots of war. See Lasch, *Haven in a Heartless World* (New York, 1979), pp. 98–99, 102. John Money labels "social engineers" psychologists who attempt "to spread the new gospel of relativism, tolerance, personal growth, and psychic maturity"—people like Harry Stack Sullivan, who urged a "worldwide mobilization of psychiatry" against class conflict and war as well as personal anxiety. See Sullivan, "Remobilization for Enduring Peace and Social Progress," *Psychiatry* 10 (1947):239, criticized in Money, "Delusion, Belief, and Fact," *Psychiatry* 11 (1948):36, 38.

147. Barbara Lerner, *Therapy in the Ghetto: Political Impotence and Personal Disintegration* (Baltimore, 1972), p. 8.

148. Justine Wise Polier, *The Rule of Law and the Role of Psychiatry* (Baltimore, 1968), pp. 74–75.

149. B. Lerner, *Therapy*, p. 20.

150. B. Lerner, *Therapy*, pp. 156–162.

151. B. Lerner, *Therapy*, pp. 14–27.

152. Chorover, *Genesis*, esp. pp. 172–173.

153. Kittrie, *Different*, pp. 6–7.

154. Thomas S. Szasz, *Law, Liberty and Psychiatry* (New York, 1963) p. vii.

155. Polier, *Rule*.

156. Szasz, *Law*, p. 168.

157. Chorover, *Genesis*, p. 113.

158. Doyal, *Health*, p. 218.

159. Ryan, *Blaming*, p. 143.

160. Tennov, *Psychotherapy*, p. 11.

161. B. Lerner, *Therapy*, pp. 6–7.

162. B. Lerner, *Therapy*, p. 11.

163. Miriam Lewin, *In the Shadow of the Past: Psychology Portrays the Sexes* (New York, 1984). See also her review article, "The Tyranny of Therapy," *Women's Review of Books* 1, 8 (May 1984):8.

164. A test administered to a group of trained professionals, female and male, asked them to

define the qualities that constitute a healthy, socially competent adult/male/female. The seventy-nine respondents overwhelmingly equated a mature healthy adult with a mature healthy male and characterized adult females as being less in control, less objective, vainer, and more likely than men to dislike math and science. The same test administered to a group of male and a group of feminist therapists showed only the males as having a double standard for mental health. I. K. Broverman, D. M. Broverman, F. E. Clarkson, P. S. Rosenkrantz, and S. R. Vogel, "Sex-role Stereotypes and Clinical Judgments of Mental Health," *Journal of Consulting and Clinical Psychology* 34, 1 (1970):1-7; A. L. Aslin, "Feminist & Community Mental Health Center Psychotherapists' Expectations of Mental Health for Women," *Sex Roles: A Journal of Research* 3, 6 (1977):537-544.

165. Barbara Wootton, *Social Science and Social Pathology* (London, 1959), p. 218.

166. John D. Owen, *School Inequality and the Welfare State* (Baltimore, 1974), pp. 121-124.

167. David J. Rothman, *The Discovery of the Asylum: Social Order and Disorder in the New Republic* (Boston, 1971), p. 188.

168. Michael Katz, *Class, Bureaucracy and Schools* (New York, 1975), p. 189.

169. Carl F. Kaestle, *The Evolution of an Urban School System: New York City, 1750–1850* (Cambridge, Mass., 1973), p. 161.

170. John Jarolimek, *The Schools in Contemporary Society* (New York, 1981), p. 11.

171. Owen, *School Inequality*, p. 121.

172. Jarolimek, *Schools*, p. 13.

173. Kaestle, *Evolution*, p. 164.

174. The speaker was Governor Clinton addressing the New York legislature; see Kaestle, *Evolution*, p. 164.

175. Ann Gibson Buis, "An Historical Study of the Role of the Federal Government in the Financial Support of Education," unpublished Ph.D. dissertation, Ohio State University, 1953, p. 55; cited by Owen, *School Inequality*, p. 122. See also David B. Tyack, *The One Best System: A History of American Urban Education* (Cambridge, Mass., 1974), pp. 75–76.

176. Tyack, *One Best System*, p. 74.

177. Herbert Gutman, "Work, Culture, and Society in Industrializing America, 1815–1919," *American Historical Review* 78 (June 1973):531–588.

178. Tyack, *One Best System*, p. 72.

179. Katz, *Class*, pp. 169, 175.

180. William Ryan, *Equality* (New York, 1981), p. 122. See also Samuel Bowles and Herbert Gintis, *Schooling in Capitalist America: Educational Reform and the Contradictions of Economic Life* (New York, 1976); and Owen, *School Inequality*, pp. 9–13.

181. Frances FitzGerald, *America Revised* (Boston, 1979), p. 184.

182. Tyack, *One Best System*, Parts I and II, pp. 13–77.

183. Tyack, *One Best System* pp. 59–60.

184. Tyack, *One Best System* p. 273; Owen, *School Inequality*, pp. 10–55.

185. Owen, *School Inequality*, Chapter 2, pp. 14–27.

186. Chorover, *Genesis*, pp. 52–53.

187. Helen Rogan, *Mixed Company: Women in the Modern Army* (New York, 1981), p. 185. In a related occurrence, twelve women were secretly tested for the Mercury space program in 1959–60. One presumes that the inclusion of women was to provide justification for their exclusion from the program if they did poorly on the tests. In fact, three women performed exceptionally. They were barred from the program and the entire affair was declared classified material.

188. Tyack, *One Best System*, p. 205.

189. Tyack, *One Best System*, p. 204.

190. Katz, *Class*, p. 171.

191. Tyack, *One Best System*, pp. 279–281.

192. Gene Maeroff, "Questions on Teachers' Skills," *New York Times*, April 12, 1983.

193. Bennett Harrison, *Education, Training, and the Urban Ghetto* (Baltimore, 1972), pp. 94, 116.

194. This is the conclusion of a Harvard study conducted by Peter B. Doeringer, "Manpower Programs for Ghetto Labor Markets," Industrial Relations Research Association: Proceedings, May 1969.

195. Harrison, *Education*, p. 68.

196. Conclusion of a study by the Manpower Demonstration Research Corp. of New York, reported by Kathleen Teltsch, "Black Teen-agers Found Eager to Work," *New York Times*, April 21, 1983.

197. Frank Friedlander and Stuart Greenberg, "Effect of Job Attitudes, Training, and Organization Climate on Performance of the Hard-Core Unemployed," *Journal of Applied Psychology*, Dec. 1971, p. 294.

198. Katz, *Class*, p. 172.

199. Quotation from John Goodlad, reported by Fred M. Hechinger, "About Education," *New York Times*, March 29, 1983. Goodlad's book, *A Place Called School*, is in press and will be published by McGraw Hill.

200. Tyack, *One Best System*, p. 197.

201. Maeroff, *New York Times*, April 12, 1983.

202. Fred M. Hechinger, "About Education," *New York Times*, April 12, 1983; "Schools Try New Ways to Improve Education," *New York Times*, April 14, 1983.

203. Robert and Helen Lynd, *Middletown in Transition* (New York, 1937), p. 241.

204. Tyack, *One Best System*, p. 282.

205. Hechinger, *New York Times*, March 29, 1983.

206. Tyack, *One Best System*, p. 275. For many years many students received excellent educations because very intelligent women became teachers; teaching was one of the few avenues of activity permitted them. They worked long hours for low pay, yet were dedicated to their students. Now that feminist activism has enabled women to enter fields formerly closed to them, they are seeking jobs offering more challenge and higher pay, and the quality of teachers is declining. Maeroff, *New York Times*, April 12, 1983.

207. Lionel S. Lewis, *Scaling the Ivory Tower: Merit and Its Limits in Academic Careers* (Baltimore, 1975), p. 185.

208. FitGerald, *Revised*, p. 184.

209. See, for instance, "Knowledge, Education, and Human Values: Toward the Recovery of Wholeness," Critical Issues Symposium Series, Charles F. Kettering Foundation, 1980.

210. Thorstein Veblen, *The Higher Learning in America* (New York, 1950).

211. Rieff, *To My Fellow Teachers* (New York, 1973), p. 193.

212. Richard J. Barnet and Ronald E. Muller, *Global Reach: The Power of the Multinational Corporations* (New York, 1974), pp. 114, 117–118, 136.

213. Lewis, *Scaling*, pp. 30–35.

214. Lewis, *Scaling*, pp. 38–39.

215. Lewis, *Scaling*, p. 187.

216. Lewis, *Scaling*, p. 55.

217. Ryan, *Equality*, pp. 157–158.

218. Lewis, *Scaling*, p. 55ff.

219. Theodore Caplow and Reece McGee, *The Academic Marketplace* (New York, 1965), pp. 111, 226.

220. Patricia Graham, "Women in Academe," *Science* 169 (Sept. 25, 1970):1284–1290.

221. David Noble, "The Selling of the University," *Nation*, Feb. 6, 1982, pp. 129ff.

222. Noble, "Selling," *Nation*, Feb. 6, 1982, p. 146.

223. Quoted by Noble, "Selling," *Nation*, Feb. 6, 1982, p. 143.

224. Noble, "Selling," *Nation*, Feb. 6, 1982, p. 143.

225. "Campus Cartels," *Nation*, March 20, 1982.

226. "Schools Study Ethics of Business-Aided Research," *New York Times*, April 8, 1983.

227. Noble, "Selling," *Nation*, Feb. 6, 1982; "Campus Cartels," *Nation*, March 20, 1982.

228. Michel Foucault, *The Birth of the Clinic*, trans. A. M. Sheridan Smith (New York, 1973), pp. 32–34.

229. Katz, *Class*, p. 183.

230. Katz, *Class*, pp. 190–191.

231. Alvin Gouldner, *The New Class* (New York, 1979); see especially pp. 96ff.

232. Gouldner, *New Class*, pp. 29, 43, and passim.

233. The director was Arthur Jaffe, quoted in *New York Times*, July 19, 1981.

234. Lasch, *Haven*, pp. 182–183.

235. J. M. Synge, *The Aran Islands and Other Writings* (New York, 1962), p. 61.

236. R. M. Dworkin, "Is Law a System of Rules?" *The Philosophy of Law*, ed. R. M. Dworkin (Oxford, 1979), pp. 41–42.

237. Michael E. Tigar and Madeleine R. Levy, *Law and the Rise of Capitalism* (New York, 1977), p. 320.

238. Tigar and Levy, *Law*, pp. 4–5.

239. Tigar and Levy, *Law*, p. 286.

240. Tigar and Levy, *Law*, p. 164.

241. Tigar and Levy, *Law,* p. 183.

242. Tigar and Levy, *Law,* p. 193.

243. Tigar and Levy, *Law,* pp. 185, 227.

244. Tigar and Levy, *Law,* pp. 297, 304–305.

245. Tigar and Levy, *Law,* p. 309.

246. Arthur Kinoy, "The Radical Lawyer and Teacher of Law," *Law Against the People,* ed. R. Lefcourt (New York, 1971).

247. Philip Green, *The Pursuit of Inequality* (New York, 1981), p. 8.

248. Tigar and Levy, *Law,* p. 279.

249. Tigar and Levy, *Law,* p. 283.

250. Iredell Jenkins, *Social Order and the Limits of Law* (Princeton, N.J., 1980), p. 11.

251. Tigar and Levy, *Law,* p. 324.

252. Martin Garbus, "Excluding Justice," *New York Times,* April 4, 1983.

253. Richard Halloran, "Secrets," *New York Times,* April 19, 1983; Leslie Maitland, "Secrecy," *New York Times,* April 25, 1983.

254. Farer, "Reaganism," *New York Review of Books,* Jan. 21, 1982; Robert Pear, "Rights Panel," *New York Times,* March 20, 1983; "U.S. Plans," *New York Times,* April 3, 1983; "Rights Unit," *New York Times,* April 12, 1983.

255. See Iver Peterson, "FBI Spy," *New York Times,* March 27, 1983; and Iver Peterson, "Judge Clears FBI of Negligence in Slaying of Rights Worker," *New York Times,* April 28, 1983.

256. Lowi, *Liberalism,* p. xvi.

257. Foucault, *Power/Knowledge,* pp. 40ff.

258. Evelyn N. Parks, "From Constabulary to Police Society: Implications for Social Control," *Catalyst* (Summer 1970):77–97.

259. Michael Specter, "Community Corrections," *Nation,* March 13, 1982.

260. "Number of Prisoners," *New York Times,* July 15, 1982.

261. Graham Hughes, "Who Should Go to Prison?" *New York Review of Books,* Jan. 1, 1982.

262. Specter, "Corrections," *Nation,* March 13, 1982.

263. Specter, "Corrections," *Nation,* March 13, 1982; and Susan Chira, "Accord Is Set on Halfway Houses to Ease Crowding in State Prisons," *New York Times,* June 16, 1983.

264. Leon Trotsky, "Their Morals and Ours," *New International,* June 1938.

265. Judge W. Don Reader of the Family Court in Canton, Ohio, as quoted by E. R. Shipp, "Issue and Debate," *New York Times,* May 22, 1982.

266. Polier, *Rule,* pp. 38, 94.

267. Polier, *Rule,* p. 37.

268. Jenkins, *Social Order,* p. 120.

269. Consider, for example, statements made by Alan Dershowitz in Stuart Taylor, Jr., "Defense Counsel to Portray 'Underside' of Justice," *New York Times,* March 22, 1982.

270. See David Margolick, "Lawyers for Poor," *New York Times,* April 3, 1983.

271. See, for a brief summary, "Put Legal Back Into Legal Services," *New York Times,* April 14, 1983.

272. Weil, "Prospects," *Oppression,* p. 9.

273. Weil, "Prospects," *Oppression,* pp. 14–16.

274. Rosabeth Moss Kanter, *Men and Women of the Corporation* (New York, 1977), p. 15.

275. Barnet and Muller, *Global,* p. 230.

276. See, for example, J. K. Galbraith, *The New Industrial State* (New York, 1967); *Economics and the Public Purpose* (Boston, 1973).

277. Neils Meyer, Helveg Petersen, and Villy Sorensen, *Revolt from the Center,* trans. Christine Hauch (London, 1981), p. 43.

278. Barnet and Muller, *Global,* p. 15.

279. Hazel Henderson, *The Politics of the Solar Age* (Garden City, N.Y., 1981), p. 98.

280. Henderson, *Solar,* p. 110.

281. Barnet and Muller, *Global,* pp. 241–242.

282. Robert Lekachman, "An Agenda for the Left," *New York Times,* Feb. 22, 1982.

283. Barnet and Muller, *Global,* p. 112.

284. Barnet and Muller, *Global,* p. 60.

285. Anthony Sampson, *The Seven Sisters: The Great Oil Companies and the World They Shaped* (New York, 1980), pp. 222–223.

286. Benjamin Barber, "A Tale of Two Capitalisms," *New York Times,* Oct. 4, 1981.

287. Leo Huberman, *We, The People* (New York, 1932), p. 217.

288. Edward S. Herman, *Corporate Control, Corporate Power*, p. 240.
289. Barnet and Muller, *Global*, pp. 32, 247.
290. Herman, *Corporate*, pp. 5, 15, 244, 245.
291. Herman, *Corporate*, p. 185.
292. Anthony Sampson, *The Sovereign State of ITT* (New York, 1980), pp. 155, 159.
293. Statement of "major impact" made by Alvin Tucker, deputy assistant inspector general in the Pentagon, quoted by Fred Hiatt, "Pentagon Board Assailed for Conflicts of Interest, Cronyism," *International Herald Tribune*, August 27–28, 1983.
294. Barnet and Muller, *Global*, pp. 252–253.
295. Ralph Miliband, *The State in Capitalist Society* (New York, 1969), pp. 63ff.
296. Henderson, *Solar*, p. 44.
297. Meyer et al., *Revolt*, p. 43.
298. Sampson, *Seven Sisters*, p. 225.
299. Barnet and Muller, *Global*, p. 15.
300. Sampson, *Seven Sisters*, p. 369.
301. Meyer et al., *Revolt*, p. 43.
302. Galbraith, *New Industrial State*, p. 59.
303. Meyer et al., *Revolt*, p. 43.
304. Barnet and Muller, *Global*, p. 22; Henderson, *Solar*, p. 97; Herman, *Corporate*, pp. 259–261.
305. Barnet and Muller, *Global*, p. 16; Henderson, *Solar*, p. 97.
306. Barnet and Muller, *Global*, p. 252.
307. See, for example, Leslie Maitland, "Top EPA Official Accused," *New York Times*, March 24, 1983.
308. Jeff Gerth, "Big Severance Payments," *New York Times*, March 16, 1983.
309. Henderson, *Solar*, p. 103.
310. Herman, *Corporate*, p. 240.
311. Sampson, *ITT*, pp. 30–37.
312. Sampson, *ITT*, p. 39.
313. Sampson, *ITT*, pp. 45–46.
314. Sampson, *Seven Sisters*, p. 94.
315. Sampson, *Seven Sisters*, p. 151.
316. Sampson, *Seven Sisters*, p. 303.
317. George W. Ball, "Brezhneved by the U.S.," *New York Times*, June 14, 1983.
318. Sampson, *Seven Sisters*, pp. 304–305.
319. Sampson, *Seven Sisters*, pp. 318–319.
320. Sampson, *Seven Sisters*, p. 384.
321. Sampson, *ITT*, p. 253.
322. Judith Miller, "Nuclear Plants," *New York Times*, Jan. 23, 1983.
323. David Burnham, "Dow Anxiety," *New York Times*, April 19, 1983.
324. Philip Shabecoff, "EPA Aide," *New York Times*, March 16, 1983.
325. See Howard Kohn, *Who Killed Karen Silkwood?* (New York, 1981).
326. Florence Falk, "Karen Silkwood: Laundered News," *Heresies* 13, 4, 1 (1981):3–4.
327. Kohn, *Silkwood*, p. 447.
328. Falk, "Silkwood," *Heresies* 13.
329. Sampson, *Seven Sisters*, p. 382. The official was Lord Kearton, chairman of the British government oil organization.
330. Barnet and Muller, *Global*, pp. 23, 28–29; Sampson, *ITT*, p. 107.
331. Quoted by Sampson, *ITT*, p. 20.
332. Sampson, *ITT*, p. 65.
333. Quoted by Herman, *Corporate*, p. 259.
334. Sampson, *Seven Sisters*, p. 370.
335. Sampson, *ITT*, p. 107.
336. Barnet and Muller, *Global*, pp. 147, 179. These figures are from the 1970s.
337. Barnet and Muller, *Global*, p. 149.
338. Barnet and Muller, *Global*, p. 190.
339. Barnet and Muller, *Global*, pp. 125, 135, 152–153.
340. Lappe and Allen, *New York Times*, May 28, 1982.
341. Barnet and Muller, *Global*, p. 182.
342. Andrée Blouin with Jean MacKellar, *My Country, Africa* (New York, 1983).
343. Doyal, *Health*, pp. 115–116, 315 n. 76.

344. Doyal, *Health*, pp. 107–123.

345. Doyal, *Health*, pp. 123–130.

346. Barnet and Muller, *Global*, pp. 30–31.

347. Barnet and Muller, *Global*, pp. 178–184; Doyal, *Health*, p. 133.

348. Barnet and Muller, *Global*, pp. 176–178.

349. Doyal, *Health*, p. 135.

350. Illich, *Shadow*, p. 9.

351. Barnet and Muller, *Global*, p. 186.

352. Herman, *Corporate*, p. 250.

353. Barnet and Muller, *Global*, pp. 149, 179.

354. Sampson, *ITT*, p. 106; Barnet and Muller, *Global*, p. 229.

355. Sampson, *ITT*, p. 105.

356. Barnet and Muller return to this theme throughout their book, but see pp. 89–111, for example.

357. Barnet and Muller, *Global*, p. 14.

358. Herman, *Corporate*, p. 259.

359. Herman, *Corporate*, p. 255.

360. Barnet and Muller, *Global*, p. 16.

361. Sampson, *ITT*, p. 138.

362. Sampson, *Seven Sisters*, pp. 134, 244–247.

363. See, for example, Kanter, *Corporation*, passim.

364. Sampson, *Seven Sisters*, pp. 371–372.

365. Barnet and Muller, *Global*, pp. 347–348.

366. Sampson, *ITT*, p. 302; *Seven Sisters*, p. 377.

367. Barnet and Muller, *Global*, pp. 355–356. The vice president was Jacques S. Gansler.

368. Barnet and Muller, *Global*, p. 54. The executive was Saadia Schorr.

369. Sampson, *ITT*, pp. 70, 99, 120–121, 123–125.

370. Earl Shorris, *The Oppressed Middle* (New York, 1981), passim.

371. Shorris, *Oppressed*, pp. 298–310.

372. Barnet and Muller, *Global*, pp. 357–358, 51.

373. Barnet and Muller, *Global*, p. 67.

374. Barnet and Muller, *Global*, p. 346.

375. Sheldon Danziger, *Wharton Quarterly* (Fall 1979).

376. Barnet and Muller, *Global*, p. 290. The distribution of wealth was last measured officially in 1962. At that time the bottom 25 percent of the population had no net worth; the top 19 percent had 76 percent of total net worth; and the middle 56 percent had 24 percent. See Lester Thurow, "The Leverage of Our Wealthiest 400," *New York Times*, Oct. 11, 1984.

377. Frances Fox Pliven and Richard A. Cloward, *Regulating the Poor: The Functions of Public Welfare* (New York, 1972), pp. xiii–xiv.

378. Ibid.

379. Michael Harrington, *The Twilight of Capitalism* (New York, 1976), p. 90.

380. Doyal, *Health*, pp. 25–26.

381. Barry Commoner, *The Closing Circle* (New York, 1971), p. 339.

382. Barnet and Muller, *Global*, p. 340.

383. Barnet and Muller, *Global*, p. 360.

384. Henderson, *Solar*, p. 377.

385. Meyer et al., *Revolt*, p. 34.

386. "Acidic Tide of Pizza Sludge," *New York Times*, Jan. 2, 1983.

387. Barnet and Muller, *Global*, pp. 360, 343.

388. Henderson, *Solar*, p. 176.

389. *Christian Science Monitor*, Nov. 5, 1979.

390. Henderson, *Solar*, p. 135; Sampson, *ITT*, p. 184.

391. Commoner, *Closing*, pp. 143–145.

392. Henderson, *Solar*, p. 25.

393. Shabecoff, *New York Times*, April 3, 1982.

394. *Mother Jones*, Nov. 1979, p. 12.

395. Barnet and Muller, *Global*, p. 360.

396. Barnet and Muller, *Global*, p. 361.

397. Barnet and Muller, *Global*, p. 325.

398. Henderson, *Solar*, pp. 44, 101.

399. Herman, *Corporate*, pp. 293–294.

400. Herman, *Corporate*, pp. 277, 280.

401. H. Perlmutter, "Super-Giant Firms in the Future," *Wharton Quarterly* (Winter 1968).

402. Barnet and Muller, *Global*, p. 214.

403. See Note 2 for this chapter.

404. Barnet and Muller, *Global*, p. 360.

405. Galbraith, *New Industrial State*, pp. 24–25.

406. "Security and Insecurity," *New York Times*, April 30, 1983.

407. Burt Neuborne, ACLU memorandum, "Current Threats to the First Amendment."

408. Judith Miller, "More U.S. Lie Tests," *New York Times*, Oct. 9, 1981.

409. "U.S. Orders Disclaimers," *New York Times*, Feb. 25, 1983; " 'P' Films Ratings Rate an 'X,' " *New York Times*, Feb. 26, 1983.

410. Barnet and Muller, *Global*, pp. 117–118.

411. Herbert I. Schiller, *Communications and Cultural Domination* (White Plains, N.Y., 1976), p. 10; Barnet and Muller, *Global*, pp. 144–145.

412. Benjamin Barber, "The Tides in New Channels," *New York Times*, April 21, 1982.

413. Paul M. Hirsch, "The Role of Television and Popular Culture in Contemporary Society," *Television: The Critical View*, ed. Horace Newcomb (New York, 1982), p. 280.

414. Quoted by Harry F. Waters, "Life According to TV," *Newsweek*, Dec. 6, 1982.

415. Barnet and Muller, *Global*, p. 136.

416. Schiller, *Communications and Cultural Domination*, p. 75.

417. Sandra Wallman, "Epistemologies of Sex," Tiger and Fowler, *Hierarchies*, pp. 50–51. For examples of the sexism of television executives see Les Brown, *Television: The Business Behind the Box* (New York, 1971), pp. 9–10.

418. Waters, "TV," *Newsweek*, Dec. 6, 1982, citing study of George Gerbner.

419. Frank J. Prial, "TV Violence," *New York Times*, April 16, 1983.

420. "A Window on Violence," *New York Times*, May 22, 1982.

421. Gerbner, quoted by Waters, "TV," *Newsweek*, Dec. 6, 1982.

422. Hirsch, "Role," Newcomb, *Television*, p. 303.

423. Bill Nichols, *Ideology and the Image* (Bloomington, Ind., 1981), pp. 170–182.

424. Todd Gitlin, "Sixteen Notes on Television and the Movement," *Literature in Revolution*, ed. George Abbott White and Charles Newman (New York, 1972), pp. 338–339.

425. Gitlin, "Notes," White and Newman, *Literature*, pp. 339, 346.

426. Gitlin, "Notes," White and Newman, *Literature*, pp. 341–345.

427. Pornography is not, strictly speaking, a television product, but sadistic and pornographic films appear on television more and more often. There is evidence that pornography leads to rape. See *Take Back the Night: Women on Pornography*, ed. Laura Lederer (New York, 1980).

428. Gitlin, "Notes," White and Newman, *Literature*, p. 360.

429. Barber, "Tides," *New York Times*, April 21, 1982.

430. Herman, *Corporate*, p. 298.

431. Stuart and Elizabeth Ewen, *Channels of Desire: Mass Images and the Shaping of American Consciousness* (New York, 1982), p. 75.

432. Ewen and Ewen, *Channels*, p. 58.

433. See Hirsch, "Role," Newcomb, *Television*, pp. 285–286; Todd Gitlin, "Prime Time Ideology," Newcomb, *Television*, p. 449.

434. Henderson, *Solar*, p. 28.

435. Barnet and Muller, *Global*, p. 341. Czechoslavakia, for example, suffers one of the world's highest levels of sulfur dioxide; its plants and animals are becoming extinct, its forests are degraded, and its water is contaminated. See James M. Markham, "Smoggy Prague Tries to Fight Growing Plague of Pollution," *New York Times*, April 9, 1984.

436. Henderson, *Solar*, p. 22.

437. Erich Kahler, *The Tower and the Abyss* (New York, 1957), p. 277.

438. Marcuse, *One-Dimensional Man*, pp. 7–8.

439. *New York Times*, Dec. 27, 1980.

440. Roy Ash, *Columbia Journal of World Business* 5, 2 (March–April 1970), p. 92.

441. Quoted by Eleanor Smeal, president, National Organization for Women, speech at National Press Club, Washington, D.C., June 25, 1981.

CHAPTER SIX

*FEMINISM*

1. Barbara Bovee Polk, "Male Power and the Women's Movement," in Freeman, *Women*, pp. 592–593.

2. All examples cited come from "Clunkers," a feature in *Think* Magazine 47, 4 (July/August 1981):14–15. *Think* is an IBM house organ, and the passages cited were selected by its editors for their opacity or awkwardness. Nevertheless, they are representative of corporate and government prose.

3. *Language in America*, ed. Neil Postman, Charles Weingartner, and Terence P. Moran (New York, 1969), p. 96.

4. Consider, for instance, the often quoted statement by an American Army major in Vietnam: "We had to destroy the town in order to save it"; or Lyndon Johnson's remark: "We'll remain in Vietnam until there is a final surrender of violence itself"; or this passage from the U.S. Marine Corps Platoon Book: "The cold skill of effectively wielded bayonet-tipped rifles in hand-to-hand combat produces a vastly demoralizing psychological effect on enemy troops." There are no humans involved in these statements, no killing or dying: the vanished town is presumably re-deemed; violence will surrender, presumably, to the peace bringers, the Americans; and cold skill of bayonets operates on its own, like a bodiless machine. Postman, Weingartner, and Moran, *Language*, pp. 21, 197.

5. Leo Kovar, M.D., "Malevolent Transformation: Limits and Extensions," *Journal of Contemporary Psychoanalysis* 14, 3 (July 1978):419–423.

6. Jane Lancaster gives the example of the male anthropologist who sees a group of female baboons with a single male and names it a "harem": in perfect "objectivity." But a female anthro-pologist sees in the same grouping a set of females who require only one male to impregnate them, and therefore limit their association to that one. Some feminists insist that the claim to objectivity is always false, always a mask for androcentric bias. As Evelyn Fox Keller puts it, refuting Galileo: "It is not true that 'the conclusions of natural science are true and necessary, and the judgement of man has nothing to do with them'; it is the judgment of woman that they have nothing to do with." Jane Lancaster, *Primate Behavior and the Emergence of Human Culture* (New York, 1975) p. 34; Evelyn Fox Keller, "Feminism and Science," *Signs* 7, 3 (Spring 1982):589–602. The refer-ence is to Galileo Galilei, *Dialogue on the Great World Systems*, trans. T. Salusbury, ed. G. de Santillana (Chicago, 1953), p. 63.

7. Jean Bethke Elshtain, "Feminist Discourse and Its Discontents: Language, Power and Meaning," *Signs* 7, 3 (Spring 1982):608, cites Luther to make the point that no women of Luther's time could use such language. But few men of our time could, either.

8. Marguerite Duras, interviewed by Susan Husserl-Kapit, *Signs* 1, 2 (Winter 1975):425–426, 434.

9. Hélène Cixous, "The Laugh of the Medusa," trans. Keith Cohen and Paula Cohen, *New French Feminisms*, ed. Elaine Marks and Isabelle de Courtivon (New York, 1981), pp. 245, 247.

10. Monique Wittig, *Les Guerrillères*, trans. David le Vay (New York, 1971), p. 9.

11. Wittig, *Guerrillères*, pp. 10–11.

12. Wittig, *Guerrillères*, p. 100.

13. Consider this passage from Luce Irigaray, "And the One Doesn't Stir Without the Other," trans. Hélène Vivienne Wenzel, *Signs* 7, 1 (Autumn 1981):60–61:

> With your milk, Mother, I swallowed ice. And here I am now, my insides frozen. And I walk with even more difficulty than you do, and I move even less. You flowed into me, and that hot liquid became poison, paralyzing me.... You take care of me, you keep watch over me. You want me always in your sight in order to protect me. You fear that something will happen to me.... I look like you, you look like me. I look at myself in you, you look at yourself in me.

14. Susan Griffin, *Woman and Nature: The Roaring Inside Her* (New York, 1978), pp. 155–156.

15. Chrystos, "I Don't Understand Those Who Have Turned Away from Me," *This Bridge Called My Back*, ed. Cherrie Moraga and Gloria Anzaldua (Watertown, Mass., 1981), p. 68. Many other authors in this anthology punctuate and capitalize in a similar way. Some also use spacing, arrangement of text on a page, as a literary device. See also "Racism Is the Issue," *Heresies* 4, 3, 15.

16. Audre Lorde, *Zami: A New Spelling of My Name* (Watertown, Mass., 1982), p. 14.

17. Gertrude Stein, "Poetry and Grammar," *Gertrude Stein: Writings and Lectures 1909–1945*, ed. Patricia Meyrowitz (Baltimore, 1974), p. 133.

18. Mary Daly, *Gyn/Ecology*, p. 29.

19. Mary Daly, *Gyn/Ecology*, p. 424.

20. Sandra M. Gilbert and Susan Gubar, "Alphabet Soup: Women, Language, Sexuality," in manuscript.

21.   Julia Kristeva, "Women's Time," trans. Alice Jardine and Harry Blake, *Signs* 7, 1 (Autumn 1981):24–25.

22.   Consider, for example, this passage chosen at random from the seventeenth-century English writer Robert Burton:

> As a long-winged hawk when he is first whistled off the fist mounts aloft, and for his pleasure fetcheth many a circuit in the air, still soaring higher and higher till he be come to his full pitch, and in the end, when the game is sprung, comes down amain and stoops upon a sudden, so will I, having come at last into these ample fields of air wherein I may freely expatiate and exercise myself for my recreation, a while rove, wander round about the world, mount aloft to those etherial orbs and celestial spheres, and so descend to my former elements again."Air Rectified. With a Digression of Air," *Anatomy of Melancholy*.

23.   *British Medical Journal*, 7 (1976), p. 787; cited by Doyal, *Health*, p. 213.

24.   The continued insistence of editors on the "man-he" formulation is another evidence of bias. The use of a plural pronoun with a singular subject, as in "Does everyone have their lunch?" is damned as solecistic by many prescriptive grammarians, although it has a long history of use by major authors and in informal speech. Moreover, use of the "man-he" formula had to be legislated in England, by Parliament, in 1850; before that "he or she" was used in legal documents. The "one-he" formulation is justified on grounds of agreement in number, that is, on the basis of an arbitrary grammatical rule, despite the fact that it violates the actual gender of many readers, making them feel excluded or invisible, and despite the fact that an alternative usage is available. What is at stake here is not correctness but male dominance. See, for instance, Jim Quinn, "Lingo," *Nation*, April 3, 1982; Anne Bodine, "Androcentrism in Prescriptive Grammar," *Language and Society* 4, 2 (August 1975):129–146.

25.   Elshtain, "Feminist Discourse," *Signs* 7, 3 (Spring 1982):621.

26.   Elshtain, "Feminist Discourse," *Signs* 7, 3 (Spring 1982):605.

27.   Catharine A. MacKinnon, "Feminism, Marxism, Method, and the State: Toward Feminist Jurisprudence," *Signs* 8, 4 (Summer 1983):635–658.

28.   Alice Jardine, "Introduction to Julia Kristeva's 'Women's Time,' " *Signs* 7, 1 (Autumn 1981):11. Jardine is alluding to Kristeva's *Pouvoirs de l'horreur*, later published in the United States as *Powers of Horror*, trans. Leon S. Roudiez (New York, 1982).

29.   Ynestra King, "Feminism and the Revolt of Nature," *Heresies* 13, 4, 1 (1982):12–16.

30.   Polk, "Power," Freeman, *Women*, p. 595.

31.   Catharine A. MacKinnon, "Feminism:Agenda," *Signs* 7, 3 (Spring 1982):515–544.

32.   MacKinnon, "Feminism:Agenda," *Signs* 7, 3 (Spring 1982):523.

33.   Alexander Szalai, "The Situation of Women in the Light of Contemporary Time-Budget Research," Background paper to U.N. Conference No. E Conf. 66/BP/6 of the International Woman's Year (1975), p. 19, discussed by Janssen-Jurreit, *Sexism*, p. 173.

34.   Study done by Institute for Economy of the Siberian Division of the Academy of Sciences of the USSR, reported in *Komsomolskaya Pravda* in 1967, discussed by Janssen-Jurreit, *Sexism*, p. 171.

35.   Magdalena Sokolowska, *Frauenemanzipation und Sozialismus* (Hamburg, 1973), discussed by Janssen-Jurreit, *Sexism*, p. 175.

36.   MacKinnon, "Feminism:Agenda," *Signs* 7, 3 (Spring 1982):523.

37.   Barbara Ehrenreich, "What Is Socialist Feminism?" *WIN* (June 3, 1976).

38.   See Chapter Three, pp. 253–254.

39.   MacKinnon, "Feminism:Agenda," *Signs* 7, 3 (Spring 1982):517–520.

40.   Barbara Ehrenreich, *The Hearts of Men* (Garden City, N.Y., 1983).

41.   The Neuwirth Law authorizing the sale of contraceptives in France was passed in December 1967. See Françoise Parturier, "An Open Letter to Men," trans. Elissa Gelfand, *New French Feminisms*, p. 60 n. 1.

42.   These accusations occur frequently in the writings of women of color. See, for example, Hull, Scott, and Smith, *Some of Us*; Moraga and Anzaldua, *Bridge*; and "Racism Is the Issue," *Heresies* 3, 4, 15.

43.   See Audre Lorde, "An Open Letter to Mary Daly," Moraga and Anzaldua, *Bridge*, pp. 94–97.

44.   Elizabeth Higginbotham, "Two Representative Issues in Contemporary Sociological Work on Black Women," Hull, Scott, and Smith, *Some of Us*, p. 95.

45.   This problem is courageously addressed in the Moraga and Anzaldua volume.

46.   Lorde, "Open Letter," Moraga and Anzaldua, *Bridge*, p. 97.

47.   "Sharp Rise in Childbearing Found Among U.S. Women in Early 30's," *New York Times*, June 10, 1983, citing Report of House Select Committee on Children, Youth and Families.

48.   "Blacks Closing Wage Gap," *Boston Globe*, May 8, 1978.

49.   "ERA and Minority Women," ERA pamphlet published by NOW, 1981, p. 3.

50.   "Real Income Down 5.5%," *New York Times*, Aug. 21, 1981.

51.   Lynn Hecht Schafran, "Reagan vs. Women," *New York Times*, Oct. 13, 1981. *Newsweek*, April 5, 1982.

52.   The prediction comes from a 1981 study by the National Advisory Council on Economic Opportunity. See for example "Women's Issues Are American Issues," *New York Times*, April 29, 1983.

53.   David Shribman, "Study Finds Women Are Systematically Underpaid," *New York Times*, April 29, 1983.

54.   Betty Friedan, *The Feminine Mystique* (New York, 1963), p. 272.

55.   "Divorce American Style," *Newsweek*, Jan. 10, 1983.

56.   See Andree Brooks, "Mothers Defending Rights of Custody," *New York Times*, Feb. 26, 1983.

57.   Nan D. Hunter, "Women and Child Support," *Families, Politics, and Public Policy*, ed. Irene Diamond (New York, 1983), p. 302. Hunter's statistics were drawn from the U.S. Dept. of Commerce, Bureau of the Census, *Child Support and Alimony: 1978*, Series P-23 (Washington, D.C.: Government Printing Office, September 1981).

58.   Ehrenreich, *Hearts*, p. 121. The statement of decline comes from Andrew Hacker, "Farewell to the Family?" *New York Review of Books*, March 18, 1982, p. 37.

59.   Statistics from Lenore Weitzman, cited in "Divorce American Style," *Newsweek*, Jan. 10, 1983.

60.   Hunter, "Women and Child Support," Diamond, *Families*, p. 203. In 1978 the mean annual child-support amount for those women who actually received support was $1800, or $150 per month. Child support represented about 20 percent of their mean total income of $8944. The annual figure broke down by number of children to mean amounts per month of $100 for one child, $164 for two children, $210 for three children, and $230 for four or more. These monetary computations exclude the three out of ten women who, after child support was awarded, were receiving nothing. U.S. Dept. of Commerce, Bureau of the Census, *Child Support and Alimony: 1978*, Series P-23 (Washington, D.C.: Government Printing Office, September 1981), pp. 1, 5. In a much smaller sample drawn from other nationwide data, Judith Cassetty found that the average annual child-support payment actually made in 1974 was $539. Judith Cassetty, *Child Support and Public Policy: Securing Support from Absent Fathers* (Lexington, Mass.: Lexington Books, 1978), p. 72. The $2110 figure is from a Census Bureau Report released in July 1983. See "Child Support Frequently Not Paid," *New York Times*, July 8, 1983.

61.   "Child Support Frequently Not Paid," *New York Times*, July 8, 1983.

62.   "Divorce American Style," *Newsweek*, Jan. 10, 1983.

63.   Schafran, "Reagan vs. Women," *New York Times*, Oct. 13, 1981.

64.   *Newsweek*, April 5, 1982; Steven V. Roberts, "Capitol Hill Battle," *New York Times*, April 8, 1981.

65.   "Private Budget Study Finds Harm to Women," *New York Times*, March 29, 1984.

66.   Ehrenreich, *Hearts*, p. 177. Economic calculations from *A Children's Defense Budget: A Response to Reagan's Black Book* (Washington, D.C.: The Children's Defense Fund, 1981), p. 61.

67.   "ILO Says Female Workers Face Wide Discrimination," *New York Times*, April 3, 1980.

68.   Henderson, *Solar*, p. 169.

69.   Saadawi, *Hidden*, p. 112.

70.   See Janssen-Jurreit, *Sexism*, pp. 156–157, for some examples.

71.   Bernard, *Female World*, p. 172.

72.   Susan Edmiston, "Hers," *New York Times*, July 1, 1982. The figures come from "Survey of Women Officers of America's Largest Corporations," by Kane, Parsons, & Associates.

73.   "Shrinking Fertility Rate," *New York Times*, May 10, 1983.

74.   Jane E. Brody, "Personal Health," *New York Times*, May 11, 1983, reports that not the act of giving birth, but the time spent caring for a baby, creates the loving bond between mother and child. The lack of a physiological "instinct" to mother is discussed by Nancy Chodorow, *The Reproduction of Mothering*, pp. 17–30.

75.   Charlotte Robinson, "Study Says Children Are Depressing," *Boston Globe*, May 18, 1979. A study conducted by Dr. Marcia Guttentag of the Harvard Graduate School of Education,

in conjunction with the National Institute of Mental Health, correlated domestic states with likelihood of depression. Least likely to be depressed were single women with upwardly mobile careers; married men were second, single men third, and married women fourth. The most unhappy were separated and divorced men, mothers with low-paying jobs, and, beyond all others, mothers with young children and low-paying jobs.

76. Frances FitzGerald, "The Triumphs of the New Right," *New York Review*, Nov. 19, 1981, describes the basic premise of New Right women as a "trade-off": "if women behave themselves sexually, then men will have to marry them, stay married, and support them." See also Andrea Dworkin, *Right-Wing Women* (New York, 1983), and Ehrenreich, *Hearts*, pp. 144–168.

77. Zillah R. Eisenstein, "The Sexual Politics of the New Right: Understanding the 'Crisis of Liberalism' for the 1980s," *Signs* 7, 3 (Spring 1982):578.

78. Zillah Eisenstein, "The State, the Patriarchal Family, and Working Mothers," Diamond, *Families*, p. 54.

79. Connie Paige, *The Right To Lifers* (New York, 1983).

80. Quoted from 1982 study of sex differences in voting, by Arthur H. Miller and Oksana Malanchuk at the University of Michigan, in Adam Clymer, "Gap Between Sexes in Voting Seen as Outlasting Recession," *New York Times*, May 22, 1983.

81. Rochelle Semmel Albin, "Has Feminism Aided Mental Health?" *New York Times*, June 16, 1981, quotes Dr. Grace Baruch and a study by the National Institute of Mental Health conducted by Dr. Frederic Ilfeld.

82. The book is David McClelland, John Atkinson, R. A. Clark, and E. L. Lowell, *The Achievement Motive* (New York, 1953). The comment is from Joanna Rohrbaugh, *Women: Psychology's Puzzle* (New York, 1979), p. 219.

83. Matina S. Horner, "Women's Need to Fail," *Psychology Today*, Nov. 1969; "Toward an Understanding of Achievement-Related Conflicts in Women," *Journal of Social Issues* 28, 9 (1972):157–175.

84. L. W. Hoffman, "Fear of Success in Males and Females: 1965 and 1972," *Journal of Consulting and Clinical Psychology* (1974).

85. Several studies are published and discussed in *Women and Achievement*, ed. Martha Mednick, Sandra Tangri, and Lois Hoffman (New York, 1975).

86. John Condry and Sharon Dyer, "Fear of Success: Attribution of Cause to the Victim," *Journal of Social Issues* 32, 3 (Summer 1976):63–83. See also Lenore J. Weitzman, "Sex-Role Socialization," in Freeman, *Women*.

87. Harriet Holter, "Sex Roles and Social Change," Mednick et al., *Women and Achievement*.

88. For an overview, see Marilyn French, "Women in Language," *Soundings* 59, 3 (Fall 1976):329–344.

89. The way people speak is called "language behavior" in the jargon. For research on this subject, see *Language and Sex*, ed. Barrie Thorne and Nancy Henley (Rowley, Mass., 1975); Mary Ritchie Key, *Male/Female Language* (Metuchen, N.J., 1975); Elizabeth Aries, "Interaction Patterns and Themes of Males, Females, and Mixed Groups," *Small Group Behavior* 7, 1 (1976):1–18; Casey Miller and Kate Swift, *Words and Women* (London, 1977); Karen Adams and Norma C. Ware, "Sexism and the English Language: The Linguistic Implications of Being a Woman," in Freeman, *Women*.

90. Peter Trudgill, "Sex, Covert Prestige and Linguistic Change in the Urban British English of Norwich," *Language in Society* 1, 2 (1973):179–195.

91. Robin Lakoff, "Language and Woman's Place," *Language in Society* 2, 1 (1973):45–79; *Language and Woman's Place* (New York, 1975).

92. Betty Lou Dubois and Isabel Crouch, "The Question of Tag Questions in Women's Speech: They Don't Really Use More of Them, Do They?" *Language in Society* 4, 4 (1975):289–294.

93. Sigmund Freud, "Some Psychical Consequences of the Anatomical Distinction Between the Sexes" (1925), *Standard Edition of the Complete Psychological Works*, trans. and ed. James Strachey (London, 1961), XIX, pp. 257–258.

94. Jean Piaget, *The Moral Judgment of the Child* (1932; reprint, New York, 1965), pp. 77–83.

95. All preceding references to Kohlberg's work are from Lawrence Kohlberg, "Stage and Sequence: The Cognitive-Developmental Approach to Socialization," in *Handbook of Socialization Theory and Research*, ed. David A. Goslin (Chicago, 1969).

96. Nancy Hartsock, *Money, Sex, and Power: Toward a Feminist Historical Materialism* (New York, 1983), pp. 41–42.

97. This is pointed out by Carol Gilligan, "In a Different Voice: Women's Conceptions of

Self and of Morality," *Harvard Educational Review* 47, 4 (Nov. 1977):481–517. The works of Erikson which discuss children's moral development are *Childhood and Society* (New York, 1950); and *Identity: Youth and Crisis* (New York, 1968).

98.   Study done by Kohlberg and Edward F. Zigler in 1967; see "Stage and Sequence," Goslin, *Handbook*, p. 372.

99.   Kohlberg, "Stage and Sequence," Goslin, *Handbook*, p. 399.

100.   Carol Gilligan, *In a Different Voice* (Cambridge, Mass., 1982).

101.   Gilligan, *Voice*, Chapter 2.

102.   Colin M. Turnbull, *The Human Cycle* (New York, 1983), pp. 44ff.

103.   Gilligan, *Voice*, pp. 59, 74.

104.   Erik H. Erikson, *Gandhi's Truth* (New York, 1969), pp. 230–231.

105.   Gilligan, *Voice*, pp. 104–105.

106.   Germaine Tillion, *Ravensbrück: An Eyewitness Account of a Women's Concentration Camp* (New York, 1975), p. xxii.

107.   Nadine Brozan, "Holocaust Women: A Study in Survival," *New York Times*, March 23, 1983. Quotation from Jolly Zeleny.

108.   Brozan, "Holocaust Women," *New York Times*, March 23, 1983. Quotation from Susan Cernyak-Spatz.

109.   Ellen Willis, *The Village Voice*, June 23, 1980; July 16–22, 1980.

CHAPTER SEVEN
*THE LONG VIEW FORWARD: HUMANITY*

1.   Turnbull, *Human Cycle*, pp. 21–22.

2.   Freud, *Civilization*, p. 33.

3.   George F. Kennan, "A Modest Proposal," *New York Review of Books*, July 16, 1981.

4.   Roy A. and Zhores A. Medvedev, "A Nuclear *Samizdat* on America's Arms Race," *Nation*, Jan. 16, 1982.

5.   Jonathan Schell gives an especially comprehensive exposition of the cost in *The Fate of the Earth* (New York, 1982).

6.   See Anthony Lewis, "Who Are the Realists?" *New York Times*, June 3, 1982.

7.   Amory B. Lovins, L. Hunter Lovins, and Leonard Ross, "Nuclear Power and Nuclear Bombs," *Foreign Affairs* 58, 5 (Spring 1980):1137–1177.

8.   Mark Hertsgaard, "Nuclear Nothing," *New York Times*, April 29, 1983.

9.   Illich, *Medical Nemesis*, p. 20.

10.   Joseph Veroff, Elizabeth Douvan, and Richard A. Kulka, *The Inner America: A Self-Portrait from 1957–1976* (New York, 1981), discuss these and other shifts in the American ethos.

11.   Foucault, *Sexuality*, p. 136.

12.   Leonard Silk, "Russian Economy Gives Andropov Huge Problems," *New York Times*, June 12, 1983.

13.   Martha Wolfenstein, "Fun Morality" (1951), *Childhood in Contemporary Cultures*, ed. Margaret Mead and Martha Wolfenstein (Chicago, 1955), pp. 168–176.

14.   A recent example is *Not in Our Genes*, the work of R. C. Lewontin, Steven Rose, and Leon Kamin (New York, 1984). See especially pp. 37–51.

15.   For discussion of this, see Lewontin, Rose, and Kamin, *Not in Genes*, pp. 42–44.

16.   Lewontin, Rose, and Kamin, *Not in Genes*, p. 44.

17.   For full discussion of this new form of discourse, see Foucault, *Order*.

18.   William Bennet, "The Science Watch," *Harvard Magazine* 64 (Sept.–Oct. 1978):23.

19.   Fritjof Capra, *The Tao of Physics* (New York, 1977), p. 56.

20.   Capra, *Tao*, p. 57.

21.   Capra, *Tao*, p. 61.

22.   Capra, *Tao*, pp. 134–147.

23.   Capra, *Tao*, p. 173.

24.   Paul Davies, *Other Worlds: Space, Superspace and the Quantum Theory* (London, 1982), p. 108.

25.   Lewis Thomas, *The Lives of a Cell* (New York, 1974).

26.   Fritjof Capra, "The Dance of Life," *Science Digest* (April 1982):30–33.

27.   Money, *Love*, pp. 1–2.

28.   For report on research conducted by Dr. Norman Geschwind, see Brody, "Left-Handed," *New York Times*, April 19, 1983; see also N. Geschwind and P. Behan, "Left-Handedness: Association with Immune Diseases, Migraine and Developmental Learning Disorder," *Proceedings of the National Academy of Sciences* 79 (1982):5097–5100.

29. See "The Business Brain," *AMA Management Digest* (April 1982):18–24.

30. Dudley Lynch, "Are You in Your Right Mind?" *AMA Management Digest* (April 1982):18–20.

31. Friedrich Nietzsche, *Briefe*, letter to Gast, Sept. 19, 1880. In Hayman, *Nietzsche*, p. 227. The emphasis is Nietzsche's.

32. MacIntyre, *After Virtue*, p. 32.

33. Jenkins, *Social Order*, p. 232.

34. "*Fundamental innovations:* In place of 'moral values,' purely naturalistic values. Naturalization of morality.

"In place of 'sociology,' a theory of the forms of domination.

"In place of 'society,' the culture complex, as my chief interest (as a whole or in its parts).

"In place of 'epistemology,' a perspective theory of affects (to which belongs a hierarchy of the affects; the affects transfigured; their superior order, their 'spirituality').

"In place of 'metaphysics' and religion, the theory of eternal recurrence (this as a means of breeding and selection)." Nietzsche, *Will to Power*, II, 462, p. 255.

35. Bertrand Russell, *Power: A New Social Analysis* (New York, 1936), p. 35.

36. Talcott Parsons, "On the Concept of Political Power," *Political Power*, ed. Roderick Bell, David B. Edwards, and R. Harrison Wagner (New York, 1969), p. 256.

37. Simone Weil, "Prospects" (1933), *Oppression and Liberty*, trans. Arthur Wills and John Petrie (Amherst, Mass., 1973), p. 16.

38. Perlmutter, *Authoritarianism*, pp. 19–20.

39. Weil, "Analysis of Oppression" (1934), *Oppression*.

40. Terence Smith, "Former Leaders Ponder Fragile Nature of Power," *International Herald Tribune*, Aug. 30, 1983. The leaders were Gerald Ford, former president of the United States; Valéry Giscard d'Estaing, former president of France; James Callaghan, former prime minister of Britain; Malcolm Fraser, former prime minister of Australia; and Helmut Schmidt, former chancellor of West Germany.

41. Weil, "Analysis," *Oppression*.

42. Foucault, *Power/Knowledge*, p. 156.

43. Weil, "Analysis," *Oppression*.

44. Foucault, *Power/Knowledge*, pp. 88, 236.

45. Foucault, *Power/Knowledge*, p. 98.

46. Douglas McGregor, *The Human Side of Enterprise* (New York, 1960) p. 21.

47. McGregor, *Enterprise*, p. 102.

48. McGregor, *Enterprise*, p. 98.

49. S. J. Gould, *Darwin*, p. 90.

50. Norman A. Graebner, "America's Limited Power in the Contemporary World," *Key Reporter* XLVII, 3 (Spring 1982):2–5.

51. Freud, *Civilization and Its Discontents*, pp. 52–62, 60, 89.

52. See Wilson, *Sociobiology*; Steven Goldberg, *The Inevitability of Patriarchy* (New York, 1974); Lionel Tiger and Robin Fox, *The Imperial Animal* (London, 1977); and Lionel Tiger, *Men in Groups* (London, 1969).

53. Lewontin, Rose, and Kamin, *Not in Genes*, pp. 153–154. See also Daniel Goleman, "Psychology Is Revising Its View of Women," *New York Times*, March 20, 1984, on a new study of children from birth on, by Carol Jacklin and Eleanor Maccoby. The study involved testing hormonal levels at birth, and careful observation of behavior. At the time the article was written, the children were entering first grade, and no connection had been found between hormones and aggression.

54. Lewontin, Rose, and Kamin, *Not in Genes*, p. 20.

55. The Arapesh, for instance, are gentle, males and females; the Mundugumor are assertive and violent, females and males; and among the Tchambuli, the males are dependent and irresponsible and the females dominant, impersonal, and managing. See Mead, *Sex and Temperament*, for discussion of these differences and others.

56. Lenore Weitzman, "Sex-Role Socialization," Freeman, *Women*, p. 153.

57. Money, *Love*, pp. 159, 175.

58. Money, *Love*, pp. 29–30.

59. Lewontin, Rose, and Kamin, *Not in Genes*, p. 90.

60. Joseph Pleck, *The Myth of Masculinity* (Cambridge, Mass., 1981), p. 170.

61. Eleanor E. Maccoby and Carol Nagy Jacklin, quoted by Bryce Nelson, "Aggression: Still a Stronger Trait for Males," *New York Times*, June 30, 1983.

62. Lewontin, Rose, and Kamin, *Not in Genes*, p. 91.

63. Wilson, *Human*, pp. 101, 107–108.

64. Weil, "The Power of Words," *Oppression*. Although Weil was writing in the 1930s, her perception remains true that modern wars are "conflicts with no definable objective." Because they have no real goal, they can be judged only by the sacrifices required to wage them, "and from this it follows that the sacrifices already incurred are a perpetual argument for new ones."

65. Tom Wicker, "Making Things Worse," *New York Times*, July 9, 1982.

66. Freud, *Civilization and Its Discontents*, pp. 52–62, 60, 89.

67. Dianne Herman, "The Rape Culture," Freeman, *Women*, pp. 45–47.

68. "Study Details Family Violence," *New York Times*, April 23, 1984.

69. See, for example, Susan Griffin, *Pornography and Silence* (New York, 1981); Andrea Dworkin, *Pornography: Men Possessing Women* (New York, 1981); and *Take Back the Night*, ed. Laura Lederer (New York, 1982).

70. Ochshorn, *Female Experience*, pp. 14–15, 34.

71. Ochshorn, *Female Experience*, pp. 107–114.

72. Philipe Ariès, *Centuries of Childhood* (New York, 1962), pp. 100–127.

73. Foucault, *Sexuality*, pp. 36–37.

74. Foucault, *Sexuality*, p. 48.

75. For discussion of such proceedings in France, see Foucault, *Sexuality*, pp. 54ff.

76. Lucien Febvre, "Sensibility and History," *A New Kind of History*, ed. Peter Burke (New York, 1973), p. 25.

77. Foucault, *Sexuality*, p. 107.

78. Stone, *Family*, p. 440.

79. Griffin, *Pornography*, p. 56.

80. Gilles Deleuze, *Présentation de Sacher-Masoch* (Paris, 1967), cited by Ronald Hayman, *Nietzsche*, p. 355.

81. For discussion of snuff films, see Lederer, *Night*, passim.

82. For connections between pornography and actual violence, drawn from police reports, see Irene Diamond, "Pornography and Repression: A Reconsideration of 'Who' and 'What,' " Lederer, *Night*, pp. 183–200; for relations between pornography and violence, see Diana E. H. Russell, "Pornography and Violence: What Does the New Research Say?" Lederer, *Night*, pp. 216–236.

83. Edmund White, "The Political Vocabulary of Homosexuality," *The State of the Language*, ed. Leonard Michaels and Christopher Ricks (Berkeley, Calif., 1980), p. 242.

84. Pat Califia, "Feminism and Sadomasochism," *Heresies* 12, 3, 4 (1981):30–34.

85. Susan Brownmiller, *Against Our Will* (New York, 1975). For descriptions of studies of rapists, see Pauline B. Bart and Margaret Jozsa, "Dirty Books, Dirty Films, and Dirty Data," Lederer, *Night*, pp. 201–215.

86. Betty Friedan, *The Second Stage* (New York, 1981), p. 154.

87. Abraham Maslow, "Self-Esteem (Dominance-Feeling) and Sexuality in Women," *Psychoanalysis and Female Sexuality*, ed. Hendrick M. Ruitenbeek (New Haven, Conn., 1966), pp. 161–197.

88. George Gilder, *Sexual Suicide* (New York, 1973), pp. 14–16.

89. Robert Stoller, *Perversion* (New York, 1975), p. 26.

90. Georges Bataille, *Death and Sensuality* (New York, 1977), p. 90. Bataille and Stoller are among the writers discussed by Hartsock, *Money, Sex, and Power*, Chapter 7.

91. Stoller, *Sexual Excitement: The Dynamics of Erotic Life* (New York, 1979), p. 113.

92. A. Dworkin, *Pornography*, p. 135.

93. Califia, "Feminism and Sadomasochism," *Heresies* 12 and "A Secret Side of Lesbian Sexuality," *The Advocate*, December 27, 1979.

94. Ibid.

95. Weil, "Theoretical Picture of a Free Society" (1934), *Oppression*, p. 96.

96. For discussion of this theory, see Salvatore Cucchiari, "The Gender Revolution and The Transition from Bisexual Horde to Patrilocal Band: The Origins of Gender Hierarchy," Ortner and Whitehead, *Sexual Meanings*; Sigmund Freud, "The Infantile Genital Organization: An Interpolation into the Theory of Sexuality" (1923), in standard edition of *Complete Psychological Works of Sigmund Freud*, ed. James Strachey (London, 1961); Robert J. Stoller, "Facts and Fancies: An Examination of Freud's Concept of Bisexuality," *Women and Analysis*, ed. Jean Strouse (New York, 1974), pp. 343–364; John Money and Patricia Tucker, *Sexual Signatures* (Boston, 1975). For discussion of compulsory heterosexuality, see Adrienne Rich, *Of Woman Born* (New York, 1976), and Rubin, "Traffic," Reiter, *Anthropology*, pp. 157–210.

97. Allan Griswold Johnson, "On the Prevalence of Rape in the United States," *Signs* 6, 2 (Winter 1980):349. Johnson was appalled at his own statistics, reported in "On the Prevalence of Rape in the United States," *Signs* 6, 1 (Autumn 1980); he reexamined his data and submitted his

analysis to demographers for review, but found his conclusion "inescapable": sexual violence against women is part of the normal functioning of the American sexual system. On the normality of rapists, see the works cited in note 85 in this chapter.

98. Michael Ignatieff, "Homo Sexualis," *London Review of Books*, March 4–17, 1982.

99. James Joyce, *A Portrait of the Artist as a Young Man* (New York, 1968), quotations from pp. 104, 124, 142.

100. Becker, *Denial of Death*, p. 162.

101. Norman O. Brown, *Life Against Death* (New York, 1959), Chapter 9.

102. Becker, *Denial of Death*, p. 163.

103. Freud, *Civilization*, pp. 51, 52.

104. Sigmund Freud, *A General Introduction to Psychoanalysis* (Garden City, N.Y., 1943), pp. 376–377.

105. Freud, *Civilization*, p. 33.

106. Evelyn Goodenough, "Interests in Persons as an Aspect of Sex Differences in the Early Years," *Genetic Psychological Monograph* 55 (1957):287–323.

107. David Lynn, *Parental and Sex Role Identification: A Theoretical Formulation* (Berkeley, Calif., 1969), p. 24.

108. David Lynn, "A Note on Sex Difference in the Development of Masculine and Feminine Identification," *Psychological Review* 66, 2 (1959):126–135.

109. D. B. Leventhal and K. M. Shember, "Sex Role Adjustment and Non-sanctioned Aggression," *Journal of Experimental Research in Personality* 3 (1969):283–286.

110. Gilligan, *Different Voice*, pp. 39–40.

111. Myron Brenton, *The American Male* (New York, 1966), p. 22.

112. Statistics taken from International Labor Organization study presented at the United Nations Women's Conference in Copenhagen, 1980, but reversed. See Chapter Six, p. 467.

113. Glennon, Linda M., *Women and Dualism* (New York, 1979), pp. 170–199, discusses some of these complaints.

114. D'Andrade, "Sex Differences," Maccoby, *Development*, p. 202.

115. D'Andrade, "Sex Differences," Maccoby, *Development*, p. 216; David A. Hamburg and Donald Munde, "Sex Hormones in the Development of Sex Differences in Human Behavior," Maccoby, *Development*, p. 19; and Jane E. Brody, "Some Disorders Appear Linked to Being Left-Handed," *New York Times*, April 19, 1983.

116. Lewontin, Rose, and Kamin, *Not in Genes*, Chapter 6.

117. John Money, "Sex, Hormones, and Other Variables in Human Eroticism"; J. L. Hampson and Joan G. Hampson, "The Ontogenesis of Sexual Behavior in Man"; both in *Sex and Internal Secretions*, Vol. ed. W. C. Young, Vol. 2 (Baltimore, Md., 1961).

118. Kanter, *Corporation*, pp. 163, 170, 255ff.

119. See David M. Potter, *American Women and the American Character*, Stetson University Bulletin LXIII (Jan. 1962), p. 21.

120. Chodorow, *Mothering*, pp. 23–30.

121. Chodorow, *Mothering*, p. 75.

122. Farrell, *Liberated*, p. 122.

123. Erving Goffman, "Gender Display," Tiger and Fowler, *Hierarchies*, p. 70.

124. Dinnerstein, *Mermaid*, especially pp. 188–191.

125. Chodorow, *Mothering*, pp. 75–76, 185, 214; Dinnerstein, *Mermaid*.

126. Sidney Bolkowsky, "The Alpha and Omega of Psychoanalysis," *Psychoanalytic Review* 69, 1 (Spring 1982):131–150. See also Stanley Diamond, "The Search for the Primitive," *In Search of the Primitive: A Critique of Civilization* (New Brunswick, N.J., 1974), pp. 116–175; and Meyer Fortes, "Mind," *The Institutions of Primitive Society*, ed. E. E. Evans-Pritchard (Glencoe, Ill., 1956), pp. 90–94.

127. Rosalyn F. Baxandall, "Who Shall Care for Our Children? The History and Development of Day Care in the United States," Freeman, *Women*, pp. 134–149. The study was conducted by Urie Brofenbrenner, *Two Worlds of Childhood: U.S. and USSR* (New York, 1970).

128. Chodorow, *Mothering*, p. 217.

129. Rubin, "Traffic," Reiter, *Anthropology*, p. 180.

130. Rubin, "Traffic," Reiter, *Anthropology*, p. 199.

131. Elshtain, *Private*, passim.

132. Dietrich Bonhoeffer, *Letters and Papers from Prison*, ed. Eberhard Bethge (New York, 1967), p. 27. The emphasis is Bonhoeffer's.

133. Slater, *Hera*, p. 8.

134. As Stephen Jay Gould points out, sharing need not be genetic, since we all learn it in our mothers' arms. *Darwin*, p. 257.

135. Margaret Mead showed that the terms *cooperative* and *competitive* are not necessarily

opposites; groups of people can work together for very different personal goals; people can compete cooperatively. The way people work together is, Mead writes, "fundamentally conditioned by the total social emphasis" of their society. The goals of individuals are "culturally determined and are not the response of the organism to an external . . . situation, like a simple scarcity of food." Mead, *Cooperation*, p. 16. Joseph Folsom distinguished between competition and rivalry, defining the former as behavior aimed at a goal which others also seek, and the latter as behavior aimed at worsting another by attaining a goal they also seek. Joseph Folsom, *Social Psychology* (New York, 1931), pp. 337–346; 370–371. And Ruth Benedict coined the term *synergy* to describe a mode of behavior that was at once cooperative and competitive. High-synergy cultures create structures through which individuals can by the same act serve their own advantage and that of the group; low-synergy cultures create structures in which acts are necessarily mutually opposed and counter-active, in which the advantage of one individual becomes the disadvantage of another. Ruth Benedict, "Synergy," *American Anthropologist* 72 (1970):320–333.

136. Robert Paul Wolff discusses sharing as a condition of personal pleasure in *The Poverty of Liberalism* (Boston, 1968), Chapter 5.

137. Gass adds that Descartes "delivered the *coup de grâce*": he removed quality from the external world and attributed it only to perception, "as though the telescope with its lenses had swallowed the stars." William Gass, *On Being Blue* (Boston, 1976), p. 64.

138. Nietzsche, *Will to Power*, II, pp. 4, 461.

139. Weil, "Analysis" (1934), *Oppression*.

140. Bergmann, *On Being Free*, p. 122.

141. Friedrich Nietzsche, "The Problem of Socrates," Section 11, *The Twilight of the Idols*, *The Portable Nietzsche*, trans. Walter Kaufmann (New York, 1954), p. 479.

142. Maslow, *Farther Reaches*, pp. 12–13.

143. Chodorow, *Mothering*, p. 76.

144. Hobsbawm, *Revolutionaries*, p. 204.

145. C. B. MacPherson, *The Political Theory of Possessive Individualism* (New York, 1964), p. 263.

146. For discussion of universal physical force, a pull felt by creatures too small to be affected by gravity, see Lewontin, Rose, and Kamin, *Not in Genes*, pp. 273–274.

147. Bergmann, *On Being Free*, p. 48.

148. This is also the definition of freedom offered by Bergmann, *On Being Free*; see especially pp. 92ff.

149. Martin Foss, *Symbol and Metaphor in Human Experience* (Princeton, N.J., 1949), pp. 1–32.

150. Cited by Wilson, *Sociobiology*, p. 23.

151. Merchant, *Death of Nature*, pp. 69–126.

152. Hartsock, *Money, Sex, and Power*, discusses community as it is conceived of by political and economic thinkers; see especially pp. 41–46.

# References Consulted

*BOOKS AND PERIODICALS*

Abernethy, Virginia. "Female Hierarchy: An Evolutionary Perspective." In Tiger and Fowler, *Hierarchies.*

Abram, A. "Women Traders in Medieval London." *Economic Journal* (London) 26 (June 1916):276–285.

Adams, Karen, and Norma C. Ware. "Sexism and the English Language: The Linguistic Implications of Being a Woman." In Freeman, *Women.*

Adkins, A. W. H. *Merit and Responsibility: A Study in Greek Values.* Oxford: Oxford Univ. Press, 1960.

Agonito, Rosemary. *History of Ideas on Women.* New York: G. P. Putnam's Sons/Paragon, 1977.

Ali, Syed Ameer. *A Short History of the Saracens.* London, 1900.

Alvarez, A. "The Background." In Battin and Mayo, *Suicide.*

Anderson, Peter. "Reproductive Role of the Human Breast." *Current Anthropology* 24, 1 (Feb. 1983): 25–43.

Anton, Ferdinand. *Woman in Pre-Columbian America.* New York: Abner Schram, 1973.

Aptheker, Herbert. *American Negro Slave Revolts.* New York: International Publishers, 1970.

Ardener, Edwin. "Belief and the Problem of Women." In Ardener, *Perceiving.*

Ardener, Shirley, ed. *Perceiving Women.* London: Malaby Press, 1975.

Arendt, Hannah. *The Origins of Totalitarianism.* New York: Harcourt Brace Jovanovich, 1968.

Aries, Elizabeth. "Interaction Patterns and Themes of Males, Females, and Mixed Groups." *Small Group Behavior* 7, 1 (1976):1–18.

Ariès, Philippe. *Centuries of Childhood.* New York: Random House, 1962.

Aristotle. *Generation of Animals.* Trans. A. L. Peck. Cambridge, Mass.: Loeb Classical Library, 1943.

——. *Politics.* Trans. T. A. Sinclair. Rev. ed. New York: Penguin Books, 1981.

Arthur, Marylin. " 'Liberated' Women: The Classical Era." In Bridenthal and Koonz, *Visible.*

Ash, Roy. *Columbia Journal of World Business* 5, 2 (March–April, 1970).

Aslin, A. L. "Feminist & Community Mental Health Center Psychotherapists' Expectations of Mental Health for Women." *Sex Roles: A Journal of Research,* 3, 6 (1977):537–544.

Athenaeus. *The Deipnosophistae,* V. Trans. Charles Burton Gulick. Cambridge, Mass: Loeb Classical Library, 1932.

Bachofen, J. J. *Das Mutterrecht* (1861). Published in English as *Myth, Religion, and Mother-Right.* Trans. Ralph Manheim. Princeton, N.J.: Princeton Univ. Press, 1967.

Bacon, Francis. *The Great Instauration.* 1620.

——. *Novum Organum.* 1620.

——. *Preface to the History of the Winds.* 1623.

Bainton, Roland H. *Women of the Reformation.* Minneapolis, Minn.: Augsburg Publishing House, 1977.

Bakan, David. *And They Took Themselves Wives.* San Francisco: Harper and Row, 1979.

Balbus, Isaac D. *Marxism and Domination.* Princeton, N.J.: Princeton Univ. Press, 1982.

Balikci, Asen. "The Netsilik Eskimos: Adaptive Process." In Lee and DeVore, *Hunter.*

Balsdon, J. P. V. D. *Roman Women: Their History and Their Habits.* Westport, Conn.: Greenwood Press, 1962.

Bamberger, Joan. "The Myth of Matriarchy: Why Men Rule in Primitive Society." In Rosaldo and Lamphere, *Woman.*

Bandel, Betty. "The English Chroniclers' Attitudes Toward Women." *Journal of the History of Ideas* 16 (1955):113–118.

Barber, Benjamin. "The Conceptual Foundations of Totalitarianism." In Friedrich, Curtis, and Barber, *Totalitarianism*.

Barnet, Richard J., and Ronald E. Muller. *Global Reach: The Power of the Multinational Corporations*. New York: Simon and Schuster, 1974.

Barrett, Jane. "Women Hold Up Half the Sky." In Young, *China*.

Bart, Pauline B., and Margaret Jozsa. "Dirty Books, Dirty Films, and Dirty Data." In Lederer, *Night*.

Bataille, Georges. *Death and Sensuality*. New York: Arno Press, 1977.

Battin, M. Pabst, and David Mayo, eds. *Suicide: The Philosophical Issues*. New York: St. Martin's Press, 1980.

Baxandall, Rosalyn F. "Who Shall Care for Our Children? The History and Development of Day Care in the United States." In Freeman, *Women*.

———, Linda Gordon, and Susan Raverby. *America's Working Women: A Documentary History, 1600 to the Present*. New York: Random House, 1976.

Beard, Mary R. *Woman as Force in History*. New York: Macmillan/Collier Books, 1971.

Becker, Ernest. *The Denial of Death*. New York: Free Press, 1973.

*Beijing Review* 25, 42 (Oct. 18, 1982) and 26, 5 (Jan. 31, 1983).

Bell, Susan Groag, ed. *Women from the Greeks to the French Revolution*. Stanford, Calif.: Stanford Univ. Press, 1973.

Bendix, Reinhard. *Work and Authority in Industry*. Berkeley: Univ. of California Press, 1974.

Benedict, Ruth. "Synergy: Some Notes of Ruth Benedict." Excerpts from lectures given in 1941. Selected by Abraham H. Maslow and John J. Honigmann. *American Anthropologist* 72 (1970):320–333.

Bennet, William. "The Science Watch." *Harvard Magazine* 64 (Sept.–Oct. 1978).

Berger, Peter. "Is History the Enemy of Progress?" Review of *Tradition*, by Edward Shils. *New York Times Book Review*, Feb. 14, 1982.

———, and Thomas Luckman. *The Social Construction of Reality: A Treatise in the Sociology of Knowledge*. Garden City, N.Y.: Anchor/Doubleday, 1977.

Bergmann, Frithjof. *On Being Free*. Notre Dame, Ind.: Univ. of Notre Dame Press, 1977.

Bernard, Jessie. *The Female World*. New York: Free Press, 1981.

———. "The Mother Role." In Freeman, *Women*.

Berndt, Catherine H. "Interpretations and 'Facts' in Aboriginal Australia." In Dahlberg, *Gatherer*.

Bettelheim, Bruno. *Freud and Man's Soul*. New York: Alfred A. Knopf, 1983.

Billigmeier, Jon-Christian, and Judy A. Turner. "The Socio-Economic Roles of Women in Mycenaean Greece: A Brief Survey from Evidence of the Linear B Tablets." *Women's Studies*, 8 (1981):3–20.

Black, C. *Married Women's Work*. London: G. Bell and Sons, 1915.

Block, Maurice, and Jean H. Block. "Women and the Dialectics of Nature in Eighteenth-Century French Thought." In MacCormack and Strathern, *Nature*.

Block, Raymond. *The Etruscans*. New York: Frederick A. Praeger, 1958.

Blouin, Andrée, with Jean MacKellar. *My Country, Africa*. New York: Frederick A. Praeger, 1983.

Blum, Lawrence A. "Kant and Hegel's Moral Rationalism: A Feminist Perspective." In *Canadian Journal of Philosophy* 12 (June 1982):287–288.

Boals, Kay. "The Politics of Cultural Liberation: Male-Female Relations in Algeria." In Carroll, *Liberating Women's History*.

Bochkaryova, Y., and S. Lyubimova. *Women of a New World*. Moscow: Progress Press, 1969.

Bodine, Anne. "Androcentrism in Prescriptive Grammar." *Language and Society* 4, 2 (Aug. 1975):129–146.

Bolkowsky, Sidney. "Alpha and Omega of Psychoanalysis." *The Psychoanalytic Review* 69, 1 (Spring 1982):131–150.

Bonhoeffer, Dietrich. *Letters and Papers from Prison*. Ed. Eberhard Bethge. New York: Macmillan, 1967.

Boswell, John. *Christianity, Social Tolerance, and Homosexuality*. Chicago: Univ. of Chicago Press, 1980.

Boulding, Elise. *The Underside of History*. Boulder, Colorado: Westview Press, 1976.

Boulting, William. *Women in Italy*. London: Methuen and Co., 1910.

Bowles, Samuel, and Herbert Gintis. *Schooling in Capitalist America: Educational Reform and the Contradictions of Economic Life*. New York: Basic Books, 1976.

Branca, Patricia. "Image and Reality: The Myth of the Idle Victorian Woman." In Hartman and Banner, *Clio*.

Brandes, Stanley. "Like Wounded Stags." In Ortner and Whitehead, *Sexual Meanings*.

Breggin, Peter E. "The Return of Lobotomy and Psycho-Surgery." *Congressional Record* 118 (Feb. 1972):5567–5577.

Bremer, Sidney. "Lost Continuities: Alternative Urban Visions in Chicago Novels, 1890–1915." *Soundings* 64, 1 (Spring 1981): 29–51.

Brenton, Myron. *The American Male.* New York: Fawcett, 1966.

Bridenthal, Renate, and Claudia Koonz, eds. *Becoming Visible: Women in European History.* Boston: Houghton Mifflin, 1977.

———. "Beyond *Kinder, Küche, Kirche:* Weimar Women in Politics and Work." In Carroll, *Liberating Women's History.*

Briffault, Robert. *The Mothers, A Study of the Origins of Sentiment and Institutions.* 3 vols. London: 1927.

———. *The Mothers.* Abridged and with an introduction by Gordon Rattray Taylor. New York: Atheneum, 1977.

*British Medical Journal,* April 3, 1976:787.

Broverman, I. K., D. M. Broverman, F. E. Clarkson, P. S. Rosenkrantz, and S. R. Vogel. "Sex-role Stereotypes and Clinical Judgments of Mental Health." *Journal of Consulting and Clinical Psychology* 34, 1 (1970):1–7.

Brown, Connie, and Jane Seitz. " 'You've Come a Long Way, Baby': Historical Perspectives." In Morgan, *Sisterhood Is Powerful.*

Brown, Judith K. "Iroquois Women: An Ethnohistoric Note." In Reiter, *Anthropology.*

Brown, Les. *Television: The Business Behind the Box.* New York: Harcourt Brace Jovanovich, 1971.

Brown, Norman O. *Life Against Death.* New York: Vintage Books, 1959.

Brown, Roy E. M.D. "China's Approach to Total Health Care." *Holy Cross Quarterly* 7, 1–4 (1975):138–147.

Brownmiller, Susan. *Against Our Will.* New York: Simon and Schuster, 1975.

Brundage, Burr Cartwright. *The Fifth Sun.* Austin, Texas: Univ. of Texas Press, 1979.

Bryant, Dorothy. *The Kin of Ata Are Waiting for You.* New York: Random House, 1971.

Bryant, Louise. *Six Months in Russia.* New York: George H. Doran Co., 1918.

Buis, Ann Gibson. "An Historical Study of the Role of the Federal Government in the Financial Support of Education." Diss., Ohio State University, 1953.

Bury, J. B., S. A. Cook, and F. E. Adcock. "The Law of Ancient Babylonia." In *Man in Adaptation: The Institutional Framework.* Ed. Y. A. Cohen. Chicago: Aldine, 1971.

"The Business Brain." *AMA Management Digest* (April 1982):18–24.

Cairns, J. "The Cancer Problem," *Scientific American* 233, 5 (1975).

Califia, Pat. "Feminism and Sadomasochism." *Heresies* 12, 3, 4 (1981):30–34.

Campbell, Joseph. *The Hero with a Thousand Faces.* Princeton, N.J.: Princeton Univ. Press, 1968.

———. *The Masks of God: Occidental Mythology.* New York: Viking Press, 1970.

"Campus Cartels." *The Nation,* March 20, 1983.

Capellanus, Andreas. *The Art of Courtly Love.* Trans. John J. Parry. New York: Columbia Univ. Press, 1941.

Caplow, Theodore, and Reece McGee. *The Academic Marketplace.* New York: Doubleday/Anchor Books, 1965.

Capra, Fritjof. "The Dance of Life." *Science Digest* (April 1982):30–33.

———. *The Tao of Physics.* New York: Bantam, 1977.

Carcopino, Jerome. *Daily Life in Ancient Rome.* Trans. E. O. Lorimer. New Haven: Yale Univ. Press, 1940.

Carroll, Berenice A., ed. *Liberating Women's History.* Urbana, Ill.: Univ. of Illinois Press, 1976.

Carter, Angela. "The Language of Sisterhood." In Michaels and Ricks, *State of the Language.*

Casey, Kathleen. "The Cheshire Cat: Reconstructing the Experience of Medieval Woman." In Carroll, *Liberating Women's History.*

Caspari, Ernst W. "The Biological Basis of Female Hierarchies." In Tiger and Fowler, *Hierarchies.*

Catt, Carrie Chapman, and Nettie Rogers Shuler. *Woman Suffrage and Politics.* New York: Charles Scribner's Sons, 1923.

Caudwell, Chistopher. *Romance and Realism.* Princeton, N.J.: Princeton Univ. Press, 1970.

Chadwick, John. *The Mycenaean World.* New York: Cambridge Univ. Press, 1976.

Chance, Michael R. A. "Sex Differences in the Structure of Attention." In Tiger and Fowler, *Hierarchies.*

———, and Clifford Jolly. *Social Groups of Monkeys, Apes, and Men.* New York: E. P. Dutton, 1970.

Cherfas, Jeremy, and John Gribbin. "Updating Man's Ancestry." *New York Times Magazine*, Aug. 29, 1982.

Chicago, Judy. *The Dinner Party*. Garden City, N.Y.: Doubleday, 1979.

Childe, V. Gordon. *Social Evolution*. Cleveland: World Publishing, 1963.

Chodorow, Nancy. *The Reproduction of Mothering*. Berkeley and Los Angeles: Univ. of California Press, 1978.

Chojnacki, Stanley. "Dowries and Kinsmen in Early Renaissance Venice." In Stuard, *Medieval*.

Chorover, Stephan. *From Genesis to Genocide*. Cambridge, Mass.: MIT Press, 1979.

Chrystos. "I Don't Understand Those Who Have Turned Away from Me." In Moraga and Anzaldua, *Bridge*.

Cixous, Hélène. "The Laugh of the Medusa." Trans. Keith Cohen and Paula Cohen. In Marks and De Courtivon, *New French Feminisms*.

Clark, Alice. *Working Life of Women in the Seventeenth Century*. 1919. Reprint, New York: A. M. Kelley, 1968.

Clark, Cathleen B. "A Preliminary Report on Weaning Among Chimpanzees of the Gombe National Park, Tanzania." In *Primate Bio-Social Development*. Eds. Suzanne Chevalier-Skolnikoff and Frank E. Poirier. New York: Garland Press, 1977.

"Clunkers." Feature in *Think* Magazine 47, 4 (July/Aug. 1981):14–15.

Cohen, Charlotte Bonny. " 'Chung-kuo Fu nu': Women of China." In Morgan, *Sisterhood Is Powerful*.

Coleman, Emily. "Infanticide in the Early Middle Ages." In Stuard, *Medieval*.

*Common Cause Magazine*, "Medical Moola," July/Aug. 1983, p. 35.

Commoner, Barry. *The Closing Circle*. New York: Knopf, 1971.

Condry, John, and Sharon Dyer. "Fear of Success: Attribution of Cause to the Victim." *Journal of Social Issues* 32, 3 (Summer 1976):63–83.

Cook, Blanche Wiesen. "Feminism, Socialism, and Sexual Freedom: The Work and Legacy of Crystal Eastman and Alexandra Kollontai." Forthcoming in *Stratégies Féminines/Stratégies Féministes*. Eds. Françoise Basch et al. Paris: Editions Tiercé. English eds. Judith Friedlander et al. Bloomington, Ind.: Indiana Univ. Press.

————. *Women and Support Networks*. New York: Out and Out Books, 1979.

Cranstone, B. A. L. "Animal Husbandry: The Evidence from Ethnography." In *The Domestication and Exploitation of Plants and Animals*. Eds. Peter J. Ucko and G. W. Dimbleby. Chicago: Aldine Publishing, 1969.

*Critical Issues Symposium Series*. "Knowledge, Education, and Human Values: Toward the Recovery of Wholeness." New York: Charles F. Kettering Foundation, 1980.

Croll, Elisabeth. *Feminism and Socialism in China*. New York: Schocken, 1980.

Crossley-Holland, Kevin. *The Norse Myths*. New York: Pantheon, 1973.

Cucchiari, Salvatore. "The Gender Revolution and The Transition from Bisexual Horde to Patrilocal Band: The Origins of Gender Hierarchy." In Ortner and Whitehead, *Sexual Meanings*.

Curtis, Michael. "Retreat from Totalitarianism." In Friedrich, Curtis, and Barber, *Totalitarianism*.

Dahlberg, Frances, ed. *Woman the Gatherer*. New Haven, Conn.: Yale Univ. Press, 1981.

Daly, Mary. *Gyn/Ecology*. Boston: Beacon Press, 1978.

D'Andrade, Roy. "Sex Differences and Cultural Institutions." In Maccoby, *Development*.

Davidson, H. R. Ellis. *Gods and Myths of Northern Europe*. Baltimore, Md.: Penguin Books, 1964.

Davies, Paul. *Other Worlds: Space, Superspace and the Quantum Theory*. London: Sphere Books, 1982.

Davin, Delia. "Women in the Liberated Areas." In Young, *China*.

Davis, Angela Y. *Women, Race, and Class*. New York: Random House, 1981.

Davis, Elizabeth Gould. *The First Sex*. New York: G. P. Putnam's Sons/Penguin Books, 1972.

De Beauvoir, Simone. *The Second Sex*. New York: Vintage Books, 1974.

De Rougemont, Denis. *Love in the Western World*. New York: Pantheon, 1956.

Diamond, Irene, ed. *Families, Politics, and Public Policy*. New York: Longman, 1983.

————. "Pornography and Repression: A Reconsideration of 'Who' and 'What.' " In Lederer, *Night*.

Diamond, Norma. "Collectivization, Kinship, and Status of Women in Rural China." In Reiter, *Anthropology*.

Diamond, Stanley. *In Search of the Primitive*. New Brunswick, N.J.: Transaction Books, 1974.

Didion, Joan. *Salvador*. New York: Simon and Schuster, 1983.

Dinnerstein, Dorothy. *The Mermaid and the Minotaur*. New York: Harper/Colophon, 1977.

Divale, William, and Marvin Harris. "Population, Warfare, and the Male Supremacist Complex." *American Anthropologist*, 78 (1976):521–538.

"Divorce American Style." *Newsweek*, Jan. 10, 1983, pp. 44, 46.

Dobzhansky, Theodosius. "Anthropology and the Natural Sciences—The Problem of Human Evolution." *Current Anthropology* 4:138, 146–148.

Douglas, Ann. *The Feminization of American Culture*. New York: Knopf, 1977.

Doyal, Lesley. *The Political Economy of Health*. Boston: South End Press, 1979.

Draenos, Stan Spyros. "Thinking Without a Ground: Hannah Arendt and the Contemporary Situation of Understanding." In Hill, *Hannah Arendt*.

Draper, Patricia. "!Kung Women: Contrasts in Sexual Egalitarianism in Foraging and Sedentary Contexts." In Reiter, *Anthropology*.

Dubois, Betty Lou, and Isabel Crouch. "The Question of Tag Questions in Women's Speech: They Don't Really Use More of Them, Do They?" *Language in Society* 4, 4 (1975): 289–294.

Dunnell, K., and A. Cartwright. *Medicine Takers, Prescribers and Hoarders*. London: Routledge and Kegan Paul, 1972.

Duvall, Susan W., J. S. Bernstein, and J. P. Gordon. "Paternity and Status in a Rhesus Monkey Group." In Tiger and Fowler, *Hierarchies*.

Dworkin, Andrea. *Pornography: Men Possessing Women*. New York: G. P. Putnam's Sons, 1981.

———. *Right-Wing Women*. New York: Perigee, 1983.

Dworkin, R. M. "Is Law a System of Rules?" In *The Philosophy of Law*. Ed. R. M. Dworkin. Oxford: Oxford Univ. Press, 1979.

Eco, Umberto. *The Name of the Rose*. New York: Harcourt Brace Jovanovich, 1983.

Edwards, Harry. *The Struggle That Must Be*. New York: Macmillan, 1980.

Ehrenreich, Barbara. *The Hearts of Men*. Garden City, N.Y.: Doubleday, 1983.

———. "What is Socialist Feminism?" *WIN* (June 3, 1976).

———, and Deirdre English. *For Her Own Good*. Garden City, N.Y.: Doubleday/Anchor, 1979.

Eisenstein, Zillah R. "The Sexual Politics of the New Right: Understanding the 'Crisis of Liberalism' for the 1980s." *Signs* 7, 3 (Spring 1982).

———. "The State, the Patriarchal Family, and Working Mothers." In Diamond, *Families*.

Elkin, A. P. "Studies in Australian Totemism: Sub-section, Section, and Moiety Totemism." *Oceania* 4, 2 (1933–34):6–90.

———. "Studies in Australian Totemism: The Nature of Australian Totemism." *Oceania* 4, 2 (1933–34):113–131.

Elshtain, Jean Bethke. "Feminist Discourse and Its Discontents: Language, Power and Meaning." *Signs* 7, 3 (Spring 1982).

———. *Public Man, Private Woman*. Princeton, N.J.: Princeton Univ. Press, 1981.

Engel, Barbara. "Women as Revolutionaries: The Case of the Russian Populists." In Bridenthal and Koonz, *Visible*.

Engels, Frederick. *The Origin of the Family, Private Property, and the State*. Reprint, ed. and with an introduction by E. Leacock. New York: International Publishers, 1978.

"ERA and Minority Women." ERA pamphlet published by NOW, 1981.

Erikson, Erik. *Childhood and Society*. New York: Norton, 1950.

———. *Gandhi's Truth*. New York: Norton, 1969.

———. *Identity: Youth and Crisis*. New York: Norton, 1968.

Estioko-Griffin, Agnes, and P. Bion Griffin. "Woman the Hunter: The Agta." In Dahlberg, *Gatherer*.

Evans, Richard J. *The Feminist Movement in Germany: 1894–1933*. London: Sage Publications, 1976.

Evans-Pritchard, E. E. *Nuer Religion*. Oxford: Clarendon Press, 1956.

Ewen, Stuart, and Elizabeth Ewen. *Channels of Desire: Mass Images and the Shaping of American Consciousness*. New York: McGraw-Hill, 1982.

Faithorn, Elizabeth. "The Concept of Pollution Among the Káfe of the Papua New Guinea Highlands." In Reiter, *Anthropology*.

Falk, Florence. "Karen Silkwood: Laundered News," *Heresies 13*, 4, 1 (1981):3–4.

Fanon, Frantz. *A Dying Colonialism*. Trans. Haakon Chevalier. New York: Grove Press, 1967.

———. *The Wretched of the Earth*. Trans. Constance Farrington. New York: Grove Press, 1963.

Farer, Tom J. "The Making of Reaganism." *New York Review of Books*, Jan. 21, 1982.

Farrell, Warren. *The Liberated Man*. New York: Random House, 1974.

Faure, Christine. "Absent from History." Trans. Lillian S. Robinson. *Signs* 7, 1 (Autumn 1981):71–86.

Febvre, Lucien. "Sensibility and History." In *A New Kind of History.* Ed. Peter Burke. New York: Random House, 1973.

Ferenczi, Sandor. "Confusion of Tongues Between Adults and the Child" (1932).

Figes, Eva. *Patriarchal Attitudes.* New York: Stein and Day, 1970.

Finley, M. I. *The World of Odysseus.* New York: Meridian, 1956.

Fiorenza, Elisabeth Schussler. *In Memory of Her: A Feminist Theological Reconstruction of Christian Origins.* New York: Crossroad, 1984.

First, Ruth, and Ann Scott. *Olive Schreiner.* London: André Deutsch, 1980.

Fisher, Elizabeth. *Woman's Creation: Sexual Evolution and the Shaping of Society.* Garden City, N.Y.: Anchor Press/Doubleday, 1979.

FitzGerald, Frances. *America Revised.* Boston: Little, Brown, 1979.

————. "The Triumphs of the New Right." *New York Review of Books,* Nov. 19, 1981, Vol. 28:19–26.

Flexner, Eleanor. *Century of Struggle: The Women's Rights Movement in the United States.* Cambridge, Mass.: Harvard Univ. Press, 1975.

Fogel, Robert William, and Stanley L. Engerman. *Time on the Cross: The Economics of American Negro Slavery.* Boston: Little, Brown, 1974.

Folsom, Joseph. *Social Psychology.* New York: Harper and Brothers, 1931.

Fortes, Meyer. "Mind." In *The Institutions of Primitive Society.* Ed. E. E. Evans-Pritchard. Glencoe, Ill.: Free Press, 1956.

Foss, Martin. *Symbol and Metaphor in Human Experience.* Princeton, N.J.: Princeton Univ. Press, 1949.

Foucault, Michel. *The Birth of the Clinic.* Trans. A. M. Sheridan Smith. New York: Pantheon, 1973.

————. *The History of Sexuality.* Trans. Robert Hurley. New York: Pantheon, 1978.

————. *Madness and Civilization.* Trans. Richard Howard. New York: Pantheon, 1965.

————. *The Order of Things.* New York: Pantheon, 1973.

————. *Power/Knowledge.* Ed. Colin Gordon. New York: Pantheon, 1980.

Fowler, Alastair. *Spenser and the Numbers of Time.* New York: Barnes and Noble, 1949.

Fox, James. *White Mischief.* New York: Random House, 1983.

Fox, Robin. *Encounter with Anthropology.* New York: Harcourt Brace Jovanovich, 1973.

————. *The Red Lamp of Incest.* New York: Dutton, 1980.

Francke, Linda Bird. "The Sons of Divorce." *New York Times Magazine.* May 22, 1983.

Freeman, Jo, ed. *Women: A Feminist Perspective.* Palo Alto, Calif.: Mayfield, 1979.

————. "The Women's Liberation Movement: Its Origins, Organizations, Activities, and Ideas." In Freeman, *Women.*

French, Marilyn. *Shakespeare's Division of Experience.* New York: Summit Books, 1981.

————. "Women in Language." *Soundings* 59, 3 (Fall 1976):329–344.

Freud, Sigmund. *Civilization and Its Discontents* (1930). Ed. and trans. James Strachey. New York: Norton, 1961.

————. *A General Introduction to Psychoanalysis* (1935). Reprint, New York: Simon and Schuster, 1963.

————. "The Infantile Genital Organization: An Interpolation into the Theory of Sexuality" (1923). In standard edition of *Complete Psychological Works of Sigmund Freud.* Ed. and trans. James Strachey. London, 1961.

————. "Letters to Wilhelm Fliess, Drafts and Notes: 1887–1902." *The Origins of Psycho-Analysis.* Eds. Marie Bonaparte, Anna Freud, and Ernst Kris. Trans. Eric Mosbacher and James Strachey. New York: Basic Books, 1954.

————. "Some Psychical Consequences of the Anatomical Distinction Between the Sexes" (1925). In Vol. 19 of the standard edition of *Complete Psychological Works.*

Friedan, Betty. *The Feminine Mystique.* New York: Norton, 1963.

————. *The Second Stage* New York: Summit Books, 1981.

Friedl, Ernestine. *Women and Men: An Anthropologist's View.* New York: Holt, Rinehart and Winston, 1975.

Friedlander, Frank, and Stuart Greenberg. "Effect of Job Attitudes, Training, and Organization Climate on Performance of the Hard-Core Unemployed." *Journal of Applied Psychology,* (December 1971).

Friedrich, Carl J. "The Evolving Theory and Practice of Totalitarianism." In Friedrich, Curtis, and Barber, *Totalitarianism.*

————, and Z. K. Brzezinski. *Totalitarian Dictatorship and Autocracy.* New York: Frederick A. Praeger, 1967.

————, Michael Curtis, and Benjamin Barber. *Totalitarianism in Perspective: Three Views.* New York: Frederick A. Praeger, 1969.

Frisch, Rose. "Critical Weights, a Critical Body Composition, Menarche and the Maintenance of Menstrual Cycles." In *Biosocial Interrelations in Population Adaptation.* Ed. Elizabeth Watts, F. Johnston, and G. Lasker. The Hague: Mouton, 1975.

————, and J. McArthur. "Menstrual Cycles: Fatness as a Determinant of Minimum Weight for Height Necessary for their Maintenance or Onset." *Science* 185 (1974):949–951.

Gabriel, Ralph. *The Course of American Democratic Thought.* New York: Ronald Press, 1956.

Gadow, Kenneth D. *Children on Medication: A Primer for School Personnel.* Reston, Va.: ERIC Clearing House on Handicapped and Gifted Children, 1979.

Gage, Matilda Joslyn. *Church and State* (1893). Reprint, New York: Arno Press, 1972.

Galbraith, J. K. "About Men: Corporate Man." *New York Times Magazine,* Jan. 22, 1984.

————. *Economics and the Public Purpose.* Boston: Houghton Mifflin, 1973.

————. *The New Industrial State.* New York: New American Library, 1967.

Galdikas, Biruté M. F., and Geza Teleki. "Variations in Subsistence Activities of Female and Male Pongids: New Perspectives on the Origins of Hominid Labor Division." *Current Anthropology* 22, 3 (June 1981):241–256.

Gass, William. *On Being Blue.* Boston: David R. Godine, 1976.

Gathorne-Hardy, Jonathan. *Marriage, Love, Sex and Divorce.* New York: Summit Books, 1981.

Geertz, Clifford. "Stir Crazy." Rev. of *Discipline and Punish,* by Michel Foucault. *New York Review of Books,* Jan. 26, 1978.

Geiger, H. Jack. "An Overdose of Power and Money." Review of *The Social Transformation of American Medicine,* by Paul Starr. *New York Times Book Review,* Jan. 9, 1983.

Genovese, Eugene. *The Political Economy of Slavery.* New York: Vintage Books/Random House, 1967.

Geschwind, N., and P. Behan. "Left-Handedness: Association with Immune Diseases, Migraine and Developmental Learning Disorder." *Proceedings of the National Academy of Sciences* 79 (1982):5097–5100.

Gilbert, Sandra M., and Susan Gubar. "Alphabet Soup: Women, Language, Sexuality." Publication pending.

Gilder, George. *Sexual Suicide.* New York: Quadrangle, 1973.

Gilligan, Carol. "In a Different Voice: Women's Conceptions of Self and of Morality." *Harvard Educational Review* 47, 4 (Nov. 1977):481–517.

————. *In a Different Voice.* Cambridge, Mass.: Harvard Univ. Press, 1982.

Gillison, Gillian. "Images of Nature in Gimi Thought." In MacCormack and Strathern, *Nature.*

Gilman, Charlotte Perkins. *Herland.* New York: Pantheon, 1979.

————. *The Home: Its Work and Influence* (1903). Reprint, New York: New York Source Book Press, 1970.

————. *The Man-Made World or Our Androcentric Culture* (1911). Reprint, New York: New York Source Book Press, 1970.

Gimbutas, Marija. *The Gods and Goddesses of Old Europe.* Berkeley, Calif.: Univ. of California Press, 1974.

Gitlin, Todd. "Prime Time Ideology." In Newcomb, *Television.*

————. "Sixteen Notes on Television and the Movement." In *Literature in Revolution.* Ed. George Abbott White and Charles Newman. New York: Holt, Rinehart and Winston, 1972.

Glennon, Lynda M. *Women and Dualism.* New York: Longman, 1979.

*Global 2000.* A Report of the President's Council on Environmental Quality. July 1980.

Goffman, Erving. "Gender Display." In Tiger and Fowler, *Hierarchies.*

————. *Stigma: Notes on the Management of Spoiled Identity.* Englewood Cliffs, N.J.: Prentice Hall, 1963.

Goldberg, Steven. *The Inevitability of Patriarchy.* New York: Morrow, 1974.

Goldman, Irving. "The Zuni Indians of New Mexico." In Mead, *Cooperation.*

Goodale, Jane C. "Gender, Sexuality and Marriage: A Kaulong Model of Nature and Culture." In MacCormack and Strathern, *Nature.*

————. *Tiwi Wives.* Seattle, Wash.: Univ. of Washington Press, 1971.

Goodall, Jane. "The Behavior of Free-Living Chimpanzees in the Gombe Stream Reserve." *Animal Behavior Monographs* 1 (1968): 161–311.

Goodenough, Evelyn. "Interests in Persons as an Aspect of Sex Differences in the Early Years." *Genetic Psychological Monograph* 55 (1957):287–323.

Goodman, Naomi. "Eve, Child Bride of Adam." In *Psychosexual Imperatives: Their Role in*

*Identity Formation.* Eds. Marie Coleman Nelson and Jean Ikenberry. New York and London: Human Sciences Press, 1979.

Gordon, Ann D., and Mari Jo Buhle. "Sex and Class in Colonial and Nineteenth-Century America." In Carroll, *Liberating Women's History.*

Gordon, Linda. *Woman's Body, Woman's Right: Birth Control in America.* New York: Penguin Books, 1976.

Gough, Kathleen. "The Origin of the Family." In Freeman, *Women.*

Gould, Carol C., and Max W. Wartofsky, eds. *Women and Philosophy.* New York: G. P. Putnam's Sons, 1976.

Gould, Richard A. *Yiwara.* New York: Scribner's, 1969.

Gould, Stephen Jay. *Ever Since Darwin.* New York: Norton, 1977.

———. *Hens' Teeth and Horses' Toes.* New York: Norton, 1983.

———. *The Mismeasure of Man.* New York: Norton, 1981.

———. *The Panda's Thumb.* New York: Norton, 1980.

Gouldner, Alvin. *The New Class.* New York: Continuum Press, 1979.

Graebner, Norman A. "America's Limited Power in the Contemporary World." *The Key Reporter* XLVII 3 (Spring 1982):2–5.

Graham, Patricia. "Women in Academe." *Science* 169 (Sept. 25, 1970):1284–1290.

Graham, Ruth. "Loaves and Liberty: Women in the French Revolution." In Bridenthal and Koonz, *Visible.*

Graves, Robert. *The Greek Myths.* Baltimore, Md.: Penguin Books, 1966.

Green, Philip. *The Pursuit of Inequality.* New York: Pantheon Books, 1981.

Griffin, Susan. *Pornography and Silence.* New York: Harper and Row, 1981.

———. *Woman and Nature: The Roaring Inside Her.* New York: Harper and Row, 1978.

Gutman, Herbert. *The Black Family in Slavery and Freedom, 1750–1925.* New York: Pantheon Books, 1976.

———. "Work, Culture, and Society in Industrializing America, 1815–1919." *American Historical Review* 78 (June 1973):531–588.

Hacker, Helen Mayer. "Women as a Minority Group." In Roszak and Roszak, *Masculine/Feminine.*

Hackett, Amy. "Feminism and Liberalism in Wilhelmine Germany, 1890–1918." In Carroll, *Liberating Women's History.*

Hale, Judith, and Ellen Levine. "The First Feminists." In Freeman, *Women.*

Halle, Fannina W. *Women in Soviet Russia.* New York: Viking, 1935.

Hamburg, David A., and Donald Munde. "Sex Hormones in the Development of Sex Differences in Human Behavior." In Maccoby, *Development.*

Hampson, J. L., and Joan G. Hampson. "The Ontogenesis of Sexual Behavior in Man." In *Sex and Internal Secretions.* Vol 2. Ed. W. C. Young. Baltimore: Williams and Wilkins, 1961.

Haraway, Donna. "Animal Sociology and a Natural Economy of the Body Politic." Parts I and II. *Signs* 4, 1 (Autumn 1978):21–60.

Harrington, Michael. *The Twilight of Capitalism.* New York: Simon and Schuster, 1976.

Harris, Marvin. *Cannibals and Kings.* New York: Random House, 1977.

Harris, Olivia. "The Power of Signs: Gender, Culture and the Wild in the Bolivian Andes." In MacCormack and Strathern, *Nature.*

Harrison, Bennett. *Education, Training, and the Urban Ghetto.* Baltimore, Md.: Johns Hopkins Univ. Press, 1972.

Harrison, Jane. *Themis: A Study of the Social Origins of Greek Religion.* New York: Meridian Books, 1962.

Hartman, Mary S., and Lois Banner, eds. *Clio's Consciousness Raised: New Perspectives on the History of Women.* New York: Harper and Row, 1974.

Hartsock, Nancy. *Money, Sex, and Power: Toward a Feminist Historical Materialism.* New York: Longman, 1983.

Hausfater, J. "Dominance and Reproduction in Baboons (Papio Cynocephalus): A Quantitative Analysis." In Tiger and Fowler, *Hierarchies.*

Hayman, Ronald. *Nietzsche: A Critical Life.* New York: Oxford Univ. Press, 1980.

Hegel, Georg Wilhelm Friedrich. "On the Assertion of the Will to Live." In *The World as Will and Idea.* Vol 3.

Heidel, Alexander. *The Babylonian Genesis.* Chicago: Univ. of Chicago Press, 1951.

Heilbroner, Robert. *An Inquiry into the Human Prospect.* New York: Norton, 1980.

Hein, Hilde. "Philosophy from a Woman's Perspective." In manuscript.

Heller, Erich. *The Artist's Journey Into the Interior.* New York: Random House, 1965.

Heller, Reinhold. *The Earthly Chimera and The Femme Fatale: Fear of Woman in Nineteenth*

*Century Art*. Catalogue of exhibit in the David and Alfred Smart Gallery, University of Chicago. May 20–June 21, 1981.

Helm, June. "The Nature of Dogrib Socioterritorial Groups." In Lee and DeVore, *Hunter*.

Henderson, Hazel. *The Politics of the Solar Age*. Garden City, N.Y.: Doubleday, 1981.

Herlihy, David. "Land, Family, and Women in Continental Europe, 701–1200." In Stuard, *Medieval*.

Herman, Dianne. "The Rape Culture." In Freeman, *Women*.

Herman, Edward S. *Corporate Control, Corporate Power*. Cambridge: Cambridge Univ. Press, 1981.

Hewitt, McM. *Wives and Mothers in Victorian Industry*. London: Rockliff, 1958.

Hiatt, L. R. "Ownership and Use of Land Among the Australian Aborigines." In Lee and DeVore, *Hunter*.

Higginbotham, Elizabeth. "Two Representative Issues in Contemporary Sociological Work on Black Women." In Hull, Scott, and Smith, *Some of Us*.

Higgins, Ronald. *The Seventh Enemy*. London: Hodder and Stoughton, 1978.

Hill, Melvyn A., ed. *Hannah Arendt: The Recovery of the Public World*. New York: St. Martin's Press, 1979.

Hirsch, Paul M. "The Role of Television and Popular Culture in Contemporary Society." In Newcomb, *Television*.

Hobbes, Thomas. "Of the Natural Condition of Mankind as Concerning Their Felicity and Misery." *Leviathan*. Chapter XII.

———. "On Man." *Leviathan*.

Hobsbawm, E. J. *Revolutionaries*. New York: Pantheon, 1973.

Hoffman, L. W. "Fear of Success in Males and Females: 1965 and 1972." *Journal of Consulting and Clinical Psychology* (1974).

Hogbin, Ian. *The Island of Menstruating Men*. San Francisco: Chandler Publishing, 1970.

Holinshed's Chronicles [604/1/55]. *Narrative and Dramatic Sources of Shakespeare. III*. Ed. Geoffrey Bullough. New York: 1960.

Holter, Harriet. "Sex Roles and Social Change." In Mednick et al., *Women and Achievement*.

Horner, Matina S. "Toward an Understanding of Achievement-Related Conflicts in Women." *The Journal of Social Issues* 28, 9 (1972):157–175.

———. "Women's Need to Fail." *Psychology Today*, November 1969.

Hrdy, Sarah Blaffer. *The Langurs of Abu*. Cambridge, Mass.: Harvard Univ. Press, 1977.

———. *The Woman That Never Evolved*. Cambridge, Mass.: Harvard Univ. Press, 1981.

Hsiao, Kung-chuan. *A History of Chinese Political Thought*. Trans. F. W. Mote. Princeton, N.J.: Princeton Univ. Press, 1978.

Huberman, Leo. *We, the People*. New York: Monthly Review Press, 1932.

Hufton, Olwen. "Women in Revolution 1789–1796." *Past and Present* 53 (November 1971):90–91.

Hughes, Graham. "Who Should Go to Prison." *New York Review of Books*, Jan. 1, 1982.

Huizinga, Johan. *Homo Ludens*. Boston: Beacon Press, 1955.

Hull, Gloria T., Patricia Bell Scott, and Barbara Smith, eds. *But Some of Us Are Brave*. Old Westbury, N.Y.: The Feminist Press, 1982.

Hunter, Nan D. "Women and Child Support." In Diamond, *Families*.

Husserl-Kapit. Interview with Marguerite Duras. *Signs* 1, 2 (Winter 1975).

Ifeka-Moller, Caroline. "Female Militancy and Colonial Revolt." In Ardener, *Perceiving*.

Ignatieff, Michael. "Homo Sexualis." *London Review of Books*, March 4–17, 1982.

Illich, Ivan. *Medical Nemesis*. New York: Pantheon Books, 1976.

———. *Shadow Work*. Boston: Marion Boyars, 1981.

Irigaray, Luce. *And the One Doesn't Stir Without the Other*. Trans. Helene Vivienne Wenzel. *Signs* 7, 1 (Autumn 1981).

Jacobs, Jane. *The Economy of Cities*. New York: Random House, 1970.

Jacoby, Robin Miller. "Feminism and Class Consciousness in the British and American Women's Trade Union Leagues, 1890–1925." In Carroll, *Liberating Women's History*.

Jaeger, Werner. *Paideia: The Ideals of Greek Culture*. New York: Oxford Univ. Press, 1944.

James, Selwyn. *South of the Congo*. New York: 1943.

Janeway, Elizabeth. *Powers of the Weak*. New York: Alfred A. Knopf, 1980.

Janssen-Jurreit, Marielouise. *Sexism: The Male Monopoly on History and Thought*. New York: Farrar, Straus and Giroux, 1982.

Jardine, Alice. "Introduction to Julia Kristeva's 'Women's Time.' " *Signs* 7, 1 (Autumn 1981).

Jarolimek, John. *The Schools in Contemporary Society*. New York: Macmillan, 1981.

Jenkins, Iredell. *Social Order and the Limits of Law*. Princeton, N.J.: Princeton Univ. Press, 1980.

Jespersen, Otto. *Growth and Structure of the English Language.* New York: D. Appleton and Co., 1923.

Johannsson, Sheila Ryan. "Sex and Death in Victorian England: An Examination of Age- and Sex-Specific Death Rates, 1840–1910." In Vicinus, *Widening Sphere.*

Johnson, Allan Griswold. "On the Prevalence of Rape in the United States." *Signs* 6, 2 (Winter 1980): 349.

Joll, James. "Why Men Do Not Revolt." *New York Review of Books.* Sept. 28, 1978.

Jones, David C. "What's Wrong with Our Defense Establishment?" *New York Times Magazine,* Nov. 7, 1982.

Jordan, Winthrop D. *White Over Black.* Chapel Hill, N.C.: Univ. of North Carolina Press, 1968.

Jordanova, L. J. "Natural Facts: A Historical Perspective on Science and Sexuality." In MacCormack and Strathern, *Nature.*

Joyce, James. *A Portrait of the Artist as a Young Man.* New York: Viking Press, 1968.

Kaberry, Phyllis. *Aboriginal Woman: Sacred and Profane.* London: Routledge and Kegan Paul, 1939.

Kaestle, Carl F. *The Evolution of an Urban School System: New York City, 1750–1850.* Cambridge, Mass.: Harvard Univ. Press, 1973.

Kahler, Erich. *The Tower and the Abyss.* New York: George Braziller, 1957.

Kanter, Rosabeth Moss. *Men and Women of the Corporation.* New York: Basic Books, 1977.

Kaplan, Temma. "Other Scenarios: Women and Spanish Anarchism." In Bridenthal and Koonz, *Visible.*

Katz, Michael. *Class, Bureaucracy and Schools.* New York: Praeger, 1975.

Keller, Evelyn Fox. "Feminism and Science." *Signs* 7, 3 (Spring 1982):589–602.

Kellner, Douglas. "Television, Ideology, and Emancipatory Popular Culture." In Newcomb, *Television.*

Kelly, Joan. "Early Feminist Theory and the *Querelle des Femmes,* 1400–1789." *Signs* 8,1 (Autumn 1982):4–28.

Kelso, Ruth. *Doctrine for the Lady of the Renaissance* (1956). Reprint, Urbana, Ill.: Univ. of Illinois Press, 1978.

Kennan, George F. "A Modest Proposal." *New York Review of Books,* July 16, 1981.

Kessler-Harris, Alice. *Women and Work.* Oxford, England: Oxford Univ. Press, 1981.

————. "Women, Work, and the Social Order." In Carroll, *Liberating Women's History.*

Key, Mary Ritchie. *Male/Female Language.* Metuchen, N.J.: Scarecrow Press, 1975.

King, Mary-Claire, and A. C. Wilson. "Evolution at Two Levels in Humans and Chimpanzees." *Science* 188 (1975).

King, Ynestra. "Feminism and the Revolt of Nature." *Heresies* 13, 4,1 (1982):12–16.

Kinoy, Arthur. "The Radical Lawyer and Teacher of Law." In *Law Against the People.* Ed. R. Lefcourt. New York: Random House, 1971.

Kirkpatrick, Clifford. "The Conquest of Women by National Socialism." In *Nazi Germany: Its Women and Family Life.* Indianapolis: 1938.

Kirkpatrick, Jeane. "Dictatorships and Double Standards." *Commentary* 68, 5 (Nov., 1979):34–45.

Kittrie, Nicholas N. *The Right to Be Different: Deviance and Enforced Therapy.* Baltimore, Md.: Johns Hopkins Univ. Press, 1971.

Klein, Viola. "The Historical Background." In Freeman, *Women.*

Kleinbaum, Abby R. "Women in the Age of Light." In Bridenthal and Koonz, *Visible.*

Kohlberg, Lawrence. "Stage and Sequence: The Cognitive-Developmental Approach to Socialization." In *Handbook of Socialization Theory and Research.* Ed. David A. Goslin. Chicago: Rand McNally, 1969.

Kohn, Howard. *Who Killed Karen Silkwood?* New York: Summit Books, 1981.

Kolata, Gina Bari. "!Kung Hunter-Gatherers: Feminism, Diet, and Birth Control." *Science* 185 (Sept. 13, 1974):932–934.

Konner, Melvin J. "Maternal Care, Infant Behavior and Development Among the !Kung." In Lee and DeVore, *Gatherers.*

Koonz, Claudia, "Mothers in the Fatherland: Women in Nazi Germany." In Bridenthal and Koonz, *Visible.*

Kors, Alan C., and Edward Peters. *Witchcraft in Europe: 1100–1700: A Documentary History.* Philadelphia: Univ. of Pennsylvania Press, 1972.

Kovar, Leo, M.D. "Malevolent Transformation: Limits and Extensions." *Journal of Contemporary Psychoanalysis* 14, 3 (July 1978):419–423.

Kraditor, Aileen. *The Ideas of the Woman Suffrage Movement, 1890–1920.* New York: Columbia Univ. Press, 1965.

————. *Up from the Pedestal.* Chicago: Quadrangle Books, 1968.

Kramer, Samuel Noah. *The Sumerians.* Chicago: Univ. of Chicago Press, 1963.

Kristeva, Julia. "Women's Time." Trans. Alice Jardine and Harry Blake. *Signs* 7,1 (Autumn 1981):13–35.

Kruuk, H. *The Spotted Hyena.* Chicago: Univ. of Chicago Press, 1972.

Lacey, W. K. *The Family in Classical Greece.* Ithaca, N.Y.: Cornell Univ. Press, 1968.

Lacroix, Paul. *History of Prostitution.* Trans. Samuel Putnam. New York: Covici-Friede, 1926.

Ladner, Joyce A. "Racism and Tradition: Black Womanhood in Historical Perspective." In Carroll, *Liberating Women's History.*

Lamphere, Louise. "Anthropology." *Signs* 2, 3 (Spring 1977):612–627.

Lancaster, Jane. *Primate Behavior and the Emergence of Human Culture.* New York: Holt, Rinehart and Winston, 1975.

Lapidus, Gail Warshofsky, ed. *Women, Work, and Family in the Soviet Union.* White Plains, N.Y.: M. E. Sharpe, 1982.

Lasch, Christopher. "The Great American Variety Show." *New York Review of Books,* Feb. 2, 1984.

————. *Haven in a Heartless World.* New York: Basic Books, 1979.

Leacock, Eleanor. "Women in Egalitarian Societies." In Bridenthal and Koonz, *Visible.*

————. "Women's Status in Egalitarian Society: Implications for Social Evolution." *Current Anthropology* 19 (1978):247–255.

Lears, T. J. Jackson. *No Place of Grace.* New York: Pantheon, 1981.

Lederer, Laura, ed. *Take Back the Night.* New York: Bantam, 1982.

Lee, Richard B. "Population Growth and the Beginnings of Sedentary Life Among the !Kung Bushmen." In *Population Growth: Anthropological Implications.* Ed. Brian Spooner. Cambridge, Mass.: M.I.T. Press, 1972.

————. "What Hunters Do for a Living." In Lee and DeVore, *Hunter.*

————, and Irven DeVore, eds. *Kalahari Hunter Gatherers.* Cambridge, Mass.: Harvard Univ. Press, 1976.

————. *Man the Hunter.* Chicago: Aldine Publishing, 1968.

Leibowitz, Leila. "Perspectives on the Evolution of Sex Differences." In Reiter, *Anthropology.*

Leith, Suzette. "Chinese Women in the Early Communist Movement." In Young, *China.*

Lender, Mark Edward, and James Kirby Martin. *Drinking in America: A History.* New York: The Free Press, 1982.

Lennane, K. J., and R. J. Lennane. "Alleged Psychogenic Disorders in Women: A Possible Manifestation of Sexual Prejudice." *New England Journal of Medicine* 288 (1973):288–292.

Lerner, Barbara. *Therapy in the Ghetto: Political Impotence and Personal Disintegration.* Baltimore, Md.: Johns Hopkins Univ. Press, 1972.

Lerner, Gerda, ed. *Black Women in White America: A Documentary History.* New York: Pantheon Books, 1972.

————. *The Grimké Sisters from South Carolina.* Boston: Houghton Mifflin, 1967.

————. *The Majority Finds Its Past.* New York: Oxford Univ. Press, 1979.

Lessing, Doris. *Canopus in Argos: Archives.* New York: Alfred A. Knopf, 1980–83.

Leventhal, D. B., and K. M. Shember. "Sex Role Adjustment and Non-sanctioned Aggression." *Journal of Experimental Research in Personality* 3 (1969):283–286.

Lévi-Strauss, Claude. *The Elementary Structures of Kinship.* Trans. J. H. Bell and J. R. von Sturmer. Boston: Beacon Press, 1969.

————. "The Family." In *Man, Culture, and Society.* Ed. Harry Shapiro. London: Oxford Univ. Press, 1956.

————. *From Honey to Ashes.* Trans. John and Doreen Weightman. New York: Harper and Row, 1973.

————. *The Raw and the Cooked.* Trans. John and Doreen Weightman. New York: Harper/Colophon, 1975.

————. *The Savage Mind.* Chicago: Univ. of Chicago Press, 1966.

————. *Totemism.* Trans. Rodney Needham. Boston: Beacon Press, 1963.

Levin, Harry. *The Myth of the Golden Age in the Renaissance.* Bloomington, Ind.: Indiana Univ. Press, 1969.

Lewin, Kurt. "Self-Hatred Among Jews." *Contemporary Jewish Record* 4 (1941):219–232.

Lewin, Miriam. *In the Shadow of the Past: Psychology Portrays the Sexes.* New York: Columbia Univ. Press, 1984.

————. "The Tyranny of Therapy." *Women's Review of Books* 1, 8 (May 1984):8.

Lewin, R. "Cancer Hazards in the Environment." *New Scientist,* Jan. 22, 1976:168–169.

Lewis, C. S. *The Allegory of Love.* Oxford: Oxford Univ. Press, 1936.

Lewis, Lionel S. *Scaling the Ivory Tower: Merit and Its Limits in Academic Careers.* Baltimore, Md.: Johns Hopkins Univ. Press, 1975.

Lewontin, R. C. "The Inferiority Complex." Review of *The Mismeasure of Man*, by Stephen Jay Gould. *New York Review of Books*, Oct. 22, 1981.

———, Steven Rose, and Leon Kamin. *Not in Our Genes.* New York: Pantheon, 1984.

Lindenbaum, Shirley. "A Wife Is the Hand of Man." In *Man and Woman in the New Guinea Highlands.* Ed. P. Brown and G. Buchbinder. American Anthropological Association Special Publication, No. 8 (1976).

Lloyd, P. C. "The Yoruba of Nigeria." In *Peoples of Africa.* Ed. James L. Gibbs. New York: Holt, Rinehart and Winston, 1965.

Lorde, Audre. "An Open Letter to Mary Daly." In Moraga and Anzaldua, *Bridge.*

———. *Zami: A New Spelling of My Name.* Watertown, Mass.: Persephone Press, 1982.

Lougee, Carolyn C. *Le Paradis des Femmes: Women, Salons, and Social Stratifications in Seventeenth-Century France.* Princeton, N.J.: Princeton Univ. Press, 1976.

Lovins, Amory B., L. Hunter Lovins, and Leonard Ross. "Nuclear Power and Nuclear Bombs." *Foreign Affairs* 58, 5 (Spring 1980):1137–1177.

Lowi, Theodore J. *The End of Liberalism.* New York: Norton, 1979.

Lynch, Dudley. "Are You in Your Right Mind?" *AMA Management Digest* (April 1982):18–20.

Lynd, Robert, and Helen Lynd. *Middletown in Transition.* New York: Harcourt Brace, 1937.

Lynn, David. "A Note on Sex Difference in the Development of Masculine and Feminine Identification." *Psychological Review* 66, 2 (1959):126–135.

———. *Parental and Sex Role Identification: A Theoretical Formulation.* Berkeley, Calif.: University of California Press, 1969.

Maccoby, Eleanor E., ed. *The Development of Sex Differences.* Stanford, Calif.: Stanford Univ. Press, 1966.

MacCormack Carol P., and Marilyn Strathern. *Nature, Culture and Gender.* New York: Cambridge Univ. Press, 1980.

MacDonald, Michael. *Mystical Bedlam.* Cambridge: Cambridge Univ. Press, 1981.

MacIntyre, Alasdair. *After Virtue.* Notre Dame, Ind.: Univ. of Notre Dame Press, 1981.

MacKenzie, Midge. *Shoulder to Shoulder.* New York: Alfred A. Knopf, 1975.

MacKinnon, Catherine A. "Feminism, Marxism, Method, and the State: An Agenda for Theory." *Signs* 7, 3 (Spring 1982).

———. "Feminism, Marxism, Method, and the State: Toward Feminist Jurisprudence." *Signs* 8, 4 (Summer 1983):635–658.

Malcolm, Janet. *In the Freud Archives.* New York: Alfred A. Knopf, 1984.

Malinowski, Bronislaw. *The Family Among the Australian Aborigines.* London: Univ. of London Press, 1913.

———. *The Sexual Life of Savages in Northwestern Melanesia.* New York: Routledge and Kegan Paul, 1929.

Mamonova, Tatyana. "The USSR: It's Time We Began with Ourselves." In Morgan, *Sisterhood Is Global.*

Mandel, William M. *Soviet Women and Their Self-Image.* Paper delivered May 1970 at Western Slavic Conference, University of Southern California. New York University Library.

Marcuse, Herbert. *One-Dimensional Man.* Boston: Beacon Press, 1964.

Marglin, Stephen. "What Do Bosses Do?" *Review of Radical Political Economics* 6 (1974), 7 (1975).

Markovic, Mihailo. "Women's Liberation and Human Emancipation." In Gould and Wartofsky, *Women and Philosophy.*

Marks, Elaine, and Isabelle de Courtivon. *New French Feminisms.* New York: Schocken Books, 1981.

Marshack, Alexander. *The Roots of Civilization.* New York: McGraw Hill, 1972.

———. "Some Implications of the Paleolithic Symbolic Evidence for the Origin of Language." In *Origins and Evolution of Language and Speech.* Ed. S. R. Harnand, H. D. Steklis, and J. Lancaster. New York Academy of Sciences Conference Proceedings. Vol. 280. September 22–25, 1975.

Martin, M. Kay, and Barbara Voorhies. *Female of the Species.* New York: Columbia Univ. Press, 1975.

Marx, Karl. *Capital.* Reprint, New York: International Publishers, 1968.

Marx, Karl. *Capital*, Vol. 1. Harmondsworth, England: Penguin, 1976.

Maslow, Abraham. *The Farther Reaches of Human Nature.* New York: Penguin, 1971.

———. "Self-Esteem (Dominance-Feeling) and Sexuality in Women." In *Psychoanalysis and*

*Female Sexuality.* Ed. Hendrick M. Ruitenbeek. New Haven, Conn.: College and Univ. Press, 1966.

Mass, Bonnie. *Population Target: The Political Economy of Population Control in Latin America.* Toronto: Women's Educational Press, 1972.

Masson, Jeffrey Moussaieff. *The Assault on Truth: Freud's Suppression of the Seduction Theory.* New York: Farrar, Straus and Giroux, 1984.

Mather, H. G., et al. "Acute Myocardial Infarction: Home and Hospital Treatment." *British Medical Journal* 3 (1971): 334–348.

McBride, Theresa M. "The Long Road Home: Women's Work and Industrialization." In Bridenthal and Koonz, *Visible.*

McDonnell, Ernest W. *Beguines and Beghards in Medieval Culture.* New Brunswick, N.J.: Rutgers Univ. Press, 1954.

McDougall, Mary Lynn. "Working-Class Women During the Industrial Revolution, 1780–1914." In Bridenthal and Koonz, *Visible.*

McGregor, Douglas. *The Human Side of Enterprise.* New York: McGraw Hill, 1960.

McGrew, W. C. "The Female Chimpanzee as a Human Evolutionary Prototype." In Dahlberg, *Gatherer.*

McNamara, JoAnn. *A New Song.* New York: Haworth Press, 1983.

———, and Suzanne F. Wemple. "The Power of Women Through the Family in Medieval Europe: 500–1100." In Hartman and Banner, *Clio.*

———. "Sanctity and Power: The Dual Pursuit of Medieval Women." In Bridenthal and Koonz, *Visible.*

Mead, Margaret, ed. *Cooperation and Competition Among Primitive Peoples.* New York: McGraw Hill, 1937.

———. *The Mountain Arapesh* (1938). Reprint, New York: William Morrow, 1971.

———. *Sex and Temperament in Three Primitive Societies* (1935). Reprint, New York: William Morrow, 1963.

Mednick, Martha, Sandra Tangri, and Lois Hoffman, eds. *Women and Achievement.* New York: Hemisphere Publishing, 1975.

Medvedev, Roy A., and Zhores A. Medvedev. "A Nuclear *Samizdat* on America's Arms Race." *The Nation,* Jan. 16, 1982.

Mellaart, James. *Catal Huyuk.* New York: McGraw-Hill, 1967.

Memmi, Albert. *The Colonizer and the Colonized.* Boston: Beacon Press, 1965.

Merchant, Carolyn. *The Death of Nature: Women, Ecology, and the Scientific Revolution.* New York: Harper & Row, 1983.

Meyer, Neils, Helveg Petersen, and Villy Sorensen. *Revolt from the Center.* Trans. Christine Hauch. London: Marion Boyars Publishers, 1981.

Michaels, Leonard, and Christopher Ricks, eds. *The State of the Language.* Berkeley, Calif.: Univ. of California Press, 1980.

Midgely, Mary. *Beast and Man: The Roots of Human Nature.* Ithaca, N.Y.: Cornell Univ. Press, 1978.

Miliband, Ralph. *The State in Capitalist Society.* New York: Basic Books, 1969.

Miller, Casey, and Kate Swift. *Words and Women.* London: Victor Gollancz, 1977.

Millet, Richard. *Guardians of the Dynasty.* Maryknoll, N.Y.: Orbis Books, 1977.

Millett, Kate. *Going to Iran.* New York: Coward, McCann and Geoghegan, 1982.

Milton, Nancy. "A Response to 'Women and Revolution.' " In Young, *China.*

Minai, Naila. *Women in Islam.* New York: Seaview Books, 1981.

Mitchell, Juliet. *Psychoanalysis and Feminism.* New York: Random House/Vintage, 1974.

———. *Woman's Estate.* New York: Random House/Vintage, 1973.

———. *Women: The Longest Revolution.* Boston: 1966.

Money, John. "Delusion, Belief, and Fact." *Psychiatry* 11 (1948):36, 38.

———. *Love and Love Sickness.* Baltimore: Johns Hopkins Univ. Press, 1980.

———. "Sex, Hormones, and Other Variables in Human Eroticism." In *Sex and Internal Secretions,* Vol 2. Ed. W. C. Young. Baltimore: Johns Hopkins Univ. Press, 1961.

———, and Patricia Tucker. *Sexual Signatures.* Boston: Little Brown, 1975.

Montagu, Ashley. *The Nature of Human Aggression.* New York: Oxford Univ. Press, 1976.

Monter, E. William. "The Pedestal and the Stake: Courtly Love and Witchcraft." In Bridenthal and Koonz, *Visible.*

———. "Women in Calvinist Geneva (1550–1800)." *Signs* 6, 2 (Winter 1980):189–209.

Moore, Barrington, Jr. *Injustice: The Social Bases of Obedience and Revolt.* White Plains, N.Y.: M. E. Sharpe, 1978.

Moraga, Cherrie, and Gloria Anzaldua, eds. *This Bridge Called My Back.* Watertown, Mass.: Persephone Press, 1981.

Morantz, Regina. "The Lady and Her Physician." In Hartman and Banner, *Clio.*

Morey-Gaines, Ann-Janine. "Of Menace and Men: The Sexual Tensions of the American Frontier Metaphor." *Soundings* 64, 2 (Summer 1981):132–149.

Morgan, Elaine. *The Descent of Woman.* New York: Stein and Day, 1972.

Morgan, Lewis Henry. *Ancient Society.* New York: H. Holt and Co., 1877.

Morgan, Robin. "The First Feminist Exiles from the USSR," *MS.,* Nov. 1980.

————, ed. *Sisterhood Is Global.* Garden City, N.Y.: Anchor Press/Doubleday, 1984.

————, ed. *Sisterhood Is Powerful.* New York: Vintage, 1970.

Morgenstern, Julien. "*Beena* Marriage (Matriarchat) in Ancient Israel and Its Historical Implications." *Zeitschrift für die Altatestamentische Wissenschaft* 47 (1929):91–110.

————. "Additional Notes on *Beena* Marriage (Matriarchat) in Ancient Israel." *Zeitschrift für die Altatestamentische Wissenschaft* 49 (1929):46–58.

Morris, Bertram. *Philosophical Aspects of Culture.* Yellow Springs, Ohio: The Antioch Press, 1961.

Moskowitz, Breyne Arlene. "The Acquisition of Language." *Scientific American* (November 1978).

*Mother Jones,* Nov. 1979, p. 12.

Murdock, G. P. *Social Structure.* New York: Macmillan, 1949.

Murray, Gilbert. *Five Stages of Greek Religion.* New York: Columbia Univ. Press, 1925.

Murray, Janet. *Strong-Minded Women.* New York: Pantheon, 1982.

Nadelson, Leslee. "Pigs, Women, and the Men's House in Amazonia." In Ortner and Whitehead, *Sexual Meanings.*

*National NOW Times.* Jan./Feb. 1982 and March 1982.

Navarro, Vincente. *Class Struggle, the State, and Medicine.* London: Martin Robertson, 1978.

Nelson, Mary. "Why Witches Were Women." In Freeman, *Women.*

Neuborne, Burt. ACLU memorandum, "Current Threats to the First Amendment." October 1982.

Nevius, Blake. *Edith Wharton: A Study of Her Fiction.* Berkeley, Calif.: Univ. of California Press, 1953.

Newcomb, Horace, ed. *Television: The Critical View.* New York: Oxford Univ. Press, 1982.

Nichols, Bill. *Ideology and the Image.* Bloomington, Ind.: Indiana Univ. Press, 1981.

Nietzsche, Friedrich. *Human-All-Too-Human.* Trans. Helen Zimmern. 2 vols. New York: Gordon Press, 1974.

————. *Nachgelassene Fragmente* (Sept. 1870–Jan. 1871). Section III. Vol. III.

————. "On Self-Overcoming." In *Thus Spake Zarathustra.* Vol. II. New York: Viking, 1966.

————. "The Problem of Socrates." *The Twilight of the Idols,* Section 11. In *The Portable Nietzsche.* Trans. Walter Kaufmann. New York: Viking/Penguin, 1954.

————. *The Wanderer and His Shadow.* Trans. Paul V. Cohn. Ed. Oscar Levy. New York: 1964.

————. *The Will to Power.* Trans. Walter Kaufmann and R. J. Hollingdale. Ed. Walter Kaufmann. New York: Vintage, 1968.

Noble, David. "The Selling of the University." *The Nation,* Feb. 6, 1982, pp. 129ff.

Nowak, Mariette. *Eve's Rib.* New York: St. Martin's Press, 1980.

Oakley, Ann. *New York Times Book Review,* May 2, 1982.

O'Brien, Mary. "Feminist Theory and Dialectical Logic." *Signs* 7, 1 (Autumn 1981):144–157.

Ochs, Carol. *Behind the Sex of God.* Boston: Beacon Press, 1977.

Ochshorn, Judith. *The Female Experience and the Nature of the Divine.* Bloomington, Ind.: Indiana Univ. Press, 1981.

Oettinger, Leon, Jr., ed. *The Psychologist, the School, and the Child with MBD/LD.* New York: Grune and Stratton, 1978.

O'Faolain, Julia, and Lauro Martines. *Not in God's Image.* London: Temple Smith, 1973.

Okely, Judith. "Gypsy Women." In Ardener, *Perceiving.*

Okin, Susan Moller. *Women in Western Political Thought.* Princeton, N.J.: Princeton Univ. Press, 1979.

O'Laughlin, Bridget. "Mediation of Contradiction: Why Mbum Women Do Not Eat Chicken." In Rosaldo and Lamphere, *Woman.*

O'Neill, William L. "Women in Politics." In Tiger and Fowler, *Hierarchies.*

Oren, Laura. "The Welfare of Women in Laboring Families: England, 1860–1950." In Hartman and Banner, *Clio.*

Ortner, Sherry. "Is Female to Male as Nature Is to Culture?" In Rosaldo and Lamphere, *Woman.*

————. "The Virgin and the State." *Feminist Studies* 4, 3 (Oct.1978):19–35.

————, and Harriet Whitehead, eds. *Sexual Meanings: The Cultural Construction of Gender and Sexuality.* Cambridge: Cambridge Univ. Press, 1981.

Ostrogarski, Mosei. *The Rights of Women.* New York: Scribner's, 1893.

Owen, John D. *School Inequality and the Welfare State.* Baltimore, Md.: Johns Hopkins Univ. Press, 1974.

Ozick, Cynthia. "Justice (Again) to Edith Wharton." *Commentary* 62, 4 (Oct. 1976):48–57.

Pagels, Elaine. *The Gnostic Gospels.* New York: Random House, 1979.

Paige, Connie. *The Right To Lifers.* New York: Summit Books, 1983.

Parish, William, and Martin Whyte. *Village and Family in Contemporary China.* Chicago: Univ. of Chicago Press, 1978.

Parks, Evelyn N. "From Constabulary to Police Society: Implications for Social Control." *Catalyst* (Summer 1970), pp. 77–97.

Parsons, Talcott. "On the Concept of Political Power." In *Political Power.* Ed. Roderick Bell, David B. Edwards, and R. Harrison Wagner. New York: Free Press, 1969.

Parturier, Françoise. "An Open Letter to Men." Trans. Elissa Gelfand. In Marks and De Courtivon, *New French Feminisms.*

Patai, Raphael. *The Hebrew Goddess.* New York: Ktav Publishing House, 1967.

Patterson, Orlando. *Slavery and Social Death.* Cambridge, Mass.: Harvard Univ. Press, 1982.

Perlmutter, Amos. *Modern Authoritarianism.* New Haven, Conn.: Yale Univ. Press, 1981.

Perlmutter, H. "Super-Giant Firms in the Future." *Wharton Quarterly,* Winter 1968.

Pfeiffer, John E. *The Emergence of Man.* New York: Harper and Row, 1969.

Phillips, Ulrich B. *American Negro Slavery* (1918). Reprint, Baton Rouge, La.: Louisiana State Univ. Press, 1966.

Piaget, Jean. *The Moral Judgment of the Child* (1932). Reprint, New York: The Free Press, 1965.

Piercy, Marge. *Woman on the Edge of Time.* New York: Alfred A. Knopf, 1976.

Piven, Frances Fox, and Richard A. Cloward. *Regulating the Poor: The Functions of Public Welfare.* New York: Vintage Books, 1972.

Pleck, Joseph. *The Myth of Masculinity.* Cambridge, Mass.: MIT Press, 1981.

Pokzovskaia, Dr. M. I. "Report on Working Conditions for Women in Russian Factories, 1914." In Riemer and Fout, *European Women.*

Polier, Justine Wise. *The Rule of Law and the Role of Psychiatry.* Baltimore, Md.: Johns Hopkins Univ. Press, 1968.

Polk, Barbara Bovee. "Male Power and the Women's Movement." In Freeman, *Women.*

Pollard, Vickie, and Donna Keck. "They Almost Seized the Time!" In *Women's Liberation.* Ed. Sookie Stambler. New York: Ace Books, 1970.

Pomeroy, Sarah B. "A Classical Scholar's Perspective on Matriarchy." In Carroll, *Liberating Women's History.*

————. *Goddesses, Whores, Wives and Slaves.* New York: Schocken Books, 1975.

Poole, FitzJohn Porter. "Transforming 'Natural' Woman: Female Ritual Leaders and Gender Ideology Among Bimin-Kuskusmin." In Ortner and Whitehead, *Sexual Meanings.*

Pope, Barbara Corrado. "Angels in the Devil's Workshop: Leisured and Charitable Women in Nineteenth-Century England and France." In Bridenthal and Koonz, *Visible.*

Postman, Neil, Charles Weingartner, and Terence P. Moran, eds. *Language in America.* New York: Bobbs Merrill, 1969.

Potter, David M. *American Women and the American Character.* Stetson University Bulletin LXIII (Jan. 1962). .

Power, Eileen. *Medieval English Nunneries.* Cambridge: Cambridge Univ. Press, 1922.

————. *Medieval People.* London and New York: University Paperbacks, 1966.

————. "The Position of Women." In *The Legacy of the Middle Ages* (1926). Ed. C. G. Crump and E. F. Jacob. Reprint, Oxford: Clarendon Press, 1962.

Prather, J., and L. S. Fidell. "Sex Differences in the Content and Style of Medical Advertisements." *Social Science and Medicine* 9, 1 (1975):23–26.

Pritchard, James B., ed. *Ancient Near Eastern Texts.* Princeton, N.J.: Princeton Univ. Press, 1973.

Pruitt, Ida. *A Daughter of Han: The Autobiography of a Chinese Working Woman.* Stanford, Calif.: Stanford Univ. Press, 1967.

Pusey, Anne E. "Inbreeding Avoidance in Chimpanzees." *Animal Behavior* 28 (1980):543–552.

Quain, B. H. "The Iroquois." In Mead, *Cooperation.*

Quataert, Jean H. *Reluctant Feminists in German Social Democracy, 1885–1917.* Princeton, N.J.: Princeton Univ. Press, 1979.

Quinn, Jim. "Lingo." *The Nation,* April 3, 1982.

Raglan, Lord (Richard Somerset FitzRoy). *The Hero: A Study in Tradition, Myth and Drama.* New York: Vintage Books, 1956.

Ralls, Katherine. "Mammals in Which Females Are Larger Than Males." *Quarterly Review of Biology* 51 (1976):245–276.

Reichel-Dolmatoff, Gerardo. *Amazonian Cosmos.* Chicago: Univ. of Chicago Press, 1971.

Reiter, Rayna R., ed. *Toward an Anthropology of Women.* New York: Monthly Review Press, 1975.

Reynolds, Peter C. *On the Evolution of Human Behavior.* Berkeley, Calif.: Univ. of California Press, 1981.

Rich, Adrienne. *Of Woman Born.* New York: Bantam Books, 1976.

Rieff, Philip. *The Triumph of the Therapeutic.* New York: Harper and Row, 1966.

Riemer, Eleanor S., and John C. Fout. *European Women: A Documentary History, 1789–1945.* New York: Schocken Books, 1980.

Riis, Jacob. *How the Other Half Lives.* New York: Dover Books, 1971.

Robinson, James M. ed., the Nag Hammadi Library. Trans. by members of the Coptic Gnostic Library project of the Institute of Antiquity and Christianity. San Francisco: Harper and Row: 1977.

Rogan, Helen. *Mixed Company: Women in the Modern Army.* New York: G. P. Putnam's Sons, 1981.

Rogers, Katharine M. *The Troublesome Helpmate: A History of Misogyny in Literature.* Seattle: Univ. of Washington Press, 1966.

Rogers, Susan Carol. "Female Forms of Power and the Myth of Male Dominance: A Model of Female/Male Interaction in Peasant Society." *American Ethnologist* 2 (1975):727–756.

Rohrbaugh, Joanna. *Women: Psychology's Puzzle.* New York: Basic Books, 1979.

Rohrlich, Ruby, and June Nash. "Patriarchal Puzzle: State Formation in Mesopotamia and Mesoamerica." *Heresies 13,* 4, 1 (1981):60–65.

Rohrlich-Leavitt, Ruby. "Women in Transition: Crete and Sumer." In Bridenthal and Koonz, *Visible.*

———, Barbara Sykes, and Elizabeth Weatherford. "Aboriginal Woman: Male and Female Anthropological Perspectives." In Reiter, *Anthropology.*

Rosaldo, Michelle. "Woman, Culture, and Society: An Overview." In Rosaldo and Lamphere, *Woman.*

———, and Louise Lamphere, eds. *Woman, Culture, and Society.* Stanford, Calif.: Stanford Univ. Press, 1974.

Rose, Frederick G. G. "Australian Marriage, Land-Owning Groups, and Initiations." In Lee and DeVore, *Hunter.*

Rose, Steven. *Against Biological Determinism.* London and New York: Allison and Busby, Schocken Books, 1982.

———. *Towards a Liberatory Biology.* London and New York: Allison and Busby, Schocken Books, 1982.

Rosenthal, Bernice Glatzer. "Love on the Tractor: Women in the Russian Revolution and After." In Bridenthal and Koonz, *Visible.*

Rossi, Alice. "A Biosocial Perspective on Parenting." *Daedalus* 106, 2 (1977):1–31.

Roszak, Betty, and Theodore, eds. *Masculine/Feminine.* New York: Harper and Row, 1969.

Rothman, Barbara Katz. "Women, Health, and Medicine." In Freeman, *Women.*

Rothman, David J. *The Discovery of the Asylum: Social Order and Disorder in the New Republic.* Boston: Little, Brown, 1971.

Rubin, Gayle. "The Traffic in Women." In Reiter, *Anthropology.*

Russell, Bertrand. *Power: A New Social Analysis.* 1936. Reprint, New York: Norton, 1969.

Russell, Diana E. H. "Pornography and Violence: What Does the New Research Say?" In Lederer, *Night.*

Ryan, William. *Blaming the Victim.* New York: Vintage, 1976.

———. *Equality.* New York: Pantheon Books, 1981.

el Saadawi, Nawal. *The Hidden Face of Eve: Women in the Arab World.* Boston: Beacon Press, 1982.

Sacks, Karen. "State Bias and Women's Status." *American Anthropologist* 78, 2 (Sept., 1976):565–569.

Sacks, Michael Paul. *Work and Equality in Soviet Society.* New York: Frederick A. Praeger, 1982.

Sahlins, Marshall. *Stone Age Economics.* Chicago: Aldine-Atherton, 1972.

Salaff, Janet, and Judith Merkle. "Women and Revolution: The Lessons of the Soviet Union and China." In Young, *China.*

Sampson, Anthony. *The Seven Sisters: The Great Oil Companies and the World They Shaped.* New York: Bantam, 1980.

————. *The Sovereign State of ITT.* New York: Stein and Day, 1980.

Sanday, Peggy Reeves. *Female Power and Male Dominance.* New York: Cambridge Univ. Press, 1981.

Schapiro, Leonard. "Under the Volcano." Review of *Stalin's Secret War,* by Nikolai Tolstoy. *New York Review of Books,* Jan. 20, 1983.

Schatzman, Morton. *Soul Murder.* New York: Random House, 1973.

Schell, Jonathan. *The Fate of the Earth.* New York: Knopf, 1982.

Schiller, Herbert I. *Communications and Cultural Domination.* White Plains, N.Y.: M. E. Sharpe, Inc., 1976.

Schlegel, Alice. "Male:Female in Hopi Thought and Action." In *Sexual Stratification.* Ed. A. Schlegel. New York: Columbia Univ. Press, 1977.

Schmidt, Dolores Barracano, and Earl Robert Schmidt. "The Invisible Woman: The Historian as Professional Magician." In Carroll, *Liberating Women's History.*

Schorske, Carl E. "Politics and Patricide in Freud's *Interpretation of Dreams."* In *Fin-de-Siècle Vienna.* Ed. C. E. Schorske. New York: Alfred A. Knopf, 1980.

Schwartz, Harry. "Toward the Conquest of Heart Disease." *New York Times Magazine,* March 27, 1983.

Scully, Diane, and Pauline Bart. "A Funny Thing Happened on the Way to the Orifice: Women in Gynaecology Textbooks." *American Journal of Sociology* 78, 4 (Jan. 1973):1045–1050.

Secor, Cynthia. "The Androgyny Papers." *Women's Studies* 2 (1974):139.

"A Secret Side of Lesbian Sexuality." *The Advocate.* December 27, 1979.

Seltman, Charles. *Women in Antiquity.* London: Thames and Hudson, 1956.

Sennett, Richard. *Authority.* New York: Alfred A. Knopf, 1980.

Sharp, Gene. *The Politics of Nonviolent Action.* Boston: Potter, Sargent, 1973.

Sharp, Henry S. "The Null Case: The Chipewyan." In Dahlberg, *Gatherer.*

Shklar, Judith N. "Putting Cruelty First." *Daedalus* III, 3 (Summer 1982):17–27.

Shorris, Earl. *The Oppressed Middle.* New York: Anchor Press/Doubleday, 1981.

Shostak, Margerie. *Nisa.* Cambridge, Mass.: Harvard Univ. Press, 1981.

Sidel, Ruth. *Women and Child Care in China.* New York: Hill and Wang, 1972.

Simmons, Adele. "Education and Ideology in Nineteenth-Century America." In Carroll, *Liberating Women's History.*

Simmons, John, and William Mares. *Working Together.* New York: Alfred A. Knopf, 1983.

Sivard, Ruth Leger. *World Military and Social Expenditures 1982.* Leesburg, Va.: World Priorities, 1982.

Slater, Philip. *The Glory of Hera.* Boston: Beacon Press, 1971.

Smith, Jane Idleman. "Women in Islam." *Connecticut Humanities Council News,* April 1982, p. 8.

Smith, M. C., and L. Griffin. "Rationality of Appeals Used in the Promotion of Psychotropic Drugs: A Comparison of Male and Female Models." *Social Science and Medicine* 11, 6 and 7 (1977):409–414.

Smith-Rosenberg, Carroll. "Beauty, the Beast and the Militant Woman: A Case Study in Sex Roles and Social Stress in Jacksonian America." *American Quarterly* xxiii, 4 (October 1971):562–584.

————. "The Female World of Love and Ritual: Relations Between Women in Nineteenth-Century America." *Signs* 1, 1 (Autumn 1975):1–29.

————. "Puberty to Menopause." In Hartman and Banner, *Clio.*

Snow, Helen. *Women of Modern China.* The Hague: Mouton, 1967.

Sontag, Susan. *Illness as Metaphor.* New York: Farrar, Straus and Giroux, 1978.

Sophocles. *Antigone.* Trans. Elizabeth Wyckoff. In *Sophocles.* Vol. I. *The Complete Greek Tragedies.* Eds. D. Grene and R. Lattimore. Chicago: Univ. of Chicago Press, 1954.

Specter, Michael. "Community Corrections." *The Nation,* March 13, 1982.

Stackhouse, Max. *Ethics and the Urban Ethos.* Boston: Beacon Press, 1972.

Stambler, Sookie, ed. *Women's Liberation: Blueprint for the Future.* New York: Ace Books, 1970.

Stampp, Kenneth M. *The Peculiar Institution.* New York: Random House, 1956.

Stanley, Steven M. *Fossils, Genes, and the Origin of Species.* New York: Basic Books, 1982.

Starobin, Robert S. *Industrial Slavery in the Old South.* New York: Oxford Univ. Press, 1970.

Stein, Gertrude. "Poetry and Grammar." In *Gertrude Stein: Writings and Lectures 1909–1945.* Ed. Patricia Meyrowitz. Baltimore, Md.: Penguin, 1974.

Stenton, Doris Mary. *The English Woman in History.* New York: Schocken, 1977.

Stetson, Erlene. "Studying Slavery." In Hull, Scott, and Smith, *Some of Us.*

Stocking, B., and S. L. Morrison. *The Image and the Reality: A Case Study of the Impact of Medical Technology,* Oxford University Press for Nuffield Provincial Hospitals Trust, 1978.

Stoller, Robert J. "Facts and Fancies: An Examination of Freud's Concept of Bisexuality." In Strouse, *Women and Analysis*.

———. *Perversion*. New York: Pantheon, 1975.

———. *Sexual Excitement: The Dynamics of Erotic Life*. New York: Pantheon, 1979.

Stone, Laurence. *The Family, Sex and Marriage in England 1500–1800*. New York: Harper and Row, 1977.

———. "Madness." Review article. *New York Review of Books*, Dec. 16, 1982.

Strathern, Marilyn. "No Nature, No Culture: The Hagen Case." In MacCormack and Strathern, *Nature*.

Strouse, Jean, ed. *Women and Analysis*. New York: Grossman Publishers, 1974.

Stuard, Susan Mosher, ed. *Women in Medieval Society*. Philadelphia: Univ. of Pennsylvania Press, 1976.

Sullivan, Harry Stack. "Remobilization for Enduring Peace and Social Progress." *Psychiatry* 10 (1947):239.

Suttles, Wayne. "Coping with Abundance: Subsistence on the Northwest Coast." In Lee and DeVore, *Hunter*.

Swerdlow, Amy. "The Greek Woman in Attic Vase Painting." *Women's Studies* 5 (1978):267–284.

Synge, J. M. *The Aran Islands and Other Writings*. New York: Random House, 1962.

Szasz, Thomas S. *Law, Liberty and Psychiatry*. New York: Collier Books, 1963.

———. *The Theology of Medicine*. Baton Rouge, La.: Louisiana State Univ. Press, 1977.

Tanner, Nancy. *On Becoming Human*. New York: Cambridge Univ. Press, 1981.

Tarn, William. *Cambridge Ancient History* Vol. X.

Tax, Meredith. *The Rising of the Women: Feminist Solidarity and Class Conflict, 1880–1917*. New York: Monthly Review Press, 1980.

Taylor, Jeremy. "Consideration of the Miseries of Man's Life." *The Rule and Exercises of Holy Dying*. Chapters I, IV.

Teleki, Geza, E. E. Hunt, Jr., and J. H. Pfifferling. "Demographic Observations (1963–1973) on the Chimpanzees of Gombe National Park, Tanzania." *Journal of Human Evolution* 5 (1976):559–598.

Tennov, Dorothy. *Psychotherapy, the Hazardous Cure*. New York: Abelard-Schuman, 1975.

Terman, L., and C. Miles. *Sex and Personality*. New York: McGraw-Hill, 1936.

Tharpar, Romila. "The History of Female Emancipation in Southern Asia." In Ward, *New Asia*.

Thomas, Keith. *Religion and the Decline of Magic*. New York: Scribner's, 1971.

———. "Women and the Civil War Sects." In *Crisis in Europe: 1560–1660*. Ed. Trevor Aston. New York: Basic Books, 1965.

Thomas, Lewis. *The Lives of a Cell*. New York: Viking Press, 1974.

Thompson, E. P. *The Making of the English Working Class*. New York: Pantheon Books, 1964.

Thompson, William Irwin. *The Time Falling Bodies Take to Light*. New York: St. Martin's Press, 1981.

Thomson, George. *The Prehistoric Aegean*. New York: Citadel, 1965.

Thorne, Barrie, and Nancy Henley. *Language and Sex*. Rowley, Mass.: Newbury House, 1975.

Thurow, Lester. "How to Rescue a Drowning Economy." *New York Review of Books*, April 1, 1982, pp. 3–4.

Tigar, Michael E., and Madeleine R. Levy. *Law and the Rise of Capitalism*. New York: Monthly Review Press, 1977.

Tiger, Lionel. *Men in Groups*. New York: Random House, 1969.

———, and Heather T. Fowler, eds. *Female Hierarchies*. Chicago: Beresford Book Service, 1978.

———, and Robin Fox. *The Imperial Animal*. London: Secker and Warburg, 1977.

Tillion, Germaine. *Ravensbrück: An Eyewitness Account of a Women's Concentration Camp*. Trans. Gerald Satterwhite. Garden City, N.Y.: Anchor Press/Doubleday, 1975.

Topley, Margery. "Marriage Resistance in Rural Kwangtung." In Wolf, *Chinese Society*.

Trevor-Roper, H. R. "Born Again." *New York Review of Books*, Nov. 5, 1981.

Trible, Phyllis. *God and the Rhetoric of Sexuality*. Philadelphia: Fortress Press, 1978.

Trotsky, Leon. "Their Morals and Ours." *New International*, June 1938.

Trudgill, Peter. "Sex, Covert Prestige and Linguistic Change in the Urban British English of Norwich." *Language in Society* 1, 2 (1973):179–195.

Turnbull, Colin M. *The Human Cycle*. New York: Simon and Schuster, 1983.

———. "The Importance of Flux in Two Hunting Societies." In Lee and DeVore, *Hunter*.

———. "Mbuti Womanhood." In Dahlberg, *Gatherer*.

Tutin, Caroline E. G. "Exceptions to Promiscuity in a Feral Chimpanzee Community." In *Contemporary Primatology*. Ed. S. Kondo, M. Kawai, and A. Ehara. Basel: 1975.

Tyack, David B. *The One Best System: A History of American Urban Education.* Cambridge, Mass.: Harvard Univ. Press, 1974.

Vaillant, G. G. *Aztecs of Mexico.* Garden City, N.Y.: Doubleday, 1950.

Vann, Richard T. "Toward a New Lifestyle: Women in Preindustrial Capitalism." In Bridenthal and Koonz, *Visible.*

Veblen, Thorstein. *The Higher Learning in America.* New York: Hill and Wang, 1950.

Vermeule, Emily. *Greece in the Bronze Age.* Chicago: Univ. of Chicago Press, 1964.

Veroff, Joseph, Elizabeth Douvan, and Richard A. Kulka. *The Inner America: A Self-Portrait from 1957–1976.* New York: Basic Books, 1981.

Vicinus, Martha, ed. *A Widening Sphere.* Bloomington, Ind.: Univ. of Indiana Press, 1977.

Von Harnack, Adolf. *The History of Dogma.* London: 1894–99.

Von Kleist, Heinrich. *An Abyss Deep Enough. Letters.* Ed. Philip B. Miller. New York: Dutton, 1983.

Walkowitz, Judith. "The Making of an Outcast Group." In Vicinus, *Widening Sphere.*

Wallman, Sandra. "Epistemologies of Sex." In Tiger and Fowler, *Hierarchies.*

Walzer, Michael. *Spheres of Justice.* New York: Basic Books, 1983.

Ward, Barbara. "Men, Women and Change." In Ward, *Asia.*

———, ed. *Women in the New Asia.* Paris: UNESCO, 1963.

Washburn, Sherwood L., and R. Moore. *Ape Into Man: A Study of Human Evolution.* Boston: Little, Brown, 1974.

———, and C. S. Lancaster. "The Evolution of Hunting." In Lee and DeVore, *Hunter.*

Watanabe, Hitoshi. "Subsistence and Ecology of Northern Food Gatherers with Special Reference to the Ainu." In Lee and DeVore, *Hunter.*

Waters, Harry F. "Life According to TV." *Newsweek,* Dec. 6, 1982.

Weil, Simone. "Analysis of Oppression" (1934). In Weil, *Oppression.*

———. *Oppression and Liberty.* Trans. Arthur Wills and John Petrie. Amherst, Mass.: Univ. of Massachusetts Press, 1973.

———. "The Power of Words" (1937). In Weil, *Oppression.*

———. "Prospects" (1933). In Weil, *Oppression.*

———. "Sketch of Contemporary Life" (1934). In Weil, *Oppression.*

———. "Theoretical Picture of a Free Society" (1934). In Weil, *Oppression.*

Weisskoff, Walter. *Alienation and Economics.* New York: Dutton, 1971.

Weitzman, Lenore J. "Sex-Role Socialization." In Freeman, *Women.*

Welter, Barbara. *Dimity Convictions.* Athens, Ohio: Ohio Univ. Press, 1976.

———. "The Feminization of American Religion." In Hartman and Banner, *Clio.*

Wendorf, Fred, Romuald Schild, and Angela E. Close. "An Ancient Harvest on the Nile." *Science* (Nov. 1982): 68–73.

Wenig, Steffan. *Women in Egyptian Art.* New York: McGraw-Hill, 1970.

Wertheimer, Barbara. " 'Union Is Power': Sketches from Women's Labor History." In Freeman, *Women.*

Wheeler, Kenneth, et al. *The Four Day Work Week.* New York: American Management Association, 1972.

White, Edmund. "The Political Vocabulary of Homosexuality." In Michaels and Ricks, *The State of the Language.*

White, Martha S. "Women in the Professions: Psychological and Social Barriers to Women in Science." In Freeman, *Women.*

Wicklein, John. *Electronic Nightmare.* Boston: Beacon Press, 1982.

Williams, Drid. "The Brides of Christ." In Ardener, *Perceiving.*

Wilson, Edmund. *To the Finland Station.* Garden City, N.Y.: Doubleday, 1953.

Wilson, Edward O. *On Human Nature.* New York: Bantam, 1979.

———. *Sociobiology.* Cambridge, Mass.: Harvard Univ. Press, 1980.

Witke, Roxanne. "Mao Tse-tung, Women and Suicide." In Young, *China.*

———. "Woman as Politician in China of the 1920s." In Young, *China.*

Wittig, Monique. *Les Guerrillères.* Trans. David le Vay. New York: Avon, 1971.

Wolf, Arthur P. "Gods, Ghosts and Ancestors." In *Studies in Chinese Society.* Ed. Arthur P. Wolf. Stanford, Calif.: Stanford Univ. Press, 1978.

Wolf, Margery. "Chinese Women: Old Skills in a New Context." In Rosaldo and Lamphere, *Woman.*

Wolfenstein, Martha. "Fun Morality" (1951). In *Childhood in Contemporary Cultures.* Ed. Margaret Mead and Martha Wolfenstein. Chicago: Univ. of Chicago Press, 1971.

Wolff, Robert Paul. *The Poverty of Liberalism.* Boston: Beacon Press, 1968.

————. "There's Nobody Here But Us Persons." In Gould and Wartofsky, *Women and Philosophy.*

Wollstonecraft, Mary. *A Vindication of the Rights of Woman.* Ed. Carol H. Poston. New York: Norton, 1975.

Wood, Ann Douglas. "The Fashionable Diseases: Women's Complaints and Their Treatment in Nineteenth-Century America." In Hartman and Banner, *Clio.*

Woodburn, James. "An Introduction to Hadza Ecology." In Lee and DeVore, *Hunter.*

————. "Stability and Flexibility in Hadza Residential Groupings." In Lee and DeVore, *Hunter.*

Woolfolk R., and F. Richardson. *Sanity, Stress, and Survival.* New York: Signet Books, 1978.

Woolley, Sir Leonard. *The Sumerians.* New York: Norton, 1965.

Wootton, Barbara. *Social Science and Social Pathology.* London: Allen and Unwin, 1959.

Wright, Louis B. *Middle-Class Culture in Elizabethan England.* Ithaca, N.Y.: Cornell Univ. Press, 1963.

Wylie, Philip. *Generation of Vipers.* New York: Holt, Rinehart and Winston, 1955.

Wyntjes, Sherrin Marshall. "Women in the Reformation Era." In Bridenthal and Koonz, *Visible.*

Young, Marilyn B., ed. *Women in China: Studies in Social Change and Feminism.* Ann Arbor, Mich.: Center for Chinese Studies, University of Michigan, 1973.

Zihlman, Adrienne L. "Women as Shapers of the Human Adaptation." In Dahlberg, *Gatherer.*

————. "Women in Evolution, II: Subsistence and Social Organization among Early Hominids." *Signs* 4, 1 (Autumn 1978):4–20.

Zimmer, Heinrich. *Philosophies of India.* Ed. Joseph Campbell. New York: Pantheon Books, 1956.

## NEWSPAPER ARTICLES

"Acidic Tide of Pizza Sludge," *New York Times,* Jan. 2, 1983.

Albin, Rochelle Semmel. "Has Feminism Aided Mental Health?" *New York Times,* June 16, 1981.

Anderson, Susan. *New York Times.*

Apple, R. W. *New York Times,* Nov. 9, 1982.

Ball, George W. "Brezhneved by the U.S.," *New York Times,* June 14, 1983.

Barber, Benjamin. "A Tale of Two Capitalisms," *New York Times,* Oct. 4, 1981.

————. "The Tides in New Channels," *New York Times,* April 21, 1982.

"Blacks Closing Wage Gap," *Boston Globe,* May 8, 1978.

Blair, William G. "Scientific Detail Overwhelms Regard for Human Needs at Medical Schools, Panel Says," *New York Times,* Oct. 21, 1982.

Blumenthal, Ralph. *New York Times,* Aug. 25, 1981.

Boffey, Philip M. "Panel Urges Preparations to Meet Big Demand for Genetic Screening," *New York Times,* Feb. 28, 1983.

Briggs, Kenneth A. *New York Times,* August 7, 1977.

Brody, Jane E. "Emotions Found to Influence Every Human Ailment," *New York Times,* May 24, 1983.

————. "Personal Health," *New York Times,* May 11, 1983.

————. "Some Disorders Appear Linked to Being Left-Handed," *New York Times,* April 19, 1983.

Brooks, Andree. "Mothers Defending Rights of Custody," *New York Times,* Feb. 26, 1983.

Brozan, Nadine. "Holocaust Women: A Study in Survival," *New York Times,* March 23, 1983.

Burnham, Burnham. "Dow Anxiety," *New York Times,* April 19, 1983.

Butterfield, Fox. *New York Times,* July 6, 1980.

"Campus Cartels," *The Nation,* March 20, 1982.

*Chicago Tribune,* March 28, 1980.

"Child Support Frequently Not Paid," *New York Times,* July 8, 1983.

Chira, Susan. "Accord Is Set on Halfway Houses to Ease Crowding in State Prisons," *New York Times,* June 16, 1983.

*Christian Science Monitor,* Nov. 5, 1979.

Clymer, Adam. "Gap Between Sexes in Voting Seen as Outlasting Recession," *New York Times,* May 22, 1983.

————. *New York Times,* Nov. 18, 1982.

Collins, Glenn. "Tribe Where Harmony Rules," *New York Times,* Sept. 19, 1983.

Dullea, Georgia. *New York Times,* Sept. 16, 1980.

Edmiston, Susan. "Hers," *New York Times,* July 1, 1982.

Farrell, William E. *New York Times,* Nov. 13, 1977.

Gamarekian, Barbara. "Politicians' Wives 'Peace Links,'" *New York Times*, May 26, 1982.

Garbus, Martin. "Excluding Justice," *New York Times*, April 4, 1983.

————. "U.S. Plans," *New York Times*, April 3, 1983.

Gerth, Jeff. "Big Severance Payments," *New York Times*, March 16, 1983.

Goleman, Daniel. "Psychology Is Revising Its View of Women," *New York Times*, March 20, 1984.

Halloran, Richard. "Secrets," *New York Times*, April 19, 1983.

Hechinger, Fred M. "About Education," *New York Times*, March 29, 1983, April 12, 1983.

————. "Schools Try New Ways to Improve Education," *New York Times*, April 14, 1983.

Herbers, John. "Citizens' Activism Gaining in Nation," *New York Times*, May 16, 1982.

Hertsgaard, Mark. "Nuclear Nothing," *New York Times*, April 29, 1983.

Hiatt, Fred. "Pentagon Board Assailed for Conflicts of Interest, Cronyism," *International Herald Tribune*, Aug. 27–28, 1983.

Hoge, Warren. "In Brazil, Mornings Belong to Feminist TV," *New York Times*, Jan. 3, 1980.

"ILO Says Female Workers Face Wide Discrimination," *New York Times*, April 3, 1980.

King, Wayne. "Microscopic Techniques Have a Gigantic Effect on Cattle Breeding Industry," *New York Times*, Dec. 6, 1982.

Lappé, Frances Moore, and Nick Allen. "Central American Victims," *New York Times*, May 28, 1982.

Lekachman, Robert. "An Agenda for the Left," *New York Times*, Feb. 22, 1982.

Lewis, Anthony. "Who Are the Realists?" *New York Times*, June 3, 1982.

Maeroff, Gene. "Questions on Teachers' Skills," *New York Times*, April 12, 1983.

Maitland, Leslie. "Secrecy," *New York Times*, April 25, 1983.

————. "Top EPA Official Accused," *New York Times*, March 24, 1983.

Margolick, David. "Lawyers for Poor," *New York Times*, April 3, 1983.

————. *New York Times*, Jan. 18, 1982.

Markham, James M. "Smoggy Prague Tries to Fight Growing Plague of Pollution," *New York Times*, April 9, 1984.

Miller, Judith. "More U.S. Lie Tests," *New York Times*, Oct. 9, 1981.

————. "Nuclear Plants," *New York Times*, Jan. 23, 1983.

————. "3 Women and the Campaign for a Nuclear Freeze," *New York Times*, May 26, 1982.

Morrison, Alan B. "N w Fed ral sm Holes," *New York Times*, Sept. 20, 1982.

Nelson, Bryce. "Aggression: Still a Stronger Trait for Males," *New York Times*, June 30, 1983.

Nies, Judith. "Women's New Issue," *New York Times*, June 9, 1983.

"Number of Prisoners," *New York Times*, July 15, 1982.

Pear, Robert. "Rights Panel," *New York Times*, March 20, 1983.

————. "Rights Unit," *New York Times*, April 12, 1983.

————. "U.S. Reports Decline in Infant Mortality Rate," *New York Times*, March 16, 1983.

" 'P' Films Ratings Rate an 'X,' " *New York Times*, Feb. 26, 1983.

Peterson, Iver. "FBI Spy," *New York Times*, March 27, 1983.

————. "Judge Clears FBI of Negligence in Slaying of Rights Worker," *New York Times*, April 28, 1983.

"Poorer, Hungrier," *New York Times*, April 10, 1983.

Prial, Frank. "Congressmen Hear Renewal of Debate Over TV Violence," *New York Times*, April 16, 1983.

"Private Budget Study Finds Harm to Women," *New York Times*, March 29, 1984.

"Put Legal Back Into Legal Services," *New York Times*, April 14, 1983.

"Real Income Down 5.5 Percent," *New York Times*, Aug. 21, 1981.

Roberts, Steven V. "Capitol Hill Battle," *New York Times*, April 8, 1981.

Robinson, Charlotte. "Study Says Children Are Depressing," *Boston Globe*, May 17, 1979.

Schafran, Lynn Hecht. "Reagan vs. Women," *New York Times*, Oct. 13, 1981.

Schmeck, Harold M., Jr. *New York Times*, Nov. 14, 1981.

"Schools Study Ethics of Business-Aided Research," *New York Times*, April 8, 1983.

"Security and Insecurity," *New York Times*, April 30, 1983.

Serrin, William. *New York Times*, Jan. 18, 1982.

Shabecoff, Philip. "EPA Aide," *New York Times*, March 16, 1983.

"Sharp Rise in Childbearing Found Among U.S. Women in Early 30's," *New York Times*, June 10, 1983.

Shipp, E. R. "Issue and Debate," *New York Times*, May 22, 1982.

Shribman, David. "Study Finds Women Are Systematically Underpaid," *New York Times*, April 29, 1983.

"Shrinking Fertility Rate," *New York Times*, May 10, 1983.

Silk, Leonard. "Russian Economy Gives Andropov Huge Problems," *New York Times*, June 12, 1983.

Smith, Terence. "Former Leaders Ponder Fragile Nature of Power," *International Herald Tribune*, Aug. 30, 1983.

"Study Details Family Violence," *New York Times*, April 23, 1984.

Sullivan, Ronald. "Health Chief for N.Y. to Act Against Misconduct by Physicians," *New York Times*, April 3, 1983.

Sullivan, Walter. "Boston Autopsies Find 1 in 4 Diagnoses Wrong," *New York Times*, April 28, 1983.

Taylor, Stuart, Jr. *New York Times*, March 22, 1982.

Teltsch, Kathleen. "Black Teen-agers Found Eager to Work," *New York Times*, April 21, 1983.

———. "Network of 'Alternative' Philanthropies Is Forming," *New York Times*, July 5, 1983.

Thurow, Lester. "The Leverage of Our Wealthiest 400," *New York Times*, Oct. 11, 1984.

Tolchin, Martin. "Reports of U.S. Aid for Anti-Sandinista Guerrillas Worrying Senators," *New York Times*, April 6, 1983.

"U.S. Orders Disclaimers," *New York Times*, Feb. 25, 1983.

Wicker, Tom. "Making Things Worse," *New York Times*, July 9, 1982.

Williams, Joseph. *New York Times*, Feb. 19, 1982.

Willis, Ellen. *The Village Voice*, June 23, 1980, July 16–22, 1980.

"A Window on Violence," *New York Times*, May 22, 1982.

"Women's Issues Are American Issues," *New York Times*, April 29, 1983.

Wren, Christopher S. *International Herald Tribune*, Aug. 6, 1982.

Zager, Robert. "A Working Model," *New York Times*, Sept. 7, 1981.

# Index